Contemporary Political Philosophy

B

BLACKWELL PHILOSOPHY ANTHOLOGIES

Each volume in this outstanding new series provides a comprehensive and authoritative collection of the essential primary readings from philosophy's main fields of study. Designed to complement the *Blackwell Companions to Philosophy* series, each volume represents an unparalleled resource in its own right, and will provide the ideal platform for course use.

Contemporary Political Philosophy

An Anthology

Edited by *Robert E. Goodin* and *Philip Pettit*
Australian National University, Canberra

BLACKWELL
Publishers

First published 1997

Reprinted 1997, 1998

Blackwell Publishers Ltd
108 Cowley Road
Oxford OX4 1JF, UK

Blackwell Publishers Inc
350 Main Street
Malden, Massachusetts 02148, USA

British Library Cataloguing in Publication Data
A CIP catalogue record for this book is available from the British Library

Library of Congress Cataloging in Publication Data
Contemporary political philosophy: an anthology / edited by Robert E.Goodin
and Philip Pettit.
p.   cm. — (Blackwell philosophy anthologies: 4)
Includes bibliographical references and index.
ISBN 1–55786–841–7 (alk. paper)
ISBN 1–55786–842–5 (pbk: alk. paper)
1. Political science—Philosophy. I. Goodin, Robert E.
II. Pettit, Philip, 1945–. III. Series
JA71.C578   1997   96–25489
320—dc20   CIP

Commissioning Editor: Steve Smith
Desk Editor: Margaret Aherne
Production Controller: Lisa Eaton

Typeset in 9 on 11pt Ehrhardt
by Wearset, Boldon, Tyne and Wear
Printed and bound in Great Britain
by T. J. International Limited, Padstow, Cornwall

This book is printed on acid-free paper

Contents

Contents

Part III   Justice   185

Part IV   Rights   289

Part V   Liberty   389

Part VI   Equality   463

Part VII   Oppression   541

Preface

The essays contained in this collection represent what seem to us to be canonical texts in contemporary political philosophy. But they only represent the contemporary canon, they do not exhaust it. Although this collection is two or perhaps three times the size of most, we nevertheless found that we had space for only a sample of the very many more texts and topics that we would like to have included.

The collection is deliberately designed as a companion to our earlier *Companion to Contemporary Political Philosophy* (Oxford: Blackwell, 1993). We attempted to retain some thing of the same flavour in this collection, much the same scope of substantive concerns and much the same diversity of analytic styles. Inevitably,

though, there is so much more surveyed in the *Companion*'s many chapters than can be reprinted here. Interested readers are referred back to the *Companion* not only to situate the texts in the present collection but also for further readings and whole other sets of concerns.

The *Companion* as a whole, and our own introduction to it, serves effectively as a preface to this collection. So we will not expound at length here upon our views as to the nature of the political philosophical enterprise. Let this one comment suffice. We have tried to select and organize the texts included here so as to show political philosophy as it truly is: as a set of ongoing conversations and disputations, arguments and debates.

Robert E. Goodin
Philip Pettit

Acknowledgements

This collection was conceived under the spur of Steve Smith's encouragement and it was shaped by the commentary that he provided at every stage of planning as well as by the commentary that he secured from anonymous readers. We are most grateful for all his efforts. We benefited also from the comments of a number of colleagues and friends on the emerging outline of the book and would like to thank, in particular, David Miller and Ian Shapiro. One of the hardest tasks with preparing any collection, however, is getting clean copies of the papers included and identifying the copyright holders. Here we must express our gratitude for the great help provided by Andrew Gleeson. He saved us many hours in the stacks.

The authors and publishers would like to thank the following for permission to use copyright material:

Beacon Press, Boston for chapter 7; Blackwell Publishers for chapters 3 (with Carole Pateman), 6, 8, 10, 12, 14, 28, 30, 34, 35; Cambridge University Press for chapters 1, 9; Ronald Dworkin for chapter 20; Nancy Fraser and Linda Gordon for chapter 38; Harvard Law Review Association for chapter 31; Harvard University Press for chapter 5; Heinemann Educational Books and Doubleday, a division of Doubleday Dell Publishing Group Inc. for chapter 18; New York University Law Review for chapter 17; New York University Press for chapter 32; Oxford University Press for chapters 23, 24; Prentice Hall for chapter 33; Princeton University Press for chapters 2, 11, 21, 22, 26; Sage Publications, Inc. for chapters 15, 37; Charles M. Taylor for chapter 25; Telos Press for chapter 4; UCLA Law Review for chapters 27, 36; University of Chicago Press for chapter 16; University of Utah Press and Amartya Sen for chapter 29.

Every effort has been made to trace the copyright holders, but if any have been inadvertently overlooked, the publishers will be pleased to make the necessary arrangement at the first opportunity.

PART I

State and Society

1

The State

Quentin Skinner

I

In the Preface to *De cive*, his first published work on government, Hobbes describes his own project as that of undertaking "a more curious search into the rights of states and duties of subjects."[1] Since that time, the idea that the confrontation between individuals and states furnishes the central topic of political theory has come to be almost universally accepted. This makes it easy to overlook the fact that, when Hobbes issued his declaration, he was self-consciously setting a new agenda for the discipline he claimed to have invented, the discipline of political science. His suggestion that the duties of subjects are owed to the state, rather than to the person of a ruler, was still a relatively new and highly contentious one. So was his implied assumption that our duties are owed exclusively to the state, rather than to a multiplicity of jurisdictional authorities, local as well as national, ecclesiastical as well as civil in character. So, above all, was his use of the term "state" to denote this highest form of authority in matters of civil government.

Hobbes's declaration can thus be viewed as marking the end of one distinct phase in the history of political theory as well as the beginning of another and more familiar one. It announces the end of an era in which the concept of public

---

Originally published in *Political Innovation and Conceptual Change*, ed. T. Ball, J. Farr and R. L. Hanson (Cambridge University Press, 1989), 90–131. Reprinted by permission of the publisher.

power had been treated in far more personal and charismatic terms. It points to a simpler and altogether more abstract vision, one that has remained with us ever since and has come to be embodied in the use of such terms as *état, stato, staat*, and state.[2] My aim in what follows will be to sketch the historical circumstances out of which these linguistic and conceptual transformations first arose.

II

As early as the fourteenth century, the Latin term *status* – together with such vernacular equivalents as *estat, stato*, and state – can already be found in general use in a variety of political contexts. During this formative period these terms appear to have been employed predominantly to refer to the state or standing of rulers themselves.[3] One important source of this usage was undoubtedly the rubric *De statu hominum* from the opening of Justinian's *Digest*. There the authority of Hermogenianus had been adduced for the fundamental claim that, "since all law is established for the sake of human beings, we first need to consider the *status* of such persons, before we consider anything else."[4] Following the revival of Roman Law studies in twelfth-century Italy, the word *status* came in consequence to designate the legal standing of all sorts and conditions of men, with rulers being described as enjoying a distinctive "estate royal," *estat du roi*, or *status regis*.[5]

When the question of a ruler's *status* was

raised, this was generally in order to emphasize that it ought to be viewed as a state of majesty, a high estate, a condition of stateliness. Within the well-established monarchies of France and England, we encounter this formula in chronicles and official documents throughout the latter half of the fourteenth century. Froissart, for example, recalls in book I of his *Chroniques* that when the young king of England held court to entertain visiting dignitaries in 1327, "the queen was to be seen there in an *estat* of great nobility."[6] The same usage recurs poignantly in the speech made by William Thirnyng to Richard II in 1399, in which he reminds his former sovereign "in what presence you renounced and ceased of the state of King, and of lordship and of all the dignity and worship that [be]longed thereto" (Topham *et al.* 1783: 424, col. 1).

Underlying the suggestion that a distinctive quality of stateliness "belongs" to kings was the prevailing belief that sovereignty is intimately connected with display, that the presence of majesty serves in itself as an ordering force. This was to prove the most enduring of the many features of charismatic leadership eventually subverted by the emergence of the modern concept of an impersonal state.[7] As late as the end of the seventeenth century, it is still common to find political writers using the word "state" to point to a conceptual connection between the stateliness of rulers and the efficacy of their rule. As one might expect, exponents of divine-right monarchy such as Bossuet continue to speak of the *état* of *majesté* in just such terms (Bossuet 1967: 69, 72). But the same assumptions also survived even among the enemies of kingship. When Milton, for example, describes in his *History of Britain* the famous scene where Canute orders the ocean to "come no further upon my land," he observes that the king sought to give force to his extraordinary command by speaking "with all the state that royalty could put into his countenance" (Milton 1971: 365).

By the end of the fourteenth century, the term *status* had also come to be regularly used to refer to the state or condition of a realm or commonwealth.[8] This conception of the *status reipublicae* was of course classical in origin, appearing frequently in the histories of Livy and Sallust, as well as in Cicero's orations and political works.[9] It can also be found in the *Digest*, most notably under the rubric *De institia et iure*, where the analysis opens with Ulpian's contention that law

is concerned with two areas, the public and the private, and that "public law is that which pertains to the *status rei Romanae*."[10]

With the revival of Roman Law, this further piece of legal terminology also passed into general currency. It became common in the fourteenth century, both in France and England, to discuss "the state of the realm" or *estat du roilme* (Post 1964: 310–22). Speaking of the year 1389, for example, Froissart remarks that the king decided at that point "to reform the country *en bon état*, so that everyone would be contented."[11] The idea of linking the good state of a king and his kingdom soon became a commonplace. By the middle of the fifteenth century, petitioners to the English parliament regularly ended their pleas by promising the king that they would "tenderly pray God for the good estate and prosperity of your most noble person of this your noble realm."[12]

If we turn from northern Europe to the Italian city-states, we encounter the same terminology at an even earlier date. The first known advice-books addressed to *podestá* and other city-magistrates in the early years of the thirteenth century already indicate that their main concern is with the *status civitatum*, the state or condition of cities as independent political entities.[13] The anonymous *Oculus pastoralis*, perhaps written as early as the 1220s,[14] repeatedly employs the phrase,[15] as does Giovanni da Viterbo in his treatise *De regimine civitatum*,[16] completed around the year 1250.[17] By the early fourteenth century we find the same concept widely expressed in the vernacular, with writers of *Dictamina* such as Filippo Ceffi offering extensive instruction to magistrates, in the form of model speeches, on how to maintain the *stato* of the city given into their charge (Giannardi 1942: 27, 47, 48, etc.).

Discussing the state or standing of such communities, the point these writers generally wish to stress is that chief magistrates have a duty to maintain their cities in a good, happy, or prosperous state.[18] This ideal of aspiring to uphold the *bonus* or even the *optimus status reipublicae* was again Roman in origin, and was largely taken over from Cicero and Seneca by the thirteenth-century writers of advice-books.[19] The author of the *Oculus pastoralis* frequently speaks of the need to uphold the happy, advantageous, honorable and prosperous *status* of one's *civitas*.[20] Giovanni da Viterbo likewise insists on the desirability of maintaining the *bonus status* of one's community,[21] while Filippo Ceffi writes with equal confidence in the vernacular of the obligation to preserve a city "in a good and peaceful *stato*," in a "good *stato* and complete peace" (Giannardi 1942: 28).

These writers also provide the first complete restatement of the classical view of what it means for a *civitas* or *respublica* to attain its best state.[22] This requires, they all agree, that our magistrates should follow the dictates of justice in all their public acts, as a result of which the common good will be promoted, the cause of peace upheld, and the general happiness of the people assured. This line of reasoning was later taken up by Aquinas and his numerous Italian disciples at the end of the thirteenth century. Aquinas himself presents the argument at several points in his *Summa*, as well as in his commentary on Aristotle's *Politics*. A judge or magistrate, he declares, "has charge of the common good, which is justice," and ought therefore to act in such a way "as to exhibit a good aspect from the point of view of the *status* of the community as a whole."[23] But the same line of reasoning can already be found a generation earlier in advice-books for city-magistrates. Giovanni da Viterbo, for example, develops precisely the same theory of the *optimus status* in his treatise *De regimine civitatum*, while Brunetto Latini reiterates and enlarges on Giovanni's arguments in his chapter "Dou gouvernement des cités" at the end of his encyclopedic *Livres dou trésor* of 1266.[24]

This vision of the *optimus status reipublicae* later became central to *quattrocento* humanist accounts of the well-ordered political life. When Giovanni Campano (1427–77)[25] analyzes the dangers of faction in his tract *De regendo magistratu*, he declares that "there is nothing I count more unfavourable than this to the *status* and safety of a *respublica*."[26] If the good *status* of a community is to be preserved, he goes on, all individual or factional advantage must be subordinated to the pursuit of justice and "the common good of the city as a whole" (Campano 1502, fo. xxxxvii^r-v). Filippo Beroaldo (1453–1505) endorses the same conclusions in a treatise to which he actually gave the title *De optimo statu*. The best state, he argues, can be attained only if our ruler or leading magistrate "remains oblivious of his own good, and ensures that he acts in everything he does in such a way as to promote the public benefit."[27]

Finally, the Erasmian humanists imported precisely the same values and vocabulary into northern Europe in the early years of the sixteenth century. Erasmus (1974:162) himself contrasts the *optimus* with the *pessimus reipublicae status* in his *Institutio* of 1516, and argues that "the happiest *status* is reached when there is a prince whom everyone obeys, when the prince obeys the laws and when the laws answer to our ideals of honesty and equity."[28] His younger contemporary Thomas Starkey (1948: 63; also 65, 66–7) offers a very similar account in his *Dialogue* of what constitutes "the most prosperous and perfect state that in any country, city or town, by policy and wisdom may be established and set." And in More's *Utopia* the figure of Hythloday, the traveller to "the new island of Utopia," likewise insists that because the Utopians live in a society where the laws embody the principles of justice, seriously aim at the common good, and in consequence enable the citizens to live "as happily as possible," we are justified in saying that the Utopians have in fact attained the *optimus status reipublicae* – which is of course the title of More's famous book (More 1965: 244).

III

I now turn to consider the process by which the above usages – all of them common throughout late-medieval Europe – eventually gave rise to recognizably modern discussions of the concept of the state. I shall argue that, if we wish to trace both the acquisition of this concept and at the same time its expression by means of such terms as *status*, *stato* or state, we ought not to focus our main attention – as medieval historians have commonly done – on the evolution of legal theories about the *status* of kings in the fourteenth and fifteenth centuries.[29] It was rare even among civil lawyers of that period to use the Latin word *status* without qualification,[30] and virtually unheard of for political writers to employ such a barbarism at all. Even when we find *status* being used in such contexts, moreover, it is almost always evident that what is at issue is simply the state or standing of the king or his kingdom, not in the least the modern idea of the state as a separate apparatus of government.

I shall instead suggest that, in order to investigate the process by which the term *status* and its vernacular equivalents first came to acquire their modern range of reference, we need to keep our main attention fixed on the early histories and advice-books for magistrates I have already singled out, as well as on the later mirror-for-princes literature to which they eventually gave rise. It was within these traditions of practical political reasoning, I shall argue, that the terms *status* and *stato* were first consistently used in new and significantly extended ways.[31]

These genres of political literature were in turn a product of the new and distinctive forms of political organization that arose within late-medieval Italy. Beginning in the early years of the twelfth century, a growing number of cities throughout the *Regnum Italicum* succeeded in acquiring for themselves the status of autonomous and self-governing republics.[32] It is true that these communities later proved unstable, and were widely reorganized in the course of the next century under the stronger and more centralized regimes of hereditary princes (Waley 1978: 128–40). But even in this later period, the great city-republics of Florence and Venice managed to preserve their traditional hostility to the idea of hereditary monarchy, and thereby carried the ideals of participatory republican government into the era of the high Renaissance.[33]

The development of these new political formations posed a new series of questions about the concept of political authority. One of the most pressing concerned the type of regime best suited to ensuring that an independent *civitas* or *respublica* is able to remain in its *optimus status* or best state. Is it wisest to opt for the rule of an hereditary *signore*, or ought one to retain an elective system of government based on a *podestá* or other such magistrate?

Although this question remained in contention throughout the history of Renaissance Italy, it is possible to distinguish two main phases of the debate. The earliest treatises intended for city-magistrates invariably assumed – in line with their Roman authorities – that the best state of a *civitas* can be attained only under an elective form of republican government. After the widespread usurpation of these regimes, however, by the rise of hereditary *signori* in the fourteenth century, this commitment increasingly gave way to the claim that the best means of ensuring the good standing of any political community must be to institute the rule of a wise prince, a *pater patriae*, whose actions will be governed by a desire to foster the common good and hence the general happiness of all his subjects.[34]

Building on this assumption, the writers of mirror-for-princes treatises in the Renaissance generally devoted themselves to considering two related points. Their loftiest aim was to explain how a good ruler can hope to reach the characteristically princely goals of honour and glory for himself while at the same time managing to promote the happiness of his subjects.[35] But their main concern was with a far more basic and urgent question of statecraft: how to advise the new *signori* of Italy, often in highly unsettled circumstances, on how to hold on to their *status principis* or *stato del principe*, their political state or standing as effectively governing rulers of their existing territories.

As a result, the use of the term *stato* to denote the political standing of rulers, together with the discussion of how such rulers should behave if they are to manage *mantenere lo stato*, began to resound through the chronicles and political literature of fourteenth-century Italy. When Giovanni Villani, for example, speaks in his *Istorie Fiorentine* of the civic dissensions that marked the city during the 1290s, he observes that they were largely directed against *il popolo in suo stato e signoria* – against the people in their positions of political power.[36] When Ranieri Sardo in his *Cronaca Pisana* describes the accession of Gherardo d'Appiano as leader of the city in 1399, he remarks that the new *capitano* continued to enjoy the same *stato e governo* – the same political standing and governmental authority – as his father had enjoyed before him (Sardo 1845: 240–1). By the time we reach such late contributions to the mirror-for-princes literature as Machiavelli's *Il principe* of 1513, the question of what a ruler must do if he wishes to maintain his political standing had become the chief topic of debate. Machiavelli's advice is almost entirely directed at new princes who wish *tenere* or *mantenere lo stato* – who wish to maintain their positions as rulers over whatever territories they may have managed to inherit or acquire.[37]

If such a ruler is to prevent the state in which he finds himself from being altered to his disadvantage, he must clearly be able to fulfil a number of preconditions of effective government. If we now turn to consider the ways in which these preconditions were formulated and discussed in the traditions of thought I am considering, we shall find the terms *status* and *stato* employed in an increasingly extended manner to refer to these various aspects of political power.[38] As an outcome of this process, we shall eventually find these writers deploying at least some elements of a recognizably modern conception of the state.

One precondition of maintaining one's standing

as a ruler is obviously that one should be able to preserve the character of one's existing regime. We accordingly find the terms *status* and *stato* being used from an early period to refer not merely to the state or condition of princes, but also to the presence of particular regimes or systems of government.

This usage in turn appears to have arisen out of the habit of employing the term *status* to classify the various forms of rule described by Aristotle. Aquinas has sometimes been credited with popularizing this development, since there are versions of his *Expositio* of Aristotle's *Politics* in which oligarchies are described as *status paucorum* and the rule of the people is identified as the *status popularis*.[39] Such usages later became widespread in humanist political thought. Filippo Beroaldo begins his *De optimo statu* with a typology of legitimate regimes, speaking of the *status popularis*, the *status paucorum* and even the *status unius* when referring to monarchy (1508, fos. xi[r] and xii[v]). Francesco Patrizi (1412–94) opens his *De regno* with a similar typology, one in which monarchy, aristocracy, and democracy are all characterized as types of *civilium status* or states of civil society (Patrizi 1594b: 16–17, 19, and esp. 21). Writing in the vernacular at the same period, Vespasiano da Bisticci (1421–98) likewise contrasts the rule of *signori* with the *stato populare*, while Guicciardini later invokes the same distinction in his *Discorsi* on the government of Florence (Vespasiano 1970–6, vol. I: 406; Guicciardini 1932: 274). Finally, Machiavelli used *stato* in just this fashion at a number of places in *Il principe*,[40] most notably in the opening sentence of the entire work, in which he informs us that "All the *stati*, all the dominions that have had or now have power over men either have been or are republics or principalities."[41]

By this stage, the term *stato* was also in widespread use as a way of referring simply to prevailing regimes. When Giovanni Villani, for example, notes that in 1308 "it was the members of the *parte Nera* who held control" in Florence, he speaks of the government they established as *lo stato de'Neri*.[42] When Ranieri Sardo (1845: 125) writes about the fall of the Nove in Siena in 1355, he describes the change of regime as the loss of *lo stato de'Nove*. When Vespasiano (1970–6, vol. II: 171, 173) relates how the enemies of Cosimo de'Medici succeeded in setting up a new government in 1434, he expresses the point by saying that "they were able to change *lo stato*." By the

time we reach a theorist such as Machiavelli's friend Francesco Vettori, writing in the early part of the sixteenth century, both these usages of *stato* were firmly established. Vettori employs the term not only to refer to different forms of government, but also to describe the prevailing regime in Florence that he wished to see defended.[43]

A second precondition of maintaining one's existing state as a ruler is obviously that one should suffer no loss or alteration in the range of territories given into one's charge. As a result of this further preoccupation we find the terms *status* and *stato* pressed into early service as a way of referring to the general area over which a ruler or chief magistrate needs to exercise control. When the author of the *Oculus pastoralis*, for example, wishes to describe the duty of chief magistrates to look after their cities and localities, he already speaks of it as a duty to promote *suos status* (Franceschi 1966: 24). When the authors of the *Gratulatio* sent to the people of Padua in 1310 wish to express the hope that the entire province may be able to live in peace, they say that they are hoping for the *tranquillitas vestri status* (Muratori 1741:131). Similarly, when Ambrogio Lorenzetti tells us, in the verses that accompany his celebrated frescoes of 1337–9 on the theme of good government, that a *signore* must cultivate the virtues if he is to succeed in levying taxes from the areas under his command, he expresses his point by saying that this is how he must act *per governare lo stato*.[44]

These early and isolated usages first begin to proliferate in the chronicles and political treatises of the high Renaissance. When Sardo (1845: 91), for example, wants to describe how the Pisans made peace throughout their territories in 1290, what he says is that the truce extended throughout *stato suo*. When Guicciardini (1933: 298) remarks in his *Ricordi* that the French revolutionized warfare in Italy after 1494, producing a situation in which the loss of a single campaign brought with it the forfeiture of all one's lands, he describes such defeats as bringing with them the loss of *lo stato*. So too with Machiavelli, who frequently uses the term *stato* in *Il principe* in order to denote the lands or territories of a prince. He clearly has this usage in mind when he talks at length in chapter 3 about the means a wise prince must adopt if he wishes to acquire new *stati*; and he evidently has in mind the same usage when he asks in chapter 24 why so many of the princes of

Italy have lost their *stati* during his own lifetime (Machiavelli 1960: 18, 22, 24, 97).

Finally, due in large measure to these Italian influences, the same usage can be found in northern Europe by the early years of the sixteenth century. Guillaume Budé, for example, in his *L'Institution du prince* of 1519, equates the range of *les pays* commanded by Caesar after his victory over Antony with the extent of *son estat*.[45] Similarly, when Thomas Starkey (1948: 167) argues in his *Dialogue* of the early 1530s that everyone living in England should be represented by a Council, he remarks that such a body "should represent the whole state." And when Lawrence Humphrey warns in his tract *The Nobles* of 1563 that evil conduct on the part of a ruler can easily set a bad example throughout an entire community, he expresses his point by saying that the vices of a ruler can easily "spread the same into the whole state" (1973, sig. Q. 8ʳ).

As the writers of advice-books always emphasized, however, by far the most important precondition of maintaining one's state as a prince must be to keep one's hold over the existing power structure and institutions of government within one's *regnum* or *civitas*. This in turn gave rise to the most important linguistic innovation that can be traced to the chronicles and political writings of Renaissance Italy. This took the form of an extension of the term *stato* not merely to denote the idea of a prevailing regime, but also, and more specifically, to refer to the institutions of government and means of coercive control that serve to organize and preserve order within political communities.

Vespasiano speaks on several occasions in his *Vite* of *lo stato* as just such an apparatus of political authority. In his life of Alessandro Sforza, for example, he describes how Alessandro conducted himself "in his government of *lo stato*" (Vespasiano 1970–6, vol. I: 426). In his life of Cosimo de'Medici he speaks of "those who hold positions of power in *stati*," and praises Cosimo for recognizing the difficulties of holding on to power in *uno stato* when faced by opposition from influential citizens.[46] Guicciardini in his *Ricordi* similarly asks why the Medici "lost control of *lo stato* in 1527," and later observes that they found it much harder than Cosimo had done "to maintain their hold over *lo stato di Firenze*," the institutions of Florentine government.[47] Finally, Castiglione in *Il cortegiano* likewise makes it clear that he thinks of *lo stato* as a distinct power structure which a prince needs to be able to control and dominate. He begins by remarking that the Italians "have greatly contributed to discussions about the government of *stati*," and later advises courtiers that "when it comes to questions about *stati*, it is necessary to be prudent and wise" in order to counsel one's ruler about the best way to behave.[48]

Of all the writers of advice-books, however, it is Machiavelli in *Il principe* who shows the most consistent willingness to distinguish the institutions of *lo stato* from those who have charge of them. He thinks of *stati* as having their own foundations, and speaks in particular of each *stato* as having its own particular laws, customs, and ordinances (Machiavelli 1960: 53; 76, 84). He is willing in consequence to speak of *lo stato* as an agent, describing it as capable, among other things, of choosing particular courses of action and of calling in times of crisis upon the loyalty of its citizens (Machiavelli 1960: 48, 92). This means, as Machiavelli makes clear at several points, that what he takes himself to be discussing in *Il principe* is not simply how princes ought to behave; he also sees himself as writing more abstractly about statecraft (*dello stato*) and about *cose di stato* or affairs of state (Machiavelli 1960: 21, 25).

IV

It has often been argued that, by the time we reach the usages I have just been examining, we are already dealing with a recognizably modern conception of the state as an apparatus of power whose existence remains independent of those who may happen to have control of it at any given time. Gaines Post and others have even suggested that this conception is already present in a number of allusions to the *status regni* in the fourteenth century.[49] A similar claim has been advanced with even greater confidence about the employment of the term *stato* by Machiavelli and some of his contemporaries. As Chiappelli puts it, for example, "the word bears the meaning of 'State' in its full maturity" in a majority of the places where Machiavelli uses it.[50]

These claims, however, are I think greatly exaggerated. It is usually clear – except in the small number of deeply ambiguous cases I have cited[51] – that even when *status* and *stato* are employed by these writers to denote an apparatus of government, the power structure in question is not in fact viewed as independent of those who have charge of it. As Post himself concedes, the usual aim in early legal discussions of the *status regni* was to insist on a far more personal view of political power,[52] a view that was later to be revived by the proponents of absolute monarchy in the seventeenth century.[53] According to this argument, the ruler or chief magistrate, so far from being distinguishable from the institutions of the state, is said to possess and even embody those institutions himself. The same point can in most cases be made about Machiavelli's invocations of *lo stato* in *Il principe*. When he uses the term to refer to an apparatus of government, he is usually at pains to emphasize that it needs to remain in the hands of the prince: that *lo stato*, as he often puts it, remains equivalent to *il suo stato*, the prince's own state or condition of rulership.[54]

Even after the reception of humanist ideas about *lo stato* in northern Europe, the belief that the powers of government should be treated as essentially personal in character was to die hard. It is clearly this assumption, for example, which underlies many of the quarrels between kings and parliaments over the issue of taxation in the course of the sixteenth century. The basis of the parliamentary case was generally an assertion of the form that, except in times of dire necessity, kings should be able "to live of their own."[55] They should be able, that is, to ensure that their personal revenues remain sufficient to uphold both their own kingly state and the good state of their government.

I conclude that, for all the importance of the writers I have been considering, they cannot in general be said to articulate a recognizable concept of the state with anything like complete self-consciousness. It would not perhaps be too bold to assert, indeed, that in all the discussions about the state and government of princes in the first half of the sixteenth century, there will be found scarcely any instance in which the *état*, *staat* or state in question is unequivocally separated from the status or standing of the prince himself.[56]

This is not to deny, however, that the crystallizing of a recognizable concept of the state was one of the legacies of Renaissance political thought. It is merely to suggest that, if we wish to follow the process by which this development took place, we need to focus not merely on the mirror-for-princes literature on which I have so far concentrated, but also on the other strand of thought about the *optimus status reipublicae* that I began by singling out. We need, that is, to turn our attention to the rival tradition of Renaissance republicanism, the tradition centring on the claim that, if there is to be any prospect of attaining the *optimus status reipublicae*, we must always institute a self-governing form of republican regime.

Among the republican theorists of Renaissance Italy, the main reason given for this basic commitment was that all power is liable to corrupt. All individuals or groups, once granted sovereignty over a community, will tend to promote their own interest at the expense of the community as a whole. It follows that the only way to ensure that the laws promote the common good must be to leave the whole body of citizens in charge of their own public affairs. If their government is instead controlled by an authority external to the community itself, that authority will be sure to subordinate the good of the community to its own purposes, thereby interfering with the liberty of individual citizens to attain their chosen goals. The same outcome will be no less likely under the rule of an hereditary prince. Since he will generally seek his own ends rather than the common good, the community will again forfeit its liberty to act in pursuit of whatever goals it may wish to set itself.

This basic insight was followed up within the republican tradition in two distinct ways. It was used in the first place to justify an assertion of civic autonomy and independence, and so to defend the *libertas* of the Italian cities against external interference. This demand was initially directed against the Empire and its claims of feudal suzerainty over the *Regnum Italicum*. It was first developed by such jurists as Azo, and later by Bartolus and his followers,[57] seeking to vindicate what Bartolus described as "the *de facto* refusal of the cities of Tuscany to recognize any superior in temporal affairs."[58] But the same demand for *libertas* was also directed against all potential rivals as sources of coercive jurisdiction within the cities themselves. It was claimed on the one hand against local feudatories, who continued to be viewed, as late as Machiavelli's *Discorsi*, as the most dangerous enemies of free government (Machiavelli 1960, 1.55: 254–8). And it was even more vehemently directed against the jurisdictional pretensions of the church. The most radical response, embodied for example in Marsilius's *Defensor pacis* of 1324, took the form of insisting that all coercive power is secular by definition, and thus that the church has no right to exercise civil jurisdictions at all (Marsilius 1956, esp. II.4: 113–26). But even in the more orthodox treatises on city government, such as that of Giovanni da Viterbo, the church is still refused any say in civic affairs. The reason, as Giovanni expresses it, is that the ends of temporal and ecclesiastical authority are completely distinct (Giovanni da Viterbo 1901: 266–7). The implication is that, if the church tries to insist on any jurisdiction in temporal matters, it will simply be "putting its sickle into another man's harvest."[59]

The other way in which the basic insight of the republican tradition was developed was in the form of a positive claim about the precise type of regime we need to institute if we are to retain our *libertas* to pursue our chosen goals. The essence of the republican case was that the only form of government under which a city can hope to remain "in a free state" will be a *res publica* in the strictest sense. The community as a whole must retain the ultimate sovereign authority, assigning its rulers or chief magistrates a status no higher than that of elected officials. Such magistrates must in turn be treated not as rulers in the full sense, but merely as agents of *ministri* of justice, charged with the duty of ensuring that the laws established by the community for the promotion of its own good are properly enforced.

This contrast between the freedom of republican regimes and the servitude implied by any form of monarchical government has often been viewed as a distinctive contribution of *quattrocento* Florentine thought.[60] But the underlying assumption that liberty can be guaranteed only within a republic can already be found in many Florentine writers of the previous century.[61] Dante speaks in the *Inferno* of the move from seigneurial to republican rule as a move from tyranny to a *stato franco*, a state or condition of civic liberty (1966, xxvii. 54: 459). Ceffi repeatedly emphasizes in his *Dicerie* that the only means of guaranteeing civic *libertá* is to ensure that one's city remains under the guidance of an elected magistrate (Giannardi 1942: 32, 35, 41, 44). And Villani in his *Istorie Florentine* likewise contrasts the free *stato* of the Florentine republic with the tyranny imposed by the Duke of Athens as *signore* in 1342 (1802–3, vol. VIII: 11).

It is certainly true, however, that the equation between living in a republic and living "in a free state" was worked out with the greatest assurance by the leading republican theorists of Venice and Florence in the course of the high Renaissance. Among the Venetian writers, Gasparo Contarini furnished the classic statement of the argument in his *De republica Venetorum* of 1543. Owing to the city's elective system of government, he declares, in which "a mixture of the *status* of the nobility and of the people" is maintained, "there is nothing less to be feared in the city of Venice than that the head of the republic will interfere with the *libertas* or the activities of any of the citizens."[62] Among Florentine theorists, it was of course Machiavelli in his *Discorsi* who provided the most famous version of the same argument. "It is easy to understand," as he explains at the start of book II, "whence the love of living under a free constitution springs up in peoples. For experience shows that no cities have ever increased in dominion or in riches except when they have been established in liberty."[63] The reason, he goes on, "is easy to perceive, for it is not the pursuit of individual advantage but of the common good that makes cities great, and there is no doubt that it is only under republican regimes that this ideal of the common good is followed out."[64]

From the point of view of my present argument, these commitments can now be seen to be crucial in two different ways. It is within this tradition of thought that we encounter, for the first time, a vindication of the idea that there is a distinct form of "civil" or "political" authority which is wholly autonomous, which exists to regulate the public affairs of an independent community, and which brooks no rivals as a source of coercive power within its own *civitas* or *respublica*. It is here, in short, that we first encounter the familiar understanding of the state as a monopolist of legitimate force.

This view of "civil government" was of course taken up in France and England at an early stage in their constitutional development. It underlies their hostility to the jurisdictional power of the church, culminating in France in the "Gallican" Concordat of 1516, in England in the Marsiglian assumptions underpinning the Act of Appeals in 1533. It also underlies their repudiation of the Holy Roman Empire's claim to exercise any jurisdictions within their territories, a repudiation founded on a reworking of Azo's and later Bartolus's theories of *imperium* into the celebrated dictum that *Rex in regno suo est Imperator*.

For the origins of this view of civil government, however, we need to turn back to thirteenth-century Italy, and specifically to the political literature engendered by the self-governing city-republics of that period. Writing in the 1250s, Giovanni da Viterbo already takes his theme to be the analysis of civil power, that form of power which upholds the *civium libertas* or liberty of those who live together as citizens (Giovanni da Viterbo 1901: 218). Writing only a decade later, Brunetto Latini goes on to add that those who study the use of such power in the government of cities are studying "politics," "the noblest and the highest of all the sciences."[65] It is this neoclassical tradition to which later theorists of popular sovereignty are ultimately alluding when they speak of an autonomous area of "civil" or "political" authority, and offer to explicate what Locke (1967: 283) was to call "the true original, extent and end of civil government."

The other way in which the republican tradition contributed to crystallizing a recognizable concept of the state is of even greater importance. According to the writers I have been considering, a city can never hope to remain in a free state unless it succeeds in imposing strict conditions on its rulers and magistrates. They must always be elected; they must always remain subject to the laws and institutions of the city which elects them; they must always act to promote the common good – and hence the peace and happiness – of the sovereign body of its citizens. As a result, the republican theorists no longer equate the idea of governmental authority with the powers of particular rulers or magistrates. Rather they think of the powers of civil government as embodied in a structure of laws and institutions which our rulers and magistrates are entrusted to administer in the name of the common good. They cease in consequence to speak of rulers "maintaining their state" in the sense of maintaining their personal ascendancy over the apparatus of government. Rather they begin to speak of the *status* or *stato* as the name of that apparatus of government which our rulers may be said to have a duty to maintain.

There are already some hints of this momentous transition in the earliest treatises and *dictamina* intended for chief magistrates of city-republics. Brunetto Latini insists in his *Trésor* of 1266 that cities must always be ruled by elected officials if the *bien commun* is to be promoted. He further insists that these *sires* must follow the laws and customs of the city in all their public acts (Latini 1948, esp. pp. 392, 408, 415; 402, 412). And he concludes that such a system is indispensable not merely to maintaining such officials in a good *estat*, but also to maintaining "the *estat* of the city itself."[66] A similar hint can be found in Giovanni da Vignano's *Flore de parlare* of the 1270s. In one of his model letters, designed for the use of city ambassadors when seeking military help, he describes the government of such communities as their *stato*, and accordingly appeals for support "in order that our good *stato* can remain in wealth, honor, greatness and peace."[67] Finally, the same hint recurs soon afterwards in Matteo dei Libri's *Arringa* on the identical theme. He sets out a very similar model speech for ambassadors to deliver, advising them to appeal for help "in order that our good *stato* may be able to remain in peace."[68]

It is only with the final flowering of Renaissance republicanism, however, that we find such usages occurring with their unequivocally modern sense. Even here, moreover, this development is largely confined to the vernacular literature. Consider, by contrast, a work such as Alamanno Rinuccini's Latin dialogue of 1479, *De libertate* (1957). This includes a classic statement of the claim that individual as well as civic liberty is possible only under the laws and institutions of a republic. But Rinuccini never stoops to using the barbarous term *status* to describe the laws and institutions involved; he always prefers to speak of the *civitas* or *respublica* itself as the locus of political authority. So too with such classic Venetian writers as Contarini in his *De republica Venetorum*. Although Contarini has a clear conception of the apparatus of government as a set of institutions independent of those who control them, he never uses the term *status* to describe them, but always prefers in a similar way to speak of their authority as embodied in the *respublica* itself.[69]

If we turn, however, to the rather less pure latinity of Francesco Patrizi's *De institutione reipublicae*, we encounter a significant development in his chapter on the duties of magistrates. He lays it down that their basic duty is to act "in such a way as to promote the common good," and argues that this above all requires them to uphold "the established laws" of the community.[70] He then summarizes his advice by saying that this is how magistrates must act "if they are to prevent the *status* of their city from being overturned."[71]

It is in the vernacular writers on republicanism of the next generation, however, that we find the term *stato* being used with something approaching full self-consciousness to express a recognizable concept of the state. Guicciardini's *Discorso* on how the Medici should act to improve their control over Florence provides a suggestive example. He advises them to gather around themselves a group of advisers who are loyal to the *stato* and willing to act on its behalf. The reason is that "every *stato*, every form of sovereign power, needs dependents" who are willing "to serve the *stato* and benefit it in everything."[72] If the Medici can manage to base their regime on such a group, they can hope to establish "the most powerful foundation for the defence of the *stato*" that anyone could aspire to set up.[73]

Finally, if we turn to Machiavelli's *Discorsi*, we find the term *stato* being used with even greater confidence to denote the same apparatus of political authority. It is of course true that Machiavelli continues largely to employ the term in the most traditional way to refer to the state or condition of a city and its way of life (Machiavelli 1960: 135, 142, 153, 192, 194, etc.). And even when he mentions *stati* in the context of describing systems of government, these usages are again largely traditional: he is generally speaking either about a species of regime,[74] or about the general area or territory over which a prince or republic holds sway.[75]

There are several occasions, however, especially in the analysis of constitutions at the start of book I, where he appears to go further. The first is when he writes in chapter 2 about the founding of Sparta. He emphasizes that the system of laws promulgated by Lycurgus remained distinct from, and served to control, the kings and magistrates entrusted with upholding the laws themselves. And he characterizes Lycurgus's achievement in creating this system by saying that "he established *uno stato* which then endured for more than eight hundred years."[76] The next instance occurs in chapter 6, where he considers whether the institutions of government in republican Rome could have been set up in such a way as to avoid the "tumults" which marked that city's political life. He puts the question in the form of asking "whether it might have been possible to establish *uno stato* in Rome" without that distinctive weakness.[77] That last and most revealing case occurs in chapter 18, where he considers the difficulty of maintaining *uno stato libero* within a corrupt city. He not only makes an explicit distinction between the authority of the magistrates under the ancient Roman republic

and the authority of the laws "by means of which, together with the magistrates, the citizens were kept under control."[78] He adds in the same passage that the latter set of institutions and practices can best be described as "the order of the government or, indeed, of *lo stato*."[79]

It has often been noted that, with the reception of Renaissance republicanism in northern Europe, we begin to encounter similar assumptions among Dutch and English protagonists of "free states" in the middle of the seventeenth century.[80] It has less often been recognized that the same assumptions, couched in the same vocabulary, can already be found more than a century earlier among the first writers who attempted to introduce the ideals of civic humanism into English political thought. Thomas Starkey, for example,[81] distinguishes at several points in his *Dialogue* between the state itself and "they which have authority and rule of the state" (Starkey 1948: 61; cf. also 57, 63). It is the "office and duty" of such rulers, he goes on, to "maintain the state established in the country" over which they hold sway, "ever looking to the profit of the whole body" rather than to their own good (Starkey 1948: 64). The only method, he concludes, of "setting forward the very and true commonweal" is for everyone to recognize, rulers and ruled alike, that they are "under the same governance and state" (Starkey 1948: 71).

The same assumptions can be found soon afterwards in John Ponet's *Short Treatise of Politic Power* of 1556. He too speaks of rulers simply as the holders of a particular kind of office, and describes the duty attaching to their office as that of upholding the state. He is thus prompted to contrast the case of "an evil person coming to the government of any state" with a good ruler who will recognize that he has been "to such office called for his virtue, to see the whole state well governed and the people defended from injuries" (Ponet 1942: 98).

Finally, and perhaps most significantly, we find the same phraseology in Tudor translations of the classic Italian treatises on republican government. When Lewes Lewkenor, for example, issued his English version of Contarini's *De republica Venetorum* in 1599, he found himself in need of an English term to render Contarini's basic assumption that the authority of the Venetian government remains inherent at all times in the *civitas* or *respublica* itself, with the Doge and Council serving merely as representatives of the citizen-body as a whole. Following standard humanist usage, he generally expresses this concept by the term "commonwealth." But in speaking of the relationship between a commonwealth and its own citizens, he sometimes prefers instead to render *respublica* as "state." When he mentions the possibility of enfranchizing additional citizens in Venice, he explains that this can take place in special circumstances when someone can be shown to have been especially "dutiful towards the state." And when he discusses the Venetian ideal of citizenship, he feels able to allude in even more general terms to "the citizens, by whom the state of the city is maintained" (Lewkenor 1969: 18, 33).

V

For all the undoubted importance of these classical republican theorists, however, it would still be misleading to conclude that their use of the term *stato* and its equivalents may be said to express our modern concept of the state. That concept has come to embody a doubly impersonal character.[82] We distinguish the state's authority from that of the rulers or magistrates entrusted with the exercise of its powers for the time being. But we also distinguish its authority from that of the whole society or community over which its powers are exercised. As Burke (1910: 93) remarks in his *Reflections* – articulating a view already well entrenched by that time – "society is indeed a contract," but "the state ought not to be considered as nothing better than a partnership agreement" of a similar nature. Rather the state must be acknowledged to be an entity with a life of its own, an entity which is at once distinct from both rulers and ruled and is able in consequence to call upon the allegiances of both parties.

The republican theorists embrace only one half of this doubly abstract notion of the state. On the one hand there is, I think, no doubt that they constitute the earliest group of political writers who insist with full self-consciousness on a categorical distinction between the state and those who have control of it, and at the same time express that distinction as a claim about the *status*, *stato* or state. But on the other hand they make no comparable distinction between the powers of the state and those of its citizens. On the contrary, the whole thrust of classical republican theory is directed towards an ultimate equation between

the two. Although this undoubtedly yields a recognizable concept of the state – one that many Marxists and exponents of direct democracy continue to espouse – it is far from being the concept we have inherited from the more conservative mainstream of early-modern political thought.

The differences can be traced most clearly in the literature in praise of "free states." Consider again, for example, one of the earliest English works of this character, John Ponet's *Short Treatise of Politic Power*. As we have seen, Ponet makes a firm distinction between the office and person of a ruler, and even uses the term "state" to describe the form of civil authority our rulers have a duty to uphold. But he makes no analogous distinction between the powers of the state and those of the people. Not only does he maintain that "kings, princes and governors have their authority of the people"; he also insists that ultimate political authority continues to reside at all times in "the body or state of the realm or commonwealth" (Ponet 1942: 106, 105). If kings or princes are found to be "abusing their office," it is for the body of the people to remove them, since the ultimate powers of sovereignty must always remain lodged within "the body of every state" (Ponet 1942: 105; cf. also pp. 111, 124).

The same commitment is upheld even by the most sophisticated defenders of "free states" in the seventeenth century. A good example is furnished by Milton's *Ready and Easy Way to Establish a Free Commonwealth*. If we are to maintain "our freedom and flourishing condition," he argues, and establish a government "for preservation of the common peace and liberty," it is indispensable that the sovereignty of the people should never be "transferred." It should be "delegated only" to a governing Council of State (Milton 1980: 432–3, 456). The institutions of the state are thus conceived as nothing more than a means of expressing the powers of the people in an administratively more convenient form. As Milton had earlier emphasized in *The Tenure of Kings and Magistrates*, whatever authority our rulers may possess is merely "committed to them in trust from the people, to the common good of them all, in whom the power yet remains fundamentally" at all times (Milton 1962: 202). As a result, Milton, Harrington, and other defenders of "free states" hardly ever use the term "state" when speaking of the institutions of civil government. Believing as they do that such institutions must remain under the control of the whole community if its members are to preserve their birthright of liberty, they almost always prefer the term "commonwealth" as a means of referring not merely to bodies of citizens, but also to the forms of political authority by which they must be governed if they are to remain "in a free state."[83]

The same is no less true of the "monarchomachs" and other contractarian opponents of early-modern absolutism who first rose to prominence in the later sixteenth century, especially in Holland and France. Deriving their arguments mainly from scholastic rather than classical republican sources, these writers are not generally republican in the strict sense of believing that the common good of a community can never be satisfactorily assured under a monarchical form of government. Usually they are quite explicit in claiming that (to cite Marsilius of Padua's terminology) as long as the ultimate powers of a *legislator humanus* within a *civitas* or *respublica* remain in the hands of the *populus*, there is no reason to doubt that – as Aristotle had taught – a variety of different constitutional forms may be equally capable of promoting the common good, and hence the peace and happiness of the community as a whole. Some writers within this tradition, such as Marsilius himself, in consequence exhibit little interest in whether a republican or a monarchical regime is established, save only for insisting that if the latter type is chosen, the *pars principans* must always be elected.[84] Others, including François Hotman and other French monarchomachs who followed his lead in the 1570s, remain content to assume that the body of the commonwealth will normally have a monarchical head, and similarly concentrate on hedging the institution of monarchy in such a way as to make it compatible with the liberty and ultimate sovereignty of the people.[85] Still others, such as Locke in his attack on Filmer's absolutism in the *Two Treatises of Government*, suppose there to be good reasons for preferring a monarchical form of government with a liberal allowance of personal prerogative, if only to mitigate the rigours of an undiluted theory of distributive justice by allowing a "power to act according to discretion for the public good."[86]

In common with the defenders of "free states," however, these writers still assume that the apparatus of government in a *civitas* or *respublica* amounts to nothing more than a reflection of, and a device for upholding, the sovereignty of the

people. Even in a theory such as Locke's, government is still viewed simply as a trust established by the members of a community for the more effective promotion of their own good, "the peace, safety and public good of the people" (Locke 1967: 371).

The effect of this commitment, in this tradition no less than in classical republicanism, is that no effective contrast is drawn between the power of the people and the powers of the state.[87] These writers do distinguish, of course, between the apparatus of government and the authority of those who may happen to have control of it at any one time. Just as strongly as the republican theorists, they insist on a complete separation between a ruler's person and his office, and argue that – as Locke puts it – even a supreme magistrate is merely a "public person" who is "vested with the power of the law" and charged with directing the legislative toward the attainment of the common good.[88] They still assume, however, that the range of powers a community establishes over itself when its members consent to become subjects of a civil government must ultimately be identified with its own powers as a community. As Locke (1967: 369, 385) insists, we never "deliver up" our fundamental liberties in establishing a commonwealth, but merely depute or delegate a known and indifferent judge to safeguard them more effectively on our own behalf. Although this means that we commit ourselves to setting up a complex apparatus of government, it also means that the powers of such a government can never amount to anything more than "the joint power of every member of the society." This is how it comes about, as Locke concludes, that "the community perpetually retains a supreme power" over its prince or legislative, "and must, by having deputed him, have still a power to discard him when he fails in his trust" (Locke 1967: 375, 385, 445).

As a result, these writers never find themselves tempted to use the terms *status* or state when describing the powers of civil government. When they envisage the members of a *civitas* or community instituting what Locke (1967: 434) calls a form of umpirage for the settlement of their controversies, they conceive of them not as entering a new state, but simply as setting up a new form of society – a civil or political society within which the wealth or welfare of the community can be better secured. So they continue to invoke the terms *civitas* or *respublica* to refer to the apparatus of civil government, usually translating these terms as "city" or "commonwealth." As Locke (1967: 373) explicitly states, "by commonwealth I must be understood all along" to mean "any independent community which the Latins signified by the word *civitas*, to which the word which best answers in our language is commonwealth."

If we wish, therefore, to trace the process by which the powers of the state finally came to be described as such, and seen at the same time as distinct from both the powers of the people and of their magistrates, we need at this juncture to turn to a strongly contrasting tradition of early-modern political thought. We need to turn to those writers who addressed themselves critically to the thesis of popular sovereignty we have just been considering, whether in its republican guise as a claim about "free states," or in its neoscholastic form as a claim about the inalienable rights of communities. We need to turn, that is, to those theorists whose aspirations included a desire to legitimize the more absolutist forms of government that began to develop in western Europe in the early part of the seventeenth century. It was as a by-product of their arguments, and in particular of their efforts to insist that the powers of government must be something other than a mere expression of the powers of the governed, that the concept of the state as we have inherited it was first articulated with complete self-consciousness.

Some of these counter-revolutionary theorists were mainly concerned with the radical scholastic thesis – associated in particular with Marsilius and his successors – to the effect that the *populus* and the *legislator humanus* can be equated. The repudiation of this doctrine became one of the chief polemical aims of later sixteenth-century Thomism, with Suarez's *De legibus* of 1612 containing the fullest and most influential summary of the alleged counter arguments.[89] Others were more disturbed by the monarchomach theories of popular sovereignty thrown up by the religious wars in the latter part of the sixteenth century. Bodin in particular seeks in his *Six livres de la république* of 1576 to refute the arguments of those who were claiming that, as Knolles's translation of 1606 puts it, "princes sent by providence to the human race must be thrust out of their kingdoms under a pretence of tyranny."[90] Still others were no less perturbed by the implications of the republican allegation that, as Hobbes (1968: 369) scornfully paraphrases it in

Leviathan, "the subjects in a popular commonwealth enjoy liberty," while "in a monarchy they are all slaves." Hobbes himself, like Grotius before him, engages with this as well as with the neoscholastic thesis of popular sovereignty, and undoubtedly offers the most systematic attempt to answer the question that preoccupies all these theorists: how to vindicate an account of civil government which at once concedes the original sovereignty of the people and is at the same time absolutist in its political allegiances.

If there is one thesis by which these writers are all especially agitated, it is the suggestion that the powers of civil government constitute nothing more than a reflection of the powers of the people. They concede, of course, that coercive authority must be justified by its capacity to ensure the common good, and in consequence the peace and happiness of the citizen-body as a whole. Hobbes believes no less firmly than Marsilius that, as he repeatedly declares in *Leviathan*, all governments must be judged by their "aptitude to produce the peace and security of the people, for which end they were instituted."[91] What none of these writers can accept, however, is the idea that the form of authority required to produce such benefits can appropriately be envisaged as nothing more than a trustee, a type of official to whom the people delegate the exercise of their own authority purely as a matter of administrative convenience. Political power, they all admit, is originally instituted by the people, but never in the form of a trust. It is instituted by means of what Suarez calls "absolute transfer" of the people's sovereignty, one that takes the form of "a kind of alienation, not a delegation at all."[92] To set up a mere "depository" or "guardian" of sovereign power, as Bodin agrees, is not to set up a genuine "possessor" of sovereignty at all.[93] For the people to perform that particular act, as Hobbes similarly stresses at several points in *Leviathan*, it is essential for them to recognize that they are "renouncing and transferring" their own original sovereignty, with the implication that it is totally "abandoned or granted away" to someone else (Hobbes 1968: 190, 192).

Civil government, they insist, cannot therefore be seen as the powers of citizens under another guise. It must be seen as a distinct form of power, for reasons that Hobbes enunciates with complete assurance in *De cive* almost a decade before giving them classic expression in *Leviathan*. "Though a government," he declares, "be constituted by the contracts of particular men with particulars, yet its right depends not on that obligation only" (Hobbes 1983: 105). By constituting such a government, "that right which every man had before to use his faculties to his own advantages is now wholly translated on some certain man or council for the common benefit" (Hobbes 1983: 105). It follows that whatever power is thereby installed in authority must be recognized "as having its own rights and properties, insomuch as neither any one citizen, nor all of them together" can now be accounted its equivalent (Hobbes 1983: 89). This, as he was later to put it, "is the generation of that great Leviathan, or rather (to speak more reverently) of that mortal God, to which we owe, under the immortal God, our peace and defence. For by this authority, given him by every particular man in the commonwealth, he hath the use of so much power and strength conferred on him, that by terror thereof, he is enabled to form the wills of them all to peace at home and mutual aid against their enemies abroad" (Hobbes 1968: 227).

It is important, however, not to conflate this form of absolutism with that of the divine-right theorists who rose to such prominence during the same period. A writer like Bossuet, for example, deliberately sets out to obliterate the distinction between the office and person of a king. Echoing the celebrated remark attributed to Louis XIV, he insists that the figure of a ruler "embodies in himself the whole of the state": *tout l'état est en lui*.[94] By contrast, even Hobbes declares as unambiguously as possible that the powers of a ruler are never personal powers at all. They are owed entirely to his standing as holder of "the office of the sovereign," the principal duty of which, as Hobbes never tires of repeating, "consisteth in the end for which he was trusted with the sovereign power, namely the procuration of the safety of the people" (Hobbes 1968: 376).

With Hobbes no less than with Bodin, Suarez, Grotius, and the whole developing tradition of natural-law absolutism, we accordingly arrive at the view that the ends of civil or political association make it indispensable to establish a single and supreme sovereign authority whose power remains distinct not merely from the people who originally instituted it, but also from whatever office-holders may be said to have the right to wield its power at any particular time. What, then, is this form of political authority to be called?

Not surprisingly, these writers at first respond by reaching for traditional names. One suggestion, much canvassed by Bodin and later adopted by Hobbes in *De cive*, was that we should think of the authority in question as embodied in the *civitas*, the *ville* or the city as opposed to either its citizens or its magistrates.[95] But the most usual proposal was that we should think of it as that form of authority which inheres in the *respublica*, the *république* or the commonwealth. Suarez and Grotius, writing in Latin, both speak of the *respublica*.[96] Bodin, writing originally in French, speaks analogously of *la république*; translating his treatise into Latin in 1586, he rendered this as *respublica*; and when Knolles issued his English version in 1606, he in turn called the work *The Six Bookes of a Commonweale*.[97] Finally, Hobbes largely comes round to this terminology in *Leviathan*, speaking far less frequently of the city, and instead describing his work on its title-page as an enquiry into "the matter, form and power of a commonwealth" (Hobbes 1968: 73).

As these writers increasingly recognized, however, none of these traditional terms really served to render their meaning adequately. One obvious difficulty with "commonwealth" was the fact that, as Raleigh (1661: 3,8) complains in his *Maxims of State*, it had come to be used "by an usurped nickname" to refer to "the government of the whole multitude." To invoke it was thus to risk confusion with one of the theories of popular sovereignty they were most anxious to repudiate. Nor was it altogether satisfactory to speak instead of the city or *civitas*. It is true that Hobbes (1983: 89) consistently does so in *De cive*, declaring that "a city therefore (that we may define it) is one person whose will, by the compact of many men, is to be received for the will of them all." But the obvious difficulty here – in the face of which even Hobbes's confidence seems to have evaporated – was the need to insist on such a purely stipulative definition so strangely at variance with the ordinary meaning of the term.

It was at this juncture, within this tradition of thought, that a number of these theorists began to resolve their difficulties by speaking instead of the *state*, while making it clear at the same time that they were consciously using the term to express their master concept of an impersonal form of political authority distinct from both rulers and ruled.

Bodin already hints at this final crystallizing of the concept at several points in his *République*.[98]

Although he continues to write in traditional terms about rulers "who maintain their *estats*," he also uses the word *estat* on several occasions as a synonym for *république*.[99] Most significantly of all, he feels able to speak of "the state in itself" (*l'estat en soi*), describing it both as a form of authority independent of particular types of government, and as the locus of "indivisible and incommunicable sovereignty."[100] It is striking, moreover, that when Knolles came to translate these passages in 1606, he not only used the word "state" in all these instances, but also in a number of other places where Bodin himself had continued to speak in a more familiar vein of the authority of the *cité* or *république*.[101]

If we turn to English writers of the next generation, and above all to those "politic" humanists who were critical of classical republicanism, we find the same terminology used with increasing confidence. Raleigh, for example, not only speaks freely of the state in his *Maxims*, but makes it clear that he thinks of the state as an impersonal form of political authority, defining it as "the frame or set order of a commonwealth" (Raleigh 1661: 2). Bacon (1972: 89) writes in the final version of his *Essays* in a way that often suggests a similar understanding of political authority. He describes rulers as well as their councillors as having a duty to consider "the weal and advancement of the state which they serve." And he writes in a number of other passages about the state and its rulers, the state and its subjects, the "founders of states" and the "subversion of states and governments" (Bacon 1972: 11, 42, 160, 165).

It is above all in Hobbes, however, and in other theorists of *de facto* sovereignty in the English revolution, that we find this new understanding of the state being articulated with complete assurance. It is true, as we have seen, that if we turn to the body of Hobbes's texts, we still find him exhibiting a preference for the traditional terminology of "city" and "commonwealth." But if we turn instead to his Prefaces, in the course of which he stands back from his own arguments and reviews their structure, we find him self-consciously presenting himself as a theorist of the state.

This transition can already be observed in the Preface to *De cive*, in the course of which he describes his project as that of explaining "what the quality of human nature is, in what matters it is, in what not, fit to make up a civil government, and how men must be agreed among themselves,

that intend to grow up into a well-grounded state" (Hobbes 1983: 22). But it is in the Introduction to *Leviathan* that he proclaims most unequivocally that the subject matter of his entire investigation has been "that great Leviathan, called a Commonwealth or State (in Latin Civitas)" (Hobbes 1968: 81). Hobbes's ambition as a political theorist had always been to demonstrate that, if there is to be any prospect of attaining civil peace, the fullest powers of sovereignty must be vested neither in the people nor in their rulers, but always in the figure of an "artificial man."[102] Surveying this final redaction of his political philosophy, he at last felt able to add that, in speaking about the need for such an impersonal form of sovereignty, what he had been speaking about all along could best be described as the state.

VI

As the above account suggests, the idea that the supreme authority within a body politic should be identified as the authority of the state was originally the outcome of one particular theory of politics, a theory at once absolutist and secular-minded in its ideological allegiances. That theory was in turn the product of the earliest major counter-revolutionary movement within modern European history, the movement of reaction against the ideologies of popular sovereignty developed in the course of the French religious wars, and, subsequently, in the English Revolution of the seventeenth century. It is perhaps not surprising, therefore, to find that both the ideology of state power and the new terminology employed to express it provoked a series of doubts and criticisms that have never been altogether stilled.

Some of the initial hostility derived from conservative theorists anxious to uphold the old ideal of *un roi, une foi, une loi*. They wished to repudiate any suggestion that the aims of public authority should be purely civil or political in character, and thereby to reinstate a closer relationship between allegiance in church and state. But much of the hostility stemmed from those who wished to uphold a more radical ideal of popular sovereignty in place of the sovereignty of the state. Contractarian writers sought in consequence to keep alive a preference for speaking about the government of civil or political society,[103] while the so-called commonwealthmen maintained their loyalty to the classical ideal of the self-governing republic throughout much of the eighteenth century.[104]

It is true that, at the end of the century, a renewed counter-revolutionary effort was made to neutralize these various populist doubts. Hegel and his followers in particular argued that the English contractarian theory of popular sovereignty merely reflected a failure to distinguish the powers of civil society from those of the state, and a consequent failure to recognize that the independent authority of the state is indispensable if the purposes of civil society are to be fulfilled. But this hardly proved an adequate reassurance. On the one hand, the anxiety of liberal theorists about the relationship between the powers of states and the sovereignty of their citizens generated confusions which have yet to be resolved. And on the other hand, a deeper criticism developed out of these Hegelian roots, insisting that the state's vaunted independence from its own agents as well as from the members of civil society amounts to nothing more than a fraud. As a result, sceptics in the tradition of Michels and Pareto, no less than socialists in the tradition of Marx, have never ceased to insist that modern states are in truth nothing more than the executive arms of their own ruling class.

Given the importance of these rival ideologies and their distinctive vocabularies, it is all the more remarkable to observe how quickly the term "state" and its equivalents nevertheless became established at the heart of political discourse throughout western Europe. By the middle of the eighteenth century the new terminology had become virtually inescapable for all schools of thought. Even so nostalgic an exponent of classical republicanism as Bolingbroke found himself constrained in his pamphleteering of the 1720s to talk about the authority of the state, and about the need for the state to be supported, protected, and above all reformed (1967a: 19, 43, 93, 131). By the time we come to Hume's essays of the 1750s,[105] or Rousseau's *Contrat social* of a decade later,[106] we find the concept of the state and the terms *état* and *state* being put to work in a consistent and completely familiar way.

The immediate outcome of this conceptual revolution was to set up a series of reverberations in the wider political vocabularies of the western European states. Once "state" came to be accepted as the master noun of political argu-ment, a number of other concepts and assumptions bearing on the analysis of sovereignty had to be reorganized or in some cases given up. To complete this survey, we need finally to examine the process of displacement and redefinition that accompanied the entrenchment of the modern idea of the state.

One concept that underwent a process of redefinition was that of political allegiance. A subject or *subditus* had traditionally sworn allegiance to his sovereign as liege lord. But with the acceptance of the idea that sovereignty is lodged not with rulers but with the state, this was replaced by the familiar view that citizens owe their basic loyalty to the state itself.

This is not to say that those who originally advanced this argument had any desire to give up speaking of citizens as *subditi* or subjects. On the contrary, the earliest theorists of the state retained a strong preference for this traditional terminology, using it as a means of countering both the contractarian inclination to speak instead about the sovereignty of the *populus* or people, and the classical republican contention that we ought to speak only of *civitates* and *cives*, of cities and their citizens. Hobbes, for example, with his usual cunning, maintains in the first published version of his political theory that he is writing specifically "about the citizen" – *de cive*. Yet he makes it one of his most important polemical claims that "each citizen, as also every subordinate civil person" ought properly to regard himself as "the subject of him who hath the chief command" (Hobbes 1983: 90).

Hobbes is in complete agreement with his radical opponents, however, when he goes on to argue that citizens ("that is to say, subjects") ought not to pay allegiance to those who exercise these rights of sovereignty, but rather to the sovereignty inherent in the state or commonwealth itself (Hobbes 1983: 151). Hotman and later "monarchomach" theorists had already insisted that even holders of offices under a monarchy must be viewed as councillors of the kingdom, not of the king, and as servants of the crown, not of the person wearing it.[107] Hobbes simply reiterates the same argument when he declares with so much emphasis in *De cive* that the "absolute and universal obedience" owed by each and every subject is due not to the person of their ruler, but rather "to the city, that is to say, to the sovereign power" (Hobbes 1983: 186).

A further and closely connected concept that

was comparably transformed was that of treason. As long as the concept of allegiance was connected with that of doing homage, the crime of treason remained that of behaving treacherously towards a sovereign lord. By the end of the sixteenth century, however, this came to seem less and less satisfactory. Even in the case of England, still bound by the Statute of 1350 which defined treason as compassing or imagining the king's death, the judges began to place increasingly wide constructions upon the meaning of the original Act. The aim in almost every case was to establish a view of treason essentially as an offence against the king in virtue of his office as head of state.[108] Meanwhile the political writers of the same period, untrammeled by the need to wrestle with precedents, had already arrived by a more direct route at the familiar view of treason as a crime not against the king but against the state. As always, Hobbes states the new understanding of the concept most unequivocally. As he declares at the end of his analysis of dominion in *De cive*, those who are guilty of treason are those who refuse to perform the duties "without which the State cannot stand"; the crime of treason is the crime of those who act "as enemies to the Government" (Hobbes 1983: 181).

Finally, the acceptance of the state as both a supreme and an impersonal form of authority brought with it a displacement of the more charismatic elements of political leadership which, as I indicated at the outset, had earlier been of central importance to the theory and practice of government throughout western Europe.

Among the assumptions that suffered displacement, the most important was the claim I began by stressing: that sovereignty is conceptually connected with display, that majesty serves in itself as an ordering force. Machiavelli, for example, still assumes that a ruler can expect to derive protection from *la maestá dello stato*, from a connection between his own high state of stateliness and his capacity to maintain his state.[109] It proved impossible, however, for such beliefs about the charisma attaching to public authority to survive the transfer of that authority to the purely impersonal agency – the "purely moral person," in Rousseau's phrase[110] – of the modern state. By the start of the eighteenth century, we already find conservative writers lamenting that, as Bolingbroke (1967b: 333) puts it, "the state is become, under ancient and known forms, an undefinable monster," with the result that a

monarchy like England finds itself left with "a king without monarchical splendour" as head of state.

It was of course possible to transfer these attributes of majesty to the state's agents, permitting them to conduct state openings of parliament, to be granted state funerals, to lie in state, and so forth. Once it became accepted, however, that even heads of state are simply holders of offices, the attribution of so much pomp and circumstance to mere functionaries came to be seen not merely as inappropriate but even absurd, a case not of genuine pomp but of sheer pomposity. This insight was first elaborated by the defenders of "free commonwealths" in their anxiety to insist that, in Milton's phrase, rulers should never be "elevated above their brethren" but should "walk the streets as other men" (1980: 425). More's *Utopia*, for example, contains an early and devastating portrayal of public magnificence as nothing more than a form of childish vanity (1965: 152–6). Ponet's *Politic Power* includes a more minatory reminder of the punishments God visited upon the Israelites for demanding "a gallant and pompous king" (1942: 87). And Milton in *The Ready and Easy Way* condemns with deep disdain those rulers who aspire "to set a pompous face upon the superficial actings of state" (1980: 426).

One outcome of distinguishing the authority of the state from that of its agents was thus to sever a time-honoured connection between the presence of majesty and the exercise of majestic powers. Displays of stateliness eventually came to be seen as mere "shows" or "trappings" of power, not as features intrinsic to the workings of power itself.[111] When Contarini concedes, for example, that the Doge of Venice is permitted to uphold the dignity of his office with a certain magnificence, he emphasizes that this is just a matter of appearances, and uses a phrase that Lewkenor translates by saying that the Doge is allowed a "royal appearing show."[112] Speaking with much greater hostility, Milton (1980: 426, 429) agrees that a monarch "sits only like a great cypher," with all his "vanity and ostentation" being completely inessential to the ordering force of public authority.

Finally, for the most self-conscious rejection of the older images of power, as well as the most unambiguous view of the state as a purely impersonal authority, we need to turn once more to Hobbes. Discussing these concepts in chapter 10 of *Leviathan*, Hobbes deploys the idea of an effective power to command in such a way as to absorb every other element traditionally associated with the notions of public honor and dignity. To hold dignities, he declares, is simply to hold "offices of command"; to be held honorable is nothing more

than "an argument and sign of power" (Hobbes 1968: 152, 155). Here, as throughout, it is Hobbes who first speaks, systematically and unapologetically, in the abstract and unmodulated tones of the modern theorist of the state.

Notes

1   Hobbes (1983: 32). *De cive* was first published in Latin in 1642, in English in 1651. See Warrender (1983: 1). Warrender argues that the translation is at least mainly Hobbes's own work (1983: 4–8). But this is disputed by Tuck (1985: 310–12). Note that, in this as in most other quotations from primary sources, I have modernized spelling and punctuation.

2   On "the state as an abstract entity," and the political transformations that underlay the emergence of the concept, see further in Shennan (1974); and cf. Maravall (1961).

3   See Hexter (1973: 155) on "the first of its medieval political meanings."

4   Mommsen (1970, 1.5.2: 35): "Cum igitur hominum causa omne ius constitutum sit, primo de personarum statu ac post de ceteris . . . dicemus."

5   For example, see Post (1964: 333–67, 368–414).

6   Froissart (1972: 116): "La [sc. the queen] peut on veoir de l'estat grand noblece."

7   For a comparison between those systems of state power in which "the ordering force of display" is proclaimed, and those in which (as in the modern West) it is deliberately obscured, see Geertz (1980: 121–3), whose formulation I have adopted.

8   See Ercole (1926: 67–8). Hexter (1973: 115) similarly notes that *status* acquired this "second political meaning during the middle ages." Cf. Rubinstein (1971: 314–15), who begins his analysis by discussing this stage.

9   See for example Livy (1962, 30.2.8: 372; 1966, 23.24.2: 78); Sallust (1921, 40.2: 68); Cicero (1913, 2.1.3: 170).

10 Mommsen (1970, I.1.2: 29): "publicum ius est quod ad statum rei Romani spectat." Ercole (1926: 69) emphasizes the importance of this passage.

11 Froissart (1824–6, vol. XII: 93): "Le roi . . . réforma le pays en bon état tant que tous s'en contentèrent."

12 Petition from the abbey of Syon in Shadwell (1912, vol. I: 64). Cf. also vol. I: 66; I: 82, etc.

13 For a survey of this literature see Hertter (1910).

14 Sorbelli (1944) discusses this claim, originally put forward by Muratori; Sorbelli prefers a date in the 1240s.

15 See Franceschi (1966: 26, 27, 28, etc.).

16 Giovanni da Viterbo (1901: 230–2, etc.).

17 For a discussion of the date of composition see Sorbelli (1944).

18 See Ercole (1926: 67–8) and the similar discussions in Post (1964: 18–24, 310–32, 377–81), Rubinstein (1971: 314–16), and Mansfield (1983: 851–2).

19 There are references to the *optimus status reipublicae* in Cicero (1914, 5.4.11: 402 and 1927, 2.11.27: 174), and to the *optimus civitatis status* in Seneca (1964, 2.20.2: 92).

20 See Franceschi (1966: 26) on the need to act "ad . . . comodum ac felicem statum civitatis" and p. 28: "ad honorabilem et prosperum statum huius comunitatis."

21 See Giovanni da Viterbo (1901: 230) on the "bonus status totius communis huius civitatis."

22 Note that they begin to discuss this issue nearly a century earlier than such chroniclers as Giovanni Villani, one of the earliest sources usually cited in this context. See Ercole (1926: 67–8), Hexter (1973: 155), and Rubinstein (1971: 314–16). For Villani on the "buono et pacifico stato" see Villani (1802–3, vol. III: 159; vol. IV: 3, etc.).

23 Aquinas (1963, I.II.19.10: 104): "Nam iudex habet curam boni communis, quod est iustitia, et ideo vult occisionem latronis, quae habet rationem boni secundum relationem ad statum commune."

24 See Giovanni da Viterbo (1901: 220–2) on the attributes and policies to be demanded of an elected *rector*, and cf. Latini (1948: 402–5), paraphrasing Giovanni's account.

25 Note that, in providing dates for the more obscure humanists, I have taken my information from Consenza (1962).

26 Campano (1502, fo. xxxxvii^r): "nihil existimem a statu et salute reipublicae alienius."

27 Beroaldo (1508, fo. xv^v): "oblitis suorum ipsius commodorum ad utilitatem publicam quicquid agit debet referre."

28 Erasmus (1974: 194): "felicissimus est status, cum principi paretur ab omnibus atque ipse princeps paret legibus, leges autem ad archetypum aequi et honesti respondent."

29 Cf. Kantorowicz (1957, esp. pp. 207–32, 268–72), Post (1964, esp. pp. 247–53, 302–9), Strayer (1970, esp. pp. 57–9), and Wahl (1977: 80). By contrast, see Ullmann (1968–9, esp. pp. 43–4) on traditional legal concepts as an obstacle to the emergence of the concept of the state.

30 Note how loftily Hotman still speaks of such usages in his *Francogallia* as late as the 1570s. Writing about the Public Council, he observes that

its powers extend "to all those matters which the common people in vulgar parlance nowadays call Affairs of State" ("de iis rebus omnibus, quae vulgus etiam nunc Negotia Statuum populari verbo appellat") (1972: 332).

31 For the thesis that "*stato*, meaning a State, derives in the main . . . from *lo stato del principe*, meaning the status or estate of an effectively sovereign prince," see Dowdall (1923: 102). Cf. also Skinner (1978, vol. II: 352–8).

32 On this development see Waley (1978: 83–330).

33 On this "moment" see Pocock (1975: 83–330). Cf. also Skinner (1978, vol. I: 139–89).

34 On the *pater patriae*, see for example Beroaldo (1508, fos. xiv^r and xv^r) and Scala (1940: 256–8, 273).

35 Petrarch already states these twin ideals (1554: 420–1, 428). They become standard during the *quattrocento*, even recurring in Machiavelli's *Il principe* (1960: 102).

36 Villani (1802–3, vol. IV: 24). Cf. also vol. IV: 190–4.

37 For these phrases see Machiavelli (1960: 16, 19, 22, 25–6, 27, 28, 35, etc.).

38 Rubinstein (1971) similarly analyzes some of these extended usages. While I have avoided duplicating his examples, I am much indebted to his account.

39 See Aquinas (1966: 136–7, 139–40, 310–11, 319–21, 328–30). Rubinstein (1971: 322) credits Aquinas with popularizing these usages. But they were largely the product of the humanist revision of his text issued in 1492. See Mansfield (1983: 851), and cf. Cranz (1978: 169–73) for a full account.

40 See for example Machiavelli (1960: 28 and 29) on the *stato di pochi*.

41 Machiavelli (1960: 15): "Tutti li stati, tutti e'- dominii che hanno avuto et hanno imperio sopra li uomini sono stati e sono o republiche o principati."

42 Villani (1802–3, vol. IV: 190–1). Cf. also vol. IV: 25; vol. VIII: 186.

43 Vettori (1842: 432, 436). Rubinstein (1971: 318) notes that these were already standard usages in late *quattrocento* Florence.

44 The verses are reproduced in Rowley (1958, vol. I: 127).

45 Budé (1966: 140). Although Budé's *Institution* was not published until 1547, it was completed by the start of 1519. See Delaruelle (1907: 201).

46 Vespasiano (1970–6, vol. I: 177, 192). On the latter passage see also Rubinstein (1971: 318).

47 Guicciardini (1933: 287, 293). Note that Guicciardini – though not Machiavelli – also speaks explicitly of *ragione di stato*. See Maffei (1964, esp. pp. 712–20). For the subsequent history of that concept in *cinquecento* Italy, see Meinecke (1957, esp. pp. 65–145).

48 Castiglione (1960: 10, 117–18). For other *cinquecento* uses see Chabod (1962, esp. pp. 153–73).

49 See Post (1964, esp. pp. viii, 247–53, 302–9, 494–8 and pp. 269, 333) for alleged "anticipations" of Machiavelli's thought. Cf. also Kantorowicz (1957, esp. pp. 207–32) on "polity-centered kingship."

50 Chiappelli (1952: 68). Cf. also Cassirer (1946: 133–7), Chabod (1962: 146–55), D'Entrèves (1967: 30–2).

51 It is important to emphasize, however, that in the cases cited in nn. 46 to 48, as in the case of Machiavelli, it would arguably be no less of an overstatement to insist that these are all unequivocally traditional usages. In the retreat from the type of overstatements cited in n. 50, this point seems in danger of being lost. Hexter in particular irons out a number of ambiguities that ought to be admitted (1973, esp. pp. 164–7 and cf. the corrective in Gilbert [1965, 329–30]). Mansfield (1983: 853) similarly concludes that we do not find anywhere in Machiavelli's writings "an instance of the impersonal modern state among his uses of *stato*." If by this he means that Machiavelli cannot unambiguously be said to express that concept, this is undoubtedly correct. My only objection is that there are several ambiguous passages; the history of the acquisition of the concept cannot be divided into such watertight compartments.

52 See Post (1964: 334), on *status* being used to stress that the king "was not only the indispensable ruler but also the essence of the territorial State which he ruled."

53 For this revival, see below, n. 94. Post claims that the medieval sources he discusses "anticipated the idea" of "l'état, c'est moi" (1964: 269; and cf. also pp. 333–5). But when this remark was uttered in seventeenth-century France (if it ever was) it was by then blankly paradoxical, and this would have been the point of uttering it. On this point see Mansfield (1983: 849) and cf. Rowen (1961) on Louis XIV as "proprietor of the state."

54 See Machiavelli (1960: 16, 47, 87, 95). Cf. on this point Mansfield (1983: 852).

55 In England this demand (and this phrase) can be found as late as early-Stuart arguments over royal revenues. See for example the parliamentary debate of 1610 quoted in Tanner (1930: 359).

56 Even in France, the country in which, after Italy, traditional assumptions about the *status* of princes first changed, this arguably remains true until the 1570s. On this point see below, section V, and cf. Lloyd (1983: 146–53). In Spain the old assumptions appear to have survived until at least the middle of the seventeenth century, *pace* Maravall (1961). See Elliot (1984: 42–5, 121–2). In Germany a purely patrimonial concept of government appears to have survived even longer. See the comments in Shennan (1974: 113–14).

57 See Calasso (1957: 83–123), and Wahl (1977). For analogous reinterpretations of the Decretals, see

Mochi Onory (1951). For a survey see Tierney (1982).

58 See Bartolus (1562, 47.22: 779) on the "civitates Tusciae, quae non recognoscunt de facto in temporalibus superiorem."

59 Giovanni da Viterbo (1901: 266): "in alterius messem falcem suam mittere."

60 This is, for example, the main thesis of Baron (1966).

61 For this assumption in *trecento* Florentine diplomacy, see Rubinstein (1952).

62 Contarini (1626: 22 and 56): "temperandam . . . ex optimatum et populari statu . . . nihil minus urbi Venetae timendum sit, quam principem reipublicae libertati ullum unquam negocium facessere posse." On Contarini see Pocock (1975: 320–8).

63 Machiavelli (1960, II.2: 280): "E facil cosa è conoscere donde nasca ne' popoli questa affezione del vivere libero: perché si vede per esperienza le cittadi non avere mai ampliato né di dominio né di ricchezza se non mentre sono state in libertà."

64 Machiavelli (1960, II.11: 280): "La ragione è facile a intendere: perché non il bene particulare ma il bene comune è quello che fa grandi le città. E sanza dubbio questo bene comune non è osservato se non nelle republiche."

65 See Latini (1948: 391) on "politique . . . la plus noble et la plus haute science."

66 Latini (1948: 403) on "l'estat de vous et de cette ville." Cf. p. 411 on the idea of remaining "en bon estat."

67 Giovanni da Vignano (1974: 247): "che il nostro bom stato porà remanere in largheça, honore, grandeça e reponso."

68 Matteo dei Libri (1974: 12): "ke 'l nostro bon stato potrà romanire in reposo."

69 See Contarini (1626, at pp. 28 and 46), two cases where, in Lewkenor (1969), *respublica* is rendered as "state." On Lewkenor's translation see Fink (1962: 41–2).

70 Patrizi (1594: 281) on the duty to uphold "veteres leges" and act "pro communi utilitate."

71 Patrizi (1594a: 292 and 279) on how to act "ne civitatis status evertatur" and "statum reipublicae everterunt."

72 Guicciardini (1932: 271–2): "ogni stato ed ogni potenzia eminente ha bisogno delle dependenzie . . . che tutti servirebbono a beneficio dello stato." Cf. also pp. 276, 279.

73 Guicciardini (1932: 273): "uno barbacane e fondamento potentissimo a difesa dello stato."

74 See for example Machiavelli (1960, I.2: 130–2, and also pp. 182, 272, 357, etc.).

75 See in particular Machiavelli (1960, II.24: 351–3).

76 Machiavelli (1960, I.2: 133): "Licurgo . . . fece uno stato che durò più che ottocento anni."

77 Machiavelli (1960, I.6: 141): "se in Roma is poteva ordinare uno stato . . ."

78 Machiavelli (1960, I.18: 180): "le leggi dipoi che con i magistrati frenavano i cittadini."

79 Ibid.: "l'ordine del governo o vero dello stato."

80 See Fink (1962: 10–20, 56–68); Raab (1964: 185–217); Pocock (1975: 333–422); Haitsma Mulier (1980: 26–76).

81 I see no justification for the claim that Starkey merely "dressed up" his *Dialogue* in civic humanist terms. See Mayer (1985: 25) and cf. Skinner (1978, vol. I: 213–42) for an attempt to place Starkey's ideas in a humanist context.

82 A point emphasized by Shennan (1974: 9, 113–14) and Mansfield (1983: 849–50).

83 See Harrington (1977: 173) for the claim that "the interest of the commonwealth is in the whole body of the people," and his invariable preference, in the "Preliminaries" to *Oceana* for speaking of "the city" or "commonwealth" as the locus of political authority. See also pp. 161, 170, 171–2, 182–3.

84 Marsilius of Padua (1956, I.8 and 9: 27–34). For the special significance of Marsilius within this tradition of thought see Condren (1985: 262–9).

85 See esp. Hotman (1972: 287–321), where he lays out his view of the French constitution as a mixed monarchy.

86 Locke (1967: 393). On Locke's *Two Treatises* essentially as an attack on Filmerian absolutism, see Laslett (1967: 50–2, 67–78) and cf. Dunn (1969: 47–57, 58–76, 87–95). On the place of this concept in Locke's theory see Dunn (1969: 148–56).

87 Howell (1983: 155), while agreeing that this is true of Hotman, argues that two other "monarchomach" theorists – Beza and the author of the *Vindiciae contra tyrannos* – "implied the existence of the secular state as an entity distinct from ruler and people." I cannot see that either writer distinguished the powers of the state from those of the people. Cf. Skinner (1978, vol. II: 318–48).

88 Locke (1967: 386). Cf. also pp. 301, 360–1, 371, 381 for the idea of rulers as mere trustees. See also Hotman (1972: 154 and 402–4) on kings as magistrates "tied" by the duties of their office.

89 On this school of thought see Hamilton (1963) and Fernandez–Santamaria (1977). On the character of their natural-law (as opposed to divine-right) theories of absolutism see Sommerville (1982 and 1986: 59–80). For a contrast with later theories of popular sovereignty see Tully (1980: 64–8 and 111–16).

90 See Bodin (1962: A71). For Bodin's concern to refute the "monarchomachs" see Franklin (1973, esp. pp. vii. 50, 93) and Salmon (1973, esp. pp. 361, 364).

91 Hobbes (1968: 241). Cf. also pp. 192, 223, 237, etc.

92 Suarez (1612: 210): "Quocirca translatio huius potestatis a republica in principem non est delegatio, sed quasi alienatio . . . simpliciter illi conceditur."

93 Bodin (1576: 125) distinguishes between "pos-

sesseurs" of sovereignty and those who "ne sont que depositaires et gardes de cette puissance."

94 Bossuet (1967: 177). On this variety of absolutism see Keohane (1980: 241–61) and Sommerville (1986: 9–50).

95 See Bodin (1576: 9 *et passim*) on the "ville" and "cité." Cf. Hobbes (1983: 89–90 *et passim*) for the concept of "a city or civil society."

96 See Suarez (1612: 351–60) on the relations between the *princeps, leges* and *respublica*, and cf. Grotius (1625: 65) on *civitas* and *respublica* and p. 84 on the *romana respublica*.

97 Cf. the full titles of Bodin (1576), Bodin (1586), and Bodin (1962).

98 See Lloyd (1983: 156–62). Fell (1983, esp. pp. 92–107, 175–205) lays all his emphasis on Bodin's contemporary Corasius, though without investigating the extent to which he used the term *status* to express his concept of "the legislative state." But by the next generation the use of the vernacular term *état* (or *estat*) to express such a concept had become well entrenched in France. See Church (1972: 13–80) and Keohane (1980: 54–82, 119–82). Dowdall (1923: 118) singles out Loyseau's discussion in his *Traité des seigneuries* (1608) of the relationship between "seigneuries souveraines" and "estats" as being of particular importance, and this point has been much developed. See Church (1972: 33–4) and Lloyd (1981 and 1983: 162–8).

99 Bodin (1576, e.g. at pp. 219, 438).

100 Bodin (1576: 282–3): "Et combien que le gouvernement d'une Republique soit plus ou moins populaire, ou Aristocratique, ou Royale, si est-que l'estat en soi ne reçoit compairison de plus ni de moins: car toujours la souveraineté indivisible et incommunicable est à un seul." Note also Bodin's use of the phrase "en matière d'estat" (1576: 281,

414).

101 See Bodin (1962: 184, 250, 451) and cf. pp. 10, 38, 409, 700 for some additional uses of "state."

102 Hobbes (1968: 82) states that the aim of *Leviathan* is "to describe the nature of this artificial man."

103 Benjamin Hoadly, for example, continues to speak about "the civil power," "civil government" and "the power of the civil magistrate" rather than about the state. See "The Original and Institution of Civil Government, Discussed" in Hoadly (1773, vol. II: 189, 191, 201, 203 *et passim*).

104 See the usages in Robbins (1959: 125, 283) and cf. Kramnick (1968, esp. pp. 236–60) and Pocock (1975, esp. pp. 423–505).

105 Hume's main discussions of state power occur in his essays "Of Commerce" and "That Politics may be Reduced to a Science." See Hume (1875, vol. I: 100, 105 and 289, 294–5).

106 See Rousseau (1966, "De l'état civil", pp. 55 6). On "état" in the political vocabulary of Rousseau and his contemporaries see Derathé (1950: 380–2) and Keohane (1980, esp. pp. 442–9).

107 See Hotman (1972, e.g. pp. 254, 298, 402).

108 On this process see Holdsworth (1925: 307–33).

109 Machiavelli (1960: 74, and cf. also pp. 76, 93). The same applies even more strongly to Machiavelli's contemporaries among "mirror-for-princes" writers. See for example Pontano (1952: 1054–6), Sacchi (1608: 68).

110 Rousseau (1966: 54) on "la personne morale qui constitue l'Etat."

111 On the distinctiveness of this conception of public power see Geertz (1980: 121–3).

112 See Lewkenor (1969: 42), translating "specie regia" from Contarini (1626: 56). For invaluable help with earlier drafts I am greatly indebted to John Dunn and Susan James.

References

Aquinas, St. Thomas. 1963. *Summa theologiae*, 3 vols., edited by P. Caramello. Turin: Marietti.
——1966. *In octo libros politicorum Aristotelis expositio*, edited by R. Spiazzi. Turin: Marietti.
Bacon, F. 1972. *Essays*, edited by M. Hawkins. London: Dent.
Baron, H. 1966. *The Crisis of the Early Italian Renaissance*, 2nd edn. Princeton, NJ: Princeton University Press.
Bartolus of Sassoferrato. 1562. *Digestum novum commentaria*. Basel.
Beroaldo, F. 1508. "Libellus de optimo statu." In *Opuscula*. Venice, fos. x–xxxiiii.
Bodin, J. 1576. *Les Six Livres de la république*. Paris.
——1586. *De republica libri sex*. Paris.
——1962. *The Six Books of a Commonweale*, translated by R. Knolles and edited by K. McRae. Cambridge, MA: Harvard University Press.
Bolingbroke, Lord. 1967a. "A Dissertation upon Parties." In *The Works*, 4 vols., vol II. London: F. Cass, pp. 5–172.
——1967b. "Letters on the Study and Use of History." In *The Works*, 4 vols., vol. II. London. F. Cass, pp. 173–334.
Bossuet, J.-B. 1967. *Politique tirée des propres paroles de l'Ecriture Sainte*, edited by J. Le Brun. Geneva: Droz.
Budé, G. 1966. *De l'institution du prince*. Farnborough: Gregg.
Burke, E. 1910. *Reflections on the Revolution in France*, Everyman edn. London: Dent.

Calasso, F. 1957. *I Glossatori e la teoria della sovranitá*. Milan: Giuffrè.

Campano, G. 1502. "De regendo magistratu." In *Opera omnia*. Venice, fos. xxxxiii–xxxxviii.

Cassirer, E. 1946. *The Myth of the State*. New Haven, CT: Yale University Press.

Castiglione, B. 1960. *Il libro del cortegiano*. In *Opere*, edited by C. Cordié. Milan: R. Ricciardi, pp. 5–361.

Chabod, F. 1962. *L'idea di nazione*, 2nd edn. Bari: G. Laterza.

Chiappelli, F. 1952. *Studi sul linguaggio del Machiavelli*. Florence: F. Le Monnier.

Church, W. 1972. *Richelieu and Reason of State*. Princeton, NJ: Princeton University Press.

Cicero, 1913. *De officiis*, translated by W. Miller. London: Heinemann.

——1914. *De Finibus*, translated by H. Rackham. London: Heinemann.

——1927. *Tusculanae Disputationes*, translated by J. King. London: Heinemann.

Condren, C. 1985. *The Status and Appraisal of Classical Texts*. Princeton, NJ: Princeton University Press.

Contarini, G. 1626. *De republica Venetorum*. Lyons.

Cosenza, M. 1962. *Biographical and Bibliographical Dictionary of the Italian Humanists*, vol. V: *Synopsis and Bibliography*. Boston, MA: G.K. Hall.

Cranz, F. 1978. "The Publishing History of the Aristotle Commentaries of Thomas Aquinas." *Traditio* 34: 157–92.

Dante Alighieri. 1966. *Inferno*, edited by G. Petrocchi. Milan: A. Mondadori.

Delaruelle, L. 1907. *Guillaume Budé*. Paris: H. Champion.

D'Entrèves, A. 1967. *The Notion of the State*. Oxford: Oxford University Press.

Derathé, R. 1950. *Jean-Jacques Rousseau et la science politique de son temps*. Paris: Presses Universitaires de France.

Dowdall, H. 1923. "The Word 'State.'" *The Law Quarterly Review* 39: 98–125.

Dunn, J. 1969. *The Political Thought of John Locke*. Cambridge: Cambridge University Press.

Elliott, J. 1984. *Richelieu and Olivares*. Cambridge: Cambridge University Press.

Erasmus, D. 1974. *Institutio christiani principis*, edited by O. Herding. In *Opera omnia*, part IV, vol. I. Amsterdam: North-Holland, pp. 95–219.

Ercole, F. 1926. *La politica di Machiavelli*. Rome: Anonima Romana Editoriale.

Fell, A. 1983. *Origins of Legislative Sovereignty and the Legislative State*, vol. I. Cambridge, MA: Atheneum.

Fernandez–Santamaria, J.A. 1977. *The State, War and Peace*. Cambridge: Cambridge University Press.

Fink, Z. 1962. *The Classical Republicans*, 2nd edn. Evanston, IL: Northwestern University Press.

Franceschi, E. 1966. "Oculus pastoralis." *Memorie dell' accademia delle scienze di Torino* 11: 19–70.

Franklin, J. 1973. *Jean Bodin and the Rise of Absolutist Theory*. Cambridge: Cambridge University Press.

Froissart, J. 1824–6. *Chroniques*, 14 vols., edited by J. Buchon. Paris: Vordière, J. Carez.

——1972. *Chroniques: début du premier libre*, edited by G. Diller. Geneva: Droz.

Geertz, C. 1980. *Negara*. Princeton, NJ: Princeton University Press.

Giannardi, G. 1942. "Le 'Dicerie' di Filippo Ceffi." *Studi di filologia italiana* 6: 27–63.

Gilbert, F. 1965. *Machiavelli and Guicciardini*. Princeton, NJ: Princeton University Press.

Giovanni da Vignano. 1974. *Flore de parlare*. In Matteo dei Libri, *Arringhe*, edited by E. Vincenti. Milan: R. Ricciardi, pp. 229–325.

Giovanni da Viterbo. 1901. *Liber de regimine civitatum*, edited by C. Salvemini. In *Bibliotheca iuridica medii aevi*, 3 vols., edited by A. Gaudenzi, vol. III. Bologna: Società Azzoguidiana, pp. 215–80.

Grotius, H. 1625. *De iure belli ac pacis*. Paris.

Guicciardini, F. 1932. *Dialogo e discorsi del reggimento di Firenze*, edited by R. Palmarocchi. Bari: G. Laterza.

——1933. *Scritti politici e ricordi*, edited by R. Palmarocchi. Bari: G. Laterza.

Haitsma Mulier, E. 1980. *The Myth of Venice and Dutch Republican Thought in the Seventeenth Century*, translated by G. T. Moran. Assen: Van Gorcum.

Hamilton, B. 1963. *Political Thought in Sixteenth-century Spain*. Oxford: Clarendon.

Harrington, J. 1977. *The Political Works of James Harrington*, edited by J. Pocock. Cambridge: Cambridge University Press.

Hertter, F. 1910. *Die Podestalitteratur Italiens im 12. und 13. Jahrhundert*. Leipzig: B.G. Teubner.

Hexter, J. 1973. *The Vision of Politics on the Eve of the Reformation*. New York: Allen Lane.

Hoadly, B. 1772. *The Works*, 3 vols. London: W. Bowyer and J. Nichols.

Hobbes, T. 1968. *Leviathan*, edited by C. Macpherson. Harmondsworth: Penguin.

——1983. *De cive: The English Version*, edited by H. Warrender. Oxford: Clarendon.

Holdsworth, W. 1925. *A History of English Law*, vol. VIII. London: Methuen.

Hotman, F. 1972. *Francogallia*, edited by R. Giesey and J. Salmon. Cambridge: Cambridge University Press.

Hume, D. 1875. *Essays*, 2 vols., edited by T. Green and T. Grose. London: Longmans Green.

Humphrey, L. 1973. *The Nobles, or Of Nobility*. In *The English Experience*, no. 534. New York: Da Capo Press.

Kantorowicz, E. 1957. *The King's Two Bodies*. Princeton, NJ: Princeton University Press.

Keohane, N. 1980. *Philosophy and the State in France*. Princeton, NJ: Princeton University Press.

Kramnick, I. 1968. *Bolingbroke and his Circle*. Cambridge, MA: Harvard University Press.

Laslett, P. 1967. "Introduction." In Locke 1967: 1–120.

Latini, B. 1948. *Li Livres dou trésor*, edited by

F. Carmody. Berkeley, CA: University of California Press.

Lewkenor, L. 1969. *The Commonwealth and Government of Venice.* In *The English Experience*, vol. 101. New York: Da Capo Press.

Livy. 1962. *Ab urbe condita*, vol. VIII, translated by F. Moore. London: Heinemann.

——1966. *Ab urbe condita*, vol. VI, translated by F. Moore, London: Heinemann.

Lloyd, H. 1981. "The Political Thought of Charles Loyseau (1564–1610)." *European Studies Review* 11: 53–82.

——1983. *The State, France and the Sixteenth Century.* London: George Allen and Unwin.

Locke, J. 1967. *Two Treatises of Government*, edited by P. Laslett, 2nd edn. Cambridge: Cambridge University Press.

Machiavelli, N. 1960. *Il principe e discorsi*, edited by S. Bertelli. Milan: Feltrinelli.

Maffei, R. de. 1964. "Il problema della 'Ragion di Stato' nei suoi primi affioramenti." *Rivista internazionale di filosofia del diritto* 41: 712–32.

Mansfield, H. 1983. "On the Impersonality of the Modern State: A Comment on Machiavelli's Use of *Stato*." *The American Political Science Review* 77: 849–57.

Maravall, J. 1961. "The Origins of the Modern State." *Journal of World History* 6: 789–808.

Marsilius of Padua. 1956. *The Defender of Peace*, translated by A. Gewirth. New York: Columbia University Press.

Matteo dei Libri. 1974. *Arringhe*, edited by E. Vincenti. Milan: R. Ricciardi.

Mayer, T. 1985. "Faction and Ideology: Thomas Starkey's *Dialogue*." *Historical Journal* 28.1–25.

Meinecke, F. 1957. *Machiavellism*, translated by D. Scott. London: Routledge and Kegan Paul.

Milton, J. 1962. *The Tenure of Kings and Magistrates.* In *Complete Prose Works*, vol. III, edited by M. Hughes. New Haven, CT: Yale University Press, pp. 190–258.

——1971. *History of Britain.* In *Complete Prose Works*, vol. V, edited by F. Fogle. New Haven, CT: Yale University Press.

——1980. *The Ready and Easy Way to Establish a Free Commonwealth.* In *Complete Prose Works*, vol. VII, edited by R. Ayers, revised edn. New Haven, CT: Yale University Press, pp. 407–63.

Mochi Onory, S. 1951. *Fonti canonistiche dell' idea moderna dello stato.* Milan: Società Editrice "Vita e pensiero."

Mommsen, T. (ed.). 1970. *Digesta*, 21st edn. Zurich: Weidmannes.

More, St. Thomas. 1965. *Utopia.* In *The Complete Works of St. Thomas More*, vol. IV, edited by E. Surtz and J. Hexter. New Haven, CT: Yale University Press.

Muratori, L. (ed.). 1741. "Gratulatio." In *Antiquitates Italicae*, vol. IV. Milan: Arretti, pp. 131–2.

Patrizi, F. 1594a. *De institutione reipublicae.* Strassburg.

——1594b. *De regno et regis institutione.* Strassburg.

Petrarch, F. 1554. *Opera quae extant omnia.* Basel.

Pocock, J. 1975. *The Machiavellian Moment.* Princeton, NJ: Princeton University Press.

Ponet, J. 1942. *A Short Treatise of Politic Power.* Reprinted in W. Hudson, *John Ponet.* Chicago, IL: University of Chicago Press, pp. 131–62.

Pontano, G. 1952. "De principe." In *Prosatori Latini del quattrocento*, edited by E. Garin. Milan: R. Ricciardi, pp. 1023–63.

Post, G. 1964. *Studies in Medieval Legal Thought.* Princeton, NJ: Princeton University Press.

Raab, F. 1964. *The English Face of Machiavelli.* London: Routledge and Kegan Paul.

Raleigh, W. 1661. "Maxims of State." In *Remains of Sir Walter Raleigh.* London: W. Sheares, pp. 1–65.

Rinuccini, A. 1957. *Dialogus de libertate*, edited by F. Adorno. In *Atti e memorie dell' accademia toscana di scienze e lettere La Colombaria* 22: 265–303.

Robbins, C. 1959. *The Eighteenth-century Commonwealthman.* Cambridge, MA: Harvard University Press.

Rousseau, J.-J. 1966. *Du contrat social*, edited by P. Burgelin. Paris: Garnier-Flammarion.

Rowen, H. 1961. " 'L'état, c'est à moi.' Louis XIV and the State." *French Historical Studies* 2: 83–98.

Rowley, G. 1958. *Ambrogio Lorenzetti*, 2 vols. Princeton, NJ: Princeton University Press.

Rubinstein, N. 1952. "Florence and the Despots. Some Aspects of Florentine Diplomacy in the Fourteenth Century." *Transactions of the Royal Historical Society*, 2: 21–45.

——1971. "Notes on the word *stato* in Florence before Machiavelli." In *Florilegium historiale*, edited by J. Rowe and W. Stockdale. Toronto: University of Toronto Press, pp. 313–26.

Sacchi, B. 1608. *De principe viro.* Frankfurt.

Sallust. 1921. *Bellum Catilinae* translated by J. Rolfe. London: Macmillan.

Salmon, J. 1973. "Bodin and the Monarchomachs." In H. Denzer (ed.), *Bodin.* Munich: Beck, pp. 359–78.

Sardo, R. 1845. *Cronaca Pisana.* In *Archivio storico italiano* 6, part II: 73–244.

Scala, B. 1940. *De legibus et iudiciis dialogus*, edited by L. Borghi. In *La Bibliofilia* 42: 256–82.

Seneca. 1964. *De beneficiis*, translated by J. Basore. London: Heinemann.

Shadwell, L. (ed.). 1912. *Enactments in Parliament Specially Concerning the Universities of Oxford and Cambridge*, 4 vols. London: Clarendon.

Shennan, J. 1974. *The Origins of the Modern European State, 1450–1725.* London: Hutchinson.

Skinner, Q. 1978. *The Foundations of Modern Political Thought*, 2 vols. Cambridge: Cambridge University Press.

Sommerville, J. 1982. "From Suarez to Filmer: A Reappraisal." *The Historical Journal* 25: 525–40.

——1986. *Politics and Ideology in England, 1603–1640*. London: Longman.

Sorbelli, A. 1944. "I teorici del reggimento comunale." *Bullettino dell' istituto storico italiano per il medio evo* 59: 31–136.

Starkey, T. 1948. *A Dialogue between Reginald Pole and Thomas Lupset*, edited by K. Burton. London: Chatto and Windus.

Strayer, J. 1970. *On the Medieval Origins of the Modern State*. Princeton, NJ: Princeton University Press.

Suarez, F. 1612. *Tractatus de legibus, ac Deo legislatore*. Coimbra.

Tanner, J. 1930. *Constitutional Documents of the Reign of James I*. Cambridge: Cambridge University Press.

Tierney, B. 1982. *Religion, Law and the Growth of Constitutional Thought, 1150–1650*. Cambridge: Cambridge University Press.

Topham, J. *et al.* (eds.). 1783. *Rotuli Parliamentorum*, vol. III. London.

Tuck, R. 1985. "Warrender's *De cive*." *Political Studies* 33: 308–15.

Tully, J. 1980. *A Discourse on Property*. Cambridge: Cambridge University Press.

Ullmann, W. 1968–9. "Juristic Obstacles to the Emergence of the Concept of the State in the Middle Ages." *Annali di storia del diritto* 12–13: 43–64.

Vespasiano da Bisticci. 1970–6. *Le vite*, 2 vols., edited by A. Greco. Florence: Nella sede dell' istituto nazionale di studi sul rinascimento.

Vettori, F. 1842. *Parero* [On the Government of Florence, 1531–2]. In *Archivio storico italiano* 1: 433–6.

Villani, G. 1802–3. *Istorie fiorentine*, 8 vols. Milan: Società tipografica dei classici italiani.

Wahl, J. 1977. "Baldus de Ubaldis and the Foundations of the Nation-State." *Manuscripta* 21: 80–96.

Waley, D. 1978. *The Italian City-republics*, 2nd edn. London: Longman.

Warrender, H. 1983. "Editor's Introduction." In Hobbes 1983.

2

The Social Contract as Ideology

David Gauthier

Author's Note (1996)

Reprinting this essay makes me somewhat uneasy, because it now seems to me that in it, I fail to distinguish clearly the underlying rationale *for society and for social relationships from the* character *of those relationships. And so I treat contractarian thought as coming to conceive all social relationships as contractual. But this is a mistake. We may appeal to a social contract – a hypothetical rational agreement on mutually beneficial terms of interaction – without supposing that what we agree to is itself contractual in character. We benefit, all of us, from the capacity to form and sustain friendships, but friendship is not a relationship conceived in terms of mutual benefit and its norms are not contractual ones. This essay should then be read as an exposition and critique of understanding social relationships as if they were contractual, and not as a discussion of the justificatory role of hypothetical rational agreement. It should not be read as impugning the view (which I hold) that the norms of friendship (but not, say, the norms of enmity) are morally binding on us because, were we in a position to agree on the terms of our interaction, we should accept the norms of friendship (but not those of enmity) among those terms.*

The conception of social relationships as contractual lies at the core of our ideology. Indeed, that

Originally published in *Philosophy and Public Affairs*, 6 (1977), 130–64. Copyright © 1977 by Princeton University Press. Reprinted by permission of Princeton University Press.

core is constituted by the intersection of this conception with the correlative conceptions of human activity as appropriative and of rationality as utility-maximizing. My concern is to clarify this thesis and to enhance its descriptive plausibility as a characterization of our ideology, but to undermine its normative plausibility as ideologically effective.

I

The thesis refers to our ideology. There are two terms here which require immediate clarification; the first is "our." Philosophers habitually use the first-person plural pronoun; its use demands specification. Who are "we"? In this essay, first-person plural references are intended to denote those persons who have inhabited Western Europe, who are descended from such inhabitants, or who live or have lived in social structures developed from those of Western Europe during the past three to four hundred years. I am supposing, without further defense, that these persons share certain ideas and certain ways of thinking and behaving that permit the attribution to them of an ideology.

"Ideology" is the second term which requires clarification. It has not been employed with great consistency or clarity by social thinkers.[1] It picks out some aspect of our consciousness, frequently pejoratively, whether because of its allegedly derivative character (superstructure) or its allegedly misleading character (false consciousness). Although the demise of ideology as a determinant of social values and practices has been widely celebrated, more recent reports suggest that the celebrations may themselves be ideological in character. My use of the term is intended to retain the place of ideology in consciousness, and indeed perhaps to ensure the permanence of that place, without pejorative commitment.

Ideology is part of the deep structure of self-consciousness.[2] By self-consciousness I understand that capacity of human beings to conceive themselves in relation to other humans, to human structures and institutions, and to the nonhuman or natural environment, and to act in the light of these conceived relationships. Exhibited in these thoughts and activities is a conception of the self-as-human. This conception need not be, and typically is not, actually expressed in self-consciousness. Rather, it must be inferred from a person's actual thoughts and activities, insofar as they concern himself, his fellows, his society, and his world, as that underlying structure of ideas which affords their most economical foundation. This conception of self-as-human is thus a theoretical construct that we attribute to the ground of self-consciousness to explain its content, the surface of overt thought and action. This theoretical construct is what I refer to as ideology.

A conception of oneself as a person may be part of the content of consciousness. But this conception is not what I refer to as ideology, for it need not be identical with that conception which is exhibited in one's other thoughts and activities. Of course, ideology must afford the foundation for one's conscious self-awareness, but this does not preclude a difference, and even a contradiction, between the content of the ideological substructure, and the content of overt self-awareness. As with language, deep structure and surface structure must be distinguished, and their characteristics may be found to be opposed.

This similarity of language and consciousness is not accidental; in my view, self-consciousness depends on the actualization of linguistic capacity. Both language and consciousness have the deceptive appearance of transparency; both conceal a deep structure which unconsciously affects conscious activity. Ideology is not, or at least need not be, false consciousness, but it is necessarily prereflective consciousness. It can be the subject of reflection; it can be brought to the surface of

our thought, as indeed this essay is intended to exhibit. But its role does not require this reflection or an assessment of its validity or truth. Whether its role can be affected by reflection – whether the deep structure of self-consciousness can be affected by surfacing it – is a matter to which I shall allude in the course of this essay, although it may be exhibited more fully by the response to an enquiry into ideology rather than by the enquiry itself.

The structure of the ideas that comprise an ideology is not idiosyncratic. Persons who differ fundamentally in the ideological grounds of their activities would find interaction and communication difficult, if not frequently impossible. Whatever their supposed purpose, one of the main functions of social institutions is, and must be, to maintain and transmit a common ideology among those who compose a society. Without the effective functioning of such institutions, a society would rapidly disintegrate as its members ceased to be able to interact.

However, I do not suppose that a single, invariant structure of ideas holds for all persons in all times and places. My basic thesis presupposes only the existence of a common structure for us, that is, for modern Western Europeans and their descendants and offshoots.

The articulation of an ideology, like the articulation of any deep structure, cannot be expected to be an easy task. Many recent studies, especially in moral philosophy but also in political philosophy, have tended to ignore it. They have focused on the language or the logic of morals and politics and on practical, moral, and political reasoning, but frequently they have examined only the surface structure, the ideas we consciously express about ourselves. John Rawls' *A Theory of Justice* is a pioneering work in many respects, but in none more important than in its awareness of the significance of deep structure, although Rawls seems to suggest that this structure is invariant for human beings and not relative only to our own society.[3] And it is most noteworthy that in articulating this deep structure, he is led to develop, once again in the history of our political thought, the theory of the social contract.

II

The theory of the social contract has been advanced in more and less embracing forms.

Thomas Hobbes and John Locke are classic exponents of these contrasting approaches. Since my concern is primarily with the Hobbist variant, I shall begin with a brief sketch of its alternative.

Locke supposes that a certain group of men, namely landed proprietors, those who have successfully appropriated or inherited real property or estate, contract together for mutual protection and wellbeing.[4] Their contract brings civil government into existence, but civil government is not, in Locke's view, the only or the primary ground for social relationships among human beings. Locke's landed proprietors are heads of households, and their household relationships – of man with wife, father with child, and master with servant – are prior to and indeed fall outside of the contractual relationship which gives rise to political society. Furthermore, although here Locke is less explicit, it seems evident that landed proprietors enter into relationships of sociability, one with another, which are neither conditions nor consequences of the contract among them. And their relations one with another, and with other human beings, explicitly fall under the divine law of nature, which regulates conduct outside political society, in the state of nature, as well as conduct within it.

Hobbes' theory affords an altogether larger scope to contractual relations.[5] Indeed, for Hobbes, relations among human beings are of two kinds only: relations of hostility, which obtain in and constitute the state of nature, and relations of contract, which obtain in and constitute the state of society. In the state of nature, every man has the right to do whatever he will in order to preserve and benefit himself; the result is the state of war "where every man is Enemy to every man." To bring this self defeating condition to an end, every man is supposed to contract with his fellows to establish a commonwealth under a single and all-powerful sovereign. Only within a commonwealth is any sociability possible. The family is itself a miniature commonwealth; the father, or sometimes the mother, is sovereign, and the children are supposed to contract with their parent to obey in return for being allowed to live, in the way in which the vanquished in war contracts with the victor. And this latter contract, of vanquished with victor, which establishes sovereignty by acquisition, is explicitly stated by Hobbes to constitute the relation between servant and master. The contractual relationship among men, in establishing political society, is thus the model on which all other human relationships are interpreted.

It is Hobbes' radical contractarianism which I am attributing to our ideology. To make this attribution is to hold that our thoughts and activities, insofar as they concern ourselves and our relationships, are best understood by supposing that we treat all of these relationships as if they were contractual. Only the relation of hostility is excluded from the scope of contract, and only it is natural to man. All other human relationships are treated as essentially similar in character, and all are conventional, the product of human agreement.

The theory of the social contract, as part of our ideology, is not concerned with the objective character of social institutions and relationships. It is not a piece of speculative, but purportedly actual, history or sociology. Contractarians do not suppose, either explicitly or implicitly, that human society originated in a contract, or is now maintained by contract. They do not suppose that children contract with their parents. To suppose that the theory of the social contract must be intended to explain the origin of actual societies is to confuse deep structure with surface structure; our contractual conception of human relationships may ground an explanation which makes no appeal to contract.

The theory itself concerns the rationale of relationships among persons, and between society and its members, rather than the cause of those relationships. The justification of rights and duties, institutions and practices, is to be found by regarding them as if they were contractual, and showing the rationality of this hypothetical contractual base. Of course, a theory of rationale does have an explanatory function. Were the theory true, then fully self-conscious beings whose social environment was entirely the product of their deliberate choice would only relate contractually one to another. For such beings the theory of the social contract, and indeed our entire ideology, would not be a theoretical construct, but rather the conscious basis of their social thought and practice. As part of our ideology, then, the contract theory rationalizes social relationships by providing an ideal, nonactual explanation of their existence.

In attributing this ideology to us, I am not defending it. I am not claiming that society is to be understood, or ought to be understood, as if it were contractual. It may well be absurd so to understand society. What I am doing is claiming that our thoughts and actions are to be understood as if we supposed that all social relationships were to be rationalized in contractual terms. Note that "as if" plays a dual role in my account: our conscious thoughts, and overt actions, are to be explained *as if* we held the theory of the social contract, that is, the theory that all social relationships are to be understood *as if* they were contractual.

I should not want to argue that radical contractarianism of a Hobbist kind has unequivocally dominated our thoughts and practices. Rather, I believe this to be the final form of the contractarian conception of society, the form towards which it develops as an ideology, gradually increasing its influence on our thoughts, and leading us to abandon earlier ideas of human relationships as natural or supernatural rather than as conventional. I believe, although I cannot fully defend this belief here, that our society is moving towards a more Hobbist position. Evidence for this may be found in political life, for example in the "social contract" proposals of the British government under former Prime Minister Harold Wilson. But the most significant recent evidence is found in the extension of contractarian thought to family and domestic life. We may cite the arguments and practices of those who seek to divest the marriage contract of its religious and moral overtones, to treat it as the ordinary contract which, they argue, it really is. We may cite those who suppose that housework should be paid for, or that childraising is but one occupation among many possible vocations, and that those who do it, too, should be remunerated. And we may cite the words of a Montreal girl on the "jock circuit" (the circuit of those who offer non-professional diversion to professional athletes): "In a way, it's a sort of business arrangement – but then, aren't all man-woman relationships?"[6]

On reflection, we may disavow contractarianism. We may insist that there is more to human relationships than the conventions which result from agreement. The contractarian can admit this, as long as he holds that these other features of human relationships are nonessential, a sentimental residue from the past, or an emotional patina which affords a more pleasing aura to an otherwise bare artifice. But the contractarian can also maintain that we delude ourselves, and that indeed our ideology induces us to preach what we do not practice. The practice of contractarianism

may indeed be most effective if it is explicitly denied. The surface structure induced by the ideology may have a content incompatible with it.

This suggests a different linkage between ideology and false consciousness than the Marxian identification. Ideology, deep structure, may give rise to false consciousness, as surface structure. If so, then presumably bringing the ideology to consciousness, surfacing it, will undermine its effectiveness, for the contradiction between the ideology and our conscious conceptions will become patent.

In appraising contractarianism in this essay, I shall not go beyond questions of logical coherence and practical effectiveness. The further question of truth or validity is a difficult one for any ideology. The problem, at least in part, is that social institutions, practices, and relationships do not exist independently of human activity and human thought. Hence the view of these relationships presented by an ideology may be confirmed, for its adherents, because they act to constitute their relationships in accordance with it, while it may be disconfirmed, for its opponents, because they act to constitute their relationships on a quite different basis. No doubt many social theorists would insist that institutions and practices have an objective character quite independent of the thought and intent of those persons involved in them, and that ideology may falsify this objective character. But it will not do simply to insist that human relationships are not, in fact, to be explained as they are ideologically conceived, since ideology concerns rationale rather than literal explanation. To say that an ideology is false or invalid must, then, be to say that the rationale it provides for society is *incompatible* with the literal truth about that society. But how are we to determine incompatibility between the "as-if" and the "is"? This question I raise only to put aside.

III

To conceive all social relationships as contractual is to suppose that men, with their particular human characteristics, are prior to society. The contract theory expresses this priority in temporal terms, giving us the picture of men in a state of nature entering society on the basis of a contract. But, as I have pointed out, the language of the theory is the language of ideal explanation; the men in the state of nature are not ourselves.

The theory does not require that actual human individuals are temporally prior to their society; here, as elsewhere, temporal priority is a metaphor for conceptual priority.

What contractarianism does require is, first of all, that individual human beings not only can, but must, be understood apart from society. The fundamental characteristics of men are not products of their social existence. Rather, in affording the motivations that underlie human activity in the state of nature and that are expressed in natural hostility, they constitute the conditions of man's social existence. Thus man is social because he is human, and not human because he is social. In particular, self-consciousness and language must be taken as conditions, not products, of society.

But more than this is implicit in contractarianism. It would be compatible with the claim that the individual is prior to society, to suppose nonetheless that human sociability is itself a natural and fundamental characteristic of individuals, which expresses itself directly in social relations among human beings. And this is denied by contract theory in its insistence upon the essentially conventional character of society. Men who were naturally sociable would not need to contract together in order to form society, and would not rationalize society in contractarian terms. Although contract might be the foundation of government, as in Locke, society would not be a purely artificial creation. Contract as the foundation of all society is required only by men who are not inherently sociable.

Furthermore, radical contractarianism is incompatible with the view that men undergo fundamental change in becoming members of society. Men's reasons for contracting one with another are supposed to arise out of their presocial needs in the state of nature. If contractarian ideology is to be effective in rationalizing social relationships, then these needs must be represented, not as only presocial, but as permanent, so that the reasons for entering the contract will also be reasons for maintaining the society created thereby. Society is thus conceived as a mere instrument for men whose fundamental motivation is presocial, nonsocial, and fixed. If men are, in fact, socialized beings, so that human nature is in part a social product, then contractarian ideology must conceal this, representing social needs as if they were the product of presocial nature. Rousseau may use the device, and even the title,

of the social contract, but the theory which he formulates tends to subvert contractarian ideology, in its overt distinction of social man from natural man.[7]

Although the contractarian cannot represent man as a social being, he need not deny, as Hobbes may seem to, that human beings as we know them, within society, do display sociable characteristics.[8] The contractarian need but insist that man is sociable only because he creates society; human sociability is the product, and not the condition, of social existence. And as the product of what is itself conventional, this sociability is but an accidental attribute of human nature, an overlay on a fundamentally and permanently nonsocial character, possessing a merely conventional existence.

The correlate of the claim that man is nonsocial by nature is, of course, the claim that society is not, and cannot be, an end in itself. Man's social existence is not self-justifying. In offering an effective rationale for society, the contractarian must face the charge that because society is conventional, it is therefore arbitrary. Thrasymachus argued this against Socrates;[9] today there is a strong tendency to extrapolate from the contractarian, conventionalist view of such fundamental human relationships as male and female, or parent and child, to the contention that such relationships are arbitrary. The debate about the relation between *physis* and *nomos* has not advanced greatly in the past twenty-four hundred years. But to suppose that what is conventional must therefore be arbitrary is entirely contrary to the spirit of contractarianism, which finds only in convention a sufficient rationale for society.

To consider society arbitrary is to suppose that it affords no sufficient fulfilment or meets no fundamental need of most or all of its members. To avoid the charge of arbitrariness, then, the contractarian must relate the conventional character of society to a natural base in human nature. He must show society to be the indirect, rationalized expression of natural and essential human characteristics. In this way, by showing that society has, and must have, instrumental value to the naturally nonsocial human being, the contractarian justifies society to the individual, and thus resolves what has been the central problem in our political philosophy.

But how does the contractarian show that society must have instrumental value to human beings? I shall argue that he relies on the view that human activity is basically appropriative, thus establishing one of the links set out in my original thesis. Before I can make this argument convincing, however, I must first sketch part of the outline of a general formal theory of human interaction. By attending to the requirements of this theory, I shall seek to develop a conception of human good which will assure to society a sufficient instrumental value.

IV

Consider any situation in which there are several persons, each with several possible actions, and in which the outcome, as it affects each person, depends on the particular combination of actions performed. I shall define the *state of nature* as that relation holding between any two persons in the situation if and only if each acts on an independently selected principle of action, and *society* as that relation holding between any two persons in the situation if and only if both act on a mutually selected principle of action.[10] Note that, so defined, the state of nature and society are exclusive, but not exhaustive, alternatives. Both exclude fundamentally unequal relationships, in which there is a one-way dependence in the selection of principles of action. (It is perhaps worth mentioning that thinkers like Thrasymachus assume such a one-way dependence in arguing for the arbitrariness of society.)

Suppose that in a given situation, every person is in the state of nature with respect to every other person. I shall call the outcome of the actions performed in this full state of nature, the *natural outcome*. That is, the natural outcome results if each person acts on a principle of action which he selects for himself independently of the others. It is evident that a society will be considered arbitrary by those persons for whom the outcome of social action is worse than the natural outcome. Hence, a nonarbitrary society must improve on the natural outcome for everyone.

The outcome of a situation is *optimal* (in the Pareto sense) if and only if any alternative outcome which would be better for some person would be worse for some other person. If the natural outcome is optimal, then every alternative must make someone worse off, and so it is not possible for society to improve on the full state of nature for everyone. A society embracing all of the persons in the situation would either bring about the natural outcome, which would make the existence of the society pointless, or some outcome worse for some persons than the natural outcome, which would make the society arbitrary from their standpoint.

A nonarbitrary society embracing all of the persons in a situation is therefore possible only if the natural outcome of the situation is not optimal. Of course, not every society conceivable in such a situation will be nonarbitrary. The mutually selected principle of action must be such that the outcome is better for some persons, and at least as good for all persons, as the outcome in the full state of nature. It is reasonable to require further that the outcome of society be itself optimal, for otherwise some persons will consider it arbitrary, not because it is worse for them than the natural outcome, but because it is worse for them than some alternative which would leave everyone else at least as well off.

In addition to optimality, the stability of an outcome is of importance in analyzing nonarbitrary societies. An outcome is *stable*, or in equilibrium, if and only if no one person can bring about an alternative outcome which is better for himself, by unilaterally changing his way of acting. If an outcome is not stable, then it is evident that some person or persons will be tempted to defect from an agreement to accept a principle of action which brings it about.

Situations in which the natural outcome is not optimal may be divided into three types, using the concept of stability. Note that in all such situations, there must be some outcome which is both optimal and no worse for anyone than the natural outcome.

A situation is of *type I* if and only if (1) there are some outcomes which are (a) stable, (b) optimal, (c) no worse for anyone than the natural outcome, and (2) there is a nonempty set of outcomes, each satisfying (1), such that no member of the set is strongly dispreferred to any outcome satisfying (1) by any person. I shall suppose that the persons in a type I situation will be prepared to act on any principle of action which has as its outcome a member of the set of outcomes specified in (2). For such an outcome will be stable and optimal, worse for no one than the state of nature, and no one will strongly disprefer it to any other outcome satisfying these conditions.

A situation is of *type II* if and only if (1) there are some outcomes which are (a) stable, (b) optimal, (c) no worse for anyone than the natural outcome, and (2) any outcome which satisfies (1) is strongly dispreferred by some person to some other outcome satisfying (1). I shall suppose that the persons in a type II situation will be prepared all to act on some member of the set of principles of mutual action each of which has, as its outcome, a state of affairs satisfying (1). But these persons will not be prepared, without further ado, to act on any member of the set, since the outcome of each will be strongly dispreferred, by some person or persons, to the outcome of some other member. Hence they will bargain with each other to select a principle of mutual action from the set.

A situation is of *type III* if and only if (1) there are some outcomes which are (a) optimal, (b) no worse for anyone than the natural outcome, but (2) no outcome satisfying (1) is stable. In such a situation, some persons will be tempted to defect from any principle of mutual action which has, as its outcome, a state of affairs satisfying (1), since these persons can bring about an outcome better for themselves by such unilateral defection. Hence I shall suppose that the persons in a type III situation will be prepared all to act on some member of the set of principles of mutual action each of which has as its outcome a state of affairs satisfying (1), *provided* these persons have some guarantee that their agreement will be effective, that is, that no person will unilaterally violate it.

The persons in a type I situation require some procedure for *coordination*, to ensure that all adhere to the same principle of action. The persons in a type II situation require some procedure for *bargaining*, to enable them to agree on a principle of action (and possibly a coordination procedure, if bargaining results in a set of principles, each of which is about equally acceptable to each member of society). The persons in a type III situation require, in addition to bargaining and perhaps coordination procedures, some *constraining* devices, both internal ("conscience") and external ("authority"), to afford them the guarantee that each will act to bring about the agreed outcome. The rationale for society, and hence for the social contract on which it is based, is thus provided by these three desiderata: coordination, bargaining, and constraint.

Following Hobbes, I shall suppose that what characterizes political society is the existence of some form of external constraint, that is, coercive authority.[11] Coercive authority induces men to conform to principles of mutual action not in

themselves maximally beneficial for all persons, by imposing costs, penalties, or punishments on failure or refusal to conform. Coercive authority will appear arbitrary from the standpoint of those subjected to it if the outcome of the coerced actions is not better than the outcome these persons would achieve in the state of nature, when they are not subject to such coercion. Were it not for type III situations, coercion would be arbitrary, and anarchism might be the only defensible form of human society. Hence it is necessary to consider further the nature of human beings and the goods which they seek, if type III situations are essential to the human condition.

V

All members of society must regard coercion as both beneficial and necessary. This imposes a severe constraint on the goods which these persons seek. Were these goods strictly competitive in nature, so that no increase in joint supply was possible and any increase in one person's good entailed a corresponding decrease in the good available to some other person, then there could be no basis for mutual improvement from the outcome of the state of nature, and coercion could not be beneficial for all. Some might better their position by coercing others, but such coercion would be totally arbitrary from the standpoint of those whose position was worsened by it.

However, were the goods sought by the members of society essentially noncompetitive, so that an increase in one person's good was generally compatible with an increase in the goods available to others, then there would be little reason for anyone to prefer one optimal outcome to another, and some optimal outcomes would be stable, so that men would face only a problem of coordination. If coercion is necessary, then there must be considerable competition for the goods sought, so that despite the possibility of mutual improvement, frequently an increase in the good of one person must entail a decrease in the good of another. Each person's good must therefore be sharply distinct from, and in some respects opposed to, the good of others. The resources available to the members of society must be insufficient to permit the full or almost full satisfaction of everyone simultaneously, so that they face extensive conflict over the distribution of goods.

What goods satisfy these conditions? Goods

such as companionship may be left aside, since only those goods which nonsocial creatures might seek can be involved. These must be goods whose supply can be increased by cooperative action, so that mutual improvement is possible. But they must be goods which are possessed or used individually, so that distributive problems can arise. And they must be goods for which the demand is unlimited, or at least always in excess of the supply, however much that supply is augmented by cooperation, so that potential distribution problems become actual.

In classifying goods, a simple Platonic schematism will serve present purposes.[12] I shall distinguish the goods of intellect, of spirit, and of desire. Men may cooperate in the pursuit of all three, but whereas the supply of such goods as knowledge and food may be increased by concerted action, only the distribution of such a good as honor is affected. Men may possess all three, but whereas the possession of food or honor is exclusive, the possession of knowledge by one person does not affect its possession by another. Hence of the three types, only goods of desire satisfy the two requirements that cooperation increase supply and that possession create distributive problems.

But are goods of desire the object of unlimited demand? Need they be in short supply? If these goods are related to physical need, to the natural appetites for food and drink, warmth, comfort, and sex, then surely they are not – as Rousseau pointed out, in criticizing Hobbes' account of the state of nature as one in which men were in constant conflict, making a coercive society the necessary instrument of peace.[13] Only a population explosion would make the goods of desire in necessarily short supply, and there is no reason to attribute that to the state of nature. Thus if man is motivated by his natural, nonsocial appetites, and material goods are considered in relation to these appetites, the demand for these goods will not usually exceed the supply, and no distribution problem will arise which only coercive authority could resolve.

Rousseau's own argument for the necessity of coercion is not available to the radical contractarian, since it depends on the introduction of competitive motivation in the process of socialization. There are, it would seem, two possible arguments consistent with contractarian premises: either the threat of scarcity inherent in the state of nature must be the basis for a necessarily competitive

endeavor to assure oneself against its actualization or further appetites, of a kind such that scarcity of the goods satisfying them is assured, must be attributed to men in the state of nature.[14]

Hobbes adopts the first alternative.[14] He argues that in the absence of coercive authority, the threat of scarcity among the goods of desire leads to competition for the goods of spirit. He characterizes men as seeking endless power, not because they always lack sufficient means to preserve and gratify themselves, but because they always lack the assurance that their means are sufficient.

The emergence of the desire for power turns a situation in which there is potential for cooperation into one which is actually increasingly competitive. Since the goods which preserve us are largely the same, I increase the assurance of my survival and well-being only by decreasing your assurance. Power is thus relative, so that men who seek only power must be engaged in a zero-sum conflict – one gains only at the expense of the other. This is the pure war of every man against every man. However, its outcome is to lessen every man's ability to assure his own preservation, so that the state of nature is far worse for everyone than what would result, were there a coercive force sufficient to deter each from the active pursuit of unlimited power, while enabling all to cooperate in increasing the supply of those goods necessary to preservation and well-being.

Hobbes' argument for the competitive drive for power is not fully convincing. For if goods of desire are in sufficient supply in the state of nature, so that the real threat of scarcity is slight, then the cost each person incurs in embarking on the search for ever greater power – the cost of being a party to the war of every man against every man – will be greater than the risk each runs in being satisfied with his present means to preserve himself. Hence some political theorists, such as C.B. Macpherson, have argued with considerable plausibility that Hobbes' real answer to the type of criticism advanced by Rousseau is to be found, not in his explicit account of the desire for power, but in his implicit acceptance of an appetite for material goods different in kind from the limited appetites for food, drink, sex, and the like, an appetite for unlimited appropriation.[15] This appetite, peculiarly characteristic of men in Hobbes' – and in our – society, is what turns the state of nature into an arena of unlimited combat. The view which explains the need for coercion is that man is by nature and necessity an appropriator.

To appropriate is to make one's own. The most complete and literal appropriation is of course appropriation into oneself – the conversion of an external object into one's body. But not all goods can be appropriated in such a way that they lose their own bodily identity; what is one's own thus extends beyond one's body to the physically distinct objects which constitute property. To appropriate is then to acquire property; the very object of appropriation is individual possession. Now there can be property in both the goods of intellect and the goods of appetite, but primarily it is the goods of desire which are appropriated and constitute property. Since the supply of these goods can be increased by cooperative action, the goods of appropriation clearly satisfy the first two conditions requisite if coercion is to be both beneficial and necessary. But do the goods of appropriation necessarily give rise to distributive problems? Are they in short supply? Why is the appetite for appropriation characteristically *unlimited*?

The natural appetites for food, drink, and sex are *satis*fiable; one eats, drinks, copulates enough, *satis*. The appetites are constantly renewed, but so are their objects, so that a balance can be achieved between supply and demand. The desire to appropriate is not similarly satisfiable; there is no natural level of satiation for appropriate activity. If one is an appropriator *by nature*, then one must continue to appropriate, or to seek to appropriate, but the objects for appropriation are not continually renewed; what one appropriates is removed from the stock of goods available for appropriation, so that, even with the increased supply of some goods made possible by cooperation, the supply is limited by the finitude of the earth, if by no previous limit of accessibility. Hence the demand for property always exceeds the supply of goods to be appropriated. The goods of desire are always scarce from the standpoint of the appropriator, and this scarcity is increased by the presence of other appropriators. Men therefore find themselves necessarily in conflict with respect to their desire for property.

The competitive search for power is easily derived from the insatiable desire for appropriation. Hence, men find themselves in an increasingly competitive situation, in which the security of their property is continually decreasing. Thus, simply in terms of the desire to appropriate and

without reference to man's other natural appetites, the state of nature leads to an outcome far worse for everyone than what would result were there a coercive force sufficient to curb each man's appetite for power and to channel his desire to appropriate into an arena which is competitive yet peaceful – the marketplace rather than the battlefield.

The market is the primary social forum for the members of a society of appropriators. Their social concern for their fellows derives from their interest in appropriation, and is expressed in the relationship of exchange, whereby they transfer the possession of appropriated objects. Exchange of property is the primary function of the market; its efficient organization enables the appropriators to contract one with another to maximize the production and determine the allocation of their goods. Hence within society, the primary relationships of appropriators are contractual.

One might suppose that much of the argument I have developed, in seeking to link the contractarian conception of social relationships with the appropriate conception of human activity, could have been avoided quite simply by noting that the desire to appropriate necessarily manifests itself socially as the desire to exchange. Appropriators think of their fellows as partners in exchange, and so they think of social relations as contractual. But this, although true, would not show that appropriators conceive of society itself as contractual. The radical contractarian supposes that the marketplace, the locus of contract, is itself the product of a social contract, and is embedded in a coercive order which is also the product of that contract. From the claim that man is by nature an appropriator, it does not follow *directly* that he finds a coercive order beneficial and necessary. My concern has been to establish this further connection, and to introduce appropriative activity as that which naturally leads to hostility among men, yet which also affords scope for mutually beneficial cooperation, thus affording sufficient rationale for coercive society.

I have not shown that conceiving human activity as essentially appropriative requires one to accept a contractarian view of society. Locke's men are primarily appropriators, but they exist within a divinely ordained framework of natural law which relates them nonconventionally to their fellows.[16] Nor have I shown that conceiving all social relationships as contractual requires one to hold that human activity is primarily appropriative, for I have not shown that no alternative account of human activity would afford nonsocial individuals with a rationale for a social contract. What I have shown is that the contractarian conception of social relationships and the appropriative conception of human activity are mutually supporting. Given the undoubted historical importance of appropriative activity in our society, I conclude that within our ideology, the ideology of Western Europeans, the conceptions of appropriation and contract intersect in the person of the individual property-owner, related only by convention to his fellows. I shall therefore take the first connection in my initial thesis to be sufficiently defended.

VI

To conceive all social relationships as contractual is to deny that reason either determines or presupposes an order, a rational order, within which men are related prior to any agreement among themselves. This severely constrains the contractarian conception of rationality; I shall argue that it requires that rationality be conceived as related instrumentally to the satisfaction of individual interests.

Hobbes offers a useful way of formulating the problem of relating rationality to the theory of the social contract. "That is done by *right*, which is not done against reason," Hobbes claims, so that "we ought to judge those actions only *wrong*, which are repugnant to right reason . . . But that *wrong* which is done, we say it is done against some law. Therefore *true reason* is a certain *law*."[17] Reason, in other words, determines a framework of rights and laws, within which all men find themselves. But surely these rights and laws must determine relationships among men, which, being grounded in reason alone, are natural rather than conventional. If this were so, then radical contractarianism would have to be abandoned in favor of the Lockean theory that contract supplements and completes man's natural social relationships. Hobbes does not accept any such relationships; how then does he accommodate reason?

Hobbes keeps his conception of rationality consistent with his contractarianism by treating reason as both individualistic and instrumental. He speaks of "that Reason, which dictateth to every man his own good," and says that "all the voluntary actions of men tend to the benefit of themselves; and those actions are most Reasonable, that conduce most to their ends."[18] Given this conception of rationality, he is able to argue that every man has an unlimited, permissive right or liberty to do all things, so that each may do as he sees fit in order to preserve and benefit himself. The laws, to which every man is naturally subject, are but "Theorems concerning what conduceth to the conservation and defence of themselves." Hence reason does not in itself determine a system of rights and laws which relate men one to another in any way other than the natural relation of hostility. The "rational" order corresponding to the unlimited right of nature is the condition of war of every man with every man.

Contrast Hobbes' conception of reason with views which suppose rational standards transcending individual interests.[19] The Stoic holds that all men, as rational, are capable of apprehending the laws of nature, in terms of which all are related as members of a cosmopolis transcending more limited, conventional societies. The medieval Christian supposes that all men, as rational, are capable of apprehending the divinely ordained laws of nature, in terms of which all are related directly to God, and indirectly to their fellows. The Kantian supposes that all men, as rational, are directly related one to another as members of a Kingdom of Ends in which each must treat his fellows, not merely as means, but as ends in themselves. In each case there is an order – the Stoic cosmopolis, the Christian Kingdom of God, the Kantian Kingdom of Ends – which is constituted either by or in accordance with reason, to which all men belong, and within which all are related. This relationship is prior to human agreement, depending solely on man's rationality. It may of course be the basis of further, contractual relationships, but these are only of secondary importance.

Each of these positions may be brought into verbal agreement with Hobbes' claim that "those actions are most Reasonable, that conduce most to their ends," but only by equivocating on "ends." Where Hobbes speaks of the ends subjectively given by men's passions, the Stoic, Christian, or Kantian speaks of the ends objectively given by Nature, God, or Reason itself. Such objective ends constitute a natural order within which all men are related, and so each of these views is incompatible with radical contractarianism.

To specify the contractarian conception of

rationality more precisely I shall relate it to the view of human activity developed in the preceding section. A person is a rational agent if and only if he acts to fulfill his (subjective) ends as far as possible. If it be agreed, as I have argued, that the contractarian ideology involves the conception of human activity as appropriative, then a person is a rational agent if and only if he acts to appropriate as much as possible. As much what? Here, our ideology exhibits a historical development. What is to be appropriated is first thought of as real property, land or estate. The distinction between land and other forms of property is then denied, and what is to be appropriated becomes the universal measure of property, money. Finally, in a triumph of abstraction, money as a particular object is replaced by the purely formal notion of utility, an object conveniently divested of all content. The rational man is, as Samuel Gompers succinctly recognized, simply the man who seeks *more*.

Thus it follows that not only the individualistic instrumental conception of rationality, but more precisely the individualistic utility-maximizing conception, is part of the ideology of the social contract, derived by means of the appropriate conception of human activity which is historically central to our ideology. But more than this may be said about reason, for it is not a merely derivative conception in contractarian thought.

I have argued that the appropriative conception of human activity, although consonant with contractarian thought, does not in itself require a contractarian interpretation of all human relationships, for it is at least possible to view man as belonging to a natural order, perhaps divinely ordained, within which he is noncontractually related to his fellows. But the instrumental conception of rationality rules out any ultimate natural or supernatural ground for human relationships. By itself, instrumental rationality does not imply any form of order or any type of relationship among human beings; it is compatible with the supposition that human existence is entirely solitary. But conjoined with the conception of human activity as appropriative, instrumental, maximizing rationality determines the hostile order of the state of nature, and this in turn makes it necessary for men to establish a conventional order among themselves by agreement or contract. Hence instrumental rationality conjoined with appropriative human nature entails contractarian society.

This concludes my exposition of the initial thesis of this essay. Radical contractarianism entails the instrumental conception of rationality; radical contractarianism together with the conception of human nature as appropriative entail more precisely the individualistic utility-maximizing conception of rationality. Conversely, instrumental rationality, together with the appropriative conception of human nature, entails the radical contractarian view that coercive society, and all social relationships, are the product of human convention. Thus society as conventional, human nature as appropriative, and rationality as maximizing cohere together at the core of our ideology.

VII

The maximizing conception of rationality is entailed by contractarianism, but it also undercuts the very possibility of rational agreement among men, and thus the very possibility of contractually based society. There is an apparent incoherence in contractarian ideology to which I now turn.

Individual appropriators find themselves naturally and necessarily in conflict one with another. But individual utility-maximizers have no direct rational means for resolving their conflicts. Hobbes expresses this point clearly: "And therefore, as when there is a controversy in an account, the parties must by their own accord, set up for right Reason, the Reason of some Arbitrator, or Judge, to whose sentence they will both stand, or their controversie must either come to blowes, or be undecided, for want of a right Reason constituted by Nature; so is it also in all debates of what kind soever . . ."[20] The Stoic, the Christian, or the Kantian may appeal to a right reason constituted by nature, as the basis of conflict resolution among human beings. But for the contractarian there is no such appeal.

Why is this important? Consider once again the functions which society must perform – coordination, bargaining, and constraint. Each of these requires procedures for decision and action which are not strictly contained in the principle of individual utility-maximization. Each then involves at least an extension in the contractarian conception of rationality. I have argued elsewhere that coordination and bargaining are fully compatible with utility-maximization.[21] These raise no problem. But constraint is not so compatible.

The necessity for constraint arises when the outcome of bargaining is not stable, so that if each person acts to maximize his own utility, some persons will not act to bring about the agreed outcome. Voluntarily to act in a constrained manner is contrary to the dictates of individual utility-maximization.

Individual appropriators must enter into contractual relationships to resolve their conflicts and to bring about an optimal state of affairs, better for each than the natural outcome. But their conception of rationality leads them to violate their contracts whenever, as must often be the case, adherence would require them to abstain from directly maximizing behavior. In section IV, I insisted that agreement in a type III situation – a situation in which no acceptable optimal outcome is stable – is possible only given some assurance that the agreement will be honored. This assurance requires external constraints, and thus I introduced the need for coercion. But it also needs internal constraints, the constraints of conscience, and these contradict the requirements of reason. The contractarian principle of rational action undercuts the internal constraints necessary to maintain contractual relationships.

This problem can be resolved only if it is possible to remedy the want of a right reason established by nature. The remedy can only be conventional. Natural reason, the reason of the individual maximizer, leads only to the natural relationship of hostility among men. A conventional rationality which upholds adherence to one's agreements even against the dictates of individual utility-maximization must therefore be accepted as the basis of the social contract, and so of social relationships among men.

Hobbes recognizes this need for a conventional standard of right reason, for he continues the passage quoted above: "And when men that think themselves wiser than all others, clamor and demand right Reason for judge; yet seek no more, but that things should be determined, by no other mens reason but their own, it is as intolerable in the society of men, as it is in play after trump is turned, to use for trump on every occasion, that suite whereof they have most in their hand." This passage contains the heart of the matter. Trump is established by the social contract, as that convention required to achieve an optimal state of affairs, better for each than the natural outcome. But each man, guided by his own reason, uses for trump his own interest. And this is intolerable,

for it undercuts the contract and makes society impossible. However, Hobbes fails to establish a conventional standard of right reason, adhering to his individualist view that "those actions are most Reasonable, that conduce most to their ends." In the state of nature this is true, but as Hobbes himself recognizes, this is exactly what is intolerable in society or, indeed, intolerable if there is to be any society.

This is the point at which the theory of the social contract seems to collapse into incoherence. As I have noted, contract – the generic relationship of which the social contract is but the focal expression – is the fundamental relationship among appropriators. Their prime concern one with another is to exchange objects of appropriation, and contracts are their necessary means. But contracts are not fully self-sustaining. The society established by the social contract, market society, is from one point of view simply the network of contracts among individual men. But this network is maintained by a legal order which enforces the contracts. The contractual relationships of appropriators must be embedded within a political framework which coerces them into remaining within the market in their actions and relationships. Contractarian ideology represents this framework as itself contractual. But the condition of the market – the condition of the network of contracts – cannot itself be the product of a contract, which would be only part of that network. If the market is not self-sustaining, then it cannot be sustained by a part of itself.

The charge of incoherence operates at two levels. The argument which I have sketched suggests that radical contractarianism is incoherent as a *theory*, in providing an account of human relationships which presupposes a noncontractual base. I shall suggest that it can answer this charge. But there is a further argument which suggests that contractarianism is incoherent as an *ideology* in providing an account of human relationships which, in practice, undermines their base. I shall suggest in section IX that this charge succeeds, that the price contractarianism must pay for theoretical coherence is too great to allow it to maintain ideological effectiveness, once its adherents come to be aware of that price.

This last clause is important. Questions about the theoretical coherence of contractarianism need not affect its ideological coherence, except insofar as they become questions in the minds of its adherents. Suppose it were true that contractual relationships, to be effectively maintained, must be embedded within a coercive order which itself were not contractually grounded. This would not prevent persons from conceiving of this coercive order as contractual, or from conceiving of all of their social relationships as contractual without attending to their framework. As long as the question of the coercive basis of contractual relationships did not arise in thought, the incoherence of the ideology would not be recognized, and its effectiveness would be unimpaired.

But now I want to defend contractarianism against the criticism that the instrumental conception of rationality, which it requires, must undermine the theory of the contractual rationale for society. What is essential, as Hobbes recognized, is a conventional standard of rational action, which will enjoin adherence to the social contract even when strict individual maximization calls for nonadherence, yet which itself is grounded in the individualistic utility-maximizing conception of rationality.

This may seem impossible. Surely any standard of rational action which is grounded in individual utility-maximization must have its same corrosive effect on adherence to agreements which require persons to refrain from maximizing behavior. But, I have argued elsewhere, this is not so.[22] A person who begins as an individual utility-maximizer will find it rational, on individualistic maximizing grounds, to change his very *conception* of rationality, and come to adopt a conventional standard of right reason, which I have termed *constrained maximization*.

The principle of constrained maximization corresponds to straightforward individual utility-maximization in its application to state-of-nature situations, but it enjoins each person to agree with his fellows on actions leading to outcomes which are optimal and better for all than the corresponding natural outcomes, and to perform such actions within society. The rationale for the adoption of this new conception of rationality by utility-maximizers is quite simple; constrained maximizers are able to make agreements which straightforward maximizers cannot, because constrained maximizers will, and straightforward maximizers will not, adhere to these agreements, and the benefits of making such agreements are greater than the costs of adhering to them. Persons who adopt the standard of constrained maximization will find that, under widely prevailing, albeit not universal, conditions, it is rational

for them to enter into and to adhere to a social contract with at least some of their fellow human beings, thereby replacing the natural relationship of hostility with the conventional relationship of sociability.

Reason itself neither determines nor presupposes any relationships among men, so that the contractarian requirement that all social relationships be conventional is not violated. But reason does lead men to enter by agreement into social relationships, and to adopt a standard of rationality which sustains these relationships rather than undermining them. Contractarian theory takes the individualistic utility-maximizing conception of rationality as the natural standard, but provides for its rational replacement by a constrained maximizing conception which grounds those mutually optimizing actions to which men agree as the basis of their society.

VIII

I have distinguished two aspects of contractarian society: the market, the locus of the particular contracts which relate men as producers and distributors of goods, and the coercive order, or state, which ensures that the market does not revert to the battlefield of the state of nature. This distinction corresponds, in an interesting and important way, to the distinction which I have introduced between straightforward utility-maximization and constrained maximization.

Straightforward maximization corresponds to the rule of self-interest. Throughout most of human history the rule of self-interest has been considered a primary threat to society, as indeed my analysis of the problem posed to contractarianism by straightforward maximization would suggest that it is. Religion, law, morality, and tradition have combined to repress the force of self-interest. The great discovery of our society is, of course, the discovery of the social value of self-interest. The triumph of the science of economics was to demonstrate that under appropriate conditions, those of perfect competition in a free market, if each person acted purely self-interestedly, to maximize his own utilities, then the outcome would necessarily be optimal, the particular optimum depending solely on the initial positions of the persons in the market. Instead of repressing self-interest, our society has harnessed it. The benefits have been striking; critics of our society would hold that the costs have been overlooked.

Within the perfectly competitive market, straightforward individual utility-maximization is an adequate rule of reason. However, the market may fail to be perfectly competitive because of the presence of externalities – free goods or uncompensated costs, and the market is never fully self-sustaining, since force and fraud always threaten it. Hence it requires to be regulated and controlled by the power of the state, and here straightforward maximization must be supplanted by constrained maximization. The distinction which I have drawn between these two conceptions of rationality parallels the distinction between the two primary sectors of contractarian society.

This may be indicated by a suitable relabeling of the two conceptions of rationality. Straightforward individual utility-maximization, the natural standard of reason, is effective in maintaining optimal productive and distributive activities for men in the market, and so may be termed the standard of *economic* rationality. Constrained individual utility-maximization, the conventional standard of reason for contractarians, is effective in maintaining the beneficial and necessary coercive order of the state against those directly maximizing actions which would restore the hostility of the state of nature, and so may be termed the standard of *political* rationality.

Since contractarian ideology is at the basis of our social thinking, it should not be surprising that the conception of society which is consonant with it proves familiar to us, in focusing on the economic, bargaining order of the market and viewing the political, coercive order of the state as sustaining the market. It should also not be surprising that contractarian society is of limited extent, and is not a single society of the human race.

Not all persons need find it mutually advantageous to leave the state of nature to establish a market and a state. Only if all can improve on their original situation can all have sufficient reason to enter the social contract. If, however, the relations among some persons, or among some groups previously established by contract, are such that a gain for one must be a loss for another, then not everyone will have reason to agree to a departure from the existing state of affairs.

The implication of this for the present world situation is worth noting. On the contractarian view, it is evident that people should enter into contractual relations only with those with whom cooperation will prove profitable. Now we – Western Europeans and offshoots whose thinking is shaped by contractarian ideology – have no reason to expect it to be profitable or beneficial to us to cooperate with the overpopulated and underdeveloped peoples of much of the rest of the world. Given the finitude of the earth's resources, their gains are our losses.

To the question, Who is my neighbor? the radical contractarian has a simple answer. My neighbor, according to our ideology, is the man with whom I can make a mutually profitable agreement. Everyone else is my enemy – to be exploited if I can, to exploit me if he can. One might take as one measure of the hold of contractarian ideology upon us the extent to which this answer determines our practice, whatever we may preach.

IX

Radical contractarianism has come more and more to dominate our thoughts and actions, or so I would contend. Correlatively, contractarianism has passed increasingly from covert to overt manifestation in our self-awareness. Institutions and practices which derive their rationale from noncontractarian considerations are being discarded or rejected. The effect of this is to throw into sharp relief the contractarian conception of rationality, and its relationship to man's appropriative desires.

Insofar as the two are mutually supportive, all is well. The supposition that all human relationships other than hostility are conventional, the product of mutually beneficial agreement, will sustain bargaining activity within the market, for here economic rationality and the desire to appropriate reinforce each other. But the coercive order of the state is a quite different matter, for here political rationality imposes a constraint on the unlimited appetite of the contractarian. However rational it may be to stand to one's advantageous agreements even against direct interest, yet reason is insufficient in practice to overcome the motivations which, on the contractarian view, direct our actions. Awareness of oneself as an appropriator undercuts one's willingness to accept the constraints of the political order.

Historically the political order, which is necessary to the maintenance of peace and security within society, has been supported by motivations quite different from those that enter the contractarian conception of human nature. As this conception comes to be both more overt and more pervasive, these other factors lose their hold on us, and the political order loses its motivational base.

To the extent to which it has not been self-enforcing, political society has rested on *patriotism* – the love of country which binds men to the coercive order because it is surrounded with the emotional trappings of fatherland or motherland (trappings which themselves are corroded as the contractarian conception of the family comes to the fore!). It is, I suggest, this attachment of individuals to their society which has generated sufficient voluntary support to enable coercion to be effective. To be sure, not all members of society have felt this attachment, but enough have been moved by it to permit the remainder to be constrained through the further motive of *fear* – fear of the coercive order itself.

In addition to patriotic feeling, familial feeling has been a fundamental motive supporting the political order. The effect of familial feeling has been primarily to strengthen society as an entity enduring in time. Since future generations have little to contribute to the wellbeing of those now alive, a contract between us and our descendants seems a tenuous basis for an enduring society. However, the transgenerational affective ties which bind together members of a family supply the motivation needed for each generation to seek the continuation of society. I shall term this motive *love*, and suggest that it operates primarily at a prerational level. By this I mean that membership in the family, and the ties of love, precede, causally if not logically, the emergence of that individual self who engages in the appropriate and contractual activities of the market, and aligns with others to create and maintain the state.

Patriotism and love thus maintain the enduring political basis of contractual market society. Because our ideology is part of the deep structure of our thought about ourselves, it has been possible for us to think in contractarian ways while acting on these quite uncontractarian motives. We may suppose that our ties to our fellows and our society are strictly contractual, and yet act on ties which are not contractual. However, as the ideology of contract comes increasingly to manifest itself at the level of conscious thought, so that we come consciously to disavow nonappropriative motivation, patriotism and love must seem more and more irrelevant and even unintelligible. The rejection by the young of America's role in the Vietnam war and the emergence of radical feminism are manifestations of this increasingly overt contractarian consciousness.

Patriotism and love have had a further effect on the development of our society. Historically they have served, together with the fear engendered by the coercive order which they sustain, to exclude most human beings from effective membership in market society, and thus from what, to the contractarian, are the essentially human activities of appropriation and exchange. Neither workers, who have lacked control over the means of production, nor women, who have engaged in reproduction rather than production, have conceived themselves, or been in a position to conceive themselves, as full human beings in the sense implicit in radical contractarian ideology.[23] Marx, mistakenly, thought religion to be the opium of the people;[24] the real opiates, in contractarian society, have been love and patriotism. By removing wide areas of human activity, and even more important, most people, from the effective scope of the ideology, love and patriotism have enabled those remaining within its scope to conduct their appropriative activities more successfully.

Indeed, this restriction of appropriation to, largely, the male bourgeoisie has been essential to the development of our society. If every person had considered himself, or herself, to be an appropriator, in competition with every other person, then, as Hobbes insisted, only an all-powerful sovereign could have prevented endless conflict. The mode of rationality which would have led every person to make and carry out an agreement to check competition and ensure mutual advantage would have been insufficient to overcome the competitive desire to appropriate.

C.B. Macpherson, in his introduction to *Leviathan*, emphasizes this when he says: "Given the postulate that the power of every man necessarily opposed and hindered the power of other men, so that every man in society necessarily sought more power over others, *and provided* that this centrifugal force was not offset by any centripetal force, it would follow that any slackening or temporary absence of a sovereign power would tend to lead to internecine strife. What Hobbes overlooked and failed to put into his model was the centripetal force of a cohesive bourgeois class within the society."[25] The male bourgeoisie have acted as a cohesive, centripetal force because they have recognized, implicitly, that they must retain appropriative activity exclusively in their hands to prevent the strife which would result from the competition of every person with every other person. But they have been able to retain appropriative activity for themselves alone, not just because of their cohesion, but because neither workers nor women have conceived of themselves as appropriators. Acceptance by workers and women of the contractarian view of human beings would lead to their refusal to remain excluded from truly human, appropriative activity.

I have suggested that the ideology of radical contractarianism is manifesting itself increasingly in our overt consciousness. And this consciousness is spreading more and more widely. In itself, the ideology embraces everyone, so that, as more and more people attain self-awareness, they do so in the terms provided by the deep structure of our thought – in the terms, then, of contractarianism.

The likely end of the current fad for liberation movements, whatever the ostensible aim of these movements, will be to extend contractarian self-awareness to new areas of human activity and new groups of human beings. Radical feminists will go the way of radical trades unionists; women will join the system rather than overthrow it. But as all persons come to consider all human relationships to be contractual, they will not achieve the happy state of ideally rational appropriators, or even the cohesive unity of the male bour-

geoisie. The absorptive capacity of the system is being overstrained, so that the effect of extending contractarian ideology is and will continue to be to corrode all of those bonds which in the real world have been the underpinning of the market. Bereft of its framework, the bargaining order will collapse into competitive chaos.

Love and patriotism are myths to the contractarian. But these myths, and not reason, have been the real support for the enduring coercive order, enabling it to enlist fear and thus assure the survival of the state. And the contractarian state, rational to the constrained maximizer but effective only because of its basis in these myths, has maintained the bargaining order of the market. Remove this basis by bringing all human beings to awareness of themselves as appropriators, and the practical incoherence of contractarian ideology manifests itself in the inability of conscious contractarians to maintain the coercive basis of their social relationships. Thus the triumph of radical contractarianism leads to the destruction, rather than the rationalization, of our society, for what real men and women who believe the ideology need to keep them from the war of all against all is not reason, but the Hobbist sovereign, and he is not available.

The ideology of radical contractarianism is, of course, but one among many possible ways of structuring our thought about man, society, and reason. We may see that this way of thinking is, from a practical point of view, bankrupt, and indeed that it will destroy us if we remain its adherents. But other ways of thinking, however possible they may be, are not produced to order. Faced with the falling of the dusk, the owl of Minerva spreads its wings – and takes flight.[26]

Notes

Earlier versions of this essay were read to the Institute on Contractarian Philosophy of the Canadian Philosophical Association, to a joint meeting of philosophers from the University of Winnipeg and the University of Manitoba, and at the University of Waterloo, the University of Wisconsin (Madison), and the University of North Carolina (Chapel Hill). I hope that I have profited from discussion on those occasions; I am certainly grateful to those who questioned, commented, and objected.

1   For some brief characterizations of ideology, see Chaim I. Waxman, ed., *The End of Ideology Debate* (New York: Simon & Schuster, 1968), pp. 3–4. Superstructure and false consciousness are, of course, part of the Marxian account of ideology. The demise of ideology was celebrated in Daniel Bell, *The End of Ideology* (New York: The Free Press, 1960), and discussed in Waxman. Note such titles as "The End of Ideology as Ideology" by Robert A. Haber, "The Anti-Ideology Ideologues" by Michael Harrington, "The End of 'The End of Ideology'" by Donald Clark Hodges.

2   My sketchy characterization of ideology needs to be amplified and embedded in a theory of con-

sciousness. There is, of course, no space for that here. What I have to say owes much to my reading of D.C. Dennett, *Content and Consciousness* (London: Routledge & Kegan Paul, 1969), especially chap. VI. But I should not want to suggest that Dennett would accept parenthood for my ideas.

3 "Now one may think of moral philosophy . . . as the attempt to describe our moral capacity; . . . This enterprise is very difficult. For by such a description is not meant simply a list of the judgments on institutions and actions that we are prepared to render, accompanied with supporting reasons when these are offered. Rather, what is required is a formulation of a set of principles which, when conjoined to our beliefs and knowledge of the circumstances, would lead us to make these judgments with their supporting reasons were we to apply these principles conscientiously and intelligently. . . . The principles which describe them [our moral capacities] must be presumed to have a complex structure, and the concepts involved will require serious study.

"A useful comparison here is with the problem of describing the sense of grammaticalness that we have for the sentences of our native language. . . . This is a difficult undertaking which . . . is known to require theoretical constructions that far outrun the ad hoc precepts of our explicit grammatical knowledge. A similar situation presumably holds in moral philosophy. . . . A correct account of moral capacities will certainly involve principles and theoretical constructions which go much beyond the norms and standards cited in everyday life; . . ." John Rawls, *A Theory of Justice* (Cambridge, Mass.: Harvard University Press, 1971), pp 46–47. Other relevant passages are on pp. 126–128, 137–138, 143 145.

4 John Locke, *Two Treatises of Government*, especially Second Treatise, chaps. VII-IX. See also chap. II for discussion of the law of nature.

5 Thomas Hobbes, *Leviathan*, especially chaps. 13, 17, and 20.

6 The source for this is one of the magazines distributed in Canada with the Saturday newspaper. The magazine has found its way from my desk into a bundle of old newspapers, leaving behind only the quote.

7 "This passage from the state of nature to civil society produces in man a very remarkable change, in substituting justice for instinct in his conduct, and giving his actions the morality which previously they lacked. . . . If the abuses of this new condition did not often degrade him below that from which he has come, he should bless unceasingly the happy moment . . . which, from a stupid and limited animal, made an intelligent being and a man." Jean-Jacques Rousseau, *Du contrat social*, book I,

chap. VIII, my translation. Also, "He who dares undertake to create a people ought to feel himself capable of changing, so to speak, human nature, of transforming each individual, who by himself is complete and solitary, into part of a larger whole from which he receives almost his very life and being, of changing his constitution to strengthen it, of substituting an interdependent and moral existence for the physical and independent existence which we all have received from nature. It is necessary, in a word, that he remove man's own powers, in order to give him ones which are foreign to him and which he can not use without the help of others." Book II. chapter VII, also my translation.

It should be noted here that Rawls subverts contractarianism in a way very similar to Rousseau. Having determined one's fundamental legitimating principle for society (for Rousseau, that social relationships respect liberty in avoiding the dependence of one man on another; for Rawls, that social relationships embody mutual respect), one then introduces a "most favored" initial situation, in which persons would rationally choose a society based on the legitimating principle. One then supposes that in society, human beings are so socialized that their self-conception comes to center on that legitimating principle; hence they will consider their social relationships to be those they would have chosen. Thus the principle acquires a contractarian rationale.

But the rationale is spurious; since the initial situation is selected to ensure the "correct" choice, the act of choice is evidently neither necessary nor sufficient to justify the legitimating principle. The real character of the theory then emerges when one asks for the grounds of the legitimating principle.

8 *Leviathan*, chap. 13, "men have no pleasure, (but on the contrary a great deal of griefe) in keeping company, where there is no power able to over-awe them all."

9 Plato, *Republic*, 338d–339a.

10 To act on a mutually selected principle of action is to act on the basis of a choice, made by each person, of a single set of actions, one for each person in the situation; until all choose the same set, no one acts.

11 *Leviathan*, chap. 17, especially "the agreement . . . of men, is by Covenant only, which is Artificiall: and therefore it is no wonder if there be somewhat else required (besides Covenant) to make their Agreement constant and lasting; which is a Common Power, to keep them in awe, and to direct their actions to the Common Benefit."

12 The classification of goods obviously corresponds to the tripartite division of the soul in *Republic*, 436a–441c.

13 Hobbes "ought to say that, the state of nature

being where the care of our own conservation is the least prejudicial to that of others, it was consequently the most conducive to peace and the most appropriate for mankind. He says precisely the opposite, having inopportunely introduced into the savage's care for his own conservation the need to satisfy a multitude of passions which are the work of society . . ." Jean-Jacques Rousseau, *Discours sur l'origine et les fondements de l'inégalité parmi les hommes*, première partie. Translation mine.

14 *Leviathan*, chaps. 13 and 11.

15 "Hobbes . . . came nearest to postulating man as an infinite appropriator (though he did not quite do so), . . ." C.B. Macpherson, *Democratic Theory: Essays in Retrieval* (Oxford: At the Clarendon Press, 1973), p. 29n.

16 *Two Treatises of Government*, Second Treatise, chap. V (on appropriation), and chap. II (on the law of nature).

17 *De Cive*, chap. II, para. I.

18 *Leviathan*, chap 15.

19 The comparisons in this paragraph are intended to be commonplace; I have not tied them to particular references to Stoics, medieval Christians, and Kant.

20 *Leviathan*, chap. 5.

21 The argument on pp. 205–206 of "Coordination," *Dialogue* 14, no. 2 (June 1975), may be transferred from the case of act-utilitarianism to that of individual utility-maximization, to show that coordination is a natural extension of maximization. Bargaining is discussed in "Rational Cooperation," *Nous* 8, no. 1 (March 1974), pp. 53–65.

22 See "Reason and Maximization," *Canadian Journal of Philosophy* 4, no. 3, (March 1975), especially pp. 427–430.

23 Lacking control over the means of production, workers have been required to sell their labor, and thus their claim to own their products, in order to survive. Thus they have been excluded from appropriative activity, an exclusion which continued even after they combined in trade unions, until those unions abandoned the goal of replacing the appropriative, competitive economy with a noncompetitive order, and adopted instead the aim of exercising power within the existing system. Reproduction, the activity of women, has been considered inferior and instrumental to true production. Being unable to engage in production, women have been required to sell *their* labor in order to survive; the husband has thus appropriated the children as products.

24 Karl Marx, *Contribution to the Critique of Hegel's Philosophy of Right*, Introduction.

25 Thomas Hobbes, *Leviathan*, edited and introduced by C.B. Macpherson (Harmondsworth, Middlesex: Penguin Books, 1968), pp. 55–56. See also pp. 61–63.

26 "One word more about giving instruction as to what the world ought to be. Philosophy in any case always comes on the scene too late to give it. As the thought of the world, it appears only when actuality is already there cut and dried after its process of formation has been completed. . . . When philosophy paints its grey in grey, then has a shape of life grown old. By philosophy's grey in grey it cannot be rejuvenated but only understood. The owl of Minerva spreads its wings only with the falling of the dusk." *Hegel's Philosophy of Right*, tr. T.M. Knox (Oxford: At the Clarendon Press, 1942), pp. 12–13.

Hegel played a larger role in earlier drafts of this essay. The discussion of property and contract in the first part of the *Philosophy of Right* is a fundamental source for any articulation of contractarian ideology, however much Hegel rejects the view that all social relationships are contractual. But the exposition of Hegel is a problem in itself, and this essay faces enough problems, so Hegel has been unfairly relegated to a footnote.

3

The Fraternal Social Contract

Carole Pateman

The sons form a conspiracy to overthrow the despot, and in the end substitute a social contract with equal rights for all . . . Liberty means equality among the brothers (sons) . . . Locke suggests that the fraternity is formed not by birth but by election, by contract . . . Rousseau would say it is based on will. (Norman O. Brown, Love's Body)

The stories of the origins of civil society found in the classic social contract theories of the seventeenth and eighteenth centuries have been repeated many times. More recently, John Rawls and his followers have given new lease of life to the story of the contract that generates political right. But in all the telling of the tales, and in the discussion and argument about the social contract, we are told only half the story. Political theorists present the familiar account of the creation of civil society as a universal realm that (at least potentially) includes everyone and of the origins of political right in the sense of the authority of government in the liberal state, or Rousseau's participatory polity. But this is not the 'original' political right. There is silence about the part of the story which reveals that the social contract is a fraternal pact that constitutes civil society as a patriarchal or masculine order. To uncover the latter, it is necessary to begin to tell the repressed story of the genesis of patriarchal political right which men exercise over women.

Originally published in *The Disorder of Women* (Polity Press, 1980), 33–57. Copyright © Carole Pateman. Reprinted by permission of Blackwell Publishers and the author.

Most discussions of contract theory accept uncritically the claim that the stories successfully show why the authority of the state is legitimate; but the critical failure to recognize the social contract as fraternal pact is of a different kind. Only half the story appears in commentaries on the classic texts or in contemporary Rawlsian arguments, because modern political theory is so thoroughly patriarchal that one aspect of its origins lies outside the analytical reach of most theorists. Political theorists argue about the individual, and take it for granted that their subject matter concerns the public world, without investigating the way in which the 'individual', 'civil society' and 'the public' have been constituted as patriarchal categories in opposition to womanly nature and the 'private' sphere. The civil body politic created through the fraternal social contract is fashioned after only one of the two bodies of humankind.

The patriarchal character of civil society is quite explicit in the classic texts – if they are read from a feminist perspective. In this chapter, I can draw attention to only a few of the implications of such a reading and to some of the most obvious omissions in standard discussions of contract theory.[1] For instance, civil society is public society, but it is not usually appreciated that feminist arguments refer to a different sense of the separation of 'public' and 'private' from that typically found in discussions of civil society.

The meaning of 'civil society' in the contract stories, and as I am using it here, is constituted through the 'original' separation and opposition between the modern, public – civil – world and the modern, private or conjugal and familial sphere: that is, in the new social world created through contract, everything that lies beyond the domestic (private) sphere is public, or 'civil', society. Feminists are concerned with *this* division. In contrast, most discussions of civil society and such formulations as 'public' regulation versus 'private' enterprise presuppose that the politically relevant separation between public and private is drawn *within* 'civil society' as constructed in the social contract stories. That is to say, 'civil society' has come to be used in a meaning closer to that of Hegel, the social contract theorists' greatest critic, who contrasts the universal, public state with the market, classes and corporations of private, civil society.

Hegel, of course, presents a threefold division between family, civil society, state – but the separation between the family and the rest of social life is invariably 'forgotten' in arguments about civil society. The shift in meaning of 'civil', 'public' and 'private' goes unnoticed because the 'original' creation of civil society through the social contract is a patriarchal construction which is also a separation of the sexes. Political theorists have repressed this part of the story from their theoretical consciousness – though it is implicit in the assumption that civil life requires a natural foundation – and thus liberals and (non-feminist) radicals alike deal only with the liberal understanding of civil society, in which 'civil' life becomes private in opposition to the public state.

Perhaps the most striking feature of accounts of the contract story is the lack of attention paid to fraternity, when liberty and equality are so much discussed. One reason for the neglect is that most discussions pass over the insights about fraternity found in Freud's versions of the contract story. Fraternity is central to socialism, and nineteenth- and twentieth-century liberalism, as a recent study has shown, relies heavily on fraternity as a crucial bond integrating individual and community. However, discussions of fraternity do not touch upon the constitution of the 'individual' through the patriarchal separation of private and public, nor upon how the division within the (masculine) 'individual' includes an opposition between fraternity and reason. Fraternity comes to the fore in liberals' attempts to formulate a more sociologically adequate account of the individual than is found in the abstract conceptions of classic liberal contract theory. But for feminists explicit recourse to liberal or socialist

fraternal bonds merely exposes the patriarchal character of ostensibly universal categories and calls attention to the fundamental problem of whether and how women could be fully incorporated into a patriarchal civil world.

A feminist reading of the contract stories is also important for another reason. The contemporary feminist movement has brought the idea of patriarchy into popular and academic currency, but confusion abounds about its meaning and implications and recently some feminists have argued that the term is best avoided. 'Patriarchy' is, to my knowledge, the only term with which to capture the specificities of the subjection and oppression of *women* and to distinguish this from other forms of domination. If we abandon the concept of patriarchy, the problem of the subjection of women and sexual domination will again vanish from view within individualist and class theories. The crucial question, therefore, is the sense in which it can be said that our own society is patriarchal.

Two popular feminist claims about patriarchy add to the confusion. The first is that the literal meaning of 'patriarchy', rule by fathers, is still relevant. To insist that patriarchy is nothing more than paternal rule is itself a patriarchal interpretation, as an examination of the classic texts reveals. The second claim is that patriarchy is a timeless, human universal, which obviously rules out the possibility that men's domination of women takes different forms in different historical periods and cultures. More precisely, neither claim about patriarchy can acknowledge that our own momentous transition from the traditional to the modern world – a transition which the contract stories encapsulate theoretically – involved a change from a traditional (paternal) form of patriarchy to a new *specifically modern* (or fraternal) form: patriarchal civil society.

Few of the participants in recent feminist debates about patriarchy seem aware of the significance of patriarchal political theory in the classic sense: that is, the patriarchalism of Sir Robert Filmer and other less well-known writers of three centuries ago. Nor have they taken account of the theoretical and practical significance of the battle waged between the patriarchalists and the social contract theorists. Zillah Eisenstein has done so, but on the other hand Jean Elshtain's references to patriarchal theory merely reiterate the standard view in political theory that patriarchalism had suffered a fatal defeat by the end of the seventeenth century.[2] This is far from the case, and an understanding of the exact sense in which, and the limits within which, the contract theorists emerged victorious over the patriarchalists is central to an appreciation of how a specifically modern form of patriarchy was brought into being.

Patriarchal political theory had little in common with the ancient tradition of patriarchalism that took the family as the general model for social order and made claims about the emergence of political society from the family, or the coming together of many families. In *Patriarchalism in Political Thought*, Schochet emphasizes that patriarchal theory was formulated explicitly as a justification for political authority and political obedience, and – as he also stresses – it was systematized in opposition to the social contract theories that were developing at the same time and challenging (one half of) the patriarchalists' most fundamental assumptions.[3] Patriarchalism developed, and was 'defeated', in a specific historical and theoretical context.

The standard interpretation of the conflict between the patriarchalists and the contract theorists treats it as a battle over paternal rule and focuses on the irreconcilable differences between the two doctrines over the political right of fathers and the natural liberty of sons. The patriarchalists claimed that kings and fathers ruled in exactly the same way (kings were fathers and vice versa); that family and polity were homologous; that sons were born naturally subject to their fathers; and that political authority and obedience and a hierarchy of inequality were natural. The contract theorists rejected all these claims: they argued that paternal and political rule were distinct; that family and polity were two different and separate forms of association; that sons were born free and equal and, as adults, were as free as their fathers before them; that political authority and obligation were conventional and political subjects were civil equals.[4] It is true that in this particular controversy the patriarchalists were defeated. The theoretical assumptions of the contract theorists were an essential part of the transformation of the traditional order and the world of father-kings into capitalist society, liberal representative government and the modern family.

However, this familiar version of the story in which the sons gain their natural liberty, make the contract and create liberal civil society, or Rousseau's participatory civil order, is only half the tale. It is a patriarchal reading of the texts which identifies patriarchy with paternal rule; it therefore omits the story of the real origin of political right. Patriarchalism has two dimensions: the paternal (father/son) and the masculine (husband/wife). Political theorists can represent the outcome of the theoretical battle as a victory for contract theory because they are silent about the sexual or conjugal aspect of patriarchy, which appears as non-political or natural and so of no theoretical consequence. But a feminist reading of the texts shows that patriarchalism was far from defeated. The contract theorists rejected paternal right, but they absorbed and simultaneously transformed conjugal, masculine patriarchal right.

To see how this came about – and hence to take a necessary first step towards elucidating some of the characteristics of modern patriarchy – it is necessary to begin with the patriarchal story of monarchical fatherhood exemplified in the writings of Sir Robert Filmer. Although Filmer's father is overthrown in the story of the social contract, his sons receive a vital inheritance that is, paradoxically, obscured by the doctrine of paternal right.

Filmer's aim was to show the awful error of the contract theorists' claim that men were by nature free and equal, a claim he saw as the 'main foundation of popular sedition'.[5] Filmer argued that all law was of necessity the product of the will of one man. All titles to rule devolved from the original divine grant of kingly right to Adam, the first father. The ground was immediately swept from under the feet of the proponents of the doctrine of the natural freedom of mankind once it was recognized that 'the natural and private dominion of Adam [is] the fountain of all government and propriety'.[6] Filmer writes that 'the title comes from the fatherhood';[7] Adam's sons, and hence all succeeding generations of sons, were born into political subjection by virtue of Adam's 'right of fatherhood', his 'fatherly power' or the 'power of the fatherhood'.[8]

At the birth of his first son, Adam became the first monarch, and his political right passed to all subsequent fathers and kings. For Filmer, fathers and kings ruled by virtue of their fatherhood and all fathers were monarchs in their families: 'the Father of a family governs by no other law than by his own will.'[9] Filmer argued that no government could be a tyranny because the king's will was law; similarly, the will of the father was the absolute, arbitrary will of the *patria potestas* who, under Roman law, had the power of life and death over his children. Laslett comments that Filmer 'did not adopt the capital punishment of children by their fathers, but he quoted examples of it from Bodin with approval.'[10]

Filmer's view of the origin of political right seems, therefore, to be unmistakable: it derives from fatherhood. But patriarchy, even in its classical formulation, is more complex than its literal meaning suggests. Fatherly power is only one dimension of patriarchy, as Filmer himself reveals. Filmer's apparently straightforward statements obscure the foundation of patriarchal right. Paternal power is not the origin of political right. The genesis of political power lies in Adam's conjugal or sex right, not in his fatherhood. Adam's political title is granted *before* he becomes a father. Sons, as Filmer caustically reminds Hobbes, do not spring up like mushrooms. If Adam was to be a father, Eve had to become a mother and if Eve was to be a mother, then Adam must have sexual access to her body. In other words, sexual or conjugal right must *necessarily precede* the right of fatherhood.

Filmer makes it clear that Adam's political right is originally established in his right as a husband over Eve: 'God gave to Adam . . . the dominion over the woman', and 'God ordained Adam to rule over his wife, and her desires were to be subject to his'.[11] However, sexual or conjugal right then fades from view in Filmer's writings. After proclaiming that Adam's first dominion or political right is over a woman, not another man (son), Filmer then subsumes conjugal right under the power of fatherhood. Eve and her desires are subject to Adam but, Filmer continues, 'here we have the original grant of government, and the fountain of all power placed in the Father of all mankind'. Recall that in the Bible story in the Book of Genesis, Eve is created only after Adam and the animals have been placed on earth. Moreover, she is not created *ab initio* but *from* Adam, who is thus in a sense her parent. Filmer is able to treat all political right as the right of a father because the patriarchal father has the creative powers of both a mother and a father. He is not just one of two parents; he is *the* parent.

The patriarchal image of political fathers (here in Locke's words) is that of 'nursing Fathers tender and careful of the publick weale'.[12] The patriarchal story is about the procreative power of a father who is complete in himself. His procreative power both gives and nurtures physical life and creates and maintains political right. Filmer is able to dismiss Adam's power over Eve so easily because, in the story, women are procreatively and politically irrelevant. The reason Adam has dominion over 'the woman' is, according to Filmer (here following a very ancient notion), that 'the man . . . is the nobler and principal agent in generation'.[13] Women are merely empty vessels for the exercise of the father's sexual and procreative power. The original political right which God gives to Adam is, so to speak, the right to fill the empty vessel.

There is therefore no question to be asked, or error to be corrected, about women's natural freedom. Filmer invokes women merely to highlight the folly of the doctrine of the natural liberty of sons. The contract theorists' argument about natural freedom entails that 'there can be no superior power'. The full absurdity of that conclusion is revealed for Filmer in its corollary that 'women, especially virgins, [would] by birth have as much natural freedom as any other, and therefore ought not to lose their liberty without their own consent.'[14]

Filmer could present the natural freedom of women as the *reductio ad absurdum* of the contract argument because there was no controversy between the patriarchalists and contract theorists about women's subjection. The contract theorists' aim was theoretical parricide, not the overthrow of the sexual right of men and husbands. Both sides agreed, first, that women (wives), unlike sons, were born and remained naturally subject to men (husbands); and, second, that the right of men over women was *not political*. Locke, for example, concurred with Filmer's view that a wife's subjection has a 'Foundation in Nature'. The husband is naturally 'the abler and the stronger', so he must rule over his wife.[15] Rousseau, the vehement critic of the fraudulent liberal social contract that brings into being a corrupt civil society of inequality and domination, is no less insistent that women must be 'subjected either to a man or to the judgements of men and they are never permitted to put themselves above these judgements'. When a woman becomes a wife, she acknowledges her husband as 'a master for the whole of life'.[16]

The contract theorists' 'victory' hinged on the separation of paternal from political power, so they could not, like Filmer, subsume sexual under paternal – that is, political – rule. Instead, the social contract story hides original political right by proclaiming sexual or conjugal right as *natural*. Men's dominion over women is held to follow from the respective natures of the sexes, and Rousseau spells out this claim in detail in Book V of *Emile*. Locke has no quarrel with Filmer about the *legitimacy* of sexual, patriarchal right; rather, he insists that it is not political. Eve's subordination:

> can be no other Subjection than what every Wife owes her Husband, . . . Adam ['s] . . . can only be a Conjugal Power, not Political, the Power that every Husband hath to order the things of private Concernment in his Family, as Proprietor of the Goods and Land there, and to have his Will take place before that of his wife in all things of their common Concernment.[17]

Both sides in the seventeenth-century controversy – unlike contemporary political theorists – were well aware that the new doctrine of natural freedom and equality had subversive implications for *all* relationships of power and subordination. The patriarchalists claimed that the doctrine was so absurd that the problems it raised of justifying, say, the power of a husband over his wife were immediately shown to be figments of the contract theorists' disordered imaginations. But if the contract theorists were content with conjugal patriarchy, the individualist language of their attack on paternal right meant that they had (as Sir Robert Filmer argued) opened the thin ends of numerous revolutionary wedges, including a feminist wedge. Women almost at once seized on the contradiction of an 'individualism' and a 'universalism' which insisted that women were born into subjection and that their subjection was natural and politically irrelevant. By the end of the seventeenth century, for example, Mary Astell was asking: 'If all Men are born Free, how is it that all Women are born Slaves?'[18]

The difficulty for the contract theorists was that given their premises, an answer to the question was impossible. Logically, there is no reason why a free and equal female individual should always (contract to) subordinate herself to another free and equal (male) individual upon marriage. The difficulty, however, was easily overcome. Political theorists, whether liberal or socialist, absorbed masculine right into their theories and 'forgot' the story of the origin of patriarchal power. Natural subjection was seen in terms of paternal power and three centuries of feminist criticism – whether written by women whose names never appear in political theory textbooks, by the cooperative or utopian socialists, or by the otherwise acceptable philosopher, John Stuart Mill – was suppressed and ignored.

The standard view that the rise of social contract theory and the development of civil society was also a defeat for patriarchalism has meant that some vital questions about the construction of the civil body politic have never been asked. One problem about the social contract that has received some attention is the question of exactly who makes the agreement. Many commentators talk uncritically of 'individuals' sealing the pact, but Schochet, for example, points out that in the seventeenth century it was taken for granted that fathers of families entered the social contract.

When I first began to think about these matters from a feminist perspective, I assumed that the social contract was a patriarchal contract because it was made by fathers whose agreement was taken to bind their families. Certainly, 'individuals', in the universal sense in which the category is usually used to mean anyone and everyone, do not make the social contract. Women have no part in it: as natural subjects they lack the requisite capacities and abilities. The 'individuals' of the stories are *men*, but they do not act as fathers. After all, the stories tell of the defeat of the father's political power. Men no longer have a political place as fathers. But fathers are also husbands – Locke's friend Tyrrell wrote that wives were 'concluded by their Husbands'[19] – and, from yet another viewpoint, the participants in the social contract are sons or brothers. The contract is made by brothers, or a *fraternity*. It is no accident that fraternity appears historically hand in hand with liberty and equality, nor that it means exactly what it says: brotherhood.

If 'patriarchy' is all too often interpreted literally, 'fraternity' is usually treated as if its literal meaning had no relevance today and as if the terms in the revolutionary slogan, 'Liberty, Equality, Fraternity', unquestionably applied to us all, not only to men joined by fraternal bonds. Bernard Crick has recently pointed out that fraternity has been relatively little analysed, even though, he says, 'fraternity with liberty is humanity's greatest dream'.[20] When it is mentioned, fraternity is usually presented as an expression of community; it is seen as 'at bottom, a certain type of social cooperation . . . a relation between a group of equals for the utmost mutual help and aid'.[21] Or as Crick argues, addressing his fellow socialists, fraternity is an ethic and social practice that 'goes with simplicity, lack of ostentation, friendliness, helpfulness, kindliness, openness, lack of restraint between individuals in everyday life and a willingness to work together in common tasks.'[22] The general acceptance that 'fraternity' is no more than a way of talking about the bonds of community illustrates how deeply patriarchal conceptions structure our political theory and practice. Feminists have long appreciated the extent to which socialist solidarity and community has meant that women are little more than auxiliaries to the comrades and that women's political demands must wait until after the revolution. But the problems women have in finding a language in which to make their demands is illustrated by the final words of Simone de Beauvoir's *The Second Sex*, where she states that 'men and women [must] unequivocally affirm their brotherhood.'[23]

The fact that the social contract is not an agreement between individuals, fathers or husbands, but a fraternal pact, becomes particularly clear in Freud's versions of the social contract story. Freud's account of the murder of the primal father by his sons is not usually considered in discussions of the social contract. Yet, as Brown states, 'the battle of books re-enacts Freud's primal crime.'[24] And Rieff treats Freud's myth of the parricide as a version of the social contract, to be considered as part of the same tradition as the theories of Hobbes, Locke or Rousseau.[25] The best warrant of all is available for this interpretation. In *Moses and Monotheism* Freud refers to the pact made by the brothers after their dreadful deed as 'a sort of social contract'.[26]

But, it could be objected, Freud's myth is about the origins of society itself. Freud claims – and this is taken at face value by Juliet Mitchell's *Psychoanalysis and Feminism*, which has been very influential among feminists – that the parricide ushers in 'civilization': that is, human society. However, the classic social contract theorists are also sometimes read in the same way; the passage from 'the state of nature' can be seen as the transition from nature or savagery to the first human social order. In neither case is there good reason

to accept a universal reading that identifies 'civilization' or 'civil society' with society itself. When the form of the laws instituted by the brothers is examined, it is clear that the stories are about the origin of a culturally and historically specific form of social life. The close connection between 'civil society' and 'civilization' is suggested too by the fact that the term 'civilization' came into general use only towards the end of the eighteenth century, 'to express a particular stage of European history, sometimes the final or ultimate stage.'[27] 'Civilization' expressed the 'sense of modernity: an achieved condition of refinement and order.'[28]

In her interpretation of Freud, Mitchell claims that the 'law of the father' is established after the parricide. On the contrary: the law of the father, the absolute rule of one father-king, holds sway before his murder. The crucial point about the contract is that it takes place after the death of the father and abolishes his arbitrary right. Instead, the brothers (sons), prompted by remorse for their dreadful deed, by love and hatred and by a desire to prevent parricide in future, establish their *own* law. They establish justice, 'the first "right" or "law"'[29] – or civil society. The law, or arbitrary will, of the father is overthrown by the combined action of the brothers, who then place mutual restrictions on themselves, establishing an equality which, Freud states, 'saved the organization which had made them strong'.[30] A contract between free and equal brothers replaces the 'law of the father' with public rules which bind all equally. As Locke makes clear, the rule of one man (father) is incompatible with civil society, which requires an impartial, impersonal set of rules promulgated by a collective body of men who stand to the law and each other as free equals, as a fraternity.

At this point the objection might be raised that even if brothers enter the contract, they cease to be brothers once the pact is concluded. In the act of contracting they constitute themselves as equal, civil 'individuals' and thus cast off familial and, hence, fraternal ties. The fundamental distinction between the traditional patriarchy of the father and modern patriarchy is precisely that the latter is created in separation from, and opposition to, the familial sphere.

However, it does not follow that all ascriptive ties are therefore abandoned and that the term 'fraternal' ceases to be appropriate. Brown claims that there is an 'inner contradiction' in the trilogy of liberty, equality, fraternity: 'without a father there can be no sons or brothers.'[31] However, as recent accounts of fraternity make clear, the concept covers much more than bonds of kinship. 'Individuals' can be part of a fraternity or a brotherhood – a 'community' – even though they are not brothers (sons of a father or kin). The father is dead and the participants in civil society have left kinship behind them, but as civil individuals they still share an ascriptive bond – a bond *as men*.

Freud's story of the parricide is important because he makes explicit what the classic tales of theoretical murder leave obscure: the motive for the brothers' collective act is not merely to claim their natural liberty and right of self-government, but *to gain access to women*. In the classic theorists' state of nature the 'family' already exists and men's conjugal right is deemed a natural right.[32] Freud's primal father, his *patria potestas*, keeps all the women of the horde for himself. The parricide eliminates the father's political right, and also his *exclusive* sexual right. The brothers inherit his patriarchal, masculine right and share the women among themselves. No man can be a primal father ever again, but by setting up rules that give all men equal access to women (compare their equality before the laws of the state) they exercise the 'original' political right of dominion over women that was once the prerogative of the father.

Freud writes of the brothers' 'renunciation of the passionately desired mothers and sisters of the horde.'[33] This is misleading. The fraternity do not renounce the women, but each gives up the desire to put himself in the place of the father. As part of the fraternal social contract the brothers institute what Freud calls the law of exogamy or kinship. In historically specific terms, the brothers create the modern system of marriage law and family and establish the modern order of conjugal or sexual right. The 'natural foundation' of civil society has been brought into being through the fraternal social contract.

The separation of 'paternal' from political rule, or the family from the public sphere, is also the separation of women from men through the subjection of women to men. The brothers establish their own law and their own form of sexual or conjugal dominion. The fraternal social contract creates a new, modern patriarchal order that is presented as divided into two spheres: civil society or the universal sphere of freedom, equality, individualism, reason, contract and impartial law – the realm of men or 'individuals'; and the private world of particularity, natural subjection, ties of blood, emotion, love and sexual passion – the world of women, in which men also rule.

In short, the contract constitutes patriarchal civil society and the modern, ascriptive rule of men over women. Ascription and contract are usually seen as standing at opposite poles, but the social contract is sexually ascriptive in both form (it is made by brothers) and content (the patriarchal right of a fraternity is established). Civil individuals have a fraternal bond because, *as men*, they share a common interest in upholding the contract which legitimizes their masculine patriarchal right and allows them to gain material and psychological benefit from women's subjection.

One important question raised by the contract stories is exactly how the 'foundation in nature', which upholds the subjection of women, should be characterized. Locke tells us that the strength and ability of the man (husband) is the natural basis of the wife's subordination; a view which becomes absorbed into patriarchal liberalism, but also opens the way for liberal feminism. Feminists began to criticize the argument from strength long ago,[34] and although the claim is still heard today, historically it has become less and less plausible to rely on strength as the criterion for masculine political right. Contemporary liberal feminists, following the lead of much earlier writers like Mary Astell and Mary Wollstonecraft, have attacked the alleged lesser ability and capacity of women as an artifact of defective education, as a matter of deliberate social contrivance, not a fact of nature.

The difficulty for the liberal feminist argument is that education cannot be equal while men and women remain differentially positioned within their 'separate spheres', but the patriarchal division between the private family and public, civil society is a central structural principle of liberalism. Moreover, the problem runs deeper than a liberal perspective suggests. Liberal feminism assumes that the relevant political problem is to show that women possess the capacities men possess and can do what men can do. However, this also assumes that there is no political significance to the fact that women have one natural ability which men lack: women, but not men, are able to give birth.

Now, it may be claimed that this provides no 'foundation in nature' for women's subjection because birth (unlike child-rearing) is ultimately irrelevant to the development of the capacities of civil beings. The difficulty with this argument is that it, too, ignores the story of the 'origin' of patriarchal political right, and thus the importance of birth for patriarchal civil society. The ability to give birth, both actually and metaphorically, is central to patriarchal theory.

Filmer's argument shows that Adam's right of domination over Eve is the right to become a father: a right to demand sexual access to Eve's body and to insist that she give birth. Eve's procreative, creative capacity is then denied and appropriated by *men* as the ability to give *political birth*, to be the 'originators' of a new form of political order. Adam and the participants in the fraternal social contract gain an amazing patriarchal ability and become the 'principal agents' in political generation. Moreover, in patriarchal argument birth also symbolizes and encapsulates all the reasons why it has been claimed that women must be bodily removed from civil society.[35]

Some of the murky depths become clearer in the stories told by Rousseau and Freud. Women, they insist, are unable to transcend their bodily natures in the manner required of 'individuals' who are to participate in civil life and uphold the universal laws of civil society. The female body, subject to uncontrollable natural processes and passions, deprives women of the reason and moral character which can be educated for civil society.[36]

Rousseau's solution is that the sexes must be segregated to the greatest possible extent, even in domestic life. Significantly, in *Emile* Rousseau allows the tutor to give only one direct command, in which he sends Emile away from Sophie for an extended period to learn about politics and citizenship before he is permitted to claim her body as a husband. Freud offers no solution but states explicitly that from the 'beginning' – from the original parricide in which women are at stake, and which is endlessly reproduced through the Oedipus complex – women continue to have 'a hostile attitude towards' civil society.[37] Or, as Mitchell interprets Freud, a woman 'cannot receive the "touch" of the law, her submission to it must be in establishing herself as its opposite.'[38]

Women are 'opposite' to and outside the fraternal social contract and its civil law in two senses. First, they are 'originally', necessarily, excluded from an agreement through which the brothers inherit their legacy of patriarchal sex right and legitimize their claim over women's bodies and ability to give birth. Second, the civil law encapsulates all that women lack. The civil law stems from a reasoned agreement that it is to the rational mutual advantage of the participants to the contract to constrain their interactions and desires through a law equally applicable to all. Women's passions render them incapable of making such a reasoned agreement or of upholding it if made. In other words, the patriarchal claim that there is a 'foundation in nature' for women's subjection to men is a claim that women's bodies must be governed by men's reason. The separation of civil society from the familial sphere is also a division between men's reason and women's bodies.

Feminist scholars are now showing how, from ancient times, political life has been conceptualized in opposition to the mundane world of necessity, the body, the sexual passions and birth: in short, in opposition to women and the disorders and creativity they symbolize.[39] In Filmer's classic patriarchalism the father is both mother and father and creates political right through his fatherhood, but Filmer's account is only one version of a long Western tradition in which the creation of political life has been seen as a masculine act of birth: as a male replica of the ability which only women possess.

The fraternal social contract is a specifically modern reformulation of this patriarchal tradition. The father is dead, but the brothers appropriate the ability specific to women; they, too, can generate new political life and political right. The social contract is the point of origin, or birth, of civil society, and simultaneously its separation from the (private) sphere of real birth and the disorder of women. The brothers give birth to an artificial body, the body politic of civil society; they create Hobbes's 'Artificial Man, we call a Commonwealth,' or Rousseau's 'artificial and collective body', or the 'one Body' of Locke's 'Body Politick'.

The 'birth' of the civil body politic, however, is an act of reason; there is no analogue to a bodily act of procreation. The social contract, as we are all taught, is not an actual event. The natural paternal body of Filmer's patriarchy is metaphorically put to death by the contract theorists, but the 'artificial' body that replaces it is a construct of the mind, not the creation of a political community by real people. Whereas the birth of a human child can produce a new male or female, the creation of civil society produces a social body fashioned after the image of only one of the two bodies of humankind. Or, more exactly, the civil body politic is fashioned after the image of the male 'individual' who is constituted through the separation of civil society from women. This individual has some singular – and largely unrecognized – aspects precisely because his defining characteristics are thrown into relief only through the contrast with the womanly nature that has been excluded from civil society.

The abstract character of the individual in liberal contract theory has been criticized from the left ever since Rousseau's initial attack. But because the critiques invariably pass silently over the separation of male reason from female body in the original creation of the civil individual, one of his most notable features has also silently been incorporated by the critics. The 'individual' is disembodied. For three centuries the figure of the individual has been presented as universal, as the embodiment of all, but it is only because he is disembodied that the 'individual' can appear universal. Like the new body politic he, too, is 'artificial': he is nothing more than a 'man of reason'.[40]

In the most recent rewriting of the liberal contract story, *A Theory of Justice*, Rawls claims that his parties in their original position know none of the essential facts about themselves. Thus it might seem that Rawls's parties are truly universal and that the original choices include a choice between the two bodies (sexes) of humankind. The fact that Rawls ignores this possibility, and writes that the parties can be seen as heads of families,[41] shows how deeply entrenched are patriarchal assumptions about the proper characteristics of the 'individual'. Moreover, the attributes of the parties and their original position illustrate the fact that Rawls stands at the logical conclusion of the fraternal contract tradition. The original position and its choices are explicitly hypothetical (logical) and the parties are nothing more than disembodied entities of reason; otherwise they could not help but know the natural facts about themselves, inseparable from their bodies, such as the facts of sex, age and colour.[42]

Ironically, the disembodiment necessary to maintain the political fiction of the universal civil individual poses profound problems for fraternity. For individualist liberals the problems are part of their wider difficulties over the self, and involve an opposition within the individual

between fraternity and reason. The opposition between reason and fraternity is an opposition between the public and the private. But this is not the patriarchal opposition between 'private' and 'public', between family (women) and civil society (men); instead, the relevant division between public and private is the other opposition to which I referred earlier: the opposition located within 'civil society' as I am using the term.[43] For liberals relying on a social view of the self or for socialist critics of liberalism the problems arise because in the 1980s an emphasis on fraternity begins to reveal the patriarchal character of their theories. To preserve universality, '*the* individual' must be abstracted even from his masculinity and fraternity, so that the individual has no body and, hence, no sex.

The creation of the 'individual' presupposes the division of rational civil order from the disorder of womanly nature. It might thus seem that the civil individual and the body politic made in his image would be unified. Indeed, they are so presented in liberal theory, but its critics from Rousseau onward argue that the individual and civil society are inherently divided, one from the other and within themselves. The individual is torn between *bourgeois* and *citoyen*, or between *Homo economicus* and *Homo civicus*, and civil society is divided between private interest and the public universal interest, or between 'civil' society and state. The point about such critiques, however, is exactly that they are concerned with extrafamilial social life and with the individual as an inhabitant of the public world.

The liberal opposition between private and public (like the patriarchal opposition between the sexes) appears in a variety of guises: for example, society, economy and freedom stand against state, public and coercion. Liberals see these dualities as posing important problems of freedom, since the private sphere of civil society must be protected from the coercive intrusions of the state, and they now spend a good deal of time and effort trying to sort out where the dividing line plausibly can be drawn. Their critics, on the other hand, argue that the opposition between private and public poses an insoluble problem; that it is an unbridgeable structural fissure at the centre of liberalism. I agree with the critics; but the criticism does not go far enough because it takes no account of the 'original' patriarchal division and thus leaves the critics' own conception of the 'individual' and 'civil society' untouched.

In *Knowledge and Politics*, Robert Unger presents a comprehensive discussion and critique of the liberal dichotomies, but even his analysis of the division between fact and theory, values and rules, desire and reason, ignores the fact that it also represents the opposition between the sexes. The 'self' is implicitly taken to be masculine. The reference to 'men' must be taken literally when he writes: 'The dichotomy of the public and private life is still another corollary of the separation of understanding and desire . . . When reasoning [men] belong to a public world. . . . When desiring, however, men are private beings.'[44] In Unger's account, the 'desire' and associated disorder represented by women and their private world has been 'forgotten'. The 'self' has become that of the male individual in civil society, an individual torn between the claims of public interest ('reason') and private or subjective interest ('desire'). The opposition between women, bodies, passion, and men, reason, rational advantage, is repressed and replaced by the dichotomy between the individual's private interest and the claims of the public interest or universal law.

In this form, the dichotomy is also expressed as an opposition between the fraternity and reason of civil individuals. The only ties between the individuals of liberal contract theory are those of self-interest. The individual is, as it were, a collection of pieces of property that can, through rational calculation of the mind, be made the subject of contract. The individual thus enters into only certain kinds of relationship and this limitation gives rise to another familiar difficulty within liberal theory: that of presenting a coherent conception of citizenship or the political. The liberal individual's political bonds with other citizens are merely another expression of the pursuit of self-interest; *Homo civicus* is absorbed into, or is nothing more than one face of, the 'private' *Homo economicus*. However, this view of the individual as citizen – as public or civil individual – systematically undermines one of the most significant expressions of fraternity.

Liberal individuals interact in a benign public world. They compete one with the other, but the competition is regulated and the rules are fair; the only coercion required is to enforce the rules. Hence the division between private and public as an opposition between society and state is often presented as between freedom and coercion. Currently this position is associated with the New

Right, but in the past *le doux commerce* could be offered as the antithesis of violence and the idealist liberals, claiming to have reconciled the oppositions, could assert that will, not force, is the basis of the state.

On the other hand, it is also clear that the individual can be required to protect his protection (as Hobbes put it) by something more than mere obedience to the law. He may have to surrender his body in defence of the state. Indeed, this has always been seen as the ultimate act of loyalty and allegiance, the truly exemplary act of citizenship. However, it is also an act which will never be to the rational advantage of a liberal individual, as Hobbes's logical working out of radical individualism reveals. In the clash between private and public interest, the private claim always has the rational advantage. It is not in the individual's self-interest to be a soldier; thus reason is torn apart from the fraternity on which citizenship, in the last analysis, depends. Of all the male clubs and associations, it is in the military and on the battlefield that fraternity finds its most complete expression.

The opposition between the figure of the soldier and the figure of the individual, or between fraternity and reason, is unique to liberal civil society. In many respects the fraternal contract story transforms ancient patriarchal themes into a specifically modern theory, but the conception of a liberal individual breaks with older traditions in which citizenship has involved a distinctive form of activity and has also been closely tied to the bearing of arms. Feminist scholars are now showing that from ancient times there has been an integral connection between the warrior and conceptions of self-identity, sexuality and masculinity, which have all been bound up with citizenship. The peculiarity of the liberal individual is that although he is male he is also defined – unlike either his predecessors in the traditional world or the 'individuals' that appear in social-liberal and socialist theory – in opposition to the political and the masculine passions that underlie the defence of the state by arms.

Although our consciousness is informed by the liberal individual's image, and many of our social practices and institutions presuppose that we are motivated by self-interest (the contemporary preoccupation with freeriders is no accident), the state has never relied on rational self-interest as the basis for socio-political order. Nor did most classic theorists, except Hobbes, have the courage of their theoretical convictions on this point. Hobbes's conclusion that Leviathan's sword was the only alternative to an inherently insecure 'artificial' ground for order was rejected in favour of such devices as natural law, sympathy, benevolence or hidden hands – and socialists have appealed to solidarity, comradeship and community or, in a word, to *fraternity*. Historically, obedience and loyalty to the state have been fostered by appeals not to individual rational advantage but to ascriptive, psychological bonds, especially to nationalism, patriotism and fraternity. These are ties of a much more full-blooded character than, for example, Rawls's sense of justice and, most importantly, they appeal directly to the masculine self's sense of identity. However, the real and ideological basis for the motivating force of self-interest means that it is hard to eliminate the opposition between fraternity and reason.

When some liberals over the past century attempted to develop an adequately social and developmental conception of individuality, one that restored the affective ties of community that had been stripped away in liberal contract theory, they also turned to the idea of fraternity. In the eyes of these liberals, Gaus states, fraternity is the 'most powerful of communal bonds'.[45] The ideal of fraternity provides the 'pre-eminent conception of communal bonds in modern liberal theory', so that Dewey, for example, wrote of a 'fraternally associated public', and Rawls sees his difference principle as a 'natural meaning of fraternity'.[46]

The explicit use of 'fraternity' in both social-liberal and socialist attempts to reintegrate the civil individual and the community (or to reintegrate the liberal division between private and public) means that the patriarchal character of civil society begins to come to the surface. Moreover, the masculine attributes of the individual begin to be exposed. The universalism of the category of the 'individual' can be maintained only as long as the abstraction from the body is maintained. 'The individual' is a fiction: individuals have one of two bodies, masculine or feminine. But how can the feminine body become part of a (liberal or socialist) fraternal body politic?

Citizenship has now been extended formally to women, raising the substantive problem of how we can become civil 'individuals' made in the masculine image. The importance, in practice, of the intimate connection between masculinity,

citizenship and bearing arms became explicit when women, taking the universalism of the principles of civil society at face value, demanded to be enfranchised. The 'jewel' in the armoury of the anti-suffragists was the argument from physical force.[47] Women, it was claimed, were naturally unable and unwilling to bear arms or use violence, so that if they became citizens, the state would inevitably be fatally weakened.

Now that women are enfranchised (and are even prime ministers) the same patriarchal view of citizenship is still found. In the British House of Commons in 1981, in a debate on the Nationality Bill, Enoch Powell argued that a woman should not pass on her citizenship to her child because 'nationality, in the last resort, is tested by fighting. A man's nation is the nation for which he will fight.' The difference between men and women, which must be expressed in citizenship, is that between 'fighting on the one hand and the creation and preservation of life on the other'.[48] It is true that women are now included as members of the armed forces but they are still excluded from combat units, which exemplify fraternities in action.[49]

'Men are born free': the rejection of (masculine) natural subjection generated the revolutionary claim that will, not force, is the basis of the state. One of the major successes of the fraternal contract story is the way it has helped to obscure coercion and violence in civil society and the manner in which 'will' is determined within relations of domination and subjection. Critics of contract theory have said a good deal about the inequality of parties to contracts and exploitation, but less about the consequences of contract and subordination. Only rarely have they discussed how contract gives the appearance of freedom to sexually ascriptive domination and subjection. Contract also hides the figure of the armed man in the shadows behind the civil individual. Foucault has counterposed a 'military dream' of a society against the original contract (what is presented as the original pact in the familiar stories), but the two are not so far apart as they may seem.

Foucault writes that the military dream looked, 'not to the state of nature, but to the meticulously subordinated cogs of a machine, not to the primal social contract, but to permanent coercions, not to fundamental rights, but to indefinitely progressive forms of training, not to the general will but to automatic docility.'[50] Automatic docility and the disciplines of the body portrayed by Foucault are part of the consequences of the fraternal social contract. Foucault states that 'the development and generalization of disciplinary mechanisms constituted the other, dark side' of the development of a 'formally egalitarian juridical framework'. However, it is less that the disciplines 'distort the contractual link systematically'[51] than that discipline in civil society, *which is also patriarchal discipline*, is typically established through contract. The forms of subjection specific to civil society are, as Foucault emphasizes, developed by the complicity of subordinates as well as by force – complicity made all the easier (as, importantly, is resistance) when consciousness is informed by patriarchal forms of liberty and equality. For example, when 'individuals' have a free choice of marriage partner, publicly recognized by a free contract, it is made harder to acknowledge that the marriage contract is a political fiction which ceremonially recognizes the patriarchal subjection of a wife and the masculine privileges of a husband.[52]

The modern discipline of the body is aided by political theory that has already separated reason from the body and the reason of men from the bodies of women. Foucault ignores the significant fact that the 'military dream' is a dream of men, whereas the fraternal social contract is also a dream of women. But the women's dream cannot be fulfilled, although the ostensibly universal categories of the contract make it always enticing. The history of liberal feminism is the history of attempts to generalize liberal liberties and rights to the whole adult population; but liberal feminism does not, and cannot, come to grips with the deeper problems of *how* women are to take an equal place in the patriarchal civil order.

Now that the feminist struggle has reached the point where women are almost formal civil equals, the opposition is highlighted between equality made after a male image and the real social position of women *as women*. Women have never, of course, been excluded entirely from civil life – the two spheres of the modern civil order are not separate in reality – but our inclusion has been singular. In a world presented as conventional, contractual and universal, women's civil position is ascriptive, defined by the natural particularity of being women; patriarchal subordination is socially and legally upheld throughout civil life, in production and citizenship as well as in the family. Thus to explore the subjection of

women is also to explore the fraternity of men. Recent feminist research has begun to uncover – despite the important divisions between men of different classes and races (and associations and clubs where fraternity is given explicit expression are usually so divided) – how men, *as men*, maintain the power and privileges of their patriarchal right throughout the whole of socio-political life.

The fraternal social contract story shows that the categories and practices of civil society cannot simply be universalized to women. The social contract is a modern patriarchal pact that establishes men's sex right over women, and the civil individual has been constructed in opposition to women and all that our bodies symbolize, so how can we become full members of civil society or parties to the fraternal contract?

The contradictory answer is that women in civil society must disavow our bodies and act as part of the brotherhood – but since we are never regarded as other than women, we must simultaneously continue to affirm the patriarchal conception of femininity, or patriarchal subjection.[53] The peculiar relation between civil society and women and our bodies is illustrated by the fact that few legal jurisdictions have abolished the right of a husband to use his wife's body against her will, that coercive sexual relations ('sexual harassment') are part of everyday working life; that women's bodies are sold in the capitalist market,[54] that women, until 1934 in the USA and 1948 in Britain, lost their citizenship if they married foreigners; that only in 1983 did all British women citizens win the right to pass on their citizenship to their husbands and so enable them to live in Britain,[55] and that welfare policies still do not fully recognize women's status as individuals.

The theoretical and social transformation required if women and men are to be full members of a free, properly democratic (or properly 'civilized') society is as far-reaching as can be imagined. The meaning of 'civil society' (in both senses discussed here) has been constructed through the exclusion of women and all that we symbolize. To 'rediscover' a patriarchal conception of civil society will do little to challenge men's patriarchal right. To create a properly democratic society, which includes women as full citizens, it is necessary to deconstruct and reassemble our understanding of the body politic. This task extends from the dismantling of the patriarchal separation of private and public, to a transformation of our individuality and sexual identities as feminine and masculine beings. These identities now stand opposed, part of the multi-faceted expression of the patriarchal dichotomy between reason and desire. The most profound and complex problem for political theory and practice is how the two bodies of humankind and feminine and masculine individuality can be fully incorporated into political life. How can the present of patriarchal domination, opposition and duality be transformed into a future of autonomous, democratic differentiation?

The traditional patriarchy of the fathers was long ago transformed into the fraternal, modern patriarchy of civil society. Perhaps there is hope, since these observations could be written only under the shadow of the owl of Minerva's wings. Alternatively, perhaps the time for optimism is past; feminism may have re-emerged at a point in the crisis of patriarchy in which the figure of the armed man – now armed not with the sword but with plastic bullets, cluster bombs, chemical, biological and nuclear weapons – has totally obliterated the figure of the civil individual. Perhaps, as Mary O'Brien suggests, 'the brotherhood have gone quite mad and lost control of their creations in some cosmic sorcerers' apprenticeship.'[56]

Notes

1 A more extensive and detailed feminist reading of the contract stories and of their significance for the marriage contract and other contracts, such as that between prostitute and client, is presented in my book, *The Sexual Contract* (Polity Press, Cambridge, 1988: Stanford University Press, Stanford, 1988).

2 Z. Eisenstein, *The Radical Future of Liberal Feminism*, (Longman, New York, 1981), chap. 3, but Eisenstein develops her argument in a different direction from my own; J. Elshtain, *Public Man, Private Woman: Women in Social and Political Thought* (Princeton University Press, Princeton, 1981), chap. 3. More recently, see L. Nicholson, *Gender and History: The Limits of Social Theory in the Age of the Family* (Columbia University Press, New York, 1986).

3 G. Schochet, *Patriarchalism in Political Thought: The Authoritarian Family and Political Speculation and Attitudes Especially in Seventeenth Century England* (Basil Blackwell, Oxford, 1975).

4 This brief summary highlights the essential points of conflict between the protagonists, and thus glosses over the differences among theorists on both sides. Hobbes, for instance, saw paternal and political rule as homologous, but rejected patriarchal claims about paternity.

5 Sir R. Filmer, *Patriarchia and Other Political Works*, ed. P. Laslett (Basil Blackwell, Oxford, 1949), p. 54.

6 Ibid., p. 71.

7 Ibid., p. 188.

8 Ibid., pp. 71, 57, 194.

9 Ibid., p. 96.

10 Laslett, 'Introduction', *Patriarchia*, p. 28. Filmer writes (p. 256): 'where there are only Father and sons, no sons can question the Father for the death of their brother.'

11 Filmer, *Patriarchia*, pp. 241, 283.

12 J. Locke, *Two Treatises of Government*, ed. P. Laslett, 2nd ed., (Cambridge University Press, Cambridge, 1967), II, §110.

13 Filmer, *Patriarchia*, p. 245.

14 Ibid., p. 287.

15 Locke, *Two Treatises*, I, §47; II, §82.

16 J.-J. Rousseau, *Emile, or On Education*, tr. A. Bloom (Basic Books, New York, 1979), pp. 370, 404.

17 Locke, *Two Treatises*, I, §48.

18 M. Astell, *Some Reflections Upon Marriage* (Source Book Press, New York, 1970), p. 107 (from the 1730 ed., first published 1700). On analogies drawn between the marriage contract and social contract and powers of husbands and kings, see M. Shanley, 'Marriage Contract and Social Contract in Seventeenth Century English Political Thought', *Western Political Quarterly*, 32(1), 1979, pp. 79–91.

19 Cited by Schochet, *Patriarchalism in Political Thought*, p. 202. I have discussed liberty, equality and the social contract in *The Problem of Political Obligation*, 2nd ed. (Polity Press, Cambridge, 1985; University of California Press, Berkeley, CA, 1985).

20 B. Crick, *In Defence of Politics* 2nd ed. (Penguin Books, Harmondsworth, Middlesex, 1982), p. 228.

21 E. Hobsbawm, 'The Idea of Fraternity', *New Society*, November 1975, cited in M. Taylor, *Community, Anarchy and Liberty* (Cambridge University Press, Cambridge, 1982) p. 31.

22 Crick, *In Defence of Politics*, p. 233. Crick (p. 230) suggests that 'sisterhood' is 'in some ways truly a less ambiguous image of what I am trying to convey by "fraternity".' Although he notes the relation between fraternity, the 'aggressive brothers' band' and 'stereotypes' of manliness, he argues that it is better to 'try to desex, even to feminize, old "fraternity", rather than to pause to rewrite

most languages'; which exactly misses the point that language expresses and forms part of the patriarchal structure of our society ('language is a form of life').

23 S. de Beauvoir, *The Second Sex*, tr. H. M. Parshley (Penguin Books, New York, 1953), p. 732. But of course we must remember that de Beauvoir was writing without the support of the organized feminist movement. Today, feminists have devoted a good deal of attention to language – and have provided some fascinating accounts of how, in practice, fraternity has shaped the working class and the labour movement, so that the 'worker' is a man and a member of the 'men's movement'; see especially C. Cockburn, *Brothers: Male Dominance and Technological Change* (Pluto Press, London, 1983), also B. Campbell, *The Road to Wigan Pier Revisited: Poverty and Politics in the 80s* (Virago Books, London, 1984). (The term 'men's movement' is Beatrix Campbell's.)

24 N. O. Brown, *Love's Body* (Vintage Books, New York, 1966), p. 4. I am grateful to Peter Breiner for drawing my attention to Brown's interpretation in *Love's Body*. A similar point is made, though its implications for patriarchy are not pursued, by M. Hulliung, 'Patriarchalism and Its Early Enemies', *Political Theory*, 2(1974), pp. 410–19. Hulliung (p. 416) notes that there is no reason why the parricide 'cannot just as well be turned into a morality play on behalf of . . . democratic ideals' and that 'the assassins are "brothers" towards each other, and brothers are equal.'

25 P. Rieff, *Freud: The Mind of the Moralist* (Methuen, London, n.d.), chap. VII.

26 S. Freud, *Moses and Monotheism*, tr. K. Jones (Vintage Books, New York, 1939), p. 104.

27 S. Rothblatt, *Tradition and Change in English Liberal Education* (Faber & Faber, London, 1976), p. 18.

28 R. Williams, *Keywords: A Vocabulary of Culture and Society*, revised ed. (Oxford University Press, New York, 1985), p. 58. I am grateful to Ross Poole for drawing my attention to the emergence of 'civilization'.

29 S. Freud, *Civilization and its Discontents* (W. W. Norton & Co., New York, n.d.), p. 53.

30 S. Freud, *Totem and Taboo*, tr. A. Brill (Vintage Books, New York, n.d.), p. 186.

31 Brown, *Love's Body*, p. 5.

32 Again, Hobbes is an exception. There are no families in his radically individualist state of nature; women are as strong as men. However, he merely assumes that in civil society women will always enter a marriage contract that places them in subjection to their husbands.

33 S. Freud, *Moses and Monotheism*, p. 153.

34 For example, Mary Astell sarcastically remarks (*Reflections Upon Marriage*, p. 86) that if 'Strength

of Mind goes along with Strength of Body, [then] 'tis only for some odd Accidents which Philosophers have not yet thought worthwhile to enquire into, that the Sturdiest Porter is not the wisest Man!' Or consider William Thompson, *Appeal of One Half of the Human Race, Women, Against the Pretensions of the Other Half, Men, to Retain them in Political, and Thence in Civil and Domestic, Slavery* (Source Book Press, New York, 1970; originally published 1825), p. 120: 'If strength be the superior title to happiness, let the knowledge and skill of man be employed in adding to the pleasurable sensations of horses, elephants, and all stronger animals. If strength be the title to happiness, let all such qualifications for voters as the capacity to read and write, or any *indirect* means to insure intellectual aptitude be abolished; and let the simple test for the exercise of political rights, both by men and women, be the capacity of carrying 300lbs weight.'

35 This helps to explain why we do not have 'a philosophy of birth'; see M. O'Brien, *The Politics of Reproduction* (Routledge & Kegan Paul, London, 1981), especially chap. 1.

36 In another chapter I began to explore one aspect of this perception of women and its corollary, that we pose a permanent threat to civil life; see Carole Pateman, *The Disorder of Women* (Oxford: Polity, 1980), chapter 1.

37 S. Freud, *Civilization and Its Discontents*, p. 56.

38 J. Mitchell, *Psychoanalysis and Feminism* (Penguin Books, Harmondsworth, Middlesex, 1975), p. 405.

39 See for example N. Hartsock, *Money, Sex and Power: Towards a Feminist Historical Materialism* (Northeastern University Press, Boston, MA, 1983), chap. 8; O'Brien, *The Politics of Reproduction*, chaps. 3, 4; Elshtain, *Public Man, Private Woman*, chap. 1; H. Pitkin, *Fortune Is A Woman: Gender and Politics in the Thought of Niccolo Machiavelli* (University of California Press, Berkeley, CA, 1984).

40 For his history, see G. Lloyd, *The Man of Reason; 'Male' and 'Female' in Western Philosophy* (Methuen, London, 1984). On the Cartesian 'drama of parturition', see S. Bordo. 'The Cartesian Masculinization of Thought', *Signs*, 11(3), (1986), pp. 439–56.

41 J. Rawls, *A Theory of Justice* (Harvard University Press, Cambridge, MA, 1971), p. 128.

42 It will probably be objected that one can look younger or older than one's real age, or be convinced that one is in the 'wrong' body, or 'pass' as white. However, these examples all depend on the knowledge of age, sexual and colour differences and the specific meaning given to them in different cultures. One cannot, say, be a transsexual without already being fully aware of what 'masculine' and 'feminine' involve and how these are integrally

connected to bodies. That Rawls's arguments, despite his apparently sexually undifferentiated 'parties', presuppose a sexually differentiated morality is shown in D. Kearns, '*A Theory of Justice* and Love: Rawls on the Family', *Politics*, 18(2), (1983), pp. 36–42.

43 This division between private and public is constituted in the second stage of the familiar story of the social contract (Locke's theory shows this clearly); see my books, *The Problem of Political Obligation*, chap. 4 and *The Disorder of Women*, chap. 6.

44 R.M. Unger, *Knowledge and Politics* (Free Press, New York, 1976), p. 45. Unger has little to say about women or the family, but his comments (like those on the division of labour) illustrate that his critique is not the 'total critique' at which he aims. He notes, for example, that the family 'draws men back into an association that competes with loyalties to all other groups' (p. 264) – but it 'draws back' only those who go into civil society.

45 G.F. Gaus, *The Modern Liberal Theory of Man* (Croom Helm, London, 1983), p. 90.

46 Gaus, *Modern Liberal Theory*, p. 94; he cites Dewey and Rawls on pp. 91 and 94.

47 The description comes from B. Harrison, *Separate Spheres: The Opposition to Women's Suffrage in Britain* (Holmes & Meier, New York, 1978), chap. 4. Women were once an essential part of armies, but by the First World War 'the once integral place of women in Western armies had faded from memory' (like so much else about women!); see B.C. Hacker, 'Women and Military Institutions in Early Modern Europe: A Reconnaissance', *Signs*, 6(4), (1981), pp. 643–71 (the quotation is from p. 671).

48 Cited in *Rights*, 4(5), (1981), p. 4.

49 On women, the military and combat, see J. Stiehm, 'The Protected, The Protector, The Defender', *Women's Studies International Forum*, 5(1982), pp. 367–76; and 'Reflections on Women and Combat', Postscript to *Bring Me Men and Women: Mandated Change at the US Air Force Academy* (University of California Press, Berkeley, CA, 1981).

50 M. Foucault, *Discipline and Punish: The Birth of the Prison*, tr. A. Sheridan (Vintage Books, New York, 1979), p. 169.

51 Foucault, *Discipline and Punish*, pp. 222–3.

52 See C. Pateman, 'The Shame of the Marriage Contract', in J. Stiehm, ed., *Women's View of the Political World of Men* (Transnational Publishers, Dobbs Ferry, NY, 1984).

53 Mrs Thatcher provides a fascinating illustration. On the one hand she is 'the best man in the Cabinet', the victor of the Falklands War, accomplice of Reagan's state terrorism against Libya, and is photographed with weapons. On the other hand she talks to the press about 'feminine' matters (such as having her hair tinted), draws headlines like 'Four Years on and looking Ten Years Younger', and uses the language of good housekeeping to talk about cuts in social welfare spending (see A. Carter, 'Masochism for the Masses', *New Statesman*, 3 June 1983, pp. 8–10).

54 For a critique of a contractarian defence of prostitution, see my 'Defending Prostitution: Charges Against Ericsson', *Ethics*, 93 (1983), pp. 561–5, and *The Sexual Contract*, chap. 7.

55 The right is still hedged with immigration restrictions that make it hard for black British women to exercise it; for an account of the interaction of sex and race in British law, see Women, Immigration and Nationality Group, *Worlds Apart: Women Under Immigration and Nationality Law* (Pluto Press, London, 1985). For the USA, see V. Sapiro, 'Women, Citizenship and Nationality. Immigration and Naturalization Policies in the United States', *Politics and Society*, 13(1) (1984), pp. 1–26.

56 O'Brien, *The Politics of Reproduction*, p. 205.

4

Theses on the Theory of the State

Claus Offe and Volker Ronge

The following notes give a brief outline of some of the theoretically relevant findings which the authors have made in two empirical studies of reformist state policies in West Germany. These studies were concerned with the reform of vocational training and with a new programmatic approach to research and development policies. We believe that such case studies of certain state policies in specific policy areas are necessary to gain both theoretical understanding and political perspectives which cannot be gained either through deductive reasoning or immediate experience. For the sake of convenience, the organization of the argument is divided into eight points. These remarks are intended to provoke discussion and debate and are, of course, tentative in nature.

1. In Marxist theories of the state, there is a cleavage between two approaches. One approach suggests that there is a particular *instrumental* relationship between the *ruling class* (capital as a whole) on the one side and the state apparatus on the other side. The state thus becomes an instrument for promoting the common interests of the ruling class. We believe that this view is gravely misleading – including the version that is offered in the doctrine of "state monopoly capitalism" with its stereotyped proposition of a "merger of the monopolies and the state apparatus." The alternative view is that the state does not patronize

Originally published in *New German Critique*, 6 (1975), 137–47. Reprinted by permission of Telos Press Ltd.

certain interests, and is not allied with certain classes. Rather, what the state protects and sanctions is a set of *rules* and *social relationships* which are presupposed by the class rule of the capitalist class. The state does not defend the interests of one class, but the *common* interest of all members of a *capitalist class society*.

2. The concept of the *capitalist state* describes an institutional form of political power which contains the following four major elements:

(a) Political power is prohibited from organizing production according to its own political criteria; property is *private* (be it property in labor power or property in means of production). Hence, it is not from political power, but from private freedom that decisions over the use of the means of production emerge.

(b) Political power depends indirectly – through the mechanisms of taxation and dependence on the capital market – on the volume of private accumulation. The occupant of a power position in a capitalist state is in fact powerless *unless* the volume of the accumulation process allows that individual to derive the material resources (through taxation) necessary to promote any political ends.

(c) Since the state *depends* on a process of accumulation which is beyond its power to *organize*, every occupant of state power is basically interested in promoting those conditions most conducive to accumulation. This interest does not result from alliance of a particular government with particular classes also interested in accumulation, nor does it result from any political power of the capitalist class which "puts pressure" on the incumbents of state power to pursue its class interest. Rather, it does result from an *institutional self-interest* of the state which is conditioned by the fact that the state is *denied* the power to control the flow of those resources which are indispensable for the *use* of state power. The agents of accumulation are not interested in "using" the power of the state, but the state must be interested – for the sake of its own power – in guaranteeing and safeguarding a "healthy" accumulation process upon which it depends.

(d) In democratic political regimes, any political group or party can win control over institutional state power only to the extent that it wins sufficient electoral support in general elections. This mechanism plays a key role in disguising the fact that the material resources of state power, and the ways in which these are used, depend upon the revenues derived from the accumulation process, and not upon the preferences of the general electorate. There is a dual determination of political power in the capitalist state: by its institutional *form* access to political power is determined through the rules of democratic and representative government, by its material *content*, the use of political power is controlled by the course and the further requirements of the accumulation process.

3. Is there any method by which these divergent constitutional requirements of the capitalist state can be reconciled through the policies of a particular government? Yes, there is *one*. If the conditions can be created through which *every* citizen becomes a participant in *commodity relationships*, all of the four structural elements of the capitalist state are taken into account. As long as every owner of a unit of value can successfully exchange his/her value as a commodity, there is no need for the state to intervene in economic decision making; there is no lack of material resources needed by the state; there is no problem in maintaining a steady process of accumulation (which is only the net result of equivalent exchange between the owners of capital and the owners of labor power); and there is no problem in maintaining political support for a political party which manages to create this universe of commodities. It is only to the extent that values fail to operate in the commodity form that the structure of the capitalist state becomes problematic. The

commodity form is the general point of equilibrium of the capitalist state. At the same time, accumulation takes place as long as every value appears in the form of a commodity. The link between the political and the economic structure of capitalist society is the commodity form. Both substructures depend upon the universalization of this form for their viability.

4. The key problem, however, lies in the fact that the dynamics of capitalist development seem to exhibit a constant tendency to *paralyze* the commodity form of value. Values cease to exist in the commodity form as soon as they cease seeking exchange for money or other values. To be sure, in an economic world consisting of commodities one can never be certain that one particular item offered on the market for sale will actually find a buyer. But in this simple case the failure of a value offered for exchange is supposed to be *self corrective*: the owner of the exchange-seeking value will either be forced to lower the price or to offer an alternative good the use value of which does have higher chances of being bought. At least in the world of Jean Baptiste Say, an economy consisting of commodities is self-perpetuating: the failure of a good as a commodity leads to other goods less likely to fail. Similarly, parts of labor and parts of capital which are, as it were, temporarily thrown out of the commodity form in the course of an economic depression, create, through the very fact of their idleness, the preconditions for a new boom (at least if there is downward flexibility of prices). The functioning of this "healthy" self-corrective mechanism, however, does not seem to be the regular case, particularly in advanced capitalist societies. Marxist economic theory has developed various, though controversial, theorems which could explain such failure of self-corrective mechanisms. For example, it is assumed that monopolization of the economy leads to downward inflexibility of prices on the one side, and, to a constant flow of what Baran and Sweezy have called "surplus profit" on the other, i.e., monopolistic profits unsuccessfully in search of investment outlets. Another explanation is based on the increasingly social character of production in capitalism. This means increasing division of labor within and among capitalist enterprises, hence increased specialization of every single unit of capital and labor, and hence diminished flexibility and adaptivity to alternative uses. Thirdly it has

been argued that the periodic destruction of large parts of value through unfettered economic crises is by itself a healthy economic mechanism which will improve chances for the remaining values to "perform" as commodities, but that the conflict associated with such "cleansing off" of superfluous values tend to become explosive to the extent that they have to be prevented by state intervention and Keynesian policies.

Whatever may be the correct and complete explanation, there is plenty of everyday evidence to the effect that both labor and capital are thrown out of the commodity form, and that there is little basis for any confidence that they will be reintegrated into exchange relationships automatically.

5. It is equally evident that the most abstract and inclusive common denominator of state activities and state intervention in advanced capitalist societies is to *guard the commodity form of individual economic actors*. This, again, does not directly mean guarding the general interests of a particular class, but guarding the general interest of all classes on the basis of capitalist exchange relationships ("*Tausch als universale Verkehrsform*"). For instance, it would be mistaken to argue that state policies of education and training are designed to provide the necessary manpower for certain industries, since no one, least of all the state bureaucracy, has any reliable information as to what industry will need what type of skills at what time, or in what numbers. Such policies are instead designed to provide a *maximum of exchange opportunities* to both labor and capital, so that individuals of both classes can enter into capitalist relationships of production with each other. Likewise, research and development policies designed and funded by the state are by no means directed towards concrete beneficiaries (e.g., industries which can use the resulting technologies, or users of specific "civilian" technologies). These policies are designed to open up new markets, to shield the domestic economy against the intrusion of foreign competitors – briefly, to create and maintain the commodity form of value, in whose absence values become non-existent in a capitalist society.

6. The overwhelming concern of all state policies with the problem of guarding the commodity form of value is a relatively *new strategy* which in some capitalist states, like the U.S., is still subject

to substantial political and ideological controversies. What are the alternative strategies open to the state in order to deal with the structural problem of failure of values to perform as commodities? The most "ancient" method seems to be *inaction*, i.e., hoping for the self-corrective mechanism in the course of which those units of value that have dropped out of the commodity form are supposed to return to the market. The assumption is that the more unpleasant unemployment (of labor or capital) is, the sooner the owners of those values will return to the marketplace. The flaw in this logic lies, however, in trusting that owners of values do *not* have another option than to return to the commodity form. They do in fact have such options, of which emigration, delinquency and political revolt are only a few historical examples.

The second method is *subsidies and alimentation*. In this case, those owners of labor power and owners of capital who have lost their chance to participate in exchange relationships are allowed to survive under conditions artificially created by the state. Their economic existence is protected although they have dropped out of the commodity form, or they are prevented from dropping out because they are granted a claim for income derived from sources other than the sale of value. The problem with this "welfare state" type of dealing with "decommodified" values is that it becomes too costly in fiscal terms, thus sharpening the fiscal crisis of the state. Subsidizing the owners of values that have become obsolete as commodities is particularly costly for the state because it implies a category of expenditures which are by no means self-financing. They do not increase, but rather diminish the basis of future state revenues.

On the basis of these considerations, we wish to argue that the more and more dominant, more and more exclusive strategy of the capitalist state is to solve the problem of the obsolescence of the commodity form by *creating* conditions under which values can function as commodities. More specifically, these attempts develop in three directions: first, the saleability of *labor power* is enhanced through measures and programs directed towards education, training, regional mobility and general adaptivity of labor power. Second, the saleability of *capital* and manufactured goods is enhanced through transnational integration of capital and product markets, research and development policies, regional development policies, etc. Third, those *sectors of the economy* (which can be specified by industry, by region, by labor market segments) which are unable to survive within the commodity form on their own strength are allowed by plan to fall victim to market pressures and at the same time they are urged to modernize, i.e., to transform themselves into "marketable" goods. We suggest that the term "*administrative recommodification*" might be an appropriate label for this most advanced strategy of the capitalist state; it is basically different from both the "laissez faire" and "welfare state-protective" types of strategy sketched out above.

7. Policies which pursue the goal of reorganizing, maintaining and generalizing exchange relationships make use of a specific sequence of *instruments*. These instruments can be categorized in the following way. First, we find *regulations and incentives* applied which are designed to control "destructive" competition and to make competitors subject to rules which allow for the economic survival of their respective market partners. Usually these regulations consist in measures and laws which try to protect the "weaker" party in an exchange relationship, or which support this party through various incentives. Second, we find the large category of *public infrastructure investment* which is designed to help broad categories of commodity owners (again: both labor and capital) to engage in exchange relationships. Typical examples are schools of all kinds, transportation facilities, energy plants, and measures for urban and regional development. Third, we find attempts to introduce *compulsory schemes of joint decision making* and joint financing which are designed to force market partners to agree upon conditions of mutually acceptable exchange in an organized way, *outside* the exchange process itself, so that the outcome is reliable for both sides. Such compulsory schemes of mutual accommodation are to be found not only in the area of wage bargaining, but equally in areas like housing, education, and environmental protection.

8. Such attempts to stabilize and universalize the commodity form and exchange process by political and administrative means leads to a number of specific structural contradictions of state capitalist societies which in turn can become the focus of social conflict and political struggle. Such contradictions can be found on the economic, political and ideological levels of society. On the *economic* level, the very state policies which are designed to maintain and promote universal exchange relationships have the effect of *threatening the continuity* of those relationships. For all three of the above-mentioned instruments of economic policy making (regulations, infrastructure and compulsive accommodation) deprive the owners of capital of value to varying degrees, either in the form of *capital* that is just "taxed away," or in the form of *labor*, or in the form of their *freedom* to utilize both of these in the way they deem most profitable. To the extent such state policies of "administrative recommodification" are "effective," they are bound to put a burden upon the owners of capital which has the paradoxical effect of making them *ineffective*. Since, in a capitalist society, all exchange relationships depend upon the willingness of owners of money capital to invest, i.e., to exchange money capital for constant capital and variable capital; since this willingness depends upon the expected profitability of investment; and since all observable state policies of recommodification do have the side-effect of depriving capital of either capital or labor power or the freedom to use both in profitable ways, the cure turns out to be worse than the illness. That is to say, reformist policies of the capitalist state by no means unequivocally "serve" the interests of the capitalist class: very often they are met by the most vigorous resistance and opposition of this class. Social conflicts and political struggles do not, of course, emerge automatically from this contradiction. They are waged by political forces which are willing and able to defend the reformist policies of the capitalist state against the obstructive resistance of the capitalist class itself.

A second structural contradiction is related to the organizational *power structures* created by such state strategies. It has often been observed by both liberal and Marxist social scientists that those sectors of the economy which are not immediately controlled by market mechanisms tend to expand (both in terms of labor power employed and value absorbed) in advanced capitalist social structures. The most obvious example is public administration and all the agencies that are created and controlled by it (like schools, transportation facilities, post offices, hospitals, public service institutions, welfare bureaucracies, the military, etc.). What is the explanation for the growth of the share of these organizations? In the most simplified form, the state's attempts to maintain and universalize the commodity form do require organizations which cease to be subject to the commodity form in their own mode of operation.

This can be demonstrated in the case of teachers. Although it is true that their labor power is *hired* for wage, it is not true that the *purpose* of their labor is to produce commodities for sale (which is the case in commercial enterprises). The purpose of their labor is, rather, to produce such use-values (skills, etc.) which put commodity owners (e.g., workers) in a position to actually sell their commodities. Therefore, schools do not *sell* their "products" (which hence do not assume the form of commodities), although they help to maintain and to *improve the saleability* of the commodities of the *recipients* of their products. But to the recipients the products of educational activities (i.e., the work of teachers) are distributed through channels different from exchange. The same is true in such organizations as public housing authorities, hospitals, transportation systems, prisons and other parts of the administrative apparatus. Although we often find nominal *fees* (as opposed to equivalent *prices*) as a mechanism playing a role in the distribution of their products and services, the prevailing mechanism is by no means *sale* but such things as legal claims, legal compulsion, acknowledged need or simply free use.

One of the most debated and most controversial issues in the fields of liberal public economics and political science is just what mechanism of production and distribution of "public goods" could be substituted for the exchange mechanism that is inapplicable in the area of public production – an increasing part of production designed to maintain and to universalize the commodity form of property.

This strategy of *maintaining* the commodity form presupposes the growth of state-organized production facilities *exempt* from the commodity form. This, again, is a contradiction only in the structural sense – a source of possible conflicts and destabilizing developments which in turn remain contingent upon political action. This contradiction can give rise to social conflicts and political struggles which try to gain popular control over exactly those "weakest links" in the world of commodities. Although it is a puzzle to many Marxists who consider themselves "orthodox," it still is hardly deniable that the major

social conflicts and political struggles that have taken place during the decade of the sixties did *not* take place within exchange relationships between labor and capital, but took place as conflicts over the control over the service organizations that *serve* the commodity form without themselves being *part* of the commodity nexus. Conflicts in schools, universities, prisons, military organizations, housing authorities and hospitals are cases in point. We suggest that an explanation of this fact can be based on the consideration that such organizations represent the most advanced forms of erosion of the commodity form within capitalist exchange relationships themselves.

A third contradiction can be located on the ideological level, or in the normative and moral infrastructure of capitalist society. The commodity form does presuppose two related norms with which individual actors must comply. First, they must be willing to utilize the opportunities open to them, and they must constantly strive to improve their exchange position (*possessiveness*); and second, they must be willing to accept whatever material outcome emerges from their particular exchange relationship – particularly if this outcome is unfavorable to them. Such outcomes must, in other words, be attributed to either natural events or to the virtues and failures of the individual (*individualism*).

For a capitalist commodity economy to function, the normative syndrome of possessive individualism must be the basis both of the behavior of the actor as well as of his interpretations of the actual and future behavior of others. Our point is now that the contradiction of state capitalism on the ideological level results in the *subversion* of this normative syndrome of possessive individualism. To the extent that exchange relationships are prepared and maintained through visible political and administrative acts of the state, the actual exchange value any unit of property (be it in labor or capital) achieves on the market can be seen as at least as much determined through *political* measures as through the *individual* way of managing one's property and resources. These resources themselves thus come to be seen as something resulting from, and contingent upon, political measures. Whether or not one receives exchange value for one's labor power, and how much of it, becomes – on the level of normative orientation – less a matter of adequate state policies in such areas as education, training, and regional development. Similarly, for the owner of capital, his market success does not depend upon his preparedness to take risks, his inventiveness and his ability to anticipate changes in demand, but instead upon state policies in such areas as tariffs, research and development, infrastructure supply and regional development. The structural weakening of the moral fiber of a capitalist commodity society — which is caused by the very attempts to stabilize and universalize the commodity form through policy measures — again does not imply any automatic tendency toward crises or the "breakdown" of capitalism. It can, however, become the focus of social conflict and political struggle which is oriented toward overcoming the obsolete commodity relationships as the organizing principle of social reproduction.

5

Invoking Civil Society

Charles Taylor

In recent years the notion of civil society has come back into circulation. The intention is to invoke something like the concept that developed at the turn of the nineteenth century, which stands in contrast to "the state." But in fact those who introduced it were trying to articulate features of the development of western civilization which go back much farther.

One of the first fields of application of the revived term was to the polities of Eastern Europe. "Civil society" defined what they had been deprived of and were struggling to recreate: a web of autonomous associations, independent of the state, which bound citizens together in matters of common concern, and by their mere existence or action could have an effect on public policy. In this sense, western liberal democracies were thought to have functioning civil societies.

"Civil society" in this sense refers to what the Leninist model of rule had essentially negated. That model arose first in the Soviet Union, then was reproduced in other "Marxist–Leninist" regimes, finally was imitated more or less completely, and sometimes caricaturally, by a number of newly independent third-world countries. The essential virtue of the model for its protagonists was that it offered a kind of total mobilization of society toward what were seen as revolutionary goals. The central instrument was a vanguard party dominated by a revolutionary elite. And a crucial feature of this system was the satellitization of all aspects of social life to this party. Trade

unions, leisure clubs, even churches, all had to be permeated and made into "transmission belts" of the party's purposes. Leninism in its heyday was one of the principal sources of modern totalitarianism.

This system has been in decay for a number of decades – since the death of Stalin in its original homeland, and somewhat later in countries that followed the Russian example with an indigenous revolutionary elite, such as China and Cuba. In fact there was a long period of retreat, where the drive to total mobilization flagged more and more visibly, but without any of the fundamental principles of the system being renounced. Future generations will probably describe this period of slow inner decay as the Age of Brezhnev. With Gorbachev, we entered a new phase, in which some of the tenets of total mobilization were themselves challenged. Unanimity was no longer an unambiguously good thing. They began to have real, if restricted, elections in Moscow. But under Brezhnev the goal was to keep the facade of unanimity unbroken. In principle no dissident opinions should be expressed, everyone should turn out for Leninist holidays, people should pass spontaneous resolutions on critical occasions denouncing U.S. imperialism; at the same time, the demands of the regime on private life were lessening. Governments like Czechoslovakia's even encouraged a kind of privatization of life. Let everyone cultivate their gardens, provided they turned out for May Day parades and otherwise kept their mouths shut. It was a Leninism of fatigue.

In these circumstances, as the furious terror of Stalinism receded, the pressure rose in certain

Originally published in *Philosophical Arguments* (1995), 204–24, 303. Copyright © 1995 by Charles Taylor. Reprinted by permission of Harvard University Press.

East European societies for reform. A total change of regime seemed, for obvious geopolitical reasons, utopian. The goal was rather to undo Leninism partially from below, to open a margin of free association out of party control but enjoying legal recognition. It is understandable that an aspiration of this kind should find expression in a distinction between civil society and the state. For on this model, the state – understood in flatly Weberian terms as the agency with the monopoly of physical force – would have an entirely different basis than society would. Its ultimate foundation would be external, in the threat of Soviet intervention, whereas the different components of the newly freed "civil society" would express indigenous social forces.

But in using this term, thinkers in both East and West wanted to express something more than the mutual independence of state and society. They wanted also to invoke something of the history and practice of the western democracies as a model. The notion was, first, that in the West there already is a civil society and, second, that this contemporary reality is heir to a centuries-long development of the distinction between society and state. There is truth in both claims, but to get at it we have to modulate the meaning of "civil society". This turns out to be a more complex and many-faceted idea than one might have thought at first. The nuances are worth exploring because they color the models of the political process we want to steer our lives by in coming decades.

To take the first claim: civil society already exists in the West. Yes, there is in western societies a web of autonomous associations, independent of the state, and these have an effect on public policy. But there has also been a tendency for these to become integrated into the state, the tendency toward what has been called (often in a slightly sneering tone, because of the origins of the term in fascist Italy) "corporatism." States like Sweden, Holland, and Germany, but also many others, have gone some way to integrating trade unions, employers' associations, and the like into government planning. To speak of integration "into the state" may be tendentious here; some people see it as a loss of government independence to special interests. But in fact what occurs is an interweaving of society and government to the point where the distinction no longer expresses an important difference in the basis of power or the dynamics of policymaking. Both government and associations draw on and are

responsive to the same public. For instance, issues of national income policy, debated between management and labor unions in tripartite negotiations with the government as third party, can also be debated in parliament, where the same social forces are represented in the form of the social-democratic and conservative parties. In fact, these two loci of negotiation and debate are generally complementary; the issue about corporatism could be phrased as a question – how much of the crucial negotiation takes place outside parliament?

Of course, there are many associations in western societies which are not involved in corporatist negotiations. Some of these are capable of having an impact on policy through lobbying or public campaigns, while others are marginal and easy to ignore. But the drift toward corporatism in modern industrial democracies consists in the first category, with strong associations being more and more integrated into the process of decisionmaking. It makes sense for a democratic government to consult before deciding, not only to determine the most popular policy, but also to soften the edges of confrontation with the losers, who will at least have the sense that they have been listened to and will be listened to again.

This style of government is roundly condemned, on the right and the left. But it is not clear that either has come up with a viable alternative. The attack from the right is mainly in evidence in the English-speaking countries. Margaret Thatcher was its best-known protagonist. She certainly upset the rules of the game as they were understood under her predecessors of both parties. She introduced a politics of conflict into what formerly had been negotiation. It has been argued by her supporters that this was necessary in order to challenge the position that the labor unions had won in British society. She had to fight a war, ending in the bruising battle of a miners' strike. But the outcome of war is generally peace restored on a new basis. Confrontation as a style of government is not sustainable in the long run in democratic countries.

Of course, right-wing politicians like Thatcher don't subscribe theoretically to endless conflict. They envisage a new dispensation after the special interests have been dealt with, and various enterprises and functions privatized. Many things that the government now orchestrates will run themselves without state interference. State and society will do their own thing without getting in each other's way. This is especially espoused by the right because of their belief in the efficacy of unadulterated market forces.

Now I believe that this hope is utopian – or dystopian, if you don't share the moral outlook of the right. Too much is at stake to allow government and society to coexist without coordination. The really successful economies in the late twentieth century are resolutely corporatist, for instance, Germany and Japan. The idea that there is another path to competitive success on world markets seems to be a nostalgic illusion of the English-speaking countries, remembering an earlier, braver era of economic purity. But those days are gone forever. The obvious failure of the Marxist policy of suppressing the market altogether can be taken only by the simple-minded as proof that total reliance on the market is the best policy. Obviously we are all going to have to live with some mix of market and state orchestration. The difficult question is what mix suits each society. In fact, right-wing governments go on orchestrating for more than they admit. And to the extent that they refrain from doing so – that, say, Britain and the United States turn their backs on industrial policy – they will probably live to rue the day.

What is the relevance of all this to the idea of civil society? It is that the anti-corporatist aspiration can very well be, and often is, expressed in this society/state distinction. So the idea that civil society is something we *have* in the West needs to be nuanced. In one sense we do; in another sense it is a goal that has to be striven for against the grain of modern democratic government.

Let's look more closely at these different senses. (1) In a minimal sense, civil society exists where there are free associations that are not under tutelage of state power. (2) In a stronger sense, civil society exists where society as a whole can structure itself and coordinate its actions through such free associations. (3) As an alternative or supplement to the second sense, we can speak of civil society wherever the ensemble of associations can significantly determine or inflect the course of state policy.

No one can deny that civil society exists in sense (1) in the West; or that it was lacking under Leninism and was a crucial aspiration of those living under Leninist regimes. But civil society as contrasted with the state in western political theory incorporated more than this; it involved (2)

and sometimes (3). It was in virtue of this that it could be referred to in the singular as civil *society*. We might say that (2) and (3) introduce a public dimension that has been crucial to the concept in the western tradition.

One aspect of the right-wing indictment of corporatism could be formulated in the charge that it has suppressed civil society in sense (2). Sense (3) might be thought to be integrally fulfilled by corporatist mechanisms of negotiation. But this will not be easily accepted by one who suspects that the associations are in fact being integrated into the state apparatus, rather than bringing to bear their independent weight on it.

This brings us to the left-wing criticism of corporatism, which also can be and sometimes is expressed in terms of civil society. Here too it is the enriched concept involving senses (2) and (3) which is in play. I'm thinking of the criticism that comes from what are sometimes called the "new social movements," and which has found expression, for instance, in Germany's green party.

On this outlook, the state and the large powerful associations it consults form a unity. They tend equally toward elite control and growing distance from the constituencies they claim to speak for. In addition, they are equally committed to increasing bureaucratic control in the name of technological efficacy over more and more aspects of human life. Even such seemingly benign features of modern society as the welfare state, originally introduced on the initiative of the left, become suspect as mechanisms of control and "normalization." To be a beneficiary of the welfare state is to submit to bureaucratic regulation, to have your life shaped by categories that may cut across those in which you want to live your life.

One response to this has been to try to open a sphere of independent self-regulation by spontaneously associating groups. Another has been to try to win for the new social movements themselves greater impact on the formation of policy. These correspond to senses (2) and (3) respectively, and so it is not surprising that this New Left has also been tempted to bring the term "civil society" into play. The sense, justified or not, of an analogy between their situation and that of dissidents in the eastern European bloc has strengthened this temptation.[1]

So the first claim mentioned above, that civil society already exists in the West, is more problematic than it appeared. But the second claim is also not simply true, and it would be worth exploring at even greater length.

The relative freedom we enjoy is seen as having sources deep in the history of the West, and in particular in conceptions of society going back to medieval Christendom. These sources can be articulated with something like the conception of civil society. In the context of contemporary Eastern Europe, the obvious pole of comparison is Russia. At successive stages, Russia took a different political path from western polities. The development of an independent noble class, of free cities, and hence of a regime of "estates" was cut short at crucial moments by the state building of Ivan the Terrible and later by Peter the Great. Subsequent initiatives aimed at joining the West were repressed by Nicholas I and then by Lenin. A mainstay of western development, that is, a church independent of political authority, never existed in the Russian Orthodox tradition.

So runs the story, and it obviously has a great deal of truth to it, and particular relevance to the situation of Eastern Europe; at least to Hungary, Poland, Czechoslovakia, East Germany. These societies developed in close cultural contact and symbiosis with western Europe. They share analogous institutional developments and some of the same ideals. For instance, republican ideals of self-rule were present in Poland and enshrined even in the name of the pre-partition state, Rzeczpospolita Polska (the Commonwealth of Poland). The poignant fate of these societies was to have been forced to accept an alien political system, in fact of Russian origin, which ran against the grain of those societies and was the cause of endless conflict. The aspiration to greater freedom is in effect synonymous with an aspiration to rejoin Europe. That is why it finds natural expression in a view of the European political tradition and in the notion of civil society.[2]

Perhaps this contrast between Russia and the West has been overdrawn. Sometimes it is put in such a way as to imply that the tragic political plight of Russia has been virtually inevitable from the Mongol conquest on. And western freedom is described in a symmetrically self-congratulatory way as flowing inevitably out of a more remote past. In fact, there were moments when things could have been reversed. Arguably, the Bolshevik takeover was a contingent political disaster for Russia, which interrupted the slow development of civil society that had been gathering pace in the last decades of tsarism. Arguably, Peter's was not the only road to modernization open to Russia. At the same time, when Peter did try to imitate Europe, he took what was seen as the latest, most effective model, the so-called absolute monarchies. Those were in fact constrained by a context of law and independent associations. But no one would then have predicted confidently that they wouldn't grow stronger, that they would give way before a totally different governing formula, then effective only in England and Holland. Western democracy was never written in the genes. At the same time, the chauvinistic idea that representative institutions can't take root outside their home culture is refuted by the existence of such societies as India and Japan (and, dare we hope, post-Gorbachev Russia and post-Deng China).

But when all this is said, it remains true that western liberal democracy has deep roots in its past, that certain socially entrenched self-conceptions greatly facilitated its rise, and that many of these were absent in Russia or were ruthlessly rooted out by earlier rulers. What were these roots, and how do they relate to the term "civil society"?

There are a number of factors worth talking about in this connection; some of them are ideas, some are institutions, but most often they are both at once: institutions and practices that incorporate their own self-interpretation. In one form or another, they seem to be part of the background of western democratic society. But the relation is sometimes more complex and ambiguous than at first appears, mainly because modern democracy itself is a more complex and tension-ridden reality than is generally acknowledged. Some of these tensions will emerge from looking at how the society/state distinction arose.

(A) The medieval notion of society is one of those which has turned out to be important in the development of the West. What is important is in a sense a negative fact: that society is not defined in terms of its political organization. The underlying issue is this: what gives a society its identity? What are the features without which it would cease to be a society, or would become a wholly different one? In many civilizations and eras, these questions are answered in terms of political structure. For both the Greeks and the Romans, the identity of society was defined by its *politeia*, its political constitution. Under the Empire unity came from a common subjection to authority, although a fiction was maintained that this authority came from an act of the people. Now to the extent that a society is defined by its political organization, to that degree it is permeable by political power. It lacks a principle of resistance to the invasive force of sovereign political authority. Just being politically defined is hardly a sufficient condition for this kind of takeover by despotic power, as the Greek polis attests. It is rather that the basis for a certain kind of limitation on this power is lacking, whenever the conditions ripen for its advance.

Now unlike the ancient conceptions, the notion that developed in the early Middle Ages was of a society where political authority was one organ among others. Royal authority, for instance, was *singulis major* but *universis minor*. This idea, that society is not identical with its political organization, can be seen as a crucial differentiation, one of the origins of the later notion of civil society and one of the roots of western liberalism.

(B) This differentiation was carried further by one of the most important features of Latin Christendom: the development of an idea of the church as an independent society. In principle, the inhabitants of Christendom were Christian. But these same people were organized in two societies, one temporal and one spiritual, of which neither could be simply subordinated to the other. This was, of course, a formula for perpetual struggle, and extravagant claims were made for one side or the other, including an arrogation of *plenitudo potestatis* by Pope Innocent III. But the underlying common understanding remained within the Gelasian definition of "two swords." There were two sources of authority, both granted for different purposes by God. Each was subordinate to the other for some purposes and supreme for others. Western Christendom was in its essence bifocal.

Alongside these two pervasive features, there were particular facets of medieval political arrangements which with hindsight appear important. (C) One is the development of a legal notion of subjective rights. This was linked to the peculiar nature of feudal relations of authority. The relations of vassalage were seen in a quasi-contractual light. The superior had obligations as well as the inferior. To repudiate these obligations was a felony, as much as for the vassal. So inferiors were seen as the beneficiaries of obligations, privileges enjoyed as a kind of property. This is the origin of the western notion of subjec-

tive rights. It starts off as a notion of purely positive law, before being transposed by the natural-rights doctrines of the seventeenth and eighteenth centuries. But it meant that medieval sovereigns faced a society that was partly defined as a skein of rights and duties, which imposed on them the necessity of winning consent for important changes. This, along with the existence of relatively independent, self-governing cities (D), brought about the standard political structures of medieval polities (E), in which a monarch ruled with the intermittent and uncertain support of a body of estates, which had to be called together from time to time to raise the resources he needed to govern and wage war. This dyarchy constituted another, purely secular dualism, linking the political structure to society at large.

We can recognize our roots in all of this. But it didn't ensure trouble-free progress for modern liberal democracy. Between us and that time lies the great early-modern attempt over most of Europe to set up absolute monarchies. Kings won the power to raise taxes without calling the estates, built standing armies on these resources, which in turn made their power harder to challenge. Around 1680 this looked like the wave of the future; it must have seemed to many that only this kind of state could be militarily effective. Moreover, influential theories justified the new model of political society. On one hand, the concepts of Roman law, favoring monarchical power, become dominant. On the other hand, Bodin and later Hobbes develop a notion of sovereignty which quite undermines or supersedes the medieval understanding of society. The notion comes to be accredited that a society, in order to exist at all, must be held together by sovereign power, that is, by a power unlimited by any other. In other words, the identification of society with its political organization returns, and in a form that is unambiguously favorable to despotism. Important vestiges of feature A emerge in social-contract doctrines, where society is accorded existence prior to government, as it is with the jurists Grotius and Pufendorf. This is the feature of contract theory that Hobbes wanted to suppress. But even with Grotius and Pufendorf in the seventeenth century, the "contract of subjection" is seen as setting up absolute power, against which society henceforth has no legal recourse.

Meanwhile, throughout this period, a satellitization of the church is taking place in a number of Protestant countries, and the very division of

Christendom undermines the idea at the heart of B, that everyone belongs to a single alternative society.

As I said above, absolute monarchies were really rather limited exercises in despotism, seen in the light of twentieth-century dictatorships. They did away with D and E, but remained limited by C, the entrenched traditions of rights. Of course, nothing assured that C in turn would not be eroded if absolutism pursued its course. The important stream of reform thinking in the eighteenth century that looked to "enlightened despotism" to reorder society on rational lines was hostile to traditional rights, wanted them swept aside in the name of reason. But absolutism couldn't run its course. What undermined it was the military, and behind that the economic success of the at-first relatively minor powers who operated on another, more consensual model, especially England and the Low Countries. In that sense, the end of the eighteenth century may have parallels with the end of the twentieth.

Around this alternative model, there crystallized a number of anti-absolutist doctrines. The most celebrated and influential was that of Locke. In a sense he transposed and renewed both A and B and brought them back into political theory. Feature A returns in the unprecedentedly strong form that defines government as a trust.[3] Society exists before government; it issues from a first contract that takes individuals out of the state of nature. The newly formed body then sets up government. This may be defined as supreme, but it is in fact in a fiduciary relation to society. Should it violate its trust, society recovers its freedom of action.

But Locke also reintroduces a version of B. Prior to all political society, mankind forms a kind of community. We are constituted as such by being under natural law, which is enjoined on us by God.[4] We are made a community, in other words, by our enjoyment of natural rights. This community is in fact defined as a transform of C, now written into the order of things rather than simply inscribed in positive law. Any particular political society has to respect this higher law, since those who set it up were bound by it, and they couldn't pass on powers they didn't have.

Locke is, of course, still using the term "civil society" in its traditional sense, where it is synonymous with "political society." But he is preparing the ground for the emergence of the new, contrastive sense a century later. This contrast arises out of the anti-absolutist doctrines of the eighteenth century, but in two rather different ways. One develops out of Locke's embryonic notion of mankind as a prepolitical community. Locke's state of nature is not the scene of devastation portrayed by Hobbes. It lacks security, which is why humans are driven to set up governments. But otherwise it is the possible scene of great progress in what was later called civilization, of economic development, the division of labor, the development of money, and the accumulation of property. This idea was developed in the eighteenth century into a picture of human social life in which much that is valuable is seen as coming about in a pre- or nonpolitical realm, at best under the protection of political authority, but by no means under its direction.

There was another source of the contrast, which we can perhaps most handily identify with Montesquieu. His portrait of monarchy in *De l'esprit des lois* offers an alternative anti-absolutist doctrine to Locke's. Unlike Locke, he assumes a strong monarchical government that is unremovable. The important issue turns on whether this government is unchecked, and veering toward despotism, or whether it is limited by law. But limitation by law is ineffective unless independent bodies exist which have a standing in this law and are there to defend it. The rule of law and the *corps intermédiares* stand and fall together. Without law, bodies like parliament and estates like the nobility have no standing; without such bodies and estates, the law has no effective defenders. The free monarchy (a pleonasm for Montesquieu, since the unfree one is despotism) is in equilibrium between a powerful central authority and an interlocking mass of agencies and associations it has to work with.

Montesquieu's theory draws on different elements of the tradition from Locke's. It is based on elements C, D, and E of the medieval constitution. Indeed, the long debate in France over the rise of absolutism was seen as one that pitted the ancient constitution, inherited originally from the Frankish conquerors, against models drawn from Roman law. Montesquieu saw himself as reformulating the "German" case. Speaking of the English constitution, which he admired, Montesquieu says that it was derived from the ancient Germans. "Ce beau système a été trouvé dans les bois."[5] What he doesn't need to draw on at all is A and B. Society is not defined independently of its political constitution. On the contrary, the free society is identified with a certain such constitution.

For all the importance of the medieval constitution to him, in this respect Montesquieu thinks more like an ancient. The polis too was defined politically. The very terms we use show this to be a tautology. This vision of things allowed no place for a distinction between civil society and the state. This would have been incomprehensible to a Greek or Roman. Montesquieu, along with many anti-absolutists of his era, was an admirer of ancient freedom. But he didn't make it an alternative model to absolute rule. His genius was rather to articulate a third standard, in some ways antithetical to the polis, which was nevertheless one of freedom and dignity for the participant. Monarchy was antithetical to the republic because the latter supposed "vertu", a dedication to the public good as well as austere mores and equality; but monarchy required a lively sense of one's own rights and privileges, and thrived on differences of status and displays of wealth and power, which were bound up with honor. Patriotic virtue was what kept society free in the ancient republic, because it led people to defend laws to the death against internal and external threats. The lively sense of one's own rights and status protected freedom in the modern monarchy, because it made the privileged resist royal encroachment and feel shame in obeying any order that derogated their code.

So while retaining a thoroughly political definition of society, like the ancients, Montesquieu laid the ground for a society/state distinction that was alien to the ancients. He did this with a view of society as poised between central power and a skein of entrenched rights.

Both anti-absolutist doctrines are reflected in the distinction eventually drawn around the turn of the century, which found its most celebrated statement in Hegel's *Philosophy of Right*. But in fact they sit uneasily together in this new concept of civil society. There is a tension between them, and between the different models for a free society which can be articulated with this new concept.

Thus two streams come together into "civil society." Let's call them the L-stream and the M-stream, after the figures I have somewhat arbitrarily chosen to represent them. What I want to do here is map the convergence and highlight some of the tensions.

The central feature of the L-stream is the elaboration of a richer view of society as an extrapolitical reality. One facet of this elaboration has dominated the discussion of civil society until quite recently: the development of a picture of society as an "economy," that is, as an entity of interrelated acts of production, exchange, and consumption which has its own internal dynamic, its own autonomous laws. This crystallizes in the eighteenth century with the work of the physiocrats and, more definitively, with Adam Smith. Just how great an intellectual revolution is involved here can be measured in the transformation of the word's meaning. "Economics" is etymologically the art of household management; it designated a particular field of prudent administration. The *nomos* was that imposed by the manager, the head of household or *oikos*. It already involved one revolution in thinking to begin to consider whole kingdoms as like households, needing to have their production and consumption "managed" in this way. This gives us the jump to "political economy." But the important change is to a view of this domain as in a sense organizing itself, following its own laws of equilibrium and change. The *nomos* in the word now comes to resemble its use in a term like "astronomy," referring us to an "autonomous" domain of causal laws. The modern "economy" is born, as a domain with its own organization.

This gives a new twist and a new force to the idea of society as enjoying an extrapolitical identity. The "economy" now defines a dimension of social life in which we function as a society potentially outside the ambit of politics. Of course, there are differences among the practitioners of the new science as to how autonomous it should be. Even Adam Smith was in favor of much more state regulation than his popular reputation allows. But this intellectual revolution allows us to raise the issue of economic autonomy; without the notion of the economic as governed by its own laws, the issue couldn't even be framed. Now everyone thinks in these terms, interventionist and free-enterpriser alike. They differ only in their assessment of the likely outcome of unregulated flow, and hence of the need or lack of it for remedial action of a more or less radical kind. Even Marx, especially Marx, has a theory of unimpeded flow. It is the disaster scenario laid out in *Capital*.

This provided an important part of the content of the new concept of civil society, at least of its

L-facet. It figures in Hegel's formulation, where the self-regulating, entrepreneurial economy is given a central place on this level of society. Marx took over Hegel's concept and reduced it almost exclusively to this, and it is partly due to Marx's influence that "civil society" was for so long defined in economic terms. But this represents an impoverishment of Hegel's concept. It also owed something to the M-stream, so that his civil society incorporated bodies engaged in conscious self-management – the corporations – which were also integrated in their own way into the state.

But I want to return to this later, when we look at the tension between the two streams. Right now it is important to see that, even in what I call the L-stream, the economy is not the only component. What is also of great importance is the development in the eighteenth century of an autonomous public with its own "opinion."

This involves a quite new use of the notion of "public." The term designates what is of common concern, and not just objectively or from an outsider's perspective, but what is commonly recognized as of common concern. So public is what matters to the whole society, or belongs to this whole society, or pertains to the instruments, institutions, or loci by which the society comes together as a body and acts. So plainly the political structure of a society is public – its executive organs, the loci of its legislative power, and whatever spaces of assembly these require – from the agora in which the citizen assembly meets to the court where a king exercises his rule. These are loci of what one might call public space.

The new notion of opinion in the eighteenth century defines a quite different model of public space. Through the circulation of newspapers, reviews, and books among the educated classes, and scattered, small-scale personal exchanges in salons, coffeehouses, and (in some cases) political assemblies, there emerges a sense of nation, or its literate segment, an opinion that deserves to be called "public." Public opinion, as originally conceived, is not just the sum of our private individual opinions, even where we spontaneously agree. It is something that has been elaborated in debate and discussion, and is recognized by everyone as something held in common. This element of common recognition is what makes it public, in the strong sense.

This is also what gives it its force, a new force in history. The novel aspect is that public opinion is elaborated entirely outside the channels and public spaces of the political structure. More radically, it is developed outside the channels and public spaces of any authority whatever, since it is also independent of that second focus of European societies, the church. Governments were used to facing the independent power of religious opinion, articulated by churches. What was new was opinion, presented as that of society, which was elaborated through no official, established, hierarchical organs of definition.[6]

Like the economy, public opinion was here to stay. And though some thinkers envisaged a kind of absolute rule which would align itself on enlightened opinion, in fact free opinion and absolute power don't consort too well. But it can't be simply forgotten, and so contemporary despotisms are forced not only to suppress public opinion, but also to counterfeit it. Official newspapers write editorials and report meetings and resolutions, all of which purportedly come spontaneously from individual authors and initiators. The orchestrated character of all this has to be hidden from view. Such is the prestige of public opinion.

The self-regulating economy and public opinion – these are two ways in which society can come to some unity or coordination outside the political structures. They give body to the Lockean idea, which in turn has medieval roots, that society has its own identity beyond the political dimension. It seems to follow from this that political authority ought to respect the autonomy of society in the spheres where it is manifest. This involves a new kind of limitation of authority. It was always understood as limited in Christendom by the church, to some degree or other; and also by rights ascribed to individuals or corporations. But the political used to be the only domain in which secular social purpose could be articulated and carried out. To the extent that these new spheres of nonpolitical social identity become recognized, this is no longer the case.

Indeed, the new space of public opinion, mediated by printed materials, can be the source of a more radical challenge, questioning the primacy of political structures on their own ground. Previously it was axiomatic that societies found their political identities and defined their political direction through the traditionally established political structures, and only there – whether these were royal courts or parliaments or some combination of the two. Unofficial pressure might be exercised through agitation and pamphleteering, but this didn't challenge the principle that the authoritative locus for defining political ends lay in the established bodies. With the development of the new space of public opinion, more far-reaching claims had to be made. It has been argued, for instance, that in early eighteenth-century America a new form of discourse emerges in newspapers and pamphlets.[7] It is a discourse that implicitly arrogates to this print-sustained space the power and duty to define the goals of the people and to call the established bodies to book for their deviations from these goals. The discourse is cast in the traditional rhetoric of republicanism, but under this familiar cover a radically new formula is being advanced. In republican societies, the people did indeed criticize and control their officers, but assembled in the *ekklesia* or general meeting. This was itself a governing body, the foundational one. Now the powers of the assembled people are being arrogated to a new print-mediated public space, unembodied in any traditional structure or, indeed, in face-to-face meetings of any kind. The political identity of society shifts to an unprecedented locus. Whether or not this analysis holds for the eighteenth-century British colonies, something like this shift plainly became central to modern democratic self-understanding.

This congeries of ideas about the economy and public space constituted one of the strands in the new notion of "civil society" as distinguished from the state. It comprised a public, but not a politically structured domain. The first feature was essential: civil society was not the private sphere. Where Aristotle distinguishes *polis* from *oikos*, and only the first is a public domain, Hegel distinguishes three terms in *Sittlichkeit*: family, civil society, and the state. Civil society is not identical with the third term, the polis, and not with the first term either. That is why I argue that any definition of civil society in sense (1), which identifies it simply with the existence of autonomous associations free from state tutelage, fails to do justice to the historical concept. This defines a pattern of public social life, and not just a collection of private enclaves.

This notion of civil society, the L-variant, can inspire radical political hopes, sometimes of an anti-political kind. Even Locke saw the political structure as an emanation of a society that in one sense was already political, because people had put in common their power to enforce the Law of Nature, but had as yet no political structure.

With the enriching of the concept, we can formulate the idea that society has its own prepolitical life and unity which the political structure must serve. Society has the right and power to make and unmake political authority, according as it does so serve or fail to serve.

This is the radical doctrine of Thomas Paine. In a somewhat less radical variant, something like this was acted on by the American colonists in their war of independence. It was less radical because the decision to rebel was taken by political authorities in the thirteen colonies. The early-modern idea, that a rebellion against a supreme authority in violation of its trust could be carried out by duly constituted subordinate authority (the central notion of *vindiciae contra tyrannos*), would also have served to justify the rebellion. Americans saw themselves as fighting for established right as against usurpation. But in fact the language they adopted, that of "We, the People," had a more radical impact. It seemed to draw the revolutionary conclusion from the L-variant: the people have an identity, they have purposes, even a will, outside any political structure. In the name of this identity, following this will, they have the right to make and unmake these structures. The duality of focus in the western concept of society, which goes back in different forms to the Middle Ages, finally takes on its most revolutionary formulation.

This has become a commonplace of modern thought. Between 1776 and now, the notion of a people's prepolitical identity has taken a new and much more powerful form, that of the nation. We now speak of this right to make and unmake structures as the right of self-determination. No one today dares deny this in principle, however suppressed it may be in practice.

But radical hopes can also take an antipolitical form. One could dream of the nonpolitical spheres of society becoming more and more autonomous, more and more self-sufficient. Taken to the extreme, this offers a vision of a society without politics, where the government of men gives way to the administration of things, as Saint-Simon articulated it, followed by Engels. In less extreme fashion, one could hope for a society in which the development of industry and commerce would serve to tie people together in peace, and thus drastically reduce the role of government, lessening its policing function and doing away with war altogether.

The eighteenth-century developments described

above, which gave us the notions of economy and public opinion, also provided a notion of "civilization." A civilized society was partly so in virtue of its political constitution – indeed, the term in some respects replaces the earlier French expression *état policé*. But "civilization" included a lot more – pacification, enlightenment, technical development, arts and sciences, polished mores. Within the self-definition of modern Europe as civilized, in contrast to other societies and to its own past, the virtues of peaceful production bulked large, and the older warrior virtues were seen in an unfavorable light. European society gained in polish as it turned its back on these and on the honor ethic behind them. But it was also the honor ethic that gave the political life intrinsic value. For the new social ethic of peaceful productivity, as we see for instance with the utilitarians, political structures had purely instrumental significance. The less we needed them, the better.

So two rather different kinds of political hopes arise from this notion of society as having a pre- or nonpolitical identity. The one moves toward the norm of self-determination; the other toward the goal of marginalizing the political. So we can see why the L stream was not the only one to feed the new concept of civil society. It was not just that these hopes each in their own way undermine the very distinction between society and state. This they did, of course. Radical self-determination swallows up the state in society, in a supposed common will; while the goal of marginalization tries to approach as closely as possible to anarchy.

But also, much more importantly, both hopes pose a threat to freedom, and the distinction was introduced in the first place in the context of counter-absolutist thought. One recurring threat to freedom has come from the politics of what would later be called the general will. This *idée force*, as elaborated by Rousseau, fuses the idea of a people's will independent of all political structure with the ethic of ancient republicanism, drawing its power from both. Rousseau invokes the prepolitical in the very unancient idea of a social contract, of society as constituted by will, as well as in his understanding of nature as inner voice. He invokes the ancient ethic of virtue in the ideal of a transparent face-to-face political society. The latter, of course, drops out of the picture as unrealizable in the modern world. What remains is the notion of popular will as the

ultimate justification for all political structures and authority.

The most thoroughgoing destruction of civil society has been carried out in the name of some variants and successors of this idea in the twentieth century, notably the nation and the proletariat. A strange and horrifying reversal has taken place, whereby an idea whose roots lie in a prepolitical concept of society can now justify the total subjection of life to an enterprise of political transformation. And in less spectacular form, the power of the state has often been enhanced by its self-definition as an instrument of the national will.

But in a more subtle way, the politics of marginalizing politics has also been seen as posing a threat to freedom. This is particularly so when the sphere of society in the name of which the political is being marginalized is that of the self-regulating economy. For in this domain the disposition of things in society as a whole is seen as arising not out of any collective will or common decision, but by way of an "invisible hand." To leave our collective fate to blind economic forces can be portrayed as a kind of alienation. On top of this, all those whose allegiance is to an ideal of the political life as good in itself will see the marginalization of politics as an abandonment of what is most valuable in life, a flight from the public into the narrower and less significant sphere of private satisfactions, the "petty and paltry pleasures" of which Tocqueville speaks in *Democracy in America*.

Marx, who developed a theory of alienation, himself subscribed to his own version of a world without politics. But Tocqueville spelled out the dangers implicit in the kinds of hopes generated by the L-theory. The modern democracy of the general will can degenerate, he argues, into a kind of mild despotism (*despotisme doux*) in which citizens fall prey to a tutelary power that dwarfs them; and this is both cause and effect of a turn away from the public to the private which, although tempting, represents a diminution of their human stature.

Those who are thus dissatisfied with the L-variant of the notion of civil society are induced to turn to Montesquieu. Tocqueville can be seen as the greatest disciple of Montesquieu in the nineteenth century. But Hegel, in his dissatisfaction with the L-variant, had already drawn on Montesquieu. Like Marx after him, Hegel couldn't believe in the benign effects of an autonomous, unregulated economic sphere. And he produced his own variant of the civic-humanist doctrine that the life of the citizen had value in itself. At the same time, his theory of modern life, in distinction from the ancients, turned on the differentiated development of this nonpolitical public sphere, which related individuals in their separate identities. The result was the Hegelian concept of civil society – a separate sphere, but not self-sufficient. Not only did its constituent economic processes need regulation, which was undertaken partly within civil society, but this society could only escape destruction by being incorporated in the higher unity of the state, that is, society as politically organized.

Hegel combines both the L- and the M-streams in his concept of civil society. If the L-concept, to repeat, turns on the idea of a nonpolitical dimension to society, Montesquieu's contribution is the picture of a society defined by its political organization, but where this is constitutionally diverse, distributing power among many independent agencies. It is important here too that there be independent associations for nonpolitical purposes. But their significance is not that they form a nonpolitical social sphere, but rather that they form the basis for the fragmentation and diversity of power *within* the political system. What is relevant is not their life outside, but the way they are integrated into the political system and the weight they have in it.

Thus the different elements of Hegel's political society take up their role in the state, make up the different estates, and form the basis for a differentiated constitution, whose formula was partly inspired by Montesquieu. In this way, we avoid both the undifferentiated homogeneity of the general-will state, which Hegel thought must lead inevitably to tyranny and terror, and also the unregulated and ultimately self-destructive play of blind economic forces, which then seemed to be menacing England.

With Tocqueville, the heritage of Montesquieu is even clearer. The only bulwark against mild despotism is free associations. Voluntary associations for all purposes are valuable. But their significance is that they give us the taste and habit of self-rule, and so they are essential for political purposes. But if they are to be real loci of self-rule, they have to be nongigantic and numerous, and exist at many levels of the polity. This itself should be decentralized, so that self-government can be practiced also at the local and not just the national level. If it dies out at the former, it is in danger at the latter. "In democratic countries the science of association is the mother of science," according to Tocqueville.

So our notion of civil society is complex. It is an amalgam of two rather different influences, which I have called the L-stream and the M-stream. It clearly goes beyond the minimal definition (1) above. But it hovers between the other two because of its dual origin. For the purposes of deconstructing a Leninist dictatorship, any one of these definitions will do. But when we come to ask how the concept of civil society relates to the freedom of western liberal democracies, we find a more complex story.

We can see now why the question discussed at the outset, whether we in fact have a functioning independent civil society in the West, was not so easy to answer. Among the other reasons is the fact that there are different definitions of what this independence involves, which have equally strong warrant in our two-streamed tradition. No easier to answer is the question of what role a concept of civil society has to play in the future defense of freedom.

It is tempting to think that it is almost guaranteed a role, just because of its place in the complex intellectual and institutional background of western liberty. The distinction between civil society and the state is indeed important to the western tradition, not just because of all the roots of the idea in earlier epochs, but more especially because it has been central to the different forms of counter-absolutist thinking. Indeed, it owes its existence and relevance to the development in the West of reforming absolutism, of "the well-ordered police state" in the seventeenth and eighteenth centuries.[8] It made no sense in the context of the polis, or in the medieval polity, no more than it did in a host of traditional nonwestern polities. It arose, one might say, as a necessary instrument of defense in face of the specific *threats* to freedom implicit in the western tradition. But precisely to the extent that the modern state is still drawn to a vocation of mobilizing and reorganizing its subjects' lives, the distinction would seem to be guaranteed a continuing relevance.

So one can argue that the distinction is essential to our conception of what it is to preserve freedom. But it has also been shouldered aside by supposedly simpler and more arresting definitions of a free society, which turn on the idea of a general will or a politics-free sphere. To make the notion of civil society central to our political discourse ought to involve a rejection of these seductively limpid formulas.

But those who find these simpler definitions unsatisfactory (as I do), and want to recur to "civil society," will find that it is not a unified idea. Both its sources are deeply woven into our political traditions and way of life. Which definition we accept of civil society will have important consequences for our picture of the free society and hence our political practice.

In fact, our choice today lies not simply between the two variants. The force of the L-idea is too great and too obtrusive to be altogether denied. The choice seems to lie between a view of

civil society almost exclusively concerned with the L-stream and one that tries to balance both. In the first category fall those critics of corporatist politics on the right who aim to roll back the power of the state. In the second are found the contemporary followers of Tocqueville, some of whom along with a bewilderingly diverse variety of utopians end up on the ecological left, but who are also found near the center of many western societies. I hope an impression has emerged that the second view, which balances both streams, is greatly superior to the first; more, that the first is in constant danger of falling victim to the simpler formulas of a prepolitical freedom that end up subverting the distinction or neutralizing its force as a counter-thrust to bureaucratic power. In any case, this is what I propose.

Notes

1. For a work in which both predicaments are discussed together in a very illuminating way, see John Keane, ed., *Civil Society and the State* (London, 1988). The civil-society tradition has been mediated to thinkers on the left partly through the work of Antonio Gramsci, who had a much richer concept than Marx, one more indebted to Hegel. It should also be said that the concern on the left with the "colonization of the life-world" by bureaucracies dedicated to technological efficacy is not confined to ecological green parties. A well-known theorist who has addressed this issue, and who is in no sense a "green," is Jürgen Habermas. See his *Theorie des kommunikativen Handelns* (Frankfurt, 1981); *The Theory of Communicative Action*, 2 vols. (Boston, 1985, 1989).

2. For a discussion of Eastern Europe in this context, see Jenö Szucs, "Three Historical Regions of Europe," and Mihaly Vajda, "East-Central European Perspectives," in Keane, *Civil Society*.

3. See *Second Treatise of Civil Government*, paras. 221–222, in Peter Laslett, ed., *Locke's Two Treatises of Government*, 2nd ed. (Cambridge, Eng., 1967), p. 430.

4. Ibid., para. 172. Locke speaks of "the common bond whereby humane kind is united into one fellowship and societie" (Laslett, p. 401).

5. Montesquieu, *De l'esprit des lois*, 11.6, in *Oeuvres complètes* (Paris, 1964), p. 590.

6. This whole development has been interestingly discussed by Jürgen Habermas in his *Strukturwandel der Öffentlichkeit* (Berlin, 1962); *Structural Transformation* (Cambridge, Mass., 1989).

7. I have drawn here on the interesting discussion in Michael Warner, *The Letters of the Republic* (Cambridge, Mass., 1989).

8. See Marc Raeff, *The Well Ordered Police State* (New Haven, 1983). Of course the term is used not in its twentieth-century sense. "Police" translates the eighteenth-century German "Polizei," which covered the state's action in ordering the lives of its subjects rather than in suppressing violence.

6

Democracy: From City-states to a Cosmopolitan Order?

David Held

This article traces the development of the idea of democracy from city-states and the early republican tradition to liberalism and Marxism. The relevance of leading conceptions of democracy to contemporary circumstances are then explored. In light of the complex interconnections among states and societies, a set of arguments are developed which offer a new agenda for democratic theory which departs from an exclusive focus on particular political communities and the nation-state. After an examination of a number of key models of the international order – the states system, the UN Charter framework – the case is made for a cosmopolitan international democracy. While such a case is fraught with difficulties, strong grounds are presented for its indispensability to the maintenance and development of democracy both within pre-established borders and across them.

Democracy seems to have scored an historic victory over alternative forms of governance.[1] Nearly everyone today professes to be a democrat. Political regimes of all kinds throughout the world claim to be democracies. Yet what these regimes say and do is often substantially different from one another. Democracy bestows an aura of legitimacy on modern political life: laws, rules and policies appear justified when they are 'democratic'. But it was not always so. The great majority of political thinkers from ancient Greece to the present day have been highly critical of the theory and practice of democracy. A uniform commitment to democracy is a very recent phenomenon. Moreover, democracy is a remarkably difficult form of government to create and sustain. The history of twentieth-century Europe alone makes this clear: fascism, Nazism and Stalinism came very close to obliterating democracy altogether.

Against this background, it is unsettling that some recent political commentators have proclaimed (by means of a phrase borrowed most notably from Hegel) the 'end of history' – the triumph of the west over all political and economic alternatives. The revolutions which swept across Central and Eastern Europe at the end of 1989 and the beginning of 1990 stimulated an atmosphere of celebration. Liberal democracy was championed as the agent of progress and capitalism as the only viable economic system: ideological conflict, it was said, is being steadily displaced by universal democratic reason and market-orientated thinking.[2] But such a view is quite inadequate in a number of respects.

In the first instance, the 'liberal' component of liberal democracy cannot be treated simply as a unity. There are distinctive liberal traditions which embody quite different conceptions from each other of the individual agent, of autonomy, of the rights and duties of subjects, and of the proper nature and form of community. In addition, the 'celebratory' view of liberal democracy

Originally published in *Political Studies*, 40, Special Issue (1992), 10–39. Copyright © Political Studies Association. Reprinted by permission of Blackwell Publishers.

neglects to explore whether there are any tensions, or even perhaps contradictions, between the 'liberal' and 'democratic' components of liberal democracy; for example, between the liberal preoccupation with individual rights or 'frontiers of freedom' which 'nobody should be permitted to cross', and the democratic concern for the regulation of individual and collective action, that is, for public accountability.[3] Those who have written at length on this question have frequently resolved it in quite different directions. Furthermore, there is not simply one institutional form of liberal democracy. Contemporary democracies have crystallized into a number of different types, which makes any appeal to a liberal position vague at best.[4] An uncritical affirmation of liberal democracy essentially leaves unanalysed the whole meaning of democracy and its possible variants.

This essay seeks to address this lacuna, first, by examining the development of different models of democracy; secondly, by considering the conditions of application of these models; thirdly, by exploring the meaning of democracy in the context of the progressive enmeshment today of states and societies in regional and global networks; and finally, by assessing the proper form and scope of democracy in relation to systems of international governance. The first two sets of issues will be examined in the next section, and the second two sets in the subsequent one. It will be argued, ultimately, that democracy can result from, and only from, a nucleus, or federation, of democratic states and societies. Or, to put the point differently, national democracies require international democracy if they are to be sustained and developed in the contemporary era. Paradoxically, perhaps, democracy has to be extended and deepened within and between countries for it to retain its relevance in the twenty-first century.

If the case for rethinking democracy in relation to the interconnectedness of states and societies is established successfully, a new agenda will have been created for democratic theory and practice. It is important to be clear about the meaning of 'new' in this context. The agenda will not be new in the sense of being without precedent; others before have sought to understand the impact of the international order on the form and operation of domestic politics within democratic states. Others before have also sought to set out the normative implications of changes in the international order for the role and nature of democratic government. Nor will the agenda be new in the sense that traditional questions of democratic theory will be wholly displaced. On the contrary, questions will remain about the proper form of citizenship, the nature of individual rights and duties and the extent of participation and representation, for instance. But the agenda will be new to the extent that the case is made that a theory of democracy (whether focusing on philosophical or empirical-analytic concerns) requires a theory of the interlocking processes and structures of the global system. For a theory of democracy must offer, it will be maintained, an account both of the changing meaning of democracy within the global order and of the impact of the global order on the development of democratic associations. Democratic institutions and practices have to be articulated with the complex arena of national and international politics, and the mutual interpenetration of the national and international must be mapped. Political understanding, and the successful pursuit of democratic political theory, is dependent on the outcome of these tasks.[5] Before pursuing them, however, the concept of democracy itself requires some clarification.

Models of Democracy

Within the history of democratic theory lies a deeply rooted conflict about whether democracy should mean some kind of popular power (a form of politics in which citizens are engaged in self-government and self-regulation) or an aid to decision-making (a means of conferring authority on those periodically voted into office). This conflict has given rise to three basic variants or models of democracy, which it is as well to bear in mind. First, there is direct or participatory democracy, a system of decision-making about public affairs in which citizens are directly involved. This was the 'original' type of democracy found in ancient Athens, among other places. Secondly, there is liberal or representative democracy, a system of rule embracing elected 'officers' who undertake to 'represent' the interests or views of citizens within the framework of the 'rule of law'. Thirdly, there is a variant of democracy based on a one-party model (although some may doubt whether this is a form of democracy at all). Until recently, the Soviet Union, East European societies and many third world countries have been dominated by this conception. The following discussion deals briefly with each of these models in turn, developing concepts and issues which will be drawn upon in later argument.

The active citizen and republican government

Athenian democracy has long been taken as a fundamental source of inspiration for modern western political thought. This is not to say that the west has been right to trace many elements of its democratic heritage exclusively to Athens; for, as recent historical and archaeological research has shown, some of the key political innovations, both conceptual and institutional, of the nominally western political tradition can be traced to older civilizations in the east. The city-state or *polis* society, for example, existed in Mesopotamia long before it emerged in the west.[6] Nonetheless, the political ideals of Athens – equality among citizens, liberty, respect for the law and justice – have been taken as integral to western political thinking, and it is for this reason that Athens constitutes a useful starting point.

The Athenian city-state, ruled as it was by citizen-governors, did not differentiate between state and society. In ancient Athens, citizens were at one and the same time subjects of political authority and the creators of public rules and regulations. The people (*demos*) engaged in legislative and judicial functions, for the Athenian concept of citizenship entailed their taking a share in these functions, participating *directly* in the affairs of 'the state.'[7] Athenian democracy required a general commitment to the principle of civic virtue: dedication to the republican city-state and the subordination of private life to public affairs and the common good. 'The public' and 'the private' were intertwined. Citizens could properly fulfil themselves and live honourably only in and through the *polis*. Of course, who was to count as a citizen was a tightly restricted matter; among the excluded were women and a substantial slave population.

The Athenian city-state – eclipsed ultimately by the rise of empires, stronger states and military regimes – shared features with republican Rome. Both were predominantly face-to-face societies and oral cultures; both had elements of popular participation in governmental affairs, and both had little, if any, centralized bureaucratic control. Furthermore, both sought to foster a deep sense of public duty, a tradition of civic virtue or responsibility to 'the republic' – to the distinctive matters of the public realm. And in both polities, the claims of the state were given a unique priority over those of the individual citizen. But if Athens was a democratic republic, contemporary scholarship generally affirms that Rome was, by comparison, an essentially oligarchical system.[8] Nevertheless, from antiquity, it was Rome which was to prove the most durable influence on the dissemination of republican ideas.

Classical republicanism received its most robust restatement in the early Renaissance, especially in the city-states of Italy. The meaning of the concept of 'active citizenship in a republic' became a leading concern. Political thinkers of this period were critical of the Athenian formulation of this notion; shaped as their views were by Aristotle, one of the most notable critics of Greek democracy, and by the centuries-long impact of republican Rome, they recast the republican tradition. While the concept of the *polis* remained central to the political theory of Italian cities, most notably in Florence, it was no longer regarded as a means to self-fulfilment.[9] Emphasis continued to be placed on the importance of civic virtue but the latter was understood as highly fragile, subject particularly to corruption if dependent solely upon the political involvement of any one major grouping: the people, the aristocracy or the monarchy. A constitution which could reflect and balance the interests of all leading political factions became an aspiration. Niccolò Machiavelli thus argued that all singular constitutional forms (monarchy, aristocracy and democracy) were unstable, and only a governmental system combining elements of each could promote the kind of political culture on which civic virtue depends.[10] The best example of such a government was, he proclaimed, Rome: Rome's mixed government (with its system of consuls, Senate and tribunes of the people) was directly linked to its sustained achievements.

The core of the Renaissance republican case was that the freedom of a political community rested upon its accountability to no authority other than that of the community itself. Self-government is the basis of liberty, together with the right of citizens to participate – within a constitutional framework which creates distinct roles for leading social forces – in the government of their own common business.[11] As one commentator put it, 'the community as a whole must retain the ultimate sovereign authority', assigning its various rulers or chief magistrates 'a status no higher than that of elected officials'.[12] Such 'rulers' must ensure the effective enforcement of the laws created by the community for the promotion of its own good; for they are not rulers in a traditional sense, but 'agents of *ministri* of justice'.

In Renaissance republicanism, as well as in Greek democratic thought, a citizen was someone who participated in 'giving judgement and holding office'.[13] Citizenship meant participation in public affairs. This definition is noteworthy because it suggests that theorists within these traditions would have found it hard to locate citizens in modern democracies, except perhaps as representatives or office holders. The limited scope in contemporary politics for the active involvement of citizens would have been regarded as most undemocratic.[14] Yet the idea that human beings should be active citizens of a political order – citizens of their states – and not merely dutiful subjects of a ruler has had few advocates from the earliest human associations to the early Renaissance.[15]

The demise in the west of the idea of the active citizen, one whose very being is affirmed in and through political action, is hard to explain fully. But it is clear enough that the antithesis of *Homo politicus* is the *Homo credens* of the Christian faith: the citizen whose active judgement is essential is displaced by the true believer.[16] Although it would be quite misleading to suggest that the rise of Christianity effectively banished secular considerations from the lives of rulers and ruled, it unquestionably shifted the source of authority and wisdom from this-worldly to other-worldly representatives. During the Middle Ages, the integration of Christian Europe came to depend above all on two theocratic authorities: the Roman Catholic Church and the Holy Roman Empire. There was no theoretical alternative to their account of the nature of power and rule.[17] Not until the end of the sixteenth century, when it became apparent that religion had become a highly divisive force and that the powers of the state would have to be separated from the duty of rulers to uphold any particular faith, did the nature and limits of political authority, law, rights and obedience become a preoccupation of European political thought from Italy to England.[18]

Liberal representative democracy

Modern liberal and liberal democratic theories have constantly sought to justify the sovereign power of the state while at the same time justifying limits on that power.[19] The history of this attempt since Thomas Hobbes is the history of arguments to balance might and right, power and law, duties and rights. On the one hand, states must have a monopoly of coercive power in order to provide a secure basis on which trade, commerce, religion and family life can prosper. On the other hand, by granting the state a regulatory and coercive capability, political theorists were aware that they had accepted a force that could, and frequently did, deprive citizens of political and social freedoms.

Liberal democrats provided the key institutional innovation to try to overcome this dilemma: representative democracy. The liberal concern with reason, law and freedom of choice could only be upheld properly by recognizing the political equality of all mature individuals. Such equality would ensure not only a secure social environment in which people would be free to pursue their private activities and interests, but also a state which, under the watchful eye of the electorate, would do what was best in the general or public interest. Thus, liberal democrats argued, the democratic constitutional state, linked to other key institutional mechanisms, particularly the free market, would resolve the problems of ensuring both authority and liberty.

Two classic statements of the new position can be found in the philosophy of James Madison and in the work of one of the key figures of nineteenth-century English liberalism: Jeremy Bentham. In Madison's account, 'pure democracies' (by which he means societies 'consisting of a small number of citizens, who assemble and administer the government in person') have always been intolerant, unjust and unstable.[20] By contrast, representative government overcomes the excesses of 'pure democracy' because regular elections force a clarification of public issues, and the elected few, able to withstand the political process, are likely to be competent and capable of 'discerning the true interest of their country'.

The central concern of Madison's argument is not the rightful place of the active citizen in the life of the political community but, instead, the legitimate pursuit by individuals of their interests, and government as a means for the enhancement of these interests. Although Madison himself sought clear ways of reconciling particular interests with what he called modern 'extended republics', his position signals a clear shift from the classical ideals of civic virtue and the public realm to liberal preoccupations.[21] He conceived the representative state as the chief mechanism to aggregate individuals' interests and to protect their rights. In such a state, he believed, security of person and property would be sustained and politics could be made compatible with the demands of large nation-states, with their complex patterns of trade, commerce and international relations.[22]

In parallel with this view, Bentham held that representative democracy 'has for its characteristic object and effect . . . securing its members against oppression and depredation at the hands of those functionaries which it employs for its defence'.[23] Democratic government is required to protect citizens from the despotic use of political power, whether it be by a monarch, the aristocracy or other groups. The representative state thus becomes an umpire or referee while individuals pursue in civil society, according to the rules of economic competition and free exchange, their own interests. The free vote and the free market are both essential, for a key presupposition is that the collective good can be properly realized in most domains of life only if individuals interact in competitive exchanges, pursuing their utility with minimal state interference. Significantly, however, this argument has another side. Tied to the advocacy of a 'minimal state', whose scope and power need to be strictly limited, there is a strong commitment to certain types of state intervention: for instance, to regulate the behaviour of the disobedient, and to reshape social relations and institutions if, in the event of the failure of *laissez-faire*, the greatest happiness of the greatest number is not achieved – the only scientifically defensible criterion, Bentham held, of the public good.

From classical antiquity to the seventeenth century, democracy was largely associated with the gathering of citizens in assemblies and public meeting places. By the early nineteenth century it was beginning to be thought of as the right of citizens to participate in the determination of the collective will through the medium of elected representatives.[24] The theory of representative democracy fundamentally shifted the terms of reference of democratic thought: the practical limits that a sizeable citizenry imposes on democracy, and which had been the focus of so much critical (anti-democratic) attention, were practically eliminated. Representative democracy could now be celebrated as both accountable and feasible government, potentially stable over great territories and time spans.[25] It could even be heralded, as James Mill put it, as 'the grand discovery of modern times' in which 'the solution of all difficulties, both speculative and practical, will be found'.[26] Accordingly, the theory and practice of popular government shook off its traditional association with small states and cities, opening itself to become the legitimating creed of the emerging world of nation-states. But who exactly was to count as a legitimate participant, or a 'citizen' or 'individual', and what his or her exact role was to be in this new order, remained either unclear or unsettled. Even in the work of the enlightened John Stuart Mill ambiguities remained: the idea that all citizens should have equal political weight in the polity remained outside his actual doctrine, along with that of most of his contemporaries.[27]

It was left by and large to the extensive and often violently suppressed struggles of working-class and feminist activists in the nineteenth and twentieth centuries to accomplish a genuinely universal suffrage in some countries. Their achievement was to remain fragile in places such as Germany, Italy and Spain, and was in practice denied to some groups; for instance, many African-Americans in the US before the civil rights movement in the 1950s and 1960s. However, through these struggles the idea that the rights of citizenship should apply equally to all adults became slowly established; many of the arguments of the liberal democrats could be turned against existing institutions to reveal the extent to which the principles and aspirations of equal political participation and equal human development remained unfulfilled. It was only with the actual achievement of citizenship for all adult men and women that liberal democracy took on its distinctively contemporary form: a cluster of rules and institutions permitting the broadest participation of the majority of citizens in the selection of representatives who alone can make political decisions (that is, decisions affecting the whole community).

This cluster includes elected government; free and fair elections in which every citizen's vote has an equal weight; a suffrage which embraces all citizens irrespective of distinctions of race, religion, class, sex and so on; freedom of conscience, information and expression on all public matters broadly defined; the right of all adults to oppose their government and stand for office; and associational autonomy – the right to form independent associations including social movements, interest groups and political parties.[28] The consolidation of representative democracy, thus understood, has been a twentieth-century phenomenon; perhaps one should even say a late twentieth-century phenomenon. For it is only in the closing decades of this century that democracy has been securely established in the west and widely adopted in principle as a suitable model of government beyond the west.

Marxism and one-party democracy

The struggle of liberalism against tyranny, and the struggle by liberal democrats for political equality, represented a major step forward in the history of human emancipation, as Karl Marx and Friedrich Engels readily acknowledged. But for them, and for the Marxist tradition more broadly, the great universal ideals of 'liberty, equality and justice' cannot be realized simply by the 'free' struggle for votes in the political system together with the 'free' struggle for profit in the market-place. Advocates of the democratic state and the market economy present these institutions as the only ones under which liberty can be sustained and inequalities minimized. However, according to the Marxist critique, the capitalist economy, by virtue of its internal dynamics, inevitably produces systematic inequality and massive restrictions on real freedom. The formal existence of certain liberties is of little value if they cannot be exercised in practice. Therefore, although each step towards formal political equality is an advance, its liberating potential is severely curtailed by inequalities of class.

In class societies the state cannot become the vehicle for the pursuit of the common good or public interest. Far from playing the role of emancipator, protective knight, umpire, or judge in the face of disorder, the agencies of the liberal representative state are enmeshed in the struggles of civil society. Marxists conceive the state as an extension of civil society, reinforcing the social order for the enhancement of particular interests. Their argument is that political emancipation is only a step towards human emancipation: that is,

the complete democratization of both society and the state. In their view, liberal democratic society fails when judged by its own promises.

Among these promises are, first, political participation, or general involvement mediated by representatives in decisions affecting the whole community; secondly, accountable government; and thirdly, freedom to protest and reform.[29] But 'really existing liberal democracy', as one Marxist recently put it, fails to deliver on any of these promises. For it is distinguished by the existence of a largely passive citizenry (significant numbers of eligible citizens do not vote in elections, for example); the erosion and displacement of parliamentary institutions by unelected centres of power (typified by the expansion of bureaucratic authority and of the role of functional representatives); and substantial structural constraints on state action and, in particular, on the possibility of the piecemeal reform of capitalism (the flight of capital, for example, is a constant threat to elected governments with strong programmes of social reform).[30]

Marx himself envisaged the replacement of the liberal democratic state by a 'commune structure': the smallest communities, which were to administer their own affairs, would elect delegates to larger administrative units (districts, towns); these in turn would elect candidates to still larger areas of administration (the national delegation).[31] This arrangement is known as the 'pyramid' structure of 'delegative democracy': all delegates are revocable, bound by the instructions of their constituency, and organized into a 'pyramid' of directly elected committees. The post-capitalist state would not, therefore, bear any resemblance to a liberal, parliamentary regime. All state agencies would be brought within the sphere of a single set of directly accountable institutions. Only when this happens will 'that self-reliance, that freedom, which disappeared from earth with the Greeks, and vanished into the blue haze of heaven with Christianity', as the young Marx put it, gradually be restored.[32]

In the Marxist-Leninist account, the system of delegative democracy is to be complemented, in principle, by a separate but somewhat similar system at the level of the Communist Party. The transition to socialism and communism necessitates the 'professional' leadership of a disciplined cadre of revolutionaries.[33] Only such a leadership has the capacity to organize the defence of the revolution against counter-revolutionary forces, to plan the expansion of the forces of production, and to supervise the reconstruction of society. Since all fundamental differences of interest are class interests, since the working-class interest (or standpoint) is the progressive interest in society, and since during and after the revolution it has to be articulated clearly and decisively, a revolutionary party is essential. The party is the instrument which can create the framework for socialism and communism. In practice, the party has to rule; and it was only in the 'Gorbachev era' in the Soviet Union (from 1984 to August 1991) that a pyramid of councils, or 'Soviets', from the central authority to those at local village and neighbourhood level, was given anything more than a symbolic or ritualistic role in the post-revolutionary period.

Democracy, the state, and civil society

What should be made of these various models of democracy in contemporary circumstances? The classical participatory model cannot easily be adapted to stretch across space and time. Its emergence in the context of city-states, and under conditions of 'social exclusivity', was an integral part of its successful development. In complex industrial societies, marked by a high degree of social, economic and political differentiation, it is very hard to envisage how a democracy of this kind could succeed on a large scale.

The significance of these reflections is reinforced by examining the fate of the conception of democracy advocated by Marx and Engels, and their followers. In the first instance, the 'deep structure' of Marxist categories – with its emphasis on the centrality of class, the universal standpoint of the proletariat, and a conception of politics which is rooted squarely in production – ignores or severely underestimates the contributions to politics of other forms of social structure, collectivity, agency, identity, interest and knowledge. Secondly, as an institutional arrangement that allows for mediation, negotiation and compromise among struggling factions, groups or movements, the Marxist model does not stand up well under scrutiny, especially in its Marxist-Leninist form. A system of institutions to promote discussion, debate and competition among divergent views – a system encompassing the formation of movements, pressure groups and/or political parties with independent leaderships to help press their cases – appears both necessary and desirable. Further, the changes in Central and Eastern Europe after 1989 seem to provide remarkable confirmatory evidence of this, with their emphasis on the importance of political and civil rights, a competitive party system, and the 'rolling back of the state', that is, the freeing of civil society from state domination.

One cannot escape the necessity, therefore, of recognizing the importance of a number of fundamental liberal tenets, concerning the centrality, in principle, of an 'impersonal' structure of public power, of a constitution to help guarantee and protect rights, of a diversity of power centres within and outside the state, and of mechanisms to promote competition and debate among alternative political platforms. What this amounts to, among other things, is confirmation of the fundamental liberal notion that the 'separation' of state from civil society must be an essential element of any democratic political order. Conceptions of democracy that depend on the assumption that the state could ever replace civil society, or vice versa, must be treated with caution.

To make these points is not, however, to affirm any one liberal democratic model as it stands, although many advocates of democracy appear to take this view. It is one thing to accept the arguments concerning the necessary protective, conflict-mediating and redistributive functions of the democratic state, quite another to accept these as prescribed in existing accounts of liberal democracy. Advocates of liberal democracy have tended to be concerned, above all else, with the proper principles and procedures of democratic government. But by focusing on 'government', they have drawn attention away from a thorough examination of the relation between formal rights and actual rights; between commitments to treat citizens as free and equal and practices which do neither sufficiently; between concepts of the state as, in principle, an independent authority, and state involvement in the reproduction of the inequalities of everyday life; between notions of political parties as appropriate structures for bridging the gap between state and society, and the array of power centres which such parties and their leaders cannot reach. To ignore these questions is to risk the establishment of 'democracy' in the context of a sea of political, economic and social inequality. And it is to risk the creation of, at best, a very partial form of democratic politics – a form of politics in which the involvement of some bears a direct relation to the limited or non-participation of others.

The implications of these points are, I believe, of considerable significance. For democracy to flourish it has to be reconceived as a double-sided phenomenon: concerned, on the one hand, with the reform of state power and, on the other hand, with the restructuring of civil society. This entails recognizing the indispensability of a process of what I have elsewhere called 'double democratization': the interdependent transformation of both state and civil society.[34] Such a process must be premised on the principles that the division between state and civil society must be a central aspect of democratic life, and that the power to make decisions must be free of the inequalities and constraints which can be imposed by an unregulated system of private capital, as Marx foresaw. But, of course, to recognize the importance of both these points is to recognize the necessity of recasting substantially their traditional connotations.[35]

In short, if democratic life involves no more than a periodic vote, citizens' activities will be largely confined to the 'private' realm of civil society and the scope of their actions will depend largely on the resources they can command. Few opportunities will exist for citizens to act as citizens, that is, as participants in public life. But if democracy is understood as a double-sided process, this state of affairs might be redressed by creating opportunities for people to establish themselves 'in their capacity of being citizens'.[36] The 'active citizen' could once again return to the centre of public life, involving him- or herself in the realms of both state and civil society. Of course, the nature of this involvement would differ in each of these realms, according to their organizational and institutional features. But opportunities will at least have been created for all those affected by the decision-making structures of their communities to participate in the latters' regulation – or so the story of democracy has so far suggested. However, democracy has another side.

Democracy, Globalization and International Governance

Throughout the nineteenth and twentieth centuries democratic theory has tended to assume a 'symmetrical' and 'congruent' relationship between political decision-makers and the recipients of political decisions.[37] In fact, symmetry and congruence have often been taken for granted at two crucial points: first, between citizen-voters and the decision-makers whom they are, in principle, able to hold to account; and secondly, between the 'output' (decisions, policies, and so on) of decision-makers and their constituents – ultimately, 'the people' in a delimited territory.

Even the critics of modern democracies have tended to share this assumption; following the narrative of democracy as conventionally told, they have thought of the problem of political accountability as, above all, a national problem. Contemporary representative structures are, they hold, insufficiently responsive to their citizens; and, in discussing various forms of participatory democracy, or contemporary interpretations of the relevance of republicanism, they place emphasis on making the political process more transparent and intelligible, more open to, and reflective of, the heterogeneous wants and needs of 'the people'.[38]

But the problem, for defenders and critics alike of modern democratic systems, is that regional and global interconnectedness contests the traditional national resolutions of the key questions of democratic theory and practice. The very process of governance can escape the reach of the nation-state. National communities by no means exclusively make and determine decisions and policies for themselves, and governments by no means determine what is right or appropriate exclusively for their own citizens.[39] To take some topical examples: a decision to increase interest rates in an attempt to stem inflation or exchange-rate instability is most often taken as a 'national' decision, although it may well stimulate economic changes in other countries. Similarly, a decision to permit the 'harvesting' of the rainforests may contribute to ecological damage far beyond the borders which formally limit the responsibility of a given set of political decision-makers. These decisions, along with policies on issues as diverse as investment, arms procurement and AIDS, are typically regarded as falling within the legitimate domain of authority of a sovereign nation-state. Yet, in a world of regional and global interconnectedness, there are major questions to be put about the coherence, viability and accountability of national decision-making entities themselves.

Further, decisions made by quasi-regional or quasi-supranational organizations such as the European Community, the North Atlantic Treaty Organization, or the International Monetary

Fund diminish the range of decisions open to given national 'majorities'. The idea of a community which rightly governs itself and determines its own future – an idea at the very heart of the democratic polity itself – is, accordingly, today deeply problematic. Any simple assumption in democratic theory that political relations are, or could be, 'symmetrical' or 'congruent' appears unjustified.

If the inadequacy of this assumption can be fully shown, issues are raised which go to the heart of democratic thought. The idea that *consent* legitimates government and the state system more generally has been central to nineteenth- and twentieth-century liberal democrats.[40] The latter have focused on the ballot box as the mechanism whereby the individual citizen expresses political preferences and citizens as a whole periodically confer authority on government to enact laws and regulate economic and social life. The principle of 'majority rule', or the principle that decisions which accrue the largest number of votes should prevail, is at the root of the claim of political decisions to be regarded as worthy or legitimate.[41] But the very idea of consent through elections, and the particular notion that the relevant constituencies of voluntary agreement are the communities of a bounded territory or a state, becomes problematic as soon as the issue of national, regional and global interconnectedness is considered and the nature of a so-called 'relevant community' is contested. Whose consent is necessary and whose participation is justified in decisions concerning, for instance, AIDS, or acid rain, or the use of nonrenewable resources? What is the relevant constituency: national, regional or international? To whom do decision-makers have to justify their decisions? To whom should they be accountable? Further, what are the implications for the idea of legitimate rule of decisions taken in polities, with potentially life-and-death consequences for large numbers of people, many of whom might have no democratic stake in the decision-making process?

Territorial boundaries demarcate the basis on which individuals are included and excluded from participation in decisions affecting their lives (however limited the participation might be), but the outcomes of these decisions most often 'stretch' beyond national frontiers. The implications of this are considerable, not only for the categories of consent and legitimacy, but for all the key ideas of democracy: the nature of a

constituency, the meaning of representation, the proper form and scope of political participation, and the relevance of the democratic nation-state, faced with unsettling patterns of relations and constraints in the international order, as the guarantor of the rights, duties and welfare of subjects. Of course, these considerations would probably come as little surprise to those nations and countries whose independence and identity have been deeply affected by the hegemonic reach of empires, old and new, but they do come as a surprise to many in the west.

In order to explore the significance of these matters further, it is necessary to examine why for most of the nineteenth and twentieth centuries democracy *in* nation-states has not been accompanied by democratic relations *among* states; why the inter-state system is now coming under pressure in a way which makes the relation between democracy within borders and democracy across borders a more urgent concern; why contemporary circumstances are creating the possibility of rethinking democracy at regional and global levels; and why democracy at such levels is an important condition for the development of democracy within local and national communities. I shall endeavour to show that democracy within a nation-state or region requires democracy within a network of interwoven international forces and relations; and that such a requirement is thwarted by the 'deep structure' of the sovereign state order and the grafting on to this structure of the United Nations system in the immediate aftermath of the second world war. Nonetheless, one can glimpse the possibility, I shall also seek to show, of an alternative to this state of affairs.

Sovereignty and the Westphalian order

The history of the modern inter-state system, and of international relations more generally, has borne little relation to any democratic principle of organization. In the arena of world politics, Hobbes's way of thinking about power and power relations has often been regarded as the most insightful account of the meaning of the state at the global level.[42] Hobbes drew a comparison between international relations and the state of nature, describing the international system of states as being in a continuous 'posture of war'.[43] A war of 'all against all' is a constant threat, since each state is at liberty to act to secure its own interests unimpeded by any higher religious or moral strictures.

In the study of international affairs, Hobbes's account has become associated with the 'realist' theory of international politics.[44] Realism posits, in the spirit of Hobbes's work, that the system of sovereign states is inescapably anarchic in character; and that this anarchy forces all states, in the inevitable absence of any supreme arbiter to enforce moral behaviour and agreed international codes, to pursue power politics in order to attain their vital interests. This *realpolitik* view of states has had a significant influence on both the analysis and practice of international relations in recent times as it offers a convincing *prima facie* explanation of the chaos and disorder of world affairs. In this account, the modern system of nation-states is a 'limiting factor' which will always thwart any attempt to conduct international relations in a manner which transcends the politics of the sovereign state.

A concomitant of each and every modern state's claim to supreme authority is a recognition that such a claim gives other states an equal entitlement to autonomy and respect within their own borders. In the context of the rapid erosion of 'Christian society' from the late sixteenth century, the development of sovereignty can be interpreted as part of a process of mutual recognition whereby states granted each other rights of jurisdiction in their respective territories and communities. Accordingly, sovereignty involved the assertion by the modern state of independence, that is, of its possession of sole rights to jurisdiction over a particular people and territory. And in the world of relations among states, the principle of the sovereign equality of all states gradually became adopted as the paramount principle governing the formal conduct of states towards one another, however representative or unrepresentative were their particular regimes.

The conception of international order which emerged to clarify and formalize the inter-state system has been referred to as the 'Westphalian' model (after the Peace of Westphalia of 1648 which brought to an end the German phase of the thirty years war).[45] The model covers a period from 1648 to 1945 (although some would argue it still holds today).[46] It depicts the emergence of a world community consisting of sovereign states which settle their differences privately and often by force; which engage in diplomatic relations but otherwise minimal cooperation; which seek to place their own national interest above all others; and which accept the logic of the principle of effectiveness, that is, the principle that might eventually makes right in the international world – appropriation becomes legitimation.[47] The model of Westphalia is summarized in Table 1.[48]

This framework of international affairs had a lasting and paradoxical quality rich in implications: an increasingly developed and interlinked states system simultaneously endorsed the right of each state to autonomous and independent action. As one commentator has aptly noted, the upshot of this was that states were 'not subject to international moral requirements because they represent separate and discrete political orders with no common authority among them'.[49] In this situation, the world consists of separate political powers, pursuing their own interests, backed ultimately by their organization of coercive power.[50]

The consolidation of the modern states system resulted from the expansion of Europe across the globe. If the Iberian monarchies led the early wave of 'European globalization', their position was eroded in the seventeenth century by the Dutch, and subsequently by the English. Key features of the modern states system – the centralization of political power, the expansion of

Table 1. The Model of Westphalia

1 The world consists of, and is divided by, sovereign states which recognize no superior authority.

2 The processes of law-making, the settlement of disputes and law-enforcement are largely in the hands of individual states subject to the logic of 'the competitive struggle for power'.

3 Differences among states are often settled by force: the principle of effective power holds sway. Virtually no legal fetters exist to curb the resort to force; international legal standards afford minimal protection.

4 Responsibility for cross border wrongful acts are a 'private matter' concerning only those affected; no collective interest in compliance with international law is recognized.

5 All states are regarded as equal before the law: legal rules do not take account of asymmetries of power.

6 International law is orientated to the establishment of minimal rules of coexistence; the creation of enduring relationships among states and peoples is an aim, but only to the extent that it allows national political objectives to be met.

7 The minimization of impediments on state freedom is the 'collective' priority.

administrative rule, the legitimation of power through claims to representation, the emergence of massed armies – which existed in Europe in embryo in the sixteenth century, were to become prevalent features of the entire global system.[51]

While the diffusion of European power mainly occurred through the medium of sea-going military and commercial endeavours, Europe became connected to a global system of trade and production relationships. At the centre of the latter were new and expanding capitalistic economic mechanisms which had their origins in the sixteenth century, or in what is sometimes called the 'long sixteenth century', running from about 1450 to 1640.[52] Capitalism was from the beginning an international affair:[53] capital never allowed its aspirations to be determined by national boundaries alone. Consequently, the emergence of capitalism ushered in a fundamental change in the world order: it made possible, for the first time, genuinely global interconnections among states and societies; it penetrated the distant corners of the world and brought far-reaching changes to the dynamics and nature of political rule.

The development of the world capitalist economy initially took the form of the expansion of market relations, driven by a growing need for raw materials and other factors of production. Capitalism stimulated this drive and was, in turn, stimulated by it. It is useful to make a distinction between the expansion of capitalist market relations based on the desire to buy, sell and accumulate mobile resources (capital), and the formation of industrial capitalism involving highly distinctive class relations – based initially on those who own and control the means of production and those who have only their labouring capacity to sell. It is only with the development of capitalism in Europe after 1500, and in particular with the formation of the capitalist organization of production from the middle of the eighteenth century, that the activities of capitalists and the capitalist system began to converge.[54] From this period, the objectives of war became linked to economic objectives: military endeavour and conquest became more directly connected with the pursuit of economic advantage than they had been in earlier periods.[55]

The globalization of economic life – broadly, the growth of complex economic interconnections among states and societies – has not by any means been, of course, a uniform process, affecting each region and country in a similar way. From the outset, this process has involved great costs for the autonomy and independence of many: for example, the progressive collapse of non-European civilizations, among them the Moslem, Indian and Chinese; the disorganizing effects of western rule on a large number of small societies; and the interlinked degradation of the non-European and European worlds caused by the slave trade. In fact, globalization has been characterized both by 'hierarchy' and 'unevenness'.[56] Hierarchy denotes the structure of economic globalization: its domination by those constellations of economic power concentrated in the west and north. With the decline of Europe's empires in the twentieth century, and the end of the cold war, economic globalization has arguably become more significant than ever as the determinant of hierarchy, and the front line of geopolitics. It is likely that the economic summits of the leading industrial countries will supplant superpower summits as the primary arena within which to discern new contours of hierarchy and power. While there may be uncertainty about the precise distribution of influence at the centre of the advanced industrial countries, the hierarchical structure of the economic processes of globalization firmly places the leading economic powers of the west or north in central positions.

The other side of hierarchy is unevenness. This refers to the asymmetrical effects of economic globalization upon the life-chances and well-being of peoples, classes, ethnic groupings, movements and the sexes. The contours of these processes of 'unevenness' are not difficult to discern, although they will not be documented here. They are broadly correlated with geography, race and gender and, accordingly, with the clusters of poverty and deprivation found among the countries of the south, among non-Whites and among women. However, the existence of significant poverty in the north (in Europe and the US), the persistence of unemployment in the most advanced industrial countries (even during periods of marked growth), and the fate of many indigenous peoples, indicates the approximate nature of conceiving unevenness in these terms alone. Unevenness is a phenomenon of both international and national development. The categories of social and political stratification must, therefore, be thought of as denoting systematic divisions within and across territories.[57]

The effective power which sovereignty bestows is, to a significant degree, connected to the economic resources at the disposal of a state or people. Clearly, the resources a polity can mobilize will vary according to its position in the global structure of economic relations, its place in the international division of labour, and the support it can muster from regional economic networks.[58] The growing awareness in many western countries that their sovereignty is under pressure from a variety of sources and forces places before them (often for the first time) issues that have been apparent to many countries for a long time. The struggle for sovereignty and autonomy in many third world countries was closely related to the struggle for freedom from colonial domination. *De jure* sovereignty has been of the utmost importance to those countries that had previously been denied it; but *de jure* sovereignty is not, of course, the same thing as *de facto* or practical sovereignty. The often weak and debt-ridden economies of many third world countries leave them vulnerable and dependent on economic forces and relations over which they have little, if any, control. Although the internationalization of production and finance places many instruments of economic control beyond even the most powerful countries, the position of those at the lower end of the globalization hierarchy, experiencing the worst effects of unevenness, is substantially worse.

Political independence often provides at best only a brief respite from the processes of marginalization in the world economy. In countries such as those of the Sub-Sahara, where the boundaries of the state (with two small exceptions) do not correspond to the boundaries of any that existed before colonization, where there has been no 'established habit' of exercising central authority and accepting its role, and where some of the most elementary human securities have often been absent, independence has been fraught with many types of difficulty.[59] Against this background, the achievement of any form of democracy is significant. Nevertheless, the achievement is handicapped by vulnerability to the international economy, by a fragile resource base which is threatening to the autonomy of political organizations, and by social groups often deeply divided by extreme poverty, hardship and ill-health as well as by ethnic, cultural and other considerations. In addition, it is handicapped by the very *structure* of the international political system which leaves individual states, locked into the competitive pursuit of their own security and interests, without systematic means to pursue the accountability and regulation of some of the most powerful forces ordering national and international affairs. It is political and economic might which ultimately determines the effective deployment of rules and resources within and beyond borders in the Westphalian world.

The international order and the United Nations Charter

The titanic struggles of the first and second world wars led to a growing acknowledgement that the nature and process of international governance would have to change if the most extreme forms of violence against humanity were to be outlawed, and the growing interconnectedness and interdependence of nations recognized. Slowly, the subject, scope and very sources of the Westphalian conception of international regulation, particularly its conception of international law, were all called into question.[60]

First and foremost, opinion moved against the doctrine that international law, as Oppenheim put it, is a 'law between states only and exclusively'.[61] Single persons and groups became recognized as subjects of international law. It is generally accepted, for example, that persons as individuals are subjects of international law on the basis of such documents as the Charters of the Nuremberg and Tokyo War Crimes Tribunals, the Universal Declaration of Human Rights of 1948, the Covenants on Civil and Political Rights of 1966, and the European Convention on Human Rights of 1950.

Opinion has also moved against the doctrine that international law is primarily about political and strategic (state) affairs. According to this position, international law is concerned progressively with orchestrating and regulating economic, social and environmental matters. Linked to substantial increases in the numbers of 'actors' in world politics – for example, the UN, the UN Economic and Social Council, UNCTAD, the World Bank, the International Monetary Fund, the Food and Agricultural Organization and the World Health Organization – there have been many pressures to increase the scope of international law. Faced with this development, there are those who characterize the changing reach of international law as being ever less concerned with the freedom or liberty of states, and ever more with the general welfare of all those in the global system who are able to make their voices count.[62]

Finally, the influential legal doctrine that the only true source of international law is the consent of states – either their expressed consent, or their implied consent – has been fundamentally challenged. Today, a number of sources of international law jostle for recognition. These include the traditional sources such as international conventions or treaties (general or particular) which are recognized by states; international custom or practice which provides evidence of an accepted rule or set of rules; and the underlying principles of law recognized by 'civilized nations'. They also include the 'will of the international community', which can assume the 'status of law' or the 'basis of international legal obligation' under certain circumstances.[63] The latter represents a break in principle with the requirement of individual state consent in the making of international rules and responsibilities.[64]

Although the Westphalian model of international law had its critics throughout the modern era, particularly during the ill-fated efforts of the League of Nations, it was not until after the second world war that a new model of international law and accountability was widely advocated and accepted, culminating in the adoption of the UN Charter. The image of international regulation projected by the Charter (and related documents) was one of 'states still jealously "sovereign"', but linked together in a 'myriad of relations'; under pressure to resolve disagreements by peaceful means and according to legal criteria; subject in principle to tight restrictions on the resort to force; and constrained to observe 'certain standards' with regard to the treatment of all persons on their territory, including their own citizens.[65] Of course, how restrictive the provisions of the Charter have been to states, and to what extent they have been actually operationalized, are important questions. Before addressing them, however, leading elements of the Charter model should be sketched (see Table 2).[66]

The shift in the structure of international regulation from the Westphalian to the UN Charter model raised fundamental questions about the nature and form of international law – questions which point to the possibility of a significant disjuncture between the law of nation-states, of the states system, and of the wider international community. At the heart of this shift lies a conflict between claims made on behalf of individual

Table 2. The UN Charter Model

1 The world community consists of sovereign states, connected through a dense network of relations, both *ad hoc* and institutionalized. Single persons and groups are regarded as legitimate actors in international relations (albeit with limited roles).

2 Certain peoples oppressed by colonial powers, racist regimes or foreign occupants are assigned rights of recognition and a determinate role in articulating their future and interests.

3 Gradual acceptance of standards and values which call into question the principle of effective power; accordingly, major violations of given international rules are not in theory to be regarded as legitimate. Restrictions are placed on the resort to force, including the unwarranted use of economic force.

4 The creation of new rules, procedures and institutions designed to aid law-making and law-enforcement in international affairs.

5 The adoption of legal principles delimiting the form and scope of the conduct of all members of the international community, and providing a set of guidelines for the structuring of international rules.

6 Fundamental concern expressed for the rights of individuals, and the creation of a corpus of international rules seeking to constrain states to observe certain standards in the treatment of all, including their own citizens.

7 The preservation of peace, the advancement of human rights and the establishment of greater social justice are the stated collective priorities; 'public affairs' include the whole of the international community. With respect to certain values – peace, the prohibition of genocide – international rules now provide in principle for the personal responsibility of state officials and the attribution of criminal acts to states.

8 The recognition of systematic inequalities among peoples and states and the establishment of new rules – including the concept of 'the common heritage of mankind'[67] – to create ways of governing the distribution, appropriation and exploitation of territory, property and natural resources.

states and those made on behalf of an alternative organizing principle of world affairs: ultimately, a democratic community of states, with equal voting rights in the General Assembly of nation-states, openly and collectively regulating international life while constrained to observe the UN Charter and a battery of human rights conventions. However, this conflict has not been settled, and it would be quite misleading to conclude that the era of the UN Charter model simply displaced the Westphalian logic of international governance. The essential reason for this is that the Charter framework represents, in many respects, an extension of the interstate system.

The organizations and procedures of the UN were designed partly to overcome weaknesses in the League of Nations. Its 'architecture', therefore, was drawn up to accommodate the international power structure as it was understood in 1945. The division of the globe into powerful nation-states, with distinctive sets of geopolitical interests, was built into the Charter conception. As a result, the UN was virtually immobilized as an autonomous actor on many pressing issues.[68] One of the most obvious manifestations of this was the special veto power accorded to the five Permanent Members of the UN Security Council. This privileged political status added authority and legitimacy to the position of each of the major powers; for although they were barred in principle from the use of force on terms contrary to the Charter, they were protected against censure and sanctions in the event of unilateral action in the form of their veto. Moreover, the Charter gave renewed credence (through Article 51) to unilateral strategic state initiatives if they were necessary in 'self defence', since there was no clear delimitation of the meaning of this phrase. In addition, while the Charter placed new obligations on states to settle disputes peacefully, and laid down certain procedures for passing judgement on alleged acts of self-defence, these procedures have rarely been used and there has been no insistence on compliance with them. The possibility of mobilizing the collective coercive measures envisaged in the Charter itself against illegitimate state action has, furthermore, never materialized, and even the UN's peacekeeping missions have been restricted generally to areas in which the consent of the territorial state in question has first been given.

The UN's susceptibility to the agendas of the most powerful states has been reinforced by its dependence on finance provided by its members. This position of vulnerability to state politics is underscored by the absence of any mechanism to confer some kind of direct UN status on regional and transnational functional or cultural forces (agencies, groups or movements) who often might have a significant perspective on international questions. In sum, the UN Charter model, despite its good intentions, failed effectively to generate a new principle of organization in the international order – a principle which might

break fundamentally with the logic of Westphalia and generate new democratic mechanisms of political coordination and change.

Nonetheless, it would be wrong simply to leave the argument here. The UN Charter system has been distinctively innovative and influential in a number of respects. It has provided an international forum in which all states are in certain respects equal, a forum of particular value to third world countries and to those seeking a basis for 'consensus' solutions to international problems. It has provided a framework for decolonization, and for the pursuit of the reform of international economic institutions. Moreover, it has provided a vision, valuable in spite of all its limitations, of a new world order based upon a meeting of governments and, under appropriate circumstances, of a supranational presence in world affairs championing human rights.[69] Further, some of the deficiencies attributed to the UN can be better placed at the door of the states system itself, with its deep structural embeddedness in the global capitalist economy.

It might, accordingly, be a considerable step forward in the cross-border regulation of world affairs if the UN system were to live up to its Charter. Among other things, this would involve pursuing measures to implement key elements of the rights Conventions, enforcing the prohibition on the discretionary right to use force, activating the collective security system envisaged in the Charter itself and, more generally, ensuring compliance with the Charter's main articles.[70] In addition, if the Charter model were extended – for example, by adding the requirement of compulsory jurisdiction in the case of disputes falling under the UN rubric, or by providing means of redress in the case of human rights violations through a new international human rights court, or by making a (near) consensus vote in the General Assembly a legitimate source of international law, or by modifying the veto arrangement in the Security Council and rethinking representation on it to allow for an adequate regional presence – a basis might be established for the Charter model to generate political resources of its own, and to act as an autonomous decision-making centre.

While each move in this direction would be significant, particularly in enhancing the prospects of world peace, it would still represent, at best, a movement towards a very partial or 'thin' form of democracy in international affairs.

Certainly, each state would enjoy formal equality in the UN system, and regional interests would be better represented. But it would still be possible for a plethora of different kinds of political regimes to participate on an equal footing in the Charter framework; the dynamics and logic of the inter-state system would still represent an immensely powerful principle of organization in global affairs, especially with its military machinery largely intact; the massive disparities of power and asymmetries of resources in the hierarchical and uneven global political economy would be left virtually unaddressed; the changing structure of the global order reflected in discussion about the proper subject, scope and sources of international law would remain marginal to the model; and transnational actors, civil associations, non-governmental organizations and social movements might still have a minimal role in this governance system. It would remain, then, a state-centred or sovereignty-centred model of international politics, and would lie at some considerable distance from what might be called a 'thicker' democratic ordering of international affairs. Furthermore, it would lie at some distance from an adequate recognition of the transformations being wrought in the wake of globalization – transformations which are placing increasing strain on both the Westphalian and Charter conceptions of international governance.

Cosmopolitan democracy and the new international order

There is a striking paradox to note about the contemporary era: from Africa to Eastern Europe, Asia to Latin America, more and more nations and groups are championing the idea of 'the rule of the people'; but they are doing so at just that moment when the very efficacy of democracy as a national form of political organization appears open to question. As substantial areas of human activity are progressively organized on a global level, the fate of democracy, and of the independent democratic nation-state in particular, is fraught with difficulty.

It could be objected that there is nothing particularly new about global interconnections, and that the significance of global interconnections for politics has, in principle, been plain for people to see for a long time. Such an objection could be elaborated by emphasizing, as I have done, that a dense pattern of global interconnections began to

emerge with the initial expansion of the world economy and the rise of the modern state from the late sixteenth century. Further, it could be suggested that domestic and international politics have been interwoven throughout the modern era: domestic politics has always to be understood against the background of international politics, and the former is often the source of the latter.[71] However, it is one thing to claim that there are elements of continuity in the formation and structure of modern states, economies and societies, quite another to claim that there is nothing new about aspects of their form and dynamics. For there is a fundamental difference between, on the one hand, the development of particular trade routes, or select military and naval operations which have an impact on certain towns, rural centres and territories, and, on the other hand, an international order involving the emergence of a global economic system which stretches beyond the control of any single state (even of dominant states); the expansion of networks of transnational relations and communications over which particular states have limited influence; the enormous growth in international organizations and regimes which can limit the scope for action of the most powerful states; the development of a global military order, and the build-up of the means of 'total' warfare as an enduring feature of the contemporary world, which can reduce the range of policies available to governments and their citizens. While trade routes and military expeditions can link distant populations together in long loops of cause and effect, contemporary developments in the international order link peoples through multiple networks of transaction and coordination, reordering the very notion of distance itself.[72]

It needs to be emphasized that processes of globalization do not necessarily lead to growing global integration; that is, to a world order marked by the progressive development of a homogenous or unified society and politics. For globalization can generate forces of both fragmentation and unification. Fragmentation or disintegrative trends are possible for several reasons. The growth of dense patterns of interconnectedness among states and societies can increase the range of developments affecting people in particular locations. By creating new patterns of transformation and change, globalization can weaken old political and economic structures without necessarily leading to the establishment of new systems of regulation. Further, the impact of global and regional processes is likely to vary under different international and national conditions – for instance, a nation's location in the international economy, its place in particular power blocs, its position with respect to the international legal system. In addition, globalization can engender an awareness of political difference as much as an awareness of common identity; enhanced international communications can highlight conflicts of interest and ideology, and not merely remove obstacles to mutual understanding.

In positive terms, globalization implies at least two distinct phenomena. First, it suggests that political, economic and social activity is becoming worldwide in scope. And, secondly, it suggests that there has been an intensification of levels of interaction and interconnectedness within and among states and societies.[73] What is new about the modern global system is the spread of globalization through new dimensions of activity – technological, organizational, administrative and legal, among others – each with their own logic and dynamics of change, and the chronic intensification of patterns of interconnectedness mediated by such phenomena as the modern communications industry and new information technology. Politics unfolds today, with all its customary uncertainty and indeterminateness, against the background of a world shaped and permeated by the movement of goods and capital, the flow of communication, the interchange of cultures and the passage of people.[74]

In this context, the meaning and place of democratic politics, and of the contending models of democracy, have to be rethought in relation to a series of overlapping local, regional and global processes and structures.[75] It is essential to recognize at least three elements of globalization: first, the way processes of economic, political, legal and military interconnectedness are changing the nature, scope and capacity of the sovereign state from above, as its 'regulatory' ability is challenged and reduced in some spheres; secondly, the way in which local groups, movements and nationalisms are questioning the nation-state from below as a representative and accountable power system; and, thirdly, the way global interconnectedness creates chains of interlocking political decisions and outcomes among states and their citizens, altering the nature and dynamics of national political systems themselves. Democracy

has to come to terms with all three of these developments and their implications for national and international power centres. If it fails to do so, it is likely to become ever less effective in determining the shape and limits of political activity. The international form and structure of politics and civil society has, accordingly, to be built into the foundations of democratic thought and practice.

Three distinct requirements arise: first, that the territorial boundaries of systems of accountability be recast so that those issues which escape the control of a nation-state – aspects of monetary management, environmental questions, elements of security, new forms of communication – can be brought under better democratic control. Secondly, that the role and place of regional and global regulatory and functional agencies be rethought so that they might provide a more coherent and useful focal point in public affairs. Thirdly, that the articulation of political institutions with the key groups, agencies, associations and organizations of international civil society be reconsidered to allow the latter to become part of a democratic process – adopting, within their very *modus operandi*, a structure of rules and principles compatible with those of democracy.

How might this approach to democracy be developed? What are its essential characteristics? Addressing these questions requires recalling earlier arguments about the need to conceive democracy as a double-sided process, while reappraising the proper domain for the application of this process.[76] For if the above arguments are correct, democracy has to become a transnational affair if it is to be possible both within a restricted geographic domain and within the wider international community. The possibility of democracy today must, in short, be linked to an expanding framework of democratic institutions and agencies. I refer to such a framework as 'the cosmopolitan model of democracy'.[77] The framework can be elaborated by focusing initially on some of its institutional requirements.

In the first instance, the 'cosmopolitan model of democracy' presupposes the creation of regional parliaments (for example, in Latin America and Africa) and the enhancement of the role of such bodies where they already exist (the European Parliament) in order that their decisions become recognized, in principle, as legitimate independent sources of regional and international law. Alongside such developments, the model anticipates the possibility of general referendums, cutting across nations and nation-states, with constituencies defined according to the nature and scope of controversial transnational issues. In addition, the opening of international governmental organizations to public scrutiny and the democratization of international 'functional' bodies (on the basis perhaps of the creation of elected supervisory boards which are in part statistically representative of their constituencies) would be significant.

Hand in hand with these changes the cosmopolitan model of democracy assumes the entrenchment of a cluster of rights, including civil, political, economic and social rights, in order to provide shape and limits to democratic decision-making.[78] This requires that they be enshrined within the constitutions of parliaments and assemblies (at the national and international level); and that the influence of international courts is extended so that groups and individuals have an effective means of suing political authorities for the enactment and enforcement of key rights, both within and beyond political associations.

In the final analysis, the formation of an authoritative assembly of all democratic states and societies – a re-formed UN, or a complement to it – would be an objective. The UN, as previously noted, combines two contradictory principles of representation: the equality of all countries (one country, one vote in the General Assembly) and deference to geopolitical strength (special veto power in the Security Council to those with current or former superpower status). An authoritative assembly of all democratic states and societies would seek unreservedly to place principles of democratic representation above those of superpower politics. Moreover, unlike the UN General Assembly, it would not, to begin with at least, be an assembly of all nations; for it would be an assembly of democratic nations which would draw in others over time, perhaps by the sheer necessity of being a member if their systems of governance are to enjoy legitimacy in the eyes of their own populations. As such, the new Assembly in its early stages can best be thought of as a complement to the UN, which it would either replace over time or accept in a modified form as a 'second chamber' – a necessary meeting place for all states irrespective of the nature of their regimes.

Of course, the idea of a new democratic international Assembly is open to a battery of objec-tions commonly put to similar schemes. Would it have any teeth to implement decisions? How would democratic international law be enforced? Would there be a centralized police and military force?[79] And so forth. These concerns are significant, but many of them can be met and countered. For instance, it needs to be stressed that any global legislative institution should be conceived above all as a 'standard-setting' institution. Although a distinction ought to be made between legal instruments which would have the status of law independently of any further negotiation or action on the part of a region or state or local government, and instruments which would require further discussion with them, implementation of the detail of a broad range of recommendations would be a matter for non-global levels of governance.[80] In addition, the question of law enforcement at a regional and global level is not beyond resolution in principle: a proportion of a nation-state's police and military (perhaps a growing proportion over time) could be 'seconded' to the new international authorities and placed at their disposal on a routine basis. To this end, avenues could be established to meet the concern that 'covenants, without the sword, are but words'.[81]

Equally, only to the extent that the new forms of 'policing' are locked into an international democratic framework would there be good grounds for thinking that a new settlement could be created between coercive power and accountability. If such a settlement seems like a fantasy, it should be emphasized that it is a fantasy to imagine that one can advocate democracy today without confronting the range of issues elaborated here. If the emerging international order is to be democratic, these issues have to be considered, even though their details are, of course, open to further specification.

The implications for international civil society of all this are in part clear. A democratic network of states and civil societies is incompatible with the existence of powerful sets of social relations and organizations which can, by virtue of the very bases of their operations, systematically distort democratic conditions and processes. At stake are, among other things, the curtailment of the power of corporations to constrain and influence the *political* agenda (through such diverse measures as the public funding of elections, the use of 'golden shares' and citizen directors), and the restriction of the activities of powerful transnational interest groups to pursue their interests unchecked (through, for example, the regulation of bargaining procedures to minimize the use of 'coercive tactics' within and between public and private associations, and the enactment of rules limiting the sponsorship of political representatives by sectional interests, whether these be particular industries or trade unions).

If individuals and peoples are to be free and equal in determining the conditions of their own existence there must be an array of social spheres – for instance, privately and cooperatively owned enterprises, independent communications media, and autonomously run cultural centres – which allow their members control of the resources at their disposal without direct interference from political agencies or other third parties.[82] At issue here is a civil society that is neither simply planned nor merely market orientated but, rather, open to organizations, associations and agencies pursuing their own projects, subject to the constraints of democratic processes and a common structure of action.[83]

The key features of this model are set out in Table 3. The cosmopolitan model of democracy presents a programme of possible transformations with short- and long-term political implications. It does not present an all-or-nothing choice, but rather lays down a direction of possible change with clear points of orientation (see Appendix I).

Would a cosmopolitan framework of democracy, assuming its details could be adequately fleshed out, have the organizational resources – procedural, legal, institutional and military – to alter the dynamics of resource production and distribution, and of rule creation and enforcement, in the contemporary era? It would be deeply misleading to suggest that it would initially have these capabilities. Nevertheless, its commitment to the extension and deepening of mechanisms of democratic accountability across major regions and international structures would help to regulate resources and forces which are already beyond the reach of national democratic mechanisms and movements. Moreover, its commitment to the protection and strengthening of human rights, and to the further development of a regional and international court system, would aid the process whereby individuals and groups could sue their governments for the enactment of key human rights.

In addition, the establishment of regional authorities as major independent voices in world

Table 3. The Cosmopolitan Model of Democracy

1   The global order consists of multiple and overlapping networks of power including the political, social and economic.

2   All groups and associations are attributed rights of self-determination specified by a commitment to individual autonomy and a specific cluster of rights. The cluster is composed of rights within and across each network of power. Together, these rights constitute the basis of an empowering legal order – a 'democratic international law'.

3   Law-making and law-enforcement can be developed within this framework at a variety of locations and levels, along with an expansion of the influence of regional and international courts to monitor and check political and social authority.

4   Legal principles are adopted which delimit the form and scope of individual and collective action within the organizations and associations of state *and* civil society. Certain standards are specified for the treatment of all, which no political regime or civil association can legitimately violate.

5   As a consequence, the principle of non-coercive relations governs the settlement of disputes, though the use of force remains a collective option in the last resort in the face of tyrannical attacks to eradicate democratic international law.

6   The defence of self-determination, the creation of a common structure of action and the preservation of the democratic good are the overall collective priorities.

7   Determinate principles of social justice follow: the *modus operandi* of the production, distribution and the exploitation of resources must be compatible with the democratic process and a common framework of action.

politics might contribute further to the erosion of the old division of the world by the US and the former USSR. Likewise, the new institutional focus at the global level on major transnational issues would go some way towards eradicating sectarian approaches to these questions, and to countering 'hierarchy' and some of the major asymmetries in life chances. Finally, new sets of regional and global rules and procedures might help prevent public affairs from becoming a quagmire of infighting among nations wholly unable to settle pressing collective issues.

Of course, there would be new possible dangers – no political scheme is free from such risks. But what would be at issue would be the beginning of the creation of a new international democratic culture and spirit – one set off from the partisan claims of the nation-state. Such developments might take years, if not decades, to become entrenched. But 1989–91 has shown that political change can take place at an extraordinary speed, itself no doubt partially a result of the process of globalization.

Conclusion

In order to avoid possible misunderstandings about the arguments offered above, it might be useful, by way of a conclusion, to emphasize the terrain they occupy and the ground they reject. This can be done by assessing critically a number of conceptual polarities frequently found in political discourse: globalism versus cultural diversity; constitutionalism versus politics; political ambition versus political feasibility; participatory or direct democracy versus liberal representative democracy and global governance from above versus the extension of grassroots associations from below. Although these polarities provide much of the tension which charges the debate about the possibility of democracy beyond borders, there are good reasons for doubting their coherence.

To begin with, globalism and cultural diversity are not simply opposites. For global interconnectedness is already forming a dense web of relations linking cultures one to another. The issue is how and in what way cultures are linked and interrelated, not how a sealed cultural diversity can persist in the face of globalization.

Secondly, the juxtaposition of constitutionalism – or the elaboration of theoretical models of principles of political organization – with politics as a practical activity sets up another false polarity. Politics typically operates within a framework – albeit a shifting framework – of rules. Politics is rarely without some pattern, and is most often about the nature of the rules which will shape and delimit political activity. For politics is at root about the ways in which rules and resources are distributed, produced and legitimated. The question is whether politics will be shaped by an explicit, formal constitution or model which might, in principle, be open and contestable, or whether politics will be subject to an unwritten constitution, which is altogether more difficult to invoke as a defence in the face of unaccountable systems of power.

Thirdly, the question of feasibility cannot simply be set up in opposition to the question of political ambition. For what is ambitious today might be feasible tomorrow. Who anticipated the remarkable changes of 1989–90 in Eastern Europe? Who foresaw the fall of communism in the Soviet Union? The growing interconnectedness between states and societies is generating consequences, intended and unintended, for the stability of regimes, governments and states. While the question of political feasibility is of the utmost significance, it would be naive to juxtapose it simply with programmes of political ambition.

Fourthly, versions of participatory democracy cannot simply be opposed to liberal representative democracy. Programmes of participatory or direct democracy are fraught with complexities and questions. Likewise, liberal representative democracy does not simply mean one set of possible institutions or forms. The nature of liberal democracy is itself an intensely contested issue. So while there seem to be good grounds for accepting the liberal distinction between state and civil society, there are not equally good grounds for uncritically accepting either of these in their liberal form. The juxtaposition of participation with liberal representative democracy leaves most of political analysis to one side.

Fifthly, the problems of global governance from above cannot be solved through the extension of grassroots democracy alone. For the questions have to be posed: which grassroots, and which democracy? There are many social movements – for instance, right-wing nationalist movements or the Eugenics movement – which highlight how the very nature of a grassroots movement can be contested and fought over. Grassroots movements are by no means merely noble or wise. Like most social, economic or political forms, they can appear in a variety of shapes, with a variety of patterns of internal organization. Appeal to the nature of inherent goodness of grassroots associations and movements bypasses the necessary work of theoretical analysis.

Today, any attempt to set out a position of what could be called 'embedded utopianism' must begin both from where we are – the existing pattern of political relations and processes – and from an analysis of what might be: desirable political forms and principles.[84] If utopia is to be embedded it must be linked into patterns and movements as they are. But if this context of embeddedness is not simply to be affirmed in the shape and patterns generated by past groups and movements, it has to be assessed according to standards, criteria and principles. These, in my view, follow from a theory of democracy.

Finally, if the history and practice of democracy has until now been centred on the idea of locality (the city-state, the community, the nation), it is likely that in the future it will be centred on the international or global domain. It would be immensely naive to claim that there are any straightforward solutions to the problems posed by global interconnectedness, with its complex and often profoundly uneven effects; but there is, without doubt, an inescapably important set of questions to be addressed. Certainly, one can find many good reasons for being optimistic about finding a path forward, and many good reasons for thinking that at this juncture democracy will face another critical test.

Appendix I
Objectives of the Cosmopolitan Model of Democracy: Illustrative Issues

Short-term	*Long-term*
Polity/governance	
1 Reform of UN Security Council (to give the third world a significant voice)	1 Global Parliament (with limited revenue-raising capacity) connected to regions, nations and localities
2 Creation of a UN second chamber (on the model of the EC?)	2 New Charter of Rights and Duties locked into different domains of power
3 Enhanced political regionalization (EC and beyond)	3 Separation of political and economic interests; public funding of electoral processes
4 Compulsory jurisdiction before the International Court. New International Criminal Court and New Human Rights Court for the pursuit of rights	4 Interconnected global legal system
5 Establishment of a small but effective, accountable, international, military force	5 Permanent 'secondment' of a growing proportion of a nation-state's coercive capability to regional and global institutions. Aim: demilitarization and transcendence of war system
Civil Society	
1 Enhancement of non-state, non-market solutions in the organization of civil society	1 Creation of a diversity of self-regulating associations and groups in civil society
2 Introduction of limits to private ownership of key 'public-shaping' institutions: media, information, etc.	2 Systematic experimentation with different democratic organizational forms in civil society
3 Provision of resources to those in the most vulnerable social positions to defend and articulate their interests	3 Multi-sectoral economy and pluralization of patterns of ownership and possession

Notes

1 I should like to thank Richard Falk, Anthony Giddens, Jack Hayward, Quentin Skinner, David Scott-Macnab, Saul Mendlovitz and John Thompson for many constructive comments on this essay. The essay seeks to draw together and expand upon a number of themes discussed in my recent writings, particularly in *Models of Democracy* (Cambridge, Polity Press, 1987), Ch. 9; 'Democracy, the nation-state and the global system', in D. Held (ed.), *Political Theory Today* (Cambridge, Polity Press, 1991); and 'Democracy and globalization', *Alternatives*, 16: 2 (1991).

2 See F. Fukuyama, 'The end of History', *The National Interest*, 16 (1989) and 'A reply to my critics', *The National Interest*, 18 (1989/90). For a more detailed commentary on these texts, cf. D. Held, 'Liberalism, Marxism and democracy', *Theory and Society* (forthcoming).

3 I. Berlin, *Four Essays on Liberty* (Oxford, Oxford University Press, 1969), pp. 164ff.

4 See, for example, A. Lijphart, *Democracies* (New Haven, CT, Yale University Press, 1984) and R. Dahl, *Democracy and Its Critics* (New Haven, CT, Yale University Press, 1989).

5 A fuller account of the nature and scope of political theory as outlined here can be found in the 'Introduction' to Held, *Political Theory Today*, pp. 1–21.

6 See M. Bernal, *Black Athena* (London, Free Association Books, 1987), Vol. I and P. Springborg, *Western Republicanism and the Oriental Prince* (Cambridge, Polity Press, 1992).

7 When referring to the Greek *polis*, some scholars prefer to use the term 'city-republic' on the grounds that the concept of the state was an early modern formulation. For some of the issues underpinning this preference see Held, *Models of Democracy*, Ch. 2.

8 M. Finley, *Politics in the Ancient World* (Cambridge, Cambridge University Press, 1983). pp. 84ff.

9 See J.G.A. Pocock, *The Machiavellian Moment: Florentine Political Thought and the Atlantic Republican Tradition* (Princeton, NJ, Princeton University Press, 1975), pp. 64–80.

10 See N. Machiavelli, *The Discourses* (Harmondsworth, Penguin, 1983), pp. 104–11.

11 The republican view emphasizes, in short, that the freedom of citizens consists above all in their unhindered pursuit of their self-chosen ends. The highest political ideal is the civic freedom of an independent, self-governing republic.

12 Q. Skinner, 'The state', in T. Ball, J. Farr and R. Hanson (eds), *Political Innovation and Conceptual Change* (Cambridge, Cambridge University Press, 1989), p. 105.

13 Aristotle, *The Politics* (Harmondsworth, Penguin, 1981), p. 169.

14 See M. Finley, *Democracy Ancient and Modern* (London, Chatto and Windus, 1973).

15 The concern with aspects of 'self-government' in Renaissance Italy had a significant influence in seventeenth- and eighteenth-century England, France and America. The problem of how civic life was to be constructed, and public life sustained, was faced by diverse thinkers. While the meaning of the ideal of active citizenship was progressively altered – and denuded of many of its most challenging implications – threads of this ideal remained and continued to have an impact. It is possible to trace 'radical' and 'conservative' strains of republicanism throughout the early modern period. Cf. Pocock, *The Machiavellian Moment* and G.S. Wood, *The Creation of the American Republic: 1776–1787* (Chapel Hill, University of North Carolina Press, 1969).

16 Pocock, *The Machiavellian Moment*, p. 550.

17 H. Bull, *The Anarchical Society* (London, Macmillan, 1977), p. 27.

18 Q. Skinner, *The Foundations of Political Thought, Vol. 1* (Cambridge, Cambridge University Press, 1978), p. 352.

19 See D. Held, 'The development of the modern state', in S. Hall and B. Gieben (eds), *Formations of Modernity* (Cambridge, Polity Press, 1992).

20 J. Madison, *The Federalist Papers*, edited by R. Fairfield (New York, Doubleday, 1966), No. 10, p. 20.

21 Madison, *The Federalist Papers*, No. 10, pp. 21–2.

22 See R.W. Krouse, 'Classical images of democracy in America: Madison and Tocqueville', in G. Duncan (ed.), *Democratic Theory and Practice* (Cambridge, Cambridge University Press, 1983), pp. 58–78.

23 J. Bentham, *Constitutional Code, Book 1*, in *The Works of Jeremy Bentham, Vol. IX* (Edinburgh, W. Tait, 1843), p. 47.

24 N. Bobbio, *Democracy and Dictatorship* (Cambridge, Polity Press, 1989), p. 144.

25 See Dahl, *Democracy and Its Critics*, pp. 28–30.

26 Quoted in G.H. Sabine, *A History of Political Theory* (London, George G. Harrap, 3rd edn, 1963), p. 695.

27 See Held, *Models of Democracy*, Ch. 3.

28 See N. Bobbio, *Which Socialism?* (Cambridge, Polity Press, 1987), p. 66 and Dahl, *Democracy and Its Critics*, pp. 221 and 233.

29 Bobbio, *Which Socialism?*, pp. 42–4.

30 A. Callinicos, *The Revenge of History: Marxism and the East European Revolutions* (Cambridge, Polity Press, 1991), pp. 108–9.

31 K. Marx, *The Civil War in France* (Peking, Foreign Languages Press, 1970), pp. 67–70.

32 Marx, Letter 2, from the *Deutsch-Französische Jahrbücher* (Paris, 1844).

33 See, for example, V.I. Lenin, *What Is To Be Done?* (Moscow, Progress Publishers, 1947).

34 Held, *Models of Democracy*, Ch. 9.

35 For texts which seek to do this, see Held, *Models of Democracy*, Chs 8 and 9; Held, 'Democracy, the nation-state and the global system', pp. 227–35; and J. Keane, *Democracy and Civil Society* (London, Verso, 1988). See also Keane's essay in *Political Studies*, 40, Special Issue (1992), 116–29.

36 H. Arendt, *On Revolution* (New York, Viking Press, 1963), p. 256.

37 Held, 'Democracy, the nation-state and the global system', p. 198. Some of the material in the following paragraphs is adapted from pp. 201–5 of that essay.

38 Cf., for example, C.B. Macpherson, *The Life and Times of Liberal Democracy* (Oxford, Oxford University Press, 1977); C. Pateman, *The Problem of Political Obligation* (Cambridge, Polity Press, 2nd edn, 1985); and B. Barber, *Strong Democracy* (Berkeley, University of California Press, 1984).

39 C. Offe, *Disorganized Capitalism* (Cambridge, Polity Press, 1985), pp. 286ff.

40 R. Hanson, 'Democracy', in T. Ball, J. Farr and R. Hanson (eds), *Political Innovation and Conceptual Change* (Cambridge, Cambridge University Press, 1989), pp. 68–9.

41 Cf. Dahl, *Democracy and Its Critics*, Chs 10 and 11.

42 See, for example, R. Aron, *Peace and War: a Theory of International Relations* (New York, Doubleday, 1966).

43 T. Hobbes, *Leviathan* (Harmondsworth, Penguin, 1968), pp. 187–8.

44 Cf. H.J. Morgenthau, *Politics Among Nations* (New York, Knopf, 1948); M. Wight, *Power Politics* (Harmondsworth, Penguin, 1986); and S. Smith, 'Reasons of state', in D. Held and C. Pollitt (eds), *New Forms of Democracy* (London, Sage, 1987).

45 See R. Falk, 'The interplay of Westphalia and Charter conceptions of the international legal order', in R. Falk and C. Black (eds), *The Future of the International Legal Order, Vol 1* (Princeton, NJ, Princeton University Press, 1969); R. Falk, *A Study of Future Worlds* (New York, The Free Press, 1975), Ch. 2; and A. Cassese, *International Law in a Divided World* (Oxford, Clarendon Press, 1986), especially pp. 393ff. While the emergence of this model can be linked directly to the Peace of Westphalia, important qualifications ought also to be noted. First, the basic conception of territorial sovereignty was outlined well before this settlement (although not generally assented to). Secondly, there were few, if any, references in the classic texts of early modern political theory to an intrinsically territorial state; as T. Baldwin put it, 'political theory had still to catch up with practice'.

On both these points see T. Baldwin, 'The territorial state', in H. Gross and T.R. Harrison, (eds), *Cambridge Essays in Jurisprudence* (Oxford, Clarendon Press, 1992).

46 By a 'model' I mean a theoretical construction designed to reveal and explain the main elements of a political form or order and its underlying structure of relations. Models in this context are 'networks' of concepts and generalizations about aspects of the political, economic and social spheres.

47 A. Cassese, 'Violence, war and the rule of law in the International Community', in D. Held (ed.), *Political Theory Today* (Cambridge, Polity Press, 1991), p. 256.

48 These points are adapted from Falk, 'The interplay of Westphalia and Charter conceptions of the international legal order', and Cassese, *International Law in a Divided World*, pp. 396–9.

49 C. Beitz, *Political Theory and International Relations* (Princeton, NJ, Princeton University Press, 1979), p. 25.

50 The resort to coercion or armed force by non-state actors is also, arguably, an almost inevitable outcome in such a world. For communities contesting established territorial boundaries have, as Baldwin succinctly wrote, 'little alternative but to resort to arms in order to establish "effective control" over the area they seek as their territory, and in that way make their case for international recognition (cf. Eritrea, East Timor, Kurdistan . . .)'. See Baldwin 'The territorial state'.

51 See G. Modelski, *Principles of World Politics* (New York, Free Press, 1972).

52 See F. Braudel, *Capitalism and Material Life* (London, Weidenfeld and Nicolson, 1973).

53 I. Wallerstein, *The Capitalist Economy* (Cambridge, Cambridge University Press, 1979), p. 19.

54 C. Tilly, *Coercion, Capital and European States, AD 990–1990* (Oxford, Blackwell, 1990), pp. 17 and 189.

55 See M. Mann, *The Sources of Social Power, Vol. 1* (Cambridge, Cambridge University Press, 1986), pp. 510–16.

56 The following analysis is indebted to R. Falk, 'Economic dimensions of global civilization: a preliminary perspective' (working paper prepared for the Cairo meeting of the Global Civilization Project, Oct. 1990), pp. 2–12.

57 See R.W. Cox, *Production, Power, and World Order: Social Forces in the Making of History* (New York, Columbia University Press, 1987), Ch. 9.

58 I do not mean this to be an 'economistic' point. There are obviously other important factors involved in determining a state's effective power. See D. Held, *Political Theory and the Modern State* (Cambridge, Polity Press, 1989), Ch. 8.

59 See G. Hawthorn, 'Sub-Saharan Africa', in D. Held (ed.), *Prospects for Democracy: North, South, East, West* (Cambridge, Polity Press, forthcoming, 1993). Cf. R.H. Jackson and C.G. Rosberg, 'Why Africa's weak states persist: the empirical and the juridical in statehood', *World Politics*, 17 (1982), 1–24.

60 For an overview see Bull, *The Anarchical Society*, Ch. 6.

61 See L. Oppenheim, *International Law, Vol. 1* (London, Longman, 1905), Ch. 1.

62 Cf., for example, B. Röling, *International Law in an Expanded World* (Amsterdam, Djambatan, 1960); W. Friedmann, *The Changing Structure of International Law* (London, Stevens and Son, 1964); and Cassese, *International Law in a Divided World*, especially Chs 7–9.

63 Cf. Bull, *The Anarchical Society*, pp. 147–58; C. Jenks, *Law, Freedom and Welfare* (London, Stevens and Son, 1963), Ch. 5; and R. Falk, *The Status of Law in International Society* (Princeton, NJ. Princeton University Press, 1970), Ch. 5.

64 It is interesting to note that the tradition of natural law thinking, which informed early modern international law in particular, recognized a certain tension between the requirement of governmental consent and the existence of international rights and duties.

65 Cassese, 'Violence, war and the rule of law', p. 256.

66 I have drawn these points from Cassese, *International Law in a Divided World*, pp. 398–400.

67 First propounded in the late 1960s, the concept of 'the common heritage of mankind' has been enshrined in two notable treaties: the Convention on the Moon and Other Celestial Bodies (1979) and the Convention on the Law of the Sea (1982). The concept has been proposed as a device to exclude a state or private right of appropriation over certain resources and to permit the development of these resources, where appropriate, for the benefit of all, with due regard paid to environmental protection.

68 See Falk, *A Study of Future Worlds*, pp. 69–72; R. Falk, *A Global Approach to National Policy* (Cambridge, MA, Harvard University Press, 1975), pp. 169–96; Cassese, *International Law in a Divided World*, pp. 142–3, 200–1, 213–14 and 246–50.

69 Cf. R. Falk, 'Reflections on democracy and the Gulf War', *Alternatives*, 16: 2 (1991), p. 272.

70 In making these proposals I do not wish to imply that the UN Charter itself is a fully coherent document. It includes some contradictory stipulations and procedures; some of its clauses are vague at best; and some of its recommendations can generate conflicting priorities. It is, in short, open to conflicts of interpretation which would have to be addressed thoroughly if it were to take on a more robust role.

71 P. Gourevitch, 'The second image reversed: the international sources of domestic politics', *International Organization*, 32 (1978).

72 Or, as Anthony Giddens usefully put it, globalization can be defined as 'the intensification of worldwide social relations which link distant localities in such a way that local happenings are shaped by events occurring many miles away and vice versa', in *Consequences of Modernity* (Cambridge, Polity Press, 1990), p. 64.

73 See A. McGrew, 'Conceptualizing global politics', in A. McGrew, P. Lewis et al., *Global Politics* (Cambridge, Polity Press, 1992), pp. 1–28.

74 C.W. Kegley and E.R. Wittkopf, *World Politics* (Basingstoke, Macmillan, 1989), p. 511.

75 I have discussed these processes and structures in 'Democracy, the nation-state and the global system', pp. 207–27 and at greater length in *Foundations of Democracy: the Principle of Autonomy and the Global Order* (Cambridge, Polity Press, 1993).

76 See above pp. 84–5.

77 In previous publications I have referred to this as 'the federal model', but given the current controversy about 'federalism' in Europe the term has become unhelpful in conveying my intentions. I would like to thank Daniele Archibugi for pressing this point. A central theme of my forthcoming work, *Foundations of Democracy*, is what I now prefer to call 'the cosmopolitan model of democracy' or, better still, of 'democratic autonomy'. Of course, anyone who seeks to use the term 'cosmopolitan' needs to clarify its meaning, especially in relation to Kant's thought. I seek to do this in *Foundations*.

78 It is beyond the scope of this essay to set out my particular conception of rights which I link to the notion of a 'common structure of action': the necessary conditions for people in principle to enjoy free and equal political participation. See Held, 'Democracy, the nation-state and global system', pp. 227–35, and, particularly, Held, *Foundations of Democracy*.

79 Among other difficulties to be faced would be the rules determining the Assembly's representative base. One country, one vote? Representatives allocated according to population size? Would major international functional organizations be represented? Cf. I. McLean, 'Forms of representation and systems of voting', in D. Held (ed.), *Political Theory Today* (Cambridge, Polity Press, 1991), pp. 190–96 and J. Burnheim, *Is Democracy Possible?* (Cambridge, Polity Press, 1985), pp. 82–124.

80 European Community law embodies a range of relevant distinctions among legal instruments and types of implementation which are helpful to reflect on in this context. However, I leave open these complex issues in this essay.

81 Hobbes, *Leviathan*, p. 223.

82 The models for the organization of such spheres are, it must be readily acknowledged, far from settled. See D. Held and C. Pollitt (eds), *New Forms of Democracy* (London, Sage, 1986).

83 The proposed European Social Charter embodies principles and rules which are compatible with the idea of generating elements of a common structure of action. If operationalized it would, in principle, alter the structure and functioning of market processes in a number of ways. While the Charter falls considerably short of what I have in mind by a common structure of action, and its details require extensive consideration which I shall not offer here, it is a useful illustration of the possibility of legislation to alter the background conditions and operations of the economic organizations of civil society.

84 Cf. R. Falk, *Positive Prescriptions for the Near Future* (Princeton, NJ, Princeton University, Center for International Studies, World Order Studies Program Occasional Paper, No. 20, 1991), pp. 8–10.

PART II

Democracy

7

The Public Sphere

Jürgen Habermas

Concept

By "public sphere" we mean first of all a domain of our social life in which such a thing as public opinion can be formed. Access to the public sphere is open in principle to all citizens. A portion of the public sphere is constituted in every conversation in which private persons come together to form a public. They are then acting neither as business nor professional people conducting their private affairs, nor as legal consociates subject to the legal regulations of a state bureaucracy and obligated to obedience. Citizens act as a public when they deal with matters of general interest without being subject to coercion; thus with the guarantee that they may assemble and unite freely, and express and publicize their opinions freely. When the public is large, this kind of communication requires certain means of dissemination and influence: today, newspapers and periodicals, radio and television are the media of the public sphere. We speak of a political public sphere (as distinguished from a literary one, for instance) when the public discussions concern objects connected with the practice of the state. The coercive power of the state is the counterpart, as it were, of the political public sphere, but it is not a part of it. State power is, to be sure, considered "public" power, but it owes the

Originally published in *Jürgen Habermas on Society and Politics*, ed. Steven Seidman (Beacon Press, 1989). Copyright © 1989 by Beacon Press. Reprinted by permission of the publisher.

attribute of publicness to its task of caring for the public, that is, providing for the common good of all legal consociates. Only when the exercise of public authority has actually been subordinated to the requirement of democratic publicness does the political public sphere acquire an institutionalized influence on the government, by way of the legislative body. The term "public opinion" refers to the functions of criticism and control of organized state authority that the public exercises informally, as well as formally during periodic elections. Regulations concerning the publicness (or publicity [*Publizität*] in its original meaning) of state-related activities, as, for instance, the public accessibility required of legal proceedings, are also connected with this function of public opinion. To the public sphere as a sphere mediating between state and society, a sphere in which the public as the vehicle of public opinion is formed, there corresponds the principle of publicness – the publicness that once had to win out against the secret politics of monarchs and that since then has permitted democratic control of state activity.

It is no accident that these concepts of the public sphere and public opinion were not formed until the eighteenth century. They derive their specific meaning from a concrete historical situation. It was then that one learned to distinguish between opinion and public opinion, or *opinion publique*. Whereas mere opinions (things taken for granted as part of a culture, normative convictions, collective prejudices and judgments) seem to persist unchanged in their quasi-natural structure as a kind of sediment of history, public opinion, in terms of its very idea, can be formed only if a public that engages in rational discussion exists. Public discussions that are institutionally protected and that take, with critical intent, the exercise of political authority as their theme have not existed since time immemorial – they developed only in a specific phase of bourgeois society, and only by virtue of a specific constellation of interests could they be incorporated into the order of the bourgeois constitutional state.

History

It is not possible to demonstrate the existence of a public sphere in its own right, separate from the private sphere, in the European society of the High Middle Ages. At the same time, however, it is not a coincidence that the attributes of authority at that time were called "public." For a public representation of authority existed at that time. At all levels of the pyramid established by feudal law, the status of the feudal lord is neutral with respect to the categories "public" and "private"; but the person possessing that status represents it publicly; he displays himself, represents himself as the embodiment of a "higher" power, in whatever degree. This concept of representation has survived into recent constitutional history. Even today the power of political authority on its highest level, however much it has become detached from its former basis, requires representation through the head of state. But such elements derive from a pre-bourgeois social structure. Representation in the sense of the bourgeois public sphere, as in "representing" the nation or specific clients, has nothing to do with *representative publicness*, which inheres in the concrete existence of a lord. As long as the prince and the estates of his realm "are" the land, rather than merely "representing" it, they are capable of this kind of representation; they represent their authority "before" the people rather than for the people.

The feudal powers (the church, the prince, and the nobility) to which this representative publicness adheres disintegrated in the course of a long process of polarization; by the end of the eighteenth century they had decomposed into private elements on the one side and public on the other. The position of the church changed in connection with the Reformation; the tie to divine authority that the church represented, that is, religion,

became a private matter. Historically, what is called the freedom of religion safeguarded the first domain of private autonomy; the church itself continued its existence as one corporate body under public law among others. The corresponding polarization of princely power acquired visible form in the separation of the public budget from the private household property of the feudal lord. In the bureaucracy and the military (and in part also in the administration of justice), institutions of public power became autonomous vis-à-vis the privatized sphere of the princely court. In terms of the estates, finally, elements from the ruling groups developed into organs of public power, into parliament (and in part also into judicial organs); elements from the occupational status groups, insofar as they had become established in urban corporations and in certain differentiations within the estates of the land, developed into the sphere of bourgeois society, which would confront the state as a genuine domain of private autonomy.

Representative publicness gave way to the new sphere of "public power" that came into being with the national and territorial states. Ongoing state activity (permanent administration, a standing army) had its counterpart in the permanence of relationships that had developed in the meantime with the stock market and the press, through traffic in goods and news. Public power became consolidated as something tangible confronting those who were subject to it and who at first found themselves only negatively defined by it. These are the "private persons" who are excluded from public power because they hold no office. "Public" no longer refers to the representative court of a person vested with authority; instead, it now refers to the competence-regulated activity of an apparatus furnished with a monopoly on the legitimate use of force. As those to whom this public power is addressed, private persons subsumed under the state form the public.

As a private domain, society, which has come to confront the state, as it were, is on the one hand clearly differentiated from public power; on the other hand, society becomes a matter of public interest insofar as with the rise of a market economy the reproduction of life extends beyond the confines of private domestic power. The *bourgeois public sphere* can be understood as the sphere of private persons assembled to form a public. They soon began to make use of the public sphere of informational newspapers, which was officially regulated, against the public power itself, using those papers, along with the morally and critically oriented weeklies, to engage in debate about the general rules governing relations in their own essentially privatized but publicly relevant sphere of commodity exchange and labor.

The Liberal Model of the Public Sphere

The medium in which this debate takes place – public discussion – is unique and without historical prototype. Previously the estates had negotiated contracts with their princes in which claims to power were defined on a case-by-case basis. As we know, this development followed a different course in England, where princely power was relativized through parliament, than on the Continent, where the estates were mediatized by the monarch. The "third estate" then broke with this mode of equalizing power, for it could no longer establish itself as a ruling estate. Given a commercial economy, a division of authority accomplished through differentiation of the rights of those possessing feudal authority (liberties belonging to the estates) was no longer possible – the power under private law of disposition of capitalist property is nonpolitical. The bourgeois are private persons; as such, they do not "rule." Thus their claims to power in opposition to public power are directed not against a concentration of authority that should be "divided" but rather against the principle of established authority. The principle of control, namely publicness, that the bourgeois public opposes to the principle of established authority aims at a transformation of authority as such, not merely the exchange of one basis of legitimation for another.

In the first modern constitutions the sections listing basic rights provide an image of the liberal model of the public sphere: they guarantee society as a sphere of private autonomy; opposite it stands a public power limited to a few functions; between the two spheres, as it were, stands the domain of private persons who have come together to form a public and who, as citizens of the state, mediate the state with the needs of bourgeois society, in order, as the idea goes, to thus convert political authority to "rational" authority in the medium of this public sphere. Under the presuppositions of a society based on the free exchange of commodities, it seemed that the general interest, which served as the criterion by which this kind of rationality was to be evaluated, would be assured if the dealings of private persons in the marketplace were emancipated from social forces and their dealings in the public sphere were emancipated from political coercion.

The political daily press came to have an important role during this same period. In the second half of the eighteenth century, serious competition to the older form of news writing as the compiling of items of information arose in the form of literary journalism. Karl Bücher describes the main outlines of this development: "From mere institutions for the publication of news, newspapers became the vehicles and guides of public opinion as well, weapons of party politics. The consequence of this for the internal organization of the newspaper enterprise was the insertion of a new function between the gathering of news and its publication: the editorial function. For the newspaper publisher, however, the significance of this development was that from a seller of new information he became a dealer in public opinion." Publishers provided the commercial basis for the newspaper without, however, commercializing it as such. The press remained an institution of the public itself, operating to provide and intensify public discussion, no longer a mere organ for the conveyance of information, but not yet a medium of consumer culture.

This type of press can be observed especially in revolutionary periods, when papers associated with the tiniest political coalitions and groups spring up, as in Paris in 1789. In the Paris of 1848 every halfway prominent politician still formed his own club, and every other one founded his own *journal*: over 150 clubs and more than 200 papers came into being there between February and May alone. Until the permanent legalization of a public sphere that functioned politically, the appearance of a political newspaper was equivalent to engagement in the struggle for a zone of freedom for public opinion, for publicness as a principle. Not until the establishment of the bourgeois constitutional state was a press engaged in the public use of reason relieved of the pressure of ideological viewpoints. Since then it has been able to abandon its polemical stance and take advantage of the earning potential of commercial activity. The ground was cleared for this development from a press of viewpoints to a commercial press at about the same time in England, France, and the United States, during the 1830s. In the course of this transformation from the journalism of writers who were private persons to the consumer services of the mass media, the sphere of publicness was changed by an influx of private interests that achieved privileged representation within it.

The Public Sphere in Mass Welfare-State Democracies

The liberal model of the public sphere remains instructive in regard to the normative claim embodied in institutionalized requirements of publicness; but it is not applicable to actual relationships within a mass democracy that is industrially advanced and constituted as a social-welfare state. In part, the liberal model had always contained ideological aspects; in part, the social presuppositions to which those aspects were linked have undergone fundamental changes. Even the forms in which the public sphere was manifested, forms which made its idea seem to a certain extent obvious, began to change with the Chartist movement in England and the February Revolution in France. With the spread of the press and propaganda, the public expanded beyond the confines of the bourgeoisie. Along with its social exclusivity the public lost the cohesion given it by institutions of convivial social intercourse and by a relatively high standard of education. Accordingly, conflicts which in the past were pushed off into the private sphere now enter the public sphere. Group needs, which cannot expect satisfaction from a self-regulating market, tend toward state regulation. The public sphere, which must now mediate these demands, becomes a field for competition among interests in the cruder form of forcible confrontation. Laws that have obviously originated under the "pressure of the streets" can scarcely continue to be understood in terms of a consensus achieved by private persons in public discussion; they correspond, in more or less undisguised form, to compromises between conflicting private interests. Today it is social organizations that act in relation to the state in the political public sphere, whether through the mediation of political parties or directly, in interplay with public administration. With the interlocking of the public and private domains, not only do political agencies take over certain functions in the sphere of commodity exchange and social labor; societal powers also take over political functions. This leads to a kind of "refeudalization" of the public sphere. Large-scale organizations strive for political compromises with the state and with one another, behind closed doors if possible; but at the same time they have to secure at least plebiscitarian approval from the mass of the population through the deployment of a staged form of publicity.

The political public sphere in the welfare state is characterized by a singular weakening of its critical functions. Whereas at one time publicness was intended to subject persons or things to the public use of reason and to make political decisions susceptible to revision before the tribunal of public opinion, today it has often enough already been enlisted in the aid of the secret policies of interest groups; in the form of "publicity" it now acquires public prestige for persons or things and renders them capable of acclamation in a climate of nonpublic opinion. The term "public relations" itself indicates how a public sphere that formerly emerged from the structure of society must now be produced circumstantially on a case-by-case basis. The central relationship of the public, political parties, and parliament is also affected by this change in function.

This existing trend towards the weakening of the public sphere, as a principle, is opposed, however, by a welfare-state transformation of the functioning of basic rights: the requirement of publicness is extended by state organs to all organizations acting in relation to the state. To the extent to which this becomes a reality, a no longer intact public of private persons acting as individuals would be replaced by a public of organized private persons. Under current circumstances, only the latter could participate effectively in a process of public communication using the channels of intra-party and intra-organizational public spheres, on the basis of a publicness enforced for the dealings of organizations with the state. It is in this process of public communication that the formation of political compromises would have to achieve legitimation. The idea of the public sphere itself, which signified a rationalization of authority in the medium of public discussions among private persons, and which has been preserved in mass welfare-state democracy, threatens to disintegrate with the structural transformation of the public sphere. Today it could be realized only on a different basis, as a rationalization of the exercise of social and political power under the mutual control of rival organizations committed to publicness in their internal structure as well as in their dealings with the state and with one another.

8

Procedural Democracy

Robert A. Dahl

If one makes certain minimal assumptions about a human association, I shall argue here, then one must also accept the reasonableness of certain criteria for evaluating how that association governs itself. These criteria specify democratic procedures, and an association that satisfied all of the criteria would be fully democratic in its procedures.

However, since their origins in classical Greece, democratic ideas have been plagued by the problem of inclusion: what persons have a rightful claim to be included as citizens with full and equal rights to participate in governing the association? My strategy will be to leave this problem initially unsolved in order to set out the assumptions and the criteria of procedural democracy. I shall then examine several well known solutions to the problem – those advanced by Schumpeter, Locke, Rousseau and Mill – and show that they are defective. I shall conclude by offering what seems to me a more satisfactory solution to the problem of inclusion.

1 Assumptions

Let me start by assuming that each of a number of persons has in mind the idea of forming an association for certain purposes, or changing an already existing association in order to adapt to conditions as they now understand them. Among

Originally published in *Philosophy, Politics and Society*, 5th series, ed. P. Laslett and J. S. Fishkin (Blackwell Publishers, 1979), 97–133. Reprinted by permission of the publisher.

other things, the association will have rules, or will make decisions about rules, that are to be binding on the members. Anyone to whom the rules apply is defined as a member. Thus being subject to the rules and decisions of the association is an essential characteristic of membership; it is sufficient to distinguish members from non-members.

Suppose one believes that the following assumptions are valid:

(A1) There is a need among the members or putative members[1] for *binding decisions* on at least some matters, and so for a process that will eventuate in binding decisions on these matters.

This condition has two aspects. First, at least some of the purposes the members have in mind can be satisfactorily attained if and only if at least some members are influenced to act, or not to act, in certain ways.[2] Second, the actions necessary to these purposes can be brought about if, and only if, there exists a procedure by means of which the members, or some of them, can decide on a rule, policy, purpose, principle, act, or pattern of conduct with which members will be obliged to act consistently. The obligation to act consistently with the rule is imposed on *all* members in the sense that even when acts by particular members or offices are specified, all members are required not to act in such a way as to impede or prevent that particular act.

In order to bring about the acts they seek, rule makers might create an expectation that violators of the rule will be punished by officials.

Conceivably, however, decisions might be binding without punishments by officials or other members. It might be enough to evoke an expectation of divine or magical sanctions. Or the mere process of enacting and announcing a rule might cause enough members to adopt it as a principle of conduct so as to produce a quite satisfactory level of compliance. In short, the need for binding decisions, and for procedures to bring them about, does not imply that the association is necessarily coercive, employs the threat of violent sanctions to bring about compliance, or possesses other characteristics that are often used to distinguish a state from other sorts of associations.

(A2) A process for making binding decisions ought to include at least two stages: setting the agenda and deciding the outcome.

Setting the agenda is the part of the process during which the matters are selected on which decisions are to be made (including a decision not to decide the matter). Deciding the outcome, or the *decisive stage*, is the time during which the process culminates in an outcome, signifying that a rule has definitely been adopted or rejected. If setting the agenda is, so to speak, the first say, the decisive stage is the last say, the final word, the controlling decision, the moment of sovereignty with respect to the matter at hand. Until the decisive stage is completed, the process of decision-making is tentative; it may lead to discussion, agreements, even outcomes of votes; but these are all preliminary, may be over-ruled at the decisive stage, and are not binding on the members. Decisions are binding only at the conclusion of the decisive stage.

(A3) Binding decisions should be made only by members.

That is, no person who is not a member is properly qualified, in the broadest sense, to make, or participate in making, decisions that will be binding on members. I say nothing about the possible grounds for such a belief, which are many. It may be, for example, that the founders of the association have managed to include among the members everyone who is considered to be fully qualified, or everyone who must be included if the rule is to be useful, or everyone whose interests are affected. But other reasons would also suffice.

(A4) Equally valid claims justify equal shares.

That is, if the claims made on behalf of A,B,C . . . to an object of value, X, are judged to be equally valid, then any procedure for allocating X to A,B,C . . . must give equal regard to the claims of each.

Because this principle seems to have well-nigh universal acceptability, one might suspect that it is tautological. I think it falls just short of a tautology, but it is close enough to being so as to make its contradiction seem quite fundamentally arbitrary. Thus suppose that Christopher, Ann, and Jane each claims the last piece of pie; they agree (or I hold) that their claims are equally valid; that is, there are no grounds for asserting that, say, Christopher's claims are superior to Ann's or Jane's; or that either Ann's or Jane's are better. Then they must also agree (or I must insist) that any procedure for allocating the piece of pie must give equal regard to the claims of each. The principle does not specify a particular procedure. Several procedures might therefore be thought to satisfy the principle equally well: The piece of pie might be divided equally among them, or awarded according to a random process, etc.

Even with the addition of this elementary principle of fairness, the conditions set out so far do not constitute grounds for asserting that an association ought to be governed by democratic procedures. If a single member were judged by all the others to be definitely more qualified than they to make decisions on all the matters which the association is to deal with, or if there were a graded hierarchy of competencies, then to say that the association ought to be governed by the one person, or by a graded hierarchy, would not be inconsistent with the judgement that all the preceding conditions also hold.

In order for democratic procedures to be required, it is sufficient to add one additional and highly crucial assumption:

(A5) The claims of a significant number of members as to the rules, policies, etc., to be adopted by binding decisions are valid and equally valid, taken all around, and no member's claims are, taken all around, superior or overriding in relation to the claims of this set of members.

This set of members I am going to call the demos. Members of the demos are citizens, though this usage is not meant to imply that they are necessarily citizens of a state.

A 'significant number' must, of course, be more than one member; otherwise democratic procedures would not be required nor could the procedures be democratic. What constitutes a sufficiently large number or proportion, however, has been an issue of great theoretical and practical importance. It is directly bound up with the question of whose claims are valid and equally valid. These issues are central to the problem of inclusion: what persons have a rightful claim to be included in the demos? Since this question is too important to be closed off merely by stipulation, I want to defer it for the time being. Meanwhile, the grounds that would properly justify having one's claims accepted as equally valid are not at issue here. I shall simply assume that one arrives at such a judgement somehow; whether the grounds are reasonable or unreasonable is not at this point a matter of concern. In this way a controversial issue in the history of democratic ideas and practices can be set aside for consideration later on.

2 Criteria

Suppose, then, some collection of persons wish to form an association, and one believes that the five assumptions described above are valid with respect to this group. Then it is reasonable to hold that the procedures by which the demos is to arrive at its decisions ought to meet certain criteria, which I am going to call the criteria of procedural democracy.

When I say that the procedures ought to meet certain criteria, I mean that if one believes in the assumptions, then one must reasonably affirm the desirability of the criteria; conversely, to reject the criteria is in effect to deny that the assumptions apply.

One additional point. The criteria do not specify any *particular* procedure, such as majority rule. Specific procedures cannot be extracted from the criteria. The criteria are standards against which proposed procedures are to be evaluated. They do not eliminate all elements of judgement in evaluation. I think it should not be surprising that democratic theory, like most other normative theories, cannot furnish completely unambiguous answers in all concrete situations in which a choice has to be made between alternative proposals.

Political equality

First, all proposed procedures for making binding decisions must be evaluated according to *the criterion of political equality*. That is, the decision rule for determining outcomes at the decisive stage must take into account, and take equally into account, the expressed preferences of each member of the demos as to the outcome. The expression of preferences as to the outcome at the decisive stage is, of course, what we usually mean by 'voting' and 'a vote'; thus the criterion of political equality specifies that at the decisive stage each citizen has an equal vote.

To reject this criterion would be to deny at least one of two premises discussed earlier. Either equally valid claims do not justify equal shares, or it is not true that the claims of a significant number of members are valid and equally valid.

However, the criterion does not explicitly embody a particular method of voting or elections. It is not reducible solely to the principle of one man one vote, or to the principle that each citizen should have an equal vote in districts of equal numbers of voters, potential voters, or residents, or to a system of proportional representation based on equal votes. To adopt the criterion implies that specific procedures like these ought to be evaluated according to the extent to which they satisfy the conclusions. How preferences may best be expressed and what the specific rules should be for taking preferences into account, and equally into account, are questions requiring additional judgements; but procedures judged to meet the criterion better ought to be preferred over those that meet it worse. Obviously the requirement that the better be preferred to the worse holds even if all the procedures proposed are in some respects defective.

Nor does the criterion explicitly specify the majority principle. It requires only that the majority principle and alternatives to it be evaluated according to the criterion, and the solution that best meets the criterion of political equality be adopted. Whether majority voting is the best, or always the best, is thus left open.

Effective participation

The second criterion according to which all proposed procedures must be evaluated is the criterion of *effective participation*. According to this criterion, throughout the process of making binding decisions, one must have an adequate opportunity, and an equal opportunity, for expressing his or her preferences as to the final outcome. Thus citizens must have adequate and equal opportunities for placing questions on the agenda, and for expressing reasons for endorsing one outcome rather than another. For to deny any citizen adequate opportunities for effective participation means that their preferences cannot be known, or cannot be correctly known, and hence cannot be taken into account. And if some citizens have less opportunity than others, then their preferences as to the final outcome are less likely to be taken equally into account. But not to take their preferences as to the final outcome equally into account is to reject the criterion of political equality, and thus to deny the condition of roughly equal qualification, taken all around.

Any specific procedures, then, must be evaluated according to the adequacy of the opportunities they provide for, and the relative costs they impose on, expression and participation by the demos in making binding decisions. Other things being equal, procedures that meet the criteria better are to be preferred over those that meet it less well. Once again, the requirement that the better be chosen over the worse clearly applies even if all the options are thought to be imperfect in some respect. Thus having the agenda for the assembly determined by a council of 500, chosen by lot, as in classical Athens, would meet the criterion better than having the agenda set single-handedly by Pericles or Creon, even if the system of selection by lot involved some minor departures from a strictly random selection in which every citizen had an exactly equal chance of being selected.

I think it is consistent with historic usage to say that any association satisfying these two criteria is, at least to that extent, *procedurally democratic*. To put it somewhat formally, in order to leave room for some important distinctions to come, I want to call such an association *procedurally democratic* (or a *procedural democracy*) in a *narrow sense*. The criteria enable one to evaluate a large number of possible procedures. They are not decisive in cases where a procedure is better according to one criterion and worse by the other. Moreover, any evaluation would ordinarily require additional judgements about the facts of the particular situation, or about general tendencies and regularities of human behaviour and action. Nonetheless, the criteria are far from vacuous.

Although I will not introduce a rigorous argument here, it would be hard to deny that procedures providing for decisions by a randomly selected sample of citizens would satisfy the criteria better than a procedure by which one citizen makes binding decisions for all the rest, or that a voting scheme allocating one vote to each citizen would be better than a scheme in which some citizens had ten votes and others none. I do not mean to imply that judgements about alternatives like these could invariably result from a perfectly rigorous argument ending in a completely unassailable conclusion.

Enlightened understanding

As I have already suggested, judgements about the existence, composition, and boundaries of a demos are highly contestable. Thus one might simply challenge such judgements outright by asserting that some citizens are more qualified than the rest to make the decisions required. This objection of course raises a fundamental challenge to procedural democracy and is generally a premise in a counter-argument for aristocracy, meritocracy, or rule by a qualified elite. It is not this fundamental objection that I wish to consider at the moment, but rather a second kind of objection which might run rather like this:

> I agree – the objector might say – that the citizens are equally well qualified, taken all around. I agree also that none among them, or among the other members, or among non-members are so definitely better qualified as to warrant their making the decisions instead of the demos. Yet for all that, I think the citizens are not as well qualified as they might be. They make mistakes about the means to the ends they want; they also choose ends they would reject if they were more enlightened. I agree then that they ought to govern themselves by procedures that are satisfactory according to the criteria of procedural democracy, narrowly defined. Yet a number of different procedures will satisfy the criteria about equally well; among these, however, some are more likely to lead to a more enlightened demos – and thus to better decisions – than others. Surely these are better procedures, and ought to be chosen over the others.

One might object, I suppose, that enlightenment has nothing to do with democracy. But I think this would be a foolish and historically false assertion. It is foolish because democracy has usually been conceived as a system in which 'rule by the people' makes it more likely that 'the people' will get what it wants, or what it believes is best, than alternative systems, like aristocracy, in which an elite determines what is best. But to know what it wants, or what is best, the people must be enlightened, at least to some degree. And because advocates of democracy have invariably recognized this, and placed great stress on the means to an informed and enlightened demos, such as education and public discussion, the objection is also historically false.

I propose therefore to amplify the doctrine of procedural democracy by adding a third criterion. Unfortunately, I do not know how to formulate the criterion except in words that are rich in meaning and correspondingly ambiguous. Let me, however, offer this formulation for *the criterion of enlightened understanding*:

> In order to express his or her preferences accurately, each citizen ought to have adequate and equal opportunities for discovering and validating, in the time permitted by the need for a decision, what his or her preferences are on the matter to be decided.

This criterion implies, then, that alternative procedures for making decisions ought to be evaluated according to the opportunities they furnish citizens for acquiring an understanding of means and ends, and of oneself and other relevant selves. Yet if the criterion is accepted, ambiguous as it may be, I think it would be hard to justify procedures that cut off or suppressed information which, were it available, might well cause citizens to arrive at a different decision; or gave some citizens much easier access than others to information of crucial importance; or presented citizens with an agenda of decisions that had to be decided without discussion, though time was available; and so on. To be sure, these may look like easy cases; but a great many political systems – perhaps most – operate according to the worse not the better procedures.

Control of the agenda

If an association were to satisfy all three criteria, it could properly be regarded as a *full procedural democracy with respect to its agenda* and *in relation*

to its demos. The criteria are to be understood as aspects of the best possible political system, from a democratic point of view; while no actual system could be expected to satisfy the criteria perfectly, systems could be judged more democratic or less, and to that extent better or worse, according to how nearly they meet the criteria.

Yet to say that a system is governed by fully democratic procedures 'with respect to an agenda' and 'in relation to a demos' suggests the possibility that the three criteria are incomplete. The two qualifying clauses imply the possibility of restrictions – of democratic decision-making processes limited to a narrow agenda, or responsive to a highly exclusive demos, or both. To judge whether a demos is appropriately inclusive and exercises control over an appropriate agenda evidently requires additional standards. The catch is that the condition of equal qualification is of indefinite range: it need apply only to certain matters or to some members of an association. Obviously, to say that some persons are sufficiently well qualified to govern themselves on some matters is not to say that all persons are sufficiently competent to govern themselves on all matters.

Thus the conditions set out earlier are no longer sufficient for generating the additional criteria we need. To remedy this defect in the conditions, I now propose a change of strategy. I shall propose a fourth criterion, and show what sort of judgement as to equality would impose this criterion.

In order to see more clearly why a fourth criterion is needed, let us suppose that Philip of Macedon, having defeated the Athenians at Chaeronea, deprives the Athenian assembly of the authority to make any decisions on matters of foreign and military policy. The citizens continue to assemble some forty times a year and decide on many matters, but on some of the most important questions they must remain silent. With respect to 'local' matters, the Athenian polis is no less democratic than before; but with respect to foreign and military affairs, the Athenians are now governed hierarchically by Philip or his minions.

Again: let us imagine that during the Nazi occupation of Norway, Hitler had allowed the Norwegians to use their democratic political institutions for one or two matters – driving speeds for civilian traffic, let us say – but nothing else. If the Norwegians had gone along with this arrangement, we might conclude that while they had retained some nominal degree of 'democracy', in a broad sense they had lost it. Save for one subject of minor importance, Norwegians would be denied the opportunity to make binding decisions on the matters they felt important and fully qualified to decide for themselves. If we were to take as valid their own judgement as to their competence, then we must also hold that the criteria of procedural democracy ought to apply to all the questions they feel are important and not merely to trivial matters. For to say that some persons outside the demos should be able to prevent the demos from deciding for itself which questions it wishes to put on the agenda of things to be decided according to the criteria of procedural democracy is to deny at least one of the original premises: binding decisions ought to be made only by members, equally valid claims justify equal shares, and no member's claims are, taken all around, superior or overriding in relation to the claims of the demos.

These considerations suggest an additional criterion, *final control of the agenda by the demos*:

> The demos must have the exclusive opportunity to make decisions that determine what matters are and are not to be decided by means of procedural democracy.

The criterion of final control is perhaps what is also meant when we say that in a democracy the people must have the final say, or must be sovereign. A system that satisfies this criterion as well as the other three could be regarded as *a full procedural democracy in relation to its demos*.

According to this criterion, a political system would be procedurally democratic even if the demos decided that it would not make every decision on every matter, but instead chose to have some decisions on some matters made, say, in a hierarchical fashion by judges or administrators. As long as the demos could effectively retrieve any matter for decision by itself, the criterion would be met. In this respect, then, the doctrine of procedural democracy allows more latitude for delegation of decision-making than would be permissible by Rousseau's eccentric definition of democracy in the *Social Contract*. By defining democracy so as to make delegation impermissible, Rousseau could hardly avoid concluding, as he did, that democracy (in his sense) would be impossible among human beings, though perhaps satisfactory for gods.

Thus the criterion of final control does not presuppose a judgement that the demos is qualified to decide *every* question requiring a binding decision. It does presuppose a judgement that the demos is qualified to decide (1) which matters do or do not require binding decisions, (2) of those that do, which matters the demos is qualified to decide for itself, and (3) the terms on which the demos delegates authority. To accept the criterion as appropriate is therefore to imply that the demos is the best judge of its own competence and limits. Consequently, to say that certain matters ought to be placed beyond the final reach of the demos – in the sense that the demos ought to be prohibited from dealing with them at all – is to say that on these matters the demos is not qualified to judge its own competence and limits.

Let me now phrase our revised assumption as follows:

> (A5.1) *The Full Condition of Equal Qualification*. With respect to all matters, citizens are qualified, and equally well qualified, taken all around, to decide which matters do or do not require binding decisions; of those that do, which matters the demos is qualified to decide for itself; and the terms on which the demos delegates authority.

By *delegation* I mean a revocable grant of authority, subject to recovery by the demos. Empirically, of course, the boundaries between delegation and alienation are not always sharp, and what begins as delegation might end as alienation. But the theoretical distinction is nonetheless crucial.

In a system of full procedural democracy decisions about delegation would be made according to democratic procedures. But alienation would clearly violate the criterion of final control, and would be inconsistent with the judgement that the full condition of equal qualification existed among a demos.[3]

The criterion of final control completes the requirements for full procedural democracy in relation to a demos. If all the members of some set of persons are judged equally qualified, in the full sense, and if the other conditions set out earlier are held to exist among them, then the procedures according to which these persons, the demos, make binding decisions ought to be evaluated according to the four criteria. If citizens were reasonable, they would select the procedures that best meet the criteria.

3 The Problem of Inclusion

The criteria of procedural democracy assume the existence of a demos of qualified citizens. However, neither the existence of a demos nor the scope of its competence can be settled satisfactorily merely by assumption. Any specific claim of either kind would surely be highly contestable. Thus the assumptions have allowed me to by-pass two inter-related problems:

(1) The problem of inclusion: What persons have a rightful claim to be included in the demos?
(2) The scope of its authority. What rightful limits are there on the control of a demos? Is alienation ever permissible?

Finding solutions is particularly difficult for two reasons. First, not only is it hard to find much direct confrontation with these problems by democratic theorists, but political and moral theory is typically expressed in universalistic terms – 'all men', 'all persons' – that belie the need for boundaries even as the theory prescribes limits on conduct. Second, the two problems are interdependent; a solution to one seems to depend on a solution to the other.

Thus the extent to which a particular demos ought to have final control over the agenda evidently depends on a prior judgement as to the scope of matters which the demos is qualified to decide. In this sense, judgements as to the scope of the agenda and the composition of the demos are interdependent. A judgement as to the competence of the demos bears on the scope of its agenda; and the nature of an agenda bears on a judgement as to the composition of the demos. The demos being given, the scope of its agenda can be determined. The scope of an agenda being given, the composition of an appropriate demos to make decisions on those matters can be determined. But in principle the one cannot be determined independently of the other.

In this essay, however, I intend to explore only the first problem. I shall argue that we cannot successfully deal with it without directly meeting the question of competence and openly confronting the view that a meritorious elite of exceptional knowledge and virtue ought to govern. This rival idea, which the Greeks called aris-

tocracy and I shall call meritocracy, seems to me to constitute the greatest challenge to democracy, both historically and in the present world. I shall show that insofar as democratic theorists like Locke and Rousseau evaded taking direct and explicit issue with the challenge of meritocracy, they allowed a lethal defect to remain in the foundations of democratic ideas.

What properly constitutes a demos? Who must be included in a properly constituted demos, and who may or must be excluded from it?

The question of inclusion in (or exclusion from) the demos would scarcely present a serious challenge if a demos could enact rules that were binding only on itself. In that case, an outsider might still argue that a demos was acting unwisely or unjustly toward itself; but this would hardly give the outsider a justifiable claim to be included. Some associations do escape the problem in this way. The rules of an association might be binding only on its demos, either because all members of the association are also citizens, in which case the association is fully inclusive, or because every member is free to leave the association at any time with no great difficulty, in which case a member who objects to a rule can simply escape the application of the rule by withdrawing from the association.

It is by no means true of every association, however, that its demos can enact rules that are binding only on itself. A trade union might enforce a rule preventing non-members from working at a particular trade or workplace. An even more obvious and certainly more important exception is of course the state. Even if a state met all four of the criteria for procedural democracy and thus were a full procedural democracy in relation to its citizens, it could enact laws that were enforceable against persons who were not citizens, did not have the right to participate in making the laws, and had not given their consent either explicitly or implicitly to the laws they were forced to obey. Indeed every state has done so in the past, and there are grounds for thinking that all states will continue to do so in the future.

If some persons are excluded from the demos of a state, and yet are compelled to obey its laws, do they have a justifiable claim to be included in the demos or else to be excluded from the domain of enforcement? How inclusive should the demos be? Are there criteria for judging when, if ever, exclusion is rightful or inclusion is obligatory?

Citizenship as wholly contingent

One response is that the grounds for deciding who ought to be included in a demos are inherently particularistic and historical, often indeed primordial, and cannot be set forth as general principles. Thus citizenship is wholly contingent on circumstances that cannot be specified in advance. This is Schumpeter's solution.

Although democratic ideas often yield rather ambiguous answers to the question of inclusion, Schumpeter was an exception. It is an 'inescapable conclusion', he asserted, that we must 'leave it to every populus to define himself' [sic]. He rested his argument on an incontestable historical fact: what had been thought and legally held to constitute a 'people' has varied enormously, even among 'democratic' countries. What is more, there are no grounds for rejecting any exclusion whatsoever as improper: 'it is not relevant whether we, the observers, admit the validity of those reasons or of the practical rules by which they are made to exclude portions of the population; all that matters is that the society in question admits it.' He pressed his argument relentlessly. The exclusion of Blacks in the American South does not allow us to say that the South was undemocratic. The rule of the 'Bolshevik party' in the Soviet Union 'would not *per se* entitle us to call the Soviet Republic undemocratic. We are entitled to call it so only if the Bolshevik party itself is managed in an undemocratic manner – as obviously it is.'[4]

The last two examples beautifully illustrate the absurdities to which we may be led by the absence of any criterion for defining the *demos*. It is undeniable that in the United States, southern Blacks were excluded from the *demos*. But surely *to that extent* the South was undemocratic: *undemocratic in relation to its Black population*. Suppose that in the South, as in Rhodesia or South Africa, Blacks had been a preponderant majority of the population. Would Schumpeter still have said that the Southern states were 'democratic'? Is there not some number or proportion of a population below which a 'people' is not a demos but rather an aristocracy, oligarchy, or despotism? If the rulers numbered 100 in a population of 100 million, would we call the rulers a demos and the system a democracy? On Schumpeter's argument, Britain was already a 'democracy' by the end of the eighteenth century – even though only one adult in twenty could vote.

Consider the monumental implications of the second example, in which Schumpeter asserts that 'the Soviet Republic' would be a democracy if only the ruling party itself were internally democratic. Schumpeter imposes no minimum limits on the relative size of the party. Suppose it were one per cent of the population? Or suppose that the Politburo were internally democratic, and ruled the party, which ruled over the State, which ruled over the people. Then the members of the Politburo would constitute the Soviet *populus*, and the Soviet State would be, on Schumpeter's interpretation, a democracy.

His definition thus leaves us with no particular reason for wanting to know whether a system is 'democratic' or not. Indeed, if a demos can be a tiny group that exercises a brutal despotism over a vast subject population, then 'democracy' is conceptually, morally, and empirically indistinguishable from autocracy. Thus Schumpeter's solution is truly no solution at all, for its upshot is that there are simply no principles for judging whether anyone is unjustly excluded from citizenship. But the argument leads, as we have seen, to absurdities.

These consequences follow because Schumpeter failed to distinguish, indeed insisted on conflating, two different kinds of propositions:

System X is democratic in relation to its own demos.

System Y is democratic in relation to everyone subject to its rules.

Perhaps because he was convinced by historical experience that no state like Y had ever existed or was likely to, he felt that any 'realistic' theory of democracy, such as he proposed, could scarcely require that a 'democracy' be a system like Y. For if this requirement were imposed, then no democratic state would, or probably ever could, exist. But by carrying historicism and moral relativism to their limits, he obliterated the possibility of any useful distinction between democracy, aristocracy, oligarchy, and one-party dictatorship.

Citizenship as a categorical right

Schumpeter's solution, or rather non-solution, was to allow a demos to draw any line it chooses between itself and other members. Suppose instead that one were to insist that no one subject to the rules of the demos should be excluded from the demos. Then the demos and the members (in the language used here) would be identical.

It is possible to interpret Locke, Rousseau, and a long succession of writers they influenced as advancing a solution along these lines.[5] The argument is grounded on the moral axiom that no person ought to be governed without his consent, or, with Rousseau, required to obey laws that are not of his own making in some genuine sense. In developing the argument writers have found it useful to distinguish between the initial act of forming the polity, (society, association, community, city, or state) and the subsequent process of making and enforcing the rules of the polity. Thus both Locke and Rousseau held that the initial formation required the agreement of everyone who has to be subject to it; thereafter, however, laws could be enacted and enforced if they were endorsed by a majority. Both sought to explain why, even though unanimity is required in the first instance, thereafter a majority is sufficient. I wish to ignore this question, for my concern here is a different one: in speaking of agreement by 'all' or a 'majority', what is the collection of persons to which they refer? Does 'the consent of every individual' and 'the determination of the *majority*' of such individuals[6] literally refer to *every* member, in the sense that a majority must be *a majority of every person subject to the laws*?

Clearly, neither Locke nor Rousseau meant to imply this conclusion. To begin with, children are of course to be excluded from the demos. The exclusion of children from the demos is so often taken as unproblematical that one hardly notices how much the claim to citizenship based on categorical right is embarrassed by this simple exclusion: for it is made on the grounds that children are not competent to govern themselves or the community. Yet if we permit the exclusion of children from the demos (and who seriously does not?) then we allow a contingent element, based on qualifications for governing, to limit the universality of the claim based on categorical right. Never mind; let us momentarily ignore this embarrassment, though I intend to return to it.

Suppose, then, that the claim based on a categorical right is revised to read: all *adults* subject to the laws of a state should be members of the demos of that state. Citizenship is no longer fully coextensive with membership; but all adult members are citizens by categorical right. Did Rousseau and Locke mean to justify such a claim?

Certainly Rousseau did not, though it is easy to see why the *Social Contract* is sometimes understood as saying so. There Rousseau occasionally appears to be asserting an unqualified right to membership in the demos.[7] But Rousseau makes it clear that he means no such thing. Thus he lauds Geneva, even though its demos consisted of only a small minority of the population. Children were, of course, excluded. But so too were women. What is more, a majority of adult males were also excluded from the Genevan demos. Rousseau was well aware of these exclusions. Yet he neither condemned them as inconsistent with his principles, nor provided grounds on which they might be justified. Rather, he seems simply to have taken them for granted.

Rousseau may, in fact, have anticipated Schumpeter's solution. In arguing that it is wrong to take the government of Venice as an instance of true aristocracy, he remarks that although the ordinary people in Venice have no part in the government, there the nobility takes the place of the people. This is Schumpeter's populus defining itself. Rousseau then goes on to show that Venice and Geneva are truly alike. Thus the government of Venice is actually no more aristocratic than that of Geneva! (Book IV, Chapter 3).

What Rousseau does not feel it important to say is that in both cities the great bulk of the people subject to the laws were not only excluded from the execution and administration of the laws (the *government*, in Rousseau's terminology) but also from any participation in *making* the laws. In neither republic were the people – that is, most people – entitled to assemble in order to vote on the laws, or even to vote for representatives who would make the laws. In both cities, most people were thus subject to laws which they had no part in making.[8] One might conclude that neither republic could be legitimate in Rousseau's eyes. But this was not his conclusion, nor did he even hint at such an inference.

What Rousseau seems to have assumed, as other advocates of democracy had done since the Greek city states of antiquity, is that a large number of persons in any republic – children, women, foreigners, and many male adult residents – will be subjects but are not qualified to be citizens. In this way, Rousseau himself undermined the categorical principle of inclusion that he appeared to set forth in the *Social Contract*.

Locke's language in *The Second Treatise* is as categorical and universalistic as Rousseau's, if not more so.[9] Yet his apparent assertion of an unqualified and categorical claim was limited both explicitly and implicitly by a requirement as to competence. Naturally, children were excluded; I shall return later to Locke's argument on 'paternal power'. It is highly doubtful that he meant women to be included as a matter of right.[10] As to adult males, he explicitly excluded 'lunatics and idiots [who] are never set free from the government of their parents.'[11] In addition, 'slaves, . . . being captives taken in a just war, are by the right of nature subjected to the absolute dominion and arbitrary power of their masters.' He probably intended to exclude servants as well.[12] Thus a claim to citizenship was not categorical but, as it turns out, contingent on a judgement as to the relative qualifications of a person for participating in the government of the commonwealth. Like Rousseau, Locke torpedoed his own view (if indeed it was his view) that every person subject to the laws made by the demos possesses a categorical and unqualified right to membership in the demos.

Citizenship as contingent on competence

Locke and Rousseau appear to have advanced two different principles on which a claim to citizenship might be grounded. One is explicit, categorical, and universal; the other is implicit, contingent, and limiting:

> *Categorical Principle*: Every person subject to a government and its laws has an unqualified right to be a member of the demos (i.e., a citizen).
> *Contingent Principle*: Only persons who are qualified to govern, but all such persons, should be members of the demos (i.e., citizens).

If some persons subject to the laws are not qualified to govern, then obviously the two principles lead to contradictory conclusions. Which principle should take precedence? As we have seen, Locke and Rousseau held, at least implicitly, that the second principle takes precedence over the first.

What was only or mainly implicit in the arguments of Locke and Rousseau was made explicit by John Stuart Mill. Mill openly confronted the conflict he believed to exist between the two principles. Like his predecessors he also insisted that in case of conflict the first must give way to the second.

To be sure, on a careless reading Mill could be interpreted as favouring the categorical principle.[13] Yet although on casual inspection his language has a universalistic tone, in fact Mill does not endorse a categorical principle of general inclusion. It is hardly surprising that he argues, not from principles of right, but rather from considerations of social utility. His judgements are meant to reflect a balancing of social utilities and disutilities. And while his argument is powerful, it does not lead him to a categorical principle but to a contingent and contestable judgement about social utility. If the question is one of social utility, however, then relative competence is also a factor to be weighed.

As every reader of *Representative Government* soon discovers, it was Mill himself who undermined his own argument for universal inclusion by posing a counterargument based on considerations of competence. In the course of his discussion, he gave explicit and careful recognition that the criterion of competence must take priority over any principle, whether categorical or utilitarian, that makes inclusion in the demos a matter of general right among all adults subject to the laws. At a minimum, he argued, to demonstrate that persons are qualified to engage in governing requires a showing that they have 'acquired the commonest and most essential requisites for taking care of themselves, for pursuing intelligently their own interests and those of the persons most nearly allied to them.' It was Mill's judgement that in the England of his day, many categories of adults could not meet this standard and ought therefore to be denied the suffrage until they acquired the competence they at that time lacked.[14]

By giving priority to the criterion of competence, recognizing the contingent and socially specific nature of judgements about competence, and accepting a restricted demos as the consequence of his own judgement as to the qualifications of fellow Englishmen, Mill brought into the open a problem that has been glossed over by some of his most illustrious predecessors. Yet in justifying an exclusionary demos Mill did no more than to make explicit what had generally been implicit in all previous democratic theory and practice.

The formal opportunities for participation available to citizens in the democratic city-states of Greece, the universalistic language in which democratic beliefs are often presented, and the emphasis on participation by Rousseau and Mill have induced some writers to interpret 'classical' democratic ideas as much less 'elitist' than they actually were.[15]

In classical Athens itself, the demos could hardly have consisted of more than a third of the free adults, a sixth of all free persons, and a seventh – or less – of the total population. In relation to its own demos, the Athenians may have come about as close as any people to procedural democracy, and possibly a good deal closer than any modern state. But the fact is that the Athenian demos, as a modern admirer rather nonchalantly admits, was 'a minority elite'.[16]

One might choose to dismiss these limits as transitory deficiencies in a revolutionary new political idea which transcended the historical limits of actual practice. But as we have seen, Locke and Rousseau accepted, and Mill defended, the principle that a demos might properly exclude large numbers of adults who are subject to laws made by the demos. Thus the attempt to ground 'participatory democracy' on Mill and his predecessors is fatally flawed. Participation indeed. But only for the qualified! And in principle the qualified might be a tiny minority. Thus it is not only Schumpeter's solution that would permit the demos to shrink into a ruling elite. Rousseau himself, as we saw, regarded Geneva and Venice both as true republics, governed 'by the people', even though in both cities the demos constituted a minority of the adults: in Venice about one-tenth of one per cent of the population!

Modern admirers of 'classical' democratic ideas seem to have reversed the relation between citizenship and competence as it was generally understood from the Greeks to Mill. In the 'classical' perspective not every adult, much less every person, was necessarily qualified to govern and thus to enter into the demos. Rather, the demos consisted of all those who *were* qualified to govern. It was precisely because citizens were a qualified minority of the whole people that they were entitled to govern and could on the whole be counted on to govern well.

As a consequence, 'classical' ideas leave the intellectual defence of procedural democracy lethally vulnerable. Consider the standing of the case for procedural democracy if the criterion of competence is given priority over a categorical and universal principle of right.

If everyone subject to law has a categorical right to participate in the process of making laws,

if the requirement of consent is universal and uncontestable, then the case for democracy is very powerful and the case against exclusionary alternatives – aristocracy, meritocracy, rule by a qualified elite, monarchy, dictatorship, and so on – is correspondingly weakened. If the claim to citizenship is a categorical and universal right of all human beings, then among any human group a demos always exists and that demos must always be inclusive. To put it in another way, among any body of persons who wish to establish or maintain an association having a government capable of making binding decisions, the condition of equal qualification, the most crucial of the conditions for procedural democracy set forth earlier, must necessarily exist.

But if the criterion of competence overrides a claim based on rights, then the argument for democracy rests on mushy grounds. Citizenship depends on contingent judgements, not categorical rights. And the contingent judgements need not lead to universal inclusion. Indeed, as we have seen, the boundaries between democracy on the one side and meritocracy on the other become fuzzy and indeterminate. The arguments for the one or the other become indistinguishable except for a crucial judgement as to the relative magnitude of the competent members, the citizenry or ruling group.

4 Towards a Criterion of Inclusiveness

Three questions arise: First, is it possible to get around the principle of competence in deciding on the inclusiveness of the demos? Second, if not, is it possible to avoid the contingent and contestable nature of a judgement as to competence? Third, if again not, can we develop strong criteria that such a judgement ought to satisfy?

That we cannot get round the principle of competence in deciding on the inclusiveness of the demos is decisively demonstrated by the exclusion of children. It is virtually never argued, no doubt because it would be so obviously untenable to do so, that children either must be members of the state's demos, or else ought not to be subject to laws made by the demos. So far as I am aware, no one seriously contends that children should be full members of the state's demos. An eight-year-old child can hardly be enlightened enough to participate equally with adults in deciding on laws to be enforced by the government of the state. Yet these laws are enforced on children – without their explicit or implied consent. It is often held – and legal systems tend to reflect the force of the argument – that because of their limited competence children should not be subject to exactly the same laws as adults; they cannot, for example, enter into legally enforceable contracts. Yet they are not wholly exempt from the enforcement of all laws.

Children therefore furnish us with a clear instance of violation of the principle that a government must rest on the consent of the governed, or that no one should be subject to a law not of one's own choosing, or subject to a law made by an association not of one's own choosing. Yet this violation is nearly always taken for granted; or else it is interpreted as not actually a violation. One way of interpreting it is to say that the principle of consent applies only to adults. But this is to admit that some persons who are subject to the rules of a state can nevertheless be properly excluded from the demos of the state.

On what grounds? The only defensible ground on which to exclude children from the demos is that they are not yet fully capable of the 'exercise of reason', to use the common phrase. The need to exclude children on this ground was of course perfectly obvious to early democratic theorists. Locke devotes a whole chapter to Paternal Power. After reminding us of 'that equal right that every man hath to his natural freedom, without being subject to the will or authority of any other man', he immediately turns to the exceptions, of which children are the most numerous, obvious, and important.[17]

The example of children is sufficient to show that the criterion of competence cannot reasonably be evaded, that any reasonable bounding of a demos must, by excluding children, necessarily exclude a large body of persons subject to the laws, and that any assertion of a universal right of *all* persons to membership in a demos cannot be sustained. It might be argued, however, that children constitute a comparatively well-defined and unique exception.[18] Thus once a distinction is allowed between children and adults, all *adults* subject to the laws must be included. The categorical principle might then be re-stated as follows:

Modified Categorical Principle: Every adult subject to a government and its laws must be presumed to be qualified as, and has an unqualified right to be, a member of the demos.

There are, however, at least two sources of difficulty with the modified categorical principle. First, the boundary between childhood and adulthood is itself something of a difficulty. There is the well known arbitrariness of imposing a dichotomy – child/adult – on what is clearly a continuous process of development; we may reasonably disagree about whether one becomes qualified at 21, or 18, or whatever. There are also the troublesome cases for which experience, even when joined with compassion, points to no clear solution. As Locke put it:

> . . . if, through defects that may happen out of ordinary course of nature, any one comes not to such a degree of Reason wherein he might be supposed capable of knowing the Law, and so living within the rules of it, he is never capable of being a Free Man, . . . but is continued under the Tuition and Government of others all the time his own understanding is incapable of that charge. And so Lunatics and Idiots are never set free from the government of their Parents . . .[19]

Thus the modified categorical principle runs the risk of circularity by defining 'adult' as persons who are presumed to be qualified to govern.

A second source of difficulty with the modified principle is caused by the presence in a country of foreigners who might be adult by any reasonable standards, who are subject to the laws of the country in which they temporarily reside, but who are not thereby qualified to participate in governing.

Suppose that France is holding an election on Sunday and I, an American, arrive in Paris on Saturday as a tourist. Would anyone argue that I should be entitled to participate in the election – much less acquire all the other political rights of French citizenship? I think not. On what grounds could I properly be excluded? On the ground that I am unqualified.[20]

To sum up:

(1) Schumpeter's solution to the problem of the composition of the demos is unacceptable because it effectively erases the distinction between democracy and a non-democratic order dominated by a collegial elite.

(2) A categorical principle of inclusion that

overrides the need for a judgement as to competence is also unacceptable, for it is rendered untenable by such cases as children, feeble-minded persons, and foreigners of temporary residence. In so far as Locke and Rousseau advanced a categorical principle, their defence of it is unconvincing. However, evidence suggests that they recognized these objections and never intended their argument to be taken as a rejection of the priority of a criterion of competence.

(3) Because a judgement as to competence is contingent on weighing evidence and making inferences as to the intellectual and moral qualifications of specific categories of persons, a decision based on competence is inherently open to question. To be sure, a reasonable argument may be presented in behalf of a particular judgement as to the proper boundaries of inclusion and exclusion. But the exact location of any boundary is necessarily a highly debatable judgement. Thus Mill presented persuasive reasons to justify the particular exclusions he advocated; yet probably few contemporary democrats would accept his exclusions as reasonable.

In short, if Schumpeter's solution leads to absurdities, those found in earlier democratic ideas, whether in classical antiquity or in the works of early modern theorists like Locke, Rousseau, and Mill, provide all too fragile a foundation for the doctrine of procedural democracy. Even though we must accept the need for, and the contingent and contestable nature of a judgement as to competence, we are in need of further criteria that will help to reduce the arbitrariness of such a judgement.

Further requirements

I now want to argue that a reasonable criterion of inclusion in a system of procedural democracy in relation to its demos must pass three tests. At the outset, a criterion of inclusion must satisfy the general principle of fairness that constitutes one of the conditions of procedural democracy: equally valid claims justify equal shares. Consequently if C_a is a citizen, and if another member, M, is about as well qualified as C_a, then either M must be included in the demos or C_a must be excluded from it. If C_a is excluded, then the same test must be applied in comparing the claims of C_a with any other citizen, C_i. And so on, until a fair boundary can be staked out.

Assuming that a boundary of inclusion and exclusion meets the general principle of fairness, several additional tests may reasonably be required. The reasonableness of these tests rests, however, on two additional principles, which I shall refer to as *equal consideration* and *burden of proof*. I do not propose to consider whether or how these principles might be derived from antecedent considerations. Although the burden of proof principle reflects a judgement as to human experience, I doubt whether it is wholly verifiable, at least as a practical matter. And the principle of equal consideration is a moral orientation so fundamental that it is hard to see how one might go about the task of demonstrating its validity to an adversary. Fortunately, the principle itself is widely accepted. I want to introduce it initially as a principle of universal application and then narrow it to include only the members of the association.

> *Equal consideration (universal inclusion).* No distribution of socially allocated entities, whether actions, forebearances, or objects, is acceptable if it violates the principle that the good or interest of each human being is entitled to equal consideration.[21]

The principle does not depend on an assumption as to whether one's good is distinguished from one's interests, or whether 'good' or 'interest' refer to want-regarding or ideal-regarding principles.[22] It simply asserts that the good or interest of each person, whatever they may be, ought to be given equal consideration in social allocations. If A and B are human beings, if some entity X is socially allocated, if X is equally beneficial to A and to B, and if no benefits to others need to be taken into account, then the principle holds that there are no grounds for upholding a claim that X ought to go to A rather than B, or B rather than A. Whatever principle of distribution is adopted, it must not incorporate a bias toward either A or B. Thus if X is indivisible, the most appropriate solution might be to toss a coin. But to claim that because A is stronger than B or A has discovered X first, then A ought to have X, would not be acceptable.

To universalize the principle of equal consideration, however, poses a host of theoretical and practical problems that I do not wish to deal with here. Moreover, universality is not necessary in order to arrive at a reasonable solution to the problem of the composition of the demos. A much less inclusive version applying only to the *members* will prove satisfactory.

> *Equal Consideration for all members*: No distribution of socially allocated entities, whether actions, forbearances, or objects, is acceptable if it violates the principle that the good or interest of each member is entitled to equal consideration.

If one accepts the principle of equal consideration of all members, then of course one must also hold that a criterion of inclusion is unacceptable if it violates this principle. However, the import of the principle is further amplified by an additional assumption that also reflects a widely held though not strictly universal judgement:

> *Burden of Proof*: In the absence of a compelling showing to the contrary everyone is assumed to be the best judge of his or her own good or interests. Thus if A holds that her good consists of X, not Y, and B insists that A's good consists of Y, not X, then A's judgement is to be accepted unless the validity of B's judgement can be satisfactorily demonstrated.[23]

For any given member, M, an association that meets the criteria of procedural democracy in relation to its demos can satisfy the principle of equal consideration in one of two ways. M may be a citizen; that is, M is already included in the demos, in which case equal consideration is insured by procedural democracy. Alternatively, if M is excluded from the demos the principle of equal consideration can be satisfied if, but only if, the citizens give as much consideration to M's good or interest as to their own. However, the demos cannot reasonably be expected to give equal consideration to M unless (1) it *knows* at least as much about M's good as about its own, and (2) it will in fact *act* on this knowledge in such a way as to give equal consideration to M's good or interests. But the burden of proof principle requires a compelling showing that the demos definitely is a better judge than M as to M's own interests. The second test that M's exclusion must meet is precisely such a showing.

If the second test is met satisfactorily, M's exclusion will still violate the principle of equal consideration if the demos cannot reasonably be expected to *act* so as to give equal consideration to M. Thus, given the burden of proof, a positive

showing is necessary that the demos has in fact given equal consideration to M's interests in the past and will continue to do so in the future; or, though it has neglected M's good in the past, there are nevertheless compelling reasons for believing that the demos has recently changed in this respect, or is about to change and will care equally for M's good in the future.

The arguments used in the past to justify the exclusions from full citizenship in the state of various categories of adults – the unpropertied, women, racial minorities, for example – would, I think, fail to meet these three tests. Experience has shown that any group of adults excluded from the demos will be lethally weakened in its own defence; and an exclusive demos will fail to protect the interests of those who are excluded.

> We need not suppose that when power resides in an exclusive class, that class will knowingly and deliberately sacrifice the other classes to themselves; it suffices that, in the absence of its natural defenders, the interest of the excluded is always in danger of being overlooked, and, when looked at, is seen with very different eyes from those of the persons whom it directly concerns.[24]

Mill was surely right. In rejecting the conclusion his own premises pointed to – the enfranchisement of the working classes – Mill's justification failed all three tests. 'Universal teaching must precede universal enfranchisement', he wrote. But it was not until *after* the extension of the suffrage in 1868 that Parliament passed the first act establishing public elementary schools. The historical record since then demonstrates even more fully that when a large class of adults is excluded from citizenship their interests will almost certainly not be given equal consideration. Perhaps the most convincing evidence is provided by the exclusion of Southern Blacks from political life in the United States until the late 1960s.

Though one might argue from numerous cases of child neglect that all too many children fall under III.2, there are reasonable grounds for holding that in general the exclusion of children meets the tests. The bonds between children and adults are unique in the human species. For one thing, while most citizens may not understand from their own direct experiences what it is like to be a member of an excluded class, race, or sex, every adult has once been a child. Moreover, many adults are closely tied to children by bonds of love, nurturance, pity, joy, compassion, and hope. Among adults these bonds are far too weak to ensure enough mutuality of interests and understanding to ensure that members of a demos will protect the interests of other adults who are excluded. Consequently, as children approach 'the age of reason' the justification for their guardianship by parents, community, and state weakens and finally fails to meet the two tests.

What then of III.2? For example, what of the child in a community of uncaring adults? In this case, it is not possible for a procedural democracy to arrive at a satisfactory solution. Yet since the existing state of affairs violates the principle of equal consideration, an obligation arises for all who accept that principle to search for and bring about changes that will remedy the situation. There is an obligation to raise the level of M's competence or the enlightenment and compassion of the demos or both. Meanwhile III.2 ought to be viewed as a morally intolerable state of affairs.

A criterion of inclusion

These considerations provide reasonable grounds for adopting a criterion that approaches universality among adults. It is not only very much less arbitrary than Schumpeter's solution but far more inclusive than the restricted demos that was accepted, implicitly or explicitly, by Mill, Rousseau, Locke, and the Greek *polis*.

(C.5) *Inclusiveness*: The demos must include all adult members of the association except transients.

Admittedly the definition of adults and transients is a potential source of ambiguity. Probably no definition of the term adult can be completely watertight. In general, however, every member ought to be considered an adult who does not suffer from a severe mental disability or whose punishment for disobeying the rules is not reduced because he or she is younger than a given age. The meaning of the criterion seems to me to be clear enough: A demos that permitted the concept of adulthood to be manipulated in order to deprive certain persons of their rights – dissenters, for example – to that degree would simply fail to meet the criterion of inclusiveness. Obviously this criterion, like others, can never be self-enforcing.

Taken with the other four criteria, inclusiveness completes the requirements for procedural democracy. To the extent that a system approaches all five criteria, it is fully democratic

Test I	Is every citizen, C_i, definitely more qualified than the member M excluded by the criterion?
Test II	Is the judgement of the demos as to M's good demonstrably superior to M's judgement?
Test III	If M is excluded, will the demos act so as to care equally for M's good?

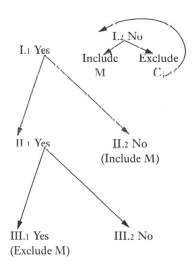

Figure 1. Three Tests for a Criterion of Inclusion

Table 1. The Argument for Procedural Democracy in Schematic Outline

If one believes that:	Then procedures for making binding decisions must satisfy the following criteria:	To the extent that procedures satisfy the criteria, then the system approaches:
A.1. A specific collection of people has a need for binding decisions.	C.1. Political equality	Procedural democracy in a narrow sense
A.2. Binding decisions involve two stages: Setting the agenda The decisive stage	C.2. Effective participation	Full procedural democracy with respect to an agenda and in relation to a demos
A.3. Binding decisions ought to be made only by persons who are subject to the decisions (i.e., by *members*)	C.3. Enlightened understanding	
A.4. Equally valid claims justify equal shares.		
A.5. The preferences of a significant number of members as to the decision are equally valid and no member's preferences are of overriding validity.		
A.5.1. The full condition of equal qualification exists.	C.4. Final control of the agenda	Full procedural democracy in relation to its demos
A.6. The good of each member is entitled to equal consideration, *and* each member is assumed to be the best judge of his or her own interests in the absence of a compelling showing to the contrary.	C.5. Inclusiveness	Full procedural democracy

in a procedural sense. The argument is summarized in Table 1.

5 Comments

The argument for procedural democracy holds that if one believes in the half dozen assumptions in Table 1, then reason requires one to hold that an association should adopt procedures for making binding decisions that will satisfy the five criteria of procedural democracy.

I take it for granted that in the real world no system will fully meet these criteria. At best any actual polity is likely to be something of an approximation to procedural democracy. My guess is that any approximation will invariably fall pretty far short of meeting the criteria. However, I have not tried to specify thresholds of attainment above which a system may properly be called a procedural democracy, for that exercise promises to be rather sterile. Instead, the criteria serve as standards against which one may compare alternative procedures in order to judge their relative merits according to the criteria of procedural democracy: to compare different systems in order to judge their relative approximations to procedural democracy; and to compare a given system over time in order to judge whether its trend, if any, is toward or away from procedural democracy. I do not hold that the criteria of procedural democracy fully define the notion of a good polity or good society. But to the extent that procedural democracy is worthwhile, then judgements of the sort I just mentioned bear directly on the relative worth or goodness of political arrangements.

The doctrine thus serves the task of clarification and prescription, of appraising and choosing among alternatives. For an example, suppose that I am a member of an association, and I believe that the conditions of procedural democracy exist among us but that my fellow members have not understood why the criteria of procedural democracy ought to apply to our processes of decision-making. My task is clarification: if we believe these things to be true, I would say to them, then we must reasonably adopt the criteria of procedural democracy. Or clarification might go in the other direction. Since you deny the validity of the criteria, I would say, then it must be that you reject one or more of these assumptions as valid among us. Which of the assumptions do you reject, and on what grounds?

Nor need I be a member of an association in order to arrive at judgements and recommendations as to the procedures the association ought to employ. If I judge that the conditions exist, then I must also conclude that the association should be procedurally democratic, whether or not I am a member.

As I have already said, I think that objections to procedural democracy will most often come to rest on a denial of the condition of equal qualification. This is why I have dealt at such length with that assumption. Sooner or later, to advocate procedural democracy requires a direct confrontation with its main alternative, which historically, today, and doubtless far into the future, is the doctrine of meritocracy. This enduring rival to democratic ideas is the view that adults in general are not qualified to govern, that the task of governing ought properly to be lodged with a meritorious minority, an elite possessing superior knowledge and virtue.

Many defences of democracy imply that democracy is always better than meritocracy. Yet even the most committed adherents of democracy have usually shrunk from insisting that every kind of human association must always follow democratic procedures.

In setting out the doctrine of procedural democracy I have not assumed that the condition of equal qualification always holds. Yet I would have to believe the doctrine irrelevant if I did not believe that the condition exists in at least some important associations.

Whether or not the state is the most important of all human associations, it is surely highly crucial. It is crucial because of its extraordinary influence, power, and authority, and thus the capacity of those who govern the state to control the resources, structures, agendas, and decisions of all other associations within the boundaries of the state. A people that alienates its final control over the agenda and decisions of the government of the state runs a very high risk of alienating its final control over other important associations as well.

I have not tried to show here what kinds of institutional arrangements procedural democracy would require for governing the state. Partly, though not wholly, in response to democratic ideas, a set of institutions for the government of the state has evolved during the last two centuries. The common features of these institutions have been called polyarchy. The institutions of polyarchy provide a much better approximation to procedural democracy among a numerous people, I believe, than the more exclusionary and authoritarian systems they replaced or serve as existing alternatives to polyarchy in the present world. Yet it seems clear to me that the institutions of polyarchy are not sufficient for a close approximation to procedural democracy.

However, I refrain here from arguing whether they are necessary, or how polyarchies might be further democratized, or whether radically different kinds of political institutions could provide a closer fit to procedural democracy.

A people that adhered to the doctrine of procedural democracy in the government of the state would also want to employ that doctrine in determining how other associations ought to be governed. For reasons I have already indicated, the doctrine bars a universalistic and *a priori* judge-ment that procedural democracy is best for all associations. But every system for governing any association ought to be tested against the doctrine, to determine whether the conditions are present; and, if they are, the relative merits of existing and alternative arrangements for satisfying the criteria.

As with the state, the question of what government is best for other associations will turn most frequently on a contestable and contingent judgement as to the relative competence of the members to govern. If, as I believe, a wise and humane people that sought to govern the state according to the criteria of procedural democracy would also employ the principles of equal consideration and burden of proof in making judgements about the relative qualifications of members to govern other associations, then it appears to me that many hierarchic or meritocratic arrangements would have to give way to procedural democracy.

Notes

1 Hereafter, in the case of an association not yet formed, member means putative member.

2 Hereafter expressions like 'acting' are meant to include not acting in certain ways.

3 In this respect the criterion comes closer to meeting Rousseau's restrictions in the *Social Contract* than might first appear. Rousseau would allow a sovereign people to grant executive power to (1) itself or a majority ('democracy'), (2) a minority ('aristocracy'), or (3) a single person ('monarchy'). What the people may not do is alienate its sovereignty, the power to make laws. Although 'democracy' in sense (1) is impractical, all three forms of delegating executive power are equally legitimate because, and as long as, the people does not alienate any of its sovereignty. Cf. particularly Book 2, Chapters 1 and 6, and Book 3, Chapter 6.

4 The whole discussion occurs in less than three pages (243–5) in Joseph A. Schumpeter, *Capitalism, Socialism, and Democracy* (New York: Harper and Bros., 1942, 1947).

5 I do not mean to suggest that Locke and Rousseau (or later writers) presented similar views on democracy, for they were of course very different. Thus Locke permitted the delegation and even the indefinite alienation by the demos of the power to make laws. (*Second Treatise*, Ch. X and Ch. XIX, par. 243.) Rousseau, as we saw above, did not. However, because their differences are not directly relevant to the argument of this section, I ignore them here.

6 The phrases are from Locke's *Second Treatise of Government*, Chapter VIII, 'Of the Beginning of Political Societies', par. 95–7, and *passim*, in John Locke, *Two Treatises of Government*, ed. by Peter Laslett, 2nd ed., (Cambridge: Cambridge University Press, 1967).

7 For example, in Book I, Chapters 4 and 6.

8 In Venice, the number of noblemen, who alone had rights to participate in the government, were from one to two per cent of the population of the city, and, if the mainland population is included, around one-tenth of one per cent. In 1797, there were 1,090 noblemen, 137,000 residents of the city, and 2.2 million people on the mainland. The number of noblemen was never larger than about 2,000. James C. Davis, *The Decline of the Venetian Nobility as a Ruling Class* (Baltimore: The Johns Hopkins Press, 1962), Table 1, p. 58.

In Geneva the percentage, though not as tiny, was small. Of the five orders subject to the laws, only males in the top two orders participated in making laws: 'at the top, the "citizens", who had the legal right to hold office, and of whom Rousseau was one; next, the "burghers", who had the right to vote but not to hold office.' Together, the citizens and burghers were 'some 1,500 in number' in a population of 25,000. Moreover, the top offices were monopolized by a few families. R. R. Palmer, *The Age of the Democratic Revolution, A Political History of Europe and America, 1760–1800* (Princeton: Princeton University Press, 1959), p. 36. Palmer remarks that 'Rousseau himself, in all the study he made of Geneva politics at Neuchatel, showed no interest in the Natives. The Natives, however, (were) three-quarters of the population who were not Burghers.' (p. 137)

9   For example, *Second Treatise*, Ch. VIII, §93.

10 See his discussion on the status of women in 'conjugal society', Ch. VIII, §§78–84. '. . . it seems highly improbable that Locke was thinking in terms of extending those rights to women.' Willmoore Kendall, *John Locke and the Doctrine of Majority Rule* (Urbana: Univ. of Illinois Press, 1941, p. 121, fn. vi.).

11 Ch. VI, §60.

12 Ch. VII, §85.

13 For example, *Considerations on Representative Government* Third Edition (1865), ed. by Currin V. Shields (New York: The Liberal Arts Press, 1958), pp. 42, 55, 131. A much fuller exposition of Mill's ideas about the conflict between 'the principle of participation' and 'the principle of competence', which draws on a wide variety of Mill's work, is Dennis F. Thompson, *John Stuart Mill and Representative Government* (Princeton: Princeton University Press, 1976).

14 Ibid., pp. 131–8.

15 For examples, see Peter Bachrach's comments on 'classical democratic theory' and its contrasts with 'elitist theory' in *The Theory of Democratic Elitism* (Boston: Little, Brown, 1967), pp. 2–9. And Carole Pateman, *Participation and Democratic Theory* (Cambridge: Cambridge University Press, 1970), who presents Rousseau and John Stuart Mill as 'two examples of "classical" democratic theorists, whose theories provide us with the basic postulates of a theory of participatory democracy'. (p. 21.)

16 M. I. Finley, *Democracy, Ancient and Modern* (New Brunswick: Rutgers University Press, 1973). The remark is made in the context of slavery; he does not mention that the exclusion of women and resident foreigners made the demos an even more restrictive 'minority elite'. All the conjectures about the relative size of the citizen body and the level of their participation in public affairs look very fragile to me. I have taken the estimates above from A.H.M. Jones, *Athenian Democracy* (Oxford: Basil Blackwell, 1969), pp. 78–9. As to actual participation, scholarly guess work looks even shakier. Though sympathetic to the Athenian democracy, Jones concludes that 'contrary to general belief, the average assembly was attended mainly by the relatively well-to-do citizens . . .' (Ibid. p. 36. See also pp. 50, 55, and the discussion 104–7). However, unlike the Assembly and the Council, the magistracies chosen by lot 'were filled by quite humble citizens'. (p. 104.) I cannot help suspecting that an Athenian Survey Research Centre would have turned up a good deal of evidence of citizen apathy and non-participation.

17 *The Second Treatise, op. cit.*, par. 55 and 63 (pp. 28, 31). In the *Social Contract*, Rousseau also recognizes, though merely in passing, the authority of the father over children 'before they reach the age

of reason'; *op. cit.*, p. 239.

18 Douglas Rae has commented that children may be thought of as having a life-time bundle of rights, some of which they become eligible for as they mature. Locke seems to make a similar point in the paragraphs cited above. By contrast, for excluded adults 'the bonds of . . . subjection' never 'quite drop off, and leave a man at his own free disposal'.

19 *Second Treatise*, par. 60, *op. cit.*, p. 30.

20 Suppose I were able to demonstrate that I had carefully studied the issues, parties, candidates, and the like. My exclusion would seem rather less justified. Still, a French citizen might say, 'you will hardly be in France long enough to justify your inclusion. Your coming here is voluntary; you acknowledge by coming your willingness to obey our laws; you will have left the country before the election will effect any changes in existing laws; consequently you will not bear any responsibility for your choices. Therefore you are, in that respect, *morally* unqualified to participate in this election.' This seems to me a powerful rebuttal to my claim. However, the force of the objection derives mainly from the fact that I may not be subject to the laws my participation might have helped to bring about. To this extent, I am not a member in the sense defined earlier, and consequently I *ought* to be excluded under the assumption (No. 3) that binding decisions should be made only by members.

21 This assumption is, I think, roughly equivalent to, though not necessarily identical with, a widespread if contestable judgement that forms a fundamental ground for a good deal of moral theory. For instance, Hugo Adam Bedau specifies a not dissimilar notion that he calls 'the doctrine of metaphysical egalitarianism' in J. Roland Pennock and John W. Chapman, *Equality* (New York: Atherton Press, 1976), p. 17. Stanley I. Benn asserts the 'principle of equal consideration of interests', ibid., p. 67. It is probably at least a second cousin to Rawls's assumption of human equality based on the capacity for moral personality, *op. cit.*, p. 506.

22 Brian Barry, *Political Argument* (London: Routledge and Kegan Paul, 1965), pp. 38–9 and 173ff.

23 The principle is analogous to, though not identical with, the first of the two principles that according to Mill are, 'of as universal truth and applicability as any general propositions which can be laid down respecting human affairs. The first is that the rights and interests of every and any person are only secure from being disregarded when the person interested is himself able, and habitually disposed, to stand up for them . . . Human beings are only secure from evil at the hands of others in proportion as they have the power of being, and are, *self-protecting . . .*' *op. cit.*, p. 43.

24 Mill, *op. cit.*, pp. 44–5.

9

The Market and the Forum: Three Varieties of Political Theory

Jon Elster

I want to compare three views of politics generally, and of the democratic system more specifically. I shall first look at social choice theory, as
an instance of a wider class of theories with certain common features. In particular, they share
the conception that the political process is instrumental rather than an end in itself, and the view
that the decisive political act is a private rather
than a public action, viz. the individual and secret
vote. With these usually goes the idea that the
goal of politics is the optimal compromise
between given, and irreducibly opposed, private
interests. The other two views arise when one
denies, first, the private character of political
behaviour and then, secondly, goes on also to
deny the instrumental nature of politics.
According to the theory of Jürgen Habermas, the
goal of politics should be rational agreement
rather than compromise, and the decisive political
act is that of engaging in public debate with a
view to the emergence of a consensus. According
to the theorists of participatory democracy, from
John Stuart Mill to Carole Pateman, the goal of
politics is the transformation and education of the
participants. Politics, on this view, is an end in
itself – indeed many have argued that it represents the good life for man. I shall discuss these
views in the order indicated. I shall present them
in a somewhat stylized form, but my critical comments will not I hope, be directed to strawmen.

Originally published in *Foundations of Social Choice
Theory*, ed. Jon Elster and Aanund Hylland (Cambridge
University Press, 1986), 103–32. Reprinted by permis-
sion of the publisher.

I

Politics, it is usually agreed, is concerned with the
common good, and notably with the cases in
which it cannot be realized as the aggregate outcome of individuals pursuing their private interests. In particular, uncoordinated private choices
may lead to outcomes that are worse for all than
some other outcome that could have been
attained by coordination. Political institutions are
set up to remedy such *market failures*, a phrase
that can be taken either in the static sense of an
inability to provide public goods or in the more
dynamic sense of a breakdown of the self-
regulating properties usually ascribed to the
market mechanism.[1] In addition there is the
redistributive task of politics – moving along the
Pareto-optimal frontier once it has been reached.[2]
According to the first view of politics, this task is
inherently one of interest struggle and compromise. The obstacle to agreement is not only that
most individuals want redistribution to be in their
favour, or at least not in their disfavour.[3] More
basically consensus is blocked because there is no
reason to expect that individuals will converge in
their views on what constitutes a just redistribution.

I shall consider social choice theory as representative of the private-instrumental view of politics, because it brings out supremely well the
logic as well as the limits of that approach. Other
varieties, such as the Schumpeterian or neo-
Schumpeterian theories, are closer to the actual
political process, but for that reason also less
suited to my purpose. For instance,

Schumpeter's insistence that voter preferences are shaped and manipulated by politicians[4] tends to blur the distinction, central to my analysis, between politics as the aggregation of given preferences and politics as the transformation of preferences through rational discussion. And although the neo-Schumpeterians are right in emphasizing the role of the political parties in the preference-aggregation process,[5] I am not here concerned with such mediating mechanisms. In any case, political problems also arise within the political parties, and so my discussion may be taken to apply to such lower-level political processes. In fact, much of what I shall say makes better sense for politics on a rather small scale – within the firm, the organization or the local community – than for nationwide political systems.

In very broad outline, the structure of social choice theory is as follows.[6] (1) We begin with a *given* set of agents, so that the issue of a normative justification of political boundaries does not arise. (2) We assume that the agents confront a *given* set of alternatives, so that for instance the issue of agenda manipulation does not arise. (3) The agents are supposed to be endowed with preferences that are similarly *given* and not subject to change in the course of the political process. They are, moreover, assumed to be causally independent of the set of alternatives. (4) In the standard version, which is so far the only operational version of the theory, preferences are assumed to be purely ordinal, so that it is not possible for an individual to express the intensity of his preferences, nor for an outside observer to compare preference intensities across individuals. (5) The individual preferences are assumed to be defined over all pairs of individuals, i.e. to be complete, and to have the formal property of transitivity, so that preference for *A* over *B* and for *B* over *C* implies preference for *A* over *C*.

Given this setting, the task of social choice theory is to arrive at a social preference ordering of the alternatives. This might appear to require more than is needed: why not define the goal as one of arriving at the choice of one alternative? There is, however, usually some uncertainty as to which alternatives are really feasible, and so it is useful to have an ordering if the top-ranked alternative proves unavailable. The ordering should satisfy the following criteria. (6) Like the individual preferences, it should be complete and transitive. (7) It should be Pareto-optimal, in the sense

of never having one option socially preferred to another which is individually preferred by everybody. (8) The social choice between two given options should depend only on how the individuals rank these two options, and thus not be sensitive to changes in their preferences concerning other options. (9) The social preference ordering should respect and reflect individual preferences, over and above the condition of Pareto-optimality. This idea covers a variety of notions, the most important of which are *anonymity* (all individuals should count equally), *non-dictatorship* (*a fortiori* no single individual should dictate the social choice), *liberalism* (all individuals should have some private domain within which their preferences are decisive), and *strategy-proofness* (it should not pay to express false preferences).

The substance of social choice theory is given in a series of impossibility and uniqueness theorems, stating either that a given subset of these conditions is incapable of simultaneous satisfaction or that they uniquely describe a specific method for aggregating preferences. Much attention has been given to the impossibility theorems, yet from the present point of view these are not of decisive importance. They stem largely from the paucity of allowable information about the preferences, i.e. the exclusive focus on ordinal preferences.[7] True, at present we do not quite know how to go beyond ordinality. Log-rolling and vote-trading may capture some of the cardinal aspects of the preferences, but at some cost.[8] Yet even should the conceptual and technical obstacles to intra- and inter-individual comparison of preference intensity be overcome,[9] many objections to the social choice approach would remain. I shall discuss two sets of objections, both related to the assumption of given preferences. I shall argue, first, that the preferences people choose to express may not be a good guide to what they really prefer, and secondly that what they really prefer may in any case be a fragile foundation for social choice.

In actual fact, preferences are never 'given', in the sense of being directly observable. If they are to serve as inputs to the social choice process, they must somehow be *expressed* by the individuals. The expression of preferences is an action, which presumably is guided by these very same preferences.[10] It is then far from obvious that the individually rational action is to express these preferences as they are. Some methods for aggregating preferences are such that it may pay the individual to express false preferences, i.e. the outcome may in some cases be better according to his real preferences if he chooses not to express them truthfully. The condition for strategy-proofness for social choice mechanisms was designed expressly to exclude this possibility. It turns out, however, that the systems in which honesty always pays are rather unattractive in other respects.[11] We then have to face the possibility that even if we require that the social preferences be Pareto-optimal with respect to the expressed preferences, they might not be so with respect to the real ones. Strategy-proofness and collective rationality, therefore, stand and fall together. Since it appears that the first must fall, so must the second. It then becomes very difficult indeed to defend the idea that the outcome of the social choice mechanism represents the common good, since there is a chance that everybody might prefer some other outcome.

Amos Tversky has pointed to another reason why choices – or expressed preferences – cannot be assumed to represent the real preferences in all cases.[12] According to his 'concealed preference hypothesis', choices often conceal rather than reveal underlying preferences. This is especially so in two sorts of cases. First, there are the cases of anticipated regret associated with a risky decision. Consider the following example (from Tversky):

On her twelfth birthday, Judy was offered a choice between spending the weekend with her aunt in the city (C), or having a party for all her friends. The party could take place either in the garden (GP) or inside the house (HP). A garden party would be much more enjoyable, but there is always the possibility of rain, in which case an inside party would be more sensible. In evaluating the consequences of the three options, Judy notes that the weather condition does not have a significant effect on C. If she chooses the party, however, the situation is different. A garden party will be a lot of fun if the weather is good, but quite disastrous if it rains, in which case an inside party will be acceptable. The trouble is that Judy expects to have a lot of regret if the party is to be held inside and the weather is very nice.

Now, let us suppose that for some reason it is no longer possible to have an outside party. In this situation, there is no longer any regret

associated with holding an inside party in good weather because (in this case) Judy has no other place for holding the party. Hence, the elimination of an available course of action (holding the party outside) removes the regret associated with an inside party, and increases its overall utility. It stands to reason, in this case, that if Judy was indifferent between C and HP, in the presence of GP, she will prefer HP to C when GP is eliminated.

What we observe here is the violation of condition (8) above, the so-called 'independence of irrelevant alternatives'. The expressed preferences depend causally on the set of alternatives. We may assume that the real preferences, defined over the set of possible outcomes, remain constant, contrary to the case to be discussed below. Yet the preferences over the *pairs* (choice, outcome) depend on the set of available choices, because the 'costs of responsibility' differentially associated with various such pairs depend on what else one 'could have done'. Although Judy could not have escaped her predicament by deliberately making it physically impossible to have an outside party,[13] she might well have welcomed an event outside her control with the same consequence.

The second class of cases in which Tversky would want to distinguish the expressed preferences from the real preferences concerns decisions that are unpleasant rather than risky. For instance, 'society may prefer to save the life of one person rather than another, and yet be unable to make this choice'. In fact, losing both lives through inaction may be preferred to losing only one life by deliberate action. Such examples are closely related to the problems involved in act utilitarianism versus outcome utilitarianism.[14] One may well judge that it would be a good thing if state A came about, and yet not want to be the person by whose agency it comes about. The reasons for not wanting to be that person may be quite respectable, or they may not. The latter would be the case if one were afraid of being blamed by the relatives of the person who was deliberately allowed to die, or if one simply confused the causal and the moral notions of responsibility. In such cases the expressed preferences might lead to a choice that in a clear sense goes against the real preferences of the people concerned.

A second, perhaps more basic, difficulty is that

the real preferences themselves might well depend causally on the feasible set. One instance is graphically provided by the fable of the fox and the sour grapes.[15] For the 'ordinal utilitarian', as Arrow for instance calls himself,[16] there would be no welfare loss if the fox were excluded from consumption of the grapes, since he thought them sour anyway. But of course the cause of his holding them to be sour was his conviction that he would in any case be excluded from consuming them, and then it is difficult to justify the allocation by invoking his preferences. Conversely, the phenomenon of 'counter-adaptive preferences' – the grass is always greener on the other side of the fence, and the forbidden fruit always sweeter – is also baffling for the social choice theorist, since it implies that such preferences, if respected, would not be satisfied – and yet the whole point of respecting them would be to give them a chance of satisfaction.

Adaptive and counter-adaptive preferences are only special cases of a more general class of desires, those which fail to satisfy some substantive criterion for acceptable preferences, as opposed to the purely formal criterion of transitivity. I shall discuss these under two headings: autonomy and morality.

Autonomy characterizes the way in which preferences are shaped rather than their actual content. Unfortunately I find myself unable to give a positive characterization of autonomous preferences, so I shall have to rely on two indirect approaches. First, autonomy is for desires what judgment is for belief. The notion of judgment is also difficult to define formally, but at least we know that there are persons who have this quality to a higher degree than others: people who are able to take account of vast and diffuse evidence that more or less clearly bears on the problem at hand, in such a way that no element is given undue importance. In such people the process of belief formation is not disturbed by defective cognitive processing, nor distorted by wishful thinking and the like. Similarly, autonomous preferences are those that have not been shaped by irrelevant causal processes – a singularly unhelpful explanation. To improve somewhat on it, consider, secondly, a short list of such irrelevant causal processes. They include adaptive and counter-adaptive preferences, conformity and anti-conformity, the obsession with novelty and the equally unreasonable resistance to novelty. In other words, preferences may be shaped by adap-

tation to what is possible, to what other people do or to what one has been doing in the past – or they may be shaped by the desire to differ as much as possible from these. In all of these cases the source of preference change is not in the person, but outside him – detracting from his autonomy.

Morality, it goes without saying, is if anything even more controversial. (Within the Kantian tradition it would also be questioned whether it can be distinguished at all from autonomy.) Preferences are moral or immoral by virtue of their content, not by virtue of the way in which they have been shaped. Fairly uncontroversial examples of unethical preferences are spiteful and sadistic desires, and arguably also the desire for positional goods, i.e. goods such that it is logically impossible for more than a few to possess them.[17] The desire for an income twice the average can lead to less welfare for everybody, so that such preferences fail to pass the Kantian generalization test.[18] Also they are closely linked to spite, since one way of getting more than others is to take care that they get less – indeed this may often be a more efficient method than trying to excel.[19]

To see how the lack of autonomy may be distinguished from the lack of moral worth, let me use *conformity* as a technical term for a desire caused by a drive to be like other people, and *conformism* for a desire to be like other people, with anti-conformity and anti-conformism similarly defined. Conformity implies that other people's desires enter into the causation of my own, conformism that they enter irreducibly into the description of the object of my desires. Conformity may bring about conformism, but it may also lead to anti-conformism, as in Theodore Zeldin's comment that among the French peasantry 'prestige is to a great extent obtained from conformity with traditions, so that the son of a non-conformist might be expected to be one too'.[20] Clearly, conformity may bring about desires that are morally laudable, yet lacking in autonomy. Conversely, I do not see how one could rule out on *a priori* grounds the possibility of autonomous spite, although I would welcome a proof that autonomy is incompatible not only with anti-conformity, but also with anti-conformism.

We can now state the objection to the political view underlying social choice theory. It is, basically, that it embodies a confusion between the kind of behaviour that is appropriate in the market place and that which is appropriate in the forum. The notion of consumer sovereignty is acceptable because, and to the extent that, the consumer chooses between courses of action that differ only in the way they affect him. In political choice situations, however, the citizen is asked to express his preference over states that also differ in the way in which they affect other people. This means that there is no similar justification for the corresponding notion of the citizen's sovereignty, since other people may legitimately object to social choice governed by preferences that are defective in some of the ways I have mentioned. A social choice mechanism is capable of resolving the market failures that would result from unbridled consumer sovereignty, but as a way of redistributing welfare it is hopelessly inadequate. If people affected each other only by tripping over each other's feet, or by dumping their garbage into one another's backyards, a social choice mechanism might cope. But the task of politics is not only to eliminate inefficiency, but also to create justice – a goal to which the aggregation of pre-political preferences is a quite incongruous means.

This suggests that the principles of the forum must differ from those of the market. A long-standing tradition from the Greek *polis* onwards suggests that politics must be an open and public activity, as distinct from the isolated and private expression of preferences that occurs in buying and selling. In the following sections I look at two different conceptions of public politics, increasingly removed from the market theory of politics. Before I go on to this, however, I should briefly consider an objection that the social choice theorist might well make to what has just been said. He could argue that the only alternative to the aggregation of given preferences is some kind of censorship or paternalism. He might agree that spiteful and adaptive preferences are undesirable, but he would add that any institutional mechanism for eliminating them would be misused and harnessed to the private purposes of power-seeking individuals. Any remedy, in fact, would be worse than the disease. This objection assumes (i) that the only alternative to aggregation of given preferences is censorship, and (ii) that censorship is always objectionable. Robert Goodin, in his paper 'Laundering preferences', challenges the second assumption, by arguing that laundering or filtering of preferences by self-censorship is an acceptable alternative to aggregation. I shall

now discuss a challenge to the first assumption, viz. the idea of a *transformation* of preferences through public and rational discussion.

II

Today this view is especially associated with the writings of Jürgen Habermas on 'the ethics of discourse' and 'the ideal speech situation'. As mentioned above, I shall present a somewhat stylized version of his views, although I hope they bear some resemblance to the original.[21] The core of the theory, then, is that rather than aggregating or filtering preferences, the political system should be set up with a view to changing them by public debate and confrontation. The input to the social choice mechanism would then not be the raw, quite possibly selfish or irrational, preferences that operate in the market, but informed and other-regarding preferences. Or rather, there would not be any need for an aggregating mechanism, since a rational discussion would tend to produce unanimous preferences. When the private and idiosyncratic wants have been shaped and purged in public discussion about the public good, uniquely determined rational desires would emerge. Not optimal compromise, but unanimous agreement is the goal of politics on this view.

There appear to be two main premises underlying this theory. The first is that there are certain arguments that simply cannot be stated publicly. In a political debate it is pragmatically impossible to argue that a given solution should be chosen just because it is good for oneself. By the very act of engaging in a public debate – by arguing rather than bargaining – one has ruled out the possibility of invoking such reasons.[22] To engage in discussion can in fact be seen as one kind of self-censorship, a pre-commitment to the idea of rational decision. Now, it might well be thought that this conclusion is too strong. The first argument only shows that in public debate one has to pay some lip-service to the common good. An additional premise states that over time one will in fact come to be swayed by considerations about the common good. One cannot indefinitely praise the common good 'du bout des lèvres', for – as argued by Pascal in the context of the wager – one will end up having the preferences that initially one was faking.[23] This is a psychological, not a conceptual premise. To explain why going through the motions of rational discussion should tend to bring about the real thing, one might argue that people tend to bring what they mean into line with what they say in order to reduce dissonance, but this is a dangerous argument to employ in the present context. Dissonance reduction does not tend to generate autonomous preferences. Rather one would have to invoke the power of reason to break down prejudice and selfishness. By speaking with the voice of reason, one is also exposing oneself to reason.

To sum up, the conceptual impossibility of expressing selfish arguments in a debate about the public good, and the psychological difficulty of expressing other-regarding preferences without ultimately coming to acquire them, jointly bring it about that public discussion tends to promote the common good. The *volonté générale*, then, will not simply be the Pareto-optimal realization of given (or expressed) preferences,[24] but the outcome of preferences that are themselves shaped by a concern for the common good. For instance, by mere aggregation of given preferences one would be able to take account of some negative externalities, but not of those affecting future generations. A social choice mechanism might prevent persons now living from dumping their garbage into one another's backyards, but not from dumping it in the future. Moreover, considerations of distributive justice within the Pareto constraint would now have a more solid foundation, especially as one would also be able to avoid the problem of strategy-proofness. By one stroke one would achieve more rational preferences, as well as the guarantee that they will in fact be expressed.

I now want to set out a series of objections – seven altogether – to the view stated above. I should explain that the goal of this criticism is not to demolish the theory, but to locate some points that need to be fortified. I am, in fact, largely in sympathy with the fundamental tenets of the view, yet fear that it might be dismissed as Utopian, both in the sense of ignoring the problem of getting from here to there, and in the sense of neglecting some elementary facts of human psychology.

The *first objection* involves a reconsideration of the issues of paternalism. Would it not, in fact, be unwarranted interference to impose on the citizens the obligation to participate in political discussion? One might answer that there is a link between the right to vote and the obligation to participate in discussion, just as rights and duties are correlative in other cases. To acquire the right to vote, one has to perform certain civic duties that go beyond pushing the voting button on the television set. There would appear to be two different ideas underlying this answer. First, only those should have the right to vote who are sufficiently *concerned* about politics to be willing to devote some of their resources – time in particular – to it. Secondly, one should try to favour *informed* preferences as inputs to the voting process. The first argument favours participation and discussion as a sign of interest, but does not give it an instrumental value in itself. It would do just as well, for the purpose of this argument, to demand that people should pay for the right to vote. The second argument favours discussion as a means to improvement – it will not only select the right people, but actually make them more qualified to participate.

These arguments might have some validity in a near-ideal world, in which the concern for politics was evenly distributed across all relevant dimensions, but in the context of contemporary politics they miss the point. The people who survive a high threshold for participation are disproportionately found in a privileged part of the population. At best this could lead to paternalism, at worst the high ideals of rational discussion could create a self-elected elite whose members spend time on politics because they want power, not out of concern for the issues. As in other cases, to be discussed later, the best can be the enemy of the good. I am not saying that it is impossible to modify the ideal in a way that allows both for rational discussion and for low-profile participation, only that any institutional design must respect the trade off between the two.

My *second objection* is that even assuming unlimited time for discussion, unanimous and rational agreement might not necessarily ensue. Could there not be legitimate and unresolvable differences of opinions over the nature of the common good? Could there not even be a plurality of ultimate values?

I am not going to discuss this objection, since it is in any case preempted by the *third objection*. Since there are in fact always time constraints on discussions – often the stronger the more important the issues – unanimity will rarely emerge. For any constellation of preferences short of unanimity, however, one would need a social choice mechanism to aggregate them. One can discuss only for so long, and then one has to make a decision, even if strong differences of opinion should remain. This objection, then, goes to show that the transformation of preferences can never do more than supplement the aggregation of preferences, never replace it altogether.

This much would no doubt be granted by most proponents of the theory. True, they would say, even if the ideal speech situation can never be fully realized, it will nevertheless improve the outcome of the political process if one goes some way towards it. The *fourth objection* questions the validity of this reply. In some cases a little discussion can be a dangerous thing, worse in fact than no discussion at all, viz. if it makes some but not all persons align themselves on the common good. The following story provides an illustration:

> Once upon a time two boys found a cake. One of them said, 'Splendid! I will eat the cake.' The other one said, 'No, that is not fair! We found the cake together, and we should share and share alike, half for you and half for me.' The first boy said, 'No, I should have the whole cake!' Along came an adult who said, 'Gentlemen, you shouldn't fight about this: you should *compromise*. Give him three quarters of the cake.'[25]

What creates the difficulty here is that the first boy's preferences are allowed to count twice in the social choice mechanism suggested by the adult: once in his expression of them and then again in the other boy's internalized ethic of sharing. And one can argue that the outcome is socially inferior to that which would have emerged had they both stuck to their selfish preferences. When Adam Smith wrote that he had never known much good done by those who affected to trade for the public good, he may only have had in mind the harm that can be done by *unilateral* attempts to act morally. The categorical imperative itself may be badly served by people acting unilaterally on it.[26] Also, an inferior outcome may result if discussion brings about partial adherence to morality in all participants rather than full adherence in some and none in others, as in the story of the two boys. Thus Serge Kolm argues that economies with moderately altruistic agents tend to work less well than economies where either everybody is selfish or everybody is altruistic.[27]

A *fifth objection* is to question the implicit assumption that the body politic as a whole is better or wiser than the sum of its parts. Could it not rather be the case that people are made more, not less, selfish and irrational by interacting politically? The cognitive analogy suggests that the rationality of beliefs may be positively as well as negatively affected by interaction. On the one hand there is what Irving Janis has called 'groupthink', i.e. mutually reinforcing bias.[28] On the other hand there certainly are many ways in which people can, and do, pool their opinions and supplement each other to arrive at a better estimate.[29] Similarly autonomy and morality could be enhanced as well as undermined by interaction. Against the pessimistic view of Reinhold Niebuhr that individuals in a group show more unrestrained egoism than in their personal relationships,[30] we may set Hannah Arendt's optimistic view:

> American faith was not all based on a semireligious faith in human nature, but on the contrary, on the possibility of checking human nature in its singularity, by virtue of human bonds and mutual promises. The hope for man in his singularity lay in the fact that not man but men inhabit the earth and form a world between them. It is human worldliness that will save men from the pitfalls of human nature.[31]

Niebuhr's argument suggests an aristocratic disdain of the *mass*, which transforms individually decent people – to use a characteristically condescending phrase – into an unthinking horde. While rejecting this as a general view, one should equally avoid the other extreme, suggested by Arendt. Neither the Greek nor the American assemblies were the paradigms of discursive reason that she makes them out to be. The Greeks were well aware that they might be tempted by demagogues, and in fact took extensive precautions against this tendency.[32] The American town surely has not always been the incarnation of collective freedom, since on occasion it could also serve as the springboard for witch hunts. The mere decision to engage in rational discussion does not ensure that the transactions will in fact be conducted rationally, since much depends on the structure and the framework of the proceedings. The random errors of selfish and private preferences may to some extent cancel each other out and thus be less to be feared than the massive and coordinated errors that may arise through group-think. On the other hand, it would be excessively stupid to rely on mutually compensating vices to bring about public benefits as a general rule. I am not arguing against the need for public discussion, only for the need to take the question of institutional and constitutional design very seriously.

A *sixth objection* is that unanimity, were it to be realized, might easily be due to conformity rather than to rational agreement. I would in fact tend to have more confidence in the outcome of a democratic decision if there was a minority that voted against it, than if it was unanimous. I am not here referring to people expressing the majority preferences against their real ones, since I am assuming that something like the secret ballot would prevent this. I have in mind that people may come to change their real preferences, as a result of seeing which way the majority goes. Social psychology has amply shown the strength of this bandwagon effect,[33] which in political theory is also known as the 'chameleon' problem.[34] It will not do to argue that the majority to which the conformist adapts his view is likely to pass the test of rationality even if his adherence to it does not, since the majority could well be made up of conformists each of whom would have broken out had there been a minority he could have espoused.

To bring the point home, consider a parallel case of non-autonomous preference formation. We are tempted to say that a man is free if he can get or do whatever it is that he wants to get or do. But then we are immediately faced with the objection that perhaps he only wants what he can get, as the result of some such mechanism as 'sour grapes'.[35] We may then add that, other things being equal, the person is freer the more things he wants to do which he is not free to do, since these show that his wants are not in general shaped by adaptation to his possibilities. Clearly, there is an air of paradox over the statement that a man's freedom is greater the more of his desires he is not free to realize, but on reflection the paradox embodies a valid argument. Similarly, it is possible to dissolve the air of paradox attached to the view that a collective decision is more trustworthy if it is less than unanimous.

My *seventh objection* amounts to a denial of the view that the need to couch one's argument in terms of the common good will purge the desires of all selfish arguments. There are in general many ways of realizing the common good, if by that phrase we now only mean some arrangement that is Pareto-superior to uncoordinated individual decisions. Each such arrangement will, in addition to promoting the general interest, bring an extra premium to some specific group, which will then have a strong interest in that particular arrangement.[36] The group may then come to prefer the arrangement because of that premium, although it will argue for it in terms of the common good. Typically the arrangement will be justified by a causal theory – an account, say, of how the economy works – that shows it to be not only *a* way, but the only way of promoting the common good. The economic theories underlying the early Reagan administration provide an example. I am not imputing insincerity to the proponents of these views, but there may well be an element of wishful thinking. Since social scientists disagree so strongly among themselves as to how societies work, what could be more human than to pick on a theory that uniquely justifies the arrangement from which one stands to profit? The opposition between general interest and special interests is too simplistic, since the private benefits may causally determine the way in which one conceives of the common good.

These objections have been concerned to bring out two main ideas. First, one cannot assume that one will in fact approach the good society by acting as if one had already arrived there. The fallacy inherent in this 'approximation assumption'[37] was exposed a long time ago in the economic 'theory of the second best':

> It is *not* true that a situation in which more, but not all, of the optimum conditions are fulfilled is necessarily, or is even likely to be, superior to a situation in which fewer are fulfilled. It follows, therefore, that in a situation in which there exist many constraints which prevent the fulfilment of the Paretian optimum conditions, the removal of any one constraint may affect welfare or efficiency either by raising it, by lowering it or by leaving it unchanged.[38]

The ethical analogue is not the familiar idea that some moral obligations may be suspended when other people act non-morally.[39] Rather it is that the nature of the moral obligation is changed in a non-moral environment. When others act non-morally, there may be an obligation to deviate not only from what they do, but also from the behaviour that would have been optimal if adopted by everybody.[40] In particular, a little discussion, like a little rationality or a little socialism, may be a dangerous thing.[41] If, as suggested by Habermas, free and rational discussion will only be possible in a society that has abolished political and economic domination, it is by no means obvious that abolition can be brought about by rational argumentation. I do not want to suggest that it could occur by force – since the use of force to end the use of force is open to obvious objections. Yet something like irony, eloquence or propaganda might be needed, involving less respect for the interlocutor than what would prevail in the ideal speech situation.

As will be clear from these remarks, there is a strong tension between two ways of looking at the relation between political ends and means. On the one hand, the means should partake of the nature of the ends, since otherwise the use of unsuitable means might tend to corrupt the end. On the other hand, there are dangers involved in choosing means immediately derived from the goal to be realized, since in a non-ideal situation these might take us away from the end rather than towards it. A delicate balance will have to be struck between these two, opposing considerations. It is in fact an open question whether there exists a ridge along which we can move to the good society, and if so whether it is like a knife-edge or more like a plateau.

The second general idea that emerges from the discussion is that even in the good society, should we hit upon it, the process of rational discussion could be fragile, and vulnerable to adaptive preferences, conformity, wishful thinking and the like. To ensure stability and robustness there is a need for structures – political institutions or constitutions – that could easily reintroduce an element of domination. We would in fact be confronted, at the political level, with a perennial dilemma of individual behaviour. How is it possible to ensure at the same time that one is bound by rules that protect one from irrational or unethical behaviour – and that these rules do not turn into prisons from which it is not possible to break out even when it would be rational to do so?[42]

III

It is clear from Habermas's theory, I believe, that rational political discussion has an *object* in terms of which it makes sense.[43] Politics is concerned with substantive decision-making, and is to that extent instrumental. True, the idea of instrumental politics might also be taken in a more narrow sense, as implying that the political process is one in which individuals pursue their selfish interests, but more broadly understood it implies only that political action is primarily a means to a non-political end, only secondarily, if at all, an end in itself. In this section I shall consider theories that suggest a reversal of this priority, and that find the main point of politics in the educative or otherwise beneficial effects on the participants. And I shall try to show that this view tends to be internally incoherent, or self-defeating. The benefits of participation are by-products of political activity. Moreover, they are *essentially* by-products, in the sense that any attempt to turn them into the main purpose of such activity would make them evaporate.[44] It can indeed be highly satisfactory to engage in political work, but only on the condition that the work is defined by a serious purpose which goes beyond that of achieving this satisfaction. If that condition is not fulfilled, we get a narcissistic view of politics – corresponding to various consciousness-raising activities familiar from the last decade or so.

My concern, however, is with political theory rather than with political activism. I shall argue that certain types of arguments for political institutions and constitutions are self-defeating, since they justify the arrangement in question by effects that are essentially by-products. Here an initial and important distinction must be drawn between the task of justifying a constitution *ex ante* and that of evaluating it *ex post* and at a distance. I argue below that Tocqueville, when assessing the American democracy, praised it for consequences that are indeed by-products. In his case, this made perfectly good sense as an analytical attitude adopted after the fact and at some distance from the system he was examining. The incoherence arises when one invokes the same arguments before the fact, in public discussion. Although the constitution-makers may secretly have such side effects in mind, they cannot coherently invoke them in public.

Kant proposed a *transcendental formula of public right*: 'All actions affecting the rights of other human beings are wrong if their maxim is not compatible with their being made public.'[45] Since Kant's illustrations of the principle are obscure, let me turn instead to John Rawls, who imposes a similar condition of publicity as a constraint on what the parties can choose in the original position.[46] He argues, moreover, that this condition tends to favour his own conception of justice, as compared to that of the utilitarians.[47] If utilitarian principles of justice were openly adopted, they would entail some loss of self-esteem, since people would feel that they were not fully being treated as ends in themselves. Other things being equal, this would also lead to a loss in average utility. It is then conceivable that public adoption of Rawls's two principles of justice would bring about a higher average utility than public adoption of utilitarianism, although a lower average than under a secret utilitarian constitution introduced from above. The latter possibility, however, is ruled out by the publicity constraint. A utilitarian could not then advocate Rawls's two principles on utilitarian grounds, although he might well applaud them on such grounds. The fact that the two principles maximize utility would essentially be a by-product, and if chosen on the grounds that they are utility-maximizing they would no longer be so. Utilitarianism, therefore, is self-defeating in Kant's sense: 'it essentially lacks openness'.[48]

Derek Parfit has raised a similar objection to act consequentialism (AC) and suggested how it could be met:

This gives to all one common aim: the best possible outcome. If we try to achieve this, we may often fail. Even when we succeed, the fact that we are disposed to try might make the outcome worse. AC might thus be indirectly self-defeating. What does this show? A consequentialist might say: 'It shows that AC should be only one part of our moral theory. It should be the part that covers successful acts. When we are certain to succeed, we should aim for the best possible outcome. Our wider theory should be this: we should have the aim and dispositions having which would make the outcome best. This wider theory would not be self-defeating. So the objection has been met.'[49]

Yet there is an ambiguity in the word 'should' in the penultimate sentence, since it is not clear whether we are told that it is good to have certain aims and dispositions, or that we should aim at having them. The latter answer immediately raises the problem that having certain aims and dispositions – i.e. being a certain kind of person – is essentially a by-product. When instrumental rationality is self-defeating, we cannot decide on instrumentalist grounds to take leave of it – no more than we can fall asleep by deciding not to try to fall asleep. Although spontaneity may be highly valuable on utilitarian grounds, 'you cannot both genuinely possess this kind of quality and also reassure yourself that while it is free and creative and uncalculative, it is also acting for the best'.[50]

Tocqueville, in a seeming paradox, suggested that democracies are less suited than aristocracies to deal with long-term planning, and yet are superior in the long-run to the latter. The paradox dissolves once it is seen that the first statement involves time at the level of the actors, the second at the level of the observer. On the one hand, 'a democracy finds it difficult to coordinate the details of a great undertaking and to fix on some plan and carry it through with determination in spite of obstacles. It has little capacity for combining measures in secret and waiting patiently for the result'.[51] On the other hand, 'in the long run government by democracy should increase the real forces of a society, but it cannot immediately assemble at one point and at a given time, forces as great as those at the disposal of an aristocratic government'.[52] The latter view is further elaborated in a passage from the chapter on 'The Real Advantages Derived by American Society from Democratic Government'·

That constantly renewed agitation introduced by democratic government into political life passes, then, into civil society. Perhaps, taking everything into consideration, that is the greatest advantage of democratic government, and I praise it much more on account of what it causes to be done than for what it does. It is incontestable that the people often manage public affairs very badly, but their concern therewith is bound to extend their mental horizon and to shake them out of the rut of ordinary routine . . . Democracy does not provide a people with the most skillful of governments, but it does that which the most skillful government often cannot do: it spreads throughout the body social a restless activity, superabundant force, and energy never found elsewhere, which, however little favoured by circumstances, can do wonders. Those are its true advantages.[53]

The advantages of democracies, in other words, are mainly and essentially by-products. The avowed aim of democracy is to be a good system of government, but Tocqueville argues that it is inferior in this respect to aristocracy, viewed purely as a decision-making apparatus. Yet the very activity of governing democratically has as a by-product a certain energy and restlessness that benefits industry and generates prosperity. Assuming the soundness of this observation, could it ever serve as a public justification for introducing democracy in a nation that had not yet acquired it? The question is somewhat more complex than one might be led to think from what I have said so far, since the quality of the decisions is not the only consideration that is relevant for the choice of a political system. The argument from *justice* could also be decisive. Yet the following conclusion seems inescapable: if the system has no inherent advantage in terms of justice or efficiency, one cannot coherently and publicly advocate its introduction because of the side effects that would follow in its wake. There must be a *point* in democracy as such. If people are motivated by such inherent advantages to throw themselves into the system, other benefits may ensue – but the latter cannot by themselves be the motivating force. If the democratic method is introduced in a society solely because of the side effects on economic prosperity, and no one believes in it on any other ground, it will not produce them.

Tocqueville, however, did not argue that political activity is an end in itself. The justification for democracy is found in its effects, although not in the intended ones, as the strictly instrumental view would have it. More to the point is Tocqueville's argument for the jury system: 'I do not know whether a jury is useful to the litigants, but I am sure that it is very good for those who have to decide the case. I regard it as one of the most effective means of popular education at society's disposal.'[54] This is still an instrumental view, but the gap between the means and the end is smaller. Tocqueville never argued that the effect of democracy was to make politicians prosperous, only that it was conducive to general prosperity. By contrast, the justification of the

jury system is found in the effect on the jurors themselves. And, as above, that effect would be spoilt if they believed that the impact on their own civic spirit was the main point of the proceedings.

John Stuart Mill not only applauded but advocated democracy on the ground of such educative effects on the participants. In current discussion he stands out both as an opponent of the purely instrumental view of politics, that of his father James Mill,[55] and as a forerunner of the theory of participatory democracy.[56] In his theory the gap between means and ends in politics is even narrower, since he saw political activity not only as a means to self-improvement, but also as a source of satisfaction and thus a good in itself. As noted by Albert Hirschman, this implies that 'the benefit of collective action for an individual is not the difference between the hoped-for result and the effort furnished by him or her, but the *sum* of these two magnitudes'.[57] Yet this very way of paraphrasing Mill's view also points to a difficulty. Could it really be the case that participation would yield a benefit even when the hoped-for results are nil, as suggested by Hirschman's formula? Is it not rather true that the effort is itself a function of the hoped-for result, so that in the end the latter is the only independent variable? When Mill refers, critically, to the limitations of Bentham, whose philosophy 'can teach the means of organising and regulating the merely *business* part of the social arrangement',[58] he seems to be putting the cart before the horse. The non-business part of politics may be the more valuable, but the value is contingent on the importance of the business part.

For a fully developed version of the non-instrumental theory of politics, we may go to the work of Hannah Arendt. Writing about the distinction between the private and the public realm in ancient Greece, she argues that:

Without mastering the necessities of life in the household, neither life nor the 'good life' is possible, but politics is never for the sake of life. As far as the members of the *polis* are concerned, household life exists for the sake of the 'good life' in the *polis*.[59]

The public realm . . . was reserved for individuality; it was the only place where men could show who they really and inexchangeably were. It was for the sake of this chance, and out of love for a body politic that it made it possible to them all, that each was more or less willing to share in the burden of jurisdiction, defence and administration of public affairs.[60]

Against this we may set the view of Greek politics found in the work of M. I. Finley. Asking why the Athenian people claimed the right of every citizen to speak and make proposals in the Assembly, yet left its exercise to a few, he finds that 'one part of the answer is that the *demos* recognised the instrumental role of political rights and were more concerned in the end with the substantive decisions, were content with their power to select, dismiss and punish their political leaders'.[61] Elsewhere he writes, even more explicitly: 'Then, as now, politics was instrumental for most people, not an interest or an end in itself.'[62] Contrary to what Arendt suggests, the possession or the possibility of exercising a political right may be more important than the actual exercise. Moreover, even the exercise derives its value from the decisions to be taken. Writing about the American town assemblies, Arendt argues that the citizens participated 'neither exclusively because of duty nor, and even less, to serve their own interests but most of all because they enjoyed the discussions, the deliberations, and the making of decisions'.[63] This, while not putting the cart before the horse, at least places them alongside each other. Although discussion and deliberation in other contexts may be independent sources of enjoyment, the satisfaction one derives from *political* discussion is parasitic on decision-making. Political debate is about what to *do* – not about what ought to be the case. It is defined by this practical purpose, not by its subject-matter.

Politics in this respect is on a par with other activities such as art, science, athletics or chess. To engage in them may be deeply satisfactory, if you have an independently defined goal such as 'getting it right' or 'beating the opposition'. A chess player who asserted that he played not to win, but for the sheer elegance of the game, would be in narcissistic bad faith – since there is no such thing as an elegant way of losing, only elegant and inelegant ways of winning. When the artist comes to believe that the process and not the end result is his real purpose, and that defects and irregularities are valuable as reminders of the struggle of creation, he similarly forfeits any claim to our interest. The same holds for E. P.

Thompson, who, when asked whether he really believed that a certain rally in Trafalgar Square would have any impact at all, answered: 'That's not really the point, is it? The point is, it shows that democracy's alive . . . A rally like that gives us self-respect. Chartism was terribly good for the Chartists, although they never got the Charter.'[64] Surely, the Chartists, if asked whether they thought they would ever get the Charter, would not have answered: 'That's not really the point, is it?' It was because they believed they might get the Charter that they engaged in the struggle for it with the seriousness of purpose that also brought them self-respect as a side effect.[65]

IV

I have been discussing three views concerning the relation between economics and politics, between the market and the forum. One extreme is 'the economic theory of democracy', most outrageously stated by Schumpeter, but in essence also underlying social choice theory. It is a market theory of politics, in the sense that the act of voting is a private act similar to that of buying and selling. I cannot accept, therefore, Alan Ryan's argument that 'On any possible view of the distinction between private and public life, voting is an element in one's public life.'[66] The very distinction between the secret and the open ballot shows that there is room for a private-public distinction within politics. The economic theory of democracy, therefore, rests on the idea that the forum should be like the market, in its purpose as well as in its mode of functioning. The purpose is defined in economic terms, and the mode of functioning is that of aggregating individual decisions.

At the other extreme there is the view that the forum should be completely divorced from the market, in purpose as well as in institutional arrangement. The forum should be more than the distributive totality of individuals queuing up for the election booth. Citizenship is a quality that can only be realized in public, i.e. in a collective joined for a common purpose. This purpose, moreover, is not to facilitate life in the material sense. The political process is an end in itself, a good or even the supreme good for those who participate in it. It may be applauded because of the educative effects on the participants, but the benefits do not cease once the education has been completed. On the contrary, the education of the citizen leads to a preference for public life as an end in itself. Politics on this view is not *about* anything. It is the agonistic display of excellence,[67] or the collective display of solidarity, divorced from decision-making and the exercise of influence on events.

In between these extremes is the view I find most attractive. One can argue that the forum should differ from the market in its mode of functioning, yet be concerned with decisions that ultimately deal with economic matters. Even higher-order political decisions concern lower-level rules that are directly related to economic matters. Hence constitutional arguments about how laws can be made and changed, constantly invoke the impact of legal stability and change on economic affairs. It is the concern with substantive decisions that lends the urgency to political debates. The ever-present constraint of *time* creates a need for focus and concentration that cannot be assimilated to the leisurely style of philosophical argument in which it may be better to travel hopefully than to arrive. Yet within these constraints arguments form the core of the political process. If thus defined as public in nature, and instrumental in purpose, politics assumes what I believe to be its proper place in society.

Notes

1. Elster (1978, Ch. 5) refers to these two varieties of market failure as *suboptimality* and *counterfinality* respectively, linking them both to collective action.

2. This is a simplification. First, as argued in Samuelson (1950), there may be political constraints that prevent one from attaining the Pareto-efficient frontier. Secondly, the very existence of several points that are Pareto-superior to the *status quo*, yet involve differential benefits to the participants, may block the realization of any of them.

3. Hammond (1976) offers a useful analysis of the consequences of selfish preferences over income distributions, showing that 'without interpersonal comparisons of some kind, any social preference ordering over the space of possible income distributions must be dictatorial'.

4. Schumpeter (1961, p. 263): 'the will of the people is the product and not the motive power of the political process'. One should not, however, conclude (as does Lively 1975, p. 38) that Schumpeter thereby abandons the market analogy, since on his view (Schumpeter 1939, p. 73) consumer preferences are no less manipulable (with some qualifications stated in Elster 1983a, Ch. 5).

5. See in particular Downs (1957).

6. For fuller statements, see Arrow (1963), Sen (1970), and Kelly (1978), as well as the contribution of Aanund Hylland to Elster and Hylland (1986).

7. Cf. d'Aspremont and Gevers (1977).

8. Riker and Ordeshook (1973, pp. 112–13).

9. Cf. the contributions of Donald Davidson and Allan Gibbard to Elster and Hylland (1986).

10. Presumably, but not obviously, since the agent might have several preference orderings and rely on higher-order preferences to determine which of the first-order preferences to express, as suggested for instance by Sen (1976).

11. Pattanaik (1978) offers a survey of the known results. The only strategy-proof mechanisms for social choice turn out to be the dictatorial one (the dictator has no incentive to misrepresent his preferences) and the randomizing one of getting the probability that a given option will be chosen equal to the proportion of voters that have it as their first choice.

12. Tversky (1981).

13. Cf. Elster (1979, Ch. II) or Schelling (1980) for the idea of deliberately restricting one's feasible set to make certain undesirable behaviour impossible at a later time. The reason this does not work here is that the regret would not be eliminated.

14. Cf. for instance Williams (1973) or Sen (1979).

15. Cf. Elster (1983b, Ch. III) for a discussion of this notion.

16. Arrow (1973).

17. Hirsch (1976)

18. Haavelmo (1970) offers a model in which everybody may suffer a loss of welfare by trying to keep up with the neighbours.

19. One may take the achievements of others as a parameter and one's own as the control variable, or conversely try to manipulate the achievements of others so that they fall short of one's own. The first of these ways of realizing positional goods is clearly less objectionable than the second, but still less pure than the non-comparative desire for a certain standard of excellence.

20. Zeldin (1973, p. 134).

21. I rely mainly on Habermas (1982). I also thank Helge Høibraaten, Rune Slagstad, and Gunnar Skirbekk for having patiently explained to me various aspects of Habermas's work.

22. Midgaard (1980).

23. For Pascal's argument, cf. Elster (1979, Ch. II. 3).

24. As suggested by Runciman and Sen (1965).

25. Smullyan (1980, p. 56).

26 Sobel (1967).
27 Kolm (1981a, b).
28 Janis (1972).
29 Cf. Hogarth (1977) and Lehrer (1978).
30 Niebuhr (1932, p. 11).
31 Arendt (1973, p. 174).
32 Finley (1973); see also Elster (1979, Ch. II.8).
33 Asch (1956) is a classic study.
34 See Goldman (1972) for discussion and further references.
35 Berlin (1969, p. xxxviii); cf. also Elster (1983b, Ch. III.3).
36 Schotter (1981, pp. 26 ff., pp. 43 ff.) has a good discussion of this predicament.
37 Margalit (1983).
38 Lipsey and Lancaster (1956–7, p. 12).
39 This is the point emphasized in Lyons (1965).
40 Cf. Hansson (1970) as well as Føllesdal and Hilpinen (1971) for discussions of 'conditional obligations' within the framework of deontic logic. It does not appear, however, that the framework can easily accommodate the kind of dilemma I am concerned with here.
41 Cf. for instance Kolm (1977) concerning the dangers of a piecemeal introduction of socialism – also mentioned by Margalit (1983) as an objection to Popper's strategy for piecemeal social engineering.
42 Cf. Ainslie (1982) and Elster (1979, Ch. II.9).
43 Indeed, Habermas (1982) is largely concerned with maxims for *action*, not with the evaluation of states of affairs.
44 Cf. Elster (1983b, Ch. III) for a discussion of the notion that some psychological or social states are

essentially by-products of actions undertaken for some other purpose.
45 Kant (1795, p. 126).
46 Rawls (1971, p. 133).
47 Rawls (1971, pp. 177 ff., esp. p. 181).
48 Williams (1973, p. 123).
49 Parfit (1981, p. 554).
50 Williams (1973, p. 131); also Elster (1983b, Ch. II. 3).
51 Tocqueville (1969, p. 229).
52 Tocqueville (1969, p. 224).
53 Tocqueville (1969, pp. 243–4).
54 Tocqueville (1969, p. 275).
55 Cf. Ryan (1972). His contrast between 'two concepts of democracy' corresponds in part to the distinction between the first and the second of the theories discussed here, in part to the distinction between the first and the third, as he does not clearly separate the public conception of politics from the non-instrumental one.
56 Pateman (1970, p. 29).
57 Hirschman (1982, p. 82).
58 Mill (1859, p. 105).
59 Arendt (1958, p. 37).
60 Arendt (1958, p. 41).
61 Finley (1976, p. 83).
62 Finley (1981, p. 31).
63 Arendt (1973, p. 119).
64 *Sunday Times*, 2 November 1980.
65 Cf. also Barry (1978, p. 47).
66 Ryan (1972, p. 105).
67 Veyne (1976) makes a brilliant statement of this non-instrumental attitude among the elite of the Ancient World.

References

Ainslie, G. (1982) 'A behavioral economic approach to the defense mechanisms', *Social Science Information* 21, 735–80.
Arendt, H. (1958) *The Human Condition*, Chicago: University of Chicago Press.
——(1973) *On Revolution*, Harmondsworth: Pelican Books.
Arrow, K. (1963) *Social Choice and Individual Values*, New York: Wiley.
——(1973) 'Some ordinal-utilitarian notes on Rawls's theory of justice', *Journal of Philosophy* 70, 245–63.
Asch, S. (1956) 'Studies of independence and conformity: I. A minority of one against a unanimous majority', *Psychology Monographs* 70.
Barry, B. (1978) 'Comment', in S. Benn et al. (eds.), *Political Participation*, Canberra: Australian National University Press, pp. 37–48.
Berlin, I. (1969) *Two Concepts of Liberty*, Oxford: Oxford University Press.
d'Aspremont, C. and Gevers, L. (1977) 'Equity and the informational basis of collective choice', *Review of Economic Studies* 44, 199–210.

Downs, A. (1957) *An Economic Theory of Democracy*, New York: Harper.
Elster, J. (1978) *Logic and Society*, Chichester: Wiley.
——(1979) *Ulysses and the Sirens*, Cambridge: Cambridge University Press.
——(1983a) *Explaining Technical Change*, Cambridge: Cambridge University Press; Oslo: Universitetsforlaget.
——(1983b) *Sour Grapes*, Cambridge: Cambridge University Press.
Elster, J. and Hylland, A. (eds.) (1986) *Foundations of Social Choice Theory*, Cambridge: Cambridge University Press.
Finley, M.I. (1973) *Democracy: Ancient and Modern*, London: Chatto and Windus.
——(1976) 'The freedom of the citizen in the Greek world', reprinted as Ch. 5 in M.I. Finley, *Economy and Society in Ancient Greece*, London: Chatto and Windus 1981.
——(1981) 'Politics', in M.I. Finley (ed.), *The Legacy of Greece*, Oxford: Oxford University Press, pp. 22–36.

Føllesdal, D. and Hilpinen, R. (1971) 'Deontic logic: an introduction', in R. Hilpinen (ed.), *Deontic Logic: Introductory and Systematic Readings*, Dordrecht: Reidel, pp. 1–35.

Goldman, A. (1972) 'Toward a theory of social power', *Philosophical Studies* 23, 221–68.

Goodin, R.E. (1986) 'Laundering preferences', in Elster and Hylland (eds, 1986), pp. 75–101.

Haavelmo, T. (1970) 'Some observations on welfare and economic growth', in W.A. Eltis, M. Scott and N. Wolfe (eds.), *Induction, Growth and Trade: Essays in Honour of Sir Roy Harrod*, Oxford: Oxford University Press, pp. 65–75.

Habermas, J. (1982) Diskursethik – notizen zu einem Begründingsprogram. Mimeographed.

Hammond, P. (1976) 'Why ethical measures need interpersonal comparisons', *Theory and Decision* 7, 263–74.

Hansson, B. (1970) 'An analysis of some deontic logics', *Nous* 3, 373–98.

Hirsch, F. (1976) *Social Limits to Growth*, Cambridge, Mass.: Harvard University Press.

Hirschman, A. (1982) *Shifting Involvements*, Princeton: Princeton University Press.

Hogarth, R.M. (1977) 'Methods for aggregating opinions', in H. Jungermann and G. de Zeeuw (eds.), *Decision Making and Change in Human Affairs*, Dordrecht: Reidel, pp. 231–56.

Janis, I. (1972) *Victims of Group-Think*, Boston: Houghton Mifflin.

Kant, I. (1795) *Perpetual Peace*, in H. Reiss (ed.), *Kant's Political Writings*, Cambridge: Cambridge University Press.

Kelly, J. (1978) *Arrow Impossibility Theorems*, New York: Academic Press.

Kolm, S.-C. (1977) *La transition socialiste*, Paris: Editions du Cerf.

——(1981a) 'Altruismes et efficacités', *Social Science Information* 20, 293–354.

——(1981b) 'Efficacité et altruisme', *Revue Economique* 32, 5–31.

Lehrer, K. (1978) 'Consensus and comparison. A theory of social rationality', in C.A. Hooker, J.J. Leach and E.F. McClennen (eds.), *Foundations and Applications of Decision Theory*. Vol. 1: *Theoretical Foundations*, Dordrecht: Reidel, pp. 283–310.

Lipsey, R.G. and Lancaster, K. (1956–7) 'The general theory of the second-best', *Review of Economic Studies* 24, 11–32.

Lively, J. (1975) *Democracy*. Oxford: Blackwell.

Lyons, D. (1965) *Forms and Limits of Utilitarianism*, Oxford, Oxford University Press.

Margalit, A. (1983) 'Ideals and second bests', in S. Fox (ed.), *Philosophy for Education*, Jerusalem: Van Leer Foundation, pp. 77–90.

Midgaard, K. (1980) 'On the significance of language and a richer concept of rationality', in L. Lewin and E. Vedung (eds.), *Politics as Rational Action*, Dordrecht: Reidel, pp. 83–97.

Mill, J.S. (1859) 'Bentham', in J.S. Mill, *Utilitarianism*, London: Fontana Books (1962), pp. 78–125.

Niebuhr, R. (1932) *Moral Man and Immoral Society*, New York: Scribner's.

Parfit, D. (1981) 'Prudence, morality and the prisoner's dilemma', *Proceedings of the British Academy*, Oxford: Oxford University Press.

Pateman, C. (1970) *Participation and Democratic Theory*, Cambridge: Cambridge University Press.

Pattanaik, P. (1978) *Strategy and Group Choice*, Amsterdam: North-Holland.

Rawls, J. (1971) *A Theory of Justice*, Cambridge, Mass.: Harvard University Press.

Riker, W. and Ordeshook, P.C. (1973) *An Introduction to Positive Political Theory*, Englewood Cliffs, N.J.: Prentice Hall.

Runciman, W.G. and Sen, A. (1965) 'Games, justice and the general will', *Mind* 74, 554–62.

Ryan, A. (1972) 'Two concepts of politics and democracy: James and John Stuart Mill', in M. Fleisher (ed.), *Machiavelli and the Nature of Political Thought*, London: Croom Helm, pp. 76–113.

Samuelson, P. (1950) 'The evaluation of real national income', *Oxford Economic Papers* 2, 1–29.

Schelling, T.C. (1980) 'The intimate contest for self-command', *The Public Interest* 60, 94–118.

Schotter, A. (1981) *The Economic Theory of Social Institutions*, Cambridge: Cambridge University Press.

Schumpeter, J. (1939) *Business Cycles*, New York: McGraw-Hill.

——(1961) *Capitalism, Socialism and Democracy*, London: Allen and Unwin.

Sen, A.K. (1970) *Collective Choice and Social Welfare*, San Francisco: Holden-Day.

——(1976) 'Liberty, unanimity and rights', *Economica* 43, 217–45.

——(1979) 'Utilitarianism and welfarism', *Journal of Philosophy* 76, 463–88.

Sobel, J.H. (1967) ' "Everyone", consequences and generalization arguments', *Inquiry* 10, 373–404.

Smullyan, R. (1980) *This Book Needs No Title*, Englewood Cliffs, N.J.: Prentice Hall.

Tocqueville, A. de (1969) *Democracy in America*, New York: Anchor Books.

Tversky, A. (1981) 'Choice, preference and welfare: some psychological observations', paper presented at a colloquium on 'Foundations of social choice theory', Ustaoset (Norway).

Williams, B.A.O. (1973) 'A critique of utilitarianism', in J.J.C. Smart and B.A.O. Williams, *Utilitarianism: For and Against*, Cambridge: Cambridge University Press, pp. 77–150.

Veyne, P. (1976) *Le pain et le cirque*, Paris: Seuil.

Zeldin, T. (1973) *France 1848–1945*, Vol. 1, Oxford: Oxford University Press.

10

Deliberation and Democratic Legitimacy

Joshua Cohen

In this essay I explore the ideal of a 'deliberative democracy'.[1] By a deliberative democracy I shall mean, roughly, an association whose affairs are governed by the public deliberation of its members. I propose an account of the value of such an association that treats democracy itself as a fundamental political ideal and not simply as a derivative ideal that can be explained in terms of the values of fairness or equality of respect.

The essay is in three sections. In section I, I focus on Rawls's discussion of democracy and use that discussion both to introduce certain features of a deliberative democracy, and to raise some doubts about whether their importance is naturally explained in terms of the notion of a fair system of social cooperation. In section II, I develop an account of deliberative democracy in terms of the notion of an *ideal deliberative procedure*. The characterization of that procedure provides an abstract model of deliberation which links the intuitive ideal of democratic association to a more substantive view of deliberative democracy. Three features of the ideal deliberative procedure figure prominently in the essay. First, it helps to account for some familiar judgements about collective decision-making, in particular about the ways that collective decision-making ought to be different from bargaining, contracting and other market-type interactions, both in its explicit attention to considerations of the common advantage and in the ways that that attention helps to form the aims of the participants. Second, it

accounts for the common view that the notion of democratic association is tied to notions of autonomy and the common good. Third, the ideal deliberative procedure provides a distinctive structure for addressing institutional questions. And in section III of the paper I rely on that distinctive structure in responding to four objections to the account of deliberative democracy.

I

The ideal of deliberative democracy is a familiar ideal. Aspects of it have been highlighted in recent discussion of the role of republican conceptions of self-government in shaping the American constitutional tradition and contemporary public law.[2] It is represented as well in radical democratic and socialist criticisms of the politics of advanced industrial societies.[3] And some of its central features are highlighted in Rawls's account of democratic politics in a just society, particularly in those parts of his account that seek to incorporate the 'liberty of the ancients' and to respond to radical democrats and socialists who argue that 'the basic liberties may prove to be merely formal'. In the discussion that follows I shall first say something about Rawls's remarks on three such features, and then consider his explanation of them.[4]

First, in a well-ordered democracy, political debate is organized around alternative conceptions of the public good. So an ideal pluralist scheme, in which democratic politics consists of fair bargaining among groups each of which pursues its particular or sectional interest, is unsuited

Originally published in *The Good Polity*, ed. Alan Hamlin and Philip Pettit (Blackwell Publishers, 1989), 17–34. Reprinted by permission of the publisher.

to a just society (Rawls 1971, pp. 360–1).[5] Citizens and parties operating in the political arena ought not to 'take a narrow or group-interested standpoint' (p. 360). And parties should only be responsive to demands that are 'argued for openly by reference to a conception of the public good' (pp. 226, 472). Public explanations and justifications of laws and policies are to be cast in terms of conceptions of the common good (conceptions that, on Rawls's view, must be consistent with the two principles of justice), and public deliberation should aim to work out the details of such conceptions and to apply them to particular issues of public policy (p. 362).

Second, the ideal of democratic order has egalitarian implications that must be satisfied in ways that are manifest to citizens. The reason is that in a just society political opportunities and powers must be independent of economic or social position – the political liberties must have a fair value[6] – and the fact that they are independent must be more or less evident to citizens. Ensuring this manifestly fair value might, for example, require public funding of political parties and restrictions on private political spending, as well as progressive tax measures that serve to limit inequalities of wealth and to ensure that the political agenda is not controlled by the interests of economically and socially dominant groups (Rawls 1971, pp. 225–6, 277–8; 1982, pp. 42–3). In principle, these distributional requirements might be more stringently egalitarian than those fixed by the difference principle (1982, p. 43).[7] This is so in part because the main point of these measures is not simply to ensure that democratic politics proceeds under fair conditions, nor only to encourage just legislation, but also to ensure that the equality of citizens is manifest and to declare a commitment to that equality 'as the public intention' (1971, p. 233).

Third, democratic politics should be ordered in ways that provide a basis for self-respect, that encourage the development of a sense of political competence, and that contribute to the formation of a sense of justice;[8] it should fix 'the foundations for civic friendship and [shape] the ethos of political culture' (Rawls 1971, p. 234). Thus the importance of democratic order is not confined to its role in obstructing the class legislation that can be expected from systems in which groups are effectively excluded from the channels of political representation and bargaining. In addition, democratic politics should also shape the ways in which the members of the society understand themselves and their own legitimate interests.

When properly conducted, then, democratic politics involves *public deliberation focused on the common good*, requires some form of *manifest equality* among citizens, and *shapes the identity and interests* of citizens in ways that contribute to the formation of a public conception of common good. How does the ideal of a fair system of social co-operation provide a way to account for the attractiveness and importance of these three features of the deliberative democratic ideal? Rawls suggests a formal and an informal line of argument. The formal argument is that parties in the original position would choose the principle of participation[9] with the proviso that the political liberties have their fair value. The three conditions are important because they must be satisfied if constitutional arrangements are to ensure participation rights, guarantee a fair value to those rights, and plausibly produce legislation that encourages a fair distribution according to the difference principle.

Rawls also suggests an informal argument for the ordering of political institutions, and I shall focus on this informal argument here:

> Justice as fairness begins with the idea that where common principles are necessary and to everyone's advantage, they are to be worked out from the viewpoint of a suitably defined initial situation of equality in which each person is fairly represented. The principle of participation transfers this notion from the original position to the constitution . . . [thus] preserv[ing] the equal representation of the original position to the degree that this is feasible. (Rawls 1971, pp. 221–2)10

Or, as he puts it elsewhere: 'The idea [of the fair value of political liberty] is to incorporate into the basic structure of society an effective political procedure which *mirrors* in that structure the fair representation of persons achieved by the original position' (1982, p. 45; emphasis added). The suggestion is that, since we accept the intuitive ideal of a fair system of co-operation, we should want our political institutions themselves to conform, in so far as it is feasible, to the requirement that terms of association be worked out under fair conditions. And so we arrive directly at the requirement of equal liberties with fair value, rather than arriving at it indirectly, through a hypothetical choice of that requirement under fair conditions. In this informal argument, the original position serves as an *abstract model* of what fair conditions are, and of what we should strive to mirror in our political institutions, rather than as an initial-choice situation in which regulative principles for those institutions are selected.

I think that Rawls is right in wanting to accommodate the three conditions. What I find less plausible is that the three conditions are natural consequences of the ideal of fairness. Taking the notion of fairness as fundamental, and aiming (as in the informal argument) to model political arrangements on the original position, it is not clear why, for example, political debate ought to be focused on the common good, or why the manifest equality of citizens is an important feature of a democratic association. The pluralist conception of democratic politics as a system of bargaining with fair representation for all groups seems an equally good mirror of the ideal of fairness.

The response to this objection is clear enough: the connection between the ideal of fairness and the three features of democratic politics depends on psychological and sociological assumptions. Those features do not follow directly from the ideal of a fair system of co-operation, or from that ideal as it is modelled in the original position. Rather, we arrive at them when we consider what is required to preserve fair arrangements and to achieve fair outcomes. For example, public political debate should be conducted in terms of considerations of the common good because we cannot expect outcomes that advance the common good unless people are looking for them. Even an ideal pluralist scheme, with equal bargaining power and no barriers to entry, cannot reasonably be expected to advance the common good as defined by the difference principle (1971, p. 360).

But this is, I think, too indirect and instrumental an argument for the three conditions. Like utilitarian defences of liberty, it rests on a series of highly speculative sociological and psychological judgements. I want to suggest that the reason why the three are attractive is not that an order with, for example, no explicit deliberation about the common good and no manifest equality would be unfair (though of course it might be). Instead it is that they comprise elements of an independent and expressly political ideal that is focused in the first instance[11] on the appropriate conduct of public affairs – on, that is, the appropriate ways of arriving at collective decisions. And to understand that ideal we ought not to proceed by seeking to 'mirror' ideal fairness in the fairness of political arrangements, but instead to proceed by seeking to mirror a system of ideal deliberation in social and political institutions. I want now to turn to this alternative.

II[12]

The notion of a deliberative democracy is rooted in the intuitive ideal of a democratic association in which the justification of the terms and conditions of association proceeds through public argument and reasoning among equal citizens. Citizens in such an order share a commitment to the resolution of problems of collective choice through public reasoning, and regard their basic institutions as legitimate in so far as they establish the framework for free public deliberation. To elaborate this ideal, I begin with a more explicit account of the ideal itself, presenting what I shall call the 'formal conception' of deliberative democracy. Proceeding from this formal conception, I pursue a more substantive account of deliberative democracy by presenting an account of an *ideal deliberative procedure* that captures the notion of justification through public argument and reasoning among equal citizens, and serves in turn as a model for deliberative institutions.

The formal conception of a deliberative democracy has five main features:

D1 A deliberative democracy is an ongoing and independent association, whose members expect it to continue into the indefinite future.

D2 The members of the association share (and it is common knowledge that they share) the view that the appropriate terms of association provide a framework for or are the results of their deliberation. They share, that is, a commitment to co-ordinating their activities within institutions that make deliberation possible and according to norms that they arrive at through their deliberation. For them, free deliberation among equals is the basis of legitimacy.

D3 A deliberative democracy is a pluralistic association. The members have diverse preferences, convictions and ideals concerning the conduct of their own lives. While sharing a commitment to the deliberative resolution of problems of collective choice (D2), they also have divergent aims, and do not think that some particular set of preferences, convictions or ideals is mandatory.

D4 Because the members of a democratic association regard deliberative procedures as the source of *legitimacy*, it is important to them that the terms of their association not merely *be* the results of their deliberation, but also be *manifest* to them as such.[13] They prefer institutions in which the connections between deliberation and outcomes are evident to ones in which the connections are less clear.

D5 The members recognize one another as having deliberative capacities, i.e. the capacities required for entering into a public exchange of reasons and for acting on the result of such public reasoning.

A theory of deliberative democracy aims to give substance to this formal ideal by characterizing the conditions that should obtain if the social order is to be manifestly regulated by deliberative forms of collective choice. I propose to sketch a view of this sort by considering an ideal scheme of deliberation, which I shall call the 'ideal deliberative procedure'. The aim in sketching this procedure is to give an explicit statement of the conditions for deliberative decision-making that are suited to the formal conception, and thereby to highlight the properties that democratic institutions should embody, so far as possible. I should emphasize that the ideal deliberative procedure is meant to provide a model for institutions to mirror – in the first instance for the institutions in which collective choices are made and social outcomes publicly justified – and not to characterize an initial situation in which the terms of association themselves are chosen.[14]

Turning then to the ideal procedure, there are three general aspects of deliberation. There is a need to decide on an agenda, to propose alternative solutions to the problems on the agenda, supporting those solutions with reasons, and to conclude by settling on an alternative. A democratic conception can be represented in terms of the requirements that it sets on such a procedure. In particular, outcomes are democratically legitimate if and only if they could be the object of a free and reasoned agreement among equals. The ideal deliberative procedure is a procedure that captures this principle.[15]

I1 Ideal deliberation is *free* in that it satisfies two conditions. First, the participants regard themselves as bound only by the results of their deliberation and by the preconditions for that deliberation. Their consideration of proposals is not constrained by the authority of prior norms or requirements. Second, the participants suppose that they can act from the results, taking the fact that a certain decision is arrived at through their deliberation as a sufficient reason for complying with it.

I2 Deliberation is *reasoned* in that the parties to it are required to state their reasons for advancing proposals, supporting them or criticizing them. They give reasons with the expectation that those reasons (and not, for example, their power) will settle the fate of their proposal. In ideal deliberation, as Habermas puts it, 'no force except that of the better argument is exercised' (1975, p. 108). Reasons are offered with the aim of bringing others to accept the proposal, given their disparate ends (D3) and their commitment (D2) to settling the conditions of their association through free deliberation among equals. Proposals may be rejected because they are not defended with acceptable reasons, even if they could be so defended. The deliberative conception emphasizes that collective choices should be *made in a deliberative way*, and not only that those choices should have a desirable fit with the preferences of citizens.

I3 In ideal deliberation parties are both formally and substantively *equal*. They are formally equal in that the rules regulating the procedure do not single out individuals. Everyone with the deliberative capacities has equal standing at each stage of the deliberative process. Each can put issues on the agenda, propose solutions, and offer reasons in support of or in criticism of proposals. And each has an equal voice in the decision. The participants are substantively equal in that the existing distribution of power and resources does not shape their chances to contribute to deliberation, nor does that distribution play an authoritative role in their deliberation. The participants in the deliberative procedure do not regard themselves as bound by the existing system of rights, except in so far as that system establishes the framework of free deliberation among equals. Instead they regard that system as a potential object of their deliberative judgement.

I4 Finally, ideal deliberation aims to arrive at a rationally motivated *consensus* – to find reasons that are persuasive to all who are committed to acting on the results of a free and reasoned assessment of alternatives by equals. Even under ideal conditions there is no promise that consensual reasons will be forthcoming. If they are not, then deliberation concludes with voting, subject to some form of majority rule.[16] The fact that it may so conclude does not, however, eliminate the distinction between deliberative forms of collective choice and forms that aggregate non-deliberative preferences. The institutional consequences are likely to be different in the two cases, and the results of voting among those who are committed to finding reasons that are persuasive to all are likely to differ from the results of an aggregation that proceeds in the absence of this commitment.

Drawing on this characterization of ideal deliberation, can we say anything more substantive about a deliberative democracy? What are the implications of a commitment to deliberative decisions for the terms of social association? In the remarks that follow I shall indicate the ways that this commitment carries with it a commitment to advance the common good and to respect individual autonomy.

Common Good and Autonomy

Consider first the notion of the common good. Since the aim of ideal deliberation is to secure agreement among all who are committed to free deliberation among equals, and the condition of pluralism obtains (D3), the focus of deliberation is on ways of advancing the aims of each party to it. While no one is indifferent to his/her own good, everyone also seeks to arrive at decisions that are acceptable to all who share the commitment to deliberation (D2). (As we shall see just below, taking that commitment seriously is likely to require a willingness to revise one's understanding of one's own preferences and convictions.) Thus the characterization of an ideal deliberative procedure links the formal notion of deliberative democracy with the more substantive ideal of a democratic association in which public debate is focused on the common good of the members.

Of course, talk about the common good is one thing; sincere efforts to advance it are another. While public deliberation may be organized around appeals to the common good, is there any reason to think that even ideal deliberation would not consist in efforts to disguise personal or class advantage as the common advantage? There are two responses to this question. The first is that in my account of the formal idea of a deliberative democracy, I stipulated (D2) that the members of the association are committed to resolving their differences through deliberation, and thus to providing reasons that they sincerely expect to be persuasive to others who share that commitment. In short, this stipulation rules out the problem. Presumably, however, the objection is best understood as directed against the plausibility of realizing a deliberative procedure that conforms to the ideal, and thus is not answerable through stipulation.

The second response, then, rests on a claim about the effects of deliberation on the motivations of deliberators.[17] A consequence of the reasonableness of the deliberative procedure (I2) together with the condition of pluralism (D3) is that the mere fact of having a preference, conviction or ideal does not by itself provide a reason in support of a proposal. While I may take my preferences as a sufficient reason for advancing a proposal, deliberation under conditions of pluralism requires that I find reasons that make the proposal acceptable to others who cannot be expected to regard my preferences as sufficient reasons for agreeing. The motivational thesis is that the need to advance reasons that persuade others will help to shape the motivations that people bring to the deliberative procedure in two ways. First, the practice of presenting reasons

Joshua Cohen

will contribute to the formation of a commitment to the deliberative resolution of political questions (D2). Given that commitment, the likelihood of a sincere representation of preferences and convictions should increase, while the likelihood of their strategic misrepresentation declines. Second, it will shape the content of preferences and convictions as well. Assuming a commitment to deliberative justification, the discovery that I can offer no persuasive reasons on behalf of a proposal of mine may transform the preferences that motivate the proposal. Aims that I recognize to be inconsistent with the requirements of deliberative agreement may tend to lose their force, at least when I expect others to be proceeding in reasonable ways and expect the outcome of deliberation to regulate subsequent action.

Consider, for example, the desire to be wealthier come what may. I cannot appeal to this desire itself in defending policies. The motivational claim is the need to find an independent justification that does not appeal to this desire and will tend to shape it into, for example, a desire to have a level of wealth that is consistent with a level that others (i.e. equal citizens) find acceptable. I am of course assuming that the deliberation is known to be regulative, and that the wealth cannot be protected through wholly non-deliberative means.

Deliberation, then, focuses debate on the common good. And the relevant conceptions of the common good are not comprised simply of interests and preferences that are antecedent to deliberation. Instead, the interests, aims and ideals that comprise the common good are those that survive deliberation, interests that, on public reflection, we think it legitimate to appeal to in making claims on social resources. Thus the first and third of the features of deliberative democracy that I mentioned in the discussion of Rawls (pp. 143f. above) comprise central elements in the deliberative conception.

The ideal deliberative scheme also indicates the importance of autonomy in a deliberative democracy. In particular, it is responsive to two main threats to autonomy. As a general matter, actions fail to be autonomous if the preferences on which an agent acts are, roughly, given by the circumstances, and not determined by the agent. There are two paradigm cases of 'external' determination. The first is what Elster (1982) has called 'adaptive preferences'.[18] These are preferences that shift with changes in the circumstances of the agent without any deliberate contribution

by the agent to that shift. This is true, for example, of the political preferences of instinctive centrists who move to the median position in the political distribution, wherever it happens to be. The second I shall call 'accommodationist preferences'. While they are deliberately formed, accommodationist preferences represent psychological adjustments to conditions of subordination in which individuals are not recognized as having the capacity for self-government. Consider Stoic slaves, who deliberately shape their desires to match their powers, with a view to minimizing frustration. Since the existing relations of power make slavery the only possibility, they cultivate desires to be slaves, and then act on those desires. While their motives are deliberately formed, and they act on their desires, the Stoic slaves do not act autonomously when they seek to be good slaves. The absence of alternatives and consequent denial of scope for the deliberative capacities that defines the condition of slaves supports the conclusion that their desires result from their circumstances, even though those circumstances shape the desires of the Stoic slaves through their deliberation.

There are then at least two dimensions of autonomy. The phenomenon of adaptive preferences underlines the importance of conditions that permit and encourage the deliberative formation of preferences; the phenomenon of accommodationist preferences indicates the need for favourable conditions for the exercise of the deliberative capacities. Both concerns are met when institutions for collective decision-making are modelled on the ideal deliberative procedure. Relations of power and subordination are neutralized (I1, I3, I4), and each is recognized as having the deliberative capacities (D5), thus addressing the problem of accommodationist preferences. Further, the requirement of reasonableness discourages adaptive preferences (I2). While preferences are 'formed' by the deliberative procedure, this type of preference formation is consistent with autonomy, since preferences that are shaped by public deliberation are not simply given by external circumstances. Instead they are the result of 'the power of reason as applied through public discussion'.[19]

Beginning, then, from the formal ideal of a deliberative democracy, we arrive at the more substantive ideal of an association that is regulated by deliberation aimed at the common good and that respects the autonomy of the members.

And so, in seeking to embody the ideal deliberative procedure in institutions, we seek, *inter alia*, to design institutions that focus political debate on the common good, that shape the identity and interests of citizens in ways that contribute to an attachment to the common good, and that provide the favourable conditions for the exercise of deliberative powers that are required for autonomy.

III

I want now to shift the focus. While I shall continue to pursue the relationship between the ideal deliberative procedure and more substantive issues about deliberative democratic association, I want to do so by considering four natural objections to the conception I have been discussing, objections to that conception for being sectarian, incoherent, unjust and irrelevant. My aim is not to provide a detailed response to the objections, but to clarify the conception of deliberative democracy by sketching the lines along which a response should proceed. Before turning to the objections, I enter two remarks about what follows.

First, as I indicated earlier, a central aim in the deliberative conception is to specify the institutional preconditions for deliberative decision-making. The role of the ideal deliberative procedure is to provide an abstract characterization of the important properties of deliberative institutions. The role of the ideal deliberative procedure is thus different from the role of an ideal social contract. The ideal deliberative procedure provides a model for institutions, a model that they should mirror, so far as possible. It is not a choice situation in which institutional principles are selected. The key point about the institutional reflection is that it should *make deliberation possible*. Institutions in a deliberative democracy do not serve simply to implement the results of deliberation, as though free deliberation could proceed in the absence of appropriate institutions. Neither the commitment to nor the capacity for arriving at deliberative decisions is something that we can simply assume to obtain independent from the proper ordering of institutions. The institutions themselves must provide the framework for the formation of the will; they determine whether there is equality, whether deliberation is free and reasoned, whether there is autonomy, and so on.

Second, I shall be focusing here on some requirements on 'public' institutions that reflect the ideal of deliberative resolution. But there is of course no reason to expect as a general matter that the preconditions for deliberation will respect familiar institutional boundaries between 'private' and 'public' and will all pertain to the public arena. For example, inequalities of wealth, or the absence of institutional measures designed to redress the consequences of those inequalities, can serve to undermine the equality required in deliberative arenas themselves. And so a more complete treatment would need to address a wider range of institutional issues (see Cohen and Rogers 1983, chs 3, 6; Cohen 1988).

Sectarianism

The first objection is that the ideal of deliberative democracy is objectionably sectarian because it depends on a particular view of the good life – an ideal of active citizenship. What makes it sectarian is not the specific ideal on which it depends, but the (alleged) fact that it depends on some specific conception at all. I do not think that the conception of deliberative democracy suffers from the alleged difficulty. In explaining why not, I shall put to the side current controversy about the thesis that sectarianism is avoidable and objectionable, and assume that it is both.[20]

Views of the good figure in political conceptions in at least two ways. First, the *justification* of some conceptions appeals to a notion of the human good. Aristotelian views, for example, endorse the claim that the exercise of the deliberative capacities is a fundamental component of a good human life, and conclude that a political association ought to be organized to encourage the realization of those capacities by its members. A second way in which conceptions of the good enter is that the *stability* of a society may require widespread allegiance to a specific conception of the good, even though its institutions can be justified without appeal to that conception. For example, a social order that can be justified without reference to ideals of national allegiance may none the less require widespread endorsement of the ideal of patriotic devotion for its stability.

A political conception is objectionably sectarian only if its *justification* depends on a particular view of the human good, and not simply because its stability is contingent on widespread agreement on the value of certain activities and aspirations. For this reason the democratic conception is not sectarian. It is organized around a view of political justification – that justification proceeds through free deliberation among equal citizens – and not a conception of the proper conduct of life. So, while it is plausible that the stability of a deliberative democracy depends on encouraging the ideal of active citizenship, this dependence does not suffice to show that it is objectionably sectarian.

Incoherence

Consider next the putative incoherence of the ideal. We find this charge in an important tradition of argument, including Schumpeter's *Capitalism, Socialism, and Democracy* and, more recently, William Riker's work on social choice and democracy. I want here to say a word about the latter, focusing on just one reason that Riker gives for thinking that the ideal of popular self-government is incoherent.[21]

Institutionalizing a deliberative procedure requires a decision rule short of consensus – for example, majority rule. But majority rule is globally unstable: as a general matter, there exists a majority-rule path leading from any element in the set of alternatives to any other element in the set. The majority, standing in for the people, wills everything and therefore wills nothing. Of course, while anything can be the result of majority decision, it is not true that everything will be the result. But, because majority rule is so unstable, the actual decision of the majority will not be determined by preferences themselves, since they do not constrain the outcome. Instead decisions will reflect the particular institutional constraints under which they are made. But these constraints are 'exogenous to the world of tastes and values' (Riker 1982, p. 190). So the ideal of popular self-government is incoherent because we are, so to speak, governed by the institutions, and not by ourselves.

I want to suggest one difficulty with this argument that highlights the structure of the deliberative conception. According to the argument I just sketched, outcomes in majority-rule institutions reflect 'exogenous' institutional constraints, and not underlying preferences. This suggests that we can identify the preferences and convictions that are relevant to collective choices apart from the

institutions through which they are formed and expressed. But that is just what the deliberative conception denies. On this conception, the relevant preferences and convictions are those that could be expressed in free deliberation, and not those that are prior to it. For this reason, popular self-government *premises* the existence of institutions that provide a framework for deliberation; these arrangements are not 'exogenous constraints' on the aggregation of preferences, but instead help to shape their content and the way that citizens choose to advance them. And, once the deliberative institutions are in place, and preferences, convictions and political actions are shaped by them, it is not clear that instability problems remain so severe as to support the conclusion that self-government is an empty and incoherent ideal.

Injustice

The third problem concerns injustice. I have been treating the ideal of democracy as the basic ideal for a political conception. But it might be argued that the ideal of democracy is not suited to the role of fundamental political ideal because its treatment of basic liberties is manifestly unacceptable. It makes those liberties dependent on judgements of majorities and thus endorses the democratic legitimacy of decisions that restrict the basic liberties of individuals. In responding to this objection I shall focus on the liberty of expression,[22] and shall begin by filling out a version of the objection which I put in the words of an imagined critic.[23]

'You embrace the ideal of a democratic order. The aim of a democratic order is to maximize the *power of the people* to secure its wants. To defend the liberty of expression you will argue that that power is diminished if the people lack the information required for exercising their will. Since expression provides information, you will conclude that abridgements of expression ought to be barred. The problem with your argument is that preventing restrictions on expression also restricts the power of the people, since the citizens may collectively prefer such restrictions. And so it is not at all clear as a general matter that the protection of expression will maximize popular power. So while you will, of course, not want to prevent everyone from speaking all the time, you cannot defend the claim that there is even a presumption in favour of the protection of expression. And this disregard for fundamental liberties is unacceptable.'

This objection has force against some conceptions on which democracy is a fundamental ideal, particularly those in which the value of expression turns exclusively on its role as a source of information about how best to advance popular ends. But it does not have any force against the deliberative conception, since the latter does not make the case for expression turn on its role in maximizing the power of the people to secure its wants. That case rests instead on a conception of collective choice, in particular on a view about how the 'wants' that are relevant to collective choice are formed and defined in the first place. The relevant preferences and convictions are those that arise from or are confirmed through deliberation. And a framework of free expression is required for the reasoned consideration of alternatives that comprises deliberation. The deliberative conception holds that free expression is required for *determining* what advances the common good, because what is good is fixed by public deliberation, and not prior to it. It is fixed by informed and autonomous judgements, involving the exercise of the deliberative capacities. So the ideal of deliberative democracy is not hostile to free expression; it rather presupposes such freedom.

But what about expression with no direct bearing on issues of public policy? Is the conception of deliberative democracy committed to treating all 'non-political expression' as second-class, and as meriting lesser protection? I do not think so. The deliberative conception construes politics as aiming in part at the formation of preferences and convictions, not just at their articulation and aggregation. Because of this emphasis on reasoning about preferences and convictions, and the bearing of expression with no political focus on such reasoning, the deliberative view draws no bright line between political speech and other sorts of expression. Forms of expression that do not address issues of policy may well bear on the formation of the interests, aims, and ideals that citizens bring to public deliberation. For this reason the deliberative conception supports protection for the full range of expression, regardless of the content of that expression.[24] It would violate the core of the ideal of free deliberation among equals to fix preferences and convictions in advance by restricting the content of expression,

or by barring access to expression, or by preventing the expression that is essential to having convictions at all. Thus the injustice objection fails because the liberties are not simply among the topics for deliberation; they help to comprise the framework that makes it possible.[25]

Irrelevance

The irrelevance objection is that the notion of public deliberation is irrelevant to modern political conditions.[26] This is the most important objection, but also the one about which it is hardest to say anything at the level of generality required by the present context. Here again I shall confine myself to one version of the objection, though one that I take to be representative.

The version that I want to consider starts from the assumption that a direct democracy with citizens gathering in legislative assemblies is the only way to institutionalize a deliberative procedure. Premising that, and recognizing that direct democracy is impossible under modern conditions, the objection concludes that we ought to be led to reject the ideal because it is not relevant to our circumstances.

The claim about the impossibility of direct democracy is plainly correct. But I see no merit in the claim that direct democracy is the uniquely suitable way to institutionalize the ideal procedure.[27] In fact, in the absence of a theory about the operations of democratic assemblies – a theory which cannot simply stipulate that ideal conditions obtain – there is no reason to be confident that a direct democracy would subject political questions to deliberative resolution, even if a direct democracy were a genuine institutional possibility.[28] In the absence of a realistic account of the functioning of citizen assemblies, we cannot simply assume that large gatherings with open-ended agendas will yield any deliberation at all, or that they will encourage participants to regard one another as equals in a free deliberative procedure. The appropriate ordering of deliberative institutions depends on issues of political psychology and political behaviour; it is not an immediate consequence of the deliberative ideal. So, far from being the only deliberative scheme, direct democracy may not even be a particularly good arrangement for deliberation. But, once we reject the idea that a direct democracy is the natural or necessary form of expression of the deliberative ideal, the straightforward argument for irrelevance no longer works. In saying how the ideal might be relevant, however, we come up against the problem I mentioned earlier. Lacking a good understanding of the workings of institutions, we are inevitably thrown back on more or less speculative judgements. What follows is some sketchy remarks on one issue that should be taken in this spirit.

At the heart of the institutionalization of the deliberative procedure is the existence of arenas in which citizens can propose issues for the political agenda and participate in debate about those issues. The existence of such arenas is a public good, and ought to be supported with public money. This is not because public support is the only way, or even the most efficient way, of ensuring the provision of such arenas. Instead, public provision expresses the basic commitment of a democratic order to the resolution of political questions through free deliberation among equals. The problem is to figure out how arenas might be organized to encourage such deliberation.

In considering that organization, there are two key points that I want to underscore. The first is that material inequalities are an important source of political inequalities. The second point – which is more speculative – is that deliberative arenas which are organized exclusively on local, sectional or issue-specific lines are unlikely to produce the open-ended deliberation required to institutionalize a deliberative procedure. Since these arenas bring together only a narrow range of interests, deliberation in them can be expected at best to produce coherent sectional interests, but no more comprehensive conception of the common good.

These two considerations together provide support for the view that political parties supported by public funds play an important role in making a deliberative democracy possible.[29] There are two reasons for this, corresponding to the two considerations I have just mentioned. In the first place, an important feature of organizations generally, and parties in particular, is that they provide a means through which individuals and groups who lack the 'natural' advantage of wealth can overcome the political disadvantages that follow on that lack. Thus they can help to overcome the inequalities in deliberative arenas that result from material inequality. Of course, to play this role, political organizations must them-

selves be freed from the dominance of private resources, and that independence must be manifest. Thus the need for public funding. Here we arrive back at the second point that I mentioned in the discussion of Rawls's view – that measures are needed to ensure manifest equality – though now as a way of displaying a shared commitment to deliberative decisions, and not simply as an expression of the commitment to fairness. Second, because parties are required to address a comprehensive range of political issues, they provide arenas in which debate is not restricted in the ways that it is in local, sectional or issue-specific organizations. They can provide the more open-ended arenas needed to form and articulate the conceptions of the common good that provide the focus of political debate in a deliberative democracy.

There is certainly no guarantee that parties will operate as I have just described. But this is not especially troubling, since there are no guarantees of anything in politics. The question is how we can best approximate the deliberative conception. And it is difficult to see how that is possible in the absence of strong parties, supported with public resources (though, of course, a wide range of other conditions are required as well).

IV

I have suggested that we take the notion of democratic association as a fundamental political ideal, and have elaborated that ideal by reference to an ideal deliberative procedure and the requirements for institutionalizing such a procedure. I have sketched a few of those requirements here. To show that the democratic ideal can play the role of fundamental organizing ideal, I should need to pursue the account of fundamental liberties and political organization in much greater detail and to address a wide range of other issues as well. Of course, the richer the requirements are for institutionalizing free public deliberation, the larger the range of issues that may need to be removed from the political agenda; that is, the larger the range of issues that form the background framework of public deliberation rather than its subject matter. And, the larger that range, the less there is to deliberate about. Whether that is good news or bad news, it is in any case a suitable place to conclude.

Notes

I have had countless discussions of the subject matter of this paper with Joel Rogers, and wish to thank him for his unfailingly sound and generous advice. For our joint treatment of the issues that I discuss here, see Cohen and Rogers (1983), ch. 6. The main differences between the treatment of issues here and the treatment in the book lies in the explicit account of the ideal deliberative procedure, the fuller treatment of the notions of autonomy and the common good, and the account of the connection of those notions with the ideal procedure. An earlier draft of this paper was presented to the Pacific Division Meetings of the American Philosophical Association. I would like to thank Loren Lomasky, Alan Hamlin and Philip Pettit for helpful comments on that draft.

1   I originally came across the term 'deliberative democracy' in Sunstein (1985). He cites (n. 26) an article by Bessette, which I have not consulted.

2   For some representative examples, see Sunstein (1984, 1985, 1986), Michelman (1986), Ackerman (1984, 1986).

3   I have in mind, in particular, criticisms which focus on the ways in which material inequalities and weak political parties restrict democracy by constraining public political debate or undermining the equality of the participants in that debate. For discussion of these criticisms, and of their connections with the ideal of democratic order, see Cohen and Rogers (1983), chs 3, 6; Unger (1987), ch. 5.

4   In the discussion that follows, I draw on Rawls (1971, esp. sections 36, 37, 43, 54; 1982).

5   This rejection is not particularly idiosyncratic. Sunstein, for example, argues (1984, 1985) that ideal pluralism has never been embraced as a political ideal in American public law.

6   Officially, the requirement of fair value is that 'everyone has a fair opportunity to hold public office and to influence the outcome of political decisions' (Rawls 1982, p. 42).

7   Whatever their stringency, these distributional requirements take priority over the difference principle, since the requirement of fair value is part of the principle of liberty; that is, the first principle of justice (Rawls 1982, pp. 41–2).

8   The importance of democratic politics in the account of the acquisition of the sense of justice is underscored in Rawls (1971), pp. 473–4.

9   The principle of participation states that 'all citizens are to have an equal right to take part in, and to determine the outcome of, the constitutional process that establishes the laws with which they are to comply' (Rawls 1971, p. 221).

10   I assume that the principle of participation should be understood here to include the requirement of the fair value of political liberty.

11   The reasons for the phrase 'in the first instance' are clarified below at pp. 146–7.

12   Since writing the first draft of this section of the paper, I have read Elster (1986a) and Manin (1987), which both present parallel conceptions. This is especially so with Elster's treatment of the psychology of public deliberation (pp. 112–13). I am indebted to Alan Hamlin for bringing the Elster article to my attention. The overlap is explained by the fact that Elster, Manin and I all draw on Habermas. See Habermas (1975, 1979, 1984). I have also found the discussion of the contractualist account of motivation in Scanlon (1982) very helpful.

13   For philosophical discussions of the importance of manifestness or publicity, see Kant (1983), pp. 135–9; Rawls (1971), p. 133 and section 29; Williams (1985), pp. 101–2, 200.

14   The distinction between the ideal procedure and an initial-choice situation will be important in the later discussion of motivation formation (see pp. 147–8) and institutions (p. 149).

15   There are of course norms and requirements on individuals that do not have deliberative justification. The conception of deliberative democracy is, in Rawls's term, a 'political conception', and not a comprehensive moral theory. On the distinction between political and comprehensive theories, see Rawls (1987), pp. 1–25.

16   For criticism of the reliance on an assumption of unanimity in deliberative views, see Manin (1987), pp. 359–61.

17   Note the parallel with Elster (1986a) indicated in note 12. See also the discussion in Habermas (1975), p. 108, about 'needs that can be communicatively shared', and Habermas (1979), ch. 2.

18   For an interesting discussion of autonomous preferences and political processes, see Sunstein (1986 pp. 1145–58; 1984, pp. 1699–700).

19   Whitney vs. California, 274 US 357 (1927).

20   For contrasting views on sectarianism, see Rawls (1987); Dworkin (1985), pt 3; MacIntyre (1981); Sandel (1982).

21   See Riker (1982); for discussion of Riker's view see Coleman and Ferejohn (1986); Cohen (1986).

22   For discussion of the connection between ideals of democracy and freedom of expression, see Meikeljohn (1948), Tribe (1978; 1985, ch. 2) and Ely (1980, pp. 93–4, 105–16). Freedom of expression is a special case that can perhaps be more straightforwardly accommodated by the democratic conception than liberties of conscience, or the liberties associated with privacy and personhood. I do think, however, that these other liberties can be given satisfactory treatment by the democratic conception, and would reject it if I did

not think so. The general idea would be to argue that other fundamental liberties must be protected if citizens are to be able to engage in and have equal standing in political deliberation without fear that such engagement puts them at risk for their convictions or personal choices. Whether this line of argument will work out on the details is a matter for treatment elsewhere.

23 This objection is suggested in Dworkin (1985), pp. 61–3. He cites the following passage from a letter of Madison's: 'And a people who mean to be their own Governors, must arm themselves with *the power which knowledge gives*' (emphasis added).

24 On the distinction between content-based and content-neutral abridgements, the complexities of drawing the distinction in particular cases, and the special reasons for hostility to content-based abridgements, see Tribe (1978), pp. 584–682; Stone (1987), pp. 46–118.

25 I am not suggesting that the deliberative view provides the only sound justification for the liberty of expression. My concern here is rather to show that the deliberative view is capable of accommodating it.

26 For an especially sharp statement of the irrelevance objection, see Schmitt (1985).

27 This view is sometimes associated with Rousseau, who is said to have conflated the notion of demo-cratic legitimacy with the institutional expression of that ideal in a direct democracy. For criticism of this interpretation, see Cohen (1986a).

28 Madison urges this point in the *Federalist Papers*. Objecting to a proposal advanced by Jefferson which would have regularly referred constitutional questions 'to the decision of the whole of society', Madison argues that this would increase 'the danger of disturbing the public tranquillity by interesting too strongly the public passions'. And 'it is the reason, alone, of the public that ought to control and regulate the government . . . [while] the passions ought to be controlled and regulated by the government'. I endorse the form of the objection, not its content. (*Federalist Papers* 1961, pp. 315–17.)

29 Here I draw on Cohen and Rogers (1983), pp. 154–7. The idea that parties are required to organize political choice and to provide a focus for public deliberation is one strand of arguments about 'responsible parties' in American political-science literature. My understanding of this view has been greatly aided by Perlman (1987), and, more generally, by the work of my colleague Walter Dean Burnham on the implications of party decline for democratic politics. See, for example, Burnham (1982).

References

Ackerman, B.A. 1984: The Storrs Lectures: Discovering the constitution. *Yale Law Journal*, 93: 1013–72.

——1986: Discovering the constitution. Unpublished manuscript.

Burnham, W.D. 1982: *The Current Crisis in American Politics*. Oxford: Oxford University Press.

Cohen, J. 1986a: Autonomy and democracy: reflections on Rousseau. *Philosophy and Public Affairs*, 15: 275–97.

——1986b: An epistemic conception of democracy. *Ethics*, 97: 26–38.

——1988: The material basis of deliberative democracy. *Social Philosophy and Policy*.

Cohen, J. and Rogers, J. 1983: *On Democracy*. Harmondsworth: Penguin.

Coleman, J. and Ferejohn, J. 1986: Democracy and social choice. *Ethics*, 97 (October): 6–25.

Dworkin, R. 1985: *A Matter of Principle*. Cambridge, Mass.: Harvard University Press.

Elster, J. 1982: Sour grapes. In A. Sen and B. Williams (eds), *Utilitarianism and Beyond*, Cambridge: Cambridge University Press, 219–38.

——1986: The market and the forum: three varieties of political theory. In J. Elster and A. Hylland (eds), *The Foundations of Social Choice Theory*. Cambridge: Cambridge University Press, 103–32.

Ely, J.H. 1980: *Democracy and Distrust: a theory of judicial review*. Cambridge, Mass.: Harvard University Press.

Federalist Papers 1961: ed. C. Rossiter. New York: New American Library.

Habermas, J. 1975: *The Legitimation Crisis of Late Capitalism*, tr. T. McCarthy. Boston, Mass.: Beacon Press; London: Heinemann.

——1979: *Communication and the Evolution of Society*, tr. T. McCarthy. Boston, Mass.: Beacon Press.

——1984: *The Theory of Communicative Action*, vol. I, tr. T. McCarthy. Boston, Mass.: Beacon Press.

Kant, I., tr. T. Humphrey 1983: To perpetual peace: a philosophical sketch. In *Perpetual Peace and other Essays*, Indianapolis: Hackett.

MacIntyre, A. 1981: *After Virtue*. Notre Dame, Ind.: University of Notre Dame Press.

Manin, B. 1987: On legitimacy and political deliberation. *Political Theory*, 15: 338–68.

Meiklejohn, A. 1948: *Free Speech and its Relation of Self-Government*. New York: Harper and Row.

Michelman, F.I. 1986: The Supreme Court, 1985 Term – Foreword: Traces of Self-Government. *Harvard Law Review*, 100: 4–77.

Perlman, L. 1987: Parties, democracy and consent. Unpublished.

Rawls, J. 1971: *A Theory of Justice*. Cambridge, Mass.: Harvard University Press; also Oxford: Clarendon Press (1972).

——1982: The basic liberties and their priority. *Tanner Lectures on Human Values*, Salt Lake City: University of Utah Press, vol. III.

——1987: The idea of an overlapping consensus. *Oxford Journal of Legal Studies*, 7: 1–25.

Riker, W. 1982: *Liberalism against Populism: a confrontation between the theory of democracy and the theory of social choice*. San Francisco: W.H. Freeman.

Sandel, M. 1982: *Liberalism and the Limits of Justice*. Cambridge: Cambridge University Press.

Scanlon, T.M. 1982: Contractualism and utilitarianism. In A.K. Sen and B. Williams (eds), *Utilitarianism and Beyond*, Cambridge: Cambridge University Press, 103–28.

Schmitt, C. 1985: *The Crisis of Parliamentary Democracy*, tr. E. Kennedy. Cambridge, Mass.: MIT Press.

Schumpeter, J.A. 1954: *Capitalism, Socialism and Democracy*, London: Unwin.

Stone, G. 1987: Content-neutral restrictions. *University of Chicago Law Review*, 54: 46–118.

Sunstein, C. 1984: Naked preferences and the constitution. *Columbia Law Review*, 84: 1689–732.

——1985: Interest groups in American public law. *Stanford Law Review*, 38: 29–87.

——1986: Legal interference with private preferences. *University of Chicago Law Review*, 53: 1129–84.

Tribe, L. 1978: *American Constitutional Law*. Mineola NY: Foundation Press.

——1985: *Constitutional Choices*. Cambridge, Mass.: Harvard University Press.

Unger, R. 1987: *False Necessity*. Cambridge: Cambridge University Press.

Williams, B. 1985: *Ethics and the Limits of Philosophy*. London: Fontana, Collins; Cambridge, Mass.: Harvard University Press.

11

Preferences and Politics

Cass R. Sunstein

The drafting of the United States Constitution, it is often said, signaled a rejection of conceptions of politics founded on classical ideals in favor of a quite different modern view.[1] The precise terms of the alleged shift are not altogether clear, but it is possible to identify the most prominent strands. The classical conception assumes a relatively homogeneous people and prizes active participation by the polity's citizenry. In the classical conception, the polity is self-consciously concerned with the character of the citizens; it seeks to inculcate in them and to profit from a commitment to the public good. Plato said that politics is the "art whose business it is to care for souls";[2] and under the classical conception, civic virtue, not private interest, is the wellspring of political behavior. Whether or not the state imposes a "comprehensive view"[3] on the nation, it relies relatively little on private rights to constrain government. The underlying vision of "republican" politics is one of frequent participation and deliberation in the service of decision, by the citizenry, about the sorts of values according to which the nation will operate.

In the modern account, by contrast, government is above all respectful of the divergent conceptions of the good held by its many constituents. People are taken as they are, not as they might be. Modern government has no concern with souls. Although electoral processes are ensured, no special premium is placed on citizen participation. Self-interest, not virtue, is understood to be the usual motivating force of political behavior. Politics is typically, if not always, an effort to aggregate private interests. It is surrounded by checks, in the form of rights, protecting private liberty and private property from public intrusion.

In this system, the goal of the polity is quite modest: the creation of the basic ground rules under which people can satisfy their desires and go about their private affairs. Much of this is famously captured in *The Federalist* No. 10, in which Madison redescribed the so-called republican problem of the corruption of virtue as the so-called liberal problem of the control of factions, which, as Madison had it, were inevitable if freedom was to be preserved.

In fact, the conventional division between the American founders and their classical predecessors is far too crude. The founders attempted to create a deliberative democracy, one in which the institutions of representation, checks and balances, and federalism would ensure a deliberative process among political equals rather than an aggregation of interests.[4] But respect for private preferences, rather than collective deliberation about public values or the good life, does seem to be a distinguishing feature of American constitutionalism. Indeed, the view that government should refuse to evaluate privately held beliefs about individual welfare, which are said to be irreducibly "subjective," links a wide range of views about both governmental structure and individual rights.

In this article I want to explore the question whether a contemporary democracy might not

Originally published in *Philosophy and Public Affairs*, 20 (1991), 3–34. Copyright © by Princeton University Press. Reprinted by permission of Princeton University Press.

sometimes override the private preferences and beliefs of its citizens, not in spite of its salutary liberalism but because of it. It is one thing to affirm competing conceptions of the good; it is quite another to suggest that political outcomes must generally be justified by, or even should always respect, private preferences. A large part of my focus here is on the phenomenon of endogenous preferences. By this term I mean to indicate that preferences are not fixed and stable, but are instead adaptive to a wide range of factors – including the context in which the preference is expressed, the existing legal rules, past consumption choices, and culture in general. The phenomenon of endogenous preferences casts doubt on the notion that a democratic government ought to respect private desires and beliefs in all or almost all contexts.[5] It bears on a number of particular problems as well, including the rationale for and extent of the constitutional protection accorded to speech; proportional representation and checks and balances; and the reasons for and limits of governmental regulation of the arts, broadcasting, and the environment. I take up these issues at several points in this article.

The argument proceeds in several stages. In Section 1, I set forth some fairly conventional ideas about welfare and autonomy, in conjunction with the endogeneity of desires, in order to argue against the idea that government ought never or rarely to override private preferences. In Section 2, I contend that in three categories of cases, private preferences, as expressed in consumption choices, should be overridden. The first category involves what I call collective judgments, including considered beliefs, aspirations for social justice, and altruistic goals; the second involves preferences that have adapted to undue limitations in available opportunities or to unjust background conditions; the third points to intrapersonal collective action problems that, over a lifetime, impair personal welfare. In all of these cases, I suggest, a democracy should be free and is perhaps obliged to override private preferences. In Section 3, I make some remarks about the relevance of these claims to several current issues of constitutional controversy. These include proportional representation in politics and governmental regulation of the speech "market," including rights of access to the media, democratic controls on the electoral process, hate speech, and pornography.

1 Against Subjective Welfarism

Should a constitutional democracy take preferences as the basis for political choice? In contemporary politics, law, and economics, the usual answer is affirmative. Modern economics, for example, is dominated by a conception of welfare based on the satisfaction of existing preferences, as measured by willingness to pay; in politics and law, something called "paternalism" is disfavored in both the public and private realms.[6] But the idea that government ought to take preferences as the basis for political decisions is a quite modern one. This is not to say that the idea is without foundations. Partly a function of the perceived (though greatly overstated) difficulty of making interpersonal comparisons of utility, the idea is also a product of the epistemological difficulties of assessing preferences in terms of their true connection with individual welfare, and, perhaps most of all, the genuine political dangers of allowing government to engage in such inquiries.

The constellation of ideas that emerges from these considerations has been exceptionally influential. It embodies a conception of political justification that might be described as "subjective welfarism."[7] On this view, the government, even or perhaps especially in a democracy, should attend exclusively to conceptions of welfare as subjectively held by its citizens. A wide range of prominent approaches to politics turn out to be versions of subjective welfarism. These include, for example, certain forms of utilitarianism; the view that some version of Paretian efficiency ought to be treated as the foundational norm for political life; opposition to paternalism in public and private life; approaches to politics modeled on bargaining theory (rational or otherwise); and conceptions of politics that see the democratic process as an effort to aggregate individual preferences.

It is important to understand that subjective welfarism, thus defined, may or may not be accompanied by a broader notion that ethical and moral questions should generally be treated in welfarism or subjectivist terms. It is as a political conception, rather than an ethical one, that subjective welfarism underlies a wide range of approaches to public life, including ideas about institutional arrangements and individual or collective rights. What I want to argue here is that subjective welfarism, even as a political conception, is unsupportable by reference to principles of autonomy or welfare, the very ideas that are said to give rise to it.

The initial objection to the view that government should take preferences "as they are," or as the basis for political choice, is one of impossibility. Whether people have a preference for a commodity, a right, or anything else is in part a function of whether the government has allocated it to them in the first instance. There is no way to avoid the task of initially allocating an entitlement, and the decision to grant an entitlement to one person frequently makes that person value that entitlement more than if the right had been allocated to someone else. (It also makes other people value it less than they would otherwise.) Government must not only allocate rights to one person or another; it must also decide whether or not to make the right alienable through markets or otherwise. The initial allocation serves to reflect, to legitimate, and to reinforce social understandings about presumptive rights of ownership, and that allocation has an important causal connection to individual perceptions of the good or right in question.

For example, a decision to give employees a right to organize, farmers a right to be free from water pollution, or women a right not to be subjected to sexual harassment will have an impact on social attitudes toward labor organization, clean water, and sexual harassment. The allocation therefore has an effect on social attitudes toward the relevant rights and on their valuation by both current owners and would-be purchasers. And when preferences are a function of legal rules, the rules cannot be justified by reference to the preferences.[8] Moreover, the initial assignment creates the basic "reference state" from which values and judgments of fairness are subsequently made, and those judgments affect preferences and private willingness to pay.[9] Of course, a decision to make an entitlement alienable or inalienable (consider the right to vote or reproductive capacities) will have preference-shaping effects. Because of the preference-shaping effects of the rules of allocation, it is difficult to see how a government might even attempt to take preferences "as given" or as the basis for decisions in any global sense.

To some degree this concern might be put to one side. Surely there is a difference between a government that concerns itself self-consciously and on an ongoing basis with private preferences and a government that sets up the basic rules of property, contract, and tort, and then lets things turn out however they may. If this distinction can be sustained, disagreements about the relationship between politics and preferences turn on competing notions of autonomy or freedom on the one hand and welfare on the other. Subjective welfarism is founded on the claim that an approach that treats preferences as sovereign is most likely to promote both individual freedom, rightly conceived, and individual or social welfare.

It will be useful to begin with welfare. Even if one accepted a purely welfarist view, one might think that the process of promoting welfare should take place not by satisfying current preferences but by promoting those preferences and satisfying them to such an extent as is consonant with the best or highest conception of human happiness. This view is connected with older (and some current) forms of utilitarianism; it also has roots in Aristotle.[10] Here one does not take existing preferences as given, and one does not put all preferences on the same plane. A criterion of welfare remains the ultimate one, but the system is not focused solely on preference satisfaction, since it insists that welfare and preference satisfaction are entirely different things.[11]

A central point here is that preferences are shifting and endogenous rather than exogenous, and as a result are a function of current information, consumption patterns, legal rules, and general social pressures. An effort to identify welfare with preference satisfaction would be easier to understand if preferences were rigidly fixed at some early age, or if learning were impossible; if this were so, democratic efforts to reflect on, change, or select preferences would breed only frustration. But because preferences are shifting and endogenous, and because the satisfaction of existing preferences might lead to unhappy or deprived lives, a democracy that treats all preferences as fixed will lose important opportunities for welfare gains.

With respect to welfare, then, the problem posed by the endogeneity of preferences is not the origin of desires but their malleability. At least if the relevant cases can be confidently identified in advance, and if collective action can be justified by reference to particular good reasons, the argument for democratic interference will be quite powerful. Respect for preferences that have resulted from unjust background conditions and that will lead to human deprivation or misery hardly appears the proper course for a liberal democracy.[12]

For example, legal rules prohibiting or discouraging addictive behavior may have significant advantages in terms of welfare. Regulation of heroin or cigarettes (at least if the regulation can be made effective) might well increase aggregate social welfare, by decreasing harmful behavior, removing the secondary effects of those harms, and producing more healthful and satisfying lives. Similarly, governmental action relating to the environment, broadcasting, or culture – encouraging or requiring, for example, protection of beautiful areas, broadcasting about public issues, high-quality programs, or public support of artistic achievement – may in the end generate (or, better, prevent obstacles to the generation of) new preferences, providing increased satisfaction and in the end producing considerable welfare gains. The same may well be true of antidiscrimination measures, which affect the desires and attitudes of discriminators and victims alike. A system that takes existing private preferences as the basis for political choice will sacrifice important opportunities for social improvement on welfarist criteria. This point was a crucial one in the early stages of utilitarian thought; it has been lost more recently with the shift from older forms of welfarism to the idea of "revealed preferences."

Moreover, the satisfaction of private preferences, whatever their content and origins, does not respond to a persuasive conception of liberty or autonomy. The notion of autonomy should refer instead to decisions reached with a full and vivid awareness of available opportunities, with reference to all relevant information, and without illegitimate or excessive constraints on the process of preference formation. When these conditions are not met, decisions should be described as unfree or nonautonomous; for this reason it is most difficult to identify autonomy with preference satisfaction. If preferences are a product of available information, existing consumption patterns, social pressures, and governmental rules, it seems odd to suggest that individual freedom lies exclusively or by definition in preference satisfaction, or that current preferences should, on grounds of autonomy, be treated as the basis for settling political issues. It seems even odder to suggest that all preferences should be treated equally, independently of their basis and consequences, or of the reasons offered in their support.

For purposes of autonomy, then, governmental interference with existing desires may be justified because of problems in the origins of those desires. Welfare-based arguments that invoke endogeneity tend to emphasize the malleability of preferences after they are formed; arguments based on autonomy stress what happens before the preferences have been created, that is, the conditions that gave rise to them. Because of this difference, the two arguments will operate along different tracks; and in some cases autonomy-based arguments will lead to conclusions different from those that would emerge from arguments based on welfare. In many cases, however, considerations of autonomy will argue powerfully against taking preferences as the basis for social choice.

Consider, for example, a decision to purchase dangerous foods, consumer products, or cigarettes by someone unaware of the (serious) health risks; an employer's decision not to hire blacks because of a background of public and private segregation or racial hostility in his community; a person who disparages or has no interest in art and literature because the culture in which he has been reared centers mainly around television; a decision of a woman to adopt a traditional gender role because of the social stigma attached to refusing to do so; a decision not to purchase cars equipped with seat belts or not to wear a motorcycle helmet produced by the social pressures imposed by one's peer group; a lack of interest in environmental diversity resulting from limitation of one's personal experiences to industrialized urban areas; a decision not to employ blacks at a restaurant because of fear of violence from whites.

These examples are different from one another. The source of the problem varies in each. But in all of them, the interest in liberty or autonomy does not call for governmental inaction, even if that were an intelligible category. Indeed, in many or perhaps all of these cases, regulation removes a kind of coercion.

One goal of a democracy, in short, is to ensure autonomy not merely in the satisfaction of preferences, but also, and more fundamentally, in the processes of preference formation. John Stuart Mill himself was emphatic on this point, going so far as to suggest that government itself should be evaluated in large measure by its effects on the character of the citizenry.[13] The view that freedom requires an opportunity to choose among alternatives finds a natural supplement in the view that people should not face unjustifiable constraints on the free development of their preferences and beliefs. It is not altogether clear what such a view would require – a point to which I will return. At the very least, however, it would see a failure of autonomy, and a reason for collective response, in beliefs and preferences based on insufficient information or opportunities.

Governmental action might also be justified on grounds of autonomy when the public seeks to implement, through democratic processes culminating in law, widely held social aspirations or collective desires. Individual consumption choices often diverge from collective considered judgments: people may seek, through law, to implement a democratic decision about what courses to pursue. If so, it is ordinarily no violation of autonomy to allow those considered judgments to be vindicated by governmental action. Collective aspirations or considered judgments, produced by a process of deliberation on which competing perspectives are brought to bear, reflect a conception of political freedom having deep roots in the American constitutional tradition. On this view, political autonomy can be found in collective self-determination, as citizens decide, not what they "want," but instead who they are, what their values are, and what those values require. What they "want" must be supported by reasons.

To summarize: On the thinnest version of the account offered thus far, the mere fact that preferences are what they are is at least sometimes and perhaps generally an insufficient justification for political action. Government decisions need not be and in some cases should not be justified by reference to preferences alone. More broadly, a democratic government should sometimes take private preferences as an object of regulation and control – an inevitable task in light of the need to define initial entitlements – and precisely in the interest of welfare and autonomy. Of course, there are serious risks of overreaching here, and there must be some constraints (usually denominated "rights") on this process. Checks laid down in advance are an indispensable part of constitutional government. Those checks will include, at a minimum, basic guarantees of political liberty and personal security, and such guarantees may not be comprised by processes of collective self-determination. I return to this point below.

2 Democratic Rejection of Revealed Preferences: A Catalogue

In this section I attempt to particularize the claims made thus far by cataloguing cases in which considerations of autonomy and welfare justify governmental action that subjective welfarism would condemn. In all of these cases, I claim that participants in a liberal government ought to be concerned with whether its citizens are experiencing satisfying lives and that the salutary liberal commitment to divergent conceptions of the good ought not to be taken to disable government from expressing that concern through law. The cases fall into three basic categories.

A. Collective judgments and aspirations

Citizens in a democratic polity might act to embody in law not the preferences that they hold as private consumers, but instead what might be described as collective judgments, including aspirations or considered reflections. Measures of this sort are a product of deliberative processes on the part of citizens and representatives. In that process, people do not simply determine what they "want." The resulting measures cannot be understood as an attempt to aggregate or trade off private preferences.

Politics, markets, and the dependence of preferences on context Frequently political choices cannot easily be understood as a process of aggregating prepolitical desires. Some people may, for example, support nonentertainment broadcasting on television, even though their own consumption patterns favor situation comedies; they may seek stringent laws protecting the environment or endangered species, even though they do not use the public parks or derive material benefits from protection of such species; they may approve of laws calling for social security and welfare even though they do not save or give to the poor; they may support antidiscrimination laws even though their own behavior is hardly race- or gender-neutral. The choices people make as political participants are different from those they make as consumers. Democracy thus calls for an intrusion on markets.

The widespread disjunction between political and consumption choices presents something of a puzzle. Indeed, it sometimes leads to the view that market ordering is undemocratic and that choices made through the political process are a preferable basis for social ordering.

A generalization of this sort is far too broad in light of the multiple breakdowns of the political process and the advantages of market ordering in many arenas. Respect for private markets is an important way of respecting divergent conceptions of the good and is thus properly associated with individual liberty. Respect for markets is also an engine of economic productivity, an important individual and collective goal. But it would be a mistake to suggest, as some do, that markets always reflect individual choice more reliably than politics; or that democratic choices differ from consumption outcomes only because of confusion, as voters fail to realize that they must ultimately bear the costs of the programs they favor; or that voting patterns merely reflect a willingness to seek certain goods so long as other people are footing the bill.

Undoubtedly, consumer behavior is sometimes a better or more realistic reflection of actual preferences than is political behavior. But in light of the fact that preferences depend on context, the very notion of a "better reflection" of "actual" preferences is a confusing one; there is no such thing as an "actual" (in the sense of unitary or acontextual) preference in these settings. Moreover, the difference might be explained by the fact that political behavior reflects a variety of influences that are distinctive to the context of politics, and that justify according additional weight to what emerges through the political setting.

These influences include four closely related phenomena. First, citizens may seek to implement individual and collective aspirations in political behavior but not in private consumption. As citizens, people may seek the aid of the law to bring about a social state that they consider to be in some sense higher than what emerges from market ordering. Second, people may, in their capacity as political actors, attempt to satisfy altruistic or other-regarding desires, which diverge from the self-interested preferences sometimes characteristic of markets.[14] Third, political decisions might vindicate what might be called metapreferences or second-order preferences. People have wishes about their wishes, and sometimes they try to vindicate those second-order wishes, including considered judgments about what is best, through law. Fourth, people

may precommit themselves, in democratic processes, to a course of action that they consider to be in the general interest. The adoption of a constitution is itself an example of a precommitment strategy.

Three qualifications are necessary here. First, some of these objections might be translated into the terms of subjective welfarism. Some preferences, after all, are most effectively expressed in democratic arenas, and that expression can be supported precisely on the grounds that they are subjectively held and connected to a certain form of individual and collective welfare. My broader point, however, is that political choices will reflect a kind of deliberation and reasoning, transforming values and perceptions of interests, that is often inadequately captured in the marketplace. It is this point that amounts to a rejection or at least a renovation of subjective welfarism as a political conception. It is here that democracy becomes something other than an aggregative mechanism, that politics is seen to be irreducible to bargaining, and that prepolitical "preferences" are not taken as the bedrock of political justification.

Second, to point to these various possibilities is not at all to deny that market or private behavior frequently reflects considered judgments, altruism, aspirations, or far more complex attitudes toward diverse goods than are captured in conventional accounts of preference structures. There are countless counterexamples to any such claim. All I mean to suggest is that divergences between market and political behavior will sometimes be attributable to phenomena of the sort I have described.

Third, a democratic system must be built on various safeguards to ensure that its decisions are in fact a reflection of deliberative processes of the sort described here. Often, of course, such processes are distorted by the fact that some groups are more organized than others, by disparities in wealth and influence, and by public and private coercion of various kinds. I am assuming here that these problems have been sufficiently overcome to allow for a favorable characterization of the process.

Explanations Thus far I have suggested that people may seek, through law, to implement collective desires that diverge from market choices. Is it possible to come up with concrete explanations for the differences? There are a number of possibilities.

First, the collective character of politics, which permits a response to collective action problems, is critical here. People may not want to implement their considered judgments, or to be altruistic, unless there is assurance that others will be bound to do so as well. More simply, people may prefer not to contribute to a collective benefit if donations are made individually, with no guarantee that others will participate; but their most favored system, obtainable only or best through democratic forms, might be one in which they contribute if (but only if) there is assurance that others will do so as well. Perhaps people feel ashamed if others are contributing and they are not. Perhaps they feel victimized if they are contributing and others are not. In any case, the satisfaction of aspirations or altruistic goals will sometimes have the characteristics of the provision of public goods or the solution of a prisoner's dilemma.

Second, the collective character of politics might overcome the problem, discussed below, of preferences and beliefs that have adapted, at least to some extent, to an unjust status quo or to limits in available opportunities.[15] Without the possibility of collective action, the status quo may seem intractable, and private behavior, and even desires, will adapt accordingly. But if people can act in concert, preferences might take on a quite different form. Consider social movements involving the environment, labor, and race and sex discrimination. The collective action problem thus interacts with aspirations, altruistic desires, second-order preferences, and precommitment strategies. All of these are most likely to be enacted into law if an apparatus such as democratic rule is available to overcome collective action problems.

Third, social and cultural norms might incline people to express aspirational or altruistic goals more often in political behavior than in markets. Such norms may press people, in their capacity as citizens, in the direction of a concern for others or for the public interest.

Fourth, the deliberative aspects of politics, bringing additional information and perspectives to bear, may affect preferences as expressed through governmental processes. A principal function of a democratic system is to ensure that through representative or participatory processes, new or submerged voices, or novel depictions of where interests lie and what they in fact are, are heard and understood. If representatives or citizens are able to participate in a collective discussion of (for example) broadcasting or levels of risk in the workplace, they might well generate a far fuller and richer picture of diverse social goods, and of how they might be served, than can be provided through individual decisions as registered in the market. It should hardly be surprising if preferences, values, and perceptions of both individual and collective welfare are changed as a result of that process.

Fifth, and finally, consumption decisions are a product of the criterion of private willingness to pay, which creates distortions of its own. Willingness to pay is a function of ability to pay, and it is an extremely crude proxy for utility or welfare. Political behavior removes this distortion – which is not to say that it does not introduce distortions of new kinds.

Qualifications Arguments from collective desires are irresistible if the measure at issue is adopted unanimously. But more serious difficulties are produced if (as is usual) the law imposes on a minority what it regards as a burden rather than a benefit. Suppose, for example, that a majority wants to require high-quality television and to ban violent and dehumanizing shows, but that a significant minority wants to see the latter. (I put the First Amendment questions to one side.) It might be thought that those who perceive a need to bind themselves, or to express an aspiration, should not be permitted to do so if the consequence is to deprive others of an opportunity to satisfy their preferences.

The foreclosure of the preferences of the minority is unfortunate, but in general it is difficult to see what argument there might be for an across-the-board rule against collective action of this sort. If the majority is prohibited from vindicating its considered judgments through legislation, an important arena for democratic self-government will be eliminated. The choice is between the considered judgments of the majority and the preferences (and perhaps judgments as well) of the minority. On the other hand, the foreclosure of the minority should probably be permitted only when less restrictive alternatives, including private arrangements, are unavailable to serve the same end.

Of course, the argument for democratic outcomes embodying collective judgments is not always decisive. It is easy to imagine cases in which that argument is weak. Consider a law forbidding atheism or agnosticism, or barring the expression of unpatriotic political displays. And while I cannot provide in this space a full discussion of the contexts in which the case for democratic outcomes is overcome, it might be useful to describe, in a preliminary way, three categories of cases in which constraints on collective judgments seem especially appropriate.

First, if the particular choice foreclosed has some special character, and especially if it is a part of deliberative democracy itself, it is appropriately considered a right, and the majority has no authority to intervene. Political expression and participation are prime examples. The equal political rights of members of the minority, as citizens, should be respected even if a general aspiration, held by the majority, argues for selective exclusions. So, too, other rights fundamental to autonomy or welfare – consider consensual sexual activity – ought generally to be off-limits to government.

Second, some collective desires might be objectionable or a product of unjust background conditions. A collective judgment that racial intermarriage is intolerable could not plausibly be justified even if it is said to reflect a collective social aspiration. To explain why, it is of course necessary to offer an argument challenging that judgment and invoking principles of justice. Such an argument might itself involve notions of autonomy or welfare. However that may be, the example suggests that the collective judgment must not be objectionable on moral grounds.

Third, some collective desires might reflect a special weakness on the part of the majority: consider a curfew law, or perhaps prohibition. In such circumstances, a legal remedy might remove desirable incentives for private self-control, have unintended side effects resulting from the "bottling-up" of desires, or prove unnecessary in light of the existence of alternative remedies. When any one of these three concerns arises, the case for protection of collective judgments is implausible. But in many contexts, these concerns are absent, and democratic controls initiated on these grounds are justified.

B. Excessive limitations in opportunities or unjust background conditions

Citizens in a democracy might override existing preferences in order to foster and promote diverse experiences, with a view to providing broad opportunities for the formation of preferences and beliefs and for distance on and critical scrutiny of current desires. This goal usually supports private ordering and freedom of contract as well. But it calls for collective safeguards when those forces push toward homogeneity and uniformity, as they often do in industrialized nations. Here the argument for governmental controls finds a perhaps ironic origin in Mill. Such controls are necessary to cultivate divergent conceptions of the good and to ensure a degree of reflection on those conceptions.

A system that took this goal seriously could start from a range of different foundations. It might find its roots in the principles that underlie a deliberative democracy itself.[16] Here the notions of autonomy and welfare would be defined by reference to the idea of free and equal persons acting as citizens in setting up the terms of democratic life. That idea will impose constraints on the sorts of preferences and beliefs that a political system would be permitted to inculcate. Perhaps more controversially, the system could be regarded as embodying a mild form of liberal perfectionism. Such a system would see the inculcation of critical and disparate attitudes toward prevailing conceptions of the good as part of the framework of a liberal democracy. Liberal education is of course the principal locus of this concern, but the principles embodied in liberal education need not be confined to the school system. Still another foundation would be Aristotelian. Here the governing goal would be to ensure that individual capacities and capabilities are promoted and not thwarted by governmental arrangements.[17] And this set of ideas, a different kind of perfectionism, is not so dramatically different from Mill's version of utilitarianism.

If government can properly respond to preferences that are based on limitations in available opportunities, it might well undertake aggressive initiatives with respect to the arts and broadcasting: subsidizing public broadcasting, ensuring a range of disparate programming, or calling for high-quality programming not sufficiently provided by the marketplace. Indeed, the need to provide diverse opportunities for preference formation suggests reasons to be quite skeptical of unrestricted markets in communication and broadcasting. There is a firm theoretical justification for governmental regulation here, including the much-criticized, and now largely abandoned, "fairness doctrine," which required broadcasters to cover controversial issues and to give equal time to competing views. In view of the inevitable effects of programming on character, beliefs, and even conduct, it is hardly clear that governmental "inaction" is always appropriate in a constitutional democracy. Indeed, the contrary seems true. I take up this issue in more detail below.

Market behavior is sometimes based on an effort to reduce cognitive dissonance by adjusting to undue limitations in current practices and opportunities. When this is so, respect for preferences seems unjustified on grounds of autonomy and under certain conditions welfare as well. Preferences might be regarded as nonautonomous insofar as they are reflexively adaptive to unjust background conditions, and collective responses to such preferences might yield welfare gains.[18] The point has significant implications. For example, workers appear to underestimate the risks of hazardous activity partly in order to reduce the dissonance that would be produced by an accurate understanding of the dangers of the workplace.[19] Democratic controls might produce gains in terms of both welfare and autonomy.

Similar ideas help account for principles of antidiscrimination. In general, the beliefs of both beneficiaries and victims of existing injustice are affected by dissonance-reducing strategies.[20] The phenomenon of blaming the victim has distinct cognitive and motivational foundations: the strategy of blaming the victim, or assuming that an injury or an inequality was deserved or inevitable, permits nonvictims or members of advantaged groups to reduce dissonance by enabling them to maintain that the world is just – a pervasively, insistently, and sometimes irrationally held belief.[21] The reduction of cognitive dissonance is a powerful motivational force, and it operates as a significant obstacle to the recognition of social injustice or irrationality.

Victims also participate in dissonance-reducing strategies, including the lowering of their own self-esteem to accommodate both the fact of victimization and the belief that the world is essentially just. Sometimes it is easier to assume that one's suffering is warranted than that it has been imposed cruelly or by chance. Consider here the astonishing fact that after a draft lottery, participants decided that the results of the purely random process, whether favorable or not, were deserved.[22] The phenomenon of blaming the victim also reflects the "hindsight effect," through which people unjustifiably perceive events as having been more predictable than they in fact were, and therefore suggest that victims or disadvantaged groups should have been able to prevent the negative outcome. All of these phenomena make reliance on existing or revealed preferences highly problematic in certain contexts.

There is suggestive evidence to this effect in the psychological literature in this area. Some work here reveals that people who engage in cruel behavior begin to devalue the objects of their cruelty; observers tend to do the same.[23] Such evidence bears on antidiscrimination law in general. Certain aspects of American labor and race discrimination law can be understood as a response to the basic problem of distorted beliefs and preferences. For example, the Supreme Court has emphatically rejected freedom-of-choice plans as a remedy for school segregation.[24] Such plans would simply permit whites and blacks to send their children to whichever school they wished. The Court's rejection of such plans might well be puzzling to proponents of subjective welfarism, but the outcome becomes more reasonable if it is seen as based in part on the fact that, in this area, preferences and beliefs have conspicuously grown up around and adapted to the segregative status quo. Under these circumstances, freedom of choice is no solution at all; indeed, in view of the background and context the term seems an oxymoron.

In labor law as well, American law rejects freedom of contract and freedom of choice in order to protect collective bargaining. Some of this legislation must stand on a belief that private preferences have been adaptive to a status quo skewed against unionization. Special steps are therefore necessary in order to encourage collective bargaining, which also, of course, overcomes the prisoner's dilemma faced by individual workers, and therefore facilitates collective deliberation on the conditions of the workplace.

Poverty itself is perhaps the most severe obstacle to the free development of preferences and beliefs. Programs that attempt to respond to the deprivations faced by poor people – most obviously by eliminating poverty, but also through broad public education and regulatory efforts designed to make cultural resources generally available regardless of wealth – are fully justified in this light. They should hardly be seen as objectionable paternalism or as unsupportable redistribution. Indeed, antipoverty efforts are tightly linked with republican efforts to promote security and independence in the interest of creating the conditions for full and equal citizenship.

Sometimes, of course, preferences are only imperfectly adapted. At some level there is a perception of injury, but a fear of social sanctions or a belief that the cause is intractable prevents people from seeking redress. Here the collective character of politics, permitting the organization of numerous people, can be exceedingly helpful.

Standing by itself, the fact that preferences are shifting and endogenous is hardly a sufficient reason for the imposition of democratic controls. All preferences are to some degree dependent on existing law and current opportunities, and that fact cannot be a reason for governmental action without creating a license for tyranny. The argument for democratic controls in the face of endogenous preferences must rely on a belief that welfare or autonomy will thereby be promoted. Usually governmental interference should be avoided. But far too often, the salutary belief in respect for divergent conceptions of the good is transformed into an unwillingness to protect people from either unjust background conditions or a sheer lack of options.

The actual content of democratic controls here will of course be controversial, and it probably should begin and usually end with efforts to provide information and to increase opportunities. Thus, for example, governmentally required disclosure of risks in the workplace is a highly laudable strategy. In a few cases, however, these milder initiatives are inadequate, and other measures are necessary. A moderately intrusive strategy could involve economic incentives, which might take the form of tax advantages or cash payments. For example, the government might give financial inducements to day-care centers as a way of relieving child-care burdens. Such a system might well be preferable to direct transfers of money to families, a policy that will predictably lead many more women to stay at home. In view of the sources and consequences of the differential distribution of child-care burdens, it is fully legitimate for the government to take steps in the direction of equalization. The most intrusive option, to be used rarely, is direct coercion, as in the case of governmentally mandated use of safety equipment.

The category of democratic responses to endogenous preferences of this sort overlaps with that of measures that attempt to protect collective aspirations. Frequently, aspirations form the basis for laws that attempt to influence processes of preference formation.

C. *Intrapersonal collective action problems*

There is also a case for democratic controls on existing preferences when such preferences are a function of past acts of consumption and when such acts alter desires or beliefs in such a way as to cause long-term harm. In such cases, the two key facts are that preferences are endogenous to past consumption decisions and that the effect of those decisions on current preferences is pernicious. For government to act in this context, it is important that it be confident of its conclusions; in the face of uncertainty, freedom of choice is appropriate here. An absence of information on the part of the private actors is usually a necessary condition for collective controls.

Regulations of addictive substances, myopic behavior, and habits are familiar examples. In the case of an addiction, the problem is that the costs of nonconsumption increase dramatically over time as the benefits of consumption remain constant or fall sharply. The result is that the aggregate costs, over time or over a life, of consumption exceed the aggregate benefits, even though the initial consumption choice provides benefits that exceed costs. Individual behavior that is rational for each individual consumption choice ultimately leads people into severely inferior social states. In such cases, people, if fully informed, would in all likelihood not want to choose the good in the first place. Governmental action is a possible response.

Menahem Yaari offers the example of a group of traders attempting to induce alcoholism in an Indian tribe.[25] At the outset, alcoholic beverages are not extremely valuable to consumers. The consumers are willing to buy only for a low price, which the traders accept. But as a result of consumption, the value of the beverages to the consumers steadily increases to the point where they are willing to pay enormous sums to obtain them. Thus the traders are able "to manoeuvre the Indian into a position where rationality conflicts with Pareto-efficiency, i.e., into a position where to be efficient is to be irrational and to be rational is to be inefficient . . . [T]he disadvantage, for an economic unit, of having endogenously changing tastes is that, even with perfect information and perfect foresight, the unit may find itself forced to follow an action which, by the unit's own standards, is Pareto-dominated."

Because of the effect over time of consumption on preferences, someone who is addicted to heroin is much worse off than he would have been had he never started, even though the original decision to consume was not irrational in terms of immediate costs and benefits. Statutes that regulate addictive substances respond to a social belief, grounded on this consideration, that the relevant preferences should not be formed in the first place.

We might describe this situation as involving an intrapersonal collective action problem, in which the costs and benefits, for a particular person, of engaging in an activity change dramatically over time.[26] A central point here is that consumption patterns induce a significant change in preferences, and in a way that makes people worse off in the long run.[27] In the case of addictions, there will also be interconnections between intrapersonal collective action problems and preferences and beliefs that are adaptive to unjust background conditions, at least as a general rule. (Yaari's own example, involving whites trading alcohol with native Americans, is a prime example.) The problem of drug addiction is hardly distributed evenly throughout the population, and the process of addiction is in large part a response to social institutions that severely limit and condition the range of options.

While addiction is the most obvious case, it is part of a far broader category. Consider, for example, myopic behavior, defined as a refusal, because the short-term costs exceed the short-term benefits, to engage in activity having long-term benefits that dwarf long-term costs. Another kind of intrapersonal collective action problem is produced by habits, in which people engage in behavior because of the subjectively high short-term costs of changing their behavior, regardless of the fact that the long-term benefits exceed the long-term costs. *Akrasia*, or weakness of the will, has a related structure, and some laws respond to its individual or collective forms.

For the most part, problems of this sort are best addressed at the individual level or through private associations, which minimize coercion; but social regulation is a possible response. Statutes that subsidize the arts or public broadcasting, or that discourage the formation of some habits and encourage the formation of others, are illustrations. There are similar arguments for compulsory recycling programs (the costs of participation in which decrease substantially over time, and often turn into benefits) and for democratic restrictions on smoking cigarettes.[28]

The problem with collective controls in this context is that they are unlikely to be fine-tuned. They will often sweep up so many people and circumstances as to create serious risks of abuse. In some settings, however, citizens will be able to say with confidence that the effect of consumption on preferences will lead to severe welfare or autonomy losses. In such cases democratic controls are justified.

3 Examples

A. The frontiers of free speech law: the fairness doctrine, campaign speech, hate speech, and pornography

The most important issues in the contemporary law of free expression have produced cleavages between groups and ideas that were previously closely allied. Thus the First Amendment has been invoked, with considerable vigor and passion, on behalf of cigarette companies seeking to advertise their products; corporations attempting to influence electoral outcomes; people engaged in racial hate speech; pornographers; and large networks objecting to a private right of access to broadcasting or to other efforts to promote quality and diversity in the media. The effort to invoke the First Amendment is increasingly resisted – often, ironically, on the theory that it runs counter to the goals of deliberative democracy and free expression itself – by individuals and groups formerly associated with an absolutist or near-absolutist position against governmental regulation of speech.

These debates raise exceedingly complex issues, and I can only touch on them briefly here. The complexities are increased by the fact that a system dedicated to freedom of expression ought to be highly sensitive to the idea that speech alters preferences and beliefs. It should also find that process to be one to which a democracy is generally quite receptive. As Justice Louis D. Brandeis wrote in what is probably the most distinguished judicial opinion in the entire history of free expression, "the fitting remedy for evil counsels is good ones . . . If there be time to expose through discussion the falsehood and fallacies, to avert the evil by the processes of education, the remedy to be applied is more speech, not enforced silence."[29]

Justice Brandeis's statement notwithstanding, I want to suggest that attention to the endogenous character of preferences and to the considerations traced thus far provides some basis for receptivity to democratic controls in this context.

The fairness doctrine There is a growing consensus that the government should not concern itself with the airwaves and that total reliance on private markets and consumer preferences is the appropriate strategy for government. On this view, broadcasting should be treated like soap, cereal, or any other commodity. Indeed, there is a growing consensus that this result is ordained by the First Amendment. But if the claims made here are persuasive, the consensus is misguided. The meaning of the First Amendment is a function of competing views about what sort of relation between government and markets will best promote democratic deliberation. Lawyers (and not a few nonlawyers) have an unfortunate habit of thinking that the meaning of the First Amendment precedes rather than postdates that inquiry.

The consequence of market-based strategies in broadcasting is a system in which most viewers see shows that rarely deal with serious problems; are frequently sensationalistic, prurient, dehumanizing, or banal; reflect and perpetuate a bland, watered-down version of the most conventional views about politics and morality; are influenced excessively by the concerns of advertisers; produce an accelerating "race to the bottom" in terms of the quality and quantity of attention that they require and encourage; and are often riddled with violence, sexism, and racism. It simply defies belief to suggest that such shows do not affect the preferences and even the character of the citizenry. Is it so clear that a constitutional democracy ought to consider itself unable to respond to this situation? Is it so clear that a First Amendment enacted in order to ensure democratic self-determination bars a democratic corrective here?

In my view, the considerations marshaled thus far suggest that citizens in a constitutional democracy ought to be conceded, and ought to exercise, the power to engage in a wide range of controls. If welfare and autonomy provide the governing criteria, large gains might be expected from such controls. All three of the categories I have described argue in favor of some form of regulation. Democratic controls would probably reflect collective desires, which deserve respect. They would respond to the fact that in spite of the large number of channels, the current regulatory regime diminishes genuine options, to the detriment of both welfare and autonomy; they would also counteract a kind of intrapersonal collective action problem faced by many of those habituated to the broadcasting status quo.

Such controls might permit the government to regulate advertising on television, certainly for children, but for others as well; to require broadcasters to pay attention to public affairs, as in, for example, an hour of compulsory programming per night; to ban gratuitous or prurient violence on television, especially when it is sexualized; to require, as a condition for licensing, a subsidy to public television; and to impose a broad fairness doctrine, in the form not only of an obligation of attention to important issues but also a chance to speak for divergent sides. The evident dangers notwithstanding, there would be a wide range of collective and external benefits from such controls, which would thus carry forward a strand of the liberal tradition that calls for governmental action in such cases.[30]

At least in principle, rights of private access to the media for differing positions and associated kinds of controls ought to be considered congenial to the free speech guarantee. Surely this is so if that guarantee is understood as a protection of a deliberative process centered on public values rather than of a "marketplace." The First Amendment need not be seen as an obstacle to such efforts. If anything, the existing system might be thought to raise serious constitutional questions. A system in which access to the media, with its inevitable consequences for the shaping of preferences and beliefs, is made dependent on private willingness to pay raises genuine problems for free expression.[31]

Campaign regulation It would not be difficult to argue that a variety of regulations on the electoral process are necessary both to promote a deliberative process among political equals and to ensure that the deliberative process is a genuine one. Properly conceived, such efforts would be highly congenial to the purposes of the free speech guarantee. Both restrictions on campaign contributions – to eliminate the distorting effects of wealth[32] – and qualitative measures to reduce the "soundbite" phenomenon and to promote more in the way of reflective discussion hold considerable promise.

Currently, however, there is a large if ironic obstacle to such efforts: the First Amendment. The Supreme Court has generally been unreceptive to governmental efforts to regulate electoral campaigns.[33] In the key passage in *Buckley v. Valeo*, the Court said that "the concept that government may restrict the speech of some elements of our society in order to enhance the relative voice of others is wholly foreign to the first amendment."[34] It is crucial to note here that the Court did not say that the effort to promote deliberation among political equals was insufficiently weighty or inadequately promoted by the legislation at hand. Instead the Court said, far more broadly, that the effort was constitutionally illegitimate.

Under the approach suggested here, campaign regulation would be treated more hospitably. In view of the effects of wealth on the formation of political beliefs, and the corrosive consequences of some forms of electioneering, democratic controls on the process might be welcomed. The First Amendment might be understood not as a guarantor of unrestricted speech "markets," and much less as a vehicle for the translation of economic inequalities into political ones, but instead as an effort to ensure a process of deliberation that would, under current conditions, be promoted rather than undermined through regulatory measures. This is so especially if citizens in a democratic polity support regulation of the electoral process in order to pursue their desire for a well-functioning deliberative process.

Of course, there are great risks here, and any regulatory efforts must be carefully monitored to ensure that they do not act as incumbent protection bills or as serious constraints on speech that should instead be encouraged. But the issue is far more complex, from the standpoint of the First Amendment itself, than existing law allows.

Violent pornography and hate speech Many Western democracies, including those firmly committed to freedom of speech, regulate speech that casts contempt on identifiable social groups (hate speech). Some such democracies also control sexually explicit speech, especially when it associates sex and violence. These controls have been justified on mixed grounds of human dig-

nity, community morality, and sexual equality. In the United States, the precise status of such restrictions remains unclear. Probably the best account of current law is that hate speech is protected, as is most speech that associates sex and violence, even if that speech is not conceivably part of a serious exchange of ideas but instead qualifies as pornography.[35]

The cases of hate speech and pornography raise somewhat different problems. Hate speech is self-consciously directed toward an issue of public concern; it is conspicuously and intentionally political in nature. Violent pornography is of course political too, in the sense that it has political origins and consequences. But it cannot be thought to be a self-conscious contribution to democratic deliberation about public issues. In this way it differs from misogynist speech of a more straightforward sort, where the political content is explicit. In terms of its connection to the First Amendment, pornography should probably be thought to fall in the same category as commercial speech, libel of private persons, bribes, and conspiracies. The reason is that most pornography does not amount to an effort to contribute to deliberation on matters of public interest, even if that category is broadly conceived, as it should be. Expression that is not central to the free speech principle counts as speech, but it is entitled to a lesser degree of protection. It may be regulated, not on a whim, but on a basis of demonstration of harm that is weaker than that required for political speech.

Should the First Amendment be taken to disable government from regulating hate speech and pornography? The affirmative answer of current law may well be unsound. Both of these forms of speech have serious and corrosive effects on beliefs and desires. Both have the additional and unusual characteristic of denying victimized groups the right to participate in the community as free and equal persons. With respect to certain kinds of violent pornography, there are especially severe consequences in terms of how men and women perceive sexuality, how men perceive women, and how women perceive themselves. One need not believe that the regulation of violent pornography would eliminate sexual violence or even do a great deal to produce sexual equality in order to recognize that the pervasiveness of material that associates sex with violence has a variety of harmful social consequences.

The case for regulation of these forms of

speech is strongest when the relevant speech is pervasive, when it causes tangible harm, and when it falls outside the category of speech that is guaranteed First Amendment protection unless there is a demonstration of unavoidable, imminent, and serious danger. The considerations marshaled here suggest that at least certain forms of violent pornography ought to be regulated, and that perhaps in certain restricted settings, hate speech may be an appropriate subject of democratic controls as well.

B. *Proportional representation*

In recent years, there has been a revival of interest in systems of proportional or group representation, both for disadvantaged groups and perhaps generally as well. There is a solid constitutional pedigree for such systems, notwithstanding the constant and emphatic rejections, by the Supreme Court, of constitutionally based arguments for representation of members of racial minority groups. Despite the rigidity of the one person-one vote formula, with its majoritarian and individualistic overtones, group representation has always been a feature of American constitutionalism.[36]

Moreover, the basic constitutional institutions of federalism, bicameralism, and checks and balances share some of the appeal of proportional representation, and owe their origins in part to notions of group representation. These institutions proliferate the points of access to government, increasing the ability of diverse groups to influence policy, multiplying perspectives in government, and improving deliberative capacities. In this respect, they ensure something in the way of group representation, at least when compared with unitary systems. Of course both the separation of powers and bicameralism grew in part out of efforts to promote representation of diverse groups: bicameralism allowed representation of both the wealthy and the masses, while the notion of separation derived from (though it also repudiated) notions of mixed government, which was designed to ensure a measure of representation of groups defined in social and economic terms.

Proportional representation might be designed, as in its Western European forms, to ensure representation in the legislature of all those groups that are able to attain more than a minimal share of the vote. In another form, the system might be

an effort to ensure that members of disadvantaged groups are given the power to exert influence on political outcomes. In America, the Voting Rights Act goes far in this direction for blacks.

There are serious problems with both of these efforts, and I do not mean to evaluate them in detail here. I do suggest that efforts to ensure proportional representation become much more acceptable if they are justified on grounds that do not take existing preferences as the basis for governmental decisions and if they emphasize the preference-shaping effects of discussion and disagreement in politics.[37] The argument here is that deliberative processes will be improved, not undermined, if mechanisms are instituted to ensure that multiple groups have access to the process and are actually present when decisions are made. Proportional or group representation, precisely by having this effect, would ensure that diverse views are expressed on an ongoing basis in the representative process, where they might otherwise be excluded.

In this respect, proportional or group representation could be regarded as a kind of second-best solution for the real-world failures of Madisonian deliberation. And the primary purpose of access is not to allow each group to have its "piece of the action" – though that is not entirely irrelevant – but instead to ensure that the process of deliberation is not distorted by the mistaken appearance of a common set of interests on the part of all concerned. In this incarnation, proportional representation is designed to increase the likelihood that political outcomes will incorporate some understanding of all perspectives. That process should facilitate the healthy expression of collective values or aspirations and the scrutiny of preferences adaptive to unjust background conditions or limited opportunities.

For this reason, proportional representation may be the functional analogue of the institutions of checks and balances and federalism, recognizing the creative functions of disagreement and multiple perspectives for the governmental process. In this sense there is continuity between recent proposals for proportional representation and some of the attractive features of the original constitutional regime. Indeed, Hamilton himself emphasized that in a system of checks and balances, the "jarring of parties . . . will promote deliberation."[38] If this is so, proportional representation is most understandable in a democracy that does not take existing preferences as the basis for social choice but instead sees the broadest form of deliberation, covering ends as well as means, as a central ingredient in democratic politics.

4 Conclusion

A constitutional democracy should not be self-consciously concerned, in a general and comprehensive way, with the souls of its citizens. Under modern conditions, liberal constraints on the operation of the public sphere and a general respect for divergent conceptions of the good are indispensable. At the same time, it would be a grave mistake to characterize liberal democracy as a system that requires existing preferences to be taken as the basis for governmental decisions and that forbids citizens, operating through democratic channels, from enacting their considered judgments into law, or from counteracting, through the provision of opportunities and information, preferences and beliefs that have adjusted to an unjust status quo. Ironically, a system that forecloses these routes – and that claims to do so in the name of liberalism or democracy – will defeat many of the aspirations that gave both liberalism and democracy their original appeal, and that continue to fuel them in so many parts of the world.

Notes

I am grateful to Jon Elster for many valuable discussions of these issues; to Elizabeth Anderson, Joshua Cohen, George Loewenstein, Jon Macey, Jane Mansbridge, Frederick Schauer, and Elisabeth Wood for helpful comments on an earlier draft; and, for their lively responses, to participants in the University of Toronto Legal Theory Workshop and the University of Chicago seminar led by Gary Becker and James Coleman on rational models in the social sciences. Some of this essay develops arguments set forth in chaps. 1 and 2 of my *After the Rights Revolution: Reconceiving the Regulatory State* (Cambridge, Mass.: Harvard University Press, 1990).

1 See Gordon Wood, *The Creation of the American Republic, 1776–1787* (New York: W.W. Norton, 1972); Thomas Pangle, *The Spirit of Modern Republicanism: The Moral Vision of the American Founders and the Philosophy of Locke* (Chicago: University of Chicago Press, 1988); and Martin Diamond, "Ethics and Politics: The American Way," in *The Moral Foundations of the American Republic*, ed. Robert Horwitz (Charlottesville: University Press of Virginia, 1986), pp. 75–106.

2 *The Laws* 650b.

3 See John Rawls, "The Idea of an Overlapping Consensus," *Oxford Journal of Legal Studies* 7 (1987): 1–25.

4 Indeed, participants in the liberal tradition, in its classical forms, emphasized the need for deliberation in government and placed a high value on political virtue. Many liberals do not take private preferences as the basis for social choice, without regard to their sources and consequences, or to the reasons that might be offered in their support. See my "Beyond the Republican Revival," *Yale Law Journal* 97 (1988): 1539–89.

5 On the limits of preference-based theories, see Amartya Sen, "Rational Fools: A Critique of the Behavioral Foundations of Economic Theory," *Philosophy & Public Affairs* 6, no. 4 (Summer 1977): 317–44; Jon Elster, *Sour Grapes* (New York: Cambridge University Press. 1983); and John Roemer, "'Rational Choice' Marxism," in *Analytical Marxism*, ed. John Roemer (New York: Cambridge University Press, 1986), pp. 191–201. Of course, the satisfaction of private preferences in markets or elsewhere may create prisoners' dilemmas or collective action problems, and here governmental controls (or social norms) are a natural solution. I will not, however, deal with this narrower problem here.

It might well be that literature, in addition to economics and political theory, is a fruitful place to explore this subject. See Martha Nussbaum, *Love's Knowledge* (New York: Oxford University Press, 1990), and "Shame, Separateness, and Political Unity: Aristotle's Criticism of Plato," in *Essays on Aristotle's Ethics*, ed. Amelie Rorty (Berkeley: University of California Press, 1980), pp. 395–435. It is thus no accident that writers in politics and economics sometimes draw on literature. See, e.g., Elster, *Sour Grapes*.

6 David Gauthier, *Morals by Agreement* (New York: Oxford University Press, 1986), contains arguments in this direction; for a representative example at the intersection of economics and law, see Richard Posner, *Economics of Justice* (Cambridge, Mass.: Harvard University Press, 1983), p. 53. There are, of course, criticisms within all of these fields. In economics, see Sen, "Rational Fools"; in politics, see Elster, *Sour Grapes*.

It is notable that the great expositors of liberalism in the nineteenth and twentieth centuries are emphatic in their rejection of the view that satisfaction of existing preferences is adequate for purposes of ethics or politics. See John Stuart Mill, *Considerations on Representative Government*, ed. C. V. Shields (1861; New York: Liberal Arts Press, 1958), and *The Subjection of Women*, ed. Susan Moller Okin (1869; Indianapolis: Hackett, 1988); and John Rawls, *A Theory of Justice* (Cambridge, Mass.: Harvard University Press, 1971). Mill's rejection of that view is especially emphatic in his essay on Bentham, where he criticizes Bentham for the view that "[t]o say either that man should, or that he should not, take pleasure in one thing, displeasure in another, appeared to him as much an act of despotism in the moralist as in the political ruler." Mill, by contrast, emphasized the need to explore the influences "on the regulation of . . . affections and desires," and pointed to "the deficiencies of a system of ethics which does not pretend to aid individuals in the formation of their own character" (*Mill on Bentham and Coleridge*, ed. F.R. Leavis [London: Chatto & Windus, 1950], pp. 68, 71, 70). Of course, there is a difference between what a system of ethics and what a system of politics should say about that question, as Mill clearly believed.

Dewey spoke in similar terms, invoking the need for critical reflection on the "conditions under which objects are enjoyed" and "the consequences of esteeming and liking them," and arguing that "judgments about values are judgments about that which should regulate the formation of our desires, affections and enjoyments" (John Dewey, *The Quest for Certainty: A Study of the Relation of Knowledge and Action* [New York: Putnam, 1960], pp. 259, 265, 272–73; emphasis in original).

7 I am grateful to Joshua Cohen for this formulation. I will not explore the complexities of the notion of "preference" here. I mean to refer simply to choices, mostly as these are observed in market behavior. This understanding of course captures the economic notion of "revealed preference" and also is a foundational part of subjective welfarism as I understand it. For a recent and interestingly offhand, example, see Ingemar Hansson and Charles Stuart, "Malthusian Selection of Preferences," *American Economic Review* 90 (1990): 529, 542: "We use natural selection to explain behavior, or equivalently, preferences." I do not explore the view, much broader than the claims defended here, that the existence of even widely held preferences, thus defined, furnishes no argument at all for governmental action.

If the notion of preference is intended to refer to an internal psychological force, or to a supposed wellspring of action, difficulties of course abound:

people have first-, second-, and *n*th-order preferences, and their desires can be organized into many different categories, ranging from whimsy to considered judgments.

8 See Elster, *Sour Grapes*, and Rawls, *A Theory of Justice*. The problem here is not the simple fact of endogeneity, but that social rules and practices cannot be justified by reference to preferences that they have produced.

The point in the text receives empirical confirmation in the "endowment effect" frequently observed in social psychology and economics. See, e.g., David Brookshire and Don Coursey, "Measuring the Value of a Public Good: An Empirical Comparison of Elicitation Procedures," *American Economic Review* 77 (1987): 554–65; David Harless, "More Laboratory Evidence on the Disparity Between Willingness to Pay and Compensation Demanded," *Journal of Economic Behavior & Organization* 11 (1989): 359–70; Richard Thaler, "Toward a Positive Theory of Consumer Choice," *Journal of Economic Behavior & Organization* 1 (1980): 39–60; and Jack Knetsch and J. A. Sinden, "Willingness to Pay and Compensation Demanded: Experimental Evidence of an Unexpected Disparity in Measures of Value," *Quarterly Journal of Economics* 99 (1984): 507–21. The endowment effect is the consequence, for preferences and willingness to pay, of the initial allocation of an entitlement. Cf. Martha Nussbaum, "Shame, Separateness, and Political Unity," and "Aristotelian Social Democracy," in *Liberalism and the Good*, ed. R. Bruce Douglas, Gerald Mara, and Henry Richardson (New York: Routledge, 1990), pp. 203–52. A similar problem occurs when preferences are produced through an effort to counter the status quo, as in the "grass is always greener" phenomenon, in which people prefer things simply because they are unavailable. There is much less, however, in the way of empirical confirmation of this phenomenon.

9 See Daniel Kahneman, Jack Knetsch, and Richard Thaler, "Fairness and the Assumptions of Economics," in *Rational Choice: The Contrast Between Economics and Psychology*, ed. Robin Hogarth and Melvin Reder (Chicago: University of Chicago Press, 1987), pp. 101–16, esp. pp. 113–14. A related phenomenon is "loss aversion," which refers to the fact that a negative change from the status quo is usually seen as more harmful than a positive change is seen as beneficial. See Daniel Kahneman and Amos Tversky, "Prospect Theory: An Analysis of Decision Under Risk," *Econometrica* 47 (1979): 263, 286–88. Loss aversion, together with the "reference state" phenomenon, may help to explain the endowment effect described in note 8 above.

10 For a modern utilitarian account along these lines,

see Richard Brandt, *A Theory of the Good and the Right* (New York: Oxford University Press, 1979). For Aristotelian accounts, see Nussbaum, "Aristotelian Social Democracy," and Amartya Sen, "Well-Being, Agency, and Freedom," *Journal of Philosophy* 82 (1985): 169–221.

11 See Amartya Sen, *The Standard of Living*, The Tanner Lectures on Human Values, ed. Geoffrey Hawthorne (Cambridge: Cambridge University Press, 1987). On various conceptions of welfare, see James Griffin, *Well-Being: Its Meaning, Measurement and Moral Significance* (Oxford: Clarendon Press, 1986).

12 The objection here is not solely that preferences are endogenous to state action of some sort. As discussed in more detail below, the fact of endogeneity is not in itself an argument for democratic control of preferences. The argument is instead that misery that is a product of unjust background conditions calls for collective change. A subjectively satisfactory status quo produced by unjust background conditions will also call for change in some settings, for reasons taken up below. I do not deal with the possibility that subjective unhappiness that is a product of just background conditions also calls for governmental action, except insofar as an intrapersonal collective action problem is involved.

Moreover, to say that a preference is endogenous is not to say that it is a mere whim or fancy, or highly malleable. Some preferences are in fact relatively stable, even if they are a function of legal rules, social pressures, or existing institutions. A high degree of stability, and great resistance to change, will counsel against efforts at changing preferences, certainly on welfare grounds, and perhaps on grounds of autonomy as well (though even stable preferences may be nonautonomous, as in the case of rigid adaptations to an unjust status quo). In the face of extremely stable preferences, democratic efforts at change will merely breed resentment and frustration on the part of the objects of those efforts.

13 See Mill, *Considerations on Representative Government*.

14 See Howard Margolis, *Selfishness, Altruism, and Rationality: A Theory of Social Choice* (New York: Cambridge University Press, 1982). Of course the work by Kenneth Arrow and his followers in social choice theory creates serious problems for all preference-based theories of politics.

15 Cf. Mill's discussion of the ability of regimes to create active or passive characters, in *Considerations on Representative Government*.

16 See Joshua Cohen, "Deliberation and Democratic Legitimacy," in *The Good Polity: Normative Analysis of the State*, ed. Alan Hamlin and Philip Pettit (Oxford: Basil Blackwell, 1989), pp. 17–34.

17 See Nussbaum, "Aristotelian Social Democracy." Here, as above, I do not attempt to choose among foundations but instead suggest that those adopting a wide range of starting points should reject subjective welfarism. To say this is not of course to deny the need to rely ultimately on some conception of the good. For these purposes a wide variety of possibilities should do, including a form of liberal perfectionism, or a thin but relatively precise conception, as in Rawls's *A Theory of Justice*, or a thick but vague one, as in "Aristotelian Social Democracy."

18 There is a difference between self-conscious adaptation to an intractable status quo and the sorts of processes I am describing. If a person without musical talent decides to counteract and revise a desire to be a world-famous pianist, it would be odd to find that (healthy) decision to be inconsistent with personal autonomy. The cases under discussion involve a reflexive process based on a socially produced absence of sufficient opportunities. Of course, the notion of sufficient opportunities itself requires a baseline; every system contains limited opportunities.

19 See George Akerlof and William Dickens, "The Economic Consequences of Cognitive Dissonance," *American Economic Review* 72 (1982): 307–18.

20 On cognitive dissonance, see Leon Festinger, *A Theory of Cognitive Dissonance* (Stanford, Calif.: Stanford University Press, 1957); on some of its implications for social theory, welfare, and autonomy, see Elster, *Sour Grapes*. See also the discussion of endowment effects and reference states in notes 8 and 9 (above) and the accompanying text.

Consider also Mary Wollstonecraft, *A Vindication of the Rights of Women*, ed. Carol Poston (1792; New York: W. W. Norton, 1975), which can be seen as an extended discussion of the social formation of preferences and the phenomenon of the adaptation of preferences, beliefs, and desires to an unjust status quo. Thus Wollstonecraft writes, "I will venture to affirm, that a girl, whose spirits have not been damped by inactivity, or innocence tainted by false shame, will always be a romp, and the doll will never excite attention unless confinement allows her no alternative" (p. 43). Similar points are made in Mill, *The Subjection of Women*, as against the claim that the existing desires of women are a product of consent.

Consider finally the discussion of women's illiteracy in Bangladesh in Nussbaum, "Aristotelian Social Democracy." Drawing on Martha Chen, *A Quiet Revolution: Women in Transition in Rural Bangladesh* (Cambridge, Mass.: Schenkman, 1983), Nussbaum explores the fact that many women in Bangladesh did not demand or even want greater education or literacy, and indeed expressed satisfaction with their current educational status. Of course, desires of this sort were a product of a lack of available opportunities and of social and cultural pressures.

21 See Melvin Lerner, *The Belief in a Just World: A Fundamental Delusion* (New York: Plenum Press, 1980).

22 Zick Rubin and Anne Peplau, "Belief in a Just World and Reaction to Another's Lot," *Journal of Social Issues* 29 (1973): 73–93.

23 See Lerner, *The Belief in a Just World*.

24 See Green v. County School Bd., 391 U.S. 430 (1968), and Paul Gewirtz, "Choice in the Transition," *Columbia Law Review* 86 (1986): 728–98.

25 Menahem Yaari, "Endogenous Changes in Tastes: A Philosophical Discussion," in *Decision Theory and Social Ethics: Issues in Social Choice*, ed. Hans Gottinger and Werner Leinfellner (Boston: D. Reidel, 1978), pp. 59–98.

26 Thomas Schelling, "Egonomics, or the Art of Self-Management," *American Economic Review* 68 (1978): 290–94; Jon Elster, "Weakness of Will and the Free-Rider Problem," *Economics and Philosophy* 1 (1985): 231–65.

27 Of course, all consumption has an effect on preferences. For example, exposure to classical music usually increases appreciation. But the pattern under discussion is a rare one: it is that pattern, producing miserable lives, to which a democracy might respond. To be sure, in practice the response might make things worse rather than better.

28 See Robert Goodin, *No Smoking: The Ethical Issues* (Chicago: University of Chicago Press, 1989).

29 Whitney v. California, 274 U.S. 357, 377 (1927).

30 See, e.g., John Stuart Mill, *Principles of Political Economy*, ed. W.J. Ashley (1871; London and New York: Longmans, Green & Co., 1929). See also Owen Fiss, "Free Speech and Social Structure," *Iowa Law Review* 71 (1986): 1405–25; this essay carries the argument considerably further than I do here.

31 The Supreme Court seemed to recognize this point in Red Lion Broadcasting Co. v. FCC, 395 U.S. 367 (1969), but the point has dropped out of the current debate. If this analysis is correct, moreover, it is by no means clear that the print media should be more immunized from regulation than broadcasting, especially now that the original scarcity rationale seems weak.

32 See John Rawls, "The Basic Liberties and Their Priority," in *The Tanner Lectures on Human Values*, ed. Sterling McMurrin (Salt Lake City: University of Utah Press, 1982), 3:76.

33 See Buckley v. Valeo, 424 U.S. 1 (1976), and First National Bank of Boston v. Bellotti, 435 U.S. 765 (1978).

34 424 U.S. at pp. 48–9.

35 I collapse some complex issues here. See Miller v. California, 413 U.S. 15 (1973), and my "Pornography and the First Amendment," *Duke Law Journal* (September 1986): 589–627.

36 At the time of the framing, for example, geography was thought to define distinct communities with distinct interests; representation of the states as such seemed only natural. It would not be impossible to argue that racial and ethnic groups (among others) are the contemporary analogues to groups that were defined in geographical terms during the founding period.

37 In part this is Mill's defense of such efforts. See *Considerations on Representative Government*. For valuable discussions, see Charles Beitz, *Political Equality: An Essay in Democratic Theory* (Princeton, N.J.: Princeton University Press, 1989), pp. 123–40; and Iris Young, "Polity and Group Difference: A Critique of the Ideal of Universal Citizenship," *Ethics* 99 (1989): 250–84. Beitz's argument that proportional representation is not a requirement of political fairness is not inconsistent with the more prudential considerations invoked here; Young's claims about the need for discussion among the differently situated are highly compatible with my account.

38 *The Federalist* No. 70.

12

Dealing with Difference: A Politics of Ideas or a Politics of Presence?[1]

Anne Phillips

In the post-communist world of the 1980s and 1990s, liberalism and liberal democracy have achieved an impressive ascendancy, and can more plausibly present themselves as the only legitimate bases for equality, justice or democracy. Critics, of course, remain, but the grounds of complaint have shifted considerably. For many years, the central arguments against liberalism fell into three broad categories: that the liberal emphasis on individual freedoms and rights reflected a self-protective and competitive egotism that refused any wider community; that the liberal focus on "merely" political equalities ignored or even encouraged gross inequalities in social and economic life; and that the liberal consolidation of representative democracy reduced the importance of more active citizen participation. None of these complaints has disappeared, but each has been reformulated in terms of diversity and difference. Feminist theorists, in particular, have identified liberalism with an abstract individualism that ignores its own gendered content, and many have criticized the homogenizing ideals of equality that require us to be or become the same.[2] Accusations of gender-blindness and race- or ethnicity-blindness have added weight to older complaints that liberalism is blind to class. At a moment when most political theorists have situated themselves more firmly in the liberal tradition, liberalism is extensively criticized for erasing diversity and difference.

From the standpoint of that much maligned

visitor from Mars (whose technical brilliance in negotiating the journey always combines with an astonishing ignorance of political ideas) it might well appear that liberals never thought about difference. Left at such a level of generality, the accusation is distinctly odd, for notions of diversity and difference have been central to liberalism from its inception and to liberal democracy throughout its formation. What gave the original impetus to liberalism was the perception that neither nature nor tradition guaranteed political order, and that the very equality of what we now see as male subjects increased the potential diversity and conflict. Hence the search for a contractual basis for political authority that would bind these different individuals into a coherent whole; hence the concern with rights and autonomies that would allow them to pursue part of their lives under their own steam. In these and subsequent developments, difference remained politically significant and theoretically important: a driving force, indeed, in the separation between public and private affairs.

The defining characteristics of liberal democracy, as Robert Dahl among others has clarified,[3] are also grounded in the heterogeneity of the societies that gave it birth. It was the diversity of the citizenry, as much as its absolute size, that made the earlier (more consensual) practices of Athenian democracy so inappropriate to the modern world. Lacking any half-credible basis for seeing citizens as united in their goals, theorists of liberal democracy took issue with the homogenizing presumptions of a common good or common purpose, and made diversity a central

Originally published in *Constellations*, 1 (1994), 74–91. Reprinted by permission of Blackwell Publishers.

organizing theme. John Stuart Mill's famous vacillations over democracy derived from a double sense of democracy as both impetus and threat to diversity: something that breaks the hold of any single notion of the good life, but can also encourage a deadening conformity. In more straightforwardly confident vein, Georg Kateb has presented constitutional and representative democracy as that system *par excellence* that encourages and disseminates diversity. The procedures of electoral competition do not merely chasten and circumscribe the powers of government. By promoting a more skeptical attitude towards the basis on which competing claims are resolved, they also cultivate "a general tolerance of, and even affection for diversity: diversity in itself, and diversity as the source of regulated contest and competition."[4]

Difference is not something we have only just noticed. What we can more usefully say is that difference has been perceived in an overly cerebral fashion as differences in opinions and beliefs, and that the resulting emphasis on what I will call a politics of ideas has proved inadequate to the problems of political exclusion. The diversity most liberals have in mind is a diversity of beliefs, opinions, preferences and goals, all of which may stem from the variety of experience, but are considered as in principle detachable from this. Even the notion of interests, which seems most thoroughly grounded in differential material conditions, lends itself to at least semi detachment. The preference for higher taxes on those with higher incomes may be stronger among those with little money, especially if they believe the proceeds will finance public provision of educational or health services that would be otherwise beyond their reach. But support for higher taxation and better public provision is not restricted to those who most directly benefit: political preferences are influenced by material circumstances without being reducible to these. The interests of pensioners or the long-term unemployed can then be championed by those who are neither retired nor out of work; the interests of geographical localities can be represented by people who no longer live in the area; the interests of mothers with young children can be represented by childless men.

One consequence for democracy is that what is to be represented then takes priority over who does the representation. Issues of political presence are largely discounted, for when difference is considered in terms of intellectual diversity, it does not much matter who represents the range of ideas. One person may easily stand in for another; there is no additional requirement for the representatives to "mirror" the characteristics of the person or people represented. What concerns us in the choice of representative is a congruity of political beliefs and ideals, combined perhaps with a superior ability to articulate and register opinions. The quality of the democracy is guaranteed by the extension of suffrage to all adults, each of whom contributes his or her vote to the opinions that gain public weight. Stripped of any pre-democratic authority, the role of the politician is to carry a message. The messages will vary, but it hardly matters if the messengers are the same. (Those who believe that men have a monopoly on the political skills of articulating policies and ideas will not be surprised that most messengers are men.)

The notion of representation as primarily a matter of ideas has not, of course, gone unchallenged. In 1789, a group of Frenchwomen laid claim to a place in the Estates General in the following terms:

> Just as a nobleman cannot represent a plebeian and the latter cannot represent a nobleman, so a man, no matter how honest he may be, cannot represent a woman. Between the representatives and the represented there must be an absolute identity of interests.[5]

Shared experience here takes precedence over shared ideas; more precisely, no amount of thought or sympathy, no matter how careful or honest, can jump the barriers of experience. This assertion came, however, at a very particular point in the development of democracy, when the challenge to privilege momentarily centered around questioning which "estates" were entitled to representation. Subsequent notions of citizenship seemed to make this an anachronism, the last gasp of a feudal tradition. Hard fought extensions of suffrage combined with the evolution of political parties as the basic medium of representation to encourage an alternative notion of politics as a battleground for contested ideas.

The socialist tradition is of interest here, not only because it threw up a politics of pressing for the "representation of labour" (which seems to echo the earlier idea of representing different estates) but because it has been persistently troubled by tensions between a politics of ideas and an alternative politics of presence. Those involved in socialist parties often argued fiercely over the relationship between intellectuals and the "authentically" working class, some feeling that a socialist politics should privilege the voices and presence of workers, others that class identities should signify less than adherence to socialist ideas. In *What Is To Be Done*, Lenin offered one classic refutation of the politics of presence. Stressing the multiplicity of arenas within which the power of capital was exerted, he argued the limits of an experience confined to any one of these, and the overriding importance of strategic links between one set of struggles and another. This privileged the all-seeing intellectual (who might in principle originate from any class position or faction), the political activist who could look beyond each specific struggle or campaign to its wider connections and ramifications, and fit the various pieces of the jigsaw together. When socialist feminists challenged such views in the 1970s, one of the things they pointed out was that they denied legitimacy to women's self-understandings; another was that they presumed an objectivity on the part of these activists that raised them to a God-like level. As Sheila Rowbotham remarked in her critique of Leninist conceptions of the vanguard party, "(t)he Party is presented as soaring above all sectional concerns without providing any guarantees that this soaring will not be in fact an expression of the particular preoccupations of the group or groups with power within it."[6] Part of what was at issue in the development of an autonomous women's movement was the arrogance of those who thought that ideas could be separated from presence.

In Hannah Pitkin's influential discussion of representation, she criticizes the mirror view as beginning and ending with who is present, setting to one side the far more important question of what the representatives actually do. "Think of the legislature as a pictorial representation or a representative sample of the nation," she argues, "and you will almost inevitably concentrate on its composition rather than its activities."[7] But looking back at her discussion from a distance of twenty-five years, what is notable is how she elides the mapping of ideas with the mapping of people, not really distinguishing between a representative sample that captures the range of ideas, the range of interests, or the range of socially

significant groups. Her emphasis throughout is on the distinction between being and doing, and her arguments are as much directed against versions of proportional representation that would more adequately reflect the multiplicity of parties and opinion as against later preoccupations with representing excluded or marginalized groups. Questions of power and inequality do not figure largely in Pitkin's account. Such questions have become central to democratic debate today.

It is no part of my intention to disparage politics as a battleground for ideas. Much of the radicalizing impetus to democracy has centered around initiatives to make ideas more rather than less important, as in efforts to bind representatives more closely to the opinions they profess to hold, or in measures to reduce the backstage manipulations of pressure groups that disrupt the higher politics of ideas. But when the politics of ideas is taken in isolation from the politics of presence, it does not deal adequately with the experiences of those social groups who by virtue of their race or ethnicity or religion or gender have felt themselves excluded from the democratic process. Political exclusion is increasingly – I believe rightly – viewed in terms that can only be met by political presence, and much of this development has depended on a more complex understanding of the relationship between ideas and experience. The separation between who and what is to be represented, and the subordination of one to the other, relies on an understanding of ideas and interests as relatively unproblematic. It is as if the field of politics is already clearly demarcated, containing with it various clusters of preferences or ideas or concerns that exist independently of any process of formation. This is in stark contrast with the preoccupations that ran through the early years of the contemporary women's movement, when women talked of the difficulties in finding a voice, the way that dominant definitions of politics blocked out alternatives, or hegemonic culture controlled what could or could not be said. The emphasis then shifted from an objectively defined set of interests (that just needed more vigorous pursuit) to a more exploratory notion of possibilities so far silenced and ideas one had to struggle to express. In this later understanding of the processes that generate needs and concerns and ideas, it is harder to sustain the primacy of ideas over political presence. If it is simply a question of representing a given range of ideas and interests, it may not much matter who does the work of representation. But if the range of ideas has been curtailed by orthodoxies that rendered alternatives invisible, there will be no satisfactory solution short of changing the people who represent and develop the ideas.

The renewed concern over the relationship between ideas and experience also figures in recent arguments over the limits of tolerance in dealing with difference. The classically liberal treatment of difference allows for private spaces within which people can get on with their own chosen affairs and a public realm ordered around a set of minimum shared presumptions. But the relegation of difference to a private world of private variation has been experienced as an injunction to keep peculiarities a secret, and the shared presumptions that control the public world have proved less than even-handed in their treatment of different groups. The separation of church from state has long been considered the solution to the problems of religious difference, but it achieves this by requiring all religions to adopt a similarly self-denying ordinance that will limit the relevance of religious precepts to practices in the private sphere. This resolution is more amenable to some religions than to others; in particular, it is more acceptable to the heavily secularized forms of Christianity that became the norm in contemporary Europe. In similar vein, we might say that the relegation of homosexuality to a private affair between consenting adults helps reduce more overt forms of discrimination, but it achieves this at the expense of any more public disruption of a heterosexual norm. Private deviation is permitted, but not equal public worth.

Part of the dissatisfaction with liberalism's treatment of difference is the feeling that toleration is a poor substitute for recognition.[8] We only tolerate what we do not like or approve of (otherwise there is no need for toleration[9]), and yet where difference is bound up with identity, this is hard for the tolerated to accept. You can put up with people thinking you a harmless freak for your membership in the flat earth society. You may even revel in people thinking you a dangerous lunatic for your belief in communist revolution. It is not so easy to live with mere tolerance of your perverted sexuality or your denial of femininity or your irrationally fundamentalist religion. Tolerance is perceived as non-egalitarian, resting in some way on a distinction between majority norms and minority deviance, and incorporating some implied preference for a particular

way of life.[10] It is perhaps one of the tributes to democracy that people do not find tolerance satisfactory for long, and that the imperatives of democratic equality seem to press on further towards the recognition of equal worth. One reflection of this pressure has been the emerging school of thought that looks to "democratic" rather than "liberal" ways of dealing with diversity[11]: instead of treating difference as something that can flourish in the private domain, it turns to public manifestations in which differences can be confronted and (hopefully) resolved. Here, too, presence becomes crucial, for any public domain marked by the systematic absence of significant groups cannot even approach this resolution.

Once raised, the issues of presence are unlikely to go away. These are questions that must be addressed if democracies are to deliver on political equality. My concern in the rest of this paper is with what happens next, and in particular, with the tensions that arise between ideas and political presence. In the caricatures of those most resistant to a politics of presence, it is frequently misrepresented as a kind of "group-think": something that is necessarily separatist, necessarily corrosive of any wider community, and falsely presuming not only that one has to be a member of a particular group in order to understand or represent that group's interests, but that all members of the group in question will think along similar lines.[12] The caricature misses its mark. Faced, for example, with that 1789 claim that "between the representatives and the represented there must be an absolute identity of interests," most contemporary theorists will shy away from the implications of an essential female subject, or an authentic black subject, that can be represented by any one of its kind. Far more dominant today is the notion of multiple identities or multiple "subject positions," each of which is subject to political transformation and change. An attention to difference does not entail an essentialist understanding of identity; nor does it demand any wholesale rejection of the politics of competing ideas. But then the very sophistication of contemporary theories of identity can paralyze development; the very distance people have traveled from the caricatures of their position can remove them from democracy as it currently exists. In both the theoretical and the movement-centered literature which I now go on to discuss, issues of difference have been construed within a robustly democratic future that bears little relationship to contemporary political life. One of the challenges of democracy is how to combine the insights from such discussion with prescriptions that can be made relevant to representative democracy as practiced today.

Democracy as Public Contestation

Much of the contemporary literature on democracy and difference operates with notions of a more active and vigorous democracy that depends crucially on public debate. Rejecting both the false harmony that stamps out difference, and the equally false essentialism that defines people through some single, authentic identity, many theorists look to a democracy which maximises citizen participation, and requires us to engage and contest with one another. In a recent essay on feminism and democracy, Susan Mendus suggests that difference is the rationale for democracy, and that "whereas traditional democratic theory tends to construe difference as an obstacle to the attainment of a truly democratic state, feminist theory should alert us to the possibility that difference is rather what necessitates the pursuit of democracy."[13] In his work on multiculturalism, Charles Taylor calls for a politics of democratic empowerment as the way of dealing with demands for equal recognition without thereby entrenching people in fragmented identities.[14] In his discussion of the republican revival, Cass Sunstein argues for a deliberative democracy to which all citizens will have equal access, and where all perspectives can be equally addressed.[15]

All such arguments assume equality of access (without necessarily exploring the conditions that would deliver this result), and all differentiate themselves from merely majoritarian decision-making by anticipating some process of transformation and change. Where the classically liberal resolution of difference relies on a combination of private spaces and majority norms (these in turn established by majority vote), the democratic resolution of difference expects us to engage more directly with each other. We bring our differences to the public stage; we revise them through public debate. Major disagreements then surface between those who anticipate a full "resolution" in some newly achieved public consensus, and those who see differences as contingent but never as "difference" going away. The first position

looks more utopian than the second, but both operate at a level of generality that barely touches on democracy as practiced today.

Consider William Connolly's arguments in *Identity/Difference*,[16] which are particularly interesting in that they both say what should happen and why it almost certainly won't. Here, a "robust" politics of democratic engagement is presented as something that neither evades nor confirms difference: a politics that enables people to disturb settled conventions and expose settled identities. All identities are formed through difference – you know who you are through your difference from some other – and all identities are simultaneously threatened by the difference(s) of the other. There is always a danger that identities will be dogmatized into some naturalistic or unchanging essence, and always a danger that difference will generate destructive resentments and fears. What keeps these at bay is a politics of mutual challenge and disruption in which we are constantly reminded of the contingent nature of our identities. This politics depends in turn on the successful permeation of a "culture of genealogy" which helps us to see our identities as ambiguous and contestable and contested. Democracy then appears as an exciting engagement with difference: the challenge of "the other"; the disruption of certainties; the recognition of ambiguities within one's self as well as one's differences with others.

All this is tremendously refreshing, and in no way relies on a future transcendence of difference. But just at the point where he has achieved the philosophical resolution, Connolly backs off from claiming any immediate relevance for today. The confidence that enables people to dispense with settled identities or to accept the contingencies of fate may not be available to those suffering from economic inequality and political exclusion. Indeed, in an environment characterized by systematic inequality, the appeals to a robust democracy in which no-one shelters behind accusations of the other could "too readily be received as yet another attack on those already excluded from democratic politics."[17]

One compelling attraction of democracy is that it enables anyone to engage in fundamental riddles of existence through participation in a public politics that periodically disturbs and denaturalizes elements governing the cultural unconscious. But these same characteristics can intensify the reactive demand to redogmatize conventional identities if a large minority of the society is already suffering under severe burden of material deprivation and effective exclusion from the good life offered to a majority.[18]

Robust democracy then becomes possible only when economic inequalities are substantially reduced. My problem with this is not that it begs the question of how we might achieve such a precondition (we all have difficulties answering this), but that so much of what currently drives a politics of identity and difference is precisely the sense of deprivation and exclusion that Connolly sees as making such a politics so dangerous. Again, this is a point Connolly himself makes, noting that against the background of U.S. neoconservatism, any politics of identity and difference tends to fuel "the energies of ressentiment and the dogmatization of identity."[19] The philosophical resolution of democracy and difference remains largely that.[20]

Democracy Inside Social Movements

The second context in which these discussions take place is as interventions into specific movements that have formed around the politics of race, gender, sexuality and ethnicity. All these movements have involved a critique of the phony essentialisms that disguised systematic difference and inequality; nearly all of them, however, have also generated their own essentialisms that at some point or other claimed a unified female or lesbian or black or some other experience. Thus feminists took issue with the gender amnesia that transformed man "into a paradigm of humankind as such"[21] but, in the further explorations of sexual difference, they often insisted on a primary distinction between men and women that obscured further differences between women. Lesbian feminists took issue with the hegemonic controls of a heterosexual norm but, in the search for an affirming identity, they often constructed "the" authentic lesbian who would not tolerate differences of sexual practice or political attitudes within the lesbian community.[22] Anti-racists took issue with the mythologies of nation that had rendered black people invisible but, in the subsequent racial dualism that focused so exclusively on differences between "black" and "white" they tended to obscure the cultural and religious pluralism that characterizes the many non-white minorities.[23]

The problems of essentialism have, as a consequence, figured largely in the internal politics and debates of these movements. Much contemporary attention is focused on the conditions that can articulate group difference without thereby "disciplining" group members into a single authentic identity; in the process, many have suggested limits to the very notion of "a" group. As Shane Phelan puts it in her discussion of lesbian feminism in the United States: "Politics that ignores our identities, that makes them 'private', is useless; but nonnegotiable identities will enslave us whether they are imposed from within or without."[24] Speaking from the British context, Stuart Hall has suggested that we should pay more attention to the ways in which black experience is a diaspora experience, one in which the constructions of history and politics and culture are therefore fundamental, and not to be captured through notions of an essential black subject.[25] He talks here of "the end of innocence," "the recognition of the extraordinary diversity of subject positions, social experiences and cultural identities which compose the category 'black',"[26] and the impossibility of grounding the black subject or black experience in the essentialisms of nature or any other such guarantee.

These arguments cut across the balder distinction between ideas and presence, for what is being identified are differences in experiences and identities within what has hitherto been seen as an all-embracing category or group. It is not simply that "black" people or women or lesbians will disagree among themselves as to the appropriate policies and ideas and goals (they will vote for different parties, for example), but that their very senses of what it means to be black or female or lesbian will necessarily vary. In the context of the political movements with which these arguments engage, there seem to be two important implications. One is that the diversity of "subject positions" should be reflected within the organizational structures that define who does or doesn't get into the conversation. There should be no privileging of some voices as more authentic than others, and no coercive imposition of a supposedly unified point of view. The other implication, however, is that there is no way of knowing in advance whether this diversity has been successfully acknowledged. Any prior setting of the boundaries risks restoring some version of the authentic subject, for even if the boundaries are significantly pluralized, they still define in advance what are the appropriate or relevant differences. Thus Stuart Hall argues that it is no longer possible to represent "the black subject" without reference to class, gender, sexuality, ethnicity. But if this were taken as a series of guidelines about the different characteristics that must be covered within the membership of some campaigning organization, that would hardly be doing justice to his critique.

This is a problem that in some way or another besets every radical initiative, whether it is a matter of deciding whom to invite to address a meeting, who is to join an editorial board, or which groups are to participate in a campaign. We have become sufficiently attuned to the politics of presence to distrust the notion that anyone can "stand in" for anyone else, and sufficiently alert to the coercive powers of homogeneity to want to reflect diversity. But the critiques of essentialism deprive us of any simple mechanism for achieving the appropriate balance, and remind us that diversity is too great to be captured in any categorical list.

In the context of political movements, this is not such a serious difficulty. At their best, such movements already enjoy the kind of robust democracy that is proposed as an ideal for the polity as a whole: allowing for, indeed incapable of containing, the kind of contestation and mutual challenge that acknowledges difference and simultaneously disrupts it. The vehemence of debate indicates both a recurrent tendency towards essentialism and a continuous challenge to this: people are tough enough to resist prior classification and far too argumentative to accept someone else's definition of their selves. It is also worth noting that the fluidity of this politics lends itself more easily to a kind of learning through trial and error, for none of the consequences that people may derive from their current understandings of identity or difference is likely to be set in stone. The larger difficulties arise where we seek out more compromised intervention into democracies that are still pretty feeble.

Political Prescriptions for the Polity as a Whole

When we turn to the political prescriptions that might flow from a new understanding of democ-

racy and difference, we are not dealing in far-off utopias: There is a range of policies already proposed or implemented; and change is neither distant nor unlikely. The problem, rather, is that because such prescriptions operate in a half-way house of remedial reform, they are less able to resolve the contradictory pressures between the politics of ideas and the politics of presence. The kinds of mechanisms I have in mind include the quota systems adopted by a number of European political parties to achieve gender parity in elected assemblies, the redrawing of boundaries around black-majority constituencies to raise the number of black politicians elected in the United States, and the longer established power-sharing practices of those European consociational democracies that have distributed executive power and economic resources between different religious and linguistic groups. In each of these instances, the initiatives operate within the framework of an existing (not very robust) democracy. Tensions that might more readily resolve themselves in a future ferment of activity and deliberation become more acute in what everyone knows is a compromised situation.

All the more immediate proposals for reform insist on deliberate intervention as necessary to break the link between social structures of inequality or exclusion and the political reflection of these in levels of participation and influence. All of them also agree in looking to specifically *political* mechanisms – rather than, or sometimes as well as, longer term social transformation. They take issue therefore with the complacencies of a free market in politics, which sees political equality as sufficiently guaranteed by the procedures of one person one vote; they also challenge the more standard radical alternative, which has focused attention on prior economic or social change. Whatever their differences on other issues, the traditions of revolutionary Marxism and welfare state social reform have tended to agree on a broadly materialist analysis of the problems of political equality, seeing equal political access as something that depends on more fundamental changes in social, economic, and sometimes educational, conditions. The current interest in achieving equal or proportionate presence reverses this, focusing instead on institutional mechanisms – its critics would say "political fixes" – that can achieve more immediate change.

The roots of this reversal lie partly in frustration with what has proved an unbelievably slow process of structural transformation (*first* eliminate the sexual division of labor . . . the racial ordering of income and education and employment . . . the class patterning that decides children's futures – is it any wonder we search for short cuts?) But political frustration is not new, and people do not normally change direction just because things take so long. The additional impetus comes from the kind of arguments already outlined, which suggest that the range of political ideas and preferences is seriously constrained by the characteristics of the people who convey them. In a more traditional base-superstructure model, we were advised to concentrate first on generating the social conditions for equal citizenship, then to enjoy the political equalization that flows from this. Such an approach, however, treats policy choices as more straightforward than they are, and fails to observe the way that strategies devised for equality reflect the limits of those currently in power.[27] Where policy initiatives are worked out *for* rather than *with* a politically excluded constituency, they rarely engage all relevant concerns. Again, it is only if we consider the field of politics as already clearly demarcated, with all possible options already in play, that we can put much confidence in such an approach.

I do not discount the criticism that regards institutional mechanisms for achieving equal or proportionate presence as a species of diversionary "political fixing," but we should not be required to choose between these and other urgent tasks of social and economic transformation. When political exclusion is such a marked feature of contemporary democratic life, it seems inappropriate to rely on distant prospects of a more robustly participatory democracy and/or structural changes in social and economic conditions. The very distance of such prospects puts a premium on political prescriptions that can be made relevant to representative democracy as currently practiced, and most of these will involve some form of affirmative action that can guarantee more equal representation in existing decision-making assemblies. Any specifically political mechanism, however, risks imposing a rigid definition of the identities that have to be included or the interests so far left out. The more complex understanding of multiple identities that change both over time and according to context is a potential casualty here, as is the continuing importance we would all want to attach to political disagreement and debate.

If we consider, for example, the mechanisms that might be appropriate in contemporary Britain to redress racial exclusions, one immediate problem is the diversity of non-white experience, and the major disagreements that have surfaced between taking race or ethnicity or religion as the basis of social identity and political exclusion. When we take race as the central indicator, this encourages a dualism of "black" or "white," a division of the universe which is often said to be closer to the political perceptions of Afro-Caribbeans than to the self-definitions of the significantly more numerous Asians. Tariq Modood, indeed, has argued that "the concept of Black is harmful to Asians and is a form of political identity that most Asians do not accept as their primary public identity."[28] But if we take ethnicity or religion instead, these are felt to be too closely associated with a politics of multiculturalism that has looked to the greater dissemination of knowledge about ethnic and religious minorities as the way of breaking down racial stereotypes, and has been thought insufficiently vigorous in its challenges to racism *per se*. Alternative ways of defining group identities or redressing group exclusions have become loaded with political significance, with an attention to cultural diversity being variously perceived as something that depoliticizes the anti-racist struggle or is a crucial corrective to the simplicities of racial dualism.[29]

What, in this context, is an appropriate mechanism for dealing with political exclusion? Can Asians be represented by Afro-Caribbeans, Hindus by Muslims, black women by black men? Or do these groups have nothing more in common than their joint experience of being excluded from power? In their recent book on *Racialized Boundaries*, Floya Anthias and Nira Yuval-Davies conclude that "the form of political representation which has grown out of identity politics and equal opportunities and which has attempted to represent social difference more genuinely, has created an impossible mission for itself,"[30] and that what is a positive diversity of overlapping identities becomes dangerously constrained in efforts towards proportional representation. But does this mean that nothing can be done: that given the risks, on the one hand, of an imposed and misleading uniformity, and the absurdities, on the other, of an endless search for sufficiently pluralized categories, we have to abandon the quest for specifically political mechanisms?

Caucuses and quotas are the most obvious political mechanisms for dealing with political exclusion, yet both of these depend on a prior categorization of the basis on which people have been excluded. Neither seems adequate to the complexity of political identities.

The politics that has developed in the United States around the strategy of black-majority, single-member constituencies might seem more straightforward, for it seems clear enough that it is race rather than ethnicity that has been at issue in the political exclusion of African-Americans, and racial bloc voting is plausibly described as "the single most salient feature of contemporary political life."[31] But even so, a political resolution that privileges race as the prime consideration can make it more difficult for people to articulate what are complex and multiple identities: can obscure tensions, for example, around gender and class, can block out major disagreements over policy preferences and political ideas. The implication that black representatives are representative merely by virtue of being black is inevitably problematic, even where "blackness" is a less contested category.

Those who consider the problems of political equality as adequately dealt with by provision for the equal right to vote will be happy to rest their case there, but criticism of the strategy of black electoral success has not been confined to these quarters. Equally powerful criticism comes from those who regard proportionate presence as a necessary but insufficient condition, and are concerned that the focus on numbers alone can reduce political accountability, limit prospects for multi-racial coalition, and undermine the urgency of policy debate.[32] There is, in other words, a strong sense of the tensions that can develop between a politics of presence and a politics of ideas. But instead of resolving this by opting for the second over the first, critics have looked to alternative patterns of representation that can make it possible to combine the two. Some of the most innovative work in this area comes from those pressing for a return to the more competitive politics of multi-member constituencies but based on forms of proportional representation and cumulative voting that would maintain the scope for electing representatives from minority groups.[33] It is felt, in other words, that mechanisms *can* be devised which continue the gains in black political presence without forcing an either/or choice between the politics of presence and the politics of ideas.

European initiatives on gender parity can also be seen as successfully negotiating the competing demands of ideas and presence – and here we enter the realm of policies already in position rather than proposals in contested debate. The favored strategy involves pressuring existing political parties to introduce a more balanced ticket of both women and men in their candidates for winnable seats, thus maintaining accountability through party policies and programs while changing the gender composition of elected assemblies. Often enough, the mechanism has been a straightforward quota, which has contributed to a remarkable increase in the numbers of women elected in the Nordic countries. Critics of such strategies usually rest their case on the paucity of "experienced" women, the potential loss of "good" men to politics, and the risk that the overall caliber of politicians (not too high in my opinion) will fall. They do not dwell particularly on the essentialist presumptions of "a" women's perspective, or the dangerous potential for women pressing only narrowly sectional concerns. There are just too many women for them to be considered as a unified or sectional group, and they are spread across every class or ethnic or religious dimension and every conceivable political persuasion. When it is applied to women, the politics of presence does not seriously disrupt the politics of competing ideas; it is relatively easy to pursue both of these together.

Outside the more established democracies of Europe and the United States, the arguments often start from the opposite direction, a feeling that *who* is to be represented has so far taken precedence over *what*, and that what is missing is the higher politics of ideas. One might think, for example, of the abuse of kinship networks and ethnic solidarities by political elites in postcolonial Africa, many of whom evacuated the terrain of contested policies and ideals to cultivate a power base around exclusionary identities. When the colonial powers retreated from Africa, they left behind societies in which the state had become the main avenue for economic and social advancement, and where the politics of patronage was almost doomed to flourish. In this context, people lived under what seemed an absence of politics, with the contrast between a civilian or military regime seeming of far less consequence than whether you had access to any of the rulers. As ethnic connections emerged as one of the main routes of access, ethnic rivalries became literally deadly, even when the ethnicities in question were relatively recent creations.[34] It is against this background that African radicals and writers have so eloquently called for a politics based on vision and ideals.[35]

Through all these examples, the biggest mistake is to set up ideas as the opposite of political presence: to treat ideas as totally separate from the people who carry them; or worry exclusively about the people without giving a thought to their policies and ideas. It should be said, however, that this is not such a frequent mistake as the caricatures suggest, and that those exploring equal or proportionate presence rarely regard it as a substitute for the politics of competing ideas. If anything, the most acute criticisms of the politics of presence have come from those most committed to challenging political exclusions, and the debate has long shifted beyond its either/or axis. What is, perhaps, emerging is that the more satisfactory ways of redressing group exclusion are those which are the less group-specific. This seems to be the case in relation to gender quotas, if only because the category of "woman" is so inclusive of other kinds of difference and division that it leaves open the necessary space for a multiplicity of political identities. It also seems to be the case in the proposals that have developed around the implementation of the Voting Rights

Act in the United States, which have moved away from the more tightly drawn voting districts that provide a "safe seat" for minority representatives towards a larger geographical constituency that can no longer pretend to contain only one voice.

Such developments acknowledge the danger in preemptive classifications of people's political identities, and are well aware that essentialist definitions of the groups that have been excluded can work to reduce political accountability and debate. They nonetheless take issue with the more traditional treatment of diversity and difference as simply a matter of contested ideas. The overly cerebral understanding of difference has not engaged sufficiently with the problems of political presence, for it has encouraged an unacceptable level of complacency over the homogeneity of political elites. We can no longer pretend that the full range of ideas and preferences and alternatives has been adequately represented when those charged with the job of representation are all white or all male or all middle class; or that democracies complete their task of political equality when they establish a free market in political ideas. One would not want to take up permanent residence in the half-way house of remedial reform, but mechanisms should be – and can be – devised that address the problems of group exclusion without fixing the boundaries or character of each group.

Notes

1   The work for this article was made possible by a Social Science Research Fellowship from the Nuffield Foundation, 1992–3, and the first version was presented as "Democracy and Difference: Changing Boundaries of the Political," Annual Conference for the Study of Political Thought at Yale University, New Haven, CT, April 1993.

2   I summarize and discuss many of these arguments in *Engendering Democracy* (Pennsylvania: University of Pennsylvania State Press, 1991). See also Jane Flax. "Beyond equality: gender, justice and difference," in G. Bock and S. James, eds., *Beyond Equality and Difference* (London: Routledge, 1992).

3   Robert A. Dahl, *Democracy and Its Critics* (New Haven: Yale University Press, 1989).

4   George Kateb, "The Moral Distinctiveness of Representative Democracy," *Ethics* 91:3 (1981): 361.

5   Cited by Silvia Vegetti Finzi, "Female identity between sexuality and maternity," in Bock and James, eds., *Beyond Equality and Difference*, 128.

6   Sheila Rowbotham, "The women's movement and organising for socialism," in S. Rowbotham, L. Segal and H. Wainwright, *Beyond the Fragments: Feminism and the making of socialism* (London: Newcastle Socialist Centre and Islington Community Press, 1979), 61.

7   Hannah F. Pitkin, *The Concept of Representation* (Berkeley: University of California Press, 1967), 226.

8   See Shane Phelan's discussion of the way that lesbian feminists in the United States came to reject liberalism. *Identity Politics: Lesbian Feminism and the Limits of Community* (Philadelphia: Temple University Press, 1989).

9   See Susan Mendus, *Toleration and the Limits of Liberalism* (London: Macmillan, 1989).

10 I do not know if this is intrinsic to tolerance, but I suspect it is. If we could imagine a world in which difference was genuinely detached from power – in which there really were multiple differences and none carried more weight than any other – then I

am not sure we would be talking of the need for toleration. See also Kirstie McClure, "Difference, Diversity and The Limits of Toleration," *Political Theory* 18:3 (1990).

11 I owe this formulation to Peter Jones's paper "Groups, Beliefs and Identities," presented at the European Consortium for Political Research, Leiden, April 1993.

12 All these points can be found in Cynthia V. Ward, "The Limits of 'Liberal Republicanism,': Why Group-Based Remedies And Republican Citizenship Don't Mix," *Columbia Law Review* 91:3 (1991). In querying the notion that *only* the members of particular disadvantaged groups can understand or represent their interests, she might usefully turn this question round to ask whether such understanding or representation is possible without the presence of *any* members of the disadvantaged groups.

13 Susan Mendus, "Losing the Faith: Feminism and Democracy" in John Dunn, ed., *Democracy: The Unfinished Journey 508BC to AD1993* (Oxford: Oxford University Press, 1992), 216.

14 Charles Taylor, *The Ethics of Authenticity* (Cambridge, Mass.: Harvard University Press, 1992); Charles Taylor and Amy Gutmann, *Multiculturalism and The Politics of Recognition* (Cambridge, Mass: Harvard University Press, 1992).

15 Cass Sunstein, "Beyond the Republican Revival," *Yale Law Journal* 97:8 (1988).

16 William Connolly, *Identity/Difference: Democratic Negotiations of Political Paradox* (Ithaca: Cornell University Press, 1991).

17 Connolly, 197.

18 Connolly, 211.

19 Connolly, 213.

20 In a review of Connolly's book, Iris Young describes his prescriptions as "therapies." *Political Theory* 20:3 (1992): 514.

21 Adriana Cavarero, "Equality and sexual difference: amnesia in political thought," in Bock and James, eds., *Beyond Equality and Difference*, 36.

22 Phelan, *Identity Politics*. Phelan notes in particular the rows that broke out over sado-masochism, and whether this was an "acceptable" part of lesbian identity.

23 See the essays in Tariq Modood, *Not Easy Being British: colour, culture and citizenship* (Stoke on Trent: Runnymede Trust and Trentham Books, 1992). The largest non-white group in Britain is Asians of Indian origin, many of whom have felt the racial dualism of anti-racist politics rendered them invisible.

24 Phelan, *Identity Politics*, 170.

25 Stuart Hall, "New Ethnicities," in J. Donald and A. Rattansi, eds., *"Race", Culture and Difference* (London: Sage and Open University Press, 1992).

26 Hall, 254.

27 Obvious examples include the post-war preoccupation with full employment as a condition for equal citizenship, where full employment was either unthinkingly equated with full employment for men, or else extended formally to include women without any serious consideration of the structural changes that would then become necessary to re-order the relationship between paid and unpaid work. Will Kymlicka provides a different example in his discussion of the Trudeau reforms which set out to promote more equal citizenship in Canada, but equated full and equal participation for the native Indian population with a color-blind constitution that would dismantle the system of segregated reserves. Though widely applauded by the country's media and even opposition parties, the proposals had to be withdrawn in the face of almost unanimous opposition from the Indians themselves. Kymlicka, *Liberalism, Community and Culture* (Oxford: Clarendon Press, 1989).

28 Modood, *Not Easy Being British*, 29.

29 For an excellent overview of these debates, and an attempt to push beyond them, see the essays in Donald and Rattansi, eds., *"Race", Culture and Difference*.

30 Floya Anthias and Nira Yuval-Davies, *Racialized Boundaries: Race, Nation, Gender, Colour and Class and the Anti-Racist Struggle* (London: Routledge, 1992), 192.

31 S. Issacharoff, "Polarized Voting and the Political Process: the Transformation of Voting Rights Jurisprudence," *Michigan Law Review* 90:7 (1992): 1855.

32 Bernard Grofman and Chandler Davidson, eds., *Controversies in Minority Voting: The Voting Rights Act in Perspective* (Washington D.C: The Brookings Institution, 1992) provides a comprehensive range of the arguments that have developed around minority representation.

33 Lani Guinier, "The Triumph of Tokenism: The Voting Rights Act and The Theory of Black Electoral Success," *Michigan Law Review* 89:5 (1991); "No Two Seats: The Elusive Quest for Political Equality," *Virginia Law Review* 77:8 (1991). I discuss this material at greater length in "Political Inclusion and Political Presence. Or, Why Does It Matter Who Our Representatives Are?" (Paper presented at the Joint Sessions of the European Consortium on Political Research, Leiden, 2–7 April, 1993).

34 Think here of the Nigerian civil war and the attempted secession of Biafra. The Ibo people who provided the ethnic basis for Biafra only came into substantial existence as a unified "people" through this war.

35 See especially Chinua Achebe's novels and essays, especially *The Anthills of The Savannah* and *The Trouble With Nigeria*.

PART III

Justice

13

Justice as Fairness[1]

John Rawls

1. It might seem at first sight that the concepts of justice and fairness are the same, and that there is no reason to distinguish them, or to say that one is more fundamental than the other. I think that this impression is mistaken. In this paper I wish to show that the fundamental idea in the concept of justice is fairness; and I wish to offer an analysis of the concept of justice from this point of view. To bring out the force of this claim, and the analysis based upon it, I shall then argue that it is this aspect of justice for which utilitarianism, in its classical form, is unable to account, but which is expressed, even if misleadingly, by the idea of the social contract.

To start with I shall develop a particular conception of justice by stating and commenting upon two principles which specify it, and by considering the circumstances and conditions under which they may be thought to arise. The principles defining this conception, and the conception itself, are, of course, familiar. It may be possible, however, by using the notion of fairness as a framework, to assemble and to look at them in a new way. Before stating this conception, however, the following preliminary matters should be kept in mind.

Throughout I consider justice only as a virtue of social institutions, or what I shall call practices.[2] The principles of justice are regarded as formulating restrictions as to how practices may define positions and offices, and assign thereto powers and liabilities, rights and duties. Justice as a virtue of particular actions or of persons I do not take up at all. It is important to distinguish these various subjects of justice, since the meaning of the concept varies according to whether it is applied to practices, particular actions, or persons. These meanings are, indeed, connected, but they are not identical. I shall confine my discussion to the sense of justice as applied to practices, since this sense is the basic one. Once it is understood, the other senses should go quite easily.

Justice is to be understood in its customary sense as representing but *one* of the many virtues of social institutions, for these may be antiquated, inefficient, degrading, or any number of other things, without being unjust. Justice is not to be confused with an all-inclusive vision of a good society; it is only one part of any such conception. It is important, for example, to distinguish that sense of equality which is an aspect of the concept of justice from that sense of equality which belongs to a more comprehensive social ideal. There may well be inequalities which one concedes are just, or at least not unjust, but which, nevertheless, one wishes, on other grounds, to do away with. I shall focus attention, then, on the usual sense of justice in which it is essentially the elimination of arbitrary distinctions and the establishment, within the structure of a practice, of a proper balance between competing claims.

Finally, there is no need to consider the principles discussed below as *the* principles of justice. For the moment it is sufficient that they are typical of a family of principles normally associated with the concept of justice. The way in which the principles of this family resemble one another, as shown by the background against which they may

Originally published in *Philosophical Review*, 67 (1958), 164–94.

be thought to arise, will be made clear by the whole of the subsequent argument.

2. The conception of justice which I want to develop may be stated in the form of two principles as follows: first, each person participating in a practice, or affected by it, has an equal right to the most extensive liberty compatible with a like liberty for all; and second, inequalities are arbitrary unless it is reasonable to expect that they will work out for everyone's advantage, and provided the positions and offices to which they attach, or from which they may be gained, are open to all. These principles express justice as a complex of three ideas: liberty, equality, and reward for services contributing to the common good.[3]

The term "person" is to be construed variously depending on the circumstances. On some occasions it will mean human individuals, but in others it may refer to nations, provinces, business firms, churches, teams, and so on. The principles of justice apply in all these instances, although there is a certain logical priority to the case of human individuals. As I shall use the term "person," it will be ambiguous in the manner indicated.

The first principle holds, of course, only if other things are equal: that is, while there must always be a justification for departing from the initial position of equal liberty (which is defined by the pattern of rights and duties, powers and liabilities, established by a practice), and the burden of proof is placed on him who would depart from it, nevertheless, there can be, and often there is, a justification for doing so. Now, that similar particular cases, as defined by a practice, should be treated similarly as they arise, is part of the very concept of a practice; it is involved in the notion of an activity in accordance with rules.[4] The first principle expresses an analogous conception, but as applied to the structure of practices themselves. It holds, for example, that there is a presumption against the distinctions and classifications made by legal systems and other practices to the extent that they infringe on the original and equal liberty of the persons participating in them. The second principle defines how this presumption may be rebutted.

It might be argued at this point that justice requires only an equal liberty. If, however, a greater liberty were possible for all without loss or conflict, then it would be irrational to settle on a lesser liberty. There is no reason for circumscribing rights unless their exercise would be incompatible, or would render the practice defining them less effective. Therefore no serious distortion of the concept of justice is likely to follow from including within it the concept of the greatest equal liberty.

The second principle defines what sorts of inequalities are permissible; it specifies how the presumption laid down by the first principle may be put aside. Now by inequalities it is best to understand not *any* differences between offices and positions, but differences in the benefits and burdens attached to them either directly or indirectly, such as prestige and wealth, or liability to taxation and compulsory services. Players in a game do not protest against there being different positions, such as batter, pitcher, catcher, and the like, nor to there being various privileges and powers as specified by the rules; nor do the citizens of a country object to there being the different offices of government such as president, senator, governor, judge, and so on, each with their special rights and duties. It is not differences of this kind that are normally thought of as inequalities, but differences in the resulting distribution established by a practice, or made possible by it, of the things men strive to attain or avoid. Thus they may complain about the pattern of honors and rewards set up by a practice (e.g., the privileges and salaries of government officials) or they may object to the distribution of power and wealth which results from the various ways in which men avail themselves of the opportunities allowed by it (e.g., the concentration of wealth which may develop in a free price system allowing large entrepreneurial or speculative gains).

It should be noted that the second principle holds that an inequality is allowed only if there is reason to believe that the practice with the inequality, or resulting in it, will work for the advantage of *every* party engaging in it. Here it is important to stress that *every* party must gain from the inequality. Since the principle applies to practices, it implies that the representative man in every office or position defined by a practice, when he views it as a going concern, must find it reasonable to prefer his condition and prospects with the inequality to what they would be under the practice without it. The principle excludes, therefore, the justification of inequalities on the grounds that the disadvantages of those in one position are outweighed by the greater advantages of those in another position. This rather simple restriction is the main modification I wish to make in the utilitarian principle as usually understood. When coupled with the notion of a practice, it is a restriction of consequence,[5] and one which some utilitarians, e.g., Hume and Mill, have used in their discussions of justice without realizing apparently its significance, or at least without calling attention to it.[6] Why it is a significant modification of principle, changing one's conception of justice entirely, the whole of my argument will show.

Further, it is also necessary that the various offices to which special benefits or burdens attach are open to all. It may be, for example, to the common advantage, as just defined, to attach special benefits to certain offices. Perhaps by doing so the requisite talent can be attracted to them and encouraged to give its best efforts. But any offices having special benefits must be won in a fair competition in which contestants are judged on their merits. If some offices were not open, those excluded would normally be justified in feeling unjustly treated, even if they benefited from the greater efforts of those who were allowed to compete for them. Now if one can assume that offices are open, it is necessary only to consider the design of practices themselves and how they jointly, as a system, work together. It will be a mistake to focus attention on the varying relative positions of particular persons, who may be known to us by their proper names, and to require that each such change, as a once for all transaction viewed in isolation, must be in itself just. It is the system of practices which is to be judged, and judged from a general point of view: unless one is prepared to criticize it from the standpoint of a representative man holding some particular office, one has no complaint against it.

3. Given these principles one might try to derive them from a priori principles of reason, or claim that they were known by intuition. These are familiar enough steps and, at least in the case of the first principle, might be made with some success. Usually, however, such arguments, made at this point, are unconvincing. They are not likely to lead to an understanding of the basis of the principles of justice, not at least as principles of justice. I wish, therefore, to look at the principles in a different way.

Imagine a society of persons amongst whom a certain system of practices is *already* well estab-

lished. Now suppose that by and large they are mutually self-interested; their allegiance to their established practices is normally founded on the prospect of self-advantage. One need not assume that, in all senses of the term "person," the persons in this society are mutually self-interested. If the characterization as mutually self-interested applies when the line of division is the family, it may still be true that members of families are bound by ties of sentiment and affection and willingly acknowledge duties in contradiction to self-interest. Mutual self-interestedness in the relations between families, nations, churches, and the like, is commonly associated with intense loyalty and devotion on the part of individual members. Therefore, one can form a more realistic conception of this society if one thinks of it as consisting of mutually self-interested families, or some other association. Further, it is not necessary to suppose that these persons are mutually self-interested under all circumstances, but only in the usual situations in which they participate in their common practices.

Now suppose also that these persons are rational: they know their own interests more or less accurately; they are capable of tracing out the likely consequences of adopting one practice rather than another; they are capable of adhering to a course of action once they have decided upon it; they can resist present temptations and the enticements of immediate gain; and the bare knowledge or perception of the difference between their condition and that of others is not, within certain limits and in itself, a source of great dissatisfaction. Only the last point adds anything to the usual definition of rationality. This definition should allow, I think, for the idea that a rational man would not be greatly downcast from knowing, or seeing, that others are in a better position than himself, unless he thought their being so was the result of injustice, or the consequence of letting chance work itself out for no useful common purpose, and so on. So if these persons strike us as unpleasantly egoistic, they are at least free in some degree from the fault of envy.[7]

Finally, assume that these persons have roughly similar needs and interests, or needs and interests in various ways complementary, so that fruitful cooperation amongst them is possible; and suppose that they are sufficiently equal in power and ability to guarantee that in normal circumstances none is able to dominate the others.

This condition (as well as the others) may seem excessively vague; but in view of the conception of justice to which the argument leads, there seems no reason for making it more exact here.

Since these persons are conceived as engaging in their common practices, which are already established, there is no question of our supposing them to come together to deliberate as to how they will set these practices up for the first time. Yet we can imagine that from time to time they discuss with one another whether any of them has a legitimate complaint against their established institutions. Such discussions are perfectly natural in any normal society. Now suppose that they have settled on doing this in the following way. They first try to arrive at the principles by which complaints, and so practices themselves, are to be judged. Their procedure for this is to let each person propose the principles upon which he wishes his complaints to be tried with the understanding that, if acknowledged, the complaints of others will be similarly tried, and that no complaints will be heard at all until everyone is roughly of one mind as to how complaints are to be judged. They each understand further that the principles proposed and acknowledged on this occasion are binding on future occasions. Thus each will be wary of proposing a principle which would give him a peculiar advantage, in his present circumstances, supposing it to be accepted. Each person knows that he will be bound by it in future circumstances the peculiarities of which cannot be known, and which might well be such that the principle is then to his disadvantage. The idea is that everyone should be required to make *in advance* a firm commitment, which others also may reasonably be expected to make, and that no one be given the opportunity to tailor the canons of a legitimate complaint to fit his own special conditions, and then to discard them when they no longer suit his purpose. Hence each person will propose principles of a general kind which will, to a large degree, gain their sense from the various applications to be made of them, the particular circumstances of which being as yet unknown. These principles will express the conditions in accordance with which each is the least unwilling to have his interests limited in the design of practices, given the competing interests of the others, on the supposition that the interests of others will be limited likewise. The restrictions which would so arise might be thought of as those a person would keep in mind if he were designing a practice in which his enemy were to assign him his place.

The two main parts of this conjectural account have a definite significance. The character and respective situations of the parties reflect the typical circumstances in which questions of justice arise. The procedure whereby principles are proposed and acknowledged represents constraints, analogous to those of having a morality, whereby rational and mutually self-interested persons are brought to act reasonably. Thus the first part reflects the fact that questions of justice arise when conflicting claims are made upon the design of a practice and where it is taken for granted that each person will insist, as far as possible, on what he considers his rights. It is typical of cases of justice to involve persons who are pressing on one another their claims, between which a fair balance or equilibrium must be found. On the other hand, as expressed by the second part, having a morality must at least imply the acknowledgment of principles as impartially applying to one's own conduct as well as to another's, and moreover principles which may constitute a constraint, or limitation, upon the pursuit of one's own interests. There are, of course, other aspects of having a morality: the acknowledgment of moral principles must show itself in accepting a reference to them as reasons for limiting one's claims, in acknowledging the burden of providing a special explanation, or excuse, when one acts contrary to them, or else in showing shame and remorse and a desire to make amends, and so on. It is sufficient to remark here that having a morality is analogous to having made a firm commitment in advance; for one must acknowledge the principles of morality even when to one's disadvantage.[8] A man whose moral judgments always coincided with his interests could be suspected of having no morality at all.

Thus the two parts of the foregoing account are intended to mirror the kinds of circumstances in which questions of justice arise and the constraints which having a morality would impose upon persons so situated. In this way one can see how the acceptance of the principles of justice might come about, for given all these conditions as described, it would be natural if the two principles of justice were to be acknowledged. Since there is no way for anyone to win special advantages for himself, each might consider it reasonable to acknowledge equality as an initial principle. There is, however, no reason why they should regard this position as final; for if there are inequalities which satisfy the second principle, the immediate gain which equality would allow can be considered as intelligently invested in view of its future return. If, as is quite likely, these inequalities work as incentives to draw out better efforts, the members of this society may look upon them as concessions to human nature: they, like us, may think that people ideally should want to serve one another. But as they are mutually self-interested, their acceptance of these inequalities is merely the acceptance of the relations in which they actually stand, and a recognition of the motives which lead them to engage in their common practices. *They* have no title to complain of one another. And so provided that the conditions of the principle are met, there is no reason why they should not allow such inequalities. Indeed, it would be short-sighted of them to do so, and could result, in most cases, only from their being dejected by the bare knowledge, or perception, that others are better situated. Each person will, however, insist on an advantage to himself, and so on a common advantage, for none is willing to sacrifice anything for the others.

These remarks are not offered as a proof that persons so conceived and circumstanced would settle on the two principles, but only to show that these principles could have such a background, and so can be viewed as those principles which mutually self-interested and rational persons, when similarly situated and required to make in advance a firm commitment, could acknowledge as restrictions governing the assignment of rights and duties in their common practices, and thereby accept as limiting their rights against one another. The principles of justice may, then, be regarded as those principles which arise when the constraints of having a morality are imposed upon parties in the typical circumstances of justice.

4. These ideas are, of course, connected with a familiar way of thinking about justice which goes back at least to the Greek Sophists, and which regards the acceptance of the principles of justice as a compromise between persons of roughly equal power who would enforce their will on each other if they could, but who, in view of the equality of forces amongst them and for the sake of their own peace and security, acknowledge certain forms of conduct insofar as prudence seems to require. Justice is thought of as a pact between rational egoists the stability of which is dependent on a balance of power and a similarity of circumstances.[9] While the previous account is connected with this tradition, and with its most recent variant, the theory of games,[10] it differs from it in several important respects which, to forestall misinterpretations, I will set out here.

First, I wish to use the previous conjectural account of the background of justice as a way of analyzing the concept. I do not want, therefore, to be interpreted as assuming a general theory of human motivation: when I suppose that the parties are mutually self-interested, and are not willing to have their (substantial) interests sacrificed to others, I am referring to their conduct and motives as they are taken for granted in cases where questions of justice ordinarily arise. Justice is the virtue of practices where there are assumed to be competing interests and conflicting claims, and where it is supposed that persons will press their rights on each other. That persons are mutually self-interested in certain situations and for certain purposes is what gives rise to the question of justice in practices covering those circumstances. Amongst an association of saints, if such a community could really exist, the disputes about justice could hardly occur; for they would all work selflessly together for one end, the glory of God as defined by their common religion, and reference to this end would settle every question of right. The justice of practices does not come up until there are several different parties (whether we think of these as individuals, associations, or nations and so on, is irrelevant) who do press their claims on one another, and who do regard themselves as representatives of interests which deserve to be considered. Thus the previous account involves no general theory of human motivation. Its intent is simply to incorporate into the conception of justice the relations of men to one another which set the stage for questions of justice. It makes no difference how wide or general these relations are, as this matter does not bear on the analysis of the concept.

Again, in contrast to the various conceptions of the social contract, the several parties do not establish any particular society or practice; they do not covenant to obey a particular sovereign body or to accept a given constitution.[11] Nor do they, as in the theory of games (in certain respects a marvelously sophisticated development of this tradition), decide on individual strategies adjusted to their respective circumstances in the game. What the parties do is to *jointly* acknowledge certain *principles* of appraisal relating to their common *practices* either as already established or merely proposed. They accede to standards of judgment, not to a given practice; they do not make any specific agreement, or bargain, or adopt a particular strategy. The subject of their acknowledgment is, therefore, very general indeed; it is simply the acknowledgment of certain principles of judgment, fulfilling certain general conditions, to be used in criticizing the arrangement of their common affairs. The relations of mutual self-interest between the parties who are similarly circumstanced mirror the conditions under which questions of justice arise, and the procedure by which the principles of judgment are proposed and acknowledged reflects the constraints of having a morality. Each aspect, then, of the preceding hypothetical account serves the purpose of bringing out a feature of the notion of justice. One could, if one liked, view the principles of justice as the "solution" of this highest order "game" of adopting, subject to the procedure described, principles of argument for all coming particular "games" whose peculiarities one can in no way foresee. But this comparison, while no doubt helpful, must not obscure the fact that this highest order "game" is of a special sort.[12] Its significance is that its various pieces represent aspects of the concept of justice.

Finally, I do not, of course, conceive the several parties as necessarily coming together to establish their common practices for the first time. Some institutions may, indeed, be set up *de novo*; but I have framed the preceding account so that it will apply when the full complement of social institutions already exists and represents the result of a long period of development. Nor is the account in any way fictitious. In any society where people reflect on their institutions they will have an idea of what principles of justice would be acknowledged under the conditions described, and there will be occasions when questions of justice are actually discussed in this way. Therefore if their practices do not accord with these principles, this will affect the quality of their social relations. For in this case there will be some recognized situations wherein the parties are mutually aware that one of them is being forced to accept what the other would concede is unjust. The foregoing analysis may then be thought of as representing the actual quality of relations between persons as defined by practices accepted as just. In such practices the parties will acknow-

ledge the principles on which it is constructed, and the general recognition of this fact shows itself in the absence of resentment and in the sense of being justly treated. Thus one common objection to the theory of the social contract, its apparently historical and fictitious character, is avoided.

5. That the principles of justice may be regarded as arising in the manner described illustrates an important fact about them. Not only does it bring out the idea that justice is a primitive moral notion in that it arises once the concept of morality is imposed on mutually self-interested agents similarly circumstanced, but it emphasizes that, fundamental to justice, is the concept of fairness which relates to right dealing between persons who are cooperating with or competing against one another, as when one speaks of fair games, fair competition, and fair bargains. The question of fairness arises when free persons, who have no authority over one another, are engaging in a joint activity and amongst themselves settling or acknowledging the rules which define it and which determine the respective shares in its benefits and burdens. A practice will strike the parties as fair if none feels that, by participating in it, they or any of the others are taken advantage of, or forced to give in to claims which they do not regard as legitimate. This implies that each has a conception of legitimate claims which he thinks it reasonable for others as well as himself to acknowledge. If one thinks of the principles of justice as arising in the manner described, then they do define this sort of conception. A practice is just or fair, then, when it satisfies the principles which those who participate in it could propose to one another for mutual acceptance under the aforementioned circumstances. Persons engaged in a just, or fair, practice can face one another openly and support their respective positions, should they appear questionable, by reference to principles which it is reasonable to expect each to accept.

It is this notion of the possibility of mutual acknowledgment of principles by free persons who have no authority over one another which makes the concept of fairness fundamental to justice. Only if such acknowledgment is possible can there be true community between persons in their common practices; otherwise their relations will appear to them as founded to some extent on force. If, in ordinary speech, fairness applies more particularly to practices in which there is a choice whether to engage or not (e.g., in games, business competition), and justice to practices in which there is no choice (e.g., in slavery), the element of necessity does not render the conception of mutual acknowledgment inapplicable, although it may make it much more urgent to change unjust than unfair institutions. For one activity in which one can always engage is that of proposing and acknowledging principles to one another supposing each to be similarly circumstanced; and to judge practices by the principles so arrived at is to apply the standard of fairness to them.

Now if the participants in a practice accept its rules as fair, and so have no complaint to lodge against it, there arises a prima facie duty (and a corresponding prima facie right) of the parties to each other to act in accordance with the practice when it falls upon them to comply. When any number of persons engage in a practice, or conduct a joint undertaking according to rules, and thus restrict their liberty, those who have submitted to these restrictions when required have the right to a similar acquiescence on the part of those who have benefited by their submission. These conditions will obtain if a practice is correctly acknowledged to be fair, for in this case all who participate in it will benefit from it. The rights and duties so arising are special rights and duties in that they depend on previous actions voluntarily undertaken, in this case on the parties having engaged in a common practice and knowingly accepted its benefits.[13] It is not, however, an obligation which presupposes a deliberate performative act in the sense of a promise, or contract, and the like.[14] An unfortunate mistake of proponents of the idea of the social contract was to suppose that political obligation does require some such act, or at least to use language which suggests it. It is sufficient that one has knowingly participated in and accepted the benefits of a practice acknowledged to be fair. This prima facie obligation may, of course, be overridden: it may happen, when it comes one's turn to follow a rule, that other considerations will justify not doing so. But one cannot, in general, be released from this obligation by denying the justice of the practice only when it falls on one to obey. If a person rejects a practice, he should, so far as possible, declare his intention in advance, and avoid participating in it or enjoying its benefits.

This duty I have called that of fair play, but it should be admitted that to refer to it in this way

is, perhaps, to extend the ordinary notion of fairness. Usually acting unfairly is not so much the breaking of any particular rule, even if the infraction is difficult to detect (cheating), but taking advantage of loop-holes or ambiguities in rules, availing oneself of unexpected or special circumstances which make it impossible to enforce them, insisting that rules be enforced to one's advantage when they should be suspended, and more generally, acting contrary to the intention of a practice. It is for this reason that one speaks of the sense of fair play: acting fairly requires more than simply being able to follow rules; what is fair must often be felt, or perceived, one wants to say. It is not, however, an unnatural extension of the duty of fair play to have it include the obligation which participants who have knowingly accepted the benefits of their common practice owe to each other to act in accordance with it when their performance falls due; for it is usually considered unfair if someone accepts the benefits of a practice but refuses to do his part in maintaining it. Thus one might say of the tax-dodger that he violates the duty of fair play: he accepts the benefits of government but will not do his part in releasing resources to it; and members of labor unions often say that fellow workers who refuse to join are being unfair: they refer to them as "free riders," as persons who enjoy what are the supposed benefits of unionism, higher wages, shorter hours, job security, and the like, but who refuse to share in its burdens in the form of paying dues, and so on.

The duty of fair play stands beside other prima facie duties such as fidelity and gratitude as a basic moral notion; yet it is not to be confused with them.[15] These duties are all clearly distinct, as would be obvious from their definitions. As with any moral duty, that of fair play implies a constraint on self-interest in particular cases; on occasion it enjoins conduct which a rational egoist strictly defined would not decide upon. So while justice does not require of anyone that he sacrifice his interests in that *general position* and procedure whereby the principles of justice are proposed and acknowledged, it may happen that in particular situations, arising in the context of engaging in a practice, the duty of fair play will often cross his interests in the sense that he will be required to forego particular advantages which the peculiarities of his circumstances might permit him to take. There is, of course, nothing surprising in this. It is simply the consequence of the firm commitment which the parties may be supposed to have made, or which they would make, in the general position, together with the fact that they have participated in and accepted the benefits of a practice which they regard as fair.

Now the acknowledgment of this constraint in particular cases, which is manifested in acting fairly or wishing to make amends, feeling ashamed, and the like, when one has evaded it, is one of the forms of conduct by which participants in a common practice exhibit their recognition of each other as persons with similar interests and capacities. In the same way that, failing a special explanation, the criterion for the recognition of suffering is helping one who suffers, acknowledging the duty of fair play is a necessary part of the criterion for recognizing another as a person with similar interests and feelings as oneself.[16] A person who never under any circumstances showed a wish to help others in pain would show, at the same time, that he did not recognize that they were in pain; nor could he have any feelings of affection or friendship for anyone; for having these feelings implies, failing special circumstances, that he comes to their aid when they are suffering. Recognition that another is a person in pain shows itself in sympathetic action; this primitive natural response of compassion is one of those responses upon which the various forms of moral conduct are built.

Similarly, the acceptance of the duty of fair play by participants in a common practice is a reflection in each person of the recognition of the aspirations and interests of the others to be realized by their joint activity. Failing a special explanation, their acceptance of it is a necessary part of the criterion for their recognizing one another as persons with similar interests and capacities, as the conception of their relations in the general position supposes them to be. Otherwise they would show no recognition of one another as persons with similar capacities and interests, and indeed, in some cases perhaps hypothetical, they would not recognize one another as persons at all, but as complicated objects involved in a complicated activity. To recognize another as a person one must respond to him and act towards him in certain ways; and these ways are intimately connected with the various prima facie duties. Acknowledging these duties in *some* degree, and so having the elements of morality, is not a matter of choice, or of intuiting moral qualities, or a matter of the expression of feelings or attitudes (the

three interpretations between which philosophical opinion frequently oscillates); it is simply the possession of one of the forms of conduct in which the recognition of others as persons is manifested.

These remarks are unhappily obscure. Their main purpose here, however, is to forestall, together with the remarks in Section 4, the misinterpretation that, on the view presented, the acceptance of justice and the acknowledgment of the duty of fair play depends in everyday life solely on there being a *de facto* balance of forces between the parties. It would indeed be foolish to underestimate the importance of such a balance in securing justice; but it is not the only basis thereof. The recognition of one another as persons with similar interests and capacities engaged in a common practice must, failing a special explanation, show itself in the acceptance of the principles of justice and the acknowledgment of the duty of fair play.

The conception at which we have arrived, then, is that the principles of justice may be thought of as arising once the constraints of having a morality are imposed upon rational and mutually self-interested parties who are related and situated in a special way. A practice is just if it is in accordance with the principles which all who participate in it might reasonably be expected to propose or to acknowledge before one another when they are similarly circumstanced and required to make a firm commitment in advance without knowledge of what will be their peculiar condition, and thus when it meets standards which the parties could accept as fair should occasion arise for them to debate its merits. Regarding the participants themselves, once persons knowingly engage in a practice which they acknowledge to be fair and accept the benefits of doing so, they are bound by the duty of fair play to follow the rules when it comes their turn to do so, and this implies a limitation on their pursuit of self-interest in particular cases.

Now one consequence of this conception is that, where it applies, there is no moral value in the satisfaction of a claim incompatible with it. Such a claim violates the conditions of reciprocity and community amongst persons, and he who presses it, not being willing to acknowledge it when pressed by another, has no grounds for complaint when it is denied; whereas he against whom it is pressed can complain. As it cannot be mutually acknowledged it is a resort to coercion;

granting the claim is possible only if one party can compel acceptance of what the other will not admit. But it makes no sense to concede claims the denial of which cannot be complained of in preference to claims the denial of which can be objected to. Thus in deciding on the justice of a practice it is not enough to ascertain that it answers to wants and interests in the fullest and most effective manner. For if any of these conflict with justice, they should not be counted, as their satisfaction is no reason at all for having a practice. It would be irrelevant to say, even if true, that it resulted in the greatest satisfaction of desire. In tallying up the merits of a practice one must toss out the satisfaction of interests the claims of which are incompatible with the principles of justice.

6. The discussion so far has been excessively abstract. While this is perhaps unavoidable, I should now like to bring out some of the features of the conception of justice as fairness by comparing it with the conception of justice in classical utilitarianism as represented by Bentham and Sidgwick, and its counterpart in welfare economics. This conception assimilates justice to benevolence and the latter in turn to the most efficient design of institutions to promote the general welfare. Justice is a kind of efficiency.[17]

Now it is said occasionally that this form of utilitarianism puts no restrictions on what might be a just assignment of rights and duties in that there might be circumstances which, on utilitarian grounds, would justify institutions highly offensive to our ordinary sense of justice. But the classical utilitarian conception is not totally unprepared for this objection. Beginning with the notion that the general happiness can be represented by a social utility function consisting of a sum of individual utility functions with identical weights (this being the meaning of the maxim that each counts for one and no more than one),[18] it is commonly assumed that the utility functions of individuals are similar in all essential respects. Differences between individuals are ascribed to accidents of education and upbringing, and they should not be taken into account. This assumption, coupled with that of diminishing marginal utility, results in a prima facie case for equality, e.g., of equality in the distribution of income during any given period of time, laying aside indirect effects on the future. But even if utilitarianism is interpreted as having such

restrictions built into the utility function, and even if it is supposed that these restrictions have in practice much the same result as the application of the principles of justice (and appear, perhaps, to be ways of expressing these principles in the language of mathematics and psychology), the fundamental idea is very different from the conception of justice as fairness. For one thing, that the principles of justice should be accepted is interpreted as the contingent result of a higher order administrative decision. The form of this decision is regarded as being similar to that of an entrepreneur deciding how much to produce of this or that commodity in view of its marginal revenue, or to that of someone distributing goods to needy persons according to the relative urgency of their wants. The choice between practices is thought of as being made on the basis of the allocation of benefits and burdens to individuals (these being measured by the present capitalized value of their utility over the full period of the practice's existence), which results from the distribution of rights and duties established by a practice.

Moreover, the individuals receiving these benefits are not conceived as being related in any way: they represent so many different directions in which limited resources may be allocated. The value of assigning resources to one direction rather than another depends solely on the preferences and interests of individuals as individuals. The satisfaction of desire has its value irrespective of the moral relations between persons, say as members of a joint undertaking, and of the claims which, in the name of these interests, they are prepared to make on one another;[19] and it is this value which is to be taken into account by the (ideal) legislator who is conceived as adjusting the rules of the system from the center so as to maximize the value of the social utility function.

It is thought that the principles of justice will not be violated by a legal system so conceived provided these executive decisions are correctly made. In this fact the principles of justice are said to have their derivation and explanation; they simply express the most important general features of social institutions in which the administrative problem is solved in the best way. These principles have, indeed, a special urgency because, given the facts of human nature, so much depends on them; and this explains the peculiar quality of the moral feelings associated with justice.[20] This assimilation of justice to a higher order executive decision, certainly a striking conception, is central to classical utilitarianism; and it also brings out its profound individualism, in one sense of this ambiguous word. It regards persons as so many *separate* directions in which benefits and burdens may be assigned; and the value of the satisfaction or dissatisfaction of desire is not thought to depend in any way on the moral relations in which individuals stand, or on the kinds of claims which they are willing, in the pursuit of their interests, to press on each other.

7. Many social decisions are, of course, of an administrative nature. Certainly this is so when it is a matter of social utility in what one may call its ordinary sense: that is, when it is a question of the efficient design of social institutions for the use of common means to achieve common ends. In this case either the benefits and burdens may be assumed to be impartially distributed, or the question of distribution is misplaced, as in the instance of maintaining public order and security or national defense. But as an interpretation of the basis of the principles of justice, classical utilitarianism is mistaken. It *permits* one to argue, for example, that slavery is unjust on the grounds that the advantages to the slaveholder as slaveholder do not counterbalance the disadvantages to the slave and to society at large burdened by a comparatively inefficient system of labor. Now the conception of justice as fairness, when applied to the practice of slavery with its offices of slaveholder and slave, would not allow one to consider the advantages of the slaveholder in the first place. As that office is not in accordance with principles which could be mutually acknowledged, the gains accruing to the slaveholder, assuming them to exist, cannot be counted as in *any* way mitigating the injustice of the practice. The question whether these gains outweigh the disadvantages to the slave and to society cannot arise, since in considering the justice of slavery these gains have no weight at all which requires that they be overridden. Where the conception of justice as fairness applies, slavery is *always* unjust.

I am not, of course, suggesting the absurdity that the classical utilitarians approved of slavery. I am only rejecting a type of argument which their view allows them to use in support of their disapproval of it. The conception of justice as derivative from efficiency implies that judging the justice of a practice is always, in principle at least, a matter of weighing up advantages and disadvantages, each having an intrinsic value or disvalue as the satisfaction of interests, irrespective of whether or not these interests necessarily involve acquiescence in principles which could not be mutually acknowledged. Utilitarianism cannot account for the fact that slavery is always unjust, nor for the fact that it would be recognized as irrelevant in defeating the accusation of injustice for one person to say to another, engaged with him in a common practice and debating its merits, that nevertheless it allowed of the greatest satisfaction of desire. The charge of injustice cannot be rebutted in this way. If justice were derivative from a higher order executive efficiency, this would not be so.

But now, even if it is taken as established that, so far as the ordinary conception of justice goes, slavery is always unjust (that is, slavery by definition violates commonly recognized principles of justice), the classical utilitarian would surely reply that these principles, as other moral principles subordinate to that of utility, are only generally correct. It is simply for the most part true that slavery is less efficient than other institutions; and while common sense may define the concept of justice so that slavery is unjust, nevertheless, where slavery would lead to the greatest satisfaction of desire, it is not wrong. Indeed, it is then right, and for the very same reason that justice, as ordinarily understood, is usually right. If, as ordinarily understood, slavery is always unjust, to this extent the utilitarian conception of justice might be admitted to differ from that of common moral opinion. Still the utilitarian would want to hold that, as a matter of moral principle, his view is correct in giving no special weight to considerations of justice beyond that allowed for by the general presumption of effectiveness. And this, he claims, is as it should be. The every day opinion is morally in error, although, indeed, it is a useful error, since it protects rules of generally high utility.

The question, then, relates not simply to the analysis of the concept of justice as common sense defines it, but the analysis of it in the wider sense as to how much weight considerations of justice, as defined, are to have when laid against other kinds of moral considerations. Here again I wish to argue that reasons of justice have a *special* weight for which only the conception of justice as fairness can account. Moreover, it belongs to the concept of justice that they do have this special weight. While Mill recognized that this was so, he thought that it could be accounted for by the special urgency of the moral feelings which naturally support principles of such high utility. But it is a mistake to resort to the urgency of feeling; as with the appeal to intuition, it manifests a failure to pursue the question far enough. The special weight of considerations of justice can be explained from the conception of justice as fairness. It is only necessary to elaborate a bit what has already been said as follows.

If one examines the circumstances in which a certain tolerance of slavery is justified, or perhaps better, excused, it turns out that these are of a rather special sort. Perhaps slavery exists as an inheritance from the past and it proves necessary to dismantle it piece by piece; at times slavery may conceivably be an advance on previous institutions. Now while there may be some excuse for slavery in special conditions, it is never an excuse for it that it is sufficiently advantageous to the slaveholder to outweigh the disadvantages to the slave and to society. A person who argues in this way is not perhaps making a wildly irrelevant remark; but he is guilty of a moral fallacy. There is disorder in his conception of the ranking of moral principles. For the slaveholder, by his own admission, has no moral title to the advantages which he receives as a slaveholder. He is no more prepared than the slave to acknowledge the principle upon which is founded the respective positions in which they both stand. Since slavery does not accord with principles which they could mutually acknowledge, they each may be supposed to agree that it is unjust: it grants claims which it ought not to grant and in doing so denies claims which it ought not to deny. Amongst persons in a general position who are debating the form of their common practices, it cannot, therefore, be offered as a reason for a practice that, in conceding these very claims that ought to be denied, it nevertheless meets existing interests more effectively. By their very nature the satisfaction of these claims is without weight and cannot enter into any tabulation of advantages and disadvantages.

Furthermore, it follows from the concept of morality that, to the extent that the slaveholder recognizes his position vis-a-vis the slave to be unjust, he would not choose to press his claims. His not wanting to receive his special advantages is one of the ways in which he shows that he thinks slavery is unjust. It would be fallacious for the legislator to suppose, then, that it is a ground for having a practice that it brings advantages greater than disadvantages, if those for whom the practice is designed, and to whom the advantages flow, acknowledge that they have no moral title to them and do not wish to receive them.

For these reasons the principles of justice have a special weight; and with respect to the principle of the greatest satisfaction of desire, as cited in the general position amongst those discussing the merits of their common practices, the principles of justice have an absolute weight. In this sense they are not contingent; and this is why their force is greater than can be accounted for by the general presumption (assuming that there is one) of the effectiveness, in the utilitarian sense, of practices which in fact satisfy them.

If one wants to continue using the concepts of classical utilitarianism, one will have to say, to meet this criticism, that at least the individual or social utility functions must be so defined that no value is given to the satisfaction of interests the representative claims of which violate the principles of justice. In this way it is no doubt possible to include these principles within the form of the utilitarian conception; but to do so is, of course, to change its inspiration altogether as a moral conception. For it is to incorporate within it principles which cannot be understood on the basis of a higher order executive decision aiming at the greatest satisfaction of desire.

It is worth remarking, perhaps, that this criticism of utilitarianism does not depend on whether or not the two assumptions, that of individuals having similar utility functions and that of diminishing marginal utility, are interpreted as psychological propositions to be supported or refuted by experience, or as moral and political principles expressed in a somewhat technical language. There are, certainly, several advantages in taking them in the latter fashion.[21] For one thing, one might say that this is what Bentham and others really meant by them, at least as shown by how they were used in arguments for social reform. More importantly, one could hold that the best way to defend the classical utilitarian view is to interpret these assumptions as moral and political principles. It is doubtful whether, taken as psychological propositions, they are true of men in general as we know them under normal conditions. On the other hand, utilitarians would not have wanted to propose them merely as practical working principles of legislation, or as expedient maxims to guide reform, given the egalitarian sentiments of modern society.[22] When pressed they might well have invoked the idea of a more or less equal capacity of men in relevant respects if given an equal chance in a just society. But if the argument above regarding slavery is correct, then granting these assumptions as moral and political principles makes no difference. To view individuals as equally fruitful lines for the allocation of benefits, even as a matter of moral principle, still leaves the mistaken notion that the satisfaction of desire has value in itself irrespective of the relations between persons as members of a common practice, and irrespective of the claims upon one another which the satisfaction of interests represents. To see the error of this idea one must give up the conception of justice as an executive decision altogether and refer to the notion of justice as fairness: that participants in a common practice be regarded as having an original and equal liberty and that their common practices be considered unjust unless they accord with principles which persons so circumstanced and related could freely acknowledge before one another, and so could accept as fair. Once the emphasis is put upon the concept of the mutual recognition of principles by participants in a common practice the rules of which are to define their several relations and give form to their claims on one another, then it is clear that the granting of a claim the principle of which could not be acknowledged by each in the general position (that is, in the position in which the parties propose and acknowledge principles before one another) is not a reason for adopting a practice. Viewed in this way, the background of the claim is seen to exclude it from consideration; that it can represent a value in itself arises from the conception of individuals as separate lines for the assignment of benefits, as isolated persons who stand as claimants on an administrative or benevolent largesse. Occasionally persons do so stand to one another; but this is not the general case, nor, more importantly, is it the case when it is a matter of the justice of practices themselves in which participants stand in various relations to be appraised in accordance with standards which they may be expected to acknowledge before one another. Thus however mistaken the notion of the social contract may be as history, and however far it may overreach itself as a general theory of social and political obligation, it does express,

suitably interpreted, an essential part of the concept of justice.[23]

8. By way of conclusion I should like to make two remarks: first, the original modification of the utilitarian principle (that it require of practices that the offices and positions defined by them be equal unless it is reasonable to suppose that the representative man in *every* office would find the inequality to his advantage), slight as it may appear at first sight, actually has a different conception of justice standing behind it. I have tried to show how this is so by developing the concept of justice as fairness and by indicating how this notion involves the mutual acceptance, from a general position, of the principles on which a practice is founded, and how this in turn requires the exclusion from consideration of claims violating the principles of justice. Thus the slight alteration of principle reveals another family of notions, another way of looking at the concept of justice.

Second, I should like to remark also that I have been dealing with the *concept* of justice. I have tried to set out the kinds of principles upon which judgments concerning the justice of practices may be said to stand. The analysis will be successful to the degree that it expresses the principles involved in these judgments when made by competent persons upon deliberation and reflection.[24] Now every people may be supposed to have the concept of justice, since in the life of every society there must be at least some relations in which the parties consider themselves to be circumstanced and related as the concept of justice as fairness requires. Societies will differ from one another not in having or in failing to have this notion but in the range of cases to which they apply it and in the emphasis which they give to it as compared with other moral concepts.

A firm grasp of the concept of justice itself is necessary if these variations, and the reasons for them, are to be understood. No study of the development of moral ideas and of the differences between them is more sound than the analysis of the fundamental moral concepts upon which it must depend. I have tried, therefore, to give an analysis of the concept of justice which should apply generally, however large a part the concept may have in a given morality, and which can be used in explaining the course of men's thoughts about justice and its relations to other moral concepts. How it is to be used for this purpose is a large topic which I cannot, of course, take up here. I mention it only to emphasize that I have been dealing with the concept of justice itself and

to indicate what use I consider such an analysis to have.

Notes

1   An abbreviated version of this paper (less than one-half the length) was presented in a symposium with the same title at the American Philosophical Association, Eastern Division, December 28, 1957, and appeared in the *Journal of Philosophy*, LIV, 653–662.
2   I use the word "practice" throughout as a sort of technical term meaning any form of activity specified by a system of rules which defines offices, roles, moves, penalties, defenses, and so on, and which gives the activity its structure. As examples one may think of games and rituals, trials and parliaments, markets and systems of property. I have attempted a partial analysis of the notion of a practice in a paper "Two Concepts of Rules," *Philosophical Review*, LXIV (1955), 3–32.
3   These principles are, of course, well-known in one form or another and appear in many analyses of justice even where the writers differ widely on other matters. Thus if the principle of equal liberty is commonly associated with Kant (see *The Philosophy of Law*, tr. by W. Hastie, Edinburgh, 1887, pp. 56 f.), it may be claimed that it can also be found in J. S. Mill's *On Liberty* and elsewhere, and in many other liberal writers. Recently H. L. A. Hart has argued for something like it in his paper "Are There Any Natural Rights?," *Philosophical Review*, LXIV (1955), 175–191. The injustice of inequalities which are not won in return for a contribution to the common advantage is, of course, widespread in political writings of all sorts. The conception of justice here discussed is distinctive, if at all, only in selecting these two principles in this form; but for another similar analysis, see the discussion by W. D. Lamont, *The Principles of Moral Judgment* (Oxford, 1946), ch. v.
4   This point was made by Sidgwick, *Methods of Ethics*, 6th ed. (London, 1901), Bk. III, ch. v, sec. 1. It has recently been emphasized by Sir Isaiah Berlin in a symposium, "Equality," *Proceedings of the Aristotelian Society*, n.s. LVI (1955–1956), 305 f.
5   In the paper referred to above, note 2, I have tried to show the importance of taking practices as the proper subject of the utilitarian principle. The criticisms of so-called "restricted utilitarianism" by J.J.C. Smart, "Extreme and Restricted Utilitarianism," *Philosophical Quarterly*, VI (1956), 344–354, and by H.J. McCloskey, "An Examination of Restricted Utilitarianism," *Philosophical Review*, LXVI (1957), 466–485, do

not affect my argument. These papers are concerned with the very general proposition, which is attributed (with what justice I shall not consider) to S.E. Toulmin and P.H. Nowell-Smith (and in the case of the latter paper, also, apparently, to me); namely, the proposition that particular moral actions are justified by appealing to moral rules, and moral rules in turn by reference to utility. But clearly I meant to defend no such view. My discussion of the concept of rules as maxims is an explicit rejection of it. What I did argue was that, in the *logically special* case of practices (although actually quite a common case) where the rules have special features and are not moral rules at all but legal rules or rules of games and the like (except, perhaps, in the case of promises), there is a peculiar force to the distinction between justifying particular actions and justifying the system of rules themselves. Even then I claimed only that restricting the utilitarian principle to practices as defined strengthened it. I did not argue for the position that this amendment alone is sufficient for a complete defense of utilitarianism as a general theory of morals. In this paper I take up the question as to how the utilitarian principle itself must be modified, but here, too, the subject of inquiry is not all of morality at once, but a limited topic, the concept of justice
6   It might seem as if J.S. Mill, in paragraph 36 of Chapter v of *Utilitarianism*, expressed the utilitarian principle in this modified form, but in the remaining two paragraphs of the chapter, and elsewhere, he would appear not to grasp the significance of the change. Hume often emphasizes that *every* man must benefit. For example, in discussing the utility of general rules, he holds that they are requisite to the "well-being of every individual"; from a stable system of property "every individual person must find himself a gainer in balancing the account . . ." "Every member of society is sensible of this interest; everyone expresses this sense to his fellows along with the resolution he has taken of squaring his actions by it, on the conditions that others will do the same." *A Treatise of Human Nature*, Bk. III, Pt. II, sec. II, par. 22.
7   It is not possible to discuss here this addition to the usual conception of rationality. If it seems peculiar, it may be worth remarking that it is analogous to the modification of the utilitarian principle which the argument as a whole is designed to explain and justify. In the same way

that the satisfaction of interests, the representative claims of which violate the principles of justice, is not a reason for having a practice (see Section 7), unfounded envy, within limits, need not be taken into account.

8 The idea that accepting a principle as a moral principle implies that one generally acts on it, failing a special explanation, has been stressed by R.M. Hare, *The Language of Morals* (Oxford, 1952). His formulation of it needs to be modified, however, along the lines suggested by P.L. Gardiner, "On Assenting to a Moral Principle," *Proceedings of the Aristotelian Society*, n.s. LV (1955), 23–44. See also C.K. Grant, "Akrasia and the Criteria of Assent to Practical Principles," *Mind*, LXV (1956), 400–407, where the complexity of the criteria for assent is discussed.

9 Perhaps the best known statement of this conception is that given by Glaucon at the beginning of Book II of Plato's *Republic*. Presumably it was, in various forms, a common view among the Sophists; but that Plato gives a fair representation of it is doubtful. See K.R. Popper, *The Open Society and Its Enemies*, rev. ed. (Princeton, 1950), pp. 112–118. Certainly Plato usually attributes to it a quality of manic egoism which one feels must be an exaggeration; on the other hand, see the Melian Debate in Thucydides, *The Peloponnesian War*, Book V, ch. VII, although it is impossible to say to what extent the views expressed there reveal any current philosophical opinion. Also in this tradition are the remarks of Epicurus on justice in *Principal Doctrines*, XXXI–XXXVIII. In modern times elements of the conception appear in a more sophisticated form in Hobbes *The Leviathan* and in Hume *A Treatise of Human Nature*, Bk. III, Pt. II, as well as in the writings of the school of natural law such as Pufendorf's *De jure naturae et gentium*. Hobbes and Hume are especially instructive. For Hobbes's argument see Howard Warrender's *The Political Philosophy of Hobbes* (Oxford, 1957). W.J. Baumol's *Welfare Economics and the Theory of the State* (London, 1952), is valuable in showing the wide applicability of Hobbes's fundamental idea (interpreting his natural law as principles of prudence), although in this book it is traced back only to Hume's *Treatise*.

10 See J. von Neumann and O. Morgenstern, *The Theory of Games and Economic Behavior*, 2nd ed. (Princeton, 1947). For a comprehensive and not too technical discussion of the developments since, see R. Duncan Luce and Howard Raiffa, *Games and Decisions: Introduction and Critical Survey* (New York, 1957). Chs. VI and XIV discuss the developments most obviously related to the analysis of justice.

11 For a general survey see J.W. Gough, *The Social Contract*, 2nd ed. (Oxford, 1957), and Otto von Gierke, *The Development of Political Theory*, tr. by B. Freyd (London, 1939), Pt. II, ch. II.

12 The difficulty one gets into by a mechanical application of the theory of games to moral philosophy can be brought out by considering among several possible examples, R.B. Braithwaite's study, *Theory of Games as a Tool for the Moral Philosopher* (Cambridge, 1955). On the analysis there given, it turns out that the fair division of playing time between Matthew and Luke depends on their preferences, and these in turn are connected with the instruments they wish to play. Since Matthew has a threat advantage over Luke, arising purely from the fact that Matthew, the trumpeter, prefers both of them playing at once to neither of them playing, whereas Luke, the pianist, prefers silence to cacophony, Matthew is alloted 26 evenings of play to Luke's 17. If the situation were reversed, the threat advantage would be with Luke. See pp. 36 f. But now we have only to suppose that Matthew is a jazz enthusiast who plays the drums, and Luke a violinist who plays sonatas, in which case it will be fair, on this analysis, for Matthew to play whenever and as often as he likes, assuming, of course, as it is plausible to assume, that he does not care whether Luke plays or not. Certainly something has gone wrong. To each according to his threat advantage is hardly the principle of fairness. What is lacking is the concept of morality, and it must be brought into the conjectural account in some way or other. In the text this is done by the form of the procedure whereby principles are proposed and acknowledged (Section 3). If one starts directly with the particular case as known, and if one accepts as given and definitive the preferences and relative positions of the parties, whatever they are, it is impossible to give an analysis of the moral concept of fairness. Braithwaite's use of the theory of games, insofar as it is intended to analyze the concept of fairness, is, I think, mistaken. This is not, of course, to criticize in any way the theory of games as a mathematical theory, to which Braithwaite's book certainly contributes, nor as an analysis of how rational (and amoral) egoists might behave (and so as an analysis of how people sometimes actually do behave). But it is to say that if the theory of games is to be used to analyze moral concepts, its formal structure must be interpreted in a special and general manner as indicated in the text. Once we do this, though, we are in touch again with a much older tradition.

13 For the definition of this prima facie duty, and the idea that it is a special duty, I am indebted to H.L.A. Hart. See his paper "Are There Any Natural Rights?," *Philosophical Review*, LXIV (1955), 185 f.

14 The sense of "performative" here is to be derived from J.L. Austin's paper in the symposium,

"Other Minds," *Proceedings of the Aristotelian Society*. Supplementary Volume (1946), pp. 170–174.

15 This, however, commonly happens. Hobbes, for example, when invoking the notion of a "tacit covenant," appeals not to the natural law that promises should be kept but to his fourth law of nature, that of gratitude. On Hobbes's shift from fidelity to gratitude, see Warrender, *The Political Philosophy of Hobbes*, (Oxford, 1957) pp. 51–52, 233–237. While it is not a serious criticism of Hobbes, it would have improved his argument had he appealed to the duty of fair play. On his premises he is perfectly entitled to do so. Similarly Sidgwick thought that a principle of justice, such as every man ought to receive adequate requital for his labor, is like gratitude universalized. See *Methods of Ethics*, Bk. III, ch. v, sec. 5. There is a gap in the stock of moral concepts used by philosophers into which the concept of the duty of fair play fits quite naturally.

16 I am using the concept of criterion here in what I take to be Wittgenstein's sense. See *Philosophical Investigations*, (Oxford, 1953); and Norman Malcolm's review, "Wittgenstein's *Philosophical Investigations*," *Philosophical Review*, LXIII (1954), 543–547. That the response of compassion, under appropriate circumstances, is part of the criterion for whether or not a person understands what "pain" means, is, I think, in the *Philosophical Investigations*. The view in the text is simply an extension of this idea. I cannot, however, attempt to justify it here. Similar thoughts are to be found, I think, in Max Scheler, *The Nature of Sympathy*, tr. by Peter Heath (New Haven, 1954). His way of writing is often so obscure that I cannot be certain.

17 While this assimilation is implicit in Bentham's and Sidgwick's moral theory, explicit statements of it as applied to justice are relatively rare. One clear instance in *The Principles of Morals and Legislation* occurs in ch. x, footnote 2 to sec XL: ". . . justice, in the only sense in which it has a meaning, is an imaginary personage, feigned for the convenience of discourse, whose dictates are the dictates of utility, applied to certain particular cases. Justice, then, is nothing more than an imaginary instrument, employed to forward on certain occasions, and by certain means, the purposes of benevolence. The dictates of justice are nothing more than a part of the dictates of benevolence, which, on certain occasions, are applied to certain subjects. . . ." Likewise in *The Limits of Jurisprudence Defined*, ed. by C.W. Everett (New York, 1945), pp. 117 f., Bentham criticizes Grotius for denying that justice derives from utility; and in *The Theory of Legislation*, ed. by C.K. Ogden (London, 1931), p. 3, he says that he uses the words "just" and "unjust" along with other words "simply as collec-

tive terms including the ideas of certain pains or pleasures." That Sidgwick's conception of justice is similar to Bentham's is admittedly not evident from his discussion of justice in Bk. III, ch. v of *Methods of Ethics*. But it follows, I think, from the moral theory he accepts. Hence C.D. Broad's criticisms of Sidgwick in the matter of distributive justice in *Five Types of Ethical Theory* (London, 1930), pp. 249–253, do not rest on a misinterpretation.

18 This maxim is attributed to Bentham by J.S. Mill in *Utilitarianism*, ch. v, par. 36. I have not found it in Bentham's writings, nor seen such a reference. Similarly James Bonar, *Philosophy and Political Economy* (London, 1893), p. 234 n. But it accords perfectly with Bentham's ideas. See the hitherto unpublished manuscript in David Baumgardt, *Bentham and the Ethics of Today* (Princeton, 1952), App. IV. For example, "the total value of the stock of pleasure belonging to the whole community is to be obtained by multiplying the number expressing the value of it as respecting any one person, by the number expressing the multitude of such individuals" (p. 556).

19 An idea essential to the classical utilitarian conception of justice. Bentham is firm in his statement of it: "It is only upon that principle [the principle of asceticism], and not from the principle of utility, that the most abominable pleasure which the vilest of malefactors ever reaped from his crime would be reprobated, if it stood alone. The case is, that it never does stand alone; but is necessarily followed by such a quantity of pain (or, what comes to the same thing, such a chance for a certain quantity of pain) that the pleasure in comparison of it, is as nothing: and this is the true and sole, but perfectly sufficient, reason for making it a ground for punishment" (*The Principles of Morals and Legislation*, ch. II, sec. iv. See also ch. x, sec. x, footnote 1). The same point is made in *The Limits of Jurisprudence Defined*, pp. 115 f. Although much recent welfare economics, as found in such important works as I.M.D. Little, *A Critique of Welfare Economics*, 2nd ed. (Oxford, 1957) and K.J. Arrow, *Social Choice and Individual Values* (New York, 1951), dispenses with the idea of cardinal utility, and uses instead the theory of ordinal utility as stated by J.R. Hicks, *Value and Capital*, 2nd ed. (Oxford, 1946), Pt. I, it assumes with utilitarianism that individual preferences have value as such, and so accepts the idea being criticized here. I hasten to add, however, that this is no objection to it as a means of analyzing economic policy, and for that purpose it may, indeed, be a necessary simplifying assumption. Nevertheless it is an assumption which cannot be made in so far as one is trying to analyze moral concepts, especially the concept of justice, as economists would, I think,

agree. Justice is usually regarded as a separate and distinct part of any comprehensive criterion of economic policy. See, for example, Tibor Scitovsky, *Welfare and Competition* (London, 1952), pp. 59–69, and Little, *A Critique of Welfare Economics*, 2nd ed., ch. VII.

20   See J.S. Mill's argument in *Utilitarianism*, ch. v, pars. 16–25.

21   See D.G. Ritchie, *Natural Rights* (London, 1894), pp. 95 ff., 249 ff. Lionel Robbins has insisted on this point on several occasions. See *An Essay on the Nature and Significance of Economic Science*, 2nd ed. (London, 1935), pp. 134–43, "Interpersonal Comparisons of Utility: A Comment," *Economic Journal*, XLVIII (1938), 635–641, and more recently, "Robertson on Utility and Scope," *Economica*, n.s. XX (1953), 108f.

22   As Sir Henry Maine suggested Bentham may have regarded them. See *The Early History of Institutions* (London, 1875), pp. 398 ff.

23   Thus Kant was not far wrong when he interpreted the original contract merely as an "Idea of Reason"; yet he still thought of it as a *general* criterion of right and as providing a general theory of political obligation. See the second part of the essay, "On the Saying 'That may be right in theory but has no value in practice'" (1793), in *Kant's Principles of Politics*, tr. by W. Hastie (Edinburgh, 1891). I have drawn on the contractarian tradition not for a general theory of political obligation but to clarify the concept of justice.

24   For a further discussion of the idea expressed here, see my paper, "Outline of a Decision Procedure for Ethics," in the *Philosophical Review*, LX (1951), 177–197. For an analysis, similar in many respects but using the notion of the ideal observer instead of that of the considered judgment of a competent person, see Roderick Firth, "Ethical Absolutism and the Ideal Observer," *Philosophy and Phenomenological Research*, XII (1952), 317–345. While the similarities between these two discussions are more important than the differences, an analysis based on the notion of a considered judgment of a competent person, as it is based on a kind of judgment, may prove more helpful in understanding the features of moral judgment than an analysis based on the notion of an ideal observer, although this remains to be shown. A man who rejects the conditions imposed on a considered judgment of a competent person could no longer profess to *judge* at all. This seems more fundamental than his rejecting the conditions of observation, for these do not seem to apply, in an ordinary sense, to making a moral judgment.

14

Distributive Justice

Robert Nozick

The minimal state is the most extensive state that can be justified. Any state more extensive violates people's rights. Yet many persons have put forth reasons purporting to justify a more extensive state. It is impossible within the compass of this book to examine all the reasons that have been put forth. Therefore, I shall focus upon those generally acknowledged to be most weighty and influential, to see precisely wherein they fail. In this chapter we consider the claim that a more extensive state is justified, because necessary (or the best instrument) to achieve distributive justice.

The term "distributive justice" is not a neutral one. Hearing the term "distribution," most people presume that some thing or mechanism uses some principle or criterion to give out a supply of things. Into this process of distributing shares some error may have crept. So it is an open question, at least, whether redistribution should take place; whether we should do again what has already been done once, though poorly. However, we are not in the position of children who have been given portions of pie by someone who now makes last minute adjustments to rectify careless cutting. There is no *central* distribution, no person or group entitled to control all the resources, jointly deciding how they are to be doled out. What each person gets, he gets from others who give to him in exchange for something, or as a gift. In a free society, diverse persons control dif-

ferent resources, and new holdings arise out of the voluntary exchanges and actions of persons. There is no more a distributing or distribution of shares than there is a distributing of mates in a society in which persons choose whom they shall marry. The total result is the product of many individual decisions which the different individuals involved are entitled to make. Some uses of the term "distribution," it is true, do not imply a previous distributing appropriately judged by some criterion (for example, "probability distribution"); nevertheless, despite the title of this chapter, it would be best to use a terminology that clearly is neutral. We shall speak of people's holdings; a principle of justice in holdings describes (part of) what justice tells us (requires) about holdings. I shall state first what I take to be the correct view about justice in holdings, and then turn to the discussion of alternate views.[1]

I

The Entitlement Theory

The subject of justice in holdings consists of three major topics. The first is the *original acquisition of holdings*, the appropriation of unheld things. This includes the issues of how unheld things may come to be held, the process, or processes, by which unheld things may come to be held, the things that may come to be held by these processes, the extent of what comes to be held by a particular process, and so on. We shall refer to the complicated truth about this topic, which we shall not formulate here, as the principle of justice in acquisition. The second topic concerns the *transfer of holdings* from one person to another. By what processes may a person transfer holdings to another? How may a person acquire a holding from another who holds it? Under this topic come general descriptions of voluntary exchange, and gift and (on the other hand) fraud, as well as reference to particular conventional details fixed upon in a given society. The complicated truth about this subject (with placeholders for conventional details) we shall call the principle of justice in transfer. (And we shall suppose it also includes principles governing how a person may divest himself of a holding, passing it into an unheld state.)

If the world were wholly just, the following inductive definition would exhaustively cover the subject of justice in holdings.

1 A person who acquires a holding in accordance with the principle of justice in acquisition is entitled to that holding.
2 A person who acquires a holding in accordance with the principle of justice in transfer, from someone else entitled to the holding, is entitled to the holding.
3 No one is entitled to a holding except by (repeated) applications of 1 and 2.

The complete principle of distributive justice would say simply that a distribution is just if everyone is entitled to the holdings they possess under the distribution.

A distribution is just if it arises from another just distribution by legitimate means. The legitimate means of moving from one distribution to another are specified by the principle of justice in transfer. The legitimate first "moves" are specified by the principle of justice in acquisition.[2] Whatever arises from a just situation by just steps is itself just. The means of change specified by the principle of justice in transfer preserve justice. As correct rules of inference are truth-preserving, and any conclusion deduced via repeated application of such rules from only true premises is itself true, so the means of transition from one situation to another specified by the principle of justice in transfer are justice-preserving, and any situation actually arising from repeated transitions in accordance with the principle from a just situation is itself just. The parallel between justice-preserving transformations and truth-preserving transformations illuminates where it fails as well as where it holds. That a conclusion could have been deduced by truth-preserving means from premises that are true suffices to show its truth. That from a just situation a situation *could* have arisen via justice-preserving means does *not* suffice to show its justice. The fact that a thief's victims voluntarily *could* have presented him with gifts does not entitle the thief to his ill-gotten gains. Justice in holdings is historical; it depends upon what actually has happened. We shall return to this point later.

Not all actual situations are generated in accordance with the two principles of justice in holdings: the principle of justice in acquisition and the principle of justice in transfer. Some people steal from others, or defraud them, or enslave them, seizing their product and preventing them from living as they choose, or forcibly exclude others from competing in exchanges. None of these are permissible modes of transition from one situation to another. And some persons acquire holdings by means not sanctioned by the principle of justice in acquisition. The existence of past injustice (previous violations of the first two principles of justice in holdings) raises the third major topic under justice in holdings: the rectification of injustice in holdings. If past injustice has shaped present holdings in various ways, some identifiable and some not, what now, if anything, ought to be done to rectify these injustices? What obligations do the performers of injustice have toward those whose position is worse than it would have been had the injustice not been done? Or, than it would have been had compensation been paid promptly? How, if at all, do things change if the beneficiaries and those made worse off are not the direct parties in the act of injustice, but, for example, their descendants? Is an injustice done to someone whose holding was itself based upon an unrectified injustice? How far back must one go in wiping clean the historical slate of injustices? What may victims of injustice permissibly do in order to rectify the injustices being done to them, including the many injustices done by persons acting through their government? I do not know of a thorough or theoretically sophisticated treatment of such issues.[3] Idealizing greatly, let us suppose theoretical investigation will produce a principle of rectification. This principle uses historical information about previous situations and injustices done in them (as defined by the first two principles of justice and rights against interference), and information about the actual course of events that flowed from these injustices, until the present, and it yields a description (or descriptions) of holdings in the society. The principle of rectification presumably will make use of its best estimate of subjunctive information about what would have occurred (or a probability distribution over what might have occurred, using the expected value) if the injustice had not taken place. If the actual description of holdings turns out not to be one of the descriptions yielded by the principle, then one of the descriptions yielded must be realized.[4]

The general outlines of the theory of justice in holdings are that the holdings of a person are just if he is entitled to them by the principles of justice in acquisition and transfer, or by the principle of rectification of injustice (as specified by the first two principles). If each person's holdings are just, then the total set (distribution) of holdings is just. To turn these general outlines into a specific theory we would have to specify the details of each of the three principles of justice in holdings: the principle of acquisition of holdings, the principle of transfer of holdings, and the principle of rectification of violations of the first two principles. I shall not attempt that task here. (Locke's principle of justice in acquisition is discussed below.)

Historical Principles and End-result Principles

The general outlines of the entitlement theory illuminate the nature and detects of other conceptions of distributive justice. The entitlement theory of justice in distribution is *historical*; whether a distribution is just depends upon how it came about. In contrast, *current time-slice principles* of justice hold that the justice of a distribution is determined by how things are distributed (who has what) as judged by some *structural* principle(s) of just distribution. A utilitarian who judges between any two distributions by seeing which has the greater sum of utility and, if the sums tie, applies some fixed equality criterion to choose the more equal distribution, would hold a current time-slice principle of justice. As would someone who had a fixed schedule of trade-offs between the sum of happiness and equality. According to a current time-slice principle, all that needs to be looked at, in judging the justice of a distribution, is who ends up with what; in

comparing any two distributions one need look only at the matrix presenting the distributions. No further information need be fed into a principle of justice. It is a consequence of such principles of justice that any two structurally identical distributions are equally just. (Two distributions are structurally identical if they present the same profile, but perhaps have different persons occupying the particular slots. My having ten and your having five, and my having five and your having ten are structurally identical distributions.) Welfare economics is the theory of current time-slice principles of justice. The subject is conceived as operating on matrices representing only current information about distribution. This, as well as some of the usual conditions (for example, the choice of distribution is invariant under relabeling of columns), guarantees that welfare economics will be a current time-slice theory, with all of its inadequacies.

Most persons do not accept current time-slice principles as constituting the whole story about distributive shares. They think it relevant in assessing the justice of a situation to consider not only the distribution it embodies, but also how that distribution came about. If some persons are in prison for murder or war crimes, we do not say that to assess the justice of the distribution in the society we must look only at what this person has, and that person has, and that person has, . . . at the current time. We think it relevant to ask whether someone did something so that he *deserved* to be punished, deserved to have a lower share. Most will agree to the relevance of further information with regard to punishments and penalties. Consider also desired things. One traditional socialist view is that workers are entitled to the product and full fruits of their labor; they have earned it; a distribution is unjust if it does not give the workers what they are entitled to. Such entitlements are based upon some past history. No socialist holding this view would find it comforting to be told that because the actual distribution A happens to coincide structurally with the one he desires D, A therefore is no less just than D; it differs only in that the "parasitic" owners of capital receive under A what the workers are entitled to under D, and the workers receive under A what the owners are entitled to under D, namely very little. This socialist rightly, in my view, holds onto the notions of earning, producing, entitlement, desert, and so forth, and he rejects current time-slice principles that look only to the structure of the resulting set of holdings. (The set of holdings resulting from what? Isn't it implausible that how holdings are produced and come to exist has no effect at all on who should hold what?) His mistake lies in his view of what entitlements arise out of what sorts of productive processes.

We construe the position we discuss too narrowly by speaking of *current* time-slice principles. Nothing is changed if structural principles operate upon a time sequence of current time-slice profiles and, for example, give someone more now to counterbalance the less he has had earlier. A utilitarian or an egalitarian or any mixture of the two over time will inherit the difficulties of his more myopic comrades. He is not helped by the fact that *some* of the information others consider relevant in assessing a distribution is reflected, unrecoverably, in past matrices. Henceforth, we shall refer to such unhistorical principles of distributive justice, including the current time-slice principles, as *end-result principles* or *end-state principles*.

In contrast to end-result principles of justice, *historical principles* of justice hold that past circumstances or actions of people can create differential entitlements or differential deserts to things. An injustice can be worked by moving from one distribution to another structurally identical one, for the second, in profile the same, may violate people's entitlements or deserts; it may not fit the actual history.

Patterning

The entitlement principles of justice in holdings that we have sketched are historical principles of justice. To better understand their precise character, we shall distinguish them from another subclass of the historical principles. Consider, as an example, the principle of distribution according to moral merit. This principle requires that total distributive shares vary directly with moral merit; no person should have a greater share than anyone whose moral merit is greater. (If moral merit could be not merely ordered but measured on an interval or ratio scale, stronger principles could be formulated.) Or consider the principle that results by substituting "usefulness to society" for "moral merit" in the previous principle. Or instead of "distribute according to moral merit," or "distribute according to usefulness to society," we might consider "distribute according to the weighted sum of moral merit, usefulness to society, and need," with the weights of the different dimensions equal. Let us call a principle of distribution *patterned* if it specifies that a distribution is to vary along with some natural dimension, weighted sum of natural dimensions, or lexicographic ordering of natural dimensions. And let us say a distribution is patterned if it accords with some patterned principle. (I speak of natural dimensions, admittedly without a general criterion for them, because for any set of holdings some artificial dimensions can be gimmicked up to vary along with the distribution of the set.) The principle of distribution in accordance with moral merit is a patterned historical principle, which specifies a patterned distribution. "Distribute according to I.Q." is a patterned principle that looks to information not contained in distributional matrices. It is not historical, however, in that it does not look to any past actions creating differential entitlements to evaluate a distribution; it requires only distributional matrices whose columns are labeled by I.Q. scores. The distribution in a society, however, may be composed of such simple patterned distributions, without itself being simply patterned. Different sectors may operate different patterns, or some combination of patterns may operate in different proportions across a society. A distribution composed in this manner, from a small number of patterned distributions, we also shall term "patterned." And we extend the use of "pattern" to include the overall designs put forth by combinations of end-state principles.

Almost every suggested principle of distributive justice is patterned: to each according to his moral merit, or needs, or marginal product, or how hard he tries, or the weighted sum of the foregoing, and so on. The principle of entitlement we have sketched is *not* patterned.[5] There is no one natural dimension or weighted sum or combination of a small number of natural dimensions that yields the distributions generated in accordance with the principle of entitlement. The set of holdings that results when some persons receive their marginal products, others win at gambling, others receive a share of their mate's income, others receive gifts from foundations, others receive interest on loans, others receive gifts from admirers, others receive returns on investment, others make for themselves much of what they have, others find things, and so on, will not be patterned. Heavy strands of patterns will run through it; significant portions of the variance in holdings will be accounted for by pattern-variables. If most people most of the time choose to transfer some of their entitlements to others only in exchange for something from them, then a large part of what many people hold will vary with what they held that others wanted. More details are provided by the theory of marginal productivity. But gifts to relatives, charitable donations, bequests to children, and the like, are not best conceived, in the first instance, in this manner. Ignoring the strands of pattern, let us suppose for the moment that a distribution actually arrived at by the operation of the principle of entitlement is random with respect to any pattern. Though the resulting set of holdings will be unpatterned, it will not be incomprehensible, for it can be seen as arising from the operation of a small number of principles. These principles specify how an initial distribution may arise (the principle of acquisition of holdings) and how distributions may be transformed into others (the principle of transfer of holdings). The process whereby the set of holdings is generated will be intelligible, though the set of holdings itself that results from this process will be unpatterned.

The writings of F.A. Hayek focus less than is usually done upon what patterning distributive justice requires. Hayek argues that we cannot know enough about each person's situation to distribute to each according to his moral merit (but would justice demand we do so if we did have this knowledge?); and he goes on to say, "our objection is against all attempts to impress upon society a deliberately chosen pattern of distribution, whether it be an order of equality or of inequality."[6] However, Hayek concludes that in a free society there will be distribution in accordance with value rather than moral merit; that is, in accordance with the perceived value of a person's actions and services to others. Despite his rejection of a patterned conception of distributive justice, Hayek himself suggests a pattern he thinks justifiable: distribution in accordance with the perceived benefits given to others, leaving room for the complaint that a free society does not realize exactly this pattern. Stating this patterned strand of a free capitalist society more precisely, we get "To each according to how much he benefits others who have the resources for benefiting those who benefit them." This will seem arbitrary unless some acceptable initial set of holdings is specified, or unless it is held that the operation of the system over time washes out any significant effects from the initial set of holdings. As an example of the latter, if almost anyone would have bought a car from Henry Ford, the supposition that it was an arbitrary matter who held the money then (and so bought) would not place Henry Ford's earnings under a cloud. In any event, *his* coming to hold it is not arbitrary. Distribution according to benefits to others *is* a major patterned strand in a free capitalist society, as Hayek correctly points out, but it is only a strand and does not constitute the whole pattern of a system of entitlements (namely, inheritance, gifts for arbitrary reasons, charity, and so on) or a standard that one should insist a society fit. Will people tolerate for long a system yielding distributions that they believe are unpatterned?[7] No doubt people will not long accept a distribution they believe is *unjust*. People want their society to be and to look just. But must the look of justice reside in a resulting pattern rather than in the underlying generating principles? We are in no position to conclude that the inhabitants of a society embodying an entitlement conception of justice in holdings will find it unacceptable. Still, it must be granted that were people's reasons for transferring some of their holdings to others always irrational or arbitrary, we would find this disturbing. (Suppose people always determined what holdings they would transfer, and to whom, by using a random device.) We feel more comfortable upholding the justice of an entitlement system if most of the transfers under it are done for reasons. This does not mean necessarily that all deserve what holdings they receive. It means only that there is a purpose or point to someone's transferring a holding to one person rather than to another; that usually we can see what the transferrer thinks he's gaining, what cause he thinks he's serving, what goals he thinks he's helping to achieve, and so forth. Since in a capitalist society people often transfer holdings to others in accordance with how much they perceive these others benefiting them, the fabric constituted by the individual transactions and transfers is largely reasonable and intelligible.[8] (Gifts to loved ones, bequests to children, charity to the needy also are nonarbitrary components of the fabric.) In stressing the large strand of distribution in accordance with benefit to others, Hayek shows the point of many transfers, and so shows that the system of transfer of entitlements is not just spinning its gears aimlessly. The system of entitlements is defensible when constituted by the individual aims of individual transactions. No overarching aim is needed, no distributional pattern is required.

To think that the task of a theory of distributive justice is to fill in the blank in "to each according to his————" is to be predisposed to search for a pattern; and the separate treatment of "from each according to his————" treats production and distribution as two separate and independent issues. On an entitlement view these are *not* two separate questions. Whoever makes something, having bought or contracted for all other held resources used in the process (transferring some of his holdings for these cooperating factors), is entitled to it. The situation is *not* one of something's getting made, and there being an open question of who is to get it. Things come into the world already attached to people having entitlements over them. From the point of view of the historical entitlement conception of justice in holdings, those who start afresh to complete "to each according to his————" treat objects as if they appeared from nowhere, out of nothing. A complete theory of justice might cover this limit case as well; perhaps here is a use for the usual conceptions of distributive justice.[9]

So entrenched are maxims of the usual form that perhaps we should present the entitlement conception as a competitor. Ignoring acquisition and rectification, we might say:

From each according to what he chooses to do, to each according to what he makes for himself (perhaps with the contracted aid of others) and what others choose to do for him and choose to give him of what they've been given previously (under this maxim) and haven't yet expended or transferred.

This, the discerning reader will have noticed, has its defects as a slogan. So as a summary and great simplification (and not as a maxim with any independent meaning) we have:

From each as they choose, to each as they are chosen.

How Liberty Upsets Patterns

It is not clear how those holding alternative conceptions of distributive justice can reject the entitlement conception of justice in holdings. For

suppose a distribution favored by one of these non-entitlement conceptions is realized. Let us suppose it is your favorite one and let us call this distribution D_1; perhaps everyone has an equal share, perhaps shares vary in accordance with some dimension you treasure. Now suppose that Wilt Chamberlain is greatly in demand by basketball teams, being a great gate attraction. (Also suppose contracts run only for a year, with players being free agents.) He signs the following sort of contract with a team: In each home game, twenty-five cents from the price of each ticket of admission goes to him. (We ignore the question of whether he is "gouging" the owners, letting them look out for themselves.) The season starts, and people cheerfully attend his team's games; they buy their tickets, each time dropping a separate twenty-five cents of their admission price into a special box with Chamberlain's name on it. They are excited about seeing him play; it is worth the total admission price to them. Let us suppose that in one season one million persons attend his home games, and Wilt Chamberlain winds up with \$250,000, a much larger sum than the average income and larger even than anyone else has. Is he entitled to this income? Is this new distribution D_2, unjust? If so, why? There is *no* question about whether each of the people was entitled to the control over the resources they held in D_1; because that was the distribution (your favorite) that (for the purposes of argument) we assumed was acceptable. Each of these persons *chose* to give twenty-five cents of their money to Chamberlain. They could have spent it on going to the movies, or on candy bars, or on copies of *Dissent* magazine, or of *Monthly Review*. But they all, at least one million of them, converged on giving it to Wilt Chamberlain in exchange for watching him play basketball. If D_1 was a just distribution, and people voluntarily moved from it to D_2, transferring parts of their shares they were given under D_1 (what was it for if not to do something with?), isn't D_2 also just? If the people were entitled to dispose of the resources to which they were entitled (under D_1), didn't this include their being entitled to give it to, or exchange it with, Wilt Chamberlain? Can anyone else complain on grounds of justice? Each other person already has his legitimate share under D_1. Under D_1, there is nothing that anyone has that anyone else has a claim of justice against. After someone transfers something to Wilt Chamberlain, third parties *still* have their legitimate shares; *their* shares are not changed. By what process could such a transfer among two persons give rise to a legitimate claim of distributive justice on a portion of what was transferred, by a third party who had no claim of justice on any holding of the others *before* the transfer?[10] To cut off objections irrelevant here, we might imagine the exchanges occurring in a socialist society, after hours. After playing whatever basketball he does in his daily work, or doing whatever other daily work he does, Wilt Chamberlain decides to put in *overtime* to earn additional money. (First his work quota is set; he works time over that.) Or imagine it is a skilled juggler people like to see, who puts on shows after hours.

Why might someone work overtime in a society in which it is assumed their needs are satisfied? Perhaps because they care about things other than needs. I like to write in books that I read, and to have easy access to books for browsing at odd hours. It would be very pleasant and convenient to have the resources of Widener Library in my back yard. No society, I assume, will provide such resources close to each person who would like them as part of his regular allotment (under D_1). Thus, persons either must do without some extra things that they want, or be allowed to do something extra to get some of these things. On what basis could the inequalities that would eventuate be forbidden? Notice also that small factories would spring up in a socialist society, unless forbidden. I melt down some of my personal possessions (under D_1) and build a machine out of the material. I offer you, and others, a philosophy lecture once a week in exchange for your cranking the handle on my machine, whose products I exchange for yet other things, and so on. (The raw materials used by the machine are given to me by others who possess them under D_1, in exchange for hearing lectures.) Each person might participate to gain things over and above their allotment under D_1. Some persons even might want to leave their job in socialist industry and work full time in this private sector. I shall say something more about these issues in the next chapter. Here I wish merely to note how private property even in means of production would occur in a socialist society that did not forbid people to use as they wished some of the resources they are given under the socialist distribution D_1.[11] The socialist society would have to forbid capitalist acts between consenting adults.

The general point illustrated by the Wilt Chamberlain example and the example of the entrepreneur in a socialist society is that no end-state principle or distributional patterned principle of justice can be continuously realized without continuous interference with people's lives. Any favored pattern would be transformed into one unfavored by the principle, by people choosing to act in various ways; for example, by people exchanging goods and services with other people, or giving things to other people, things the transferrers are entitled to under the favored distributional pattern. To maintain a pattern one must either continually interfere to stop people from transferring resources as they wish to, or continually (or periodically) interfere to take from some persons resources that others for some reason chose to transfer to them. (But if some time limit is to be set on how long people may keep resources others voluntarily transfer to them, why let them keep these resources for *any* period of time? Why not have immediate confiscation?) It might be objected that all persons voluntarily will choose to refrain from actions which would upset the pattern. This presupposes unrealistically (1) that all will most want to maintain the pattern (are those who don't, to be "reeducated" or forced to undergo "self-criticism"?), (2) that each can gather enough information about his own actions and the ongoing activities of others to discover which of his actions will upset the pattern, and (3) that diverse and far-flung persons can coordinate their actions to dovetail into the pattern. Compare the manner in which the market is neutral among persons' desires, as it reflects and transmits widely scattered information via prices, and coordinates persons' activities.

It puts things perhaps a bit too strongly to say that every patterned (or end-state) principle is liable to be thwarted by the voluntary actions of the individual parties transferring some of their shares they receive under the principle. For perhaps some *very* weak patterns are not so thwarted.[12] Any distributional pattern with any egalitarian component is overturnable by the voluntary actions of individual persons over time; as is every patterned condition with sufficient content so as actually to have been proposed as presenting the central core of distributive justice. Still, given the possibility that some weak conditions or patterns may not be unstable in this way, it would be better to formulate an explicit description of the kind of interesting and contentful patterns under discussion, and to prove a theorem about their instability. Since the weaker the patterning, the more likely it is that the entitlement system itself satisfies it, a plausible conjecture is that any patterning either is unstable or is satisfied by the entitlement system.

Sen's Argument

Our conclusions are reinforced by considering a recent general argument of Amartya K. Sen.[13] Suppose individual rights are interpreted as the right to choose which of two alternatives is to be more highly ranked in a social ordering of the alternatives. Add the weak condition that if one alternative unanimously is preferred to another then it is ranked higher by the social ordering. If there are two different individuals each with individual rights, interpreted as above, over different pairs of alternatives (having no members in common), then for some possible preference rankings of the alternatives by the individuals, there is no linear social ordering. For suppose that person A has the right to decide among (X, Y) and person B has the right to decide among (Z, W); and suppose their individual preferences are as follows (and that there are no other individuals). Person A prefers W to X to Y to Z, and person B prefers Y to Z to W to X. By the unanimity condition, in the social ordering W is preferred to X (since each individual prefers it to X), and Y is preferred to Z (since each individual prefers it to Z). Also in the social ordering, X is preferred to Y, by person A's right of choice among these two alternatives. Combining these three binary rankings, we get W preferred to X preferred to Y preferred to Z, in the social ordering. However, by person B's right of choice, Z must be preferred to W in the social ordering. There is no transitive social ordering satisfying all these conditions, and the social ordering, therefore, is nonlinear. Thus far, Sen.

The trouble stems from treating an individual's right to choose among alternatives as the right to determine the relative ordering of these alternatives within a social ordering. The alternative which has individuals rank *pairs* of alternatives, and separately rank the individual alternatives is no better; their ranking of pairs feeds into some method of amalgamating preferences to yield a social ordering of pairs; and the choice among the alternatives in the highest

ranked pair in the social ordering is made by the individual with the right to decide between this pair. This system also has the result that an alternative may be selected although *everyone* prefers some other alternative; for example, A selects X over Y, where (X, Y) somehow is the highest ranked *pair* in the social ordering of pairs, although everyone, including A, prefers W to X. (But the choice person A was given, however, was only between X and Y.)

A more appropriate view of individual rights is as follows. Individual rights are co-possible; each person may exercise his rights as he chooses. The exercise of these rights fixes some features of the world. Within the constraints of these fixed features, a choice may be made by a social choice mechanism based upon a social ordering; if there are any choices left to make! Rights do not determine a social ordering but instead set the constraints within which a social choice is to be made, by excluding certain alternatives, fixing others, and so on. (If I have a right to choose to live in New York or in Massachusetts, and I choose Massachusetts, then alternatives involving my living in New York are not appropriate objects to be entered in a social ordering.) Even if all possible alternatives are ordered first, apart from anyone's rights, the situation is not changed: for then the highest ranked alternative *that is not excluded by anyone's exercise of his rights* is instituted. Rights do not determine the position of an alternative or the relative position of two alternatives in a social ordering; they *operate upon* a social ordering to constrain the choice it can yield.

If entitlements to holdings are rights to dispose of them, then social choice must take place *within* the constraints of how people choose to exercise these rights. If any patterning is legitimate, it falls within the domain of social choice, and hence is constrained by people's rights. *How else can one cope with Sen's result?* The alternative of first having a social ranking with rights exercised within *its* constraints is no alternative at all. Why not just select the top-ranked alternative and forget about rights? If that top-ranked alternative itself leaves some room for individual choice (and here is where "rights" of choice is supposed to enter in) there must be something to stop these choices from transforming it into another alternative. Thus Sen's argument leads us again to the result that patterning requires continuous interference with individuals' actions and choices.[14]

Redistribution and Property Rights

Apparently, patterned principles allow people to choose to expend upon themselves, but not upon others, those resources they are entitled to (or rather, receive) under some favored distributional pattern D_1. For if each of several persons chooses to expend some of his D_1 resources upon one other person, then that other person will receive more than his D_1 share, disturbing the favored distributional pattern. Maintaining a distributional pattern is individualism with a vengeance! Patterned distributional principles do not give people what entitlement principles do, only better distributed. For they do not give the right to choose what to do with what one has; they do not give the right to choose to pursue an end involving (intrinsically, or as a means) the enhancement of another's position. To such views, families are disturbing; for within a family occur transfers that upset the favored distributional pattern. Either families themselves become units to which distribution takes place, the column occupiers (on what rationale?), or loving behavior is forbidden. We should note in passing the ambivalent position of radicals toward the family. Its loving relationships are seen as a model to be emulated and extended across the whole society, at the same time that it is denounced as a suffocating institution to be broken and condemned as a focus of parochial concerns that interfere with achieving radical goals. Need we say that it is not appropriate to enforce across the wider society the relationships of love and care appropriate within a family, relationships which are voluntarily undertaken?[15] Incidentally, love is an interesting instance of another relationship that is historical, in that (like justice) it depends upon what actually occurred. An adult may come to love another because of the other's characteristics; but it is the other person, and not the characteristics, that is loved.[16] The love is not transferrable to someone else with the same characteristics, even to one who "scores" higher for these characteristics. And the love endures through changes of the characteristics that gave rise to it. One loves the particular person one actually encountered. Why love is historical, attaching to persons in this way and not to characteristics, is an interesting and puzzling question.

Proponents of patterned principles of distributive justice focus upon criteria for determining who is to receive holdings; they consider the reasons for which someone should have something, and also the total picture of holdings. Whether or not it is better to give than to receive, proponents of patterned principles ignore giving altogether. In considering the distribution of goods, income, and so forth, their theories are theories of recipient justice; they completely ignore any right a person might have to give something to someone. Even in exchanges where each party is simultaneously giver and recipient, patterned principles of justice focus only upon the recipient role and its supposed rights. Thus discussions tend to focus on whether people (should) have a right to inherit, rather than on whether people (should) have a right to bequeath or on whether persons who have a right to hold also have a right to choose that others hold in their place. I lack a good explanation of why the usual theories of distributive justice are so recipient oriented; ignoring givers and transferrers and their rights is of a piece with ignoring producers and their entitlements. But why is it *all* ignored?

Patterned principles of distributive justice necessitate *re*distributive activities. The likelihood is small that any actual freely-arrived-at set of holdings fits a given pattern; and the likelihood is nil that it will continue to fit the pattern as people exchange and give. From the point of view of an entitlement theory, redistribution is a serious matter indeed, involving, as it does, the violation of people's rights. (An exception is those takings that fall under the principle of the rectification of injustices.) From other points of view, also, it is serious.

Taxation of earnings from labor is on a par with forced labor.[17] Some persons find this claim obviously true: taking the earnings of n hours labor is like taking n hours from the person; it is like forcing the person to work n hours for another's purpose. Others find the claim absurd. But even these, *if* they object to forced labor, would oppose forcing unemployed hippies to work for the benefit of the needy.[18] And they would also object to forcing each person to work five extra hours each week for the benefit of the needy. But a system that takes five hours' wages in taxes does not seem to them like one that forces someone to work five hours, since it offers the person forced a wider range of choice in activities than does taxation in kind with the particular labor specified. (But we can imagine a gradation of systems of forced labor, from one that specifies a particular activity, to one that gives a choice among two activities, to . . .; and so on up.) Furthermore, people envisage a system with something like a proportional tax on everything above the amount necessary for basic needs. Some think this does not force someone to work extra hours, since there is no fixed number of extra hours he is forced to work, and since he can avoid the tax entirely by earning only enough to cover his basic needs. This is a very uncharacteristic view of forcing for those who *also* think people are forced to do something *whenever* the alternatives they face are considerably worse. However, *neither* view is correct. The fact that others intentionally intervene, in violation of a side constraint against aggression, to threaten force to limit the alternatives, in this case to paying taxes or (presumably the worse alternative) bare subsistence, makes the taxation system one of forced labor and distinguishes it from other cases of limited choices which are not forcings.[19]

The man who chooses to work longer to gain an income more than sufficient for his basic needs prefers some extra goods or services to the leisure and activities he could perform during the possible nonworking hours; whereas the man who chooses not to work the extra time prefers the leisure activities to the extra goods or services he could acquire by working more. Given this, if it would be illegitimate for a tax system to seize some of a man's leisure (forced labor) for the purpose of serving the needy, how can it be legitimate for a tax system to seize some of a man's goods for that purpose? Why should we treat the man whose happiness requires certain material goods or services differently from the man whose preferences and desires make such goods unnecessary for his happiness? Why should the man who prefers seeing a movie (and who has to earn money for a ticket) be open to the required call to aid the needy, while the person who prefers looking at a sunset (and hence need earn no extra money) is not? Indeed, isn't it surprising that redistributionists choose to ignore the man whose pleasures are so easily attainable without extra labor, while adding yet another burden to the poor unfortunate who must work for his pleasures? If anything, one would have expected the reverse. Why is the person with the nonmaterial or nonconsumption desire allowed to proceed unimpeded to his most favored feasible alternative, whereas the man whose pleasures or desires involve material things and who must work for extra money (thereby serving whomever consid-

ers his activities valuable enough to pay him) is constrained in what he can realize? Perhaps there is no difference in principle. And perhaps some think the answer concerns merely administrative convenience. (These questions and issues will not disturb those who think that forced labor to serve the needy or to realize some favored end-state pattern is acceptable.) In a fuller discussion we would have (and want) to extend our argument to include interest, entrepreneurial profits, and so on. Those who doubt that this extension can be carried through, and who draw the line here at taxation of income from labor, will have to state rather complicated patterned *historical* principles of distributive justice, since end-state principles would not distinguish *sources* of income in any way. It is enough for now to get away from end-state principles and to make clear how various patterned principles are dependent upon particular views about the sources or the illegitimacy or the lesser legitimacy of profits, interest, and so on; which particular views may well be mistaken.

What sort of right over others does a legally institutionalized end-state pattern give one? The central core of the notion of a property right in X, relative to which other parts of the notion are to be explained, is the right to determine what shall be done with X; the right to choose which of the constrained set of options concerning X shall be realized or attempted.[20] The constraints are set by other principles or laws operating in the society; in our theory, by the Lockean rights people possess (under the minimal state). My property rights in my knife allow me to leave it where I will, but not in your chest. I may choose which of the acceptable options involving the knife is to be realized. This notion of property helps us to understand why earlier theorists spoke of people as having property in themselves and their labor. They viewed each person as having a right to decide what would become of himself and what he would do, and as having a right to reap the benefits of what he did.

This right of selecting the alternative to be realized from the constrained set of alternatives may be held by an *individual* or by a *group* with some procedure for reaching a joint decision; or the right may be passed back and forth, so that one year I decide what's to become of X, and the next year you do (with the alternative of destruction, perhaps, being excluded). Or, during the same time period, some types of decisions about X may be made by me, and others by you. And so on. We lack an adequate, fruitful, analytical apparatus for classifying the *types* of constraints on the set of options among which choices are to be made, and the *types* of ways decision powers can be held, divided, and amalgamated. A *theory* of property would, among other things, contain such a classification of constraints and decision modes, and from a small number of principles would follow a host of interesting statements about the *consequences* and effects of certain combinations of constraints and modes of decision.

When end-result principles of distributive justice are built into the legal structure of a society, they (as do most patterned principles) give each citizen an enforceable claim to some portion of the total social product; that is, to some portion of the sum total of the individually and jointly made products. This total product is produced by individuals laboring, using means of production others have saved to bring into existence, by people organizing production or creating means to produce new things or things in a new way. It is on this batch of individual activities that patterned distributional principles give each individual an enforceable claim. Each person has a claim to the activities and the products of other persons, independently of whether the other persons enter into particular relationships that give rise to these claims, and independently of whether they voluntarily take these claims upon themselves, in charity or in exchange for something.

Whether it is done through taxation on wages or on wages over a certain amount, or through seizure of profits, or through there being a big *social pot* so that it's not clear what's coming from where and what's going where, patterned principles of distributive justice involve appropriating the actions of other persons. Seizing the results of someone's labor is equivalent to seizing hours from him and directing him to carry on various activities. If people force you to do certain work, or unrewarded work, for a certain period of time, they decide what you are to do and what purposes your work is to serve apart from your decisions. This process whereby they take this decision from you makes them a *part-owner* of you; it gives them a property right in you. Just as having such partial control and power of decision, by right, over an animal or inanimate object would be to have a property right in it.

End-state and most patterned principles of distributive justice institute (partial) ownership by others of people and their actions and labor. These principles involve a shift from the classical liberals' notion of self-ownership to a notion of (partial) property rights in *other* people.

Considerations such as these confront end-state and other patterned conceptions of justice with the question of whether the actions necessary to achieve the selected pattern don't themselves violate moral side constraints. Any view holding that there are moral side constraints on actions, that not all moral considerations can be built into end states that are to be achieved, must face the possibility that some of its goals are not achievable by any morally permissible available means. An entitlement theorist will face such conflicts in a society that deviates from the principles of justice for the generation of holdings, if and only if the only actions available to realize the principles themselves violate some moral constraints. Since deviation from the first two principles of justice (in acquisition and transfer) will involve other persons' direct and aggressive intervention to violate rights, and since moral constraints will not exclude defensive or retributive action in such cases, the entitlement theorist's problem rarely will be pressing. And whatever difficulties he has in applying the principle of rectification to persons who did not themselves violate the first two principles are difficulties in balancing the conflicting considerations so as correctly to formulate the complex principle of rectification itself; he will not violate moral side constraints by applying the principle. Proponents of patterned conceptions of justice, however, often will face head-on clashes (and poignant ones if they cherish each party to the clash) between moral side constraints on how individuals may be treated and their patterned conception of justice that presents an end state or other pattern that *must* be realized.

May a person emigrate from a nation that has institutionalized some end-state or patterned distributional principle? For some principles (for example, Hayek's) emigration presents no theoretical problem. But for others it is a tricky matter. Consider a nation having a compulsory scheme of minimal social provision to aid the neediest (or one organized so as to maximize the position of the worst-off group); no one may opt out of participating in it. (None may say, "Don't compel me to contribute to others and don't provide for me via this compulsory mechanism if I am in need.") Everyone above a certain level is forced to contribute to aid the needy. But if emigration from the country were allowed, anyone could choose to move to another country that did not have compulsory social provision but otherwise was (as much as possible) identical. In such a case, the person's *only* motive for leaving would be to avoid participating in the compulsory scheme of social provision. And if he does leave, the needy in his initial country will receive no (compelled) help from him. What rationale yields the result that the person be permitted to emigrate, yet forbidden to stay and opt out of the compulsory scheme of social provision? If providing for the needy is of overriding importance, this does militate against allowing internal opting out; but it also speaks against allowing external emigration. (Would it also support, to some extent, the kidnapping of persons living in a place without compulsory social provision, who could be forced to make a contribution to the needy in your community?) Perhaps the crucial component of the position that allows emigration solely to avoid certain arrangements, while not allowing anyone internally to opt out of them, is a concern for fraternal feelings within the country. "We don't want anyone here who doesn't contribute, who doesn't care enough about the others to contribute." That concern, in this case, would have to be tied to the view that forced aiding tends to produce fraternal feelings between the aided and the aider (or perhaps merely to the view that the knowledge that someone or other voluntarily is not aiding produces unfraternal feelings).

Locke's Theory of Acquisition

Before we turn to consider other theories of justice in detail, we must introduce an additional bit of complexity into the structure of the entitlement theory. This is best approached by considering Locke's attempt to specify a principle of justice in acquisition. Locke views property rights in an unowned object as originating through someone's mixing his labor with it. This gives rise to many questions. What are the boundaries of what labor is mixed with? If a private astronaut clears a place on Mars, has he mixed his labor with (so that he comes to own) the whole planet, the whole uninhabited universe, or just a particular plot? Which plot does an act bring under ownership? The minimal (possibly disconnected) area such that an act decreases entropy in that area, and not elsewhere? Can virgin land (for the purposes of ecological investigation by high-flying airplane) come under ownership by a Lockean process? Building a fence around a territory presumably would make one the owner of only the fence (and the land immediately underneath it).

Why does mixing one's labor with something make one the owner of it? Perhaps because one owns one's labor, and so one comes to own a previously unowned thing that becomes permeated with what one owns. Ownership seeps over into the rest. But why isn't mixing what I own with what I don't own a way of losing what I own rather than a way of gaining what I don't? If I own a can of tomato juice and spill it in the sea so that its molecules (made radioactive, so I can check this) mingle evenly throughout the sea, do I thereby come to own the sea, or have I foolishly dissipated my tomato juice? Perhaps the idea, instead, is that laboring on something improves it and makes it more valuable; and anyone is entitled to own a thing whose value he has created. (Reinforcing this, perhaps, is the view that laboring is unpleasant. If some people made things effortlessly, as the cartoon characters in *The Yellow Submarine* trail flowers in their wake, would they have lesser claim to their own products whose making didn't *cost* them anything?) Ignore the fact that laboring on something may make it less valuable (spraying pink enamel paint on a piece of driftwood that you have found). Why should one's entitlement extend to the whole object rather than just to the *added value* one's labor has produced? (Such reference to value might also serve to delimit the extent of ownership; for example, substitute "increases the value of" for "decreases entropy in" in the above entropy criterion.) No workable or coherent value-added property scheme has yet been devised, and any such scheme presumably would fall to objections (similar to those) that fell the theory of Henry George.

It will be implausible to view improving an object as giving full ownership to it, if the stock of unowned objects that might be improved is limited. For an object's coming under one person's ownership changes the situation of all others. Whereas previously they were at liberty (in Hohfeld's sense) to use the object, they now no longer are. This change in the situation of others (by removing their liberty to act on a previously unowned object) need not worsen their situation. If I appropriate a grain of sand from Coney Island, no one else may now do as they will with *that* grain of sand. But there are plenty of other grains of sand left for them to do the same with. Or if not grains of sand, then other things. Alternatively, the things I do with the grain of sand I appropriate might improve the position of others, counterbalancing their loss of the liberty to use that grain. The crucial point is whether appropriation of an unowned object worsens the situation of others.

Locke's proviso that there be "enough and as good left in common for others" (sect. 27) is meant to ensure that the situation of others is not worsened. (If this proviso is met is there any motivation for his further condition of nonwaste?) It is often said that this proviso once held but now no longer does. But there appears to be an argument for the conclusion that if the proviso no longer holds, then it cannot ever have held so as to yield permanent and inheritable property rights. Consider the first person *Z* for whom there is not enough and as good left to appropriate. The last person *Y* to appropriate left *Z* without his previous liberty to act on an object, and so worsened *Z*'s situation. So *Y*'s appropriation is not allowed under Locke's proviso. Therefore the next to last person *X* to appropriate left *Y* in a worse position, for *X*'s act ended permissible appropriation. Therefore *X*'s appropriation wasn't permissible. But then the appropriator two from last, *W*, ended permissible appropriation and so, since it worsened *X*'s position, *W*'s appropriation wasn't permissible. And so on back to the first person *A* to appropriate a permanent property right.

This argument, however, proceeds too quickly. Someone may be made worse off by another's appropriation in two ways: first, by losing the opportunity to improve his situation by a particular appropriation or any one; and second, by no longer being able to use freely (without appropriation) what he previously could. A *stringent* requirement that another not be made worse off by an appropriation would exclude the first way if nothing else counterbalances the diminution in opportunity, as well as the second. A *weaker* requirement would exclude the second way, though not the first. With the weaker requirement, we cannot zip back so quickly from *Z* to *A*, as in the above argument; for though person *Z* can no longer *appropriate*, there may remain some for him to *use* as before. In this case *Y*'s appropriation would not violate the weaker Lockean condition. (With less remaining that people are at

liberty to use, users might face more inconvenience, crowding, and so on; in that way the situation of others might be worsened, unless appropriation stopped far short of such a point.) It is arguable that no one legitimately can complain if the weaker provision is satisfied. However, since this is less clear than in the case of the more stringent proviso, Locke may have intended this stringent proviso by "enough and as good" remaining, and perhaps he meant the nonwaste condition to delay the end point from which the argument zips back.

Is the situation of persons who are unable to appropriate (there being no more accessible and useful unowned objects) worsened by a system allowing appropriation and permanent property? Here enter the various familiar social considerations favoring private property: it increases the social product by putting means of production in the hands of those who can use them most efficiently (profitably); experimentation is encouraged, because with separate persons controlling resources, there is no one person or small group whom someone with a new idea must convince to try it out; private property enables people to decide on the pattern and types of risks they wish to bear, leading to specialized types of risk bearing; private property protects future persons by leading some to hold back resources from current consumption for future markets; it provides alternate sources of employment for unpopular persons who don't have to convince any one person or small group to hire them, and so on. These considerations enter a Lockean theory to support the claim that appropriation of private property satisfies the intent behind the "enough and as good left over" proviso, *not* as a utilitarian justification of property. They enter to rebut the claim that because the proviso is violated no natural right to private property can arise by a Lockean process. The difficulty in working such an argument to show that the proviso is satisfied is in fixing the appropriate base line for comparison. Lockean appropriation makes people no worse off than they would be *how*?[21] This question of fixing the baseline needs more detailed investigation than we are able to give it here. It would be desirable to have an estimate of the general economic importance of original appropriation in order to see how much leeway there is for differing theories of appropriation and of the location of the baseline. Perhaps this importance can be measured by the percentage of all income that is based upon untransformed raw materials and given resources (rather than upon human actions), mainly rental income representing the unimproved value of land, and the price of raw material *in situ*, and by the percentage of current wealth which represents such income in the past.[22]

We should note that it is not only persons favoring *private* property who need a theory of how property rights legitimately originate. Those believing in collective property, for example those believing that a group of persons living in an area jointly own the territory, or its mineral resources, also must provide a theory of how such property rights arise; they must show why the persons living there have rights to determine what is done with the land and resources there that persons living elsewhere don't have (with regard to the same land and resources).

The Proviso

Whether or not Locke's particular theory of appropriation can be spelled out so as to handle various difficulties, I assume that any adequate theory of justice in acquisition will contain a proviso similar to the weaker of the ones we have attributed to Locke. A process normally giving rise to a permanent bequeathable property right in a previously unowned thing will not do so if the position of others no longer at liberty to use the thing is thereby worsened. It is important to specify *this* particular mode of worsening the situation of others, for the proviso does not encompass other modes. It does not include the worsening due to more limited opportunities to appropriate (the first way above, corresponding to the more stringent condition), and it does not include how I "worsen" a seller's position if I appropriate materials to make some of what he is selling, and then enter into competition with him. Someone whose appropriation otherwise would violate the proviso still may appropriate provided he compensates the others so that their situation is not thereby worsened; unless he does compensate these others, his appropriation will violate the proviso of the principle of justice in acquisition and will be an illegitimate one.[23] A theory of appropriation incorporating this Lockean proviso will handle correctly the cases (objections to the theory lacking the proviso) where someone appropriates the total supply of something necessary for life.[24]

A theory which includes this proviso in its principle of justice in acquisition must also contain a more complex principle of justice in transfer. Some reflection of the proviso about appropriation constrains later actions. If my appropriating all of a certain substance violates the Lockean proviso, then so does my appropriating some and purchasing all the rest from others who obtained it without otherwise violating the Lockean proviso. If the proviso excludes someone's appropriating all the drinkable water in the world, it also excludes his purchasing it all. (More weakly, and messily, it may exclude his charging certain prices for some of his supply.) This proviso (almost?) never will come into effect; the more someone acquires of a scarce substance which others want, the higher the price of the rest will go, and the more difficult it will become for him to acquire it all. But still, we can imagine, at least, that something like this occurs: someone makes simultaneous secret bids to the separate owners of a substance, each of whom sells assuming he can easily purchase more from the other owners; or some natural catastrophe destroys all of the supply of something except that in one person's possession. The total supply could not be permissibly appropriated by one person at the beginning. His later acquisition of it all does not show that the original appropriation violated the proviso (even by a reverse argument similar to the one above that tried to zip back from Z to A). Rather, it is the combination of the original appropriation *plus* all the later transfers and actions that violates the Lockean proviso.

Each owner's title to his holding includes the historical shadow of the Lockean proviso on appropriation. This excludes his transferring it into an agglomeration that does violate the Lockean proviso and excludes his using it in a way, in coordination with others or independently of them, so as to violate the proviso by making the situation of others worse than their baseline situation. Once it is known that someone's ownership runs afoul of the Lockean proviso, there are stringent limits on what he may do with (what it is difficult any longer unreservedly to call) "his property." Thus a person may not appropriate the only water hole in a desert and charge what he will. Nor may he charge what he will if he possesses one, and unfortunately it happens that all the water holes in the desert dry up, except for his. This unfortunate circumstance, admittedly no fault of his, brings into operation the Lockean proviso and limits his property rights.[25] Similarly, an owner's property right in the only island in an area does not allow him to order a castaway from a shipwreck off his island as a trespasser, for this would violate the Lockean proviso.

Notice that the theory does not say that owners do have these rights, but that the rights are over-ridden to avoid some catastrophe. (Overridden rights do not disappear; they leave a trace of a sort absent in the cases under discussion.)[26] There is no such external (and *ad hoc?*) overrid-ing. Considerations internal to the theory of property itself, to its theory of acquisition and appropriation, provide the means for handling such cases. The results, however, may be coex-tensive with some condition about catastrophe, since the baseline for comparison is so low as compared to the productiveness of a society with private appropriation that the question of the Lockean proviso being violated arises only in the case of catastrophe (or a desert-island situation).

The fact that someone owns the total supply of something necessary for others to stay alive does *not* entail that his (or anyone's) appropriation of anything left some people (immediately or later) in a situation worse than the baseline one. A med-ical researcher who synthesizes a new substance that effectively treats a certain disease and who refuses to sell except on his terms does not worsen the situation of others by depriving them of whatever he has appropriated. The others eas-ily can possess the same materials he appropri-ated; the researcher's appropriation or purchase of chemicals didn't make those chemicals scarce in a way so as to violate the Lockean proviso. Nor would someone else's purchasing the total supply of the synthesized substance from the medical researcher. The fact that the medical researcher uses easily available chemicals to synthesize the drug no more violates the Lockean proviso than does the fact that the only surgeon able to per-form a particular operation eats easily obtainable food in order to stay alive and to have the energy to work. This shows that the Lockean proviso is not an "end-state principle"; it focuses on a par-ticular way that appropriative actions affect oth-ers, and not on the structure of the situation that results.[27]

Intermediate between someone who takes all of the public supply and someone who makes the total supply out of easily obtainable substances is someone who appropriates the total supply of something in a way that does not deprive the oth-ers of it. For example, someone finds a new sub-stance in an out-of-the-way place. He discovers that it effectively treats a certain disease and appropriates the total supply. He does not worsen the situation of others; if he did not stumble upon the substance no one else would have, and the others would remain without it. However, as time passes, the likelihood increases that others would have come across the substance; upon this fact might be based a limit to his property right in the substance so that others are not below their base-line position; for example, its bequest might be limited. The theme of someone worsening another's situation by depriving him of some-thing he otherwise would possess may also illumi-nate the example of patents. An inventor's patent does not deprive others of an object which would not exist if not for the inventor. Yet patents would have this effect on others who indepen-dently invent the object. Therefore, these inde-pendent inventors, upon whom the burden of proving independent discovery may rest, should not be excluded from utilizing their own inven-tion as they wish (including selling it to others). Furthermore, a known inventor drastically lessens the chances of actual independent inven-tion. For persons who know of an invention usu-ally will not try to reinvent it, and the notion of independent discovery here would be murky at best. Yet we may assume that in the absence of the original invention, sometime later someone else would have come up with it. This suggests placing a time limit on patents, as a rough rule of thumb to approximate how long it would have taken, in the absence of knowledge of the inven-tion, for independent discovery.

I believe that the free operation of a market system will not actually run afoul of the Lockean proviso. (Recall that crucial to our story in Part I of *Anarchy, State and Utopia* of how a protective agency becomes dominant and a *de facto* mono-poly is the fact that it wields force in situations of conflict, and is not merely in competition, with other agencies. A similar tale cannot be told about other businesses.) If this is correct, the proviso will not play a very important role in the activities of protective agencies and will not provide a sig-nificant opportunity for future state action. Indeed, were it not for the effects of previous *ille-gitimate* state action, people would not think the possibility of the proviso's being violated as of more interest than any other logical possibility.

(Here I make an empirical historical claim; as does someone who disagrees with this). This completes our indication of the complication in the entitlement theory introduced by the Lockean proviso.

II

Rawls' Theory

We can bring our discussion of distributive justice into sharper focus by considering in some detail John Rawls' recent contribution to the subject. *A Theory of Justice*[28] is a powerful, deep, subtle, wide-ranging, systematic work in political and moral philosophy which has not seen its like since the writings of John Stuart Mill, if then. It is a fountain of illuminating ideas, integrated together into a lovely whole. Political philosophers now must either work within Rawls' theory or explain why not. The considerations and distinctions we have developed are illuminated by, and help illuminate, Rawls' masterful presentation of an alternative conception. Even those who remain unconvinced after wrestling with Rawls' systematic vision will learn much from closely studying it. I do not speak only of the Millian sharpening of one's views in combating (what one takes to be) error. It is impossible to read Rawls' book without incorporating much, perhaps transmuted, into one's own deepened view. And it is impossible to finish his book without a new and inspiring vision of what a moral theory may attempt to do and unite; of how *beautiful* a whole theory can be. I permit myself to concentrate here on disagreements with Rawls only because I am confident that my readers will have discovered for themselves its many virtues.

Social Cooperation

I shall begin by considering the role of the principles of justice. Let us assume, to fix ideas, that a society is a more or less self-sufficient association of persons who in their relations to one another recognize certain rules of conduct as binding and who for the most part act in accordance with them. Suppose further that these rules specify a system of cooperation designed to advance the good of those taking part in it. Then, although a society is a cooperative venture for mutual advantage, it is typically marked by a conflict as well as by an identity of interests. There is an identity of interests since social cooperation makes possible a better life for all than any would have if each were to live solely by his own efforts. There is a conflict of interests since persons are not indifferent as to how the greater benefits produced by their collaboration are distributed, for in order to pursue their ends they each prefer a larger to a lesser share. A set of principles is required for choosing among the various social arrangements which determine this division of advantages and for underwriting an agreement on the proper distributive shares. These principles are the principles of social justice: they provide a way of assigning rights and duties in the basic institutions of society and they define the appropriate distribution of the benefits and burdens of social cooperation.[29]

Let us imagine n individuals who do not cooperate together and who each live solely by their own efforts. Each person i receives a payoff, return, income, and so forth, S_i; the sum total of what each individual gets acting separately is

$$S = \sum_{i=i}^{n} S_i.$$

By cooperating together they can obtain a larger sum total T. The problem of distributive social justice, according to Rawls, is how these benefits of cooperation are to be distributed or allocated. This problem might be conceived of in two ways: how is the total T to be allocated? Or, how is the incremental amount due to social cooperation, that is the benefits of social cooperation T – S, to be allocated? The latter formulation assumes that each individual i receives from the subtotal S of T, his share S_i. The two statements of the problem differ. When combined with the noncooperative distribution of S (each i getting S_i), a "fair-looking" distribution of T – S under the second version may not yield a "fair-looking" distribution of T (the first version). Alternatively, a fair-looking distribution of T may give a particular individual i less than his share S_i. (The constraint $T_i \geqslant S_i$ on the answer to the first formulation of the problem, where T_i is the share in T of the ith individual, would exclude this possibility.) Rawls, without distinguishing these two formulations of the problem, writes as though his concern is the first one, that is, how the total sum

T is to be distributed. One might claim, to support a focus on the first issue, that due to the enormous benefits of social cooperation, the noncooperative shares S_i are so small in comparison to any cooperative ones T_i that they may be ignored in setting up the problem of social justice. Though we should note that this certainly is not how people entering into cooperation with one another would agree to conceive of the problem of dividing up cooperation's benefits.

Why does social cooperation *create* the problem of distributive justice? Would there be no problem of justice and no need for a theory of justice, if there was no social cooperation at all, if each person got his share solely by his own efforts? If we suppose, as Rawls seems to, that this situation does *not* raise questions of distributive justice, then in virtue of what facts about social cooperation do these questions of justice emerge? What is it about social cooperation that gives rise to issues of justice? It cannot be said that there will be conflicting claims only where there is social cooperation; that individuals who produce independently and (initially) fend for themselves will not make claims of justice on each other. If there were ten Robinson Crusoes, each working alone for two years on separate islands, who discovered each other and the facts of their different allotments by radio communication via transmitters left twenty years earlier, could they not make claims on each other, supposing it were possible to transfer goods from one island to the next?[30] Wouldn't the one with least make a claim on ground of need, or on the ground that his island was naturally poorer, or on the ground that he was naturally least capable of fending for himself? Mightn't he say that justice demanded he be given some more by the others, claiming it unfair that he should receive so much less and perhaps be destitute, perhaps starving? He might go on to say that the different individual noncooperative shares stem from differential natural endowments, which are not deserved, and that the task of justice is to rectify these arbitrary facts and inequities. Rather than its being the case that no one *will* make such claims in the situation lacking social cooperation, perhaps the point is that such claims clearly would be without merit. Why would they clearly be without merit? In the social noncooperation situation, it might be said, each individual deserves what he gets unaided by his own efforts; or rather, no one else can make a claim *of justice* against this holding. It is pellucidly clear in this situation who is entitled to what, so no theory of justice is needed. On this view social cooperation introduces a muddying of the waters that makes it unclear or indeterminate who is entitled to what. Rather than saying that no theory of justice applies to this noncooperative case (wouldn't it be unjust if someone stole another's products in the noncooperative situation?), I would say that it is a clear case of application of the correct theory of justice: the entitlement theory.

How does social cooperation change things so that the same entitlement principles that apply to the noncooperative cases become inapplicable or inappropriate to cooperative ones? It might be said that one cannot disentangle the contributions of distinct individuals who cooperate; everything is everyone's joint product. On this joint product, or on any portion of it, each person plausibly will make claims of equal strength; all have an equally good claim, or at any rate no person has a distinctly better claim than any other. Somehow (this line of thought continues), it must be decided how this total product of joint social cooperation (to which individual entitlements do not apply differentially) is to be divided up: this is the problem of distributive justice.

Don't individual entitlements apply to parts of the cooperatively produced product? First, suppose that social cooperation is based upon division of labor, specialization, comparative advantage, and exchange; each person works singly to transform some input he receives, contracting with others who further transform or transport his product until it reaches its ultimate consumer. People cooperate in making things but they work separately, each person is a miniature firm.[31] The products of each person are easily identifiable, and exchanges are made in open markets with prices set competitively, given informational constraints, and so forth. In such a system of social cooperation, what is the task of a theory of justice? It might be said that whatever holdings result will depend upon the exchange ratios or prices at which exchanges are made, and therefore that the task of a theory of justice is to set criteria for "fair prices." This is hardly the place to trace the serpentine windings of theories of a just price. It is difficult to see why these issues should even arise here. People are choosing to make exchanges with other people and to transfer entitlements, with no restrictions on their freedom to trade with any other party at any mutually acceptable ratio.[32] Why does such sequential social cooperation, linked together by people's voluntary exchanges, raise any special problems about how things are to be distributed? Why isn't the appropriate (a not inappropriate) set of holdings just the one which *actually occurs* via this process of mutually-agreed-to exchanges whereby people choose to give to others what they are entitled to give or hold?

Let us now drop our assumption that people work independently, cooperating only in sequence via voluntary exchanges, and instead consider people who work together jointly to produce something. Is it now impossible to disentangle people's respective contributions? The question here is not whether marginal productivity theory is an appropriate theory of fair or just shares, but whether there is some coherent notion of identifiable marginal product. It seems unlikely that Rawls' theory rests on the strong claim that there is no such reasonably serviceable notion. Anyway, once again we have a situation of a large number of bilateral exchanges: owners of resources reaching separate agreements with entrepreneurs about the use of their resources, entrepreneurs reaching agreements with individual workers, or groups of workers first reaching some joint agreement and then presenting a package to an entrepreneur, and so forth. People transfer their holdings or labor in free markets, with the exchange ratios (prices) determined in the usual manner. If marginal productivity theory is reasonably adequate, people will be receiving, in these voluntary transfers of holdings, roughly their marginal products.[33]

But if the notion of marginal product were so ineffective that factors' marginal products in actual situations of joint production could not be identified by hirers or purchasers of the factors, then the resulting distribution to factors would not be patterned in accordance with marginal product. Someone who viewed marginal productivity theory, where it was applicable, *as a patterned theory of justice*, might think that such situations of joint production and indeterminate marginal product provided an opportunity for some theory of justice to enter to determine appropriate exchange ratios. But an entitlement theorist would find acceptable whatever distribution resulted from the party's voluntary exchanges.[34] The questions about the workability of marginal productivity theory are intricate ones.[35] Let us merely note here the strong personal incentive for owners of resources to con-

verge to the marginal product, and the strong market pressures tending to produce this result. Employers of factors of productions are not all dolts who don't know what they're doing, transferring holdings they value to others on an irrational and arbitrary basis. Indeed, Rawls' position on inequalities requires that separate contributions to joint products be isolable, to some extent at least. For Rawls goes out of his way to argue that inequalities are justified if they serve to raise the position of the worst-off group in the society, if without the inequalities the worst-off group would be even more worse off. These serviceable inequalities stem, at least in part, from the necessity to provide incentives to certain people to perform various activities or fill various roles that not everyone can do equally well. (Rawls is *not* imagining that inequalities are needed to fill positions that everyone can do equally well, or that the most drudgery-filled positions that require the least skill will command the highest income.) But *to whom* are the incentives to be paid? To which performers of what activities? When it is necessary to provide incentives to some to perform their productive activities, there is no talk of a joint social product from which no individual's contribution can be disentangled. If the product was all that inextricably joint, it couldn't be known that the extra incentives were going to the crucial persons; and it couldn't be known that the additional product produced by these now motivated people is greater than the expenditure to them in incentives. So it couldn't be known whether the provision of incentives was efficient or not, whether it involved a net gain or a net loss. But Rawls' discussion of justifiable inequalities presupposes that these things can be known. And so the claim we have imagined about the indivisible, nonpartitionable nature of the joint product is seen to dissolve, leaving the reasons for the view that social cooperation creates special problems of distributive justice otherwise not present, unclear if not mysterious.

Terms of Cooperation and the Difference Principle

Another entry into the issue of the connection of social cooperation with distributive shares brings us to grips with Rawls' actual discussion. Rawls imagines rational, mutually disinterested individuals meeting in a certain situation, or abstracted from their other features not provided for in this situation. In this hypothetical situation of choice, which Rawls calls "the original position," they choose the first principles of a conception of justice that is to regulate all subsequent criticism and reform of their institutions. While making this choice, no one knows his place in society, his class position or social status, or his natural assets and abilities, his strength, intelligence, and so forth.

The principles of justice are chosen behind a veil of ignorance. This ensures that no one is advantaged or disadvantaged in the choice of principles by the outcome of natural chance or the contingency of social circumstances. Since all are similarly situated and no one is able to design principles to favor his particular condition, the principles of justice are the result of a fair agreement or bargain.[36]

What would persons in the original position agree to?

Persons in the initial situation would choose two . . . principles: the first requires equality in the assignment of basic rights and duties, while the second holds that social and economic inequalities, for example, inequalities of wealth and authority are just only if they result in compensating benefits for everyone, and in particular for the least advantaged members of society. These principles rule out justifying institutions on the grounds that the hardships of some are offset by a greater good in the aggregate. It may be expedient but it is not just that some should have less in order that others may prosper. But there is no injustice in the greater benefits earned by a few provided that the situation of persons not so fortunate is thereby improved. The intuitive idea is that since everyone's well-being depends upon a scheme of cooperation without which no one could have a satisfactory life, the division of advantages should be such as to draw forth the willing cooperation of everyone taking part in it, including those less well situated. Yet this can be expected only if reasonable terms are proposed. The two principles mentioned seem to be a fair agreement on the basis of which those better endowed, or more fortunate in their social position, neither of which we can be said to deserve, could expect the willing cooperation of others when some workable scheme is a necessary condition of the welfare of all.[37]

This second principle, which Rawls specifies as the difference principle, holds that the institutional structure is to be so designed that the worst-off group under it is at least as well off as the worst-off group (not necessarily the same group) would be under any alternative institutional structure. If persons in the original position follow the minimax policy in making the significant choice of principles of justice, Rawls argues, they will choose the difference principle. Our concern here is not whether persons in the position Rawls describes actually would minimax and actually would choose the particular principles Rawls specifies. Still, we should question why individuals in the original position would choose a principle that focuses upon groups, rather than individuals. Won't application of the minimax principle lead each person in the original position to favor maximizing the position of the worst-off *individual?* To be sure, this principle would reduce questions of evaluating social institutions to the issue of how the unhappiest depressive fares. Yet avoiding this by moving the focus to groups (or representative individuals) seems *ad hoc*, and is inadequately motivated for those in the individual position.[38] Nor is it clear which groups are appropriately considered; why exclude the group of depressives or alcoholics or the representative paraplegic?

If the difference principle is not satisfied by some institutional structure J, then under J some group G is worse off than it would be under another institutional structure I that satisfies the principle. If another group F is better off under J than it would be under the I favored by the difference principle, is this sufficient to say that under J "some . . . have less in order that others may prosper"? (Here one would have in mind that G has less in order that F prosper. Could one also make the same statement about I? Does F have less under I in order that G may prosper?) Suppose that in a society the following situation prevailed:

1 Group G has amount A and group F has amount B, with B greater than A. Also things could be arranged differently so that G would have more than A, and F would have less than B. (The different arrangement might involve a mechanism to transfer some holdings from F to G.)

Is this sufficient to say

2 *G* is badly off *because F* is well off; *G* is badly off *in order that F* be well off; *F*'s being well off makes *G* badly off; *G* is badly off *on account of F*'s being well off; *G* is not better off *because of* how well off *F* is.

If so, does the truth of statement 2 depend on *G*'s being in a worse position than *F*? There is yet another possible institutional structure *K* that transfers holdings from the worse-off group *G* to *F*, making *G* even more worse off. Does the possibility of *K* make it true to say that, under *J*, *F* is not (even) better off because of how well off *G* is?

We do not normally hold that the truth of a subjunctive (as in 1) is alone sufficient for the truth of some indicative causal statement (as in 2). It would improve my life in various ways if you were to choose to become my devoted slave, supposing I could get over the initial discomfort. Is the cause of my present state your not becoming my slave? Because your enslaving yourself to a poorer person would improve his lot and worsen yours, are we to say that the poor person is badly off because you are as well off as you are; has he less in order that you may prosper? From

3 If *P* were to do act *A* then *Q* would not be in situation *S*.

we will conclude

4 *P*'s not doing *A* is responsible for *Q*'s being in situation *S*; *P*'s not doing *A* causes *Q* to be in *S*.

only if we *also* believe that

5 *P* ought to do act *A*, or *P* has a duty to do act *A*, or *P* has an obligation to do act *A*, and so forth.[39]

Thus the inference from 3 to 4, in this case, *presupposes* 5. One cannot argue from 3 to 4 as one step in order *to get to* 5. The statement that in a particular situation some have less in order that others may prosper is often based upon the very evaluation of a situation or an institutional framework that it is introduced to support. Since this evaluation does *not* follow merely from the subjunctive (for example, 1 or 3) an *independent* argument must be produced for it.[40]

Rawls holds, as we have seen, that

since everyone's well-being depends upon a scheme of cooperation without which no one could have a satisfactory life, the division of advantages should be such as to draw forth the willing cooperation of everyone taking part in it, including those less well situated. Yet this can be expected only if reasonable terms are proposed. The two principles mentioned seem to be a fair agreement on the basis of which those better endowed or more fortunate in their social position . . . could expect the willing cooperation of others when some workable scheme is a necessary condition of the welfare of all.[41]

No doubt, the difference principle presents terms on the basis of which those less well endowed would be willing to cooperate. (What *better* terms could they propose for themselves?) But is this a fair agreement on the basis of which those *worse* endowed could expect the *willing* cooperation of others? With regard to the existence of gains from social cooperation, the situation is symmetrical. The better endowed gain by cooperating with the worse endowed, *and* the worse endowed gain by cooperating with the better endowed. Yet the difference principle is not neutral between the better and the worse endowed. Whence the asymmetry?

Perhaps the symmetry is upset if one asks *how much* each gains from the social cooperation. This question might be understood in two ways. How much do people benefit from social cooperation, as compared to their individual holdings in a *non* cooperative scheme? That is, how much is $T_i - S_i$, for each individual *i*? Or, alternatively, how much does each individual gain from general social cooperation, as compared, not with *no* cooperation, but with *more limited* cooperation? The latter is the more appropriate question with regard to general social cooperation. For failing general agreement on the principles to govern how the benefits of general social cooperation are to be held, not everyone will remain in a noncooperative situation if there is some other beneficial cooperative arrangement involving some, but not all, people, whose participants *can* agree. These people will participate in this more narrow cooperative arrangement. To focus upon the benefits of the better and the worse endowed cooperating together, we must try to imagine less extensive schemes of partitioned social cooperation in which the better endowed cooperate only among themselves and the worse endowed cooperate only among themselves, with no cross-cooperation. The members of both groups gain from the internal cooperation within their respective groups and have larger shares than they would if there were no social cooperation at all. An individual benefits from the wider system of extensive cooperation between the better and the worse endowed to the extent of his incremental gain from this wider cooperation; namely, the amount by which his share under a scheme of general cooperation is greater than it would be under one of limited intragroup (but not cross-group) cooperation. *General* cooperation will be of more benefit to the better or to the worse endowed if (to pick a simple criterion) the mean incremental gain from general cooperation (when compared with limited intragroup cooperation) is greater in one group than it is in the other.

One might speculate about whether there is an inequality between the groups' mean incremental gains and, if so, which way it goes. If the better-endowed group includes those who manage to accomplish something of great economic advantage to others, such as new inventions, new ideas about production or ways of doing things, skill at economic tasks, and so on,[42] it is difficult to avoid concluding that the *less* well endowed gain *more* than the better endowed do from the scheme of general cooperation. What follows from this conclusion? I do *not* mean to imply that the better endowed should get even more than they get under the entitlement system of general social cooperation.[43] What *does* follow from the conclusion is a deep suspicion of imposing, in the name of fairness, constraints upon voluntary social cooperation (and the set of holdings that arises from it) so that those already benefiting most from this general cooperation benefit even more!

Rawls would have us imagine the worse-endowed persons say something like the following: "Look, better endowed: you gain by cooperating with us. If you want our cooperation you'll have to accept reasonable terms. We suggest these terms: We'll cooperate with you only if we get *as much as possible*. That is, the terms of our cooperation should give us that maximal share such that, if it was tried to give us more, we'd end up with less." How generous these proposed terms are might be seen by imagining that the better endowed make the almost symmetrical opposite proposal: "Look, worse endowed: you gain by cooperating with *us*. If you want our cooperation you'll have to accept reasonable terms. We propose these terms: We'll cooperate with you so long as *we* get as much as possible.

That is, the terms of our cooperation should give us the maximal share such that, if it was tried to give us more, we'd end up with less." If these terms seem outrageous, as they are, why don't the terms proposed by those worse endowed seem the same? Why shouldn't the better endowed treat this latter proposal as beneath consideration, supposing someone to have the nerve explicitly to state it?

Rawls devotes much attention to explaining why those less well favored should not complain at receiving less. His explanation, simply put, is that because the inequality works for his advantage, someone less well favored shouldn't complain about it; he receives *more* in the unequal system than he would in an equal one. (Though he might receive still more in another unequal system that placed someone else below him.) But Rawls discusses the question of whether those *more* favored will or should find the terms satisfactory *only* in the following passage, where *A* and *B* are any two representative men with *A* being the more favored:

> The difficulty is to show that *A* has no grounds for complaint. Perhaps he is required to have less than he might since his having more would result in some loss to *B*. Now what can be said to the more favored man? To begin with, it is clear that the well-being of each depends on a scheme of social cooperation without which no one could have a satisfactory life. Secondly, we can ask for the willing cooperation of everyone only if the terms of the scheme are reasonable. The difference principle, then, seems to be a fair basis on which those better endowed, or more fortunate in their social circumstances, could expect others to collaborate with them when some workable arrangement is a necessary condition of the good of all.[44]

What Rawls imagines being said to the more favored men does *not* show that these men have no grounds for complaint, nor does it at all diminish the weight of whatever complaints they have. That the well-being of all depends on social cooperation without which no one could have a satisfactory life could also be said to the less well endowed by someone proposing any other principle, including that of maximizing the position of the best endowed. Similarly for the fact that we can ask for the willing cooperation of everyone only if the terms of the scheme are reasonable.

The question is: What terms *would be* reasonable? What Rawls imagines being said thus far merely sets up his problem; it doesn't distinguish his proposed difference principle from the almost symmetrical counterproposal that we imagined the better endowed making, or from any other proposal. Thus, when Rawls continues, "The difference principle, then, seems to be a fair basis on which those best endowed, or more fortunate in their social circumstances, could expect others to collaborate with them when some workable arrangement is a necessary condition of the good of all," the presence of the "then" in his sentence is puzzling. Since the sentences which precede it are neutral between his proposal and any other proposal, the conclusion that the difference principle presents a fair basis for cooperation *cannot* follow from what precedes it in this passage. Rawls is merely repeating that it seems reasonable; hardly a convincing reply to anyone to whom it doesn't seem reasonable.[45] Rawls has not shown that the more favored man *A* has no grounds for complaint at being required to have less in order that another *B* might have more than he otherwise would. And he can't show this, since *A does* have grounds for complaint. Doesn't he?

The Original Position and End-result Principles

How can it have been supposed that these terms offered by the less well endowed are fair? Imagine a social pie somehow appearing so that *no one* has any claim at all on any portion of it, no one has any more of a claim than any other person; yet there must be unanimous agreement on how it is to be divided. Undoubtedly, apart from threats or holdouts in bargaining, an equal distribution would be suggested and found plausible as a solution. (It is, in Schelling's sense, a focal point solution.) If *somehow* the size of the pie wasn't fixed, and it was realized that pursuing an equal distribution somehow would lead to a smaller total pie than otherwise might occur, the people might well agree to an unequal distribution which raised the size of the least share. But in any actual situation, wouldn't this realization reveal something about differential claims on parts of the pie? Who is it that could make the pie larger, and would do it if given a larger share, but not if given an equal share under the scheme of equal distribution? To whom is an incentive to be provided to make this

larger contribution? (There's no talk here of inextricably entangled joint product; it's known *to whom* incentives are to be offered, or at least to whom a bonus is to be paid after the fact.) Why doesn't this identifiable differential contribution lead to some differential entitlement?

If things fell from heaven like manna, and no one had any special entitlement to any portion of it, and no manna would fall unless all agreed to a particular distribution, and somehow the quantity varied depending on the distribution, then it is plausible to claim that persons placed so that they couldn't make threats, or hold out for specially large shares, would agree to the difference principle rule of distribution. But is *this* the appropriate model for thinking about how the things people produce are to be distributed? Why think the same results should obtain for situations where there *are* differential entitlements as for situations where there are not?

A procedure that founds principles of distributive justice on what rational persons who know nothing about themselves or their histories would agree to *guarantees that end-state principles of justice will be taken as fundamental.* Perhaps some historical principles of justice are derivable from end-state principles, as the utilitarian tries to derive individual rights, prohibitions on punishing the innocent, and so forth, from *his* end-state principle; perhaps such arguments can be constructed even for the entitlement principle. But no historical principle, it seems, could be agreed to in the first instance by the participants in Rawls' original position. For people meeting together behind a veil of ignorance to decide who gets what, knowing nothing about any special entitlements people may have, will treat anything to be distributed as manna from heaven.[46]

Suppose there were a group of students who have studied during a year, taken examinations, and received grades between 0 and 100 which they have not yet learned of. They are now gathered together, having no idea of the grade any one of them has received, and they are asked to allocate grades among themselves so that the grades total to a given sum (which is determined by the sum of the grades they actually have received from the teacher). First, let us suppose they are to decide jointly upon a particular distribution of grades; they are to give a particular grade to each identifiable one of them present at the meeting. Here, given sufficient restrictions on their ability to threaten each other, they probably would agree to each person receiving the same grade, to each person's grade being equal to the total divided by the number of people to be graded. Surely they would *not* chance upon the particular set of grades they already have received. Suppose next that there is posted on a bulletin board at their meeting a paper headed ENTITLEMENTS, which lists each person's name with a grade next to it, the listing being identical to the instructor's gradings. Still, this particular distribution will not be agreed to by those having done poorly. Even if they know what "entitlement" means (which perhaps we must suppose they don't, in order to match the absence of moral factors in the calculations of persons in Rawls' original position), why should they agree to the instructor's distribution? What self-interested reason to agree to it would they have?

Next suppose that they are unanimously to agree not to a *particular* distribution of grades, but rather to general principles to govern the distribution of grades. What principle would be selected? The equality principle, which gives each person the same grade, would have a prominent chance. And if it turned out that the total was variable depending upon how they divided it, depending on which of them got what grade, and a higher grade was desirable though they were not competing among each other (for example, each of them was competing for some position with the members of separate distinct groups), then the principle of distributing grades so as to maximize the lowest grades *might* seem a plausible one. Would these people agree to the non-end-state *historical* principle of distribution: give people grades according to how their examinations were evaluated by a qualified and impartial observer?[47] If all the people deciding knew the particular distribution that would be yielded by this historical principle, they wouldn't agree to it. For the situation then would be equivalent to the earlier one of their deciding upon a particular distribution, in which we already have seen they would not agree to the entitlement distribution. Suppose then that the people do not know the particular distribution actually yielded by this historical principle. They cannot be led to select this historical principle because it looks just, or fair, to them; for no such notions are allowed to be at work in the original position. (Otherwise people would argue there, like here, about what justice requires.) Each person engages in a calculation to decide whether it will be in his own

interests to accept this historical principle of distribution. Grades, under the historical principle, depend upon nature and developed intelligence, how hard the people have worked, accident, and so on, factors about which people in the original position know almost nothing. (It would be risky for someone to think that since he is reasoning so well in thinking about the principles, he must be one of the intellectually better endowed. Who knows what dazzling argument the others are reasoning their way through, and perhaps keeping quiet about for strategic reasons.) Each person in the original position will do something like assigning probability distributions to his place along these various dimensions. It seems unlikely that each person's probability calculations would lead to the historical-entitlement principle, in preference to every other principle. Consider the principle we may call the reverse-entitlement principle. It recommends drawing up a list of the historical entitlements in order of magnitude, and giving the most anyone is entitled to, to the person entitled to the least; the second most to the person entitled to the second least, and so on.[48] Any probability calculations of self-interested persons in Rawls' original position, or any probability calculations of the students we have considered, will lead them to view the entitlement and the reverse-entitlement principles as ranked equally insofar as their own self-interest is concerned! (What calculations could lead them to view one of the principles as superior to the other?) Their calculations will not lead them to select the entitlement principle.

The nature of the decision problem facing persons deciding upon principles in an original position behind a veil of ignorance limits them to end-state principles of distribution. The self-interested person evaluates any non end state principle on the basis of how it works out for him; his calculations about any principle focus on how he ends up under the principle. (These calculations include consideration of the labor he is yet to do, which does not appear in the grading example except as the sunk cost of the labor already done.) Thus for any principle, an occupant of the original position will focus on the distribution D of goods that it leads to, or a probability distribution over the distributions $D_1, \ldots, D_n$ it may lead to, and upon his probabilities of occupying each position in each D_i profile, supposing it to obtain. The point would remain the same if, rather than using personal probabilities, he uses some other decision rule of the sort discussed by decision theorists. In these calculations, the only role played by the principle is that of generating a distribution of goods (or whatever else they care about) or of generating a probability distribution over distributions of goods. Different principles are compared solely by comparing the alternative distributions they generate. Thus the principles drop out of the picture, and each self-interested person makes a choice among alternative end-state distributions. People in the original position either directly agree to an end-state distribution or they agree to a principle; if they agree to a principle, they do it solely on the basis of considerations about end-state distributions. The *fundamental* principles they agree to, the ones they can all converge in agreeing upon, *must* be end-state principles.

Rawls' construction is incapable of yielding an entitlement or historical conception of distributive justice. The end-state principles of justice yielded by his procedure might be used in an attempt to *derive*, when conjoined with factual information, historical-entitlement principles, as derivative principles falling under a nonentitlement conception of justice.[49] It is difficult to see how such attempts could derive and account for the *particular* convolutions of historical-entitlement principles. And any derivations from end-state principles of approximations of the principles of acquisition, transfer, and rectification would strike one as similar to utilitarian contortions in trying to derive (approximations of) usual precepts of justice; they do not yield the particular result desired, and they produce the wrong reasons for the sort of result they try to get. If historical-entitlement principles are fundamental, then Rawls' construction will yield approximations of them at best; it will produce the wrong sorts of reasons for them, and its derived results sometimes will conflict with the precisely correct principles. The whole procedure of persons choosing principles in Rawls' original position presupposes that no historical-entitlement conception of justice is correct.

It might be objected to our argument that Rawls' procedure is designed to *establish* all facts about justice; there is no independent notion of entitlement, not provided by his theory, to stand on in criticizing his theory. But we do not need any *particular* developed historical-entitlement theory as a basis from which to criticize Rawls' construction. If *any* such fundamental historical-entitlement view is correct, then Rawls' theory is not. We are thus able to make this structural criticism of the type of theory Rawls presents and the type of principles it must yield, without first having formulated fully a particular historical-entitlement theory as an alternative to his. We would be ill advised to accept Rawls' theory and his construal of the problem as one of which principles would be chosen by rational self-interested individuals behind a veil of ignorance, unless we were sure that no adequate historical-entitlement theory was to be gotten.

Since Rawls' construction doesn't yield a historical or entitlement conception of justice, there will be some feature(s) of his construction in virtue of which it doesn't. Have we done anything other than focus upon the particular feature(s), and say that this makes Rawls' construction incapable in principle of yielding an entitlement or historical conception of justice? This would be a criticism without any force at all, for in this sense we would have to say that the construction is incapable in principle of yielding any conception other than the one it actually yields. It seems clear that our criticism goes deeper than this (and I hope it is clear to the reader); but it is difficult to formulate the requisite criterion of depth. Lest this appear lame, let us add that as Rawls states the root idea underlying the veil of ignorance, that feature which is the most prominent in excluding agreement to an entitlement conception, it is to prevent someone from tailoring principles to his own advantage, from designing principles to favor his particular condition. But not only does the veil of ignorance do this; it ensures that no shadow of entitlement considerations will enter the rational calculations of ignorant, nonmoral individuals constrained to decide in a situation reflecting some formal conditions of morality.[50] Perhaps, in a Rawls-*like* construction, some condition weaker than the veil of ignorance could serve to exclude the special tailoring of principles, or perhaps some other "structural-looking" feature of the choice situation could be formulated to mirror entitlement considerations. But as it stands there is no reflection of entitlement considerations in any form in the situation of those in the original position; these considerations do not enter even to be overridden or outweighed or otherwise put aside. Since no glimmer of entitlement principles is built into the structure of the situation of persons in the original position, there is no way these principles could be selected; and Rawls' construction is incapable in principle of yielding them. This is not to say, of course, that the entitlement principle (or "the principle of natural liberty") couldn't be *written* on the list of principles to be considered by those in the original position. Rawls doesn't do even this, perhaps because it is so transparently clear that there would be no point in including it to be considered *there*.

Macro and Micro

We noted earlier the objection which doubted whether there is any independent notion of entitlement. This connects with Rawls' insistence that the principles he formulates are to be applied only to the fundamental macrostructure of the whole society, and that no micro counterexample to them will be admissible. The difference principle is, on the face of it, *unfair* (though that will be of no concern to anyone deciding in the original position); and a wide gamut of counterexamples to it can be produced that focus on small situations that are easy to take in and manage. But Rawls does *not* claim the difference principle is to apply to every situation; only to the basic structure of the society. How are we to decide if it applies to that? Since we may have only weak confidence in our intuitions and judgments about the justice of the whole structure of society, we may attempt to aid our judgment by focusing on microsituations that we do have a firm grasp of. For many of us, an important part of the process of arriving at what Rawls calls "reflective equilibrium" will consist of thought experiments in which we try out principles in hypothetical microsituations. If, in our considered judgment, they don't apply there then they are not universally applicable. And we may think that since correct principles of justice *are* universally applicable, principles that fail for microsituations cannot be correct. Since Plato, at any rate, that has been our tradition; principles may be tried out in the large and in the small. Plato thought that writ large the principles are easier to discern; others may think the reverse.

Rawls, however, proceeds as though distinct principles apply to macro and micro contexts, to the basic structure of society and to the situations we can take in and understand. Are the fundamental principles of justice *emergent* in this fashion, applying only to the largest social structure

yet not to its parts? Perhaps one thinks of the possibility that a whole social structure is just, even though none of its parts is, because the injustice in each part somehow balances out or counteracts another one, and the total injustice ends up being balanced out or nullified. But can a part satisfy the most fundamental principle of justice yet still clearly be unjust, apart from its failure to perform any supposed task of counterbalancing another existing injustice? Perhaps so, if a part involves some special domain. But surely a regular, ordinary, everyday part, possessing no very unusual features, should turn out to be just when it satisfies the fundamental principles of justice; otherwise, special explanations must be offered. One cannot say merely that one is speaking of principles to apply only to the fundamental structure, so that micro counterexamples do not tell. In virtue of what features of the basic structure, features not possessed by microcases, do special moral principles apply that would be unacceptable elsewhere?

There are special disadvantages to proceeding by focusing only on the intuitive justice of described complex wholes. For complex wholes are not easily scanned; we cannot easily keep track of everything that is relevant. The justice of a whole society may depend on its satisfying a number of distinct principles. These principles, though individually compelling (witness their application to a wide range of particular microcases), may yield surprising results when combined together. That is, one may be surprised at which, and only which, institutional forms satisfy all the principles (Compare the surprise at discovering what, and only what, satisfies a number of distinct and individually compelling conditions of adequacy; and how illuminating such discoveries are.) Or perhaps it is one simple principle which is to be writ large, and what things look like when this is done is very surprising, at first. I am not claiming that new *principles* emerge in the large, but that how the old microprinciples turn out to be satisfied in the large may surprise. If this is so, then one should not depend upon judgments about the whole as providing the only or even the major body of data against which to check one's principles. One major path to changing one's intuitive judgments about some complex whole is through seeing the larger and often surprising implications of principles solidly founded at the micro level. Similarly, discovering that one's judgments are wrong or mistaken often surely will involve overturning them by stringent applications of principles grounded on the micro level. For these reasons it is undesirable to attempt to protect principles by excluding microtests of them.

The only reason I have thought of for discounting microtests of the fundamental principles is that microsituations have particular entitlements built into them. Of course, continues the argument, the fundamental principles under consideration will run afoul of these entitlements, for the principles are to operate at a deeper level than such entitlements. Since they are to operate at the level that underlies such entitlements, no microsituation that includes entitlements can be introduced as an example by which to test these fundamental principles. Note that this reasoning grants that Rawls' procedure assumes that no fundamental entitlement view is correct, that it assumes there is some level so deep that no entitlements operate that far down.

May all entitlements be relegated to relatively superficial levels? For example, people's entitlements to the parts of their own bodies? An application of the principle of maximizing the position of those worst off might well involve forceable redistribution of bodily parts ("You've been sighted for all these years; now one – or even both – of your eyes is to be transplanted to others"), or killing some people early to use their bodies in order to provide material necessary to save the lives of those who otherwise would die young.[51] To bring up such cases is to sound slightly hysterical. But we are driven to such extreme examples in examining Rawls' prohibition on micro counterexamples. That not all entitlements in microcases are plausibly construed as superficial, and hence as illegitimate material by which to test out suggested principles, is made especially clear if we focus on those entitlements and rights that most clearly are not socially or institutionally based. On what grounds are such cases, whose detailed specifications I leave to the ghoulish reader, ruled inadmissible? On what grounds can it be claimed that the fundamental principles of justice need apply only to the fundamental institutional structure of a society? (And couldn't we build such redistributive practices concerning bodily parts or the ending of people's lives into the fundamental structure of a society?)

It is ironic that we criticize Rawls' theory for its fundamental incompatibility with historical-entitlement conceptions of justice. For Rawls' theory itself describes a process (abstractly conceived) with a result. He does not present a direct deductive argument for his two principles of justice from other statements that entail them. Any deductive formulation of Rawls' argument would contain metastatements, statements about principles: such as, any principles agreed to by persons in a certain situation are correct. Combined with an argument showing that persons in that situation would agree to principles P, one can deduce that P is correct, and then deduce that P. At some places in the argument, "P" appears in quotes, distinguishing the argument from a direct deductive argument for the truth of P. Instead of a direct deductive argument, a situation and process are specified, and *any* principles that would emerge from that situation and process are held to constitute the principles of justice. (Here I ignore the complicated interplay between which principles of justice one wants to derive and which initial situation one specifies.) Just as for an entitlement theorist any set of holdings that emerges from a legitimate process (specified by the principle of transfer) is just, so for Rawls any set of principles that emerges from the original position by the constrained process of unanimous agreement is the set of (correct) principles of justice. Each theory specifies starting points and processes of transformation, and each accepts whatever comes out. According to each theory, whatever comes out is to be accepted because of its pedigree, its history. Any theory which gets to a process must start with something which is not *itself* justified by being the outcome of a process (otherwise, it should start farther back) – namely, either with general statements arguing for the fundamental priority of the process, or with the process itself. Entitlement theory and Rawls' theory each get to a process. Entitlement theory specifies a process for generating sets of holdings. The three principles of justice (in acquisition, transfer, and rectification) that underlie this process, having this process as their subject matter, are themselves process principles rather than end-state principles of distributive justice. They specify an ongoing process, *without* fixing how it is to turn out, *without* providing some external patterned criterion it must meet. Rawls' theory arrives at a process P for generating principles of justice. This process P involves people in the original position agreeing to principles of justice behind a veil of ignorance. According to Rawls, any principles emerging from this process P will be the principles of justice. But this process P for generating principles of justice cannot, we already have argued, itself generate process principles as the fundamental principles of justice. P must generate end-state or end-result principles. Even though the difference principle, in Rawls' theory, is to apply to an ongoing and continuing institutional process (one that includes *derived* entitlements based upon institutional expectations under the principle, and derived elements of pure procedural justice, and so on), it is an end-result principle (but not a *current* time-slice principle). The difference principle fixes how the ongoing process is to turn out and provides an external patterned criterion it must meet; any process is rejected which fails to meet the test of the criterion. The mere fact that a principle regulates an ongoing institutional process does not make it a process principle. If it did, the utilitarian principle would also be a process principle, rather than the end-result principle it is.

The structure of Rawls' theory thus presents a dilemma. If processes are so great, Rawls' theory is defective because it is incapable of yielding process principles of justice. If processes are not so great, then insufficient support has been provided for the principles yielded by Rawls' process P for arriving at principles. Contract arguments embody the assumption that anything that emerges from a certain process is just. Upon the force of this fundamental assumption rests the force of a contract argument. Surely then no contract argument should be structured so as to preclude process principles being the fundamental principles of distributive justice by which to judge the institutions of a society; no contract argument should be structured so as to make it impossible that its results be of the same sort as the assumptions upon which it rests.[52] If processes are good enough to found a theory upon, they are good enough to be the possible result of the theory. One can't have it both ways.

We should note that the difference principle is an especially strong kind of patterned end-state principle. Let us say that a principle of distribution is *organic* if an unjust distribution, according to the principle, can be gotten from one the principle deems just, by deleting (in imagination) some people and their distributive shares. Organic principles focus on features dependent upon the *overall* pattern. In contrast, patterned principles of the form "to each according to his score on a particular natural dimension D" are *not*

organic principles. If a distribution satisfies this principle, it will continue to do so when some people and their holdings are deleted, for this deletion will not affect the ratios of the remaining people's holdings, or the ratios of their scores along the dimension D. These unchanged ratios will continue to be the same and will continue to satisfy the principle.

The difference principle *is* organic. If the least well-off group and their holdings are deleted from a situation, there is no guarantee that the resulting situation and distribution will maximize the position of the new least well-off group. Perhaps that new bottom group could have more if the top group had even less (though there was no way to transfer from the top group to the previous bottom group).[53]

Failure to satisfy the deletion condition (that a distribution remains just under deletion of people and their holdings) marks off organic principles. Consider also the addition condition, which holds that if two distributions (over disjoint sets of individuals) are just then so is the distribution which consists of the combination of these two just distributions. (If the distribution on earth is just, and that on some planet of a distant star is just, then so is the sum distribution of the two.) Principles of distribution of the form "to each according to his score on natural dimension D" violate this condition, and therefore (let us say) are *nonaggregative*. For though within each group all ratios of shares match ratios of scores on D, they needn't match *between* the groups.[54] The entitlement principle of justice in holdings satisfies both the deletion and the addition conditions; the entitlement principle is nonorganic and aggregative.

We should not leave the subject of the properties of the difference principle without mentioning the interesting but I think mistaken speculation of Thomas Scanlon that "there is no plausible principle which is distinct from the Difference Principle and intermediate between it and strict equality."[55] How can it be that no plausible egalitarian principle short of absolute equality would exclude great inequalities in order to achieve a *slight* benefit for the worst-off representative man? For the egalitarian, inequality is a cost, a minus-factor. The strict egalitarian doesn't allow any inequality at all, treating the cost of an inequality as infinite. The difference principle allows *any* amount of this cost provided there is *some* benefit (to the worst-off group) however small. This doesn't treat inequality as a significant cost. I have phrased my comments so that the following principle, call it Egalitarian General Principle 1, will leap to mind: An inequality is justified only if its benefits outweigh its costs. Following Rawls, suppose its benefits are only those to the worst-off group. How shall we measure its costs (and in a way so that they are comparable to its benefits)? The costs should represent the total amount of inequality in the society, which might be variously treated. So let us consider as the measure of inequality in a particular system (and hence its cost) the difference between the situation of the best-off representative man and the worst-off representative man. Let X_W be the share of the worst-off representative man under System X; let X_B be the share of the best-off representative man under X. Let E be an efficient system of equality (in which everyone gets no less a share than in any other equal system). ($E_B = E_W$) Thus we get the following First Specification of Egalitarian General Principle 1. (Other specifications would use other measures of inequality.) An unequal system U is unjustified if $U_B - U_W > U_W - E_W$. (Or should it be $\geq$?) An inequality is justified only if its benefit to the worst-off group ($U_w - E_w$) is greater than (or equal to?) the cost of the inequality ($U_B - U_W$). (Note that this involves measurement on an interval scale, and interpersonal comparisons.) This is an intermediate position the egalitarian might find attractive, and it is a stronger egalitarian principle than the difference principle.

There is an even *more* stringent egalitarian principle short of strict egalitarianism, supported by considerations similar to those which lead to the rejection of a simple cost-benefit principle for moral contexts.[56] This would give us Egalitarian General Principle 2: An unequal system U is justified only if a) its benefits outweigh its costs, *and* b) there is no *other* unequal system S, with lesser inequality, such that the *extra* benefits of U over S do not outweigh the extra costs of U over S. As before, treating $X_B - X_w$ as the costs of the inequality in a system X, we get the following First Specification of Egalitarian General Principle 2: An unequal system U is justified only if:

a) $U_W - E_W > U_B - U_W$ *and*

b) There is no system S such that $S_B - S_W < U_B - U_W$, and

$U_W - S_W \leq (U_B - U_W) - (S_B - S_W)$.

(Notice b) comes to: There is no system S with less inequality than U, such that the extra benefits of U over S are less than or equal to its extra costs.)

In *increasing* order of egalitarian stringency we have: the difference principle, the first specification of General Egalitarian Principle 1, the first specification of General Egalitarian Principle 2, and the principle of strict equality (choose E). Surely an egalitarian would find the middle two more attractive than the difference principle. (Such an egalitarian might want to consider what changes in the structure of the Original Position or the nature of the persons in it, would lead to one of these egalitarian principles being chosen.) I do not myself, of course, suggest that these egalitarian principles are correct. But their consideration helps illuminate exactly how egalitarian the difference principle is, and make it implausible to claim it stands as the most egalitarian plausible principle short of strict equality. (However, perhaps Scanlon means that any more stringent egalitarian principle would have to ascribe a cost to inequality, and no theoretical justification has been given which would enable one to ascribe a precise cost.)

There is one way we should mention whereby even more egalitarian principles might be gotten from Rawls' original position. Rawls imagines rational self-interested persons behind a veil of ignorance choosing principles to govern their institutions. He further imagines, in the third part of his book, that when raised in a society which embodies these principles, people thereby develop a sense of justice and a particular psychology (attitudes towards others, etc.). Call this Stage I of the argument. Stage II of the argument would involve taking *these* people who are the result of Stage I and the operation of a society in accordance with Stage I principles, and placing *them* in an original position. The Stage II original position contains individuals with the psychology and sense of justice which is the product of Stage I, rather than individuals who are (merely) rational and self-interested. Now these persons choose principles to govern the society they are to live in. Will the principles they choose in Stage II be the same principles chosen by the others in Stage I? If not, imagine people raised in a society embodying the Stage II principles, determine what psychology *they* would develop, and place *these* individuals, who are the products of Stage II, in a Stage III original position, and continue as before to iterate the process. We shall say that the iterated original position yields particular principles P if 1) there is a Stage n original position wherein P is chosen, and P is also chosen in the Stage n + 1 original position, or 2) if new principles are chosen in each new stage of the original position, these principles converge to P at the limit. Otherwise, no particular principles are yielded by the iterated original position, e.g., succeeding stages of the original position oscillate between two sets of principles.

Are Rawls' two principles in fact yielded by the iterated original position, that is, at Stage II do the people with the psychology Rawls describes as resulting from the operation of his two principles of justice, themselves choose those very principles when *they* are placed in an original position? If so, this would strengthen Rawls' result. If not, we face the question of whether any principles are yielded by the original position; at what stage they are yielded (or are they yielded at the limit); and what precisely *those* principles are. This would seem to be an interesting area of investigation for those souls who choose to work, despite my arguments, within the Rawlsian framework.

Natural Assets and Arbitrariness

Rawls comes closest to considering the entitlement system in his discussion of what he terms the system of natural liberty:

The system of natural liberty selects an efficient distribution roughly as follows. Let us suppose that we know from economic theory that under the standard assumptions defining a competitive market economy, income and wealth will be distributed in an efficient way, and that the particular efficient distribution which results in any period of time is determined by the initial distribution of assets, that is, by the initial distribution of income and wealth, and of natural talents and abilities. With each initial distribution, a definite efficient outcome is arrived at. Thus it turns out that if we are to accept the outcome as just, and not merely as efficient, we must accept the basis upon which over time the initial distribution of assets is determined.

In the system of natural liberty the initial distribution is regulated by the arrangements implicit in the conception of careers open to talents. These arrangements presuppose a background of equal liberty (as specified by the first principle) and a free market economy. They require a formal equality of opportunity in that all have at least the same legal rights of access to all advantaged social positions. But since there is no effort to preserve an equality or similarity, of social conditions, except insofar as this is necessary to preserve the requisite background institutions, the initial distribution of assets for any period of time is strongly influenced by natural and social contingencies. The existing distribution of income and wealth, say, is the cumulative effect of prior distributions of natural assets – that is, natural talents and abilities – as these have been developed or left unrealized, and their use favored or disfavored over time by social circumstances and such chance contingencies as accident and good fortune. Intuitively, the most obvious injustice of the system of natural liberty is that it permits distributive shares to be improperly influenced by these factors so arbitrary from a moral point of view.[57]

Here we have *Rawls'* reason for rejecting a system of natural liberty: it "permits" distributive shares to be improperly influenced by factors that are so arbitrary from a moral point of view. These factors are: "prior distribution . . . of natural talents and abilities as these have been developed over time by social circumstances and such chance contingencies as accident and good fortune." Notice that there is no mention *at all* of how persons have chosen to develop their own natural assets. Why is that simply left out? Perhaps because such choices also are viewed as being the products of factors outside the person's control, and hence as "arbitrary from a moral point of view." "The assertion that a man deserves the superior character that enables him to make the effort to cultivate his abilities is equally problematic; for his character depends in large part upon fortunate family and social circumstances for which he can claim no credit."[58] (What view is presupposed here of character and its relation to action?) "The initial endowment of natural assets and the contingencies of their growth and nurture in early life are arbitrary from a moral point of view . . . the effort a person is willing to make is influenced by his natural abilities and skills and the alternatives open to him. The better endowed are more likely, other things equal, to strive con- scientiously. . . ."[59] This line of argument can succeed in blocking the introduction of a person's autonomous choices and actions (and their results) only by attributing *everything* noteworthy about the person completely to certain sorts of "external" factors. So denigrating a person's autonomy and prime responsibility for his actions is a risky line to take for a theory that otherwise wishes to buttress the dignity and self-respect of autonomous beings; especially for a theory that founds so much (including a theory of the good) upon persons' choices. One doubts that the unexalted picture of human beings Rawls' theory presupposes and rests upon can be made to fit together with the view of human dignity it is designed to lead to and embody.

Before we investigate Rawls' reasons for rejecting the system of natural liberty, we should note the situation of those in the original position. The system of natural liberty is *one* interpretation of a principle that (according to Rawls) they *do* accept: social and economic inequalities are to be arranged so that they both are reasonably expected to be to everyone's advantage, and are attached to positions and offices open to all. It is left unclear whether the persons in the original position explicitly consider and choose among *all* the various interpretations of this principle, though this would seem to be the most reasonable construal. (Rawls' chart on page 124 listing the conceptions of justice considered in the original position does *not* include the system of natural liberty.) Certainly they explicitly consider one interpretation, the difference principle. Rawls does not state why persons in the original position who considered the system of natural liberty would reject it. Their reason cannot be that it makes the resulting distribution depend upon a *morally* arbitrary distribution of natural assets. What we must suppose, as we have seen before, is that the self-interested calculation of persons in the original position does not (and cannot) lead them to adopt the entitlement principle. We, however, and Rawls, base our evaluations on different considerations.

Rawls has explicitly *designed* the original position and its choice situation so as to embody and realize his negative reflective evaluation of allowing shares in holdings to be affected by natural assets: "Once we decide to look for a conception of justice that nullifies the accidents of natural endowment and the contingencies of social cir- cumstance. . . ."[60] (Rawls makes many scattered references to this theme of nullifying the accidents of natural endowment and the contingencies of social circumstance.) This quest crucially shapes Rawls' theory, and it underlies his delineation of the original position. It is not that persons who *did* deserve their natural endowments would choose differently if placed in Rawls' original position, but rather that, presumably, for such persons, Rawls would not hold that the principles of justice to govern *their* mutual relations were fixed by what they would choose in the original position. It is useful to remember how much of Rawls' construction rests upon this foundation. For example, Rawls argues that certain egalitarian demands are not motivated by envy but rather, because they are in accord with his two principles of justice, by resentment of injustice.[61] This argument can be undercut, as Rawls realizes,[62] if the very considerations which underlie the original position (yielding Rawls' two principles of justice) themselves embody or are based upon envy. So in addition to wanting to understand Rawls' rejection of alternative conceptions and to assess how powerful a criticism he makes of the entitlement conception, reasons internal to his theory provide motivation to explore the basis of the requirement that a conception of justice be geared to nullify differences in social circumstances and in natural assets (and any differences in social circumstances they result in).

Why shouldn't holdings partially depend upon natural endowments? (They will also depend on how these are developed and on the uses to which they are put.) Rawls' reply is that these natural endowments and assets, being undeserved, are "arbitrary from a moral point of view." There are two ways to understand the relevance of this reply: It might be part of an argument to establish that the distributive effects of natural differences ought to be nullified, which I shall call the positive argument; or it might be part of an argument to rebut a possible counterargument holding that the distributive effects of natural differences oughtn't to be nullified, which I shall call the negative argument. Whereas the positive argument attempts to establish that the distributive effects of natural differences ought to be nullified, the negative one, by merely rebutting *one* argument that the differences oughtn't to be nullified, leaves open the possibility that (for other reasons) the differences oughtn't to be nullified. (The negative argument also leaves it possibly a matter of moral *indifference* whether the distributive effects of natural differences are to be nullified; note the difference between saying that something ought to be the case and saying that it's not that it oughtn't to be the case.)

The Positive Argument

We shall begin with the positive argument. How might the point that differences in natural endowments are arbitrary from a moral point of view function in an argument meant to establish that differences in holdings stemming from differences in natural assets ought to be nullified? We shall consider four possible arguments; the first, the following argument A:

1 Any person should morally deserve the holdings he has; it shouldn't be that persons have holdings they don't deserve.
2 People do not morally deserve their natural assets.
3 If a person's X partially determines his Y, and his X is undeserved then so is his Y.

Therefore,

4 People's holdings shouldn't be partially determined by their natural assets.

This argument will serve as a surrogate for other similar, more complicated ones.[63] But Rawls explicitly and emphatically *rejects* distribution according to moral desert.

> There is a tendency for common sense to suppose that income and wealth, and the good things in life generally, should be distributed according to moral desert. Justice is happiness according to virtue. While it is recognized that this ideal can never be fully carried out, it is the appropriate conception [according to common sense] of distributive justice, at least as a *prima facie* principle, and society should try to realize it as circumstances permit. Now justice as fairness rejects this conception. Such a principle would not be chosen in the original position.[64]

Rawls could not, therefore, accept any premiss like the first premiss in argument A, and so no variant of this argument underlies his rejection of differences in distributive shares stemming from undeserved differences in natural assets. Not only does Rawls reject premiss 1, his theory is not

coextensive with it. He favors giving incentives to persons if this most improves the lot of the least well off, and it often will be because of their natural assets that these persons will receive incentives and have larger shares. We noted earlier that the entitlement conception of justice in holdings, not being a patterned conception of justice, does not accept distribution in accordance with moral desert either. Any person may give to anyone else any holding he is entitled to, independently of whether the recipient morally deserves to be the recipient. To each according to the legitimate entitlements that legitimately have been transferred to him, is not a patterned principle.

If argument A and its first premiss are rejected, it is not obvious how to construct the positive argument. Consider next argument B:

1 Holdings ought to be distributed according to some pattern that is not arbitrary from a moral point of view.
2 That persons have different natural assets *is* arbitrary from a moral point of view.

Therefore,

3 Holdings ought not to be distributed according to natural assets.

But differences in natural assets might be *correlated* with other differences that are not arbitrary from a moral point of view and that are clearly of some possible moral relevance to distributional questions. For example, Hayek argued that under capitalism distribution generally is in accordance with perceived service to others. Since differences in natural assets will produce differences in ability to serve others, there will be some correlation of differences in distribution with differences in natural assets. The principle of the system is *not* distribution in accordance with natural assets; but differences in natural assets will lead to differences in holdings under a system whose principle is distribution according to perceived service to others. If conclusion 3 above is to be interpreted in extension so as to exclude this, it should be made explicit. But to add the premiss that any pattern that has some roughly coextensive description that is arbitrary from a moral point of view is itself arbitrary from a moral point of view would be far too strong, because it would yield the result that *every* pattern is arbitrary from a moral point of view. Perhaps the crucial thing to be avoided is not mere coextensiveness, but rather some morally arbitrary feature's *giving rise to* differences in distributive shares. Thus consider argument C:

1 Holdings ought to be distributed according to some pattern that is not arbitrary from a moral point of view.
2 That persons have different natural assets is arbitrary from a moral point of view.
3 If part of the explanation of why a pattern contains differences in holdings is that other differences in persons give rise to these differences in holdings, and if these other differences are arbitrary from a moral point of view, then the pattern also is arbitrary from a moral point of view.

Therefore,

4 Differences in natural assets should not give rise to differences in holdings among persons.

Premiss 3 of this argument holds that any moral arbitrariness that underlies a pattern infects the pattern and makes it too morally arbitrary. But any pattern will have some morally arbitrary facts as part of the explanation of how it arises, including the pattern proposed by Rawls. The difference principle operates to give some persons larger distributive shares than others; which persons receive these larger shares will depend, at least partially, on differences between these persons and others, differences that are arbitrary from a moral point of view, for some persons with special natural assets will be offered larger shares as an incentive to use these assets in certain ways. Perhaps some premiss similar to 3 can be formulated so as to exclude what Rawls wishes to exclude while not excluding his *own* view. Still, the resulting argument would *assume* that the set of holdings should realize some pattern.

Why should the set of holdings be patterned? Patterning is *not* intrinsic to a theory of justice, as we have seen in our presentation of the entitlement theory: a theory that focuses upon the underlying principles that generate sets of holdings rather than upon the pattern a set of holdings realizes. If it be denied that the theory of these underlying principles *is* a separate theory of distributive justice, rather than merely a collection of diverse considerations from other areas, then the question becomes one of whether there *is* any separate subject of distributive justice which requires a separate theory.

On the manna-from-heaven model given earlier, there might be a more compelling reason to search for a pattern. But since things come into being already held (or with agreements already made about how they are to be held), there is no need to search for some pattern for unheld holdings to fit; and since the process whereby holdings actually come into being or are shaped, itself needn't realize any particular pattern, there is no reason to expect any pattern to result. The situation is not an appropriate one for wondering, "After all, what is to become of these things; what are we to do with them." In the non-manna-from-heaven world in which things have to be made or produced or transformed by people, there is no separate process of distribution for a theory of distribution to be a theory of. The reader will recall our earlier argument that (roughly) any set of holdings realizing a particular pattern may be transformed by the voluntary exchanges, gifts, and so forth, of the persons having the holdings under the pattern into *another* set of holdings that does not fit the pattern. The view that holdings *must* be patterned perhaps will seem less plausible when it is seen to have the consequence that people may not choose to do acts that upset the patterning, even with things they legitimately hold.

There is another route to a patterned conception of justice that, perhaps, should be mentioned. Suppose that each morally legitimate fact has a "unified" explanation that shows it is morally legitimate, and that *conjunctions* fall into the domain of facts to be explained as morally legitimate. If p and q are each morally legitimate facts, with their respective explanations as morally legitimate being P, and Q, then if $p \wedge q$ is also to be explained as morally legitimate, and if $P \wedge Q$ does not constitute a "unified" explanation (but is a mere conjunction of different explanations), then some further explanation will be needed. Applying this to holdings, suppose there are separate entitlement explanations showing the legitimacy of my having my holdings, and of your having yours, and the following question is asked: "Why is it legitimate that I hold what I do *and* you hold what you do; why is that joint fact *and all the relations contained within it* legitimate?" If the conjunction of the two separate explanations will not be held to explain in a unified manner the legitimacy of the joint fact (whose legitimacy is not viewed as being constituted by the legitimacy of its constituent parts), then some patterned principles of distribution would appear to be necessary to show its legitimacy, and to legitimate any nonunit set of holdings.

With scientific explanation of particular facts, the usual practice is to consider some conjunctions of explained facts as not requiring separate explanation, but as being explained by the conjunctions of the explanations of the conjuncts. (If E_1 explains e_1 and E_2 explains e_2 then $E_1 \wedge E_2$ explains $e_1 \wedge e_2$.) If we required that any two conjuncts and any n-place conjunction had to be explained in some unified fashion, and not merely by the conjunction of separate and disparate explanations, then we would be driven to reject most of the usual explanations and to search for an underlying pattern to explain what appear to be separate facts. (Scientists, of course, often do offer a unified explanation of apparently separate facts.) It would be well worth exploring the interesting consequences of refusing to treat, even in the first instance, any two facts as legitimately separable, as having separate explanations whose conjunction is all there is to the explanation of them. What would our theories of the world look like if we required unified explanations of *all* conjunctions? Perhaps an extrapolation of how the world looks to paranoid persons. Or, to put it undisparagingly, the way it appears to persons having certain sorts of dope experiences. (For example, the way it sometimes appears to me after smoking marijuana.) Such a vision of the world differs fundamentally from the way we normally look at it; it is surprising at first that a simple condition on the adequacy of explanations of conjunctions leads to it, until we realize that such a condition of adequacy must lead to a view of the world as deeply and wholly patterned.

A similar condition of adequacy on explanations of the moral legitimacy of conjunctions of separate morally legitimate facts would lead to a view that requires sets of holdings to exhibit an overall patterning. It seems unlikely that there will be compelling arguments for imposing such a principle of adequacy. Some may find such a unified vision plausible for only one realm; for example, in the moral realm concerning sets of holdings, but not in the realm of ordinary nonmoral explanation, or vice versa. For the case of explaining nonmoral facts, the challenge would be to produce such a unified theory. Were one produced that introduced novel considerations and explained no *new* facts (other than conjunctions of old ones) the decision as to its acceptability might be a difficult one and would depend largely on how explanatorily satisfying was the new way we saw the old facts. In the case of moral explanations and accounts which show the moral legitimacy of various facts, the situation is somewhat different. First, there is even less reason (I believe) to suppose a unified explanation appropriate and necessary. There is less need for a *greater* degree of explanatory unity than that provided when the same underlying principles for generating holdings appear in different explanations. (Rawls' theory, which contains elements of what he calls pure procedural justice, does not satisfy a strong condition of adequacy for explaining conjunctions and entails that such a condition cannot be satisfied.) Secondly, there is more danger than in the scientific case that the demand for a unified explanation will shape the "moral facts" to be explained. ("It can't be that both of those *are* facts for there's no unified patterned explanation that would yield them both.") Hence success in finding a unified explanation of such seriously primed facts will leave it unclear how well supported the explanatory theory is.

I turn now to our final positive argument which purports to derive the conclusion that distributive shares shouldn't depend upon natural assets from the statement that the distribution of natural assets is morally arbitrary. This argument focuses on the notion of equality. Since a large part of Rawls' argument serves to justify or show acceptable a particular deviation from equal shares (some may have more if this serves to improve the position of those worst off), perhaps a reconstruction of his underlying argument that places equality at its center will be illuminating. Differences between persons (the argument runs) are arbitrary from a moral point of view if there is no moral argument for the conclusion that there ought to be the differences. Not all such differences will be morally objectionable. That there is no such moral argument will seem important only in the case of those differences we believe oughtn't to obtain unless there is a moral reason establishing that they ought to obtain. There is, so to speak, a presumption against certain differences that can be overridden (can it merely be neutralized?) by moral reasons; in the absence of any such moral reasons of sufficient weight, there ought to be equality. Thus we have argument D:

1 Holdings ought to be equal, unless there is a (weighty) moral reason why they ought to be unequal.

2 People do not deserve the ways in which they differ from other persons in natural assets;

there is no moral reason why people ought to differ in natural assets.

3 If there is no moral reason why people differ in certain traits, then their actually differing in these traits does not provide, and cannot give rise to, a moral reason why they should differ in other traits (for example, in holdings).

Therefore,

4 People's differing in natural assets is not a reason why holdings ought to be unequal.
5 People's holdings ought to be equal unless there is some other moral reason (such as, for example, raising the position of those worst off) why their holdings ought to be unequal.

Statements similar to the third premiss will occupy us shortly. Here let us focus on the first premiss, the equality premiss. Why ought people's holdings to be equal, in the absence of special moral reason to deviate from equality? (Why think there *ought* to be *any* particular pattern in holdings?) Why is equality the rest (or rectilinear motion) position of the system, deviation from which may be caused only by moral forces? Many "arguments" for equality merely *assert* that differences between persons are arbitrary and must be justified. Often writers state a presumption in favor of equality in a form such as the following: "Differences in treatment of persons need to be justified."[65] The most favored situation for this sort of assumption is one in which there is one person (or group) treating everyone, a person (or group) having *no* right or entitlement to bestow the particular treatment as they wish or even whim. But if I go to one movie theater rather than to another adjacent to it, need I justify my different treatment of the two theater owners? Isn't it enough that I felt like going to one of them? That differences in treatment need to be justified *does* fit contemporary *governments*. Here there is a centralized process treating all, with no entitlement to bestow treatment according to whim. The major portion of distribution in a free society does not, however, come through the actions of the government, nor does failure to overturn the results of the localized individual exchanges constitute "state action." When there is no *one* doing the treating, and all are entitled to bestow their holdings as they wish, it is not clear why the maxim that differences in treatment must be justified should be thought to have extensive application. Why must differences between persons be

justified? Why think that we must change, or remedy, or compensate for any inequality which can be changed, remedied, or compensated for? Perhaps here is where social cooperation enters in: though there is no presumption of equality (in, say, primary goods, or things people care about) among all persons, perhaps there is one among persons cooperating together. But it is difficult to see an argument for this; surely not all persons who cooperate together explicitly agree to this presumption as one of the terms of their mutual cooperation. And its acceptance would provide an unfortunate incentive for well-off persons to refuse to cooperate with, or to allow any of their number to cooperate with, some distant people who are less well off than any among them. For entering into such social cooperation, beneficial to those less well off, would seriously worsen the position of the well-off group by creating relations of presumptive equality between themselves and the worse-off group. In the next chapter I shall consider the major recent argument for equality, one which turns out to be unsuccessful. Here we need only note that the connection argument D forges between not deserving natural assets and some conclusion about distributive shares *assumes* equality as a norm (that can be deviated from with, and only with, moral reason); and hence argument D itself cannot be used to establish any such conclusion about equality.

The Negative Argument

Unsuccessful in our quest for a convincing positive argument to connect the claim that people don't deserve their natural assets with the conclusion that differences in holdings ought not to be based upon differences in natural assets, we now turn to what we called the negative argument: the use of the claim that people don't deserve their natural assets to rebut a possible counterargument to Rawls' view. (If the equality argument D were acceptable, the negative task of rebutting possible counterconsiderations would form part of the positive task of showing that a presumption for equality holds unoverridden in a particular case.) Consider the following possible counterargument E to Rawls:

1 People deserve their natural assets.
2 If people deserve X, they deserve any Y that flows from X.

3 People's holdings flow from their natural assets.

Therefore,

4 People deserve their holdings.
5 If people deserve something, then they ought to have it (and this overrides any presumption of equality there may be about that thing).

Rawls would rebut this counterargument to his position by denying its first premiss. And so we see *some* connection between the claim that the distribution of natural assets is arbitrary and the statement that distributive shares should not depend upon natural assets. However, no great weight can be placed upon *this* connection. For there are other counterarguments, in a similar vein; for example the argument F that begins:

1 If people have X, and their having X (whether or not they deserve to have it) does *not* violate anyone else's (Lockean) right or entitlement to X, and Y flows from (arises out of, and so on) X by a process that does not itself violate anyone's (Lockean) rights or entitlements,[66] then the person is entitled to Y.
2 People's having the natural assets they do does not violate anyone else's (Lockean) entitlements or rights.

and goes on to argue that people are entitled to what they make, to the products of their labor, to what others give them or exchange. It is not true, for example, that a person earns Y (a right to keep a painting he's made, praise for writing *A Theory of Justice*, and so on) only if he's earned (or otherwise *deserves*) whatever he used (including natural assets) in the process of earning Y. Some of the things he uses he just may *have*, not illegitimately. It needn't be that the foundations underlying desert are themselves deserved, *all the way down*.

At the very least, we can parallel these statements about desert with ones about entitlements. And if, correctly, we describe people as entitled to their natural assets even if it's not the case that they can be said to deserve them, then the argument parallel to E above, with "are entitled to" replacing "deserve" throughout, *will* go through. This gives us the acceptable argument G:

1 People are entitled to their natural assets.
2 If people are entitled to something, they are entitled to whatever flows from it (via specified types of processes).

3 People's holdings flow from their natural assets.

Therefore,

4 People are entitled to their holdings.
5 If people are entitled to something, then they ought to have it (and this overrides any presumption of equality there may be about holdings).

Whether or not people's natural assets are arbitrary from a moral point of view, they are entitled to them, and to what flows from them.[67]

A recognition of people's entitlements to their natural assets (the first premiss of argument G) might be necessary to avoid the stringent application of the difference principle which would lead, we already have seen, to even stronger property rights in other persons than redistributive theories usually yield. Rawls feels that he avoids this[68] because people in his original position rank the principle of liberty as lexicographically prior to the difference principle, applied not only to economic well-being but to health, length of life, and so on. (However, see note 51 above.)

We have found no cogent argument to (help) establish that differences in holding arising from differences in natural assets should be eliminated or minimized. Can the theme that people's natural assets are arbitrary from a moral point of view be used differently, for example, to justify a certain *shaping* of the original position? Clearly if the shaping is designed to nullify differences in holdings due to differences in natural assets, we need an argument for this goal, and we are back to our unsuccessful quest for the route to the conclusion that such differences in holdings ought to be nullified. Instead, the shaping might take place by excluding the participants in the original position from knowing of their own natural endowments. In this way the fact that natural endowments are arbitrary from a moral point of view would help to impose and to justify the veil of ignorance. But how does it do this; why should knowledge of natural endowments be excluded from the original position? Presumably the underlying principle would be that if any particular features are arbitrary from a moral point of view, then persons in the original position should not know they possess them. But this would exclude their knowing *anything* about themselves, for each of their features (including rationality, the ability to make choices, having a life span of more than three days, having a memory, being able to communicate with other organisms like themselves) will be based upon the fact that the sperm and ovum which produced them contained particular genetic material. The physical fact that those particular gametes contained particular organized chemicals (the genes for people rather than for muskrats or trees) is arbitrary *from a moral point of view*; it is, from a moral point of view, an accident. Yet the persons in the original position are to know some of their attributes.

Perhaps we are too quick when we suggest excluding knowledge of rationality, and so forth, merely because these features *arise from* morally arbitrary facts. For these features also have moral significance; that is, moral facts depend upon or arise from them. Here we see an ambiguity in saying that a fact is arbitrary from a moral point of view. It might mean that there is no moral reason why the fact ought to be that way, or it might mean that the fact's being that way is of no moral significance and has no moral consequences. Rationality, the ability to make choices, and so on, are not morally arbitrary in this second sense. But if they escape exclusion on this ground, now the problem is that the natural assets, knowledge of which Rawls wishes to exclude from the original position, are not morally arbitrary in this sense either. At any rate, the entitlement theory's claim that moral entitlements may arise from or be partially based upon such facts is what is now at issue. Thus, in the absence of an argument to the effect that differences in holdings due to differences in natural assets ought to be nullified, it is not clear how anything about the original position can be based upon the (ambiguous) claim that differences in natural assets are arbitrary from a moral point of view.

Collective Assets

Rawls' view seems to be that everyone has some entitlement or claim on the totality of natural assets (viewed as a pool), with no one having differential claims. The distribution of natural abilities is viewed as a "collective asset."[69]

> We see then that the difference principle represents, in effect, an agreement to regard the distribution of natural talents as a common asset and to share in the benefits of this distrib-

ution whatever it turns out to be. Those who have been favored by nature, whoever they are, may gain from their good fortune only on terms that improve the situation of those who have lost out. . . . No one deserves his greater natural capacity nor merits a more favorable starting place in society. But it does not follow that one should eliminate these distinctions. There is another way to deal with them. The basic structure can be arranged so that these contingencies work for the good of the least fortunate.[70]

People will differ in how they view regarding natural talents as a common asset. Some will complain, echoing Rawls against utilitarianism,[71] that this "does not take seriously the distinction between persons"; and they will wonder whether any reconstruction of Kant that treats people's abilities and talents as resources for others can be adequate. "The two principles of justice . . . rule out even the tendency to regard men as means to one another's welfare."[72] Only if one presses *very* hard on the distinction between men and their talents, assets, abilities, and special traits. Whether any coherent conception of a person remains when the distinction is so pressed is an open question. Why we, thick with particular traits, should be cheered that (only) the thus purified men within us are not regarded as means is also unclear.

People's talents and abilities *are* an asset to a free community; others in the community benefit from their presence and are better off because they are there rather than elsewhere or nowhere. (Otherwise they wouldn't choose to deal with them.) Life, over time, is not a constant-sum game, wherein if greater ability or effort leads to some getting more, that means that others must lose. In a free society, people's talents do benefit others, and not only themselves. Is it the extraction of even more benefit to others that is supposed to justify treating people's natural assets as a collective resource? What justifies this extraction?

> No one deserves his greater natural capacity nor merits a more favorable starting place in society. But it does not follow that one should eliminate these distinctions. There is another way to deal with them. The basic structure can be arranged so that these contingencies work for the good of the least fortunate.[73]

And if there weren't "another way to deal with them"? Would it then follow that one should eliminate these distinctions? What exactly would be contemplated in the case of natural assets? If people's assets and talents *couldn't* be harnessed to serve others, would something be done to remove these exceptional assets and talents, or to forbid them from being exercised for the person's own benefit or that of someone else he chose, even though this limitation wouldn't improve the absolute position of those somehow unable to harness the talents and abilities of others for their own benefit? Is it so implausible to claim that envy underlies this conception of justice, forming part of its root notion?[74]

We have used our entitlement conception of justice in holdings to probe Rawls' theory, sharpening our understanding of what the entitlement conception involves by bringing it to bear upon an alternative conception of distributive justice, one that is deep and elegant. Also, I believe, we have probed deep-lying inadequacies in Rawls' theory. I am mindful of Rawls' reiterated point that a theory cannot be evaluated by focusing upon a single feature or part of it; instead the whole theory must be assessed (the reader will not know how whole a theory can be until he has read all of Rawls' book), and a perfect theory is not to be expected. However we have examined an important part of Rawls' theory, and its crucial underlying assumptions. I am as well aware as anyone of how sketchy my discussion of the entitlement conception of justice in holdings has been. But I no more believe we need to have formulated a complete alternative theory in order to reject Rawls' undeniably great advance over utilitarianism, than Rawls needed a complete alternative theory before he could reject utilitarianism. What more does one need or can one have, in order to begin progressing toward a better theory, than a sketch of a plausible alternative view, which from its very different perspective highlights the inadequacies of the best existing well-worked-out theory? Here, as in so many things, we learn from Rawls.

We began this chapter's investigation of distributive justice in order to consider the claim that a state more extensive than the minimal state could be justified on the grounds that it was necessary, or the most appropriate instrument, to achieve distributive justice. According to the entitlement conception of justice in holdings that we have presented, there is no argument based upon the first two principles of distributive justice, the principles of acquisition and of transfer, for such a more extensive state. If the set of holdings is properly generated, there is no argument for a more extensive state based upon distributive justice.[75] (Nor, we have claimed, will the Lockean proviso actually provide occasion for a more extensive state.) If, however, these principles are violated, the principle of rectification comes into play. Perhaps it is best to view some patterned principles of distributive justice as rough rules of thumb meant to approximate the general results of applying the principle of rectification of injustice. For example lacking much historical information, and assuming (1) that victims of injustice generally do worse than they otherwise would and (2) that those from the least well-off group in the society have the highest probabilities of being the (descendants of) victims of the most serious injustice who are owed compensation by those who benefited from the injustices (assumed to be those better off, though sometimes the perpetrators will be others in the worst-off group), then a *rough* rule of thumb for rectifying injustices might seem to be the following: organize society so as to maximize the position of whatever group ends up least well-off in the society. This particular example may well be implausible, but an important question for each society will be the following: given *its* particular history, what operable rule of thumb best approximates the results of a detailed application in that society of the principle of rectification? These issues are very complex and are best left to a full treatment of the principle of rectification. In the absence of such a treatment applied to a particular society, one *cannot* use the analysis and theory presented here to condemn any particular scheme of transfer payments, unless it is clear that no considerations of rectification of injustice could apply to justify it. Although to introduce socialism as the punishment for our sins would be to go too far, past injustices might be so great as to make necessary in the short run a more extensive state in order to rectify them.

Notes

1 The reader who has looked ahead and seen that the second part of this chapter discusses Rawls' theory mistakenly may think that every remark or argument in the first part against alternative theories of justice is meant to apply to, or anticipate, a criticism of Rawls' theory. This is not so; there are other theories also worth criticizing.

2 Applications of the principle of justice in acquisition may also occur as part of the move from one distribution to another. You may find an unheld thing now and appropriate it. Acquisitions also are to be understood as included when, to simplify, I speak only of transitions by transfers.

3 See, however, the useful book by Boris Bittker, *The Case for Black Reparations* (New York: Random House, 1973).

4 If the principle of rectification of violations of the first two principles yields more than one description of holdings, then some choice must be made as to which of these is to be realized. Perhaps the sort of considerations about distributive justice and equality that I argue against play a legitimate role in *this* subsidiary choice. Similarly, there may be room for such considerations in deciding which otherwise arbitrary features a statute will embody, when such features are unavoidable because other considerations do not specify a precise line; yet a line must be drawn.

5 One might try to squeeze a patterned conception of distributive justice into the framework of the entitlement conception, by formulating a gimmicky obligatory "principle of transfer" that would lead to the pattern. For example, the principle that if one has more than the mean income one must transfer everything one holds above the mean to persons below the mean so as to bring them up to (but not over) the mean. We can formulate a criterion for a "principle of transfer" to rule out such obligatory transfers, or we can say that no correct principle of transfer, no principle of transfer in a free society will be like this. The former is probably the better course, though the latter also is true.

Alternatively, one might think to make the entitlement conception instantiate a pattern, by using matrix entries that express the relative strength of a person's entitlements as measured by some real-valued function. But even if the limitation to natural dimensions failed to exclude this function, the resulting edifice would *not* capture our system of entitlements to *particular* things.

6 F. A. Hayek, *The Constitution of Liberty* (Chicago: University of Chicago Press, 1960), p. 87.

7 This question does not imply that they will tolerate any and every patterned distribution. In discussing Hayek's views, Irving Kristol has recently speculated that people will not long tolerate a system that yields distributions patterned in accordance with value rather than merit. ("'When Virtue Loses All Her Loveliness' – Some Reflections on Capitalism and 'The Free Society,'" *The Public Interest*, Fall 1970, pp. 3–15.) Kristol, following some remarks of Hayek's, equates the merit system with justice. Since some case can be made for the external standard of distribution in accordance with benefit to others, we ask about a weaker (and therefore, more plausible) hypothesis.

8 We certainly benefit because great economic incentives operate to get others to spend much time and energy to figure out how to serve us by providing things we will want to pay for. It is not mere paradox mongering to wonder whether capitalism should be criticized for most rewarding and hence encouraging, not individualists like Thoreau who go about their own lives, but people who are occupied with serving others and winning them as customers. But to defend capitalism one need not think businessmen are the finest human types. (I do not mean to join here the general maligning of businessmen, either.) Those who think the finest should acquire the most can try to convince their fellows to transfer resources in accordance with *that* principle.

9 Varying situations continuously from that limit situation to our own would force us to make explicit the underlying rationale of entitlements and to consider whether entitlement considerations lexicographically precede the considerations of the usual theories of distributive justice, so that the *slightest* strand of entitlement outweighs the considerations of the usual theories of distributive justice.

10 Might not a transfer have instrumental effects on a third party, changing his feasible options? (But what if the two parties to the transfer independently had used their holdings in this fashion?) I discuss this question below, but note here that this question concedes the point for distributions of ultimate intrinsic noninstrumental goods (pure utility experiences, so to speak) that are transferable. It also might be objected that the transfer might make a third party more envious because it worsens his position relative to someone else. I find it incomprehensible how this can be thought to involve a claim of justice. On envy, see Chapter 8 of *Anarchy, State and Utopia*.

Here and elsewhere in this chapter, a theory which incorporates elements of pure procedural justice might find what I say acceptable, *if* kept in its proper place; that is, if background institutions exist to ensure the satisfaction of certain conditions on distributive shares. But if these institutions are not themselves the sum or invisible-hand result of people's voluntary (nonaggressive) actions, the constraints they impose require justification. At no point does *our* argument assume any background institutions more extensive than those of the minimal night-watchman state, a state limited to protecting persons against murder, assault, theft, fraud, and so forth.

11 See the selection from John Henry MacKay's novel, *The Anarchists*, reprinted in Leonard Krimmerman and Lewis Perry, eds., *Patterns of Anarchy* (New York: Doubleday Anchor Books, 1966), in which an individualist anarchist presses upon a communist anarchist the following question: "Would you, in the system of society which you call 'free Communism' prevent individuals from exchanging their labor among themselves by means of their own medium of exchange? And further: Would you prevent them from occupying land for the purpose of personal use?" The novel continues: "[the] question was not to be escaped. If he answered 'Yes!' he admitted that society had the right of control over the individual and threw overboard the autonomy of the individual which he had always zealously defended; if on the other hand, he answered 'No!' he admitted the right of private property which he had just denied so emphatically. . . . Then he answered 'In Anarchy any number of men must have the right of forming a voluntary association, and so realizing their ideas in practice. Nor can I understand how any one could justly be driven from the land and house which he uses and occupies . . . every serious man must declare himself: for Socialism, and thereby for force and against liberty, or for Anarchism, and thereby for liberty and against force.'" In contrast, we find Noam Chomsky writing, "Any consistent anarchist must oppose private ownership of the means of production," "the consistent anarchist then . . . will be a socialist . . . of a particular sort." Introduction to Daniel Guerin, *Anarchism: From Theory to Practice* (New York: Monthly Review Press, 1970), pages xiii, xv.

12 Is the patterned principle stable that requires merely that a distribution be Pareto-optimal? One person might give another a gift or bequest that the second could exchange with a third to their mutual benefit. Before the second makes this exchange, there is not Pareto-optimality. Is a stable pattern presented by a principle choosing that among the Pareto-optimal positions that satisfies some further condition C? It may seem that there cannot be a counterexample, for won't any voluntary exchange made away from a situation show that the first situation wasn't Pareto-optimal? (Ignore the implausibility of this last claim for the case of bequests.) But principles are to be satisfied

over time, during which new possibilities arise. A distribution that at one time satisfies the criterion of Pareto-optimality might not do so when some new possibilities arise (Wilt Chamberlain grows up and starts playing basketball); and though people's activities will tend to move then to a new Pareto-optimal position, *this* new one need not satisfy the contentful condition C. Continual interference will be needed to insure the continual satisfaction of C. (The theoretical possibility of a pattern's being maintained by some invisible-hand process that brings it back to an equilibrium that fits the pattern when deviations occur should be investigated.)

13 *Collective Choice and Social Welfare*, Holden-Day, Inc., 1970, chaps. 6 and 6*.

14 Oppression will be less noticeable if the background institutions do not prohibit certain actions that upset the patterning (various exchanges or transfers of entitlement), but rather prevent them from being done, by nullifying them.

15 One indication of the stringency of Rawls' difference principle, which we attend to in the second part of this chapter, is its inappropriateness as a governing principle even within a family of individuals who love one another. Should a family devote its resources to maximizing the position of its least well off and least talented child, holding back the other children or using resources for their education and development only if they will follow a policy through their lifetimes of maximizing the position of their least fortunate sibling? Surely not. How then can this even be considered as the appropriate policy for enforcement in the wider society? (I discuss below what I think would be Rawls' reply: that some principles apply at the macro level which do not apply to microsituations.)

16 See Gregory Vlastos, "The Individual as an Object of Love in Plato" in his *Platonic Studies* (Princeton: Princeton University Press, 1973), pp. 3–34.

17 I am unsure as to whether the arguments I present below show that such taxation merely *is* forced labor; so that "is on a par with" means "is one kind of." Or alternatively, whether the arguments emphasize the great similarities between such taxation and forced labor, to show it is plausible and illuminating to view such taxation in the light of forced labor. This latter approach would remind one of how John Wisdom conceives of the claims of metaphysicians.

18 Nothing hangs on the fact that here and elsewhere I speak loosely of *needs*, since I go on, each time, to reject the criterion of justice which includes it. If, however, something did depend upon the notion, one would want to examine it more carefully. For a skeptical view, see Kenneth Minogue, *The Liberal*

Mind, (New York: Random House, 1963), pp. 103–112.

19 Further details which this statement should include are contained in my essay "Coercion," in *Philosophy, Science, and Method*, ed. S. Morgenbesser, P. Suppes, and M. White (New York: St. Martin, 1969).

20 On the themes in this and the next paragraph, see the writings of Armen Alchian.

21 Compare this with Robert Paul Wolff's "A Refutation of Rawls' Theorem on Justice," *Journal of Philosophy*, March 31, 1966, sect. 2. Wolff's criticism does not apply to Rawls' conception under which the baseline is fixed by the difference principle.

22 I have not seen a precise estimate. David Friedman, *The Machinery of Freedom* (N.Y.: Harper & Row, 1973), pp. xiv, xv, discusses this issue and suggests 5 percent of U.S. national income as an upper limit for the first two factors mentioned. However he does not attempt to estimate the percentage of current wealth which is based upon such income in the past. (The vague notion of "based upon" merely indicates a topic needing investigation.)

23 Fourier held that since the process of civilization had deprived the members of society of certain liberties (to gather, pasture, engage in the chase), a socially guaranteed minimum provision for persons was justified as compensation for the loss (Alexander Gray, *The Socialist Tradition* (New York: Harper & Row, 1968), p. 188). But this puts the point too strongly. This compensation would be due those persons, if any, for whom the process of civilization was a *net loss*, for whom the benefits of civilization did not counterbalance being deprived of these particular liberties.

24 For example, Rashdall's case of someone who comes upon the only water in the desert several miles ahead of others who also will come to it and appropriates it all. Hastings Rashdall, "The Philosophical Theory of Property," in *Property, its Duties and Rights* (London: Macmillan, 1915).

We should note Ayn Rand's theory of property rights ("Man's Rights" in *The Virtue of Selfishness* (New York: New American Library, 1964), p. 94), wherein these follow from the right to life, since people need physical things to live. But a right to life is not a right to whatever one needs to live; other people may have rights over these other things. At most, a right to life would be a right to have or strive for whatever one needs to live, provided that having it does not violate anyone else's rights. With regard to material things, the question is whether having it does violate any right of others. (Would appropriation of all unowned things do so? Would appropriating the water hole in Rashdall's example?) Since special considerations (such as the Lockean proviso) may enter with regard to material property, one *first* needs a theory of property rights before one can apply any supposed right to life (as amended above). Therefore the right to life cannot provide the foundation for a theory of property rights.

25 The situation would be different if his water hole didn't dry up, due to special precautions he took to prevent this. Compare our discussion of the case in the text with Hayek, *The Constitution of Liberty*, p. 136; and also with Ronald Hamowy, "Hayek's Concept of Freedom; A Critique," *New Individualist Review*, April 1961, pp. 28–31.

26 I discuss overriding and its moral traces in "Moral Complications and Moral Structures," *Natural Law Forum*, 1968, pp. 1–50.

27 Does the principle of compensation (Chapter 4) introduce patterning considerations? Though it requires compensation for the disadvantages imposed by those seeking security from risks, it is not a patterned principle. For it seeks to remove only those disadvantages which prohibitions inflict on those who might present risks to others, not all disadvantages. It specifies an obligation on those who impose the prohibition, which stems from their own particular acts, to remove a particular complaint those prohibited may make against them.

28 Cambridge, Mass.: Harvard University Press, 1971.

29 Rawls, *Theory of Justice*, p. 4.

30 See Milton Friedman, *Capitalism and Freedom* (Chicago: University of Chicago Press, 1962), p. 165.

31 On the question of why the economy contains firms (of more than one person), and why each individual does not contract and recontract with others, see Ronald H. Coase, "The Nature of the Firm," in *Readings in Price Theory*, ed. George Stigler and Kenneth Boulding (Homewood, Ill.: Irwin, 1952); and Armen A. Alchian and Harold Demsetz, "Production, Information Costs and Economic Organization," *American Economic Review*, 1972, 777–795.

32 We do not, however, assume here or elsewhere the satisfaction of those conditions specified in economists' artificial model of so-called "perfect competition." One appropriate mode of analysis is presented in Israel M. Kirzner, *Market Theory and the Price System* (Princeton, N.J.: Van Nostrand, 1963); see also his *Competition and Entrepreneurship* (Chicago: University of Chicago Press, 1973).

33 Receiving this, we should note, is not the same as receiving the equivalent of what the person *causes* to exist, or *produces*. The marginal product of a unit of F_1 with respect to factor $F_2, \ldots, F_n$ is a *subjunctive* notion; it is the difference between the total product of $F_1, \ldots, F_n$ used most efficiently (as

efficiently as known how, given prudence about many costs in finding out the most efficient use of factors) and the total product of the most efficient use of $F_2, \ldots, F_n$ along with a unit less of F_1. But these two different most efficient uses of $F_2, \ldots, F_n$ along with a unit less of F_1 (one with the additional unit of F_1, the other without it) will use them differently. And F_1's marginal product (with respect to the other factors), what everyone reasonably would pay for an additional unit of F_1, will not be what it *causes* (*it* causes) combined with $F_2, \ldots, F_n$ and the other units of F_1, but rather the difference it makes, the difference there would be if this unit of F_1 were absent and the remaining factors were organized most efficiently to cope with its absence. Thus marginal productivity theory is not best thought of as a theory of actual produced product, of those things whose causal pedigree includes the unit of the factor, but rather as a theory of the difference (subjunctively defined) made by the presence of a factor. *If* such a view were connected with justice, it would seem to fit best with an entitlement conception.

34 Readers who believe that Marx's analysis of exchange relations between owners of capital and laborers undercuts the view that the set of holdings which results from voluntary exchange is legitimate, or who believe it a distortion to term such exchanges "voluntary," will find some relevant considerations adduced in Chapter 8.

35 See Marc Blaug, *Economic Theory in Retrospect* (Homewood, Ill.: Irwin, 1968), chap. 11, and the references cited therein. For a recent survey of issues about the marginal productivity of capital, see G.C. Harcourt, "Some Cambridge Controversies in the Theory of Capital," *Journal of Economic Literature*, 7, no. 2 (June 1969), 369–405.

36 Rawls, *Theory of Justice*, p. 12.

37 Rawls, *Theory of Justice*, pp. 14–15.

38 Rawls, *Theory of Justice*, sect. 16, especially p. 98.

39 Here we simplify the content of 5, but not to the detriment of our present discussion. Also, of course, beliefs other than 5, when conjoined with 3 would justify the inference to 4; for example belief in the material conditional "If 3, then 4." It is something like 5, though, that is relevant to our discussion here.

40 Though Rawls does not clearly distinguish 2 from 1 and 4 from 3, I do not claim that he makes the illegitimate step of sliding from the latter subjunctive to the former indicative. Even so, the mistake is worth pointing out because it is an easy one to fall into, and it might appear to prop up positions we argue against.

41 Rawls, *Theory of Justice*, p. 15.

42 They needn't be *better endowed*, from birth. In the context in which Rawls uses it, all "better endowed" means is: accomplishes more of economic value, able to do this, has a high marginal product, and so forth. (The role that unpredictable factors play in this complicates imagining a prior partitioning of the two groups.) The text follows Rawls in categorizing persons as "better" and "worse" endowed only in order to criticize the considerations *he* adduces for his theory. The entitlement theory does not rest upon any assumption that the classification is an important one, or even a possible one, or upon any elitist presupposition.

Since the entitlement theorist does not accept the patterned principle "to each according to his natural endowment," he can easily grant that what an exercised endowment brings in the market will depend upon the endowments of others and how they choose to exercise them, upon the market-expressed desires of buyers, upon the alternate supply of what he offers and of what others may substitute for what he offers, and upon other circumstances summing the myriad choices and actions of others. Similarly, we saw earlier that the similar considerations Rawls adduces about the social factors upon which the marginal product of labor depends (*Theory of Justice*, p. 308) will not faze an entitlement theorist, even though they might undercut the rationale put forth by a proponent of the patterned principle of distribution according to marginal product.

43 Supposing they could identify themselves and each other, they might *try* to exact a larger share by banding together as a group and bargaining jointly with the others. Given the large numbers of persons involved and the incentive for some of the better-endowed individuals to break ranks and reach separate agreements with the worse endowed, if such a coalition of the better endowed is unable to impose sanctions on its defectors it will dissolve. The better endowed remaining in the coalition may use boycott as a "sanction," and refuse to cooperate with a defector. To break the coalition, those less well endowed would have to (be able to) offer someone better endowed sufficient incentive to defect to make up for his loss through no longer being able to cooperate with the other better-endowed persons. Perhaps it would pay for someone to defect from the coalition only as part of a sizable group of defectors, which defecting group the initial coalition might try to keep small by special offers to individuals to defect *from it*, and so on. The problem is a complicated one, further complicated by the obvious fact (despite our use of Rawls' classificatory terminology) that there is no sharp line of cleavage between the endowments of people to determine which groups would form.

44 Rawls, *Theory of Justice*, p. 103.

45 I treat Rawls' discussion here as one concerning better- and worse-endowed individuals who know

they are so. Alternatively, one might imagine that *these* considerations are to be weighed by someone in the original position. ("If I turn out to be better endowed then . . .; if I turn out to be worse endowed then. . . .") But this construal will not do. Why would Rawls bother saying, "The two principles . . . seem to be a fair agreement on the basis of which those better endowed or more fortunate in their social position could expect the willing cooperation of others" (*Theory of Justice*, p. 15). Who is doing the expecting when? How is this to be translated into subjunctives to be contemplated by someone in the original position? Similarly, questions arise about Rawls' saying, "The difficulty is to show that *A* has no grounds for complaint. Perhaps he is required to have less than he might since his having more would result in some loss to *B. Now what can be said to the more favored man?* . . . The difference principle then seems to be a fair basis on which those better endowed . . . could expect others to collaborate with them . . ." (*Theory of Justice*, p. 103, my italics). Are we to understand this as: someone in the original position wonders what to say to himself as he then thinks of the possibility that he will turn out to be one of the better endowed? And does he then say that the difference principle *then* seems a fair basis for cooperation despite the fact that, and even while, he is contemplating the possibility that he is better endowed? Or does he say then that even later if and when he knows he is better endowed the difference principle will seem fair to him at that later time? And when are we to imagine him possibly complaining? Not while in the original position, for then he is agreeing to the difference principle. Nor does he worry, while in the process of deciding in the original position, that he will complain later. For he knows that he will have no cause to complain later at the effects of whatever principle he himself rationally will choose soon in the original position. Are we to imagine him complaining against himself? And isn't the answer to any later complaint, "You agreed to it (or you would have agreed to it if so originally positioned)"? What "difficulty" does Rawls concern himself with here? Trying to squeeze it into the original position makes it completely mysterious. And what is thinking of what is a "fair agreement" (sect. 3) or a "fair basis" (p. 103) doing here anyway, in the midst of the rational self-interested calculations of persons in the original position, who do not then knowingly possess, or at any rate utilize, particular moral notions?

I see no coherent way to incorporate how Rawls treats and speaks of the issue of the terms of cooperation between the better and the worse endowed into the structure and perspective of the original position. Therefore my discussion considers Rawls here as addressing himself to individuals *outside* the original position, either to better-endowed individuals or to his readers, to convince *them* that the difference principle which Rawls extracts from the original position is fair. It is instructive to compare how Rawls imagines justifying the social order to a person in the worst-off group in an unequal society. Rawls wants to tell this person that the inequalities work out to his advantage. This is told to someone who knows who he is: "The social order can be justified to everyone, and in particular to those who are least favored" (p. 103). Rawls does not want to say, "You would have gambled, and you lost," or any such thing, even "You chose it then in the original position"; nor does he wish merely to address someone in the original position. He also wants a consideration apart from the original position that will convince someone who knows of his inferior position in an unequal society. To say, "You have less in order that I may prosper," would *not* convince someone who knows of his inferior position, and Rawls rightly rejects it, even though its subjunctive analogue for someone in the original position, if we could make sense of this, would not be without force.

46 Do the people in the original position ever wonder whether *they* have the *right* to decide how everything is to be divided up? Perhaps they reason that since they are deciding this question, they must assume they are entitled to do so; and so particular people can't have particular entitlements to holdings (for then they wouldn't have the right to decide together on how all holdings are to be divided); and hence everything legitimately may be treated like manna from heaven.

47 I do not mean to assume that all teachers are such, nor even that learning in universities should be graded. All I need is some example of entitlement, the details of which the reader will have some familiarity with, to use to examine decision making in the original position. Grading is a simple example, though not a perfect one, entangled as it is with whatever ultimate social purposes the ongoing practice serves. We may ignore this complication, for their selecting the historical principle on the grounds that it effectively serves those purposes would illustrate our point below that their fundamental concerns and fundamental principles are end-state ones.

48 But recall the reasons why using magnitudes of entitlement does not capture accurately the entitlement principle (note 5).

49 Some years ago, Hayek argued (*The Constitution of Liberty*, chap. 3) that a free capitalist society, over time, raises the position of those worst off more than any alternative institutional structure; to use present terminology, he argued that *it* best satisfies

the end-state principle of justice formulated by the difference principle.

50 Someone might think entitlement principles count as specially tailored in a morally objectionable way, and so he might reject my claim that the veil of ignorance accomplishes more than its stated purpose. Since to specially tailor principles is to tailor them *unfairly* for one's own advantage, and since the question of the fairness of the entitlement principle is precisely the issue, it is difficult to decide which begs the question: my criticism of the strength of the veil of ignorance, or the defense against this criticism which I imagine in this note.

51 This is especially serious in view of the weakness of Rawls' reasons (sect. 82) for placing the liberty principle prior to the difference principle in a lexicographic ordering.

52 "The idea of the original position is to set up a fair procedure so that any principle agreed to will be just. The aim is to use the notion of pure procedural justice as a basis for theory." Rawls, *Theory of Justice*, p. 136.

53 The difference principle thus creates *two* conflicts of interest: between those at the top and those at bottom; *and* between those in the middle and those at bottom, for if those at bottom were gone the difference principle might apply to improve the position of those in the middle, who would become the new bottom group whose position is to be maximized.

54 Let the second group have individuals who score half as much on D and have shares twice as large as the corresponding individuals in the first group, where in the first group the ratios between any two individuals' shares and their scores on D are the same. It follows that *within* the second group, the ratio of any two individuals' shares will be the same as the ratio of their scores. Yet between groups this identity of ratios will *not* hold.

55 Thomas Scanlon, Jr., "Rawls' Theory of Justice," *University of Pennsylvania Law Review*, 121, No. 5, May 1973, p. 1064.

56 See my "Moral Complications and Moral Structures," *Natural Law Forum*, 13, 1968, especially pp. 11–21.

57 Rawls, *Theory of Justice*, p. 72. Rawls goes on to discuss what he calls a liberal interpretation of his two principles of justice, which is designed to eliminate the influence of social contingencies, but which "intuitively, still appears defective . . . [for] it still permits the distribution of wealth and income to be determined by the natural distribution of abilities and talents . . . distributive shares are decided by the outcome of the natural lottery; and this outcome is arbitrary from a moral perspective. There is no more reason to permit the distribution of income and wealth to be settled by the distribution of natural assets than by historical

and social fortune" (pp. 73–74).

58 Rawls, *Theory of Justice*, p. 104.

59 Rawls, *Theory of Justice*, pp. 311–312.

60 Rawls, *Theory of Justice*, p. 15.

61 Rawls, *Theory of Justice*, pp. 538–541.

62 "In order to show that the principles of justice are based in part on envy it would have to be established that one or more of the conditions of the original position arose from this propensity." *Theory of Justice*, p. 538.

63 For example:

1 Differences between any two persons' holdings should be morally deserved; morally undeserved differences should not exist.

2 Differences between persons in natural assets are morally undeserved.

3 Differences between persons partially determined by other differences that are undeserved are themselves undeserved.

Therefore,

4 Differences between persons' holdings shouldn't be partially determined by differences in their natural assets.

64 Rawls, *Theory of Justice*, p. 310. In the remainder of this section, Rawls goes on to criticize the conception of distribution according to moral desert.

65 "No reason need be given for . . . an equal distribution of benefits – for that is 'natural' – self-evidently right and just, and needs no justification, since it is in some sense conceived as being self-justified. . . . The assumption is that equality needs no reasons, only inequality does so; that uniformity, regularity, similarity, symmetry, . . . need not be specially accounted for, whereas differences, unsystematic behavior, changes in conduct, need explanation and, as a rule, justification. If I have a cake and there are ten persons among whom I wish to divide it, then if I give exactly one-tenth to each, this will not, at any rate automatically, call for justification; whereas if I depart from this principle of equal division I am expected to produce a special reason. It is some sense of this, however latent, that makes equality an idea which has never seemed intrinsically eccentric. . . . ," Isaiah Berlin, "Equality," reprinted in Frederick A. Olafson, ed. *Justice and Social Policy* (Englewood Cliffs, N.J.: Prentice-Hall, 1961), p. 131. To pursue the analogy with mechanics further, note that it is a substantive theoretical position which specifies a particular state or situation as one which requires no explanation whereas deviations from it are to be explained in terms of external forces. See Ernest Nagel's discussion of D'Alembert's attempt to provide an *a priori* argument for Newton's first law of motion. [*The Structure of Science* (New York: Harcourt, Brace, and World, 1961), pp. 175–177.]

66 A process, we might strengthen the antecedent by

adding, of the sort that would create an entitlement to Y if the person were entitled to X. I use "Lockean" rights and entitlements to refer to those (discussed in Part I) against force, fraud, and so on, which are to be recognized in the minimal state. Since I believe these are the only rights and entitlements people possess (apart from those they specially acquire), I needn't have included the specification to Lockean rights. One who believes some have a right to the fruits of others' labor will deny the truth of the first premiss as stated. If the Lockean specification were not included, he might grant the truth of 1, while denying that of 2 or of later steps.

67 If nothing of moral significance could flow from what was arbitrary, then no particular person's existence could be of moral significance, since which of the many sperm cells succeeds in fertilizing the egg cell is (so far as we know) arbitrary from a moral point of view. This suggests another, more vague, remark directed to the spirit of Rawls' position rather than to its letter. Each existing person is the product of a process wherein the one sperm cell which succeeds is no more deserving than the millions that fail. Should we wish that process had been "fairer" as judged by Rawls' standards, that all "inequities" in it had been rectified? We should be apprehensive about any principle that would condemn morally the very sort of process that brought us to be, a principle that therefore would undercut the legitimacy of our very existing.

68 But see also our discussion below of Rawls' view of natural abilities as a collective asset.

69 Rawls, *Theory of Justice*, p. 179.

70 Rawls, *Theory of Justice*, p. 102.

71 Rawls, *Theory of Justice*, p. 27.

72 Rawls, *Theory of Justice*, p. 183.

73 Rawls, *Theory of Justice*, p. 102.

74 Will the lexicographic priority that Rawls claims for liberty in the original position prevent the difference principle from requiring a head tax on assets and abilities? The legitimacy of a head tax is *suggested* by Rawls' speaking of "collective assets" and "common assets." Those underutilizing their assets and abilities are misusing a public asset. (Squandering public property?) Rawls may intend no such strong inferences from his terminology, but we need to hear more about why those in the original position wouldn't accept the strong interpretation. The notion of liberty needs elaboration which is to exclude a head tax and yet allow the other taxation schemes. Assets and abilities can be harnessed without a head tax; and "harnessing" is an appropriate term – as it would be for a horse harnessed to a wagon which doesn't *have* to move ever, but if it does, it must draw the wagon along.

With regard to envy, the difference principle, applied to the choice between either A having ten and B having five or A having eight and B having five, would favor the latter. Thus, despite Rawls' view (pp. 79–80), the difference principle is inefficient in that it sometimes will favor a status quo against a Pareto-better but more unequal distribution. The inefficiency could be removed by shifting from the simple difference principle to a staggered difference principle, which recommends the maximization of the position of the least well-off group, and *subject to that constraint*, the maximization of the position of the next least well-off group, and this point also is made by A.K. Sen (*Collective Choice and Social Welfare*, p. 138, note) and is acknowledged by Rawls (p. 83). But such a staggered principle does not embody a presumption in favor of equality of the sort used by Rawls. How then could Rawls justify an inequality *special* to the staggered principle to someone in the least well-off group? Perhaps these issues underlie the unclarity (see p. 83) as to whether Rawls accepts the staggered principle.

75 "But isn't justice to be tempered with compassion?" Not by the guns of the state. When private persons choose to transfer resources to help others, this fits within the entitlement conception of justice.

15

The Procedural Republic and the Unencumbered Self

Michael J. Sandel

Political philosophy seems often to reside at a distance from the world. Principles are one thing, politics another, and even our best efforts to "live up" to our ideals typically founder on the gap between theory and practice.[1]

But if political philosophy is unrealizable in one sense, it is unavoidable in another. This is the sense in which philosophy inhabits the world from the start; our practices and institutions are embodiments of theory. To engage in a political practice is already to stand in relation to theory.[2] For all our uncertainties about ultimate questions of political philosophy – of justice and value and the nature of the good life – the one thing we know is that we live *some* answer all the time.

In this essay I will try to explore the answer we live now, in contemporary America. What is the political philosophy implicit in our practices and institutions? How does it stand, as philosophy? And how do tensions in the philosophy find expression in our present political condition?

It may be objected that it is a mistake to look for a single philosophy, that we live no "answer," only answers. But a plurality of answers is itself a kind of answer. And the political theory that affirms this plurality is the theory I propose to explore.

The Right and the Good

We might begin by considering a certain moral and political vision. It is a liberal vision, and like

most liberal visions gives pride of place to justice, fairness, and individual rights. Its core thesis is this: a just society seeks not to promote any particular ends, but enables its citizens to pursue their own ends, consistent with a similar liberty for all; it therefore must govern by principles that do not presuppose any particular conception of the good. What justifies these regulative principles above all is not that they maximize the general welfare, or cultivate virtue, or otherwise promote the good, but rather that they conform to the concept of *right*, a moral category given prior to the good, and independent of it.

This liberalism says, in other words, that what makes the just society just is not the *telos* or purpose or end at which it aims, but precisely its refusal to choose in advance among competing purposes and ends. In its constitution and its laws, the just society seeks to provide a framework within which its citizens can pursue their own values and ends, consistent with a similar liberty for others.

The ideal I've described might be summed up in the claim that the right is prior to the good, and in two senses: The priority of the right means first, that individual rights cannot be sacrificed for the sake of the general good (in this it opposes utilitarianism), and second, that the principles of justice that specify these rights cannot be premised on any particular vision of the good life. (In this it opposes teleological conceptions in general.)

This is the liberalism of much contemporary moral and political philosophy, most fully elaborated by Rawls, and indebted to Kant for its philosophical foundations.[3] But I am concerned here less with the lineage of this vision than with what seem to me three striking facts about it.

First, it has a deep and powerful philosophical appeal. Second, despite its philosophical force, the claim for the priority of the right over the good ultimately fails. And third, despite its philosophical failure, this liberal vision is the one by which we live. For us in late twentieth century America, it is our vision, the theory most thoroughly embodied in the practices and institutions most central to our public life. And seeing how it goes wrong as philosophy may help us to diagnose our present political condition. So first, its philosophical power; second, its philosophical failure; and third, however briefly, its uneasy embodiment in the world.

But before taking up these three claims, it is worth pointing out a central theme that connects them. And that is a certain conception of the person, of what it is to be a moral agent. Like all political theories, the liberal theory I have described is something more than a set of regulative principles. It is also a view about the way the world is, and the way we move within it. At the heart of this ethic lies a vision of the person that both inspires and undoes it. As I will try to argue now, what make this ethic so compelling, but also, finally, vulnerable, are the promise and the failure of the unencumbered self.

Kantian Foundations

The liberal ethic asserts the priority of right, and seeks principles of justice that do not presuppose any particular conception of the good.[4] This is what Kant means by the supremacy of the moral law, and what Rawls means when he writes that "justice is the first virtue of social institutions."[5] Justice is more than just another value. It provides the framework that *regulates* the play of competing values and ends; it must therefore have a sanction independent of those ends. But it is not obvious where such a sanction could be found.

Theories of justice, and for that matter, ethics, have typically founded their claims on one or another conception of human purposes and ends. Thus Aristotle said the measure of a *polis* is the good at which it aims, and even J.S. Mill, who in the nineteenth century called "justice the chief part, and incomparably the most binding part of all morality," made justice an instrument of utilitarian ends.[6]

This is the solution Kant's ethic rejects. Different persons typically have different desires and ends, and so any principle derived from them can only be contingent. But the moral law needs a *categorical* foundation, not a contingent one. Even so universal a desire as happiness will not do. People still differ in what happiness consists of, and to install any particular conception as regulative would impose on some the conceptions of others, and so deny at least to some the freedom to choose their *own* conceptions. In any case, to govern ourselves in conformity with desires and inclinations, given as they are by nature or circumstance, is not really to be *self*-governing at all. It is rather a refusal of freedom, a capitulation to determinations given outside us.

According to Kant, the right is "derived entirely from the concept of freedom in the external relationships of human beings, and has nothing to do with the end which all men have by nature [i.e., the aim of achieving happiness] or with the recognized means of attaining this end."[7] As such, it must have a basis prior to all empirical ends. Only when I am governed by principles that do not presuppose any particular ends am I free to pursue my own ends consistent with a similar freedom for all.

But this still leaves the question of what the basis of the right could possibly be. If it must be a basis prior to all purposes and ends, unconditioned even by what Kant calls "the special circumstances of human nature,"[8] where could such a basis conceivably be found? Given the stringent demands of the Kantian ethic, the moral law would seem almost to require a foundation in nothing, for any empirical precondition would undermine its priority. "Duty!" asks Kant at his most lyrical, "What origin is there worthy of thee, and where is to be found the root of thy noble descent which proudly rejects all kinship with the inclinations?"[9]

His answer is that the basis of the moral law is to be found in the *subject*, not the object of practical reason, a subject capable of an autonomous will. No empirical end, but rather "a subject of ends, namely a rational being himself, must be made the ground for all maxims of action."[10] Nothing other than what Kant calls "the subject of all possible ends himself" can give rise to the right, for only this subject is also the subject of an autonomous will. Only this subject could be that "something which elevates man above himself as part of the world of sense" and enables him to participate in an ideal, unconditioned realm wholly independent of our social and psychological inclinations. And only this thoroughgoing independence can afford us the detachment we need if we are ever freely to choose for ourselves, unconditioned by the vagaries of circumstance.[11]

Who or what exactly *is* this subject? It is, in a certain sense, *us*. The moral law, after all, is a law we give *ourselves*; we don't *find* it, we *will* it. That is how it (and we) escape the reign of nature and circumstance and merely empirical ends. But what is important to see is that the "we" who do the willing are not "we" qua particular persons, you and me, each for ourselves – the moral law is not up to us as individuals – but "we" qua participants in what Kant calls "pure practical reason," "we" qua participants in a transcendental subject.

Now what is to guarantee that I *am* a subject of this kind, capable of exercising pure practical reason? Well, strictly speaking, there *is* no guarantee, the transcendental subject is only a possibility. But it is a possibility I must *presuppose* if I am to think of myself as a free moral agent. Were I wholly an empirical being, I would not be capable of freedom, for every exercise of will would be conditioned by the desire for some object. All choice would be heteronomous choice, governed by the pursuit of some end. My will could never be a first cause, only the effect of some prior cause, the instrument of one or another impulse or inclination. "When we think of ourselves as free," writes Kant, "we transfer ourselves into the intelligible world as members and recognize the autonomy of the will."[12] And so the notion of a subject prior to and independent of experience, such as the Kantian ethic requires, appears not only possible but indispensable, a necessary presupposition of the possibility of freedom.

How does all of this come back to politics? As the subject is prior to its ends, so the right is prior to the good. Society is best arranged when it is governed by principles that do not presuppose any particular conception of the good, for any other arrangement would fail to respect persons as being capable of choice; it would treat them as objects rather than subjects, as means rather than ends in themselves.

We can see in this way how Kant's notion of the subject is bound up with the claim for the priority of right. But for those in the Anglo-American tradition, the transcendental subject will seem a strange foundation for a familiar ethic. Surely, one may think, we can take rights seriously and affirm the primacy of justice without embracing the *Critique of Pure Reason*. This, in any case, is the project of Rawls.

He wants to save the priority of right from the obscurity of the transcendental subject. Kant's idealist metaphysic, for all its moral and political advantage, cedes too much to the transcendent, and wins for justice its primacy only by denying it its human situation. "To develop a viable Kantian conception of justice," Rawls writes, "the force and content of Kant's doctrine must be detached from its background in transcendental idealism" and recast within the "canons of a reasonable empiricism."[13] And so Rawls' project is to preserve Kant's moral and political teaching by replacing Germanic obscurities with a domesticated metaphysic more congenial to the Anglo-American temper. This is the role of the original position.

From Transcendental Subject to Unencumbered Self

The original position tries to provide what Kant's transcendental argument cannot – a foundation for the right that is prior to the good, but still situated in the world. Sparing all but essentials, the original position works like this: It invites us to imagine the principles we would choose to govern our society if we were to choose them in advance, before we knew the particular persons we would be – whether rich or poor, strong or weak, lucky or unlucky – before we knew even our interests or aims or conceptions of the good. These principles – the ones we would choose in that imaginary situation – are the principles of justice. What is more, if it works, they are principles that do not presuppose any particular ends.

What they *do* presuppose is a certain picture of the person, of the way we must be if we are beings for whom justice is the first virtue. This is the picture of the unencumbered self, a self understood as prior to and independent of purposes and ends.

Now the unencumbered self describes first of all the way we stand toward the things we have, or want, or seek. It means there is always a distinction between the values I *have* and the person I *am*. To identify any characteristics as *my* aims, ambitions, desires, and so on, is always to imply some subject "me" standing behind them, at a certain distance, and the shape of this "me" must be given prior to any of the aims or attributes I bear. One consequence of this distance is to put the self *itself* beyond the reach of its experience, to secure its identity once and for all. Or to put the point another way, it rules out the possibility of what we might call *constitutive* ends. No role or commitment could define me so completely that I could not understand myself without it. No project could be so essential that turning away from it would call into question the person I am.

For the unencumbered self, what matters above all, what is most essential to our personhood, are not the ends we choose but our capacity to choose them. The original position sums up this central claim about us. "It is not our aims that primarily reveal our nature," writes Rawls, "but rather the principles that we would acknowledge to govern the background conditions under which these aims are to be formed . . . We should therefore reverse the relation between the right and the good proposed by teleological doctrines and view the right as prior."[14]

Only if the self is prior to its ends can the right be prior to the good. Only if my identity is never tied to the aims and interests I may have at any moment can I think of myself as a free and independent agent, capable of choice.

This notion of independence carries consequences for the kind of community of which we are capable. Understood as unencumbered selves, we are of course free to join in voluntary association with others, and so are capable of community in the cooperative sense. What is denied to the unencumbered self is the possibility of membership in any community bound by moral ties antecedent to choice; he cannot belong to any community where the self *itself* could be at stake. Such a community – call it constitutive as against merely cooperative – would engage the identity as well as the interests of the participants, and so implicate its members in a citizenship more thoroughgoing than the unencumbered self can know.

For justice to be primary, then, we must be creatures of a certain kind, related to human circumstance in a certain way. We must stand to our circumstance always at a certain distance, whether as transcendental subject in the case of Kant, or as unencumbered selves in the case of Rawls. Only in this way can we view ourselves as subjects as well as objects of experience, as agents and not just instruments of the purposes we pursue.

The unencumbered self and the ethic it inspires, taken together, hold out a liberating vision. Freed from the dictates of nature and the sanction of social roles, the human subject is installed as sovereign, cast as the author of the only moral meanings there are. As participants in pure practical reason, or as parties to the original position, we are free to construct principles of justice unconstrained by an order of value antecedently given. And as actual, individual selves, we are free to choose our purposes and ends unbound by such an order, or by custom or tradition or inherited status. So long as they are not unjust, our conceptions of the good carry weight, whatever they are, simply in virtue of our having chosen them. We are, in Rawls' words, "self-originating sources of valid claims."[15]

This is an exhilarating promise, and the liberalism it animates is perhaps the fullest expression of the Enlightenment's quest for the self-defining subject. But is it true? Can we make sense of our moral and political life by the light of the self-image it requires? I do not think we can, and I will try to show why not by arguing first within the liberal project, then beyond it.

Justice and Community

We have focused so far on the foundations of the liberal vision, on the way it derives the principles it defends. Let us turn briefly now to the substance of those principles, using Rawls as our example. Sparing all but essentials once again, Rawls' two principles of justice are these: first, equal basic liberties for all, and second, only those social and economic inequalities that benefit the least-advantaged members of society (the difference principle).

In arguing for these principles, Rawls argues against two familiar alternatives – utilitarianism and libertarianism. He argues against utilitarianism that it fails to take seriously the distinction between persons. In seeking to maximize the general welfare, the utilitarian treats society as a whole as if it were a single person; it conflates our many, diverse desires into a single system of desires, and tries to maximize. It is indifferent to the distribution of satisfactions among persons, except insofar as this may affect the overall sum. But this fails to respect our plurality and distinctness. It uses some as means to the happiness of all, and so fails to respect each as an end in himself. While utilitarians may sometimes defend individual rights, their defense must rest on the calculation that respecting those rights will serve utility in the long run. But this calculation is contingent and uncertain. So long as utility is what Mill said it is, "the ultimate appeal on all ethical questions,"[16] individual rights can never be secure. To avoid the danger that their life prospects might one day be sacrificed for the greater good of others, the parties to the original position therefore insist on certain basic liberties for all, and make those liberties prior.

If utilitarians fail to take seriously the distinctness of persons, libertarians go wrong by failing to acknowledge the arbitrariness of fortune. They define as just whatever distribution results from an efficient market economy, and oppose all redistribution on the grounds that people are entitled to whatever they get, so long as they do not cheat or steal or otherwise violate someone's rights in getting it. Rawls opposes this principle on the ground that the distribution of talents and assets and even efforts by which some get more and others get less is arbitrary from a moral point of view, a matter of good luck. To distribute the good things in life on the basis of these differences is not to do justice, but simply to carry over into human arrangements the arbitrariness of social and natural contingency. We deserve, as individuals, neither the talents our good fortune may have brought, nor the benefits that flow from them. We should therefore regard these talents as common assets, and regard one another as common beneficiaries of the rewards they bring. "Those who have been favored by nature, whoever they are, may gain from their good fortune only on terms that improve the situation of those who have lost out . . . In justice as fairness, men agree to share one another's fate."[17]

This is the reasoning that leads to the difference principle. Notice how it reveals, in yet another guise, the logic of the unencumbered self. I cannot be said to deserve the benefits that flow from, say, my fine physique and good looks, because they are only accidental, not essential facts about me. They describe attributes I *have*, not the person I *am*, and so cannot give rise to a claim of desert. Being an unencumbered self, this is true of *everything* about me. And so I cannot, as an individual, deserve anything at all.

However jarring to our ordinary understandings this argument may be, the picture so far remains intact; the priority of right, the denial of desert, and the unencumbered self all hang

impressively together.

But the difference principle requires more, and it is here that the argument comes undone. The difference principle begins with the thought, congenial to the unencumbered self, that the assets I have are only accidentally mine. But it ends by assuming that these assets are therefore *common* assets and that society has a prior claim on the fruits of their exercise. But this assumption is without warrant. Simply because I, as an individual, do not have a privileged claim on the assets accidentally residing "here," it does not follow that everyone in the world collectively does. For there is no reason to think that their location in society's province or, for that matter, within the province of humankind, is any *less* arbitrary from a moral point of view. And if their arbitrariness within *me* makes them ineligible to serve *my* ends, there seems no obvious reason why their arbitrariness within any particular society should not make them ineligible to serve that society's ends as well.

To put the point another way, the difference principle, like utilitarianism, is a principle of sharing. As such, it must presuppose some prior moral tie among those whose assets it would deploy and whose efforts it would enlist in a common endeavor. Otherwise, it is simply a formula for using some as means to others' ends, a formula this liberalism is committed to reject.

But on the cooperative vision of community alone, it is unclear what the moral basis for this sharing could be. Short of the constitutive conception, deploying an individual's assets for the sake of the common good would seem an offense against the "plurality and distinctness" of individuals this liberalism seeks above all to secure.

If those whose fate I am required to share really are, morally speaking, *others*, rather than fellow participants in a way of life with which my identity is bound, the difference principle falls prey to the same objections as utilitarianism. Its claim on me is not the claim of a constitutive community whose attachments I acknowledge, but rather the claim of a concatenated collectivity whose entanglements I confront.

What the difference principle requires, but cannot provide, is some way of identifying those *among* whom the assets I bear are properly regarded as common, some way of seeing ourselves as mutually indebted and morally engaged to begin with. But as we have seen, the constitutive aims and attachments that would save and situate the difference principle are precisely the ones denied to the liberal self; the moral encumbrances and antecedent obligations they imply would undercut the priority of right.

What, then, of those encumbrances? The point so far is that we cannot be persons for whom justice is primary, and also be persons for whom the difference principle is a principle of justice. But which must give way? Can we view ourselves as independent selves, independent in the sense that our identity is never tied to our aims and attachments?

I do not think we can, at least not without cost to those loyalties and convictions whose moral force consists partly in the fact that living by them is inseparable from understanding ourselves as the particular persons we are – as members of this family or community or nation or people, as bearers of that history, as citizens of this republic. Allegiances such as these are more than values I happen to have, and to hold, at a certain distance. They go beyond the obligations I voluntarily incur and the "natural duties" I owe to human beings as such. They allow that to some I owe more than justice requires or even permits, not by reason of agreements I have made but instead in virtue of those more or less enduring attachments and commitments that, taken together, partly define the person I am.

To imagine a person incapable of constitutive attachments such as these is not to conceive an ideally free and rational agent, but to imagine a person wholly without character, without moral depth. For to have character is to know that I move in a history I neither summon nor command, which carries consequences nonetheless for my choices and conduct. It draws me closer to some and more distant from others; it makes some aims more appropriate, others less so. As a self-interpreting being, I am able to reflect on my history and in this sense to distance myself from it, but the distance is always precarious and provisional, the point of reflection never finally secured outside the history itself. But the liberal ethic puts the self beyond the reach of its experience, beyond deliberation and reflection. Denied the expansive self-understandings that could shape a common life, the liberal self is left to lurch between detachment on the one hand, and entanglement on the other. Such is the fate of the unencumbered self, and its liberating promise.

The Procedural Republic

But before my case can be complete, I need to consider one powerful reply. While it comes from a liberal direction, its spirit is more practical than philosophical. It says, in short, that I am asking too much. It is one thing to seek constitutive attachments in our private lives; among families and friends, and certain tightly knit groups, there may be found a common good that makes justice and rights less pressing. But with public life – at least today, and probably always – it is different. So long as the nation-state is the primary form of political association, talk of constitutive community too easily suggests a darker politics rather than a brighter one; amid echoes of the moral majority, the priority of right, for all its philosophical faults, still seems the safer hope.

This is a challenging rejoinder, and no account of political community in the twentieth century can fail to take it seriously. It is challenging not least because it calls into question the status of political philosophy and its relation to the world. For if my argument is correct, if the liberal vision we have considered is not morally self-sufficient but parasitic on a notion of community it officially rejects, then we should expect to find that the political practice that embodies this vision is not *practically* self-sufficient either – that it must draw on a sense of community it cannot supply and may even undermine. But is that so far from the circumstance we face today? Could it be that through the original position darkly, on the far side of the veil of ignorance, we may glimpse an intimation of our predicament, a refracted vision of ourselves?

How does the liberal vision – and its failure – help us make sense of our public life and its predicament? Consider, to begin, the following paradox in the citizen's relation to the modern welfare state. In many ways, we in the 1980s stand near the completion of a liberal project that has run its course from the New Deal through the Great Society and into the present. But notwithstanding the extension of the franchise and the expansion of individual rights and entitlements in recent decades, there is a widespread sense that, individually and collectively, our control over the forces that govern our lives is receding rather than increasing. This sense is deepened by what appear simultaneously as the power and the powerlessness of the nation-state. On the one hand, increasing numbers of citizens view the state as an overly intrusive presence, more likely to frustrate their purposes than advance them. And yet, despite its unprecedented role in the economy and society, the modern state seems itself disempowered, unable effectively to control the domestic economy, to respond to persisting social ills, or to work America's will in the world.

This is a paradox that has fed the appeals of recent politicians (including Carter and Reagan), even as it has frustrated their attempts to govern. To sort it out, we need to identify the public philosophy implicit in our political practice, and to reconstruct its arrival. We need to trace the advent of the procedural republic, by which I mean a public life animated by the liberal vision and self-image we've considered.

The story of the procedural republic goes back in some ways to the founding of the republic, but its central drama begins to unfold around the turn of the century. As national markets and large-scale enterprise displaced a decentralized economy, the decentralized political forms of the early republic became outmoded as well. If democracy was to survive, the concentration of economic power would have to be met by a similar concentration of political power. But the Progressives understood, or some of them did, that the success of democracy required more than the centralization of government; it also required the nationalization of politics. The primary form of political community had to be a recast on a national scale. For Herbert Croly, writing in 1909, the "nationalizing of American political, economic, and social life" was "an essentially formative and enlightening political transformation." We would become more of a democracy only as we became "more of a nation . . . in ideas, in institutions, and in spirit."[18]

This nationalizing project would be consummated in the New Deal, but for the democratic tradition in America, the embrace of the nation was a decisive departure. From Jefferson to the populists, the party of democracy in American political debate had been, roughly speaking, the party of the provinces, of decentralized power, of small-town and small-scale America. And against them had stood the party of the nation – first Federalists, then Whigs, then the Republicans of Lincoln – a party that spoke for the consolidation of the union. It was thus the historic achievement of the New Deal to unite, in a single party and political program, what Samuel Beer has called "liberalism and the national idea."[19]

What matters for our purpose is that, in the twentieth century, liberalism made its peace with concentrated power. But it was understood at the start that the terms of this peace required a strong sense of national community, morally and politically to underwrite the extended involvements of a modern industrial order. If a virtuous republic of small-scale, democratic communities was no longer a possibility, a national republic seemed democracy's next best hope. This was still, in principle at least, a politics of the common good. It looked to the nation, not as a neutral framework for the play of competing interests, but rather as a formative community, concerned to shape a common life suited to the scale of modern social and economic forms.

But this project failed. By the mid- or late twentieth century, the national republic had run its course. Except for extraordinary moments, such as war, the nation proved too vast a scale across which to cultivate the shared self-understandings necessary to community in the formative, or constitutive sense. And so the gradual shift, in our practices and institutions, from a public philosophy of common purposes to one of fair procedures, from a politics of good to a politics of right, from the national republic to the procedural republic.

Our Present Predicament

A full account of this transition would take a detailed look at the changing shape of political institutions, constitutional interpretation, and the terms of political discourse in the broadest sense. But I suspect we would find in the *practice* of the procedural republic two broad tendencies foreshadowed by its philosophy: first, a tendency to crowd out democratic possibilities; second, a tendency to undercut the kind of community on which it nonetheless depends.

Where liberty in the early republic was understood as a function of democratic institutions and dispersed power,[20] liberty in the procedural republic is defined in opposition to democracy, as an individual's guarantee against what the majority might will. I am free insofar as I am the bearer of rights, where rights are trumps.[21] Unlike the liberty of the early republic, the modern version permits – in fact even requires – concentrated power. This has to do with the universalizing logic of rights. Insofar as I have a right, whether to free speech or a minimum income, its provision cannot be left to the vagaries of local preferences but must be assured at the most comprehensive level of political association. It cannot be one thing in New York and another in Alabama. As rights and entitlements expand, politics is therefore displaced from smaller forms of association and relocated at the most universal form – in our case, the nation. And even as politics flows to the nation, power shifts away from democratic institutions (such as legislatures and political parties) and toward institutions designed to be insulated from democratic pressures, and hence better equipped to dispense and defend individual rights (notably the judiciary and bureaucracy).

These institutional developments may begin to account for the sense of powerlessness that the welfare state fails to address and in some ways doubtless deepens. But it seems to me a further clue to our condition that recalls even more directly the predicament of the unencumbered self – lurching, as we left it, between detachment on the one hand, the entanglement on the other. For it is a striking feature of the welfare state that it offers a powerful promise of individual rights, and also demands of its citizens a high measure of mutual engagement. But the self-image that attends the rights cannot sustain the engagement.

As bearers of rights, where rights are trumps, we think of ourselves as freely choosing, individual selves, unbound by obligations antecedent to rights, or to the agreements we make. And yet, as citizens of the procedural republic that secures these rights, we find ourselves implicated willy-nilly in a formidable array of dependencies and expectations we did not choose and increasingly reject.

In our public life, we are more entangled, but less attached, than ever before. It is as though the unencumbered self presupposed by the liberal ethic had begun to come true – less liberated than disempowered, entangled in a network of obligations and involvements unassociated with any act of will, and yet unmediated by those common identifications or expansive self-definitions that would make them tolerable. As the scale of social and political organization has become more comprehensive, the terms of our collective identity have become more fragmented, and the forms of political life have outrun the common purpose needed to sustain them.

Something like this, it seems to me, has been unfolding in America for the past half-century or so. I hope I have said at least enough to suggest the shape a fuller story might take. And I hope in any case to have conveyed a certain view about politics and philosophy and the relation between them – that our practices and institutions are themselves embodiments of theory, and to unravel their predicament is, at least in part, to seek after the self-image of the age.

Notes

Author's Note: An earlier version of this article was presented to the Political Philosophy Colloquium at Princeton University, and to the Legal Theory Workshop at Columbia Law School. I am grateful to the participants, and also to the Editor, William Connolly, for helpful comments and criticisms. I would also like to thank the Ford Foundation for support of a larger project of which this essay is a first installment.

1   An excellent example of this view can be found in Samuel Huntington, *American Politics: The Promise of Disharmony* (Cambridge: Harvard University Press, 1981). See especially his discussion of the "ideals versus institutions" gap, pp. 10–12, 39–41, 61–84, 221–262.

2   See, for example, the conceptions of a "practice" advanced by Alasdair MacIntyre and Charles Taylor. MacIntyre, *After Virtue* (Notre Dame: University of Notre Dame Press, 1981), pp. 175–209. Taylor, "Interpretation and the Sciences of Man," *Review of Metaphysics* 25, (1971) pp. 3–51.

3   John Rawls, *A Theory of Justice* (Oxford: Oxford University Press, 1972). Immanuel Kant, *Groundwork of the Metaphysics of Morals*, trans. H. J. Paton. (1785; New York: Harper and Row, 1956). Kant, *Critique of Pure Reason*, trans. Norman Kemp Smith (1781, 1787; London: Macmillan, 1929). Kant, *Critique of Practical Reason*, trans. L. W. Beck (1788; Indianapolis: Bobbs-Merrill, 1956). Kant, "On the Common Saying: 'This May Be True in Theory, But It Does Not Apply in Practice,'" in Hans Reiss, ed., *Kant's Political Writings* (1793; Cambridge: Cambridge University Press, 1970). Other recent versions of the claim for the priority of the right over good can be found in Robert Nozick, *Anarchy, State and Utopia* (New York: Basic Books, 1974); Ronald Dworkin, *Taking Rights Seriously* (London: Duckworth, 1977); Bruce

Ackerman, *Social Justice in the Liberal State* (New Haven: Yale University Press, 1980).

4   This section, and the two that follow, summarize arguments developed more fully in Michael Sandel, *Liberalism and the Limits of Justice* (Cambridge: Cambridge University Press, 1982).

5   Rawls (1971), p. 3.

6   John Stuart Mill, *Utilitarianism*, in *The Utilitarians* (1893; Garden City: Doubleday, 1973), p. 465. Mill, *On Liberty*, in *The Utilitarians*, p. 485 (Originally published 1849).

7   Kant (1793), p. 73.

8   Kant (1785), p. 92.

9   Kant (1788), p. 89.

10 Kant (1785), p. 105.

11 Kant (1788), p. 89.

12 Kant (1785), p. 121.

13 Rawls, "The Basic Structure as Subject," *American Philosophical Quarterly* (1977), p. 165.

14 Rawls (1971), p. 560.

15 Rawls, "Kantian Constructivism in Moral Theory," *Journal of Philosophy* 77 (1980), p. 543.

16 Mill (1849), p. 485.

17 Rawls (1971), pp. 101–102.

18 Croly, *The Promise of American Life* (Indianapolis: Bobbs-Merrill, 1965), pp. 270–273.

19 Beer, "Liberalism and the National Idea," *The Public Interest*, Fall (1966), pp. 70–82.

20 See, for example, Laurence Tribe, *American Constitutional Law* (Mineola: The Foundation Press, 1978), pp. 2–3.

21 See Ronald Dworkin, "Liberalism," in Stuart Hampshire, ed., *Public and Private Morality* (Cambridge: Cambridge University Press, 1978), p. 136.

16

Polity and Group Difference: A Critique of the Ideal of Universal Citizenship

Iris Marion Young

An ideal of universal citizenship has driven the emancipatory momentum of modern political life. Ever since the bourgeoisie challenged aristocratic privileges by claiming equal political rights for citizens as such, women, workers, Jews, blacks, and others have pressed for inclusion in that citizenship status. Modern political theory asserted the equal moral worth of all persons, and social movements of the oppressed took this seriously as implying the inclusion of all persons in full citizenship status under the equal protection of the law.

Citizenship for everyone, and everyone the same qua citizen. Modern political thought generally assumed that the universality of citizenship in the sense of citizenship for all implies a universality of citizenship in the sense that citizenship status transcends particularity and difference. Whatever the social or group differences among citizens, whatever their inequalities of wealth, status, and power in the everyday activities of civil society, citizenship gives everyone the same status as peers in the political public. With equality conceived as sameness, the ideal of universal citizenship carries at least two meanings in addition to the extension of citizenship to everyone: (*a*) universality defined as general in opposition to particular; what citizens have in common as opposed to how they differ, and (*b*) universality in the sense of laws and rules that say the same

for all and apply to all in the same way; laws and rules that are blind to individual and group differences.

During this angry, sometimes bloody, political struggle in the nineteenth and twentieth centuries, many among the excluded and disadvantaged thought that winning full citizenship status, that is, equal political and civil rights, would lead to their freedom and equality. Now in the late twentieth century, however, when citizenship rights have been formally extended to all groups in liberal capitalist societies, some groups still find themselves treated as second-class citizens. Social movements of oppressed and excluded groups have recently asked why extension of equal citizenship rights has not led to social justice and equality. Part of the answer is straightforwardly Marxist: those social activities that most determine the status of individuals and groups are anarchic and oligarchic; economic life is not sufficiently under the control of citizens to affect the unequal status and treatment of groups. I think this is an important and correct diagnosis of why equal citizenship has not eliminated oppression, but in this article I reflect on another reason more intrinsic to the meaning of politics and citizenship as expressed in much modern thought.

The assumed link between citizenship for everyone, on the one hand, and the two other senses of citizenship – having a common life with and being treated in the same way as the other citizens – on the other, is itself a problem. Contemporary social movements of the oppressed

Originally published in *Ethics*, 99 (1989), 250–74. Copyright © by the University of Chicago. Reprinted by permission of the University of Chicago Press.

have weakened the link. They assert a positivity and pride in group specificity against ideals of assimilation. They have also questioned whether justice always means that law and policy should enforce equal treatment for all groups. Embryonic in these challenges lies a concept of *differentiated* citizenship as the best way to realize the inclusion and participation of everyone in full citizenship.

In this article I argue that far from implying one another, the universality of citizenship, in the sense of the inclusion and participation of everyone, stands in tension with the other two meanings of universality embedded in modern political ideas: universality as generality, and universality as equal treatment. First, the ideal that the activities of citizenship express or create a general will that transcends the particular differences of group affiliation, situation, and interest has in practice excluded groups judged not capable of adopting that general point of view; the idea of citizenship as expressing a general will has tended to enforce a homogeneity of citizens. To the degree that contemporary proponents of revitalized citizenship retain that idea of a general will and common life, they implicitly support the same exclusions and homogeneity. Thus I argue that the inclusion and participation of everyone in public discussion and decision making requires mechanisms for group representation. Second, where differences in capacities, culture, values, and behavioral styles exist among groups, but some of these groups are privileged, strict adherence to a principle of equal treatment tends to perpetuate oppression or disadvantage. The inclusion and participation of everyone in social and political institutions therefore sometimes requires the articulation of special rights that attend to group differences in order to undermine oppression and disadvantage.

1 Citizenship as Generality

Many contemporary political theorists regard capitalist welfare society as depoliticized. Its interest group pluralism privatizes policy-making, consigning it to back-room deals and autonomous regulatory agencies and groups. Interest group pluralism fragments both policy and the interests of the individual, making it difficult to assess issues in relation to one another and set priorities. The fragmented and privatized nature of the political process, moreover, facilitates the dominance of the more powerful interests.[1]

In response to this privatization of the political process, many writers call for a renewed public life and a renewed commitment to the virtues of citizenship. Democracy requires that citizens of welfare corporate society awake from their privatized consumerist slumbers, challenge the experts who claim the sole right to rule, and collectively take control of their lives and institutions through processes of active discussion that aim at reaching collective decisions.[2] In participatory democratic institutions citizens develop and exercise capacities of reasoning, discussion, and socializing that otherwise lie dormant, and they move out of their private existence to address others and face them with respect and concern for justice. Many who invoke the virtues of citizenship in opposition to the privatization of politics in welfare capitalist society assume as models for contemporary public life the civic humanism of thinkers such as Machiavelli or, more often, Rousseau.[3]

With these social critics I agree that interest group pluralism, because it is privatized and fragmented, facilitates the domination of corporate, military, and other powerful interests. With them I think democratic processes require the institutionalization of genuinely public discussion. There are serious problems, however, with uncritically assuming as a model the ideals of the civic public that come to us from the tradition of modern political thought.[4] The ideal of the public realm of citizenship as expressing a general will, a point of view and interest that citizens have in common which transcends their differences, has operated in fact as a demand for homogeneity among citizens. The exclusion of groups defined as different was explicitly acknowledged before this century. In our time, the excluding consequences of the universalist ideal of a public that embodies a common will are more subtle, but they still obtain.

The tradition of civic republicanism stands in critical tension with the individualist contract theory of Hobbes or Locke. Where liberal individualism regards the state as a necessary instrument to mediate conflict and regulate action so that individuals can have the freedom to pursue their private ends, the republican tradition locates freedom and autonomy in the actual public activities of citizenship. By participating in public discussion and collective decision making, citizens transcend their particular self-interested lives and the pursuit of private interests to adopt a general point of view from which they agree on the common good. Citizenship is an expression of the universality of human life; it is a realm of rationality and freedom as opposed to the heteronomous realm of particular need, interest, and desire.

Nothing in this understanding of citizenship as universal as opposed to particular, common as opposed to differentiated, implies extending full citizenship status to all groups. Indeed, at least some modern republicans thought just the contrary. While they extolled the virtues of citizenship as expressing the universality of humanity, they consciously excluded some people from citizenship on the grounds that they could not adopt the general point of view, or that their inclusion would disperse and divide the public. The ideal of a common good, a general will, a shared public life leads to pressures for a homogeneous citizenry.

Feminists in particular have analyzed how the discourse that links the civic public with fraternity is not merely metaphorical. Founded by men, the modern state and its public realm of citizenship paraded as universal values and norms which were derived from specifically masculine experience: militarist norms of honor and homoerotic camaraderie; respectful competition and bargaining among independent agents; discourse framed in unemotional tones of dispassionate reason.

Several commentators have argued that in extolling the virtues of citizenship as participation in a universal public realm, modern men expressed a flight from sexual difference, from having to recognize another kind of existence that they could not entirely understand, and from the embodiment, dependency on nature, and morality that women represent.[5] Thus the opposition between the universality of the public realm of citizenship and the particularity of private interest became conflated with oppositions between reason and passion, masculine and feminine.

The bourgeois world instituted a moral division of labor between reason and sentiment, identifying masculinity with reason and femininity with sentiment, desire, and the needs of the body. Extolling a public realm of manly virtue and citizenship as independence, generality, and dispassionate reason entailed creating the private sphere of the family as the place to which emotion, senti-

ment, and bodily needs must be confined.[6] The generality of the public thus depends on excluding women, who are responsible for tending to that private realm, and who lack the dispassionate rationality and independence required of good citizens.

In his social scheme, for example, Rousseau excluded women from the public realm of citizenship because they are the caretakers of affectivity, desire, and the body. If we allowed appeals to desires and bodily needs to move public debates, we would undermine public deliberation by fragmenting its unity. Even within the domestic realm, moreover, women must be dominated. Their dangerous, heterogeneous sexuality must be kept chaste and confined to marriage. Enforcing chastity on women will keep each family a separated unity, preventing the chaos and blood mingling that would be produced by illegitimate children. Chaste, enclosed women in turn oversee men's desire by tempering its potentially disruptive impulses through moral education. Men's desire for women itself threatens to shatter and disperse the universal, rational realm of the public, as well as to disrupt the neat distinction between the public and private. As guardians of the private realm of need, desire, and affectivity, women must ensure that men's impulses do not subvert the universality of reason. The moral neatness of the female-tended hearth, moreover, will temper the possessively individualistic impulses of the particularistic realm of business and commerce, since competition, like sexuality, constantly threatens to explode the unity of the polity.[7]

It is important to recall that universality of citizenship conceived as generality operated to exclude not only women, but other groups as well. European and American republicans found little contradiction in promoting a universality of citizenship that excluded some groups, because the idea that citizenship is the same for all translated in practice to the requirement that all citizens be the same. The white male bourgeoisie conceived republican virtue as rational, restrained, and chaste, not yielding to passion or desire for luxury, and thus able to rise above desire and need to a concern for the common good. This implied excluding poor people and wage workers from citizenship on the grounds that they were too motivated by need to adopt a general perspective. The designers of the American constitution were no more egalitarian than their European brethren in this respect; they specifically intended to restrict the access of the laboring class to the public, because they feared disruption of commitment to the general interests.

These early American republicans were also quite explicit about the need for the homogeneity of citizens, fearing that group differences would tend to undermine commitment to the general interest. This meant that the presence of blacks and Indians, and later Mexicans and Chinese, in the territories of the republic posed a threat that only assimilation, extermination, or dehumanization could thwart. Various combinations of these three were used, of course, but recognition of these groups as peers in the public was never an option. Even such republican fathers as Jefferson identified the red and black people in their territories with wild nature and passion, just as they feared that women outside the domestic realm were wanton and avaricious. They defined moral, civilized republican life in opposition to this backward-looking, uncultivated desire that they identified with women and nonwhites.[8] A similar logic of exclusion operated in Europe, where Jews were particular targets.[9]

These republican exclusions were not accidental, nor were they inconsistent with the ideal of universal citizenship as understood by these theorists. They were a direct consequence of a dichotomy between public and private that defined the public as a realm of generality in which all particularities are left behind, and defined the private as the particular, the realm of affectivity, affiliation, need, and the body. As long as that dichotomy is in place, the inclusion of the formerly excluded in the definition of citizenship – women, workers, Jews, blacks, Asians, Indians, Mexicans – imposes a homogeneity that suppresses group differences in the public and in practice forces the formerly excluded groups to be measured according to norms derived from and defined by privileged groups.

Contemporary critics of interest group liberalism who call for a renewed public life certainly do not intend to exclude any adult persons or groups from citizenship. They are democrats, convinced that only the inclusion and participation of all citizens in political life will make for wise and fair decisions and a polity that enhances rather than inhibits the capacities of its citizens and their relations with one another. The emphasis by such participatory democrats on generality and commonness, however, still threatens to suppress differences among citizens.

I shall focus on the text of Benjamin Barber, who, in his book *Strong Democracy*, produces a compelling and concrete vision of participatory democratic processes. Barber recognizes the need to safeguard a democratic public from intended or inadvertent group exclusions, though he offers no proposals for safeguarding the inclusion and participation of everyone. He also argues fiercely against contemporary political theorists who construct a model of political discourse purified of affective dimensions. Thus Barber does not fear the disruption of the generality and rationality of the public by desire and the body in the way that nineteenth-century republican theorists did. He retains, however, a conception of the civic public as defined by generality, as opposed to group affinity and particular need and interest. He makes a clear distinction between the public realm of citizenship and civic activity, on the one hand, and a private realm of particular identities, roles, affiliations, and interests on the other. Citizenship by no means exhausts people's social identities, but it takes moral priority over all social activities in a strong democracy. The pursuit of particular interests, the pressing of the claims of particular groups, all must take place within a framework of community and common vision established by the public realm. Thus Barber's vision of participatory democracy continues to rely on an opposition between the public sphere of a general interest and a private sphere of particular interest and affiliation.[10]

While recognizing the need for majority rule procedures and means of safeguarding minority rights, Barber asserts that "the strong democrat regrets every division and regards the existence of majorities as a sign that mutualism has failed" (p. 207). A community of citizens, he says, "owes the character of its existence to what its constituent members have in common" (p. 232), and this entails transcending the order of individual needs and wants to recognize that "we are a moral body whose existence depends on the common ordering of individual needs and wants into a single vision of the future in which all can share" (p. 224). This common vision is not imposed on individuals from above, however, but is forged by them in talking and working together. Barber's models of such common projects, however, reveal his latent biases: "Like players on a team or soldiers at war, those who practice a common politics may come to feel ties that they never felt before they commenced their common activity. This sort of bonding, which emphasizes common procedures, common work, and a shared sense of what a community needs to succeed, rather than monolithic purposes and ends, serves strong democracy most successfully" (p. 244).

The attempt to realize an ideal of universal citizenship that finds the public embodying generality as opposed to particularity, commonness versus difference, will tend to exclude or to put at a disadvantage some groups, even when they have formally equal citizenship status. The idea of the public as universal and the concomitant identification of particularity with privacy makes homogeneity a requirement of public participation. In exercising their citizenship, all citizens should assume the same impartial, general point of view transcending all particular interests, perspectives, and experiences.

But such an impartial general perspective is a myth.[11] People necessarily and properly consider public issues in terms influenced by their situated experience and perception of social relations. Different social groups have different needs, cultures, histories, experiences, and perceptions of social relations which influence their interpretation of the meaning and consequences of policy proposals and influence the form of their political reasoning. These differences in political interpretation are not merely or even primarily a result of differing or conflicting interests, for groups have differing interpretations even when they seek to promote justice and not merely their own self-regarding ends. In a society where some groups are privileged while others are oppressed, insisting that as citizens persons should leave behind their particular affiliations and experiences to adopt a general point of view serves only to reinforce that privilege; for the perspectives and interests of the privileged will tend to dominate this unified public, marginalizing or silencing those of other groups.

Barber asserts that responsible citizenship requires transcending particular affiliations, commitments, and needs, because a public cannot function if its members are concerned only with their private interests. Here he makes an important confusion between plurality and privatization. The interest group pluralism that he and others criticize indeed institutionalizes and encourages an egoistic, self-regarding view of the political process, one that sees parties entering the political competition for scarce goods and privileges only in order to maximize their own gain, and therefore they need not listen to or respond to the claims of others who have their own point of view. The processes and often the outcomes of interest group bargaining, moreover, take place largely in private; they are neither revealed nor discussed in a forum that genuinely involves all those potentially affected by decisions.

Privacy in this sense of private bargaining for the sake of private gain is quite different from plurality, in the sense of the differing group experiences, affiliations, and commitments that operate in any large society. It is possible for persons to maintain their group identity and to be influenced by their perceptions of social events derived from their group-specific experience, and at the same time to be public spirited, in the sense of being open to listening to the claims of others and not being concerned for their own gain alone. It is possible and necessary for people to take a critical distance from their own immediate desires and gut reactions in order to discuss public proposals. Doing so, however, cannot require that citizens abandon their particular affiliations, experiences, and social location. As I will discuss in the next section, having the voices of particular group perspectives other than one's own explicitly represented in public discussion best fosters the maintenance of such critical distance without the pretense of impartiality.

A repoliticization of public life should not require the creation of a unified public realm in which citizens leave behind their particular group affiliations, histories, and needs to discuss a general interest or common good. Such a desire for unity suppresses but does not eliminate differences and tends to exclude some perspectives from the public.[12] Instead of a universal citizenship in the sense of this generality, we need a group differentiated citizenship and a heterogeneous public. In a heterogeneous public, differences are publicly recognized and acknowledged as irreducible, by which I mean that persons from one perspective or history can never completely understand and adopt the point of view of those with other group-based perspectives and histories. Yet commitment to the need and desire to decide together the society's policies fosters communication across those differences.

2 Differentiated Citizenship as Group Representation

In her study of the functioning of a New England Town Meeting government, Jane Mansbridge discusses how women, blacks, working-class people, and poor people tend to participate less and have their interests represented less than whites, middle-class professionals, and men. Even though all citizens have the right to participate in the decision-making process, the experience and perspectives of some groups tend to be silenced for many reasons. White middle-class men assume authority more than others and they are more practiced at speaking persuasively; mothers and old people often find it more difficult than others to get to meetings.[13] Amy Gutmann also discusses how participatory democratic structures tend to silence disadvantaged groups. She offers the example of community control of schools, where increased democracy led to increased segregation in many cities because the more privileged and articulate whites were able to promote their perceived interests against blacks' just demand for equal treatment in an integrated system.[14] Such cases indicate that when participatory democratic structures define citizenship in universalistic and unified terms, they tend to reproduce existing group oppression.

Gutmann argues that such oppressive consequences of democratization imply that social and economic equality must be achieved before political equality can be instituted. I cannot quarrel with the value of social and economic equality, but I think its achievement depends on increasing political equality as much as the achievement of political equality depends on increasing social and economic equality. If we are not to be forced to trace a utopian circle, we need to solve now the "paradox of democracy" by which social power makes some citizens more equal than others, and equality of citizenship makes some people more powerful citizens. That solution lies at least in part in providing institutionalized means for the explicit recognition and representation of oppressed groups. Before discussing principles and practices involved in such a solution, however, it is necessary to say something about what a group is and when a group is oppressed.

The concept of a social group has become politically important because recent emancipatory and leftist social movements have mobilized around group identity rather than exclusively class or economic interests. In many cases such mobilization has consisted in embracing and positively defining a despised or devalued ethnic or racial identity. In the women's movement, gay rights movement, or elders' movements, differential social status based on age, sexuality, physical capacity, or the division of labor has been taken up as a positive group identity for political mobilization.

I shall not attempt to define a social group here, but I shall point to several marks which distinguish a social group from other collectivities of people. A social group involves first of all an affinity with other persons by which they identify with one another, and by which other people identify them. A person's particular sense of history, understanding of social relations and personal possibilities, her or his mode of reasoning, values, and expressive styles are constituted at least partly by her or his group identity. Many group definitions come from the outside, from other groups that label and stereotype certain people. In such circumstances the despised group members often find their affinity in their oppression. The concept of social group must be distinguished from two concepts with which it might be confused: aggregate and association.

An aggregate is any classification of persons according to some attribute. Persons can be aggregated according to any number of attributes, all of them equally arbitrary – eye color, the make of car we drive, the street we live on. At times the groups that have emotional and social salience in our society are interpreted as aggregates, as arbitrary classifications of persons according to attributes of skin color, genitals, or years lived. A social group, however, is not defined primarily by a set of shared attributes, but by the sense of identity that people have. What defines black Americans as a social group is not primarily their skin color; this is exemplified by the fact that some persons whose skin color is fairly light, for example, identify as black. Though sometimes objective attributes are a necessary condition for classifying oneself or others as a member of a certain social group, it is the identification of certain persons with a social status, a common history that social status produces, and a self-identification that defines the group as a group.

Political and social theorists tend more often to elide social groups with associations rather than aggregates. By an association I mean a collectivity of persons who come together voluntarily – such as a club, corporation, political party, church, college, union, lobbying organization, or interest group. An individualist contract model of society applies to associations but not to groups. Individuals constitute associations; they come together as already formed persons and set them up, establishing rules, positions, and offices.

Since one joins an association, even if membership in it fundamentally affects one's life, one does not take that association membership to define one's very identity in the way, for example, being Navajo might. Group affinity, on the other hand, has the character of what Heidegger calls "thrownness": one finds oneself as a member of a group, whose existence and relations one experiences as always already having been. For a person's identity is defined in relation to how others identify him or her, and others do so in terms of groups which always already have specific attributes, stereotypes, and norms associated with them, in reference to which a person's identity will be formed. From the thrownness of group affinity it does not follow that one cannot leave groups and enter new ones. Many women become lesbian after identifying as heterosexual, and anyone who lives long enough becomes old. These cases illustrate thrownness precisely in that such changes in group affinity are experienced as a transformation in one's identity.

A social group should not be understood as an essence or nature with a specific set of common attributes. Instead, group identity should be understood in relational terms. Social processes generate groups by creating relational differentiations, situations of clustering and affective bonding in which people feel affinity for other people. Sometimes groups define themselves by despising or excluding others whom they define as other, and whom they dominate and oppress. Although social processes of affinity and separation define groups, they do not give groups a substantive identity. There is no common nature that members of a group have.

As products of social relations, groups are fluid; they come into being and may fade away. Homosexual practices have existed in many societies and historical periods, for example, but gay male group identification exists only in the West in the twentieth century. Group identity may become salient only under specific circumstances, when in interaction with other groups. Most people in modern societies have multiple group identifications, moreover, and therefore groups

themselves are not discrete unities. Every group has group differences cutting across it.

I think that group differentiation is an inevitable and desirable process in modern societies. We need not settle that question, however. I merely assume that ours is now a group differentiated society, and that it will continue to be so for some time to come. Our political problem is that some of our groups are privileged and others are oppressed.

But what is oppression? In another place I give a fuller account of the concept of oppression.[15] Briefly, a group is oppressed when one or more of the following conditions occurs to all or a large portion of its members: (1) the benefits of their work or energy go to others without those others reciprocally benefiting them (exploitation); (2) they are excluded from participation in major social activities, which in our society means primarily a workplace (marginalization); (3) they live and work under the authority of others, and have little work autonomy and authority over others themselves (powerlessness); (4) as a group they are stereotyped at the same time that their experience and situation is invisible in the society in general, and they have little opportunity and little audience for the expression of their experience and perspective on social events (cultural imperialism); (5) group members suffer random violence and harassment motivated by group hatred or fear. In the United States today at least the following groups are oppressed in one or more of these ways: women, blacks, Native Americans, Chicanos, Puerto Ricans and other Spanish-speaking Americans, Asian Americans, gay men, lesbians, working-class people, poor people, old people, and mentally and physically disabled people.

Perhaps in some utopian future there will be a society without group oppression and disadvantage. We cannot develop political principles by starting with the assumption of a completely just society, however, but must begin from within the general historical and social conditions in which we exist. This means that we must develop participatory democratic theory not on the assumption of an undifferentiated humanity, but rather on the assumption that there are group differences and that some groups are actually or potentially oppressed or disadvantaged.

I assert, then, the following principle: a democratic public, however that is constituted, should provide mechanisms for the effective representation and recognition of the distinct voices and perspectives of those of its constituent groups that are oppressed or disadvantaged within it. Such group representation implies institutional mechanisms and public resources supporting three activities: (1) self-organization of group members so that they gain a sense of collective empowerment and a reflective understanding of their collective experience and interests in the context of the society; (2) voicing a group's analysis of how social policy proposals affect them, and generating policy proposals themselves, in institutionalized contexts where decision makers are obliged to show that they have taken these perspectives into consideration; (3) having veto power regarding specific policies that affect a group directly, for example, reproductive rights for women, or use of reservation lands for Native Americans.

The principles call for specific representation only for oppressed or disadvantaged groups, because privileged groups already are represented. Thus the principle would not apply in a society entirely without oppression. I do not regard the principle as merely provisional, or instrumental, however, because I believe that group difference in modern complex societies is both inevitable and desirable, and that wherever there is group difference, disadvantage or oppression always looms as a possibility. Thus a society should always be committed to representation for oppressed or disadvantaged groups and ready to implement such representation when it appears. These considerations are rather academic in our own context, however, since we live in a society with deep group oppressions the complete elimination of which is only a remote possibility.

Social and economic privilege means, among other things, that the groups which have it behave as though they have a right to speak and be heard, that others treat them as though they have that right, and that they have the material, personal, and organizational resources that enable them to speak and be heard in public. The privileged are usually not inclined to protect and further the interests of the oppressed partly because their social position prevents them from understanding those interests, and partly because to some degree their privilege depends on the continued oppression of others. So a major reason for explicit representation of oppressed groups in discussion and decision making is to undermine oppression. Such group representation also

exposes in public the specificity of the assumptions and experience of the privileged. For unless confronted with different perspectives on social relations and events, different values and language, most people tend to assert their own perspective as universal.

Theorists and politicians extol the virtues of citizenship because through public participation persons are called on to transcend merely self-centered motivation and acknowledge their dependence on and responsibility to others. The responsible citizen is concerned not merely with interests but with justice, with acknowledging that each other person's interest and point of view is as good as his or her own, and that the needs and interests of everyone must be voiced and be heard by the others, who must acknowledge, respect, and address those needs and interests. The problem of universality has occurred when this responsibility has been interpreted as transcendence into a general perspective.

I have argued that defining citizenship as generality avoids and obscures this requirement that all experiences, needs, and perspectives on social events have a voice and are respected. A general perspective does not exist which all persons can adopt and from which all experiences and perspectives can be understood and taken into account. The existence of social groups implies different, though not necessarily exclusive, histories, experiences, and perspectives on social life that people have, and it implies that they do not entirely understand the experience of other groups. No one can claim to speak in the general interest, because no one of the groups can speak for another, and certainly no one can speak for them all. Thus the only way to have all group experience and social perspectives voiced, heard, and taken account of is to have them specifically represented in the public.

Group representation is the best means to promote just outcomes to democratic decision-making processes. The argument for this claim relies on Habermas's conception of communicative ethics. In the absence of a Philosopher King who reads transcendent normative verities, the only ground for a claim that a policy or decision is just is that it has been arrived at by a public which has truly promoted free expression of all needs and points of view. In his formulation of a communicative ethic, Habermas retains inappropriately an appeal to a universal or impartial point of view from which claims in a public should be addressed. A communicative ethic that does not merely articulate a hypothetical public that would justify decisions, but proposes actual conditions tending to promote just outcomes of decision-making processes, should promote conditions for the expression of the concrete needs of all individuals in their particularity.[16] The concreteness of individual lives, their needs and interests, and their perception of the needs and interests of others, I have argued, are structured partly through group-based experience and identity. Thus full and free expression of concrete needs and interests under social circumstances where some groups are silenced or marginalized requires that they have a specific voice in deliberation and decision making.

The introduction of such differentiation and particularity into democratic procedures does not encourage the expression of narrow self-interest; indeed, group representation is the best antidote to self-deceiving self-interest masked as an impartial or general interest. In a democratically structured public where social inequality is mitigated through group representation, individuals or groups cannot simply assert that they want something; they must say that justice requires or allows that they have it. Group representation provides the opportunity for some to express their needs or interests who would not likely be heard without that representation. At the same time, the test of whether a claim on the public is just, or a mere expression of self-interest, is best made when persons making it must confront the opinion of others who have explicitly different, though not necessarily conflicting, experiences, priorities, and needs. As a person of social privilege, I am not likely to go outside of myself and have a regard for social justice unless I am forced to listen to the voice of those my privilege tends to silence.

Group representation best institutionalizes fairness under circumstances of social oppression and domination. But group representation also maximizes knowledge expressed in discussion, and thus promotes practical wisdom. Group differences not only involve different needs, interests, and goals, but probably more important different social locations and experiences from which social facts and policies are understood. Members of different social groups are likely to know different things about the structure of social relations and the potential and actual effects of social policies. Because of their history,

their group-specific values or modes of expression, their relationship to other groups, the kind of work they do, and so on, different groups have different ways of understanding the meaning of social events, which can contribute to the others' understanding if expressed and heard.

Emancipatory social movements in recent years have developed some political practices committed to the idea of a heterogeneous public, and they have at least partly or temporarily instituted such publics. Some political organizations, unions, and feminist groups have formal caucuses for groups (such as blacks, Latinos, women, gay men and lesbians, and disabled or old people) whose perspectives might be silenced without them. Frequently these organizations have procedures for caucus voice in organization discussion and caucus representation in decision making, and some organizations also require representation of members of specific groups in leadership bodies. Under the influence of these social movements asserting group difference, during some years even the Democratic party, at both national and state levels, has instituted delegate rules that include provisions for group representation.

Though its realization is far from assured, the ideal of a "rainbow coalition" expresses such a heterogeneous public with forms of group representation. The traditional form of coalition corresponds to the idea of a unified public that transcends particular differences of experience and concern. In traditional coalitions, diverse groups work together for ends which they agree interest or affect them all in a similar way, and they generally agree that the differences of perspective, interests, or opinion among them will not surface in the public statements and actions of the coalition. In a rainbow coalition, by contrast, each of the constituent groups affirms the presence of the others and affirms the specificity of its experience and perspective on social issues.[17] In the rainbow public, blacks do not simply tolerate the participation of gays, labor activists do not grudgingly work alongside peace movement veterans, and none of these paternalistically allow feminist participation. Ideally, a rainbow coalition affirms the presence and supports the claims of each of the oppressed groups or political movements constituting it, and it arrives at a political program not by voicing some "principles of unity" that hide differences but rather by allowing each constituency to analyze economic and social issues from the perspective of its experience. This implies that each group maintains autonomy in relating to its constituency, and that decision-making bodies and procedures provide for group representation.

To the degree that there are heterogeneous publics operating according to the principles of group representation in contemporary politics, they exist only in organizations and movements resisting the majority politics. Nevertheless, in principle participatory democracy entails commitment to institutions of a heterogeneous public in all spheres of democratic decision making. Until and unless group oppression or disadvantages are eliminated, political publics, including democratized workplaces and government decision-making bodies, should include the specific representation of those oppressed groups, through which those groups express their specific understanding of the issues before the public and register a group based vote. Such structures of group representation should not replace structures of regional or party representation but should exist alongside them.

Implementing principles of group representation in national politics in the United States, or in restructured democratic publics within particular institutions such as factories, offices, universities, churches, and social service agencies, would require creative thinking and flexibility. There are no models to follow. European models of consociational democratic institutions, for example, cannot be taken outside of the contexts in which they have evolved, and even within them they do not operate in a very democratic fashion. Reports of experiments with publicly institutionalized self-organization among women, indigenous peoples, workers, peasants, and students in contemporary Nicaragua offer an example closer to the conception I am advocating.[18]

The principle of group representation calls for such structures of representation for oppressed or disadvantaged groups. But what groups deserve representation? Clear candidates for group representation in policy making in the United States are women, blacks, Native Americans, old people, poor people, disabled people, gay men and lesbians, Spanish-speaking Americans, young people, and nonprofessional workers. But it may not be necessary to ensure specific representation of all these groups in all public contexts and in all policy discussions. Representation should be designated whenever the group's history and social situation provide a particular perspective on the

issues, when the interests of its members are specifically affected, and when its perceptions and interests are not likely to receive expression without that representation.

An origin problem emerges in proposing a principle such as this, which no philosophical argument can solve. To implement this principle a public must be constituted to decide which groups deserve specific representation in decision-making procedures. What are the principles guiding the composition of such a "constitutional convention"? Who should decide what groups should receive representation, and by what procedures should this decision take place? No program or set of principles can found a politics, because politics is always a process in which we are already engaged; principles can be appealed to in the course of political discussion, they can be accepted by a public as guiding their action. I propose a principle of group representation as a part of such potential discussion, but it cannot replace that discussion or determine its outcome.

What should be the mechanisms of group representation? Earlier I stated that the self-organization of the group is one of the aspects of a principle of group representation. Members of the group must meet together in democratic forums to discuss issues and formulate group positions and proposals. This principle of group representation should be understood as part of a larger program for democratized decision-making processes. Public life and decision-making processes should be transformed so that all citizens have significantly greater opportunities for participation in discussion and decision making. All citizens should have access to neighborhood or district assemblies where they participate in discussion and decision making. In such a more participatory democratic scheme, members of oppressed groups would also have group assemblies, which would delegate group representatives.

One might well ask how the idea of a heterogeneous public which encourages self-organization of groups and structures of group representation in decision making is different from the interest group pluralism criticism which I endorsed earlier in this article. First, in the heterogeneous public not any collectivity of persons that chooses to form an association counts as a candidate for group representation. Only those groups that describe the major identities and major status relationships constituting the society or particular institution, and which are oppressed or disadvantaged, deserve specific representation in a heterogeneous public. In the structures of interest group pluralism, Friends of the Whales, the National Association for the Advancement of Colored People, the National Rifle Association, and the National Freeze Campaign all have the same status, and each influences decision making to the degree that their resources and ingenuity can win out in the competition for policymakers' ears. While democratic politics must maximize freedom of the expression of opinion and interest, that is a different issue from ensuring that the perspective of all groups has a voice.

Second, in the heterogeneous public the groups represented are not defined by some particular interest or goal, or some particular political position. Social groups are comprehensive identities and ways of life. Because of their experiences their members may have some common interests that they seek to press in the public. Their social location, however, tends to give them distinctive understandings of all aspects of the society and unique perspectives on social issues. For example, many Native Americans argue that their traditional religion and relation to land gives them a unique and important understanding of environmental problems.

Finally, interest group pluralism operates precisely to forestall the emergence of public discussion and decision making. Each interest group promotes only its specific interest as thoroughly and forcefully as it can, and it need not consider the other interests competing in the political marketplace except strategically, as potential allies or adversaries in the pursuit of its own. The rules of interest group pluralism do not require justifying one's interest as right or as compatible with social justice. A heterogeneous public, however, is a *public*, where participants discuss together the issues before them and are supposed to come to a decision that they determine as best or most just.

3 Universal Rights and Special Rights

A second aspect of the universality of citizenship is today in tension with the goal of full inclusion and participation of all groups in political and social institutions: universality in the formulation of law and policies. Modern and contemporary liberalism hold as basic the principle that the rules and policies of the state, and in contemporary liberalism also the rules of private institutions, ought to be blind to race, gender, and other group differences. The public realm of the state and law properly should express its rules in general terms that abstract from the particularities of individual and group histories, needs, and situations to recognize all persons equally and treat all citizens in the same way.

As long as political ideology and practice persisted in defining some groups as unworthy of equal citizenship status because of supposedly natural differences from white male citizens, it was important for emancipatory movements to insist that all people are the same in respect of their moral worth and deserve equal citizenship. In this context, demands for equal rights that are blind to group differences were the only sensible way to combat exclusion and degradation.

Today, however, the social consensus is that all persons are of equal moral worth and deserve equal citizenship. With the near achievement of equal rights for all groups, with the important exception of gay men and lesbians, group inequalities nevertheless remain. Under these circumstances many feminists, black liberation activists, and others struggling for the full inclusion and participation of all groups in this society's institutions and positions of power, reward, and satisfaction, argue that rights and rules that are universally formulated and thus blind to differences of race, culture, gender, age, or disability, perpetuate rather than undermine oppression.

Contemporary social movements seeking full inclusion and participation of oppressed and disadvantaged groups now find themselves faced with a dilemma of difference.[19] On the one hand, they must continue to deny that there are any essential differences between men and women, whites and blacks, able-bodied and disabled people, which justify denying women, blacks, or disabled people the opportunity to do anything that others are free to do or to be included in any institution or position. On the other hand, they have found it necessary to affirm that there are often group-based differences between men and women, whites and blacks, able-bodied and disabled people that make application of a strict principle of equal treatment, especially in competition for positions, unfair because these differences put those groups at a disadvantage. For example, white middle-class men as a group are socialized into the behavioral styles of a particular kind of articulateness, coolness, and competent authoritativeness that are most rewarded in professional and managerial life. To the degree that there are group differences that disadvantage, fairness seems to call for acknowledging rather than being blind to them.

Though in many respects the law is now blind to group differences, the society is not, and some groups continue to be marked as deviant and as the other. In everyday interactions, images, and decision making, assumptions continue to be made about women, blacks, Latinos, gay men, lesbians, old people, and other marked groups, which continue to justify exclusions, avoidances, paternalism, and authoritarian treatment. Continued racist, sexist, homophobic, ageist, and ableist behaviors and institutions create particular circumstances for these groups, usually disadvantaging them in their opportunity to develop their capacities and giving them particular experiences and knowledge. Finally, in part because they have been segregated and excluded from one another, and in part because they have particular histories and traditions, there are cultural differences among social groups – differences in language, style of living, body comportment and gesture, values, and perspectives on society.

Acknowledging group difference in capacities, needs, culture, and cognitive styles poses a problem for those seeking to eliminate oppression only if difference is understood as deviance or deficiency. Such understanding presumes that some capacities, needs, culture, or cognitive styles are normal. I suggested earlier that their privilege allows dominant groups to assert their experience of and perspective on social events as impartial and objective. In a similar fashion, their privilege allows some groups to project their group-based capacities, values, and cognitive and behavioral styles as the norm to which all persons should be expected to conform. Feminists in particular have argued that most contemporary workplaces, especially the most desirable, presume a life rhythm and behavioral style typical of men, and that women are expected to accommodate to the workplace expectations that assume those norms.

Where group differences in capacities, values, and behavioral or cognitive styles exist, equal treatment in the allocation of reward according to rules of merit composition will reinforce and perpetuate disadvantage. Equal treatment requires everyone to be measured according to the same norms, but in fact there are no "neutral" norms of

behavior and performance. Where some groups are privileged and others oppressed, the formulation of law, policy, and the rules of private institutions tend to be biased in favor of the privileged groups, because their particular experience implicitly sets the norm. Thus where there are group differences in capacities, socialization, values, and cognitive and cultural styles, only attending to such differences can enable the inclusion and participation of all groups in political and economic institutions. This implies that instead of always formulating rights and rules in universal terms that are blind to difference, some groups sometimes deserve special rights.[20] In what follows, I shall review several contexts of contemporary policy debate where I argue such special rights for oppressed or disadvantaged groups are appropriate.

The issue of a right to pregnancy and maternity leave, and the right to special treatment for nursing mothers, is highly controversial among feminists today. I do not intend here to wind through the intricacies of what has become a conceptually challenging and interesting debate in legal theory. As Linda Krieger argues, the issue of rights for pregnant and birthing mothers in relation to the workplace has created a paradigm crisis for our understanding of sexual equality, because the application of a principle of equal treatment on this issue has yielded results whose effects on women are at best ambiguous and at worst detrimental.[21]

In my view an equal treatment approach on this issue is inadequate because it either implies that women do not receive any right to leave and job security when having babies, or it assimilates such guarantees under a supposedly gender neutral category of "disability." Such assimilation is unacceptable because pregnancy and childbirth are normal conditions of normal women, they themselves count as socially necessary work, and they have unique and variable characteristics and needs.[22] Assimilating pregnancy into disability gives a negative meaning to these processes as "unhealthy." It suggests, moreover, that the primary or only reason that a woman has a right to leave and job security is that she is physically unable to work at her job, or that doing so would be more difficult than when she is not pregnant and recovering from childbirth. While these are important reasons, depending on the individual woman, another reason is that she ought to have the time to establish breastfeeding and develop a relationship and routine with her child, if she chooses.

The pregnancy leave debate has been heated and extensive because both feminists and non-feminists tend to think of biological sex difference as the most fundamental and ineradicable difference. When difference slides into deviance, stigma, and disadvantage, this impression can engender the fear that sexual equality is not attainable. I think it is important to emphasize that reproduction is by no means the only context in which issues of same versus different treatment arise. It is not even the only context where it arises for issues involving bodily difference. The last twenty years have seen significant success in winning special rights for persons with physical and mental disabilities. Here is a clear case where promoting equality in participation and inclusion requires attending to the particular needs of different groups.

Another bodily difference which has not been as widely discussed in law and policy literature, but should be, is age. With increasing numbers of willing and able old people marginalized in our society, the issue of mandatory retirement has been increasingly discussed. This discussion has been muted because serious consideration of working rights for all people able and willing to work implies major restructuring of the allocation of labor in an economy with already socially volatile levels of unemployment. Forcing people out of their workplaces solely on account of their age is arbitrary and unjust. Yet I think it is also unjust to require old people to work on the same terms as younger people. Old people should have different working rights. When they reach a certain age they should be allowed to retire and receive income benefits. If they wish to continue working, they should be allowed more flexible and part-time schedules than most workers currently have.

Each of these cases of special rights in the workplace – pregnancy and birthing, physical disability, and being old – has its own purposes and structures. They all challenge, however, the same paradigm of the "normal, healthy" worker and "typical work situation." In each case the circumstance that calls for different treatment should not be understood as lodged in the differently treated workers, per se, but in their interaction with the structure and norms of the workplace. Even in cases such as these, that is, difference does not have its source in natural, unalterable, biological

attributes, but in the relationship of bodies to conventional rules and practices. In each case the political claim for special rights emerges not from a need to compensate for an inferiority, as some would interpret it, but from a positive assertion of specificity in different forms of life.[23]

Issues of difference arise for law and policy not only regarding bodily being, but just as importantly for cultural integrity and invisibility. By culture I mean group-specific phenomena of behavior, temperament, or meaning. Cultural differences include phenomena of language, speaking style or dialect, body comportment, gesture, social practices, values, group-specific socialization, and so on. To the degree that groups are culturally different, however, equal treatment in many issues of social policy is unjust because it denies these cultural differences or makes them a liability. There are a vast number of issues where fairness involves attention to cultural differences and their effects, but I shall briefly discuss three: affirmative action, comparable worth, and bilingual, bicultural education and service.

Whether they involve quotas or not, affirmative action programs violate a principle of equal treatment because they are race or gender conscious in setting criteria for school admissions, jobs, or promotions. These policies are usually defended in one of two ways. Giving preference to race or gender is understood either as just compensation for groups that have suffered discrimination in the past, or as compensation for the present disadvantage these groups suffer because of that history of discrimination and exclusion.[24] I do not wish to quarrel with either of these justifications for the differential treatment based on race or gender implied by affirmative action policies. I want to suggest that in addition we can understand affirmative action policies as compensating for the cultural biases of standards and evaluators used by the schools or employers. These standards and evaluators reflect at least to some degree the specific life and cultural experience of dominant groups – whites, Anglos, or men. In a group-differentiated society, moreover, the development of truly neutral standards and evaluations is difficult or impossible, because female, black, or Latino cultural experience and the dominant cultures are in many respects not reducible to a common measure. Thus affirmative action policies compensate for the dominance of one set of cultural attributes. Such an interpretation of affirmative action locates the "problem" that affirmative action solves partly in the understandable biases of evaluators and their standards, rather than only in specific differences of the disadvantaged group.

Although they are not a matter of different treatment as such, comparable worth policies similarly claim to challenge cultural biases in traditional evaluation in the worth of female-dominated occupations, and in doing so require attending to differences. Schemes of equal pay for work of comparable worth require that predominantly male and predominantly female jobs have similar wage structures if they involve similar degrees of skill, difficulty, stress, and so on. The problem in implementing these policies, of course, lies in designing methods of comparing the jobs, which often are very different. Most schemes of comparison choose to minimize sex differences by using supposedly gender-neutral criteria, such as educational attainment, speed of work, whether it involves manipulation of symbols, decision making, and so on. Some writers have suggested, however, that standard classifications of job traits may be systematically biased to keep specific kinds of tasks involved in many female-dominated occupations hidden.[25] Many female-dominated occupations involve gender-specific kinds of labor – such as nurturing, smoothing over social relations, or the exhibition of sexuality – which most task observation ignores.[26] A fair assessment of the skills and complexity of many female-dominated jobs may therefore involve paying explicit attention to gender differences in kinds of jobs rather than applying gender blind categories of comparison.

Finally, linguistic and cultural minorities ought to have the right to maintain their language and culture and at the same time be entitled to all the benefits of citizenship, as well as valuable education and career opportunities. This right implies a positive obligation on the part of governments and other public bodies to print documents and to provide services in the native language of recognized linguistic minorities, and to provide bilingual instruction in schools. Cultural assimilation should not be a condition of full social participation, because it requires a person to transform his or her sense of identity, and when it is realized on a group level it means altering or annihilating the group's identity. This principle does not apply to any persons who do not identify with majority language or culture within a society, but only to sizeable linguistic or cultural minorities living in distinct though not necessarily segregated communities. In the United States, then, special rights for cultural minorities applies at least to Spanish-speaking Americans and Native Americans.

The universalist finds a contradiction in asserting both that formerly segregated groups have a right to inclusion and that these groups have a right to different treatment. There is no contradiction here, however, if attending to difference is necessary in order to make participation and inclusion possible. Groups with different circumstances or forms of life should be able to participate together in public institutions without shedding their distinct identities or suffering disadvantage because of them. The goal is not to give special compensation to the deviant until they achieve normality, but rather to denormalize the way institutions formulate their rules by revealing the plural circumstances and needs that exist, or ought to exist, within them.

Many opponents of oppression and privilege are wary of claims for special rights because they fear a restoration of special classifications that can justify exclusion and stigmatization of the specially marked groups. Such fear has been particularly pronounced among feminists who oppose affirming sexual and gender difference in law and policy. It would be foolish for me to deny that this fear has some significant basis.

Such fear is founded, however, on accession to traditional identification of group difference with deviance, stigma, and inequality. Contemporary movements of oppressed groups, however, assert a positive meaning to group difference, by which a group claims its identity as a group and rejects the stereotypes and labeling by which others mark it as inferior or inhuman. These social movements engage the meaning of difference itself as a terrain of political struggle, rather than leave difference to be used to justify exclusion and subordination. Supporting policies and rules that attend to group difference in order to undermine oppression and disadvantage is, in my opinion, a part of that struggle.

Fear of claims to special rights points to a connection of the principle of group representation with the principle of attending to difference in policy. The primary means of defense from the use of special rights to oppress or exclude groups is the self-organization and representation of those groups. If oppressed and disadvantaged groups are able to discuss among themselves what procedures and policies they judge will best further their social and political equality, and have access to mechanisms to make their judgments known to the larger public, then policies that attend to difference are less likely to be used against them than for them. If they have the institutionalized right to veto policy proposals that directly affect them, and them primarily, moreover, such danger is further reduced.

In this article I have distinguished three meanings of universality that have usually been collapsed in discussions of the universality of citizenship and the public realm. Modern politics properly promotes the universality of citizenship in the sense of the inclusion and participation of everyone in public life and democratic processes. The realization of genuinely universal citizenship in this sense today is impeded rather than furthered by the commonly held conviction that when they exercise their citizenship, persons should adopt a universal point of view and leave behind the perceptions they derive from their particular experience and social position. The full inclusion and participation of all in law and public life is also sometimes impeded by formulating laws and rules in universal terms that apply to all citizens in the same way.

In response to these arguments, some people have suggested to me that such challenges to the ideal of universal citizenship threaten to leave no basis for rational normative appeals. Normative reason, it is suggested, entails universality in a Kantian sense: when a person claims that something is good or right he or she is claiming that everyone in principle could consistently make that claim, and that everyone should accept it. This refers to a fourth meaning of universality, more epistemological than political. There may indeed be grounds for questioning a Kantian-based theory of the universality of normative reason, but this is a different issue from the substantive political issues I have addressed here, and the arguments in this paper neither imply nor exclude such a possibility. In any case, I do not believe that challenging the ideal of a unified public or the claim that rules should always be formally universal subverts the possibility of making rational normative claims.

Notes

1   Theodore Lowi's classic analysis of the privatized operations of interest group liberalism remains descriptive of American politics; see *The End of Liberalism* (New York: Norton, 1969). For more recent analyses, see Jürgen Habermas, *Legitimation Crisis* (Boston: Beacon, 1973); Claus Offe, *Contradictions of the Welfare State* (Cambridge, Mass.: MIT Press, 1984); John Keane, *Public Life in Late Capitalism* (Cambridge, Mass.: MIT Press, 1984); Benjamin Barber, *Strong Democracy* (Berkeley: University of California Press, 1984).

2   For an outstanding recent account of the virtues of and conditions for such democracy, see Philip Green, *Retrieving Democracy* (Totowa, N.J.: Rowman & Allanheld, 1985).

3   Barber and Keane both appeal to Rousseau's understanding of civic activity as a model for contemporary participatory democracy, as does Carole Pateman in her classic work, *Participation and Democratic Theory* (Cambridge: Cambridge University Press, 1970). (Pateman's position has, of course, changed.) See also James Miller, *Rousseau: Dreamer of Democracy* (New Haven, Conn.: Yale University Press, 1984).

4   Many who extol the virtues of the civic public, of course, appeal also to a model of the ancient polis. For a recent example, see Murray Bookchin, *The Rise of Urbanization and the Decline of Citizenship* (San Francisco: Sierra Club Books, 1987). In this article, however, I choose to restrict my claims to modern political thought. The idea of the ancient Greek polis often functions in both modern and contemporary discussion as a myth of lost origins, the paradise from which we have fallen and to which we desire to return; in this way, appeals to the ancient Greek polis are often contained within appeals to modern ideas of civic humanism.

5   Hannah Pitkin performs a most detailed and sophisticated analysis of the virtues of the civic public as a flight from sexual difference through a reading of the texts of Machiavelli; see *Fortune Is a Woman* (Berkeley: University of California Press, 1984). Carole Pateman's recent writing also focuses on such analysis. See, e.g., Carole Pateman, *The Social Contract* (Stanford, Calif.: Stanford University Press, 1988). See also Nancy Hartsock, *Money, Sex and Power* (New York: Longman, 1983), chaps. 7 and 8.

6   See Susan Okin, "Women and the Making of the Sentimental Family," *Philosophy and Public Affairs* 11 (1982): 65–88; see also Linda Nicholson, *Gender and History: The Limits of Social Theory in the Age of the Family* (New York: Columbia University Press, 1986).

7   For analyses of Rousseau's treatment of women, see Susan Okin, *Women in Western Political Thought* (Princeton, N.J.: Princeton University Press, 1978); Lynda Lange, "Rousseau: Women and the General Will," in *The Sexism of Social and Political Theory*, ed. Lorenne M. G. Clark and Lynda Lange (Toronto: University of Toronto Press, 1979); Jean Bethke Elshtain, *Public Man, Private Woman* (Princeton, N.J.: Princeton University Press, 1981), chap. 4. Mary Dietz develops an astute critique of Elshtain's "maternalist" perspective on political theory; in so doing, however, she also seems to appeal to a universalist ideal of the civic public in which women will transcend their particular concerns and become general; see "Citizenship with a Feminist Face: The Problem with Maternal Thinking," *Political Theory* 13 (1985): 19–37. On Rousseau on women, see also Joel Schwartz, *The Sexual Politics of Jean-Jacques Rousseau* (Chicago: University of Chicago Press, 1984).

8   See Ronald Takaki, *Iron Cages: Race and Culture in 19th Century America* (New York: Knopf, 1979). Don Herzog discusses the exclusionary prejudices of some other early American republicans; see "Some Questions for Republicans," *Political Theory* 14 (1986): 473–93.

9   George Mosse, *Nationalism and Sexuality* (New York: Fertig, 1985).

10 Barber, chaps. 8 and 9. Future page references in parentheses are to this book.

11 I have developed this account more thoroughly in my paper, Iris Marion Young, "Impartiality and the Civic Public: Some Implications of Feminist Critiques of Moral and Political Theory," in *Feminism as Critique*, ed. S. Benhabib and D. Cornell (Oxford: Polity Press, 1987), pp. 56–76.

12 On feminism and participatory democracy, see Pateman.

13 Jane Mansbridge, *Beyond Adversarial Democracy* (New York: Basic Books, 1980)

14 Amy Gutmann, *Liberal Equality* (Cambridge: Cambridge University Press, 1980), pp. 191–202.

15 See Iris Marion Young, "Five Faces of Oppression," *Philosophical Forum* (1988).

16 Jürgen Habermas, *Reason and the Rationalization of Society* (Boston: Beacon, 1983), pt. 3. For criticism of Habermas as retaining too universalist a conception of communicative action, see Seyla Benhabib, *Critique, Norm and Utopia* (New York: Columbia University Press, 1986); and Young, "Impartiality and the Civic Public."

17 The Mel King for mayor campaign organization exhibited the promise of such group representation in practice, which was only partially and haltingly realized; see special double issue of *Radical America* 17, no. 6, and 18, no. 1 (1984). Sheila Collins discusses how the idea of a rainbow coalition challenges traditional American political assumptions of a "melting pot," and she shows how lack of coordination between the national level rainbow departments and the grassroots campaign committees prevented the 1984 Jackson campaign from realizing the promise of group representation; see *The Rainbow Challenge: The Jackson Campaign and the Future of U.S. Politics* (New York: Monthly Review Press, 1986).

18 See Gary Ruchwarger, *People in Power: Forging a Grassroots Democracy in Nicaragua* (Hadley, Mass.: Bergin & Garvey, 1985).

19 Martha Minow, "Learning to Live with the Dilemma of Difference: Bilingual and Special Education," *Law and Contemporary Problems*, no. 48 (1985), pp. 157–211.

20 I use the term "special rights" in much the same way as Elizabeth Wolgast, in *Equality and the Rights of Women* (Ithaca, N.Y.: Cornell University Press, 1980). Like Wolgast, I wish to distinguish a class of rights that all persons should have, general rights, and a class of rights that categories of persons should have by virtue of particular circumstances. That is, the distinction should refer only to different levels of generality, where "special" means only "specific." Unfortunately, "special rights" tends to carry a connotation of *exceptional*, that is, specially marked and deviating from the norm. As I assert below, however, the goal is not to compensate for deficiencies in order to help people be "normal," but to denormalize, so that in certain contexts and at certain levels of abstraction everyone has "special" rights.

21 Linda J. Krieger, "Through a Glass Darkly: Paradigms of Equality and the Search for a Women's Jurisprudence," *Hypatia: A Journal of Feminist Philosophy* 2 (1987): 45–62. Deborah Rhode provides an excellent synopsis of the dilemmas involved in this pregnancy debate in feminist legal theory in "Justice and Gender" (typescript), chap. 9.

22 See Ann Scales, "Towards a Feminist Jurisprudence," *Indiana Law Journal* 56 (1980): 375–444. Christine Littleton provides a very good analysis of the feminist debate about equal vs. different treatment regarding pregnancy and childbirth, among other legal issues for women, in "Reconstructing Sexual Equality," *California Law Review* 25 (1987): 1279–1337. Littleton suggests, as I have stated above, that only the dominant male conception of work keeps pregnancy and birthing from being conceived of as work.

23 Littleton suggests that difference should be understood not as a characteristic of particular sorts of people, but of the interaction of particular sorts of people with specific institutional structures. Minow expresses a similar point by saying that dif-

ference should be understood as a function of the relationship among groups, rather than located in attributes of a particular group.

24 For one among many discussions of such "backward looking" and "forward looking" arguments, see Bernard Boxill, *Blacks and Social Justice* (Totowa, N.J.: Rowman & Allanheld, 1984), chap. 7.

25 See R.W. Beatty and J.R. Beatty, "Some Problems with Contemporary Job Evaluation Systems," and Ronnie Steinberg, "A Want of Harmony: Perspectives on Wage Discrimination and Comparable Worth," both in *Comparable Worth and Wage Discrimination: Technical Possibilities and Political Realities*, ed. Helen Remick (Philadelphia: Temple University Press, 1981); D.J. Treiman and H.I. Hartmann, eds., *Women, Work and Wages* (Washington, D.C.: National Academy Press, 1981), p. 81.

26 David Alexander, "Gendered Job Traits and Women's Occupations" (Ph.D. diss., University of Massachusetts, Department of Economics, 1987).

17

The Domain of the Political and Overlapping Consensus

John Rawls

In a society marked by a pluralism of comprehensive moral views, the ability of a constitutional regime to maintain widespread allegiance is due to "overlapping consensus." Those with divergent comprehensive views may nonetheless agree on a given political conception of justice. However, the idea of an overlapping consensus, as used in Professor Rawls's earlier works, has caused some misgivings. It seems to suggest that political philosophy is "political" in the wrong way. Professor Rawls answers these misgivings. A political conception of justice, such as Rawls's "justice as fairness" in A Theory of Justice, *is not merely tailored by the dominant group to justify favored results. Nor does it presuppose any particular comprehensive doctrine, whether religious or philosophical. Rather, as supported by an overlapping consensus, justice as fairness falls into a special domain of the political. It gives the framework of a stable constitutional regime by resting on the consensus of citizens who share an understanding of the role of certain basic rights and liberties, even though they may not agree on comprehensive doctrines.*

Introduction

In this Article, I shall examine the idea of an overlapping consensus[1] and its role in a political conception of justice for a constitutional regime. A political conception, I shall suppose, views the

Originally published in *New York University Law Review*, 233 (1989), 233–55. Reprinted by permission of New York University Law Review.

political as a special domain with distinctive features that call for the articulation within the conception of the characteristic values that apply to that domain. Justice as fairness, the conception presented in my book *A Theory of Justice* [*Theory*][2] is an example of a political conception and I refer to it to fix ideas. By going over these matters I hope to allay misgivings about the idea of an overlapping consensus, especially the misgiving that it makes political philosophy political in the wrong way.[3] That is, this idea may suggest to some the view that consensus politics is to be taken as regulative and that the content of first principles of justice should be adjusted to the claims of the dominant political and social interests.

This misgiving may have resulted from my having used the idea of an overlapping consensus without distinguishing between two stages in the exposition of justice as fairness and without stressing that the idea of an overlapping consensus is used only in the second. To explain: in the first stage justice as fairness should be presented as a free-standing political conception that articulates the very great values applicable to the special domain of the political, as marked out by the basic structure of society. The second stage consists of an account of the stability of justice as fairness, that is, its capacity to generate its own support,[4] in view of the content of its principles and ideals as formulated in the first stage. In this second stage the idea of an overlapping consensus is introduced to explain how, given the plurality of conflicting comprehensive religious, philosophical, and moral doctrines always found in a democratic society – the kind of society that justice as fairness itself enjoins – free institutions may gain the allegiance needed to endure over time.

1 Four General Facts

I begin with some background. Any political conception of justice presupposes a view of the political and social world, and recognizes certain general facts of political sociology and human psychology. Four general facts are especially important.

The first fact is that the diversity of comprehensive religious, philosophical, and moral doctrines found in modern democratic societies is not a mere historical condition that may soon pass away; it is a permanent feature of the public culture of democracy. Under the political and social conditions that the basic rights and liberties of free institutions secure, a diversity of conflicting and irreconcilable comprehensive doctrines will emerge, if such diversity does not already exist. Moreover, it will persist and increase. The fact about free institutions is the fact of pluralism.

A second and related general fact is that only the oppressive use of state power can maintain a continuing common affirmation of one comprehensive religious, philosophical, or moral doctrine. If we think of political society as a community when it is united in affirming one and the same comprehensive doctrine, then the oppressive use of state power is necessary to maintain a political community. In the society of the Middle Ages, more or less united in affirming the Catholic faith, the Inquisition was not an accident; preservation of a shared religious belief demanded the suppression of heresy. The same holds, I believe, for any comprehensive philosophical and moral doctrine, even for secular ones. A society united on a form of utilitarianism, or on the liberalism of Kant or Mill, would likewise require the sanctions of state power to remain so.

A third general fact is that an enduring and secure democratic regime, one not divided into contending doctrinal confessions and hostile social classes, must be willingly and freely supported by at least a substantial majority of its politically active citizens. Together with the first general fact, this means that for a conception of justice to serve as the public basis of justification for a constitutional regime, it must be one that

widely different and even irreconcilable comprehensive doctrines can endorse. Otherwise the regime will not be enduring and secure. As we shall see later, this suggests the need for what I have referred to as a political conception of justice.[5]

A fourth fact is that the political culture of a reasonably stable democratic society normally contains, at least implicitly, certain fundamental intuitive ideas from which it is possible to work up a political conception of justice suitable for a constitutional regime. This fact is important when we come to specify the general features of a political conception of justice and to elaborate justice as fairness as such a view.

2 The Burdens of Reason

These facts, especially the first two – namely, the fact that a diversity of comprehensive doctrines is a permanent feature of a society with free institutions, and that this diversity can be overcome only by the oppressive use of state power – call for explanation. For why should free institutions with their basic rights and liberties lead to diversity, and why should state power be required to suppress it? Why does our sincere and conscientious attempt to reason with one another fail to lead us to agreement? It seems to lead to agreement in science, or if disagreement in social theory and economics often seems intractable, at least – in the long run – in natural science.

There are, of course, several possible explanations. We might suppose that most people hold views that advance their own more narrow interests; and since their interests are different, so are their views. Or perhaps people are often irrational and not very bright, and this mixed with logical errors leads to conflicting opinions.

But such explanations are too easy, and not the kind we want. We want to know how reasonable disagreement is possible, for we always work at first within ideal theory. Thus we ask: how might reasonable disagreement come about?

One explanation is this. We say that reasonable disagreement is disagreement between reasonable persons, that is, between persons who have realized their two moral powers[6] to a degree sufficient to be free and equal citizens in a democratic regime, and who have an enduring desire to be fully cooperating members of society over a complete life. We assume such persons share a common human reason, similar powers of thought and judgment, a capacity to draw inferences and to weigh evidence and to balance competing considerations, and the like.

Now the idea of reasonable disagreement involves an account of the sources, or causes, of disagreement between reasonable persons. These sources I shall refer to as the "burdens of reason." The account of these burdens must be such that it is fully compatible with, and so does not impugn, the reasonableness of those who disagree among themselves.

What, then, goes wrong? If we say it is the presence of prejudice and bias, of self- and group-interest, of blindness and willfulness – not to mention irrationality and stupidity (often main causes of the decline and fall of nations)   we impugn the reasonableness of at least some of those who disagree. We must discover another explanation.

An explanation of the right kind is that the burdens of reason, the sources of reasonable disagreement among reasonable persons, are the many hazards involved in the correct (and conscientious) exercise of our powers of reason and judgment in the ordinary course of political life. Except for the last two sources below, the ones I mention now are not peculiar to reasoning about values; nor is the list I give complete. It covers only the more obvious sources of reasonable disagreement:

(a) The evidence – empirical and scientific – bearing on the case may be conflicting and complex, and hence hard to assess and evaluate.

(b) Even where we agree fully about the kinds of considerations that are relevant, we may disagree about their weight, and so arrive at different judgments.

(c) To some extent all of our concepts, not only our moral and political concepts, are vague and subject to hard cases; this indeterminacy means that we must rely on judgment and interpretation (and on judgments about interpretations) within some range (not itself sharply specifiable) wherein reasonable persons may differ.

(d) To some unknown extent, our total experience, our whole course of life up to now, shapes the way we assess evidence and weigh moral and political values, and our total experiences surely differ. Thus, in a modern society with its numerous offices and positions, its various divisions of labor, its many social groups and often their ethnic variety, the total experiences of citizens are

disparate enough for their judgments to diverge, at least to some degree, on many if not most cases of any significant complexity.

(e) Often there are different kinds of normative considerations of different force on both sides of a question and it is difficult to make an overall assessment.[7]

(f) Finally, since any system of social institutions can admit only a limited range of values, some selection must be made from the full range of moral and political values that might be realized. This is because any system of institutions has, as it were, but a limited social space. In being forced to select among cherished values, we face great difficulties in setting priorities, and other hard decisions that may seem to have no clear answer.[8]

These are some sources of the difficulties in arriving at agreement in judgment, sources that are compatible with the full reasonableness of those judging. In noting these sources – these burdens of reason – we do not, of course, deny that prejudice and bias, self- and group-interest, blindness and willfulness, play an all-too-familiar part in political life. But these sources of unreasonable disagreement stand in marked contrast to sources of disagreement compatible with everyone's being fully reasonable.

I conclude by stating a fifth general fact: we make many of our most important judgments subject to conditions which render it extremely unlikely that conscientious and fully reasonable persons, even after free discussion, can exercise their powers of reason so that all arrive at the same conclusion.

3 Precepts of Reasonable Discussion

Next I consider how, if we are reasonable, we should conduct ourselves in view of the plain facts about the burdens of reason. I suppose that, as reasonable persons, we are fully aware of these burdens, and try to take them into account. On this basis we recognize certain precepts to govern deliberation and discussion. A few of these follow.

First, the political discussion aims to reach reasonable agreement, and hence so far as possible it should be conducted to serve that aim. We should not readily accuse one another of self- or group-interest, prejudice or bias, and of such deeply entrenched errors as ideological blindness and delusion. Such accusations arouse resentment and hostility, and block the way to reasonable agreement. The disposition to make such accusations without compelling grounds is plainly unreasonable, and often a declaration of intellectual war.

Second, when we are reasonable we are prepared to find substantive and even intractable disagreements on basic questions. The first general fact means that the basic institutions and public culture of a democratic society specify a social world within which opposing general beliefs and conflicting comprehensive doctrines are likely to flourish and may increase in number. It is unreasonable, then, not to recognize the likelihood – indeed the practical certainty – of irreconcilable reasonable disagreements on matters of the first significance. Even when it seems that agreement should in principle be possible, it may be unattainable in the present case, at least in the foreseeable future.[9]

Third, when we are reasonable, we are ready to enter discussion crediting others with a certain good faith. We expect deep differences of opinion, and accept this diversity as the normal state of the public culture of a democratic society. To hate that fact is to hate human nature, for it is to hate the many not unreasonable expressions of human nature that develop under free institutions.[10]

I have suggested that the burdens of reason sufficiently explain the first two general facts – the facts of pluralism, given free institutions, and the necessity of the oppressive use of state power to maintain a political community (a political society united on a comprehensive doctrine) – whatever further causes those facts might have. Those facts are not, then, mere historical contingencies. Rather, they are rooted in the difficulties of exercising our reason under the normal conditions of human life.

4 Features of a Political Conception of Justice

Recall that the third general fact was that an enduring and stable democratic regime is one that at least a substantial majority of its politically active citizens freely support. Given this fact, what are the more general features of a political doctrine underlying a regime able to gain such allegiance? Plainly, it must be a doctrine that a

diversity of comprehensive religious, philosophical, and moral doctrines can endorse, each from its own point of view.[11] This follows not only from the third general fact but also from the first, the fact of pluralism: for a democratic regime will eventually, if not from the outset, lead to a pluralism of comprehensive doctrines.

Let us say that a political conception of justice (in contrast to a political regime) is stable if it meets the following condition: those who grow up in a society well-ordered by it – a society whose institutions are publicly recognized to be just, as specified by that conception itself – develop a sufficient allegiance to those institutions, that is, a sufficiently strong sense of justice guided by appropriate principles and ideals, so that they normally act as justice requires, provided they are assured that others will act likewise.[12]

Now what more general features of a political conception of justice does this definition of stability suggest? The idea of a political conception of justice includes three such features.[13]

First, while a political conception of justice is, of course, a moral conception, it is worked out for a specific subject, namely, the basic structure of a constitutional democratic regime. This structure consists in society's main political, social, and economic institutions, and how they fit together into one unified system of social cooperation.

Second, accepting a political conception of justice does not presuppose accepting any particular comprehensive doctrine. The conception presents itself as a reasonable conception for the basic structure alone.[14]

Third, a political conception of justice is formulated so far as possible solely in terms of certain fundamental intuitive ideas viewed as implicit in the public political culture of a democratic society. Two examples are the idea of society as a fair system of social cooperation over time from one generation to the next, and the idea of citizens as free and equal persons fully capable of engaging in social cooperation over a complete life. (That there are such ideas is the fourth general fact.) Such ideas of society and citizen are normative and political ideas; they belong to a normative political conception, and not to metaphysics or psychology.[15]

Thus the distinction between political conceptions of justice and other moral conceptions is a matter of scope, that is, of the range of subjects to which a conception applies, and of the wider content which a wider range requires. A conception is said to be general when it applies to a wide range of subjects (in the limit to all subjects); it is comprehensive when it includes conceptions of what is of value in human life, ideals of personal virtue and character, and the like, that inform much of our nonpolitical conduct (in the limit, our life as a whole).

Religious and philosophical conceptions tend to be general and fully comprehensive; indeed, their being so is sometimes regarded as a philosophical ideal to be attained. A doctrine is fully comprehensive when it covers all recognized values and virtues within one rather precisely articulated scheme of thought; whereas a doctrine is partially comprehensive when it comprises certain, but not all, nonpolitical values and virtues and is rather loosely articulated. By definition, then, for a conception to be even partially comprehensive it must extend beyond the political and include nonpolitical values and virtues.

Keeping these points in mind, political liberalism tries to articulate a workable political conception of justice. The conception consists in a view of politics and of the kind of political institutions which would be most just and appropriate when we take into account the five general facts. From these facts rises the need to found social unity on a political conception that can gain the support of a diversity of comprehensive doctrines. Political liberalism is not, then, a view of the whole of life: it is not a (fully or partially) comprehensive doctrine.

Of course, as a liberalism, it has the kind of content we historically associate with liberalism. It affirms certain basic political and civil rights and liberties, assigns them a certain priority, and so on. Justice as fairness begins with the fundamental intuitive idea of a well-ordered society as a fair system of cooperation between citizens regarded as free and equal. This idea together with the five general facts shows the need for a political conception of justice, and such a conception in turn leads to the idea of "constitutional essentials," as we may refer to them.

A specification of the basic rights and liberties of citizens – rights and liberties they are to have in their status as free and equal – falls under those essentials. For such rights and liberties concern the fundamental principles that determine the structure of the political process – the powers of the legislative, executive and the judiciary, the limits and scope of majority rule, as well as the basic political and civil rights and liberties legisla-

tive majorities must respect, such as the right to vote and to participate in politics, freedom of thought and liberty of conscience, and also the protections of the rule of law.

These matters are a long story; I merely mention them here. The point is that a political understanding of the constitutional essentials is of utmost urgency in securing a workable basis of fair political and social cooperation between citizens viewed as free and equal. If a political conception of justice provides a reasonable framework of principles and values for resolving questions concerning these essentials – and this must be its minimum objective – then a diversity of comprehensive doctrines may endorse it. In this case a political conception of justice is already of great significance, even though it may have little specific to say about innumerable economic and social issues that legislative bodies must regularly consider.

5 The Special Domain of the Political

The three features of a political conception[16] make clear that justice as fairness is not applied moral philosophy. That is, its content – its principles, standards, and values – is not presented as an application of an already elaborated moral doctrine, comprehensive in scope and general in range. Rather, it is a formulation of a family of highly significant (moral) values that properly apply to basic political institutions; it gives a specification of those values which takes account of certain special features of the political relationship, as distinct from other relationships.

The political relationship has at least two significant features:

First, it is a relationship of persons within the basic structure of society, a structure of basic institutions we enter only by birth and exit only by death (or so we may appropriately assume[17]). Political society is closed, as it were; and we do not, and indeed cannot, enter or leave it voluntarily.

Second, the political power exercised within the political relationship is always coercive power backed by the state's machinery for enforcing its laws. In a constitutional regime political power is also the power of equal citizens as a collective body. It is regularly imposed on citizens as individuals, some of whom may not accept the reasons widely thought to justify the general structure of political authority (the constitution), some of whom accept that structure, but do not regard as well grounded many of the statutes and other laws to which they are subject.

Political liberalism holds, then, that there is a special domain of the political identified by at least these features. So understood, the political is distinct from the associational, which is voluntary in ways that the political is not; it is also distinct from the personal and the familial, which are affectional domains, again in ways the political is not.[18]

Taking the political as a special domain, let us say that a political conception formulating its basic values is a "free-standing" view. It is a view for the basic structure that formulates its values independent of non-political values and of any specific relationship to them. Thus a political conception does not deny that there are other values that apply to the associational, the personal, and the familial; nor does it say that the political is entirely separate from those values. But our aim is to specify the special domain of the political in such a way that its main institutions can gain the support of an overlapping consensus.

As a form of political liberalism, then, justice as fairness holds that, with regard to the constitutional essentials, and given the existence of a reasonably well-ordered constitutional regime, the family of very great political values expressed by its principles and ideals normally will have sufficient weight to override all other values that may come into conflict with them. Justice as fairness also holds, again with respect to constitutional essentials, that so far as possible, questions about those essentials should be settled by appeal to those political values alone. For it is on those questions that agreement among citizens who affirm opposing comprehensive doctrines is most urgent.

Now, in holding these convictions we clearly imply some relation between political and non-political values. Thus, if it is said that outside the church there is no salvation,[19] and that hence a constitutional regime, with its guarantees of freedom of religion, cannot be accepted unless it is unavoidable, we must make some reply. From the point of view of political liberalism, the appropriate reply is to say that the conclusion is unreasonable;[20] it proposes to use the public's political power – a power in which citizens have an equal share – to enforce a view affecting constitutional essentials about which citizens as reasonable persons, given the burdens of reason, are bound to differ uncompromisingly in judgment.

It is important to stress that this reply does not say that a doctrine *Extra ecclesiam nulla salus* is not true. Rather, it says that it is unreasonable to use the public's political power to enforce it. A reply from within an alternative comprehensive view – the kind of reply we should like to avoid in political discussion – would say that the doctrine in question is incorrect and rests on a misapprehension of the divine nature. If we do reject the enforcement by the state of a doctrine as unreasonable we may of course also regard that doctrine itself as untrue. And there may be no way entirely to avoid implying its lack of truth, even when considering constitutional essentials.[21]

Note, however, that in saying it is unreasonable to enforce a doctrine, we do not necessarily reject it as incorrect, though we may do so. Indeed, it is vital to the idea of political liberalism that we may with perfect consistency hold that it would be unreasonable to use political power to enforce our own comprehensive religious, philosophical or moral views – views which we must, of course, affirm as true or reasonable (or at least as not unreasonable).

6 How is Political Liberalism Possible?

The question now arises, how, as I have characterized it, is political liberalism possible? That is, how can the values of the special domain of the political – the values of a sub-domain of the realm of all values – normally outweigh any values that may conflict with them? Or put another way: how can we affirm our comprehensive doctrines as true or reasonable and yet hold that it would not be reasonable to use the state's power to gain the allegiance of others to them?[22]

The answer to this question has two complementary parts. The first part says that values of the political are very great values indeed and hence not easily overridden. These values govern the basic framework of social life, "the very groundwork of our existence,"[23] and specify the fundamental terms of political and social cooperation. In justice as fairness some of these great values are expressed by the principles of justice for the basic structure: the values of equal political and civil liberty, of fair equality of opportunity, of economic reciprocity, the social bases of mutual respect among citizens, and so on.

Other great values fall under the idea of free public reason, and are expressed in the guidelines for public inquiry and in the steps taken to secure that such inquiry is free and public, as well as informed and reasonable. These values include not only the appropriate use of the fundamental concepts of judgment, inference, and evidence, but also the virtues of reasonableness and fair-mindedness as shown in the adherence to the criteria and procedures of common sense knowledge, and to the methods and conclusions of science when not controversial, as well as respect for the precepts governing reasonable political discussion.[24]

Together these values give expression to the liberal political ideal that since political power is the coercive power of free and equal citizens as a corporate body, this power should be exercised, when constitutional essentials are at stake, only in ways that all citizens can reasonably be expected to endorse publicly in the light of their own common, human reason.[25]

So far as possible, political liberalism tries to present a free-standing account of these values as those of a special domain – the political. It is left to citizens individually, as part of their liberty of conscience, to settle how they think the great values of the political domain relate to other values within their comprehensive doctrine. We hope that by doing this we can, in working political practice, firmly ground the constitutional essentials in those political values alone, and that these values will provide a satisfactory shared basis of public justification.

The second part of the answer as to how political liberalism is possible complements the first. This part says that the history of religion and philosophy shows that there are many reasonable ways in which the wider realm of values can be understood so as to be either congruent with, or supportive of, or else not in conflict with, the values appropriate to the special domain of the political as specified by a political conception of justice for a democratic regime. History tells of a plurality of not unreasonable comprehensive doctrines. That these comprehensive doctrines are divergent makes an overlapping consensus necessary. That they are not unreasonable makes it possible. A model case of an overlapping consensus of the kind I have considered elsewhere shows how this is so.[26] Many other such cases could make the same point.

7 The Question of Stability

Justice as fairness, as I have said, is best presented in two stages.[27] In the first stage it is worked out as a free-standing political (but of course moral) conception for the basic structure of society. Only when this is done and its content – its principles of justice and ideals – is provisionally on hand do we take up, in the second stage, the problem of stability and introduce the idea of an overlapping consensus: a consensus in which a diversity of conflicting comprehensive doctrines endorse the same political conception, in this case, justice as fairness.

In describing the second stage, let us agree that a political conception must be practicable, that is, must fall under the art of the possible. This contrasts with a moral conception that is not political; a moral conception may condemn the world and human nature as too corrupt to be moved by its precepts and ideals.

There are, however, two ways in which a political conception may be concerned with stability.[28] In one way, we suppose that stability is a purely practical matter: if a conception fails to be stable, it is futile to try to base a political structure upon it. Perhaps we think there are two separate tasks: one is to work out a political conception that seems sound, or reasonable, at least to us; the other is to find ways to bring others who reject the conception to share it in due course, or failing that, to act in accordance with it, prompted if need be by penalties enforced by state power. As long as the means of persuasion or enforcement can be found, the conception is viewed as stable; it is not utopian in the pejorative sense.

But as a liberal conception, justice as fairness is concerned with stability in a second, very different way. Finding a stable conception is not simply a matter of avoiding futility. Rather, what counts is the kind of stability and the nature of the forces that secure it. The idea is that, given certain assumptions specifying a reasonable human psychology[29] and the normal conditions of human life, those who grow up under basic institutions that are just – institutions that justice as fairness itself enjoins – acquire a reasoned and informed allegiance to those institutions sufficient to render the institutions stable. Put another way, the sense of justice of citizens, in view of their traits of character and interests as formed by living under a just basic structure, is strong enough to resist the normal tendencies to injustice. Citizens act willingly so as to give one another justice over time. Stability is secured by sufficient motivation of the appropriate kind acquired under just institutions.[30]

The kind of stability required of justice as fairness is based, then, on its being a liberal political view, one that aims at being acceptable to citizens as reasonable and rational, as well as free and equal, and so addressed to their free public reason. Earlier we saw how this feature of liberalism connects with the feature of political power in a constitutional regime, namely, that it is the power of equal citizens as a collective body. It follows that if justice as fairness were not expressly designed to gain the reasoned support of citizens who affirm reasonable although conflicting comprehensive doctrines – the existence of such conflicting doctrines being a feature of the kind of public culture which that conception itself encourages – it would not be liberal.[31]

The point, then, is that, as a liberal conception, justice as fairness must not merely avoid futility; the explanation of why it is practicable must be of a special kind. The problem of stability is not the problem of bringing others who reject a conception to share it, or to act in accordance with it, by workable sanctions if necessary – as if the task were to find ways to impose that conception on others once we are ourselves convinced it is sound. Rather, as a liberal political conception, justice as fairness relies for its reasonableness in the first place upon generating its own support in a suitable way by addressing each citizen's reason, as explained within its own framework.[32]

Only in this manner is justice as fairness an account of political legitimacy. Only so does it escape being a mere account of how those who hold political power can satisfy themselves, in the light of their own convictions, whether political or fully comprehensive, that they are acting properly – satisfy themselves, that is, and not citizens generally.[33] A conception of political legitimacy aims for a public basis of justification and appeals to free public reason, and hence to all citizens viewed as reasonable and rational.

8 Comparison with *A Theory of Justice*

It may seem that the idea of an overlapping consensus and related topics are a significant departure from *Theory*. They are some departure

certainly; but how much? *Theory* never discusses whether justice as fairness is meant as a comprehensive moral doctrine or as a political conception of justice. In one place it says that if justice as fairness succeeds reasonably well, a next step would be to study the more general view suggested by the name "rightness as fairness."[34]

But *Theory* holds that even this view would not be fully comprehensive: it would not cover, for example, our relations to other living things and to the natural order itself.[35] *Theory* emphasizes the limited scope of justice as fairness, and the limited scope of the kind of view it exemplifies; the book leaves open the question of how far its conclusions might need revision once these other matters are taken into account. There is, however, no mention of the distinction between a political conception of justice and a comprehensive doctrine. The reader might reasonably conclude, then, that justice as fairness is set out as part of a comprehensive view that may be developed later were success to invite.

This conclusion is supported by the discussion of the well-ordered society of justice as fairness in Part III of *Theory*.[36] There it is assumed that the members of any well-ordered society, whether it be a society of justice as fairness or of some other view, accept the same conception of justice and also, it seems, the same comprehensive doctrine of which that conception is a part, or from which it can be derived. Thus, for example, all the members of a well-ordered society associated with utilitarianism (classical or average), are assumed to affirm the utilitarian view, which is by its nature (unless expressly restricted) a comprehensive doctrine.

Although the term was introduced in another context,[37] the idea of an overlapping consensus was first introduced to think of the well-ordered society of justice as fairness in a different and more realistic way.[38] Given the free institutions which that conception itself enjoins, we can no longer assume that citizens generally, even if they accept justice as fairness, also accept the particular comprehensive view in which it might seem to be embedded in *Theory*. We now assume citizens hold two distinct views; or perhaps better, we assume their overall view has two parts. One part can be seen to be, or to coincide with, a political conception of justice, the other part is a (fully or partially) comprehensive doctrine to which the political conception is in some manner related.[39]

The political conception may be simply a part

of, or an adjunct to, a partially comprehensive view; or it may be endorsed because it can be derived within a fully articulated comprehensive doctrine. It is left to citizens individually to decide for themselves in what way their shared political conception is related to their wider and more comprehensive views. A society is well-ordered by justice as fairness so long as, first, citizens who affirm reasonable comprehensive doctrines generally endorse justice as fairness as giving the content of their political judgments; and second, unreasonable comprehensive doctrines do not gain enough currency to compromise the essential justice of basic institutions.

This is a better and no longer utopian way of thinking of the well-ordered society of justice as fairness. It corrects the view in *Theory*, which fails to take into account the condition of pluralism to which its own principles lead.

Moreover, because justice as fairness is now seen as a free-standing political conception that articulates fundamental political and constitutional values, endorsing it involves far less than is contained in a comprehensive doctrine. Taking such a well-ordered society as the aim of reform and change does not seem altogether impracticable; under the reasonably favorable conditions that make a constitutional regime possible, that aim is a reasonable guide and may be in good part realized. By contrast, a free democratic society well-ordered by any comprehensive doctrine, religious or secular, is surely utopian in a pejorative sense. Achieving it would, in any case, require the oppressive use of state power. This is as true of the liberalism of rightness as fairness, as it is of the Christianity of Aquinas or Luther.

9 In What Sense Political?

To trace our steps, I put before you this brief summary.[40] I have suggested that once we recognize the five general facts[41] and the inevitable burdens of reason even under favorable conditions,[42] and once we reject the oppressive use of state power to impose a single comprehensive doctrine as the way to achieve social unity, then we are led to democratic principles and must accept the fact of pluralism as a permanent feature of political life. Hence, to achieve social unity for a well-ordered democratic regime, what I have called political liberalism introduces the idea of an overlapping consensus and along with it the further

idea of the political as a special domain. Political liberalism does this not only because its content includes the basic rights and liberties the securing of which leads to pluralism, but also because of the liberal ideal of political legitimacy, namely, that social cooperation, at least as it concerns the constitutional essentials, is to be conducted so far as possible on terms both intelligible and acceptable to all citizens as reasonable and rational. Those terms are best stated by reference to the fundamental political and constitutional values (expressed by a political conception of justice) that, given the diversity of comprehensive doctrines, all citizens may still be reasonably expected to endorse.

We must, however, be careful that a political conception is not political in the wrong way. It should aim to formulate a coherent view of the very great (moral) values applying to the political relationship and to set out a public basis of justification for free institutions in a manner accessible to free public reason. It must not be political in the sense of merely specifying a workable compromise between known and existing interests, nor political in looking to the particular comprehensive doctrines known to exist in society and in then being tailored to gain their allegiance.

In this connection let us ensure that the assumptions about pluralism do not make justice as fairness political in the wrong way. Consider first the five general facts reviewed in Parts 1 and 2. These we suppose are accepted from the point of view of you and me as we try to develop justice as fairness. When the original position is viewed as a device of representation, these facts are made available to the parties in that position as they decide which principles of justice to select. So if principles that require free democratic institutions are accepted in the first stage, then the account of the stability in the second stage must show how justice as fairness can be endorsed by an overlapping consensus. As we have seen, this follows because free institutions themselves lead to pluralism.

The crucial question, then, is whether the five general facts, along with other premises allowed by the constraints of the original position in the first stage, suffice to lead the parties to select the two principles of justice,[43] or whether certain further assumptions related to pluralism are also needed, assumptions that make justice as fairness political in the wrong way. I cannot settle this matter here; it would require a survey of the argument from the original position.

I believe we need only suppose in the first stage that the parties assume the fact of pluralism to obtain, that is, that a plurality of comprehensive doctrines exists in society.[44] The parties must then protect against the possibility that the person each party represents may be a member of a religious, ethnic, or other minority. This suffices for the argument for the equal basic liberties to get going. In the second stage, when stability is considered, the parties again assume that pluralism obtains. They confirm principles leading to a social world that allows free play to human nature and thus, we hope, encourages a diversity of reasonable rather than unreasonable comprehensive doctrines, given the burdens of reason.[45] This makes stability possible.

Now it is often said that the politician looks to the next election, the statesman to the next generation. To this we add that the student of philosophy looks to the standing conditions of human life, and how these affect the burdens of reason. Political philosophy must take into account the five general facts we noted, among them the fact that free institutions encourage a diversity of comprehensive doctrines. But in doing this we abstract from the particular content of these doctrines, whatever it may be, and from the many contingencies under which the doctrines exist. A political conception so arrived at is not political in the wrong way but suitably adapted to the public political culture that its own principles shape and sustain. And although such a conception may not apply to all societies at all times and places, this does not make it historicist, or relativist; rather, it is universal in virtue of its extending appropriately to specify a reasonable conception of justice among all nations.[46]

10 Concluding Remarks

The foregoing shows, I think, that the freedoms discussed have a dual role. On the one hand, they are the result of the working out, at the most basic level (in what I called the first stage of justice as fairness), of the fundamental ideas of a democratic society as a fair system of cooperation between citizens as free and equal. On the other hand, in the second stage, we know on the basis of general facts and the historical condition of the age that a conception of political justice leading to free institutions must be acceptable to a plurality of opposing comprehensive doctrines. That conception must, therefore, present itself as independent of any particular comprehensive view and must firmly guarantee for all citizens the basic rights and liberties as a condition of their sense of security and their peaceful, mutual recognition.

As the first role is perhaps clearer than the second, I comment on the latter. We know from the burdens of reason that even in a well-ordered society, where the basic freedoms are secure, sharp political disagreement will persist on their more particular interpretation. For instance, where exactly should the line be drawn between church and state? Or, granting there is no such crime as seditious libel, who precisely belongs to the class of public persons in regard to whom the law of libel is relaxed? Or, what are the limits of protected speech? So the question arises: if disagreements on such constitutional essentials always remain, what is gained by a publicly recognized political conception? Isn't the aim – to underwrite the basic rights and liberties of citizens by achieving an overlapping consensus, thereby giving everyone the sense that their rights are indeed secure – still unresolved?

There are two replies to this. First, by securing the basic rights and liberties, and assigning them a due priority, the most divisive questions are taken off the political agenda. This means that they are publicly recognized as politically settled, once and for all, and so contrary views on those questions are emphatically rejected by all political parties.[47] Though disagreements remain, as they must, they occur in areas of less central significance, where reasonable citizens equally attached to the political conception may reasonably be expected to differ. If liberty of conscience is guaranteed and separation of church and state is enjoined, we still expect there to be differences about what more exactly these provisions mean. Differences in judgement on the details in matters of any complexity even among reasonable persons are a condition of human life. But with the most divisive questions off the political agenda, it should be possible to reach a peaceful settlement within the framework of democratic institutions.

A second reply, complementing the first, is that the political conception, when properly formulated, should guide reflective judgment both to an agreed enumeration of the basic rights and liberties and to an agreement about their central range of significance. This it can do by its fundamental intuitive idea of society as a fair system of cooperation between citizens as free and equal persons, and by its idea of such persons as having the two moral powers, one a capacity for a sense of justice and the other a capacity for a conception of the good, that is, a conception of what is worthy of their devoted pursuit over a complete life.[48] Basic rights and liberties secure the conditions for the adequate development and exercise of those powers by citizens viewed as fully cooperating members of society. Citizens are thought to have and to want to exercise these powers whatever their more comprehensive religious, philosophical, or moral doctrine may be. Thus, the equal political liberties and freedom of speech and thought enable us to develop and exercise these powers by participating in society's political life and by assessing the justice and effectiveness of its laws and social policies; and liberty of conscience and freedom of association enable us to develop and exercise our moral powers in forming, revising, and rationally pursuing our conceptions of the good that belong to our comprehensive doctrines, and affirming them as such.[49]

But in view of the truism that no conception, whether in law, morals, or science, interprets and applies itself, we should expect various interpretations of even the constitutional essentials to gain currency. Does this jeopardize the rule of law? Not necessarily. The idea of the rule of law has numerous elements and it can be specified in a variety of ways. But however this is done, it cannot depend on the idea of a clear, unambiguous directive that informs citizens, or legislators, or judges what the constitution enjoins in all cases. There can be no such thing. The rule of law is not put in jeopardy by the circumstance that citizens, and even legislators and judges, may often hold conflicting views on questions of interpretation.

Rather, the rule of law means the regulative role of certain institutions and their associated legal and judicial practices. It may mean, among other things, that all officers of the government, including the executive, are under the law and that their acts are subject to judicial scrutiny, that the judiciary is suitably independent, and that

civilian authority is supreme over the military. Moreover, it may mean that judges' decisions rest on interpreting existing law and relevant precedents, that judges must justify their verdicts by reference thereto and adhere to a consistent reading from case to case, or else find a reasonable basis for distinguishing them, and so on. Similar constraints do not bind legislators; while they may not defy basic law and can try politically to change it only in ways the constitution permits, they need not explain or justify their vote, though their constituents may call them to account. The rule of law exists so long as such legal institutions and their associated practices (variously specified) are conducted in a reasonable way in accordance with the political values that apply to them: impartiality and consistency, adherence to law and respect for precedent, all in the light of a coherent understanding of recognized constitutional norms viewed as controlling the conduct of all government officers.[50]

Two conditions underwrite the rule of law so understood: first, the recognition by politically engaged citizens of the dual role of the basic rights and liberties; and second, its being the case that the main interpretations of those constitutional essentials take the most divisive matters off the political agenda and specify the central range of significance of the basic liberties in roughly the same way. The ideas of the domain of the political and of an overlapping consensus indicate how these conditions strengthen the stability of a political conception.

It is important for the viability of a just democratic regime over time for politically active citizens to understand those ideas. For in the long run, the leading interpretations of constitutional essentials are settled politically. A persistent majority, or an enduring alliance of strong enough interests, can make of the Constitution what it wants.[51] This fact is simply a corollary to the third general fact – that an enduring democratic regime must be freely supported by a substantial majority of its politically active citizens. As a fact, we must live with it and see it as specifying further one of the conditions of achieving a well-ordered constitutional state.

Notes

James B. Conant University Professor, Harvard University. A.B., 1943, Ph.D., 1950, Princeton University. An earlier version of this Article was the John Dewey Lecture in Jurisprudence, given at New York University School of Law, November 15, 1988.

1   An overlapping consensus exists in a society when

the political conception of justice that regulates its basic institutions is endorsed by each of the main religious, philosophical, and moral doctrines likely to endure in that society from one generation to the next. I have used this idea mainly in Rawls, Justice as Fairness: Political not Metaphysical, 14 Phil. & Pub. Aff. 223 (1985) [hereinafter Justice as Fairness] and Rawls, The Idea of an Overlapping Consensus, 7 Oxford J. Legal Stud. 1 (1987) [hereinafter Overlapping Consensus]. The idea is introduced in J. Rawls, A Theory of Justice 387–88 (1971) [hereinafter Theory].

2 Theory, note 1 (above).

3 For an awareness of these misgivings I am indebted to the comments of G.A. Cohen and Paul Seabright (soon after the lecture "Overlapping Consensus" was given at Oxford in May 1986), see Overlapping Consensus, note 1 (above), and to discussions with Jürgen Habermas (at Harvard the following October). For a better understanding of and suggestions for how to deal with the misgivings, I am greatly indebted to Ronald Dworkin, Thomas Nagel, and T.M. Scanlon. I also have gained much from Wilfried Hinsch, to whom I owe the important idea of a reasonable comprehensive doctrine, which I have simply elaborated a bit. This idea, when joined with suitable companion ideas such as the burdens of reason, see Part 2, and the precepts of reasonable discussion, see Part 3, imposes an appropriate limit on the comprehensive doctrines we may reasonably expect to be included in an overlapping consensus.

4 See Part 8.

5 See Part 7.

6 These powers are those of a capacity for a sense of justice and a capacity for a conception of the good. Theory, note 1 (above); at 505; Justice as Fairness, note 1 (above), at 232–34.

7 This source of disagreement I have expressed in a somewhat flat way. It could be put more strongly by saying, as Thomas Nagel does, that there are basic conflicts of value in which there seem to be decisive and sufficient (normative) reasons for two or more incompatible courses of action; and yet some decision must be made. See T. Nagel, Mortal Questions 128–41 (1979). Moreover, these normative reasons are not evenly balanced, and so it matters greatly what decision is made. The lack of even balance holds because in such cases the values are incomparable. They are each specified by one of the several irreducibly different perspectives within which values arise, in particular, the perspectives that specify obligations, rights, utility, perfectionist ends, and personal commitments. Put another way, these values have different bases which their different formal features reflect. These basic conflicts reveal what Nagel thinks of as the fragmentation of value. See id. I find much in

Nagel's discussion very plausible, and I might endorse it were I stating my own (partially) comprehensive moral doctrine; since I am not doing that, but rather trying so far as possible to avoid controversial philosophical theses and to give an account of the difficulties of reason that rest on the plain facts open to all, I refrain from any statement stronger than (e).

8 This point has often been stressed by Sir Isaiah Berlin, most recently in his article, On the Pursuit of the Ideal, N.Y. Rev. Books, Mar. 17, 1988, at 11.

9 For instance, consider the questions of the causes of unemployment and the more effective ways to reduce it.

10 I have adapted this idea from Pliny the Younger's remark, "He who hates vice, hates mankind," quoted in J. Shklar, Ordinary Vices 192 (1984).

11 Here I assume that any substantial majority will include citizens who hold conflicting comprehensive doctrines.

12 Note that this is a definition of stability for a political conception of justice. It is not to be mistaken for a definition of stability, or of what I call the security, of a political regime (as a system of institutions).

13 The features of a political conception of justice are discussed in more detail in Justice as Fairness, note 1 (above), at 224–34.

14 A political conception for the basic structure must also generalize to, or else fit in with, a political conception for an international society of constitutionally democratic states; but here I put this important matter aside. See note 46 below.

15 See Justice as Fairness note 1 (above) at 239–40 & n. 22 (discussing a "political conception of the person").

16 See Part 4.

17 The appropriateness of this assumption rests in part on a point I shall only mention here, namely, that the right of emigration does not make the acceptance of political authority voluntary in the way that freedom of thought and liberty of conscience make the acceptance of ecclesiastical authority voluntary. This brings out a further feature of the domain of the political, one that distinguishes it from the associational.

18 The associational, the personal, and the familial are only three examples of the non-political; there are others.

19 The common medieval maxim *Extra ecclesiam nulla salus* ("Outside the church there is no salvation") was used, for example, in the famous bull "Unam sanctam" of Nov. 18, 1302, by Pope Boniface VIII, reprinted in Enchiridion symbolorum definitionum et declarationum de rebus fidei et morum 870 at 279 (33rd ed. H. Denzinger and A. Schönmetzer eds. 1965).

20 For clarity on this point I owe thanks to Wilfried Hinsch and Peter de Marneffe.

21 See Rawls, Overlapping Consensus, note 1 (above), at 14.

22 Recall here the formulation of political liberalism a few lines back, namely, given the existence of a well-ordered constitutional democratic regime, the family of great values expressed by its principles and ideals, and realized in its basic institutions, normally has sufficient weight to override whatever other values may come into conflict with them. See Part 4.

23 J.S. Mill, Utilitarianism, ch. 5, ¶ 25 (3rd ed. 1867), reprinted in John Stuart Mill: A Selection of His Works 216 (J. Robson ed. 1982).

24 See Part 3.

25 On this point see the instructive discussion by Jeremy Waldron, Theoretical Foundations of Liberalism, 37 Phil. Q. 127 (1987).

26 See Justice as Fairness, note 1 (above), at 250. The model case of an overlapping consensus is one in which the political conception is endorsed by three comprehensive doctrines: the first endorses justice as fairness, say, because its religious beliefs and understanding of faith lead to the principle of toleration and support the basic equal liberties; the second doctrine affirms justice as fairness as a consequence of a comprehensive liberal conception such as that of Kant or Mill; while the third affirms justice as fairness as a political conception, that is, not as a consequence of a wider doctrine but as in itself sufficient to express very great values that normally outweigh whatever other values might oppose them, at least under reasonably favorable conditions. Id. See also Overlapping Consensus, note 1 (above), Section III, at 9–12 (more fully discussing this model case).

27 These two stages correspond to the two parts of the argument from the original position for the two principles of justice contained in Theory, note 1 (above). In the first part the parties select principles without taking the effects of the special psychologies into account. Id. at 118–93. In the second part they ask whether a society well-ordered by the principles selected in the first part would be stable, that is, would generate in its members a sufficiently strong sense of justice to counteract tendencies to injustice. Id. at 395–587. The argument for the principles of justice is not complete until the principles selected in the first part are shown in the second part to be sufficiently stable. So in *Theory* the argument is not complete until the next to last section, section 86. Id. at 567–77. For these two parts, see id. at 144, 530–31.

28 In this and the next several paragraphs I am indebted to a very helpful discussion with T.M. Scanlon.

29 The assumptions of such a psychology are noted briefly in Overlapping Consensus, note 1 (above), at 22–23. In Section VI of the same essay I also consider the way in which a political conception can gain an allegiance to itself that may to some degree shape comprehensive doctrines to conform to its requirements. Id. at 18–22. This is plainly an important aspect of stability and strengthens the second part of the answer as to how political liberalism is possible. See Part 6.

I wish to thank Francis Kamm for pointing out to me several significant complications in the relation between a political conception and the comprehensive doctrines it shapes to accord with it, and how far as a result the viability of political liberalism depends on the support of such doctrines. It seems best not to pursue these matters here but to postpone them until a more complete account of stability can be given.

30 As stated in *Theory*, the question is whether the just and the good are congruent. Theory, note 1 (above), at 395, 567–77. In section 86 of *Theory*, it is argued that a person who grows up in a society well-ordered by justice as fairness, and who has a rational plan of life, and who also knows, or reasonably believes, that everyone else has an effective sense of justice, has sufficient reason, founded on that person's good (and not on justice) to comply with just institutions. Id. at 567–77. These institutions are stable because the just and the good are congruent. That is, no reasonable and rational person in the well-ordered society of justice as fairness is moved by rational considerations of the good not to honor what justice requires.

31 Recall that reasonable comprehensive doctrines are ones that recognize the burdens of reason and accept the fact of pluralism as a condition of human life under free democratic institutions, and hence accept freedom of thought and liberty of conscience. See Parts 2 and 3.

32 The force of the phrase "within its own framework" as used in the text emerges in the two parts of the argument from the original position in Theory, note 1 (above). Both parts are carried out within the same framework and subject to the same conditions embedded in the original position as a device of representation.

33 For this distinction, see Nagel, What Makes Political Theory Utopian? 56 Social Research 903 (1989).

34 Theory, note 1 (above), at 17.

35 Id. at 512.

36 Id. at 453–62.

37 Id. at 387–88.

38 Justice as Fairness, note 1 (above), at 248–51.

39 For example, in the well-ordered society of justice as fairness, some may hold a form of utilitarianism as their comprehensive doctrine, provided they understand that doctrine, as I believe J.S. Mill did,

so as to coincide in its requirements with justice as fairness, at least for the most part. See J.S. Mill, note 23 (above), ch. 3 ¶ 10.

40 I am grateful to Erin Kelley for valuable discussion about how to put this summary.

41 See Parts 1 and 2.

42 See Part 2.

43 These two principles are:

1 Each person has an equal right to a fully adequate scheme of equal basic rights and liberties, which scheme is compatible with a similar scheme for all.

2 Social and economic inequalities are to satisfy two conditions: first, they must be attached to offices and positions open to all under conditions of fair equality of opportunity; and second, they must be to the greatest benefit of the least advantaged members of society.

Justice as Fairness, note 1 (above), at 227.

44 I should like to thank David Chow for very helpful comments on this point.

45 The reasons for thinking reasonable rather than unreasonable doctrines are encouraged are sketched briefly in Overlapping Consensus, note 1 (above), at 18–23.

46 Perhaps I should explain briefly that the political conception so arrived at may not apply to some societies because the general facts we have assumed may not appropriately obtain in their case. Nevertheless, those facts do obtain widely in the modern world, and hence the political conception applies. Its not applying in some cases, however, does not make that conception relativist or historicist so long as it provides grounds for judging the basic institutions of different societies and their social policies. Thus, the appropriate test of a conception's universality is whether it can be extended to, or developed into, a reasonable political conception of justice for an international society of nation-states. In Theory, note 1(above), at 377–79, I noted briefly how, after the principles of justice have been adopted for the basic structure of society (viewed as a closed scheme of cooperation), the idea of the original position can be used once more at the higher level. The parties are now seen as representatives of states. We start with (closed) societies and build up to the international society of states. Doing this locates us where we are and follows the historical tendencies of democratic societies. Others may want to begin with an original position in which the parties are seen as representatives of citizens of the world society. I supposed that in any case the outcome would be something like the familiar principles of international justice governing a society of states rather than a world state, for example, a principle of equality among peoples as organized into states, although states who recognize certain duties towards other states. For I think that Kant is right that a world state would likely be either highly oppressive if not autocratic, or else torn by civil strife as separate peoples and cultures tried to win their autonomy. I. Kant, Perpetual Peace: A Philosophical Sketch (1795; L. Beck trans. 1949). If so, the principles of international justice will include a principle of equality among peoples as organized into states; and there will also be, I think, principles for forming and regulating loose confederations of states, and standards of fairness for various cooperative arrangements between them, and so on. In such a confederation or arrangement, one role of the state, however arbitrary its boundaries may appear from a historical point of view, is to be the representative of a people as they take responsibility for their territory and the numbers they put on it, and especially for maintaining its environmental integrity and its capacity to sustain them in perpetuity.

Theory does not pursue these larger matters but only mentions the extension to the international system as background for discussing conscientious refusal in section 58. Theory, note 1 (above), at 377–82. But given this extension, as briefly indicated, we can see that justice as fairness as a political conception is universal in at least two ways. First, its principles extend to the international society and bind all its members, the nation-states; and second, insofar as certain of a society's domestic institutions and policies are likely to lead to war or to expansionist aims, or to render a people unreliable and untrustworthy as partners in a confederation of states or in a cooperative arrangement, those institutions and policies are open to censure and sanctions of varying degrees of severity by the principles of international justice. Here violations of what are recognized as human rights may be particularly serious. Thus, the requirements of a just international society may reflect back and impose constraints downwards on the domestic institutions of states generally. But these constraints will already be met, I assume, by a just constitutional regime.

I cannot pursue these matters further here, and have appended this footnote only to indicate why I think the political conception of justice as fairness is in a suitable way universal, and not relativist or historicist, even though it may not apply to all societies at all times and places. Thomas Pogge's *Realizing Rawls* (1989) includes an account of international justice from within a conception much like justice as fairness, but very importantly revised and extended in a different way to the global sphere. His much fuller discussion will sustain, I believe, the same general point about the universality of such a conception, although his approach to international justice is very different.

47 For example, it is not on the political agenda whether certain groups are to have the vote, or whether certain religious or philosophical views have the protections of liberty of conscience and freedom of thought.

48 This conception of the person, which characterizes citizens, is also a political conception. Justice as Fairness, note 1 (above), at 239–44. I add that persons understand their own conceptions of the good against the background of their own comprehensive doctrines.

49 For further discussion of the basic rights and liberties, see Rawls, Basic Liberties and Their Priority, in 3 Tanner Lectures on Human Values 1 (S. McMurrin ed. 1982).

50 I owe thanks to T.M. Scanlon for helpful discussion of the rule of law as summarized in the last two paragraphs.

51 On this point, see A. Bickel, The Least Dangerous Branch 244–72 (1962) (discussing politics of Dred Scott v. Sanford. 60 U.S. (19 Haw.) 393 (1857), and the school segregation cases, notably Brown v. Board of Educ., 347 U.S. 483 (1954).

PART IV

Rights

18

Citizenship and Social Class

T.H. Marshall

The invitation to deliver these lectures[1] gave me both personal and professional pleasure. But, whereas my personal response was a sincere and modest appreciation of an honour I had no right to expect, my professional reaction was not modest at all. Sociology, it seemed to me, had every right to claim a share in this annual commemoration of Alfred Marshall, and I considered it a sign of grace that a University which has not yet accepted sociology as an inmate should nevertheless be prepared to welcome her as a visitor. It may be – and the thought is a disturbing one – that sociology is on trial here in my person. If so, I am sure I can rely on you to be scrupulously fair in your judgement, and to regard any merit you may find in my lectures as evidence of the academic value of the subject I profess, while treating everything in them that appears to you paltry, common or ill-conceived as the product of qualities peculiar to myself and not to be found in any of my colleagues.

I will not defend the relevance of my subject to the occasion by claiming Marshall as a sociologist. For, once he had deserted his first loves of metaphysics, ethics and psychology, he devoted his life to the development of economics as an independent science and to the perfection of its own special methods of investigation and analysis. He deliberately chose a path markedly different from that followed by Adam Smith and John Stuart

Mill, and the mood in which he made this choice is indicated in the inaugural lecture which he delivered here in Cambridge in 1885. Speaking of Comte's belief in a unified social science, he said: 'No doubt if that existed economics would gladly find shelter under its wing. But it does not exist; it shows no signs of coming into existence. There is no use in waiting idly for it; we must do what we can with our present resources.'[2] He therefore defended the autonomy and the superiority of the economic method, a superiority due mainly to its use of the measuring rod of money, which 'is so much the best measure of motives that no other can compete with it'.[3]

Marshall was, as you know, an idealist; so much so that Keynes has said of him that he 'was too anxious to do good'.[4] The last thing I wish to do is to claim him for sociology on that account. It is true that some sociologists have suffered from a similar affliction of benevolence, often to the detriment of their intellectual performance, but I should hate to distinguish the economist from the sociologist by saying that the one should be ruled by his head while the other may be swayed by his heart. For every honest sociologist, like every honest economist, knows that the choice of ends or ideals lies outside the field of social science and within the field of social philosophy. But idealism made Marshall passionately eager to put the science of economics at the service of policy by using it – as a science may legitimately be used – to lay bare the full nature and content of the problems with which policy has to deal and to assess the relative efficacy of alternative means for the achievement of given ends. And he realized that, even in the case of what would naturally be regarded as economic problems, the science of economics was not of itself able fully to render these two services. For they involved the consideration of social forces which are as immune to attack by the economist's tape-measure as was the croquet ball to the blows which Alice tried in vain to strike with the head of her flamingo. It was, perhaps, on this account that, in certain moods, Marshall felt a quite unwarranted disappointment at his achievements, and even expressed regret that he had preferred economics to psychology, a science which might have brought him nearer to the pulse and life-blood of society and given him a deeper understanding of human aspirations.

It would be easy to cite many passages in which Marshall was drawn to speak of these elusive factors of whose importance he was so firmly convinced, but I prefer to confine my attention to one essay whose theme comes very near to that which I have chosen for these lectures. It is a paper he read to the Cambridge Reform Club in 1873 on *The Future of the Working Classes*, and it has been republished in the memorial volume edited by Professor Pigou. There are some textual differences between the two editions which, I understand, are to be attributed to corrections made by Marshall himself after the original version had appeared in print as a pamphlet.[5] I was reminded of this essay by my colleague, Professor Phelps Brown, who made use of it in his inaugural lecture.[6] It is equally well suited to my purpose today, because in it Marshall, while examining one facet of the problem of social equality from the point of view of economic cost, came right up to the frontier beyond which lies the territory of sociology, crossed it, and made a brief excursion on the other side. His action could be interpreted as a challenge to sociology to send an emissary to meet him at the frontier, and to join with him in the task of converting no-man's-land into common ground. I have been presumptuous enough to answer the challenge by setting out to travel, as historian and sociologist, towards a point on the economic frontier of that same general theme, the problem of social equality.

In his Cambridge paper Marshall posed the question 'whether there be valid ground for the opinion that the amelioration of the working classes has limits beyond which it cannot pass'. 'The question', he said, 'is not whether all men will ultimately be equal – that they certainly will not – but whether progress may not go on

steadily, if slowly, till, by occupation at least, every man is a gentleman. I hold that it may, and that it will.'[7] His faith was based on the belief that the distinguishing feature of the working classes was heavy and excessive labour, and that the volume of such labour could be greatly reduced. Looking round he found evidence that the skilled artisans, whose labour was not deadening and soul-destroying, were already rising towards the condition which he foresaw as the ultimate achievement of all. They are learning, he said, to value education and leisure more than 'mere increase of wages and material comforts'. They are 'steadily developing independence and a manly respect for themselves and, therefore, a courteous respect for others; they are steadily accepting the private and public duties of a citizen; steadily increasing their grasp of the truth that they are men, and not producing machines. They are steadily becoming gentlemen.'[8] When technical advance has reduced heavy labour to a minimum, and that minimum is divided in small amounts among all, then, 'in so far as the working classes are men who have such excessive work to do, in so far will the working classes have been abolished.'[9]

Marshall realized that he might be accused of adopting the ideas of the socialists, whose works, as he has himself told us, he had, during this period of his life, been studying with great hopes and with greater disappointment. For, he said: 'The picture to be drawn will resemble in some respects those which have been shown to us by the Socialists, that noble set of untutored enthusiasts who attributed to all men an unlimited capacity for those self-forgetting virtues that they found in their own breasts.'[10] His reply was that his system differed fundamentally from socialism in that it would preserve the essentials of a free market. He held, however, that the State would have to make some use of its power of compulsion, if his ideals were to be realized. It must compel children to go to school, because the uneducated cannot appreciate, and therefore freely choose, the good things which distinguish the life of gentlemen from that of the working classes. 'It is bound to compel them and to help them to take the first step upwards; and it is bound to help them, if they will, to make many steps upwards.'[11] Notice that only the first step is compulsory. Free choice takes over as soon as the capacity to choose has been created.

Marshall's paper was built round a sociological

hypothesis and an economic calculation. The calculation provided the answer to his initial question, by showing that world resources and productivity might be expected to prove sufficient to provide the material bases needed to enable every man to be a gentleman. In other words, the cost of providing education for all and of eliminating heavy and excessive labour could be met. There was no impassable limit to the amelioration of the working classes – at least on this side of the point that Marshall described as the goal. In working out these sums Marshall was using the ordinary techniques of the economist, though admittedly he was applying them to a problem which involved a high degree of speculation.

The sociological hypothesis does not lie so completely on the surface. A little excavation is needed to uncover its total shape. The essence of it is contained in the passages I have quoted, but Marshall gives us an additional clue by suggesting that, when we say a man belongs to the working classes, 'we are thinking of the effect that his work produces on him rather than the effect that he produces on his work'.[12] This is certainly not the sort of definition we should expect from an economist, and, in fact, it would hardly be fair to treat it as a definition at all or to subject it to close and critical examination. The phrase was intended to catch the imagination, and to point to the general direction in which Marshall's thoughts were moving. And that direction was away from a quantitative assessment of standards of living in terms of goods consumed and services enjoyed towards a qualitative assessment of life as a whole in terms of the essential elements in civilization or culture. He accepted as right and proper a wide range of quantitative or economic inequality, but condemned the qualitative inequality or difference between the man who was, 'by occupation at least, a gentleman' and the man who was not. We can, I think, without doing violence to Marshall's meaning, replace the word 'gentleman' by the word 'civilized'. For it is clear that he was taking as the standard of civilized life the conditions regarded by his generation as appropriate to a gentleman. We can go on to say that the claim of all to enjoy these conditions is a claim to be admitted to a share in the social heritage, which in turn means a claim to be accepted as full members of the society, that is, as citizens.

Such, I think, is the sociological hypothesis latent in Marshall's essay. It postulates that there

is a kind of basic human equality associated with the concept of full membership of a community – or, as I should say, of citizenship – which is not inconsistent with the inequalities which distinguish the various economic levels in the society. In other words, the inequality of the social class system may be acceptable provided the equality of citizenship is recognized. Marshall did not identify the life of a gentleman with the status of citizenship. To do so would have been to express his ideal in terms of legal rights to which all men were entitled. That, in turn, would have put the responsibility for granting those rights fair and square on the shoulders of the State, and so led, step by step, to acts of State interference which he would have deplored. When he mentioned citizenship as something which skilled artisans learned to appreciate in the course of developing into gentlemen, he mentioned only its duties and not its rights. He thought of it as a way of life growing within a man, not presented to him from without. He recognized only one definite right, the right of children to be educated, and in this case alone did he approve the use of compulsory powers by the State to achieve his object. He could hardly go further without imperilling his own criterion for distinguishing his system from socialism in any form – the preservation of the freedom of the competitive market.

Nevertheless, his sociological hypothesis lies as near to the heart of our problem today as it did three-quarters of a century ago – in fact nearer. The basic human equality of membership, at which I maintain that he hinted, has been enriched with new substance and invested with a formidable array of rights. It has developed far beyond what he foresaw, or would have wished. It has been clearly identified with the status of citizenship. And it is time we examined his hypothesis and posed his questions afresh, to see if the answers are still the same. Is it still true that basic equality, when enriched in substance and embodied in the formal rights of citizenship, is consistent with the inequalities of social class? I shall suggest that our society today assumes that the two are still compatible, so much so that citizenship has itself become, in certain respects, the architect of legitimate social inequality. Is it still true that the basic equality can be created and preserved without invading the freedom of the competitive market? Obviously it is not true. Our modern system is frankly a Socialist system, not one whose authors are, as Marshall was, eager to distinguish it from socialism. But it is equally obvious that the market still functions – within limits. Here is another possible conflict of principles which demands examination. And thirdly, what is the effect of the marked shift of emphasis from duties to rights? Is this an inevitable feature of modern citizenship – inevitable and irreversible? Finally, I want to put Marshall's initial question again in a new form. He asked if there were limits beyond which the amelioration of the working classes could not pass, and he was thinking of limits set by natural resources and productivity. I shall ask whether there appear to be limits beyond which the modern drive towards social equality cannot, or is unlikely to, pass, and I shall be thinking, not of the economic cost (I leave that vital question to the economists), but of the limits inherent in the principles that inspire the drive. But the modern drive towards social equality is, I believe, the latest phase of an evolution of citizenship which has been in continuous progress for some 250 years. My first task, therefore, must be to prepare the ground for an attack on the problems of today by digging for a while in the subsoil of past history.

The Development of Citizenship to the End of the Nineteenth Century

I shall be running true to type as a sociologist if I begin by saying that I propose to divide citizenship into three parts. But the analysis is, in this case, dictated by history even more clearly than by logic. I shall call these three parts, or elements, civil, political and social. The civil element is composed of the rights necessary for individual freedom – liberty of the person, freedom of speech, thought and faith, the right to own property and to conclude valid contracts, and the right to justice. The last is of a different order from the others, because it is the right to defend and assert all one's rights on terms of equality with others and by due process of law. This shows us that the institutions most directly associated with civil rights are the courts of justice. By the political element I mean the right to participate in the exercise of political power, as a member of a body invested with political authority or as an elector of the members of such a body. The corresponding institutions are parliament and councils of local government. By the social element I mean the whole range from the right to a modicum of

economic welfare and security to the right to share to the full in the social heritage and to live the life of a civilized being according to the standards prevailing in the society. The institutions most closely connected with it are the educational system and the social services.[13]

In early times these three strands were wound into a single thread. The rights were blended because the institutions were amalgamated. As Maitland said: 'The further back we trace our history the more impossible it is for us to draw strict lines of demarcation between the various functions of the State: the same institution is a legislative assembly, a governmental council and a court of law . . . Everywhere, as we pass from the ancient to the modern, we see what the fashionable philosophy calls differentiation.'[14] Maitland is speaking here of the fusion of political and civil institutions and rights. But a man's social rights, too, were part of the same amalgam, and derived from the status which also determined the kind of justice he could get and where he could get it, and the way in which he could take part in the administration of the affairs of the community of which he was a member. But this status was not one of citizenship in our modern sense. In feudal society status was the hall-mark of class and the measure of inequality. There was no uniform collection of rights and duties with which all men – noble and common, free and serf – were endowed by virtue of their membership of the society. There was, in this sense, no principle of the equality of citizens to set against the principle of the inequality of classes. In the medieval towns, on the other hand, examples of genuine and equal citizenship can be found. But its specific rights and duties were strictly local, whereas the citizenship whose history I wish to trace is, by definition, national.

Its evolution involved a double process, of fusion and of separation. The fusion was geographical, the separation functional. The first important step dates from the twelfth century, when royal justice was established with effective power to define and defend the civil rights of the individual – such as they then were – on the basis, not of local custom, but of the common law of the land. As institutions the courts were national, but specialized. Parliament followed, concentrating in itself the political powers of national government and shedding all but a small residue of the judicial functions which formerly belonged to the Curia Regis, that 'sort of constitutional protoplasm out of which will in time be evolved the various councils of the crown, the houses of parliament, and the courts of law'.[15] Finally, the social rights which had been rooted in membership of the village community, the town and the gild, were gradually dissolved by economic change until nothing remained but the Poor Law, again a specialized institution which acquired a national foundation, although it continued to be locally administered.

Two important consequences followed. First, when the institutions on which the three elements of citizenship depended parted company, it became possible for each to go its separate way, travelling at its own speed under the direction of its own peculiar principles. Before long they were spread far out along the course, and it is only in the present century, in fact I might say only within the last few months, that the three runners have come abreast of one another.

Secondly, institutions that were national and specialized could not belong so intimately to the life of the social groups they served as those that were local and of a general character. The remoteness of parliament was due to the mere size of its constituency; the remoteness of the courts, to the technicalities of their law and their procedure, which made it necessary for the citizen to employ legal experts to advise him as to the nature of his rights and to help him to obtain them. It has been pointed out again and again that, in the Middle Ages, participation in public affairs was more a duty than a right. Men owed suit and service to the court appropriate to their class and neighbourhood. The court belonged to them and they to it, and they had access to it because it needed them and because they had knowledge of its affairs. But the result of the twin process of fusion and separation was that the machinery giving access to the institutions on which the rights of citizenship depended had to be shaped afresh. In the case of political rights the story is the familiar one of the franchise and the qualifications for membership of parliament. In the case of civil rights the issue hangs on the jurisdiction of the various courts, the privileges of the legal profession, and above all on the liability to meet the costs of litigation. In the case of social rights the centre of the stage is occupied by the Law of Settlement and Removal and the various forms of means test. All this apparatus combined to decide, not merely what rights were recognized in principle, but also to what extent rights recog-

nized in principle could be enjoyed in practice.

When the three elements of citizenship parted company, they were soon barely on speaking terms. So complete was the divorce between them that it is possible, without doing too much violence to historical accuracy, to assign the formative period in the life of each to a different century – civil rights to the eighteenth, political to the nineteenth and social to the twentieth. These periods must, of course, be treated with reasonable elasticity, and there is some evident overlap, especially between the last two.

To make the eighteenth century cover the formative period of civil rights it must be stretched backwards to include Habeas Corpus, the Toleration Act, and the abolition of the censorship of the press; and it must be extended forwards to include Catholic Emancipation, the repeal of the Combination Acts, and the successful end of the battle for the freedom of the press associated with the names of Cobbett and Richard Carlile. It could then be more accurately, but less briefly, described as the period between the Revolution and the first Reform Act. By the end of that period, when political rights made their first infantile attempt to walk in 1832, civil rights had come to man's estate and bore, in most essentials, the appearance that they have today.[16] 'The specific work of the earlier Hanoverian epoch', writes Trevelyan, 'was the establishment of the rule of law; and that law, with all its grave faults, was at least a law of freedom. On that solid foundation all our subsequent reforms were built.'[17] This eighteenth-century achievement, interrupted by the French Revolution and completed after it, was in large measure the work of the courts, both in their daily practice and also in a series of famous cases in some of which they were fighting against parliament in defence of individual liberty. The most celebrated actor in this drama was, I suppose, John Wilkes, and, although we may deplore the absence in him of those noble and saintly qualities which we should like to find in our national heroes, we cannot complain if the cause of liberty is sometimes championed by a libertine.

In the economic field the basic civil right is the right to work, that is to say the right to follow the occupation of one's choice in the place of one's choice, subject only to legitimate demands for preliminary technical training. This right had been denied by both statute and custom; on the one hand by the Elizabethan Statute of Artificers, which confined certain occupations to certain social classes, and on the other by local regulations reserving employment in a town to its own members and by the use of apprenticeship as an instrument of exclusion rather than of recruitment. The recognition of the right involved the formal acceptance of a fundamental change of attitude. The old assumption that local and group monopolies were in the public interest, because 'trade and traffic cannot be maintained or increased without order and government',[18] was replaced by the new assumption that such restrictions were an offence against the liberty of the subject and a menace to the prosperity of the nation. As in the case of the other civil rights, the courts of law played a decisive part in promoting and registering the advance of the new principle. The Common Law was elastic enough for the judges to apply it in a manner which, almost imperceptibly, took account of gradual changes in circumstances and opinion and eventually installed the heresy of the past as the orthodoxy of the present. The Common Law is largely a matter of common sense, as witness the judgement given by Chief Justice Holt in the case of Mayor of Winton *v.* Wilks (1705): 'All people are at liberty to live in Winchester, and how can they be restrained from using the lawful means of living there? Such a custom is an injury to the party and a prejudice to the public.'[19] Custom was one of the two great obstacles to the change. But, when ancient custom in the technical sense was clearly at variance with contemporary custom in the sense of the generally accepted way of life, its defences began to crumble fairly rapidly before the attacks of a Common Law which had, as early as 1614, expressed its abhorrence of 'all monopolies which prohibit any from working in any lawful trade'.[20] The other obstacle was statute law, and the judges struck some shrewd blows even against this doughty opponent. In 1756 Lord Mansfield described the Elizabethan Statute of Artificers as a penal law, in restraint of natural right and contrary to the Common Law of the kingdom. He added that 'the policy upon which the Act was made is, from experience, become doubtful'.[21]

By the beginning of the nineteenth century this principle of individual economic freedom was accepted as axiomatic. You are probably familiar with the passage quoted by the Webbs from the report of the Select Committee of 1811, which states that:

no interference of the legislature with the freedom of trade, or with the perfect liberty of every individual to dispose of his time and of his labour in the way and on the terms which he may judge most conducive to his own interest, can take place without violating general principles of the first importance to the prosperity and happiness of the community.[22]

The repeal of the Elizabethan statutes followed quickly, as the belated recognition of a revolution which had already taken place.

The story of civil rights in their formative period is one of the gradual addition of new rights to a status that already existed and was held to appertain to all adult members of the community – or perhaps one should say to all male members, since the status of women, or at least of married women, was in some important respects peculiar. This democratic, or universal, character of the status arose naturally from the fact that it was essentially the status of freedom, and in seventeenth-century England all men were free. Servile status, or villeinage by blood, had lingered on as a patent anachronism in the days of Elizabeth, but vanished soon afterwards. This change from servile to free labour has been described by Professor Tawney as 'a high landmark in the development both of economic and political society', and as 'the final triumph of the common law' in regions from which it had been excluded for four centuries. Henceforth the English peasant 'is a member of a society in which there is, nominally at least, one law for all men'.[23] The liberty which his predecessors had won by fleeing into the free towns had become his by right. In the towns the terms 'freedom' and 'citizenship' were interchangeable. When freedom became universal, citizenship grew from a local into a national institution.

The story of political rights is different both in time and in character. The formative period began, as I have said, in the early nineteenth century, when the civil rights attached to the status of freedom had already acquired sufficient substance to justify us in speaking of a general status of citizenship. And, when it began, it consisted, not in the creation of new rights to enrich a status already enjoyed by all, but in the granting of old rights to new sections of the population. In the eighteenth century political rights were defective, not in content, but in distribution – defective, that is to say, by the standards of democratic citizenship. The Act of 1832 did little, in a purely quantitative sense, to remedy that defect. After it was passed the voters still amounted to less than one-fifth of the adult male population. The franchise was still a group monopoly, but it had taken the first step towards becoming a monopoly of a kind acceptable to the ideas of nineteenth-century capitalism – a monopoly which could, with some degree of plausibility, be described as open and not closed. A closed group monopoly is one into which no man can force his way by his own efforts; admission is at the pleasure of the existing members of the group. The description fits a considerable part of the borough franchise before 1832; and it is not too wide of the mark when applied to the franchise based on freehold ownership of land. Freeholds are not always to be had for the asking, even if one has the money to buy them, especially in an age in which families look on their lands as the social, as well as the economic, foundation of their existence. Therefore the Act of 1832, by abolishing rotten boroughs and by extending the franchise to leaseholders and occupying tenants of sufficient economic substance, opened the monopoly by recognizing the political claims of those who could produce the normal evidence of success in the economic struggle.

It is clear that, if we maintain that in the nineteenth century citizenship in the form of civil rights was universal, the political franchise was not one of the rights of citizenship. It was the privilege of a limited economic class, whose limits were extended by each successive Reform Act. It can nevertheless be argued that citizenship in this period was not politically meaningless. It did not confer a right, but it recognized a capacity. No sane and law-abiding citizen was debarred by personal status from acquiring and recording a vote. He was free to earn, to save, to buy property or to rent a house, and to enjoy whatever political rights were attached to these economic achievements. His civil rights entitled him, and electoral reform increasingly enabled him, to do this.

It was, as we shall see, appropriate that nineteenth-century capitalist society should treat political rights as a secondary product of civil rights. It was equally appropriate that the twentieth century should abandon this position and attach political rights directly and independently to citizenship as such. This vital change of principle was put into effect when the Act of 1918, by adopting manhood suffrage, shifted the basis of political rights from economic substance to personal status. I say 'manhood' deliberately in order to emphasize the great significance of this reform quite apart from the second, and no less important, reform introduced at the same time – namely the enfranchisement of women. But the Act of 1918 did not fully establish the political equality of all in terms of the rights of citizenship. Remnants of an inequality based on differences of economic substance lingered on until, only last year, plural voting (which had already been reduced to dual voting) was finally abolished.

When I assigned the formative periods of the three elements of citizenship each to a separate century – civil rights to the eighteenth, political to the nineteenth and social to the twentieth – I said that there was a considerable overlap between the last two. I propose to confine what I have to say now about social rights to this overlap, in order that I may complete my historical survey to the end of the nineteenth century, and draw my conclusions from it, before turning my attention to the second half of my subject, a study of our present experiences and their immediate antecedents. In this second act of the drama social rights will occupy the centre of the stage.

The original source of social rights was membership of local communities and functional associations. This source was supplemented and progressively replaced by a Poor Law and a system of wage regulation which were nationally conceived and locally administered. The latter – the system of wage regulation – was rapidly decaying in the eighteenth century, not only because industrial change made it administratively impossible, but also because it was incompatible with the new conception of civil rights in the economic sphere, with its emphasis on the right to work where and at what you pleased under a contract of your own making. Wage regulation infringed this individualist principle of the free contract of employment.

The Poor Law was in a somewhat ambiguous position. Elizabethan legislation had made of it something more than a means for relieving destitution and suppressing vagrancy, and its constructive aims suggested an interpretation of social welfare reminiscent of the more primitive, but more genuine, social rights which it had largely superseded. The Elizabethan Poor Law was, after all, one item in a broad programme of economic planning whose general object was, not to create a new social order, but to preserve the existing one with the minimum of essential change. As the pattern of the old order dissolved under the blows of a competitive economy, and the plan disintegrated, the Poor Law was left high and dry as an isolated survival from which the idea of social rights was gradually drained away. But at the very end of the eighteenth century there occurred a final struggle between the old and the new, between the planned (or patterned) society and the competitive economy. And in this battle citizenship was divided against itself; social rights sided with the old and civil with the new.

In his book *Origins of Our Time*, Karl Polanyi attributes to the Speenhamland system of poor relief an importance which some readers may find surprising. To him it seems to mark and symbolize the end of an epoch. Through it the old order rallied its retreating forces and delivered a spirited attack into the enemy's country. That, at least, is how I should describe its significance in the history of citizenship. The Speenhamland system offered, in effect, a guaranteed minimum wage and family allowances, combined with the right to work or maintenance. That, even by modern standards, is a substantial body of social rights, going far beyond what one might regard as the proper province of the Poor Law. And it was fully realized by the originators of the scheme that the Poor Law was being invoked to do what wage regulation was no longer able to accomplish. For the Poor Law was the last remains of a system which tried to adjust real income to the social needs and status of the citizen and not solely to the market value of his labour. But this attempt to inject an element of social security into the very structure of the wage system through the instrumentality of the Poor Law was doomed to failure, not only because of its disastrous practical consequences, but also because it was utterly obnoxious to the prevailing spirit of the times.

In this brief episode of our history we see the Poor Law as the aggressive champion of the social rights of citizenship. In the succeeding phase we find the attacker driven back far behind his original position. By the Act of 1834 the Poor Law renounced all claim to trespass on the territory of the wages system, or to interfere with the forces of the free market. It offered relief only to those who, through age or sickness, were incapable of continuing the battle, and to those other weaklings who gave up the struggle, admitted defeat, and cried for mercy. The tentative move towards the concept of social security was reversed. But

more than that, the minimal social rights that remained were detached from the status of citizenship. The Poor Law treated the claims of the poor, not as an integral part of the rights of the citizen, but as an alternative to them – as claims which could be met only if the claimants ceased to be citizens in any true sense of the word. For paupers forfeited in practice the civil right of personal liberty, by internment in the workhouse, and they forfeited by law any political rights they might possess. This disability of defranchisement remained in being until 1918, and the significance of its final removal has, perhaps, not been fully appreciated. The stigma which clung to poor relief expressed the deep feelings of a people who understood that those who accepted relief must cross the road that separated the community of citizens from the outcast company of the destitute.

The Poor Law is not an isolated example of this divorce of social rights from the status of citizenship. The early Factory Acts show the same tendency. Although in fact they led to an improvement of working conditions and a reduction of working hours to the benefit of all employed in the industries to which they applied, they meticulously refrained from giving this protection directly to the adult male – the citizen *par excellence*. And they did so out of respect for his status as a citizen, on the grounds that enforced protective measures curtailed the civil right to conclude a free contract of employment. Protection was confined to women and children, and champions of women's rights were quick to detect the implied insult. Women were protected because they were not citizens. If they wished to enjoy full and responsible citizenship, they must forgo protection. By the end of the nineteenth century such arguments had become obsolete, and the factory code had become one of the pillars in the edifice of social rights.

The history of education shows superficial resemblances to that of factory legislation. In both cases the nineteenth century was, for the most part, a period in which the foundations of social rights were laid, but the principle of social rights as an integral part of the status of citizenship was either expressly denied or not definitely admitted. But there are significant differences. Education, as Marshall recognized when he singled it out as a fit object of State action, is a service of a unique kind. It is easy to say that the recognition of the right of children to be educated does not affect the status of citizenship any more than does the recognition of the right of children to be protected from overwork and dangerous machinery, simply because children, by definition, cannot be citizens. But such a statement is misleading. The education of children has a direct bearing on citizenship, and, when the State guarantees that all children shall be educated, it has the requirements and the nature of citizenship definitely in mind. It is trying to stimulate the growth of citizens in the making. The right to education is a genuine social right of citizenship, because the aim of education during childhood is to shape the future adult. Fundamentally it should be regarded, not as the right of the child to go to school, but as the right of the adult citizen to have been educated. And there is here no conflict with civil rights as interpreted in an age of individualism. For civil rights are designed for use by reasonable and intelligent persons, who have learned to read and write. Education is a necessary prerequisite of civil freedom.

But, by the end of the nineteenth century, elementary education was not only free, it was compulsory. This signal departure from *laissez faire* could, of course, be justified on the grounds that free choice is a right only for mature minds, that children are naturally subject to discipline, and that parents cannot be trusted to do what is in the best interests of their children. But the principle goes deeper than that. We have here a personal right combined with a public duty to exercise the right. Is the public duty imposed merely for the benefit of the individual – because children cannot fully appreciate their own interests and parents may be unfit to enlighten them? I hardly think that this can be an adequate explanation. It was increasingly recognized, as the nineteenth century wore on, that political democracy needed an educated electorate, and that scientific manufacture needed educated workers and technicians. The duty to improve and civilize oneself is therefore a social duty, and not merely a personal one, because the social health of a society depends upon the civilization of its members. And a community that enforces this duty has begun to realize that its culture is an organic unity and its civilization a national heritage. It follows that the growth of public elementary education during the nineteenth century was the first decisive step on the road to the re-establishment of the social rights of citizenship in the twentieth.

When Marshall read his paper to the Cambridge Reform Club, the State was just preparing to shoulder the responsibility he attributed to it when he said that it was 'bound to compel them (the children) and help them to take the first step upwards'. But this would not go far towards realizing his ideal of making every man a gentleman, nor was that in the least the intention. And as yet there was little sign of any desire 'to help them, if they will, to make many steps upwards'. The idea was in the air, but it was not a cardinal point of policy. In the early nineties the L.C.C., through its Technical Education Board, instituted a scholarship system which Beatrice Webb obviously regarded as epoch-making. For she wrote of it:

> In its popular aspect this was an educational ladder of unprecedented dimensions. It was, indeed, among educational ladders the most gigantic in extent, the most elaborate in its organization of 'intakes' and promotions, and the most diversified in kinds of excellence selected and in types of training provided that existed anywhere in the world.[24]

The enthusiasm of these words enables us to see how far we have advanced our standards since those days.

The Early Impact of Citizenship on Social Class

So far my aim has been to trace in outline the development of citizenship in England to the end of the nineteenth century. For this purpose I have divided citizenship into three elements, civil, political and social. I have tried to show that civil rights came first, and were established in something like their modern form before the first Reform Act was passed in 1832. Political rights came next, and their extension was one of the main features of the nineteenth century, although the principle of universal political citizenship was not recognized until 1918. Social rights, on the other hand, sank to vanishing point in the eighteenth and early nineteenth centuries. Their revival began with the development of public elementary education, but it was not until the twentieth century that they attained to equal partnership with the other two elements in citizenship.

I have as yet said nothing about social class,

and I should explain here that social class occupies a secondary position in my theme. I do not propose to embark on the long and difficult task of examining its nature and analysing its components. Time would not allow me to do justice to so formidable a subject. My primary concern is with citizenship, and my special interest is in its impact on social inequality. I shall discuss the nature of social class only so far as is necessary for the pursuit of this special interest. I have paused in the narrative at the end of the nineteenth century because I believe that the impact of citizenship on social inequality after that date was fundamentally different from what it had been before it. That statement is not likely to be disputed. It is the exact nature of the difference that is worth exploring. Before going any further, therefore, I shall try to draw some general conclusions about the impact of citizenship on social inequality in the earlier of the two periods.

Citizenship is a status bestowed on those who are full members of a community. All who possess the status are equal with respect to the rights and duties with which the status is endowed. There is no universal principle that determines what those rights and duties shall be, but societies in which citizenship is a developing institution create an image of an ideal citizenship against which achievement can be measured and towards which aspiration can be directed. The urge forward along the path thus plotted is an urge towards a fuller measure of equality, an enrichment of the stuff of which the status is made and an increase in the number of those on whom the status is bestowed. Social class, on the other hand, is a system of inequality. And it too, like citizenship, can be based on a set of ideals, beliefs and values. It is therefore reasonable to expect that the impact of citizenship on social class should take the form of a conflict between opposing principles. If I am right in my contention that citizenship has been a developing institution in England at least since the latter part of the seventeenth century, then it is clear that its growth coincides with the rise of capitalism, which is a system, not of equality, but of inequality. Here is something that needs explaining. How is it that these two opposing principles could grow and flourish side by side in the same soil? What made it possible for them to be reconciled with one another and to become, for a time at least, allies instead of antagonists? The question is a pertinent one, for it is clear that, in the twentieth century, citizenship and the capitalist class system have been at war.

It is at this point that a closer scrutiny of social class becomes necessary. I cannot attempt to examine all its many and varied forms, but there is one broad distinction between two different types of class which is particularly relevant to my argument. In the first of these class is based on a hierarchy of status, and the difference between one class and another is expressed in terms of legal rights and of established customs which have the essential binding character of law. In its extreme form such a system divides a society into a number of distinct, hereditary human species – patricians, plebeians, serfs, slaves and so forth. Class is, as it were, an institution in its own right, and the whole structure has the quality of a plan, in the sense that it is endowed with meaning and purpose and accepted as a natural order. The civilization at each level is an expression of this meaning and of this natural order, and differences between social levels are not differences in standard of living, because there is no common standard by which they can be measured. Nor are there any rights – at least none of any significance – which all share in common.[25] The impact of citizenship on such a system was bound to be profoundly disturbing, and even destructive. The rights with which the general status of citizenship was invested were extracted from the hierarchical status system of social class, robbing it of its essential substance. The equality implicit in the concept of citizenship, even though limited in content, undermined the inequality of the class system, which was in principle a total inequality. National justice and a law common to all must inevitably weaken and eventually destroy class justice, and personal freedom, as a universal birthright, must drive out serfdom. No subtle argument is needed to show that citizenship is incompatible with medieval feudalism.

Social class of the second type is not so much an institution in its own right as a by-product of other institutions. Although we may still refer to 'social status', we are stretching the term beyond its strict technical meaning when we do so. Class differences are not established and defined by the laws and customs of the society (in the medieval sense of that phrase), but emerge from the interplay of a variety of factors related to the institutions of property and education and the structure of the national economy. Class cultures dwindle to a minimum, so that it becomes possible, though admittedly not wholly satisfactory, to measure the different levels of economic welfare by reference to a common standard of living. The working classes, instead of inheriting a distinctive though simple culture, are provided with a cheap and shoddy imitation of a civilization that has become national.

It is true that class still functions. Social inequality is regarded as necessary and purposeful. It provides the incentive to effort and designs the distribution of power. But there is no overall pattern of inequality, in which an appropriate value is attached, *a priori*, to each social level. Inequality therefore, though necessary, may become excessive. As Patrick Colquhoun said, in a much-quoted passage: 'Without a large proportion of poverty there could be no riches, since riches are the offspring of labour, while labour can result only from a state of poverty. . . . Poverty therefore is a most necessary and indispensable ingredient in society, without which nations and communities could not exist in a state of civilization.'[26] But Colquhoun, while accepting poverty, deplored 'indigence', or, as we should say, destitution. By 'poverty' he meant the situation of a man who, owing to lack of any economic reserves, is obliged to work, and to work hard, in order to live. By 'indigence' he meant the situation of a family which lacks the minimum necessary for decent living. The system of inequality which allowed the former to exist as a driving force inevitably produced a certain amount of the latter as well. Colquhoun, and other humanitarians, regretted this and sought means to alleviate the suffering it caused. But they did not question the justice of the system of inequality as a whole. It could be argued, in defence of its justice, that, although poverty might be necessary, it was not necessary that any particular family should remain poor, or quite as poor as it was. The more you look on wealth as conclusive proof of merit, the more you incline to regard poverty as evidence of failure — but the penalty for failure may seem to be greater than the offence warrants. In such circumstances it is natural that the more unpleasant features of inequality should be treated, rather irresponsibly, as a nuisance, like the black smoke that used to pour unchecked from our factory chimneys. And so in time, as the social conscience stirs to life, class-abatement, like smoke-abatement, becomes a desirable aim to be pursued as far as is compatible with the continued efficiency of the social machine.

But class-abatement in this form was not an attack on the class system. On the contrary it aimed, often quite consciously, at making the class system less vulnerable to attack by alleviating its less defensible consequences. It raised the floor-level in the basement of the social edifice, and perhaps made it rather more hygienic than it was before. But it remained a basement, and the upper stories of the building were unaffected. And the benefits received by the unfortunate did not flow from an enrichment of the status of citizenship. Where they were given officially by the State, this was done by measures which, as I have said, offered alternatives to the rights of citizenship, rather than additions to them. But the major part of the task was left to private charity, and it was the general, though not universal, view of charitable bodies that those who received their help had no personal right to claim it.

Nevertheless it is true that citizenship, even in its early forms, was a principle of equality, and that during this period it was a developing institution. Starting at the point where all men were free and, in theory, capable of enjoying rights, it grew by enriching the body of rights which they were capable of enjoying. But these rights did not conflict with the inequalities of capitalist society; they were, on the contrary, necessary to the maintenance of that particular form of inequality. The explanation lies in the fact that the core of citizenship at this stage was composed of civil rights. And civil rights were indispensable to a competitive market economy. They gave to each man, as part of his individual status, the power to engage as an independent unit in the economic struggle and made it possible to deny to him social protection on the ground that he was equipped with the means to protect himself. Maine's famous dictum that 'the movement of the progressive societies has hitherto been a movement from Status to Contract'[27] expresses a profound truth which has been elaborated, with varying terminology, by many sociologists, but it requires qualification. For both status and contract are present in all but the most primitive societies. Maine himself admitted this when, later in the same book, he wrote that the earliest feudal communities, as contrasted with their archaic predecessors, 'were neither bound together by mere sentiment nor recruited by a fiction. The tie which united them was Contract.'[28] But the contractual element in feudalism co-existed with a class system based on status and, as contract hardened into custom, it helped to perpetuate class status. Custom retained the form of mutual undertakings, but not the reality of a free agreement. Modern contract did not grow out of feudal contract; it marks a new development to whose progress feudalism was an obstacle that had to be swept aside. For modern contract is essentially an agreement between men who are free and equal in status, though not necessarily in power. Status was not eliminated from the social system. Differential status, associated with class, function and family, was replaced by the single uniform status of citizenship, which provided the foundation of equality on which the structure of inequality could be built.

When Maine wrote, this status was clearly an aid, and not a menace, to capitalism and the free-market economy, because it was dominated by civil rights, which confer the legal capacity to strive for the things one would like to possess but do not guarantee the possession of any of them. A property right is not a right to possess property, but a right to acquire it, if you can, and to protect it, if you can get it. But, if you use these arguments to explain to a pauper that his property rights are the same as those of a millionaire, he will probably accuse you of quibbling. Similarly, the right to freedom of speech has little real substance if, from lack of education, you have nothing to say that is worth saying, and no means of making yourself heard if you say it. But these blatant inequalities are not due to defects in civil rights, but to lack of social rights, and social rights in the mid-nineteenth century were in the doldrums. The Poor Law was an aid, not a menace, to capitalism, because it relieved industry of all social responsibility outside the contract of employment, while sharpening the edge of competition in the labour market. Elementary schooling was also an aid, because it increased the value of the worker without educating him above his station.

But it would be absurd to contend that the civil rights enjoyed in the eighteenth and nineteenth centuries were free from defects, or that they were as egalitarian in practice as they professed to be in principle. Equality before the law did not exist. The right was there, but the remedy might frequently prove to be out of reach. The barriers between rights and remedies were of two kinds: the first arose from class prejudice and partiality, the second from the automatic effects of the unequal distribution of wealth, working through the price system. Class prejudice, which undoubtedly coloured the whole administration of justice in the eighteenth century, cannot be eliminated by law, but only by social education and the building of a tradition of impartiality. This is a slow and difficult process, which presupposes a change in the climate of thought throughout the upper ranks of society. But it is a process which I think it is fair to say has been successfully accomplished, in the sense that the tradition of impartiality as between social classes is firmly established in our civil justice. And it is interesting that this should have happened without any fundamental change in the class structure of the legal profession. We have no exact knowledge on this point, but I doubt whether the picture has radically altered since Professor Ginsberg found that the proportion of those admitted to Lincoln's Inn whose fathers were wage-earners had risen from 0.4 per cent in 1904–8 to 1.8 per cent in 1923–7, and that at this latter date nearly 72 per cent were sons of professional men, high-ranking businessmen and gentlemen.[29] The decline of class prejudice as a barrier to the full enjoyment of rights is, therefore, due less to the dilution of class monopoly in the legal profession than to the spread in all classes of a more humane and realistic sense of social equality.

It is interesting to compare with this the corresponding development in the field of political rights. Here too class prejudice, expressed through the intimidation of the lower classes by the upper, prevented the free exercise of the right to vote by the newly enfranchised. In this case a practical remedy was available, in the secret ballot. But that was not enough. Social education, and a change of mental climate, were needed as well. And, even when voters felt free from undue influence, it still took some time to break down the idea, prevalent in the working as well as other classes, that the representatives of the people, and still more the members of the government, should be drawn from among the *élites* who were born, bred and educated for leadership. Class monopoly in politics, unlike class monopoly in law, has definitely been overthrown. Thus, in these two fields, the same goal has been reached by rather different paths.

The removal of the second obstacle, the effects of the unequal distribution of wealth, was technically a simple matter in the case of political rights, because it costs little or nothing to register a vote.

Nevertheless, wealth can be used to influence an election, and a series of measures was adopted to reduce this influence. The earlier ones, which go back to the seventeenth century, were directed against bribery and corruption, but the later ones, especially from 1883 onwards, had the wider aim of limiting election expenses in general, in order that candidates of unequal wealth might fight on more or less equal terms. The need for such equalizing measures has now greatly diminished, since working-class candidates can get financial support from party and other funds. Restrictions which prevent competitive extravagance are, therefore, probably welcomed by all. It remained to open the House of Commons to men of all classes, regardless of wealth, first by abolishing the property qualification for members, and then by introducing payment of members in 1911.

It has proved far more difficult to achieve similar results in the field of civil rights, because litigation, unlike voting, is very expensive. Court fees are not high, but counsel's fees and solicitor's charges may mount up to very large sums indeed. Since a legal action takes the form of a contest, each party feels that his chances of winning will be improved if he secures the services of better champions than those employed on the other side. There is, of course, some truth in this, but not as much as is popularly believed. But the effect in litigation, as in elections, is to introduce an element of competitive extravagance which makes it difficult to estimate in advance what the costs of an action will amount to. In addition, our system by which costs are normally awarded to the winner increases the risk and the uncertainty. A man of limited means, knowing that, if he loses, he will have to pay his opponent's costs (after they have been pruned by the Taxing Master) as well as his own, may easily be frightened into accepting an unsatisfactory settlement, especially if his opponent is wealthy enough not to be bothered by any such considerations. And even if he wins, the taxed costs he recovers will usually be less than his actual expenditure, and often considerably less. So that, if he has been induced to fight his case expensively, the victory may not be worth the price paid.

What, then, has been done to remove these barriers to the full and equal exercise of civil rights? Only one thing of real substance, the establishment in 1846 of the County Courts to provide cheap justice for the common people. This important innovation has had a profound and beneficial effect on our legal system, and done much to develop a proper sense of the importance of the case brought by the small man – which is often a very big case by his standards. But County Court costs are not negligible, and the jurisdiction of the County Courts is limited. The second major step taken was the development of a poor person's procedure, under which a small fraction of the poorer members of the community could sue *in forma pauperis*, practically free of all cost, being assisted by the gratuitous and voluntary services of the legal profession. But, as the income limit was extremely low (£2 a week since 1919), and the procedure did not apply in the County Courts, it has had little effect except in matrimonial causes. The supplementary service of free legal advice was, until recently, provided by the unaided efforts of voluntary bodies. But the problem has not been overlooked, nor the reality of the defects in our system denied. It has attracted increasing attention during the last hundred years. The machinery of the Royal Commission and the Committee has been used repeatedly, and some reforms of procedure have resulted. Two such Committees are at work now, but it would be most improper for me to make any reference to their deliberations.[30] A third, which started earlier, issued a report on which is based the Legal Aid and Advice Bill laid before parliament just three months ago.[31] This is a bold measure, going far beyond anything previously attempted for the assistance of the poorer litigants, and I shall have more to say about it later on.

It is apparent from the events I have briefly narrated that there developed, in the latter part of the nineteenth century, a growing interest in equality as a principle of social justice and an appreciation of the fact that the formal recognition of an equal capacity for rights was not enough. In theory even the complete removal of all the barriers that separated civil rights from their remedies would not have interfered with the principles or the class structure of the capitalist system. It would, in fact, have created a situation which many supporters of the competitive market economy falsely assumed to be already in existence. But in practice the attitude of mind which inspired the efforts to remove these barriers grew out of a conception of equality which overstepped these narrow limits, the conception of equal social worth, not merely of equal natural rights. Thus although citizenship, even by the end of the nineteenth century, had done little to reduce social inequality, it had helped to guide progress into the path which led directly to the egalitarian policies of the twentieth century.

It also had an integrating effect, or, at least, was an important ingredient in an integrating process. In a passage I quoted just now Maine spoke of pre-feudal societies as bound together by a sentiment and recruited by a fiction. He was referring to kinship, or the fiction of common descent. Citizenship requires a bond of a different kind, a direct sense of community membership based on loyalty to a civilization which is a common possession. It is a loyalty of free men endowed with rights and protected by a common law. Its growth is stimulated both by the struggle to win those rights and by their enjoyment when won. We see this clearly in the eighteenth century, which saw the birth, not only of modern civil rights, but also of modern national consciousness. The familiar instruments of modern democracy were fashioned by the upper classes and then handed down, step by step, to the lower: political journalism for the intelligentsia was followed by newspapers for all who could read, public meetings, propaganda campaigns and associations for the furtherance of public causes. Repressive measures and taxes were quite unable to stop the flood. And with it came a patriotic nationalism, expressing the unity underlying these controversial outbursts. How deep or widespread this was it is difficult to say, but there can be no doubt about the vigour of its outward manifestation. We still use those typically eighteenth-century songs, 'God Save the King' and 'Rule Britannia', but we omit the passages which would offend our modern, and more modest, sensibilities. This jingo patriotism, and the 'popular and parliamentary agitation' which Temperley found to be 'the main factor in causing the war' of Jenkins's era,[32] were new phenomena in which can be recognized the first small trickle which grew into the broad stream of the national war efforts of the twentieth century.

This growing national consciousness, this awakening public opinion, and these first stirrings of a sense of community membership and common heritage did not have any material effect on class structure and social inequality for the simple and obvious reason that, even at the end of the nineteenth century, the mass of the working people did not wield effective political power. By that time the franchise was fairly wide, but those who had recently received the vote had not yet learned how to use it. The political rights of citizenship, unlike the civil rights, were full of potential danger to the capitalist system, although those who were cautiously extending them down the social scale probably did not realize quite how great the danger was. They could hardly be expected to foresee what vast changes could be brought about by the peaceful use of political power, without a violent and bloody revolution. The Planned Society and the Welfare State had not yet risen over the horizon or come within the view of the practical politician. The foundations of the market economy and the contractual system seemed strong enough to stand against any probable assault. In fact, there were some grounds for expecting that the working classes, as they became educated, would accept the basic principles of the system and be content to rely for their protection and progress on the civil rights of citizenship, which contained no obvious menace to competitive capitalism. Such a view was encouraged by the fact that one of the main achievements of political power in the later nineteenth century was the recognition of the right of collective bargaining. This meant that social progress was being sought by strengthening civil rights, not by creating social rights; through the use of contract in the open market, not through a minimum wage and social security.

But this interpretation underrates the significance of this extension of civil rights in the economic sphere. For civil rights were in origin intensely individual, and that is why they harmonized with the individualistic phase of capitalism. By the device of incorporation groups were enabled to act legally as individuals. This important development did not go unchallenged, and limited liability was widely denounced as an infringement of individual responsibility. But the position of trade unions was even more anomalous, because they did not seek or obtain incorporation. They can, therefore, exercise vital civil rights collectively on behalf of their members without formal collective responsibility, while the individual responsibility of the workers in relation to contract is largely unenforceable. These civil rights became, for the workers, an instrument for raising their social and economic status, that is to say, for establishing the claim that they, as citizens, were entitled to certain social rights. But the normal method of establishing social rights is by the exercise of political power, for social rights imply an absolute right to a certain standard of civilization which is conditional only on the discharge of the general duties of citizenship. Their content does not depend on the economic value of the individual claimant. There is therefore a significant difference between a genuine collective bargain through which economic forces in a free market seek to achieve equilibrium and the use of collective civil rights to assert basic claims to the elements of social justice. Thus the acceptance of collective bargaining was not simply a natural extension of civil rights; it represented the transfer of an important process from the political to the civil sphere of citizenship. But 'transfer' is, perhaps, a misleading term, for at the time when this happened the workers either did not possess, or had not yet learned to use, the political right of the franchise. Since then they have obtained and made full use of that right. Trade unionism has, therefore, created a secondary system of industrial citizenship parallel with and supplementary to the system of political citizenship.

It is interesting to compare this development with the history of parliamentary representation. In the early parliaments, says Pollard, 'representation was no wise regarded as a means of expressing individual right or forwarding individual interests. It was communities, not individuals, who were represented.'[33] And, looking at the position on the eve of the Reform Act of 1918, he added: 'Parliament, instead of representing communities or families, is coming to represent nothing but individuals.'[34] A system of manhood and womanhood suffrage treats the vote as the voice of the individual. Political parties organize these voices for group action, but they do so nationally and not on the basis of function, locality or interest. In the case of civil rights the movement has been in the opposite direction, not from the representation of communities to that of individuals, but from the representation of individuals to that of communities. And Pollard makes another point. It was a characteristic of the early parliamentary system, he says, that the representatives were those who had the time, the means and the inclination to do the job. Election by a majority of votes and strict accountability to the electors was not essential. Constituencies did not instruct their members, and election promises were unknown. Members 'were elected to bind their constituents, and not to be bound by them'.[35] It is not too fanciful to suggest that some of these

features are reproduced in modern trade unions, though, of course, with many profound differences. One of these is that trade union officials do not undertake an onerous unpaid job, but enter on a remunerative career. This remark is not meant to be offensive, and, indeed, it would hardly be seemly for a university professor to criticize a public institution on the ground that its affairs are managed largely by its salaried employees.

All that I have said so far has been by way of introduction to my main task. I have not tried to put before you new facts culled by laborious research. The limit of my ambition has been to regroup familiar facts in a pattern which may make them appear to some of you in a new light. I thought it necessary to do this in order to prepare the ground for the more difficult, speculative and controversial study of the contemporary scene, in which the leading role is played by the social rights of citizenship. It is to the impact of these on social class that I must now turn my attention.

Social Rights in the Twentieth Century

The period of which I have hitherto been speaking was one during which the growth of citizenship, substantial and impressive though it was, had little direct effect on social inequality. Civil rights gave legal powers whose use was drastically curtailed by class prejudice and lack of economic opportunity. Political rights gave potential power whose exercise demanded experience, organization and a change of ideas as to the proper functions of government. All these took time to develop. Social rights were at a minimum and were not woven into the fabric of citizenship. The common purpose of statutory and voluntary effort was to abate the nuisance of poverty without disturbing the pattern of inequality of which poverty was the most obviously unpleasant consequence.

A new period opened at the end of the nineteenth century, conveniently marked by Booth's survey of Life and Labour of the People in London and the Royal Commission on the Aged Poor. It saw the first big advance in social rights, and this involved significant changes in the egalitarian principle as expressed in citizenship. But there were other forces at work as well. A rise of money incomes unevenly distributed over the social classes altered the economic distance which separated these classes from one another, diminishing the gap between skilled and unskilled labour and between skilled labour and non-manual workers, while the steady increase in small savings blurred the class distinction between the capitalist and the propertyless proletarian. Secondly, a system of direct taxation, ever more steeply graduated, compressed the whole scale of disposable incomes. Thirdly, mass production for the home market and a growing interest on the part of industry in the needs and tastes of the common people enabled the less well-to-do to enjoy a material civilization which differed less markedly in quality from that of the rich than it had ever done before. All this profoundly altered the setting in which the progress of citizenship took place. Social integration spread from the sphere of sentiment and patriotism into that of material enjoyment. The components of a civilized and cultured life, formerly the monopoly of the few, were brought progressively within reach of the many, who were encouraged thereby to stretch out their hands towards those that still eluded their grasp. The diminution of inequality strengthened the demand for its abolition, at least with regard to the essentials of social welfare.

These aspirations have in part been met by incorporating social rights in the status of citizenship and thus creating a universal right to real income which is not proportionate to the market value of the claimant. Class-abatement is still the aim of social rights, but it has acquired a new meaning. It is no longer merely an attempt to abate the obvious nuisance of destitution in the lowest ranks of society. It has assumed the guise of action modifying the whole pattern of social inequality. It is no longer content to raise the floor-level in the basement of the social edifice, leaving the superstructure as it was. It has begun to remodel the whole building, and it might even end by converting a skyscraper into a bungalow. It is therefore important to consider whether any such ultimate aim is implicit in the nature of this development, or whether, as I put it at the outset, there are natural limits to the contemporary drive towards greater social and economic equality. To answer this question I must survey and analyse the social services of the twentieth century.

I said earlier that the attempts made to remove the barriers between civil rights and their remedies gave evidence of a new attitude towards the problem of equality. I can therefore conveniently begin my survey by looking at the latest example

of such an attempt, the Legal Aid and Advice Bill, which offers a social service designed to strengthen the civil right of the citizen to settle his disputes in a court of law. It also brings us face to face at once with one of the major issues of our problem, the possibility of combining in one system the two principles of social justice and market price. The State is not prepared to make the administration of justice free for all. One reason for this – though not, of course, the only one – is that costs perform a useful function by discouraging frivolous litigation and encouraging the acceptance of reasonable settlements. If all actions which are started went to trial, the machinery of justice would break down. Also, the amount that it is appropriate to spend on a case depends largely on what it is worth to the parties, and of this, it is argued, they themselves are the only judges. It is very different in a health service, where the seriousness of the disease and the nature of the treatment required can be objectively assessed with very little reference to the importance the patient attaches to it. Nevertheless, though some payment is demanded, it must not take a form which deprives the litigant of his right to justice or puts him at a disadvantage *vis-à-vis* his opponent.

The main provisions of the scheme are as follows. The service will be confined to an economic class – those whose disposable income and capital do not exceed £420 and £500 respectively.[36] 'Disposable' means the balance after considerable deductions have been allowed for dependants, rent, ownership of house and tools, and so forth. The maximum contributable by the litigant towards his own costs is limited to half the excess of his disposable income over £156 plus the excess of his disposable capital above £75. His liability towards the costs of the other side, if he loses, is entirely in the discretion of the court. He will have the professional assistance of solicitor and counsel drawn from a panel of volunteers, and they will be remunerated for their services, in the High Court (and above) at rates 15 per cent below what the Taxing Master would regard as reasonable in the free market, and in the County Court according to uniform scales not yet fixed.

The scheme, it will be seen, makes use of the principles of the income limit and the means test, which have just been abandoned in the other major social services. And the means test will be applied, or the maximum contribution assessed, by the National Assistance Board, whose officers, in addition to making the allowances prescribed in the regulations, 'will have general discretionary powers to enable them to deduct from income any sums which they normally disregard in dealing with an application for assistance under the National Assistance Act, 1948'.[37] It will be interesting to see whether this link with the old Poor Law will make Legal Aid unsavoury to many of those entitled to avail themselves of it, who will include persons with gross incomes up to £600 or £700 a year. But, quite apart from the agents employed to enforce it, the reason for introducing a means test is clear. The price payable for the service of the court and of the legal profession plays a useful part by testing the urgency of the demand. It is, therefore, to be retained. But the impact of price on demand is to be made less unequal by adjusting the bill to the income out of which it must be met. The method of adjustment resembles the operation of a progressive tax. If we consider income only, and ignore capital, we see that a man with a disposable income of £200 would be liable to contribute £22, or 11 per cent of that income, and a man with a disposable income of £420 would have a maximum contribution of £132, or over 31 per cent of that income.

A system of this kind may work quite well (assuming the scale of adjustment to be satisfactory) provided the market price of the service is a reasonable one for the smallest income that does not qualify for assistance. Then the price scale can taper down from this pivotal point until it vanishes where the income is too small to pay anything. No awkward gap will appear at the top between the assisted and the unassisted. The method is in use for State scholarships to universities. The cost to be met in this case is the standardized figure for maintenance plus fees. Deductions are made from the gross income of the parents on lines similar to those proposed for Legal Aid, except that income tax is not deducted. The resulting figure is known as the 'scale income'. This is applied to a table which shows the parental contribution at each point on the scale. Scale incomes up to £600 pay nothing, and the ceiling above which parents must pay the full costs, without subsidy, is £1,500. A Working Party has recently recommended that the ceiling should be raised 'to at least £2,000' (before tax),[38] which is a fairly generous poverty line for a social service. It is not unreasonable to assume that, at that income level, the market cost of a university education can be met by the family without undue hardship.

The Legal Aid Scheme will probably work in much the same way for County Court cases, where costs are moderate. Those with incomes at the top of the scale will not normally receive any subsidy towards their own costs, even if they lose their case. The contribution they can be called on to make out of their own funds will usually be enough to cover them. They will thus be in the same position as those just outside the scheme, and no awkward gap will appear. Litigants coming within the scheme will, however, get professional legal assistance at a controlled and reduced price, and that is in itself a valuable privilege. But in a heavy High Court case the maximum contribution of the man at the top of the scale would be far from sufficient to meet his own costs if he was defeated. His liability under the scheme could, therefore, be many times less than that of a man, just outside the scheme, who fought and lost an identical action. In such cases the gap may be very noticeable, and this is particularly serious in litigation, which takes the form of a contest. The contest may be between an assisted litigant and an unassisted one, and they will be fighting under different rules. One will be protected by the principle of social justice, while the other is left to the mercy of the market and the ordinary obligations imposed by contract and the rules of the court. A measure of class-abatement may, in some cases, create a form of class privilege. Whether this will happen depends largely on the content of regulations which have not yet been issued, and on the way in which the court uses its discretion in awarding costs against assisted litigants who lose their actions.

This particular difficulty could be overcome if the system were made universal, or nearly so, by carrying the scale of maximum contributions up to much higher income levels. In other words, the means test could be preserved, but the income limit dropped. But this would mean bringing all, or practically all, legal practitioners into the scheme, and subjecting them to controlled prices for their services. It would amount almost to the nationalization of the profession, so far as litigation is concerned, or so it would probably appear to the barristers, whose profession is inspired by a strong spirit of individualism. And the disappearance of private practice would deprive the Taxing Masters of a standard by which to fix the controlled price.

I have chosen this example to illustrate some of the difficulties that arise when one tries to combine the principles of social equality and the price system. Differential price adjustment by scale to different incomes is one method of doing this. It was widely used by doctors and hospitals until the National Health Service made this unnecessary. It frees real income, in certain forms, from its dependence on money income. If the principle were universally applied, differences in money income would become meaningless. The same result could be achieved by making all gross incomes equal, or by reducing unequal gross incomes to equal net incomes by taxation. Both processes have been going on, up to a point. Both are checked by the need to preserve differential incomes as a source of economic incentive. But, when different methods of doing much the same thing are combined, it may be possible to carry the process much further without upsetting the economic machine, because their various consequences are not easily added together, and the total effect may escape notice in the general confusion. And we must remember that gross money incomes provide the measuring-rod by which we traditionally assess social and economic achievement and prestige. Even if they lost all meaning in terms of real income, they might still function, like orders and decorations, as spurs to effort and badges of success.

But I must return to my survey of the social services. The most familiar principle in use is not, of course, the scaled price (which I have just been discussing), but the guaranteed minimum. The State guarantees a minimum supply of certain essential goods and services (such as medical attention and supplies, shelter and education) or a minimum money income available to be spent on essentials – as in the case of Old Age Pensions, insurance benefits and family allowances. Anyone able to exceed the guaranteed minimum out of his own resources is at liberty to do so. Such a system looks, on the face of it, like a more generous version of class-abatement in its original form. It raises the floor-level at the bottom, but does not automatically flatten the superstructure. But its effects need closer examination.

The degree of equalization achieved depends on four things – whether the benefit is offered to all or to a limited class; whether it takes the form of money payment or service rendered; whether the minimum is high or low; and how the money to pay for the benefit is raised. Cash benefits sub-ject to income limit and means test had a simple and obvious equalizing effect. They achieved class-abatement in the early and limited sense of the term. The aim was to ensure that all citizens should attain at least to the prescribed minimum, either by their own resources or with assistance if they could not do it without. The benefit was given only to those who needed it, and thus inequalities at the bottom of the scale were ironed out. The system operated in its simplest and most unadulterated form in the case of the Poor Law and Old Age Pensions. But economic equalization might be accompanied by psychological class discrimination. The stigma which attached to the Poor Law made 'pauper' a derogatory term defining a class. 'Old Age Pensioner' may have had a little of the same flavour, but without the taint of shame.

The general effect of social insurance, when confined to an income group, was similar. It differed in that there was no means test. Contribution gave a right to benefit. But, broadly speaking, the income of the group was raised by the excess of benefits over total expenditure by the group in contributions and additional taxes, and the income gap between this group and those above it was thereby reduced. The exact effect is hard to estimate, because of the wide range of incomes within the group and the varying incidence of the risks covered. When the scheme was extended to all, this gap was reopened, though again we have to take account of the combined effects of the regressive flat-rate levy and the, in part, progressive taxation which contributed to the financing of the scheme. Nothing will induce me to embark on a discussion of this problem. But a total scheme is less specifically class-abating in a purely economic sense than a limited one, and social insurance is less so than a means-test service. Flat-rate benefits do not reduce the gaps between different incomes. Their equalizing effect depends on the fact that they make a bigger percentage addition to small incomes than to large. And, even though the concept of diminishing marginal utility (if one may still refer to it) can strictly be applied only to the rising income of one unchanging individual, that remains a matter of some significance. When a free service, as in the case of health, is extended from a limited income group to the whole population, the direct effect is in part to increase the inequality of disposable incomes, again subject to modification by the incidence of taxes. For members of the middle classes, who used to pay their doctors, find this part of their income released for expenditure on other things.

I have been skating gingerly over this very thin ice in order to make one point. The extension of the social services is not primarily a means of equalizing incomes. In some cases it may, in others it may not. The question is relatively unimportant; it belongs to a different department of social policy. What matters is that there is a general enrichment of the concrete substance of civilized life, a general reduction of risk and insecurity, an equalization between the more and the less fortunate at all levels – between the healthy and the sick, the employed and the unemployed, the old and the active, the bachelor and the father of a large family. Equalization is not so much between classes as between individuals within a population which is now treated for this purpose as though it were one class. Equality of status is more important than equality of income.

Even when benefits are paid in cash, this class fusion is outwardly expressed in the form of a new common experience. All learn what it means to have an insurance card that must be regularly stamped (by somebody), or to collect children's allowances or pensions from the post office. But where the benefit takes the form of a service, the qualitative element enters into the benefit itself, and not only into the process by which it is obtained. The extension of such services can therefore have a profound effect on the qualitative aspects of social differentiation. The old elementary schools, though open to all, were used by a social class (admittedly a very large and varied one) for which no other kind of education was available. Its members were brought up in segregation from the higher classes and under influences which set their stamp on the children subjected to them. 'Ex-elementary schoolboy' became a label which a man might carry through life, and it pointed to a distinction which was real, and not merely conventional, in character. For a divided educational system, by promoting both intra-class similarity and inter-class difference, gave emphasis and precision to a criterion of social distance. As Professor Tawney has said, translating the views of educationalists into his own inimitable prose: 'The intrusion into educational organization of the vulgarities of the class system is an irrelevance as mischievous in effect as it is odious in conception.'[39] The limited service was class-making at the same time as it was

class-abating. Today the segregation still takes place, but subsequent education, available to all, makes it possible for a re-sorting to take place. I shall have to consider in a moment whether class intrudes in a different way into this re-sorting.

Similarly the early health service added 'panel patient' to our vocabulary of social class, and many members of the middle classes are now learning exactly what the term signifies. But the extension of the service has reduced the social importance of the distinction. The common experience offered by a general health service embraces all but a small minority at the top and spreads across the important class barriers in the middle ranks of the hierarchy. At the same time the guaranteed minimum has been raised to such a height that the term 'minimum' becomes a misnomer. The intention, at least, is to make it approximate so nearly to the reasonable maximum that the extras which the rich are still able to buy will be no more than frills and luxuries. The provided service, not the purchased service, becomes the norm of social welfare. Some people think that, in such circumstances, the independent sector cannot survive for long. If it disappears, the skyscraper will have been converted into a bungalow. If the present system continues and attains its ideals, the result might be described as a bungalow surmounted by an architecturally insignificant turret.

Benefits in the form of a service have this further characteristic that the rights of the citizen cannot be precisely defined. The qualitative element is too great. A modicum of legally enforceable rights may be granted, but what matters to the citizen is the superstructure of legitimate expectations. It may be fairly easy to enable every child below a certain age to spend the required number of hours in school. It is much harder to satisfy the legitimate expectation that the education should be given by trained teachers in classes of moderate size. It may be possible for every citizen who wishes it to be registered with a doctor. It is much harder to ensure that his ailments will be properly cared for. And so we find that legislation, instead of being the decisive step that puts policy into immediate effect, acquires more and more the character of a declaration of policy that it is hoped to put into effect some day. We think at once of County Colleges and Health Centres. The rate of progress depends on the magnitude of the national resources and their distribution between competing claims. Nor can the State easily foresee what it will cost to fulfil its obligations, for, as the standard expected of the service rises – as it inevitably must in a progressive society – the obligations automatically get heavier. The target is perpetually moving forward, and the State may never be able to get quite within range of it. It follows that individual rights must be subordinated to national plans.

Expectations officially recognized as legitimate are not claims that must be met in each case when presented. They become, as it were, details in a design for community living. The obligation of the State is towards society as a whole, whose remedy in case of default lies in parliament or a local council, instead of to individual citizens, whose remedy lies in a court of law, or at least in a quasi-judicial tribunal. The maintenance of a fair balance between these collective and individual elements in social rights is a matter of vital importance to the democratic socialist State.

The point I have just made is clearest in the case of housing. Here the tenure of existing dwellings has been protected by firm legal rights, enforceable in a court of law. The system has become very complicated, because it has grown piecemeal, and it cannot be maintained that the benefits are equally distributed in proportion to real need. But the basic right of the individual citizen to have a dwelling at all is minimal. He can claim no more than a roof over his head, and his claim can be met, as we have seen in recent years, by a shake-down in a disused cinema converted into a rest centre. Nevertheless, the general obligation of the State towards society collectively with regard to housing is one of the heaviest it has to bear. Public policy has unequivocally given the citizen a legitimate expectation of a home fit for a family to live in, and the promise is not now confined to heroes. It is true that, in dealing with individual claims, authorities work as far as possible on a priority scale of needs. But, when a slum is being cleared, an old city remodelled, or a new town planned, individual claims must be subordinated to the general programme of social advance. An element of chance, and therefore of inequality, enters. One family may be moved ahead of its turn into a model dwelling, because it is part of a community due for early treatment. A second will have to wait, although its physical conditions may be worse than those of the first. As the work goes on, though in many places inequalities vanish, in others they become

more apparent. Let me give you one small example of this. In the town of Middlesbrough, part of the population of a blighted area had been moved to a new housing estate. It was found that, among the children living on this estate, one in eight of those who competed for places in secondary schools were successful. Among the section of the same original population that had been left behind the proportion was one in one hundred and fifty-four.[40] The contrast is so staggering that one hesitates to offer any precise explanation of it, but it remains a striking example of inequality between individuals appearing as the interim result of the progressive satisfaction of collective social rights. Eventually, when the housing programme has been completed, such inequalities should disappear.

There is another aspect of housing policy which, I believe, implies the intrusion of a new element into the rights of citizenship. It comes into play when the design for living, to which I have said individual rights must be subordinated, is not limited to one section at the bottom of the social scale nor to one particular type of need, but covers the general aspects of the life of a whole community. Town planning is total planning in this sense. Not only does it treat the community as a whole, but it affects and must take account of all social activities, customs and interests. It aims at creating new physical environments which will actively foster the growth of new human societies. It must decide what these societies are to be like, and try to provide for all the major diversities which they ought to contain. Town planners are fond of talking about a 'balanced community' as their objective. This means a society that contains a proper mixture of all social classes, as well as of age and sex groups, occupations and so forth. They do not want to build working-class neighbourhoods and middle-class neighbourhoods, but they do propose to build working-class houses and middle-class houses. Their aim is not a classless society, but a society in which class differences are legitimate in terms of social justice, and in which, therefore, the classes co-operate more closely than at present to the common benefit of all. When a planning authority decides that it needs a larger middle-class element in its town (as it very often does) and makes designs to meet its needs and fit its standards, it is not, like a speculative builder, merely responding to a commercial demand. It must re-interpret the demand in harmony with its total plan and then give it the sanction of its authority as the responsible organ of a community of citizens. The middle-class man can then say, not 'I will come if you pay the price I feel strong enough to demand', but 'If you want me as a citizen, you must give me the status which is due as of right to the kind of citizen I am'. This is one example of the way in which citizenship is itself becoming the architect of social inequality.

The second, and more important, example is in the field of education, which also illustrates my earlier point about the balance between individual and collective social rights. In the first phase of our public education, rights were minimal and equal. But, as we have observed, a duty was attached to the right, not merely because the citizen has a duty to himself, as well as a right, to develop all that is in him – a duty which neither the child nor the parent may fully appreciate – but because society recognized that it needed an educated population. In fact the nineteenth century has been accused of regarding elementary education solely as a means of providing capitalist employers with more valuable workers, and higher education merely as an instrument to increase the power of the nation to compete with its industrial rivals. And you may have noticed that recent studies of educational opportunity in the pre-war years have been concerned to reveal the magnitude of social waste quite as much as to protest against the frustration of natural human rights.

In the second phase of our educational history, which began in 1902, the educational ladder was officially accepted as an important, though still small, part of the system. But the balance between collective and individual rights remained much the same. The State decided what it could afford to spend on free secondary and higher education, and the children competed for the limited number of places provided. There was no pretence that all who could benefit from more advanced education would get it, and there was no recognition of any absolute natural right to be educated according to one's capacities. But in the third phase, which started in 1944, individual rights have ostensibly been given priority. Competition for scarce places is to be replaced by selection and distribution into appropriate places, sufficient in number to accommodate all, at least at the secondary school level. In the Act of 1944 there is a passage which says that the supply of secondary schools will not be considered ade-

quate unless they 'afford for all pupils opportunities for education offering such variety of instruction and training as may be desirable in view of their different ages, abilities and aptitudes'. Respect for individual rights could hardly be more strongly expressed. Yet I wonder whether it will work out like that in practice.

If it were possible for the school system to treat the pupil entirely as an end in himself, and to regard education as giving him something whose value he could enjoy to the full whatever his station in after-life, then it might be possible to mould the educational plan to the shape demanded by individual needs, regardless of any other considerations. But, as we all know, education today is closely linked with occupation, and one, at least, of the values the pupil expects to get from it is a qualification for employment at an appropriate level. Unless great changes take place, it seems likely that the educational plan will be adjusted to occupational demand. The proportion between Grammar, Technical and Modern Secondary Schools cannot well be fixed without reference to the proportion between jobs of corresponding grades. And a balance between the two systems may have to be sought in justice to the pupil himself. For if a boy who is given a Grammar School education can then get nothing but a Modern School job, he will cherish a grievance and feel that he has been cheated. It is highly desirable that this attitude should change, so that a boy in such circumstances will be grateful for his education and not resentful at his job. But to accomplish such a change is no easy task.

I see no signs of any relaxation of the bonds that tie education to occupation. On the contrary, they appear to be growing stronger. Great and increasing respect is paid to certificates, matriculation, degrees and diplomas as qualifications for employment, and their freshness does not fade with the passage of the years. A man of forty may be judged by his performance in an examination taken at the age of fifteen. The ticket obtained on leaving school or college is for a life journey. The man with a third-class ticket who later feels entitled to claim a seat in a first-class carriage will not be admitted, even if he is prepared to pay the difference. That would not be fair to the others. He must go back to the start and re-book, by passing the prescribed examination. And it is unlikely that the State will offer to pay his return fare. This is not, of course, true of the whole field of employment, but it is a fair description of a large and significant part of it, whose extension is being constantly advocated. I have, for instance, recently read an article in which it is urged that every aspirant to an administrative or managerial post in business should be required to qualify 'by passing the matriculation or equivalent examination'.[41] This development is partly the result of the systematization of techniques in more and more professional, semi-professional and skilled occupations, though I must confess that some of the claims of so-called professional bodies to exclusive possession of esoteric skill and knowledge appear to me to be rather thin. But it is also fostered by the refinement of the selective process within the educational system itself. The more confident the claim of education to be able to sift human material during the early years of life, the more is mobility concentrated within those years, and consequently limited thereafter.

The right of the citizen in this process of selection and mobility is the right to equality of opportunity. Its aim is to eliminate hereditary privilege. In essence it is the equal right to display and develop differences, or inequalities; the equal right to be recognized as unequal. In the early stages of the establishment of such a system the major effect is, of course, to reveal hidden equalities – to enable the poor boy to show that he is as good as the rich boy. But the final outcome is a structure of unequal status fairly apportioned to unequal abilities. The process is sometimes associated with ideas of *laissez faire* individualism, but within the educational system it is a matter, not of *laissez faire*, but of planning. The process through which abilities are revealed, the influences to which they are subjected, the tests by which they are measured, and the rights given as a result of the tests are all planned. Equality of opportunity is offered to all children entering the primary schools, but at an early age they are usually divided into three streams – the best, the average and the backward. Already opportunity is becoming unequal, and the children's range of chances limited. About the age of eleven they are tested again, probably by a team of teachers, examiners and psychologists. None of these is infallible, but perhaps sometimes three wrongs may make a right. Classification follows for distribution into the three types of secondary school. Opportunity becomes still more unequal, and the chance of further education has already been limited to a select few. Some of these, after being tested again, will go on to receive it. In the end

the jumble of mixed seed originally put into the machine emerges in neatly labelled packets ready to be sown in the appropriate gardens.

I have deliberately couched this description in the language of cynicism in order to bring out the point that, however genuine may be the desire of the educational authorities to offer enough variety to satisfy all individual needs, they must, in a mass service of this kind, proceed by repeated classification into groups, and this is followed at each stage by assimilation within each group and differentiation between groups. That is precisely the way in which social classes in a fluid society have always taken shape. Differences within each class are ignored as irrelevant; differences between classes are given exaggerated significance. Thus qualities which are in reality strung out along a continuous scale are made to create a hierarchy of groups, each with its special character and status. The main features of the system are inevitable, and its advantages, in particular the elimination of inherited privilege, far outweigh its incidental defects. The latter can be attacked and kept within bounds by giving as much opportunity as possible for second thoughts about classification, both on the educational system itself and in after-life.

The conclusion of importance to my argument is that, through education in its relations with occupational structure, citizenship operates as an instrument of social stratification. There is no reason to deplore this, but we should be aware of its consequences. The status acquired by education is carried out into the world bearing the stamp of legitimacy, because it has been conferred by an institution designed to give the citizen his just rights. That which the market offers can be measured against that which the status claims. If a large discrepancy appears, the ensuing attempts to eliminate it will take the form, not of a bargain about economic value, but of a debate about social rights. And it may be that there is already a serious discrepancy between the expectations of those who reach the middle grades in education and the status of the non-manual jobs for which they are normally destined.

I said earlier that in the twentieth century citizenship and the capitalist class system have been at war. Perhaps the phrase is rather too strong, but it is quite clear that the former has imposed modifications on the latter. But we should not be justified in assuming that, although status is a principle that conflicts with contract, the stratified status system which is creeping into citizenship is an alien element in the economic world outside. Social rights in their modern form imply an invasion of contract by status, the subordination of market price to social justice, the replacement of the free bargain by the declaration of rights. But are these principles quite foreign to the practice of the market today, or are they there already, entrenched within the contract system itself? I think it is clear that they are.

As I have already pointed out, one of the main achievements of political power in the nineteenth century was to clear the way for the growth of trade unionism by enabling the workers to use their civil rights collectively. This was an anomaly, because hitherto it was political rights that were used for collective action, through parliament and local councils, whereas civil rights were intensely individual, and had therefore harmonized with the individualism of early capitalism. Trade unionism created a sort of secondary industrial citizenship, which naturally became imbued with the spirit appropriate to an institution of citizenship. Collective civil rights could be used, not merely for bargaining in the true sense of the term, but for the assertion of basic rights. The position was an impossible one and could only be transitional. Rights are not a proper matter for bargaining. To have to bargain for a living wage in a society which accepts the living wage as a social right is as absurd as to have to haggle for a vote in a society which accepts the vote as a political right. Yet the early twentieth century attempted to make sense of this absurdity. It fully endorsed collective bargaining as a normal and peaceful market operation, while recognizing in principle the right of the citizen to a minimum standard of civilized living, which was precisely what the trade unions believed, and with good reason, that they were trying to win for their members with the weapon of the bargain.

In the outburst of big strikes immediately before the First World War this note of a concerted demand for social rights was clearly audible. The government was forced to intervene. It professed to do so entirely for the protection of the public, and pretended not to be concerned with the issues in dispute. In 1912 Mr Askwith, the chief negotiator, told Mr Asquith, the Prime Minister, that intervention had failed and government prestige had suffered. To which the Prime Minister replied: 'Every word you have spoken endorses the opinion I have formed. It is a degra-dation of government.'[42] History soon showed that such a view was a complete anachronism. The government can no longer stand aloof from industrial disputes, as though the level of wages and the standard of living of the workers were matters with which it need not concern itself. And government intervention in industrial disputes has been met from the other side by trade union intervention in the work of government. This is both a significant and a welcome development, provided its implications are fully realized. In the past trade unionism had to assert social rights by attacks delivered from outside the system in which power resided. Today it defends them from inside, in cooperation with government. On major issues crude economic bargaining is converted into something more like a joint discussion of policy.

The implication is that decisions reached in this way must command respect. If citizenship is invoked in the defence of rights, the corresponding duties of citizenship cannot be ignored. These do not require a man to sacrifice his individual liberty or to submit without question to every demand made by government. But they do require that his acts should be inspired by a lively sense of responsibility towards the welfare of the community. Trade union leaders in general accept this implication, but this is not true of all members of the rank and file. The traditions built up at a time when trade unions were fighting for their existence, and when conditions of employment depended wholly on the outcome of unequal bargaining, make its acceptance very difficult. Unofficial strikes have become very frequent, and it is clear that one important element in industrial disputes is discord between trade union leaders and certain sections of trade union members. Now duties can derive either from status or from contract. Leaders of unofficial strikes are liable to reject both. The strikes usually involve breach of contract or the repudiation of agreements. Appeal is made to some allegedly higher principle – in reality, though this may not be expressly asserted, to the status rights of industrial citizenship. There are many precedents today for the subordination of contract to status. Perhaps the most familiar are to be found in our handling of the housing problem. Rents are controlled and the rights of occupants protected after their contracts have expired, houses are requisitioned, agreements freely entered into are set aside or modified by tribunals applying the principles of social equity and the just price. The sanctity of contract gives way to the requirements of public policy, and I am not suggesting for a moment that this ought not to be so. But if the obligations of contract are brushed aside by an appeal to the rights of citizenship, then the duties of citizenship must be accepted as well. In some recent unofficial strikes an attempt has, I think, been made to claim the rights both of status and of contract while repudiating the duties under both these heads.

But my main concern is not with the nature of strikes, but rather with the current conception of what constitutes a fair wage. I think it is clear that this conception includes the notion of status. It enters into every discussion of wage rates and professional salaries. What *ought* a medical specialist or a dentist to earn, we ask? Would twice the salary of a university professor be about right, or is that not enough? And, of course, the system envisaged is one of stratified, not uniform, status. The claim is not merely for a basic living wage with such variations above that level as can be extracted by each grade from the conditions in the market at the moment. The claims of status are to a hierarchical wage structure, each level of which represents a social right and not merely a market value. Collective bargaining must involve, even in its elementary forms, the classification of workers into groups, or grades, within which minor occupational differences are ignored. As in mass schooling, so in mass employment, questions of rights, standards, opportunities and so forth can be intelligibly discussed and handled only in terms of a limited number of categories and by cutting up a continuous chain of differences into a series of classes whose names instantly ring the appropriate bell in the mind of the busy official. As the area of negotiation spreads, the assimilation of groups necessarily follows on the assimilation of individuals, until the stratification of the whole population of workers is, as far as possible, standardized. Only then can general principles of social justice be formulated. There must be uniformity within each grade, and difference between grades. These principles dominate the minds of those discussing wage claims, even though rationalization produces other arguments, such as that profits are excessive and the industry can afford to pay higher wages, or that higher wages are necessary to maintain the supply of suitable labour or to prevent its decline.

The White Paper on Personal Incomes[43] flashed a beam of light into these dark places of the mind, but the end result has been only to make the process of rationalization more intricate and laborious. The basic conflict between social rights and market value has not been resolved. One labour spokesman said: 'An equitable relationship must be established between industry and industry.'[44] An equitable relationship is a social, not an economic, concept. The General Council of the T.U.C. approved the principles of the White Paper to the extent that 'they recognize the need to safeguard those wage differentials which are essential elements in the wages structure of many important industries, and are required to sustain those standards of craftsmanship, training and experience that contribute directly to industrial efficiency and higher productivity'.[45] Here market value and economic incentive find a place in an argument which is fundamentally concerned with status. The White Paper itself took a rather different, and possibly a truer, view of differentials. 'The last hundred years have seen the growth of certain traditional or customary relationships between personal incomes – including wages and salaries – in different occupations. . . . These have no necessary relevance to modern conditions.' Tradition and custom are social, not economic, principles, and they are old names for the modern structure of status rights.

The White Paper stated frankly that differentials based on these social concepts could not satisfy current economic requirements. They did not provide the incentives needed to secure the best distribution of labour. 'Relative income levels must be such as to encourage the movement of labour to those industries where it is most needed, and should not, as in some cases they still do, tempt it in a contrary direction.' Notice that it says '*still* do'. Once again the modern conception of social rights is treated as a survival from the dark past. As we go on, the confusion thickens. 'Each claim for an increase in wages or salaries must be considered on its national merits', that is, in terms of national policy. But this policy cannot be directly enforced by the exercise of the political rights of citizenship through government, because that would involve 'an incursion by the Government into what has hitherto been regarded as a field of free contract between individuals and organizations', that is, an invasion of the civil rights of the citizen. Civil rights are therefore to assume political responsibility, and free contract is to act as the instrument of national policy. And there is yet another paradox. The incentive that operates in the free contract system of the open market is the incentive of personal gain. The incentive that corresponds to social rights is that of public duty. To which is the appeal being made? The answer is, to both. The citizen is urged to respond to the call of duty by allowing some scope to the motive of individual self-interest. But these paradoxes are not the invention of muddled brains; they are inherent in our contemporary social system. And they need not cause us undue anxiety, for a little common sense can often move a mountain of paradox in the world of action, though logic may be unable to surmount it in the world of thought.

Conclusions

I have tried to show how citizenship, and other forces outside it, have been altering the pattern of social inequality. To complete the picture I ought now to survey the results as a whole on the structure of social class. They have undoubtedly been profound, and it may be that the inequalities permitted, and even moulded, by citizenship do not any longer constitute class distinctions in the sense in which that term is used for past societies. But to examine this question I should require another lecture, and it would probably consist of a mixture of dry statistics of uncertain meaning and meaningful judgements of doubtful validity. For our ignorance of this matter is profound. It is therefore perhaps fortunate for the reputation of sociology that I should be obliged to confine myself to a few tentative observations, made in an attempt to answer the four questions which I posed at the end of my introduction to my theme.

We have to look for the combined effects of three factors. First, the compression, at both ends, of the scale of income distribution. Second, the great extension of the area of common culture and common experience. And third, the enrichment of the universal status of citizenship, combined with the recognition and stabilization of certain status differences chiefly through the linked systems of education and occupation. The first two have made the third possible. Status differences can receive the stamp of legitimacy in terms of democratic citizenship provided they do not cut too deep, but occur within a population

united in a single civilization; and provided they are not an expression of hereditary privilege. This means that inequalities can be tolerated within a fundamentally egalitarian society provided they are not dynamic, that is to say that they do not create incentives which spring from dissatisfaction and the feeling that 'this kind of life is not good enough for me', or 'I am determined that my son shall be spared what I had to put up with'. But the kind of inequality pleaded for in the White Paper can be justified only if it *is* dynamic, and if it *does* provide an incentive to change and betterment. It may prove, therefore, that the inequalities permitted, and even moulded, by citizenship will not function in an economic sense as forces influencing the free distribution of manpower. Or that social stratification persists, but social ambition ceases to be a normal phenomenon, and becomes a deviant behaviour pattern – to use some of the jargon of sociology.

Should things develop to such lengths, we might find that the only remaining drive with a consistent distributive effect – distributive, that is, of manpower through the hierarchy of economic levels – was the ambition of the schoolboy to do well in his lessons, to pass his examinations, and to win promotion up the educational ladder. And if the official aim of securing 'parity of esteem' between the three types of secondary school were realized, we might lose the greater part even of that. Such would be the extreme result of establishing social conditions in which every man was content with the station of life to which it had pleased citizenship to call him.

In saying this I have answered two of my four questions, the first and the last. I asked whether the sociological hypothesis latent in Marshall's essay is valid today, the hypothesis, namely, that there is a kind of basic human equality, associated with full community membership, which is not inconsistent with a superstructure of economic inequality. I asked, too, whether there was any limit to the present drive towards social equality inherent in the principles governing the movement. My answer is that the preservation of economic inequalities has been made more difficult by the enrichment of the status of citizenship. There is less room for them, and there is more and more likelihood of their being challenged. But we are certainly proceeding at present on the assumption that the hypothesis is valid. And this assumption provides the answer to the second question. We are not aiming at absolute equality. There are limits inherent in the egalitarian movement. But the movement is a double one. It operates partly through citizenship and partly through the economic system. In both cases the aim is to remove inequalities which cannot be regarded as legitimate, but the standard of legitimacy is different. In the former it is the standard of social justice, in the latter it is social justice combined with economic necessity. It is possible, therefore, that the inequalities permitted by the two halves of the movement will not coincide. Class distinctions may survive which have no appropriate economic function, and economic differences which do not correspond with accepted class distinctions.

My third question referred to the changing balance between rights and duties. Rights have been multiplied, and they are precise. Each individual knows just what he is entitled to claim. The duty whose discharge is most obviously and immediately necessary for the fulfilment of the right is the duty to pay taxes and insurance contributions. Since these are compulsory, no act of will is involved, and no keen sentiment of loyalty. Education and military service are also compulsory. The other duties are vague, and are included in the general obligation to live the life of a good citizen, giving such service as one can to promote the welfare of the community. But the community is so large that the obligation appears remote and unreal. Of paramount importance is the duty to work, but the effect of one man's labour on the well-being of the whole society is so infinitely small that it is hard for him to believe that he can do much harm by withholding or curtailing it.

When social relations were dominated by contract, the duty to work was not recognized. It was a man's own affair whether he worked or not. If he chose to live idly in poverty, he was at liberty to do so, provided he did not become a nuisance. If he was able to live idly in comfort, he was regarded, not as a drone, but as an aristocrat – to be envied and admired. When the economy of this country was in process of transformation into a system of this kind, great anxiety was felt whether the necessary labour would be forthcoming. The driving forces of group custom and regulation had to be replaced by the incentive of personal gain, and grave doubts were expressed whether this incentive could be relied upon. This explains Colquhoun's views on poverty, and the pithy remark of Mandeville, that labourers 'have nothing to stir them up to be serviceable but their wants, which it is prudence to relieve but folly to cure'.[46] And in the eighteenth century their wants were very simple. They were governed by established class habits of living, and no continuous scale of rising standards of consumption existed to entice the labourers to earn more in order to spend more on desirable things hitherto just beyond their reach – like radio sets, bicycles, cinemas or holidays by the sea. The following comment by a writer in 1728, which is but one example from many in the same sense, may well have been based on sound observation. 'People in low life', he said, 'who work only for their daily bread, if they can get it by three days work in the week, will many of them make holiday the other three, or set their own price on their labour.'[47] And, if they adopted the latter course, it was generally assumed that they would spend the extra money on drink, the only easily available luxury. The general rise in the standard of living has caused this phenomenon, or something like it, to reappear in contemporary society, though cigarettes now play a more important role than drink.

It is no easy matter to revive the sense of the personal obligation to work in a new form in which it is attached to the status of citizenship. It is not made any easier by the fact that the essential duty is not to have a job and hold it, since that is relatively simple in conditions of full employment, but to put one's heart into one's job and work hard. For the standard by which to measure hard work is immensely elastic. A successful appeal to the duties of citizenship can be made in times of emergency, but the Dunkirk spirit cannot be a permanent feature of any civilization. Nevertheless, an attempt is being made by trade union leaders to inculcate a sense of this general duty. At a conference on November 18 of last year Mr Tanner referred to 'the imperative obligation on both sides of industry to make their full contribution to the rehabilitation of the national economy and world recovery'.[48] But the national community is too large and remote to command this kind of loyalty and to make of it a continual driving force. That is why many people think that the solution of our problem lies in the development of more limited loyalties, to the local community and especially to the working group. In this latter form industrial citizenship, devolving its obligations down to the basic units of production, might supply some of the vigour that citizenship in general appears to lack.

I come finally to the second of my original four questions, which was not, however, so much a question as a statement. I pointed out that Marshall stipulated that measures designed to raise the general level of civilization of the workers must not interfere with the freedom of the market. If they did, they might become indistinguishable from socialism. And I said that obviously this limitation on policy had since been abandoned. Socialist measures in Marshall's sense have been accepted by all political parties. This led me to the platitude that the conflict between egalitarian measures and the free market must be examined in the course of any attempt to carry Marshall's sociological hypothesis over into the modern age.

I have touched on this vast subject at several points, and in the concluding summary I will confine myself to one aspect of the problem. The unified civilization which makes social inequalities acceptable, and threatens to make them economically functionless, is achieved by a progressive divorce between real and money incomes. This is, of course, explicit in the major social services, such as health and education, which give benefits in kind without any *ad hoc* payment. In scholarships and legal aid, prices scaled to money incomes keep real income relatively constant, in so far as it is affected by these particular needs. Rent restriction, combined with security of tenure, achieves a similar result by different means. So, in varying degrees, do rationing, food subsidies, utility goods and price controls. The advantages obtained by having a larger money income do not disappear, but they are confined to a limited area of consumption.

I spoke just now of the conventional hierarchy of the wage structure. Here importance is attached to differences in money income and the higher earnings are expected to yield real and substantial advantages – as, of course, they still do in spite of the trend towards the equalization of real incomes. But the importance of wage differentials is, I am sure, partly symbolic. They operate as labels attached to industrial status, not only as instruments of genuine economic stratification. And we also see signs that the acceptance of this system of economic inequality by the workers themselves – especially those fairly low down in the scale – is sometimes counteracted by claims to greater equality with respect to those forms of real enjoyment which are not paid for out of wages. Manual workers may accept it as right and proper that they should earn less money than certain clerical grades, but at the same time wage-earners may press for the same general amenities as are enjoyed by salaried employees, because these should reflect the fundamental equality of all citizens and not the inequalities of earnings or occupational grades. If the manager can get a day off for a football match, why not the workman? Common enjoyment is a common right.

Post-war studies of adult and child opinion have found that, when the question is posed in general terms, there is a declining interest in the earning of big money. This is not due, I think, only to the heavy burden of progressive taxation, but to an implicit belief that society should, and will, guarantee all the essentials of a decent and secure life at every level, irrespective of the amount of money earned. In a population of secondary schoolboys examined by the Bristol Institute of Education, 86 per cent wanted an interesting job at a reasonable wage and only 9 per cent a job in which they could make a lot of money. And the average intelligence quotient of the second group was 16 points lower than that of the first.[49] In a poll conducted by the British Institute of Public Opinion, 23 per cent wanted as high wages as possible, and 73 per cent preferred security at lower wages.[50] But at any given moment, and in response to a particular question about their present circumstances, most people, one would imagine, would confess to a desire for more money than they are actually getting. Another poll, taken in November 1947, suggests that even this expectation is exaggerated. For 51 per cent said their earnings were at or above a level adequate to cover family needs, and only 45 per cent that they were inadequate. The attitude is bound to vary at different social levels. The classes which have gained most from the social services, and in which real income in general has been rising, might be expected to be less preoccupied with differences in money income. But we should be prepared to find other reactions in that section of the middle classes in which the pattern of money incomes is at the moment most markedly incoherent, while the elements of civilized living traditionally most highly prized are becoming unattainable with the money incomes available – or by any other means.

The general point is one to which Professor Robbins referred when he lectured here two years ago. 'We are following', he said, 'a policy which is self-contradictory and self-frustrating. We are relaxing taxation and seeking, wherever possible, to introduce systems of payments which fluctuate with output. And, at the same time, our price fixing and the consequential rationing system are inspired by egalitarian principles. The result is that we get the worst of both worlds.'[51] And again: 'The belief that, in normal times, it is particularly sensible to try to mix the principles and run an egalitarian real income system side by side with an inegalitarian money income system seems to me somewhat *simpliste*.'[52] Yes, to the economist perhaps, if he tries to judge the situation according to the logic of a market economy. But not necessarily to the sociologist, who remembers that social behaviour is not governed by logic, and that a human society can make a square meal out of a stew of paradox without getting indigestion – at least for quite a long time. The policy, in fact, may not be *simpliste* at all, but subtle; a newfangled application of the old maxim *divide et impera* – play one off against the other to keep the peace. But, more seriously, the word *simpliste* suggests

that the antinomy is merely the result of the muddled thinking of our rulers and that, once they see the light, there is nothing to prevent them altering their line of action. I believe, on the contrary, that this conflict of principles springs from the very roots of our social order in the present phase of the development of democratic citizenship. Apparent inconsistencies are in fact a source of stability, achieved through a compromise which is not dictated by logic. This phase will not continue indefinitely. It may be that some of the conflicts within our social system are becoming too sharp for the compromise to achieve its purpose much longer. But, if we wish to assist in their resolution, we must try to understand their deeper nature and to realize the profound and disturbing effects which would be produced by any hasty attempt to reverse present and recent trends. It has been my aim in these lectures to throw a little light on one element which I believe to be of fundamental importance, namely the impact of a rapidly developing concept of the rights of citizenship on the structure of social inequality.

Notes

1   The Marshall Lectures, Cambridge 1949.
2   *Memorials of Alfred Marshall*, ed. A.C. Pigou, p. 164.
3   ibid., p. 158.
4   ibid., p. 37.
5   Privately printed by Thomas Tofts. The page references are to this edition.
6   Published under the title 'Prospects of Labour' in *Economica*, February, 1949.
7   *Memorials of Alfred Marshall*, pp. 3 and 4.
8   *The Future of the Working Classes*, p. 6.
9   ibid., p. 16.
10 ibid., p. 9. The revised version of this passage is significantly different. It runs: 'The picture to be drawn will resemble in many respects those which have been shown to us by some socialists, who attributed to all men . . . ' etc. The condemnation is less sweeping and Marshall no longer speaks of the Socialists, *en masse* and with a capital 'S', in the past tense. *Memorials*, p. 109.
11 ibid., p. 15.
12 ibid., p. 5.
13 By this terminology, what economists sometimes call 'income from civil rights' would be called 'income from social rights'. Cf. H. Dalton: *Some Aspects of the Inequality of Incomes in Modern Communities*, Part 3, Chapters 3 and 4.
14 F. Maitland: *Constitutional History of England*, p. 105.
15 A.F. Pollard: *Evolution of Parliament*, p. 25.
16 The most important exception is the right to strike, but the conditions which made this right vital for the workman and acceptable to political opinion had not yet fully come into being.
17 G.M. Trevelyan: *English Social History*, p. 351.
18 City of London Case, 1610. See E.F. Heckscher: *Mercantilism*, Vol. 1, pp. 269–325, where the whole story is told in considerable detail.
19 *King's Bench Reports* (Holt), p. 1002.
20 Heckscher, *Mercantilism*, Vol. 1, p. 283.
21 ibid., p. 316.
22 Sidney and Beatrice Webb: *History of Trade Unionism* (1920), p. 60.
23 R.H. Tawney: *Agrarian Problem in the Sixteenth Century* (1916), pp. 43–4.
24 *Our Partnership*, p. 79.
25 See the admirable characterization given by R.H. Tawney in *Equality*, pp. 121–2.
26 *A Treatise on Indigence* (1806), pp. 7–8.
27 H.S. Maine: *Ancient Law* (1878), p. 170.
28 ibid., p. 365.
29 M. Ginsberg: *Studies in Sociology*, p. 171.
30 The Austin Jones Committee on County Court Procedure and the Evershed Committee on Supreme Court Practice and Procedure. The report of the former and an interim report of the latter have since been published.
31 The Rushcliffe Committee on Legal Aid and Legal

Advice in England and Wales.

32   C. Grant Robertson: *England under the Hanoverians*, p. 491.

33   R.W. Pollard: *The Evolution of Parliament*, p. 155.

34   ibid., p. 165.

35   ibid., p. 152.

36   Where disposable capital exceeds £500, legal aid may still be granted, at the discretion of the local committee, if disposable income does not exceed £420.

37   Cmd. 7563: Summary of the Proposed New Service, p. 7, para 17.

38   Ministry of Education: *Report of the Working Party on University Awards*, 1948, para. 60. The general account of the present system is taken from the same source.

39   R.H. Tawney: *Secondary Education for All*, p. 64.

40   Ruth Glass: *The Social Background of a Plan*, p. 129.

41   J.A. Bowie, in *Industry* (January 1949), p. 17.

42   Lord Askwith: *Industrial Problems and Disputes*, p. 228.

43   Cmd. 7321, 1948.

44   As reported in *The Times*.

45   Recommendations of the Special Committee on the Economic Situation as accepted by the General Council at their Special Meeting on 18 February 1948.

46   B. Mandeville: *The Fable of the Bees*, 6th ed. (1732), p. 213.

47   E.S. Furniss: *The Position of the Laborer in a System of Nationalism*, p. 125.

48   *The Times*, 19 November 1948.

49   *Research Bulletin*, No. 11, p. 23.

50   January 1946.

51   L. Robbins: *The Economic Problem in Peace and War*, p. 9.

52   ibid., p. 16.

19

Are There Any Natural Rights?[1]

H.L.A. Hart

I shall advance the thesis that if there are any moral rights at all, it follows that there is at least one natural right, the equal right of all men to be free. By saying that there is this right, I mean that in the absence of certain special conditions which are consistent with the right being an equal right, any adult human being capable of choice (1) has the right to forbearance on the part of all others from the use of coercion or restraint against him save to hinder coercion or restraint and (2) is at liberty to do (i.e., is under no obligation to abstain from) any action which is not one coercing or restraining or designed to injure other persons.[2]

I have two reasons for describing the equal right of all men to be free as a *natural* right; both of them were always emphasized by the classical theorists of natural rights. (1) This right is one which all men have if they are capable of choice; they have it *qua* men and not only if they are members of some society or stand in some special relation to each other. (2) This right is not created or conferred by men's voluntary action; other moral rights are.[3] Of course, it is quite obvious that my thesis is not as ambitious as the traditional theories of natural rights; for although on my view all men are *equally* entitled to be free in the sense explained, no man has an absolute or unconditional right to do or not to do any particular thing or to be treated in any particular way; coercion or restraint of any action may be justified in special conditions consistently with the general principle. So my argument will not show

that men have any right (save the equal right of all to be free) which is "absolute," "indefeasible," or "imprescriptible." This may for many reduce the importance of my contention, but I think that the principle that all men have an equal right to be free, meager as it may seem, is probably all that the political philosophers of the liberal tradition need have claimed to support any program of action even if they have claimed more. But my contention that there is this one natural right may appear unsatisfying in another respect; it is only the conditional assertion that *if* there are any moral rights then there must be this one natural right. Perhaps few would now deny, as some have, that there are moral rights; for the point of that denial was usually to object to some philosophical claim as to the "ontological status" of rights, and this objection is now expressed not as a denial that there are any moral rights but as a denial of some assumed logical similarity between sentences used to assert the existence of rights and other kinds of sentences. But it is still important to remember that there may be codes of conduct quite properly termed moral codes (though we can of course say they are "imperfect") which do not employ the notion of *a* right, and there is nothing contradictory or otherwise absurd in a code or morality consisting wholly of prescriptions or in a code which prescribed only what should be done for the realization of happiness or some ideal of personal perfection.[4] Human actions in such systems would be evaluated or criticised as compliances with prescriptions or as *good* or *bad, right* or *wrong, wise* or *foolish, fitting* or *unfitting*, but no one in such a system would have, exercise, or claim rights, or violate or

Originally published in *Philosophical Review*, 64 (1955), 175–91.

infringe them. So those who lived by such systems could not of course be committed to the recognition of the equal right of all to be free; nor, I think (and this is one respect in which the notion of a right differs from other moral notions), could any parallel argument be constructed to show that, from the bare fact that actions were recognized as ones which ought or ought not to be done, as right, wrong, good or bad, it followed that some specific kind of conduct fell under these categories.

I

(A) Lawyers have for their own purposes carried the dissection of the notion of a legal right some distance, and some of their results[5] are of value in the elucidation of statements of the form "X has a right to . . ." outside legal contexts. There is of course no simple identification to be made between moral and legal rights, but there is an intimate connection between the two, and this itself is one feature which distinguishes a moral right from other fundamental moral concepts. It is not merely that as a matter of fact men speak of their moral rights mainly when advocating their incorporation in a legal system, but that the concept of a right belongs to that branch of morality which is specifically concerned to determine when one person's freedom may be limited by another's[6] and so to determine what actions may appropriately be made the subject of coercive legal rules. The words *"droit," "diritto,"* and *"Recht,"* used by continental jurists, have no simple English translation and seem to English jurists to hover uncertainly between law and morals, but they do in fact mark off an area of morality (the morality of law) which has special characteristics. It is occupied by the concepts of justice, fairness, rights, and obligation (if this last is not used as it is by many moral philosophers as an obscuring general label to cover every action that morally we ought to do or forbear from doing). The most important common characteristic of this group of moral concepts is that there is no incongruity, but a special congruity in the use of force or the threat of force to secure that what is just or fair or someone's right to have done shall in fact be done; for it is in just these circumstances that coercion of another human being is legitimate. Kant, in the *Rechtslehre,* discusses the obligations which arise in this branch of morality

under the title of *officia juris,* "which do not require that respect for duty shall be of itself the determining principle of the will," and contrasts them with *officia virtutis,* which have no moral worth unless done for the sake of the moral principle. His point is, I think, that we must distinguish from the rest of morality those principles regulating the proper distribution of human freedom which alone make it morally legitimate for one human being to determine by his choice how another should act; and a certain specific moral value is secured (to be distinguished from moral virtue in which the good will is manifested) if human relationships are conducted in accordance with these principles even though coercion has to be used to secure this, for only if these principles are regarded will freedom be distributed among human beings as it should be. And it is I think a very important feature of a moral right that the possessor of it is conceived as having a moral justification for limiting the freedom of another and that he has this justification not because the action he is entitled to require of another has some moral quality but simply because in the circumstances a certain distribution of human freedom will be maintained if he by his choice is allowed to determine how that other shall act.

(B) I can best exhibit this feature of a moral right by reconsidering the question whether moral rights and "duties"[7] are correlative. The contention that they are means, presumably, that every statement of the form "X has a right to . . ." entails and is entailed by "Y has a duty (not) to . . .," and at this stage we must not assume that the values of the name variables "X" and "Y" must be different persons. Now there is certainly one sense of "a right" (which I have already mentioned) such that it does not follow from X's having a right that X or someone else has any duty. Jurists have isolated rights in this sense and have referred to them as "liberties" just to distinguish them from rights in the centrally important sense of "right" which has "duty" as a correlative. The former sense of "right" is needed to describe those areas of social life where competition is at least morally unobjectionable. Two people walking along both see a ten-dollar bill in the road twenty yards away, and there is no clue as to the owner. Neither of the two are under a "duty" to allow the other to pick it up; each has in this sense a right to pick it up. Of course there may be many things which each has a "duty" not to do in the course of the race to the spot – neither may kill or wound the other – and corresponding to these "duties" there are rights to forbearances. The moral propriety of all economic competition implies this minimum sense of "a right" in which to say that "X has a right to" means merely that X is under no "duty" not to. Hobbes saw that the expression "a right" could have this sense but he was wrong if he thought that there is no sense in which it does follow from X's having a right that Y has a duty or at any rate an obligation.

(C) More important for our purpose is the question whether for all moral "duties" there are correlative moral rights, because those who have given an affirmative answer to this question have usually assumed without adequate scrutiny that to have a right is simply to be capable of benefiting by the performance of a "duty"; whereas in fact this is not a sufficient condition (and probably not a necessary condition) of having a right. Thus animals and babies who stand to benefit by our performance of our "duty" not to ill-treat them are said *therefore* to have rights to proper treatment. The full consequence of this reasoning is not usually followed out; most have shrunk from saying that we have rights against ourselves because we stand to benefit from our performance of our "duty" to keep ourselves alive or develop our talents. But the moral situation which arises from a promise (where the legal-sounding terminology of rights and obligations is most appropriate) illustrates most clearly that the notion of having a right and that of benefiting by the performance of a "duty" are not identical. X promises Y in return for some favor that he will look after Y's aged mother in his absence. Rights arise out of this transaction, but it is surely Y to whom the promise has been made and not his mother who *has* or *possesses* these rights. Certainly Y's mother is a person concerning whom X has an obligation and a person who will benefit by its performance, but the person *to whom* he has an obligation to look after her is Y. This is something *due to* or *owed to* Y, so it is Y, not his mother, whose right X will disregard and to whom X will have done *wrong* if he fails to keep his promise, though the mother may be physically injured. And it is Y who has a moral *claim* upon X, is *entitled* to have his mother looked after, and who can *waive* the claim and *release* Y from the obligation. Y is, in other words, morally in a position to determine by his choice how X shall act and in this way to limit X's freedom of choice; and it is this fact, not the fact that he stands to benefit, that

makes it appropriate to say that he has *a right*. Of course often the person to whom a promise has been made will be the only person who stands to benefit by its performance, but this does not justify the identification of "having a right" with "benefiting by the performance of a duty." It is important for the whole logic of rights that, while the person who stands to benefit by the performance of a duty is discovered by considering what will happen if the duty is not performed, the person who has a right (to whom performance is *owed* or *due*) is discovered by examining the transaction or antecedent situation or relations of the parties out of which the "duty" arises. These considerations should incline us not to extend to animals and babies whom it is wrong to ill-treat the notion of a right to proper treatment, for the moral situation can be simply and adequately described here by saying that it is wrong or that we ought not to ill-treat them or, in the philosopher's generalized sense of "duty," that we have a duty not to ill-treat them.[8] If common usage sanctions talk of the rights of animals or babies it makes an idle use of the expression "a right," which will confuse the situation with other different moral situations where the expression "a right" has a specific force and cannot be replaced by the other moral expressions which I have mentioned. Perhaps some clarity on this matter is to be gained by considering the force of the preposition "to" in the expression "having a duty to Y" or "being under an obligation to Y" (where "Y" is the name of a person); for it is significantly different from the meaning of "to" in "doing something to Y" or "doing harm to Y," where it indicates the person affected by some action. In the first pair of expressions, "to" obviously does not have this force, but indicates the person to whom the person morally bound is bound. This is an intelligible development of the figure of a bond (*vinculum juris: obligare*); the precise figure is not that of two persons bound by a chain, but of *one* person bound, the other end of the chain lying in the hands of another to use if he chooses.[9] So it appears absurd to speak of having "duties" or owing obligations to ourselves – of course we may have "duties" not to do harm to ourselves, but what could be meant (once the distinction between these different meanings of "to" has been grasped) by insisting that we have duties or obligations *to* ourselves not to do harm to ourselves?

(D) The essential connection between the notion of a right and the justified limitation of one person's freedom by another may be thrown into relief if we consider codes of behavior which do not purport to confer rights but only to prescribe what shall be done. Most natural law thinkers down to Hooker conceived of natural law in this way: there were natural duties compliance with which would certainly benefit man – things to be done to achieve man's natural end – but not natural rights. And there are of course many types of codes of behavior which only prescribe what is to be done, e.g., those regulating certain ceremonies. It would be absurd to regard these codes as conferring rights, but illuminating to contrast them with rules of games, which often create rights, though not, of course, moral rights. But even a code which is plainly a moral code need not establish rights; the Decalogue is perhaps the most important example. Of course, quite apart from heavenly rewards human beings stand to benefit by general obedience to the Ten Commandments: disobedience is wrong and will certainly harm individuals. But it would be a surprising interpretation of them that treated them as conferring rights. In such an interpretation obedience to the Ten Commandments would have to be conceived as due to or owed to individuals, not merely to God, and disobedience not merely as wrong but as *a wrong to* (as well as harm to) individuals. The Commandments would cease to read like penal statutes designed only to rule out certain types of behavior and would have to be thought of as rules placed at the disposal of individuals and regulating the extent to which *they* may demand certain behavior from others. Rights are typically conceived of as *possessed* or *owned by* or *belonging to* individuals, and these expressions reflect the conception of moral rules as not only prescribing conduct but as forming a kind of moral property of individuals to which they are as individuals entitled; only when rules are conceived in this way can we speak of *rights* and *wrongs* as well as right and wrong actions.[10]

II

So far I have sought to establish that to have a right entails having a moral justification for limiting the freedom of another person and for determining how he should act; it is now important to see that the moral justification must be of a special kind if it is to constitute a right, and this will emerge most clearly from an examination of the circumstances in which rights are asserted with the typical expression "I have a right to. . . ." It is I think the case that this form of words is used in two main types of situations: (A) when the claimant has some special justification for interference with another's freedom which other persons do not have ("*I* have a right to be paid what you promised for my services"); (B) when the claimant is concerned to resist or object to some interference by another person as having no justification ("*I* have a right to say what I think").

(A) *Special rights.* When rights arise out of special transactions between individuals or out of some special relationship in which they stand to each other, both the persons who have the right and those who have the corresponding obligation are limited to the parties to the special transaction or relationship. I call such rights special rights to distinguish them from those moral rights which are thought of as rights against (i.e., as imposing obligations upon)[11] everyone, such as those that are asserted when some unjustified interference is made or threatened as in (B) above.

(i) The most obvious cases of special rights are those that arise from promises. By promising to do or not to do something, we voluntarily incur obligations and create or confer rights on those to whom we promise, we alter the existing moral independence of the parties' freedom of choice in relation to some action and create a new moral relationship between them, so that it becomes morally legitimate for the person to whom the promise is given to determine how the promisor shall act. The promisee has a temporary authority or sovereignty in relation to some specific matter over the other's will which we express by saying that the promisor is under an obligation *to* the promisee to do what he has promised. To some philosophers the notion that moral phenomena – rights and duties or obligations – can be brought into existence by the voluntary action of individuals has appeared utterly mysterious; but this I think has been so because they have not clearly seen how special the moral notions of a right and an obligation are, nor how peculiarly they are connected with the distribution of freedom of choice; it would indeed be mysterious if we could make actions morally good or bad by voluntary choice. The simplest case of promising illustrates two points characteristic of all special rights: (1) the right and obligation arise not because the promised action has itself any particular moral quality, but just because of the voluntary transaction between the parties; (2) the identity of the parties concerned is vital – only *this* person (the promisee) has the moral justification for determining how the promisor shall act. It is *his* right; only in relation to him is the promisor's freedom of choice diminished, so that if he chooses to release the promisor no one else can complain.

(ii) But a promise is not the only kind of transaction whereby rights are conferred. They may be *accorded* by a person consenting or authorizing another to interfere in matters which but for this consent or authorization he would be free to determine for himself. If I consent to your taking precautions for my health or happiness or authorize you to look after my interests, then you have a right which others have not, and I cannot complain of your interference if it is within the sphere of your authority. This is what is meant by a person surrendering his rights to another; and again the typical characteristics of a right are present in this situation: the person authorized has the right to interfere not because of its intrinsic character but because *these* persons have stood in *this* relationship. No one else (not similarly authorized) has any *right*[12] to interfere in theory even if the person authorized does not exercise his right.

(iii) Special rights are not only those created by the deliberate choice of the party on whom the obligation falls, as they are when they are accorded or spring from promises, and not all obligations to other persons are deliberately incurred, though I think it is true of all special rights that they arise from previous voluntary actions. A third very important source of special rights and obligations which we recognize in many spheres of life is what may be termed mutuality of restrictions, and I think political obligation is intelligible only if we see what precisely this is and how it differs from the other right-creating transactions (consent, promising) to which philosophers have assimilated it. In its bare schematic outline it is this: when a number of persons conduct any joint enterprise according to rules and thus restrict their liberty, those who have submitted to these restrictions when required have a right to a similar submission from those who have benefited by their submission. The rules may provide that officials should have authority to enforce obedience and make further rules, and this will create a structure of legal rights and duties, but the moral obligation to obey the rules in such circumstances is *due to* the co-operating members of the society, and they have the correlative moral right to obedience. In social situations of this sort (of which political society is the most complex example) the obligation to obey the rules is something distinct from whatever other moral reasons there may be for obedience in terms of good consequences (e.g., the prevention of suffering); the obligation is due to the co-operating members of the society as such and not because they are human beings on whom it would be wrong to inflict suffering. The utilitarian explanation of political obligation fails to take account of this feature of the situation both in its simple version that the obligation exists because and only if the direct consequences of a particular act of disobedience are worse than obedience, and also in its more sophisticated version that the obligation exists even when this is not so, if disobedience increases the probability that the law in question or other laws will be disobeyed on other occasions when the direct consequences of obedience are better than those of disobedience.

Of course to say that there is such a moral obligation upon those who have benefited by the submission of other members of society to restrictive rules to obey these rules in their turn does not entail either that this is the only kind of moral reason for obedience or that there can be no cases where disobedience will be morally justified. There is no contradiction or other impropriety in saying "I have an obligation to do X, someone has a right to ask me to, but I now see I ought not to do it." It will in painful situations sometimes be the lesser of two moral evils to disregard what really are people's rights and not perform our obligations to them. This seems to me particularly obvious from the case of promises: I may promise to do something and thereby incur an obligation just because that is one way in which obligations (to be distinguished from other forms of moral reasons for acting) are created; reflection may show that it would in the circumstances be wrong to keep this promise because of the suffering it might cause, and we can express this by saying "*I ought not* to do it though *I have an obligation to him* to do it" just because the italicized expressions are not synonyms but come from different dimensions of morality. The attempt to explain this situation by saying that our real obligation here is to avoid the suffering and that there is only a prima facie obligation to keep the promise seems to me to confuse two quite different kinds of moral reason, and in practice such a terminology obscures the precise character of what is at stake when "for some greater good" we infringe people's rights or do not perform our obligations to them.

The social-contract theorists rightly fastened on the fact that the obligation to obey the law is not merely a special case of benevolence (direct or indirect), but something which arises between members of a particular political society out of their mutual relationship. Their mistake was to identify *this* right-creating situation of mutual restrictions with the paradigm case of promising; there are of course important similarities, and these are just the points which all special rights have in common, viz., that they arise out of special relationships between human beings and not out of the character of the action to be done or its effects.

(iv) There remains a type of situation which may be thought of as creating rights and obligations: where the parties have a special natural relationship, as in the case of parent and child. The parent's moral right to obedience from his child would I suppose now be thought to terminate when the child reaches the age "of discretion," but the case is worth mentioning because some political philosophies have had recourse to analogies with this case as an explanation of political obligation, and also because even this case has some of the features we have distinguished in special rights, viz., the right arises out of the special relationship of the parties (though it is in this case a natural relationship) and not out of the character of the actions to the performance of which there is a right.

(v) To be distinguished from special rights, of course, are special liberties, where, exceptionally, one person is *exempted* from obligations to which most are subject but does not thereby acquire a *right* to which there is a correlative obligation. If you catch me reading your brother's diary, you say, "You have no right to read it." I say, "I have a right to read it – your brother said I might unless he told me not to, and he has not told me not to." Here I have been specially *licensed* by your brother who had a right to require me not to read his diary, so I am exempted from the moral obligation not to read it, but your brother is under no obligation to let me go on reading it. Cases where *rights*, not liberties, are accorded to manage or interfere with another person's affairs are those where the license is not revocable at will by the person according the right.

(B) *General rights*. In contrast with special rights, which constitute a justification peculiar to the holder of the right for interfering with another's freedom, are general rights, which are asserted defensively, when some unjustified interference is anticipated or threatened, in order to point out that the interference is unjustified. "I have the right to say what I think."[13] "I have the right to worship as I please." Such rights share two important characteristics with special rights. (1) To have them is to have a moral justification for determining how another shall act, viz., that he shall not interfere.[14] (2) The moral justification does not arise from the character of the particular action to the performance of which the claimant has a right; what justifies the claim is simply – there being no special relation between him and those who are threatening to interfere to justify that interference – that this is a particular exemplification of the equal right to be free. But there are of course striking differences between such defensive general rights and special rights. (1) General rights do not arise out of any special relationship or transaction between men. (2) They are not rights which are peculiar to those who have them but are rights which all men capable of choice have in the absence of those special conditions which give rise to special rights. (3) General rights have as correlatives obligations not to interfere to which everyone else is subject and not merely the parties to some special relationship or transaction, though of course they will often be asserted when some particular persons threaten to interfere as a moral objection to that interference. To assert a general right is to claim in relation to some particular action the equal right of all men to be free in the absence of any of those special conditions which constitute a special right to limit another's freedom; to assert a special right is to assert in relation to some particular action a right constituted by such special conditions to limit another's freedom. The assertion of general rights directly invokes the principle that all men equally have the right to be free; the assertion of a special right (as I attempt to show in Section III) invokes it indirectly.

III

It is, I hope, clear that unless it is recognized that interference with another's freedom requires a moral justification the notion of a right could have no place in morals; for to assert a right is to assert that there is such a justification. The characteristic function in moral discourse of those sentences in which the meaning of the expression "a right" is to be found – "I have a right to . . .," "You have no right to . . .," "What right have you to . . .?" – is to bring to bear on interferences with another's freedom, or on claims to interfere, a type of moral evaluation or criticism specially appropriate to interference with freedom and characteristically different from the moral criticism of actions made with the use of expressions like "right," "wrong," "good," and "bad." And this is only one of many different types of moral ground for saying "You ought . . ." or "You ought not. . . ." The use of the expression "What right have you to . . .?" shows this more clearly, perhaps, than the others; for we use it, just at the point where interference is actual or threatened, to call for the moral *title* of the person addressed to interfere; and we do this often without any suggestion at all that what he proposes to do is otherwise wrong and sometimes with the implication that the same interference on the part of another person would be unobjectionable.

But though our use in moral discourse of "a right" does presuppose the recognition that interference with another's freedom requires a moral justification, this would not itself suffice to establish, except in a sense easily trivialized, that in the recognition of moral rights there is implied the recognition that all men have a right to equal freedom; for unless there is some restriction inherent in the meaning of "a right" on the type of moral justification for interference which can constitute a right, the principle could be made wholly vacuous. It would, for example, be possible to adopt the principle and then assert that some characteristic or behavior of some human beings (that they are improvident, or atheists, or Jews, or Negroes) constitutes a moral justification for interfering with their freedom; *any* differences between men could, so far as my argument has yet gone, be treated as a moral justification for interference and so constitute a right, so that the equal right of all men to be free would be compatible with gross inequality. It may well be that the expression "moral" itself imports some restriction on what can constitute a moral justification for interference which would avoid this consequence, but I cannot myself yet show that this is so. It is, on the other hand, clear to me that the moral justification for interference

which is to constitute a *right* to interfere (as distinct from merely making it morally good or desirable to interfere) is restricted to certain special conditions and that this is inherent in the meaning of "a right" (unless this is used so loosely that it could be replaced by the other moral expressions mentioned). Claims to interfere with another's freedom based on the general character of the activities interfered with (e.g., the folly or cruelty of "native" practices) or the general character of the parties ("We are Germans; they are Jews") even when well founded are not matters of moral right or obligation. Submission in such cases even where proper is not *due to* or *owed to* the individuals who interfere; it would be equally proper whoever of the same class of persons interfered. Hence other elements in our moral vocabulary suffice to describe this case, and it is confusing here to talk of rights. We saw in Section II that the types of justification for interference involved in special rights was independent of the character of the action to the performance of which there was a right but depended upon certain previous transactions and relations between individuals (such as promises, consent, authorization, submission to mutual restrictions). Two questions here suggest themselves: (1) On what intelligible principle could these bare forms of promising, consenting, submission to mutual restrictions, be either necessary or sufficient, irrespective of their content, to justify interference with another's freedom? (2) What characteristics have these types of transaction or relationship in common? The answer to both these questions is I think this: If we justify interference on such grounds as we give when we claim a moral right, we are in fact indirectly invoking as our justification the principle that all men have an equal right to be free. For we are in fact saying in the case of promises and consents or authorizations that this claim to interfere with another's freedom is justified because he has, in exercise of his equal right to be free, freely chosen to create this claim; and in the case of mutual restrictions we are in fact saying that this claim to interfere with another's freedom is justified because it is fair; and it is fair because only so will there be an equal distribution of restrictions and so of freedom among this group of men. So in the case of special rights as well as of general rights recognition of them implies the recognition of the equal right of all men to be free.

Notes

1   I was first stimulated to think along these lines by Mr. Stuart Hampshire, and I have reached by different routes a conclusion similar to his.

2   Further explanation of the perplexing terminology of freedom is, I fear, necessary. *Coercion* includes, besides preventing a person from doing what he chooses, making his choice less eligible by threats; *restraint* includes any action designed to make the exercise of choice impossible and so includes killing or enslaving a person. But neither coercion nor restraint includes *competition*. In terms of the distinction between "having a right to" and "being at liberty to," used above and further discussed in Section I, B, all men may have, consistently with the obligation to forbear from coercion, the *liberty* to satisfy if they can such at least of their desires as are not designed to coerce or injure others, even though in fact, owing to scarcity, one man's satisfaction causes another's frustration. In conditions of extreme scarcity this distinction between competition and coercion will not be worth drawing; natural rights are only of importance "where peace is possible" (Locke). Further, freedom (the absence of coercion) can be *valueless* to those victims of unrestricted competition too poor to make use of it; so it will be pedantic to point out to them that though starving they are free. This is the truth exaggerated by the Marxists whose *identification* of poverty with lack of freedom confuses two different evils.

3   Save those general rights (cf. Section II, B) which are particular exemplifications of the right of all men to be free.

4   Is the notion of *a* right found in either Plato or Aristotle? There seems to be no Greek word for it as distinct from "right" or "just" (δικαίον), though expressions like τὰ ἐμὰ δικαία are I believe fourth-century legal idioms. The natural expressions in Plato are τὸ ἑαυτοῦ (ἔχειν) or τὰ τινὶ ὀφειλόμενα, but these seem confined to property or debts. There is no place for a moral right unless the moral value of individual freedom is recognized.

5   As W.D. Lamont has seen: cf. his *Principles of Moral Judgment* (Oxford, 1946); for the jurists, cf. Hohfeld's *Fundamental Legal Conceptions* (New Haven, 1923).

6   Here and subsequently I use "interfere with another's freedom," "limit another's freedom," "determine how another shall act," to mean either the use of coercion or demanding that a person shall do or not do some action. The connection between these two types of "interference" is too complex for discussion here; I think it is enough for present purposes to point out that having a justification for demanding that a person shall or shall not do some action is a necessary though not a sufficient condition for justifying coercion.

7   I write "duties" here because one factor obscuring the nature of a right is the philosophical use of "duty" and "obligation" for all cases where there are moral reasons for saying an action ought to be done or not done. In fact "duty," "obligation," "right," and "good" come from different segments of morality, concern different types of conduct, and make different types of moral criticism or evaluation. Most important are the points (1) that obligations may be voluntarily incurred or created, (2) that they are *owed to* special persons (who have rights), (3) that they do not arise out of the character of the actions which are obligatory but out of the relationship of the parties. Language roughly though not consistently confines the use of "having an obligation" to such cases.

8   The use here of the generalized "duty" is apt to prejudice the question whether animals and babies have rights.

9   Cf. A.H. Campbell, *The Structure of Stair's Institutes* (Glasgow, 1954), p. 31.

10   Continental jurists distinguish between "*subjektives*" and "*objektives Recht*," which corresponds very well to the distinction between *a* right, which an individual has, and what it is right to do.

11   Cf. Section (B).

12   Though it may be *better* (the lesser of two evils) that he should: cf. item iii below.

13   In speech the difference between general and special rights is often marked by stressing the pronoun where a special right is claimed or where the special right is denied. "You have no right to stop him reading that book" refers to the reader's general right. "*You* have no right to stop him reading that book" denies that the person addressed has a special right to interfere though others may have.

14   Strictly, in the assertion of a general right both the *right* to forbearance from coercion and the *liberty* to do the specified action are asserted, the first in the face of actual or threatened coercion, the second as an objection to an actual or anticipated demand that the action should not be done. The first has as its correlative an obligation upon everyone to forbear from coercion; the second the absence in any one of a justification for such a demand. Here, in Hohfeld's words, the correlative is not an obligation but a "no-right."

20

Taking Rights Seriously[1]

Ronald Dworkin

1 The Rights of Citizens

The language of rights now dominates political debate in the United States. Does the Government respect the moral and political rights of its citizens? Or does the Government's war policy, or its race policy, fly in the face of these rights? Do the minorities whose rights have been violated have the right to violate the law in return? Or does the silent majority itself have rights, including the right that those who break the law be punished? It is not surprising that these questions are now prominent. The concept of rights, and particularly the concept of rights against the Government, has its most natural use when a political society is divided, and appeals to co-operation or a common goal are pointless.

The debate does not include the issue of whether citizens have *some* moral rights against their Government. It seems accepted on all sides that they do. Conventional lawyers and politicians take it as a point of pride that our legal system recognizes, for example, individual rights of free speech, equality, and due process. They base their claim that our law deserves respect, at least in part, on that fact, for they would not claim that totalitarian systems deserve the same loyalty.

Some philosophers, of course, reject the idea that citizens have rights apart from what the law happens to give them. Bentham thought that the idea of moral rights was 'nonsense on stilts'. But that view has never been part of our orthodox political theory, and politicians of both parties appeal to the rights of the people to justify a great part of what they want to do. I shall not be concerned, in this essay, to defend the thesis that citizens have moral rights against their governments; I want instead to explore the implications of that thesis for those, including the present United States Government, who profess to accept it.

It is much in dispute, of course, what *particular* rights citizens have. Does the acknowledged right to free speech, for example, include the right to participate in nuisance demonstrations? In practice the Government will have the last word on what an individual's rights are, because its police will do what its officials and courts say. But that does not mean that the Government's view is necessarily the correct view; anyone who thinks it does must believe that men and women have only such moral rights as Government chooses to grant, which means that they have no moral rights at all.

All this is sometimes obscured in the United States by the constitutional system. The American Constitution provides a set of individual *legal* rights in the First Amendment, and in the due process, equal protection, and similar clauses. Under present legal practice the Supreme Court has the power to declare an act of Congress or of a state legislature void if the Court finds that the act offends these provisions. This practice has led some commentators to suppose that individual moral rights are fully protected by this system, but that is hardly so, nor could it be so.

The Constitution fuses legal and moral issues, by making the validity of a law depend on the

Originally published in *New York Review of Books*, 18 December 1970. Reprinted by permission of the author.

answer to complex moral problems, like the problem of whether a particular statute respects the inherent equality of all men. This fusion has important consequences for the debates about civil disobedience; I have described these elsewhere[2] and I shall refer to them later. But it leaves open two prominent questions. It does not tell us whether the Constitution, even properly interpreted, recognizes all the moral rights that citizens have, and it does not tell us whether, as many suppose, citizens would have a duty to obey the law even if it did invade their moral rights.

Both questions become crucial when some minority claims moral rights which the law denies, like the right to run its local school system, and which lawyers agree are not protected by the Constitution. The second question becomes crucial when, as now, the majority is sufficiently aroused so that Constitutional amendments to eliminate rights, like the right against self-incrimination, are seriously proposed. It is also crucial in nations, like the United Kingdom, that have no constitution of a comparable nature.

Even if the Constitution were perfect, of course, and the majority left it alone, it would not follow that the Supreme Court could guarantee the individual rights of citizens. A Supreme Court decision is still a legal decision, and it must take into account precedent and institutional considerations like relations between the Court and Congress, as well as morality. And no judicial decision is necessarily the right decision. Judges stand for different positions on controversial issues of law and morals and, as the fights over Nixon's Supreme Court nominations showed, a President is entitled to appoint judges of his own persuasion, provided that they are honest and capable.

So, though the constitutional system adds something to the protection of moral rights against the Government, it falls far short of guaranteeing these rights, or even establishing what they are. It means that, on some occasions, a department other than the legislature has the last word on these issues, which can hardly satisfy someone who thinks such a department profoundly wrong.

It is of course inevitable that some department of government will have the final say on what law will be enforced. When men disagree about moral rights, there will be no way for either side to prove its case, and some decision must stand if

there is not to be anarchy. But that piece of orthodox wisdom must be the beginning and not the end of a philosophy of legislation and enforcement. If we cannot insist that the Government reach the right answers about the rights of its citizens, we can insist at least that it try. We can insist that it take rights seriously, follow a coherent theory of what these rights are, and act consistently with its own professions. I shall try to show what that means, and how it bears on the present political debates.

2 Rights and the Right to Break the Law

I shall start with the most violently argued issue. Does an American ever have the moral right to break a law? Suppose someone admits a law is valid; does he therefore have a duty to obey it? Those who try to give an answer seem to fall into two camps. The conservatives, as I shall call them, seem to disapprove of any act of disobedience; they appear satisfied when such acts are prosecuted, and disappointed when convictions are reversed. The other group, the liberals, are much more sympathetic to at least some cases of disobedience; they sometimes disapprove of prosecutions and celebrate acquittals. If we look beyond these emotional reactions, however, and pay attention to the arguments the two parties use, we discover an astounding fact. Both groups give essentially the same answer to the question of principle that supposedly divides them.

The answer that both parties give is this. In a democracy, or at least a democracy that in principle respects individual rights, each citizen has a general moral duty to obey all the laws, even though he would like some of them changed. He owes that duty to his fellow citizens, who obey laws that they do not like, to his benefit. But this general duty cannot be an absolute duty, because even a society that is in principle just may produce unjust laws and policies, and a man has duties other than his duties to the State. A man must honour his duties to his God and to his conscience, and if these conflict with his duty to the State, then he is entitled, in the end, to do what he judges to be right. If he decides that he must break the law, however, then he must submit to the judgment and punishment that the State imposes, in recognition of the fact that his duty to his fellow citizens was overwhelmed but not extinguished by his religious or moral obligation.

Of course this common answer can be elaborated in very different ways. Some would describe the duty to the State as fundamental, and picture the dissenter as a religious or moral fanatic. Others would describe the duty to the State in grudging terms, and picture those who oppose it as moral heroes. But these are differences in tone, and the position I described represents, I think, the view of most of those who find themselves arguing either for or against civil disobedience in particular cases.

I do not claim that it is everyone's view. There must be some who put the duty to the State so high that they do not grant that it can ever be overcome. There are certainly some who would deny that a man ever has a moral duty to obey the law, at least in the United States today. But these two extreme positions are the slender tails of a bell curve, and all those who fall in between hold the orthodox position I described – that men have a duty to obey the law but have the right to follow their consciences when it conflicts with that duty.

But if that is so, then we have a paradox in the fact that men who give the same answer to a question of principle should seem to disagree so much, and to divide so fiercely, in particular cases. The paradox goes even deeper, for each party, in at least some cases, takes a position that seems flatly inconsistent with the theoretical position they both accept. This position is tested, for example, when someone evades the draft on grounds of conscience, or encourages others to commit this crime. Conservatives argue that such men must be prosecuted, even though they are sincere. Why must they be prosecuted? Because society cannot tolerate the decline in respect for the law that their act constitutes and encourages. They must be prosecuted, in short, to discourage them and others like them from doing what they have done.

But there seems to be a monstrous contradiction here. If a man has a right to do what his conscience tells him he must, then how can the State be justified in discouraging him from doing it? Is it not wicked for a state to forbid and punish what it acknowledges that men have a right to do?

Moreover, it is not just conservatives who argue that those who break the law out of moral conviction should be prosecuted. The liberal is notoriously opposed to allowing Southern school officials to go slow on desegregation, even though he acknowledges that these school officials think

they have a moral right to do what the law forbids. The liberal does not often argue, it is true, that the desegregation laws must be enforced to encourage general respect for law. He argues instead that the desegregation laws must be enforced because they are right. But his position also seems inconsistent: can it be right to prosecute men for doing what their conscience requires, when we acknowledge their right to follow their conscience?

We are therefore left with two puzzles. How can two parties to an issue of principle, each of which thinks it is in profound disagreement with the other, embrace the same position on that issue? How can it be that each side urges solutions to particular problems which seem flatly to contradict the position of principle that both accept? One possible answer is that some or all of those who accept the common position are hypocrites, paying lip service to rights of conscience which in fact they do not grant.

There is some plausibility in this charge. A sort of hypocrisy must be involved when public officials who claim to respect conscience deny Muhammad Ali the right to box in their states. If Ali, in spite of his religious scruples, had joined the Army, he would have been allowed to box even though, on the principles these officials say they honour, he would have been a worse human being for having done so. But there are few cases that seem so straightforward as this one, and even here the officials do not seem to recognize the contradiction between their acts and their principles. So we must search for some explanation beyond the truth that men often do not mean what they say.

The deeper explanation lies in a set of confusions that often embarrass arguments about rights. These confusions have clouded all the issues I mentioned at the outset and have crippled attempts to develop a coherent theory of how a government that respects rights must behave.

In order to explain this, I must call attention to the fact, familiar to philosophers but often ignored in political debate, that the word 'right' has different force in different contexts. In most cases when we say that someone has a 'right' to do something, we imply that it would be wrong to interfere with his doing it, or at least that some special grounds are needed for justifying any interference. I use this strong sense of right when I say that you have the right to spend your money gambling, if you wish, though you ought to spend it in a more worthwhile way. I mean that it would be wrong for anyone to interfere with you even though you propose to spend your money in a way that I think is wrong.

There is a clear difference between saying that someone has a right to do something in this sense and saying that it is the 'right' thing for him to do, or that he does no 'wrong' in doing it. Someone may have the right to do something that is the wrong thing for him to do, as might be the case with gambling. Conversely, something may be the right thing for him to do and yet he may have no right to do it, in the sense that it would not be wrong for someone to interfere with his trying. If our army captures an enemy soldier, we might say that the right thing for him to do is to try to escape, but it would not follow that it is wrong of us to try to stop him. We might admire him for trying to escape, and perhaps even think less of him if he did not. But there is no suggestion here that it is wrong of us to stand in his way; on the contrary, if we think our cause is just, we think it right for us to do all we can to stop him.

Ordinarily this distinction, between the issues of whether a man has a right to do something and whether it is the right thing for him to do, causes no trouble. But sometimes it does, because sometimes we say that a man has a right to do something when we mean only to deny that it is the wrong thing for him to do. Thus we say that the captured soldier has a 'right' to try to escape when we mean, not that we do wrong to stop him, but that he has no duty not to make the attempt. We use 'right' this way when we speak of someone having the 'right' to act on his own principles, or the 'right' to follow his own conscience. We mean that he does no wrong to proceed on his honest convictions, even though we disagree with these convictions, and even though, for policy or other reasons, we must force him to act contrary to them.

Suppose a man believes that welfare payments to the poor are profoundly wrong, because they sap enterprise, and so declares his full income-tax each year but declines to pay half of it. We might say that he has a right to refuse to pay, if he wishes, but that the Government has a right to proceed against him for the full tax, and to fine or jail him for late payment if that is necessary to keep the collection system working efficiently. We do not take this line in most cases; we do not say that the ordinary thief has a right to steal, if he wishes, so long as he pays the penalty. We say that

a man has the right to break the law, even though the State has a right to punish him, only when we think that, because of his convictions, he does no wrong in doing so.[3]

These distinctions enable us to see an ambiguity in the orthodox question: Does a man ever have a right to break the law? Does that question mean to ask whether he ever has a right to break the law in the strong sense, so that the Government would do wrong to stop him, by arresting and prosecuting him? Or does it mean to ask whether he ever does the right thing to break the law, so that we should all respect him even though the Government should jail him?

If we take the orthodox position to be an answer to the first — and most important — question, then the paradoxes I described arise. But if we take it as an answer to the second, they do not. Conservatives and liberals do agree that sometimes a man does not do the wrong thing to break a law, when his conscience so requires. They disagree, when they do, over the different issue of what the State's response should be. Both parties do think that sometimes the State should prosecute. But this is not inconsistent with the proposition that the man prosecuted did the right thing in breaking the law.

The paradoxes seem genuine because the two questions are not usually distinguished, and the orthodox position is presented as a general solution to the problem of civil disobedience. But once the distinction is made, it is apparent that the position has been so widely accepted only because, when it is applied, it is treated as an answer to the second question but not the first. The crucial distinction is obscured by the troublesome idea of a right to conscience; this idea has been at the centre of most recent discussions of political obligation, but it is a red herring drawing us away from the crucial political questions. The state of a man's conscience may be decisive, or central, when the issue is whether he does something morally wrong in breaking the law; but it need not be decisive or even central when the issue is whether he has a right, in the strong sense of that term, to do so. A man does not have the right, in that sense, to do whatever his conscience demands, but he may have the right, in that sense, to do something even though his conscience does not demand it.

If that is true, then there has been almost no serious attempt to answer the questions that almost everyone means to ask. We can make a fresh start by stating these questions more clearly. Does an American ever have the right, in a strong sense, to do something which is against the law? If so, when? In order to answer these questions put in that way, we must try to become clearer about the implications of the idea, mentioned earlier, that citizens have at least some rights against their government.

I said that in the United States citizens are supposed to have certain fundamental rights against their Government, certain moral rights made into legal rights by the Constitution. If this idea is significant, and worth bragging about, then these rights must be rights in the strong sense I just described. The claim that citizens have a right to free speech must imply that it would be wrong for the Government to stop them from speaking, even when the Government believes that what they will say will cause more harm than good. The claim cannot mean, on the prisoner-of-war analogy, only that citizens do no wrong in speaking their minds, though the Government reserves the right to prevent them from doing so.

This is a crucial point, and I want to labour it. Of course a responsible government must be ready to justify anything it does, particularly when it limits the liberty of its citizens. But normally it is a sufficient justification, even for an act that limits liberty, that the act is calculated to increase what the philosophers call general utility – that it is calculated to produce more over-all benefit than harm. So, though the New York City government needs a justification for forbidding motorists to drive up Lexington Avenue, it is sufficient justification if the proper officials believe, on sound evidence, that the gain to the many will outweigh the inconvenience to the few. When individual citizens are said to have rights against the Government, however, like the right of free speech, that must mean that this sort of justification is not enough. Otherwise the claim would not argue that individuals have special protection against the law when their rights are in play, and that is just the point of the claim.

Not all legal rights, or even Constitutional rights, represent moral rights against the Government. I now have the legal right to drive either way on Fifty-seventh Street, but the Government would do no wrong to make that street one-way if it thought it in the general interest to do so. I have a Constitutional right to vote for a congressman every two years, but the

national and state governments would do no wrong if, following the amendment procedure, they made a congressman's term four years instead of two, again on the basis of a judgment that this would be for the general good.

But those Constitutional rights that we call fundamental, like the right of free speech, are supposed to represent rights against the Government in the strong sense; that is the point of the boast that our legal system respects the fundamental rights of the citizen. If citizens have a moral right of free speech, then governments would do wrong to repeal the First Amendment that guarantees it, even if they were persuaded that the majority would be better off if speech were curtailed.

I must not overstate the point. Someone who claims that citizens have a right against the Government need not go so far as to say that the State is *never* justified in overriding that right. He might say, for example, that although citizens have a right to free speech, the Government may override that right when necessary to protect the rights of others, or to prevent a catastrophe, or even to obtain a clear and major public benefit (though if he acknowledged this last as a possible justification he would be treating the right in question as not among the most important or fundamental). What he cannot do is to say that the Government is justified in overriding a right on the minimal grounds that would be sufficient if no such right existed. He cannot say that the Government is entitled to act on no more than a judgment that its act is likely to produce, overall, a benefit to the community. That admission would make his claim of a right pointless, and would show him to be using some sense of 'right' other than the strong sense necessary to give his claim the political importance it is normally taken to have.

But then the answers to our two questions about disobedience seem plain, if unorthodox. In our society a man does sometimes have the right, in the strong sense, to disobey a law. He has that right whenever that law wrongly invades his rights against the Government. If he has a moral right to free speech, that is, then he has a moral right to break any law that the Government, by virtue of his right, had no right to adopt. The right to disobey the law is not a separate right, having something to do with conscience, additional to other rights against the Government. It is simply a feature of these rights against the

Government, and it cannot be denied in principle without denying that any such rights exist.

These answers seem obvious once we take rights against the Government to be rights in the strong sense I described. If I have a right to speak my mind on political issues, then the Government does wrong to make it illegal for me to do so, even if it thinks this is in the general interest. If, nevertheless, the Government does make my act illegal, then it does a further wrong to enforce that law against me. My right against the Government means that it is wrong for the Government to stop me from speaking; the Government cannot make it right to stop me just by taking the first step.

This does not, of course, tell us exactly what rights men do have against the Government. It does not tell us whether the right of free speech includes the right of demonstration. But it does mean that passing a law cannot affect such rights as men do have, and that is of crucial importance, because it dictates the attitude that an individual is entitled to take toward his personal decision when civil disobedience is in question.

Both conservatives and liberals suppose that in a society which is generally decent everyone has a duty to obey the law, whatever it is. That is the source of the 'general duty' clause in the orthodox position, and though liberals believe that this duty can sometimes be 'overridden', even they suppose, as the orthodox position maintains, that the duty of obedience remains in some submerged form, so that a man does well to accept punishment in recognition of that duty. But this general duty is almost incoherent in a society that recognizes rights. If a man believes he has a right to demonstrate, then he must believe that it would be wrong for the Government to stop him, with or without benefit of a law. If he is entitled to believe that, then it is silly to speak of a duty to obey the law as such, or of a duty to accept the punishment that the State has no right to give.

Conservatives will object to the short work I have made of their point. They will argue that even if the Government was wrong to adopt some law, like a law limiting speech, there are independent reasons why the Government is justified in enforcing the law once adopted. When the law forbids demonstration, then, so they argue, some principle more important than the individual's right to speak is brought into play, namely the principle of respect for law. If a law, even a bad law, is left unenforced, then respect for law is

weakened, and society as a whole suffers. So an individual loses his moral right to speak when speech is made criminal, and the Government must, for the common good and for the general benefit, enforce the law against him.

But this argument, though popular, is plausible only if we forget what it means to say that an individual has a right against the State. It is far from plain that civil disobedience lowers respect for law, but even if we suppose that it does, this fact is irrelevant. The prospect of utilitarian gains cannot justify preventing a man from doing what he has a right to do, and the supposed gains in respect for law are simply utilitarian gains. There would be no point in the boast that we respect individual rights unless that involved some sacrifice, and the sacrifice in question must be that we give up whatever marginal benefits our country would receive from overriding these rights when they prove inconvenient. So the general benefit cannot be a good ground for abridging rights, even when the benefit in question is a heightened respect for law.

But perhaps I do wrong to assume that the argument about respect for law is only an appeal to general utility. I said that a state may be justified in overriding or limiting rights on other grounds, and we must ask, before rejecting the conservative position, whether any of these apply. The most important – and least well understood – of these other grounds invokes the notion of *competing rights* that would be jeopardized if the right in question were not limited. Citizens have personal rights to the State's protection as well as personal rights to be free from the State's interference, and it may be necessary for the Government to choose between these two sorts of rights. The law of defamation, for example, limits the personal right of any man to say what he thinks, because it requires him to have good grounds for what he says. But this law is justified, even for those who think that it does invade a personal right, by the fact that it protects the right of others not to have their reputations ruined by a careless statement.

The individual rights that our society acknowledges often conflict in this way, and when they do it is the job of government to discriminate. If the Government makes the right choice, and protects the more important at the cost of the less, then it has not weakened or cheapened the notion of a right; on the contrary it would have done so had it failed to protect the more important of the two.

So we must acknowledge that the Government has a reason for limiting rights if it plausibly believes that a competing right is more important.

May the conservative seize on this fact? He might argue that I did wrong to characterize his argument as one that appeals to the general benefit, because it appeals instead to competing rights, namely the moral right of the majority to have its laws enforced, or the right of society to maintain the degree of order and security it wishes. These are the rights, he would say, that must be weighed against the individual's right to do what the wrongful law prohibits.

But this new argument is confused, because it depends on yet another ambiguity in the language of rights. It is true that we speak of the 'right' of society to do what it wants, but this cannot be a 'competing right' of the sort that may justify the invasion of a right against the Government. The existence of rights against the Government would be jeopardized if the Government were able to defeat such a right by appealing to the right of a democratic majority to work its will. A right against the Government must be a right to do something even when the majority thinks it would be wrong to do it, and even when the majority would be worse off for having it done. If we now say that society has a right to do whatever is in the general benefit, or the right to preserve whatever sort of environment the majority wishes to live in, and we mean that these are the sort of rights that provide justification for overruling any rights against the Government that may conflict, then we have annihilated the latter rights.

In order to save them, we must recognize as competing rights only the rights of other members of the society as individuals. We must distinguish the 'rights' of the majority as such, which cannot count as a justification for overruling individual rights, and the personal rights of members of a majority, which might well count. The test we must use is this. Someone has a competing right to protection, which must be weighed against an individual right to act, if that person would be entitled to demand that protection from his government on his own title, as an individual, without regard to whether a majority of his fellow citizens joined in the demand.

It cannot be true, on this test, that anyone has a right to have all the laws of the nation enforced. He has a right to have enforced only those criminal laws, for example, that he would have a right to have enacted if they were not already law. The

laws against personal assault may well fall into that class. If the physically vulnerable members of the community – those who need police protection against personal violence – were only a small minority, it would still seem plausible to say that they were entitled to that protection. But the laws that provide a certain level of quiet in public places, or that authorize and finance a foreign war, cannot be thought to rest on individual rights. The timid lady on the streets of Chicago is not entitled to just the degree of quiet that now obtains, nor is she entitled to have boys drafted to fight in wars she approves. There are laws – perhaps desirable laws – that provide these advantages for her, but the justification for these laws, if they can be justified at all, is the common desire of a large majority, not her personal right. If, therefore, these laws do abridge someone else's moral right to protest, or his right to personal security, she cannot urge a competing right to justify the abridgement. She has no personal right to have such laws passed, and she has no competing right to have them enforced either.

So the conservative cannot advance his argument much on the ground of competing rights, but he may want to use another ground. A government, he may argue, may be justified in abridging the personal rights of its citizens in an emergency, or when a very great loss may be prevented, or, perhaps, when some major benefit can clearly be secured. If the nation is at war, a policy of censorship may be justified even though it invades the right to say what one thinks on matters of political controversy. But the emergency must be genuine. There must be what Oliver Wendell Holmes described as a clear and present danger, and the danger must be one of magnitude.

Can the conservative argue that when any law is passed, even a wrongful law, this sort of justification is available for enforcing it? His argument might be something of this sort. If the Government once acknowledges that it may be wrong – that the legislature might have adopted, the executive approved, and the courts left standing, a law that in fact abridges important rights – then this admission will lead not simply to a marginal decline in respect for law, but to a crisis of order. Citizens may decide to obey only those laws they personally approve, and that is anarchy. So the Government must insist that whatever a citizen's rights may be before a law is passed and upheld by the courts, his rights thereafter are determined by that law.

But this argument ignores the primitive distinction between what may happen and what will happen. If we allow speculation to support the justification of emergency or decisive benefit, then, again, we have annihilated rights. We must, as Learned Hand said, discount the gravity of the evil threatened by the likelihood of reaching that evil. I know of no genuine evidence to the effect that tolerating some civil disobedience, out of respect for the moral position of its authors, will increase such disobedience, let alone crime in general. The case that it will must be based on vague assumptions about the contagion of ordinary crimes, assumptions that are themselves unproved, and that are in any event largely irrelevant. It seems at least as plausible to argue that tolerance will increase respect for officials and for the bulk of the laws they promulgate, or at least retard the rate of growing disrespect.

If the issue were simply the question whether the community would be marginally better off under strict law enforcement, then the Government would have to decide on the evidence we have, and it might not be unreasonable to decide, on balance, that it would. But since rights are at stake, the issue is the very different one of whether tolerance would destroy the community or threaten it with great harm, and it seems to me simply mindless to suppose that the evidence makes that probable or even conceivable.

The argument from emergency is confused in another way as well. It assumes that the Government must take the position either that a man never has the right to break the law, or that he always does. I said that any society that claims to recognize rights at all must abandon the notion of a general duty to obey the law that holds in all cases. This is important, because it shows that there are no short cuts to meeting a citizen's claim of right. If a citizen argues that he has a moral right not to serve in the Army, or to protest in a way he finds effective, then an official who wants to answer him, and not simply bludgeon him into obedience, must respond to the particular point he makes, and cannot point to the draft law or a Supreme Court decision as having even special, let alone decisive, weight. Sometimes an official who considers the citizen's moral arguments in good faith will be persuaded that the citizen's claim is plausible, or even right. It does not follow, however, that he will always be persuaded or that he always should be.

I must emphasize that all these propositions concern the strong sense of right, and they therefore leave open important questions about the right thing to do. If a man believes he has the right to break the law, he must then ask whether he does the right thing to exercise that right. He must remember that reasonable men can differ about whether he has a right against the Government, and therefore the right to break the law, that he thinks he has; and therefore that reasonable men can oppose him in good faith. He must take into account the various consequences his acts will have, whether they involve violence, and such other considerations as the context makes relevant; he must not go beyond the rights he can in good faith claim, to acts that violate the rights of others.

On the other hand, if some official, like a prosecutor, believes that the citizen does *not* have the right to break the law, then *he* must ask whether he does the right thing to enforce it. In the article I mentioned earlier I argued that certain features of our legal system, and in particular the fusion of legal and moral issues in our Constitution, mean that citizens often do the right thing in exercising what they take to be moral rights to break the law, and that prosecutors often do the right thing in failing to prosecute them for it. I will not repeat those arguments here; instead I want to ask whether the requirement that Government take its citizens' rights seriously has anything to do with the crucial question of what these rights are.

3 Controversial Rights

The argument so far has been hypothetical: if a man has a particular moral right against the Government, that right survives contrary legislation or adjudication. But this does not tell us what rights he has, and it is notorious that reasonable men disagree about that. There is wide agreement on certain clear-cut cases; almost everyone who believes in rights at all would admit, for example, that a man has a moral right to speak his mind in a non-provocative way on matters of political concern, and that this is an important right that the State must go to great pains to protect. But there is great controversy as to the limits of such paradigm rights, and the so-called 'anti-riot' law involved in the Chicago Seven trial is a case in point.

The defendants were accused of conspiring to

cross state lines with the intention of causing a riot. This charge is vague – perhaps unconstitutionally vague – but the law apparently defines as criminal emotional speeches which argue that violence is justified in order to secure political equality. Does the right of free speech protect this sort of speech? That, of course, is a legal issue, because it invokes the free-speech clause of the First Amendment of the Constitution. But it is also a moral issue, because, as I said, we must treat the First Amendment as an attempt to protect a moral right. It is part of the job of governing to 'define' moral rights through statutes and judicial decisions, that is, to declare officially the extent that moral rights will be taken to have in law. Congress faced this task in voting on the anti-riot bill, and the Supreme Court will face it if the Chicago Seven case goes that far. How should the different departments of government go about defining moral rights?

They should begin with a sense that whatever they decide might be wrong. History and their descendants may judge that they acted unjustly when they thought they were right. If they take their duty seriously, they must try to limit their mistakes, and they must therefore try to discover where the dangers of mistake lie.

They might choose one of two very different models for this purpose. The first model recommends striking a balance between the rights of the individual and the demands of society at large. If the Government *infringes* on a moral right (for example, by defining the right of free speech more narrowly than justice requires), then it has done the individual a wrong. On the other hand, if the Government *inflates* a right (by defining it more broadly than justice requires) then it cheats society of some general benefit, like safe streets, that it is perfectly entitled to have. So a mistake on one side is as serious as a mistake on the other. The course of government is to steer to the middle, to balance the general good and personal rights, giving to each its due.

When the Government, or any of its branches, defines a right, it must bear in mind, according to the first model, the social cost of different proposals and make the necessary adjustments. It must not grant the same freedom to noisy demonstrations as it grants to calm political discussion, for example, because the former causes much more trouble than the latter. Once it decides how much of a right to recognize, it must enforce its decision to the full. That means permitting an individual to act within his rights, as the Government has defined them, but not beyond, so that if anyone breaks the law, even on grounds of conscience, he must be punished. No doubt any government will make mistakes, and will regret decisions once taken. That is inevitable. But this middle policy will ensure that errors on one side will balance out errors on the other over the long run.

The first model, described in this way, has great plausibility, and most laymen and lawyers, I think, would respond to it warmly. The metaphor of balancing the public interest against personal claims is established in our political and judicial rhetoric, and this metaphor gives the model both familiarity and appeal. Nevertheless, the first model is a false one, certainly in the case of rights generally regarded as important, and the metaphor is the heart of its error.

The institution of rights against the Government is not a gift of God, or an ancient ritual, or a national sport. It is a complex and troublesome practice that makes the Government's job of securing the general benefit more difficult and more expensive, and it would be a frivolous and wrongful practice unless it served some point. Anyone who professes to take rights seriously, and who praises our Government for respecting them, must have some sense of what that point is. He must accept, at the minimum, one or both of two important ideas. The first is the vague but powerful idea of human dignity. This idea, associated with Kant, but defended by philosophers of different schools, supposes that there are ways of treating a man that are inconsistent with recognizing him as a full member of the human community, and holds that such treatment is profoundly unjust.

The second is the more familiar idea of political equality. This supposes that the weaker members of a political community are entitled to the same concern and respect of their government as the more powerful members have secured for themselves, so that if some men have freedom of decision whatever the effect on the general good, then all men must have the same freedom. I do not want to defend or elaborate these ideas here, but only to insist that anyone who claims that citizens have rights must accept ideas very close to these.[4]

It makes sense to say that a man has a fundamental right against the Government, in the strong sense, like free speech, if that right is necessary to protect his dignity, or his standing as equally entitled to concern and respect, or some other personal value of like consequence. It does not make sense otherwise.

So if rights make sense at all, then the invasion of a relatively important right must be a very serious matter. It means treating a man as less than a man, or as less worthy of concern than other men. The institution of rights rests on the conviction that this is a grave injustice, and that it is worth paying the incremental cost in social policy or efficiency that is necessary to prevent it. But then it must be wrong to say that inflating rights is as serious as invading them. If the Government errs on the side of the individual, then it simply pays a little more in social efficiency than it has to pay; it pays a little more, that is, of the same coin that it has already decided must be spent. But if it errs against the individual it inflicts an insult upon him that, on its own reckoning, it is worth a great deal of that coin to avoid.

So the first model is indefensible. It rests, in fact, on a mistake I discussed earlier, namely the confusion of society's rights with the rights of members of society. 'Balancing' is appropriate when the Government must choose between competing claims of right – between the Southerner's claim to freedom of association, for example, and the black man's claim to an equal education. Then the Government can do nothing but estimate the merits of the competing claims, and act on its estimate. The first model assumes that the 'right' of the majority is a competing right that must be balanced in this way; but that, as I argued before, is a confusion that threatens to destroy the concept of individual rights. It is worth noticing that the community rejects the first model in that area where the stakes for the individual are highest, the criminal process. We say that it is better that a great many guilty men go free than that one innocent man be punished, and that homily rests on the choice of the second model for government.

The second model treats abridging a right as much more serious than inflating one, and its recommendations follow from that judgment. It stipulates that once a right is recognized in clear-cut cases, then the Government should act to cut off that right only when some compelling reason is presented, some reason that is consistent with the suppositions on which the original right must be based. It cannot be an argument for curtailing a right, once granted, simply that society would

pay a further price in extending it. There must be something special about that further cost, or there must be some other feature of the case, that makes it sensible to say that although great social cost is warranted to protect the original right, this particular cost is not necessary. Otherwise, the Government's failure to extend the right will show that its recognition of the right in the original case is a sham, a promise that it intends to keep only until that becomes inconvenient.

How can we show that a particular cost is not worth paying without taking back the initial recognition of a right? I can think of only three sorts of grounds that can consistently be used to limit the definition of a particular right. First, the Government might show that the values protected by the original right are not really at stake in the marginal case, or are at stake only in some attenuated form. Second, it might show that if the right is defined to include the marginal case, then some competing right, in the strong sense I described earlier, would be abridged. Third, it might show that if the right were so defined, then the cost to society would not be simply incremental, but would be of a degree far beyond the cost paid to grant the original right, a degree great enough to justify whatever assault on dignity or equality might be involved.

It is fairly easy to apply these grounds to one problem the Supreme Court has recently faced, and must face soon again. The draft law provides an exemption for conscientious objectors, but this exemption, as interpreted by the draft boards, has been limited to those who object to *all* wars on *religious* grounds. If we suppose that the exemption is justified on the ground that an individual has a moral right not to kill in violation of his own principles, then the question is raised whether it is proper to exclude those whose morality is not based on religion, or whose morality is sufficiently complex to distinguish among wars. The Court has just held that the draft boards are wrong to exclude the former, and it will soon be asked to decide whether they are wrong to exclude the latter as well.

None of the three grounds I listed can justify either of these exclusions. The invasion of personality in forcing men to kill when they believe killing immoral is just as great when these beliefs are based on secular grounds, or take account of the fact that wars differ in morally relevant ways, and there is no pertinent difference in competing rights or in national emergency. There are differences among the cases, of course, but they are insufficient to justify the distinction. A government that is secular on principle cannot prefer a religious to a non-religious morality as such. There are utilitarian arguments in favour of limiting the exception to religious or universal grounds – an exemption so limited may be less expensive to administer, and may allow easier discrimination between sincere and insincere applicants. But these utilitarian reasons are irrelevant, because they cannot count as grounds for limiting a right.

What about the anti-riot law, as applied in the Chicago trial? Does that law represent an improper limitation of the right to free speech, supposedly protected by the First Amendment? If we were to apply the first model for government to this issue, the argument for the anti-riot law would look strong. But if we set aside talk of balancing as inappropriate, and turn to the proper grounds for limiting a right, then the argument becomes a great deal weaker. The original right of free speech must suppose that it is an assault on human personality to stop a man from expressing what he honestly believes, particularly on issues affecting how he is governed. Surely the assault is greater, and not less, when he is stopped from expressing those principles of political morality that he holds most passionately, in the face of what he takes to be outrageous violations of these principles.

It may be said that the anti-riot law leaves him free to express these principles in a non-provocative way. But that misses the point of the connection between expression and dignity. A man cannot express himself freely when he cannot match his rhetoric to his outrage, or when he must trim his sails to protect values he counts as nothing next to those he is trying to vindicate. It is true that some political dissenters speak in ways that shock the majority, but it is arrogant for the majority to suppose that the orthodox methods of expression are the proper ways to speak, for this is a denial of equal concern and respect. If the point of the right is to protect the dignity of dissenters, then we must make judgments about appropriate speech with the personalities of the dissenters in mind, not the personality of the 'silent' majority for whom the anti-riot law is no restraint at all.

So the argument fails, that the personal values protected by the original right are less at stake in this marginal case. We must consider whether competing rights, or some grave threat to society, nevertheless justify the anti-riot law. We can consider these two grounds together, because the only plausible competing rights are rights to be free from violence, and violence is the only plausible threat to society that the context provides.

I have no right to burn your house, or stone you or your car, or swing a bicycle chain against your skull, even if I find these to be natural means of expression. But the defendants in the Chicago trial were not accused of direct violence; the argument runs that the acts of speech they planned made it likely that others would do acts of violence, either in support of or out of hostility to what they said. Does this provide a justification?

The question would be different if we could say with any confidence how much and what sort of violence the anti-riot law might be expected to prevent. Will it save two lives a year, or two hundred, or two thousand? Two thousand dollars of property, or two hundred thousand, or two million? No one can say, not simply because prediction is next to impossible, but because we have no firm understanding of the process by which demonstration disintegrates into riot, and in particular of the part played by inflammatory speech, as distinct from poverty, police brutality, blood lust, and all the rest of human and economic failure. The Government must try, of course, to reduce the violent waste of lives and property, but it must recognize that any attempt to locate and remove a cause of riot, short of a reorganization of society, must be an exercise in speculation, trial, and error. It must make its decisions under conditions of high uncertainty, and the institution of rights, taken seriously, limits its freedom to experiment under such conditions.

It forces the Government to bear in mind that preventing a man from speaking or demonstrating offers him a certain and profound insult, in return for a speculative benefit that may in any event be achieved in other if more expensive ways. When lawyers say that rights may be limited to protect other rights, or to prevent catastrophe, they have in mind cases in which cause and effect are relatively clear, like the familiar example of a man falsely crying 'Fire!' in a crowded theatre.

But the Chicago story shows how obscure the causal connections can become. Were the speeches of Hoffman or Rubin necessary conditions of the riot? Or had thousands of people come to Chicago for the purposes of rioting anyway, as the Government also argues? Were they in any case sufficient conditions? Or could the police have contained the violence if they had not been so busy contributing to it, as the staff of the President's Commission on Violence said they were?

These are not easy questions, but if rights mean anything, then the Government cannot simply assume answers that justify its conduct. If a man has a right to speak, if the reasons that support that right extend to provocative political speech, and if the effects of such speech on violence are unclear, then the Government is not entitled to make its first attack on that problem by denying that right. It may be that abridging the right to speak is the least expensive course, or the least damaging to police morale, or the most popular politically. But these are utilitarian arguments in favour of starting one place rather than another, and such arguments are ruled out by the concept of rights.

This point may be obscured by the popular belief that political activists look forward to violence and 'ask for trouble' in what they say. They can hardly complain, in the general view, if they are taken to be the authors of the violence they expect, and treated accordingly. But this repeats the confusion I tried to explain earlier between having a right and doing the right thing. The speaker's motives may be relevant in deciding whether he does the right thing in speaking passionately about issues that may inflame or enrage the audience. But if he has a right to speak, because the danger in allowing him to speak is speculative, his motives cannot count as independent evidence in the argument that justifies stopping him.

But what of the individual rights of those who will be destroyed by a riot, of the passer-by who will be killed by a sniper's bullet or the shopkeeper who will be ruined by looting? To put the issue in this way, as a question of competing rights, suggests a principle that would undercut the effect of uncertainty. Shall we say that some rights to protection are so important that the Government is justified in doing all it can to maintain them? Shall we therefore say that the Government may abridge the rights of others to act when their acts might simply increase the risk, by however slight or speculative a margin, that some person's right to life or property will be violated?

Some such principle is relied on by those who oppose the Supreme Court's recent liberal rulings on police procedure. These rulings increase the chance that a guilty man will go free, and therefore marginally increase the risk that any particular member of the community will be murdered, raped, or robbed. Some critics believe that the Court's decisions must therefore be wrong.

But no society that purports to recognize a variety of rights, on the ground that a man's dignity or equality may be invaded in a variety of ways, can accept such a principle. If forcing a man to testify against himself, or forbidding him to speak, does the damage that the rights against self-incrimination and the right of free speech assume, then it would be contemptuous for the State to tell a man that he must suffer this damage against the possibility that other men's risk of loss may be marginally reduced. If rights make sense, then the degrees of their importance cannot be so different that some count not at all when others are mentioned.

Of course the Government may discriminate and may stop a man from exercising his right to speak when there is a clear and substantial risk that his speech will do great damage to the person or property of others, and no other means of preventing this are at hand, as in the case of the man shouting 'Fire!' in a theatre. But we must reject the suggested principle that the Government can simply ignore rights to speak when life and property are in question. So long as the impact of speech on these other rights remains speculative and marginal, it must look elsewhere for levers to pull.

4 Why Take Rights Seriously?

I said at the beginning of this essay that I wanted to show what a government must do that professes to recognize individual rights. It must dispense with the claim that citizens never have a right to break its law, and it must not define citizens' rights so that these are cut off for supposed reasons of the general good. The present Government's policy towards civil disobedience, and its campaign against vocal protest, may therefore be thought to count against its sincerity.

One might well ask, however, whether it is wise to take rights all that seriously after all. America's genius, at least in her own legend, lies in not taking any abstract doctrine to its logical extreme. It may be time to ignore abstractions, and concentrate instead on giving the majority of our citizens a new sense of their Government's concern for their welfare, and of their title to rule.

That, in any event, is what Vice-President Agnew seems to believe. In a recent policy statement on the issue of 'weirdos' and social misfits, he said that the liberals' concern for individual rights was a headwind blowing in the face of the ship of state. That is a poor metaphor, but the philosophical point it expresses is very well taken. He recognizes, as many liberals do not, that the majority cannot travel as fast or as far as it would like if it recognizes the rights of individuals to do what, in the majority's terms, is the wrong thing to do.

The Vice-President supposes that rights are divisive, and that national unity and a new respect for law may be developed by taking them more sceptically. But he is wrong. America will continue to be divided by its social and foreign policy, and if the economy grows weaker the divisions will become more bitter. If we want our laws and our legal institutions to provide the ground rules within which these issues will be contested, then these ground rules must not be the conqueror's law that the dominant class imposes on the weaker, as Marx supposed the law of a capitalist society must be. The bulk of the law – that part which defines and implements social, economic, and foreign policy – cannot be neutral. It must state, in its greatest part, the majority's view of the common good. The institution of rights is therefore crucial, because it represents the majority's promise to the minorities that their dignity and equality will be respected. When the divisions among the groups are most violent, then this gesture, if law is to work, must be most sincere.

The institution requires an act of faith on the part of the minorities, because the scope of their rights will be controversial whenever they are important, and because the officers of the majority will act on their own notions of what these rights really are. Of course these officials will disagree with many of the claims that a minority makes. That makes it all the more important that they take their decisions gravely. They must show that they understand what rights are, and they must not cheat on the full implications of the doctrine. The Government will not re-establish respect for law without giving the law some claim to respect. It cannot do that if it neglects the one feature that distinguishes law from ordered brutality. If the Government does not take rights seriously, then it does not take law seriously either.

Notes

1   First published in the *New York Review of Books*, 18 December 1970.

2   'On Not Prosecuting Civil Disobedience', *NYR*, 6 June 1968.

3   It is not surprising that we sometimes use the concept of having a right to say that others must not interfere with an act and sometimes to say that the act is not the wrong thing to do. Often, when someone has *no* right to do something, like attacking another man physically, it is true *both* that it is the wrong thing to do and that others are entitled to stop it, by demand, if not by force. It is therefore natural to say that someone has a right when we mean to deny *either* of these consequences, as well as when we mean to deny both.

4   He need not consider these ideas to be axiomatic. He may, that is, have reasons for insisting that dignity or equality are important values, and these reasons may be utilitarian. He may believe, for example, that the general good will be advanced, *in the long run*, only if we treat indignity or inequality as very great injustices, and never allow our *opinions* about the general good to justify them. I do not know of any good arguments for or against this sort of 'institutional' utilitarianism, but it is consistent with my point, because it argues that we must treat violations of dignity and equality as special moral crimes, beyond the reach of ordinary utilitarian justification.

21

Basic Rights

Henry Shue

"Negative" Rights and "Positive" Rights

Many Americans would probably be initially inclined to think that rights to subsistence are at least slightly less important than rights to physical security, even though subsistence is at least as essential to survival as security is and even though questions of security do not even arise when subsistence fails. Much official U.S. government rhetoric routinely treats all "economic rights," among which basic subsistence rights are buried amidst many non-basic rights, as secondary and deferrable, although the fundamental enunciation of policy concerning human rights by the then Secretary of State did appear to represent an attempt to correct the habitual imbalance.[1] Now that the same argument in favor of basic rights to both aspects of personal survival, subsistence and security, is before us, we can examine critically some of the reasons why it sometimes appears that although people have basic security rights, the right, if any, to even the physical necessities of existence like minimal health care, food, clothing, shelter, unpolluted water, and unpolluted air is somehow less urgent or less basic.

Frequently it is asserted or assumed that a highly significant difference between rights to physical security and rights to subsistence is that they are respectively "negative" rights and "positive" rights.[2] This position, which I will now try to refute, is considerably more complex than it at

first appears. I will sometimes refer to it as the position that subsistence rights are *positive* and *therefore secondary*. Obviously taking the position involves holding that subsistence rights are positive in some respect in which security rights are negative and further claiming that this difference concerning positive/negative is a good enough reason to assign priority to negative rights over positive rights. I will turn shortly to the explanation of this assumed positive/negative distinction. But first I want to lay out all the premises actually needed by the position that subsistence rights are positive and therefore secondary, although I need to undercut only some – strictly speaking, only one – of them in order to cast serious doubt upon the position's conclusions.

The alleged lack of priority for subsistence rights compared to security rights assumes:

1. The distinction between subsistence rights and security rights is (a) sharp and (b) significant.[3]
2. The distinction between positive rights and negative rights is (a) sharp and (b) significant.
3. Subsistence rights are positive.
4. Security rights are negative.

I am not suggesting that anyone has ever laid out this argument in all the steps it actually needs. On the contrary, a full statement of the argument is the beginning of its refutation – this is an example of the philosophical analogue of the principle that sunlight is the best antiseptic.[4]

In this chapter I will concentrate on establishing that premises 3 and 4 are both misleading. Then I will suggest a set of distinctions among duties that accurately transmits the insight distorted by 3 and 4. Insofar as 3 and 4 are

Originally published in *Basic Rights* (1980), 35–46, 51–64. Copyright © 1980 by Princeton University Press. Reprinted by permission of Princeton University Press.

inaccurate, considerable doubt is cast upon 2, although it remains possible that someone can specify some sharply contrasting pair of rights that actually are examples of 2.[5] I will not directly attack premise 1.[6]

Now the basic idea behind the general suggestion that there are positive rights and negative rights seems to have been that one kind of rights (the positive ones) require other people to act positively – to "do something" – whereas another kind of rights (the negative ones) require other people merely to refrain from acting in certain ways – to do nothing that violates the rights. For example, according to this picture, a right to subsistence would be positive because it would require other people, in the last resort, to supply food or clean air to those unable to find, produce, or buy their own; a right to security would be negative because it would require other people merely to refrain from murdering or otherwise assaulting those with the right. The underlying distinction, then, is between acting and refraining from acting; and positive rights are those with correlative duties to act in certain ways and negative rights are those with correlative duties to refrain from acting in certain ways. Therefore, the moral significance, if any, of the distinction between positive rights and negative rights depends upon the moral significance, if any, of the distinction between action and omission of action.[7]

The ordinarily implicit argument for considering rights to subsistence to be secondary would, then, appear to be basically this. Since subsistence rights are positive and require other people to do more than negative rights require – perhaps more than people can actually do – negative rights, such as those to security, should be fully guaranteed first. Then, any remaining resources could be devoted, as long as they lasted, to the positive – and perhaps impossible – task of providing for subsistence. Unfortunately for this argument, neither rights to physical security nor rights to subsistence fit neatly into their assigned sides of the simplistic positive/negative dichotomy. We must consider whether security rights are purely negative and then whether subsistence rights are purely positive. I will try to show (1) that security rights are more "positive" than they are often said to be, (2) that subsistence rights are more "negative" than they are often said to be, and, given (1) and (2), (3) that the distinctions between security rights and subsistence

rights, though not entirely illusory, are too fine to support any weighty conclusions, especially the very weighty conclusion that security rights are basic and subsistence rights are not.

In the case of rights to physical security, it may be possible *to avoid violating* someone's rights to physical security yourself by merely refraining from acting in any of the ways that would constitute violations. But it is impossible to *protect* anyone's rights to physical security without taking, or making payments toward the taking of, a wide range of positive actions. For example, at the very least the protection of rights to physical security necessitates police forces; criminal courts; penitentiaries; schools for training police, lawyers, and guards; and taxes to support an enormous system for the prevention, detection, and punishment of violations of personal security.[8] All these activities and institutions are attempts at providing social guarantees for individuals' security so that they are not left to face alone forces that they cannot handle on their own. How much more than these expenditures one thinks would be necessary in order for people actually to be reasonably secure (as distinguished from merely having the cold comfort of knowing that the occasional criminal is punished after someone's security has already been violated) depends on one's theory of violent crime, but it is not unreasonable to believe that it would involve extremely expensive, "positive" programs. Probably no one knows how much positive action would have to be taken in a contemporary society like the United States significantly to reduce the levels of muggings, rapes, murders, and other assaults that violate personal security, and in fact to make people reasonably secure.

Someone might suggest that this blurs rights to physical security with some other type of rights, which might be called rights-to-be-protected-against-assaults-upon-physical-security. According to this distinction, rights to physical security are negative, requiring others only to refrain from assaults, while rights-to-be-protected-against-assaults-upon-physical-security are positive, requiring others to take positive steps to prevent assaults.

Perhaps if one were dealing with some wilderness situation in which individuals' encounters with each other were infrequent and irregular, there might be some point in noting to someone: I am not asking you to cooperate with a system of guarantees to protect me from third parties, but only to refrain from attacking me yourself. But in an organized society, insofar as there were any such things as rights to physical security that were distinguishable from some other rights-to-be-protected-from-assaults-upon-physical-security, no one would have much interest in the bare rights to physical security. What people want and need, as even Mill partly recognized, is the protection of their rights.[9] Insofar as this frail distinction holds up, it is the rights-to-be-protected-against-assaults that any reasonable person would demand from society. A demand for physical security is not normally a demand simply to be left alone, but a demand to be protected against harm.[10] It is a demand for positive action, or, in the words of our initial account of a right, a demand for social guarantees against at least the standard threats.

So it would be very misleading to say simply that physical security is a negative matter of other people's refraining from violations. Ordinarily it is instead a matter of some people refraining from violations and of third parties being prevented from violations by the positive steps taken by first and second parties. The "negative" refraining may in a given case be less significant than the "positive" preventing – it is almost never the whole story. The end-result of the positive preventative steps taken is of course an enforced refraining from violations, not the performance of any positive action. The central core of the right is a right that others not act in certain ways. But the mere core of the right indicates little about the social institutions needed to secure it, and the core of the right does not contain its whole structure. The protection of "negative rights" requires positive measures, and therefore their actual enjoyment requires positive measures. In any imperfect society enjoyment of a right will depend to some extent upon protection against those who do not choose not to violate it.

Rights to subsistence too are in their own way considerably more complex than simply labeling them "positive" begins to indicate. In fact, their fulfillment involves at least two significantly different types of action. On the one hand, rights to subsistence sometimes do involve correlative duties on the part of others to provide the needed commodities when those in need are helpless to secure a supply for themselves, as, for example, the affluent may have a duty to finance food supplies and transportation and distribution facilities in the case of famine. Even the satisfaction of

subsistence rights by such positive action, however, need not be any more expensive or involve any more complex governmental programs than the effective protection of security rights would. A food stamp program, for example, could be cheaper or more expensive than, say, an anti-drug program aimed at reducing muggings and murders by addicts. Which program was more costly or more complicated would depend upon the relative dimensions of the respective problems and would be unaffected by any respect in which security is "negative" and subsistence is "positive." Insofar as any argument for giving priority to the fulfillment of "negative rights" rests on the assumption that actually securing "negative rights" is usually cheaper or simpler than securing "positive rights," the argument rests on an empirical speculation of dubious generality.

The other type of action needed to fulfill subsistence rights is even more difficult to distinguish sharply from the action needed to fulfill security rights. Rights to physical subsistence often can be completely satisfied without the provision by others of any commodities to those whose rights are in question. All that is sometimes necessary is to protect the persons whose subsistence is threatened from the individuals and institutions that will otherwise intentionally or unintentionally harm them. A demand for the fulfillment of rights to subsistence may involve not a demand to be provided with grants of commodities but merely a demand to be provided some opportunity for supporting oneself.[11] The request is not to be supported but to be allowed to be self-supporting on the basis of one's own hard work.

What is striking is the similarity between protection against the destruction of the basis for supporting oneself and protection against assaults upon one's physical security. We can turn now to some examples that clearly illustrate that the honoring of subsistence rights sometimes involves action no more positive than the honoring of security rights does. Some cases in which all that is asked is protection from harm that would destroy the capacity to be self-supporting involve threats to subsistence of a complexity that is not usually noticed with regard to security, although the adequate protection of security would involve analyses and measures more complex than a preoccupation with police and prisons. The complexity of the circumstances of subsistence should not, however, be allowed to obscure the basic fact that essentially all that is being asked in the name of subsistence rights in these examples is protection from destructive acts by other people.

Subsistence Rights and Scarcity

The choice of examples for use in an essentially theoretical discussion that does nevertheless have implications for public policy presents an intractable dilemma. Hypothetical cases and actual cases each have advantages and disadvantages that are mirror images of each other's. A description of an actual case has the obvious advantage that it is less susceptible to being tailored to suit the theoretical point it is adduced to support, especially if the description is taken from the work of someone other than the proponent of the theoretical point. Its disadvantage is that if the description is in fact an inaccurate account of the case in question, the mistake about what is happening in that case may appear to undercut the theoretical point that is actually independent of what is happening in any single case. Thus the argument about the theoretical point may become entangled in arguments about an individual instance that was at most only one supposed illustration of the more general point.

Hypothetical cases are immune to disputes about whether they accurately depict an independent event, since, being explicitly hypothetical, they are not asserted to correspond to any one real case. But precisely because they are not constrained by the need to remain close to an independent event, they may be open to the suspicion of having been streamlined precisely in order to fit the theoretical point they illustrate and having thereby become atypical of actual cases.

The only solution I can see is to offer, when a point is crucial, an example of each kind. It is vital to the argument of this book to establish that many people's lack of the substance of their subsistence rights – of, that is, the means of subsistence like food – is a deprivation caused by standard kinds of threats that could be controlled by some combination of the mere restraint of second parties and the maintenance of protective institutions by first and third parties, just as the standard threats that deprive people of their physical security could be controlled by restraint and protection against non-restraint. So I will start with a hypothetical case in order to clarify the theoretical point before introducing the partly

extraneous complexity of actual events, and then in *Basic Rights* I go on to quote a description of some actual current economic policies that deprive people of subsistence. The hypothetical case is at the level of a single peasant village, and the actual case concerns long-term national economic strategies. Anyone familiar with the causes of malnutrition in underdeveloped countries today will recognize that the following hypothetical case is in no way unusual.[12]

Suppose the largest tract of land in the village was the property of the descendant of a family that had held title to the land for as many generations back as anyone could remember. By absolute standards this peasant was by no means rich, but his land was the richest in the small area that constituted the universe for the inhabitants of this village. He grew, as his father and grandfather had, mainly the black beans that are the staple (and chief – and adequate – source of protein) in the regional diet. His crop usually constituted about a quarter of the black beans marketed in the village. Practically every family grew part of what they needed, and the six men he hired during the seasons requiring extra labor held the only paid jobs in the village – everyone else just worked his own little plot.

One day a man from the capital offered this peasant a contract that not only guaranteed him annual payments for a 10-year lease on his land but also guaranteed him a salary (regardless of how the weather, and therefore the crops, turned out – a great increase in his financial security) to be the foreman for a new kind of production on his land. The contract required him to grow flowers for export and also offered him the opportunity, which was highly recommended, to purchase through the company, with payments in installments, equipment that would enable him to need to hire only two men. The same contract was offered to, and accepted by, most of the other larger landowners in the general region to which the village belonged.

Soon, with the sharp reduction in supply, the price of black beans soared. Some people could grow all they needed (in years of good weather) on their own land, but the families that needed to supplement their own crop with purchases had to cut back their consumption. In particular, the children in the four families headed by the laborers who lost their seasonal employment suffered severe malnutrition, especially since the parents had originally worked as laborers only because their own land was too poor or too small to feed their families.

Now, the story contains no implication that the man from the capital or the peasants-turned-foremen were malicious or intended to do anything worse than single-mindedly pursue their own respective interests. But the outsider's offer of the contract was one causal factor, and the peasant's acceptance of the contract was another causal factor, in producing the malnutrition that would probably persist, barring protective intervention, for at least the decade the contract was to be honored. If the families in the village had rights to subsistence, their rights were being violated. Society, acting presumably by way of the government, ought to protect them from a severe type of active harm that eliminates their ability even to feed themselves.

But was anyone actually harming the villagers, or were they simply suffering a regrettable decline in their fortunes? If someone was violating their rights, who exactly was the violator? Against whom specifically should the government be protecting them? For, we normally make a distinction between violating someone's rights and allowing someone's rights to be violated while simply minding our own business. It makes a considerable difference – to take an example from another set of basic rights – whether I myself assault someone or I merely carry on with my own affairs while allowing a third person to assault someone when I could protect the victim and end the assault. Now, I may have a duty not to allow assaults that I can without great danger to myself prevent or stop, as well as a duty not to assault people myself, but there are clearly two separable issues here. And it is perfectly conceivable that I might have the one duty (to avoid harming) and not the other (to protect from harm by third parties), because they involve two different types of action.[13]

The switch in land-use within the story might then be described as follows. Even if one were willing to grant tentatively that the villagers all seemed to have rights to subsistence, some of which were violated by the malnutrition that some suffered after the switch in crops, no individual or organization can be identified as the violator: not the peasant-turned-foreman, for example, because – let us assume – he did not foresee the "systemic" effects of his individual choice; not the business representative from the capital because – let us assume – although he was

knowledgeable enough to know what would probably happen, it would be unrealistically moralistic to expect him to forgo honest gains for himself and the company he represented because the gains had undesired, even perhaps regretted, "side-effects"; not any particular member of the governmental bureaucracy because – let us assume – no one had been assigned responsibility for maintaining adequate nutrition in this particular village. The local peasant and the business representative were both minding their own business in the village, and no one in the government had any business with this village. The peasant and the representative may have attended to their own affairs while harm befell less fortunate villagers, but allowing harm to occur without preventing it is not the same as directly inflicting it yourself. The malnutrition was just, literally, unfortunate: bad luck, for which no one could fairly be blamed. The malnutrition was, in effect, a natural disaster – was, in the obnoxious language of insurance law, an act of God. Perhaps the village was, after all, becoming overpopulated.[14]

But, of course, the malnutrition resulting from the new choice of crop was not a natural disaster. The comforting analogy does not hold. The malnutrition was a social disaster. The malnutrition was the product of specific human decisions permitted by the presence of specific social institutions and the absence of others, in the context of the natural circumstances, especially the scarcity of land upon which to grow food, that were already given before the decisions were made. The harm in question, the malnutrition, was not merely allowed to happen by the parties to the flower-growing contract. The harm was partly caused by the requirement in the contract for a switch away from food, by the legality of the contract, and by the performance of the required switch in crops. If there had been no contract or if the contract had not required a switch away from food for local consumption, there would have been no malnutrition as things were going.[15] In general, when persons take an action that is sufficient in some given natural and social circumstances to bring about an undesirable effect, especially one that there is no particular reason to think would otherwise have occurred, it is perfectly normal to consider their action to be one active cause of the harm. The parties to the contract partly caused the malnutrition.

But the society could have protected the

villagers by countering the initiative of the contracting parties in any one of a number of ways that altered the circumstances, and the absence of the appropriate social guarantees is another cause of the malnutrition. Such contracts could, for example, have already been made illegal. Or they could have been allowed but managed or taxed in order to compensate those who would otherwise predictably be damaged by them. Exactly what was done would be, *for the most part*, an economic and political question.[16] But it is possible to have social guarantees against the malnutrition that is repeatedly caused in such standard, predictable ways.

Is a right to subsistence in such a case, then, a positive right in any important ways that a right to security is not? Do we actually find a contrast of major significance? No. As in the cases of the threats to physical security that we normally consider, the threat to subsistence is human activity with largely predictable effects.[17] Even if, as we tend to assume, the motives for deprivations of security tend to be vicious while the motives for deprivations of subsistence tend to be callous, the people affected usually need protection all the same. The design, building, and maintenance of institutions and practices that protect people's subsistence against the callous – and even the merely over-energetic – is no more and no less positive than the conception and execution of programs to control violent crimes against the person. It is not obvious which, if either, it is more realistic to hope for or more economical to pursue. It is conceivable, although I doubt if anyone really knows, that the two are more effectively and efficiently pursued together. Neither looks simple, cheap, or "negative."

This example of the flower contract is important in part because, at a very simple level, it is in fact typical of much of what is happening today among the majority of the people in the world, who are poor and rural, and are threatened by forms of "economic development" that lower their own standard of living.[18] But it is also important because, once again in a very simple way, it illustrates the single most critical fact about rights to subsistence; where subsistence depends upon tight supplies of essential commodities (like food), a change in supply can have, often by way of intermediate price effects, an indirect but predictable and devastating effect on people's ability to survive. A change in supply can transport self-supporting people into helplessness and, if no protection against the change is provided, into malnutrition or death. Severe harm to some people's ability to maintain themselves can be caused by changes in the use to which other people put vital resources (like land) they control. In such cases even someone who denied that individuals or organizations have duties to supply commodities to people who are helpless to obtain them for themselves, might grant that the government ought to execute the society's duty of protecting people from having their ability to maintain their own survival destroyed by the actions of others. If this protection is provided, there will be much less need later to provide commodities themselves to compensate for deprivations.

What transmits the effect in such cases is the local scarcity of the vital commodity. Someone might switch thousands of acres from food to flowers without having any effect on the diet of anyone else where the supply of food was adequate to prevent a significant price rise in response to the cut in supply. And it goes without saying that the price rises are vitally important only if the income and wealth of at least some people is severely limited, as of course it is in every society, often for the rural majority. It is as if an abundant supply sometimes functions as a sponge to absorb the otherwise significant effect on other people, but a tight supply (against a background of limited income and wealth) sometimes functions as a conductor to transmit effects to others, who feel them sharply.

It is extremely difficult merely to mind one's own business amidst a scarcity of vital commodities. It is illusory to think that this first commandment of liberalism can always be obeyed. The very scarcity draws people into contact with each other, destroys almost all area for individual maneuver, and forces people to elbow each other in order to move forward. The tragedy of scarcity, beyond the deprivations necessitated by the scarcity itself, is that scarcity tends to make each one's gain someone else's loss. One can act for oneself only by acting against others, since there is not enough for all. Amidst abundance of food a decision to grow flowers can be at worst a harmless act and quite likely a socially beneficial one. But amidst a scarcity of food, due partly to a scarcity of fertile land, an unmalicious decision to grow flowers can cause death – unless there are social guarantees for adequate nutrition. A call for social guarantees for subsistence in situations of scarcity is not a call for intervention in what were formerly private affairs.

Avoidance, Protection, and Aid

Still, it is true that sometimes fulfilling a right does involve transferring commodities to the person with the right and sometimes it merely involves not taking commodities away. Is there not some grain of truth obscured by the dichotomy between negative and positive rights? Are there not distinctions here that it is useful to make?

The answer, I believe, is: yes, there are distinctions, but they are not distinctions between rights. The useful distinctions are among duties, and there are no one-to-one pairings between kinds of duties and kinds of rights. The complete fulfillment of each kind of right involves the performance of multiple kinds of duties. This conceptual change has, I believe, important practical implications, although it will be only in chapter 7 that the implications can begin to be illustrated. In the remainder of this chapter I would like to tender a very simple tripartite typology of duties. For all its own simplicity, it goes considerably beyond the usual assumption that for every right there is a single correlative duty, and suggests instead that for every basic right – and many other rights as well – there are three types of duties, all of which must be performed if the basic right is to be fully honored but not all of which must necessarily be performed by the same individuals or institutions. This latter point opens the possibility of distributing each of the three kinds of duty somewhat differently and perhaps confining any difficulties about the cor relativity of subsistence rights and their accompanying duties to fewer than all three kinds of duties.

So I want to suggest that with every basic right, three types of duties correlate:

I. Duties to *avoid* depriving.
II. Duties to *protect* from deprivation.
III. Duties to *aid* the deprived.

This may be easier to see in the case of the more familiar basic right, the right to physical security (the right not to be tortured, executed, raped, assaulted, etc.). For every person's right to physical security, there are three correlative duties:

I. Duties not to eliminate a person's security – duties to *avoid* depriving.
II. Duties to protect people against deprivation of security by other people – duties to *protect* from deprivation.

III. Duties to provide for the security of those unable to provide for their own – duties to *aid* the deprived.

Similarly, for every right to subsistence there are:

I. Duties not to eliminate a person's only available means of subsistence – duties to *avoid* depriving.
II. Duties to protect people against deprivation of the only available means of subsistence by other people – duties to *protect* from deprivation.
III. Duties to provide for the subsistence of those unable to provide for their own – duties to *aid* the deprived.

If this suggestion is correct, the common notion that *rights* can be divided into rights to forbearance (so-called negative rights), as if some rights have correlative duties only to avoid depriving, and rights to aid (so-called positive rights), as if some rights have correlative duties only to aid, is thoroughly misguided. This misdirected simplification is virtually ubiquitous among contemporary North Atlantic theorists and is, I think, all the more pernicious for the degree of unquestioning acceptance it has now attained. It is duties, not rights, that can be divided among avoidance and aid, and protection. And – this is what matters – every basic right entails duties of all three types. Consequently the attempted division of rights, rather than duties, into forbearance and aid (and protection, which is often understandably but unhelpfully blurred into avoidance, since protection is partly, but only partly, the enforcement of avoidance) can only breed confusion.

It is impossible for any basic right – however "negative" it has come to seem – to be fully guaranteed unless all three types of duties are fulfilled. The very most "negative"-seeming right to liberty, for example, requires positive action by society to protect it and positive action by society to restore it when avoidance and protection both fail. This by no means implies, as I have already mentioned, that all three types of duties fall upon everyone else or even fall equally upon everyone upon whom they do fall. Although this tripartite analysis of duties is, I believe, perfectly general, I will focus here upon the duties correlative to subsistence rights: subsistence duties.

The Generality of the Tripartite Analysis

However, perhaps a brief word on the general issue is useful before turning to a fairly detailed analysis of the threefold duties correlative to the rights that most concern us: subsistence rights. Obviously theses of three ascending degrees of generality might be advanced:

All subsistence rights involve threefold correlative duties.

All basic rights involve threefold correlative duties.

Most moral rights involve threefold correlative duties.

I subscribe to all three theses. But naturally the support will be most thorough for the first thesis and least thorough for the last. For the most part I am content to leave matters at that, because the only point that I am concerned fully to establish is the priority of subsistence rights, that is, their equal priority with all other basic rights. Consequently, the arguments need, strictly speaking, to be thorough only for subsistence rights. But a contrasting pair of observations are also in order.

On the one hand, the argument here is from the particular to the general, not the converse. It is not because I assumed that normal rights involve some, or threefold, duties that I concluded that subsistence rights involve some, and threefold, duties. I explored subsistence rights, as we are about to do, and found that they can be fully accounted for only by means of admitting three kinds of correlated duties. I looked at the same time at security rights and, in Chapter 3 of *Basic Rights*, at rights to liberty and found again that an adequate explanation involves all three kinds of multiply interrelated duties, thus coming to suspect that all basic rights, at the very least, require the same tripartite analysis of the duty side of the coin.

On the other hand, on the basis of these detailed examinations of these three rights I am indeed tempted to recommend that the most general thesis be made analytically true, that is, that any right not involving the threefold duties be acknowledged to be an exceptional case. If the account of a right given at the beginning of chapter I of *Basic Rights* were made a strict definition, then it would do just this. If a right provides the rational basis for a justified demand that the actual enjoyment of the substance of the right be socially guaranteed against standard threats, then a right provides the rational basis for insisting upon the performance, as needed, of duties to avoid, duties to protect, and duties to aid, as they will shortly be explained. This picture does seem to me to fit all the standard cases of moral rights.[19] If, however, someone can give clear counter-examples to the final step of generalization (the move from duties for basic rights to duties for moral rights generally), I can see little cause for concern, provided the admission of rights that lack some kinds of correlative duties, to the realm of non-basic rights, is not allowed to devalue the coinage of rights generally.

Subsistence Duties

The first type of subsistence duty is neither a duty to provide help nor a duty to protect against harm by third parties but is the most nearly "negative" or passive kind of duty that is possible: a duty simply not to take actions that deprive others of a means that, but for one's own harmful actions, would have satisfied their subsistence rights or enabled them to satisfy their own subsistence rights, where the actions are not necessary to the satisfaction of one's own basic rights and where the threatened means is the only realistic one.[20] Duties to avoid depriving require merely that one refrain from making an unnecessary gain for oneself by a means that is destructive for others.

Part of the relation between these subsistence duties to avoid depriving (type I) and subsistence duties to protect from deprivation (type II) is quite straightforward. If everyone could be counted upon voluntarily to fulfill duties to avoid, duties to protect would be unnecessary. But since it would be naive to expect everyone to fulfill his or her duties to avoid and since other people's very survival is at stake, it is clearly necessary that some individuals or institutions have the duty of enforcing the duty to avoid. The duty to protect is, then, in part a secondary duty of enforcing the primary duty of avoiding the destruction of people's means of subsistence. In this respect it is analogous to, for example, the duty of the police to enforce the duty of parents not to starve their children.

The natural institution in many societies to have the task of enforcing those primary duties that need enforcement is the executive branch of some level of government, acting on behalf of the members of society other than the offending individuals or institutions. Which level of government takes operating responsibility is largely a practical matter and might vary among societies. Where the source of harm is, for example, a transnational corporation, protection may need to be provided by the home government or even by multilateral government action.[21] But clearly if duties to avoid depriving people of their last means of subsistence are to be taken seriously, some provision must be made for enforcing this duty on behalf of the rest of humanity upon those who would not otherwise fulfill it. Perhaps it would be worth considering non-governmental enforcement institutions as the bearers in some cases of the secondary duty to protect, but the primary institution would normally appear to be the government of the threatened person's own nation. It is normally taken to be a central function of government to prevent irreparable harm from being inflicted upon some members of society by other individual members, by institutions, or by interactions of the two. It is difficult to imagine why anyone should pay much attention to the demands of any government that failed to perform this function, if it were safe to ignore its demands.

Duties to aid (type III) are in themselves fairly complicated, and only one kind will be discussed here. At least three sub-categories of duties to aid need to be recognized. What they have in common is the requirement that resources be transferred to those who cannot provide for their own survival. First are duties to aid (III–1) that are attached to certain roles or relationships and rest therefore upon only those who are in a particular role or relationship and are borne toward only those other persons directly involved. Some central cases are the duties of parents toward their own young children and the duties of grown children toward their own aged parents. Naturally, important issues can arise even with regard to such relatively clear duties as the duty to provide food to the helplessly young and to the helplessly old, but I have nothing to add here regarding these duties, which are not universal. By their not being universal I mean that although all parents may normally have certain duties toward their own children, no child can justifiably hold that all people, or even all parents, have *this* sort of duty toward it. All people may of course have other

duties toward the child, including universal ones, and possibly including one of the other two sub-categories of duties to aid that are to be mentioned next.

The only difference between the second and third sub-categories of duties to aid is the source of the deprivation because of which aid is needed. In the second case (III–2) the deprivation is the result of failures to fulfill duties to avoid depriving and duties to protect from deprivation – some people have acted in such a way as to eliminate the last available means of subsistence for other people and the responsible government has failed to protect the victims. Thus, the need for assistance is the result of a prior twofold failure to perform duties, and the victims have been harmed by both actions and omissions of actions by other people.

In the third case (III–3) the deprivation is not the result of failures in duty and, in just this sense, the deprivation is "natural," that is, the deprivation suffered is not a case of harm primarily caused by other people. The clearest case of a natural deprivation calling for aid is a natural disaster like a hurricane or an earthquake. As always, questions arise at the borderline between cases – for example, was the death toll increased because the weather bureau or civil defense organization failed to protect with timely warnings? But uncontroversial central cases in which no human beings are much to blame are perfectly familiar, even if not so frequent as we might like to believe.

Where supplies of the necessities of life, or of the resources needed to grow or make the necessities, are scarce, duties of types I and II take on increased importance. The results of the fulfillment only of I and II would already be dramatic in the poorer areas of the world, in which most of the earth's inhabitants eke out their existences. It is easy to underestimate the importance of these two kinds of subsistence duties, which together are intended to prevent deprivation. But to eliminate the only realistic means a person has for obtaining food or other physical necessities is to cause that person, for example, the physical harm of malnutrition or of death by starvation. When physical harm but not death is caused, the effect of eliminating the only means of support can be every degree as serious as the effect of a violation of physical security by means of a bodily assault. The physical effects of malnutrition can be irreversible and far more profound than the physical effects of many an assault in fact are. And when starvation is caused, the ultimate effect of eliminating the only means of support is precisely the same as the effect of murder. Those who are helpless in the face of insuperable obstacles to their continued existence are at least one level worse off than those who are defenseless in the face of assaults upon their physical security. The defenseless will at least be able to maintain themselves if they are provided with protection against threatening assaults. If protected but otherwise left alone, they will manage. But the helpless, if simply left alone – even if they should be protected against all assaults upon their security – will die for lack of the means of subsistence. They will merely, in Coleridge's phrase, "die so slowly that none call it murder."[22]

Now of course differences between deprivations of security and deprivations of subsistence can also be noted, as already mentioned. Normally in a violation of physical security by means of assault or murder, the human agent's central intention is indeed to bring about, or at least includes bringing about, the physical harm or death that is caused for the victim, although obviously one also can injure or kill inadvertently. In the case of the elimination of the means of physical subsistence, the human agent's central intention may at least sometimes be focussed on other consequences of his or her action, such as the increased security of income that would result from a multi-year salaried contract to grow flowers rather than a precarious annual attempt to grow food. The harm to the victims may be entirely unintended. Such difference in intention between the two cases is undoubtedly relevant to any assessment of the moral stature respectively of the two persons who partly cause the harm in the two cases. But for the two victims the difference between intended physical harm and unintended physical harm may matter little, since the harmfulness of the action taken may be the same in both cases and may be even greater where unintended.

Nevertheless, it may be arbitrary to assign a role of *the* perpetrator to any one person or group in a case of the deprivation of subsistence. The deprivations in question may in fact be "systemic": the product of the joint workings of individual actions and social institutions no one of which by itself caused the harm. But what follows from this is not that no one is responsible (since everyone is). What follows is that the distinction between duties to avoid (I) and duties to protect (II), which is relatively clear in the abstract, blurs considerably in concrete reality.[23] The division of labor between individual restraint and institutional protection can be worked out in any of several acceptable ways, the full details of which would go considerably beyond the scope of this book, but between the two kinds of duties, individuals ought not to be deprived by the actions (intentional or unintentional) of others of all hope of sustaining themselves.

This means, however, that duties to protect (II) are not simply secondary duties to enforce the primary duty to avoid (I). We can mark as II–1 the duties to protect that are merely secondary duties to enforce the duty to avoid. But duties to protect also encompass the design of social institutions that do not leave individuals with duties to avoid, the fulfillment of which would necessitate super-human qualities. This task of constructing institutions can be marked as II–2. In the original example of the flower contract, some would judge that the peasant receiving the offer to switch out of food production, in the circumstances stipulated, could reasonably have been expected to foresee the consequences of the switch and to refrain from making it. But it is probably more realistic neither to expect him to have the information and comprehension necessary to foresee the consequences nor to expect him to choose not to reduce his own insecurity – and certainly an example could readily be constructed in which an individual could not reasonably be expected to know in advance the probable bad consequences for others of his or her action or to give them more weight than improvements in his or her own precarious situation.[24]

For such cases, in which individual restraint would be too much to ask, the duty to protect (II–2) includes the design of laws and institutions that avoid reliance upon unreasonable levels of individual self-control. Many actions that are immoral ought nevertheless not to be made illegal. But one of the best possible reasons for making an act illegal is its contributing to harm as fundamental as the deprivation of someone's last available means of subsistence. And a number of intermediate steps between total prohibition and complete tolerance of an action are possible, such as tax laws that create disincentives of various strengths against the kind of action that would contribute to the deprivation of subsistence from others and create alternative sources of increased economic security for oneself. Social institutions must, at the very least, be designed to enable ordinary human beings, who are neither saints nor geniuses, to do each other a minimum of serious harm.

In sum, then, we find that the fulfillment of a basic right to subsistence involves at least the following kinds of duties:

I.   To avoid depriving.
II.   To protect from deprivation

    1. By enforcing duty (I) and
    2. By designing institutions that avoid the creation of strong incentives to violate duty (I).

III. To aid the deprived

    1. Who are one's special responsibility,
    2. Who are victims of social failures in the performance of duties (I), (II–1), (II–2) and
    3. Who are victims of natural disasters.

The Systematic Interdependence of Duties

Fulfillment of a basic right (and, I think, of most other moral rights as well) requires, then, performance by some individuals or institutions of each of these three general kinds of correlative duties. Duties to avoid depriving possibly come closest to failing to be essential, because duties to protect provide for the enforcement of duties to avoid. Even if individuals, organizations, and governments were otherwise inclined to violate rights to security, for example, by failing to fulfill their respective duties to avoid, forceful fulfillment of duties to protect by whomever they fell upon – presumably a national government – could probably produce behavior in compliance with duties to avoid. But reliance on duties to protect rather than duties to avoid would constitute heavy reliance on something like national police power rather than self-restraint by individuals, corporations, and lower-level governments, and would involve obvious disadvantages even if – probably, especially if – the police power were adequate actually to enforce duties to avoid upon a generally reluctant society. Unfortunately this much power to protect would also be enormous power to deprive, which is a lesson about police that even dictators sometimes have to learn the hard way.

Since duties to avoid and duties to protect taken together have only one purpose, to prevent deprivations, the reverse of what was just described is obviously also possible: if everyone who ought to fulfill duties to avoid did so, performance of duties to protect might not be necessary. Law-enforcement agencies could perhaps be disbanded in a society of restrained organizational and individual behavior. But although reliance entirely upon duties to protect is undesirable even if possible, a safe complete reliance upon duties to avoid is most improbable in the absence of at least minimal performance of duties to protect. Organizations and individuals who will voluntarily avoid deprivation that would otherwise be advantageous to them because they know that their potential victims are protected, cannot be expected to behave in the same way when they know their potential victims are without protection.

The general conclusions about duties to avoid and duties to protect, then, are, first, that strictly speaking it is essential for the guarantee of any right only that either the one or the other be completely fulfilled, but, second, that for all practical purposes it is essential to insist upon the fulfillment of both, because complete reliance on either one alone is probably not feasible and, in the case of duties to protect, almost certainly not desirable.

What division of labor is established by one's account of duties between self-restraint and restraint by others, such as police forces, will obviously have an enormous effect upon the quality of life of those living in the social system in question. I do not want to pursue the questions involved in deciding upon the division, except to note that if either duties to avoid or duties to protect are construed too narrowly, the other duty then becomes unrealistically broad. For example, if a government, in the exercise of its duty to protect, fails to impose constraints upon agribusinesses designed to prevent them from creating malnutrition, the prevention of malnutrition will then depend upon the self-restraint of the agribusinesses. But much evidence suggests that individual agribusinesses are unwilling or unable to take into account the nutritional effect of their decisions about the use of land, local credit and capital, water, and other resources. This is especially true if the agribusiness is producing export crops and most especially if it is investing in a foreign country, the nutritional level of whose people is easily considered irrelevant.[25] If indeed a particular type of corporation has demonstrated an inability to forgo projects that produce malnutrition, given their setting, it is foolish to rely on corporate restraint, and whichever governments have responsibility to protect those who are helpless to resist the corporation's activity – host governments, home government or both – will have to fulfill their duties to protect. If, on the other hand, the corporations would restrain themselves, the governments could restrain them less. How to work this out is difficult and important. The present point is simply that between the bearers of the two duties, the job of preventing deprivation ought to get done, if there is a right not to be deprived of whatever is threatened. And the side that construes its own role too narrowly, if it actually has the power to act, may be as much at fault for contributing to the violation of rights as the side that fails to take up all the resulting slack.

However, as I have already indicated, the duty to protect ought not to be understood only in terms of the maintenance of law-enforcement, regulatory, and other closely related agencies. A major and more constructive part of the duty to protect is the duty to design social institutions that do not exceed the capacity of individuals and organizations, including private and public corporations, to restrain themselves. Not only the kinds of acute threats of deprivation that police can prevent, but the kinds of chronic threats that require imaginative legislation and, sometimes, long-term planning fall under the duty to protect.[26]

Nevertheless, it is duties to aid that often have the highest urgency, because they are often owed to persons who are suffering the consequences of failures to fulfill both duties to avoid and duties to protect, that is, they are duties of type III–2. These people will have been totally deprived of their rights to subsistence if they are then not aided either. This greater urgency does not, of course, mean that duties to aid are more compelling overall than the first two types of duty, and indeed it is specifically against duties to aid that complaints that the correlative duties accompanying subsistence rights are too burdensome may seem most plausible. It is important to notice that to the extent that duties to avoid and to protect are fulfilled, duties to assist will be less burdensome. If the fulfillment of duties to protect is sufficiently inadequate, duties to assist may be overwhelming and may seem unrealistically great,

as they do today to many people. For example, because the Dutch colonial empire failed to protect the people of Java against the effects of the Dutch schemes for agricultural exports, the nutritional problems of the majority of Indonesians today strike some people as almost beyond all solution.[27] The colossal failure of the Dutch colonial government in its duties to protect (or, even, to avoid deprivation) has created virtually Sisyphean duties to aid. These presumably fall to some degree upon the Dutch people who are today still profiting from their centuries of spoils. But whoever precisely has these duties to aid – there are plenty to go around – their magnitude has clearly been multiplied by past dereliction in the performance of the other two kinds of duties by the Dutch among others. . . .

This much, however, is already clear. The account of correlative duties is for the most part a more detailed specification of what the account of rights calls social guarantees against standard threats. Provisions for avoidance, protection, and aid are what are needed for a reasonable level of social guarantees. Making the necessary provisions for the fulfillment of subsistence rights may sometimes be burdensome, especially when the task is to recover from past neglect of basic duties. But we have no reason to believe, as proponents of the negative/positive distinction typically assert, that the performance of the duties correlative to subsistence rights would always or usually be more difficult, more expensive, less practicable, or harder to "deliver" than would the actual performance of the duties correlative to the rights that are conventionally labeled negative and that are more often announced than in fact fulfilled. And the burdens connected with subsistence rights do not fall primarily upon isolated individuals who would be expected quietly to forgo advantages to themselves for the sake of not threatening others, but primarily upon human communities that can work cooperatively to design institutions that avoid situations in which people are confronted by subsistence-threatening forces they cannot themselves handle. In spite of the sometimes useful terminology of third parties helping first parties against second parties, etc., it is worth noting, while assessing the burden of subsistence duties, that the third-party bearers of duties can also become the first-party bearers of rights when situations change. No one is assured of living permanently on one side of the rights/duties coin.

Notes

1 See introduction to Henry Shue, *Basic Rights* (Princeton, Princeton University Press, 1980).

2 For a forceful re-affirmation of this view in the current political context (and further references), see Hugo Adam Bedau, "Human Rights and Foreign Assistance Programs," in *Human Rights and U.S. Foreign Policy*, ed. by Peter G. Brown and Douglas MacLean (Lexington, Mass: Lexington Books, 1979), pp. 29–44. Also see Charles Frankel, *Human Rights and Foreign Policy*, Headline Series No. 241 (New York: Foreign Policy Association, 1978), especially pp. 36–49, where Frankel advanced a "modest list of fundamental rights" that explicitly excluded economic rights as "dangerously utopian." A version of the general distinction has recently been re-affirmed by Thomas Nagel – see "Equality," in *Mortal Questions* (New York: Cambridge University Press, 1979), pp. 114–115. An utterly unrealistic but frequently invoked version of the distinction is in Maurice Cranston, *What Are Human Rights?* (London: The Bodley Head, 1973), chapter VIII. An interesting attempt to show that the positive/negative distinction is compatible with economic rights is John Langan, "Defining Human Rights: A Revision of the Liberal Tradition," Working Paper (Washington: Woodstock Theological Center, 1979) For a provocative and relevant discussion of "negative responsibility" (responsibility for what one fails to prevent), see Bernard Williams, "A Critique of Utilitarianism," in *Utilitarianism: For & Against* (New York: Cambridge University Press, 1973), pp. 93ff.

3 Naturally my use of the same argument for the basic status of both security and subsistence is at least an indirect challenge to (1)(b). No question is raised here, however, about (1)(a): the thesis that subsistence and security are sharply distinguishable. People who should be generally sympathetic to my fundamental thesis that subsistence rights are basic rights, do sometimes try to reach the same conclusion by the much shorter seeming route of denying that security and subsistence are importantly different from each other. For example, it is correctly observed that both security and subsistence are needed for survival and then maintained that both are included in a right to survival, or right to life. Though I am by no means hostile to this approach, it does have three difficulties that I believe can be avoided by my admittedly somewhat more circuitous path of argument. First, it is simply not correct that one cannot maintain a clear and useful distinction between security and subsistence, as, in fact, I hope to have done up to this point. Second, arguments for a general right to life that includes subsistence rights appear to need some premise to the effect that the right to life entails rights to at least some of the means of life. Thus, they face the same "weakness of too much strength" – straining credulity by implying more than most people are likely to be able to believe – that we tried to avoid at the end of chapter 1 of *Basic Rights*. A right-to-the-means-of-life argument might be able to skirt the problem equally well by using a notion of a standard threat to life, analogous to our notion of a standard threat to the enjoyment of rights, but this alternative tack seems, at best, no better off. Third, the concept of a right to life is now deeply infected with ambiguities concerning whether it is a purely negative right, a purely positive right, or, as I shall soon be maintaining with regard to both security and subsistence, an inseparable mixture of positive and negative elements. The appeal for many people of a right to life seems to depend, however, upon its being taken to be essentially negative, while it can fully include subsistence rights only if it has major positive elements.

4 I think one can often show the implausibility of an argument by an exhaustive statement of all the assumptions it needs. I have previously attempted this in the case of one of John Rawls's arguments for the priority of liberty – see "Liberty and Self-Respect," *Ethics*, 85:3 (April 1975), pp. 195–203.

5 I have given a summary of the argument against 3 and arguments against thinking that either the right to a fair trial or the right not to be tortured are negative rights in "Rights in the Light of Duties," in Brown and MacLean, pp. 65–81. I have also argued directly against what is here called 2b and briefly introduced the account of duties presented in the final sections of this chapter. My goal, which I have no illusions about having attained, has been to do as definitive a job on positive and negative rights as Gerald C. MacCallum, Jr. did on positive and negative liberty in his splendid article, "Negative and Positive Freedom," *Philosophical Review*, 76:3 (July 1967), pp. 312–334.

6 See note 3 above.

7 Elsewhere I have briefly queried the moral significance of the action/omission distinction – see the essay cited in note 5 above. For a fuller discussion, see Judith Lichtenberg, "On Being Obligated to Give Aid: Moral and Political Arguments," Diss., City University of New York, 1978.

8 In FY 1975 in the United States the cost of the "criminal justice system" was $17 billion, or $71 per capita, *New York Times*, July 21, 1977, p. A3. In several countries that year the total annual income was less than $71 per capita. Obviously such isolated statistics prove nothing, but they are

suggestive. One thing they suggest is that adequate provisions for this supposedly negative right would not necessarily be less costly than adequate provisions for some rights supposed to be positive. Nor is it evident that physical security does any better on what Frankel called the test of being "realistically deliverable" (45) and Cranston called "the test of practicability" (66). On Cranston's use of the latter, see chapter 4 of *Basic Rights*.

9   "To have a right, then, is, I conceive, to have something which society ought to defend me in the possession of" – John Stuart Mill, *Utilitarianism* (Indianapolis: Bobbs-Merrill Co., 1957), p. 66 (chapter V, 14th paragraph from the end).

10   This is not a point about ordinary language, in which there is obviously a significant difference between "leave me alone" and "protect me against people who will not leave me alone." My thesis is that people who are not already grinding axes for minimal government will naturally and reasonably think in terms of enjoying a considerable degree of security, will want to have done whatever within reason is necessary, and will recognize that more is necessary than refraining campaigns – campaigns urging self-restraint upon would-be murderers, muggers, rapists, et al. I am of course not assuming that existing police and penal institutions are the best forms of social guarantees for security; I am assuming only that more effective institutions would probably be at least equally complex and expensive.

11   Therefore, as we shall see below, the complete fulfillment of a subsistence right may involve not the actual provision of any aid at all but only the performance of duties to avoid depriving and to protect against deprivation.

12   The literature on underdeveloped countries in fact abounds in actual cases that have the essential features of the so-called hypothetical case, and I have simply presented a stylized sketch of a common pattern. Most anecdotes are in the form of "horror stories" about transnational corporations switching land out of the production of the food consumed by the local poor. See, for example, Robert J. Ledogar, *Hungry for Profits: U.S. Food and Drug Multinationals in Latin America* (New York: IDOC, 1976), pp. 92–98 (Ralston Purina in Colombia) and Richard J. Barnet and Ronald E. Müller, *Global Reach: The Power of the Multinational Corporations* (New York: Simon and Schuster, 1974), p. 182 (carnations in Colombia). For a gargantuan case on a regional scale involving cattle-ranching, see Shelton H. Davis, *Victims of the Miracle: Development and the Indians of Brazil* (New York: Cambridge University Press, 1977). To a considerable extent the long-term development policy of Mexico for at least thirty of the last forty years has followed this basic pattern of

depriving the rural poor of food for subsistence for the sake of greater agricultural production of other crops – see the extremely careful and balanced study by Cynthia Hewitt de Alcantara, *Modernizing Mexican Agriculture: Socioeconomic Implications of Technological Change 1940–1970*. Report No. 76.5 (Geneva: United Nations Research Institute for Social Development, 1976); and Judith Adler Hellman, *Mexico in Crisis* (New York: Holmes & Meier Publishers, Inc., 1978), chapter 3. For a sophisticated theoretical analysis of some of the underlying dynamics, see Jeffery M. Paige, *Agrarian Revolution: Social Movements and Export Agriculture in the Underdeveloped World* (New York: Free Press, 1975), which has case studies of Angola, Peru, and Vietnam.

13   That is, they are conceptually distinct; whether this distinction makes any moral difference is another matter. See above, note 7, and the distinctions at the beginning of this chapter.

14   The increasingly frequent and facile appeal to "overpopulation" as a reason not to prevent preventable starvation is considered in chapter 4 of *Basic Rights*.

15   This much of the analysis is derived from the following important article: Onora O'Neill, "Lifeboat Earth," in *World Hunger and Moral Obligation*, edited by William Aiken and Hugh La Follette (Englewood Cliffs: Prentice-Hall, Inc., 1977), pp. 140–164. I return to discussion of the causal complexity of such cases at the end of my discussion of "Subsistence Duties" below.

16   For example, land-use laws might prohibit removing prime agricultural land from food production. Alternatively, land might be allowed to be used in the manner most beneficial to the national balance of payments with tax laws designed to guarantee compensating transfers to increase the purchasing power of the villagers (e.g., food stamps), etc. I discuss the question of how to apportion the duties to prevent social disasters in chapter 5 of *Basic Rights*.

17   There are of course non-human threats to both security and subsistence, like floods, as well. And we expect a minimally adequate society also to make arrangements to prevent, to control, or to minimize the ill effects of floods and other destructive natural forces. However, for an appreciation of the extent to which supposedly natural famines are the result of inadequate social arrangements, see Richard G. Robbins, *Famine in Russia 1891–92* (New York: Columbia University Press, 1975); and Michael F. Lofchie, "Political and Economic Origins of African Hunger," *Journal of Modern African Studies*, 13:4 (December 1975), pp. 551–567. As Lofchie says: "The point of departure for a political understanding of African hunger is so obvious it is almost always over-

looked: the distinction between drought and famine. . . . To the extent that there is a connection between drought and famine, it is mediated by the political and economic arrangements of a society. These can either minimize the human consequences of drought or accentuate its effects" (553). For a demonstration that the weather and other natural factors actually played fairly minor roles in the Great Bengal Famine, see the analysis by Amartya Sen, *Poverty and Famines* (Oxford: Clarendon Press, 1981) and, more generally, chapter 4 of my *Basic Rights*. To treat the *absence* of adequate social arrangements as a cause of a famine precipitated by a natural event like a drought or a flood, as these writers and I do, is to assume that it is reasonable to have expected the absent arrangements to have been present.

18 See note 12 above.

19 On whether an adequate definition can be literally exceptionless, see note 2 to chapter 1 of *Basic Rights*.

20 I take the need for the qualification "not necessary to the satisfaction of one's own basic rights" to be fairly obvious. However admirable self-sacrifice may be, it is surely not a basic duty owed to people generally, and the surrender of one's right to subsistence – or security – would in many circumstances constitute a literal sacrifice of oneself, that is, one's life. Unfortunately, the content of a duty does not dictate the identity of its bearers. Chapter 5 of *Basic Rights* discusses how to assign in a reasonable way the responsibility for fulfilling various duties.

21 How to bring transnational corporations under some constraints in order to prevent great social harms, like violations of basic rights, is one of our great political challenges. See the discussion of recommendation (4) in *Basic Rights*, chapter 7 and the relevant notes.

22 I am, of course, not proposing that we start calling it murder, but I am proposing that we acknowledge the parallels and act in appropriately parallel ways.

23 Without becoming anti-intellectual, or even atheoretical, we theorists might remember that a crystal-clear abstract distinction may not only have no

positive practical value but may sometimes contribute to vice. Writing about an entirely different matter, Barrie A. Paskins has put the general point eloquently: "We can imagine and describe cases in which we would think torture justified and unjustified. We can state the grounds on which we are making the discrimination. But what we cannot do is this: *we cannot provide for ourselves, or for those who must act for us in real situations, any way of making our notional distinctions in reality.* What might be claimed about the imaginary example is not that something significantly analogous could not occur but that in reality we cannot enable those who must act to recognize the case for what it is and other cases, by contrast, for what they are. In a real situation we can never be certain that the case in hand is of this kind rather than another. A too vivid imagination blinds us to the dust of war that drifts into the interrogation centre." Barrie A. Paskins, "What's Wrong with Torture?" *British Journal of International Studies*, 2 (1976), p. 144. I think this is a profound methodological point with strong implications concerning the now virtually incorrigible habit among moral and political philosophers of relying upon imaginary cases and concerning the "strict compliance" situations and "ideal theory" discussed by John Rawls and Kantians generally. I am trying to develop the methodological point in an essay with the working title, "Extreme Cases."

24 On the rationality of peasants, see James C. Scott, *The Moral Economy of the Peasant: Rebellion and Subsistence in Southeast Asia* (New Haven: Yale University Press, 1976), chapters 1 and 2.

25 See note 12 above.

26 I am indebted to John Langan for having emphasized this point. For a different argument, see his paper cited in note 2 above, p. 25.

27 For the classic account, see Clifford Geertz, *Agricultural Involution: The Processes of Ecological Change in Indonesia* (Berkeley: University of California Press for the Association of Asian Studies, 1963), chapters 4 and 5. Although various aspects of Geertz's analysis are naturally no longer accepted, the main points relevant here still stand.

22

A Defense of Abortion[1]

Judith Jarvis Thomson

Most opposition to abortion relies on the premise that the fetus is a human being, a person, from the moment of conception. The premise is argued for, but, as I think, not well. Take, for example, the most common argument. We are asked to notice that the development of a human being from conception through birth into childhood is continuous; then it is said that to draw a line, to choose a point in this development and say "before this point the thing is not a person, after this point it is a person" is to make an arbitrary choice, a choice for which in the nature of things no good reason can be given. It is concluded that the fetus is, or anyway that we had better say it is, a person from the moment of conception. But this conclusion does not follow. Similar things might be said about the development of an acorn into an oak tree, and it does not follow that acorns are oak trees, or that we had better say they are. Arguments of this form are sometimes called "slippery slope arguments" – the phrase is perhaps self-explanatory – and it is dismaying that opponents of abortion rely on them so heavily and uncritically.

I am inclined to agree, however, that the prospects for "drawing a line" in the development of the fetus look dim. I am inclined to think also that we shall probably have to agree that the fetus has already become a human person well before birth. Indeed, it comes as a surprise when one first learns how early in its life it begins to acquire human characteristics. By the tenth week, for example, it already has a face, arms and legs, fingers and toes; it has internal organs, and brain activity is detectable.[2] On the other hand, I think that the premise is false, that the fetus is not a person from the moment of conception. A newly fertilized ovum, a newly implanted clump of cells, is no more a person than an acorn is an oak tree. But I shall not discuss any of this. For it seems to me to be of great interest to ask what happens if, for the sake of argument, we allow the premise. How, precisely, are we supposed to get from there to the conclusion that abortion is morally impermissible? Opponents of abortion commonly spend most of their time establishing that the fetus is a person, and hardly any time explaining the step from there to the impermissibility of abortion. Perhaps they think the step too simple and obvious to require much comment. Or perhaps instead they are simply being economical in argument. Many of those who defend abortion rely on the premise that the fetus is not a person, but only a bit of tissue that will become a person at birth; and why pay out more arguments than you have to? Whatever the explanation, I suggest that the step they take is neither easy nor obvious, that it calls for closer examination than it is commonly given, and that when we do give it this closer examination we shall feel inclined to reject it.

I propose, then, that we grant that the fetus is a person from the moment of conception. How does the argument go from here? Something like this, I take it. Every person has a right to life. So the fetus has a right to life. No doubt the mother has a right to decide what shall happen in and to

Originally published in *Philosophy and Public Affairs*, 1 (1971), 47–66. Copyright © 1971 by Princeton University Press. Reprinted by permission of Princeton University Press.

her body; everyone would grant that. But surely a person's right to life is stronger and more stringent than the mother's right to decide what happens in and to her body, and so outweighs it. So the fetus may not be killed; an abortion may not be performed.

It sounds plausible. But now let me ask you to imagine this. You wake up in the morning and find yourself back to back in bed with an unconscious violinist. A famous unconscious violinist. He has been found to have a fatal kidney ailment, and the Society of Music Lovers has canvassed all the available medical records and found that you alone have the right blood type to help. They have therefore kidnapped you, and last night the violinist's circulatory system was plugged into yours, so that your kidneys can be used to extract poisons from his blood as well as your own. The director of the hospital now tells you, "Look, we're sorry the Society of Music Lovers did this to you – we would never have permitted it if we had known. But still, they did it, and the violinist now is plugged into you. To unplug you would be to kill him. But never mind, it's only for nine months. By then he will have recovered from his ailment, and can safely be unplugged from you." Is it morally incumbent on you to accede to this situation? No doubt it would be very nice of you if you did, a great kindness. But do you *have* to accede to it? What if it were not nine months, but nine years? Or longer still? What if the director of the hospital says, "Tough luck, I agree, but you've now got to stay in bed, with the violinist plugged into you, for the rest of your life. Because remember this. All persons have a right to life, and violinists are persons. Granted you have a right to decide what happens in and to your body, but a person's right to life outweighs your right to decide what happens in and to your body. So you cannot ever be unplugged from him." I imagine you would regard this as outrageous, which suggests that something really is wrong with that plausible-sounding argument I mentioned a moment ago.

In this case, of course, you were kidnapped; you didn't volunteer for the operation that plugged the violinist into your kidneys. Can those who oppose abortion on the ground I mentioned make an exception for a pregnancy due to rape? Certainly. They can say that persons have a right to life only if they didn't come into existence because of rape; or they can say that all persons have a right to life, but that some have less of a

right to life than others, in particular, that those who came into existence because of rape have less. But these statements have a rather unpleasant sound. Surely the question of whether you have a right to life at all, or how much of it you have, shouldn't turn on the question of whether or not you are the product of a rape. And in fact the people who oppose abortion on the ground I mentioned do not make this distinction, and hence do not make an exception in case of rape.

Nor do they make an exception for a case in which the mother has to spend the nine months of her pregnancy in bed. They would agree that would be a great pity, and hard on the mother; but all the same, all persons have a right to life, the fetus is a person, and so on. I suspect, in fact, that they would not make an exception for a case in which, miraculously enough, the pregnancy went on for nine years, or even the rest of the mother's life.

Some won't even make an exception for a case in which continuation of the pregnancy is likely to shorten the mother's life; they regard abortion as impermissible even to save the mother's life. Such cases are nowadays very rare, and many opponents of abortion do not accept this extreme view. All the same, it is a good place to begin: a number of points of interest come out in respect to it.

1. Let us call the view that abortion is impermissible even to save the mother's life "the extreme view." I want to suggest first that it does not issue from the argument I mentioned earlier without the addition of some fairly powerful premises. Suppose a woman has become pregnant, and now learns that she has a cardiac condition such that she will die if she carries the baby to term. What may be done for her? The fetus, being a person, has a right to life, but as the mother is a person too, so has she a right to life. Presumably they have an equal right to life. How is it supposed to come out that an abortion may not be performed? If mother and child have an equal right to life, shouldn't we perhaps flip a coin? Or should we add to the mother's right to life her right to decide what happens in and to her body, which everybody seems to be ready to grant – the sum of her rights now outweighing the fetus' right to life?

The most familiar argument here is the following. We are told that performing the abortion would be directly killing[3] the child, whereas doing nothing would not be killing the mother, but only letting her die. Moreover, in killing the child, one would be killing an innocent person, for the child has committed no crime, and is not aiming at his mother's death. And then there are a variety of ways in which this might be continued. (1) But as directly killing an innocent person is always and absolutely impermissible, an abortion may not be performed. Or, (2) as directly killing an innocent person is murder, and murder is always and absolutely impermissible, an abortion may not be performed.[4] Or, (3) as one's duty to refrain from directly killing an innocent person is more stringent than one's duty to keep a person from dying, an abortion may not be performed. Or, (4) if one's only options are directly killing an innocent person or letting a person die, one must prefer letting the person die, and thus an abortion may not be performed.[5]

Some people seem to have thought that these are not further premises which must be added if the conclusion is to be reached, but that they follow from the very fact that an innocent person has a right to life.[6] But this seems to me to be a mistake, and perhaps the simplest way to show this is to bring out that while we must certainly grant that innocent persons have a right to life, the theses in (1) through (4) are all false. Take (2), for example. If directly killing an innocent person is murder, and thus is impermissible, then the mother's directly killing the innocent person inside her is murder, and thus is impermissible. But it cannot seriously be thought to be murder if the mother performs an abortion on herself to save her life. It cannot seriously be said that she *must* refrain, that she *must* sit passively by and wait for her death. Let us look again at the case of you and the violinist. There you are, in bed with the violinist, and the director of the hospital says to you, "It's all most distressing, and I deeply sympathize, but you see this is putting an additional strain on your kidneys, and you'll be dead within the month. But you *have* to stay where you are all the same. Because unplugging you would be directly killing an innocent violinist, and that's murder, and that's impermissible." If anything in the world is true, it is that you do not commit murder, you do not do what is impermissible, if you reach around to your back and unplug yourself from that violinist to save your life.

The main focus of attention in writings on abortion has been on what a third party may or may not do in answer to a request from a woman for an abortion. This is in a way understandable.

Things being as they are, there isn't much a woman can safely do to abort herself. So the question asked is what a third party may do, and what the mother may do, if it is mentioned at all, is deduced, almost as an afterthought, from what it is concluded that third parties may do. But it seems to me that to treat the matter in this way is to refuse to grant to the mother that very status of person which is so firmly insisted on for the fetus. For we cannot simply read off what a person may do from what a third party may do. Suppose you find yourself trapped in a tiny house with a growing child. I mean a very tiny house, and a rapidly growing child – you are already up against the wall of the house and in a few minutes you'll be crushed to death. The child on the other hand won't be crushed to death; if nothing is done to stop him from growing he'll be hurt, but in the end he'll simply burst open the house and walk out a free man. Now I could well understand it if a bystander were to say, "There's nothing we can do for you. We cannot choose between your life and his, we cannot be the ones to decide who is to live, we cannot intervene." But it cannot be concluded that you too can do nothing, that you cannot attack it to save your life. However innocent the child may be, you do not have to wait passively while it crushes you to death. Perhaps a pregnant woman is vaguely felt to have the status of house, to which we don't allow the right of self-defense. But if the woman houses the child, it should be remembered that she is a person who houses it.

I should perhaps stop to say explicitly that I am not claiming that people have a right to do anything whatever to save their lives. I think, rather, that there are drastic limits to the right of self-defense. If someone threatens you with death unless you torture someone else to death, I think you have not the right, even to save your life, to do so. But the case under consideration here is very different. In our case there are only two people involved, one whose life is threatened, and one who threatens it. Both are innocent: the one who is threatened is not threatened because of any fault, the one who threatens does not threaten because of any fault. For this reason we may feel that we bystanders cannot intervene. But the person threatened can.

In sum, a woman surely can defend her life against the threat to it posed by the unborn child, even if doing so involves its death. And this shows not merely that the theses in (1) through

(4) are false; it shows also that the extreme view of abortion is false, and so we need not canvass any other possible ways of arriving at it from the argument I mentioned at the outset.

2. The extreme view could of course be weakened to say that while abortion is permissible to save the mother's life, it may not be performed by a third party, but only by the mother herself. But this cannot be right either. For what we have to keep in mind is that the mother and the unborn child are not like two tenants in a small house which has, by an unfortunate mistake, been rented to both: the mother *owns* the house. The fact that she does adds to the offensiveness of deducing that the mother can do nothing from the supposition that third parties can do nothing. But it does more than this: it casts a bright light on the supposition that third parties can do nothing. Certainly it lets us see that a third party who says "I cannot choose between you" is fooling himself if he thinks this is impartiality. If Jones has found and fastened on a certain coat, which he needs to keep him from freezing, but which Smith also needs to keep him from freezing, then it is not impartiality that says "I cannot choose between you" when Smith owns the coat. Women have said again and again "This body is *my* body!" and they have reason to feel angry, reason to feel that it has been like shouting into the wind. Smith, after all, is hardly likely to bless us if we say to him, "Of course it's your coat, anybody would grant that it is. But no one may choose between you and Jones who is to have it."

We should really ask what it is that says "no one may choose" in the face of the fact that the body that houses the child is the mother's body. It may be simply a failure to appreciate this fact. But it may be something more interesting, namely the sense that one has a right to refuse to lay hands on people, even where it would be just and fair to do so, even where justice seems to require that somebody do so. Thus justice might call for somebody to get Smith's coat back from Jones, and yet you have a right to refuse to be the one to lay hands on Jones, a right to refuse to do physical violence to him. This, I think, must be granted. But then what should be said is not "no one may choose," but only "*I* cannot choose," and indeed not even this, but "*I* will not *act*," leaving it open that somebody else can or should, and in particular that anyone in a position of authority, with the job of securing people's rights, both can and should. So this is no difficulty. I have not been arguing that any given third party must accede to the mother's request that he perform an abortion to save her life, but only that he may.

I suppose that in some views of human life the mother's body is only on loan to her, the loan not being one which gives her any prior claim to it. One who held this view might well think it impartiality to say "I cannot choose." But I shall simply ignore this possibility. My own view is that if a human being has any just, prior claim to anything at all, he has a just, prior claim to his own body. And perhaps this needn't be argued for here anyway, since, as I mentioned, the arguments against abortion we are looking at do grant that the woman has a right to decide what happens in and to her body.

But although they do grant it, I have tried to show that they do not take seriously what is done in granting it. I suggest the same thing will reappear even more clearly when we turn away from cases in which the mother's life is at stake, and attend, as I propose we now do, to the vastly more common cases in which a woman wants an abortion for some less weighty reason than preserving her own life.

3. Where the mother's life is not at stake, the argument I mentioned at the outset seems to have a much stronger pull. "Everyone has a right to life, so the unborn person has a right to life." And isn't the child's right to life weightier than anything other than the mother's own right to life, which she might put forward as ground for an abortion?

This argument treats the right to life as if it were unproblematic. It is not, and this seems to me to be precisely the source of the mistake.

For we should now, at long last, ask what it comes to, to have a right to life. In some views having a right to life includes having a right to be given at least the bare minimum one needs for continued life. But suppose that what in fact is the bare minimum a man needs for continued life is something he has no right at all to be given? If I am sick unto death, and the only thing that will save my life is the touch of Henry Fonda's cool hand on my fevered brow, then all the same, I have no right to be given the touch of Henry Fonda's cool hand on my fevered brow. It would be frightfully nice of him to fly in from the West Coast to provide it. It would be less nice, though no doubt well meant, if my friends flew out to the West Coast and carried Henry Fonda back with them. But I have no right at all against anybody that he should do this for me. Or again, to return to the story I told earlier, the fact that for continued life that violinist needs the continued use of your kidneys does not establish that he has a right to be given the continued use of your kidneys. He certainly has no right against you that *you* should give him continued use of your kidneys. For nobody has any right to use your kidneys unless you give him such a right; and nobody has the right against you that you shall give him this right – if you do allow him to go on using your kidneys, this is a kindness on your part, and not something he can claim from you as his due. Nor has he any right against anybody else that *they* should give him continued use of your kidneys. Certainly he had no right against the Society of Music Lovers that they should plug him into you in the first place. And if you now start to unplug yourself, having learned that you will otherwise have to spend nine years in bed with him, there is nobody in the world who must try to prevent you, in order to see to it that he is given something he has a right to be given.

Some people are rather stricter about the right to life. In their view, it does not include the right to be given anything, but amounts to, and only to, the right not to be killed by anybody. But here a related difficulty arises. If everybody is to refrain from killing that violinist, then everybody must refrain from doing a great many different sorts of things. Everybody must refrain from slitting his throat, everybody must refrain from shooting him – and everybody must refrain from unplugging you from him. But does he have a right against everybody that they shall refrain from unplugging you from him? To refrain from doing this is to allow him to continue to use your kidneys. It could be argued that he has a right against us that *we* should allow him to continue to use your kidneys. That is, while he had no right against us that we should give him the use of your kidneys, it might be argued that he anyway has a right against us that we shall not now intervene and deprive him of the use of your kidneys. I shall come back to third-party interventions later. But certainly the violinist has no right against you that *you* shall allow him to continue to use your kidneys. As I said, if you do allow him to use them, it is a kindness on your part, and not something you owe him.

The difficulty I point to here is not peculiar to the right to life. It reappears in connection with all the other natural rights; and it is something

which an adequate account of rights must deal with. For present purposes it is enough just to draw attention to it. But I would stress that I am not arguing that people do not have a right to life – quite to the contrary, it seems to me that the primary control we must place on the acceptability of an account of rights is that it should turn out in that account to be a truth that all persons have a right to life. I am arguing only that having a right to life does not guarantee having either a right to be given the use of or a right to be allowed continued use of another person's body – even if one needs it for life itself. So the right to life will not serve the opponents of abortion in the very simple and clear way in which they seem to have thought it would.

4. There is another way to bring out the difficulty. In the most ordinary sort of case, to deprive someone of what he has a right to is to treat him unjustly. Suppose a boy and his small brother are jointly given a box of chocolates for Christmas. If the older boy takes the box and refuses to give his brother any of the chocolates, he is unjust to him, for the brother has been given a right to half of them. But suppose that, having learned that otherwise it means nine years in bed with that violinist, you unplug yourself from him. You surely are not being unjust to him, for you gave him no right to use your kidneys, and no one else can have given him any such right. But we have to notice that in unplugging yourself, you are killing him; and violinists, like everybody else, have a right to life, and thus in the view we were considering just now, the right not to be killed. So here you do what he supposedly has a right you shall not do, but you do not act unjustly to him in doing it.

The emendation which may be made at this point is this: the right to life consists not in the right not to be killed, but rather in the right not to be killed unjustly. This runs a risk of circularity, but never mind: it would enable us to square the fact that the violinist has a right to life with the fact that you do not act unjustly toward him in unplugging yourself, thereby killing him. For if you do not kill him unjustly, you do not violate his right to life, and so it is no wonder you do him no injustice.

But if this emendation is accepted, the gap in the argument against abortion stares us plainly in the face: it is by no means enough to show that the fetus is a person, and to remind us that all persons have a right to life – we need to be shown also that killing the fetus violates its right to life, i.e., that abortion is unjust killing. And is it?

I suppose we may take it as a datum that in a case of pregnancy due to rape the mother has not given the unborn person a right to the use of her body for food and shelter. Indeed, in what pregnancy could it be supposed that the mother has given the unborn person such a right? It is not as if there were unborn persons drifting about the world, to whom a woman who wants a child says "I invite you in."

But it might be argued that there are other ways one can have acquired a right to the use of another person's body than by having been invited to use it by that person. Suppose a woman voluntarily indulges in intercourse, knowing of the chance it will issue in pregnancy, and then she does become pregnant; is she not in part responsible for the presence, in fact the very existence, of the unborn person inside her? No doubt she did not invite it in. But doesn't her partial responsibility for its being there itself give it a right to the use of her body?[7] If so, then her aborting it would be more like the boy's taking away the chocolates, and less like your unplugging yourself from the violinist – doing so would be depriving it of what it does have a right to, and thus would be doing it an injustice.

And then, too, it might be asked whether or not she can kill it even to save her own life: If she voluntarily called it into existence, how can she now kill it, even in self-defense?

The first thing to be said about this is that it is something new. Opponents of abortion have been so concerned to make out the independence of the fetus, in order to establish that it has a right to life, just as its mother does, that they have tended to overlook the possible support they might gain from making out that the fetus is *dependent* on the mother, in order to establish that she has a special kind of responsibility for it, a responsibility that gives it rights against her which are not possessed by any independent person – such as an ailing violinist who is a stranger to her.

On the other hand, this argument would give the unborn person a right to its mother's body only if her pregnancy resulted from a voluntary act, undertaken in full knowledge of the chance a pregnancy might result from it. It would leave out entirely the unborn person whose existence is due to rape. Pending the availability of some further argument, then, we would be left with the conclusion that unborn persons whose existence is due to rape have no right to the use of their mothers' bodies, and thus that aborting them is not depriving them of anything they have a right to and hence is not unjust killing.

And we should also notice that it is not at all plain that this argument really does go even as far as it purports to. For there are cases and cases, and the details make a difference. If the room is stuffy, and I therefore open a window to air it, and a burglar climbs in, it would be absurd to say: "Ah, now he can stay, she's given him a right to the use of her house – for she is partially responsible for his presence there, having voluntarily done what enabled him to get in, in full knowledge that there are such things as burglars, and that burglars burgle." It would be still more absurd to say this if I had had bars installed outside my windows, precisely to prevent burglars from getting in, and a burglar got in only because of a defect in the bars. It remains equally absurd if we imagine it is not a burglar who climbs in, but an innocent person who blunders or falls in. Again, suppose it were like this: people-seeds drift about in the air like pollen, and if you open your windows, one may drift in and take root in your carpets or upholstery. You don't want children, so you fix up your windows with fine mesh screens, the very best you can buy. As can happen, however, and on very, very rare occasions does happen, one of the screens is defective; and a seed drifts in and takes root. Does the person-plant who now develops have a right to the use of your house? Surely not – despite the fact that you voluntarily opened your windows, you knowingly kept carpets and upholstered furniture, and you knew that screens were sometimes defective. Someone may argue that you are responsible for its rooting, that it does have a right to your house, because after all you *could* have lived out your life with bare floors and furniture, or with sealed windows and doors. But this won't do – for by the same token anyone can avoid a pregnancy due to rape by having a hysterectomy, or anyway by never leaving home without a (reliable!) army.

It seems to me that the argument we are looking at can establish at most that there are *some* cases in which the unborn person has a right to the use of its mother's body, and therefore *some* cases in which abortion is unjust killing. There is room for much discussion and argument as to precisely which, if any. But I think we should sidestep this issue and leave it open, for at any rate the argument certainly does not establish that all abortion is unjust killing.

5. There is room for yet another argument here, however. We surely must all grant that there may be cases in which it would be morally indecent to detach a person from your body at the cost of his life. Suppose you learn that what the violinist needs is not nine years of your life, but only one hour: all you need do to save his life is to spend one hour in that bed with him. Suppose also that letting him use your kidneys for that one hour would not affect your health in the slightest. Admittedly you were kidnapped. Admittedly you did not give anyone permission to plug him into you. Nevertheless it seems to me plain you *ought* to allow him to use your kidneys for that hour – it would be indecent to refuse.

Again, suppose pregnancy lasted only an hour, and constituted no threat to life or health. And suppose that a woman becomes pregnant as a result of rape. Admittedly she did not voluntarily do anything to bring about the existence of a child. Admittedly she did nothing at all which would give the unborn person a right to the use of her body. All the same it might well be said, as in the newly emended violinist story, that she *ought* to allow it to remain for that hour – that it would be indecent in her to refuse.

Now some people are inclined to use the term "right" in such a way that it follows from the fact that you ought to allow a person to use your body for the hour he needs, that he has a right to use your body for the hour he needs, even though he has not been given that right by any person or act. They may say that it follows also that if you refuse, you act unjustly toward him. This use of the term is perhaps so common that it cannot be called wrong; nevertheless it seems to me to be an unfortunate loosening of what we would do better to keep a tight rein on. Suppose that box of chocolates I mentioned earlier had not been given to both boys jointly, but was given only to the older boy. There he sits, stolidly eating his way through the box, his small brother watching enviously. Here we are likely to say "You ought not to be so mean. You ought to give your brother some of those chocolates." My own view is that it just does not follow from the truth of this that the brother has any right to any of the chocolates. If the boy refuses to give his brother any, he is greedy, stingy, callous – but not unjust. I suppose that the people I have in mind will say it does follow that the brother has a right to some of the

chocolates, and thus that the boy does act unjustly if he refuses to give his brother any. But the effect of saying this is to obscure what we should keep distinct, namely the difference between the boy's refusal in this case and the boy's refusal in the earlier case, in which the box was given to both boys jointly, and in which the small brother thus had what was from any point of view clear title to half.

A further objection to so using the term "right" that from the fact that A ought to do a thing for B, it follows that B has a right against A that A do it for him, is that it is going to make the question of whether or not a man has a right to a thing turn on how easy it is to provide him with it; and this seems not merely unfortunate, but morally unacceptable. Take the case of Henry Fonda again. I said earlier that I had no right to the touch of his cool hand on my fevered brow, even though I needed it to save my life. I said it would be frightfully nice of him to fly in from the West Coast to provide me with it, but that I had no right against him that he should do so. But suppose he isn't on the West Coast. Suppose he has only to walk across the room, place a hand briefly on my brow – and lo, my life is saved. Then surely he ought to do it, it would be indecent to refuse. Is it to be said "Ah, well, it follows that in this case she has a right to the touch of his hand on her brow, and so it would be an injustice in him to refuse"? So that I have a right to it when it is easy for him to provide it, though no right when it's hard? It's rather a shocking idea that anyone's rights should fade away and disappear as it gets harder and harder to accord them to him.

So my own view is that even though you ought to let the violinist use your kidneys for the one hour he needs, we should not conclude that he has a right to do so – we should say that if you refuse, you are, like the boy who owns all the chocolates and will give none away, self-centered and callous, indecent in fact, but not unjust. And similarly, that even supposing a case in which a woman pregnant due to rape ought to allow the unborn person to use her body for the hour he needs, we should not conclude that he has a right to do so; we should conclude that she is self-centered, callous, indecent, but not unjust, if she refuses. The complaints are no less grave; they are just different. However, there is no need to insist on this point. If anyone does wish to deduce "he has a right" from "you ought," then all the same he must surely grant that there are cases in which it is not morally required of you that you allow that violinist to use your kidneys, and in which he does not have a right to use them, and in which you do not do him an injustice if you refuse. And so also for mother and unborn child. Except in such cases as the unborn person has a right to demand it – and we were leaving open the possibility that there may be such cases – nobody is morally *required* to make large sacrifices, of health, of all other interests and concerns, of all other duties and commitments, for nine years, or even for nine months, in order to keep another person alive.

6. We have in fact to distinguish between two kinds of Samaritan: the Good Samaritan and what we might call the Minimally Decent Samaritan. The story of the Good Samaritan, you will remember, goes like this:

> A certain man went down from Jerusalem to Jericho, and fell among thieves, which stripped him of his raiment, and wounded him, and departed, leaving him half dead.
>
> And by chance there came down a certain priest that way; and when he saw him, he passed by on the other side.
>
> And likewise a Levite, when he was at the place, came and looked on him, and passed by on the other side.
>
> But a certain Samaritan, as he journeyed, came where he was; and when he saw him he had compassion on him.
>
> And went to him, and bound up his wounds, pouring in oil and wine, and set him on his own beast, and brought him to an inn, and took care of him.
>
> And on the morrow, when he departed, he took out two pence, and gave them to the host, and said unto him, "Take care of him; and whatsoever thou spendest more, when I come again, I will repay thee." (Luke 10.30–35)

The Good Samaritan went out of his way, at some cost to himself, to help one in need of it. We are not told what the options were, that is, whether or not the priest and the Levite could have helped by doing less than the Good Samaritan did, but assuming they could have, then the fact they did nothing at all shows they were not even Minimally Decent Samaritans, not because they were not Samaritans, but because they were not even minimally decent.

These things are a matter of degree, of course,

but there is a difference, and it comes out perhaps most clearly in the story of Kitty Genovese, who, as you will remember, was murdered while thirty-eight people watched or listened, and did nothing at all to help her. A Good Samaritan would have rushed out to give direct assistance against the murderer. Or perhaps we had better allow that it would have been a Splendid Samaritan who did this, on the ground that it would have involved a risk of death for himself. But the thirty-eight not only did not do this, they did not even trouble to pick up a phone to call the police. Minimally Decent Samaritanism would call for doing at least that, and their not having done it was monstrous.

After telling the story of the Good Samaritan, Jesus said "Go, and do thou likewise." Perhaps he meant that we are morally required to act as the Good Samaritan did. Perhaps he was urging people to do more than is morally required of them. At all events it seems plain that it was not morally required of any of the thirty-eight that he rush out to give direct assistance at the risk of his own life, and that it is not morally required of anyone that he give long stretches of his life – nine years or nine months – to sustaining the life of a person who has no special right (we were leaving open the possibility of this) to demand it.

Indeed, with one rather striking class of exceptions, no one in any country in the world is *legally* required to do anywhere near as much as this for anyone else. The class of exceptions is obvious. My main concern here is not the state of the law in respect to abortion, but it is worth drawing attention to the fact that in no state in this country is any man compelled by law to be even a Minimally Decent Samaritan to any person; there is no law under which charges could be brought against the thirty-eight who stood by while Kitty Genovese died. By contrast, in most states in this country women are compelled by law to be not merely Minimally Decent Samaritans, but Good Samaritans to unborn persons inside them. This doesn't by itself settle anything one way or the other, because it may well be argued that there should be laws in this country – as there are in many European countries – compelling at least Minimally Decent Samaritanism.[8] But it does show that there is a gross injustice in the existing state of the law. And it shows also that the groups currently working against liberalization of abortion laws, in fact working toward having it declared unconstitutional for a state to permit abortion, had better start working for the adoption of Good Samaritan laws generally, or earn the charge that they are acting in bad faith.

I should think, myself, that Minimally Decent Samaritan laws would be one thing, Good Samaritan laws quite another, and in fact highly improper. But we are not here concerned with the law. What we should ask is not whether anybody should be compelled by law to be a Good Samaritan, but whether we must accede to a situation in which somebody is being compelled – by nature, perhaps – to be a Good Samaritan. We have, in other words, to look now at third-party interventions. I have been arguing that no person is morally required to make large sacrifices to sustain the life of another who has no right to demand them, and this even where the sacrifices do not include life itself; we are not morally required to be Good Samaritans or anyway Very Good Samaritans to one another. But what if a man cannot extricate himself from such a situation? What if he appeals to us to extricate him? It seems to me plain that there are cases in which we can, cases in which a Good Samaritan would extricate him. There you are, you were kidnapped, and nine years in bed with that violinist lie ahead of you. You have your own life to lead. You are sorry, but you simply cannot see giving up so much of your life to the sustaining of his. You cannot extricate yourself, and ask us to do so. I should have thought that – in light of his having no right to the use of your body – it was obvious that we do not have to accede to your being forced to give up so much. We can do what you ask. There is no injustice to the violinist in our doing so.

7. Following the lead of the opponents of abortion, I have throughout been speaking of the fetus merely as a person, and what I have been asking is whether or not the argument we began with, which proceeds only from the fetus being a person, really does establish its conclusion. I have argued that it does not.

But of course there are arguments and arguments, and it may be said that I have simply fastened on the wrong one. It may be said that what is important is not merely the fact that the fetus is a person, but that it is a person for whom the woman has a special kind of responsibility issuing from the fact that she is its mother. And it might be argued that all my analogies are therefore irrelevant – for you do not have that special kind of responsibility for that violinist, Henry Fonda

does not have that special kind of responsibility for me. And our attention might be drawn to the fact that men and women both *are* compelled by law to provide support for their children.

I have in effect dealt (briefly) with this argument in section 4 above; but a (still briefer) recapitulation now may be in order. Surely we do not have any such "special responsibility" for a person unless we have assumed it, explicitly or implicitly. If a set of parents do not try to prevent pregnancy, do not obtain an abortion, and then at the time of birth of the child do not put it out for adoption, but rather take it home with them, then they have assumed responsibility for it, they have given it rights, and they cannot *now* withdraw support from it at the cost of its life because they now find it difficult to go on providing for it. But if they have taken all reasonable precautions against having a child, they do not simply by virtue of their biological relationship to the child who comes into existence have a special responsibility for it. They may wish to assume responsibility for it, or they may not wish to. And I am suggesting that if assuming responsibility for it would require large sacrifices, then they may refuse. A Good Samaritan would not refuse – or anyway, a Splendid Samaritan, if the sacrifices that had to be made were enormous. But then so would a Good Samaritan assume responsibility for that violinist; so would Henry Fonda, if he is a Good Samaritan, fly in from the West Coast and assume responsibility for me.

8. My argument will be found unsatisfactory on two counts by many of those who want to regard abortion as morally permissible. First, while I do argue that abortion is not impermissible, I do not argue that it is always permissible. There may well be cases in which carrying the child to term requires only Minimally Decent Samaritanism of the mother, and this is a standard we must not fall below. I am inclined to think it a merit of my account precisely that it does *not* give a general yes or a general no. It allows for and supports our sense that, for example, a sick and desperately frightened fourteen-year-old schoolgirl, pregnant due to rape, may *of course* choose abortion, and that any law which rules this out is an insane law. And it also allows for and supports our sense that in other cases resort to abortion is even positively indecent. It would be indecent in the woman to request an abortion, and indecent in a doctor to perform it, if she is in her seventh month, and wants the

abortion just to avoid the nuisance of postponing a trip abroad. The very fact that the arguments I have been drawing attention to treat all cases of abortion, or even all cases of abortion in which the mother's life is not at stake, as morally on a par ought to have made them suspect at the outset.

Secondly, while I am arguing for the permissibility of abortion in some cases, I am not arguing for the right to secure the death of the unborn child. It is easy to confuse these two things in that up to a certain point in the life of the fetus it is not able to survive outside the mother's body; hence removing it from her body guarantees its death. But they are importantly different. I have argued that you are not morally required to spend nine months in bed, sustaining the life of that violinist; but to say this is by no means to say that if, when you unplug yourself, there is a miracle and he survives, you then have a right to turn round and slit his throat. You may detach yourself even if this costs him his life; you have no

right to be guaranteed his death, by some other means, if unplugging yourself does not kill him. There are some people who will feel dissatisfied by this feature of my argument. A woman may be utterly devastated by the thought of a child, a bit of herself, put out for adoption and never seen or heard of again. She may therefore want not merely that the child be detached from her, but more, that it die. Some opponents of abortion are inclined to regard this as beneath contempt – thereby showing insensitivity to what is surely a powerful source of despair. All the same, I agree that the desire for the child's death is not one which anybody may gratify, should it turn out to be possible to detach the child alive.

At this place, however, it should be remembered that we have only been pretending throughout that the fetus is a human being from the moment of conception. A very early abortion is surely not the killing of a person, and so is not dealt with by anything I have said here.

Notes

1   I am very much indebted to James Thomson for discussion, criticism, and many helpful suggestions.

2   Daniel Callahan, *Abortion: Law, Choice and Morality* (New York, 1970), p. 373. This book gives a fascinating survey of the available information on abortion. The Jewish tradition is surveyed in David M. Feldman, *Birth Control in Jewish Law* (New York, 1968), Part 5; the Catholic tradition in John T. Noonan, Jr., "An Almost Absolute Value in History," in *The Morality of Abortion*, ed. John T. Noonan, Jr. (Cambridge, Mass., 1970).

3   The term "direct" in the arguments I refer to is a technical one. Roughly, what is meant by "direct killing" is either killing as an end in itself, or killing as a means to some end, for example, the end of saving someone else's life. See note 6, below, for an example of its use.

4   Cf. *Encyclical Letter of Pope Pius XI on Christian Marriage*, St. Paul Editions (Boston, n.d.), p. 32: "however much we may pity the mother whose health and even life is gravely imperiled in the performance of the duty allotted to her by nature, nevertheless what could ever be a sufficient reason for excusing in any way the direct murder of the innocent? This is precisely what we are dealing with here." Noonan (*The Morality of Abortion*, p. 43) reads this as follows: "What cause can ever avail to excuse in any way the direct killing of the innocent? For it is a question of that."

5   The thesis in (4) is in an interesting way weaker than those in (1), (2), and (3): they rule out abortion even in cases in which both mother *and* child will die if the abortion is not performed. By contrast, one who held the view expressed in (4) could consistently say that one needn't prefer letting two persons die to killing one.

6   Cf. the following passage from Pius XII, *Address to the Italian Catholic Society of Midwives*: "The baby in the maternal breast has the right to life immediately from God. – Hence there is no man, no human authority, no science, no medical, eugenic, social, economic or moral "indication" which can establish or grant a valid juridical ground for a direct deliberate disposition of an innocent human life, that is a disposition which looks to its destruction either as an end or as a means to another end perhaps in itself not illicit. – The baby, still not born, is a man in the same degree and for the same reason as the mother" (quoted in Noonan, *The Morality of Abortion*, p. 45).

7   The need for a discussion of this argument was brought home to me by members of the Society for Ethical and Legal Philosophy, to whom this paper was originally presented.

8   For a discussion of the difficulties involved, and a survey of the European experience with such laws, see *The Good Samaritan and the Law*, ed. James M. Ratcliffe (New York, 1966).

23

Justice and Minority Rights

Will Kymlicka

1 Three Forms of Group-Differentiated Rights

Virtually all liberal democracies are either multinational or polyethnic, or both. The 'challenge of multiculturalism' is to accommodate these national and ethnic differences in a stable and morally defensible way (Gutmann 1993). In this section, I will discuss some of the most important ways in which democracies have responded to the demands of national minorities and ethnic groups.

In all liberal democracies, one of the major mechanisms for accommodating cultural differences is the protection of the civil and political rights of individuals. It is impossible to overstate the importance of freedom of association, religion, speech, mobility, and political organization for protecting group difference. These rights enable individuals to form and maintain the various groups and associations which constitute civil society, to adapt these groups to changing circumstances, and to promote their views and interests to the wider population. The protection afforded by these common rights of citizenship is sufficient for many of the legitimate forms of diversity in society.

Various critics of liberalism – including some Marxists, communitarians, and feminists – have argued that the liberal focus on individual rights reflects an atomistic, materialistic, instrumental,

or conflictual view of human relationships. I believe that this criticism is profoundly mistaken, and that individual rights can be and typically are used to sustain a wide range of social relationships. Indeed, the most basic liberal right – freedom of conscience – is primarily valuable for the protection it gives to intrinsically social (and non-instrumental) activities.[1]

However, it is increasingly accepted in many countries that some forms of cultural difference can only be accommodated through special legal or constitutional measures, above and beyond the common rights of citizenship. Some forms of group difference can only be accommodated if their members have certain group-specific rights – what Iris Young calls 'differentiated citizenship' (I. Young 1989: 258).

For example, a recent government publication in Canada noted that:

> In the Canadian experience, it has not been enough to protect only universal individual rights. Here, the Constitution and ordinary laws also protect other rights accorded to individuals as members of certain communities. This accommodation of both types of rights makes our constitution unique and reflects the Canadian value of equality that accommodates difference. The fact that community rights exist alongside individual rights goes to the very heart of what Canada is all about. (Government of Canada 1991a: 3)

It is quite misleading to say that Canada is unique in combining universal individual rights and group-specific 'community rights'. Such a combination exists in many other federal systems in Europe, Asia, and Africa. As I noted earlier, even the constitution of the United States, which is often seen as a paradigm of individualism, allows for various group-specific rights, including the special status of American Indians and Puerto Ricans.

It is these special group-specific measures for accommodating national and ethnic differences that I will focus on. There are at least three forms of group-specific rights: (1) self-government rights; (2) polyethnic rights; and (3) special representation rights. I will say a few words about each, before considering some of the issues they raise for liberal-democratic theory in subsequent chapters.

1. Self-government rights. In most multination states, the component nations are inclined to demand some form of political autonomy or territorial jurisdiction, so as to ensure the full and free development of their cultures and the best interests of their people. At the extreme, nations may wish to secede, if they think their self-determination is impossible within the larger state.

The right of national groups to self-determination is given (limited) recognition in international law. According to the United Nations' Charter, 'all peoples have the right to self-determination'. However, the UN has not defined 'peoples', and it has generally applied the principle of self-determination only to overseas colonies, not internal national minorities, even when the latter were subject to the same sort of colonization and conquest as the former. This limitation on self-determination to overseas colonies (known as the 'salt-water thesis') is widely seen as arbitrary, and many national minorities insist that they too are 'peoples' or 'nations', and, as such, have the right of self-determination. They demand certain powers of self-government which they say were not relinquished by their (often involuntary) incorporation into a larger state.[2]

One mechanism for recognizing claims to self-government is federalism, which divides powers between the central government and regional sub-units (provinces/states/cantons). Where national minorities are regionally concentrated, the boundaries of federal subunits can be drawn so that the national minority forms a majority in one of the subunits. Under these circumstances, fed-

eralism can provide extensive self-government for a national minority, guaranteeing its ability to make decisions in certain areas without being outvoted by the larger society.

For example, under the federal division of powers in Canada, the province of Quebec (which is 80 per cent francophone) has extensive jurisdiction over issues that are crucial to the survival of the French culture, including control over education, language, culture, as well as significant input into immigration policy. The other nine provinces also have these powers, but the major impetus behind the existing division of powers, and indeed behind the entire federal system, is the need to accommodate the Québécois. At the time of Confederation, most English Canadian leaders were in favour of a unitary state, like Britain, and agreed to a federal system primarily to accommodate French Canadians.

One difficulty in a federal system is maintaining the balance between centralization and decentralization. While most Quebecers want an even more decentralized division of powers, most English Canadians favour a stronger central government. One of the challenges facing Canada, therefore, is finding an acceptable form of 'asymmetrical federalism' which grants Quebec powers not given to other provinces. Other federal states face a similar problem.[3]

Federalism is often used to accommodate national diversity, and so some commentators include the rights and powers attached to federal units amongst the 'collective rights' of national minorities (e.g. F. Morton 1985: 77; Van Dyke 1982: 24–31). Of course, many federal systems arose for reasons quite unrelated to cultural diversity. Federalism is often simply a form of administrative decentralization (as in Germany), or the result of historical accidents of colonization (as in Australia). There is no inherent connection between federalism and cultural diversity. But federalism is one common strategy of accommodating national minorities. It is not surprising that countries which are 'a federation of peoples' should also form a political federation.[4]

In the United States, however, a deliberate decision was made not to use federalism to accommodate the self-government rights of national minorities. It would have been quite possible in the nineteenth century to create states dominated by the Navaho, for example, or by Chicanos, Puerto Ricans, and native Hawaiians. At the time these groups were incorporated into the United States, they formed majorities in their homelands. However, a deliberate decision was made not to accept any territory as a state unless these national groups were outnumbered. In some cases, this was achieved by drawing boundaries so that Indian tribes or Hispanic groups were outnumbered (Florida). In other cases, it was achieved by delaying statehood until anglophone settlers swamped the older inhabitants (e.g. Hawaii; the south-west). In cases where the national minority was not likely to be outnumbered, a new type of non-federal political unit was created, such as the 'commonwealth' of Puerto Rico, or the 'Protectorate' of Guam.[5]

As a result, none of the fifty states can be seen as ensuring self-government for a national minority, the way that Quebec ensures self-government for the Québécois. Self-government is instead achieved through political institutions located inside existing states (e.g. Indian reservations), or entirely outside the federal system (e.g. Puerto Rico, Guam). This has tended to make national minorities in the United States more vulnerable, since their self-government powers do not have the same constitutional protection as states' rights. On the other hand, it has provided greater flexibility in redefining those powers so as to suit the needs and interests of each minority. It is much easier to negotiate new self-government provisions for the Navaho or Puerto Ricans than to modify the powers of individual states.

Federalism can only serve as a mechanism for self-government if the national minority forms a majority in one of the federal subunits, as the Québécois do in Quebec. This is not true of most indigenous peoples in North America, who are fewer in number and whose communities are often dispersed across state/provincial lines. Moreover, with few exceptions (such as the Navaho), no redrawing of the boundaries of these federal subunits would create a state, province, or territory with an indigenous majority. It would have been possible to create a state or province dominated by an Indian tribe in the nineteenth century, but, given the massive influx of settlers since then, it is now virtually inconceivable.

One exception concerns the Inuit in the north of Canada, who wish to divide the Northwest Territories into two, so that they will form the majority in the eastern half (to be called 'Nunavut'). This redrawing of federal boundaries is seen as essential to the implementation of the Inuit's right of self-government, and has recently been approved by the federal government.

For the other indigenous peoples in North America, however, self-government has been primarily tied to the system of reserved lands (known as tribal 'reservations' in the United States, and band 'reserves' in Canada). Substantial powers have been devolved from the federal government to the tribal/band councils which govern each reserve. Indian tribes/bands have been acquiring increasing control over health, education, family law, policing, criminal justice, and resource development. They are becoming, in effect, a third order of government, with a collection of powers that is carved out of both federal and state/provincial jurisdictions.[6] However, the administrative difficulties are daunting. Indian tribes/bands differ enormously in the sorts of powers they desire. Moreover, they are territorially located within existing states/provinces, and must co-ordinate their self-government with state/provincial agencies. The exact scope and mechanisms of indigenous self-government in Canada and the United States therefore remain unclear.

Similar systems of self-government exist, or are being sought, by many other indigenous peoples. A recent international declaration regarding the rights of indigenous peoples emphasizes the importance of political self-government. In many parts of the world, however, the hope for political powers is almost utopian, and the more immediate goal is simply to secure the existing land base from further erosion by settlers and resource developers. Indeed, a recent study showed that the single largest cause of ethnic conflict in the world today is the struggle by indigenous peoples for the protection of their land rights.[7]

Self-government claims, then, typically take the form of devolving political power to a political unit substantially controlled by the members of the national minority, and substantially corresponding to their historical homeland or territory. It is important to note that these claims are not seen as a temporary measure, nor as a remedy for a form of oppression that we might (and ought) someday to eliminate. On the contrary, these rights are often described as 'inherent', and so permanent (which is one reason why national minorities seek to have them entrenched in the constitution).

2. Polyethnic rights. As I noted earlier, immigrant groups in the last thirty years have successfully challenged the 'Anglo-conformity' model which assumed that they should abandon all aspects of their ethnic heritage and assimilate to existing cultural norms and customs. At first, this challenge simply took the form of demanding the right freely to express their particularity without fear of prejudice or discrimination in the mainstream society. It was the demand, as Walzer put it, that 'politics be separated from nationality – as it was already separated from religion' (Walzer 1982: 6–11).

But the demands of ethnic groups have expanded in important directions. It became clear that positive steps were required to root out discrimination and prejudice, particularly against visible minorities.

For this reason, anti-racism policies are considered part of the 'multiculturalism' policy in Canada and Australia, as are changes to the education curriculum to recognize the history and contribution of minorities. However, these policies are primarily directed at ensuring the effective exercise of the common rights of citizenship, and so do not really qualify as group-differentiated citizenship rights.

Some ethnic groups and religious minorities have also demanded various forms of public funding of their cultural practices. This includes the funding of ethnic associations, magazines, and festivals. Given that most liberal states provide funding to the arts and museums, so as to preserve the richness and diversity of our cultural resources, funding for ethnic studies and ethnic associations can be seen as falling under this heading. Indeed, some people defend this funding simply as a way of ensuring that ethnic groups are not discriminated against in state funding of art and culture. Some people believe that public funding agencies have traditionally been biased in favour of European-derived forms of cultural expression, and programmes targeted at ethnic groups remedy this bias. A related demand – discussed at length in Chapter 5[8] – is for the provision of immigrant language education in schools.

Perhaps the most controversial demand of ethnic groups is for exemptions from laws and regulations that disadvantage them, given their religious practices. For example, Jews and Muslims in Britain have sought exemption from Sunday closing or animal slaughtering legislation; Sikh men in Canada have sought exemption from motorcycle helmet laws and from the official dress-codes of police forces, so that they can wear their turban; Orthodox Jews in the United States have sought the right to wear the yarmulka during military service; and Muslim girls in France have sought exemption from school dress-codes so that they can wear the *chador*.[9]

These group-specific measures – which I call 'polyethnic rights' – are intended to help ethnic groups and religious minorities express their cultural particularity and pride without it hampering their success in the economic and political institutions of the dominant society. Like self-government rights, these polyethnic rights are not seen as temporary, because the cultural differences they protect are not something we seek to eliminate. But, as I discuss in Chapters 5 and 9, unlike self-government rights, polyethnic rights are usually intended to promote integration into the larger society, not self-government.

3. Special representation rights. While the traditional concern of national minorities and ethnic groups has been with either self-government or polyethnic rights, there has been increasing interest by these groups, as well as other non-ethnic social groups, in the idea of special representation rights.

Throughout the Western democracies, there is increasing concern that the political process is 'unrepresentative', in the sense that it fails to reflect the diversity of the population. Legislatures in most of these countries are dominated by middle-class, able-bodied, white men. A more representative process, it is said, would include members of ethnic and racial minorities, women, the poor, the disabled, etc. The under-representation of historically disadvantaged groups is a general phenomenon. In the United States and Canada, women, racial minorities, and indigenous peoples all have under one third of the seats they would have based on their demographic weight. People with disabilities and the economically disadvantaged are also significantly under-represented.[10]

One way to reform the process is to make political parties more inclusive, by reducing the barriers which inhibit women, ethnic minorities, or the poor from becoming party candidates or party leaders; another way is to adopt some form of proportional representation, which has historically been associated with greater inclusiveness of candidates.

However, there is increasing interest in the idea that a certain number of seats in the legislature should be reserved for the members of disadvantaged or marginalized groups. During the debate in Canada over the Charlottetown Accord, for example, a number of recommendations were made for the guaranteed representation of women, ethnic minorities, official language minorities, and Aboriginals.

Group representation rights are often defended as a response to some systemic disadvantage or barrier in the political process which makes it impossible for the group's views and interests to be effectively represented. In so far as these rights are seen as a response to oppression or systemic disadvantage, they are most plausibly seen as a temporary measure on the way to a society where the need for special representation no longer exists – a form of political 'affirmative action'. Society should seek to remove the oppression and disadvantage, thereby eliminating the need for these rights.

However, the issue of special representation rights for groups is complicated, because special representation is sometimes defended, not on grounds of oppression, but as a corollary of self-government. A minority's right to self-government would be severely weakened if some external body could unilaterally revise or revoke its powers, without consulting the minority or securing its consent. Hence it would seem to be a corollary of self-government that the national minority be guaranteed representation on any body which can interpret or modify its powers of self-government (e.g. the Supreme Court). Since the claims of self-government are seen as inherent and permanent, so too are the guarantees of representation which flow from it (unlike guarantees grounded on oppression).[11]

2 The Equality Argument

Many defenders of group-specific rights for ethnic and national minorities insist that they are needed to ensure that all citizens are treated with genuine equality. On this view, 'the accommodation of differences is the essence of true equality',[12] and group-specific rights are needed to accommodate our differences. I think this argument is correct, within certain limits.

Proponents of 'benign neglect' will respond that individual rights already allow for the accommodation of differences, and that true equality requires equal rights for each individual regardless of race or ethnicity.[13] As I noted in Chapter 4, this assumption that liberal equality precludes group-specific rights is relatively recent, and arose in part as an (over-)generalization of the racial desegregation movement in the United States. It has some superficial plausibility. In many cases, claims for group-specific rights are simply an attempt by one group to dominate and oppress another.

But some minority rights eliminate, rather than create, inequalities. Some groups are unfairly disadvantaged in the cultural market-place, and political recognition and support rectify this disadvantage. I will start with the case of national minorities. The viability of their societal cultures may be undermined by economic and political decisions made by the majority. They could be outbid or outvoted on resources and policies that are crucial to the survival of their societal cultures. The members of majority cultures do not face this problem. Given the importance of cultural membership, this is a significant inequality which, if not addressed, becomes a serious injustice.

Group-differentiated rights – such as territorial autonomy, veto powers, guaranteed representation in central institutions, land claims, and language rights – can help rectify this disadvantage, by alleviating the vulnerability of minority cultures to majority decisions. These external protections ensure that members of the minority have the same opportunity to live and work in their own culture as members of the majority.

As I discussed in Chapter 3, these rights may impose restrictions on the members of the larger society, by making it more costly for them to move into the territory of the minority (e.g. longer residency requirements, fewer government services in their language), or by giving minority members priority in the use of certain land and resources (e.g. indigenous hunting and fishing rights). But the sacrifice required of non-members by the existence of these rights is far less than the sacrifice members would face in the absence of such rights.

Where these rights are recognized, members of the majority who choose to enter the minority's homeland may have to forgo certain benefits they are accustomed to. This is a burden. But without such rights, the members of many minority cultures face the loss of their culture, a loss which we cannot reasonably ask people to accept.

Any plausible theory of justice should recognize the fairness of these external protections for national minorities. They are clearly justified, I believe, within a liberal egalitarian theory, such as Rawls's and Dworkin's, which emphasizes the importance of rectifying unchosen inequalities. Indeed inequalities in cultural membership are just the sort which Rawls says we should be concerned about, since their effects are 'profound and pervasive and present from birth' (Rawls 1971: 96; cf. Dworkin 1981).[14]

This equality-based argument will only endorse special rights for national minorities if there actually is a disadvantage with respect to cultural membership, and if the rights actually serve to rectify the disadvantage. Hence the legitimate scope of these rights will vary with the circumstances. In North America, indigenous groups are more vulnerable to majority decisions than the Québécois or Puerto Ricans, and so their external protections will be more extensive. For example, restrictions on the sale of land which are necessary in the context of indigenous peoples are not necessary, and hence not justified, in the case of Quebec or Puerto Rico.[15]

At some point, demands for increased powers or resources will not be necessary to ensure the same opportunity to live and work in one's culture. Instead, they will simply be attempts to gain benefits denied to others, to have more resources to pursue one's way of life than others have. This was clearly the case with apartheid, where whites constituting under 20 per cent of the population controlled 87 per cent of the land mass of the country, and monopolized all the important levers of state power.

One could imagine a point where the amount of land reserved for indigenous peoples would not be necessary to provide reasonable external protections, but rather would simply provide unequal opportunities to them. Justice would then require that the holdings of indigenous peoples be subject to the same redistributive taxation as the wealth of other advantaged groups, so as to assist the less well off in society. In the real world, of course, most indigenous peoples are struggling to maintain the bare minimum of land needed to sustain the viability of their communities. But it is possible that their land holdings could exceed what justice allows.[16]

The legitimacy of certain measures may also depend on their timing. For example, many people have suggested that a new South African constitution should grant a veto power over certain important decisions to some or all of the major national groups. This sort of veto power is a familiar feature of various 'consociational democracies' in Europe, and, as I discuss in the next chapter, under certain circumstances it can promote justice. But it would probably be unjust to give privileged groups a veto power before there has been a dramatic redistribution of wealth and opportunities (Adam 1979: 295). A veto power can promote justice if it helps protect a minority from unjust policies that favour the majority; but it is an obstacle to justice if it allows a privileged group the leverage to maintain its unjust advantages.

So the ideal of 'benign neglect' is not in fact benign. It ignores the fact that the members of a national minority face a disadvantage which the members of the majority do not face. In any event, the idea that the government could be neutral with respect to ethnic and national groups is patently false. As I noted in Chapter 5, one of the most important determinants of whether a culture survives is whether its language is the language of government – i.e. the language of public schooling, courts, legislatures, welfare agencies, health services, etc. When the government decides the language of public schooling, it is providing what is probably the most important form of support needed by societal cultures, since it guarantees the passing on of the language and its associated traditions and conventions to the next generation. Refusing to provide public schooling in a minority language, by contrast, is almost inevitably condemning that language to ever-increasing marginalization.

The government therefore cannot avoid deciding which societal cultures will be supported. And if it supports the majority culture, by using the majority's language in schools and public agencies, it cannot refuse official recognition to minority languages on the ground that this violates 'the separation of state and ethnicity'. This shows that the analogy between religion and culture is mistaken. As I noted earlier, many liberals say that just as the state should not recognize, endorse, or support any particular church, so it should not recognize, endorse, or support any particular cultural group or identity (Ch. 1, s. 1). But the analogy does not work. It is quite possible for a state not to have an established church. But the state cannot help but give at least partial establishment to a culture when it decides which language is to be used in public schooling, or in the provision of state services. The state can (and should) replace religious oaths in courts with secular oaths, but it cannot replace the use of English in courts with no language.

This is a significant embarrassment for the 'benign neglect' view, and it is remarkable how rarely language rights are discussed in contemporary liberal theory.[17] As Brian Weinstein put it, political theorists have had a lot to say about 'the language of politics' – that is, the symbols, metaphors, and rhetorical devices of political discourse – but have had virtually nothing to say about 'the politics of language' – that is, the decisions about which languages to use in political, legal, and educational forums (Weinstein 1983: 7–13). Yet language rights are a fundamental cause of political conflict, even violence, throughout the world, including Canada, Belgium, Spain, Sri Lanka, the Baltics, Bulgaria, Turkey, and many other countries (Horowitz 1985: 219–24).

One could argue that decisions about the language of schooling and public services should be determined, not by officially recognizing the existence of various groups, but simply by allowing each political subunit to make its own language policy on a democratic basis. If a national minority forms a majority in the relevant unit, they can decide to have their mother tongue adopted as an official language in that unit. But this is because they are a local majority, not because the state has officially recognized them as a 'nation'.

This is sometimes said to be the American approach to language rights, since there is no constitutional definition of language rights in the United States. But in fact the American government has historically tried to make sure that such 'local' decisions are always made by political units that have an anglophone majority. As discussed in Chapter 2, decisions about state borders, or about when to admit territories as states, have been explicitly made with the aim of ensuring that there will be an anglophone majority. States in the American south-west and Hawaii were only offered statehood when the national minorities residing in those areas were outnumbered by settlers and immigrants. And some people oppose offering statehood to Puerto Rico precisely on the grounds that it will never have an anglophone majority (Rubinstein 1993; Glazer 1983: 280).

This illustrates a more general point. Leaving decisions about language to political subunits just pushes back the problem. What are the relevant political units – what level of government should make these decisions? Should each neighbourhood be able to decide on the language of public schooling and public services in that neighbourhood? Or should this decision be left to larger units, such as cities or provinces? And how do we decide on the boundaries of these subunits? If we draw municipal or provincial boundaries in one way, then a national minority will not form even a local majority. But if we draw the boundaries another way, then the national minority will form a local majority. In a multination state, decisions on boundaries and the division of powers are inevitably decisions about which national group will have the ability to use which state powers to sustain its culture.[18]

For example, as I noted in Chapter 2, the Inuit in Canada wish to divide the Northwest Territories into two, so that they will form the majority in the eastern half. This is seen as essential to the implementation of their right of self-government. Some liberals object that this proposal violates the separation of state and ethnicity by distributing public benefits and state powers so as to make it easier for a specific group to preserve its culture. But all decisions regarding boundaries and the distribution of powers in multination states have this effect. We can draw boundaries and distribute legislative powers so that a national minority has an increased ability within a particular region to protect its social culture; or we can draw boundaries and distribute legislative powers so that the majority nation controls decisions regarding language, education, immigration, etc. on a country-wide basis.

The whole idea of 'benign neglect' is incoherent, and reflects a shallow understanding of the relationship between states and nations. In the areas of official languages, political boundaries, and the division of powers, there is no way to avoid supporting this or that societal culture, or deciding which groups will form a majority in political units that control culture-affecting decisions regarding language, education, and immigration.

So the real question is, what is a fair way to recognize languages, draw boundaries, and distribute powers? And the answer, I think, is that we should aim at ensuring that all national groups have the opportunity to maintain themselves as a distinct culture, if they so choose. This ensures that the good of cultural membership is equally protected for the members of all national groups.

In a democratic society, the majority nation will always have its language and societal culture supported, and will have the legislative power to protect its interests in culture-affecting decisions. The question is whether fairness requires that the same benefits and opportunities should be given to national minorities. The answer, I think, is clearly yes.

Hence group-differentiated self-government rights compensate for unequal circumstances which put the members of minority cultures at a systemic disadvantage in the cultural marketplace, regardless of their personal choices in life. This is one of many areas in which true equality requires not identical treatment, but rather differential treatment in order to accommodate differential needs.[19]

This does not mean that we should entirely reject the idea of the cultural market-place. Once the societal cultures of national groups are protected, through language rights and territorial autonomy, then the cultural market-place does have an important role to play in determining the character of the culture. Decisions about which particular aspects of one's culture are worth maintaining and developing should be left to the choices of individual members. For the state to intervene at this point to support particular options or customs within the culture, while penalizing or discouraging others, would run the risk of unfairly subsidizing some people's choices (Kymlicka 1989b). But that is not the aim or effect of many rights for national minorities, which are instead concerned with external protections (see Ch. 3, s. 1).

Let me now turn to polyethnic rights for ethnic groups. I believe there is an equality-based argument for these rights as well, which also invokes the impossibility of separating state from ethnicity, but in a different way. I argued in Chapter 5 that the context of choice for immigrants, unlike national minorities, primarily involves equal access to the mainstream culture(s). Having uprooted themselves from their old culture, they are expected to become members of the national societies which already exist in their new country. Hence promoting the good of cultural membership for immigrants is primarily a matter of enabling integration, by providing language training and fighting patterns of discrimination and prejudice. Generally speaking, this is more a matter of rigorously enforcing the common rights of citizenship than providing group-differentiated rights. In so far as common rights of citizenship in fact create equal access to mainstream culture, then equality with respect to cultural membership is achieved.

But even here equality does justify some group-specific rights. Consider the case of public holidays. Some people object to legislation that exempts Jews and Muslims from Sunday closing legislation, on the ground that this violates the separation of state and ethnicity. But almost any decision on public holidays will do so. In the major immigration countries, public holidays currently reflect the needs of Christians. Hence government offices are closed on Sunday, and on the major religious holidays (Easter, Christmas). This need not be seen as a deliberate decision to promote Christianity and discriminate against other faiths (although this was undoubtedly part of the original motivation). Decisions about government holidays were made when there was far less religious diversity, and people just took it for granted that the government work-week should accommodate Christian beliefs about days of rest and religious celebration.

But these decisions can be a significant disadvantage to the members of other religious faiths. And having established a work-week that favours Christians, one can hardly object to exemptions for Muslims or Jews on the ground that they violate the separation of state and ethnicity. These groups are simply asking that their religious needs be taken into consideration in the same way that the needs of Christians have always been taken into account. Public holidays are another significant embarrassment for the 'benign neglect' view, and it is interesting to note how rarely they are discussed in contemporary liberal theory.

Similar issues arise regarding government uniforms. Some people object to the idea that Sikhs or Orthodox Jews should be exempted from requirements regarding headgear in the police or military. But here again it is important to recognize how the existing rules about government uniforms have been adopted to suit Christians. For example, existing dress-codes do not prohibit the wearing of wedding rings, which are an important religious symbol for many Christians (and Jews). And it is virtually inconceivable that designers of government dress-codes would have ever considered designing a uniform that prevented people from wearing wedding rings, unless this was strictly necessary for the job. Again, this should not be seen as a deliberate attempt to promote Christianity. It simply would have been taken for granted that uniforms should not unnecessarily conflict with Christian religious beliefs. Having adopted dress-codes that meet Christian needs, one can hardly object to exemptions for Sikhs and Orthodox Jews on the ground that they violate 'benign neglect'.

One can multiply the examples. For example, many state symbols such as flags, anthems, and mottoes reflect a particular ethnic or religious background ('In God We Trust'). The demand by ethnic groups for some symbolic affirmation of the value of polyethnicity (e.g. in government declarations and documents) is simply a demand that their identity be given the same recognition as the original Anglo-Saxon settlers.

It may be possible to avoid some of these issues by redesigning public holidays, uniforms, and state symbols. It is relatively easy to replace religious oaths with secular ones, and so we should. It would be more difficult, but perhaps not impossible, to replace existing public holidays and work-weeks with more 'neutral' schedules for schools and government offices.[20]

But there is no way to have a complete 'separation of state and ethnicity'. In various ways, the ideal of 'benign neglect' is a myth. Government decisions on languages, internal boundaries, public holidays, and state symbols unavoidably involve recognizing, accommodating, and supporting the needs and identities of particular ethnic and national groups. Nor is there any reason to regret this fact. There is no reason to regret the existence of official languages and public holidays, and no one gains by creating unnecessary conflicts between government regulations and religious beliefs. The only question is how to ensure that these unavoidable forms of support for particular ethnic and national groups are provided fairly – that is, how to ensure that they do not privilege some groups and disadvantage others. In so far as existing policies support the language, culture, and identity of dominant nations and ethnic groups, there is an argument of equality for ensuring that some attempts are made to provide similar support for minority groups, through self-government and polyethnic rights.

3 The Role of Historical Agreements

A second argument in defence of group-differentiated rights for national minorities is that they are the result of historical agreements, such as the treaty rights of indigenous peoples, or the agreement by which two or more peoples agreed to federate.

There are a variety of such agreements in Western democracies, although their provisions have often been ignored or repudiated. For example, the American government has unilaterally abrogated certain treaties with Indian tribes, and the Canadian government proposed in 1969 to extinguish all of its Indian treaties. The language rights guaranteed to Chicanos in the American south-west under the 1848 Treaty of Guadelupe Hidalgo were rescinded by the anglophone settlers as soon as they formed a majority. The language and land rights guaranteed to the Métis under the Manitoba Act of 1870 suffered the same fate in Canada. Yet many treaties and historical agreements between national groups continue to be recognized, and some have considerable legal force. For example, the 1840 Treaty of Waitangi signed by Maori chiefs and British colonists in New Zealand, declared a 'simple nullity' in 1877, has re-emerged as a central legal and political document (Sharp 1990).

The importance of honouring historical agreements is emphasized by proponents of group-differentiated rights, but has had little success convincing opponents. Those people who think that group-differentiated rights are unfair have not been appeased by pointing to agreements that were made by previous generations in different circumstances, often undemocratically and in conditions of substantial inequality in bargaining power. Surely some historical agreements are out of date, while others are patently unfair, signed under duress or ignorance. Why should governments not do what principles of equality require now, rather than what outdated and often unprincipled agreements require?[21]

One answer is to reconsider an underlying assumption of the equality argument. The equality argument assumes that the state must treat its citizens with equal respect. But there is the prior question of determining which citizens should be governed by which states. For example, how did the American government acquire the legitimate authority to govern Puerto Rico or the Navaho? And how did the Canadian government acquire legitimate authority over the Québécois and the Métis?

As I noted in Chapter 2, United Nations declarations state that all 'peoples' are entitled to 'self-determination' – i.e. an independent state. Obviously this principle is not reflected in existing boundaries, and it would be destabilizing, and indeed impossible, to fulfil. Moreover, not all peoples want their own state. Hence it is not uncommon for two or more peoples to decide to form a federation. And if the two communities are of unequal size, it is not uncommon for the smaller culture to demand various group-differentiated rights as part of the terms of federation. Forming a federation is one way of exercising a people's right of self-determination, and the historical terms of federation reflect the group's judgement about how best to exercise that right.

For example, the group-differentiated rights accorded French Canadians in the original confederation agreement in 1867, and the group-differentiated rights accorded Indians under various treaties, reflect the terms under which these communities joined Canada. It can be argued that these agreements define the terms under which the Canadian state acquired authority over these groups. These communities could have exercised their self-determination in other ways, but chose to join Canada, because they were given certain promises. If the Canadian government reneges on these promises, then it voids (morally, if not legally) the agreement which made those communities part of Canada.[22] Because these agreements define the terms under which various groups agreed to federate with Canada, the authority of the Canadian state over these groups flows from, but is also limited by, these agreements (Chartrand 1991; 1993: 240–1).

In short, the way in which a national minority was incorporated often gives rise to certain group differentiated rights. If incorporation occurred through a voluntary federation, certain rights might be spelled out in the terms of federation (e.g. in treaties), and there are legal and moral arguments for respecting these agreements. If incorporation was involuntary (e.g. colonization), then the national minority might have a claim of self-determination under international law which can be exercised by renegotiating the terms of federation so as to make it a more voluntary federation (Macklem 1993; Danley 1991).

This historical argument may justify the same rights as the equality argument. Many of the group-differentiated rights which are the result of historical agreements can be seen as providing the sort of protection required by the equality argument. For example, the right to local autonomy

for Indian tribes/bands could be justified on the equality argument, if it helps the larger state show equal concern for the members of Indian communities. Autonomy is also justified on the historical argument, in so far as Indian peoples never gave the federal government jurisdiction over certain issues.

Indeed, it is likely that the equality and historical arguments will yield similar policies. If local autonomy is required to ensure that members of a minority are not disadvantaged, then it is likely that the minority would have demanded autonomy as part of the terms of federation (had the negotiations been fair).

The negotiations between English and French regarding the terms of federation in Canada provide a clear example of this. The Québécois realized that if they agreed to enter the Canadian state in 1867, they would become a permanent minority in the country, and so could be outvoted on decisions made at the federal level. They therefore faced the question whether they should remain outside Confederation, maintaining their status as a separate colony within the British Empire, and hoping one day to become a separate country with a francophone majority.

Québécois leaders agreed to join Canada, even though they would be a minority in the federal parliament. But in return they insisted that jurisdiction over language and education be guaranteed to the provinces, not the federal government. This was 'the non-negotiable condition in return for which they were prepared to concede the principle of representation by population' in the new parliament, a principle that 'would institutionalize their minority position' within the new country (J. Smith 1993: 75). In deciding whether to accept the terms of federation, therefore, Québécois leaders were explicitly concerned about equality – that is, how to ensure that they would not be disadvantaged in the new country. Since they had considerable bargaining power in the negotiations, they were able to ensure their equality in the agreement, through guarantees of language rights and provincial autonomy.

While the equality and historical arguments often lead to the same result, they are none the less quite distinct. On the historical argument, the question is not how should the state treat 'its' minorities, but rather what are the terms under which two or more peoples decided to become partners? The question is not how should the state act fairly in governing its minorities, but what are the limits to the state's right to govern them?

For example, the two arguments may generate different answers to the question of federal funding of self-government rights. Under the equality argument, fairness may require positive state support for the measures required to maintain the viability of the national group. If fairness requires recognizing self-government in certain areas of jurisdiction, then presumably fairness will also require providing the resources needed to make self-government meaningful. The historical argument, however, may only generate a negative right to non-interference from the federal state. If the members of the national minority never gave the federal government the authority to govern them in certain areas, the federal government is unlikely to accept responsibility for funding minority self-government (unless this is itself part of the historical agreement). Any federal obligation to support self-government might be seen more as a form of humanitarian foreign aid than as a matter of domestic egalitarian justice.[23]

Contemporary political philosophers have had very little to say about the moral status of such historical agreements. For example, while Rawls recognizes a moral duty to respect treaties between countries (Rawls 1971: 378), he does not say anything about treaties or other agreements between nations within a country. This is surprising, because such agreements played a vital role in the creation and expansion of many countries, including the United States and Canada.

Respect for such agreements is important, I believe, not only to respect the self-determination of the minority, but also to ensure that citizens have trust in the actions of government. Historical agreements signed in good faith give rise to legitimate expectations on the part of citizens, who come to rely on the agreements made by governments, and it is a serious breach of trust to renege on them.

One difficulty with historical agreements is that they are often hard to interpret. For example, the Canadian government claims Quebec's 'right to be different' was implicitly recognized in the original Confederation agreement (Government of Canada 1991a: p. vi). But others deny this, and insist that Confederation was a union of provinces, not a compact between two cultures. Similar disputes arise over the interpretation of some Indian treaties. Moreover, some Indian tribes did not sign treaties, or signed them

under duress. It seems arbitrary and unfair that some groups signed historical agreements while others, through no fault of their own, did not.

Where historical agreements are absent or disputed, groups are likely to appeal to the equality argument. Indian tribes/bands which have clear treaty rights often rest their claim for group-differentiated status on historical agreement; groups who did not sign treaties are more likely to appeal to the equality argument. It is often quite arbitrary whether a particular group happened to sign a particular agreement. However, the equality argument can help those groups which, for whatever reason, lack historical rights.[24]

Historical agreements are much less common in the case of ethnic groups, since immigrants are rarely promised any special rights before arriving in their new country. Indeed, opponents of polyethnic rights sometimes say that ethnic groups should not expect any new group-differentiated rights, precisely because they agreed to come knowing full well that such rights did not exist. Yet there are some cases of polyethnic rights based on historical agreement. For example, the Hutterites (a Christian sect) were explicitly promised by Canadian immigration officials that they would be exempted from certain laws regarding education, land ownership, and military service if they settled in western Canada. (The Canadian government was anxious at the time to settle the newly opened up western frontier.)

This now seems like an anomalous case of an immigrant group given privileges denied to other citizens, and attempts have been made to eliminate these historical rights. On the other hand, solemn promises were given to the Hutterites, who would have emigrated elsewhere had these promises not been made. In this sense, they too can claim that the historical agreement defines the terms under which the Canadian government acquired authority over them.

In assessing group-differentiated rights claims, therefore, we need to know whether the rights being claimed are rectifying disadvantages, or recognizing historical agreements arising from the terms of federation. Both of these are legitimate grounds for group-differentiated rights, I believe, but both raise some difficult issues.

For example, how should we respond to agreements that are now unfair, due to changing conditions? The land claims recognized in various treaties may be too much, or too little, given changes in the size and lifestyle of indigenous communities. The powers given to Quebec in 1867 may no longer be appropriate in an age of telecommunications. To stick to the letter of historical agreements when they no longer meet the needs of minorities seems wrong.

Because of these changing circumstances, and because the original agreements are hard to interpret, many minority communities want to renegotiate their historical agreements. They want to make their group-differentiated rights more explicit in the constitution, and often more expansive. This is a major cause of the current constitutional crisis in Canada. For it has given those Canadians who see group-differentiated rights as unfair a chance to restrict, rather than entrench, such rights.

This suggests that, if we wish to defend group-differentiated rights, we should not rely solely on historical agreements. Since historical agreements must always be interpreted, and inevitably need to be updated and revised, we must be able to ground the historical agreements in a deeper theory of justice. The historical and equality arguments must work together.

4 The Value of Cultural Diversity

A third defence of group-differentiated rights for national minorities appeals to the value of cultural diversity. As I have discussed, liberals extol the virtue of having a diversity of lifestyles within a culture, so presumably they also endorse the additional diversity which comes from having two or more cultures in the same country. Surely intercultural diversity contributes to the richness of people's lives, as well as intracultural diversity (Schwartz 1986: ch. 1).

This argument is attractive to many people because it avoids relying solely on the interests of group members, and instead focuses on how the larger society also benefits from group-differentiated rights. As Richard Falk puts it, 'societal diversity enhances the quality of life, by enriching our experience, expanding cultural resources'. Hence protecting minority cultures 'is increasingly recognized to be an expression of overall enlightened self-interest' (Falk 1988: 23). Whereas the first two arguments appeal to the *obligations* of the majority, this third argument appeals to the *interests* of the majority, and

defends rights in terms of self-interest not justice.

Cultural diversity is said to be valuable, both in the quasi-aesthetic sense that it creates a more interesting world, and because other cultures contain alternative models of social organization that may be useful in adapting to new circumstances.[25] This latter point is often made with respect to indigenous peoples, whose traditional lifestyles provide a model of a sustainable relationship to the environment. As Western attitudes towards nature are increasingly recognized to be unsustainable and self-destructive, indigenous peoples 'may provide models, inspiration, guidance in the essential work of world order redesign' (Falk 1988: 23; cf. Clay 1989: 233; O'Brien 1987: 358).

There is some truth in this argument about the value of cultural diversity. None the less, I think it is a mistake to put much weight on it as a defence of national rights. First, one of the basic reasons for valuing intracultural diversity has less application to intercultural diversity. The value of diversity within a culture is that it creates more options for each individual, and expands her range of choices. But protecting national minorities does not expand the range of choices open to members of the majority in the same way. As I explained in the last chapter, choosing to leave one's culture is qualitatively different from choosing to move around within one's culture. The former is a difficult and painful prospect for most people, and very few people in the mainstream choose to assimilate into a minority culture. Indeed, measures to protect national minorities may actually reduce diversity within the majority culture, compared with a situation where minorities, unable to maintain their own societal culture, are forced to integrate and add their distinctive contribution to the diversity of the mainstream culture. Having two or more cultures within a state does expand choices for each individual, but only to a limited degree, and it would be implausible to make this the primary justification for minority rights.

There are other aesthetic and educational benefits from cultural diversity, apart from the value of expanding individual choice. But it is not clear that any of these values by themselves can justify minority rights. One problem is that the benefits of diversity to the majority are spread thinly and widely, whereas the costs for particular members of the majority are sometimes quite high. Every one may benefit, in a diffuse way, from having flourishing minority cultures in Quebec and Puerto Rico. But some members of the majority culture are asked to pay a significant price so that others can gain this diffuse benefit. For example, unilingual anglophones residing in Quebec or Puerto Rico are unlikely to get government employment or publicly funded education in English – benefits which they would take for granted elsewhere. Similarly, non-Indians residing on Indian lands may be discriminated against in terms of their access to natural resources, or their right to vote in local elections. It is not clear that the diffuse benefits of diversity for society as a whole justify imposing these sorts of sacrifices on particular people. It seems to me that these sacrifices are only consistent with justice if they are needed, not to promote benefits to the members of the majority, but to prevent even greater sacrifices to the members of the national minority.

Moreover, there are many ways of promoting diversity, and it seems likely that protecting national minorities involves more cost to the majority than other possible ways. For example, a society could arguably gain more diversity at less cost by increasing immigration from a variety of countries than by protecting national minorities. The diversity argument cannot explain why we have an obligation to sustain the particular sort of diversity created by the presence of a viable, self-governing national minority.

There is one further problem with the diversity argument. Let us say that the aesthetic or educational value of diversity does justify imposing certain costs on people in the majority culture. Why then does the value of diversity not also justify imposing a duty on the members of the minority to maintain their traditional culture? If the benefits of cultural diversity to the larger society can justify restricting individual liberties or opportunities, why does it matter whether these restrictions are imposed on people inside or outside the group? I noted earlier that a liberal theory of minority rights can accept external protections, but not internal restrictions. It is difficult to see how the diversity argument can make this distinction. Because it appeals to the interests of the larger society, it cannot explain why minorities should be able to decide for themselves whether or how to maintain their culture.

So it seems to me that the diversity argument is insufficient, by itself, to justify the rights of national minorities. Protecting national minorities

does provide benefits to the majority, and these are worth pointing out. But these diffuse benefits are better seen as a desirable by-product of national rights, rather than their primary justification. To date, most majority cultures have not seen it in their 'enlightened self-interest' to maintain minority cultures. No doubt this is due in part to ethnocentric prejudice, but we must recognize the powerful interests that majority nations often have in rejecting self-government rights for national minorities – e.g. increased access to the minority's land and resources, increased individual mobility, political stability, etc. It is unlikely that majorities will accept national rights solely on the basis of self-interest, without some belief that they have an obligation of justice to accept them. Conversely, it is unlikely that majorities will accept their obligations of justice towards national minorities without a belief that they gain something in the process. The diversity argument works best, therefore, when it is combined with arguments of justice.

The diversity argument is more plausible as a defence of polyethnic rights for ethnic groups. Unlike national self-government, these rights do contribute directly to diversity within the majority culture. Moreover, they do not involve the same sort of restrictions on the mobility or economic opportunities of the majority. Indeed, certain polyethnic policies can be seen as natural extensions of state policies regarding the funding of the arts, museums, educational television, etc.[26] Yet here again the problem arises that there are many ways of promoting diversity. Teaching children to be bilingual promotes diversity, but this cannot explain why we should teach immigrant languages in particular. Hence the diversity argument supplements, but cannot replace, justice arguments based on equality or historical agreement.

5 The Analogy with States

So far, I have been assuming that the burden of proof lies on those who wish to find room for group-differentiated rights within the liberal tradition. But we can and should question this assumption. In many ways, it is opponents of group-differentiated rights who are proposing a revision of liberal theory and practice. As I discussed in Chapter 4, certain group-differentiated rights have been a long-established part of the liberal tradition. Moreover, such rights are logically presupposed by existing liberal practice.

For example, most liberal theorists accept without question that the world is, and will remain, composed of separate states, each of which is assumed to have the right to determine who can enter its borders and acquire citizenship. I believe that this assumption can only be justified in terms of the same sorts of values which ground group-differentiated rights within each state. I believe that the orthodox liberal view about the right of states to determine who has citizenship rests on the same principles which justify group-differentiated citizenship within states, and that accepting the former leads logically to the latter.

This point is worth exploring in some depth. The existence of states, and the right of governments to control entry across state borders, raises a deep paradox for liberals. Most liberal theorists defend their theories in terms of 'equal respect for persons', and the 'equal rights of individuals'. This suggests that all 'persons' or 'individuals' have an equal right to enter a state, participate in its political life, and share in its natural resources.

In fact, however, these rights are typically reserved for *citizens*. And not everyone can become a citizen, even if they are willing to swear allegiance to liberal principles. On the contrary, there are millions of people who want to gain citizenship in various liberal democracies, but who are refused. Even the most open Western country in terms of immigration accepts only a fraction of the number of people who would come if there were genuinely open borders. Indeed, would-be immigrants are often refused entry, turned back at the border by armed border guards. These people are refused the right to enter and participate in the state because they were not born into the right group.

Citizenship, therefore, is an inherently group-differentiated notion. Unless one is willing to accept either a single world-government or completely open borders between states – and very few liberal theorists have endorsed either of these – then distributing rights and benefits on the basis of citizenship is to treat people differentially on the basis of their group membership.[27]

This creates a profound contradiction within most liberal theories. As Samuel Black notes, liberal theorists often begin by talking about the moral equality of 'persons', but end up talking about the equality of 'citizens', without explaining or even noticing the shift (Black 1991). What can justify restricting the rights of citizenship to members of a particular group, rather than all persons who desire it?

Some critics have argued that liberals cannot justify this restriction, and that the logic of liberalism requires open borders, except perhaps for temporary restrictions in the name of public order.[28] And surely that is right if we cling to the idea that liberalism should be indifferent to people's cultural membership and national identity. Open borders would dramatically increase the mobility and opportunities of individuals, and, if liberalism requires treating people solely 'as individuals' without regard for their group membership, then open borders clearly are preferable from a liberal point of view.

I believe, however, that some limits on immigration can be justified if we recognize that liberal states exist, not only to protect standard rights and opportunities of individuals, but also to protect people's cultural membership. Liberals implicitly assume that people are members of societal cultures, that these cultures provide the context for individual choice, and that one of the functions of having separate states is to recognize the fact that people belong to separate cultures. I noted examples of this in the liberal tradition in Chapter 4, and with Rawls's discussion of citizenship and the bonds of culture in Chapter 5. Once we make these assumptions explicit, however, it is clear that, in multination states, some people's cultural membership can only be recognized and protected by endorsing group-differentiated rights within the state.

Liberal theorists invariably limit citizenship to the members of a particular group, rather than all persons who desire it. The most plausible reason for this – namely, to recognize and protect our membership in distinct cultures – is also a reason for allowing group-differentiated citizenship within a state. There may be other reasons for restricting citizenship to a particular group which do not make any reference to the importance of cultural groups. It is difficult to say, since few liberals actually discuss the shift from 'equality of persons' to 'equality of citizens'. But I think it is fair to say this: in so far as liberal theorists accept the principle that citizenship can be restricted to the members of a particular group, the burden of proof lies on them to explain why they are not also committed to accepting group-differentiated rights within a state.[29] So long as liberals believe in separate states with restricted citizenship, the burden of proof lies as much with opponents of group-differentiated rights as with their defenders.

6 Conclusion

In the last two chapters, I have tried to show that liberals can and should accept a wide range of group-differentiated rights for national minorities and ethnic groups, without sacrificing their core commitments to individual freedom and social equality.

It may be useful briefly to summarize my argument. I have tried to show how freedom of choice is dependent on social practices, cultural meanings, and a shared language. Our capacity to form and revise a conception of the good is intimately tied to our membership in a societal culture, since the context of individual choice is the range of options passed down to us by our culture. Deciding how to lead our lives is, in the first instance, a matter of exploring the possibilities made available by our culture.

However, minority cultures in multination states may need protection from the economic or political decisions of the majority culture if they are to provide this context for their members. For example, they may need self-governing powers or veto rights over certain decisions regarding language and culture, and may need to limit the mobility of migrants or immigrants into their homelands.

While these group-differentiated rights for national minorities may seem discriminatory at first glance, since they allocate individual rights and political powers differentially on the basis of group membership, they are in fact consistent with liberal principles of equality. They are indeed required by the view, defended by Rawls and Dworkin, that justice requires removing or compensating for undeserved or 'morally arbitrary' disadvantages, particularly if these are 'profound and pervasive and present from birth' (Rawls 1971: 96). Were it not for these group-differentiated rights, the members of minority cultures would not have the same ability to live and work in their own language and culture that the members of majority cultures take for granted. This, I argued, can be seen as just as profound and morally arbitrary a disadvantage as the inequalities in race and class that liberals more standardly worry about.

This equality-based argument for group-differentiated rights for national minorities is further strengthened by appeals to historical agreements and the value of cultural diversity. And it is confirmed by the way that liberals implicitly invoke cultural membership to defend existing state borders and restrictions on citizenship. I have also argued that polyethnic rights for ethnic groups can be justified in terms of promoting equality and cultural diversity within the mainstream culture.

These claims are by no means uncontroversial, and there are many places where they could be challenged. One could deny that cultural meanings are dependent on a societal culture, or that individuals are closely tied to their own particular societal culture. One could also deny that minority cultures are vulnerable to the decisions of the larger society; or that this vulnerability constitutes an injustice; or that historical agreements have any moral weight; or that cultural diversity is worth promoting.

Yet I think each of these claims is plausible. Anyone who disputes them would be required to provide some alternative account of what makes meaningful choices available to people, or what justice requires in terms of language rights, public holidays, political boundaries, and the division of powers. Moreover, one would also have to offer an alternative account of the justification for restricting citizenship to the members of a particular group, rather than making it available to anyone who desires it. It is not enough to simply assert that a liberal state should respond to ethnic and national differences with benign neglect. That is an incoherent position that avoids addressing the inevitable connections between state and culture.

The idea that group-differentiated rights for national and ethnic groups can and should be accepted by liberals is hardly a radical suggestion. In fact, many multination liberal democracies already accept such an obligation, and provide public schooling and government services in the language of national minorities. Many have also adopted some form of federalism, so that national minorities will form a majority in one of the federal units (states, provinces, or cantons). And many polyethnic liberal states have adopted various forms of polyethnic policies and group-specific rights or exemptions for immigrant groups. Like Jay Sigler, I believe that providing a liberal defence of minority rights 'does not create a mandate for vast change. It merely ratifies and explains changes that have taken place in the absence of theory' (Sigler 1983: 196).

But if there are strong arguments in favour of group-differentiated rights, why have liberals so often rejected them? As I noted in Chapter 4, the explanation cannot be that liberalism is premissed on 'abstract individualism', on a conception of the individual as a solitary atom who is independent of her cultural environment. I hope that Chapters 4 and 5 have dispelled any perception that liberals ignore individuals' dependence on society and culture.

But this raises a puzzle. If individual autonomy and self-identity are tied to membership in one's societal culture, developing a theory of the rights of minority cultures would seem to be one of the very first tasks of any liberal theory. Why then have so few contemporary liberal theorists supported measures to protect cultural groups, such as group-specific language rights, land claims, or federal autonomy? I have explored some of the historical reasons in Chapter 4. Another part of the explanation, I think, is that contemporary liberal theorists implicitly assume that countries contain only one nation. They are well aware that modern states are culturally diverse – indeed, the pluralistic nature of modern liberal democracies is a pervasive theme in their writings. But they implicitly assume that this diversity is the sort that comes either from variations in people's conceptions of the good or from immigration – that is, they focus on philosophical, religious, and ethnic diversity within a single culture based on a shared language.[10] They do not recognize or discuss the existence of states that are multinational, with a diversity of societal cultures, languages, and national groups.

For example, Dworkin notes that 'in the modern world of immigration and boundary shifts', citizens do not share a racial or ethnic background, and that the communal life of the political community cannot include a single 'ethnic allegiance' (1989: 497). But, as I noted earlier, he does assume a common 'cultural structure' based on a 'shared language' (1985: 230, 233; 1989: 488). Similarly, while Rawls emphasizes the 'fact of pluralism' – particularly religious pluralism – he equates the political community with a single 'complete culture', and with a single 'people' who belong to the same 'society and culture' (1978: 70 n. 8; 1993a: 18, 222, 277; 1993b: 48).

This implicit assumption that states are uni-national is rarely explained or defended. It is not as if these theorists explicitly reject the possibility that national minorities have special rights, or directly criticize the arguments of equality or history in defence of these rights. On the contrary, they simply ignore the issue entirely. There is no discussion by contemporary liberal theorists of the differences between nation-states and poly-ethnic or multination states, or of the arguments for modifying liberal principles in countries which are a 'federation of peoples'.

This shows, I think, that it is a mistake to subsume the issue of minority rights under one of the more familiar debates in contemporary political philosophy – e.g. the debate between 'individualists' and 'communitarians', or between 'universalists' and 'contextualists', or between 'impartialists' and 'difference theorists', or between 'rationalists' and 'postmodernists'. This is a very common tendency (see e.g. I. Young 1993a; Gochnauer 1991; Galenkamp 1993; Trakman 1992; Torres 1991; Addis 1991; cf. Todorov 1993: 392–9). But it stems from an oversimplified view of the issues involved in minority rights. According to many commentators, the central question in assessing minority rights is whether one accepts in principle the idea of giving political recognition to communities or group differences. Defenders of individualism and universalism are then said to be opposed in principle to such recognition, whereas defenders of community and difference are in principle supportive of them. But, as I have emphasized, all political theories must accord recognition to certain forms of group differences and support certain cultural communities. This is inevitable in any theory which confronts issues of language policy, public holidays, political boundaries, and immigration rules. This is as true of liberal individualists and socialist internationalists as of conservatives, communitarians, and postmodernists.

So the debate over minority rights is not about whether it is ever legitimate to support 'communities' or to recognize 'difference'. Rather, the debate is whether to support the particular sort of cultural difference and community exhibited by national minorities. And, as I have noted, some liberals, despite their 'individualism' and 'universalism', recognize that justice requires extending the same support to national minorities that majority nations receive. Conversely, some communitarians and particularists, despite their commitment to 'community' and 'difference', have been reluctant to accept the demands of national minorities. They view national minorities in the same way they view ethnic groups or new social movements – that is, as forms of difference and community that can and should be accommodated by group-specific rights within the larger society. They are unwilling to accept that national minorities require recognition as separate and self-governing societies alongside the mainstream society.[31]

As I noted in Chapter 4, the history of minority rights suggests that there is little or no correlation between meta-ethical debates and support for the rights of national minorities. People's views on minority rights are shaped, not only by their foundational moral or philosophical premisses, but by more concrete factors, including ethnocentric prejudice, fears about international peace and superpower relations, and concerns about the preconditions of democratic consensus and social harmony. These considerations do not correlate in any simple or consistent way with people's underlying philosophical and moral premisses.

These larger philosophical debates are not irrelevant to the policy debate over minority rights. But the connection between the two debates is mediated by many additional assumptions about the nature of ethnic and national differences, and their role in domestic and international politics. It is these additional assumptions that largely account for the actual position endorsed by particular theorists, whatever their deeper philosophical premisses.

For this reason, the demands of national minorities and ethnic groups raise a deep challenge to all Western political traditions. All of these traditions have been shaped, implicitly or explicitly, by the same historical influences which have shaped liberal thinking. The task of developing a consistent and principled theory of minority rights is not one that liberals face alone.

Notes

1   On the importance of individual rights to the protection of groups, see Buchanan 1989; Walzer 1990; Macdonald 1989: 122–3; Tomasi 1991; Kymlicka 1990: chs. 4–6.

2   Some indigenous peoples have argued before the UN that they too have a right to self-determination under the UN Charter (see *Mikmaq Tribal Society v Canada* (1984) UN Doc. E/CN.4/Sub.2/204; Grand Council of the Crees 1992). For discussions of the salt-water thesis, and the right of self-determination under international law, see Pomerance 1982; Thornberry 1991: 13–21, 214–18; Crawford 1988; Makinson 1988.

3   On English Canadian opposition to nationalist demands for decentralization, see Stark 1992. A certain amount of *de facto* asymmetry in powers has been a long-standing aspect of Canadian federalism. However, many Canadians are unwilling to recognize this asymmetry formally in the constitution (see Gagnon and Garcea 1988; Taylor 1991; Cairns 1991). This is one reason why the 1992 Charlottetown Accord was defeated in the national referendum. Some people have claimed that a federal system cannot survive if it accords special status, but this is refuted by the experience of many countries. For a survey of various forms of asymmetrical federalism, see Elazar 1987: 54–7.

4   In Germany, federalism was imposed by the Allies after World War II to help prevent the rise of nationalist or authoritarian movements. For helpful discussions of the relationship between federalism and cultural diversity, see Howse and Knop 1993; Minow 1990; Majone 1990; Gagnon 1993; Long 1991; Duchacek 1977; Elkins 1992; Norman 1994.

5   Hence Nathan Glazer is quite wrong when he says that the division of the United States into federal units preceded its ethnic diversity (Glazer 1983 276–7). This is true of the original thirteen colonies, but decisions about the admission and boundaries of new states were made after the incorporation of national minorities, and these decisions were deliberately made so as to avoid creating states dominated by national minorities.

6   For a comparative review of these developments, see Fleras and Elliot 1992. A proposal to entrench Aboriginal self-government constitutionally as a third order of government in Canada was included in the 1992 Charlottetown Accord. This would have covered both the 'ethnic self-government' exercised by band councils on Indian reserves, and the 'public self-government' exercised by the Inuit majority within the new territory of Nunavut (see Asch 1984: ch. 7). For the relation of Indian self-government to federalism, see Resnik 1989; Cassidy and Bish 1989; Long 1991.

7   Gurr 1993: viii; cf. Nietschmann 1987.

8   Unless otherwise stated, all chapter cross-references in this chapter are to *Multicultural Citizenship* (Oxford, Clarendon Press, 1995).

9   For a discussion of these rights in the British context, see Parekh 1990: 705; 1991: 197–204; Modood

1992; Poulter 1987. In Canada, see E. Kallen 1987: 325–31. In the USA, see Minow 1990; Sandel 1990. For the Muslim girls in France, see Galeotti 1993. It is sometimes said that these measures are purely 'symbolic'. But measures relating to employment are very material, affecting people's 'life chances' not just their 'lifestyles'.

10 For statistics on the (under-)representation of blacks and Hispanics in the United States, see C. Davidson 1992: 46. For statistics on the representation of various social groups in Canada, see RCERPF 1991: 93–6 and 192.

11 While self-government may entail guaranteed representation on intergovernmental bodies which negotiate, interpret, and modify the division of powers, it may also entail *reduced* representation on federal bodies which legislate in areas of purely federal jurisdiction, in so far as the self-governing group is not governed by the decisions of these federal bodies. I discuss the relationship between self-government and representation in Ch. 7.

12 This phrase is from the judgement of the Canadian Supreme Court in explaining its interpretation of the equality guarantees under the Canadian Charter of Rights (*Andrews v. Law Society of British Columbia* 1 SCR 143; 56 DLR (4th) 1). See also Government of Canada 1991*b*: 10.

13 For examples of this view, see Knopff 1979; F. Morton 1985; Kukathas 1992; Hindess 1993; Maré 1992: 107–10; Rawls 1975: 88, 93, and the references cited in Ch. 1 n. 4.

14 I explored this relationship between national rights and liberal egalitarian justice in Kymlicka 1989*a*: ch. 9. For what it is worth, I continue to endorse the argument in that chapter, but I should have been clearer about its scope. I would now describe the argument in that chapter as an equality-based defence of certain external protections for national minorities. I did not use those terms at the time, in part because I did not have a very clear conception of the variety of rights, groups, and moral justifications that are involved in the debate.

15 I am here disagreeing with Tamir, who argues that the larger a national minority is, the more rights it should have (1993: 75). On my view, if a binational group is large enough, it may have little need for group-differentiated rights, since it can ensure its survival and development through the usual operation of the economic market-place and democratic decision-making. (This might be true, for example, if a national state contained two nations of roughly equal size and wealth.)

16 On the role of indigenous land claims in a liberal egalitarian framework, see Kymlicka 1995; Penz 1992; 1993; Russell 1993; Tully 1994. It is important to note that the equality argument for land claims is not based on notions of compensatory justice. The compensatory argument says that because indigenous peoples were the legal owners of their traditional lands, and because their lands were taken away illegally, they should be compensated for this historical wrong. Since the debate over land claims is often couched in the language of compensatory justice, I should say a word about this. I take it as given that indigenous peoples have suffered terrible wrongs in being dispossessed of their lands, and that they should be compensated for this in some way. Moreover, I believe that indigenous peoples continue to have certain property rights under the common law (in former British colonies), wherever these have not been explicitly extinguished by legislation. (That is to say, the *terra nullius* doctrine is wrong in terms both of morality and the common law.) But it is a mistake, I think, to put too much weight on historical property rights. For one thing, these claims do not, by themselves, explain why indigenous peoples have rights of self-government. Many groups have been wrongfully dispossessed of property and other economic opportunities, including women, blacks, and Japanese immigrants in the United States and Canada during World War II. Each of these groups may be entitled to certain forms of compensatory justice, but this does not by itself explain or justify granting powers of self-government (rather than compensatory programmes to promote integration and equal opportunity within the mainstream). Suffering historical injustice is neither necessary nor sufficient for claiming self-government rights (see Ch. 2, s. 2).

Moreover, the idea of compensating for historical wrongs, taken to its logical conclusion, implies that all the land which was wrongly taken from indigenous peoples in the Americas or Australia or New Zealand should be returned to them. This would create massive unfairness, given that the original European settlers and later immigrants have now produced hundreds of millions of descendants, and this land is the only home they know. Changing circumstances often make it impossible and undesirable to compensate for certain historical wrongs. As Jeremy Waldron puts it, certain historical wrongs are 'superseded' (Waldron 1992). Also, the land held by some indigenous groups at the time of contact was itself the result of the conquest or coercion of other indigenous groups (Mulgan 1989: 30–1; Crowe 1974: 65–81). The compensatory argument would presumably require rectifying these pre-contact injustices as well. (For other difficulties with compensatory claims, see Brilmayer 1992.)

The equality argument does not try to turn back the historical clock, nor to restore groups to the situation they would have been in in the absence of any historical injustice. (These compensatory aims actually fit more comfortably with Nozick's libertarian theory of entitlement than with a liberal egalitarian theory of distributive justice – see Lyons 1981.) The aim of the equality argument is to provide the sort of land base needed to sustain the viability of self-governing minority communities, and hence to prevent unfair disadvantages with respect to cultural membership now and in the future. In short, the equality argument situates land claims within a theory of distributive justice, rather than compensatory justice.

Waldron assumes that indigenous land claims are all based on claims for compensatory justice (Waldron 1992). In fact, however, most indigenous groups focus, not on reclaiming all of what they had before European settlement, but on what they need now to sustain themselves as distinct societies (see the declaration of the World Council of Indigenous Peoples, quoted in Nettheim 1988: 115; Sharp 1990: 150–3). Historical factors are, of course, relevant in other ways. The 'historical agreement' argument I discuss below is very much history-based.

17 The only attempt I know of to reconcile official languages with 'benign neglect' is by Rainer Knopff. He argues that language has two functions: it can function as the vehicle for the transmission of a particular culture, but it can also function as 'a culturally neutral, or utilitarian, means of communication which allows those of different cultures to participate in the same political community' (Knopff 1979: 67). By placing the emphasis on the utilitarian function, governments 'can enact official languages without at the same time legislating official cultures . . . in enacting 'official languages', one does not necessarily imply that the cultures which these languages transmit and represent thereby become 'official cultures' (Knopff 1979: 67). Culture, Knopff argues, 'remains a purely private affair' in Canada, for while English and French have official backing as the 'utilitarian' languages, all languages compete on equal terms for 'cultural' allegiance. It is the 'task of the individual members of a culture to show the excellence of their product on the cultural market-place, as it were. If they succeed, the language of that culture will become attractive to others . . . if [a] culture, and hence, language, cannot show itself to be worthy of choice in the light of standards of the good, then it deserves to disappear' (Knopff 1979: 70). This view of language as a 'culturally neutral medium' has been thoroughly discredited in the literature. In any event, it is simply not true that teaching in the English language in public schools is totally divorced from the teaching of the history and customs of the anglophone society.

18 Some commentators say that governments should draw boundaries and distribute powers so as to protect the viability of national minorities, but that they should not state in law that they are doing this. This enables the state to continue claiming that it treats all ethnic and national differences with 'benign neglect'. For example, van den Berghe argues that deliberately designing or revising federal units to protect minority cultures is consistent with 'benign neglect',

so long as it does not involve the explicit legal recognition of groups. He thinks it is one thing to define the powers and boundaries of a political subunit so as to ensure the protection of a minority culture (what he calls 'indirect consociationalism'), but quite another for the constitution or statute law to cite the existence of that minority as the reason for those arrangements (what he calls 'group rights') (van den Berghe 1981: 348). But surely this is hypocritical. If the agreed purpose of indirect consociationalism is to protect minority cultures, then anyone who values honesty and transparency in government (as liberals claim to do) should want that justification to be clear to everyone. Van den Berghe's solution violates the 'publicity condition' which Rawls imposes on liberal theories of justice (Rawls 1971: 133). None the less, this attitude seems to be widely shared. While most Canadians accept that the powers and boundaries of Quebec were fixed to accommodate the needs of the francophone minority in Canada, many objected to the government's proposal to state in the constitution that Quebec formed a 'distinct society' as the homeland of the French Canadian nation, because they saw this as violating the principle that the constitution should not recognize particular ethnic or national groups. Quebecers, however, are no longer willing to have their special status hidden away. They view it as a matter of basic respect that their separate identity be recognized and affirmed at the level of constitutional principle (Taylor 1991: 64).

19 This is similar to the debate over affirmative action for women or people with disabilities. Like self-government rights, affirmative action programmes asymmetrically distribute rights or opportunities on the basis of group membership. Proponents argue that they are required for genuine equality. Critics respond that the economic market-place (like the cultural market-place) already respects equality, by treating job applicants without regard for their group membership. However, an equality-based argument for group-specific affirmative action can be made if the actual operation of the economic market-place works to the disadvantage of certain groups. As with self-government rights, the equality argument for affirmative action seeks to show how the structure of common individual rights is intended to treat all people equally, but in fact works to the disadvantage of the members of a particular collectivity. Many group-specific claims can be seen in this way – that is, as compensating for the disadvantages and vulnerabilities of certain groups within the structure of common individual rights.

Of course, as I discussed in Ch. 1, affirmative action for women or people with disabilities differs in many ways from self-government rights for national minorities, since they are compensating for very different kinds of injustices. The former is intended to help disadvantaged groups integrate into society, by breaking down unjust barriers to full integration. The latter is intended to help cultural communities maintain their distinctiveness, by protecting against external decisions. This means that the former are (in theory) temporary, whereas the latter are permanent, barring dramatic shifts in population.

20 Imagine that schools and government offices (and presumably private businesses as well) were open seven days a week all year round, including Christmas and Easter, and that each student and employee was allowed to choose two days off per week, two weeks' vacation per year, plus, say, five additional holidays per year. This would maximize each individual's ability to adapt their schedule to their religious beliefs. But I do not know whether this is realistic or even desirable, given the extent to which social life is built around common weekends and holidays. As an atheist, I have no commitment to resting on the sabbath or celebrating religious holidays. But I do like the fact that most of my friends and family, regardless of their religion, language, and ethnicity, do not work on the weekends or on certain public holidays. Maintaining friendships and other voluntary associations would be much more difficult if society (including schools and other government institutions) were not organized in this way. Perhaps a better solution would be to have one major holiday from each of the largest religious groups in the country. We could have one Christian holiday (say, Christmas), but replace Easter and Thanksgiving with a Muslim and Jewish holiday. This would maintain the value of common holidays, and would also encourage people of each faith to learn something about the beliefs of other faiths.

21 E.g. the Canadian government justified its proposal to eliminate the treaty rights of Indians on the grounds that 'we can only be just in our time' (Trudeau 1969. 295). Trudeau was paraphrasing John F. Kennedy's famous quote about justice for blacks in the United States.

22 Chartrand argues that this is the current situation with respect to the Métis in Canada, who agreed to join Canada on the basis of promises made to them under the Manitoba Act 1870, which have since been broken (Chartrand 1993: 241).

23 It is interesting to note that some Aboriginal groups in Canada insist that their demands for federal funding of self-government are based solely on historical compensation for the wrongful taking of land, not on appeals to distributive justice between citizens (Lyon 1984: 13–14).

24 For a subtle discussion of the complex interaction between the equality and treaty arguments in the New Zealand context, see Sharp 1990: 135–6; Mulgan 1989: ch. 4. As Sharp notes, there is a tendency to read principles of equality back into the historical treaties.

25 These arguments parallel common arguments for

the protection of endangered plant and animal species, which are seen both as enriching the world aesthetically, and as providing potential sources of valuable genetic material or other substances that might be of human benefit.

26 Many liberals defend state funding of the arts or museums on the ground that the state has a responsibility to ensure an adequate range of options for future generations, which the cultural market-place may fail to protect (Dworkin 1985: ch. 11; Raz 1986: 162; Black 1992; Kymlicka 1989b: 893–5). If we accept that active measures are justified to preserve the richness and diversity of our cultural resources, then programmes such as the funding of ethnic festivals or immigrant language classes can be seen as falling under this heading. Indeed, as I noted in Chapter 2, some people defined this funding simply as a way of ensuring that ethnic groups are not discriminated against in state funding of art and culture. (I should note that other liberals view any such state funding as illegitimate (e.g. Rawls 1971: 331–2; Waldron 1989).)

27 Hence the popular contrast between 'consociational' and 'universal' modes of incorporating individuals into the state is misleading (e.g. Asch 1990). There is a distinction between models of citizenship that incorporate citizens on a uniform basis or through membership in some group. But uniform citizenship is not *universal* citizenship. No country allows for universal citizenship.

28 See the references in Ch. 5 n. 17.

29 One theorist who has attempted to square the circle is Michael Walzer. He argues that restricting citizenship in a state to the members of a particular group is justified in the name of protecting a distinct culture (what he calls a 'community of character'). He recognizes that this same argument can be given for group-differentiated rights *within* a state, but rejects such rights because they violate our 'shared understandings' (Walzer 1983: ch. 2). I have argued elsewhere that Walzer's argument is unsuccessful (Kymlicka 1989a: ch. 11). See also Ch. 4. I should emphasize again that my defence of the legitimacy of partially closed borders is not intended to defend the right of national groups to maintain more than their fair share of resources. On the contrary, I would argue that a country forfeits its right to restrict immigration if it has failed to live up to its obligations to share its wealth with the poorer countries of the world. See Bader 1995; Ackerman 1980: 256–7.

30 On the tendency of liberals to treat diversity as a matter of variations in individual values and beliefs, see A. Phillips 1993; Galeotti 1993: 590. For an example of this 'overly cerebral' conception of diversity, see Rawls 1993a: pp. xxvii–xxix, where he treats modern conflicts of race, ethnicity, and gender as if they were analogous to conflict over religious belief during the Reformation – i.e.

as conflicts over individuals' beliefs about 'the meaning, value and purposes of human life'.

31 This is true of Young's postmodernist account of minority rights. According to her view of 'relational difference', cultural groups must 'understand themselves as participating in the same society', and as 'part of a single polity', whose common decision-making procedures are seen as 'legitimately binding' on all

people equally. Cultural difference within a state should be accommodated by group-differentiated rights within a single society – e.g. by group representation within the mainstream polity – rather than by establishing two or more separate and self-governing societies within a state (I. Young 1993a: 135). Like many liberals, she fears the impact of national rights on other political movements or on domestic peace.

References

Ackerman, Bruce (1980), *Social Justice in the Liberal State* (Yale University Press, New Haven, Conn.).

Adam, Heribert (1979), 'The Failure of Political Liberalism', in H. Adam and H. Giliomee (eds.), *Ethnic Power Mobilized: Can South Africa Change?* (Yale University Press, New Haven, Conn.), 258–85.

Addis, Adeno (1991), 'Individualism, Communitarianism and the Rights of Ethnic Minorities', *Notre Dame Law Review*, 67/3: 615–76.

Asch, Michael (1984), *Home and Native Land: Aboriginal Rights and the Canadian Constitution* (Methuen, Toronto).

——(1990), 'Consociation and the Resolution of Aboriginal Political Rights', *Culture*, 10/1: 93–102.

Bader, Veit (1995), 'Citizenship and Exclusion: Radical Democracy, Community and Justice', *Political Theory*, forthcoming.

Black, Samuel (1991), 'Individualism at an Impasse', *Canadian Journal of Philosophy*, 21/3: 347–77.

——(1992), 'Revisionist Liberalism and the Decline of Culture', *Ethics*, 102/2: 244–67.

Brilmayer, Lea (1992), 'Groups, Histories and International Law', *Cornell International Law Journal*, 25/3: 555–63.

Buchanan, Allen (1989), 'Assessing the Communitarian Critique of Liberalism', *Ethics*, 99/4: 852–82.

Cairns, Alan (1991), 'Constitutional Change and the Three Equalities', in Ronald Watts and Douglas Brown (eds.), *Options for a New Canada* (University of Toronto Press, Toronto), 77–110.

Cassidy, Frank, and Bish, Robert (1989), *Indian Government: Its Meaning in Practice* (Institute for Research on Public Policy, Halifax).

Chartrand, Paul (1991), *Manitoba's Métis Settlement Scheme of 1870* (University of Saskatchewan Native Law Centre, Saskatoon).

——(1993), 'Aboriginal Self-Government: The Two Sides of Legitimacy', in Susan Phillips (ed.), *How Ottawa Spends: 1993–1994* (Carleton University Press, Ottawa), 231–56.

Clay, Jason (1989), 'Epilogue: The Ethnic Future of Nations', *Third World Quarterly*, 11/4: 223–33.

Crawford, James (1988), 'The Rights of Peoples', in James Crawford (ed.), *The Rights of Peoples* (Oxford University Press, Oxford), 159–75.

Crowe, Keith (1974), *A History of the Original Peoples of Northern Canada* (McGill-Queen's University Press, Montreal).

Danley, John (1991), 'Liberalism, Aboriginal Rights and Cultural Minorities', *Philosophy and Public Affairs*, 20/2: 168–85.

Davidson, Chandler (1992), 'The Voting Rights Act: A Brief History', in B. Grofman and C. Davidson (eds.), *Controversies in Minority Voting: The Voting Rights Act in Perspective* (Brookings Institute, Washington, DC), 7–51.

Duchacek, I.D. (1977), 'Federalist Responses to Ethnic Demands: An Overview', in Daniel Elazar (ed.), *Federalism and Political Integration* (Turtledove Publishing, Ramat Gan), 59–71.

Dworkin, Ronald (1981), 'What is Equality? Part II: Equality of Resources', *Philosophy and Public Affairs*, 10/4: 283–345.

——(1985), *A Matter of Principle* (Harvard University Press, London).

——(1989), 'Liberal Community', *California Law Review*, 77/3: 479–504.

Elazar, Daniel (1987), *Exploring Federalism* (University of Alabama, Tuscaloosa, Ala.).

Elkins, David (1992), *Where Should the Majority Rule? Reflections on Non-territorial Provinces and Other Constitutional Proposals* (Centre for Constitutional Studies, University of Alberta, Edmonton).

Falk, Richard (1988), 'The Rights of Peoples (in Particular Indigenous Peoples)', in James Crawford (ed.), *The Rights of Peoples* (Oxford University Press, Oxford), 17–37.

Fleras, Augie and Elliot, Jean Leonard (1992), *The Nations within: Aboriginal-State Relations in Canada, the United States and New Zealand* (Oxford University Press, Toronto).

Gagon, Alain-G. (1993), 'The Political Uses of Federation', in Michael Burgess and Alain-G. Gagon (eds.), *Comparative Federalism and Federation* (University of Toronto Press, Toronto), 15–44.

Gagon, Alain-G. and Garcea, Joseph (1988), 'Quebec and the Pursuit of Special Status', in R.D. Olling and M.W. Westmacott (eds.), *Perspectives on Canadian Federalism* (Prentice-Hall, Scarborough), 304–25.

Galenkamp, Marlies (1993), *Individualism and Collectivism: The Concept of Collective Rights* (Rotterdamse Filosofische Studies, Rotterdam).

Galeotti, Anna (1993), 'Citizenship and Equality: The Place for Toleration', *Political Theory*, 21/4: 585–605.

Glazer, Nathan (1983), *Ethnic Dilemmas: 1964–1982* (Harvard University Press, Cambridge, Mass.).

Gochnauer, Myron (1991), 'Philosophical Musings on Persons, Groups, and Rights', *University of New Brunswick Law Journal*, 40/1: 1–20.

Government of Canada (1991a), *Shaping Canada's Future Together: Proposals* (Supply and Services, Ottawa).

——(1991b), *Shared Values: The Canadian Identity* (Supply and Services, Ottawa).

Gurr, Ted (1993), *Minorities at Risk: A Global View of Ethnopolitical Conflict* (Institute of Peace Press, Washington, DC).

Gutmann, Amy (1993), 'The Challenge of Multiculturalism to Political Ethics', *Philosophy and Public Affairs*, 22/3: 171–206.

Hindess, Barry (1993), 'Multiculturalism and Citizenship', in Chandran Kukathas (ed.), *Multicultural Citizens: The Philosophy and Politics of Identity* (Centre for Independent Studies, St Leonards), 33–45.

Horowitz, D.L. (1985), *Ethnic Groups in Conflict* (University of California Press, Berkeley, Calif.).

Howse, Robert, and Knop, Karen (1993), 'Federalism, Secession, and the Limits of Ethnic Accommodation: A Canadian Perspective', *New Europe Law Review*, 1/2: 269–320.

Kallen, Evelyn (1987), 'Ethnicity and Collective Rights in Canada', in L. Driedger (ed.), *Ethnic Canada* (Copp Clark, Toronto), 318–36.

Knopff, Rainer (1979), 'Language and Culture in the Canadian Debate: The Battle of the White Papers', *Canadian Review of Studies in Nationalism*, 6/1: 66–82.

Kukathas, Chandran (1992), 'Are There Any Cultural Rights?', *Political Theory*, 20/1: 105–39.

Kymlicka, Will (1989a), *Liberalism, Community, and Culture* (Oxford University Press, Oxford).

——(1989b), 'Liberal Individualism and Liberal Neutrality', *Ethics*, 99/4: 883–905.

——(1990), *Contemporary Political Philosophy: An Introduction* (Oxford University Press, Oxford).

——(1995), 'Concepts of Community and Social Justice', in Fen Hampson and Judith Reppy (eds.), *Global Environmental Change and Social Justice*, forthcoming.

Long, J. A. (1991), 'Federalism and Ethnic Self-Determination: Native Indians in Canada', *Journal of Commonwealth and Comparative Politics*, 29/2: 192–211.

Lyon, Noel (1984), *Aboriginal Self-Government* (Institute of Intergovernmental Relations, Kingston).

Lyons, David (1981), 'The New Indian Claims and Original Rights to Land', in J. Paul (ed.), *Reading Nozick* (Rowman & Littlefield, Totowa, NJ).

Macdonald, Ian (1989), 'Group Rights', *Philosophical Papers*, 28/2: 117–36.

Macklem, Patrick (1993), 'Distributing Sovereignty: Indian Nations and Equality of Peoples', *Stanford Law Review*, 45/5: 1311–67.

Majone, Giandomenico (1990), 'Preservation of Cultural Diversity in a Federal System: The Role of the Regions', in Mark Tushnet (ed.), *Comparative Constitutional Federalism* (Greenwood Press, New York), 67–76.

Makinson, David (1988), 'Rights of Peoples: Point of View of a Logician', in James Crawford (ed.), *The Rights of Peoples* (Oxford University Press, Oxford), 69–92.

Maré, Gerhard (1992), *Brothers Born of Warrior Blood: Politics and Ethnicity and South Africa* (Raven Press, Johannesburg).

Minow, Martha (1990), 'Putting up and Putting down: Tolerance Reconsidered', in Mark Tushnet (ed.), *Comparative Constitutional Federalism* (Greenwood Press, New York), 77–113.

Modood, Tariq (1992), *Not Easy Being British: Colour, Culture and Citizenship* (Trentham Books, Stoke-on-Trent).

Morton, F. L. (1985), 'Group Rights versus Individual Rights in the Charter: The Special Cases of Natives and the Québécois', in N. Nevitte and A. Kornberg (eds.), *Minorities and the Canadian State* (Mosaic Press, Oakville): 71–85.

Mulgan, Richard (1989), *Maori, Pākehā and Democracy* (Oxford University Press, Auckland).

Nettheim, Garth (1988), ' "Peoples" and "Populations": Indigenous Peoples and the Rights of Peoples', in James Crawford (ed.), *The Rights of Peoples* (Oxford University Press, Oxford), 107–26.

Nietschmann, Bernard (1987), 'The Third World War', *Cultural Survival Quarterly*, 11/3: 1–16.

Norman, W. J. (1994), 'Towards a Normative Theory of Federalism', in Judith Baker (ed.), *Group Rights* (University of Toronto Press, Toronto), 79–99.

O'Brien, Sharon (1987), 'Cultural Rights in the United States: A Conflict of Values', *Law and Inequality Journal*, 5: 267–358.

Parekh, Bhikhu (1990), 'The Rushdie Affair: Research Agenda for Political Philosophy', *Political Studies*, 38: 695–709.

——(1991), 'British Citizenship and Cultural Difference', in Geoff Andrews (ed.), *Citizenship* (Lawrence & Wishart, London), 183–204.

——(1994), 'Decolonizing Liberalism', in Aleksandras Shtromas (ed.), *The End of 'Isms'? Reflections on the Fate of Ideological Politics after Communism's Collapse* (Blackwell, Oxford), 85–103.

Penz, Peter (1992), 'Development Refugees and Distributive Justice: Indigenous Peoples, Land and the Developmentalist State', *Public Affairs Quarterly*, 6/1: 105–31.

——(1993), 'Colonization of Tribal Lands in Bangladesh and Indonesia: State Rationales, Rights to Land, and Environmental Justice', in Michael Howard (ed.), *Asia's Environmental Crisis* (Westview Press, Boulder, Col.), 37–72.

Phillips, Anne (1993), *Democracy and Difference* (Pennsylvania State University Press, Philadelphia).

Pomerance, Michla (1982), *Self-Determination in Law*

and Practice: The New Doctrine in the United Nations (Martinus Nijhoff Publishers, The Hague).

Poulter, Sebastian (1987), 'Ethnic Minority Customs, English Law, and Human Rights', International and Comparative Law Quarterly, 36/3: 589–615.

Rawls, John (1971), A Theory of Justice (Oxford University Press, London).

——(1975), 'Fairness to Goodness', Philosophical Review, 84: 536–54.

——(1978), 'The Basic Structure as Subject', in A. Goldman and J. Kim (eds.), Values and Morals (Reidel, Dordrecht).

——(1993a), Political Liberalism (Columbia University Press, New York).

——(1993b), 'The Law of Peoples', in S. Shute and S. Hurley (eds.), On Human Rights: The Oxford Amnesty Lectures 1993 (Basic Books, New York), 41–82.

Raz, Joseph (1986), The Morality of Freedom (Oxford University Press, Oxford).

RCERPF – see Royal Commission on Electoral Reform and Party Financing.

Resnik, Judith (1989), 'Dependent Sovereigns: Indian Tribes, States, and the Federal Courts', University of Chicago Law Review, 56: 671–759.

Royal Commission on Electoral Reform and Party Financing (1991). Reforming Electoral Democracy: Final Report, vols. i and ii (Supply and Services, Ottawa).

Rubinstein, Alvin (1993), 'Is Statehood for Puerto Rico in the National Interest?', In Depth: A Journal for Values and Public Policy, Spring: 87–99.

Russell, John (1993), 'Nationalistic Minorities and Liberal Traditions', in Philip Bryden et al. (eds.), Protecting Rights and Liberties: Essays on the Charter and Canada's Political, Legal and Intellectual Life (University of Toronto Press, Toronto), 205–41.

Sandel, Michael (1990), 'Freedom of Conscience or Freedom of Choice', in James Hunter and O. Guinness (eds.), Articles of Faith, Articles of Peace (Brookings Institute, Washington, DC), 74–92.

Schwartz, Brian (1986), First Principles, Second Thoughts: Aboriginal Peoples, Constitutional Reform and Canadian Statecraft (Institute for Research on Public Policy, Montreal).

Sharp, Andrew (1990), Justice and the Maori: Maori Claims in New Zealand Political Argument in the 1980s (Oxford University Press, Auckland).

Sigler, Jay (1983), Minority Rights: A Comparative Analysis (Greenwood, Westport, Conn.).

Smith, Jennifer (1993), 'Canadian Confederation and the Influence of American Federalism', in Marian McKenna (ed.), The Canadian and American Constitutions in Comparative Perspective (University of Calgary Press, Calgary), 65–85.

Stark, Andrew (1992), 'English-Canadian Opposition to Quebec Nationalism', in R. Kent Weaver (ed.), The Collapse of Canada? (Brookings Institute, Washington, DC), 123–58.

Tamir, Yael (1993), Liberal Nationalism (Princeton University Press, Princeton, NJ).

Taylor, Charles (1991), 'Shared and Divergent Values', in Ronald Watts and D. Brown (eds.), Options for a New Canada (University of Toronto Press, Toronto), 53–76.

Thornberry, Patrick (1991), International Law and the Rights of Minorities (Oxford University Press, Oxford).

Todorov, Tzvetan (1993), On Human Diversity: Nationalism, Racism and Exoticism in French Thought (Harvard University Press, Cambridge, Mass.).

Tomasi, John (1991), 'Individual Rights and Community Virtues', Ethics, 101/3: 521–36.

Torres, Gerald (1991), 'Critical Race Theory: The Decline of the Universalist Ideal and the Hope of Plural Justice', Minnesota Law Review, 75: 993–1007.

Trakman, Leon (1992), 'Group Rights: A Canadian Perspective', New York University Journal of International Law and Politics, 24/4: 1579–650.

Trudeau, P.E. (1969), speech of 8 Aug. 1969, repr. as 'Justice in our Time', in Eldon Soifer (ed.), Ethical Issues: Perspectives for Canadians (Broadview Press, Peterborough, 1992), 295–7.

Tully, James (1994), 'Aboriginal Property and Western Theory: Recovering a Middle Ground', Social Philosophy and Policy, 11/2: 153–80.

Van den Berghe, Pierre (1981), The Ethnic Phenomenon (Elsevier, New York).

Van Dyke, Vernon (1982), 'Collective Entities and Moral Rights: Problems in Liberal-Democratic Thought', Journal of Politics, 44: 21–40.

Waldron, Jeremy (1989), 'Autonomy and Perfectionism in Raz's Morality of Freedom', Southern California Law Review, 62/3–4: 1097–152.

——(1992), 'Superseding Historic Injustice', Ethics, 103/1: 4–28.

Walzer, Michael (1982), 'Pluralism in Political Perspective', in M. Walzer (ed.), The Politics of Ethnicity (Harvard University Press, Cambridge. Mass.), 1–28.

——(1983), Spheres of Justice: A Defence of Pluralism and Equality (Blackwell, Oxford).

——(1990), 'The Communitarian Critique of Liberalism', Political Theory, 18/1: 6–23.

Weinstein, Brian (1983), The Civic Tongue: Political Consequences of Language Choices (Longman, New York).

Young, Iris Marion (1989), 'Polity and Group Difference: A Critique of the Ideal of Universal Citizenship', Ethics, 99/2: 250–74.

——(1990), Justice and the Politics of Difference (Princeton University Press, Princeton, NJ).

——(1993a), 'Together in Difference: Transforming the Logic of Group Political Conflict', in Judith Squires (ed.), Principled Positions: Postmodernism and the Rediscovery of Value (Lawrence and Wishart, London), 121–50.

——(1993b), 'Justice and Communicative Democracy', in Roger Gottlieb (ed.), Radical Democracy: Tradition, Counter-tradition, Politics (Temple University Press, Philadelphia), 123–43.

PART V

Liberty

24

Two Concepts of Liberty[1]

Isaiah Berlin

If men never disagreed about the ends of life, if our ancestors had remained undisturbed in the Garden of Eden, the studies to which the Chichele Chair of Social and Political Theory is dedicated could scarcely have been conceived. For these studies spring from, and thrive on, discord. Someone may question this on the ground that even in a society of saintly anarchists, where no conflicts about ultimate purpose can take place, political problems, for example constitutional or legislative issues, might still arise. But this objection rests on a mistake. Where ends are agreed, the only questions left are those of means, and these are not political but technical, that is to say, capable of being settled by experts or machines like arguments between engineers or doctors. That is why those who put their faith in some immense, world-transforming phenomenon, like the final triumph of reason or the proletarian revolution, must believe that all political and moral problems can thereby be turned into technological ones. That is the meaning of Saint-Simon's famous phrase about 'replacing the government of persons by the administration of things', and the Marxist prophecies about the withering away of the state and the beginning of the true history of humanity. This outlook is called utopian by those for whom speculation about this condition of perfect social harmony is the play of idle fancy. Nevertheless, a visitor from Mars to any British – or American – university today might perhaps be forgiven if he sustained

the impression that its members lived in something very like this innocent and idyllic state, for all the serious attention that is paid to fundamental problems of politics by professional philosophers.

Yet this is both surprising and dangerous. Surprising because there has, perhaps, been no time in modern history when so large a number of human beings, both in the East and West, have had their notions, and indeed their lives, so deeply altered, and in some cases violently upset, by fanatically held social and political doctrines. Dangerous, because when ideas are neglected by those who ought to attend to them – that is to say, those who have been trained to think critically about ideas – they sometimes acquire an unchecked momentum and an irresistible power over multitudes of men that may grow too violent to be affected by rational criticism. Over a hundred years ago, the German poet Heine warned the French not to underestimate the power of ideas: philosophical concepts nurtured in the stillness of a professor's study could destroy a civilization. He spoke of Kant's *Critique of Pure Reason* as the sword with which European deism had been decapitated, and described the works of Rousseau as the blood-stained weapon which, in the hands of Robespierre, had destroyed the old régime; and prophesied that the romantic faith of Fichte and Schelling would one day be turned, with terrible effect, by their fanatical German followers, against the liberal culture of the West. The facts have not wholly belied this prediction; but if professors can truly wield this fatal power, may it not be that only other professors, or, at least, other thinkers (and not governments or

Reprinted from Isaiah Berlin, *Four Essays on Liberty* (1969), 118–72. Copyright © 1958 Isaiah Berlin. Reprinted by permission of Oxford University Press.

Congressional committees), can alone disarm them?

Our philosophers seem oddly unaware of these devastating effects of their activities. It may be that, intoxicated by their magnificent achievements in more abstract realms, the best among them look with disdain upon a field in which radical discoveries are less likely to be made, and talent for minute analysis is less likely to be rewarded. Yet, despite every effort to separate them, conducted by a blind scholastic pedantry, politics has remained indissolubly intertwined with every other form of philosophical inquiry. To neglect the field of political thought, because its unstable subject-matter, with its blurred edges, is not to be caught by the fixed concepts, abstract models, and fine instruments suitable to logic or to linguistic analysis – to demand a unity of method in philosophy, and reject whatever the method cannot successfully manage – is merely to allow oneself to remain at the mercy of primitive and uncriticized political beliefs. It is only a very vulgar historical materialism that denies the power of ideas, and says that ideals are mere material interests in disguise. It may be that, without the pressure of social forces, political ideas are stillborn: what is certain is that these forces, unless they clothe themselves in ideas, remain blind and undirected.

This truth has not escaped every Oxford teacher, even in our own day. It is because he has grasped the importance of political ideas in theory and practice, and has dedicated his life to their analysis and propagation, that the first holder of this Chair has made so great an impact upon the world in which he has lived. The name of Douglas Cole is known wherever men have political or social issues at heart. His fame extends far beyond the confines of this university and country. A political thinker of complete independence, honesty, and courage, a writer and speaker of extraordinary lucidity and eloquence, a poet and a novelist, a uniquely gifted teacher and *animateur des idées*, he is, in the first place, a man who has given his life to the fearless support of principles not always popular, and to the unswerving and passionate defence of justice and truth, often in circumstances of great difficulty and discouragement. These are the qualities for which this most generous and imaginative English socialist is today chiefly known to the world. Not the least remarkable, and perhaps the most characteristic, fact about

him is that he has achieved this public position without sacrificing his natural humanity, his spontaneity of feeling, his inexhaustible personal goodness, and above all his deep and scrupulous devotion – a devotion reinforced by many-sided learning and a fabulous memory – to his vocation as a teacher of anyone who wishes to learn. It is a source of deep pleasure and pride to me to attempt to put on record what I, and many others, feel about this great Oxford figure whose moral and intellectual character is an asset to his country and to the cause of justice and human equality everywhere.

It is from him, at least as much as from his writings, that many members of my generation at Oxford have learnt that political theory is a branch of moral philosophy, which starts from the discovery, or application, of moral notions in the sphere of political relations. I do not mean, as I think some Idealist philosophers may have believed, that all historical movements or conflicts between human beings are reducible to movements or conflicts of ideas or spiritual forces, nor even that they are effects (or aspects) of them. But I do mean (and I do not think that Professor Cole would disagree) that to understand such movements or conflicts is, above all, to understand the ideas or attitudes to life involved in them, which alone make such movements a part of human history, and not mere natural events. Political words and notions and acts are not intelligible save in the context of the issues that divide the men who use them. Consequently our own attitudes and activities are likely to remain obscure to us, unless we understand the dominant issues of our own world. The greatest of these is the open war that is being fought between two systems of ideas which return different and conflicting answers to what has long been the central question of politics – the question of obedience and coercion. 'Why should I (or anyone) obey anyone else?' 'Why should I not live as I like?' 'Must I obey?' 'If I disobey, may I be coerced? By whom, and to what degree, and in the name of what, and for the sake of what?'

Upon the answers to the question of the permissible limits of coercion opposed views are held in the world today, each claiming the allegiance of very large numbers of men. It seems to me, therefore, that any aspect of this issue is worthy of examination.

I

To coerce a man is to deprive him of freedom – freedom from what? Almost every moralist in human history has praised freedom. Like happiness and goodness, like nature and reality, the meaning of this term is so porous that there is little interpretation that it seems able to resist. I do not propose to discuss either the history or the more than two hundred senses of this protean word recorded by historians of ideas. I propose to examine no more than two of these senses – but those central ones, with a great deal of human history behind them, and, I dare say, still to come. The first of these political senses of freedom or liberty (I shall use both words to mean the same), which (following much precedent) I shall call the 'negative' sense, is involved in the answer to the question 'What is the area within which the subject – a person or group of persons – is or should be left to do or be what he is able to do or be, without interference by other persons?' The second, which I shall call the positive sense, is involved in the answer to the question 'What, or who, is the source of control or interference that can determine someone to do, or be, this rather than that?' The two questions are clearly different, even though the answers to them may overlap.

The Notion of 'Negative' Freedom

I am normally said to be free to the degree to which no man or body of men interferes with my activity. Political liberty in this sense is simply the area within which a man can act unobstructed by others. If I am prevented by others from doing what I could otherwise do, I am to that degree unfree; and if this area is contracted by other men beyond a certain minimum, I can be described as being coerced, or, it may be, enslaved. Coercion is not, however, a term that covers every form of inability. If I say that I am unable to jump more than ten feet in the air, or cannot read because I am blind, or cannot understand the darker pages of Hegel, it would be eccentric to say that I am to that degree enslaved or coerced. Coercion implies the deliberate interference of other human beings within the area in which I could otherwise act. You lack political liberty or freedom only if you are prevented from attaining a goal by human beings.[2] Mere incapacity to attain a goal is not

lack of political freedom.[3] This is brought out by the use of such modern expressions as 'economic freedom' and its counterpart, 'economic slavery'. It is argued, very plausibly, that if a man is too poor to afford something on which there is no legal ban – a loaf of bread, a journey round the world, recourse to the law courts – he is as little free to have it as he would be if it were forbidden him by law. If my poverty were a kind of disease, which prevented me from buying bread, or paying for the journey round the world or getting my case heard, as lameness prevents me from running, this inability would not naturally be described as a lack of freedom, least of all political freedom. It is only because I believe that my inability to get a given thing is due to the fact that other human beings have made arrangements whereby I am, whereas others are not, prevented from having enough money with which to pay for it, that I think myself a victim of coercion or slavery. In other words, this use of the term depends on a particular social and economic theory about the causes of my poverty or weakness. If my lack of material means is due to my lack of mental or physical capacity, then I begin to speak of being deprived of freedom (and not simply about poverty) only if I accept the theory.[4] If, in addition, I believe that I am being kept in want by a specific arrangement which I consider unjust or unfair, I speak of economic slavery or oppression. 'The nature of things does not madden us, only ill will does', said Rousseau. The criterion of oppression is the part that I believe to be played by other human beings, directly or indirectly, with or without the intention of doing so, in frustrating my wishes. By being free in this sense I mean not being interfered with by others. The wider the area of non-interference the wider my freedom.

This is what the classical English political philosophers meant when they used this word.[5] They disagreed about how wide the area could or should be. They supposed that it could not, as things were, be unlimited, because if it were, it would entail a state in which all men could boundlessly interfere with all other men; and this kind of 'natural' freedom would lead to social chaos in which men's minimum needs would not be satisfied; or else the liberties of the weak would be suppressed by the strong. Because they perceived that human purposes and activities do not automatically harmonize with one another, and because (whatever their official doctrines) they put high value on other goals, such as justice, or happiness, or culture, or security, or varying degrees of equality, they were prepared to curtail freedom in the interests of other values and, indeed, of freedom itself. For, without this, it was impossible to create the kind of association that they thought desirable. Consequently, it is assumed by these thinkers that the area of men's free action must be limited by law. But equally it is assumed, especially by such libertarians as Locke and Mill in England, and Constant and Tocqueville in France, that there ought to exist a certain minimum area of personal freedom which must on no account be violated; for if it is overstepped, the individual will find himself in an area too narrow for even that minimum development of his natural faculties which alone makes it possible to pursue, and even to conceive, the various ends which men hold good or right or sacred. It follows that a frontier must be drawn between the area of private life and that of public authority. Where it is to be drawn is a matter of argument, indeed of haggling. Men are largely interdependent, and no man's activity is so completely private as never to obstruct the lives of others in any way. 'Freedom for the pike is death for the minnows'; the liberty of some must depend on the restraint of others. 'Freedom for an Oxford don', others have been known to add, 'is a very different thing from freedom for an Egyptian peasant.'

This proposition derives its force from something that is both true and important, but the phrase itself remains a piece of political claptrap. It is true that to offer political rights, or safeguards against intervention by the state, to men who are half-naked, illiterate, underfed, and diseased is to mock their condition; they need medical help or education before they can understand, or make use of, an increase in their freedom. What is freedom to those who cannot make use of it? Without adequate conditions for the use of freedom, what is the value of freedom? First things come first: there are situations, as a nineteenth-century Russian radical writer declared, in which boots are superior to the works of Shakespeare; individual freedom is not everyone's primary need. For freedom is not the mere absence of frustration of whatever kind; this would inflate the meaning of the word until it meant too much or too little. The Egyptian peasant needs clothes or medicine before, and more than, personal liberty, but the minimum freedom that he needs today, and the greater degree of freedom that he may need tomorrow, is not some species of freedom peculiar to him, but identical with that of professors, artists, and millionaires.

What troubles the consciences of Western liberals is not, I think, the belief that the freedom that men seek differs according to their social or economic conditions, but that the minority who possess it have gained it by exploiting, or, at least, averting their gaze from, the vast majority who do not. They believe, with good reason, that if individual liberty is an ultimate end for human beings, none should be deprived of it by others; least of all that some should enjoy it at the expense of others. Equality of liberty; not to treat others as I should not wish them to treat me; repayment of my debt to those who alone have made possible my liberty or prosperity or enlightenment; justice, in its simplest and most universal sense – these are the foundations of liberal morality. Liberty is not the only goal of men. I can, like the Russian critic Belinsky, say that if others are to be deprived of it – if my brothers are to remain in poverty, squalor, and chains – then I do not want it for myself, I reject it with both hands and infinitely prefer to share their fate. But nothing is gained by a confusion of terms. To avoid glaring inequality or widespread misery I am ready to sacrifice some, or all, of my freedom: I may do so willingly and freely: but it is freedom that I am giving up for the sake of justice or equality or the love of my fellow men. I should be guilt-stricken, and rightly so, if I were not, in some circumstances, ready to make this sacrifice. But a sacrifice is not an increase in what is being sacrificed, namely freedom, however great the moral need or the compensation for it. Everything is what it is: liberty is liberty, not equality or fairness or justice or culture, or human happiness or a quiet conscience. If the liberty of myself or my class or nation depends on the misery of a number of other human beings, the system which promotes this is unjust and immoral. But if I curtail or lose my freedom, in order to lessen the shame of such inequality, and do not thereby materially increase the individual liberty of others, an absolute loss of liberty occurs. This may be compensated for by a gain in justice or in happiness or in peace, but the loss remains, and it is a confusion of values to say that although my 'liberal', individual freedom may go by the board, some other kind of freedom – 'social' or 'economic' – is increased. Yet it remains true that the freedom of some must at times be curtailed to secure the freedom of others. Upon what principle should this be done? If freedom is a sacred, untouchable value, there can be no such principle. One or other of these conflicting rules or principles must, at any rate in practice, yield: not always for reasons which can be clearly stated, let alone generalized into rules or universal maxims. Still, a practical compromise has to be found.

Philosophers with an optimistic view of human nature and a belief in the possibility of harmonizing human interests, such as Locke or Adam Smith and, in some moods, Mill, believed that social harmony and progress were compatible with reserving a large area for private life over which neither the state nor any other authority must be allowed to trespass. Hobbes, and those who agreed with him, especially conservative or reactionary thinkers, argued that if men were to be prevented from destroying one another and making social life a jungle or a wilderness, greater safeguards must be instituted to keep them in their places; he wished correspondingly to increase the area of centralized control and decrease that of the individual. But both sides agreed that some portion of human existence must remain independent of the sphere of social control. To invade that preserve, however small, would be despotism. The most eloquent of all defenders of freedom and privacy, Benjamin Constant, who had not forgotten the Jacobin dictatorship, declared that at the very least the liberty of religion, opinion, expression, property, must be guaranteed against arbitrary invasion. Jefferson, Burke, Paine, Mill, compiled different catalogues of individual liberties, but the argument for keeping authority at bay is always substantially the same. We must preserve a minimum area of personal freedom if we are not to 'degrade or deny our nature'. We cannot remain absolutely free, and must give up some of our liberty to preserve the rest. But total self-surrender is self-defeating. What then must the minimum be? That which a man cannot give up without offending against the essence of his human nature. What is this essence? What are the standards which it entails? This has been, and perhaps always will be, a matter of infinite debate. But whatever the principle in terms of which the area of non-interference is to be drawn, whether it is that of natural law or natural rights, or of utility or the pronouncements of a categorical imperative, or the sanctity of the social contract, or any other concept with which men have sought

to clarify and justify their convictions, liberty in this sense means liberty *from*; absence of interference beyond the shifting, but always recognizable, frontier. 'The only freedom which deserves the name is that of pursuing our own good in our own way', said the most celebrated of its champions. If this is so, is compulsion ever justified? Mill had no doubt that it was. Since justice demands that all individuals be entitled to a minimum of freedom, all other individuals were of necessity to be restrained, if need be by force, from depriving anyone of it. Indeed, the whole function of law was the prevention of just such collisions: the state was reduced to what Lassalle contemptuously described as the functions of a night-watchman or traffic policeman.

What made the protection of individual liberty so sacred to Mill? In his famous essay he declares that, unless men are left to live as they wish 'in the path which merely concerns themselves', civilization cannot advance; the truth will not, for lack of a free market in ideas, come to light; there will be no scope for spontaneity, originality, genius, for mental energy, for moral courage. Society will be crushed by the weight of 'collective mediocrity'. Whatever is rich and diversified will be crushed by the weight of custom, by men's constant tendency to conformity, which breeds only 'withered capacities', 'pinched and hidebound', 'cramped and warped' human beings. 'Pagan self-assertion is as worthy as Christian self-denial.' 'All the errors which a man is likely to commit against advice and warning are far outweighed by the evil of allowing others to constrain him to what they deem is good.' The defence of liberty consists in the 'negative' goal of warding off interference. To threaten a man with persecution unless he submits to a life in which he exercises no choices of his goals, to block before him every door but one, no matter how noble the prospect upon which it opens, or how benevolent the motives of those who arrange this, is to sin against the truth that he is a man, a being with a life of his own to live. This is liberty as it has been conceived by liberals in the modern world from the days of Erasmus (some would say of Occam) to our own. Every plea for civil liberties and individual rights, every protest against exploitation and humiliation, against the encroachment of public authority, or the mass hypnosis of custom or organized propaganda, springs from this individualistic, and much disputed, conception of man.

Three facts about this position may be noted. In the first place Mill confuses two distinct notions. One is that all coercion is, in so far as it frustrates human desires, bad as such, although it may have to be applied to prevent other, greater evils; while non-interference, which is the opposite of coercion, is good as such, although it is not the only good. This is the 'negative' conception of liberty in its classical form. The other is that men should seek to discover the truth, or to develop a certain type of character of which Mill approved – critical, original, imaginative, independent, non-conforming to the point of eccentricity, and so on – and that truth can be found, and such character can be bred, only in conditions of freedom. Both these are liberal views, but they are not identical, and the connexion between them is, at best, empirical. No one would argue that truth or freedom of self-expression could flourish where dogma crushes all thought. But the evidence of history tends to show (as, indeed, was argued by James Stephen in his formidable attack on Mill in his *Liberty, Equality, Fraternity*) that integrity, love of truth, and fiery individualism grow at least as often in severely disciplined communities among, for example, the puritan Calvinists of Scotland or New England, or under military discipline, as in more tolerant or indifferent societies; and if this is so, Mill's argument for liberty as a necessary condition for the growth of human genius falls to the ground. If his two goals proved incompatible, Mill would be faced with a cruel dilemma, quite apart from the further difficulties created by the inconsistency of his doctrines with strict utilitarianism, even in his own humane version of it.[6]

In the second place, the doctrine is comparatively modern. There seems to be scarcely any discussion of individual liberty as a conscious political ideal (as opposed to its actual existence) in the ancient world. Condorcet had already remarked that the notion of individual rights was absent from the legal conceptions of the Romans and Greeks; this seems to hold equally of the Jewish, Chinese, and all other ancient civilizations that have since come to light.[7] The domination of this ideal has been the exception rather than the rule, even in the recent history of the West. Nor has liberty in this sense often formed a rallying cry for the great masses of mankind. The desire not to be impinged upon, to be left to oneself, has been a mark of high civilization both on the part of individuals and communities. The sense of privacy itself, of the area of personal relationships as something sacred in its own right, derives from a conception of freedom which, for all its religious roots, is scarcely older, in its developed state, than the Renaissance or the Reformation.[8] Yet its decline would mark the death of a civilization, of an entire moral outlook.

The third characteristic of this notion of liberty is of greater importance. It is that liberty in this sense is not incompatible with some kinds of autocracy, or at any rate with the absence of self-government. Liberty in this sense is principally concerned with the area of control, not with its source. Just as a democracy may, in fact, deprive the individual citizen of a great many liberties which he might have in some other form of society, so it is perfectly conceivable that a liberal-minded despot would allow his subjects a large measure of personal freedom. The despot who leaves his subjects a wide area of liberty may be unjust, or encourage the wildest inequalities, care little for order, or virtue, or knowledge; but provided he does not curb their liberty, or at least curbs it less than many other régimes, he meets with Mill's specification.[9] Freedom in this sense is not, at any rate logically, connected with democracy or self-government. Self-government may, on the whole, provide a better guarantee of the preservation of civil liberties than other régimes, and has been defended as such by libertarians. But there is no necessary connexion between individual liberty and democratic rule. The answer to the question 'Who governs me?' is logically distinct from the question 'How far does government interfere with me?' It is in this difference that the great contrast between the two concepts of negative and positive liberty, in the end, consists.[10] For the 'positive' sense of liberty comes to light if we try to answer the question, not 'What am I free to do or be?', but 'By whom am I ruled?' or 'Who is to say what I am, and what I am not, to be or do?' The connexion between democracy and individual liberty is a good deal more tenuous than it seemed to many advocates of both. The desire to be governed by myself, or at any rate to participate in the process by which my life is to be controlled, may be as deep a wish as that of a free area for action, and perhaps historically older. But it is not a desire for the same thing. So different is it, indeed, as to have led in the end to the great clash of ideologies that dominates our world. For it is this – the 'positive' conception of liberty: not freedom from, but freedom to – to lead one prescribed form of life – which the adherents of the 'negative' notion represent as being, at times, no better than a specious disguise for brutal tyranny.

II

The Notion of Positive Freedom

The 'positive' sense of the word 'liberty' derives from the wish on the part of the individual to be his own master. I wish my life and decisions to depend on myself, not on external forces of whatever kind. I wish to be the instrument of my own, not of other men's, acts of will. I wish to be a subject, not an object; to be moved by reasons, by conscious purposes, which are my own, not by causes which affect me, as it were, from outside. I wish to be somebody, not nobody; a doer – deciding, not being decided for, self-directed and not acted upon by external nature or by other men as if I were a thing, or an animal, or a slave incapable of playing a human role, that is, of conceiving goals and policies of my own and realizing them. This is at least part of what I mean when I say that I am rational, and that it is my reason that distinguishes me as a human being from the rest of the world. I wish, above all, to be conscious of myself as a thinking, willing, active being, bearing responsibility for my choices and able to explain them by references to my own ideas and purposes. I feel free to the degree that I believe this to be true, and enslaved to the degree that I am made to realize that it is not.

The freedom which consists in being one's own master, and the freedom which consists in not being prevented from choosing as I do by other men, may, on the face of it, seem concepts at no great logical distance from each other – no more than negative and positive ways of saying much the same thing. Yet the 'positive' and 'negative' notions of freedom historically developed in divergent directions not always by logically reputable steps, until, in the end, they came into direct conflict with each other.

One way of making this clear is in terms of the independent momentum which the, initially perhaps quite harmless, metaphor of self-mastery acquired. 'I am my own master'; 'I am slave to no man'; but may I not (as Platonists or Hegelians tend to say) be a slave to nature? Or to my own 'unbridled' passions? Are these not so many species of the identical genus 'slave' – some political or legal, others moral or spiritual? Have not men had the experience of liberating themselves from spiritual slavery, or slavery to nature, and do they not in the course of it become aware, on the one hand, of a self which dominates, and, on the other, of something in them which is brought to heel? This dominant self is then variously identified with reason, with my 'higher nature', with the self which calculates and aims at what will satisfy it in the long run, with my 'real', or 'ideal', or 'autonomous' self, or with my self 'at its best'; which is then contrasted with irrational impulse, uncontrolled desires, my 'lower' nature, the pursuit of immediate pleasures, my 'empirical' or 'heteronomous' self, swept by every gust of desire and passion, needing to be rigidly disciplined if it is ever to rise to the full height of its 'real' nature. Presently the two selves may be represented as divided by an even larger gap: the real self may be conceived as something wider than the individual (as the term is normally understood), as a social 'whole' of which the individual is an element or aspect: a tribe, a race, a church, a state, the great society of the living and the dead and the yet unborn. This entity is then identified as being the 'true' self which, by imposing its collective, or 'organic', single will upon its recalcitrant 'members', achieves its own, and therefore their, 'higher' freedom. The perils of using organic metaphors to justify the coercion of some men by others in order to raise them to a 'higher' level of freedom have often been pointed out. But what gives such plausibility as it has to this kind of language is that we recognize that it is possible, and at times justifiable, to coerce men in the name of some goal (let us say, justice or public health) which they would, if they were more enlightened, themselves pursue, but do not, because they are blind or ignorant or corrupt. This renders it easy for me to conceive of myself as coercing others for their own sake, in their, not my, interest. I am then claiming that I know what they truly need better than they know it themselves. What, at most, this entails is that they would not resist me if they were rational and as wise as I and understood their interests as I do. But I may go on to claim a good deal more than this. I may declare that they are actually aiming at what in their benighted state they consciously resist, because there exists within them an occult entity – their latent rational will, or their 'true' purpose – and that this entity, although it is belied by all that they overtly feel and do and say, is their 'real' self, of which the poor empirical self in space and time may know nothing or little; and that this inner spirit is the only self that deserves to have its wishes taken into account.[11] Once I take this view, I am in a position to ignore the actual wishes of men or societies, to bully, oppress, torture them in the name, and on behalf, of their 'real' selves, in the secure knowledge that whatever is the true goal of man (happiness, performance of duty, wisdom, a just society, self-fulfilment) must be identical with his freedom – the free choice of his 'true', albeit often submerged and inarticulate, self.

This paradox has been often exposed. It is one thing to say that I know what is good for X, while he himself does not; and even to ignore his wishes for its – and his – sake; and a very different one to say that he has *eo ipso* chosen it, not indeed consciously, not as he seems in everyday life, but in his role as a rational self which his empirical self may not know – the 'real' self which discerns the good, and cannot help choosing it once it is revealed. This monstrous impersonation, which consists in equating what X would choose if he were something he is not, or at least not yet, with what X actually seeks and chooses, is at the heart of all political theories of self-realization. It is one thing to say that I may be coerced for my own good which I am too blind to see: this may, on occasion, be for my benefit; indeed it may enlarge the scope of my liberty. It is another to say that if it is my good, then I am not being coerced, for I have willed it, whether I know this or not, and am free (or 'truly' free) even while my poor earthly body and foolish mind bitterly reject it, and struggle against those who seek however benevolently to impose it, with the greatest desperation.

This magical transformation, or sleight of hand (for which William James so justly mocked the Hegelians), can no doubt be perpetrated just as easily with the 'negative' concept of freedom, where the self that should not be interfered with is no longer the individual with his actual wishes and needs as they are normally conceived, but the 'real' man within, identified with the pursuit of some ideal purpose not dreamed of by his empirical self. And, as in the case of the 'positively' free self, this entity may be inflated into some super-personal entity – a state, a class, a nation, or the march of history itself, regarded as a more 'real' subject of attributes than the empirical self. But the 'positive' conception of freedom as self-

mastery, with its suggestion of a man divided against himself, has, in fact, and as a matter of history, of doctrine and of practice, lent itself more easily to this splitting of personality into two: the transcendent, dominant controller, and the empirical bundle of desires and passions to be disciplined and brought to heel. It is this historical fact that has been influential. This demonstrates (if demonstration of so obvious a truth is needed) that conceptions of freedom directly derive from views of what constitutes a self, a person, a man. Enough manipulation with the definition of man, and freedom can be made to mean whatever the manipulator wishes. Recent history has made it only too clear that the issue is not merely academic.

The consequences of distinguishing between two selves will become even clearer if one considers the two major forms which the desire to be self-directed – directed by one's 'true' self – has historically taken: the first, that of self-abnegation in order to attain independence; the second, that of self-realization, or total self-identification with a specific principle or ideal in order to attain the selfsame end.

III

The Retreat to the Inner Citadel

I am the possessor of reason and will; I conceive ends and I desire to pursue them; but if I am prevented from attaining them I no longer feel master of the situation. I may be prevented by the laws of nature, or by accidents, or the activities of men, or the effect, often undesigned, of human institutions. These forces may be too much for me. What am I to do to avoid being crushed by them? I must liberate myself from desires that I know I cannot realize. I wish to be master of my kingdom, but my frontiers are long and insecure, therefore I contract them in order to reduce or eliminate the vulnerable area. I begin by desiring happiness, or power, or knowledge, or the attainment of some specific object. But I cannot command them. I choose to avoid defeat and waste, and therefore decide to strive for nothing that I cannot be sure to obtain. I determine myself not to desire what is unattainable. The tyrant threatens me with the destruction of my property, with imprisonment, with the exile or death of those I love. But if I no longer feel attached to property, no longer care whether or not I am in prison, if I have killed within myself my natural affections, then he cannot bend me to his will, for all that is left of myself is no longer subject to empirical fears or desires. It is as if I had performed a strategic retreat into an inner citadel – my reason, my soul, my 'noumenal' self – which, do what they may, neither external blind force, nor human malice, can touch. I have withdrawn into myself; there, and there alone, I am secure. It is as if I were to say: 'I have a wound in my leg. There are two methods of freeing myself from pain. One is to heal the wound. But if the cure is too difficult or uncertain, there is another method. I can get rid of the wound by cutting off my leg. If I train myself to want nothing to which the possession of my leg is indispensable, I shall not feel the lack of it.' This is the traditional self-emancipation of ascetics and quietists, of stoics or Buddhist sages, men of various religions or of none, who have fled the world, and escaped the yoke of society or public opinion, by some process of deliberate self-transformation that enables them to care no longer for any of its values, to remain, isolated and independent, on its edges, no longer vulnerable to its weapons.[12] All political isolationism, all economic autarky, every form of autonomy, has in it some element of this attitude. I eliminate the obstacles in my path by abandoning the path; I retreat into my own sect, my own planned economy, my own deliberately insulated territory, where no voices from outside need be listened to, and no external forces can have effect. This is a form of the search for security; but it has also been called the search for personal or national freedom or independence.

From this doctrine, as it applies to individuals, it is no very great distance to the conceptions of those who, like Kant, identify freedom not indeed with the elimination of desires, but with resistance to them, and control over them. I identify myself with the controller and escape the slavery of the controlled. I am free because, and in so far as, I am autonomous. I obey laws, but I have imposed them on, or found them in, my own uncoerced self. Freedom is obedience, but 'obedience to a law which we prescribe to ourselves', and no man can enslave himself. Heteronomy is dependence on outside factors, liability to be a plaything of the external world that I cannot myself fully control, and which *pro tanto* controls and 'enslaves' me. I am free only to the degree to which my person is 'fettered' by nothing that

obeys forces over which I have no control; I cannot control the laws of nature; my free activity must therefore, *ex hypothesi*, be lifted above the empirical world of causality. This is not the place in which to discuss the validity of this ancient and famous doctrine; I only wish to remark that the related notions of freedom as resistance to (or escape from) unrealizable desire, and as independence of the sphere of causality, have played a central role in politics no less than in ethics.

For if the essence of men is that they are autonomous beings – authors of values, of ends in themselves, the ultimate authority of which consists precisely in the fact that they are willed freely – then nothing is worse than to treat them as if they were not autonomous, but natural objects, played on by causal influences, creatures at the mercy of external stimuli, whose choices can be manipulated by their rulers, whether by threats of force or offers of rewards. To treat men in this way is to treat them as if they were not self-determined. 'Nobody may compel me to be happy in his own way', said Kant. 'Paternalism is the greatest despotism imaginable.' This is so because it is to treat men as if they were not free, but human material for me, the benevolent reformer, to mould in accordance with my own, not their, freely adopted purpose. This is, of course, precisely the policy that the early utilitarians recommended. Helvétius (and Bentham) believed not in resisting, but in using, men's tendency to be slaves to their passions; they wished to dangle rewards and punishments before men – the acutest possible form of heteronomy – if by this means the 'slaves' might be made happier.[13] But to manipulate men, to propel them towards goals which you – the social reformer – see, but they may not, is to deny their human essence, to treat them as objects without wills of their own, and therefore to degrade them. That is why to lie to men, or to deceive them, that is, to use them as means for my, not their own, independently conceived ends, even if it is for their own benefit, is, in effect, to treat them as sub-human, to behave as if their ends are less ultimate and sacred than my own. In the name of what can I ever be justified in forcing men to do what they have not willed or consented to? Only in the name of some value higher than themselves. But if, as Kant held, all values are made so by the free acts of men, and called values only so far as they are this, there is no value higher than the individual. Therefore to do this is to coerce men in the name of something less ultimate than themselves – to bend them to my will, or to someone else's particular craving for (his or their) happiness or expediency or security or convenience. I am aiming at something desired (from whatever motive, no matter how noble) by me or my group, to which I am using other men as means. But this is a contradiction of what I know men to be, namely ends in themselves. All forms of tampering with human beings, getting at them, shaping them against their will to your own pattern, all thought control and conditioning,[14] is, therefore, a denial of that in men which makes them men and their values ultimate.

Kant's free individual is a transcendent being, beyond the realm of natural causality. But in its empirical form – in which the notion of man is that of ordinary life – this doctrine was the heart of liberal humanism, both moral and political, that was deeply influenced both by Kant and by Rousseau in the eighteenth century. In its *a priori* version it is a form of secularized Protestant individualism, in which the place of God is taken by the conception of the rational life, and the place of the individual soul which strains towards union with Him is replaced by the conception of the individual, endowed with reason, straining to be governed by reason and reason alone, and to depend upon nothing that might deflect or delude him by engaging his irrational nature. Autonomy, not heteronomy: to act and not to be acted upon. The notion of slavery to the passions is – for those who think in these terms – more than a metaphor. To rid myself of fear, or love, or the desire to conform is to liberate myself from the despotism of something which I cannot control. Sophocles, whom Plato reports as saying that old age alone has liberated him from the passion of love – the yoke of a cruel master – is reporting an experience as real as that of liberation from a human tyrant or slave owner. The psychological experience of observing myself yielding to some 'lower' impulse, acting from a motive that I dislike, or of doing something which at the very moment of doing I may detest, and reflecting later that I was 'not myself', or 'not in control of myself', when I did it, belongs to this way of thinking and speaking. I identify myself with my critical and rational moments. The consequences of my acts cannot matter, for they are not in my control; only my motives are. This is the creed of the solitary thinker who has defied the world and emancipated himself from the chains of men and

things. In this form, the doctrine may seem primarily an ethical creed, and scarcely political at all; nevertheless, its political implications are clear, and it enters into the tradition of liberal individualism at least as deeply as the 'negative' concept of freedom.

It is perhaps worth remarking that in its individualistic form the concept of the rational sage who has escaped into the inner fortress of his true self seems to arise when the external world has proved exceptionally arid, cruel, or unjust. 'He is truly free', said Rousseau, 'who desires what he can perform, and does what he desires.' In a world where a man seeking happiness or justice or freedom (in whatever sense) can do little, because he finds too many avenues of action blocked to him, the temptation to withdraw into himself may become irresistible. It may have been so in Greece, where the Stoic ideal cannot be wholly unconnected with the fall of the independent democracies before centralized Macedonian autocracy. It was so in Rome, for analogous reasons, after the end of the Republic.[15] It arose in Germany in the seventeenth century, during the period of the deepest national degradation of the German states that followed the Thirty Years War, when the character of public life, particularly in the small principalities, forced those who prized the dignity of human life, not for the first or last time, into a kind of inner emigration. The doctrine that maintains that what I cannot have I must teach myself not to desire; that a desire eliminated, or successfully resisted, is as good as a desire satisfied, is a sublime, but, it seems to me, unmistakable, form of the doctrine of sour grapes: what I cannot be sure of, I cannot truly want.

This makes it clear why the definition of negative liberty as the ability to do what one wishes – which is, in effect, the definition adopted by Mill – will not do. If I find that I am able to do little or nothing of what I wish, I need only contract or extinguish my wishes, and I am made free. If the tyrant (or 'hidden persuader') manages to condition his subjects (or customers) into losing their original wishes and embrace ('internalize') the form of life he has invented for them, he will, on this definition, have succeeded in liberating them. He will, no doubt, have made them *feel* free – as Epictetus feels freer than his master (and the proverbial good man is said to feel happy on the rack). But what he has created is the very antithesis of political freedom.

Ascetic self-denial may be a source of integrity

or serenity and spiritual strength, but it is difficult to see how it can be called an enlargement of liberty. If I save myself from an adversary by retreating indoors and locking every entrance and exit, I may remain freer than if I had been captured by him, but am I freer than if I had defeated or captured him? If I go too far, contract myself into too small a space, I shall suffocate and die. The logical culmination of the process of destroying everything through which I can possibly be wounded is suicide. While I exist in the natural world, I can never be wholly secure. Total liberation in this sense (as Schopenhauer correctly perceived) is conferred only by death.[16]

I find myself in a world in which I meet with obstacles to my will. Those who are wedded to the 'negative' concept of freedom may perhaps be forgiven if they think that self-abnegation is not the only method of overcoming obstacles; that it is also possible to do so by removing them: in the case of non-human objects, by physical action; in the case of human resistance, by force or persuasion, as when I induce somebody to make room for me in his carriage, or conquer a country which threatens the interests of my own. Such acts may be unjust, they may involve violence, cruelty, the enslavement of others, but it can scarcely be denied that thereby the agent is able in the most literal sense to increase his own freedom. It is an irony of history that this truth is repudiated by some of those who practise it most forcibly, men who, even while they conquer power and freedom of action, reject the 'negative' concept of it in favour of its 'positive' counterpart. Their view rules over half our world; let us see upon what metaphysical foundation it rests.

IV

Self-realization

The only true method of attaining freedom, we are told, is by the use of critical reason, the understanding of what is necessary and what is contingent. If I am a schoolboy, all but the simplest truths of mathematics obtrude themselves as obstacles to the free functioning of my mind, as theorems whose necessity I do not understand; they are pronounced to be true by some external authority, and present themselves to me as foreign bodies which I am expected mechanically to absorb into my system. But when I understand the functions of the symbols, the axioms, the formation and transformation rules – the logic whereby the conclusions are obtained – and grasp that these things cannot be otherwise, because they appear to follow from the laws that govern the processes of my own reason,[17] then mathematical truths no longer obtrude themselves as external entities forced upon me which I must receive whether I want it or not, but as something which I now freely will in the course of the natural functioning of my own rational activity. For the mathematician, the proof of these theorems is part of the free exercise of his natural reasoning capacity. For the musician, after he has assimilated the pattern of the composer's score, and has made the composer's ends his own, the playing of the music is not obedience to external laws, a compulsion and a barrier to liberty, but a free, unimpeded exercise. The player is not bound to the score as an ox to the plough, or a factory worker to the machine. He has absorbed the score into his own system, has, by understanding it, identified it with himself, has changed it from an impediment to free activity into an element in that activity itself. What applies to music or mathematics must, we are told, in principle apply to all other obstacles which present themselves as so many lumps of external stuff blocking free self-development. That is the programme of enlightened rationalism from Spinoza to the latest (at times unconscious) disciples of Hegel. *Sapere aude*. What you know, that of which you understand the necessity – the rational necessity – you cannot, while remaining rational, want to be otherwise. For to want something to be other than what it must be is, given the premisses – the necessities that govern the world – to be *pro tanto* either ignorant or irrational. Passions, prejudices, fears, neuroses, spring from ignorance, and take the form of myths and illusions. To be ruled by myths, whether they spring from the vivid imaginations of unscrupulous charlatans who deceive us in order to exploit us, or from psychological or sociological causes, is a form of heteronomy, of being dominated by outside factors in a direction not necessarily willed by the agent. The scientific determinists of the eighteenth century supposed that the study of the sciences of nature, and the creation of sciences of society on the same model, would make the operation of such causes transparently clear, and thus enable individuals to recognize their own part in the working of a rational world, frustrating only when misunderstood.

Knowledge liberates, as Epicurus taught long ago, by automatically eliminating irrational fears and desires.

Herder, Hegel, and Marx substituted their own vitalistic models of social life for the older, mechanical ones, but believed, no less than their opponents, that to understand the world is to be freed. They merely differed from them in stressing the part played by change and growth in what made human beings human. Social life could not be understood by an analogy drawn from mathematics or physics. One must also understand history, that is, the peculiar laws of continuous growth, whether by 'dialectical' conflict or otherwise, that govern individuals and groups, in their interplay with each other and with nature. Not to grasp this is, according to these thinkers, to fall into a particular kind of error, namely the belief that human nature is static, that its essential properties are the same everywhere and at all times, that it is governed by unvarying natural laws, whether they are conceived in theological or materialistic terms, which entails the fallacious corollary that a wise lawgiver can, in principle, create a perfectly harmonious society at any time by appropriate education and legislation, because rational men, in all ages and countries, must always demand the same unaltering satisfactions of the same unaltering basic needs. Hegel believed that his contemporaries (and indeed all his predecessors) misunderstood the nature of institutions because they did not understand the laws – the rationally intelligible laws, since they spring from the operation of reason – that create and alter institutions and transform human character and human action. Marx and his disciples maintained that the path of human beings was obstructed not only by natural forces, or the imperfections of their own character, but, even more, by the workings of their own social institutions, which they had originally created (not always consciously) for certain purposes, but whose functioning they systematically came to misconceive[18], and which thereupon became obstacles in their creators' progress. He offered social and economic hypotheses to account for the inevitability of such misunderstanding, in particular of the illusion that such man-made arrangements were independent forces, as inescapable as the laws of nature. As instances of such pseudo-objective forces, he pointed to the laws of supply and demand, or of the institution of property, or of the eternal division of society into rich and poor, or owners and workers, as so many unaltering human categories. Not until we had reached a stage at which the spells of these illusions could be broken, that is, until enough men reached a social stage that alone enabled them to understand that these laws and institutions were themselves the work of human minds and hands, historically needed in their day, and later mistaken for inexorable, objective powers, could the old world be destroyed, and more adequate and liberating social machinery substituted.

We are enslaved by despots – institutions or beliefs or neuroses – which can be removed only by being analysed and understood. We are imprisoned by evil spirits which we have ourselves – albeit not consciously – created, and can exorcize them only by becoming conscious and acting appropriately: indeed, for Marx understanding *is* appropriate action. I am free if, and only if, I plan my life in accordance with my own will; plans entail rules; a rule does not oppress me or enslave me if I impose it on myself consciously, or accept it freely, having understood it, whether it was invented by me or by others, provided that it is rational, that is to say, conforms to the necessities of things. To understand why things must be as they must be is to will them to be so. Knowledge liberates not by offering us more open possibilities amongst which we can make our choice, but by preserving us from the frustration of attempting the impossible. To want necessary laws to be other than they are is to be prey to an irrational desire – a desire that what must be X should also be not X. To go further, and believe these laws to be other than what they necessarily are, is to be insane. That is the metaphysical heart of rationalism. The notion of liberty contained in it is not the 'negative' conception of a field (ideally) without obstacles, a vacuum in which nothing obstructs me, but the notion of self-direction or self-control. I can do what I will with my own. I am a rational being; whatever I can demonstrate to myself as being necessary, as incapable of being otherwise in a rational society – that is, in a society directed by rational minds, towards goals such as a rational being would have – I cannot, being rational, wish to sweep out of my way. I assimilate it into my substance as I do the laws of logic, of mathematics, of physics, the rule of art, the principles that govern everything of which I understand, and therefore will, the rational purpose, by which I can never be thwarted, since I cannot want it to be other than it is.

This is the positive doctrine of liberation by reason. Socialized forms of it, widely disparate and opposed to each other as they are, are at the heart of many of the nationalist, communist, authoritarian, and totalitarian creeds of our day. It may, in the course of its evolution, have wandered far from its rationalist moorings. Nevertheless, it is this freedom that, in democracies and in dictatorships, is argued about, and fought for, in many parts of the earth today. Without attempting to trace the historical evolution of this idea, I should like to comment on some of its vicissitudes.

V

The Temple of Sarastro

Those who believed in freedom as rational self-direction were bound, sooner or later, to consider how this was to be applied not merely to a man's inner life, but to his relations with other members of his society. Even the most individualistic among them – and Rousseau, Kant, and Fichte certainly began as individualists – came at some point to ask themselves whether a rational life not only for the individual, but also for society, was possible, and if so, how it was to be achieved. I wish to be free to live as my rational will (my 'real self') commands, but so must others be. How am I to avoid collisions with their wills? Where is the frontier that lies between my (rationally determined) rights and the identical rights of others? For if I am rational, I cannot deny that what is right for me must, for the same reasons, be right for others who are rational like me. A rational (or free) state would be a state governed by such laws as all rational men would freely accept; that is to say, such laws as they would themselves have enacted had they been asked what, as rational beings, they demanded; hence the frontiers would be such as all rational men would consider to be the right frontiers for rational beings. But who, in fact, was to determine what these frontiers were? Thinkers of this type argued that if moral and political problems were genuine – as surely they were – they must in principle be soluble; that is to say, there must exist one and only one true solution to any problem. All truths could in principle be discovered by any rational thinker, and demonstrated so clearly that all other rational men could not but accept them; indeed, this was

already to a large extent the case in the new natural sciences. On this assumption, the problem of political liberty was soluble by establishing a just order that would give to each man all the freedom to which a rational being was entitled. My claim to unfettered freedom can prima facie at times not be reconciled with your equally unqualified claim; but the rational solution of one problem cannot collide with the equally true solution of another, for two truths cannot logically be incompatible; therefore a just order must in principle be discoverable – an order of which the rules make possible correct solutions to all possible problems that could arise in it. This ideal, harmonious state of affairs was sometimes imagined as a Garden of Eden before the Fall of Man, from which we were expelled, but for which we were still filled with longing; or as a golden age still before us, in which men, having become rational, will no longer be 'other-directed', nor 'alienate' or frustrate one another. In existing societies justice and equality are ideals which still call for some measure of coercion, because the premature lifting of social controls might lead to the oppression of the weaker and the stupider by the stronger or abler or more energetic and unscrupulous. But it is only irrationality on the part of men (according to this doctrine) that leads them to wish to oppress or exploit or humiliate one another. Rational men will respect the principle of reason in each other, and lack all desire to fight or dominate one another. The desire to dominate is itself a symptom of irrationality, and can be explained and cured by rational methods. Spinoza offers one kind of explanation and remedy, Hegel another, Marx a third. Some of these theories may perhaps, to some degree, supplement each other, others are not combinable. But they all assume that in a society of perfectly rational beings the lust for domination over men will be absent or ineffective. The existence of, or craving for, oppression will be the first symptom that the true solution to the problems of social life has not been reached.

This can be put in another way. Freedom is self-mastery, the elimination of obstacles to my will, whatever these obstacles may be – the resistance of nature, of my ungoverned passions, of irrational institutions, of the opposing wills or behaviour of others. Nature I can, at least in principle, always mould by technical means, and shape to my will. But how am I to treat recalcitrant human beings? I must, if I can, impose my will on them too, 'mould' them to my pattern, cast parts for them in my play. But will this not mean that I alone am free, while they are slaves? They will be so if my plan has nothing to do with their wishes or values, only with my own. But if my plan is fully rational, it will allow for the full development of their 'true' natures, the realization of their capacities for rational decisions 'for making the best of themselves' – as a part of the realization of my own 'true' self. All true solutions to all genuine problems must be compatible: more than this, they must fit into a single whole: for this is what is meant by calling them all rational and the universe harmonious. Each man has his specific character, abilities, aspirations, ends. If I grasp both what these ends and natures are, and how they all relate to one another, I can, at least in principle, if I have the knowledge and the strength, satisfy them all, so long as the nature and the purposes in question are rational. Rationality is knowing things and people for what they are: I must not use stones to make violins, nor try to make born violin players play flutes. If the universe is governed by reason, then there will be no need for coercion; a correctly planned life for all will coincide with full freedom – the freedom of rational self-direction – for all. This will be so if, and only if, the plan is the true plan – the one unique pattern which alone fulfils the claims of reason. Its laws will be the rules which reason prescribes: they will only seem irksome to those whose reason is dormant, who do not understand the true 'needs' of their own 'real' selves. So long as each player recognizes and plays the part set him by reason – the faculty that understands his true nature and discerns his true ends – there can be no conflict. Each man will be a liberated, self-directed actor in the cosmic drama. Thus Spinoza tells us that 'children, although they are coerced, are not slaves', because 'they obey orders given in their own interests', and that 'The subject of a true commonwealth is no slave, because the common interests must include his own.' Similarly, Locke says 'Where there is no law there is no freedom', because rational laws are directions to a man's 'proper interests' or 'general good'; and adds that since such laws are what 'hedges us from bogs and precipices' they 'ill deserve the name of confinement', and speaks of desires to escape from such laws as being irrational, forms of 'licence', as 'brutish', and so on. Montesquieu, forgetting his liberal moments, speaks of political liberty as

being not permission to do what we want, or even what the law allows, but only 'the power of doing what we ought to will', which Kant virtually repeats. Burke proclaims the individual's 'right' to be restrained in his own interest, because 'the presumed consent of every rational creature is in unison with the predisposed order of things'. The common assumption of these thinkers (and of many a schoolman before them and Jacobin and Communist after them) is that the rational ends of our 'true' natures must coincide, or be made to coincide, however violently our poor, ignorant, desire-ridden, passionate, empirical selves may cry out against this process. Freedom is not freedom to do what is irrational, or stupid, or wrong. To force empirical selves into the right pattern is no tyranny, but liberation.[19] Rousseau tells me that if I freely surrender all the parts of my life to society, I create an entity which, because it has been built by an equality of sacrifice of all its members, cannot wish to hurt any one of them; in such a society, we are informed, it can be nobody's interest to damage anyone else. 'In giving myself to all, I give myself to none', and get back as much as I lose, with enough new force to preserve my new gains. Kant tells us that when 'the individual has entirely abandoned his wild, lawless freedom, to find it again, unimpaired, in a state of dependence according to law', that alone is true freedom, 'for this dependence is the work of my own will acting as a lawgiver'. Liberty, so far from being incompatible with authority, becomes virtually identical with it. This is the thought and language of all the declarations of the rights of man in the eighteenth century, and of all those who look upon society as a design constructed according to the rational laws of the wise lawgiver, or of nature, or of history, or of the Supreme Being. Bentham, almost alone, doggedly went on repeating that the business of laws was not to liberate but to restrain: 'Every law is an infraction of liberty' – even if such 'infraction' leads to an increase of the sum of liberty.

If the underlying assumptions had been correct – if the method of solving social problems resembled the way in which solutions to the problems of the natural sciences are found, and if reason were what rationalists said that it was, all this would perhaps follow. In the ideal case, liberty coincides with law: autonomy with authority. A law which forbids me to do what I could not, as a sane being, conceivably wish to do is not a restraint of my freedom. In the ideal society, composed of wholly responsible beings, rules, because I should scarcely be conscious of them, would gradually wither away. Only one social movement was bold enough to render this assumption quite explicit and accept its consequences – that of the Anarchists. But all forms of liberalism founded on a rationalist metaphysics are less or more watered-down versions of this creed.

In due course, the thinkers who bent their energies to the solution of the problem on these lines came to be faced with the question of how in practice men were to be made rational in this way. Clearly they must be educated. For the uneducated are irrational, heteronomous, and need to be coerced, if only to make life tolerable for the rational if they are to live in the same society and not be compelled to withdraw to a desert or some Olympian height. But the uneducated cannot be expected to understand or co-operate with the purposes of their educators. Education, says Fichte, must inevitably work in such a way that 'you will later recognize the reasons for what I am doing now'. Children cannot be expected to understand why they are compelled to go to school, nor the ignorant – that is, for the moment, the majority of mankind – why they are made to obey the laws that will presently make them rational. 'Compulsion is also a kind of education.' You learn the great virtue of obedience to superior persons. If you cannot understand your own interests as a rational being, I cannot be expected to consult you, or abide by your wishes, in the course of making you rational. I must, in the end, force you to be protected against smallpox, even though you may not wish it. Even Mill is prepared to say that I may forcibly prevent a man from crossing a bridge if there is not time to warn him that it is about to collapse, for I know, or am justified in assuming, that he cannot wish to fall into the water. Fichte knows what the uneducated German of his time wishes to be or do better than he can possibly know them for himself. The sage knows you better than you know yourself, for you are the victim of your passions, a slave living a heteronomous life, purblind, unable to understand your true goals. You want to be a human being. It is the aim of the state to satisfy your wish. 'Compulsion is justified by education for future insight.' The reason within me, if it is to triumph, must eliminate and suppress my 'lower' instincts, my passions and desires, which render me a slave; similarly (the fatal transition from individual to social concepts is almost imperceptible) the higher elements in society – the better educated, the more rational, those who 'possess the highest insight of their time and people' – may exercise compulsion to rationalize the irrational section of society. For – so Hegel, Bradley, Bosanquet have often assured us – by obeying the rational man we obey ourselves: not indeed as we are, sunk in our ignorance and our passions, weak creatures afflicted by diseases that need a healer, wards who require a guardian, but as we could be if we were rational; as we could be even now, if only we would listen to the rational element which is, *ex hypothesi*, within every human being who deserves the name.

The philosophers of 'Objective Reason', from the tough, rigidly centralized, 'organic' state of Fichte, to the mild and humane liberalism of T.H. Green, certainly supposed themselves to be fulfilling, and not resisting, the rational demands which, however inchoate, were to be found in the breast of every sentient being. But I may reject such democratic optimism, and turning away from the teleological determinism of the Hegelians towards some more voluntarist philosophy, conceive the idea of imposing on my society – for its own betterment – a plan of my own, which in my rational wisdom I have elaborated; and which, unless I act on my own, perhaps against the permanent wishes of the vast majority of my fellow citizens, may never come to fruition at all. Or, abandoning the concept of reason altogether, I may conceive myself as an inspired artist, who moulds men into patterns in the light of his unique vision, as painters combine colours or composers sounds; humanity is the raw material upon which I impose my creative will; even though men suffer and die in the process, they are lifted by it to a height to which they could never have risen without my coercive – but creative – violation of their lives. This is the argument used by every dictator, inquisitor, and bully who seeks some moral, or even aesthetic, justification for his conduct. I must do for men (or with them) what they cannot do for themselves, and I cannot ask their permission or consent, because they are in no condition to know what is best for them; indeed, what they will permit and accept may mean a life of contemptible mediocrity, or perhaps even their ruin and suicide. Let me quote from the true progenitor of the heroic doctrine, Fichte, once again: 'No one has . . . rights against reason.' 'Man is afraid of subordinating his subjectivity to the laws of reason. He prefers tradition or arbitrariness.' Nevertheless, subordinated he must be.[20] Fichte puts forward the claims of what he called reason; Napoleon, or Carlyle, or romantic authoritarians may worship other values, and see in their establishment by force the only path to 'true' freedom.

The same attitude was pointedly expressed by Auguste Comte, who asked 'If we do not allow free thinking in chemistry or biology, why should we allow it in morals or politics?' Why indeed? If it makes sense to speak of political truths – assertions of social ends which all men, because they are men, must, once they are discovered, agree to be such; and if, as Comte believed, scientific method will in due course reveal them; then what case is there for freedom of opinion or action – at least as an end in itself, and not merely as a stimulating intellectual climate, either for individuals or for groups? Why should any conduct be tolerated that is not authorized by appropriate experts? Comte put bluntly what had been implicit in the rationalist theory of politics from its ancient Greek beginnings. There can, in principle, be only one correct way of life; the wise lead it spontaneously, that is why they are called wise. The unwise must be dragged towards it by all the social means in the power of the wise; for why should demonstrable error be suffered to survive and breed? The immature and untutored must be made to say to themselves: 'Only the truth liberates, and the only way in which I can learn the truth is by doing blindly today, what you, who know it, order me, or coerce me, to do, in the certain knowledge that only thus will I arrive at your clear vision, and be free like you.'

We have wandered indeed from our liberal beginnings. This argument, employed by Fichte in his latest phase, and after him by other defenders of authority, from Victorian schoolmasters and colonial administrators to the latest nationalist or communist dictator, is precisely what the Stoic and Kantian morality protests against most bitterly in the name of the reason of the free individual following his own inner light. In this way the rationalist argument, with its assumption of the single true solution, has led by steps which, if not logically valid, are historically and psychologically intelligible, from an ethical doctrine of individual responsibility and individual self-perfection to an authoritarian state obedient to the directives of an *élite* of Platonic guardians.

What can have led to so strange a reversal – the transformation of Kant's severe individualism into something close to a pure totalitarian doctrine on the part of thinkers, some of whom claimed to be his disciples? This question is not of merely historical interest, for not a few contemporary liberals have gone through the same peculiar evolution. It is true that Kant insisted, following Rousseau, that a capacity for rational self-direction belonged to all men; that there could be no experts in moral matters, since morality was a matter not of specialized knowledge (as the utilitarians and *philosophes* had maintained), but of the correct use of a universal human faculty; and consequently that what made men free was not acting in certain self-improving ways, which they could be coerced to do, but knowing why they ought to do so, which nobody could do for, or on behalf of, anyone else. But even Kant, when he came to deal with political issues, conceded that no law, provided that it was such that I should, if I were asked, approve it as a rational being, could possibly deprive me of any portion of my rational freedom. With this the door was opened wide to the rule of experts. I cannot consult all men about all enactments all the time. The government cannot be a continuous plebiscite. Moreover, some men are not as well attuned to the voice of their own reason as others: some seem singularly deaf. If I am a legislator or a ruler, I must assume that if the law I impose is rational (and I can only consult my own reason) it will automatically be approved by all the members of my society so far as they are rational beings. For if they disapprove, they must, *pro tanto*, be irrational; then they will need to be repressed by reason: whether their own or mine cannot matter, for the pronouncements of reason must be the same in all minds. I issue my orders, and if you resist, take it upon myself to repress the irrational element in you which opposes reason. My task would be easier if you repressed it in yourself; I try to educate you to do so. But I am responsible for public welfare, I cannot wait until all men are wholly rational. Kant may protest that the essence of the subject's freedom is that he, and he alone, has given himself the order to obey. But this is a counsel of perfection. If you fail to discipline yourself, I must do so for you; and you cannot complain of lack of freedom, for the fact that Kant's rational judge has sent you to prison is evidence that you have not listened to your own inner reason, that, like a child, a savage, an idiot, you are not ripe for self-direction or permanently incapable of it.[21]

If this leads to despotism, albeit by the best or the wisest – to Sarastro's temple in the *Magic Flute* – but still despotism, which turns out to be identical with freedom, can it be that there is something amiss in the premises of the argument? that the basic assumptions are themselves somewhere at fault? Let me state them once more: first, that all men have one true purpose, and one only, that of rational self-direction; second, that the ends of all rational beings must of necessity fit into a single universal, harmonious pattern, which some men may be able to discern more clearly than others; third, that all conflict, and consequently all tragedy, is due solely to the clash of reason with the irrational or the insufficiently rational – the immature and undeveloped elements in life – whether individual or communal, and that such clashes are, in principle, avoidable, and for wholly rational beings impossible; finally, that when all men have been made rational, they will obey the rational laws of their own natures, which are one and the same in them all, and so be at once wholly law-abiding and wholly free. Can it be that Socrates and the creators of the central Western tradition in ethics and politics who followed him have been mistaken, for more than two millennia, that virtue is not knowledge, nor freedom identical with either? That despite the fact that it rules the lives of more men than ever before in its long history, not one of the basic assumptions of this famous view is demonstrable, or, perhaps, even true?

VI

The Search for Status

There is yet another historically important approach to this topic, which, by confounding liberty with her sisters, equality and fraternity, leads to similarly illiberal conclusions. Ever since the issue was raised towards the end of the eighteenth century, the question of what is meant by 'an individual' has been asked persistently, and with increasing effect. In so far as I live in society, everything that I do inevitably affects, and is affected by, what others do. Even Mill's strenuous effort to mark the distinction between the spheres of private and social life breaks down under examination. Virtually all Mill's critics

have pointed out that everything that I do may have results which will harm other human beings. Moreover, I am a social being in a deeper sense than that of interaction with others. For am I not what I am, to some degree, in virtue of what others think and feel me to be? When I ask myself what I am, and answer: an Englishman, a Chinese, a merchant, a man of no importance, a millionaire, a convict – I find upon analysis that to possess these attributes entails being recognized as belonging to a particular group or class by other persons in my society, and that this recognition is part of the meaning of most of the terms that denote some of my most personal and permanent characteristics. I am not disembodied reason. Nor am I Robinson Crusoe, alone upon his island. It is not only that my material life depends upon interaction with other men, or that I am what I am as a result of social forces, but that some, perhaps all, of my ideas about myself, in particular my sense of my own moral and social identity, are intelligible only in terms of the social network in which I am (the metaphor must not be pressed too far) an element. The lack of freedom about which men or groups complain amounts, as often as not, to the lack of proper recognition. I may be seeking not for what Mill would wish me to seek, namely security from coercion, arbitrary arrest, tyranny, deprivation of certain opportunities of action, or for room within which I am legally accountable to no one for my movements. Equally, I may not be seeking for a rational plan of social life, or the self-perfection of a dispassionate sage. What I may seek to avoid is simply being ignored, or patronized, or despised, or being taken too much for granted – in short, not being treated as an individual, having my uniqueness insufficiently recognized, being classed as a member of some featureless amalgam, a statistical unit without identifiable, specifically human features and purposes of my own. This is the degradation that I am fighting against – not equality of legal rights, nor liberty to do as I wish (although I may want these too), but for a condition in which I can feel that I am, because I am taken to be, a responsible agent, whose will is taken into consideration because I am entitled to it, even if I am attacked and persecuted for being what I am or choosing as I do. This is a hankering after status and recognition: 'The poorest he that is in England hath a life to live as the greatest he.' I desire to be understood and recognized, even if this means to be unpopular and disliked. And the only persons who can so recognize me, and thereby give me the sense of being someone, are the members of the society to which, historically, morally, economically, and perhaps ethnically, I feel that I belong.[22] My individual self is not something which I can detach from my relationship with others, or from those attributes of myself which consist in their attitude towards me. Consequently, when I demand to be liberated from, let us say, the status of political or social dependence, what I demand is an alteration of the attitude towards me of those whose opinions and behaviour help to determine my own image of myself. And what is true of the individual is true of groups, social, political, economic, religious, that is, of men conscious of needs and purposes which they have as members of such groups. What oppressed classes or nationalities, as a rule, demand is neither simply unhampered liberty of action for their members, nor, above everything, equality of social or economic opportunity, still less assignment of a place in a frictionless, organic state devised by the rational lawgiver. What they want, as often as not, is simply recognition (of their class or nation, or colour or race) as an independent source of human activity, as an entity with a will of its own, intending to act in accordance with it (whether it is good or legitimate, or not), and not to be ruled, educated, guided, with however light a hand, as being not quite fully human, and therefore not quite fully free. This gives a far wider than a purely rationalist sense to Kant's 'paternalism is the greatest despotism imaginable'. Paternalism is despotic, not because it is more oppressive than naked, brutal, unenlightened tyranny, nor merely because it ignores the transcendental reason embodied in me, but because it is an insult to my conception of myself as a human being, determined to make my own life in accordance with my own (not necessarily rational or benevolent) purposes, and, above all, entitled to be recognized as such by others. For if I am not so recognized, then I may fail to recognize, I may doubt, my own claim to be a fully independent human being. For what I am is, in large part, determined by what I feel and think; and what I feel and think is determined by the feeling and thought prevailing in the society to which I belong, of which, in Burke's sense, I form not an isolable atom, but an ingredient (to use a perilous but indispensable metaphor) in a social pattern. I may feel unfree in the sense of not being recognized as a self-governing individual human being; but I may feel it also as a member of an unrecognized or insufficiently respected group: then I wish for the emancipation of my entire class, or community, or nation, or race, or profession. So much can I desire this, that I may, in my bitter longing for status, prefer to be bullied and misgoverned by some member of my own race or social class, by whom I am, nevertheless, recognized as a man and a rival – that is as an equal – to being well and tolerantly treated by someone from some higher and remoter group, who does not recognize me for what I wish to feel myself to be. This is the heart of the great cry for recognition on the part of both individuals and groups, and in our own day, of professions and classes, nations and races. Although I may not get 'negative' liberty at the hands of the members of my own society, yet they are members of my own group; they understand me, as I understand them; and this understanding creates within me the sense of being somebody in the world. It is this desire for reciprocal recognition that leads the most authoritarian democracies to be, at times, consciously preferred by its members to the most enlightened oligarchies, or sometimes causes a member of some newly liberated Asian or African state to complain less today, when he is rudely treated by members of his own race or nation, than when he was governed by some cautious, just, gentle, well-meaning administrator from outside. Unless this phenomenon is grasped, the ideals and behaviour of entire peoples who, in Mill's sense of the word, suffer deprivation of elementary human rights, and who, with every appearance of sincerity, speak of enjoying more freedom than when they possessed a wider measure of these rights, becomes an unintelligible paradox.

Yet it is not with individual liberty, in either the 'negative' or in the 'positive' senses of the word, that this desire for status and recognition can easily be identified. It is something no less profoundly needed and passionately fought for by human beings – it is something akin to, but not itself, freedom; although it entails negative freedom for the entire group, it is more closely related to solidarity, fraternity, mutual understanding, need for association on equal terms, all of which are sometimes – but misleadingly – called social freedom. Social and political terms are necessarily vague. The attempt to make the vocabulary of politics too precise may render it useless. But it is no service to the truth to loosen usage beyond necessity. The essence of the notion of liberty, both in the 'positive' and the 'negative' senses, is the holding off of something or someone – of others who trespass on my field or assert their authority over me, or of obsessions, fears, neuroses, irrational forces – intruders and despots of one kind or another. The desire for recognition is a desire for something different: for union, closer understanding, integration of interests, a life of common dependence and common sacrifice. It is only the confusion of desire for liberty with this profound and universal craving for status and understanding, further confounded by being identified with the notion of social self-direction, where the self to be liberated is no longer the individual but the 'social whole', that makes it possible for men, while submitting to the authority of oligarchy or dictators, to claim that this in some sense liberates them.

Much has been written on the fallacy of regarding social groups as being literally persons or selves, whose control and discipline of their members is no more than self-discipline, voluntary self-control which leaves the individual agent free. But even on the 'organic' view, would it be natural or desirable to call the demand for recognition and status a demand for liberty in some third sense? It is true that the group from which recognition is sought must itself have a sufficient measure of 'negative' freedom – from control by any outside authority – otherwise recognition by it will not give the claimant the status he seeks. But is the struggle for higher status, the wish to escape from an inferior position, to be called a struggle for liberty? Is it mere pedantry to confine this word to the main senses discussed above, or are we, as I suspect, in danger of calling any improvement of his social situation favoured by a human being an increase of his liberty, and will this not render this term so vague and distended as to make it virtually useless? And yet we cannot simply dismiss this case as a mere confusion of the notion of freedom with that of status, or solidarity, or fraternity, or equality, or some combination of these. For the craving for status is, in certain respects, very close to the desire to be an independent agent.

We may refuse this goal the title of liberty; yet it would be a shallow view that assumed that analogies between individuals and groups, or organic metaphors, or several senses of the word liberty, are mere fallacies, due either to assertions of likeness between entities in respects in which they are unlike, or simple semantic confusion. What is wanted by those who are prepared to barter their own and others' liberty of individual action for the status of their group, and their own status within the group, is not simply a surrender of liberty for the sake of security, of some assured place in a harmonious hierarchy in which all men and all classes know their place, and are prepared to exchange the painful privilege of choosing – 'the burden of freedom' – for the peace and comfort and relative mindlessness of an authoritarian or totalitarian structure. No doubt, there are such men and such desires, and no doubt such surrenders of individual liberty can occur, and, indeed, have often occurred. But it is a profound misunderstanding of the temper of our times to assume that this is what makes nationalism or Marxism attractive to nations which have been ruled by alien masters, or to classes whose lives were directed by other classes in a semi-feudal, or some other hierarchically organized, régime. What they seek is more akin to what Mill called 'pagan self-assertion', but in a collective, socialized form. Indeed, much of what he says about his own reasons for desiring liberty – the value that he puts on boldness and nonconformity, on the assertion of the individual's own values in the face of the prevailing opinion, on strong and self-reliant personalities free from the leading strings of the official law-givers and instructors of society – has little enough to do with his conception of freedom as non-interference, but a great deal with the desire of men not to have their personalities set at too low a value, assumed to be incapable of autonomous, original, 'authentic' behaviour, even if such behaviour is to be met with opprobrium, or social restrictions, or inhibitive legislation. This wish to assert the 'personality' of my class, or group or nation, is connected both with the answer to the question 'What is to be the area of authority?' (for the group must not be interfered with by outside masters), and, even more closely, with the answer to the question 'Who is to govern us?' – govern well or badly, liberally or oppressively – but above all 'who?' And such answers as: 'by representatives elected by my own and others' untrammelled choice', or 'all of us gathered together in regular assemblies', or 'the best', or 'the wisest', or 'the nation as embodied in these or those persons or institutions', or 'the divine leader', are answers that are logically, and at times also politically and socially, independent of what extent of 'negative' liberty I demand for my own or my group's activities. Provided the answer to 'Who shall govern me?' is somebody or something which I can represent as 'my own', as something which belongs to me, or to whom I belong, I can, by using words which convey fraternity and solidarity, as well as some part of the connotation of the 'positive' sense of the word freedom (which it is difficult to specify more precisely), describe it as a hybrid form of freedom; at any rate as an ideal which is perhaps more prominent than any other in the world today, yet one which no existing term seems precisely to fit. Those who purchase it at the price of their 'negative', Millian freedom certainly claim to be 'liberated' by this means, in this confused, but ardently felt, sense. 'Whose service is perfect freedom' can in this way be secularized, and the state, or the nation, or the race, or an assembly, or a dictator, or my family or milieu, or I myself, can be substituted for the Deity, without thereby rendering the word 'freedom' wholly meaningless.[23]

No doubt every interpretation of the word liberty, however unusual, must include a minimum of what I have called 'negative' liberty. There must be an area within which I am not frustrated. No society literally suppresses all the liberties of its members; a being who is prevented by others from doing anything at all on his own is not a moral agent at all, and could not either legally or morally be regarded as a human being, even if a physiologist or a biologist, or even a psychologist, felt inclined to classify him as a man. But the fathers of liberalism – Mill and Constant – want more than this minimum: they demand a maximum degree of non-interference compatible with the minimum demands of social life. It seems unlikely that this extreme demand for liberty has ever been made by any but a small minority of highly civilized and self-conscious human beings. The bulk of humanity has certainly at most times been prepared to sacrifice this to other goals: security, status, prosperity, power, virtue, rewards in the next world; or justice, equality, fraternity, and many other values which appear wholly, or in part, incompatible with the attainment of the greatest degree of individual liberty, and certainly do not need it as a pre-condition for their own realization. It is not a demand for *Lebensraum* for each individual that has stimulated the rebellions and wars of liberation for which men were ready to die in the past, or, indeed, in the present. Men who have fought for freedom have commonly fought for the right to

be governed by themselves or their representatives – sternly governed, if need be, like the Spartans, with little individual liberty, but in a manner which allowed them to participate, or at any rate to believe that they were participating, in the legislation and administration of their collective lives. And men who have made revolutions have, as often as not, meant by liberty no more than the conquest of power and authority by a given sect of believers in a doctrine, or by a class, or by some other social group, old or new. Their victories certainly frustrated those whom they ousted, and sometimes repressed, enslaved, or exterminated vast numbers of human beings. Yet such revolutionaries have usually felt it necessary to argue that, despite this, they represented the party of liberty, or 'true' liberty, by claiming universality for their ideal, which the 'real selves' of even those who resisted them were also alleged to be seeking, although they were held to have lost the way to the goal, or to have mistaken the goal itself owing to some moral or spiritual blindness. All this has little to do with Mill's notion of liberty as limited only by the danger of doing harm to others. It is the non-recognition of this psychological and political fact (which lurks behind the apparent ambiguity of the term 'liberty') that has, perhaps, blinded some contemporary liberals to the world in which they live. Their plea is clear, their cause is just. But they do not allow for the variety of basic human needs. Nor yet for the ingenuity with which men can prove to their own satisfaction that the road to one ideal also leads to its contrary.

VII

Liberty and Sovereignty

The French Revolution, like all great revolutions, was, at least in its Jacobin form, just such an eruption of the desire for 'positive' freedom of collective self-direction on the part of a large body of Frenchmen who felt liberated as a nation, even though the result was, for a good many of them, a severe restriction of individual freedoms. Rousseau had spoken exultantly of the fact that the laws of liberty might prove to be more austere than the yoke of tyranny. Tyranny is service to human masters. The law cannot be a tyrant. Rousseau does not mean by liberty the 'negative' freedom of the individual not to be interfered with within a defined area, but the possession by all, and not merely by some, of the fully qualified members of a society of a share in the public power which is entitled to interfere with every aspect of every citizen's life. The liberals of the first half of the nineteenth century correctly foresaw that liberty in this 'positive' sense could easily destroy too many of the 'negative' liberties that they held sacred. They pointed out that the sovereignty of the people could easily destroy that of individuals. Mill explained, patiently and unanswerably, that government by the people was not, in his sense, necessarily freedom at all. For those who govern are not necessarily the same 'people' as those who are governed, and democratic self-government is not the government 'of each by himself' but, at best, of 'each by the rest'. Mill and his disciples spoke of the tyranny of the majority and of the tyranny of 'the prevailing feeling and opinion', and saw no great difference between that and any other kind of tyranny which encroaches upon men's activities beyond the sacred frontiers of private life.

No one saw the conflict between the two types of liberty better, or expressed it more clearly, than Benjamin Constant. He pointed out that the transference by a successful rising of the unlimited authority, commonly called sovereignty, from one set of hands to another does not increase liberty, but merely shifts the burden of slavery. He reasonably asked why a man should deeply care whether he is crushed by a popular government or by a monarch, or even by a set of oppressive laws. He saw that the main problem for those who desire 'negative', individual freedom is not who wields this authority, but how much authority should be placed in any set of hands. For unlimited authority in anybody's grasp was bound, he believed, sooner or later, to destroy somebody. He maintained that usually men protested against this or that set of governors as oppressive, when the real cause of oppression lay in the mere fact of the accumulation of power itself, wherever it might happen to be, since liberty was endangered by the mere existence of absolute authority as such. 'It is not the arm that is unjust', he wrote, 'but the weapon that is too heavy – some weights are too heavy for the human hand.' Democracy may disarm a given oligarchy, a given privileged individual or set of individuals, but it can still crush individuals as mercilessly as any previous ruler. In an essay comparing the liberty of the moderns with that of the ancients he said that an equal right to oppress – or interfere – is not equivalent to liberty. Nor does universal consent to loss of liberty somehow miraculously preserve it merely by being universal, or by being consent. If I consent to be oppressed, or acquiesce in my condition with detachment or irony, am I the less oppressed? If I sell myself into slavery, am I the less a slave? If I commit suicide, am I the less dead because I have taken my own life freely? 'Popular government is a spasmodic tyranny, monarchy a more efficiently centralized despotism.' Constant saw in Rousseau the most dangerous enemy of individual liberty, because he had declared that 'by giving myself to all I give myself to none'. Constant could not see why, even though the sovereign is 'everybody', it should not oppress one of the 'members' of its indivisible self, if it so decided. I may, of course, prefer to be deprived of my liberties by an assembly, or a family, or a class, in which I am a minority. It may give me an opportunity one day of persuading the others to do for me that to which I feel I am entitled. But to be deprived of my liberty at the hands of my family or friends or fellow citizens is to be deprived of it just as effectively. Hobbes was at any rate more candid: he did not pretend that a sovereign does not enslave: he justified this slavery, but at least did not have the effrontery to call it freedom.

Throughout the nineteenth century liberal thinkers maintained that if liberty involved a limit upon the powers of any man to force me to do what I did not, or might not, wish to do, then, whatever the ideal in the name of which I was coerced, I was not free; that the doctrine of absolute sovereignty was a tyrannical doctrine in itself. If I wish to preserve my liberty, it is not enough to say that it must not be violated unless someone or other – the absolute ruler, or the popular assembly, or the King in Parliament, or the judges, or some combination of authorities, or the laws themselves – for the laws may be oppressive – authorizes its violation. I must establish a society in which there must be some frontiers of freedom which nobody should be permitted to cross. Different names or natures may be given to the rules that determine these frontiers: they may be called natural rights, or the word of God, or Natural Law, or the demands of utility or of the 'permanent interests of man'; I may believe them to be valid a priori, or assert them to be my own ultimate ends, or the ends of my society or culture. What these rules or commandments will have in common is that they are accepted so widely, and are grounded so deeply in the actual nature of men as they have developed through history, as to be, by now, an essential part of what we mean by being a normal human being. Genuine belief in the inviolability of a minimum extent of individual liberty entails some such absolute stand. For it is clear that it has little to hope for from the rule of majorities; democracy as such is logically uncommitted to it, and historically has at times failed to protect it, while remaining faithful to its own principles. Few governments, it has been observed, have found much difficulty in causing their subjects to generate any will that the government wanted. 'The triumph of despotism is to force the slaves to declare themselves free.' It may need no force; the slaves may proclaim their freedom quite sincerely: but they are none the less slaves. Perhaps the chief value for liberals of political – 'positive' – rights, of participating in the government, is as a means for protecting what they hold to be an ultimate value, namely individual – 'negative' – liberty.

But if democracies can, without ceasing to be democratic, suppress freedom, at least as liberals have used the word, what would make a society truly free? For Constant, Mill, Tocqueville, and the liberal tradition to which they belong, no society is free unless it is governed by at any rate two interrelated principles: first, that no power, but only rights, can be regarded as absolute, so that all men, whatever power governs them, have an absolute right to refuse to behave inhumanly; and, second, that there are frontiers, not artificially drawn, within which men should be inviolable, these frontiers being defined in terms of rules so long and widely accepted that their observance has entered into the very conception of what it is to be a normal human being, and, therefore, also of what it is to act inhumanly or insanely; rules of which it would be absurd to say, for example, that they could be abrogated by some formal procedure on the part of some court or sovereign body. When I speak of a man as being normal, a part of what I mean is that he could not break these rules easily, without a qualm of revulsion. It is such rules as these that are broken when a man is declared guilty without trial, or punished under a retroactive law; when children are ordered to denounce their parents, friends to betray one another, soldiers to use methods of barbarism; when men are tortured or murdered, or minorities are massacred because

they irritate a majority or a tyrant. Such acts, even if they are made legal by the sovereign, cause horror even in these days, and this springs from the recognition of the moral validity – irrespective of the laws – of some absolute barriers to the imposition of one man's will on another.[24] The freedom of a society, or a class or a group, in this sense of freedom, is measured by the strength of these barriers, and the number and importance of the paths which they keep open for their members – if not for all, for at any rate a great number of them.[25]

This is almost at the opposite pole from the purposes of those who believe in liberty in the 'positive' – self-directive – sense. The former want to curb authority as such. The latter want it placed in their own hands. That is a cardinal issue. These are not two different interpretations of a single concept, but two profoundly divergent and irreconcilable attitudes to the ends of life. It is as well to recognize this, even if in practice it is often necessary to strike a compromise between them. For each of them makes absolute claims. These claims cannot both be fully satisfied. But it is a profound lack of social and moral understanding not to recognize that the satisfaction that each of them seeks is an ultimate value which, both historically and morally, has an equal right to be classed among the deepest interests of mankind.

VIII

The One and the Many

One belief, more than any other, is responsible for the slaughter of individuals on the altars of the great historical ideals – justice or progress or the happiness of future generations, or the sacred mission or emancipation of a nation or race or class, or even liberty itself, which demands the sacrifice of individuals for the freedom of society. This is the belief that somewhere, in the past or in the future, in divine revelation or in the mind of an individual thinker, in the pronouncements of history or science, or in the simple heart of an uncorrupted good man, there is a final solution. This ancient faith rests on the conviction that all the positive values in which men have believed must, in the end, be compatible, and perhaps even entail one another. 'Nature binds truth, happiness, and virtue together as by an indissoluble chain', said one of the best men who ever lived, and spoke in similar terms of liberty, equality, and justice.[26] But is this true? It is a commonplace that neither political equality nor efficient organization nor social justice is compatible with more than a modicum of individual liberty, and certainly not with unrestricted *laissez-faire*; that justice and generosity, public and private loyalties, the demands of genius and the claims of society, can conflict violently with each other. And it is no great way from that to the generalization that not all good things are compatible, still less all the ideals of mankind. But somewhere, we shall be told, and in some way, it must be possible for all these values to live together, for unless this is so, the universe is not a cosmos, not a harmony; unless this is so, conflicts of values may be an intrinsic, irremovable element in human life. To admit that the fulfilment of some of our ideals may in principle make the fulfilment of others impossible is to say that the notion of total human fulfilment is a formal contradiction, a metaphysical chimaera. For every rationalist metaphysician, from Plato to the last disciples of Hegel or Marx, this abandonment of the notion of a final harmony in which all riddles are solved, all contradictions reconciled, is a piece of crude empiricism, abdication before brute facts, intolerable bankruptcy of reason before things as they are, failure to explain and to justify, to reduce everything to a system, which 'reason' indignantly rejects. But if we are not armed with an *a priori* guarantee of the proposition that a total harmony of true values is somewhere to be found – perhaps in some ideal realm the characteristics of which we can, in our finite state, not so much as conceive – we must fall back on the ordinary resources of empirical observation and ordinary human knowledge. And these certainly give us no warrant for supposing (or even understanding what would be meant by saying) that all good things, or all bad things for that matter, are reconcilable with each other. The world that we encounter in ordinary experience is one in which we are faced with choices between ends equally ultimate, and claims equally absolute, the realization of some of which must inevitably involve the sacrifice of others. Indeed, it is because this is their situation that men place such immense value upon the freedom to choose; for if they had assurance that in some perfect state, realizable by men on earth, no ends pursued by them would ever be in conflict, the necessity and agony of choice would disappear, and with it the central importance of the freedom to choose. Any method of bringing this final state nearer would then seem fully justified, no matter how much freedom were sacrificed to forward its advance. It is, I have no doubt, some such dogmatic certainty that has been responsible for the deep, serene, unshakeable conviction in the minds of some of the most merciless tyrants and persecutors in history that what they did was fully justified by its purpose. I do not say that the ideal of self-perfection – whether for individuals or nations or churches or classes – is to be condemned in itself, or that the language which was used in its defence was in all cases the result of a confused or fraudulent use of words, or of moral or intellectual perversity. Indeed, I have tried to show that it is the notion of freedom in its 'positive' sense that is at the heart of the demands for national or social self-direction which animate the most powerful and morally just public movements of our time, and that not to recognize this is to misunderstand the most vital facts and ideas of our age. But equally it seems to me that the belief that some single formula can in principle be found whereby all the diverse ends of men can be harmoniously realized is demonstrably false. If, as I believe, the ends of men are many, and not all of them are in principle compatible with each other, then the possibility of conflict – and of tragedy – can never wholly be eliminated from human life, either personal or social. The necessity of choosing between absolute claims is then an inescapable characteristic of the human condition. This gives its value to freedom as Acton had conceived of it – as an end in itself, and not as a temporary need, arising out of our confused notions and irrational and disordered lives, a predicament which a panacea could one day put right.

I do not wish to say that individual freedom is, even in the most liberal societies, the sole, or even the dominant, criterion of social action. We compel children to be educated, and we forbid public executions. These are certainly curbs to freedom. We justify them on the ground that ignorance, or a barbarian upbringing, or cruel pleasures and excitements are worse for us than the amount of restraint needed to repress them. This judgment in turn depends on how we determine good and evil, that is to say, on our moral, religious, intellectual, economic, and aesthetic values; which are, in their turn, bound up with our conception of man, and of the basic demands of his nature. In other words, our solution of such problems is based on our vision, by which we are consciously or unconsciously guided, of what constitutes a fulfilled human life, as contrasted with Mill's 'cramped and warped', 'pinched and hidebound' natures. To protest against the laws governing censorship or personal morals as intolerable infringements of personal liberty presupposes a belief that the activities which such laws forbid are fundamental needs of men as men, in a good (or, indeed, any) society. To defend such laws is to hold that these needs are not essential, or that they cannot be satisfied without sacrificing other values which come higher – satisfy deeper needs – than individual freedom, determined by some standard that is not merely subjective, a standard for which some objective status – empirical or *a priori* – is claimed.

The extent of a man's, or a people's, liberty to choose to live as they desire must be weighed against the claims of many other values, of which equality, or justice, or happiness, or security, or public order are perhaps the most obvious examples. For this reason, it cannot be unlimited. We are rightly reminded by R.H. Tawney that the liberty of the strong, whether their strength is physical or economic, must be restrained. This maxim claims respect, not as a consequence of some *a priori* rule, whereby the respect for the liberty of one man logically entails respect for the liberty of others like him; but simply because respect for the principles of justice, or shame at gross inequality of treatment, is as basic in men as the desire for liberty. That we cannot have everything is a necessary, not a contingent, truth. Burke's plea for the constant need to compensate, to reconcile, to balance; Mill's plea for novel 'experiments in living' with their permanent possibility of error, the knowledge that it is not merely in practice but in principle impossible to reach clear-cut and certain answers, even in an ideal world of wholly good and rational men and wholly clear ideas – may madden those who seek for final solutions and single, all-embracing systems, guaranteed to be eternal. Nevertheless, it is a conclusion that cannot be escaped by those who, with Kant, have learnt the truth that out of the crooked timber of humanity no straight thing was ever made.

There is little need to stress the fact that monism, and faith in a single criterion, has always proved a deep source of satisfaction both to the intellect and to the emotions. Whether the stan-dard of judgment derives from the vision of some future perfection, as in the minds of the *philosophes* in the eighteenth century and their technocratic successors in our own day, or is rooted in the past – *la terre et les morts* – as maintained by German historicists or French theocrats, or neo-Conservatives in English-speaking countries, it is bound, provided it is inflexible enough, to encounter some unforeseen and unforeseeable human development, which it will not fit; and will then be used to justify the *a priori* barbarities of Procrustes – the vivisection of actual human societies into some fixed pattern dictated by our fallible understanding of a largely imaginary past or a wholly imaginary future. To preserve our absolute categories or ideals at the expense of human lives offends equally against the principles of science and of history; it is an attitude found in equal measure on the right and left wings in our days, and is not reconcilable with the principles accepted by those who respect the facts.

Pluralism, with the measure of 'negative' liberty that it entails, seems to me a truer and more humane ideal than the goals of those who seek in the great, disciplined, authoritarian structures the ideal of 'positive' self-mastery by classes, or peoples, or the whole of mankind. It is truer, because it does, at least, recognize the fact that human goals are many, not all of them commensurable, and in perpetual rivalry with one another. To assume that all values can be graded on one scale, so that it is a mere matter of inspection to determine the highest, seems to me to falsify our knowledge that men are free agents, to represent moral decision as an operation which a slide-rule could, in principle, perform. To say that in some ultimate, all-reconciling, yet realizable synthesis, duty *is* interest, or individual freedom *is* pure democracy or an authoritarian state, is to throw a metaphysical blanket over either self-deceit or deliberate hypocrisy. It is more humane because it does not (as the system builders do) deprive men, in the name of some remote, or incoherent, ideal, of much that they have found to be indispensable to their life as unpredictably self-transforming human beings.[27] In the end, men choose between ultimate values; they choose as they do, because their life and thought are determined by fundamental moral categories and concepts that are, at any rate over large stretches of time and space, a part of their being and thought and sense of their own identity; part of what makes them human.

It may be that the ideal of freedom to choose ends without claiming eternal validity for them, and the pluralism of values connected with this, is only the late fruit of our declining capitalist civilization: an ideal which remote ages and primitive societies have not recognized, and one which posterity will regard with curiosity, even sympathy, but little comprehension. This may be so; but no sceptical conclusions seem to me to follow. Principles are not less sacred because their duration cannot be guaranteed. Indeed, the very desire for guarantees that our values are eternal and secure in some objective heaven is perhaps only a craving for the certainties of childhood or the absolute values of our primitive past. 'To realise the relative validity of one's convictions', said an admirable writer of our time, 'and yet stand for them unflinchingly, is what distinguishes a civilised man from a barbarian.' To demand more than this is perhaps a deep and incurable metaphysical need; but to allow it to determine one's practice is a symptom of an equally deep, and more dangerous, moral and political immaturity.

Notes

1   This Inaugural Lecture was delivered before the University of Oxford on 31 October 1958, and published by the Clarendon Press in the same year.

2   I do not, of course, mean to imply the truth of the converse.

3   Helvétius made this point very clearly: 'The free man is the man who is not in irons, nor imprisoned in a gaol, nor terrorized like a slave by the fear of punishment . . . it is not lack of freedom not to fly like an eagle or swim like a whale.'

4   The Marxist conception of social laws is, of course, the best-known version of this theory, but it forms a large element in some Christian and utilitarian, and all socialist, doctrines.

5   'A free man', said Hobbes, 'is he that . . . is not hindered to do what he hath the will to do.' Law is always a 'fetter', even if it protects you from being bound in chains that are heavier than those of the law, say, some more repressive law or custom, or arbitrary despotism or chaos. Bentham says much the same.

6   This is but another illustration of the natural tendency of all but a very few thinkers to believe that all the things they hold good must be intimately connected, or at least compatible, with one another. The history of thought, like the history of nations, is strewn with examples of inconsistent, or at least disparate, elements artificially yoked together in a despotic system, or held together by the danger of some common enemy. In due course the danger passes, and conflicts between the allies arise, which often disrupt the system, sometimes to the great benefit of mankind.

7   See the valuable discussion of this in Michel Villey, *Leçons d'histoire de la philosophie du droit*, who traces the embryo of the notion of subjective rights to Occam.

8   Christian (and Jewish or Moslem) belief in the absolute authority of divine or natural laws, or in the equality of all men in the sight of God, is different from belief in freedom to live as one prefers.

9   Indeed, it is arguable that in the Prussia of Frederick the Great or in the Austria of Josef II men of imagination, originality, and creative genius, and, indeed, minorities of all kinds, were less persecuted and felt the pressure, both of institutions and custom, less heavy upon them than in many an earlier or later democracy.

10   'Negative liberty' is something the extent of which, in a given case, it is difficult to estimate. It might, prima facie, seem to depend simply on the power to choose between at any rate two alternatives. Nevertheless, not all choices are equally free, or free at all. If in a totalitarian state I betray my friend under threat of torture, perhaps even if I act from fear of losing my job, I can reasonably say that I did not act freely. Nevertheless, I did, of course, make a choice, and could, at any rate in theory, have chosen to be killed or tortured or imprisoned. The mere existence of alternatives is not, therefore, enough to make my action free (although it may be voluntary) in the normal sense of the word. The extent of my freedom seems to depend on (*a*) how many possibilities are open to me (although the method of counting these can never be more than impressionistic. Possibilities of action are not discrete entities, like apples, which can be exhaustively enumerated); (*b*) how easy or difficult each of these possibilities is to actualize; (*c*) how important in my plan of life, given my character and circumstances, these possibilities are when compared with each other; (*d*) how far they are closed and opened by deliberate human acts; (*e*) what value not merely the agent, but the general sentiment of the society in which he lives, puts on the various possibilities. All these magnitudes must be 'integrated', and a conclusion, necessarily never precise, or indisputable, drawn from this process. It may well be that there are many incommensurable kinds and degrees of freedom, and that

they cannot be drawn up on any single scale of magnitude. Moreover, in the case of societies, we are faced by such (logically absurd) questions as 'Would arrangement X increase the liberty of Mr. A more than it would that of Messrs. B, C, and D between them, added together?' The same difficulties arise in applying utilitarian criteria. Nevertheless, provided we do not demand precise measurement, we can give valid reasons for saying that the average subject of the King of Sweden is, on the whole, a good deal freer today than the average citizen of Spain or Albania. Total patterns of life must be compared directly as wholes, although the method by which we make the comparison, and the truth of the conclusions, are difficult or impossible to demonstrate. But the vagueness of the concepts, and the multiplicity of the criteria involved, is an attribute of the subject-matter itself, not of our imperfect methods of measurement, or incapacity for precise thought.

11   'The ideal of true freedom is the maximum of power for all the members of human society alike to make the best of themselves', said T.H. Green in 1881. Apart from the confusion of freedom with equality, this entails that if a man chose some immediate pleasure – which (in whose view?) would not enable him to make the best of himself (what self?) – what he was exercising was not 'true' freedom: and if deprived of it, would not lose anything that mattered. Green was a genuine liberal: but many a tyrant could use this formula to justify his worse acts of oppression.

12   'A wise man, though he be a slave, is at liberty, and from this it follows that though a fool rule, he is in slavery', said St. Ambrose. It might equally well have been said by Epictetus or Kant.

13   'Proletarian coercion, in all its forms, from executions to forced labour, is, paradoxical as it may sound, the method of moulding communist humanity out of the human material of the capitalist period.' These lines by the Bolshevik leader Nikolai Bukharin, in a work which appeared in 1920, especially the term 'human material', vividly convey this attitude.

14   Kant's psychology, and that of the Stoics and Christians too, assumed that some element in man – the 'inner fastness of his mind' – could be made secure against conditioning. The development of the techniques of hypnosis, 'brain washing', subliminal suggestion, and the like, has made this *a priori* assumption, at least as an empirical hypothesis, less plausible.

15   It is not perhaps far-fetched to assume that the quietism of the Eastern sages was, similarly, a response to the despotism of the great autocracies, and flourished at periods when individuals were apt to be humiliated, or at any rate ignored or ruthlessly managed, by those possessed of the instruments of physical coercion.

16   It is worth remarking that those who demanded – and fought for – liberty for the individual or for the nation in France during this period of German quietism did not fall into this attitude. Might this not be precisely because, despite the despotism of the French monarchy and the arrogance and arbitrary behaviour of privileged groups in the French state, France was a proud and powerful nation, where the reality of political power was not beyond the grasp of men of talent, so that withdrawal from battle into some untroubled heaven above it, whence it could be surveyed dispassionately by the self-sufficient philosopher, was not the only way out? The same holds for England in the nineteenth century and well after it, and for the United States today.

17   Or, as some modern theorists maintain, because I have, or could have, invented them for myself, since the rules are man-made.

18   In practice even more than in theory.

19   On this Bentham seems to me to have said the last word: 'Is not liberty to do evil, liberty? If not, what is it? Do we not say that it is necessary to take liberty from idiots and bad men, because they abuse it?' Compare with this a typical statement made by a Jacobin club of the same period: 'No man is free in doing evil. To prevent him is to set him free.' This is echoed in almost identical terms by British Idealists at the end of the following century.

20   'To compel men to adopt the right form of government, to impose Right on them by force, is not only the right, but the sacred duty of every man who has both the insight and the power to do so.'

21   Kant came nearest to asserting the 'negative' ideal of liberty when (in one of his political treatises) he declared that 'the greatest problem of the human race, to the solution of which it is compelled by nature, is the establishment of a civil society universally administering right according to law. It is only in a society which possesses the greatest liberty . . . – with . . . the most exact determination and guarantee of the limits of [the] liberty [of each individual] in order that it may co-exist with the liberty of others – that the highest purpose of nature, which is the development of all her capacities, can be attained in the case of mankind.' Apart from the teleological implications, this formulation does not at first appear very different from orthodox liberalism. The crucial point, however, is how to determine the criterion for 'the exact determination and guarantee of the limits' of individual liberty. Most modern liberals, at their most consistent, want a situation in which as many individuals as possible can realize as many of their ends as possible, without assessment of the value of these ends as such, save in so far as they may frustrate the purposes of others. They wish the

frontiers between individuals or groups of men to be drawn solely with a view to preventing collisions between human purposes, all of which must be considered to be equally ultimate, uncriticizable ends in themselves. Kant, and the rationalists of his type, do not regard all ends as of equal value. For them the limits of liberty are determined by applying the rules of 'reason', which is much more than the mere generality of rules as such, and is a faculty that creates or reveals a purpose identical in, and for, all men. In the name of reason anything that is non-rational may be condemned, so that the various personal aims which their individual imagination and idiosyncrasies lead men to pursue – for example aesthetic and other non-rational kinds of self-fulfilment – may, at least in theory, be ruthlessly suppressed to make way for the demands of reason. The authority of reason and of the duties it lays upon men is identified with individual freedom, on the assumption that only rational ends can be the 'true' objects of a 'free' man's 'real' nature.

I have never, I must own, understood what 'reason' means in this context; and here merely wish to point out that the *a priori* assumptions of this philosophical psychology are not compatible with empiricism: that is to say, with any doctrine founded on knowledge derived from experience of what men are and seek.

22 This has an obvious affinity with Kant's doctrine of human freedom; but it is a socialized and empirical version of it, and therefore almost its opposite. Kant's free man needs no public recognition for his inner freedom. If he is treated as a means to some external purpose, that is a wrong act on the part of his exploiters, but his own 'noumenal' status is untouched, and he is fully free, and fully a man, however he may be treated. The need spoken of here is bound up wholly with the relation that I have with others; I am nothing if I am unrecognized. I cannot ignore the attitude of others with Byronic disdain, fully conscious of my own intrinsic worth and vocation, or escape into my inner life, for I am in my own eyes as others see me. I identify myself with the point of view of my milieu: I feel myself to be somebody or nobody in terms of my position and function in the social whole; this is the most 'heteronomous' condition imaginable.

23 This argument should be distinguished from the traditional approach of some of the disciples of Burke or Hegel who say that, since I am made what I am by society or history, to escape from them is impossible and to attempt it irrational. No doubt I cannot leap out of my skin, or breathe outside my proper element; it is a mere tautology to say that I am what I am, and cannot want to be liberated from my essential characteristics, some of which are social. But it does not follow that all my attributes are intrinsic and inalienable, and that I cannot seek to alter my status within the 'social network', or 'cosmic web', which determines my nature; if this were the case, no meaning could be attached to such words as 'choice' or 'decision' or 'activity'. If they are to mean anything, attempts to protect myself against authority, or even to escape from my 'station and its duties', cannot be excluded as automatically irrational or suicidal.

24 But see Berlin, 'Introduction', *Four Essays on Liberty* (Oxford: Oxford University Press, 1969), p. x.

25 In Great Britain such legal power is, of course, constitutionally vested in the absolute sovereign – the King in Parliament. What makes this country comparatively free, therefore, is the fact that this theoretically omnipotent entity is restrained by custom or opinion from behaving as such. It is clear that what matters is not the form of these restraints on power – whether they are legal, or moral, or constitutional – but their effectiveness.

26 Condorcet, from whose *Esquisse* these words are quoted, declares that the task of social science is to show 'by what bonds Nature has united the progress of enlightenment with that of liberty, virtue, and respect for the natural rights of man; how these ideals, which alone are truly good, yet so often separated from each other that they are even believed to be incompatible, should, on the contrary, become inseparable, as soon as enlightenment has reached a certain level simultaneously among a large number of nations'. He goes on to say that: 'Men still preserve the errors of their childhood, of their country, and of their age long after having recognized all the truths needed for destroying them.' Ironically enough, his belief in the need and possibility of uniting all good things may well be precisely the kind of error he himself so well described.

27 On this also Bentham seems to me to have spoken well: 'Individual interests are the only real interests . . . can it be conceived that there are men so absurd as to . . . prefer the man who is not to him who is; to torment the living, under pretence of promoting the happiness of them who are not born, and who may never be born?' This is one of the infrequent occasions when Burke agrees with Bentham; for this passage is at the heart of the empirical, as against the metaphysical, view of politics.

25

What's Wrong with Negative Liberty?

Charles Taylor

This is an attempt to resolve one of the issues that separate 'positive' and 'negative' theories of freedom, as these have been distinguished in Isaiah Berlin's seminal essay, 'Two Concepts of Liberty'.[1] Although one can discuss almost endlessly the detailed formulation of the distinction, I believe it is undeniable that there are two such families of conceptions of political freedom abroad in our civilisation.

Thus there clearly are theories, widely canvassed in liberal society, which want to define freedom exclusively in terms of the independence of the individual from interference by others, be these governments, corporations or private persons; and equally clearly these theories are challenged by those who believe that freedom resides at least in part in collective control over the common life. We unproblematically recognise theories descended from Rousseau and Marx as fitting in this category.

There is quite a gamut of views in each category. And this is worth bearing in mind, because it is too easy in the course of polemic to fix on the extreme, almost caricatural variants of each family. When people attack positive theories of freedom, they generally have some Left totalitarian theory in mind, according to which freedom resides exclusively in exercising collective control over one's destiny in a classless society, the kind of theory which underlies, for instance, official Communism. This view, in its caricaturally

extreme form, refuses to recognise the freedoms guaranteed in other societies as genuine. The destruction of 'bourgeois freedoms' is no real loss of freedom, and coercion can be justified in the name of freedom if it is needed to bring into existence the classless society in which alone men are properly free. Men can, in short, be forced to be free.

Even as applied to official Communism, this portrait is a little extreme, although it undoubtedly expresses the inner logic of this kind of theory. But it is an absurd caricature if applied to the whole family of positive conceptions. This includes all those views of modern political life which owe something to the ancient republican tradition, according to which men's ruling themselves is seen as an activity valuable in itself, and not only for instrumental reasons. It includes in its scope thinkers like Tocqueville, and even arguably the J.S. Mill of *On Representative Government*. It has no necessary connection with the view that freedom consists *purely and simply* in the collective control over the common life, or that there is no freedom worth the name outside a context of collective control. And it does not therefore generate necessarily a doctrine that men can be forced to be free.

On the other side, there is a corresponding caricatural version of negative freedom which tends to come to the fore. This is the tough-minded version, going back to Hobbes, or in another way to Bentham, which sees freedom simply as the absence of external physical or legal obstacles. This view will have no truck with other less immediately obvious obstacles to freedom, for instance, lack of awareness, or false conscious-

Originally published in *The Idea of Freedom*, ed. Alan Ryan (Oxford University Press, 1979), 175–93. Copyright © 1979 by Charles Taylor. Reprinted by permission of the author.

ness, or repression, or other inner factors of this kind. It holds firmly to the view that to speak of such inner factors as relevant to the issue about freedom, to speak for instance of someone's being less free because of false consciousness, is to abuse words. The only clear meaning which can be given to freedom is that of the absence of external obstacles.

I call this view caricatural as a representative portrait of the negative view, because it rules out of court one of the most powerful motives behind the modern defence of freedom as individual independence, viz., the post-Romantic idea that each person's form of self-realisation is original to him/her, and can therefore only be worked out independently. This is one of the reasons for the defence of individual liberty by among others J.S. Mill (this time in his *On Liberty*). But if we think of freedom as including something like the freedom of self-fulfilment, or self-realisation according to our own pattern, then we plainly have something which can fail for inner reasons as well as because of external obstacles. We can fail to achieve our own self-realisation through inner fears, or false consciousness, as well as because of external coercion. Thus the modern notion of negative freedom which gives weight to the securing of each person's right to realise him/herself in his/her own way cannot make do with the Hobbes/Bentham notion of freedom. The moral psychology of these authors is too simple, or perhaps we should say too crude, for its purposes.

Now there is a strange asymmetry here. The extreme caricatural views tend to come to the fore in the polemic, as I mentioned above. But whereas the extreme 'forced-to-be-free' view is one which the opponents of positive liberty try to pin on them, as one would expect in the heat of argument, the proponents of negative liberty themselves often seem anxious to espouse their extreme, Hobbesian view. Thus even Isaiah Berlin, in his eloquent exposition of the two concepts of liberty, seems to quote Bentham[2] approvingly and Hobbes[3] as well. Why is this?

To see this we have to examine more closely what is at stake between the two views. The negative theories, as we saw, want to define freedom in terms of individual independence from others; the positive also want to identify freedom with collective self-government. But behind this lie some deeper differences of doctrines.

Isaiah Berlin points out that negative theories are concerned with the area in which the subject should be left without interference, whereas the positive doctrines are concerned with who or what controls. I should like to put the point behind this in a slightly different way. Doctrines of positive freedom are concerned with a view of freedom which involves essentially the exercising of control over one's life. On this view, one is free only to the extent that one has effectively determined oneself and the shape of one's life. The concept of freedom here is an exercise-concept.

By contrast, negative theories can rely simply on an opportunity-concept, where being free is a matter of what we can do, of what it is open to us to do, whether or not we do anything to exercise these options. This certainly is the case of the crude, original Hobbesian concept. Freedom consists just in there being no obstacle. It is a sufficient condition of one's being free that nothing stand in the way.

But we have to say that negative theories *can* rely on an opportunity-concept, rather than that they necessarily do so rely, for we have to allow for that part of the gamut of negative theories mentioned above which incorporates some notion of self-realisation. Plainly this kind of view can't rely simply on an opportunity-concept. We can't say that someone is free, on a self-realisation view, if he is totally unrealised, if for instance he is totally unaware of his potential, if fulfilling it has never even arisen as a question for him, or if he is paralysed by the fear of breaking with some norm which he has internalised but which does not authentically reflect him. Within this conceptual scheme, some degree of exercise is necessary for a man to be thought free. Or if we want to think of the internal bars to freedom as obstacles on all fours with the external ones, then being in a position to exercise freedom, having the opportunity, involves removing the internal barriers; and this is not possible without having to some extent realised myself. So that with the freedom of self-realisation, having the opportunity to be free requires that I already be exercising freedom. A pure opportunity-concept is impossible here.

But if negative theories can be grounded on either an opportunity- or an exercise-concept, the same is not true of positive theories. The view that freedom involves at least partially collective self-rule is essentially grounded on an exercise-concept. For this view (at least partly) identifies freedom with self-direction, i.e., the actual exercise of directing control over one's life.

Charles Taylor

But this already gives us a hint towards illuminating the above paradox, that while the extreme variant of positive freedom is usually pinned on its protagonists by their opponents, negative theorists seem prone to embrace the crudest versions of their theory themselves. For if an opportunity-concept is incombinable with a positive theory, but either it or its alternative can suit a negative theory, then one way of ruling out positive theories in principle is by firmly espousing an opportunity-concept. One cuts off the positive theories by the root, as it were, even though one may also pay a price in the atrophy of a wide range of negative theories as well. At least by taking one's stand firmly on the crude side of the negative range, where only opportunity concepts are recognised, one leaves no place for a positive theory to grow.

Taking one's stand here has the advantage that one is holding the line around a very simple and basic issue of principle, and one where the negative view seems to have some backing in common sense. The basic intuition here is that freedom is a matter of being able to do something or other, of not having obstacles in one's way, rather than being a capacity that we have to realise. It naturally seems more prudent to fight the Totalitarian Menace at this last-ditch position, digging in behind the natural frontier of this simple issue, rather than engaging the enemy on the open terrain of exercise-concepts, where one will have to fight to discriminate the good from the bad among such concepts; fight, for instance, for a view of individual self-realisation against various notions of collective self-realisation, of a nation, or a class. It seems easier and safer to cut all the nonsense off at the start by declaring all self-realisation views to be metaphysical hog-wash. Freedom should just be tough-mindedly defined as the absence of external obstacles.

Of course, there are independent reasons for wanting to define freedom tough-mindedly. In particular there is the immense influence of the anti-metaphysical, materialist, natural-science-oriented temper of thought in our civilisation. Something of this spirit at its inception induced Hobbes to take the line that he did, and the same spirit goes marching on today. Indeed, it is because of the prevalence of this spirit that the line is so easy to defend, forensically speaking, in our society.

Nevertheless, I think that one of the strongest motives for defending the crude Hobbes-Bentham concept, that freedom is the absence of external obstacles, physical or legal, is the strategic one above. For most of those who take this line thereby abandon many of their own intuitions, sharing as they do with the rest of us in a post-Romantic civilisation which puts great value on self-realisation, and values freedom largely because of this. It is fear of the Totalitarian Menace, I would argue, which has led them to abandon this terrain to the enemy.

I want to argue that this not only robs their eventual forensic victory of much of its value, since they become incapable of defending liberalism in the form we in fact value it, but I want to make the stronger claim that this Maginot Line mentality actually ensures defeat, as is often the case with Maginot Line mentalities. The Hobbes-Bentham view, I want to argue, is indefensible as a view of freedom.

To see this, let's examine the line more closely, and the temptation to stand on it. The advantage of the view that freedom is the absence of external obstacles is its simplicity. It allows us to say that freedom is being able to do what you want, where what you want is unproblematically understood as what the agent can identify as his desires. By contrast an exercise-concept of freedom requires that we discriminate among motivations. If we are free in the exercise of certain capacities, then we are not free, or less free, when these capacities are in some way unfulfilled or blocked. But the obstacles can be internal as well as external. And this must be so, for the capacities relevant to freedom must involve some self-awareness, self-understanding, moral discrimination and self-control, otherwise their exercise couldn't amount to freedom in the sense of self-direction; and this being so, we can fail to be free because these internal conditions are not realised. But where this happens, where, for example, we are quite self-deceived, or utterly fail to discriminate properly the ends we seek, or have lost self-control, we can quite easily be doing what we want in the sense of what we can identify as our wants, without being free; indeed, we can be further entrenching our unfreedom.

Once one adopts a self-realisation view, or indeed, any exercise-concept of freedom, then being able to do what one wants can no longer be accepted as a sufficient condition of being free. For this view puts certain conditions on one's motivation. You are not free if you are motivated, through fear, inauthentically internalised standards, or false consciousness, to thwart your self-realisation. This is sometimes put by saying that for a self-realisation view, you have to be able to do what you really want, or to follow your real will, or to fulfil the desires of your own true self. But these formulas, particularly the last, may mislead, by making us think that exercise concepts of freedom are tied to some particular metaphysic, in particular that of a higher and lower self. We shall see below that this is far from being the case, and that there is a much wider range of bases for discriminating authentic and inauthentic desires.

In any case, the point for our discussion here is that for an exercise-concept of freedom, being free can't just be a question of doing what you want in the unproblematic sense. It must also be that what you want doesn't run against the grain of your basic purposes, or your self-realisation. Or to put the issue in another way, which converges on the same point, the subject himself can't be the final authority on the question whether he is free; for he cannot be the final authority on the question whether his desires are authentic, whether they do or do not frustrate his purposes.

To put the issue in this second way is to make more palpable the temptation for defenders of the negative view to hold their Maginot Line. For once we admit that the agent himself is not the final authority on his own freedom, do we not open the way to totalitarian manipulation? Do we not legitimate others, supposedly wiser about his purposes than himself, redirecting his feet on the right path, perhaps even by force, and all this in the name of freedom?

The answer is that of course we don't. Not by this concession alone. For there may also be good reasons for holding that others are not likely to be in a better position to understand his real purposes. This indeed plausibly follows from the post-Romantic view above that each person has his/her own original form of realisation. Some others, who know us intimately, and who surpass us in wisdom, are undoubtedly in a position to advise us, but no official body can possess a doctrine or a technique whereby they could know how to put us on the rails, because such a doctrine or technique cannot in principle exist if human beings really differ in their self-realisation.

Or again, we may hold a self-realisation view of freedom, and hence believe that there are certain conditions on my motivation necessary to my being free, but also believe that there are other necessary conditions which rule out my being forcibly led towards some definition of my self-realisation by external authority. Indeed, in these last two paragraphs I have given a portrait of what I think is a very widely held view in liberal society, a view which values self-realisation, and accepts that it can fail for internal reasons, but which believes that no valid guidance can be provided in principle by social authority, because of human diversity and originality, and holds that the attempt to impose such guidance will destroy other necessary conditions of freedom.

It is however true that totalitarian theories of positive freedom do build on a conception which involves discriminating between motivations. Indeed, one can represent the path from the negative to the positive conceptions of freedom as consisting of two steps: the first moves us from a notion of freedom as doing what one wants to a notion which discriminates motivations and equates freedom with doing what we really want, or obeying our real will, or truly directing our lives. The second step introduces some doctrine purporting to show that we cannot do what we really want, or follow our real will, outside of a society of a certain canonical form, incorporating true self-government. It follows that we can only be free in such a society, and that being free is governing ourselves collectively according to this canonical form.

We might see an example of this second step in Rousseau's view that only a social contract society in which all give themselves totally to the whole preserves us from other-dependence and ensures that we obey only ourselves; or in Marx's doctrine of man as a species-being who realises his potential in a mode of social production, and who must thus take control of this mode collectively.

Faced with this two-step process, it seems safer and easier to stop it at the first step, to insist firmly that freedom is just a matter of the absence of external obstacles, that it therefore involves no discrimination of motivation and permits in principle no second-guessing of the subject by any one else. This is the essence of the Maginot Line strategy. It is very tempting. But I want to claim that it is wrong. I want to argue that we cannot defend a view of freedom which doesn't involve at least some qualitative discrimination as to motive, i.e., which doesn't put some restrictions on motivation among the necessary conditions of freedom, and hence which could rule out second-guessing in principle.

There are some considerations one can put forward straight off to show that the pure Hobbesian concept won't work, that there are some discriminations among motivations which are essential to the concept of freedom as we use it. Even where we think of freedom as the absence of external obstacles, it is not the absence of such obstacles *simpliciter*. For we make discriminations between obstacles as representing more or less serious infringements of freedom. And we do this, because we deploy the concept against a background understanding that certain goals and activities are more significant than others.

Thus we could say that my freedom is restricted if the local authority puts up a new traffic light at an intersection close to my home; so that where previously I could cross as I liked, consistently with avoiding collision with other cars, now I have to wait until the light is green. In a philosophical argument, we might call this a restriction of freedom, but not in a serious political debate. The reason is that it is too trivial, the activity and purposes inhibited here are not really significant. It is not just a matter of our having made a trade-off, and considered that a small loss of liberty was worth fewer traffic accidents, or less danger for the children; we are reluctant to speak here of a loss of liberty at all; what we feel we are trading off is convenience against safety.

By contrast a law which forbids me from worshipping according to the form I believe in is a serious blow to liberty; even a law which tried to restrict this to certain times (as the traffic light restricts my crossing of the intersection to certain times) would be seen as a serious restriction. Why this difference between the two cases? Because we have a background understanding, too obvious to spell out, of some activities and goals as highly significant for human beings and others as less so. One's religious belief is recognised, even by atheists, as supremely important, because it is that by which the believer defines himself as a moral being. By contrast my rhythm of movement through the city traffic is trivial. We don't want to speak of these two in the same breath. We don't even readily admit that liberty is at stake in the traffic light case. For *de minimis non curat libertas*.

But this recourse to significance takes us beyond a Hobbesian scheme. Freedom is no longer just the absence of external obstacle *tout court*, but the absence of external obstacle to significant action, to what is important to man. There are discriminations to be made; some restrictions are more serious than others, some are utterly trivial. About many, there is of course controversy. But what the judgement turns on is some sense of what is significant for human life. Restricting the expression of people's religious and ethical convictions is more significant than restricting their movement around uninhabited parts of the country; and both are more significant than the trivia of traffic control.

But the Hobbesian scheme has no place for the notion of significance. It will allow only for purely quantitative judgements. On the toughest-minded version of his conception, where Hobbes seems to be about to define liberty in terms of the absence of physical obstacles, one is presented with the vertiginous prospect of human freedom being measurable in the same way as the degrees of freedom of some physical object, say a lever. Later we see that this won't do, because we have to take account of legal obstacles to my action. But in any case, such a quantitative conception of freedom is a non-starter.

Consider the following diabolical defence of Albania as a free country. We recognise that religion has been abolished in Albania, whereas it hasn't been in Britain. But on the other hand there are probably far fewer traffic lights per head in Tirana than in London. (I haven't checked for myself, but this is a very plausible assumption.) Suppose an apologist for Albanian Socialism were nevertheless to claim that this country was freer than Britain, because the number of acts restricted was far smaller. After all, only a minority of Londoners practise some religion in public places, but all have to negotiate their way through traffic. Those who do practise a religion generally do so on one day of the week, while they are held up at traffic lights every day. In sheer quantitative terms, the number of acts restricted by traffic lights must be greater than that restricted by a ban on public religious practice. So if Britain is considered a free society, why not Albania?

So the application even of our negative notion of freedom requires a background conception of what is significant, according to which some restrictions are seen to be without relevance for freedom altogether, and others are judged as being of greater and lesser importance. So some discrimination among motivations seems essential to our concept of freedom. A minute's reflection shows why this must be so. Freedom is important to us because we are purposive beings. But then there must be distinctions in the significance of different kinds of freedom based on the distinction in the significance of different purposes.

But of course, this still doesn't involve the kind of discrimination mentioned above, the kind which would allow us to say that someone who was doing what he wanted (in the unproblematic sense) wasn't really free, the kind of discrimination which allows us to put conditions on people's motivations necessary to their being free, and hence to second-guess them. All we have shown is that we make discriminations between more or less significant freedoms, based on discriminations among the purposes people have.

This creates some embarrassment for the crude negative theory, but it can cope with it by simply adding a recognition that we make judgements of significance. Its central claim that freedom just is the absence of external obstacles seems untouched, as also its view of freedom as an opportunity-concept. It is just that we now have to admit that not all opportunities are equal.

But there is more trouble in store for the crude view when we examine further what these qualitative discriminations are based on. What lies behind our judging certain purposes/feelings as more significant than others? One might think that there was room here again for another quantitative theory; that the more significant purposes are those we want more. But this account is either vacuous or false.

It is true but vacuous if we take wanting more just to mean being more significant. It is false as soon as we try to give wanting more an independent criterion, such as, for instance, the urgency or force of a desire, or the prevalence of one desire over another, because it is a matter of the most banal experience that the purposes we know to be more significant are not always those which we desire with the greatest urgency to encompass, nor the ones that actually always win out in cases of conflict of desires.

When we reflect on this kind of significance, we come up against what I have called elsewhere the fact of strong evaluation, the fact that we human subjects are not only subjects of first-order desires, but of second-order desires, desires about desires. We experience our desires and purposes as qualitatively discriminated, as higher or lower, noble or base, integrated or fragmented, significant or trivial, good and bad. This means that we experience some of our desires and goals as intrinsically more significant than others: some passing comfort is less important than the fulfilment of our lifetime vocation, our *amour propre* less important than a love relationship; while we experience some others as bad, not just comparatively, but absolutely: we desire not to be moved by spite, or some childish desire to impress at all costs. And these judgements of significance are quite independent of the strength of the respective desires: the craving for comfort may be overwhelming at this moment, we may be obsessed with our *amour propre*, but the judgement of significance stands.

But then the question arises whether this fact of strong evaluation doesn't have other consequences for our notion of freedom, than just that it permits us to rank freedoms in importance. Is freedom not at stake when we find ourselves carried away by a less significant goal to override a highly significant one? Or when we are led to act out of a motive we consider bad or despicable?

The answer is that we sometimes do speak in this way. Suppose I have some irrational fear, which is preventing me from doing something I very much want to do. Say the fear of public speaking is preventing me from taking up a career that I should find very fulfilling, and that I should be quite good at, if I could just get over this 'hang-up'. It is clear that we experience this fear as an obstacle, and that we feel we are less than we would be if we could overcome it.

Or again, consider the case where I am very attached to comfort. To go on short rations, and to miss my creature comforts for a time, makes me very depressed. I find myself making a big thing of this. Because of this reaction I can't do certain things that I should like very much to do, such as going on an expedition over the Andes, or a canoe trip in the Yukon. Once again, it is quite understandable if I experience this attachment as an obstacle, and feel that I should be freer without it.

Or I could find that my spiteful feelings and reactions which I almost can't inhibit are undermining a relationship which is terribly important to me. At times, I feel as though I am almost assisting as a helpless witness at my own destructive behaviour, as I lash out again with my unbridled tongue at her. I long to be able not to feel this spite. As long as I feel it, even control is not an option, because it just builds up inside until it either bursts out, or else the feeling somehow communicates itself, and queers things between us. I long to be free of this feeling.

These are quite understandable cases, where we can speak of freedom or its absence without strain. What I have called strong evaluation is essentially involved here. For these are not just cases of conflict, even cases of painful conflict. If the conflict is between two desires with which I have no trouble identifying, there can be no talk of lesser freedom, no matter how painful or fateful. Thus if what is breaking up my relationship is my finding fulfilment in a job which, say, takes me away from home a lot, I have indeed a terrible conflict, but I would have no temptation to speak of myself as less free.

Even seeing a great difference in the significance of the two terms doesn't seem to be a sufficient condition of my wanting to speak of freedom and its absence. Thus my marriage may be breaking up because I like going to the pub and playing cards on Saturday nights with the boys. I may feel quite unequivocally that my marriage is much more important than the release and comradeship of the Saturday night bash. But nevertheless I wouldn't want to talk of my being freer if I could slough off this desire.

The difference seems to be that in this case, unlike the ones above, I still identify with the less important desire, I still see it as expressive of myself, so that I couldn't lose it without altering who I am, losing something of my personality. Whereas my irrational fear, my being quite distressed by discomfort, my spite – these are all things which I can easily see myself losing without any loss whatsoever to what I am. This is why I can see them as obstacles to my purposes, and hence to my freedom, even though they are in a sense unquestionably desires and feelings of mine.

Before exploring further what's involved in this, let's go back and keep score. It would seem that these cases make a bigger breach in the crude negative theory. For they seem to be cases in which the obstacles to freedom are internal; and if this is so, then freedom can't simply be interpreted as the absence of *external* obstacles; and the fact that I'm doing what I want, in the sense of following my strongest desire, isn't sufficient to establish that I'm free. On the contrary, we have to make discriminations among motivations, and accept that acting out of some motivations, for example irrational fear or spite, or this too great need for comfort, is not freedom, is even a negation of freedom.

But although the crude negative theory can't be sustained in the face of these examples, perhaps something which springs from the same concerns can be reconstructed. For although we have to admit that there are internal, motivational, necessary conditions for freedom, we can perhaps still avoid any legitimation of what I called above the second-guessing of the subject. If our negative theory allows for strong evaluation, allows that some goals are really important to us, and that other desires are seen as not fully ours, then can it not retain the thesis that freedom is being able to do what I want, that is, what I can identify myself as wanting, where this means not just what I identify as my strongest desire, but what I identify as my true, authentic desire or purpose? The subject would still be the final arbiter of his being free/unfree, as indeed he is clearly capable of discerning this in the examples above, where I relied precisely on the subject's own experience of constraint, of motives with which he can't identify. We should have sloughed off the untenable Hobbesian reductive-materialist metaphysics, according to which only external obstacles count, as though action were just movement, and there could be no internal, motivational obstacles to our deeper purposes. But we would be retaining the basic concern of the negative theory, that the subject is still the final authority as to what his freedom consists in, and cannot be second-guessed by external authority. Freedom would be modified to read: the absence of internal or external obstacle to what I truly or authentically want. But we would still be holding the Maginot Line. Or would we?

I think not, in fact. I think that this hybrid or middle position is untenable, where we are willing to admit that we can speak of what we truly want, as against what we most strongly desire, and of some desires as obstacles to our freedom, while we still will not allow for second-guessing. For to rule this out in principle is to rule out in principle that the subject can ever be wrong about what he truly wants. And how can he never, in principle, be wrong, unless there is nothing to be right or wrong about in this matter?

That in fact is the thesis our negative theorist will have to defend. And it is a plausible one for the same intellectual (reductive-empiricist) tradition from which the crude negative theory springs. On this view, our feelings are brute facts about us; that is, it is a fact about us that we are affected in such and such a way, but our feelings can't themselves be understood as involving some perception or sense of what they relate to, and hence as potentially veridical or illusory, authentic or inauthentic. On this scheme, the fact that a certain desire represented one of our fundamental purposes, and another a mere force with which we cannot identify, would concern merely the brute quality of the affect in both cases. It would be a matter of the raw feel of these two desires that this was their respective status.

In such circumstances, the subject's own classification would be incorrigible. There is no such thing as an imperceptible raw feel. If the subject failed to experience a certain desire as fundamental, and if what we meant by 'fundamental' applied to desire was that the felt experience of it has a certain quality, then the desire couldn't be fundamental. We can see this if we look at those feelings which we can agree are brute in this sense: for instance, the stab of pain I feel when the dentist jabs into my tooth, or the crawling unease when someone runs his fingernail along the blackboard. There can be no question of misperception here. If I fail to 'perceive' the pain, I am not in pain. Might it not be so with our fundamental desires, and those which we repudiate?

The answer is clearly no. For first of all, many of our feelings and desires, including the relevant ones for these kinds of conflicts, are not brute. By contrast with pain and the fingernail-on-blackboard sensation, shame and fear, for instance, are emotions which involve our experiencing the situation as bearing a certain import for us, as being dangerous or shameful. This is why shame and fear can be inappropriate, or even irrational, where pain and a frisson cannot. Thus we can be in error in feeling shame or fear. We can even be consciously aware of the unfounded nature of our feelings, and this is when we castigate them as irrational.

Thus the notion that we can understand all our feelings and desires as brute, in the above sense, is not on. But more, the idea that we could discriminate our fundamental desires, or those which we want to repudiate, by the quality of brute affect is grotesque. When I am convinced that some career, or an expedition in the Andes, or a love relationship, is of fundamental importance to me (to recur to the above examples), it cannot be just because of the throbs, *élans* or tremors I feel; I must also have some sense that these are of great significance for me, meet important, long-lasting needs, represent a fulfil-

ment of something central to me, will bring me closer to what I really am, or something of the sort. The whole notion of our identity, whereby we recognise that some goals, desires, allegiances are central to what we are, while others are not or are less so, can make sense only against a background of desires and feelings which are not brute, but what I shall call import-attributing, to invent a term of art for the occasion.

Thus we have to see our emotional life as made up largely of import-attributing desires and feelings, that is, desires and feelings which we can experience mistakenly. And not only can we be mistaken in this, we clearly must accept, in cases like the above where we want to repudiate certain desires, that we are mistaken.

For let us consider the distinction mentioned above between conflicts where we feel fettered by one desire, and those where we do not, where, for instance, in the example mentioned above, a man is torn between his career and his marriage. What made the difference was that in the case of genuine conflict both desires are the agent's, whereas in the cases where he feels fettered by one, this desire is one he wants to repudiate.

But what is it to feel that a desire is not truly mine? Presumably, I feel that I should be better off without it, that I don't lose anything in getting rid of it, I remain quite complete without it. What could lie behind this sense?

Well, one could imagine feeling this about a brute desire. I may feel this about my addiction to smoking, for instance – wish I could get rid of it, experience it as a fetter, and believe that I should be well rid of it. But addictions are a special case; we understand them to be unnatural, externally-induced desires. We couldn't say in general that we are ready to envisage losing our brute desires without a sense of diminution. On the contrary, to lose my desire for, and hence delectation in, oysters, mushroom pizza, or Peking duck would be a terrible deprivation. I should fight against such a change with all the strength at my disposal.

So being brute is not what makes desires repudiable. And besides, in the above examples the repudiated desires aren't brute. In the first case, I am chained by unreasoning fear, an import-attributing emotion, in which the fact of being mistaken is already recognised when I identify the fear as irrational or unreasoning. Spite, too, which moves me in the third case, is an import-attributing emotion. To feel spite is to see oneself and the target of one's resentment in a certain light; it is to feel in some way wounded, or damaged, by his success or good fortune, and the more hurt the more he is fortunate. To overcome feelings of spite, as against just holding them in, is to come to see self and other in a different light, in particular, to set aside self-pity, and the sense of being personally wounded by what the other does and is.

(I should also like to claim that the obstacle in the second example, the too great attachment to comfort, while not itself import-attributing, is also bound up with the way we see things. The problem is here not just that we dislike discomfort, but that we are too easily depressed by it; and this is something which we overcome only by sensing a different order of priorities, whereby small discomforts matter less. But if this is thought too dubious, we can concentrate on the other two examples.)

Now how can we feel that an import-attributing desire is not truly ours? We can do this only if we see it as mistaken, that is, the import or the good it supposedly gives us a sense of is not a genuine import or good. The irrational fear is a fetter, because it is irrational; spite is a fetter because it is rooted in a self-absorption which distorts our perspective on everything, and the pleasures of venting it preclude any genuine satisfaction. Losing these desires we lose nothing, because their loss deprives us of no genuine good or pleasure or satisfaction. In this they are quite different from my love of oysters, mushroom pizza and Peking duck.

It would appear from this that to see our desires as brute gives us no clue as to why some of them are repudiable. On the contrary it is precisely their not being brute which can explain this. It is because they are import-attributing desires which are mistaken that we can feel that we would lose nothing in sloughing them off. Everything which is truly important to us would be safeguarded. If they were just brute desires, we couldn't feel this unequivocally, as we certainly do not when it comes to the pleasures of the palate. True, we also feel that our desire to smoke is repudiable, but there is a special explanation here, which is not available in the case of spite.

Thus we can experience some desires as fetters, because we can experience them as not ours. And we can experience them as not ours because we see them as incorporating a quite erroneous appreciation of our situation and of what matters to us. We can see this again if we contrast the case of spite with that of another emotion which partly overlaps, and which is highly considered in some societies, the desire for revenge. In certain traditional societies this is far from being considered a despicable emotion. On the contrary, it is a duty of honour on a male relative to avenge a man's death. We might imagine that this too might give rise to conflict. It might conflict with the attempts of a new regime to bring some order to the land. The government would have to stop people taking vengeance, in the name of peace.

But short of a conversion to a new ethical outlook, this would be seen as a trade-off, the sacrifice of one legitimate goal for the sake of another. And it would seem monstrous were one to propose reconditioning people so that they no longer felt the desire to avenge their kin. This would be to unman them.[4]

Why do we feel so different about spite (and for that matter also revenge)? Because the desire for revenge for an ancient Icelander was his sense of a real obligation incumbent on him, something it would be dishonourable to repudiate; while for us, spite is the child of a distorted perspective on things.

We cannot therefore understand our desires and emotions as all brute, and in particular we cannot make sense of our discrimination of some desires as more important and fundamental, or of our repudiation of others, unless we understand our feelings to be import-attributing. This is essential to there being what we have called strong evaluation. Consequently the half-way position which admits strong evaluation, admits that our desires may frustrate our deeper purposes, admits therefore that there may be inner obstacles to freedom, and yet will not admit that the subject may be wrong or mistaken about these purposes – this position doesn't seem tenable. For the only way to make the subject's assessment incorrigible in principle would be to claim that there was nothing to be right or wrong about here; and that could only be so if experiencing a given feeling were a matter of the qualities of brute feeling. But this it cannot be if we are to make sense of the whole background of strong evaluation, more significant goals, and aims that we repudiate. This whole scheme requires that we understand the emotions concerned as import-attributing, as, indeed, it is clear that we must do on other grounds as well.

But once we admit that our feelings are import-attributing, then we admit the possibility of error, or false appreciation. And indeed, we have to admit a kind of false appreciation which the agent himself detects in order to make sense of the cases where we experience our own desires as fetters. How can we exclude in principle that there may be other false appreciations which the agent does not detect? That he may be profoundly in error, that is, have a very distorted sense of his fundamental purposes? Who can say that such people can't exist? All cases are, of course, controversial; but I should nominate Charles Manson and Andreas Baader for this category, among others. I pick them out as people with a strong sense of some purposes and goals as incomparably more fundamental than others, or at least with a propensity to act as having such a sense so as to take in even themselves a good part of the time, but whose sense of fundamental purpose was shot through with confusion and error. And once we recognise such extreme cases, how do we avoid admitting that many of the rest of mankind can suffer to a lesser degree from the same disabilities?

What has this got to do with freedom? Well, to resume what we have seen: our attributions of freedom make sense against a background sense of more and less significant purposes, for the question of freedom/unfreedom is bound up with the frustration/fulfilment of our purposes. Further, our significant purposes can be frustrated by our own desires, and where these are sufficiently based on misappreciation, we consider them as not really ours, and experience them as fetters. A man's freedom can therefore be hemmed in by internal, motivational obstacles, as well as external ones. A man who is driven by spite to jeopardise his most important relationships, in spite of himself, as it were, or who is prevented by unreasoning fear from taking up the career he truly wants, is not really made more free if one lifts the external obstacles to his venting his spite or acting on his fear. Or at best he is liberated into a very impoverished freedom.

If through linguistic/ideological purism one wants to stick to the crude definition, and insist that men are equally freed from whom the same external obstacles are lifted, regardless of their motivational state, then one will just have to introduce some other term to mark the distinction, and say that one man is capable of taking proper advantage of his freedom, and the other

(the one in the grip of spite, or fear) is not. This is because in the meaningful sense of 'free', that for which we value it, in the sense of being able to act on one's important purposes, the internally fettered man is not free. If we choose to give 'free' a special (Hobbesian) sense which avoids this issue, we'll just have to introduce another term to deal with it.

Moreover since we have already seen that we are always making judgements of degrees of freedom, based on the significance of the activities or purposes which are left unfettered, how can we deny that the man, externally free but still stymied by his repudiated desires, is less free than one who has no such inner obstacles?

But if this is so, then can we not say of the man with a highly distorted view of his fundamental purpose, the Manson or Baader of my discussion above, that he may not be significantly freer when we lift even the internal barriers to his doing what is in line with this purpose, or at best may be liberated into a very impoverished freedom? Should a Manson overcome his last remaining compunction against sending his minions to kill on caprice, so that he could act unchecked, would we consider him freer, as we should undoubtedly consider the man who had done away with spite or unreasoning fear? Hardly, and certainly not to the same degree. For what he sees as his purpose here partakes so much of the nature of spite and unreasoning fear in the other cases, that is, it is an aspiration largely shaped by confusion, illusion and distorted perspective.

Once we see that we make distinctions of degree and significance in freedoms depending on the significance of the purpose fettered/enabled, how can we deny that it makes a difference to the degree of freedom not only whether one of my basic purposes is frustrated by my own desires but also whether I have grievously misidentified this purpose? The only way to avoid this would be to hold that there is no such thing as getting it wrong, that your basic purpose is just what you feel it to be. But there is such a thing as getting it wrong, as we have seen, and the very distinctions of significance depend on this fact.

But if this is so, then the crude negative view of freedom, the Hobbesian definition, is untenable. Freedom can't just be the absence of external obstacles, for there may also be internal ones. And nor may the internal obstacles be just confined to those that the subject identifies as such, so that he is the final arbiter; for he may be profoundly mistaken about his purposes and about what he wants to repudiate. And if so, he is less capable of freedom in the meaningful sense of the word. Hence we cannot maintain the incorrigibility of the subject's judgements about his freedom, or rule out second-guessing, as we put it above. And at the same time, we are forced to abandon the pure opportunity-concept of freedom.

For freedom now involves my being able to recognise adequately my more important purposes, and my being able to overcome or at least neutralise my motivational fetters, as well as my way being free of external obstacles. But clearly the first condition (and, I would argue, also the second) require me to have become something, to have achieved a certain condition of self-clairvoyance and self-understanding. I must be actually exercising self-understanding in order to be truly or fully free. I can no longer understand freedom just as an opportunity-concept.

In all these three formulations of the issue – opportunity- versus exercise-concept; whether freedom requires that we discriminate among motivations; whether it allows of second-guessing the subject – the extreme negative view shows up as wrong. The idea of holding the Maginot Line before this Hobbesian concept is misguided not only because it involves abandoning some of the most inspiring terrain of liberalism, which is concerned with individual self-realisation, but also because the line turns out to be untenable. The first step from the Hobbesian definition to a positive notion, to a view of freedom as the ability to fulfil my purposes, and as being greater the more significant the purposes, is one we cannot help taking. Whether we must also take the second step, to a view of freedom which sees it as realisable or fully realisable only within a certain form of society; and whether in taking a step of this kind one is necessarily committed to justifying the excesses of totalitarian oppression in the name of liberty; these are questions which must now be addressed. What is certain is that they cannot simply be evaded by a philistine definition of freedom which relegates them by fiat to the limbo of metaphysical pseudo-questions. This is altogether too quick a way with them.

Notes

1   *F.E.L.*, pp. 118–72.
2   Ibid., p. 148, note 1.
3   Ibid., p. 164.

4   Compare the unease we feel at the reconditioning of the hero of Anthony Burgess's *A Clockwork Orange*.

26

The Structure of Proletarian Unfreedom

G.A. Cohen

I

According to Karl Marx, a member of a social class belongs to it by virtue of his position within social relations of production. In keeping with this formula, Marx defined the proletarian as the producer who has (literally or in effect) nothing to sell but his own labor power.[1] He inferred that the worker is *forced* to sell his labor power (on pain of starvation).

In this article I am not concerned with the adequacy of Marx's definition of working class membership. I propose instead to assess the truth of the consequence he rightly or wrongly inferred from that definition. Is it true that workers are forced to sell their labor power?

This question is debated in the real world, by nonacademic people. Supporters and opponents of the capitalist system tend to disagree about the answer to it. There is a familiar right-wing answer to it which I think has a lot of power. In this article I argue against leftists who do not see the answer's power and against rightists who do not see the answer's limitations.

II

Some would deny that workers are forced to sell their labor power, on the ground that they have other choices: the worker can go on the dole, or

Originally published in *Philosophy and Public Affairs*, 12 (1983), 3–33. Copyright © 1983 by Princeton University Press. Reprinted by permission of Princeton University Press.

beg, or simply make no provision for himself and trust to fortune.

It is true that the worker is free to do these other things. The acknowledgment that he is free to starve to death gets its sarcastic power from the fact that he *is* free to starve to death: no one threatens to *make* him stay alive by, for example, force-feeding him. But to infer that he is therefore not forced to sell his labor power is to employ a false account of what it is to be forced to do something. When I am forced to do something I have no *reasonable* or *acceptable* alternative course. It need not be true that I have no alternative whatsoever. At least usually, when a person says, "I was forced to do it, I had no other choice," the second part of the statement is elliptical for something like "I had no other choice worth considering." For in the most familiar sense of "X is forced to do A," it is entailed that X is forced to *choose* to do A, and the claim that the worker is forced to sell his labor power is intended in that familiar sense. Hence the fact that he is free to starve or beg instead is not a refutation of the mooted claim: the claim entails that there are other (unacceptable) things he is free to do.

III

Robert Nozick might grant that many workers have no acceptable alternative to selling their labor power, and he recognizes that they need not have no alternative at all in order to count as forced to do so. But he denies that having no acceptable alternative but to do A entails being forced to do A, no matter how bad A is, and no

429

matter how much worse the alternatives are, since he thinks that to have no acceptable alternative means to be forced only when unjust actions help to explain the absence of acceptable alternatives. Property distributions reflecting a history of acquisition and exchange may leave the worker with no other acceptable option, but is he nevertheless not forced to sell his labor power, if the acquiring and exchanging were free of injustice.

Nozick's objection to the thesis under examination rests upon a moralized account of what it is to be forced to do something. It is a false account, because it has the absurd upshot that if a criminal's imprisonment is morally justified, he is then not forced to be in prison. We may therefore set Nozick's objection aside.[2]

IV

There is, however, an objection to the claim that workers are forced to sell their labor power which does not depend upon a moralized view of what being forced involves. But before we come to it, in Section V, I must explain how I intend the predicate "is forced to sell his labor power." The claim in which it figures here comes from Karl Marx. Now I noted that Marx characterized classes by reference to social relations of production, and the claim is intended to satisfy that condition: it purports to say something about the proletarian's position in capitalist relations of production. But relations of production are, for Marxism, *objective*: what relations of production a person is in does not turn on his consciousness. It follows that if the proletarian is forced to sell his labor power in the relevant Marxist sense, then this must be because of his objective situation, and not because of his attitude to himself, his level of self-confidence, his cultural attainment, and so on. It is in any case doubtful that limitations in those subjective endowments can be sources of what interests us: unfreedom, as opposed to something similar to it but also rather different: incapacity. But even if diffidence and the like could be said to force a person to sell his labor power, that would be an irrelevant case here (except, perhaps, where personal subjective limitations are caused by capitalist relations of production, a possibility considered in Section XV below).

To be forced to do *A* by one's objective situation is to do it because of factors other than the subjective ones just mentioned. Many would

insist that the proper source of force, and a *a fortiori* of objective force, is action by other people, what they have done, or are doing, or what they would do were one to try to do *A*. I agree with Harry Frankfurt[3] that this insistence is wrong, but I shall accede to it in the present article, for two reasons. The first is that the mooted restriction makes it harder, and therefore more interesting, to show that workers are forced to sell their labor power. The second is that, as I shall now argue, where relations of production force people to do things, people force people to do things, so the "no force without a forcing agent" condition is satisfied here, even if it does not hold generally.

The relations of production of a society may be identified with the powers its differently situated persons have with respect to the society's productive forces, that is, the labor capacities of its producers and the means of production they use.[4] We can distinguish between standard and deviant uses of the stated powers. Let me then propose that a worker is forced to sell his labor power in the presently required sense if and only if the constraint is a result of standard exercises of the powers constituting relations of production.

If a millionaire is forced by a blackmailer to sell his labor power, he is not forced to do so in the relevant Marxist sense, since the blackmailer does not use economic power to get him to do so. The relevant constraint must reflect use of economic power, and not, moreover, just any use of it, but a *standard* exercise of it. I do not yet know how to define "standard," but it is not hard to sort out cases in an intuitive way. If, for example, a capitalist forces people to work for him by hiring gunmen to get them to do so, the resulting constraint is due to a nonstandard exercise of economic power. And one can envisage similarly irrelevant cases of relaxation of constraint: a philanthropic capitalist might be willing to transfer large shares in the ownership of his enterprise to workers, on a "first come first served" basis. That would not be a standard use of capitalist power.

Suppose, however, that economic structural constraint does not, as just proposed, operate through the regular exercise by persons of the powers constituting the economic structure, but in some more *im*personal way, as Althusserians seem to imagine. It might still be said, for a different reason, that if the structure of capitalism leaves the worker no choice but to sell his labor power, then he is forced to do so by actions of persons. For the structure of capitalism is not in all senses self-sustaining. It is sustained by a great deal of deliberate human action, notably on the part of the state. And if, as I often think, the state functions on behalf of the capitalist class, then any structural constraint by virtue of which the worker must sell his labor power has enough human will behind it to satisfy the stipulation that where there is force, there are forcing human beings.

The stipulation might be satisfied by doctrine weaker than that which presents the state as an instrument of the capitalist class. Suppose that the state upholds the capitalist order not because it is a *capitalist* order, but because it is the prevailing order, and the state is dedicated to upholding whatever order prevails. Then, too, one might be justified in speaking of human forcing.

V

Under the stated interpretation of "is forced to sell his labor power," a serious problem arises for the thesis under examination. For if there are persons whose objective position is identical with that of proletarians but who are not forced to sell their labor power, then proletarians are not relevantly so forced, and the thesis is false. And there do seem to be such persons.

I have in mind those proletarians who, initially possessed of no greater resources than most, secure positions in the petty bourgeoisie and elsewhere, thereby rising above the proletariat. Striking cases in Britain are members of certain immigrant groups, who arrive penniless, and without good connections, but who propel themselves up the class hierarchy with effort, skill, and luck. One thinks – it is a contemporary example – of those who are willing to work very long hours in shops bought from native British bourgeois, shops which used to close early. Their initial capital is typically an amalgam of savings, which they accumulated, perhaps painfully, while still in the proletarian condition, and some form of external finance. *Objectively speaking*, most[5] British proletarians are in a position to obtain these. Therefore most British proletarians are not forced to sell their labor power.

VI

I now refute two predictable objections to the above argument.

The first says that the recently mentioned persons were, *while they were proletarians*, forced to sell their labor power. Their cases do not show that proletarians are not forced to sell their labor power. They show something different: that proletarians are not forced to remain proletarians.

This objection embodies a misunderstanding of what Marxists intend when they say that workers are forced to sell their labor power. But before I say what Marxists intend by that statement, I must defend this general claim about freedom and constraint: *fully explicit attributions of freedom and constraint contain two temporal indexes*. To illustrate: I may now be in a position truly to say that I am free to attend a concert tomorrow night, since nothing has occurred, up to now, to prevent my doing so. If so, I am *now* free to attend a concert *tomorrow night*. In similar fashion, the time when I am constrained to perform an action need not be identical with the time of the action: I might *already* be forced to attend a concert *tomorrow night* (since you might already have ensured that if I do not, I shall suffer some great loss).

Now when Marxists say that proletarians are forced to sell their labor power, they do not mean: "X is a proletarian at time t only if X is at t forced to sell his labor power at t" for that would be compatible with his not being forced to at time $t + n$, no matter how small n is. X might be forced on Tuesday to sell his labor power on Tuesday, but if he is not forced on Tuesday to sell his labor power on Wednesday (if, for example, actions open to him on Tuesday would bring it about that on Wednesday he need not do so), then, though still a proletarian on Tuesday, he is not then someone who is forced to sell his labor power in the relevant Marxist sense. The manifest intent of the Marxist claim is that the proletarian is forced at t to *continue* to sell his labor power, throughout a period from t to $t + n$, for some considerable n. It follows that because there is a route out of the proletariat, which our counterexamples travelled, reaching their destination in, as I would argue, an amount of time less than n,[6] they were, though proletarians, not forced to sell their labor power in the required Marxist sense.

Proletarians who have the option of class ascent are not forced to sell their labor power, just because they do have that option. Most proletarians have it as much as our counterexamples did. Therefore most proletarians are not forced to sell their labor power.

VII

But now I face a second objection. It is that necessarily not more than few proletarians can exercise the option of upward movement. For capitalism requires a substantial hired labor force, which would not exist if more than just a few workers rose.[7] Put differently, there are necessarily only enough petty bourgeois and other non-proletarian positions for a small number of the proletariat to leave their estate.

I agree with the premise, but does it defeat the argument against which it is directed? Does it refute the claim that most proletarians are not forced to sell their labor power? I think not.

An analogy will indicate why. Ten people are placed in a room the only exit from which is a huge and heavy locked door. At various distances from each lies a single heavy key. Whoever picks up this key – and each is physically able, with varying degrees of effort, to do so – and takes it to the door will find, after considerable self-application, a way to open the door and leave the room. But if he does so he alone will be able to leave it. Photoelectric devices installed by a jailer ensure that it will open only just enough to permit one exit. Then it will close, and no one inside the room will be able to open it again.

It follows that, whatever happens, at least nine people will remain in the room.

Now suppose that not one of the people is inclined to try to obtain the key and leave the room. Perhaps the room is no bad place, and they do not want to leave it. Or perhaps it is pretty bad, but they are too lazy to undertake the effort needed to escape. Or perhaps no one believes he would be able to secure the key in face of the capacity of the others to intervene (though no one would in fact intervene, since, being so diffident each also believes that he would be unable to remove the key from anyone else). Suppose that, whatever may be their reasons, they are all so indisposed to leave the room that if, counterfactually, one of them were to try to leave, the rest would not interfere. The universal inaction is relevant to my argument, but the explanation of it is not.

Then whomever we select, it is true of the other nine that not one of them is going to try to get the key. Therefore it is true of the selected person that he is free to obtain the key, and to use it.[8] He is therefore not forced to remain in the room. But all this is true of whomever we select.

Therefore it is true of each person that he is not forced to remain in the room, even though necessarily at least nine will remain in the room, and in fact all will.

Consider now a slightly different example, a modified version of the situation just described. In the new case there are two doors and two keys. Again, there are ten people, but this time one of them does try to get out, and succeeds, while the rest behave as before. Now necessarily eight will remain in the room, but it is true of each of the nine who do stay that he or she is free to leave it. The pertinent general feature, present in both cases, is that there is at least one means of egress which none will attempt to use, and which each is free to use, since, *ex hypothesi*, no one would block his way.

By now the application of the analogy may be obvious. The number of exits from the proletariat is, as a matter of objective circumstance, small. But most proletarians are not trying to escape, and, as a result, *it is false that each exit is being actively attempted by some proletarian.* Therefore for most[9] proletarians there exists a means of escape. So even though necessarily most proletarians will remain proletarians, and will sell their labor power, perhaps none, and at most a minority, are forced to do so.

In reaching this conclusion, which is about the proletariat's *objective* position, I used some facts of consciousness, regarding workers' aspirations and intentions. That is legitimate. For if the workers are objectively forced to sell their labor power, then they are forced to do so whatever their subjective situation may be. But their actual subjective situation brings it about that they are not forced to sell their labor power. Hence they are not objectively forced to sell their labor power.

VIII

One could say, speaking rather broadly, that we have found more freedom in the proletariat's situation than classical Marxism asserts. But if we return to the basis on which we affirmed that most proletarians are not forced to sell their labor power, we shall arrive at a more refined description of the objective position with respect to force and freedom. What was said will not be withdrawn, but we shall add significantly to it.

That basis was the reasoning originally applied

to the case of the people in the locked room. Each is free to seize the key and leave. But note the conditional nature of his freedom. He is free not only *because* none of the others tries to get the key, but *on condition* that they do not (a condition which, in the story, is fulfilled). Then *each is free only on condition that the others do not exercise their similarly conditional freedom.* Not more than one can exercise the liberty they all have. If, moreover, any one were to exercise it, then, because of the structure of the situation, all the others would lose it.

Since the freedom of each is contingent on the others not exercising their similarly contingent freedom, we can say that there is a great deal of unfreedom in their situation. Though each is individually free to leave, he suffers with the rest from what I shall call *collective unfreedom*.

In defense of this description, let us reconsider the question why the people do not try to leave. None of the reasons suggested earlier – lack of desire, laziness, diffidence – go beyond what a person wants and fears for himself alone. But the annals of human motivation show that sometimes people care about the fate of others, and they sometimes have that concern when they share a common oppression. Suppose, then, not so wildly, that there is a sentiment of solidarity in that room. A fourth possible explanation of the absence of attempt to leave now suggests itself. It is that no one will be satisfied with a personal escape which is not part of a general liberation.[10]

The new supposition does not upset the claim that each is free to leave, for we may assume that it remains true of each person that he would suffer no interference if, counterfactually, he sought to use the key (assume the others would have contempt for him, but not try to stop him). Each remains free to leave. Yet we can envisage members of the group communicating to their jailer a demand for freedom, to which he could hardly reply that they are free already (even though, individually, they are). The hypothesis of solidarity makes the collective unfreedom evident. But unless we say, absurdly, that the solidarity creates the unfreedom to which it is a response, we must say that there is collective unfreedom whether or not solidarity obtains.

Returning to the proletariat, we can conclude, by parity of reasoning, that although most proletarians are free to escape the proletariat, and, indeed, even if every one is, the proletariat is collectively unfree, an imprisoned class.

Marx often maintained that the worker is forced to sell his labor power not to any particular capitalist, but just to some capitalist or other, and he emphasized the ideological value of this distinction.[11] The present point is that, although, in a collective sense, workers are forced to sell their labor power, scarcely any particular proletarian is forced to sell himself even to some capitalist or other. And this too has ideological value. It is part of the genius of capitalist exploitation that, by contrast with exploitation which proceeds by "extra-economic coercion,"[12] it does not require the unfreedom of specified individuals. There is an ideologically valuable anonymity on *both* sides of the relationship of exploitation.

IX

It was part of the argument for affirming the freedom to escape of proletarians, taken individually, that not every exit from the proletariat is crowded with would-be escapees. Why should this be so? Here are some of the reasons:

1 It is possible to escape, but it is not easy, and often people do not attempt what is possible but hard.
2 There is also what Marx called the "dull compulsion of economic relations."[13] Long occupancy, for example from birth, of a subordinate class position nurtures the illusion, as important for the stability of the system as the myth of easy escape, that one's class position is natural and inescapable.
3 Finally, there is the fact that not all workers would like to be petty or transpetty bourgeois. Eugene Debs said, "I do not want to rise above the working class, I want to rise with them," thereby evincing an attitude like the one lately attributed to the people in the locked room. It is sometimes true of the worker that, in Brecht's words,

> He wants no servants under him
> And no boss over his head.[14]

Those lines envisage a better liberation: not just from the working class, but from class society.

X

In the rest of this article I consider objections to the arguments of Sections VII and VIII, which I shall henceforth call argument 7 and argument 8, after the numbers of the Sections in which they were presented. Shorn of explanatory detail, the arguments are as follows:

7: There are more exits from the British proletariat than there are workers trying to leave it. Therefore, British workers are individually free to leave the proletariat.
8: There are very few exits from the British proletariat and there are very many workers in it. Therefore, British workers are collectively unfree to leave the proletariat.

In the useful language of the medieval schoolmen, the workers are not forced to sell their labor power *in sensu diviso*, but they are forced to in *sensu composito*.

The arguments are consistent with one another. Hillel Steiner has pointed to a potential conflict between them, but it is unlikely to materialize. The potential conflict relates to my attribution to Marxism (see Section VI) of the claim that the worker is forced to remain a worker for some considerable amount of time *n*, a claim which the conclusion of argument 7 is intended to deny. Now, the larger *n* is, the easier it is to refute the Marxist claim and affirm argument 7's conclusion. But as *n* grows larger, the number of exits from the proletariat increases, and the conclusion of argument 8 becomes correspondingly less secure. To sustain both arguments without equivocation one must choose an intuitively plausible *n* under these opposite pressures. But it is not hard to meet that requirement: five years, for example, will do.

Right-wing readers will applaud argument 7, but they will want to resist argument 8. Left-wing readers will have, in each case, the opposite reaction. In the remaining seven Sections I deal first with four right-wing objections to argument 8, and then with three left-wing objections to argument 7.

A one-premise argument may be challenged in respect of its premise, its inference, and, independently of the way it is drawn, its conclusion. Section XI considers the inference of argument 8; Sections XII and XIII examine whether its conclusion is true, or, if true, interesting; and Section XIV investigates its premise. In Sections XV and XVI the inference of argument 7 is challenged, and in Section XVII its premise is subjected to scrutiny.

XI

Someone who, unlike Frankfurt, believes that only human action can force people to do things, might object as follows to the derivation of the conclusion of argument 8, that British workers are collectively unfree:

The prisoners in the room are collectively unfree, since the availability of only one exit is a result of a jailer's action. If they had wandered into a cave from which, for peculiar reasons, only one could leave, then, though *unable*, collectively, to leave, they would not have been *unfree* to, since there would have been no one forcing them to stay. It is true that, *in sensu composito*, most proletarians must remain proletarians, but this is due to a numerical relationship which does not reflect human design. It is therefore not correct to speak of the proletariat as collectively *unfree* to leave, as opposed to collectively *unable*. In short, the admitted restrictions on proletarian ascent are not caused by factors which would justify application of the concepts of force and unfreedom.

I have four replies to this objection.

First, what was said about the cave, if it illustrates the thesis that people are forced only when people force them, also shows how unlikely a thesis that is. For it seems false that the hapless wanderers are forced to remain in the cave only if someone put them there, or keeps them there.

It is, moreover, arguable that the (anyhow questionable) requirement of a forcing human agency is met in the cave case. I say that there is collective unfreedom to leave in that as soon as one person left, the rest would be prevented from doing so. And just as there is individual unfreedom when a person's attempt to do *A* would be blocked by someone else doing it, so there is collective unfreedom when an attempt by more than *n* to do *A* would be blocked by that subset of *n* which succeeded in doing it. This applies to the proletariat, when the number of exits is limited. They are collectively unfree since, were more to try to escape than there are exits, the successful would ensure the imprisonment of those who failed.

But apart from the mutual constraint arising out of the surplus of persons over exits, there is the fact that the adverse numerical relationship reflects the structure of capitalism which, we saw in Section IV, is sufficiently connected, in various ways, with human actions to satisfy the un-Frankfurtian scruples motivating the present objection. Proletarians suffer restricted access to means of liberation because the rights of private property are enforced by exercise of capitalist power.

Finally, even if we should have to abandon the claim that workers are collectively unfree to escape and embrace instead the idea that they are collectively unable to, the withdrawal would be only a tactical one. For anyone concerned about human freedom and the prospect of expanding it must also care about structurally induced disability (or whatever he chooses to call it), which he refuses to regard as absence of freedom. Even if he is right that the wanderers are not *forced* to stay in the cave, he surely cannot deny that whoever released them would be *liberating* them.

XII

The objector of Section XI doubted that the situation of the proletariat could be described as one of collective freedom, but he did not challenge the very concept of a collective unfreedom distinct from individual unfreedom. I now deal with a differently inspired skepticism. Set aside the question of what causes the restriction on the number of nonproletarian positions. Does the resulting lack of access justify my description of the workers as lacking collective freedom? I argued that there is some sense in which they are not all free to escape, and, since they are free *in sensu diviso*, I called their unfreedom collective unfreedom.

Collective unfreedom can be defined as follows: a group suffers collective unfreedom with respect to a type of action A if and only if performance of A by all members of the group is impossible.[15] Collective unfreedom comes in varying amounts, and it is greater the smaller the ratio of the maximum that could perform A to the total number in the group. Collective unfreedom is particularly interesting when, as in our example, there is more freedom for a set of individuals taken individually than for the same individuals when they are taken as members of a group: collective unfreedom, we might say, is *irreducibly* collective when more can perform A *in sensu diviso* than can perform it *in sensu composito*. And collective unfreedom matters more the smaller

the ratio mentioned above is, and the more important or desirable action A is.

A person shares in a collective unfreedom when, to put it roughly, he is among those who are so situated that if enough others exercise the corresponding individual freedom, then they lose their individual freedoms. More precisely: X shares in a collective unfreedom with respect to a type of action A if and only if X belongs to a set of n persons which is such that:

1 no more than m of them (where $m < n$) are free (*sensu composito*) to perform A, and
2 no matter which m members performed A, the remaining $n - m$ would then be unfree (*sensu diviso*) to perform A.[16]

Using both expressions as terms of art, one might distinguish between *collective* unfreedom and *group* unfreedom, and I am not here concerned with the latter. In the preferred definition of collective unfreedom the relevant agents are individuals, not a group as such. We are not discussing freedom and the lack of it which groups have *qua* groups, but which individuals have as members of groups. Thus, for example, the freedom or lack of it which the proletariat has to overthrow capitalism falls outside our scope,[17] since no individual proletarian could ever be free to overthrow capitalism, even when the proletariat is free to do so.

Another form of essentially interpersonal freedom is that canonically reported in sentences of the form "X is free to do A with Y," where Y is another agent, and where if X does A with Y, then Y does A with X (the last condition is needed to exclude such actions as wiping the floor with Y. "with" means "together with" in sentences of the indicated form). This can be called *freedom-to act-with*, or *relational freedom*.[18] Note that the relevant relation is neither symmetrical nor transitive. If I am free to do A with you, it does not follow that you are free to do A with me, since, for example, doing A might be seeing a film which you would love to see with me but which I do not want to see. And if I am free to make love with you and you are free to make love with him, it does not follow that I am free to make love with him. Freedom-to-act-with figured implicitly in the argument of Section VIII, when I hypothesized a sentiment of solidarity which moved each person in the room to regret that (though free to leave) he was not free to leave with the others. But freedom-to-act-with is different from what is here meant by collective freedom: in the case of the latter there need be no reference to another person in the description of the action people are free or unfree to perform.

Now someone might say: since interesting collective unfreedom obtains only when individuals are free, why should it be a source of concern? Why should we care about anything other than the freedom of individuals?[19] The question forgets that it is a fact touching each individual in the group, namely, the mutually conditional nature of their freedom, which licenses the idea of collective unfreedom. As soon as enough people exercise the coexisting individual freedoms, collective unfreedom generates individual unfreedoms. If, though free to do A, I share in a collective unfreedom with respect to A, I am less free than I otherwise would be.

But it might be claimed that there are structures manifesting what I defined as collective unfreedom which would not normally be regarded as examples of lack of freedom. Suppose, for instance, that a hotel, at which one hundred tourists are staying, lays on a coach trip for the first forty who apply, since that is the number of seats in the coach. And suppose that only thirty want to go. Then, on my account, each of the hundred is free to go, but their situation displays a collective unfreedom. Yet it seems wrong, the objector says, to speak of unfreedom here.

I do not agree. For suppose all of the tourists did want to go. Then it would seem appropriate to say that they are not all free to go. But in the case of individual freedom, while there is less reason to regret an unfreedom to do what I have no desire to do,[20] I am not less unfree for lacking that desire.[21] Why should the position be different in the case of collective unfreedom? Thwarted desire throws unfreedom into relief, and sometimes thwarted desire is needed to make unfreedom deserving of note, but it is not a necessary condition of unfreedom.

The coach case is a rather special one. For we tend to suppose that the management lay on only one coach because they correctly anticipate that one will be enough to meet the demand. Accordingly, we also suppose that if more had wanted to go, there would have been an appropriately larger number of seats available. If all that is true, then the available amount of collective freedom nonaccidentally accords with the tourists' desires, and though there still is a collective unfreedom, it is, as it were, a purely technical one. But if we assume that there is only one coach

in town, and some such assumption is required for parity with the situation of proletarians, then the tourists' collective unfreedom is more than merely technical.

There are two significantly different variants of the merely technical version of the coach case. In the first the management decide how many coaches to order after first asking each tourist whether or not he wants to go. In that case there is a time at which all are free to go, even *in sensu composito*, though they cease to be after they have declared themselves.[22] But the management might order one coach without consulting the tourists, out of knowledge of the normal distribution of tourist desire. In that case there is no time at which all are free to go, *in sensu composito*, but the collective unfreedom is still purely technical and singularly unregrettable.

Now someone who accepts my concept of collective unfreedom might argue that it is not in general a lamentable thing, and that it need not be lamentable even when the amount of collective unfreedom is not, as above, directly or indirectly causally connected, in a benign way, with people's desires. There is at present (or was when I first wrote this) a shortage of bus conductors in London, so that there is a good deal of individual freedom to become one, but also a large amount of collective unfreedom, since not more than very few of us can be bus conductors. But so what?

The rhetorical question is apposite in this case, but it is out of place when there is unfreedom to abstain from selling one's labor power to another. As I remarked earlier, the extent to which collective unfreedom with respect to an action matters depends upon the nature of the action. I grant that collective unfreedom with respect to the sale of labor power is not lamentable merely because it is collective unfreedom, since some collective unfreedom, like some individual unfreedom, is not lamentable. It is what this particular collective unfreedom forces workers to do which makes it a proper object of regret and protest. They are forced to subordinate themselves to others who thereby gain control over their, the workers', productive existence. The contrast between them and those others is the subject of the next section.

XIII

In an argument which does not challenge the concept of collective unfreedom, Hillel Steiner and

Jan Narveson[23] say that if there is a sense in which capitalism renders workers unfree, then it does the same to capitalists. For if having no choice but to sell his labor power makes the worker unfree, then the capitalist is similarly unfree, since he has no choice but to invest his capital. Sometimes authors sympathetic to Marx say similar things. Thus Gary Young argues that the "same line of reasoning" which shows that "the worker is compelled to sell his labor power to some capitalist . . . shows equally that the capitalist is compelled to obtain labor power from the worker."[24]

I shall presently question the claim that capitalists are forced to invest their capital. But even if we suppose that they are, the disanalogy between them and the workers remains so great that the Steiner/Narveson challenge must be judged rather insensitive.

For the worker is more closely connected with his labor power than the capitalist is with his capital. When I sell my labor power, I put *myself* at the disposal of another, and that is not true when I invest my capital. I come with my labor power, I am part of the deal.[25] That is why some people call wage labor wage slavery, and that is why John Stuart Mill said that "to work at the bidding and for the profit of another . . . is not . . . a satisfactory state to human beings of educated intelligence, who have ceased to think themselves naturally inferior to those whom they serve."[26] I am sure that many will think it is an irresponsible exaggeration to call wage labor wage slavery. But note that no one would say, even by way of exaggeration, that having to invest one's capital is a form of slavery.

But Steiner and Narveson are not, in any case, entitled to say that capitalists are forced to invest their capital. To begin with, some are so rich that they could devote the rest of their days to spending it on consumer goods. But let us focus on the more modestly situated remainder. When Marxists claim that workers are forced to sell their labor power, they mean that they have no acceptable alternative, if they want to stay alive. But capitalists, some might say, do have an acceptable alternative to investing their capital: they are free to sell their labor power instead.[27] Of course, Steiner and Narveson, in order to defend their thesis, might deny that that is an acceptable alternative, and I, for other reasons, might agree. But if they take that line, then they should not have proposed their analogy in the first place. So

either the capitalist is not forced to invest his capital, since he could, after all, sell his labor power; or, if he is, then that is because of how bad selling one's labor power is, in comparison with investing one's capital.[28]

It might be said that the capitalist is, *qua* capitalist, forced to invest his capital: insofar as he acts in that capacity, he has no other choice. But even if that is so – and I am not sure that it is – it is irrelevant. For while it is sometimes appropriate to deal with individuals "only in so far as they are the personifications of economic categories,"[29] that form of abstraction is out of place here. We are not here interested in the freedom and bondage of abstract characters, such as the capitalist *qua* capitalist. We are interested in *human* freedom, and hence in the human being who is a capitalist; and if the capitalist *qua* capitalist is forced to invest his capital, it does not follow that the human being who is a capitalist is forced to. It is also irrelevant, if true, that the capitalist is forced to invest his capital as long as he wants to be a capitalist. Note that, in order to confer plausibility on the claim that the worker is forced to sell his labor power, it is not necessary to stick in such phrases as "*qua* worker" or "as long as he wants to be a worker."

Those capitalists who are not dizzily rich are forced to invest their capital or sell their labor power. So they have an alternative to selling their labor power which the worker lacks. But they are not gods. Like the worker, they "enter into relations that are indispensable and independent of their will."[30] Everyone has to take capitalism as it is. But people have different amounts of choice about where to enter the set of relations it imposes, and capitalists typically have vastly more such choice than workers do.

In the foregoing discussion I did not observe the distinction between the freedom of capitalists *in sensu diviso* and their freedom *in sensu composito*, since the Steiner/Narveson objection is presented without reference to that distinction. We can, however, imagine an objection of the same general style which does make use of it:

The individual capitalist may have more freedom of choice than the individual worker, but your own emphasis is not on the unfreedom of the worker taken as an individual, but on the unfreedom he shares with other members of his class. And if we look at capitalists as a class, we find a similar collective unfreedom. They could not *all* become sellers of labor power, since for there to be sellers of it there have to be buyers of it. Capitalists consequently suffer from a collective unfreedom parallel to that of workers.

I have three replies to this objection.

Recall, first, that collective unfreedom comes in varying amounts (see Sec XII). Then note that even if the objection is otherwise sound, it demonstrates much less collective unfreedom for capitalists than can be attributed to workers, since the members of any group of all but any (say) two or three of the capitalists are not structurally prevented from giving their wealth to those two or three. Mass escape from the proletariat, leaving only two or three workers behind, is, by contrast, structurally impossible.

But one can go further. It is unlikely that capitalists suffer *any* collective unfreedom with respect to becoming wage workers, since if literally all capitalists wanted to do so, so that none of their number was willing to play the role of hirer, it would probably be easy to find workers willing and able to fill it.

Finally, the objection ignores a way in which capitalists could stop being capitalists *without* becoming wage workers: by yielding their wealth not, as above, to particular others, but to society at large. I do not propose this as a new road to socialism, since it is a practical certainty that capitalists will not travel it.[31] My point is that there is no structural barrier against complete self-extinction of the capitalist class, whereas there is a structural barrier to mass exit from the proletariat: the capitalists own the means of production.

XIV

The final challenge from the Right to be considered here concerns the premise of the argument of Section VIII: that there are not very many exits from the proletariat. The objector I have in mind grants that there cannot be general escape in the direction of the petty (and more than petty) bourgeoisie: workers could not become, *en masse*, shopkeepers and employers of other workers, if only because there would then be too few left to produce what shopkeepers sell. But the objector draws attention to a way out which has not yet been mentioned in this article: proletarians can form workers' cooperatives. There is enormous scope for the creation of such entities, and therefore virtually unlimited exit prospects. If, then, exiting is not widespread, the reason must be the fecklessness of workers, their unwillingness to undertake risks, and so on.[32]

Note that this objection is not intended to support the conclusion of argument 7, that workers are individually free to escape, which is a thesis I not only grant but defend. Fresh support for it comes from the plausible claim that there exist unexploited opportunities to form cooperatives. But the opportunities have to be very extensive indeed for the premise of argument 8 to be affected, and hence for collective proletarian unfreedom to be substantially smaller than I have maintained. So when, in due course, I reply to the objection, by describing obstacles to the formation of cooperatives (such as the hostility to them of the capitalist class, which has a lot of power), my aim is not to deny that there are a goodly number of unexploited exits of this kind, but to assert that there are not, and could not be, enough to permit *mass* escape from the proletariat through them.

The objector might develop his case as follows: "The rules of capitalism do not prohibit the formation of cooperatives. They confer on everyone the right to contract with whomsoever he pleases howsoever he pleases; they therefore give workers the right to contract with one another instead of with bosses, and the great recommendation of capitalism is that it (and not a society of workers' cooperatives) is what results when free contracting is allowed to proceed. Workers in a capitalist society are free to transform it into a society without capitalists, within the rules of capitalism itself (as opposed to through political revolution), but they choose not to do so."

The first thing to say in reply is that procedures permitted by the rules might be extremely difficult to carry out, for objective reasons. There is, for example, a serious problem of coordination affecting the initial formation of cooperatives. There might be many workers each of whom would be willing and able to prosper cooperatively with the rest, did he but know who they were and how to unite with them. The high costs of search and trial attending the formation of new enterprises create a need for initial capital which workers cannot easily supply. That is one reason why there is more tendency to convert existing firms into cooperatives than to found them from scratch. But the conversions are often ill-fated, since they are least resisted when commercial failure is actual or imminent.

Widespread exiting through cooperatives would require substantial external finance, but financiers are reluctant to back even commercially viable cooperative ventures, since dispensing with the capitalist owner sets a bad example: "the capitalist economy reacts like an organism on which one grafts a foreign organ: it spontaneously rejects the graft."[33] Towards commercially viable ventures that reaction is irrational, in the terms of bourgeois economics, but capitalists are less blinkered than economists about what is rational, all things considered. And there are also purely economic reasons for withholding finance, since special risks attach to investment in self-managed firms, such as the danger that the workers will "plunder" it, that is, pay themselves such handsome wages that the cooperative will be unable to meet its obligations to investors. To forestall their anxieties investors might be offered a measure of control over the firm, but that would tend to turn the cooperators into sellers of labor power, in effect if not in form.[34]

There is a general reply to the position of the bourgeois ideologist expounded immediately above. It is that a capitalist society is not a set of rules, but a set of relations conforming to them, an economic structure. And transformations permitted by the rules might be blocked by the structure. Creation of workers' cooperatives on the extensive scale required to secure the right-wing objection would, after all, mean the demise of great capitalist fortunes and institutions, whose agents are in an excellent position to frustrate transition to a cooperative market society. When the Labour government of 1974–79 denied support to workers' cooperatives of a kind routinely given to private industry,[35] the City of London did not rush in to fill the breach.

Recall that I do not deny that (despite the obstacles) there exist unexploited opportunities for exit through cooperation. My different point is that those opportunities are not, and could not be, extensive enough to constitute a means of extinguishing capitalism within the rules of the capitalist system. That is why the most enthusiastic proponents of the cooperative market economy rely on the state to promote a transition to that form of society.[36]

XV

One left-wing objection to the argument of Section VII does not question its premise, that there are more exits from the proletariat than there are workers trying to leave it. The objection is that it is unrealistic to infer that the great majority of workers are individually free to leave. For most lack the requisite assets of character and personality: they have no commercial shrewdness, they do not know how to present themselves well, and so on.[37]

To assess this objection, we must distinguish between the freedom to do something and the capacity to do it.

Suppose that the world's best long-distance swimmer has just begun to serve a long prison sentence. Then he has the capacity to swim the English Channel, but he is not free to do so. My situation is the opposite of his. I am free to swim it, but I lack the capacity.

One might suggest, by way of generalization, that a person is unfree to do A if and only if, were he to try to do A, he would fail to do A as a result of the action(s) of one or more other persons; and that a person lacks the capacity to do A if and only if, were he to try to do A, then, even if circumstances were maximally favorable, he would fail to do A. If a person does A, then he has both the capacity to do it and the freedom to do it (at the time when he does it).[38]

The suggested analysis of "X is unfree to do A" is both controversial and difficult to interpret. Some would strengthen it by requiring that the freedom-removing action be *intended* to cause removal of freedom. I do not accept that. I think that if you get in my way you make me unfree even if you are there by accident. Others, such as Harry Frankfurt, would defend a weaker *analysans*: for Frankfurt, natural obstacles restrict freedom. I think he is right, but I resolved (see Sec IV) to proceed as if he were not.

On the given definitions the left-wing objection, as presented above, fails, since deficiencies of character and personality that make the worker incapable of leaving his class do not therefore make him unfree to leave it. But the definitions, when put together, possess an entailment which might enable the left-wing objection to be presented in a more persuasive form. It follows from the definitions that if one lacks the capacity to do A as a result of the action of others, then one is not only incapable of doing A but also unfree to do it. To see how this entailment might be used on behalf of the left-wing objection, let us first return to the case of the prisoners in the locked room.

Each is (conditionally) free to escape, and I stipulated that each has the capacity to seize and wield the key, so each, in addition, has the capacity to escape. The stipulation was not required to prove that they are free to escape, but it made the exhibition of their freedom more vivid. Suppose now that some or all lack the capacity to escape, because they cannot pick up the key; and that they cannot pick it up because they are too weak, since the jailer gives them low-grade food, in order to make it difficult or impossible for anyone to escape. Then our definitions entail that those without the capacity to use the key are not free to escape.

Now if workers cannot escape the proletariat because of personal deficiency, then this need not, on the given definitions, detract from their freedom to escape, *but it does if the deficiency is appropriately attributable to human action* (if, for example, it is due to needlessly bad education?). If a worker suffers from an appropriately generated or maintained deficiency of a sufficiently severe kind, then he is not free to escape the proletariat, and he is forced to sell his labor power. Is he, in addition, forced to sell his labor power in the required Marxist sense? That depends on whether the causation of the deficiency is suitably connected with the prevailing relations of production (see Section V). Positive answers to these questions would upset the argument of Section VII. If it is plausible to say that capitalism *makes* most workers incapable of being anything else, then it is false that most workers are free, *in sensu diviso*, not to be proletarians.

XVI

Argument 7 says that (most) British workers are not forced to sell their labor power, since they have the reasonable alternative of setting up as petty bourgeois instead, it being false that all petty bourgeois positions are already occupied. The inference turns on the principle that *a person is not forced to do* A *if he has a reasonable or acceptable alternative course.* The objection of Section XV can be treated as a challenge to that principle. It says that even if an acceptable alternative lies before an agent, he is forced to do A if he is (or,

in the improved version of the objection, if he has been made) incapable of seizing it.

A different left-wing objection to the inference of argument 7 is substantially due to Chaim Tannenbaum. Tannenbaum accepts the italicized principle. That is, he agrees that a person is not forced to do A if he has an acceptable alternative course; and he also does not deny that petty bourgeois existence is relevantly superior to proletarian.[39] His objection is that for most workers the existence of petty bourgeois exits does not, as I have supposed, generate an acceptable alternative course to remaining a worker. For one must consider, as I did not, the risk attached to the attempt to occupy a petty bourgeois position, which, to judge by the rate at which fledgling enterprises fail, is very high; and also the costs of failure, since often a worker who has tried and failed to become a petty bourgeois is worse off than if he had not tried at all. The Tannenbaum objection does not challenge the premise of argument 7. The exits may exist but, so the objection goes, it is difficult to know where they are, and the price of fruitless search for them is considerable. Accordingly, the expected utility[40] of attempting the petty bourgeois alternative is normally too low to justify the statement that most workers are not forced to sell their labor power.

Attention to expected utility also illuminates the case of the immigrant petty bourgeois (Section V), on whom argument 7 was founded. For their lot within the working class is usually worse than that of native proletarians, who are not victims of racism and who are consequently less prone to superexploitation. Hence a smaller probability of success is required to make immigrant attempts at escape rational. The disproportionately high number of immigrants in the petty bourgeoisie is therefore less due to differences in expertise and attitude and more due to objective circumstances than seems at first to be the case.

To assess the soundness of the Tannenbaum argument, let us state it as it would apply to one whom we shall think of as a typical worker, and whom I shall call *W*:

1 The expected utility to *W* of trying the petty bourgeois course is less than the expected utility of remaining a worker (even if the utility of becoming and remaining a petty bourgeois is greater than that of remaining a worker).

2 An alternative to a given course is acceptable in the relevant sense if and only if it has at least as

much expected utility as the given course. (The relevant sense of acceptability is that in which a person is forced to do A if he has no acceptable alternative to doing A.) Therefore,

3 The existence of petty bourgeois exits does not show that W has an acceptable alternative course. Therefore,

4 The existence of petty bourgeois exits does not show that W is not forced to sell his labor power. Therefore,

5 The conclusion of argument 7 does not follow from its premise.

The first premise is a (more or less) factual claim, and the second is conceptual. In assessing the truth of the factual premise, we must discount that part of the probability of failure in attempts at petty bourgeois enterprise which is due to *purely* personal deficiencies: see Section XV. Even if we could carry out the needed discounting, it would remain extremely difficult to tell whether the factual premise is true, since the answer would involve many matters of judgment, and also information which is not a matter of judgment but which happens to be unavailable: the frequency with which enterprises founded by exworkers succeed in the United Kingdom is not given in the bankruptcy statistics, which do not distinguish those new enterprises from other ones. I shall, however, assume that the factual premise is true, in order to focus on the conceptual claim embodied in premise 2.

If a person is forced to do A if he has no acceptable alternative, then what makes for acceptability in the required sense? Suppose I am doing A, and doing B is an alternative to that. In order to see whether it is an acceptable one, do I consider only the utility of the best possible outcome of B, or do I take into account all its possible outcomes, summing the products of the utility and probability of each, so that I can compare the result with the expected utility of doing A, and thereby obtain an answer?

It seems clear that the best possible outcome of doing B cannot be all that counts since, if it were, then I would not be forced to hand over my money at gunpoint where there was a minute probability that the gun would misfire. People are regularly forced to do things to which there are alternatives with low probabilities of very high rewards.

So it appears that expected utility must figure in the calculus of constraint. But I think it figures in a more complex way than premise 2 of the Tannenbaum objection allows. An alternative to a given course can be acceptable even if it has less expected utility than the given course. Illustration: "You're not forced to go to Brighton, since you can go to Margate, though you're less likely to have a good time there."

Premise 2 of the Tannenbaum objection is false, but something similar to it may be true. Reflection on the intuitive data leads me to propose the following characterization of acceptability, at any rate as a first approximation:

B is not an acceptable alternative to A iff
  EITHER A is particularly bad
    and B is worse than A
  OR A is not particularly bad
    but B is,

which simplifies to:

B is not an acceptable alternative to A iff
  B is worse than A and B is
    particularly bad.

Expected utility is the standard for judging courses good and bad here, and in order to apply the analysis one has to make not only relative judgments of courses of action but also ones which are absolute *in some sense* (I shall not try to specify it): that is how I intend "particularly bad." If we were allowed only relative judgments, we would risk concluding that whenever someone does what is unambiguously the best thing for him to do, he is forced to do that thing. Unflaggingly rational people are not perpetually constrained.

Some consequences of the definition are worth mentioning.

First, even if A is an extremely desirable course, one might be forced to take it, since all the alternatives to it are so bad. You could be forced to go to the superb restaurant because all the others are awful. It would then be unlikely that you are going to it (only) *because* you are forced to, but that is another matter. It is not true that you do everything you are forced to do *because* you are forced to do it.

Secondly, all the alternatives to A might be absolutely terrible, and no better than A, and yet one might still not be forced to do A, since some of the alternatives might be no worse than A. To be sure, there would be constraint in such a situation. One would be forced to do A or B or C. . . . But one would not be forced to do any given one of them.

Thirdly, the extreme difficulty of assessing probabilities and utilities in real life means that it will often be intractably moot whether or not someone is forced to do something. But that is not an objection to this account, since the matter often is intractably moot.

We supposed that the expected utility of trying the petty bourgeois course is less than that of remaining a worker. Then if my account of acceptability in alternatives is correct, the substance of the Tannenbaum objection is saved if and only if trying the petty bourgeois alternative is a particularly bad thing to do.

I cannot say whether or not it is, because the facts are hard to get at and hard to organize in an informative way, and also because of an indeterminacy in the ordinary concept of constraint, on which I have relied: when estimating the goodness and badness of courses of action with a view to judging whether or not an agent is forced to do something, should we consider his preferences only, or apply more objective criteria? The ordinary concept appears to let us judge either way. It seems to have the defect that neither party to the following exchange is misusing it:

"I'm forced to go to the Indian restaurant, since I hate Chinese food."

"Since there's nothing wrong with Chinese food, you're not forced to go to the Indian restaurant."

XVII

Tannenbaum accepted the premise of argument 7 – that there are exits from the proletariat through which no worker is trying to move – but denied that it showed that workers are (individually) free to leave the proletariat, on the ground that the escape routes from it are too dangerous. I now want to consider an objection to the premise of the argument. I adduced in support of it the remarkable growth in immigrant petty bourgeois commerce in recent years. But I might be asked, How do you know that immigrants have taken places which would otherwise have been unfilled? Perhaps they prevented others from occupying them by getting there first.

With respect to some instances of ascent this skepticism is justified. But not in all cases. Often enough the nonproletarian position occupied by an immigrant demands, initially, longer hours and stronger commitment than native British tend to find worthwhile, so that it would have gone unfilled had some nonnative not filled it. And there must still be unoccupied places of that kind. (Note that an unoccupied place does not have to be describable in some such terms as "the empty shop around the corner which someone could make a go of." It suffices for the existence of an unoccupied place that there is a course of conduct such that if a worker engaged in it, he would become a nonproletarian, even though no one had ceased to be one.)

But I do concede that there are not as many vacancies as one might at first think. Much ascent into the petty bourgeoisie involves transfer of a secure place in the economic structure from one person to another, on the death, retirement, or collapse into the proletariat of the previous occupant. A good deal of immigrant ascent takes this form, and here it is plausible to say that the new occupant beat others to the place, and did not fill a place others would not have taken.

I argued the thesis of individual freedom to escape for the United Kingdom only. It could be that there is more crowding at the exits in other capitalist societies, and therefore less truth in the premise of argument 7 when it is asserted of those societies. There is, after all, no "British Dream," and in more pervasively capitalist cultures it might be only barely true that there is individual freedom to escape, and it might be, though false, nearly true that the overwhelming majority of the proletariat are forced to sell their labor power, even *in sensu diviso*, not for Tannenbaum-type reasons, but because there are virtually no exits available at any given time.

With respect to societies, what is nearly true (though false) may be more important than what is strictly true, since what is strictly true may be only barely true.[41] When considering such theses as that workers are individually free to escape the proletariat, we should beware of arguments which would at best show them to be barely true.

Notes

Sections I–IX of this article constitute a much revised version of pp. 18–25 of "Capitalism, Freedom and the Proletariat," which appeared in *The Idea of Freedom:*

Essays in Honour of Isaiah Berlin, ed. Alan Ryan (Oxford: Oxford University Press, 1979).

1 For elaboration of this definition, and a defense of

its attribution to Marx, see my *Karl Marx's Theory of History* (Oxford: Oxford University Press and Princeton: Princeton University Press, 1978), pp. 63–77, 222–23, 333–36. This book is henceforth referred to as *KMTH*.

2   For Nozick's view, see his *Anarchy, State and Utopia* (New York: Basic Books, 1974), pp. 262–64, which I criticize at p. 151 of "Robert Nozick and Wilt Chamberlain," in *Justice and Economic Distribution*, ed. John Arthur and William Shaw (Englewood Cliffs, NJ: Prentice-Hall, 1978). For more discussion of false-because-moralized definitions of freedom, see my "Capitalism, Freedom and Proletariat," *The Idea of Freedom*, pp. 12–14; "Illusions about Private Property and Freedom," in *Issues in Marxist Philosophy*, ed. John Mepham and David Ruben (Hassocks, 1981), 4:228–29; "Freedom, Justice and Capitalism," *New Left Review*, no. 126 (March/April 1981): 10–11. A partly similar critique of moralized accounts of force and freedom is given by David Zimmerman at pp. 121–31 of his "Coercive Wage Offers," *Philosophy & Public Affairs* 10, no. 2 (Spring 1981).

3   Frankfurt points out that natural things and processes operating independently of human action also force people to do things. See his "Coercion and Moral Responsibility," in *Essays on Freedom of Action*, ed. Ted Honderich (London: Routledge & Kegan Paul, 1973), pp. 83–84.

Note that one can agree with Frankfurt while denying that lack of capacity restricts freedom: the question whether internal obstacles restrict it is distinct from the question which kinds of external obstacles do.

4   See *KMTH*, pp. 31–35, 63–65, 217–25.

5   At least most: it could be argued that *all* British proletarians are in such a position, but I stay with "most" lest some ingenious person discover objective proletarian circumstances worse than the worst once suffered by now prospering immigrants. But see also note 6.

6   This might well be challenged, since the size of *n* is a matter of judgment. I would defend mine by reference to the naturalness of saying to a worker that he is not forced to (continue to) sell his labor power, since he can take steps to set himself up as a shopkeeper. Those who judge otherwise might be able, at a pinch, to deny that most proletarians are not forced to sell their labor power, but they cannot dispose of the counterexamples to the generalization that *all* are forced to. For our prospective petty bourgeois is a proletarian on the eve of his ascent when, unless, absurdly, we take *n* as 0, he is not forced to sell his labor power.

7   "The truth is this, that in this bourgeois society every workman, if he is an exceedingly clever and shrewd fellow, and gifted with bourgeois instincts and favoured by an exceptional fortune, can possibly convert himself into an *exploiteur du travail d'autrui*. But if there were no *travail* to be *exploité*, there would be no capitalist nor capitalist production" (Karl Marx, "Results of the Immediate Process of Production," *Capital*, tran. Ben Fowkes [Harmondsworth: Penguin Books, 1976], 1:1079). For commentary on similar texts see *KMTH*, p. 243.

8   For whatever may be the correct analysis of "*X* is free to do *A*," it is clear that *X* is free to do *A* if *X* would do *A* if he tried to do *A*, and that sufficient condition of freedom is all that we need here.

Some have objected that the stated condition is not sufficient: a person, they say, may do something he is not free to do, since he may do something he is not legally, or morally, free to do. Those who agree with that unhelpful remark can take it that I am interested in the non-normative use of "free," which is distinguished by the sufficient condition just stated.

9   See notes 5 and 6.

10 In a stimulating commentary on the argument of Sections VII and VIII, Jon Elster notes that it involves avoidance of two fallacies, that of composition ("What is true of each must be true of all") and that of division ("What is true of all must be true of each"): "It is true of any individual worker that he is free to leave the class, but not of all workers simultaneously. And the reason why the individual worker is free to leave the class is that the others do not want to leave it; and the reason why the others do not want to leave it is that whatever is desirable if it happens to all members simultaneously is not necessarily desirable if it happens to one member separately and exclusively" (first draft of paper on "Freedom and Power." p. 63). Elster shows that such structures pervade social life.

11 See *KMTH*, p. 223, for exposition and references.

12 The phrase comes from Marx, *Capital* (London, 1962), 1:899. See *KMTH*, pp. 82–84, for a discussion of different modes of exploitation.

13 Marx, *Capital*, 1:899.

14 From his "Song of the United Front."

15 That is, if and only if it is not possible that, for all *X*, *X* performs *A* (even if for all *X*, it is possible that *X* performs *A*).

One might also have to specify the kind of cause that makes it impossible, a complication discussed in Section XI and here set aside.

16 The concept of sharing in a collective unfreedom might be used in an attempt to define the proletariat, for example, as the largest group in a society all members of which share a collective unfreedom with respect to the sale of labor power. Unlike the definition I described and rejected at p. 25 of "Capitalism, Freedom and the Proletariat," this

one would have the virtue of keeping Sir Keith Joseph out of the working class.

17 See *KMTH*, pp. 243–45 for remarks on that issue.

18 Robert Ware brought the important concept of relational freedom to my attention.

19 One might reply: because there are some things which we may hope groups are free to do which we would not expect, or would not want, individuals to be free to do. But that answer is out of place here, because of the distinction just drawn between group and collective freedom.

20 Less reason, but not no reason, since the desire for freedom is not reducible to the desire to do what one would be free to do if one had it. I may resent my lack of freedom to do what I have no wish to do: Soviet citizens who dislike restrictions on foreign travel need not want to go abroad. And subtler reasons for valuing the freedom to do what I do not want to do are presented by Jon Elster in "Sour Grapes," in *Utilitarianism and Beyond*, ed. A. Sen and B. Williams (Cambridge: Cambridge University Press, 1982).

21 See Isaiah Berlin, *Four Essays on Liberty* (Oxford: Oxford University Press, 1969), pp. xxxviiiff., 139–40 and also Hillel Steiner, "Individual Liberty," *Proceedings of the Aristotelian Society*, 1974–75, p. 34. The point was originally made by Richard Wollheim in a review of Berlin's "Two Concepts of Liberty." But see Elster, "Sour Grapes," *Utilitarianism and Beyond*, for a good challenge to the claim defended by these authors.

22 That is, there is a time t at which they are all free to go at $t + n$, and a time $t + (n - m)$ at which they are not all free to go at $t + n$, where $n > m > 0$. See Section VI on the need to refer twice to time in fully explicit specifications of freedom.

23 In separate personal correspondence.

24 From p. 448 of his valuable article on "Justice and Capitalist Production," *Canadian Journal of Philosophy* 8, no. 3 (1978).

25 "The fact that labour and the labourer are inseparable creates certain difficulties," David O'Mahoney declares, but he reassures us that "analytically labour is no different from any other resource the owners of which contract with the entrepreneur to use it for his purposes." See "Labour Management and the Market Economy," *Irish Journal of Business and Administrative Research*, April 1979, p. 30.

26 *Principles of Political Economy* (Toronto: University of Toronto Press, 1965), p. 766.

27 We can set aside the special case of a wholly infirm capitalist. If capitalists were in general unable to live except by investing their capital, their bargaining position vis-à-vis workers would be rather different.

28 And not only in comparison with investing capital, but also absolutely, if the account of acceptability in alternatives at the end of Sec XVI below is right.

29 Marx, *Capital*, 1:92.

30 Marx, Preface to *A Contribution to the Critique of Political Economy*.

31 "A proposition is a practical certainty if its probability is so high as to allow us to reason, in *any* decision problem, as if its probability were 1" (R.C. Jeffrey, "Statistical Explanation vs. Statistical Inference," in N. Rescher *et alia*, *Essays in Honor of Carl G. Hempel* [Dordrecht: Reidel, 1970], p. 105).

32 See Nozick, *Anarchy, State and Utopia*, pp. 255–56.

33 Branko Horvat, "Plan de socialisation progressive du capital," in *Solutions Socialistes*, ed. S-C. Kolm (Paris: Editions Ramsay, 1978), p. 183.

34 See Jaroslav Vanek, *The General Theory of Labor-Managed Market Economies* (Ithaca: Cornell University Press, 1970), pp. 291ff., and pp. 317–18 (on "the dilemma of the collateral"); and also O'Mahoney, "Labour Management," pp. 33ff.

35 The first Minister of Industry in that government, Tony Benn, favored cooperatives, which is one reason why he was replaced in the summer of 1975 by Eric Varley, who interpreted Labour's semi-socialist election manifesto commitments in an un-socialist way. See *The New Worker Co-operatives*, ed. Ken Coates (Nottingham: Spokesman Books, 1976), pp. 6, 95, 218; and Ken Coates, *Work-ins, Sit-ins and Industrial Democracy* (Nottingham: Spokesman Books, 1981), pp. 140ff.

For a lucid presentation of the record of business and government hostility to cooperatives in my native Quebec, see Pauline Vaillancourt and Jean-Guy Vaillancourt, "Government Aid to Worker Production Cooperatives," *Synthesis*, Spring 1978.

36 Vanek (*General Theory*, p. 317) says that there is not "much real possibility . . . in a liberal capitalist environment" for developing a cooperative market economy, and Horvat (*Solutions Socialistes*, pp. 165ff.) proposes what amounts to expropriation without compensation as a means of instituting it.

37 See the requirements listed by Marx in the passage quoted in note 7.

38 One might say that one is *able* to do *A* if and only if one has both the capacity and the freedom to do *A*.

Some would reject the above definition of incapacity on the ground that it entails that someone who does *A* by fluke has the capacity to do *A*. I reply that if someone does *A* by fluke, then he shows a capacity to do *A*, to wit by fluke, which other people might not have. Unlike a six-month-old child, I have the capacity to hit the bull's-eye by fluke. For the view I am opposing here, see

Anthony Kenny, *Will, Freedom and Power* (Oxford: Basil Blackwell, 1975), p. 136.

39 Unlike some leftists, who resist the inference of argument 7 by urging that petty bourgeois life is no better than proletarian, because of its long hours, short holidays, financial risk, and so on. I reply (1) that the petty bourgeois, being "his own boss," has an autonomy leftists are ill-placed to disparage, since they so strongly emphasize the loss of it entailed by "proletarianization"; and (2) that it is in any case possible to base the conclusion of argument 7 on the availability of higher grade, not-so-petty, bourgeois positions, into which workers also from time to time rise.

40 The expected utility of a course of action is the sum of the products of the utility and probability of each of its possible outcomes.

41 To get an uncontroversial illustration of the sort of truth value I have in mind, suppose that each year in the past over one hundred people came to my birthday party, and you ask me whether as many as one hundred came this year, and I say No, since in fact ninety-nine came, though I do not tell you that. It is more important that it is nearly true (though false) that one hundred came than that it is strictly true that fewer than one hundred came.

This paper has been read at more places than it seems reasonable to list, and I am indebted to many commentators, but above all to Robert Brenner, Ken Coates, Jon Elster, Arthur Fine, Keith Graham, Alan Haworth, Grahame Lock, David Lloyd-Thomas, John McMurtry, Jan Narveson, Chris Provis, John Roemer, William Shaw, Hillel Steiner, Chaim Tannenbaum, Robert van der Veen, Robert Ware, and Arnold Zuboff. I also thank the Editors of *Philosophy & Public Affairs* for their characteristically acute and helpful criticisms.

27

Homelessness and the Issue of Freedom

Jeremy Waldron

Introduction

There are many facets to the nightmare of homelessness. In this essay, I want to explore just one of them: the relation between homelessness, the rules of public and private property, and the underlying freedom of those who are condemned by poverty to walk the streets and sleep in the open. Unlike some recent discussions, my concern is not with the constitutionality of various restrictions on the homeless (though that, of course, is important).[1] I want to address a prior question – a more fundamental question – of legal and moral philosophy: how should we think about homelessness, how should we conceive of it, in relation to a value like freedom?

The discussion that follows is, in some ways, an abstract one. This is intentional. The aim is to refute the view that, on abstract liberal principles, there is no reason to be troubled by the plight of the homeless, and that one has to come down to the more concrete principles of a communitarian ethic in order to find a focus for that concern. Against this view, I shall argue that homelessness is a matter of the utmost concern in relation to some of the most fundamental and abstract principles of liberal value. That an argument is abstract should not make us think of it as thin or watery. If homelessness raises questions even in regard to the most basic principles of liberty, it is an issue that ought to preoccupy liberal theorists

every bit as much as more familiar worries about torture, the suppression of dissent, and other violations of human rights. That the partisans of liberty in our legal and philosophical culture have not always been willing to see this (or say it) should be taken as an indication of the consistency and good faith with which they espouse and proclaim their principles.

1 Location and Property

Some truisms to begin with. Everything that is done has to be done somewhere. No one is free to perform an action unless there is somewhere he is free to perform it. Since we are embodied beings, we always have a location. Moreover, though everyone has to be somewhere, a person cannot always choose any location he likes. Some locations are physically inaccessible. And, physical inaccessibility aside, there are some places one is simply not allowed to be.

One of the functions of property rules, particularly as far as land is concerned, is to provide a basis for determining who is allowed to be where. For the purposes of these rules, a country is divided up into spatially defined regions or, as we usually say, places. The rules of property give us a way of determining, in the case of each place, who is allowed to be in that place and who is not. For example, if a place is governed by a private property rule, then there is a way of identifying an individual whose determination is final on the question of who is and who is not allowed to be in that place. Sometimes that individual is the owner of the land in question, and sometimes (as

Originally published in *UCLA Law Review*, 39 (1991), 295–324. Copyright © 1991 by The Regents of the University of California. Reprinted by permission of UCLA Law Review.

in a landlord-tenant relationship) the owner gives another person the power to make that determination (indeed to make it, for the time being, even as against the owner). Either way, it is characteristic of a private ownership arrangement that some individual (or some other particular legal person) has this power to determine who is allowed to be on the property.

The actual rules of private property are, of course, much more complicated than this and they involve much besides this elementary power of decision.[2] However, to get the discussion going, it is enough to recognize that there is something like this individual power of decision in most systems of private ownership. Private ownership of land exists when an individual person may determine who is, and who is not, allowed to be in a certain place, without answering to anyone else for that decision. I say who is allowed to be in my house. He says who is to be allowed in his restaurant. And so on.

The concept of *being allowed* to be in a place is fairly straightforward. We can define it negatively. An individual who is in a place where he is not allowed to be may be removed, and he may be subject to civil or criminal sanctions for trespass or some other similar offense. No doubt people are sometimes physically removed from places where they *are* allowed to be. But if a person is in a place where he is not allowed to be, not only may he be physically removed, but there is a social rule to the effect that his removal may be facilitated and aided by the forces of the state. In short, the police may be called and he may be dragged away.

I said that one function of property rules is to indicate procedures for determining who is allowed and not allowed (in this sense) to be in a given place, and I gave the example of a private property rule. However, not all rules of property are like private property rules in this regard. We may use a familiar classification and say that, though many places in this country are governed by private property rules, some are governed by rules of collective property, which divide further into rules of state property and rules of common property (though neither the labels nor the exact details of this second distinction matter much for the points I am going to make).[3]

If a place is governed by a *collective* property rule, then there is no private person in the position of owner. Instead, the use of collective property is determined by people, usually officials, acting in the name of the whole community.

Common property may be regarded as a subclass of collective property. A place is common property if part of the point of putting it under collective control is to allow anyone in the society to make use of it without having to secure the permission of anybody else. Not all collective property is like this: places like military firing ranges, nationalized factories, and government offices are off-limits to members of the general public unless they have special permission or a legitimate purpose for being there. They are held as collective property for purposes other than making them available for public use. However, examples of common property spring fairly readily to mind: they include streets, sidewalks, subways, city parks, national parks, and wilderness areas. These places are held in the name of the whole society in order to make them fairly accessible to everyone. As we shall see, they are by no means unregulated as to the nature or time of their use. Still, they are relatively open at most times to a fairly indeterminate range of uses by anyone. In the broadest terms, they are places where anyone may be.

Sometimes the state may insist that certain places owned by private individuals or corporations should be treated rather like common property if they fulfill the function of public places. For example, shopping malls in the United States are usually on privately owned land. However, because of the functions such places serve, the state imposes considerable restrictions on the owners' powers of exclusion (people may not be excluded from a shopping mall on racial grounds, for example) and on their power to limit the activities (such as political pamphleteering) that may take place there.[4] Though this is an important development, it does not alter the analysis I am developing in this Essay, and for simplicity I shall ignore it in what follows.

Property rules differ from society to society. Though we describe some societies (like the United States) as having systems of private property, and others (like the USSR – at least until recently) as having collectivist systems, clearly all societies have some places governed by private property rules, some places governed by state property rules, and some places governed by common property rules. Every society has private houses, military bases, and public parks. So if we want to categorize whole societies along these lines, we have to say it is a matter of balance and emphasis. For example, we say the USSR is (or used to be) a collectivist society and that the USA is not, not because there was no private property in the USSR, but because most industrial and agricultural land there was held collectively whereas most industrial and agricultural land in the United States is privately owned. The distinction is one of degree. Even as between two countries that pride themselves on having basically capitalist economies, for example, New Zealand and Britain, we may say that the former is "communist" to a greater extent (i.e. is more a system of common property) than the latter because more places (for example, all river banks) are held as common property in New Zealand than are held as common property in Britain. Of course, these propositions are as vague as they are useful. If we are measuring the "extent" to which a country is collectivist, that measure is ambiguous as between the quantitative proportion of land that is governed by rules of collective property and some more qualitative assessment of the importance of the places that are governed in this way.[5]

2 Homelessness

Estimates of the number of homeless people in the United States range from 250,000 to three million.[6] A person who is homeless is, obviously enough, a person who has no home. One way of describing the plight of a homeless individual might be to say that there is no place governed by a private property rule where he is allowed to be.

In fact, that is not quite correct. Any private proprietor may invite a homeless person into his house or onto his land, and if he does there *will* be some private place where the homeless person is allowed to be. A technically more accurate description of his plight is that there is no place governed by a private property rule where he is allowed to be whenever *he* chooses, no place governed by a private property rule from which he may not at any time be excluded as a result of someone else's say-so. As far as being on private property is concerned – in people's houses or gardens, on farms or in hotels, in offices or restaurants – the homeless person is utterly and at all times at the mercy of others. And we know enough about how this mercy is generally exercised to figure that the description in the previous paragraph is more or less accurate as a matter of

fact, even if it is not strictly accurate as a matter of law.[7]

For the most part the homeless are excluded from *all* of the places governed by private property rules, whereas the rest of us are, in the same sense, excluded from *all but one* (or maybe all but a few) of those places. That is another way of saying that each of us has at least one place to be in a country composed of private places, whereas the homeless person has none.

Some libertarians fantasize about the possibility that *all* the land in a society might be held as private property ("Sell the streets!").[8] This would be catastrophic for the homeless. Since most private proprietors are already disposed to exclude him from their property, the homeless person might discover in such a libertarian paradise that there was literally *nowhere* he was allowed to be. Wherever he went he would be liable to penalties for trespass and he would be liable to eviction, to being thrown out by an owner or dragged away by the police. Moving from one place to another would involve nothing more liberating than moving from one trespass liability to another. Since land is finite in any society, there is only a limited number of places where a person can (physically) be, and such a person would find that he was legally excluded from all of them. (It would not be entirely mischievous to add that since, in order to exist, a person has to be *somewhere*, such a person would not be permitted to exist.)

Our society saves the homeless from this catastrophe only by virtue of the fact that some of its territory is held as collective property and made available for common use. The homeless are allowed to *be* – provided they are on the streets, in the parks, or under the bridges. Some of them are allowed to crowd together into publicly provided "shelters" after dark (though these are dangerous places and there are not nearly enough shelters for all of them). But in the daytime and, for many of them, all through the night, wandering in public places is their only option. When all else is privately owned, the sidewalks are their salvation. They are allowed to *be* in our society only to the extent that our society is communist.

This is one of the reasons why most defenders of private property are uncomfortable with the libertarian proposal, and why that proposal remains sheer fantasy.[9] But there is a modified form of the libertarian catastrophe in prospect with which moderate and even liberal defenders of ownership seem much more comfortable. This is the increasing regulation of the streets, subways, parks, and other public places to restrict the activities that can be performed there. What is emerging – and it is not just a matter of fantasy – is a state of affairs in which a million or more citizens have no place to perform elementary human activities like urinating, washing, sleeping, cooking, eating, and standing around. Legislators voted for by people who own private places in which they can do all these things are increasingly deciding to make public places available only for activities other than these primal human tasks. The streets and subways, they say, are for commuting from home to office. They are not for sleeping; sleeping is something one does at home. The parks are for recreations like walking and informal ball-games, things for which one's own yard is a little too confined. Parks are not for cooking or urinating; again, these are things one does at home. Since the public and the private are complementary, the activities performed in public are to be the complement of those appropriately performed in private. This complementarity works fine for those who have the benefit of both sorts of places. However, it is disastrous for those who must live their whole lives on common land. If I am right about this, it is one of the most callous and tyrannical exercises of power in modern times by a (comparatively) rich and complacent majority against a minority of their less fortunate fellow human beings.

3 Locations, Actions and Freedom

The points made so far can be restated in terms of freedom. Someone who is allowed to be in a place is, in a fairly straightforward sense, free to be there. A person who is not allowed to be in a place is unfree to be there. However, the concept of freedom usually applies to actions rather than locations: one is free or unfree to do X or to do Y. What is the connection, then, between freedom to be somewhere and freedom to do something?

At the outset I recited the truism that anything a person does has to be done somewhere. To that extent, all actions involve a spatial component (just as many actions involve, in addition, a material component like the use of tools, implements, or raw materials). It should be fairly obvious that, if one is not free to be in a certain place, one is not free to do anything at that place. If I am not

allowed to be in your garden (because you have forbidden me) then I am not allowed to eat my lunch, make a speech, or turn a somersault in your garden. Though I may be free to do these things somewhere else, I am not free to do them there. It follows, strikingly, that a person who is not free to be in any place is not free to do anything; such a person is comprehensively unfree. In the libertarian paradise we imagined in the previous section, this would be the plight of the homeless. They would be simply without freedom (or, more accurately, any freedom they had would depend utterly on the forbearance of those who owned the places that made up the territory of the society in question).

Fortunately, our society is not such a libertarian paradise. There are places where the homeless may be and, by virtue of that, there are actions they may perform; they are free to perform actions on the streets, in the parks, and under the bridges. Their freedom depends on common property in a way that ours does not. Once again, the homeless have freedom in our society only to the extent that our society is communist.

That conclusion may sound glib and provocative. But it is meant as a reflection on the cold and awful reality of the experience of men, women, and children who are homeless in America. For them the rules of private property are a series of fences that stand between them and somewhere to be, somewhere to act. The only hope they have so far as freedom is concerned lies in the streets, parks, and public shelters, and in the fact that those are collectivized resources made available openly to all.

It is sometimes said that freedom means little or nothing to a cold and hungry person. We should focus on the material predicament of the homeless, it is said, not on this abstract liberal concern about freedom. That may be an appropriate response to someone who is talking high-mindedly and fatuously about securing freedom of speech or freedom of religion for people who lack the elementary necessities of human life.[10] But the contrast between liberty and the satisfaction of material needs must not be drawn too sharply, as though the latter had no relation at all to what one is free or unfree to do. I am focusing on freedoms that are intimately connected with food, shelter, clothing, and the satisfaction of basic needs. When a person is needy, he does not cease to be preoccupied with freedom; rather, his preoccupation tends to focus on freedom to perform certain actions in particular. The free-dom that means most to a person who is cold and wet is the freedom that consists in staying under whatever shelter he has found. The freedom that means most to someone who is exhausted is the freedom not to be prodded with a nightstick as he tries to catch a few hours sleep on a subway bench.

There is a general point here about the rather *passive* image of the poor held by those who say we should concern ourselves with their needs, not their freedom.[11] People remain agents, with ideas and initiatives of their own, even when they are poor. Indeed, since they are on their own, in a situation of danger, without any place of safety, they must often be more resourceful, spend more time working out how to live, thinking things through much more carefully, taking much less for granted, than the comfortable autonomous agent that we imagine in a family with a house and a job in an office or university. And – when they are allowed to – the poor do find ways of using their initiative to rise to these challenges. They have to; if they do not, they die.

Even the most desperately needy are not always paralyzed by want. There are certain things they are physically capable of doing for themselves. Sometimes they find shelter by occupying an empty house or sleeping in a sheltered spot. They gather food from various places, they light a fire to cook it, and they sit down in a park to eat. They may urinate behind bushes, and wash their clothes in a fountain. Their physical condition is certainly not comfortable, but they are *capable* of acting in ways that make things a little more bearable for themselves. Now one question we face as a society – a broad question of justice and social policy – is whether we are willing to tolerate an economic system in which large numbers of people are homeless. Since the answer is evidently, "Yes," the question that remains is whether we are will-ing to allow those who are in this predicament to act as free agents, looking after their own needs, in public places – the only space available to them. It is a deeply frightening fact about the modern United States that those who *have* homes and jobs are willing to answer "Yes" to the first question and "No" to the second.

Negative freedom

Before going on, I want to say something about the conception of freedom I am using in this essay. Those who argue that the homeless (or the poor generally) have less freedom than the rest of us are often accused of appealing to a controver-sial, dangerous, and question-begging conception of "positive" freedom.[12] It is commonly thought that one has to step outside the traditional liberal idea of "negative" freedom in order to make these points.

However, there is no need to argue about that here. The definition of freedom with which I have been working so far is as "negative" as can be. There is nothing unfamiliar about it (except perhaps the consistency with which it is being deployed). I am saying that a person is free to be someplace just in case he is not legally liable to be physically removed from that place or penalized for being there. At the very least, negative free-dom is freedom from obstructions such as some-one else's forceful effort to prevent one from doing something.[13] In exactly this negative sense (absence of forcible interference), the homeless person is unfree to be in any place governed by a private property rule (unless the owner for some reason elects to give him his permission to be there). The familiar claim that, in the negative sense of "freedom," the poor are as free as the rest of us – and that you have to move to a posi-tive definition in order to dispute that – is simply false.[14]

That private property limits freedom seems obvious.[15] If I own a piece of land, others have a duty not to use it (without my consent) and there is a battery of legal remedies which I can use to enforce this duty as I please. The right correlative to this duty is an essential incident of ownership, and any enforcement of the duty necessarily amounts to a deliberate interference with some-one else's action. It is true that the connection between property and the restriction of liberty is in some ways a contingent one: as Andrew Reeve notes, "even if I am entitled to use my property to prevent you from taking some action, I will not necessarily do so."[16] But there is a similar contin-gency in any juridical restriction. A repressive state may have laws entitling officials to crush dissent. In theory, they might choose to refrain from doing so on certain occasions; but we would still describe the law as a restriction on freedom if dissidents had to take into account the likelihood of its being used against them. Indeed we often say that the unpredictable element of official dis-cretion "chills" whatever freedom remains in the interstices of its enforcement. Thus, in exactly the way in which we call repressive political laws restrictions on freedom, we can call property rights restrictions on freedom. We do not need any special definition of freedom over and above the negative one used by liberals in contexts that are more ideologically congenial.

The definitional objection is sometimes based on a distinction between freedom and ability.[17] The homeless, it is said, are in the relevant sense *free* to perform the same activities as the rest of us; but the sad fact is that they do not have the *means* or the *power* or the *ability* to exercise these freedoms. This claim is almost always false. With the exception of a few who are so weakened by their plight that they are incapable of anything, the homeless are not *unable* to enter the privately owned places from which they are banned. They can climb walls, open doors, cross thresholds, break windows, and so on, to gain entry to the premises from which the laws of property exclude them. What stands in their way is simply what stands in the way of anyone who is negatively unfree: the likelihood that someone else will forcibly prevent their action. Of course, the rich do try to make it impossible as well as illegal for the homeless to enter their gardens: they build their walls as high as possible and top them with broken glass. But that this does not constitute mere inability as opposed to unfreedom is indicated by the fact that the homeless are not permitted even to *try* to overcome these physical obstacles. They may be dragged away and penalized for attempting to scale the walls.

A second line that is sometimes taken is this: one should regard the homeless as less free than the rest of us only if one believes that some human agency (other than their own) is responsible for their plight.[18] However, the idea of someone else's being responsible for the plight of the homeless is an ambiguous one. It may well be the case that people are homeless as a result of earlier deliberate and heartless actions by landlords, employers, or officials, or as a result of a deliberate capitalist strategy to create and sustain a vast reserve industrial army of the unemployed.[19] That *may* be the case. But even if it is not, even if their being homeless cannot be laid at anyone's door or attributed to anything over and above their own choices or the impersonal workings of the market, my point remains. Their homelessness *consists* in unfreedom. Though it may not be anyone's fault that there is no place they can go without being dragged away, still their being

removed from the places they are not allowed to be is itself a derogation from their freedom, a derogation constituted by the deliberate human action of property-owners, security guards, and police officers. To repeat, their having nowhere to go *is* their being unfree (in a negative sense) to be anywhere; it is identical with the fact that others are authorized deliberately to drag them away from wherever they choose to be. We do not need any further account of the *cause* of this state of affairs to describe it as, in itself, a situation of unfreedom.

Thirdly, someone may object that a person is not made unfree if he is prevented from doing something wrong – something he has a duty not to do. Since entering others' property and abusing common property are wrong, it is not really a derogation from freedom to enforce a person's duties in these respects. Ironically, this "moralization" of the concept of freedom certainly *would* amount to a shift in the direction of a positive definition.[20] It was precisely the identification of freedom with virtue (and the inference that a restriction on vice was no restriction at all) that most troubled liberals about theories of positive liberty.[21]

In any case, the "moralization" of freedom is confusing and question begging in the present context. It elides the notions of a restriction on freedom and an unjustified restriction on freedom, closing off certain questions that common sense regards as open. It seems to rest on a sense – elsewhere repudiated by many liberals – that all our moral and political concerns fit together in a tidy package, so that we need not ever worry about trade-offs between freedom (properly understood) and other values, such as property and justice.[22]

To say – as I have insisted we should say – that property rules limit freedom, is not to say they are *eo ipso* wrong.[23] It is simply to say that they engage a concern about liberty, and that anyone who values liberty should put himself on alert when questions of property are being discussed. (The argument I have made about the homeless is a striking illustration of the importance of our not losing sight of that.)

Above all, by building the morality of a given property system (rights, duties, and the current distribution) into the concept of freedom, the moralizing approach precludes the use of that concept as a basis for arguing about property. If when we use the words "free" and "unfree," we are already assuming that it is wrong for A to use something that belongs to B, we cannot appeal to "freedom" to explain why B's ownership of the resource is justified. We cannot even extol our property system as the basis of a "free" society, for such a boast would be nothing more than tautological. It is true that if we have independent grounds of justification for our private property system, then we *can* say that interfering with property rights is wrong without appealing to the idea of freedom. In that case, there is nothing question-begging about the claim that preventing someone from violating property rights does not count as a restriction on his freedom. But the price of this strategy is high. It not only transforms our conception of freedom into a moralized definition of positive liberty (so that the only freedom that is relevant is the freedom to do what is right), but it also excludes the concept of freedom altogether from the debate about the justification of property rights. Since most theorists of property do not want to deprive themselves of the concept of freedom as a resource in that argument, the insistence that the enforcement of property rules should not count as a restriction on freedom is, at the very least, a serious strategic mistake.

General prohibitions and particular freedoms

I think the account I have given is faithful to the tradition of negative liberty. One is free to do something only if one is not liable to be forcibly prevented from or penalized for doing it. However, the way I have applied this account may seem a little disconcerting. The issue has to do with the level of generality at which actions are described.

The laws we have usually mention general *types* of actions, rather than particular actions done by particular people at specific times and places. Statutes do not say, "Jane Smith is not to assault Sarah Jones on Friday, November 24, on the corner of College Avenue and Bancroft." They say, "Assault is prohibited," or some equivalent, and it is understood that the prohibition applies to all such actions performed by anyone anywhere. A prohibition on a general type of action is understood to be a prohibition on all tokens of that type. Jurists say we ought to value this generality in our laws; it is part of what is involved in the complex ideal of "The Rule of Law." It makes the laws more predictable and

more learnable. It makes them a better guide for the ordinary citizen who needs to have a rough and ready understanding (rather than a copious technical knowledge) of what he is and is not allowed to do as he goes about his business. A quick checklist of prohibited acts, formulated in general terms, serves that purpose admirably.[24] It also serves moral ideals of universalizability and rationality: a reason for restraining any particular act ought to be a reason for restraining any other act of the same type, unless there is a relevant difference between them (which can be formulated also in general terms).[25]

All that is important. However, there is another aspect of "The Rule of Law" ideal that can lead one into difficulties if it is combined with this insistence on generality. Legal systems of the kind we have pride themselves on the following feature: "Everything which is not explicitly prohibited is permitted." If the law does not formulate any prohibition on singing or jogging, for example, that is an indication to the citizen that singing and jogging are permitted, that he is free to perform them. To gauge the extent of his freedom, all he needs to know are the prohibitions imposed by the law. His freedom is simply the complement of that.[26]

The difficulty arises if it is inferred from this that a person's freedom is the complement of the *general* prohibitions that apply to him. For although it is possible to infer particular prohibitions from prohibitions formulated at a general level ("All murder is wrong" implies "This murder by me today is wrong"), it is not possible to infer particular permissions from the absence of any general prohibition. In our society, there is no general prohibition on cycling, but one cannot infer from this that any particular act of riding a bicycle is permitted. It depends (among other things) on whether the person involved has the right to use the particular bicycle he is proposing to ride.

This does not affect the basic point about complementarity. Our freedoms *are* the complement of the prohibitions that apply to us. The mistake arises from thinking that the only prohibitions that apply to us are general prohibitions. For, in addition to the general prohibitions laid down (say) in the criminal law, there are also the prohibitions on using particular objects and places that are generated by the laws of property. Until we know how these latter laws apply, we do not know whether we are free to perform a particular action.

It is *not* a telling response to this point to say that the effect of the laws of property can be stated in terms of a general principle – "No one is to use the property of another without his permission." They *can* be so stated; but in order to apply that principle, we need particular knowledge, not just general knowledge.[27] A person needs to know that *this* bicycle belongs to him, whereas *those* bicycles belong to other people. He needs that particular knowledge about specific objects as well as his general knowledge about the types of actions that are and are not permitted.

At any rate, the conclusions about freedom that I have reached depend on taking the prohibitions relating to particular objects generated by property laws as seriously as we take the more general prohibitions imposed by the criminal law. No doubt these different types of prohibition are imposed for different reasons. But if freedom means simply the absence of deliberate interference with one's actions, we will not be in a position to say how free a person is until we know everything about the universe of legal restraints that may be applied to him. After all, it is not freedom in the abstract that people value, but freedom to perform particular actions. If the absence of a general prohibition tells us nothing about anyone's concrete freedom, then we should be wary of using only the checklist of general prohibitions to tell us how free or unfree a person or a society really is.

These points can readily be applied to the homeless. There are no general prohibitions in our society on actions like sleeping or washing. However, we cannot infer from this that anyone may sleep or wash wherever he chooses. In order to work out whether a particular person is free to sleep or wash, we must also ask whether there are any prohibitions *of place* that apply to his performance of actions of this type. As a matter of fact, all of us face a formidable battery of such prohibitions. Most private places, for example, are off limits to us for these (or any other) activities. Though I am a well-paid professor, there are only a couple of private places where I am allowed to sleep or wash (without having someone's specific permission): my home, my office, and whatever restaurant I am patronizing. Most homeless people do not have jobs and few of them are allowed inside restaurants. ("Bathrooms for the use of customers only.") Above all, they have no homes. So there is literally no private place where they are free to sleep or wash.

For them, that is a desperately important fact about their freedom, one that must preoccupy much of every day. Unlike us, they have no private place where they can take it for granted that they will be allowed to sleep or wash. Since everyone needs to sleep and wash regularly, homeless people have to spend time searching for non-private places – like public restrooms (of which there are precious few in America, by the standards of most civilized countries) and shelters (available, if at all, only at night) – where these actions may be performed without fear of interference. If we regard freedom as simply the complement of the general prohibitions imposed by law, we are in danger of overlooking this fact about the freedom of the homeless. Most of us can afford to overlook it, because we have homes to go to. But without a home, a person's freedom is his freedom to act in public, in places governed by common property rules. That is the difference between our freedom and the freedom of the homeless.

Public places

What then are we to say about public places? If there is anywhere the homeless are free to act, it is in the streets, the subways and the parks. These regions are governed by common property rules. Since these are the only places they are allowed to be, these are the only places they are free to act.

However, a person is not allowed to do just whatever he likes in a public place. There are at least three types of prohibition that one faces in a place governed by rules of common property.

(1) If there are any general prohibitions on types of action in a society, like the prohibition on murder or the prohibition on selling narcotics, then they apply to all tokens of those types performed anywhere, public or private. And these prohibitions apply to everyone: though it is only the homeless who have no choice but to be in public places, the law forbids the rich as well as the poor from selling narcotics, and *a fortiori* from selling narcotics on the streets and in the parks.

(2) Typically, there are also prohibitions that are specific to public places and provide the basis of their commonality. Parks have curfews; streets and sidewalks have rules that govern the extent to which one person's use of these places may interfere with another's; there are rules about obstruction, jaywalking, and so on. Many of these rules can be characterized and justified as rules of

fairness. If public places are to be available for everyone's use, then we must make sure that their use by some people does not preclude or obstruct their use by others.

(3) However, some of the rules that govern behavior in public places are more substantive than that: they concern particular forms of behavior that are not to be performed in public whether there is an issue of fairness involved or not. For example, many states and municipalities forbid the use of parks for making love. It is not that there is any general constraint on lovemaking as a type of action (though some states still have laws against fornication). Although sexual intercourse between a husband and wife is permitted and even encouraged by the law, it is usually forbidden in public places. The place for that sort of activity, we say, is the privacy of the home.

Other examples spring to mind. There is no law against urinating – it is a necessary and desirable human activity. However, there is a law against urinating in public, except in the specially designated premises of public restrooms. In general, it is an activity which, if we are free to do it, we are free to do it mainly at home or in some other private place (a bathroom in a restaurant) where we have an independent right to be. There is also no law against sleeping – again a necessary and desirable human activity. To maintain their physical and mental health, people need to sleep for a substantial period every day. However, states and municipalities are increasingly passing ordinances to prohibit sleeping in public places like streets and parks.[28] The decision of the Transit Authority in New York to enforce prohibitions on sleeping in the subways attracted national attention a year or two ago.[29]

Such ordinances have and are known and even intended to have a specific effect on the homeless which is different from the effect they have on the rest of us. We are all familiar with the dictum of Anatole France: "[L]a majestueuse égalité des lois . . . interdit au riche comme au pauvre de coucher sous les ponts. . . ."[30] We might adapt it to the present point, noting that the new rules in the subway will prohibit anyone from sleeping or lying down in the cars and stations, whether they are rich or poor, homeless or housed. They will be phrased with majestic impartiality, and indeed their drafters know that they would be struck down immediately by the courts if they were formulated specifically to target those who have no homes. Still everyone is perfectly well aware of

the point of passing these ordinances, and any attempt to defend them on the basis of their generality is quite disingenuous. Their point is to make sleeping in the subways off limits to those who have nowhere else to sleep.[31]

Four facts are telling in this regard. First, it is well known among those who press for these laws that the subway is such an unpleasant place to sleep that almost no one would do it if they had anywhere else to go. Secondly, the pressure for these laws comes as a response to what is well known to be "the problem of homelessness." It is not as though people suddenly became concerned about *sleeping* in the subway as such (as though that were a particularly dangerous activity to perform there, like smoking or jumping onto a moving train). When people write to the Transit Authority and say, "Just get them out. I don't care. Just get them out any way you can," we all know who the word "them" refers to.[32] People do not want to be confronted with the sight of the homeless – it is uncomfortable for the well-off to be reminded of the human price that is paid for a social structure like theirs – and they are willing to deprive those people of their last opportunity to sleep in order to protect themselves from this discomfort. Thirdly, the legislation is called for and promoted by people who are secure in the knowledge that they themselves have some place where they are permitted to sleep. Because *they* have some place to sleep which is not the subway, they infer that the subway is not a place for sleeping. The subway is a place where those who have some other place to sleep may do things besides sleeping.

Finally, and most strikingly, those who push for these laws will try to amend them or reformulate them if they turn out to have an unwelcome impact on people who are not homeless. For example, a city ordinance in Clearwater, Florida, prohibiting sleeping in public, was struck down as too broad because it would have applied even to a person sleeping in his car.[33] Most people who have cars also have homes, and we would not want a statute aimed at the homeless to prevent car owners from sleeping in public.

Though we all know what the real object of these ordinances is, we may not have thought very hard about their cumulative effect. That effect is as follows.

For a person who has no home, and has no expectation of being allowed into something like a private office building or a restaurant, prohibitions on things like sleeping that apply particularly to public places pose a special problem. For although there is no *general* prohibition on acts of these types, still they are effectively ruled out altogether for anyone who is homeless and who has no shelter to go to. The prohibition is comprehensive in effect because of the cumulation, in the case of the homeless, of a number of different bans, differently imposed. The rules of property prohibit the homeless person from doing any of these acts in private, since there is no private place that he has a right to be. And the rules governing public places prohibit him from doing any of these acts in public, since that is how we have decided to regulate the use of public places. So what is the result? Since private places and public places between them exhaust all the places that there are, there is nowhere that these actions may be performed by the homeless person. And since freedom to perform a concrete action requires freedom to perform it at some place, it follows that the homeless person does not have the freedom to perform them. If sleeping is prohibited in public places, then sleeping is comprehensively prohibited to the homeless. If urinating is prohibited in public places (and if there are no public lavatories) then the homeless are simply unfree to urinate. These are not altogether comfortable conclusions, and they are certainly not comfortable for those who have to live with them.

4 Intention, Responsibility and Blame

I said the predicament is cumulative. I argued that if an action X is prohibited (to everyone) in public places *and* if a person A has no access to a private place wherein to perform it, then action X is effectively prohibited to A *everywhere*, and so A is comprehensively unfree to do X.

However, people may balk at this point. They may argue:

> Surely prohibition is an intentional notion, and nobody is intending that A not be permitted to do X. We do intend that he should be prohibited from X-ing in public, but we don't intend that he should be prohibited from X-ing in private. That's just the way the distribution of property turns out. We don't intend as a society – and certainly the state does not intend – that there should be *no* place where A is permitted to do X. It just happens that way.[34]

We have already seen that this point about intention cannot be sustained at the level of individual acts. If a homeless tramp tries to urinate in a rich person's yard, the rich person may try to prevent that, and he is authorized to do so. There is no doubt about the intentionality of this particular restraint on this particular violation of property rules. However, the point of the present objection is that the rich person does not intend that there should be nowhere the tramp is allowed to urinate (indeed, he probably hopes that there is somewhere – provided it is not in his back yard). And similarly for each proprietor in turn. None of them intends that the tramp should never be allowed to urinate. That just happens, in an invisible hand sort of way, as a result of each proprietor saying, in effect, "Anywhere but here." Though each particular unfreedom involves an intentional restraint, their cumulation is not in itself the product of anyone's intention.

The objection can be conceded. We can tie judgments about freedom and unfreedom this closely to intentionality if we like. On that approach, all we can say about the homeless person's freedom is that he is unfree to urinate in place X *and* he is unfree to urinate in place Y *and* he is unfree to urinate in place Z *and* . . . so on, for each place that there is. We refrain from the inference: "So he is unfree to urinate (anywhere)." However, even if we are scrupulous about not making that generalization, still there is *something* we can say at a general level about his predicament. We can say, for example, "There is no place where he is free to urinate." The logic of such a quantified sentence (i.e. "There is no place p such that he is free to urinate at p") does not commit us to any cumulation of unfreedoms, and it is an accurate statement of his position. Anyway, even if no one has intended that there be no place this person is free to urinate, it cannot be said that his predicament, so described, is a matter of no concern. It is hard to imagine how anyone could think freedom important in relation to each particular restraint, but yet have no concern about the cumulative effect of such restraints. Moreover, even if our concern about the cumulation is not directly expressed in terms of freedom because freedom is taken to be an intentional notion, still it is at least in part freedom *related*. If we value freedom in each particular case because of the importance of choice and of not being constrained in the choices one makes, then that value ought to lead us to pay some attention to how many choices a person has left after each constraint has been exercised. From any point of view that values choice and freedom of action, it ought to be a matter of concern that the choices left open to a person are being progressively closed off, one by one, and that he is nearing a situation where there is literally nowhere he can turn.

The fact that no one intended his overall predicament may mean that there is no one to *blame* for it. However, for one thing, each private proprietor will have a pretty good idea about how others may be expected to exercise their rights in this regard. It would be quite disingenuous for any of them to say. "I thought some of the other owners would let him use their property." Moral philosophers have developed interesting models of joint and collective responsibility for outcomes like these, and those models seem quite applicable here.[35] For another thing, those who impose a ban on these activities in public places certainly do know very well what the result of *that* will be: that the homeless will have almost nowhere to go, in the territory subject to their jurisdiction. Indeed the aim – again, as we all know – is often to drive them out of the jurisdiction so that some other city or state has to take care of the problem. Even where this is not intentional, still the intentional infliction of harm is not the only thing we blame people for. "I didn't mean to," is not the all-purpose excuse it is often taken to be. We blame people for recklessness and negligence, and certainly the promoters of these ordinances are quite reckless whether they leave the homeless anywhere to go or not. ("Just get them out. I do not care. Just get them out any way you can.")[36]

In any case, our concern about freedom and unfreedom is not principally a concern to find someone to blame. An intentional attack on freedom is blameworthy in part because the freedom of those who are attacked matters. If freedom is sufficiently important to sustain moral blame for those who attack it, it ought to matter also in other cases where blame is not the issue. Sometimes we can promote freedom, or make people more free, or organize our institutions so that there are fewer ways in which their freedom is restricted, and we may want to do this even in cases where we are not responding with outrage to the moral culpability of an attack on freedom. Freedom is a multifaceted concern in our political morality. Sure, we blame those who attack it deliberately or recklessly. But we are also solici-

tous for it and do our best to make it flourish, even when there is no evil freedom-hater obstructing our efforts. Blame, and the intentionality that blame is sometimes thought to presuppose, are not the only important things in the world.

5 Freedom and Important Freedoms

I have argued that a rule against performing an act in a public place amounts *in effect* to a *comprehensive* ban on that action so far as the homeless are concerned. If that argument is accepted, our next question should be: "How serious is this limitation on freedom?" Freedom in any society is limited in all sorts of ways: I have no freedom to pass through a red light nor to drive east on Bancroft Avenue. Any society involves a complicated array of freedoms and unfreedoms, and our assessment of *how free* a given society is (our assessment, for example, that the United States is a freer society than Albania) involves some assessment of the balance in that array.

Such assessments are characteristically qualitative as well as quantitative. We do not simply ask, "How many actions are people free or unfree to perform?" Indeed, such questions are very difficult to answer or even to formulate coherently.[37] Instead we often ask qualitative questions: "How important are the actions that people are prohibited from performing?" One of the tasks of a theory of human rights is to pick out a set of actions that it is thought particularly important from a moral point of view that people should have the freedom to perform, choices that it is thought particularly important that they should have the freedom to make, whatever other restrictions there are on their conduct.[38] For example, the Bill of Rights picks out things like religious worship, political speech, and the possession of firearms as actions or choices whose restriction we should be specially concerned about. A society that places restrictions on activities of these types is held to be worse, in point of freedom, than a society that merely restricts activities like drinking, smoking, or driving.

The reason for the concern has in part to do with the special significance of these actions. Religious worship is where we disclose and practice our deepest beliefs. Political speech is where we communicate with one another as citizens of a republic. Even bearing arms is held, by those who defend its status as a right, to be a special assertion of dignity, mature responsibility, civic participation, and freedom from the prospect of tyranny. And people occasionally disagree about the contents of these lists of important freedoms. Is it really important to have the right to bear arms, in a modern democratic society? Is commercial advertising as important as individual political discourse? These are disputes about which choices have this high ethical import, analogous to that attributed, say, to religious worship. They are disputes about which liberties should be given special protection in the name of human dignity or autonomy, and which attacks on freedom should be viewed as particularly inimical to the identity of a person as a citizen and as a moral agent.

On the whole, the actions specified by Bills of Rights are not what are at stake in the issue of homelessness. Certainly there would be an uproar if an ordinance was passed making it an offense to pray in the subway or to pass one's time there in political debate.[39] There has been some concern in America about the restriction of free speech in public and quasi-public places[40] (since it is arguable that the whole point of free speech is that it take place in the public realm). However, the actions that are being closed off to the homeless are, for the most part, not significant in this high-minded sense. They are significant in another way: they are actions basic to the sustenance of a decent or healthy life, in some cases basic to the sustenance of life itself. There may not seem anything particularly autonomous or self-assertive or civically republican or ethically ennobling about sleeping or cooking or urinating. You will not find them listed in any Charter. However, that does not mean it is a matter of slight concern when people are prohibited from performing such actions, a concern analogous to that aroused by a traffic regulation or the introduction of a commercial standard.

For one thing, the regular performance of such actions is a precondition for all other aspects of life and activity. It is a precondition for the sort of autonomous life that is celebrated and affirmed when Bills of Rights are proclaimed. I am not making the crude mistake of saying that if we value autonomy, we must value its preconditions in exactly the same way. But if we value autonomy we should regard the satisfaction of its preconditions as a matter of importance; otherwise, our values simply ring hollow so far as real people are concerned.

Moreover, though we say there is nothing particularly dignified about sleeping or urinating, there is certainly something deeply and inherently *un*dignified about being prevented from doing so. Every torturer knows this: to break the human spirit, focus the mind of the victim through petty restrictions pitilessly imposed on the banal necessities of human life. We should be ashamed that we have allowed our laws of public and private property to reduce a million or more citizens to something approaching this level of degradation.

Increasingly, in the way we organize common property, we have done all we can to prevent people from taking care of these elementary needs themselves, quietly, with dignity, as ordinary human beings. If someone needs to urinate, what he needs above all as a dignified person is the *freedom* to do so in privacy and relative independence of the arbitrary will of anyone else. But we have set things up so that either the street person must *beg* for this opportunity, several times every day, as a favor from people who recoil from him in horror, or, if he wants to act independently on his own initiative, he must break the law and risk arrest. The generous provision of public lavatories would make an immense difference in this regard – and it would be a difference to freedom and dignity, not just a matter of welfare.

Finally we need to understand that any restriction on the performance of these basic acts has the feature of being not only uncomfortable and degrading, but more or less literally *unbearable* for the people concerned. People need sleep, for example, not just in the sense that sleep is necessary for health, but also in the sense that they will eventually fall asleep or drop from exhaustion if it is denied them. People simply cannot bear a lack of sleep, and they will do themselves a great deal of damage trying to bear it. The same, obviously, is true of bodily functions like urinating and defecating. These are things that people simply have to do; any attempt voluntarily to refrain from doing them is at once painful, dangerous, and finally impossible. That our social system might in effect deny them the right to do these things, by prohibiting their being done in each and every place, ought to be a matter of the gravest concern.[41]

It may seem sordid or in bad taste to make such a lot of these elementary physical points in a philosophical discussion of freedom. But if freedom is important, it is as freedom for human beings, that is, for the embodied and needy organisms that we are. The point about the activities I have mentioned is that they are both urgent and quotidian. They are urgent because they are basic to all other functions. They are actions that have to be performed, if one is to be free to do anything else without distraction and distress. And they are quotidian in the sense that they are actions that have to be done every day. They are not actions that a person can *wait* to perform until he acquires a home. Every day, he must eat and excrete and sleep. Every day, if he is homeless, he will face the overwhelming task of trying to find somewhere where he is allowed to do this.

6 Homes and Opportunities

That last point is particularly important as an answer to a final objection that may be made. Someone might object that I have so far said nothing at all about the fact that our society gives everyone the *opportunity* to acquire a home, and that we are all – the homeless and the housed – equal in *this* regard even if we are unequal in our actual ownership of real estate.

There is something to this objection, but not much. Certainly a society that denied a caste of persons the right (or juridical power) to own or lease property would be even worse than ours. The opportunity to acquire a home (even if it is just the juridical power) is surely worth having. But, to put it crudely, one cannot pee in an opportunity. Since the homeless, like us, are real people, they need some real place to be, not just the notional reflex of an Hohfeldian power.[42]

We also know enough about how the world works to see that one's need for somewhere to sleep and wash is, if anything, greatest during the time that one is trying to consummate this opportunity to find a home. The lack of liberty that homelessness involves makes it harder to impress, appeal to, or deal with the people who might eventually provide one with a job and with the money to afford housing. The irony of opportunity, in other words, is that the longer it remains unconsummated, for whatever reason, the more difficult it is to exploit.

In the final analysis, whether or not a person really has the *opportunity* to obtain somewhere to live is a matter of his position in a society; it is a matter of his ability to deal with the people around him and of there being an opening in social and economic structures so that his wants and abilities can be brought into relation with others.[43] That position, that ability, and that opening do not exist magically as a result of legal status. The juridical fact that a person is not legally barred from becoming a tenant or a proprietor does not mean that there is any realistic prospect of that happening. Whether it happens depends, among other things, on how he can present himself, how reliable and respectable he appears, what skills and abilities he can deploy, how much time, effort, and mobility he can invest in a search for housing, assistance, and employment, and so on.

Those are abstract formulations. We could say equally that it is hard to get a job when one appears filthy, that many of the benefits of social and economic interaction cannot be obtained without an address or without a way of receiving telephone calls, that a person cannot take *all* his possessions with him in a shopping cart when he goes for an interview but he may have nowhere to leave them, that those who have become homeless become so because they have run out of cash altogether and so of course do not have available the up-front fees and deposits that landlords require from potential tenants, and so on.

Everything we call a social or economic opportunity depends cruelly on a person's being able to *do* certain things – for example, his being able to wash, to sleep, and to base himself somewhere. When someone is homeless he is, as we have seen, effectively *banned* from doing these things; these are things he is *not allowed* to do. So long as that is the case, it is a contemptible mockery to reassure the victims of such coercion that they have the *opportunity* to play a full part in social and economic life, for the rules of property are such that they are *prohibited* from doing the minimum that would be necessary to take advantage of that opportunity.[44]

Conclusion

Lack of freedom is not all there is to the nightmare of homelessness. There is also the cold, the hunger, the disease and lack of medical treatment, the danger, the beatings, the loneliness, and the shame and despair that may come from being unable to care for oneself, one's child, or a friend. By focusing on freedom in this essay, I have not wanted to detract from any of that.

But there are good reasons to pay attention to the issue of freedom. They are not merely strategic, though in a society that prides itself as "the land of the free," this may be one way of shaming a people into action and concern. Homelessness is partly about property and law, and freedom provides the connecting term that makes those categories relevant. By considering not only what a person is allowed to do, but where he is allowed to do it, we can see a system of property for what it is: rules that provide freedom and prosperity for some by imposing restrictions on others. So long as everyone enjoys some of the benefits as well as some of the restrictions, that correlativity is bearable. It ceases to be so when there is a class of persons who bear *all* of the restrictions and nothing else, a class of persons for whom property is nothing but a way of limiting their freedom.

Perhaps the strongest argument for thinking about homelessness as an issue of freedom is that it forces us to see people in need as *agents*. Destitution is not necessarily passive; and public provision is not always a way of compounding passivity. By focusing on what we allow people to do to satisfy their own basic needs on their own initiative, and by scrutinizing the legal obstacles that we place in their way (the doors we lock, the ordinances we enforce, and the night-sticks we raise), we get a better sense that what we are dealing with here is not just "the problem of homelessness," but a million or more *persons* whose activity and dignity and freedom are at stake.

Notes

Jeremy Waldron is Professor of Law, Jurisprudence and Social Policy Program, School of Law (Boalt Hall), University of California, Berkeley. B.A. 1974, LL.B. 1978, University of Otago, New Zealand; D. Phil. 1986, Oxford University. An earlier version of this essay was presented at faculty workshops at Cornell University and at Boalt Hall. I am grateful to all who participated in those discussions, but particularly to Gary Gleb, Carol Sanger, and Henry Shue for the very detailed suggestions they have offered.

1   *See, e.g.*, Siebert, *Homeless People: Establishing Rights to Shelter*, 4 Law & Inequality 393 (1986) (no constitutional guarantee of adequate housing): Comment, *The Unconstitutionality of "Anti homeless" Laws: Ordinances Prohibiting Sleeping in Outdoor Public Areas as a Violation of the Right to Travel*, 77 Calif. L. Rev. 595 (1989) (authored by Ades) (arguing that laws that proscribe sleeping in outdoor public areas violate the right to travel).

2   The best discussion remains Honoré, *Ownership*, in Oxford Essays in Jurisprudence 107 (A.G. Guest ed. 1961); *see also* S. Munzer, A Theory of Property 21–61 (1990); J. Waldron, The Right to Private Property 15–36 (1988).

3   *See* J. Waldron, note 2 (above), at 40–42; Macpherson, *The Meaning of Property*, in Property: Mainstream and Critical Positions 1, 4–6 (C. Macpherson ed. 1978).

4   In Pruneyard Shopping Center v. Robins, 447 U.S. 74 (1980), the United States Supreme Court held that the California courts may reasonably require the owners of a shopping mall to allow persons to exercise rights of free speech on their premises under the California Constitution, and that such a requirement does not constitute a taking for the purposes of the Fifth Amendment to the Constitution of the United States.

5   For a more complete discussion, see J. Waldron, note 2 (above), at 42–46.

6   Diluliu, *There But For Fortune*, New Republic, June 24, 1991, at 27, 28.

7   But this ignores the fact that a large number of people with no home of their own are kept from having to wander the streets only by virtue of the fact that friends and relatives are willing to let them share their homes, couches, and floors. If this generosity were less forthcoming, the number of "street people" would be much greater. Still, this generosity is contingent and precarious: those who offer it are often under great strain themselves. So the situation affords precious little security: at the first family crisis, the friend or relative may have to move out.

8   *See, e.g.*, M. Rothbard, For a New Liberty 201–2 (1973) (emphasis in original):

The ultimate libertarian program may be summed up in one phrase: the *abolition* of the public sector, the conversion of all operations and services performed by the government into activities performed voluntarily by the private enterprise economy. . . . Abolition of the public sector means, of course, that *all* pieces of land, all land areas, including streets and roads, would be owned privately, by individuals, corporations, cooperatives, or any other voluntary groupings of individuals and capital. . . . What we need to do is to reorient our thinking to consider a world in which all land areas are privately owned.

9   Herbert Spencer was so disconcerted by the possibility that he thought it a good reason to prohibit the private ownership of land altogether.

> For if *one* portion of the earth's surface may justly become the possession of an individual, and may be held by him for his sole use and benefit, as a thing to which he has an exclusive right, then *other* portions of the earth's surface may be so held; and eventually the *whole* of the earth's surface may be so held; and our planet may thus lapse altogether into private hands. . . . Supposing the entire habitable globe be so enclosed, it follows that if the landowners have a valid right to its surface, all who are not landowners, have no right at all to its surface. Hence, such can exist on the earth by sufferance only. They are all trespassers. Save by permission of the lords of the soil, they can have no room for the soles of their feet. Nay, should others think fit to deny them a resting-place, these landless men might equitably be expelled from the planet altogether.
> A. Reeve, Property 85 (1986) (quoting H. Spencer, Social Statics 114–15 (1851)).

10 For a useful discussion, see I. Berlin, *Introduction*, in Four Essays on Liberty i, xlv–lv (1969).

11 *See also* Waldron, *Welfare and the Images of Charity*, 36 Phil. Q. 463 (1986)

12 For the contrast between "positive" and "negative" conceptions of freedom, see I. Berlin, *Two Concepts of Liberty*, in Four Essays on Liberty 118 (1969).

13 The *locus classicus* of negative liberty, defined in this way, is T. Hobbes, Leviathan 261–74 (C.B. Macpherson ed. 1968).

14 The claim that the poor are as free as the rest of us is sometimes associated with the view that they have the same *opportunity* as the rest of us to acquire property and become, if not rich, then at least well-off. This line of argument is discussed in Part VI. For the moment, it does not affect the point that *being* poor amounts to being unfree, even if there are ways of extricating oneself from that predicament. (An analogy may help here: a prisoner who has the opportunity to obtain parole and fails to take advantage of that opportunity still remains unfree inasmuch as he remains imprisoned.)

15 For a particularly clear statement, see Cohen, *Capitalism, Freedom and the Proletariat*, in The Idea of Freedom 9, 11–14 (A. Ryan ed. 1979).

16 A. Reeve, note 9 (above), at 107.

17 This distinction is found in Hobbes's discussion: he defines liberty as the absence of "external impediments." and adds that "when the impediment of motion, is in the constitution of the thing it selfe, we use not to say, it wants the Liberty; but the Power to move; as when a stone lyeth still, or a man is fastned to his bed by sicknesse." T. Hobbes, note 13 (above), at 262. It is found also in Berlin's account: "If I say that I am unable to jump more than ten feet in the air, or cannot read because I am blind, or cannot understand the darker pages of Hegel, it would be eccentric to say that I am to that degree enslaved or coerced." I. Berlin, note 12 (above), at 122.

18 Cf. I. Berlin, note 12 (above), at 123:

> It is only because I believe that my inability to get a given thing is due to the fact that other human beings have made arrangements whereby I am, whereas others are not, prevented from having enough money with which to pay for it, that I think myself a victim of coercion or slavery. In other words, this use of the term depends on a particular social and economic theory about the causes of my poverty or weakness.

19 *See* 1 K. Marx, Capital, 781–802 (B. Fowkes trans. 1976).

20 For the idea of a "moralized" definition of freedom, see Cohen, note 15 (above), at 12–14.

21 Cf. I. Berlin, note 12 (above), at 133:

> Once I take this view, I am in a position to ignore the actual wishes of men or societies, to bully, oppress, torture them in the name, and on behalf, of their "real" selves, in the secure knowledge that whatever is the true goal of man (happiness, performance of duty, wisdom, a just society, self-fulfilment) must be identical with his freedom . . .

22 The whole burden of Isaiah Berlin's work has been that such tidy packaging is not to be expected.

23 It is not even to deny that they may enlarge the amount of freedom overall. Isaiah Berlin put the point precisely: "Every law seems to me to curtail *some* liberty, although it may be a means to increasing another. Whether it increases the total sum of attainable liberty will of course depend on the particular situation." I. Berlin, note 10 (above), at xlix n. 1 (emphasis in original).

24 For the connection between generality, predictability, and the rule of law, see F. Hayek, The Constitution of Liberty 148–61 (1960).

25 *See* R. Hare, Freedom and Reason 10–21 (1963).

26 For example, Dicey puts forward the following as the first principle of "the rule of law": "no man is punishable or can be lawfully made to suffer in body or goods except for a distinct breach of law established in the ordinary legal manner before the ordinary courts of the land." A. Dicey, Introduction to the Study of the Law of the Constitution 188 (10th ed. 1959). Hobbes stated

the same doctrine more succinctly: "As for other Lyberties, they depend on the silence of the Law. In cases where the Soveraign has prescribed no rule, there the Subject hath the liberty to do, or forbeare, according to his own discretion." T. Hobbes, note 13 (above), at 271.

27 For a discussion of how a lay person applies the rules of property, see B. Ackerman, Private Property and the Constitution 116–18 (1977).

28 Here are some examples. The City Code of Phoenix, Arizona provides: "It shall be unlawful for any person to use a public street, highway, alley, lane, parkway, [or] sidewalk . . . for lying [or] sleeping . . . except in the case of a physical emergency or the administration of medical assistance." A St. Petersburg, Florida ordinance similarly provides that: "No person shall sleep upon or in any street, park, wharf or other public place." I am indebted to Paul Ades for these examples. Comment, note 1(above), at 595 n. 5, 596 n. 7 (quoting Phoenix, Ariz., City Code § 23–48.01 (1981); St. Petersburg, Fla., Ordinance 25.57 (1973)).

29 And New Yorkers have grown tired of confronting homeless people every day on the subway, at the train station and at the entrances to supermarkets and apartment buildings.

"People are tired of stepping over bodies," the advocacy director for the Coalition for the Homeless, Keith Summa, said.

Lynette Thompson, a Transit Authority official who oversees the outreach program for the homeless in the subway, said there had been a marked change this year in letters from riders.

"At the beginning of last year, the tenor of those letters was, 'Please do something to help the homeless,'" Ms. Thompson said. "But since August and September, they've been saying: 'Just get them out. I don't care. Just get them out any way you can.' It got worse and people got fed up."

. . .

For the homeless, the new restrictions mean it is more difficult than ever to find a place to rest. Charles Lark, 29 years old, who said he had spent the last three years sleeping on subway trains and platforms, left New York on the day the subway-enforcement program began: "This is a cold-hearted city," he said. "I'm going to Washington. I hope it'll be better there."

Doors Closing as Mood on the Homeless Sours, N.Y. Times, Nov. 18, 1989; at 1, col. 2, 32, col. 1, col. 2.

30 A. France, Le Lys Rouge 117–18 (rev. ed. 1923) ("The law in its majestic equality forbids the rich as well as the poor to sleep under the bridges.").

31 See M. Davis, City of Quartz: Excavating the Future in Los Angeles 232–36 (1990) for an excellent account of similar devices designed to render public spaces in downtown Los Angeles "off-limits" to the homeless, as well as Davis's *Afterword – A Logic Like Hell's: Being Homeless in Los Angeles,* 39 UCLA L. Rev. 325 (1991).

32 See note 29 (above).

33 Bracing for the annual influx of homeless people fleeing the Northern cold, the police here [in Miami, Florida] have proposed an emergency ordinance that would allow them to arrest some street people as a way of keeping them on the move.

. . .

The new measure would replace a century-old law against sleeping in public that was abandoned after a similar statute in Clearwater, Fla., was struck down by Federal courts in January. The courts said the statute was too broad and would have applied even to a person sleeping in his car.

The new proposal seeks to get around the court's objection by being more specific. But it would also be more far-reaching than the original law, applying to such activities as cooking and the building of temporary shelters.

Terry Cunningham, a 23-year-old who lives on the steps of the Federal Courthouse, asked of the police, "Where do they expect me to sleep?"

City and county officials had no answer. "That's a good question," Sergeant Rivero of the Police Department said, "No one is willing to address the problem."

Miami Police Want to Control Homeless by Arresting Them, N.Y. Times, Nov. 4, 1988, at A1, col. 1. A16, col. 4.

34 Cf. 2 F. Hayek, Law, Legislation and Liberty: The Mirage of Social Justice 64 (1976):

It has of course to be admitted that the manner in which the benefits and burdens are apportioned by the market mechanism would in many instances have to be regarded as very unjust *if* it were the result of a deliberate allocation to particular people. But this is not the case. Those shares are the outcome of a process the effect of which on particular people was neither intended nor foreseen by anyone . . .

35 See D. Parfit, Reasons and Persons 67–86 (1984); D. Regan, Utilitarianism and Cooperation (1980). The tenor of these works is that each person should pay attention, not only to the immediate consequences of her individual actions, but also to the consequences of a certain set of actions (which includes actions by her and actions by others). As Parfit puts it:

It is not enough to ask. "Will my act harm other people?" Even if the answer is No, my act may still be wrong, *because* of its effects on other people. I should ask. "Will my act be one of a set of acts that will *together* harm other people?" The answer may be Yes. And the harm to others may be great.

D. Parfit at 86 (above), (emphasis in original).

36 *See* note 29 (above).
37 For a critique of the purely quantitative approach, see Taylor, *What's Wrong with Negative Liberty?* in The Idea of Freedom, note 15 (above), at 183.
38 Cf. R. Dworkin, Taking Rights Seriously 270–72 (rev. ed. 1978) (discussion of the theory that a right to certain liberties can be derived from the "special character" of the liberties).
39 The failure of First Amendment challenges to restrictions on panhandling does not bode well for the survival of even these protections. *See* Young v. New York City Transit Auth., 903 F.2d 146 (2d Cir.), *cert. denied*, 111 S. Ct. 516 (1990). *But see* Hershkoff and Cohen, *Begging to Differ: The First Amendment and the Right to Beg*, 104 Harv. L. Rev. 896 (1991) (arguing that begging is protected speech).
40 *See* note 4 (above).
41 I hope it will not be regarded as an attempt at humor if I suggest that the Rawlsian doctrine of "the strains of commitment" is directly relevant here. J. Rawls, A Theory of Justice 175–76 (1971). If the effect of a principle would be literally unbearable to some of those to whom it applies, it must be rejected by the parties in Rawls's contractarian thought-experiment, known as the "original position": "They cannot enter into agreements that may have consequences they cannot accept. They will avoid those that they can adhere to only with great difficulty." *Id*. at 176. As Rawls emphasizes, this is a matter of the *bona fides* of bargaining, not of any particular psychology of risk-aversion.
42 See also the discussion in J. Waldron, note 2 (above), at 390–422.
43 This idea is sometimes expressed in terms of "social citizenship." *See* King & Waldron, *Citizenship, Social Citizenship, and the Defense of Welfare Provision*, 18 Brit. J. Pol. Sci. 415 (1988); *see also* R. Dahrendorf, The Modern Social Conflict: An Essay on the Politics of Liberty 29–47 (1988).
44 And this is to say nothing about the appalling deprivation of ordinary opportunity that will be experienced by those tens of thousands of *children* growing up homeless in America. To suggest that a child sleeping on the streets or in a dangerous, crowded shelter, with no place to store toys or books, and no sense of hope or security, has an opportunity equal to that of anyone in our society is simply a mockery.

PART VI

Equality

28

The Idea of Equality

Bernard Williams

The idea of equality is used in political discussion both in statements of fact, or what purport to be statements of fact – that men *are* equal – and in statements of political principles or aims – that men *should be* equal, as at present they are not. The two can be, and often are, combined: the aim is then described as that of securing a state of affairs in which men are treated as the equal beings which they in fact already are, but are not already treated as being. In both these uses, the idea of equality notoriously encounters the same difficulty: that on one kind of interpretation the statements in which it figures are much too strong, and on another kind much too weak, and it is hard to find a satisfactory interpretation that lies between the two.[1]

To take first the supposed statement of fact: it has only too often been pointed out that to say that all men are equal in all those characteristics in respect of which it makes sense to say that men are equal or unequal, is a patent falsehood; and even if some more restricted selection is made of these characteristics, the statement does not look much better. Faced with this obvious objection, the defender of the claim that all men are equal is likely to offer a weaker interpretation. It is not, he may say, in their skill, intelligence, strength or virtue that men are equal, but merely in their being men: it is their common humanity that constitutes their equality. On this interpretation, we should not seek for some special characteristics in

respect of which men are equal, but merely remind ourselves that they are all men. Now to this it might be objected that being men is not a respect in which men can strictly speaking be said to be *equal*, but, leaving that aside, there is the more immediate objection that if all that the statement does is to remind us that men are men, it does not do very much, and in particular does less than its proponents in political argument have wanted it to do. What looked like a paradox has turned into a platitude.

I shall suggest in a moment that even in this weak form the statement is not so vacuous as this objection makes it seem; but it must be admitted that when the statement of equality ceases to claim more than is warranted, it rather rapidly reaches the point where it claims less than is interesting. A similar discomfiture tends to overcome the practical maxim of equality. It cannot be the aim of this maxim that all men should be treated alike in all circumstances, or even that they should be treated alike as much as possible. Granted that, however, there is no obvious stopping point before the interpretation which makes the maxim claim only that men should be treated alike in similar circumstances; and since 'circumstances' here must clearly include reference to what a man is, as well as to his purely external situation, this comes very much to saying that for every difference in the way men are treated, some general reason or principle of differentiation must be given. This may well be an important principle; some indeed have seen in it, or in something very like it, an essential element of morality itself.[2] But it can hardly be enough to constitute the principle that was advanced in the

Originally published in *Philosophy, Politics and Society*, 2nd series, ed. P. Laslett and W. G. Runciman (Blackwell Publishers, 1979), 110–31. Reprinted by permission of the publisher.

name of *equality*. It would be in accordance with this principle, for example, to treat black men differently from others just because they were black, or poor men differently just because they were poor, and this cannot accord with anyone's idea of equality.

In what follows I shall try to advance a number of considerations that can help to save the political notion of equality from these extremes of absurdity and of triviality. These considerations are in fact often employed in political argument, but are usually bundled together into an unanalysed notion of equality in a manner confusing to the advocates, and encouraging to the enemies, of that ideal. These considerations will not enable us to define a distinct third interpretation of the statements which use the notion of equality; it is rather that they enable us, starting with the weak interpretations, to build up something that in practice can have something of the solidity aspired to by the strong interpretations. In this discussion, it will not be necessary all the time to treat separately the supposedly factual application of the notion of equality, and its application in the maxim of action. Though it is sometimes important to distinguish them, and there are clear grounds for doing so, similar considerations often apply to both. The two go significantly together: on the one hand, the point of the supposedly factual assertion is to back up social ideals and programmes of political action; on the other hand – a rather less obvious point, perhaps – those political proposals have their force because they are regarded not as gratuitously egalitarian, aiming at equal treatment for reasons, for instance, of simplicity or tidiness, but as affirming an equality which is believed in some sense already to exist, and to be obscured or neglected by actual social arrangements.

1. *Common humanity*. The factual statement of men's equality was seen, when pressed, to retreat in the direction of merely asserting the equality of men as men; and this was thought to be trivial. It is certainly insufficient, but not, after all, trivial. That all men are human is, if a tautology, a useful one, serving as a reminder that those who belong anatomically to the species *homo sapiens*, and can speak a language, use tools, live in societies, can interbreed despite racial differences, etc., are also alike in certain other respects more likely to be forgotten. These respects are notably the capacity to feel pain, both from immediate physical causes and from various situations represented in perception and in thought; and the capacity to feel affection for others, and the consequences of this, connected with the frustration of this affection, loss of its objects, etc. The assertion that men are alike in the possession of these characteristics is, while indisputable and (it may be) even necessarily true, not trivial. For it is certain that there are political and social arrangements that systematically neglect these characteristics in the case of some groups of men, while being fully aware of them in the case of others; that is to say, they treat certain men as though they did not possess these characteristics, and neglect moral claims that arise from these characteristics and which would be admitted to arise from them.

Here it may be objected that the mere fact that ruling groups in certain societies treat other groups in this way does not mean that they neglect or overlook the characteristics in question. For, it may be suggested, they may well recognize the presence of these characteristics in the worse-treated group, but claim that in the case of that group, the characteristics do not give rise to any moral claim; the group being distinguished from other members of society in virtue of some further characteristic (for instance, by being black), this may be cited as the ground of treating them differently, whether they feel pain, affection, etc., or not.

This objection rests on the assumption, common to much moral philosophy that makes a sharp distinction between fact and value, that the question whether a certain consideration is *relevant* to a moral issue is an evaluative question: to state that a consideration is relevant or irrelevant to a certain moral question is, on this view, itself to commit oneself to a certain kind of moral principle or outlook. Thus, in the case under discussion, to say (as one would naturally say) that the fact that a man is black is, by itself, quite irrelevant to the issue of how he should be treated in respect of welfare, etc., would, on this view, be to commit oneself to a certain sort of moral principle. This view, taken generally, seems to me quite certainly false. The principle that men should be differentially treated in respect of welfare merely on grounds of their colour is not a special sort of moral principle, but (if anything) a purely arbitrary assertion of will, like that of some Caligulan ruler who decided to execute everyone whose name contained three 'R's.

This point is in fact conceded by those who practise such things as colour discrimination.

Few can be found who will explain their practice merely by saying, 'But they're black: and it is my moral principle to treat black men differently from others'. If any reasons are given at all, they will be reasons that seek to correlate the fact of blackness with certain other considerations which are at least candidates for relevance to the question of how a man should be treated: such as insensitivity, brute stupidity, ineducable irresponsibility, etc. Now these reasons are very often rationalizations, and the correlations claimed are either not really believed, or quite irrationally believed, by those who claim them. But this is a different point; the argument concerns what counts as a moral reason, and the rationalizer broadly agrees with others about what counts as such – the trouble with him is that his reasons are dictated by his policies, and not conversely. The Nazis' 'anthropologists' who tried to construct theories of Aryanism were paying, in very poor coin, the homage of irrationality to reason.

The question of relevance in moral reasons will arise again, in a different connexion, in this paper. For the moment its importance is that it gives a force to saying that those who neglect the moral claims of certain men that arise from their human capacity to feel pain, etc., are *overlooking* or *disregarding* those capacities; and are not just operating with a special moral principle, conceding the capacities to these men, but denying the moral claim. Very often, indeed, they have just persuaded themselves that the men in question have those capacities in a lesser degree. Here it is certainly to the point to assert the apparent platitude that these men are also human.

I have discussed this point in connexion with very obvious human characteristics of feeling pain and desiring affection. There are, however, other and less easily definable characteristics universal to humanity, which may all the more be neglected in political and social arrangements. For instance, there seems to be a characteristic which might be called 'a desire for self-respect'; this phrase is perhaps not too happy, in suggesting a particular culturally limited, bourgeois value, but I mean by it a certain human desire to be identified with what one is doing, to be able to realize purposes of one's own, and not to be the instrument of another's will unless one has willingly accepted such a role. This is a very inadequate and in some ways rather empty specification of a human desire; to a better speci-

fication, both philosophical reflection and the evidences of psychology and anthropology would be relevant. Such investigations enable us to understand more deeply, in respect of the desire I have gestured towards and of similar characteristics, what it is to be human; and of what it is to be human, the apparently trivial statement of men's equality as men can serve as a reminder.

2. *Moral capacities.* So far we have considered respects in which men can be counted as all alike, which respects are, in a sense, negative: they concern the capacity to suffer, and certain needs that men have, and these involve men in moral relations as the recipients of certain kinds of treatment. It has certainly been a part, however, of the thought of those who asserted that men were equal, that there were more positive respects in which men were alike: that they were equal in certain things that they could do or achieve, as well as in things that they needed and could suffer. In respect of a whole range of abilities, from weight-lifting to the calculus, the assertion is, as was noted at the beginning, not plausible, and has not often been supposed to be. It has been held, however, that there are certain other abilities, both less open to empirical test and more essential in moral connexions, for which it is true that men are equal. These are certain sorts of moral ability or capacity, the capacity for virtue or achievement of the highest kind of moral worth.

The difficulty with this notion is that of identifying any purely moral capacities. Some human capacities are more relevant to the achievement of a virtuous life than others: intelligence, a capacity for sympathetic understanding, and a measure of resoluteness would generally be agreed to be so. But these capacities can all be displayed in non-moral connexions as well, and in such connexions would naturally be thought to differ from man to man like other natural capacities. That this is the fact of the matter has been accepted by many thinkers, notably, for instance, by Aristotle. But against this acceptance, there is a powerful strain of thought that centres on a feeling of ultimate and outrageous absurdity in the idea that the achievement of the highest kind of moral worth should depend on natural capacities, unequally and fortuitously distributed as they are; and this feeling is backed up by the observation that these natural capacities are not themselves the bearers of the moral worth, since those that have them are as gifted for vice as for virtue.

This strain of thought has found many types of

religious expression; but in philosophy it is to be found in its purest form in Kant. Kant's view not only carries to the limit the notion that moral worth cannot depend on contingencies, but also emphasizes, in its picture of the Kingdom of Ends, the idea of *respect* which is owed to each man as a rational moral agent – and, since men are equally such agents, is owed equally to all, unlike admiration and similar attitudes, which are commanded unequally by men in proportion to their unequal possession of different kinds of natural excellence. These ideas are intimately connected in Kant, and it is not possible to understand his moral theory unless as much weight is given to what he says about the Kingdom of Ends as is always given to what he says about duty.

The very considerable consistency of Kant's view is bought at what would generally be agreed to be a very high price. The detachment of moral worth from all contingencies is achieved only by making man's characteristic as a moral or rational agent a transcendental characteristic; man's capacity to will freely as a rational agent is not dependent on any empirical capacities he may have – and, in particular, is not dependent on empirical capacities which men may possess unequally – because, in the Kantian view, the capacity to be a rational agent is not itself an empirical capacity at all. Accordingly, the respect owed equally to each man as a member of the Kingdom of Ends is not owed to him in respect of any empirical characteristics that he may possess, but solely in respect of the transcendental characteristic of being a free and rational will. The ground of the respect owed to each man thus emerges in the Kantian theory as a kind of secular analogue of the Christian conception of the respect owed to all men as equally children of God. Though secular, it is equally metaphysical: in neither case is it anything empirical *about* men that constitutes the ground of equal respect.

This transcendental, Kantian conception cannot provide any solid foundation for the notions of equality among men, or of equality of respect owed to them. Apart from the general difficulties of such transcendental conceptions, there is the obstinate fact that the concept of 'moral agent', and the concepts allied to it such as that of responsibility, do and must have an empirical basis. It seems empty to say that all men are equal as moral agents, when the question, for instance, of men's responsibility for their actions is one to which empirical considerations are clearly relevant, and one which moreover receives answers in terms of different degrees of responsibility and different degrees of rational control over action. To hold a man responsible for his actions is presumably the central case of treating him as a moral agent, and if men are not treated as equally responsible, there is not much left to their equality as moral agents.

If, without its transcendental basis, there is not much left to men's equality as moral agents, is there anything left to the notion of the *respect* owed to all men? This notion of 'respect' is both complex and unclear, and I think it needs, and would repay, a good deal of investigation. Some content can, however, be attached to it; even if it is some way away from the ideas of moral agency. There certainly is a distinction, for instance, between regarding a man's life, actions or character from an aesthetic or technical point of view, and regarding them from a point of view which is concerned primarily with what it is *for him* to live that life and do those actions in that character. Thus from the technological point of view, a man who has spent his life in trying to make a certain machine which could not possibly work is merely a failed inventor, and in compiling a catalogue of those whose efforts have contributed to the sum of technical achievement, one must 'write him off': the fact that he devoted himself to this useless task with constant effort and so on, is merely irrelevant. But from a human point of view, it is clearly not irrelevant: we are concerned with him, not merely as 'a failed inventor', but as a man who wanted to be a successful inventor. Again, in professional relations and the world of work, a man operates, and his activities come up for criticism, under a variety of professional or technical titles, such as 'miner' or 'agricultural labourer' or 'junior executive'. The technical or professional attitude is that which regards the man solely under that title, the human approach that which regards him as *a man who has* that title (among others), willingly, unwillingly, through lack of alternatives, with pride, etc.

That men should be regarded from the human point of view, and not merely under these sorts of titles, is part of the content that might be attached to Kant's celebrated injunction 'treat each man as an end in himself, and never as a means only'. But I do not think that this is all that should be seen in this injunction, or all that is concerned in the notion of 'respect'. What is involved in the examples just given could be explained by saying that each man is owed an effort at identification: that he should not be regarded as the surface to which a certain label can be applied, but one should try to see the world (including the label) from his point of view. This injunction will be based on, though not of course fully explained by, the notion that men are conscious beings who necessarily have intentions and purposes and see what they are doing in a certain light. But there seem to be further injunctions connected with the Kantian maxim, and with the notion of 'respect', that go beyond these considerations. There are forms of exploiting men or degrading them which would be thought to be excluded by these notions, but which cannot be excluded merely by considering how the exploited or degraded men see the situation. For it is precisely a mark of extreme exploitation or degradation that those who suffer it do *not* see themselves differently from the way they are seen by the exploiters; either they do not see themselves as anything at all, or they acquiesce passively in the role for which they have been cast. Here we evidently need something more than the precept that one should respect and try to understand another man's consciousness of his own activities; it is also that one may not suppress or destroy that consciousness.

All these I must confess to be vague and inconclusive considerations, but we are dealing with a vague notion. one, however, that we possess, and attach value to. To try to put these matters properly in order would be itself to try to reach conclusions about several fundamental questions of moral philosophy. What we must ask here is what these ideas have to do with equality. We started with the notion of men's equality as moral agents. This notion appeared unsatisfactory, for different reasons, in both an empirical and a transcendental interpretation. We then moved, *via* the idea of 'respect', to the different notion of regarding men not merely under professional, social or technical titles, but with consideration of their own views and purposes. This notion has at least this much to do with equality: that the titles which it urges us to look behind are the conspicuous bearers of social, political and technical *inequality*, whether they refer to achievement (as in the example of the inventor), or to social roles (as in the example of work titles). It enjoins us not to let our fundamental attitudes to men be dictated by the criteria of technical success or social position, and not to take them at the value carried by these titles and by the structures in which these titles place them. This does not mean, of course, that the more fundamental view that should be taken of men is in the case of every man the same: on the contrary. But it does mean that each man is owed the effort of understanding, and that in achieving it, each man is to be (as it were) abstracted from certain conspicuous structures of inequality in which we find him.

These injunctions are based on the proposition that men are beings who are necessarily to some extent conscious of themselves and of the world they live in. (I omit here, as throughout the discussion, the clinical cases of people who are mad or mentally defective, who always constitute special exceptions to what is in general true of men.) This proposition does not assert that men are equally conscious of themselves and of their situation. It was precisely one element in the notion of exploitation considered above that such consciousness can be decreased by social action and the environment; we may add that it can similarly be increased. But men are at least potentially conscious, to an indeterminate degree, of their situation and of what I have called their 'titles', are capable of reflectively standing back from the roles and positions in which they are cast; and this reflective consciousness may be enhanced or diminished by their social condition.

It is this last point that gives these considerations a particular relevance to the political aims of egalitarianism. The mere idea of regarding men from 'the human point of view', while it has a good deal to do with politics, and a certain amount to do with equality, has nothing specially to do with political equality. One could, I think, accept this as an ideal, and yet favour, for instance, some kind of hierarchical society, so long as the hierarchy maintained itself without compulsion, and there was human understanding between the orders. In such a society, each man would indeed have a very conspicuous title which related him to the social structure; but it might be that most people were aware of the human beings behind the titles, and found each other for the most part content, or even proud, to have the titles that they had. I do not know whether anything like this has been true of historical hierarchical societies; but I can see no inconsistency in someone's espousing it as an ideal, as some (influenced in many cases by a sentimental picture of the Middle Ages) have done. Such a person would be one who accepted the notion of 'the human view', the view of each man as something more than his title, as a valuable ideal, but rejected the ideals of political equality.

Once, however, one accepts the further notion that the degree of man's consciousness about such things as his role in society is itself in some part the product of social arrangements, and that it can be increased, this ideal of a stable hierarchy must, I think, disappear. For what keeps stable hierarchies together is the idea of necessity, that it is somehow foreordained or inevitable that there should be these orders; and this idea of necessity must be eventually undermined by the growth of people's reflective consciousness about their role, still more when it is combined with the thought that what they and the others have always thought about their roles in the social system was the product of the social system itself.

It might be suggested that a certain man who admitted that people's consciousness of their roles was conditioned in this way might nevertheless believe in the hierarchical ideal: but that in order to preserve the society of his ideal, he would have to make sure that the idea of the conditioning of consciousness did not get around to too many people, and that their consciousness about their roles did not increase too much. But such a view is really a very different thing from its naïve predecessor. Such a man, no longer himself 'immersed' in the system, is beginning to think in terms of compulsion, the deliberate *prevention* of the growth of consciousness, which is a poisonous element absent from the original ideal. Moreover, his attitude (or that of rulers similar to himself) towards the other people in the ideal society must now contain an element of condescension or contempt, since he will be aware that their acceptance of what they suppose to be necessity is a delusion. This is alien to the spirit of human understanding on which the original ideal was based. The hierarchical idealist cannot escape the fact that certain things which can be done decently without self-consciousness can, with self-consciousness, be done only hypocritically. This is why even the rather hazy and very general notions that I have tried to bring together in this section contain some of the grounds of the ideal of political equality.

3. *Equality in unequal circumstances*. The notion of equality is invoked not only in connexions where men are claimed in some sense all to be equal, but in connexions where they are agreed to be unequal, and the question arises of the distribution of, or access to, certain goods to which their inequalities are relevant. It may be objected that the notion of equality is in fact misapplied in these connexions, and that the appropriate ideas are those of fairness or justice, in the sense of what Aristotle called 'distributive justice', where (as Aristotle argued) there is no question of regarding or treating everyone as equal, but solely a question of distributing certain goods in proportion to men's recognized inequalities.

I think it is reasonable to say against this objection that there is some foothold for the notion of equality even in these cases. It is useful here to make a rough distinction between two different types of inequality, inequality of *need* and inequality of *merit*, with a corresponding distinction between goods – on the one hand, goods demanded by the need, and on the other, goods that can be earned by the merit. In the case of needs, such as the need for medical treatment in case of illness, it can be presumed for practical purposes that the persons who have the need actually desire the goods in question, and so the question can indeed be regarded as one of distribution in a simple sense, the satisfaction of an existing desire. In the case of merit, such as for instance the possession of abilities to profit from a university education, there is not the same presumption that everyone who has the merit has the desire for the goods in question, though it may, of course, be the case. Moreover, the good of a university education may be legitimately, even if hopelessly, desired by those who do not possess the merit; while medical treatment or unemployment benefit are either not desired, or not legitimately desired, by those who are not ill or unemployed, i.e. do not have the appropriate need. Hence the distribution of goods in accordance with merit has a competitive aspect lacking in the case of distribution according to need. For these reasons, it is appropriate to speak, in the case of merit, not only of the distribution of the good, but of the distribution of the opportunity of achieving the good. But this, unlike the good itself, can be said to be distributed equally to everybody, and so one does encounter a notion of *general* equality, much vaunted in our society today, the notion of equality of opportunity.

Before considering this notion further, it is worth noticing certain resemblances and differences between the cases of need and of merit. In both cases, we encounter the matter (mentioned before in this paper) of the relevance of reasons. Leaving aside preventive medicine, the proper ground of distribution of medical care is ill health: this is a necessary truth. Now in very many societies, while ill health may work as a necessary condition of receiving treatment, it does not work as a sufficient condition, since such treatment costs money, and not all who are ill have the money; hence the possession of sufficient money becomes in fact an additional necessary condition of actually receiving treatment. Yet more extravagantly, money may work as a sufficient condition by itself, without any medical need, in which case the reasons that actually operate for the receipt of this good are just totally irrelevant to its nature; however, since only a few hypochondriacs desire treatment when they do not need it, this is, in this case, a marginal phenomenon.

When we have the situation in which, for instance, wealth is a further necessary condition of the receipt of medical treatment, we can once more apply the notions of equality and inequality: not now in connexion with the inequality between the well and the ill, but in connexion with the inequality between the rich ill and the poor ill, since we have straightforwardly the situation of those whose needs are the same not receiving the same treatment, though the needs are the ground of the treatment. This is an irrational state of affairs.

It may be objected that I have neglected an important distinction here. For, it may be said, I have treated the ill health and the possession of money as though they were regarded on the same level, as 'reasons for receiving medical treatment', and this is a muddle. The ill health is, at most, a ground of the *right* to receive medical treatment; whereas the money is, in certain circumstances, the causally necessary condition of securing the right, which is a different thing. There is something in the distinction that this objection suggests: there is a distinction between a man's rights, the reasons why he should be treated in a certain way, and his power to secure those rights, the reasons why he can in fact get what he deserves. But this objection does not make it inappropriate to call the situation of inequality an 'irrational' situation: it just makes it clearer what is meant by so calling it. What is meant is that it is a situation in which reasons are insufficiently *operative*; it is a situation insufficiently controlled by reasons – and hence by reason itself. The same

point arises with another form of equality and equal rights, equality before the law. It may be said that in a certain society, men have equal rights to a fair trial, to seek redress from the law for wrongs committed against them, etc. But if a fair trial or redress from the law can be secured in that society only by moneyed and educated persons, to insist that everyone *has* this right, though only these particular persons can *secure* it, rings hollow to the point of cynicism: we are concerned not with the abstract existence of rights, but with the extent to which those rights govern what actually happens.

Thus when we combine the notions of the *relevance* of reasons, and the *operativeness* of reasons, we have a genuine moral weapon, which can be applied in cases of what is appropriately called unequal treatment, even where one is not concerned with the equality of people as a whole. This represents a strengthening of the very weak principle mentioned at the beginning of this paper, that for every difference in the way men are treated, a reason should be given: when one requires further that the reasons should be relevant, and that they should be socially operative, this really says something.

Similar considerations will apply to cases of merit. There is, however, an important difference between the cases of need and merit, in respect of the relevance of reasons. It is a matter of logic that particular sorts of needs constitute a reason for receiving particular sorts of good. It is, however, in general a much more disputable question whether certain sorts of merit constitute a reason for receiving certain sorts of good. For instance, let it be agreed, for the sake of argument, that the public school system provides a superior type of education, which it is a good thing to receive. It is then objected that access to this type of education is unequally distributed, because of its cost: among boys of equal promise or intelligence, only those from wealthy homes will receive it, and, indeed, boys of little promise or intelligence will receive it, if from wealthy homes; and this, the objection continues, is irrational.

The defender of the public school system might give two quite different sorts of answer to this objection; besides, that is, the obvious type of answer which merely disputes the facts alleged by the objector. One is the sort of answer already discussed in the case of need: that we may agree, perhaps, that boys of promise and intelligence have a right to a superior education, but in actual economic circumstances, this right cannot always be secured, etc. The other is more radical: this would dispute the premise of the objection that intelligence and promise are, at least by themselves, the grounds for receiving this superior type of education. While perhaps not asserting that wealth itself constitutes the ground, the defender of the system may claim that other characteristics significantly correlated with wealth are such grounds; or, again, that it is the purpose of this sort of school to maintain a tradition of leadership, and the best sort of people to maintain this will be people whose fathers were at such schools. We need not try to pursue such arguments here. The important point is that, while there can indeed be genuine disagreements about what constitutes the relevant sort of merit in such cases, such disagreements must also be disagreements about the nature of the good to be distributed. As such, the disagreements do not occur in a vacuum, nor are they logically free from restrictions. There is only a limited number of reasons for which education could be regarded as a good, and a limited number of purposes which education could rationally be said to serve; and to the limitations on this question, there correspond limitations on the sorts of merit or personal characteristic which could be rationally cited as grounds of access to this good. Here again we encounter a genuine strengthening of the very weak principle that, for differences in the way that people are treated, reasons should be given.

We may return now to the notion of equality of opportunity; understanding this in the normal political sense of equality of opportunity for *everyone in society* to secure certain goods. This notion is introduced into political discussion when there is question of the access to certain goods which, first, even if they are not desired by everyone in society, are desired by large numbers of people in all sections of society (either for themselves, or, as in the case of education, for their children), or would be desired by people in all sections of society if they knew about the goods in question and thought it possible for them to attain them; second, are goods which people may be said to earn or achieve; and third, are goods which not all the people who desire them can have. This third condition covers at least three different cases, however, which it is worth distinguishing. Some desired goods, like positions of prestige, management, etc., are *by their very nature* limited: whenever there are some

people who are in command or prestigious positions, there are necessarily others who are not. Other goods are *contingently* limited, in the sense that there are certain conditions of access to them which in fact not everyone satisfies, but there is no intrinsic limit to the numbers who might gain access to it by satisfying the conditions: university education is usually regarded in this light nowadays, as something which requires certain conditions of admission to it which in fact not everyone satisfies, but which an indefinite proportion of people might satisfy. Third, there are goods which are *fortuitously* limited, in the sense that although everyone or large numbers of people satisfy the conditions of access to them, there is just not enough of them to go round; so some more stringent conditions or system of rationing have to be imposed, to govern access in an imperfect situation. A good can, of course, be both contingently and fortuitously limited at once: when, due to shortage of supply, not even the people who are qualified to have it, limited in numbers though they are, can in every case have it. It is particularly worth distinguishing those kinds of limitation, as there can be significant differences of view about the way in which a certain good is limited. While most would now agree that high education is contingently limited, a Platonic view would regard it as necessarily limited.

Now the notion of equality of opportunity might be said to be the notion that a limited good shall in fact be allocated on grounds which do not *a priori* exclude any section of those that desire it. But this formulation is not really very clear. For suppose grammar school education (a good perhaps contingently, and certainly fortuitously, limited) is allocated on grounds of ability as tested at the age of 11; this would normally be advanced as an example of equality of opportunity, as opposed to a system of allocation on grounds of parents' wealth. But does not the criterion of ability exclude *a priori* a certain section of people, viz. those that are not able – just as the other excludes *a priori* those who are not wealthy? Here it will obviously be said that this was not what was meant by *a priori* exclusion: the present argument just equates this with exclusion of anybody, i.e. with the mere existence of some condition that has to be satisfied. What then is *a priori* exclusion? It must mean exclusion on grounds *other* than those appropriate or rational for the good in question. But this still will not do as it stands. For it would follow from this that so long as those allocating grammar school education on grounds of wealth thought that such grounds were appropriate or rational (as they might in one of the ways discussed above in connexion with public schools), they could sincerely describe their system as one of equality of opportunity – which is absurd.

Hence it seems that the notion of equality of opportunity is more complex than it first appeared. It requires not merely that there should be no exclusion from access on grounds other than those appropriate or rational for the good in question, but that the grounds considered appropriate for the good should themselves be such that people from all sections of society have an equal chance of satisfying them. What now is a 'section of society'? Clearly we cannot include under this term sections of the populace identified just by the characteristics which figure in the grounds for allocating the good – since, once more, any grounds at all must exclude some section of the populace. But what about sections identified by characteristics which are *correlated* with the grounds of exclusion? There are important difficulties here: to illustrate this, it may help first to take an imaginary example.

Suppose that in a certain society great prestige is attached to membership of a warrior class, the duties of which require great physical strength. This class has in the past been recruited from certain wealthy families only; but egalitarian reformers achieve a change in the rules, by which warriors are recruited from all sections of the society, on the results of a suitable competition. The effect of this, however, is that the wealthy families still provide virtually all the warriors, because the rest of the populace is so undernourished by reason of poverty that their physical strength is inferior to that of the wealthy and well nourished. The reformers protest that equality of opportunity has not really been achieved; the wealthy reply that in fact it has, and that the poor now have the opportunity of becoming warriors – it is just bad luck that their characteristics are such that they do not pass the test. 'We are not,' they might say, 'excluding anyone *for* being poor; we exclude people for being weak, and it is unfortunate that those who are poor are also weak.'

This answer would seem to most people feeble, and even cynical. This is for reasons similar to those discussed before in connexion with equality before the law; that the supposed equality of opportunity is quite empty – indeed, one may say

that it does not really exist – unless it is made more effective than this. For one knows that it could be made more effective; one knows that there is a causal connexion between being poor and being undernourished, and between being undernourished and being physically weak. One supposes further that something could be done – subject to whatever economic conditions obtain in the imagined society – to alter the distribution of wealth. All this being so, the appeal by the wealthy to the 'bad luck' of the poor must appear as disingenuous.

It seems then that a system of allocation will fall short of equality of opportunity if the allocation of the good in question in fact works out unequally or disproportionately between different sections of society, if the unsuccessful sections are under a disadvantage which could be removed by further reform or social action. This was very clear in the imaginary example that was given, because the causal connexions involved are simple and well known. In actual fact, however, the situations of this type that arise are more complicated, and it is easier to overlook the causal connexions involved. This is particularly so in the case of educational selection, where such slippery concepts as 'intellectual ability' are involved. It is a known fact that the system of selection for grammar schools by the '11+' examination favours children in direct proportion to their social class, the children of professional homes having proportionately greater success than those from working class homes. We have every reason to suppose that these results are the product, in good part, of environmental factors; and we further know that imaginative social reform, both of the primary educational system and of living conditions, would favourably effect those environmental factors. In these circumstances, this system of educational selection falls short of equality of opportunity.[3]

This line of thought points to a connexion between the idea of equality of opportunity, and the idea of equality of persons, which is stronger than might at first be suspected. We have seen that one is not really offering equality of opportunity to Smith and Jones if one contents oneself with applying the same criteria to Smith and Jones at, say, the age of 11; what one is doing there is to apply the same criteria to Smith as affected by favourable conditions and to Jones as affected by unfavourable but curable conditions. Here there is a necessary pressure to equal up the conditions: to give *Smith* and *Jones* equality of opportunity involves regarding their conditions, where curable, as themselves part of what is done to Smith and Jones, and not part of Smith and Jones themselves. Their identity, for these purposes, does not include their curable environment, which is itself unequal and a contributor of inequality. This abstraction of persons in themselves from unequal environments is a way, if not of regarding them as equal, at least of moving recognizably in that direction; and is itself involved in equality of opportunity.

One might speculate about how far this movement of thought might go. The most conservative user of the notion of equality of opportunity is, if sincere, prepared to abstract the individual from some effects of his environment. We have seen that there is good reason to press this further, and to allow that the individuals whose opportunities are to be equal should be abstracted from more features of social and family background. Where should this stop? Should it even stop at the boundaries of heredity? Suppose it were discovered that when all curable environmental disadvantages had been dealt with, there was a residual genetic difference in brain constitution, for instance, which was correlated with differences in desired types of ability; but that the brain constitution could in fact be changed by an operation.[4] Suppose further that the wealthier classes could afford such an operation for their children, so that they always came out top of the educational system; would we then think that poorer children did not have equality of opportunity, because they had no opportunity to get rid of their genetic disadvantages?

Here we might think that our notion of personal identity itself was beginning to give way; we might well wonder *who were* the people whose advantages and disadvantages were being discussed in this way. But it would be wrong, I think, to try to solve this problem simply by saying that in the supposed circumstances our notion of personal identity would have collapsed in such a way that we could no longer speak of the individuals involved – in the end, we could still pick out the individuals by spatio-temporal criteria, if no more. Our objections against the system suggested in this fantasy must, I think, be moral rather than metaphysical. They need not concern us here. What is interesting about the fantasy, perhaps, is that if one reached this state of affairs, the individuals would be regarded as in all respects equal in themselves – for in themselves they would be, as it were, pure subjects or bearers of predicates, everything else about them, including their genetic inheritance, being regarded as a fortuitous and changeable characteristic. In these circumstances, where everything about a person is controllable, equality of opportunity and absolute equality seem to coincide; and this itself illustrates something about the notion of equality of opportunity.

I said that we need not discuss here the moral objections to the kind of world suggested in this fantasy. There is, however, one such point that is relevant to the different aspects of equality that have been discussed in this paper as a whole. One objection that we should instinctively feel about the fantasy world is that far too much emphasis was being placed on achieving high ability; that the children were just being regarded as locations of abilities. I think we should still feel this even if everybody (with results hard to imagine) was treated in this way; when not everybody was so treated, the able would also be more successful than others, and those very concerned with producing the ability would probably also be over-concerned with success. The moral objections to the excessive concern with such aims are, interestingly, not unconnected with the ideal of equality itself; they are connected with equality in the sense discussed in the earlier sections of this paper, the equality of human beings despite their differences, and in particular with the complex of notions considered in the second section under the heading of 'respect'.

This conflict within the ideals of equality arises even without resort to the fantasy world. It exists today in the feeling that a thorough-going emphasis on equality of opportunity must destroy a certain sense of common humanity which is itself an ideal of equality.[5] The ideals that are felt to be in conflict with equality of opportunity are not necessarily other ideals of equality – there may be an independent appeal to the values of community life, or to the moral worth of a more integrated and less competitive society. Nevertheless, the idea of equality itself is often invoked in this connexion, and not, I think, inappropriately.

If the idea of equality ranges as widely as I have suggested, this type of conflict is bound to arise with it. It is an idea which, on the one hand, is invoked in connexion with the distribution of certain goods, some at least of which are bound to confer on their possessors some preferred status or prestige. On the other hand, the idea of equality of respect is one which urges us to give less consideration to those structures in which people enjoy status or prestige, and to consider people independently of those goods, on the distribution of which equality of opportunity precisely focuses our, and their, attention. There is perhaps nothing formally incompatible in these two applications of the idea of equality: one might hope for a society in which there existed both a fair, rational and appropriate distribution of these goods, and no contempt, condescension or lack of human communication between persons who were more and less successful recipients of the distribution. Yet in actual fact, there are deep psychological and social obstacles to the realization of this hope; as things are, the competitiveness and considerations of prestige that surround the first application of equality certainly militate against the second. How far this situation is inevitable, and how far in an economically developed and dynamic society, in which certain skills and talents are necessarily at a premium, the obstacles to a wider realization of equality might be overcome, I do not think that we know: these are in good part questions of psychology and sociology, to which we do not have the answers.

When one is faced with the spectacle of the various elements of the idea of equality pulling in these different directions, there is a strong temptation, if one does not abandon the idea altogether, to abandon some of its elements: to claim, for instance, that equality of opportunity is the only ideal that is at all practicable, and equality of respect a vague and perhaps nostalgic illusion; or, alternatively, that equality of respect is genuine equality, and equality of opportunity an inegalitarian betrayal of the ideal – all the more so if it were thoroughly pursued, as now it is not. To succumb to either of these simplifying formulae would, I think, be a mistake. Certainly, a highly rational and efficient application of the ideas of equal opportunity, unmitigated by the other considerations, could lead to a quite inhuman society (if it worked – which, granted a well-known desire of parents to secure a position for their children at least as good as their own, is unlikely). On the other hand, an ideal of equality of respect that made no contact with such things as the economic needs of society for certain skills, and human desire for some sorts of prestige, would be condemned to a futile Utopianism, and to having no rational effect on the distribution of goods, position and power that would inevitably proceed. If, moreover, as I have suggested, it is not really known how far, by new forms of social structure and of education, these conflicting claims might be reconciled, it is all the more obvious that we should not throw one set of claims out of the window; but should rather seek, in each situation, the best way of eating and having as much cake as possible. It is an uncomfortable situation, but the discomfort is just that of genuine political thought. It is no greater with equality than it is with liberty, or any other noble and substantial political ideal.

Notes

1   For an illuminating discussion of this and related questions, see R. Wollheim and I. Berlin, *Equality*, Proceedings of the Aristotelian Society, Vol. LVI (1955–6), p. 281 seq.

2   For instance, R.M. Hare: see his *Language of Morals*, Oxford: The Clarendon Press, 1952.

3   See on this C.A.R. Crosland, *Public Schools and English Education, Encounter*, July 1961.

4   A yet more radical situation – but one more likely to come about – would be that in which an individual's characteristics could be *pre-arranged* by interference with the genetic material. The dizzying consequences of this I shall not try to explore.

5   See, for example, Michael Young, *The Rise of the Meritocracy*, London: Thames and Hudson, 1958.

29

Equality of What?

Amartya Sen

Discussions in moral philosophy have offered us a wide menu in answer to the question: equality of what? In this lecture I shall concentrate on three particular types of equality, viz., (i) utilitarian equality, (ii) total utility equality, and (iii) Rawlsian equality. I shall argue that all three have serious limitations, and that while they fail in rather different and contrasting ways, an adequate theory cannot be constructed even on the *combined* grounds of the three. Towards the end I shall try to present an alternative formulation of equality which seems to me to deserve a good deal more attention than it has received, and I shall not desist from doing some propaganda on its behalf.

First a methodological question. When it is claimed that a certain moral principle has shortcomings, what can be the basis of such an allegation? There seem to be at least two different ways of grounding such a criticism, aside from just checking its *direct* appeal to moral intuition. One is to check the *implications* of the principle by taking up particular cases in which the results of employing that principle can be seen in a rather stark way, and then to examine these implications against our intuition. I shall call such a critique a *case-implication critique*. The other is to move not from the general to the particular, but from the general to the *more* general. One can examine the consistency of the principle with another principle that is acknowledged to be more fundamental.

Such prior principles are usually formulated at a rather abstract level, and frequently take the form of congruence with some very general procedures. For example, what could be reasonably assumed to have been chosen under the *as if* ignorance of the Rawlsian "original position," a hypothetical primordial state in which people decide on what rules to adopt without knowing who they are going to be – as if they could end up being any one of the persons in the community.[1] Or what rules would satisfy Richard Hare's requirement of "universalizability" and be consistent with "giving equal weights to the equal interests of the occupants of all the roles."[2] I shall call a critique based on such an approach a *prior-principle critique*. Both approaches can be used in assessing the moral claims of each type of equality, and will indeed be used here.

1 Utilitarian Equality

Utilitarian equality is the equality that can be derived from the utilitarian concept of goodness applied to problems of distribution. Perhaps the simplest case is the "pure distribution problem": the problem of dividing a given homogeneous cake among a group of persons.[3] Each person gets more utility the larger his share of the cake, and gets utility *only* from his share of the cake; his utility increases at a diminishing rate as the amount of his share goes up. The utilitarian objective is to maximize the sum-total of utility irrespective of distribution, but that requires the *equality* of the *marginal* utility of everyone – marginal utility being the incremental utility each

Originally published in *The Tanner Lectures on Human Values*, ed. S. M. McMurrin, 1 (Cambridge University Press, 1980), 195–220. Reprinted by permission of the author and the University of Utah Press.

person would get from an additional unit of cake.[4] According to one interpretation, this equality of marginal utility embodies equal treatment of everyone's interests.[5]

The position is a bit more complicated when the total size of the cake is not independent of its distribution. But even then maximization of the total utility sum requires that transfers be carried to the point at which the marginal utility gain of the gainers equals the marginal utility loss of the losers, after taking into account the effect of the transfer on the size and distribution of the cake.[6] It is in this wider context that the special type of equality insisted upon by utilitarianism becomes assertively distinguished. Richard Hare has claimed that "giving equal weight to the equal interests of all the parties" would "lead to utilitarianism" – thus satisfying the prior-principle requirement of universalizability.[7] Similarly, John Harsanyi shoots down the non-utilitarians (including this lecturer, I hasten to add), by claiming for utilitarianism an exclusive ability to avoid "unfair discrimination" between "one person's and another person's equally urgent human needs."[8]

The moral importance of needs, on this interpretation, is based exclusively on the notion of utility. This is disputable, and having had several occasions to dispute it in the past,[9] I shall not shy away from disputing it in this particular context. But while I will get on to this issue later, I want first to examine the nature of utilitarian equality without – for the time being – questioning the grounding of moral importance entirely on utility. Even when utility is the sole basis of importance there is still the question as to whether the size of *marginal* utility, irrespective of *total* utility enjoyed by the person, is an adequate index of moral importance. It is, of course, possible to define a metric on utility characteristics such that each person's utility scale is coordinated with everyone else's in a way that equal social importance is simply "scaled" as equal marginal utility. If interpersonal comparisons of utility are taken to have no descriptive content, then this can indeed be thought to be a natural approach. No matter how the relative social importances are arrived at, the marginal utilities attributed to each person would then simply reflect these values. This can be done explicitly by appropriate interpersonal scaling,[10] or implicitly through making the utility numbering reflect choices in situations of *as if* uncertainty associated with the "original

position" under the additional assumption that ignorance be interpreted as equal probability of being anyone.[11] This is not the occasion to go into the technical details of this type of exercise, but the essence of it consists in using a scaling procedure such that marginal utility measures are automatically identified as indicators of social importance.

This route to utilitarianism may meet with little resistance, but it is non-controversial mainly because it says so little. A problem arises the moment utilities and interpersonal comparisons thereof are taken to have some independent descriptive content, as utilitarians have traditionally insisted that they do. There could then be conflicts between these descriptive utilities and the appropriately scaled, essentially normative, utilities in terms of which one is "forced" to be a utilitarian. In what follows I shall have nothing more to say on utilitarianism through appropriate interpersonal scaling, and return to examining the traditional utilitarian position, which takes utilities to have interpersonally comparable descriptive content. How moral importance should relate to these descriptive features must, then, be explicitly faced.

The position can be examined from the prior-principle perspective as well as from the case-implication angle. John Rawls's criticism as a preliminary to presenting his own alternative conception of justice took mostly the prior-principle form. This was chiefly in terms of acceptability in the "original position," arguing that in the postulated situation of *as if* ignorance people would not choose to maximize the utility sum. But Rawls also discussed the violence that utilitarianism does to our notions of liberty and equality. Some replies to Rawls's arguments have reasserted the necessity to be a utilitarian by taking the "scaling" route, which was discussed earlier, and which – I think – is inappropriate in meeting Rawls's critique. But I must confess that I find the lure of the "original position" distinctly resistible since it seems very unclear what precisely would be chosen in such a situation. It is also far from obvious that prudential choice under *as if* uncertainty provides an adequate basis for moral judgment in *un*original, i.e., real-life, positions.[12] But I believe Rawls's more direct critiques in terms of liberty and equality do remain powerful.

Insofar as one is concerned with the *distribution* of utilities, it follows immediately that utilitarianism would in general give one little comfort. Even the minutest gain in total utility *sum* would be taken to outweigh distributional inequalities of the most blatant kind. This problem would be avoidable under certain assumptions, notably the case in which everyone has the *same* utility function. In the pure distribution problem, with this assumption the utilitarian best would require absolute equality of everyone's total utilities.[13] This is because when the marginal utilities are equated, so would be the total utilities if everyone has the same utility function. This is, however, egalitarianism by serendipity: just the accidental result of the marginal tail wagging the total dog. More importantly, the assumption would be very frequently violated, since there are obvious and well-discussed variations between human beings. John may be easy to please, but Jeremy not. If it is taken to be an acceptable prior-principle that the equality of the distribution of total utilities has some value, then the utilitarian conception of equality – marginal as it is – must stand condemned.

The recognition of the fundamental diversity of human beings does, in fact, have very deep consequences, affecting not merely the utilitarian conception of social good, but others as well, including (as I shall argue presently) even the Rawlsian conception of equality. If human beings are identical, then the application of the prior-principle of universalizability in the form of "giving equal weight to the equal interest of all parties" simplifies enormously. Equal marginal utilities of all – reflecting one interpretation of the equal treatment of needs – coincides with equal total utilities – reflecting one interpretation of serving their overall interests equally well. With diversity, the two can pull in opposite directions, and it is far from clear that "giving equal weight to the equal interest of all parties" would require us to concentrate only on one of the two parameters – taking no note of the other.

The case-implication perspective can also be used to develop a related critique, and I have tried to present such a critique elsewhere.[14] For example, if person A as a cripple gets half the utility that the pleasure-wizard person B does from any given level of income, then in the pure distribution problem between A and B the utilitarian would end up giving the pleasure-wizard B more income than the cripple A. The cripple would then be doubly worse off: both since he gets less utility from the same level of income,

and since he will also get less income. Utilitarianism must lead to this thanks to its single-minded concern with maximizing the utility sum. The pleasure-wizard's superior efficiency in producing utility would pull income away from the less efficient cripple.

Since this example has been discussed a certain amount,[15] I should perhaps explain what is being asserted and what is not. First, it is *not* being claimed that anyone who has lower total utility (e.g., the cripple) at any given level of income must of necessity have lower marginal utility also. This must be true for some levels of income, but need not be true everywhere. Indeed, the opposite could be the case when incomes are equally distributed. If that were so, then of course even utilitarianism would give the cripple more income than the non-cripple, since at that point the cripple would be the more efficient producer of utility. My point is that there is no guarantee that this will be the case, and more particularly, if it were the case that the cripple were not only worse off in terms of total utility but could convert income into utility less efficiently everywhere (or even just at the point of equal income division), then utilitarianism would compound his disadvantage by settling him with less income on top of lower efficiency in making utility out of income. The point, of course, is not about cripples in general, nor about all people with total utility disadvantage, but concerns people – including cripples – with disadvantage in terms of both total *and* marginal utility at the relevant points.

Second, the descriptive content of utility is rather important in this context. Obviously, if utilities were scaled to reflect moral importance, then wishing to give priority to income for the cripple would simply amount to attributing a higher "marginal utility" to the cripple's income; but this – as we have already discussed – is a very special sense of utility – quite devoid of descriptive content. In terms of descriptive features, what is being assumed in our example is that the cripple can be helped by giving him income, but the increase in his utility as a consequence of a marginal increase in income is less – in terms of the accepted descriptive criteria – than giving that unit of income to the pleasure-wizard, when both have initially the same income.

Finally, the problem for utilitarianism in this case-implication argument is not dependent on an implicit assumption that the claim to more income arising from disadvantage must dominate over the claim arising from high marginal utility.[16] A system that gives some weight to both claims would still fail to meet the utilitarian formula of social good, which demands an exclusive concern with the latter claim. It is this narrowness that makes the utilitarian conception of equality such a limited one. Even when utility is accepted as the only basis of moral importance, utilitarianism fails to capture the relevance of overall advantage for the requirements of equality. The prior-principle critiques can be supplemented by case-implication critiques using this utilitarian lack of concern with distributional questions except at the entirely marginal level.

2 Total Utility Equality

Welfarism is the view that the goodness of a state of affairs can be judged entirely by the goodness of the utilities in that state.[17] This is a less demanding view than utilitarianism in that it does not demand – in addition – that the goodness of the utilities must be judged by their sum-total. Utilitarianism is, in this sense, a special case of welfarism, and provides one illustration of it. Another distinguished case is the criterion of judging the goodness of a state by the utility level of the worst-off person in that state – a criterion often attributed to John Rawls. (*Except* by John Rawls! He uses social primary goods rather than utility as the index of advantage, as we shall presently discuss.) One can also take some other function of the utilities – other than the sum-total or the minimal element.

Utilitarian equality is one type of welfarist equality. There are others, notably the equality of total utility. It is tempting to think of this as some kind of an analogue of utilitarianism shifting the focus from marginal utility to total utility. This correspondence is, however, rather less close than it might first appear. First of all, while we economists often tend to treat the marginal and the total as belonging to the same plane of discourse, there is an important difference between them. Marginal is an essentially *counter-factual* notion: marginal utility is the additional utility that *would be* generated if the person had one more unit of income. It contrasts what is observed with what allegedly would be observed if something else were different: in this case if the income had been one unit greater. Total is not, however, an inher-

ently counter-factual concept; whether it is or is not would depend on the variable that is being totalled. In case of utilities, if they are taken to be observed facts, total utility will not be counter-factual. Thus total utility equality is a matter for direct observation, whereas utilitarian equality is not so, since the latter requires hypotheses as to what things would have been under different postulated circumstances. The contrast can be easily traced to the fact that utilitarian equality is essentially a consequence of sum *maximization*, which is itself a counter-factual notion, whereas total utility equality is an equality of some directly observed magnitudes.

Second, utilitarianism provides a complete ordering of all utility distributions – the ranking reflecting the order of the sums of individual utilities – but as specified so far, total utility equality does not do more than just point to the case of absolute equality. In dealing with two cases of non-equal distributions, something more has to be said so that they could be ranked. The ranking can be completed in many different ways.

One way to such a complete ranking is provided by the lexicographic version of the maximin rule, which is associated with the Rawlsian Difference Principle, but interpreted in terms of utilities as opposed to primary goods. Here the goodness of the state of affairs is judged by the level of utility of the worst-off person in that state; but if the worst-off persons in two states respectively have the same level of utility, then the states are ranked according to the utility levels of the second worst-off. If they too tie, then by the utility levels of the third worst-off, and so on. And if two utility distributions are matched at each rank all the way from the worst off to the best off, then the two distributions are equally good. Following a convention established in social choice theory, I shall call this *leximin*.

In what way does total utility equality lead to the leximin? It does this when combined with some other axioms, and in fact the analysis closely parallels the recent axiomatic derivations of the Difference Principle by several authors.[18] Consider four utility levels a, b, c, d, in decreasing order of magnitude. One can argue that in an obvious sense the pair of extreme points (a, d) displays greater inequality than the pair of intermediate points (b, c). Note that this is a purely *ordinal* comparison based on ranking only, and the exact magnitudes of a, b, c, and d make no difference to the comparison in question. If one were *solely* concerned with equality, then it could be argued that (b, c) is superior – or at least non-inferior – to (a, d). This requirement may be seen as a strong version of preferring equality of utility distributions, and may be called "utility equality preference." It is possible to combine this with an axiom due to Patrick Suppes which captures the notion of *dominance* of one utility distribution over another, in the sense of each element of one distribution being at least as large as the corresponding element in the other distribution.[19] In the two-person case this requires that state x must be regarded as at least as good as y, *either* if each person in state x has at least as much utility as himself in state y, *or* if each person in state x has at least as much utility as the *other* person in state y. *If*, in addition, at least one of them has strictly more, then of course x could be declared to be strictly better (and not merely at least as good). If this Suppes principle and the "utility equality preference" are combined, then we are pushed in the direction of leximin. Indeed, leximin can be fully derived from these two principles by requiring that the approach must provide a complete ordering of all possible states no matter what the interpersonally comparable individual utilities happen to be (called "unrestricted domain"), and that the ranking of any two states must depend on utility information concerning *those* states only (called "independence").

Insofar as the requirements other than utility equality preference (i.e., the Suppes principle, unrestricted domain, and independence) are regarded as acceptable – and they have indeed been widely used in the social choice literature – leximin can be seen as the natural concomitant of giving priority to the conception of equality focussing on total utility.

It should be obvious, however, that leximin can be fairly easily criticised from the prior-principle perspective as well as the case-implication perspective. Just as utilitarianism pays no attention to the force of one's claim arising from one's disadvantage, leximin ignores claims arising from the *intensity* of one's needs. The *ordinal* characteristic that was pointed out while presenting the axiom of utility equality preference makes the approach insensitive to the magnitudes of potential utility gains and losses. While in the critique of utilitarianism that was presented earlier I argued against treating these potential gains and losses as the only basis of moral judgment, it was *not* of course alleged that these have no moral

relevance at all. Take the comparison of (a, d) vis-a-vis (b, c), discussed earlier, and let (b, c) stand for $(3, 2)$. Utility equality preference would assert the superiority of $(3, 2)$ over $(10, 1)$ as well as $(4, 1)$. Indeed, it would not distinguish between the two cases at all. It is this lack of concern with "how much" questions that makes leximin rather easy to criticise *either* by showing its failure to comply with such prior-principles as "giving equal weight to the equal interest of all parties," *or* by spelling out its rather austere implications in specific cases.

Aside from its indifference to "how much" questions, leximin also has little interest in "how many" questions – paying no attention at all to the number of people whose interests are overridden in the pursuit of the interests of the worst off. The worst-off position rules the roost, and it does not matter whether this goes against the interests of one other person, or against those of a million or a billion other persons. It is sometimes claimed that leximin would not be such an extreme criterion if it could be modified so that this innumeracy were avoided, and if the interests of *one* worse-off position were given priority over the interests of exactly *one* better-off position, but not necessarily against the interests of *more than one* better-off position. In fact, one can define a less demanding version of leximin, which can be called leximin-2, which takes the form of applying the leximin principle *if* all persons other than two are indifferent between the alternatives, but not necessarily otherwise. Leximin-2, as a compromise, will be still unconcerned with "how much" questions on the magnitudes of utilities of the two non-indifferent persons, but need not be blinkered about "how many" questions dealing with numbers of people: the priority applies to one person over exactly one other.[20]

Interestingly enough, a consistency problem intervenes here. It can be proved that given the regularity conditions, viz., unrestricted domain and independence, leximin-2 logically entails leximin in general.[21] That is, given these regularity conditions, there is no way of retaining moral sensitivity to the number of people on each side by choosing the limited requirement of leximin-2 without going all the way to leximin itself. It appears that indifference to *how much* questions concerning utilities implies indifference to *how many* questions concerning the number of people on different sides. One innumeracy begets another.

Given the nature of these critiques of utilitarian equality and total utility equality respectively, it is natural to ask whether some *combination* of the two should not meet both sets of objections. If utilitarianism is attacked for its unconcern with inequalities of the utility distribution, and leximin is criticised for its lack of interest in the magnitudes of utility gains and losses, and even in the numbers involved, then isn't the right solution to choose some mixture of the two? It is at this point that the long-postponed question of the relation between utility and moral worth becomes crucial. While utilitarianism and leximin differ sharply from each other in the use that they respectively make of the utility information, both share an exclusive concern with utility data. If non-utility considerations have any role in either approach, this arises from the part they play in the determination of utilities, or possibly as surrogates for utility information in the absence of adequate utility data. A combination of utilitarianism and leximin would still be confined to the box of welfarism, and it remains to be examined whether welfarism as a general approach is *itself* adequate.

One aspect of the obtuseness of welfarism was discussed clearly by John Rawls.

> In calculating the greatest balance of satisfaction it does not matter, except indirectly, what the desires are for. We are to arrange institutions so as to obtain the greatest sum of satisfactions; we ask no questions about their source or quality but only how their satisfaction would affect the total of well-being. . . . Thus if men take a certain pleasure in discriminating against one another, in subjecting others to a lesser liberty as a means of enhancing their self-respect, then the satisfaction of these desires must be weighed in our deliberations according to their intensity, or whatever, along with other desires. . . . In justice as fairness, on the other hand, persons accept in advance a principle of equal liberty and they do this without a knowledge of their more particular ends. . . . An individual who finds that he enjoys seeing others in positions of lesser liberty understands that he has no claim whatever to this enjoyment. The pleasure he takes in other's deprivation is wrong in itself: it is a satisfaction which requires the violation of a principle to which he would agree in the original position.[22]

It is easily seen that this is an argument not merely against utilitarianism, but against the adequacy of utility information for moral judgments of states of affairs, and is, thus, an attack on welfarism in general. Second, it is clear that as a criticism of welfarism – and *a fortiori* as a critique of utilitarianism – the argument uses a principle that is unnecessarily strong. If it were the case that pleasures taken "in other's deprivation" were not taken to be wrong in itself, but simply *disregarded*, even then the rejection of welfarism would stand. Furthermore, even if such pleasures were regarded as valuable, but *less* valuable than pleasures arising from other sources (e.g., enjoying food, work, or leisure), welfarism would still stand rejected. The issue – as John Stuart Mill had noted – is the lack of "parity" between one source of utility and another.[23] Welfarism requires the endorsement not merely of the widely shared intuition that any pleasure has some value – and one would have to be a bit of a kill-joy to dissent from this – but also the much more dubious proposition that pleasures must be relatively weighed *only* according to their respective intensities, irrespective of the source of the pleasure and the nature of the activity that goes with it. Finally, Rawls's argument takes the form of an appeal to the prior-principle of equating moral rightness with prudential acceptability in the original position. Even those who do not accept that prior principle could reject the welfarist no-nonsense counting of utility irrespective of all other information by reference to other prior principles, e.g., the irreducible value of liberty.

The relevance of non-utility information to moral judgments is the central issue involved in disputing welfarism. Libertarian considerations point towards a particular class of non-utility information, and I have argued elsewhere that this may require even the rejection of the so-called Pareto principle based on utility dominance.[24] But there are also other types of non-utility information which have been thought to be intrinsically important. Tim Scanlon has recently discussed the contrast between "urgency" and utility (or intensity of preference). He has also argued that "the criteria of well-being that we actually employ in making moral judgments are objective," and a person's level of well-being is taken to be "independent of that person's tastes and interests."[25] These moral judgments could thus conflict with utilitarian – and more generally (Scanlon could have argued) with welfarist – moralities, no matter whether utility is interpreted as pleasure, or – as is increasingly common recently – as desire-fulfilment.

However, acknowledging the relevance of objective factors does not require that well-being be taken to be independent of tastes, and Scanlon's categories are *too* pure. For example, a lack of "parity" between utility from self-regarding actions and that from other-regarding actions will go beyond utility as an index of well-being and will be fatal to welfarism, but the contrast is not, of course, independent of tastes and subjective features. "Objective" considerations can count along with a person's tastes. What is required is the denial that a person's well-being be judged *exclusively* in terms of his or her utilities. If such judgments take into account a person's pleasures and desire-fulfilments, but also certain objective factors, e.g., whether he or she is hungry, cold, or oppressed, the resulting calculus would still be non-welfarist. Welfarism is an extremist position, and its denial can take many different forms – pure and mixed – so long as totally ignoring non-utility information is avoided.

Second, it is also clear that the notion of urgency need not work only *through* the determinants of personal well-being – however broadly conceived. For example, the claim that one should not be *exploited* at work is not based on making exploitation an additional parameter in the specification of well-being on top of such factors as income and effort, but on the moral view that a person deserves to get what he – according to one way of characterizing production – has produced. Similarly, the urgency deriving from principles such as "equal pay for equal work" hits directly at discrimination without having to redefine the notion of personal well-being to take note of such discriminations. One could, for example, say: "She must be paid just as much as the men working in that job, not primarily because she would otherwise have a lower level of well-being than the others, but simply because she is doing the *same* work as the men there, and why should she be paid less?" These moral claims, based on non-welfarist conceptions of equality, have played important parts in social movements, and it seems difficult to sustain the hypothesis that they are purely "instrumental" claims – ultimately justified by their indirect impact on the fulfilment of welfarist, or other well-being-based, objectives.

Thus the dissociation of urgency from utility can arise from two different sources. One disentangles the notion of personal well-being from utility, and the other makes urgency not a function only of well-being. But, at the same time, the former does not require that well-being be independent of utility, and the latter does not necessitate a notion of urgency that is independent of personal well-being. Welfarism is a purist position and must avoid any contamination from either of these sources.

3 Rawlsian Equality

Rawls's "two principles of justice" characterize the need for equality in terms of – what he has called – "primary social goods."[26] These are "things that every rational man is presumed to want," including "rights, liberties and opportunities, income and wealth, and the social bases of self-respect." Basic liberties are separated out as having priority over other primary goods, and thus priority is given to the principle of liberty which demands that "each person is to have an equal right to the most extensive basic liberty compatible with a similar liberty for others." The second principle supplements this, demanding efficiency and equality, judging advantage in terms of an index of primary goods. Inequalities are condemned unless they work out to everyone's advantage. This incorporates the "Difference Principle" in which priority is given to furthering the interests of the worst-off. And that leads to maximin, or to leximin, defined not on individual utilities but on the index of primary goods. But given the priority of the liberty principle, no trade-offs are permitted between basic liberties and economic and social gain.

Herbert Hart has persuasively disputed Rawls's arguments for the priority of liberty,[27] but with that question I shall not be concerned in this lecture. What is crucial for the problem under discussion is the concentration on bundles of primary social goods. Some of the difficulties with welfarism that I tried to discuss will not apply to the pursuit of Rawlsian equality. Objective criteria of well-being can be directly accommodated within the index of primary goods. So can be Mill's denial of the parity between pleasures from different sources, since the sources can be discriminated on the basis of the nature of the goods. Furthermore, while the Difference Principle is egalitarian in a way similar to leximin, it avoids the much-criticized feature of leximin of giving more income to people who are hard to please and who have to be deluged in champagne and buried in caviar to bring them to a normal level of utility, which you and I get from a sandwich and beer. Since advantage is judged not in terms of utilities at all, but through the index of primary goods, expensive tastes cease to provide a ground for getting more income. Rawls justifies this in terms of a person's responsibility for his own ends.

But what about the cripple with utility disadvantage, whom we discussed earlier? Leximin will give him more income in a pure distribution problem. Utilitarianism, I had complained, will give him *less*. The Difference Principle will give him neither more nor less on grounds of his being a cripple. His utility disadvantage will be irrelevant to the Difference Principle. This may seem hard, and I think it is. Rawls justifies this by pointing out that "hard cases" can "distract our moral perception by leading us to think of people distant from us whose fate arouses pity and anxiety."[28] This can be so, but hard cases do exist, and to take disabilities, or special health needs, or physical or mental defects, as morally irrelevant, or to leave them out for fear of making a mistake, may guarantee that the *opposite* mistake will be made.

And the problem does not end with hard cases. The primary goods approach seems to take little note of the diversity of human beings. In the context of assessing utilitarian equality, it was argued that if people were fundamentally similar in terms of utility functions, then the utilitarian concern with maximizing the sum-total of utilities would push us simultaneously also in the direction of equality of utility levels. Thus utilitarianism could be rendered vastly more attractive if people really were similar. A corresponding remark can be made about the Rawlsian Difference Principle. If people were basically very similar, then an index of primary goods might be quite a good way of judging advantage. But, in fact, people seem to have very different needs varying with health, longevity, climatic conditions, location, work conditions, temperament, and even body size (affecting food and clothing requirements). So what is involved is not merely ignoring a few hard cases, but overlooking very widespread and real differences. Judging advantage purely in terms of primary goods leads to a partially blind morality.

Indeed, it can be argued that there is, in fact, an element of "fetishism" in the Rawlsian frame-

work. Rawls takes primary goods as the embodiment of advantage, rather than taking advantage to be a *relationship* between persons and goods. Utilitarianism, or leximin, or – more generally – welfarism does not have this fetishism, since utilities are reflections of one type of relation between persons and goods. For example, income and wealth are not valued under utilitarianism as physical units, but in terms of their capacity to create human happiness or to satisfy human desires. Even if utility is not thought to be the right focus for the person-good relationship, to have an entirely good-oriented framework provides a peculiar way of judging advantage.

It can also be argued that while utility in the form of happiness or desire-fulfilment may be an *inadequate* guide to urgency, the Rawlsian framework asserts it to be *irrelevant* to urgency, which is, of course, a much stronger claim. The distinction was discussed earlier in the context of assessing welfarism, and it was pointed out that a rejection of welfarism need not take us to the point in which utility is given no role whatsoever. That a person's interest should have nothing directly to do with his happiness or desire-fulfilment seems difficult to justify. Even in terms of the prior-principle of prudential acceptability in the "original position," it is not at all clear why people in that primordial state should be taken to be so indifferent to the joys and sufferings in occupying particular positions, or if they are not, why their concern about these joys and sufferings should be taken to be morally irrelevant.

4 Basic Capability Equality

This leads to the further question: Can we not construct an adequate theory of equality on the *combined* grounds of Rawlsian equality and equality under the two welfarist conceptions, with some trade-offs among them? I would now like to argue briefly why I believe this too may prove to be informationally short. This can, of course, easily be asserted *if* claims arising from considerations other than well-being were acknowledged to be legitimate. Non-exploitation, or non-discrimination, requires the use of information not fully captured either by utility or by primary goods. Other conceptions of entitlements can also be brought in going beyond concern with personal well-being only. But in what follows I shall not introduce these concepts. My contention is that *even* the concept of *needs* does not get adequate coverage through the information on primary goods and utility.

I shall use a case-implication argument. Take the cripple again with marginal utility disadvantage. We saw that utilitarianism would do nothing for him; in fact it will give him *less* income than to the physically fit. Nor would the Difference Principle help him; it will leave his physical disadvantage severely alone. He did, however, get preferential treatment under leximin, and more generally, under criteria fostering total equality. His low level of total utility was the basis of his claim. But now suppose that he is no worse off than others in utility terms despite his physical handicap because of certain other utility features. This could be because he has a jolly disposition. Or because he has a low aspiration level and his heart leaps up whenever he sees a rainbow in the sky. Or because he is religious and feels that he will be rewarded in after-life, or cheerfully accepts what he takes to be just penalty for misdeeds in a past incarnation. The important point is that despite his marginal utility disadvantage, he has no longer a total utility deprivation. Now not even leximin – or any other notion of equality focussing on total utility – will do much for him. If we still think that he has needs as a cripple that should be catered to, then the basis of that claim clearly rests neither in high marginal utility, nor in low total utility, nor – of course – in deprivation in terms of primary goods.

It is arguable that what is missing in all this framework is some notion of "basic capabilities": a person being able to do certain basic things. The ability to move about is the relevant one here, but one can consider others, e.g., the ability to meet one's nutritional requirements, the wherewithal to be clothed and sheltered, the power to participate in the social life of the community. The notion of urgency related to this is not fully captured by either utility or primary goods, or any combination of the two. Primary goods suffers from fetishist handicap in being concerned with goods, and even though the list of goods is specified in a broad and inclusive way, encompassing rights, liberties, opportunities, income, wealth, and the social basis of self-respect, it still is concerned with good things rather than with what these good things *do* to human beings. Utility, on the other hand, *is* concerned with what these things do to human beings, but uses a metric that focusses not on the person's capabilities but on his mental reaction. There is something still missing in the combined list of primary goods and utilities. If it is argued that resources should be devoted to remove or substantially reduce the handicap of the cripple despite there being no marginal utility argument (because it is expensive), despite there being no total utility argument (because he is so contented), and despite there being no primary goods deprivation (because he has the goods that others have), the case must rest on something else. I believe what is at issue is the interpretation of needs in the form of basic capabilities. This interpretation of needs and interests is often implicit in the demand for equality. This type of equality I shall call "basic capability equality."

The focus on basic capabilities can be seen as a natural extension of Rawls's concern with primary goods, shifting attention from goods to what goods do to human beings. Rawls himself motivates judging advantage in terms of primary goods by referring to capabilities, even though his criteria end up focussing on goods as such: on income rather than on what income does, on the "social bases of self-respect" rather than on self-respect itself, and so on. If human beings were very like each other, this would not have mattered a great deal, but there is evidence that the conversion of goods to capabilities varies from person to person substantially, and the equality of the former may still be far from the equality of the latter.

There are, of course, many difficulties with the notion of "basic capability equality." In particular, the problem of indexing the basic capability bundles is a serious one. It is, in many ways, a problem comparable with the indexing of primary good bundles in the context of Rawlsian equality. This is not the occasion to go into the technical issues involved in such an indexing, but it is clear that whatever partial ordering can be done on the basis of broad uniformity of personal preferences must be supplemented by certain established conventions of relative importance.

The ideas of relative importance are, of course, conditional on the nature of the society. The notion of the equality of basic capabilities is a very general one, but any application of it must be rather culture-dependent, especially in the weighting of different capabilities. While Rawlsian equality has the characteristic of being both culture-dependent and fetishist, basic capability equality avoids fetishism, but remains culture-dependent. Indeed, basic capability equality can be seen as essentially an extension of the Rawlsian approach in a non-fetishist direction.

5 Concluding Remarks

I end with three final remarks. First, it is not my contention that basic capability equality can be the sole guide to the moral good. For one thing morality is not concerned only with equality. For another, while it is my contention that basic capability equality has certain clear advantages over other types of equality, I did not argue that the others were morally irrelevant. Basic capability equality is a partial guide to the part of moral goodness that is associated with the idea of equality. I have tried to argue that as a partial guide it has virtues that the other characterizations of equality do not possess.

Second, the index of basic capabilities, like utility, can be used in many different ways. Basic capability equality corresponds to total utility equality, and it can be extended in different directions, e.g., to leximin of basic capabilities.

On the other hand, the index can be used also in a way similar to utilitarianism, judging the strength of a claim in terms of incremental contribution to *enhancing* the index value. The main departure is in focussing on a *magnitude* different from utility as well as the primary goods index. The new dimension can be utilized in different ways, of which basic capability equality is only one.

Last, the bulk of this lecture has been concerned with rejecting the claims of utilitarian equality, total utility equality, and Rawlsian equality to provide a sufficient basis for the equality-aspect of morality – indeed, even for that part of it which is concerned with needs rather than deserts. I have argued that none of these three is sufficient, nor is any combination of the three.

This is my main thesis. I have also made the constructive claim that this gap can be narrowed by the idea of basic capability equality, and more generally by the use of basic capability as a morally relevant dimension taking us beyond utility and primary goods. I should end by pointing out that the validity of the main thesis is not conditional on the acceptance of this constructive claim.

Notes

For helpful comments I am most grateful to Derek Parfit, Jim Griffin, and John Perry.

1 Rawls, *A Theory of Justice* (Cambridge: Harvard University Press, 1971), pp. 17–22. See also W. Vickrey, "Measuring Marginal Utility by Reactions to Risk," *Econometrica* 13 (1945), and J.C. Harsanyi, "Cardinal Welfare, Individualistic Ethics, and Interpersonal Comparisons of Utility," *Journal of Political Economy* 63 (1955).

2 R.M. Hare, *The Language of Morals* (Oxford: Clarendon Press, 1952); "Ethical Theory and Utilitarianism," in H.D. Lewis, ed., *Contemporary British Philosophy* (London: Allen and Unwin, 1976), pp. 116–17

3 I have tried to use this format for an axiomatic contrast of the Rawlsian and utilitarian criteria in "Rawls versus Bentham: An Axiomatic Examination of the Pure Distribution Problem," in *Theory and Decision* 4 (1974); reprinted in N. Daniels, ed., *Reading Rawls* (Oxford: Blackwell, 1975). See also L. Kern, "Comparative Distributive Ethics: An Extension of Sen's Examination of the Pure Distribution Problem," in H.W. Gottinger and W. Leinfellner, eds., *Decision Theory and Social Ethics* (Dordrecht: Reidel, 1978), and J.P. Griffin, "Equality: On Sen's Equity Axiom," Keble College, Oxford, 1978, mimeographed.

4 The equality condition would have to be replaced by a corresponding combination of inequality requirements when the appropriate "continuity" properties do not hold. Deeper difficulties are raised by "non-convexities" (e.g., increasing marginal utility).

5 J. Harsanyi, "Can the Maximin Principle Serve as a Basis for Morality? A Critique of John Rawls' Theory," *American Political Science Review* 64 (1975).

6 As mentioned in note 1, the equality conditions would require modification in the absence of continuity of the appropriate type. Transfers must be carried to the point at which the marginal utility gain of the gainers from any further transfer is *no more than* the marginal utility loss of the losers.

7 Hare (1976), pp. 116–17.

8 John Harsanyi, "Non-linear Social Welfare Functions: A Rejoinder to Professor Sen," in R.E. Butts and J. Hintikka, eds., *Foundational Problems in the Special Sciences* (Dordrecht: Reidel, 1977), pp. 294–95.

9 *Collective Choice and Social Welfare* (San Francisco: Holden-Day, 1970), chapter 6 and section 11.4; "On Weights and Measures: Informational Constraints in Social Welfare Analysis," *Econometrica* 45 (1977). See also T.M. Scanlon's arguments against identifying utility with "urgency" in his "Preference and Urgency," *Journal of Philosophy* 72 (1975).

10 For two highly ingenious examples of such an exercise, see Peter Hammond, "Dual Interpersonal Comparisons of Utility and the Welfare Economics of Income Distribution," *Journal of Public Economics* 6 (1977): 51–57; and Menahem Yaari, "Rawls, Edgeworth, Shapley and Nash: Theories of Distributive Justice Re-examined," Research Memorandum No. 33, Center for Research in Mathematical Economics and Game Theory, Hebrew University, Jerusalem, 1978.

11 See Harsanyi (1955, 1975, 1977).

12 On this, see Thomas Nagel, "Rawls on Justice", *Philosophical Review* 83 (1973), and "Equality" in his *Mortal Questions* (Cambridge: Cambridge University Press, 1979).

13 The problem is much more complex when the total cake is not fixed, and where the maximization of utility sum need not lead to the equality of total utilities unless some additional assumptions are made, e.g., the absence of incentive arguments for inequality.

14 *On Economic Inequality* (Oxford: Clarendon Press, 1973), pp. 16–20.

15 See John Harsanyi, "Non-linear Social Welfare Functions," *Theory and Decision* 6 (1976): 311–12; Harsanyi (1977); Kern (1978); Griffin (1978); Richard B. Brandt, *A Theory of the Good and the Right* (Oxford: Clarendon Press, 1979), chapter 16.

16 Such an assumption is made in my Weak Equity Axiom, proposed in Sen (1973), but it is unnecessarily demanding for rejecting utilitarianism. See Griffin (1978) for a telling critique of the Weak Equity Axiom, in this exacting form.

17 See Sen (1977), and also my "Welfarism and Utilitarianism", *Journal of Philosophy* 76 (1979).

18 See P.J. Hammond, "Equity, Arrow's Conditions and Rawls' Difference Principle," *Econometrica* 44 (1976); S. Strasnick, "Social Choice Theory and the Derivation of Rawls' Difference Principle,"

Journal of Philosophy 73 (1976); C. d'Aspremont and L. Gevers, "Equity and Informational Basis of Collective Choice," *Review of Economic Studies* 44 (1977); K.J. Arrow, "Extended Sympathy and the Possibility of Social Choice," *American Economic Review* 67 (1977); A.K. Sen, "On Weights and Measures: Informational Constraints in Social Welfare Analysis," *Econometrica* 45 (1977); R. Deschamps and L. Gevers, "Leximin and Utilitarian Rules: A Joint Characterization," *Journal of Economic Theory* 17 (1978); K.W.S. Roberts, "Possibility Theorems with Interpersonally Comparable Welfare Levels," *Review of Economic Studies* 47 (1980); P.J. Hammond, "Two Person Equity," *Econometrica* 47 (1979).

19 P. Suppes, "Some Formal Models of Grading Principles," *Synthese* 6 (1966).

20 Leximin – and maximin – are concerned with conflicts between positional priorities, i.e., between ranks (such as the "worst-off position," "second worst-off position," etc.), and not with interpersonal priorities. When positions coincide with persons (e.g., the *same* person being the worst off in each state), then positional conflicts translate directly into personal conflicts.

21 Theorem 8, Sen (1977). See also Hammond (1979) for extensions of this result.

22 Rawls (1971), pp. 30–31.

23 John Stuart Mill, *On Liberty* (1859), p. 140.

24 Sen (1970), especially chapter 6. Also Sen (1979).

25 T.M. Scanlon (1975), pp. 658–59.

26 Rawls (1971), pp. 60–65.

27 H.L.A. Hart, "Rawls on Liberty and Its Priority," *University of Chicago Law Review* 40 (1973); reprinted in N. Daniels, ed., *Reading Rawls* (Oxford: Blackwell, 1975).

28 John Rawls, "A Kantian Concept of Equality," *Cambridge Review* (February 1975), p. 96.

30

Complex Equality

Michael Walzer

Pluralism

Distributive justice is a large idea. It draws the entire world of goods within the reach of philosophical reflection. Nothing can be omitted; no feature of our common life can escape scrutiny. Human society is a distributive community. That's not all it is, but it is importantly that: we come together to share, divide, and exchange. We also come together to make the things that are shared, divided, and exchanged; but that very making – work itself – is distributed among us in a division of labor. My place in the economy, my standing in the political order, my reputation among my fellows, my material holdings: all these come to me from other men and women. It can be said that I have what I have rightly or wrongly, justly or unjustly; but given the range of distributions and the number of participants, such judgments are never easy.

The idea of distributive justice has as much to do with being and doing as with having, as much to do with production as with consumption, as much to do with identity and status as with land, capital, or personal possessions. Different political arrangements enforce, and different ideologies justify, different distributions of membership, power, honor, ritual eminence, divine grace, kinship and love, knowledge, wealth, physical security, work and leisure, rewards and punishments,

Originally published in *Spheres of Justice: A Defense of Pluralism and Equality* (Martin Robertson, 1983), 3–30. Copyright © 1983 by Basic Books, Inc., a division of HarperCollins, Inc. Reprinted by permission of Blackwell Publishers.

and a host of goods more narrowly and materially conceived – food, shelter, clothing, transportation, medical care, commodities of every sort, and all the odd things (paintings, rare books, postage stamps) that human beings collect. And this multiplicity of goods is matched by a multiplicity of distributive procedures, agents, and criteria. There are such things as simple distributive systems – slave galleys, monasteries, insane asylums, kindergartens (though each of these, looked at closely, might show unexpected complexities); but no full-fledged human society has ever avoided the multiplicity. We must study it all, the goods and the distributions, in many different times and places.

There is, however, no single point of access to this world of distributive arrangements and ideologies. There has never been a universal medium of exchange. Since the decline of the barter economy, money has been the most common medium. But the old maxim according to which there are some things that money can't buy is not only normatively but also factually true. What should and should not be up for sale is something men and women always have to decide and have decided in many different ways. Throughout history, the market has been one of the most important mechanisms for the distribution of social goods; but it has never been, it nowhere is today, a complete distributive system.

Similarly, there has never been either a single decision point from which all distributions are controlled or a single set of agents making decisions. No state power has ever been so pervasive as to regulate all the patterns of sharing, dividing, and exchanging out of which a society takes shape. Things slip away from the state's grasp; new patterns are worked out – familial networks, black markets, bureaucratic alliances, clandestine political and religious organizations. State officials can tax, conscript, allocate, regulate, appoint, reward, punish, but they cannot capture the full range of goods or substitute themselves for every other agent of distribution. Nor can anyone else do that: there are market coups and cornerings, but there has never been a fully successful distributive conspiracy.

And finally, there has never been a single criterion, or a single set of interconnected criteria, for all distributions. Desert, qualification, birth and blood, friendship, need, free exchange, political loyalty, democratic decision: each has had its place, along with many others, uneasily coexisting, invoked by competing groups, confused with one another.

In the matter of distributive justice, history displays a great variety of arrangements and ideologies. But the first impulse of the philosopher is to resist the displays of history, the world of appearances, and to search for some underlying unity: a short list of basic goods, quickly abstracted to a single good; a single distributive criterion or an interconnected set; and the philosopher himself standing, symbolically at least, at a single decision point. I shall argue that to search for unity is to misunderstand the subject matter of distributive justice. Nevertheless, in some sense the philosophical impulse is unavoidable. Even if we choose pluralism, as I shall do, that choice still requires a coherent defense. There must be principles that justify the choice and set limits to it, for pluralism does not require us to endorse every proposed distributive criteria or to accept every would-be agent. Conceivably, there is a single principle and a single legitimate kind of pluralism. But this would still be a pluralism that encompassed a wide range of distributions. By contrast, the deepest assumption of most of the philosophers who have written about justice, from Plato onward, is that there is one, and only one, distributive system that philosophy can rightly encompass.

Today this system is commonly described as the one that ideally rational men and women would choose if they were forced to choose impartially, knowing nothing of their own situation, barred from making particularist claims, confronting an abstract set of goods.[1] If these constraints on knowing and claiming are suitably shaped, and if the goods are suitably defined, it is probably true that a singular conclusion can be produced. Rational men and women, constrained this way or that, will choose one, and only one, distributive system. But the force of that singular conclusion is not easy to measure. It is surely doubtful that those same men and women, if they were transformed into ordinary people, with a firm sense of their own identity, with their own goods in their hands, caught up in everyday troubles, would reiterate their hypothetical choice or even recognize it as their own. The problem is not, most importantly, with the particularism of interest, which philosophers have always assumed they could safely – that is, uncontroversially – set aside. Ordinary people can do that too, for the sake, say, of the public interest. The greater problem is with the particularism of history, culture, and membership. Even if they are committed to impartiality, the question most likely to arise in the minds of the members of a political community is not, What would rational individuals choose under universalizing conditions of such-and-such a sort? But rather, What would individuals like us choose, who are situated as we are, who share a culture and are determined to go on sharing it? And this is a question that is readily transformed into, What choices have we already made in the course of our common life? What understandings do we (really) share?

Justice is a human construction, and it is doubtful that it can be made in only one way. At any rate, I shall begin by doubting, and more than doubting, this standard philosophical assumption. The questions posed by the theory of distributive justice admit of a range of answers, and there is room within the range for cultural diversity and political choice. It's not only a matter of implementing some singular principle or set of principles in different historical settings. No one would deny that there is a range of morally permissible implementations. I want to argue for more than this: that the principles of justice are themselves pluralistic in form; that different social goods ought to be distributed for different reasons, in accordance with different procedures, by different agents; and that all these differences derive from different understandings of the social goods themselves – the inevitable product of historical and cultural particularism.

A Theory of Goods

Theories of distributive justice focus on a social process commonly described as if it had this form:

People distribute goods to (other) people.

Here, "distribute" means give, allocate, exchange, and so on, and the focus is on the individuals who stand at either end of these actions: not on producers and consumers, but on distributive agents and recipients of goods. We are as always interested in ourselves, but, in this case, in a special and limited version of ourselves, as people who give and take. What is our nature? What are our rights? What do we need, want, deserve? What are we entitled to? What would we accept under ideal conditions? Answers to these questions are turned into distributive principles, which are supposed to control the movement of goods. The goods, defined by abstraction, are taken to be movable in any direction.

But this is too simple an understanding of what actually happens, and it forces us too quickly to make large assertions about human nature and moral agency – assertions unlikely, ever, to command general agreement. I want to propose a more precise and complex description of the central process:

People conceive and create goods, which they then distribute among themselves.

Here, the conception and creation precede and control the distribution. Goods don't just appear in the hands of distributive agents who do with them as they like or give them out in accordance with some general principle.[2] Rather, goods with their meanings – because of their meanings – are the crucial medium of social relations; they come into people's minds before they come into their hands; distributions are patterned in accordance with shared conceptions of what the goods are and what they are for. Distributive agents are constrained by the goods they hold; one might almost say that goods distribute themselves among people.

> Things are in the saddle
> And ride mankind.[3]

But these are always particular things and particular groups of men and women. And, of course,

we make the things – even the saddle. I don't want to deny the importance of human agency, only to shift our attention from distribution itself to conception and creation: the naming of the goods, and the giving of meaning, and the collective making. What we need to explain and limit the pluralism of distributive possibilities is a theory of goods. For our immediate purposes, that theory can be summed up in six propositions.

1. All the goods with which distributive justice is concerned are social goods. They are not and they cannot be idiosyncratically valued. I am not sure that there are any other kinds of goods; I mean to leave the question open. Some domestic objects are cherished for private and sentimental reasons, but only in cultures where sentiment regularly attaches to such objects. A beautiful sunset, the smell of new-mown hay, the excitement of an urban vista: these perhaps are privately valued goods, though they are also, and more obviously, the objects of cultural assessment. Even new inventions are not valued in accordance with the ideas of their inventors; they are subject to a wider process of conception and creation. God's goods, to be sure, are exempt from this rule – as in the first chapter of Genesis: "and God saw every thing that He had made, and, behold, it was very good" (1:31). That evaluation doesn't require the agreement of mankind (who might be doubtful), or of a majority of men and women, or of any group of men and women meeting under ideal conditions (though Adam and Eve in Eden would probably endorse it). But I can't think of any other exemptions. Goods in the world have shared meanings because conception and creation are social processes. For the same reason, goods have different meanings in different societies. The same "thing" is valued for different reasons, or it is valued here and disvalued there. John Stuart Mill once complained that "people like in crowds," but I know of no other way to like or to dislike social goods.[4] A solitary person could hardly understand the meaning of the goods or figure out the reasons for taking them as likable or dislikable. Once people like in crowds, it becomes possible for individuals to break away, pointing to latent or subversive meanings, aiming at alternative values – including the values, for example, of notoriety and eccentricity. An easy eccentricity has sometimes been one of the privileges of the aristocracy: it is a social good like any other.

2. Men and women take on concrete identities

because of the way they conceive and create, and then possess and employ social goods. "The line between what is me and mine," wrote William James, "is very hard to draw."[5] Distributions can not be understood as the acts of men and women who do not yet have particular goods in their minds or in their hands. In fact, people already stand in a relation to a set of goods; they have a history of transactions, not only with one another but also with the moral and material world in which they live. Without such a history, which begins at birth, they wouldn't be men and women in any recognizable sense, and they wouldn't have the first notion of how to go about the business of giving, allocating, and exchanging goods.

3. There is no single set of primary or basic goods conceivable across all moral and material worlds – or, any such set would have to be conceived in terms so abstract that they would be of little use in thinking about particular distributions. Even the range of necessities, if we take into account moral as well as physical necessities, is very wide, and the rank orderings are very different. A single necessary good, and one that is always necessary – food, for example – carries different meanings in different places. Bread is the staff of life, the body of Christ, the symbol of the Sabbath, the means of hospitality, and so on. Conceivably, there is a limited sense in which the first of these is primary, so that if there were twenty people in the world and just enough bread to feed the twenty, the primacy of bread-as-staff-of-life would yield a sufficient distributive principle. But that is the only circumstance in which it would do so; and even there, we can't be sure. If the religious uses of bread were to conflict with its nutritional uses – if the gods demanded that bread be baked and burned rather than eaten – it is by no means clear which use would be primary. How, then, is bread to be incorporated into the universal list? The question is even harder to answer, the conventional answers less plausible, as we pass from necessities to opportunities, powers, reputations, and so on. These can be incorporated only if they are abstracted from every particular meaning – hence, for all practical purposes, rendered meaningless.

4. But it is the meaning of goods that determines their movement. Distributive criteria and arrangements are intrinsic not to the good-in-itself but to the social good. If we understand what it is, what it means to those for whom it is a good, we understand how, by whom, and for what reasons it ought to be distributed. All distributions are just or unjust relative to the social meanings of the goods at stake. This is in obvious ways a principle of legitimation, but it is also a critical principle.[6] When medieval Christians, for example, condemned the sin of simony, they were claiming that the meaning of a particular social good, ecclesiastical office, excluded its sale and purchase. Given the Christian understanding of office, it followed – I am inclined to say, it necessarily followed – that office holders should be chosen for their knowledge and piety and not for their wealth. There are presumably things that money can buy, but not this thing. Similarly, the words *prostitution* and *bribery*, like *simony*, describe the sale and purchase of goods that, given certain understandings of their meaning, ought never to be sold or purchased.

5. Social meanings are historical in character; and so distributions, and just and unjust distributions, change over time. To be sure, certain key goods have what we might think of as characteristic normative structures, reiterated across the lines (but not all the lines) of time and space. It is because of this reiteration that the British philosopher Bernard Williams is able to argue that goods should always be distributed for "relevant reasons" – where relevance seems to connect to essential rather than to social meanings.[7] The idea that offices, for example, should go to qualified candidates – though not the only idea that has been held about offices – is plainly visible in very different societies where simony and nepotism, under different names, have similarly been thought sinful or unjust. (But there has been a wide divergence of views about what sorts of position and place are properly called "offices.") Again, punishment has been widely understood as a negative good that ought to go to people who are judged to deserve it on the basis of a verdict, not of a political decision. (But what constitutes a verdict? Who is to deliver it? How, in short, is justice to be done to accused men and women? About these questions there has been significant disagreement.) These examples invite empirical investigation. There is no merely intuitive or speculative procedure for seizing upon relevant reasons.

6. When meanings are distinct, distributions must be autonomous. Every social good or set of goods constitutes, as it were, a distributive sphere within which only certain criteria and arrangements are appropriate. Money is inappropriate in

the sphere of ecclesiastical office; it is an intrusion from another sphere. And piety should make for no advantage in the marketplace, as the marketplace has commonly been understood. Whatever can rightly be sold ought to be sold to pious men and women and also to profane, heretical, and sinful men and women (else no one would do much business). The market is open to all comers; the church is not. In no society, of course, are social meanings entirely distinct. What happens in one distributive sphere affects what happens in the others; we can look, at most, for relative autonomy. But relative autonomy, like social meaning, is a critical principle – indeed, as I shall be arguing throughout this book, a radical principle. It is radical even though it doesn't point to a single standard against which all distributions are to be measured. There is no single standard. But there are standards (roughly knowable even when they are also controversial) for every social good and every distributive sphere in every particular society; and these standards are often violated, the goods usurped, the spheres invaded, by powerful men and women.

Dominance and Monopoly

In fact, the violations are systematic. Autonomy is a matter of social meaning and shared values, but it is more likely to make for occasional reformation and rebellion than for everyday enforcement. For all the complexity of their distributive arrangements, most societies are organized on what we might think of as a social version of the gold standard: one good or one set of goods is dominant and determinative of value in all the spheres of distribution. And that good or set of goods is commonly monopolized, its value upheld by the strength and cohesion of its owners. I call a good dominant if the individuals who have it, because they have it, can command a wide range of other goods. It is monopolized whenever a single man or woman, a monarch in the world of value – or a group of men and women, oligarchs – successfully hold it against all rivals. Dominance describes a way of using social goods that isn't limited by their intrinsic meanings or that shapes those meanings in its own image. Monopoly describes a way of owning or controlling social goods in order to exploit their dominance. When goods are scarce and widely needed, like water in the desert, monopoly itself will make them domi-

nant. Mostly, however, dominance is a more elaborate social creation, the work of many hands, mixing reality and symbol. Physical strength, familial reputation, religious or political office, landed wealth, capital, technical knowledge: each of these, in different historical periods, has been dominant; and each of them has been monopolized by some group of men and women. And then all good things come to those who have the one best thing. Possess that one, and the others come in train. Or, to change the metaphor, a dominant good is converted into another good, into many others, in accordance with what often appears to be a natural process but is in fact magical, a kind of social alchemy.

No social good ever entirely dominates the range of goods; no monopoly is ever perfect. I mean to describe tendencies only, but crucial tendencies. For we can characterize whole societies in terms of the patterns of conversion that are established within them. Some characterizations are simple: in a capitalist society, capital is dominant and readily converted into prestige and power; in a technocracy, technical knowledge plays the same part. But it isn't difficult to imagine, or to find, more complex social arrangements. Indeed, capitalism and technocracy are more complex than their names imply, even if the names do convey real information about the most important forms of sharing, dividing, and exchanging. Monopolistic control of a dominant good makes a ruling class, whose members stand atop the distributive system – much as philosophers, claiming to have the wisdom they love, might like to do. But since dominance is always incomplete and monopoly imperfect, the rule of every ruling class is unstable. It is continually challenged by other groups in the name of alternative patterns of conversion.

Distribution is what social conflict is all about. Marx's heavy emphasis on productive processes should not conceal from us the simple truth that the struggle for control of the means of production is a distributive struggle. Land and capital are at stake, and these are goods that can be shared, divided, exchanged, and endlessly converted. But land and capital are not the only dominant goods; it is possible (it has historically been possible) to come to them by way of other goods – military or political power, religious office and charisma, and so on. History reveals no single dominant good and no naturally dominant good, but only different kinds of magic and competing bands of magicians.

The claim to monopolize a dominant good – when worked up for public purposes – constitutes an ideology. Its standard form is to connect legitimate possession with some set of personal qualities through the medium of a philosophical principle. So aristocracy, or the rule of the best, is the principle of those who lay claim to breeding and intelligence: they are commonly the monopolists of landed wealth and familial reputation. Divine supremacy is the principle of those who claim to know the word of God: they are the monopolists of grace and office. Meritocracy, or the career open to talents, is the principle of those who claim to be talented: they are most often the monopolists of education. Free exchange is the principle of those who are ready, or who tell us they are ready, to put their money at risk: they are the monopolists of movable wealth. These groups – and others, too, similarly marked off by their principles and possessions – compete with one another, struggling for supremacy. One group wins, and then a different one; or coalitions are worked out, and supremacy is uneasily shared. There is no final victory, nor should there be. But that is not to say that the claims of the different groups are necessarily wrong, or that the principles they invoke are of no value as distributive criteria; the principles are often exactly right within the limits of a particular sphere. Ideologies are readily corrupted, but their corruption is not the most interesting thing about them.

It is in the study of these struggles that I have sought the guiding thread of my own argument. The struggles have, I think, a paradigmatic form. Some group of men and women – class, caste, strata, estate, alliance, or social formation – comes to enjoy a monopoly or a near monopoly of some dominant good; or, a coalition of groups comes to enjoy, and so on. This dominant good is more or less systematically converted into all sorts of other things – opportunities, powers, and reputations. So wealth is seized by the strong, honor by the well-born, office by the well educated. Perhaps the ideology that justifies the seizure is widely believed to be true. But resentment and resistance are (almost) as pervasive as belief. There are always some people, and after a time there are a great many, who think the seizure is not justice but usurpation. The ruling group does not possess, or does not uniquely possess, the qualities it claims; the conversion process violates the common understanding of the goods at stake. Social conflict is intermittent, or it is endemic; at some point, counterclaims are put for-

ward. Though these are of many different sorts, three general sorts are especially important:

1 The claim that the dominant good, whatever it is, should be redistributed so that it can be equally or at least more widely shared: this amounts to saying that monopoly is unjust.
2 The claim that the way should be opened for the autonomous distribution of all social goods: this amounts to saying that dominance is unjust.
3 The claim that some new good, monopolized by some new group, should replace the currently dominant good: this amounts to saying that the existing pattern of dominance and monopoly is unjust.

The third claim is, in Marx's view, the model of every revolutionary ideology – except, perhaps, the proletarian or last ideology. Thus, the French Revolution in Marxist theory: the dominance of noble birth and blood and of feudal landholding is ended, and bourgeois wealth is established in its stead. The original situation is reproduced with different subjects and objects (this is never unimportant), and then the class war is immediately renewed. It is not my purpose here to endorse or to criticize Marx's view. I suspect, in fact, that there is something of all three claims in every revolutionary ideology, but that, too, is not a position that I shall try to defend here. Whatever its sociological significance, the third claim is not philosophically interesting – unless one believes that there is a naturally dominant good, such that its possessors could legitimately claim to rule the rest of us. In a sense, Marx believed exactly that. The means of production is the dominant good throughout history, and Marxism is a historicist doctrine insofar as it suggests that whoever controls the prevailing means legitimately rules.[8] After the communist revolution, we shall all control the means of production: at that point, the third claim collapses into the first. Meanwhile, Marx's model is a program for ongoing distributive struggle. It will matter, of course, who wins at this or that moment, but we won't know why or how it matters if we attend only to the successive assertions of dominance and monopoly.

Simple Equality

It is with the first two claims that I shall be concerned, and ultimately with the second alone, for that one seems to me to capture best the plurality of social meanings and the real complexity of distributive systems. But the first is the more common among philosophers; it matches their own search for unity and singularity; and I shall need to explain its difficulties at some length.

Men and women who make the first claim challenge the monopoly but not the dominance of a particular social good. This is also a challenge to monopoly in general; for if wealth, for example, is dominant and widely shared, no other good can possibly be monopolized. Imagine a society in which everything is up for sale and every citizen has as much money as every other. I shall call this the "regime of simple equality." Equality is multiplied through the conversion process, until it extends across the full range of social goods. The regime of simple equality won't last for long, because the further progress of conversion, free exchange in the market, is certain to bring inequalities in its train. If one wanted to sustain simple equality over time, one would require a "monetary law" like the agrarian laws of ancient times or the Hebrew sabbatical, providing for a periodic return to the original condition. Only a centralized and activist state would be strong enough to force such a return; and it isn't clear that state officials would actually be able or willing to do that, if money were the dominant good. In any case, the original condition is unstable in another way. It's not only that monopoly will reappear, but also that dominance will disappear.

In practice, breaking the monopoly of money neutralizes its dominance. Other goods come into play, and inequality takes on new forms. Consider again the regime of simple equality. Everything is up for sale, and everyone has the same amount of money. So everyone has, say, an equal ability to buy an education for his children. Some do that, and others don't. It turns out to be a good investment: other social goods are, increasingly, offered for sale only to people with educational certificates. Soon everyone invests in education; or, more likely, the purchase is universalized through the tax system. But then the school is turned into a competitive world within which money is no longer dominant. Natural talent or family upbringing or skill in writing examinations is dominant instead, and educational success and certification are monopolized by some new group. Let's call them (what they call themselves) the "group of the talented." Eventually the members of this group claim that the good they control

should be dominant outside the school: offices, titles, prerogatives, wealth too, should all be possessed by themselves. This is the career open to talents, equal opportunity, and so on. This is what fairness requires; talent will out; and in any case, talented men and women will enlarge the resources available to everyone else. So Michael Young's meritocracy is born, with all its attendant inequalities.[9]

What should we do now? It is possible to set limits to the new conversion patterns, to recognize but constrain the monopoly power of the talented. I take this to be the purpose of John Rawls's difference principle, according to which inequalities are justified only if they are designed to bring, and actually do bring, the greatest possible benefit to the least advantaged social class.[10] More specifically, the difference principle is a constraint imposed on talented men and women, once the monopoly of wealth has been broken. It works in this way: Imagine a surgeon who claims more than his equal share of wealth on the basis of the skills he has learned and the certificates he has won in the harsh competitive struggles of college and medical school. We will grant the claim if, and only if, granting it is beneficial in the stipulated ways. At the same time, we will act to limit and regulate the sale of surgery – that is, the direct conversion of surgical skill into wealth.

This regulation will necessarily be the work of the state, just as monetary laws and agrarian laws are the work of the state. Simple equality would require continual state intervention to break up or constrain incipient monopolies and to repress new forms of dominance. But then state power itself will become the central object of competitive struggles. Groups of men and women will seek to monopolize and then to use the state in order to consolidate their control of other social goods. Or, the state will be monopolized by its own agents in accordance with the iron law of oligarchy. Politics is always the most direct path to dominance, and political power (rather than the means of production) is probably the most important, and certainly the most dangerous, good in human history.[11] Hence the need to constrain the agents of constraint, to establish constitutional checks and balances. These are limits imposed on political monopoly, and they are all the more important once the various social and economic monopolies have been broken.

One way of limiting political power is to distribute it widely. This may not work, given the well-canvassed dangers of majority tyranny; but these dangers are probably less acute than they are often made out to be. The greater danger of democratic government is that it will be weak to cope with re-emerging monopolies in society at large, with the social strength of plutocrats, bureaucrats, technocrats, meritocrats, and so on. In theory, political power is the dominant good in a democracy, and it is convertible in any way the citizens choose. But in practice, again, breaking the monopoly of power neutralizes its dominance. Political power cannot be widely shared without being subjected to the pull of all the other goods that the citizens already have or hope to have. Hence democracy is, as Marx recognized, essentially a reflective system, mirroring the prevailing and emerging distribution of social goods.[12] Democratic decision making will be shaped by the cultural conceptions that determine or underwrite the new monopolies. To prevail against these monopolies, power will have to be centralized, perhaps itself monopolized. Once again, the state must be very powerful if it is to fulfill the purposes assigned to it by the difference principle or by any similarly interventionist rule.

Still, the regime of simple equality might work. One can imagine a more or less stable tension between emerging monopolies and political constraints, between the claim to privilege put forward by the talented, say, and the enforcement of the difference principle, and then between the agents of enforcement and the democratic constitution. But I suspect that difficulties will recur, and that at many points in time the only remedy for private privilege will be statism, and the only escape from statism will be private privilege. We will mobilize power to check monopoly, then look for some way of checking the power we have mobilized. But there is no way that doesn't open opportunities for strategically placed men and women to seize and exploit important social goods.

These problems derive from treating monopoly, and not dominance, as the central issue in distributive justice. It is not difficult, of course, to understand why philosophers (and political activists, too) have focused on monopoly. The distributive struggles of the modern age begin with a war against the aristocracy's singular hold on land, office, and honor. This seems an especially pernicious monopoly because it rests upon birth and blood, with which the individual has nothing to do, rather than upon wealth, or power, or education, all of which – at least in principle – can be earned. And when every man and woman becomes, as it were, a smallholder in the sphere of birth and blood, an important victory is indeed won. Birthright ceases to be a dominant good; henceforth, it purchases very little; wealth, power, and education come to the fore. With regard to these latter goods, however, simple equality cannot be sustained at all, or it can only be sustained subject to the vicissitudes I have just described. Within their own spheres, as they are currently understood, these three tend to generate natural monopolies that can be repressed only if state power is itself dominant and if it is monopolized by officials committed to the repression. But there is, I think, another path to another kind of equality.

Tyranny and Complex Equality

I want to argue that we should focus on the reduction of dominance – not, or not primarily, on the break-up or the constraint of monopoly. We should consider what it might mean to narrow the range within which particular goods are convertible and to vindicate the autonomy of distributive spheres. But this line of argument, though it is not uncommon historically, has never fully emerged in philosophical writing. Philosophers have tended to criticize (or to justify) existing or emerging monopolies of wealth, power, and education. Or, they have criticized (or justified) particular conversions – of wealth into education or of office into wealth. And all this, most often, in the name of some radically simplified distributive system. The critique of dominance will suggest instead a way of reshaping and then living with the actual complexity of distributions.

Imagine now a society in which different social goods are monopolistically held – as they are in fact and always will be, barring continual state intervention – but in which no particular good is generally convertible. As I go along, I shall try to define the precise limits on convertibility, but for now the general description will suffice. This is a complex egalitarian society. Though there will be many small inequalities, inequality will not be multiplied through the conversion process. Nor will it be summed across different goods, because the autonomy of distributions will tend to produce a variety of local monopolies, held by different groups of men and women. I don't want to claim that complex equality would necessarily be more stable than simple equality, but I am inclined to think that it would open the way for more diffused and particularized forms of social conflict. And the resistance to convertibility would be maintained, in large degree, by ordinary men and women within their own spheres of competence and control, without large-scale state action.

This is, I think, an attractive picture, but I have not yet explained just why it is attractive. The argument for complex equality begins from our understanding – I mean, our actual, concrete, positive, and particular understanding – of the various social goods. And then it moves on to an account of the way we relate to one another through those goods. Simple equality is a simple distributive condition, so that if I have fourteen hats and you have fourteen hats, we are equal. And it is all to the good if hats are dominant, for then our equality is extended through all the spheres of social life. On the view that I shall take here, however, we simply have the same number of hats, and it is unlikely that hats will be dominant for long. Equality is a complex relation of persons, mediated by the goods we make, share, and divide among ourselves; it is not an identity of possessions. It requires then, a diversity of distributive criteria that mirrors the diversity of social goods.

The argument for complex equality has been beautifully put by Pascal in one of his *Pensées*.

The nature of tyranny is to desire power over the whole world and outside its own sphere.

There are different companies – the strong, the handsome, the intelligent, the devout – and each man reigns in his own, not elsewhere. But sometimes they meet, and the strong and the handsome fight for mastery – foolishly, for their mastery is of different kinds. They misunderstand one another, and make the mistake of each aiming at universal dominion. Nothing can win this, not even strength, for it is powerless in the kingdom of the wise . . . .

Tyranny. The following statements, therefore, are false and tyrannical: "Because I am handsome, so I should command respect." "I am strong, therefore men should love me. . . ." "I am . . . et cetera."

Tyranny is the wish to obtain by one means what can only be had by another. We owe different duties to different qualities: love is the proper response to charm, fear to strength, and belief to learning.[13]

Marx made a similar argument in his early manuscripts; perhaps he had this *pensée* in mind:

Let us assume man to be man, and his relation to the world to be a human one. Then love can only be exchanged for love, trust for trust, etc. If you wish to enjoy art you must be an artistically cultivated person; if you wish to influence other people, you must be a person who really has a stimulating and encouraging effect upon others. . . . If you love without evoking love in return, i.e., if you are not able, by the manifestation of yourself as a loving person, to make yourself a beloved person – then your love is impotent and a misfortune.[14]

These are not easy arguments, and most of my book is simply an exposition of their meaning. But here I shall attempt something more simple and schematic: a translation of the arguments into the terms I have already been using.

The first claim of Pascal and Marx is that personal qualities and social goods have their own spheres of operation, where they work their effects freely, spontaneously, and legitimately. There are ready or natural conversions that follow from, and are intuitively plausible because of, the social meaning of particular goods. The appeal is to our ordinary understanding and, at the same time, against our common acquiescence in illegitimate conversion patterns. Or, it is an appeal from our acquiescence to our resentment. There is something wrong, Pascal suggests, with the conversion of strength into belief. In political terms, Pascal means that no ruler can rightly command my opinions merely because of the power he wields. Nor can he, Marx adds, rightly claim to influence my actions: if a ruler wants to do that, he must be persuasive, helpful, encouraging, and so on. These arguments depend for their force on some shared understanding of knowledge, influence, and power. Social goods have social meanings, and we find our way to distributive justice through an interpretation of those meanings. We search for principles internal to each distributive sphere.

The second claim is that the disregard of these principles is tyranny. To convert one good into another, when there is no intrinsic connection between the two, is to invade the sphere where another company of men and women properly rules. Monopoly is not inappropriate within the spheres. There is nothing wrong, for example, with the grip that persuasive and helpful men and women (politicians) establish on political power. But the use of political power to gain access to other goods is a tyrannical use. Thus, an old description of tyranny is generalized: princes become tyrants, according to medieval writers, when they seize the property or invade the family of their subjects.[15] In political life – but more widely, too – the dominance of goods makes for the domination of people.

The regime of complex equality is the opposite of tyranny. It establishes a set of relationships such that domination is impossible. In formal terms, complex equality means that no citizen's standing in one sphere or with regard to one social good can be undercut by his standing in some other sphere, with regard to some other good. Thus, citizen X may be chosen over citizen Y for political office, and then the two of them will be unequal in the sphere of politics. But they will not be unequal generally so long as X's office gives him no advantages over Y in any other sphere – superior medical care, access to better schools for his children, entrepreneurial opportunities, and so on. So long as office is not a dominant good, is not generally convertible, office holders will stand, or at least can stand, in a relation of equality to the men and women they govern.

But what if dominance were eliminated, the autonomy of the spheres established – and the same people were successful in one sphere after another, triumphant in every company, piling up goods without the need for illegitimate conversions? This would certainly make for an inegalitarian society, but it would also suggest in the strongest way that a society of equals was not a lively possibility. I doubt that any egalitarian argument could survive in the face of such evidence. Here is a person whom we have freely chosen (without reference to his family ties or personal wealth) as our political representative. He is also a bold and inventive entrepreneur. When he was younger, he studied science, scored amazingly high grades in every exam, and made important discoveries. In war, he is surpassingly brave and wins the highest honors. Himself compassionate and compelling, he is loved by all who know him. Are there such people? Maybe so, but

I have my doubts. We tell stories like the one I have just told, but the stories are fictions, the conversion of power or money or academic talent into legendary fame. In any case, there aren't enough such people to constitute a ruling class and dominate the rest of us. Nor can they be successful in every distributive sphere, for there are some spheres to which the idea of success doesn't pertain. Nor are their children likely, under conditions of complex equality, to inherit their success. By and large, the most accomplished politicians, entrepreneurs, scientists, soldiers, and lovers will be different people; and so long as the goods they possess don't bring other goods in train, we have no reason to fear their accomplishments.

The critique of dominance and domination points toward an open-ended distributive principle. *No social good x should be distributed to men and women who possess some other good y merely because they possess y and without regard to the meaning of x.* This is a principle that has probably been reiterated, at one time or another, for every *y* that has ever been dominant. But it has not often been stated in general terms. Pascal and Marx have suggested the application of the principle against all possible *y*'s, and I shall attempt to work out that application. I shall be looking, then, not at the members of Pascal's companies – the strong or the weak, the handsome or the plain – but at the goods they share and divide. The purpose of the principle is to focus our attention; it doesn't determine the shares or the division. The principle directs us to study the meaning of social goods, to examine the different distributive spheres from the inside.

Three Distributive Principles

The theory that results is unlikely to be elegant. No account of the meaning of a social good, or of the boundaries of the sphere within which it legitimately operates, will be uncontroversial. Nor is there any neat procedure for generating or testing different accounts. At best, the arguments will be rough, reflecting the diverse and conflict-ridden character of the social life that we seek simultaneously to understand and to regulate – but not to regulate until we understand. I shall set aside, then, all claims made on behalf of any single distributive criterion, for no such criterion can possibly match the diversity of social goods.

Three criteria, however, appear to meet the requirements of the open-ended principle and have often been defended as the beginning and end of distributive justice, so I must say something about each of them. Free exchange, desert, and need: all three have real force, but none of them has force across the range of distributions. They are part of the story, not the whole of it.

Free exchange

Free exchange is obviously open-ended; it guarantees no particular distributive outcome. At no point in any exchange process plausibly called "free" will it be possible to predict the particular division of social goods that will obtain at some later point.[16] (It may be possible, however, to predict the general structure of the division.) In theory at least, free exchange creates a market within which all goods are convertible into all other goods through the neutral medium of money. There are no dominant goods and no monopolies. Hence the successive divisions that obtain will directly reflect the social meanings of the goods that are divided. For each bargain, trade, sale, and purchase will have been agreed to voluntarily by men and women who know what that meaning is, who are indeed its makers. Every exchange is a revelation of social meaning. By definition, then, no x will ever fall into the hands of someone who possesses y, merely because he possesses y and without regard to what x actually means to some other member of society. The market is radically pluralistic in its operations and its outcomes, infinitely sensitive to the meanings that individuals attach to goods. What possible restraints can be imposed on free exchange, then, in the name of pluralism?

But everyday life in the market, the actual experience of free exchange, is very different from what the theory suggests. Money, supposedly the neutral medium, is in practice a dominant good, and it is monopolized by people who possess a special talent for bargaining and trading – the green thumb of bourgeois society. Then other people demand a redistribution of money and the establishment of the regime of simple equality, and the search begins for some way to sustain that regime. But even if we focus on the first untroubled moment of simple equality – free exchange on the basis of equal shares – we will still need to set limits on what can be exchanged for what. For free exchange leaves distributions entirely in the hands of individuals, and social meanings are not subject, or are not always subject, to the interpretative decisions of individual men and women.

Consider an easy example, the case of political power. We can conceive of political power as a set of goods of varying value, votes, influence, offices, and so on. Any of these can be traded on the market and accumulated by individuals willing to sacrifice other goods. Even if the sacrifices are real, however, the result is a form of tyranny – petty tyranny, given the conditions of simple equality. Because I am willing to do without my hat, I shall vote twice; and you who value the vote less than you value my hat, will not vote at all. I suspect that the result is tyrannical even with regard to the two of us, who have reached a voluntary agreement. It is certainly tyrannical with regard to all the other citizens who must now submit to my disproportionate power. It is not the case that votes can't be bargained for; on one interpretation, that's what democratic politics is all about. And democratic politicians have certainly been known to buy votes, or to try to buy them, by promising public expenditures that benefit particular groups of voters. But this is done in public, with public funds, and subject to public approval. Private trading is ruled out by virtue of what politics, or democratic politics, is – that is, by virtue of what we did when we constituted the political community and of what we still think about what we did.

Free exchange is not a general criterion, but we will be able to specify the boundaries within which it operates only through a careful analysis of particular social goods. And having worked through such an analysis, we will come up at best with a philosophically authoritative set of boundaries and not necessarily with the set that ought to be politically authoritative. For money seeps across all boundaries – this is the primary form of illegal immigration; and just where one ought to try to stop it is a question of expediency as well as of principle. Failure to stop it at some reasonable point has consequences throughout the range of distributions, but consideration of these belongs in a later chapter.

Desert

Like free exchange, desert seems both open-ended and pluralistic. One might imagine a single neutral agency dispensing rewards and punishments, infinitely sensitive to all the forms of individual desert. Then the distributive process would indeed be centralized, but the results would still be unpredictable and various. There would be no dominant good. No *x* would ever be distributed without regard to its social meaning; for, without attention to what *x* is, it is conceptually impossible to say that *x* is deserved. All the different companies of men and women would receive their appropriate reward. How this would work in practice, however, is not easy to figure out. It might make sense to say of this charming man, for example, that he deserves to be loved. It makes no sense to say that he deserves to be loved by this (or any) particular woman. If he loves her while she remains impervious to his (real) charms, that is his misfortune. I doubt that we would want the situation corrected by some outside agency. The love of particular men and women, on our understanding of it, can only be distributed by themselves, and they are rarely guided in these matters by considerations of desert.

The case is exactly the same with influence. Here, let's say, is a woman widely thought to be stimulating and encouraging to others. Perhaps she deserves to be an influential member of our community. But she doesn't deserve that I be influenced by her or that I follow her lead. Nor would we want my followership, as it were, assigned to her by any agency capable of making such assignments. She may go to great lengths to stimulate and encourage me, and do all the things that are commonly called stimulating or encouraging. But if I (perversely) refuse to be stimulated or encouraged, I am not denying her anything that she deserves. The same argument holds by extension for politicians and ordinary citizens. Citizens can't trade their votes for hats; they can't individually decide to cross the boundary that separates the sphere of politics from the marketplace. But within the sphere of politics, they do make individual decisions; and they are rarely guided, again, by considerations of desert. It's not clear that offices can be deserved – another issue that I must postpone; but even if they can be, it would violate our understanding of democratic politics were they simply distributed to deserving men and women by some central agency.

Similarly, however we draw the boundaries of the sphere within which free exchange operates, desert will play no role within those boundaries. I am skillful at bargaining and trading, let's say, and so accumulate a large number of beautiful pictures. If we assume, as painters mostly do, that pictures are appropriately traded in the market, then there is nothing wrong with my having the pictures. My title is legitimate. But it would be odd to say that I deserve to have them simply because I am good at bargaining and trading. Desert seems to require an especially close connection between particular goods and particular persons, whereas justice only sometimes requires a connection of that sort. Still, we might insist that only artistically cultivated people, who deserve to have pictures, should actually have them. It's not difficult to imagine a distributive mechanism. The state could buy all the pictures that were offered for sale (but artists would have to be licensed, so that there wouldn't be an endless number of pictures), evaluate them, and then distribute them to artistically cultivated men and women, the better pictures to the more cultivated. The state does something like this, sometimes, with regard to things that people need – medical care, for example – but not with regard to things that people deserve. There are practical difficulties here, but I suspect a deeper reason for this difference. Desert does not have the urgency of need, and it does not involve having (owning and consuming) in the same way. Hence, we are willing to tolerate the separation of owners of paintings and artistically cultivated people, or we are unwilling to require the kinds of interference in the market that would be necessary to end the separation. Of course, public provision is always possible alongside the market, and so we might argue that artistically cultivated people deserve not pictures but museums. Perhaps they do, but they don't deserve that the rest of us contribute money or appropriate public funds for the purchase of pictures and the construction of buildings. They will have to persuade us that art is worth the money; they will have to stimulate and encourage our own artistic cultivation. And if they fail to do that, their own love of art may well turn out to be "impotent and a misfortune."

Even if we were to assign the distribution of love, influence, offices, works of art, and so on, to some omnipotent arbiters of desert, how would we select them? How could anyone deserve such a position? Only God, who knows what secrets lurk in the hearts of men, would be able to make the necessary distributions. If human beings had to do the work, the distributive mechanism would be seized early on by some band of aristocrats (so they would call themselves) with a fixed conception of what is best and most deserving, and insensitive to the diverse excellences of their fellow citizens. And then desert would cease to be a pluralist criterion; we would find ourselves face to face with a new set (of an old sort) of tyrants. We do, of course, choose people as arbiters of desert – to serve on juries, for example, or to award prizes; it will be worth considering later what the prerogatives of a juror are. But it is important to stress here that he operates within a narrow range. Desert is a strong claim, but it calls for difficult judgments; and only under very special conditions does it yield specific distributions.

Need

Finally, the criterion of need. "To each according to his needs" is generally taken as the distributive half of Marx's famous maxim: we are to distribute the wealth of the community so as to meet the necessities of its members.[17] A plausible proposal, but a radically incomplete one. In fact, the first half of the maxim is also a distributive proposal, and it doesn't fit the rule of the second half. "From each according to his ability" suggests that jobs should be distributed (or that men and women should be conscripted to work) on the basis of individual qualifications. But individuals don't in any obvious sense need the jobs for which they are qualified. Perhaps such jobs are scarce, and there are a large number of qualified candidates: which candidates need them most? If their material needs are already taken care of, perhaps they don't need to work at all. Or if, in some non-material sense, they all need to work, then that need won't distinguish among them, at least not to the naked eye. It would in any case be odd to ask a search committee looking, say, for a hospital director to make its choice on the basis of the needs of the candidates rather than on those of the staff and the patients of the hospital. But the latter set of needs, even if it isn't the subject of political disagreement, won't yield a single distributive decision.

Nor will need work for many other goods. Marx's maxim doesn't help at all with regard to the distribution of political power, honor and fame, sailboats, rare books, beautiful objects of every sort. These are not things that anyone, strictly speaking, needs. Even if we take a loose view and define the verb *to need* the way children do, as the strongest form of the verb *to want*, we still won't have an adequate distributive criterion. The sorts of things that I have listed cannot be distributed equally to those with equal wants because some of them are generally, and some of them are necessarily, scarce, and some of them can't be possessed at all unless other people, for reasons of their own, agree on who is to possess them.

Need generates a particular distributive sphere, within which it is itself the appropriate distributive principle. In a poor society, a high proportion of social wealth will be drawn into this sphere. But given the great variety of goods that arises out of any common life, even when it is lived at a very low material level, other distributive criteria will always be operating alongside of need, and it will always be necessary to worry about the boundaries that mark them off from one another. Within its sphere, certainly, need meets the general distributive rule about x and y. Needed goods distributed to needy people in proportion to their neediness are obviously not dominated by any other goods. It's not having y, but only lacking x that is relevant. But we can now see, I think, that every criterion that has any force at all meets the general rule within its own sphere, and not elsewhere. This is the effect of the rule: different goods to different companies of men and women for different reasons and in accordance with different procedures. And to get all this right, or to get it roughly right, is to map out the entire social world.

Hierarchies and Caste Societies

Or, rather, it is to map out a particular social world. For the analysis that I propose is imminent and phenomenological in character. It will yield not an ideal map or a master plan but, rather, a map and a plan appropriate to the people for whom it is drawn, whose common life it reflects. The goal, of course, is a reflection of a special kind, which picks up those deeper understandings of social goods which are not necessarily mirrored in the everyday practice of dominance and monopoly. But what if there are no such understandings? I have been assuming all along that social meanings call for the autonomy, or the relative autonomy, of distributive spheres; and so they do much of the time. But it's not impossible to imagine a society where dominance and monopoly are not violations but enactments of meaning, where social goods are conceived in hierarchical terms. In feudal Europe, for example, clothing was not a commodity (as it is today) but a badge of rank. Rank dominated dress. The meaning of clothing was shaped in the image of the feudal order. Dressing in finery to which one wasn't entitled was a kind of lie; it made a false statement about who one was. When a king or a prime minister dressed as a commoner in order to learn something about the opinions of his subjects, this was a kind of politic deceit. On the other hand, the difficulties of enforcing the clothing code (the sumptuary laws) suggests that there was all along an alternative sense of what clothing meant. At some point, at least, one can begin to recognize the boundaries of a distinct sphere within which people dress in accordance with what they can afford or what they are willing to spend or how they want to look. The sumptuary laws may still be enforced, but now one can make – and ordinary men and women do, in fact, make – egalitarian arguments against them.

Can we imagine a society in which all goods are hierarchically conceived? Perhaps the caste system of ancient India had this form (though that is a far-reaching claim, and it would be prudent to doubt its truth: for one thing, political power seems always to have escaped the laws of caste). We think of castes as rigidly segregated groups, of the caste system as a "plural society," a world of boundaries.[18] But the system is constituted by an extraordinary integration of meanings. Prestige, wealth, knowledge, office, occupation, food, clothing, even the social good of conversation: all are subject to the intellectual as well as to the physical discipline of hierarchy. And the hierarchy is itself determined by the single value of ritual purity. A certain kind of collective mobility is possible, for castes or subcastes can cultivate the outward marks of purity and (within severe limits) raise their position in the social scale. And the system as a whole rests upon a religious doctrine that promises equality of opportunity, not in this life but across the lives of the soul. The individual's status here and now "is the result of his conduct in his last incarnation . . . and if unsatisfactory can be remedied by acquiring merit in his present life which will raise his status in the next."[19] We should not assume that men and women are ever entirely content with radical inequality. Nevertheless, distributions here and now are part of a single system, largely unchallenged, in which purity is dominant over other

goods – and birth and blood are dominant over purity. Social meanings overlap and cohere.

The more perfect the coherence, the less possible it is even to think about complex equality. All goods are like crowns and thrones in a hereditary monarchy. There is no room, and there are no criteria, for autonomous distributions. In fact, however, even hereditary monarchies are rarely so simply constructed. The social understanding of royal power commonly involves some notion of divine grace, or magical gift, or human insight; and these criteria for office holding are potentially independent of birth and blood. So it is for most social goods: they are only imperfectly integrated into larger systems; they are understood, at least sometimes, in their own terms. The theory of goods explicates understandings of this sort (where they exist), and the theory of complex equality exploits them. We say, for example, that it is tyrannical for a man without grace or gift or insight to sit upon the throne. And this is only the first and most obvious kind of tyranny. We can search for many other kinds.

Tyranny is always specific in character: a particular boundary crossing, a particular violation of social meaning. Complex equality requires the defense of boundaries; it works by differentiating goods just as hierarchy works by differentiating people. But we can only talk of a *regime* of complex equality when there are many boundaries to defend; and what the right number is cannot be specified. There is no right number. Simple equality is easier: one dominant good widely distributed makes an egalitarian society. But complexity is hard: how many goods must be autonomously conceived before the relations they mediate can become the relations of equal men and women? There is no certain answer and hence no ideal regime. But as soon as we start to distinguish meanings and mark out distributive spheres, we are launched on an egalitarian enterprise.

The Setting of the Argument

The political community is the appropriate setting for this enterprise. It is not, to be sure, a self-contained distributive world: only the world is a self-contained distributive world, and contemporary science fiction invites us to speculate about a time when even that won't be true. Social goods are shared, divided, and exchanged across political frontiers. Monopoly and dominance operate almost as easily beyond the frontiers as within them. Things are moved, and people move themselves, back and forth across the lines. Nevertheless, the political community is probably the closest we can come to a world of common meanings. Language, history, and culture come together (come more closely together here than anywhere else) to produce a collective consciousness. National character, conceived as a fixed and permanent mental set, is obviously a myth; but the sharing of sensibilities and intuitions among the members of a historical community is a fact of life. Sometimes political and historical communities don't coincide, and there may well be a growing number of states in the world today where sensibilities and intuitions aren't readily shared; the sharing takes place in smaller units. And then, perhaps, we should look for some way to adjust distributive decisions to the requirements of those units. But this adjustment must itself be worked out politically, and its precise character will depend upon understandings shared among the citizens about the value of cultural diversity, local autonomy, and so on. It is to these understandings that we must appeal when we make our arguments – all of us, not philosophers alone; for in matters of morality, argument simply is the appeal to common meanings.

Politics, moreover, establishes its own bonds of commonality. In a world of independent states, political power is a local monopoly. These men and women, we can say, under whatever constraints, shape their own destiny. Or they struggle as best they can to shape their own destiny. And if their destiny is only partially in their own hands, the struggle is entirely so. They are the ones whose decision it is to tighten or loosen distributive criteria, to centralize or decentralize procedures, to intervene or refuse to intervene in this or that distributive sphere. Probably, some set of leaders make the actual decisions, but the citizens should be able to recognize the leaders as their own. If the leaders are cruel or stupid or endlessly venal, as they often are, the citizens or some of the citizens will try to replace them, fighting over the distribution of political power. The fight will be shaped by the institutional structures of the community – that is, by the outcomes of previous fights. Politics present is the product of politics past. It establishes an unavoidable setting for the consideration of distributive justice.

There is one last reason for adopting the view of the political community as setting, a reason that I shall elaborate on at some length in the next chapter. The community is itself a good – conceivably the most important good – that gets distributed. But it is a good that can only be distributed by taking people in, where all the senses of that latter phrase are relevant: they must be physically admitted and politically received. Hence membership cannot be handed out by some external agency; its value depends upon an internal decision. Were there no communities capable of making such decisions, there would in this case be no good worth distributing.

The only plausible alternative to the political community is humanity itself, the society of nations, the entire globe. But were we to take the globe as our setting, we would have to imagine what does not yet exist: a community that included all men and women everywhere. We would have to invent a set of common meanings for these people, avoiding if we could the stipulation of our own values. And we would have to ask the members of this hypothetical community (or their hypothetical representatives) to agree among themselves on what distributive arrangements and patterns of conversion are to count as just. Ideal contractualism or undistorted communication, which represents one approach – not my own – to justice in particular communities, may well be the only approach for the globe as a whole.[20] But whatever the hypothetical agreement, it could not be enforced without breaking the political monopolies of existing states and centralizing power at the global level. Hence the agreement (or the enforcement) would make not for complex but for simple equality – if power was dominant and widely shared – or simply for tyranny – if power was seized, as it probably would be, by a set of international bureaucrats. In the first case, the people of the world would have to live with the difficulties I have described: the continual reappearance of local privilege, the continual reassertion of global statism. In the second case, they would have to live with difficulties that are considerably worse. I will have a little more to say about these difficulties later. For now I take them to be reasons enough to limit myself to cities, countries, and states that have, over long periods of time, shaped their own internal life.

With regard to membership, however, important questions arise between and among such communities, and I shall try to focus on them and to draw into the light all those occasions when ordinary citizens focus on them. In a limited way, the theory of complex equality can be extended from particular communities to the society of nations, and the extension has this advantage: it will not run roughshod over local understandings and decisions. Just for that reason, it also will not yield a uniform system of distributions across the

globe, and it will only begin to address the problems raised by mass poverty in many parts of the globe. I don't think the beginning unimportant; in any case, I can't move beyond it. To do that would require a different theory, which would take as its subject not the common life of citizens but the more distanced relations of states: a different theory, a different book, another time.

Notes

1 See John Rawls, *A Theory of Justice* (Cambridge, Mass., 1971); Jürgen Habermas, *Legitimation Crisis*, trans. Thomas McCarthy (Boston, 1975), esp. p. 113; Bruce Ackerman, *Social Justice in the Liberal State* (New Haven, 1980).

2 Robert Nozick makes a similar argument in *Anarchy, State, and Utopia* (New York, 1974), pp. 149–50, but with radically individualistic conclusions that seem to me to miss the social character of production.

3 Ralph Waldo Emerson, "Ode," in *The Complete Essays and Other Writings*, ed. Brooks Atkinson (New York, 1940), p. 770.

4 John Stuart Mill, *On Liberty*, in *The Philosophy of John Stuart Mill*, ed. Marshall Cohen (New York, 1961), p. 255. For an anthropological account of liking and not liking social goods, see Mary Douglas and Baron Isherwood, *The World of Goods* (New York, 1979).

5 William James, quoted in C.R. Snyder and Howard Fromkin, *Uniqueness: The Human Pursuit of Difference* (New York, 1980), p. 108.

6 Aren't social meanings, as Marx said, nothing other than "the ideas of the ruling class," "the dominant material relationships grasped as ideas"? (Karl Marx, *The German Ideology*, ed. R. Pascal (New York, 1947), p. 89). I don't think that they are ever only that or simply that, though the members of the ruling class and the intellectuals they patronize may well be in a position to exploit and distort social meanings in their own interests. When they do that, however, they are likely to encounter resistance, rooted (intellectually) in those same meanings. A people's culture is always a joint, even if it isn't an entirely cooperative, production; and it is always a complex production. The common understanding of particular goods incorporates principles, procedures, conceptions of agency, that the rulers would not choose if they were choosing *right now* – and so provides the terms of social criticism. The appeal to what I shall call "internal" principles against the usurpations of powerful men and women is the ordinary form of critical discourse.

7 Bernard Williams, *Problems of the Self:*

Philosophical Papers, 1956–1972 (Cambridge, England, 1973), pp. 230–49 ("The Idea of Equality"). This essay is one of the starting points of my own thinking about distributive justice. See also the critique of Williams's argument (and of an earlier essay of my own) in Amy Gutmann, *Liberal Equality* (Cambridge, England, 1980), chap. 4.

8 See Alan W. Wood, "The Marxian Critique of Justice," *Philosophy and Public Affairs* 1 (1972): 244–82.

9 Michael Young, *The Rise of the Meritocracy, 1870–2033* (Harmondsworth, England, 1961) – a brilliant piece of social science fiction.

10 Rawls, *Theory of Justice*, pp. 75ff.

11 I should note here what will become more clear as I go along, that political power is a special sort of good. It has a twofold character. First, it is like the other things that men and women make, value, exchange, and share: sometimes dominant, sometimes not; sometimes widely held, sometimes the possession of a very few. And, second, it is unlike all the other things because, however it is had and whoever has it, political power is the regulative agency for social goods generally. It is used to defend the boundaries of all the distributive spheres, including its own, and to enforce the common understandings of what goods are and what they are for. (But it can also be used, obviously, to invade the different spheres and to override those understandings.) In this second sense, we might say, indeed, that political power is always dominant – at the boundaries, but not within them. The central problem of political life is to maintain that crucial distinction between "at" and "in." But this is a problem that cannot be solved given the imperatives of simple equality.

12 See Marx's comment, in his "Critique of the Gotha Program," that the democratic republic is the "form of state" within which the class struggle will be fought to a conclusion: the struggle is immediately and without distortion reflected in political life (Marx and Engels, *Selected Works* [Moscow, 1951], vol. II, p. 31).

13 Blaise Pascal, *The Pensées*, trans. J.M. Cohen

(Harmondsworth, England, 1961), p. 96 (no. 244).

14 Karl Marx, *Economic and Philosophical Manuscripts*, in *Early Writings*, ed. T.B. Bottomore (London, 1963), pp. 193–94. It is interesting to note an earlier echo of Pascal's argument in Adam Smith's *Theory of Moral Sentiments* (Edinburgh, 1813), vol. I, pp. 378–79; but Smith seems to have believed that distributions in his own society actually conformed to this view of appropriateness – a mistake neither Pascal nor Marx ever made.

15 See the summary account in Jean Bodin, *Six Books of a Commonweale*, ed. Kenneth Douglas McRae (Cambridge, Mass., 1962), pp. 210–18.

16 Cf. Nozick on "patterning," *Anarchy, State, and Utopia* [2], pp. 155ff.

17 Marx, "Gotha Program", (above) p. 23.

18 J.H. Hutton, *Caste in India: Its Nature, Function, and Origins* (4th ed., Bombay, 1963), pp. 127–28. I have also drawn on Célestin Bouglé, *Essays on the Caste System*, trans. D.F. Pocock (Cambridge, England, 1971), esp. Part III, chaps. 3 and 4; and Louis Dumont, *Homo Hierarchus: The Caste System and Its Implications* (revised English ed., Chicago, 1980).

19 Hutton, *Caste in India*, (above) p. 125.

20 See Charles Beitz, *Political Theory and International Relations* (Princeton, 1979), part III, for an effort to apply Rawlsian ideal contractualism to international society.

31

Justice Engendered

Martha Minow

1 Introduction

A What's the difference?

The use of anesthesia in surgery spread quickly once discovered. Yet the nineteenth-century doctors who adopted anesthesia selected which patients needed it and which deserved it. Both the medical literature and actual medical practices distinguished people's need for painkillers based on race, gender, ethnicity, age, temperament, personal habits, and economic class. Some people's pain was thought more serious than others; some people were thought to be hardy enough to withstand pain. Doctors believed that women, for example, needed painkillers more than men and that the rich and educated needed painkillers more than the poor and uneducated. How might we, today, evaluate these examples of discrimination? What differences between people should matter, and for what purposes?

The endless variety of our individualism means that we suffer different kinds of pain and may well experience pain differently. But when professionals use categories like gender, race, ethnicity, and class to presume real differences in people's pain and entitlement to help, I worry. I worry that unfairness will result under the guise of objectivity and neutrality. I worry that a difference assigned by someone with power over a more vulnerable person will become endowed

Originally published in *Harvard Law Review*, 101 (1987), 10–95. Copyright © 1987 by Harvard Law Review Association. Reprinted by permission of Harvard Law Review Association.

with an apparent reality, despite powerful competing views. If no one can really know another's pain, who shall decide how to treat pain, and along what calculus? These are questions of justice, not science. These are questions of complexity, not justifications for passivity, because failing to notice another's pain is an act with significance.

B The problem and the argument

Each term, the Supreme Court and the nation confront problems of difference in this heterogeneous society. The cases that present these problems attract heightened media attention and reenact continuing struggles over the meanings of subgroup identity in a nation committed to an idea called equality. The drama of these cases reveals the enduring grip of "difference" in the public imagination, and the genuine social and economic conflicts over what particular differences come to mean over time. During the 1986 term, litigators framed for the Court issues about the permissible legal meanings of difference in the lives of individuals, minority groups, and majority groups in cases involving gender, race, ethnicity, religion, and handicap.

Uniting these questions is the dilemma of difference. The dilemma of difference has three versions. The first version is the dilemma that we may recreate difference either by noticing it or by ignoring it. Decisions about employment, benefits, and treatment in society should not turn on an individual's race, gender, religion, or membership in any other group about which some have deprecating or hostile attitudes. Yet refusing to acknowledge these differences may make them continue to matter in a world constructed with some groups, but not others, in mind. If women's biological differences from men justify special benefits for women in the workplace, are women thereby helped or hurt? Are negative active stereotypes reinforced, and does that matter? Focusing on differences poses the risk of recreating them. Especially when used by decision makers who award benefits and distribute burdens, traits of difference can carry meanings uncontrolled and unwelcomed by those to whom they are assigned. Yet denying those differences undermines the value they may have to those who cherish them as part of their own identity.

The second version of the dilemma is the riddle of neutrality. If the public schools must remain neutral toward religion, do they do so by balancing the teaching of evolution with the teaching of scientific arguments about divine creation – or does this accommodation of a religious view depart from the requisite neutrality? Governmental neutrality may freeze in place the past consequences of differences. Yet any departure from neutrality in governmental standards uses governmental power to make those differences matter and thus symbolically reinforces them.

The third version of the dilemma is the choice between broad discretion, which permits individualized decisions, and formal rules that specify categorical decisions for the dispensing of public – or private – power. If the criminal justice system must not take the race of defendants or victims into account, is this goal achieved by granting discretion to prosecutors and jurors, who can then make individualized decisions but may also introduce racial concerns, or should judges impose formal rules specifying conditions under which racial concerns must be made explicit to guard against them? By granting discretion to officials or to private decision makers, legislators and judges disengage themselves from directly endorsing the use of differences in decisions; yet this grant of discretion also allows those decision makers to give significance to differences. Formal rules constrain public or private discretion, but their very specificity may make differences significant.

I believe these dilemmas arise out of powerful unstated assumptions about whose point of view matters and about what is given and what is mutable in the world. "Difference" is only meaningful as a comparison. I am no more different from you than you are from me. A short person is different only in relation to a tall one. Legal treatment of difference tends to take for granted an assumed point of comparison: Women are compared to the unstated norm of men, "minority" races to whites, handicapped persons to the able-bodied, and "minority" religions to "majorities." Such assumptions work in part through the very structure of our language, which embeds the unstated points of comparison inside categories that bury their perspective and wrongly imply a natural fit with the world. The term *working mother* modifies the general category *mother*, revealing that the general term carries some unstated common meanings (that is, a woman who cares for her children full time without pay), which, even if unintended, must expressly be modified. Legal treatment of difference thus tends to treat as unproblematic the point of view from which difference is seen, assigned, or ignored, rather than acknowledging that the problem of difference can be described and understood from multiple points of view.

Noticing the unstated point of comparison and point of view used in assessments of difference does not eliminate the dilemma of difference; instead, more importantly, it links problems of difference to questions of vantage point. I will argue that what initially may seem to be an objective stance may appear partial from another point of view. Furthermore, what initially appears to be a fixed and objective difference may seem from another viewpoint like the subordination or exclusion of some people by others. Regardless of which perspective ultimately seems persuasive, the possibility of multiple viewpoints challenges the assumption of objectivity and shows how claims to knowledge bear the imprint of those making the claims.

Difference may seem salient not because of a trait intrinsic to the person but instead because the dominant institutional arrangements were designed without that trait in mind. Consider the difference between buildings built without considering the needs of people in wheelchairs and buildings that are accessible to people in wheelchairs. Institutional arrangements define whose reality is to be the norm and make what is known as different seem natural. By asking how power influences knowledge, we can address the question of whether difference was assigned as an expression of domination or as a remedy for past domination. In so doing, we can determine the risks of creating a new pattern of domination while remedying unequal power relationships.

The commitment to seek out and to appreciate a perspective other than one's own animates the reasoning of some Supreme Court justices, some of the time. It is a difficult commitment to make and to fulfill. Aspects of language, social structure, and political culture steer in the opposite direction: toward assertions of absolute categories transcending human choice or perspective. It is not only that justice is created by, and defeated by, people who have genders, races, ethnicities, religions – people who are themselves situated in relation to the differences they discuss. It is also the case that justice is made by people who live in a world already made. Existing institutions and language already carve the world and already express and recreate attitudes about what counts as a difference and who or what is the relevant point of comparison. Once we see that any point of view, including one's own, *is* a point of view, we will realize that every difference we see is seen in relation to something already assumed as the starting point. Then we can expose for debate what the starting points should be. The task for judges is to identify vantage points, to learn how to adopt contrasting vantage points, and to decide which vantage points to embrace in given circumstances.

A difficulty here, as always, is who is "we." Writing not just for judges, but for all who judge, I mean to invoke a broad array of people in the exploration of justice. Yet the perspective I advance cannot escape my own critique of the partiality of every perspective. The very focus on the "difference" problem selects that problem rather than others (for example, the loss of coherence and tradition in society) as the point of discussion. My use of "we," then, represents an invitation to the reader to assent, to disagree, but above all, to engage with this focus. I use "we," moreover, to emphasize the human authorship of the problems and solutions at hand, and to avoid locutions that eliminate human pronouns.

In Part 2, I explore three versions of the dilemma of difference, illustrating how they arose in the contexts of religion, ethnicity, race, gender, and handicapping conditions in cases before the Supreme Court during the 1986 term. Next, in Part 3, I turn to the influence in these cases of unstated assumptions about points of reference and starting points for analysis, assumptions that are continually reinforced by established modes of thought, language, and patterns of legal reasoning.

In Part 4, I first identify how members of the Court periodically challenge these assumptions by seeking the perspective of individuals and groups unlike themselves. Unfortunately, the justices are not always successful in their efforts. Feminist scholars have done much to reveal the persistence of these assumptions, particularly the assumption that men – their needs and experiences – are the standard for individual rights, and in Part 4 I go on to develop and pursue this basic feminist insight. In so doing, I also explore ways in which some feminist analyses have recreated the problems they sought to address, elaborating the idea of "woman's experience," leaving unstated the race, ethnicity, religion, and bodily condition presumed in the identification of woman's point of view.

What, then, is to be done? In Part 5, I urge the judiciary to make a perpetual commitment to approach questions of difference by seeking out unstated assumptions about difference and typically unheard points of view. There will not be a rule, a concept, a norm, or a test to apply to these problems. The very yearning for simple and clear solutions is part of the difference problem. The allure of this simplicity reflects our dangerous tendency to assign differences, to pretend that they are natural, and to use categorical solutions to cut off rather than to promote understanding. Instead of a new solution, I urge struggles over descriptions of reality. Litigation in the Supreme Court should be an opportunity to endow rival vantage points with the reality that power enables, to redescribe and remake the meanings of difference in a world that has treated only some vantage points on difference as legitimate.

Far from being unmanageable, this approach describes what happens already in the best practices of justice. Justice, in this view, is not abstract, universal, or neutral. Instead, justice is the quality of human engagement with multiple perspectives framed by, but not limited to, the relationships of power in which they are formed. Decisions, then, can and must be made. Despite the distortions sometimes injected by a language of objectivity and neutrality, the Supreme Court has "engendered" justice in many cases. These cases show the commitment in contemporary statutory and constitutional law to give equality meaning for people once thought to be "different" from those in charge. From the work of this term, which is the last for Justice Powell, the first for Justice Scalia, and the first for Chief Justice Rehnquist as head of the Court, I hope to demonstrate how our common humanity wins when the Court struggles with our differences.

2 A Case of Differences

Arguments before the Supreme Court engage all three versions of the difference dilemma and cut across cases otherwise differentiated by doctrine and contexts. The dilemma arises in both equality and religion cases, and in statutory and constitutional contexts. This section explicitly draws connections across these seemingly disparate cases and explores the dilemma in cases decided in the 1986 term.

A The dilemma of recreating difference both by ignoring it and by noticing it

California Federal Savings & Loan Association v. Guerra (Cal Fed)[1] presented in classic form the dilemma of recreating difference through both noticing and ignoring it. Petitioners, a collection of employers, argued that a California statute[2] mandating a qualified right to reinstatement following an unpaid pregnancy disability leave amounted to special preferential treatment, in violation of Title VII's prohibition of discrimination on the basis of pregnancy.[3] Writing an opinion announcing the judgment for the Court, Justice Marshall transformed the question presented by the plaintiffs: Instead of asking whether the federal ban against discrimination on the basis of pregnancy precluded a state's decision to require special treatment for pregnancy, the majority asked whether the state could adopt a minimum protection for pregnant workers while still permitting employers to avoid treating pregnant workers differently by extending similar benefits to nonpregnant workers. Framing the problem this way, the majority ruled that "Congress intended the PDA to be 'a floor beneath which pregnancy disability benefits may not drop – not a ceiling above which they may not rise.'"[4] The majority acknowledged the risk that recognizing the difference of pregnancy could recreate its stigmatizing effects, but noted that "a State could not mandate special treatment of pregnant workers based on stereotypes or gen-

eralizations about their needs and abilities."[5] Thus, despite the federal antidiscrimination requirement, the majority found that states could direct employers to take the sheer physical disability of the pregnancy difference into account, but not any stereotyped views associated with that difference. The majority gave two responses to the problem of difference: First, accommodating pregnant workers would secure a workplace that would equally enable both female and male employees to work and have a family; second, the federal and state statutes should be construed as inviting employers to provide the same benefits to men and women in comparable situations of disability.[6]

Writing for the dissenters, Justice White maintained that the California statute required disability leave policies for pregnant workers even in the absence of similar policies for men. It thus violated the PDA, which "leaves no room for preferential treatment of pregnant workers."[7] In the face of this conflict, the federal statute must preempt the state law. The commands of nondiscrimination prohibit taking differences into account, Justice White argued, regardless of the impact of this neglect on people with the difference. Justice White acknowledged the majority's argument that preferential treatment would revive nineteenth-century protective legislation, perpetuating sex role stereotypes and "imped[ing] women in their efforts to take their rightful place in the workplace."[8] For Justice White, however, such arguments were irrelevant, because the Court's role was restricted to interpreting congressional intent and thus would not permit consideration of the arguments about stereotyping. Yet to some extent, the issue of stereotypes was unavoidable: The dilemma in the case, from one point of view, was whether women could secure a benefit that would eliminate a burden connected with their gender, without at the same time reactivating negative meanings about their gender.

In two other cases in the 1986 term, the Court confronted the dilemma of recreating difference in situations in which individuals claimed to be members of minority races in order to obtain special legal protections. By claiming an identity in order to secure some benefit from it, the individuals faced the dilemma that they might fuel negative meanings of that identity, meanings beyond their control. Although racial identification under federal civil rights statutes provides a means of legal redress, it also runs the risk of recreating stigmatizing associations, thereby stimulating prejudice.

In *Saint Francis College v. Al-Khazraji*,[9] a man from Iraq who had failed to secure tenure from his employer, a private college, brought a claim of racial discrimination under 42 U.S.C. section 1981. His case foundered, however, when the lower courts rejected his claim that his Arab identity constituted racial membership of the sort protected by the federal statute.

In *Shaare Tefila Congregation v. Cobb*,[10] members of a Jewish congregation whose synagogue was defaced by private individuals alleged violations of the federal guarantee against interference with property rights on racial grounds. The difference dilemma appeared on the face of the complaint: The petitioners argued that Jews are not a racially distinct group, and yet they claimed that Jews should be entitled to protection against racial discrimination because others treat them as though they were distinct. The petitioners thus demonstrated their reluctance to have a difference identified in a way that they themselves could not control, while simultaneously expressing their desire for protection against having that difference assigned to them by others. To gain this protection, the petitioners had to identify themselves through the very category they rejected as a definition of themselves. Both the district court and the court of appeals refused to allow the petitioners to be included in the protected group on the basis of the attitudes of others, without some proof of well-established traits internal to the group. The court of appeals reasoned:

> Although we sympathize with appellant's position, we conclude that it cannot support a claim of racial discrimination solely on the basis of defendants' perception of Jews as being members of a racially distinct group. To allow otherwise would permit charges of racial discrimination to arise out of nothing more than the subjective, irrational perceptions of defendants.[11]

In contrast, one member of the appeals panel, dissenting on this point, argued: "Misperception lies at the heart of prejudice, and the animus formed of such ignorance sows malice and hatred wherever it operates without restriction."[12]

Is the cause of individualized treatment advanced by allowing groups to claim legal protections by dint of group membership, however erroneously assigned by others? Conversely, may denying these claims of legal protection against assigned difference allow the Supreme Court to avoid addressing the dilemma and thereby reenact it? In both *Shaare Tefila* and *Saint Francis*, the Court asked only whether the legislators adopting the antidiscrimination legislation shortly after the Civil War viewed Jews and Arabs as distinct races. The Court answered the question affirmatively in both cases but based its conclusion on a review of the legislative histories and contemporaneous dictionaries and encyclopedias instead of tackling the difference dilemma directly.

The Court's historical test for membership in a minority race effectively revitalized not just categorical thinking in general, but the specific categorical thinking about race prevailing in the 1860s, despite considerable changes in scientific and moral understandings of the use of abstract categories to label people and solve problems. Whether the issue is gender, religion, or race, reviving old sources for defining group difference may reinvigorate older attitudes about the meanings of group traits. Denying the presence of those traits, however, and their significance in society, deprives individuals of protection against discrimination due to outmoded or unsubstantiated conceptions of group difference.

B Neutrality and nonneutrality: the dilemma of government embroilment in difference

The dilemma of difference appears especially acute for a government committed to acting neutrally. Neutral means might not produce neutral results, given historic practices and social arrangements that have not been neutral. For example, securing neutrality toward religious differences is the explicit goal of both the First Amendment's ban against the establishment of religion and its protection of the free exercise of religion. Thus to be truly neutral, the government must walk a narrow path between promoting or endorsing religion and failing to make room for religious exercise. Accommodation of religious practices may look nonneutral, but failure to accommodate may also seem nonneutral by burdening the religious minority whose needs were not built into the structure of mainstream institutions.

The "creation science" case, *Edwards v.*

Aguillard,[13] raised the question of how the government, in the form of public schools, can respect religious differences while remaining neutral toward them. In *Edwards*, parents and students claimed that a Louisiana statute requiring public schools to teach creation science whenever they taught the theory of evolution violated the establishment clause. Community members subscribing to fundamentalist religious beliefs, however, have argued that public school instruction in evolution alone is not neutral, because it gives a persuasive advantage to views that undermine their own religious beliefs. Relying on similar arguments, the state avowed a neutral, nonreligious purpose for its statute.[14]

The majority, in an opinion by Justice Brennan, concluded that the legislation was actually intended to "provide persuasive advantage to a particular religious doctrine that rejects the factual basis of evolution in its entirety."[15] By contrast, the dissenting opinion by Justice Scalia, which was joined by Chief Justice Rehnquist, expressly tangled with the neutrality problem, noting the difficult tensions between antiestablishment and free exercise concerns and between neutrality through indifference and neutrality through accommodation. In the end, the dissent was moved by the state's attempt to avoid undermining the different views of fundamentalist Christian students, while the majority was persuaded that the statute gave an illegal preference to a particular religious view. For both sides, however, the central difficulty was how to find a neutral position between these two risks.

In a second case, *Hobbie v. Unemployment Appeals Commission*,[16] the neutrality problem arose when the Court reviewed a state's decision to deny unemployment benefits to a woman under an apparently neutral scheme. Hobbie was discharged from her job when she refused to work during her religious Sabbath. The state argued that Hobbie's refusal to work amounted to misconduct related to her work and rendered her ineligible for unemployment benefits under a statute limiting compensation to persons who become "unemployed through no fault of their own."[17] The Court rejected this emphasis on the cause of the conflict, because the "salient inquiry" was whether the denial of unemployment benefits unlawfully burdened Hobbie's free exercise right. The Court also rejected the state's claim that making unemployment benefits available to Hobbie would unconstitutionally establish religion by easing eligibility requirements for religious adherents.[18] By requiring accommodation for free exercise, despite charges of establishing religion, the Court's solution thus framed a dilemma of neutrality: How can the government's means be neutral in a world that is not itself neutral?

A facially neutral state policy on unemployment compensation also figured in *Wimberly v. Labor & Industrial Relations Commission*.[19] Wimberly had taken a pregnancy leave from her job with no guarantee of reinstatement, and upon her return the employer told her that there were no positions available. Her application for unemployment benefits was denied under a state law disqualifying applicants unless their reasons for leaving were directly attributable to the work or to the employer. Wimberly argued that a federal statute forbidding discrimination in unemployment compensation "solely on the basis of pregnancy or termination of pregnancy"[20] required accommodation for women who leave work because of pregnancy.

The Supreme Court unanimously rejected Wimberly's claim that this denial of benefits contravened the federal statute. The Court found that the state had not singled out pregnancy as the reason for withholding unemployment benefits; instead, pregnancy fell within a broad class of reasons for unemployment unrelated to work or to the employer. The Court interpreted the federal statute to forbid discrimination but not to mandate preferential treatment. In the Court's eyes, then, it was neutral to have a general rule denying unemployment benefits to anyone unemployed for reasons unrelated to the workplace or the employer.[21]

In essence, the Court interpreted the federal statutory scheme as granting discretion to state legislatures to define their own terms for disqualification from eligibility for benefits. Although many states provide unemployment benefits for women who leave their jobs because of pregnancy, subsuming it under terms like "good cause," along with other compelling personal reasons, injury, illness, or the federal ban against refusing benefits "solely on the basis of pregnancy" does not, according to the Court, compel such coverage. A state choosing to define its unemployment eligibility narrowly enough to disqualify not just those who leave work due to pregnancy but also those who leave work for good cause, illness, or compelling personal reasons may thus do so without violating federal law.

The Court in *Wimberly* rejected the argument that ignoring the difference of pregnancy produces illicit discrimination under an apparently neutral unemployment benefits rule. In *Hobbie*, on the other hand, the Court embraced the view that ignoring a religious difference produces illicit discrimination under an apparently neutral unemployment benefits rule. In both cases, the Court grappled with the dilemma of whether to give meaning to neutrality by recognizing or not recognizing difference.

C Discretion and formality: the dilemma of using power to differentiate

The Court's commitment to the rule of law often leads it to specify, in formal terms, the rules that govern the decisions of others. This practice can secure adherence to the goals of equality and neutrality by ensuring that differences are not taken into account except in the manner explicitly specified by the Court. Although likely to promote accountability, this solution of formal rules has drawbacks. Making and enforcing specific rules engages the Court in the problem of reinvesting differences with significance by noticing them. Specifically requiring the Court to articulate permissible and impermissible uses of difference may enshrine categorical analysis and move further away from the ideal of treating persons as individuals. One way for the Court to resolve the difference dilemma is to grant or cede discretion to other decision makers. Then the problems from both noticing and ignoring difference, and from risking nonneutrality in means and results, are no longer problems for the Court but, instead, matters within the discretion of other private or public decision makers. This approach simply moves the problem to another forum, allowing the decision maker with the discretion to take difference into account in an impermissible manner. The tension between formal, predictable rules and individualized judgments under discretionary standards thus assumes heightened significance in dilemmas of difference.

This dilemma of discretion and formality most vividly occupied the Court in *McCleskey v. Kemp*,[22] in which the Court evaluated charges of racial discrimination in the administration of the death penalty in Georgia's criminal justice system. A statistical study of over two thousand murder cases in Georgia during the 1970s, submitted by the defendant and assumed by the Court to be valid, demonstrated that the likelihood of a defendant's receiving the death sentence was correlated with the victim's race and, to a lesser extent, the defendant's race. According to the study, black defendants convicted of killing white victims "have the greatest likelihood of receiving the death penalty." Should the Court treat a sentencing "discrepancy that appears to correlate with race" as a defect requiring judicial constraints on prosecutorial and jury discretion, or as an unavoidable consequence of such discretion? In making this choice, the majority and the dissenters each latched onto opposing sides of the dilemma about discretion and formality.

Justice Powell, for the majority, began by asserting that the discretion of the jury is critical to the criminal justice system and operates to the advantage of criminal defendants because it permits individualized treatment rather than arbitrary application of rules. Because of the importance of discretion, unexplained racial discrepancies in the sentencing process should not be assumed to be invidious or unconstitutional. In the majority's view, recognizing claims such as McCleskey's would open the door "to claims based on unexplained discrepancies that correlate to membership in other minority groups, and even to gender" or physical appearance. This argument, perhaps meant in part to trivialize the dissent's objections by linking physical appearance with race, sex, and ethnicity, implied that discrepancies in criminal sentences are random and too numerous to control. Furthermore, in the majority's view, any attempt to channel discretion runs the risk of undermining it altogether: "It is difficult to imagine guidelines that would produce the predictability sought by the dissent without sacrificing the discretion essential to a humane and fair system of criminal justice."[23]

Justice Brennan, in dissent, approached the problem of discretion and formality from the other direction. Like the majority, Justice Brennan asserted that imposition of the death penalty must be based on an "individualized moral inquiry." To Justice Brennan, however, the statistical correlation between death sentences and the race of defendants and victims showed that participants in the state criminal justice system had, in fact, considered race and produced judgments "completely at odds with [the] concern that an individual be evaluated as a unique human being." Justice Brennan argued that "discretion is a means, not an end" and that, under the circumstances, the Court must monitor the discretion of others. Justice Brennan also responded to the majority's fear of widespread challenges to all aspects of criminal sentencing: "Taken on its face, such a statement seems to suggest a fear of too much justice. . . . The prospect that there may be more widespread abuse than McCleskey documents may be dismaying, but it does not justify complete abdication of our judicial role."[24]

Justice Stevens, also in dissent, argued that there remains a middle road between forbidding the death penalty and ignoring, in the name of prosecutorial and jury discretion, the correlation between the death penalty and the defendant's and victim's races. He urged a specific rule: The class of defendants eligible for the death penalty should be narrowed to the category of cases, identified by the study, in which "prosecutors consistently seek, and juries consistently impose, the death penalty without regard to the race of the victim or the race of the offender."[25]

For the majority in *McCleskey*, constricting prosecutorial and jury discretion would push toward so regulated a world that the criminal justice system would no longer produce particularized, individualized decisions about defendants. For the dissenters, the Court's acquiescence in unmonitored prosecutorial and jury discretion, in the face of sentencing disparities correlated with race, condoned and perpetuated racial discrimination and thereby allowed racial stereotyping to be substituted for individualized justice.

Debate among the justices last term in an entirely different context exposed a similar tension between rules and discretion. In *Corporation of the Presiding Bishop of the Church of Jesus Christ of Latter-Day Saints v. Amos (Presiding Bishop)*,[26] the Court considered whether the federal statute exempting religious organizations from nondiscrimination requirements in their employment decisions arising out of nonprofit activities violated the establishment clause. The Court's majority endorsed the legislative grant of discretion to religious organizations while rejecting the discharged engineer's claims that such state accommodation unconstitutionally promotes religion.

The opinions in the case clearly illustrate the dilemma of discretion. The majority reasoned that under the exemption the preference for religion was not exercised by the government but, rather, by the church. Justice O'Connor, how-

ever, pointed out in her concurring opinion that allowing discretion to the private decision maker to use religion in his decisions inevitably engaged the government in that differentiation. The Court could not, simply by protecting the discretion of religious organizations, escape consideration of the tension between the constitutional command against promoting religion and the constitutional demand for free exercise of religion. Instead, Justice O'Connor argued, in distinguishing constitutional accommodation of religion from unconstitutional assistance to religious organizations, the Court must evaluate the message of the government's policy as perceived by an "objective observer."[27]

Justice Brennan's separate opinion also treated this tension as unavoidable. Yet Justice Brennan focused on the risk that case-by-case review by the Court would chill the very freedom assured to religious organizations. He therefore endorsed a categorical exemption from the ban against religious discrimination in employment for the nonprofit activities of religious organizations but argued for reserving judgment as to profit-making activities. Like Justice Stevens in *McCleskey*, Justice Brennan searched for a formal rule that could preserve discretion for other decision makers while also implementing the Court's special commitment to protect individuals from categorical, discriminatory treatment.

D The dilemmas in sum

Other cases before the Court have raised one or more aspects of the difference dilemma. The Court's voluntary affirmative action cases, during the 1986 term and earlier, directly present dilemmas about recreating difference, risking nonneutral means to transform nonneutral ends, and choosing between rules and discretion in an effort to avoid categorical decisions. Decisions about handicapped persons also raise perplexing issues about when the Court should permit public and private decision makers to make the difference of handicap matter. The Court comes down one way or another in each case, but the splits between majority and minority views persist and recreate the dilemmas. The next section argues that assumptions buried within the dilemmas make them seem more difficult than they need be. The task, then, is to articulate those assumptions and to evaluate the choices that remain for decision makers.

3 Behind and Beyond the Dilemma

The dilemma of difference appears unresolvable. The risk of nonneutrality – the risk of discrimination – accompanies efforts both to ignore and to recognize difference in equal treatment and special treatment; in color blindness or gender blindness and in affirmative action; in governmental neutrality and in governmental preferences; and in decision makers' discretion and in formal constraints on discretion. Yet the dilemma is not as intractable as it seems. What makes it seem so difficult are unstated assumptions about the nature of difference. Once articulated and examined, these assumptions can take their proper place among other choices about how to treat difference. I will explore here the assumptions underlying the dilemma of difference, assumptions that usually go without saying.

A The five unstated assumptions

Assumption 1: difference is intrinsic, not relational

[M]any of us have never conceived of ourselves only as somebody's other. (Barbara Christian)[28]

Can and should the questions about who is different be resolved by a process of discovering intrinsic differences? Is difference an objective, verifiable matter rather than something constructed by social attitudes? By posing legal claims through the difference dilemma, litigants and judges treat the problem of difference as what society or a given decision maker should do about the "different person" – a formulation that implicitly assigns the label of difference to that person.

The difference inquiry functions by pigeonholing people into sharply distinguished categories based on selected facts and features. Categorization helps people cope with complexity and understand each other. The legal analyst tends to treat the difference question as one of discovery rather than of choice. The judge asks: "Into what category does a given person or feature belong?" The categories then determine the significance of the persons or features situated within them. The distinguishing features behind critical perceptions and behind the categories themselves appear natural rather than chosen. It is hard, if not impossible, to find commonalities across differences and to argue for the same treatment across difference. Responsibility for the consequences of identifying difference, then, is dispersed through the process of perception and categorization, even as the process of categorization itself can create new perceptions and realities.

Assumption 2: the unstated norm

Anyone who deviates from the official norm, whatever that is, anyone who fails to bear a likeness to the Standard Product, is simply not viewed as fully human, and then becomes at best invisible, at worst a threat to the national security. (Giles Gunn)[29]

To treat someone as different means to accord them treatment that is different from treatment of someone else; to describe someone as "the same" implies "the same as" someone else. When differences are discussed without explicit reference to the person or trait on the other side of the comparison, an unstated norm remains. Usually, this default reference point is so powerful and well established that it need not be specified.

Some remedial statutes explicitly state the norm: In 42 U.S.C. section 1981, the norm is "white citizens" – with an emphasis on both terms, implicitly establishing the terms of sameness and difference in this very statement of the norm. Claimants invoking the statute must show themselves to be relatively similar to "white citizens." Hence, these cases focus on whether the claimant is a member of a race.

When women argue for rights, the implicit reference point used in discussions of sameness and difference is the privilege accorded some males. This reference point can present powerful arguments for overcoming the exclusion of women from activities and opportunities available to men. For example, reform efforts on behalf of women during both the nineteenth and the twentieth centuries asserted women's fundamental similarities to privileged, white men as a tactic for securing equal treatment. Unfortunately for the reformers, embracing the theory of "sameness" meant that any sign of difference between women and men could be used to justify treating women differently from men. Men remained the unstated norm.

Jerome Bruner wrote, "There is no seeing without looking, no hearing without listening, and both looking and listening are shaped by expectancy, stance, and intention."[30] Unstated reference points lie hidden in legal discourse, which is full of the language of abstract universalism. Legal language seeks universal applicability, regardless of the particular traits of an individual. Yet abstract universalism often "takes the part for the whole, the particular for the universal and essential, the present for the eternal."[31] Making explicit the unstated points of reference is the first step in addressing this problem; the next is challenging the presumed neutrality of the observer who in fact sees from an unacknowledged perspective.

Assumption 3: the observer can see without a perspective

Inevitably, "seeing" entails a form of subjectivity, an act of imagination, a way of looking that is necessarily in part determined by some private perspective. Its results are never simple "facts," amenable to "objective" judgments, but facts or pictures that are dependent on the internal visions that generate them. (Evelyn Fox Keller)[32]

If differences are intrinsic, then anyone can see them; if there is an objective reality, then any impartial observer can make judgments unaffected and untainted by his or her own perspective or experience. Once rules are selected, regardless of disputes over the rules themselves, a distinct aspiration is that they will be applied evenhandedly. This aspiration to impartiality, however, is just that – an aspiration rather than a description – because it may suppress the inevitability of the existence of a perspective and thus make it harder for the observer, or anyone else, to challenge the absence of objectivity.

What interests us, given who we are and where we stand, affects our ability to perceive. Philosophers such as A.J. Ayer and W.V. Quine note that although we can alter the theory we use to frame our perceptions of the world, we cannot see the world unclouded by preconceptions. The impact of the observer's perspective may be crudely oppressive. Yet we continue to believe in neutrality.

Judges often see difference in relation to some unstated norm or point of comparison and fail to acknowledge their own perspective and its influence on the assignment of difference. This failure

prevents us from discovering who is doing the labeling, but it does not negate the effect of the labeling of difference itself. Veiling the standpoint of the observer conceals its impact on our perception of the world. This leads to the next unstated assumption: that all other perspectives are either presumptively identical to the observer's own or are irrelevant.

Assumption 4: the irrelevance of other perspectives

We have seen the blindness and deadness to each other which are our natural inheritance. (William James)[33]

Glimpsing contrasting perspectives helps resolve problems of difference. Several of the justices have tried, on different occasions, to glimpse the point of view of a minority group or a person quite different from themselves; some have articulated eloquently the difficulty or even impossibility of knowing another's perspective and have developed legal positions that take into account this difficulty. Others have rejected as irrelevant or relatively unimportant the experience of "different" people and have denied their own partiality, often by using stereotypes as though they were real.

Thus, some justices, on some occasions, have tried to see beyond the dominant perspective and reach an alternative construction of reality. In many other instances, however, the justices presume that the perspective they adopt is either universal or superior to others. A perspective may go unstated because it is so powerful and pervasive that it may be presumed without defense; it may also go unstated because it is so unknown to those in charge that they do not recognize it as a perspective. Presumptions about whose perspective matters ultimately may be embedded in the final, typically unstated assumption: When in doubt, the status quo is preferred and is indeed presumed natural and free from coercion.

Assumption 5: the status quo is natural, uncoerced, and good

To settle for the constitutionalization of the status quo is to bequeath a petrified forest. (Aviam Soifer)[34]

Connected with many of the other assumptions is

the idea that critical features of the status quo – general social and economic arrangements – are natural and desirable. From this assumption follow three propositions: First, the goal of governmental neutrality demands the status quo because existing societal arrangements are assumed to be neutral. Second, governmental actions that change the status quo have a different status than omissions, or failures to act, that maintain the status quo. Third, prevailing social and political arrangements are not forced on anyone. Individuals are free to make choices and to assume responsibility for those choices. These propositions are rarely stated, both because they are deeply entrenched and because they view the status quo as good, natural, and freely chosen. At times, however, the justices have engaged in debate that exposes the status quo assumption.

For the most part, unstated assumptions work in subtle and complex ways. Assumptions fill the basic human need to simplify and to make our world familiar and unsurprising. Yet, by their very simplification, assumptions exclude contrasting views. Moreover, they contribute to the dilemma of difference by frustrating legislative and constitutional commitments to change the treatment of differences in race, gender, ethnicity, religion, and handicap. Before justice can be done, judges need to hear and understand contrasting points of view about the treatment of difference.

4 Perspectives on Perspectives

The difference dilemma seems paralyzing if framed by the unstated assumptions described in Part 3. Those assumptions so entrench one point of view as natural and orderly that any conscious decision to notice or to ignore difference breaks the illusion of a legal world free of perspective. The assumptions make it seem that departures from unstated norms violate commitments to neutrality. Yet adhering to the unstated norms undermines commitments to neutrality – and to equality. Is it possible to proceed differently, putting these assumptions into question?

I will suggest that it is possible, even if difficult, to move beyond the constricting assumptions. At times in the past term, members of the Court have employed the most powerful device to expose and challenge the unstated assump-

tions: looking at an issue from another point of view. By asking how a member of a religious group might experience a seemingly neutral rule or how a nonmember might experience the discretion of a religious group, Justices O'Connor, Brennan, and White made an effort in several cases to understand a different perspective.[35] Justice Marshall and the majority in *Cal Fed* tried to assume the perspective of pregnant women by considering how treatment of pregnancy affects women's abilities to work outside the home while having a family. The dissenting justices in *McCleskey* asked how defendants would react to the statistical disparity in capital sentencing by race, breaking out of the tendency to see the challenge only as a threat to the discretion and manageability of the criminal justice system. In *Saint Francis College, Shaare Tefila*, and *Arline*, members of the Court struggled over whose perspective should count for purposes of defining a race and a handicap, reaching conclusions that refused to take the usual answers for granted.

Efforts to adopt or imagine alternate perspectives are also reflected in opinions from previous terms. For example, Justice Stevens assessed an equal protection challenge to a zoning restriction burdening mentally retarded people by expressing sensitivity to a point of view other than his own: "I cannot believe that a rational member of this disadvantaged class could ever approve of the discriminatory application of the city's ordinance in this case."[36] Still earlier, Justice Douglas invited inquiry into the experience of non-English-speaking students sitting in a public school classroom conducted entirely in English.[37] Similarly, litigants have sometimes tried to convince the Court to adopt their perspective, Justice Harlan's dissent in *Plessy v. Ferguson*[38] may have been assisted by Homer Plessy's attorney, who had urged the justices to imagine themselves in the shoes of a black person:

Suppose a member of this court, nay, suppose every member of it, by some mysterious dispensation of providence should wake tomorrow with a black skin and curly hair . . . and in traveling through that portion of the country where the "Jim Crow Car" abounds, should be ordered into it by the conductor. It is easy to imagine what would be the result . . . What humiliation, what rage would then fill the judicial mind![39]

It may be ultimately impossible to take the perspective of another completely, but the effort to do so may help us recognize that our perspective is partial and that the status quo is not inevitable or ideal. After shaking free of these unstated assumptions and developing a sense of alternative perspectives, judges must then choose. The process of looking through other perspectives does not itself yield an answer, but it may lead to an answer different from the one that the judge would otherwise have reached. Seen in this light, the difference dilemma is hard but not impossible.

Historians have described how a conception of reality, when it triumphs, convinces even those injured by it of its actuality. Accordingly, political and cultural success itself submerges the fact that conceptions of reality represent a perspective of some groups, not a picture of reality free from any perspective. At the turn of the century, for example, a new middle class justified industrialism and the control of immigrants by spreading understandings of science, technology, and bureaucracy as neutral and progressive.[40] Similarly, studies have shown how groups with relatively little social and economic power internalize the views of those with more power – often at the cost of personal conflict and damaged self-respect.[41] Taking minority perspectives seriously calls for a process of dialogue in which the listener actually tries to reach beyond the assumption of one reality, one version of the truth. There is no neutrality, no escape from choice. But it is possible to develop better abilities to name and grasp competing perspectives and to make more knowing choices thereafter. In the next section, I suggest that efforts along these lines are central to the challenge of engendering justice.

5 Engendering Justice

The problem of freedom is the problem of how to divest our categories of their halo of eternal truth. (Mary Douglas)[42]

The truth is that we are all responsible, even if we are not to blame. (Sarah Burns)[43]

The nineteenth-century American legal system recognized only three races: "white," "Negro," and "Indian." Californian authorities faced an influx of Chinese and Mexicans and were forced to confront the now complicated question of racial categorization. They solved the problem of categorizing Mexicans by defining them as "whites" and by according them the rights of free white persons. Chinese, however, were labeled "Indian" and denied the political and legal rights of white persons. Similarly, in 1922, a unanimous Supreme Court concluded that Japanese persons were not covered by a federal naturalization statute applicable to "free white persons," "aliens of African nativity," and "persons of African descent."[44]

In retrospect, these results seem arbitrary. The legal authorities betrayed a striking inability to reshape their own categories for people who did not fit. Of course, it is impossible to know what might have happened if some piece of history had been otherwise. Still, it is tempting to wonder: What if the California legal authorities had changed their racial scheme, rather than forcing the Chinese and Mexican applicants into it? The officials then might have noticed that nationality, not race, distinguished these groups. What if these officials and the justices in 1922 had tried to take the point of view of the people they were labeling? Perhaps, from this vantage point, the justices would have realized the need for reasons – beyond racial classification – for granting or withholding legal rights and privileges.

In this chapter, I have argued that trying to take seriously the point of view of people labeled *different* is a way to move beyond current difficulties in the treatment of differences in our society. This last statement, like much of the chapter, is addressed to people in positions of sufficient power to label others *different* and to make choices about how to treat difference. If you have such power, you may realize the dilemma of difference: By taking another person's difference into account in awarding goods or distributing burdens, you risk reiterating the significance of that difference and, potentially, its stigma and stereotyping consequences. But if you do not take another person's difference into account – in a world that has made that difference matter – you may also recreate and reestablish both the difference and its negative implications. If you draft or enforce laws, you may worry that the effects of the laws will not be neutral whether you take difference into account or you ignore it. If you employ people, judge guilt or innocence, or make other decisions affecting lives, you may want and need the discretion to make an individualized assessment, free from any focus on categorical differences. But if that discretion is exercised without constraint, difference may be taken into account in a way that does not treat that person as an individual – and in a way that disguises this fact from view.

These dilemmas, I have argued, become less paralyzing if you try to break out of unstated assumptions and take the perspective of the person you have called *different*. Once you do that, you may glimpse that your patterns for organizing the world are both arbitrary and foreclose their own reconsideration. You may find that the categories you take for granted do not well serve features you had not focused upon in the past. You may see an injury that you had not noticed or take more seriously a harm that you had otherwise discounted. If you try to take the view of the other person, you will find that the "difference" you notice is part of the relationship or comparison you draw between that person and someone else, with reference to a norm, and you will then get the chance to examine the reference point you usually take for granted. Maybe you will conclude that the reference point itself should change. Employers do not have to treat pregnancy and parenthood as a disability, but instead as a part of the lives of valued workers. You may find that you had so much ignored the point of view of others that you did not realize that you were mistaking your point of view for reality. Perhaps you will find that the way things are is not the only way things could be – that changing the way you classify, evaluate, reward, and punish may make the differences you had noticed less significant, or even irrelevant, to the way you run your life.

I have also argued, however, that we often forget how to take the perspective of another. We forget even that our point of view is not reality and that our conceptual schemes are simplifications, serving some interests and uses rather than others. We forget because our minds – and probably our hearts – cannot contain the whole world, and so we reduce the world to shorthand that we can handle. Our shorthand – because it is our shorthand – reflects what we thought we needed, where we stood, and who we are. We treat our divisions of the world as though they were real and universal. We do not see that they embody our early experiences of discovering how we are both the same as and different from our parents. We forget how we learned from them to encode the world into the same classifications they used to serve their own needs. We forget that things

may appear frightful only because they are unfamiliar. We look at people we do not know and think they are different from us in important ways. We forget that even if they are different, in a way that matters to them, too, they also have a view of reality, and ours is as different from theirs as theirs is from ours.

We think we know what is real, what differences are real, and what really matters, even though sometimes we realize that our perceptions and desires are influenced by others. Sometimes we realize that television, radio, classes we had in school, or the attitudes of people who matter to us, affect our inclinations. Every time we wear an item of clothing that we now think is fashionable but used to think was ugly, we brush up against the outside influences on what we think inside. Yet we think that we think independently. We forget that widely held beliefs may be the ones most influenced from the outside.

The more powerful we are, the less we may be able to see that the world coincides with our view precisely because we shaped it in accordance with those views. That is just one of our privileges. Another is that we are able to put and hear questions in ways that do not question ourselves. In contrast, the more marginal we feel from the world, from the groups we know, the more likely we are to glimpse a contrast between some people's perceptions of reality and our own. Yet we still may slip into the world view of the more powerful, because it is more likely to be validated. We prefer to have our perceptions validated; we need to feel acknowledged and confirmed. But when we fail to take the perspective of another, we deny that very acknowledgment and confirmation in return.

If we want to preserve justice, we need to develop a practice for more knowing judgments about problems of difference. We must stop seeking to get close to the "truth" and instead seek to get close to other people's truths. The question is, how do we do this? In this section, I argue that we must persuade others as much as they must persuade us about the reality we should construct. Justice can be impartial only if judges acknowledge their own partiality. Justice depends on the possibility of conflicts among the values and perspectives that justice pursues. Courts, and especially the Supreme Court, provide a place for the contest over realities that govern us – if we open ourselves to the chance that a reality other than our own may matter. Justice can be engendered when we overcome our pretended indifference to difference and instead people our world with individuals who surprise one another about difference.

A Impartiality and partial truths

It is a paradox. Only by admitting our partiality can we strive for impartiality. Impartiality is the guise partiality takes to seal bias against exposure. It looks neutral to apply a rule denying unemployment benefits to anyone who cannot fulfill the work schedule, but it is not neutral if the work schedule was devised with one religious Sabbath, and not another, in mind. The idea of impartiality implies human access to a view beyond human experience, a "God's eye" point of view. Not only do humans lack this inhuman perspective, but humans who claim it are untruthful, trying to exercise power to cut off conversation and debate. Doris Lessing argues that a single absolute truth would mean the end of human discourse but that we are happily saved from that end because any truth, once uttered, becomes immediately one truth among many, subject to more discourse and dispute. If we treat other points of view as irritants in the way of our own vision, we are still hanging on to faulty certainty. Even if we admit the limits of our view, while treating those limits as gaps and leaving the rest in place, we preserve the pretense that our view is sufficiently rooted in reality to resist any real change prompted by another.

Acknowledging partiality may cure the pretense of impartiality. But unless we have less capacity to step outside our own skins than I think we do, we then have a choice of which partial view to advance or accept. Whose partial view should resolve conflicts over how to treat assertions of difference, whether assigned or claimed? Preferring the standpoint of an historically deni grated group can reveal truths obscured by the dominant view, but it can also reconfirm the underlying conceptual scheme of the dominant view by focusing on it. Similarly, the perspective of those who are labeled *different* may offer an important challenge to the view of those who imposed the label, but it is a corrective lens, another partial view, not absolute truth.[45] We then fight over whether to prefer it. "Standpoint theories" may also deny the multiple experiences of members of the denigrated group and create a new claim of essentialism.

Instead of an impartial view, we should strive for the standpoint of someone who is committed to the moral relevance of contingent particulars.[46] Put in personal terms, if I pretend to be impartial, I hide my partiality; however, if I embrace partiality, I risk ignoring you, your needs, and your alternative reality – or, conversely, embracing and appropriating your view into yet another rigid, partial view. I conclude that I must acknowledge and struggle against my partiality by making an effort to understand your reality and what it means for my own. I need to stop seeking certainty and acknowledge the complexity of our shared and colliding realities, as well as the tragic impossibility of all prevailing at once. It is this complexity that constitutes our reciprocal realities, and it is the conflict between our realities that constitutes us, whether we engage in it overtly or submerge it under a dominant view.

Moral action, then, takes place in a field of complexity, and we act ethically when we recognize what we give up as well as what we embrace. The solution is not to adopt and cling to some new standpoint but, instead, to strive to become and remain open to perspectives and claims that challenge our own. Justice, like philosophy, ought

> to trust rather to the multitude and variety of its arguments than to the conclusiveness of any one. Its reasoning should not form a chain which is no stronger than its weakest link, but a cable whose fibers may be ever so slender, provided they are sufficiently numerous and intimately connected.[47]

We who judge should remove the removal of ourselves when we either ignore or notice a difference. We can and should confront our involvement in and responsibility for what happens when we act in a reality we did not invent but still have latitude to discredit or affirm. We should have the humility and the courage to act in each situation anew, rather than applying what we presume to know already, as though each case were merely a repetition of an episode from the past.

Two exercises can help those who judge to glimpse the perspectives of others and to avoid a false impartiality. The first is to explore our own stereotypes, our own attitudes toward people we treat as different – and, indeed, our own categories for organizing the world. Audre Lorde put it powerfully: "I urge each one of us here to reach down into that deep place of knowledge inside herself and touch that terror and loathing of any difference that lives there. See whose face it wears. Then the personal as the political can begin to illuminate all our choices."[48] This is a call for applying "strict scrutiny" not just to a defendant's reasons for burdening a protected minority group but also to ourselves when we judge those reasons. It is a process that even we who see ourselves as victims of oppression need to undertake, for devices of oppression are buried within us. We must also examine and retool our methods of classification and consider how they save us from questioning our instincts, ourselves, and our existing social arrangements. Putting ourselves in the place of those who look different can push us to challenge our ignorance and fear and to investigate our usual categories for making sense of the world. This is an opportunity to enlarge judges' understanding and abilities to become better practitioners in the business of solving problems.

The second exercise is to search out differences and celebrate them by constructing new bases for connection. We can pursue the possibilities of difference behind seeming commonalities and seek out commonalities across difference, thereby confronting the ready association of sameness with equality and difference with inferiority. One route is to emphasize our common humanity, despite our different traits. Another tack is to disentangle difference from the allocation of benefits and burdens in society – a tack that may well require looking at difference to alter how people use it. The Court's effort to ensure equality for women and men in the conjunction of work and family life in *Cal Fed* represents such an effort to disentangle institutional arrangements from the difference they create. A third approach is to cherish difference and welcome anomaly. Still another is to understand that which initially seems strange and to learn about sense and reason from this exercise – just as philosophers, anthropologists and psychologists have urged us to take seriously the self-conceptions and perceptions of others. In the process of trying to understand how another person understands, we may even remake our categories of understanding. Other persons may not even define "self" the same way we do, and glimpsing their "self-concepts" thus challenges us to step beyond our operating assumptions. A further skill to practice is to recognize commonality in dif-

ference itself: in the relationships within which we construct difference and connect and distinguish ourselves from one another.

These exercises in taking the perspective of the other will deepen and broaden anyone's perspective. For judges, who debate the use of the coercive forces of the law in relation to issues of difference, these exercises are critical. Judges can and should act as representatives, standing in for others and symbolizing society itself. Judicial acts of representation must also be responsive to the demands of the people they govern, in order to secure apparent legitimacy and, ultimately, to remain effective. One judge explained that law's coercive power must be applied to ensure "the viability of a pluralistic democracy," which "depends upon the willingness to accept all of the 'thems' as 'us'" Whether the motives of the framers be considered moralistic or pragmatic, the structure of the Constitution rests on the foundational principle that successful self-governance can be achieved only through public institutions following egalitarian policies.[49]

This exhortation – that we must take the perspective of another while remembering that we cannot really know what another sees and must put our own categories up for challenge, without ceding the definition of reality over the others – sounds quite complicated. What do we do with the sense of complexity?

B Complexity, passivity, and the status quo: the problem of deference

We are mistaken when we hold onto simple certainties. Yet complexity seems both overwhelming and incapacitating. By bearing into complexity rather than turning away from it, by listening to the variety of voices implicated in our problems, we may lose a sense of ready solutions and steady certainties. But clear answers have been false gods, paid homage to in the coinage of other people's opportunities, and also at cost to our own character. We harden ourselves when we treat our categories as though they were real, closing off responses to new facts and to challenges to how we live and think. Our certainties also leave unresolved conflicts among incompatible but deeply held values. In the face of complexity, "the politics of difference can all too easily degenerate into the politics of 'mutual indifference'"[50] If we care about justice, the biggest mistake would be to respond to complexity with passivity. That response is not impartial; it favors the status quo, those benefited by it, and the conception of reality it fosters.

1. Forms of Passivity. Four forms of judicial passivity may be tempting in the face of complexity: deference, intent requirements, reliance on apparent choices or concessions of the parties, and reliance on doctrine. I will consider each in turn.

Respect for other institutions and persons is a critical part of judging, but there are particular risks when the Court, while acknowledging the complexity of a problem of difference, defers to other branches or levels of government, to private actors, or even to the parties before the Court. One risk is that the Court will pretend that it has no power over or responsibility for what results. When the Court defers to Congress, the executive, a state government, or a private actor, the justices are saying, Let's not make a decision, let's leave it to others, or let's endorse the freedom or respect the power of others. It is surely important for the justices to understand their relationship with other people or institutions with interests in a matter, but such understanding is quite different from ceding responsibility for what ensues. This principle is important for everybody, but especially for a judicial body, which has parties with genuine conflicts before it. As Frank Michelman put it, "Attention [to other branches of government] cannot mean deference, or talismanic invocation of authority. The norm of justice to parties itself commands that no other norm should ever take a form that preempts questions or exempts from reason-giving."[51]

Problems also arise when the Court takes on the second form of passivity: focusing on the intentions of the parties before it. When the Court demands evidence of intentional discrimination before upholding a plaintiff's charges, the justices are deferring to and thereby entrenching the perspective of the defendant, thus rejecting the perspective of the plaintiff-victim. Asking only about the sincerity of the motive behind a statute whose effect is challenged is also an act that takes sides, defines which reality will govern, and avoids the real challenge of responding to the perspective of the plaintiff.

It is equally problematic for the Court, in a third form of passivity, to point to apparent choices made by plaintiffs, victims, or members of minority groups, as Justice Scalia did in *Johnson*[52] as a justification for holding against them. The Court may presume incorrectly that the choices are free and uncoerced, or the Court may wrongly attribute certain meanings to a choice. Similarly, judicial references to litigants' concessions during litigation, including during oral argument, are not without risk. Although the Court may be trying to take the perspective of others seriously, its reliance on litigants' concessions as the peg for a judicial decision may also be the Court's way of reducing the task of deciding on its own. Reliance on concessions of the lawyer may be especially troubling in cases involving the rights of minorities, because it is unclear for whom the lawyer speaks at that moment: the client, the cause, or others unrepresented there who will be affected in the future by the Court's ruling.

The fourth form of passivity is perhaps one of the most effective circumventions of responsibility: the Court's reliance on its own doctrinal boundaries and categories to resolve the cases before it. This chapter has demonstrated that the difference dilemma poses similar problems in a wide variety of contexts, including cases involving religion, gender, race, and sexual preference. Yet when the Court takes the boundaries between doctrines as given, filling the doctrines with operative tests and lines of precedent, it obscures these potential similarities across contexts. By the time a case reaches an appellate court, the adversary process has so focused on specific issues of doctrinal disagreement that the competing arguments have come under one framework, not under competing theories. Legal analogy is typically inseparable from precedential reasoning, telescoping the creative potential of a search for surprising similarities into a narrow focus on prior rulings that could "control" the instant case. The Court's practice vividly demonstrates how fabricated categories can assume the status of immutable reality. Of course, law would be overwhelming without doctrinal categories and separate lines of precedent. Yet by holding to rigid categories, the Court denies the existence of tensions and portrays a false simplicity amid a rabbit warren of complexity. The Court's strict segregation of doctrine also cloisters lines of thought and insights, thereby restricting the Court's ability to use larger frames of judgment.

2. Avoiding Passivity. Besides resisting tempting forms of passivity – which do not lessen judicial responsibility – the Court can and should challenge rigid patterns of thought. What if litigants argued more emphatically across contexts and reminded members of the Court, "You have seen something like this before?" Litigants can help the Court to avoid the dangers of complacency and complexity by searching out analogies and developing unfamiliar perspectives. At the same time, litigants may gain a tactical advantage, because they may persuade a member of the Court of their point of view by analogizing to something the justice has glimpsed elsewhere. This practice also has some support in epistemology. The difficulties each of us has in seeing around the bend of our own thought can be eased with the help of insights from others who are positioned differently. Given the relationship between knowledge and power, those with less privilege may well see better than those with more.

Surprisingly, traditional legal techniques actually provide fruitful starting points for avoiding passivity. One noted feature of the legal system that can be used to mount this challenge is analogical reasoning.[53] The existence of encrusted practices and categories however, frustrates the full use of these tools. Litigants and judges should search out unexpected analogies to scrape off barnacles of thought and to challenge views so settled that they are not thought to be views. This process may persuade particular judges, in particular cases, to see a different angle on a problem. It also holds promise as a method for finding surprising commonalities that can nudge us all to reassess well-established categories of thought.

The promise of reasoning by analogy is lost if it becomes an arid conceptualist enterprise. Yet when immersed in the particulars of a problem, we sometimes are able to think up analogies that break out of ill-fitting conceptual schemes. As one observer of creative processes in art, science, and philosophy has commented, "In the history of human thinking the most fruitful developments frequently take place at those points where two different lines of thought meet."[54] By seeing something in a new light, seeing its similarity to something else once thought quite different, we are able to attribute different meanings and consequences to what we see. A glimpse of difference in one context may enable litigants and judges better to appreciate it in another context.

The adversarial process is another feature of the legal system that, with some modification, can be used to challenge judicial complacency. In fact, the values of thinking through analogies bear a striking similarity to the virtues of reasoning in

dialogue. The dialogue form puts the student in a position to follow the connections and divergences in argument and invent for herself ways to think anew, rather than simply internalizing the monologue of inherited knowledge. Barbara Johnson notes that "learning seems to take place most rapidly when the student must respond to the contradiction between *two* teachers. And what the student learns in the process is both the power of ambiguity and the non-innocence of ignorance."[55] Similarly, dialogue in legal briefs and courtroom arguments can stretch the minds of listeners, especially if they are actively forming their own position and not simply picking between the ones before them.

The introduction of additional voices may enable adversary dialogue to expand beyond a stylized, either/or mode, prompting new and creative insights. Consequently, the Court can, and should seek out alternative views in *amicus* briefs. Inventive approaches can bring the voices of those who are not present before the Court, as in the recent brief filed with the Court that collected the autobiographical accounts of men and women who believed their lives had been changed by the availability of legalized abortion.[56] Similarly, the famous "Brandeis brief" in *Muller v. Oregon*[57] marked a creative shift for the Court, introducing the use of vivid, factual detail as a way to break out of the formalist categories dominating the analysis. Seeking unusual perspectives enables justices to avail themselves of the "partial superiority" of other people's views and to reach for what is unfamiliar and perhaps suppressed under the dominant ways of seeing. Bringing in a wider variety of views can also make the so-called countermajoritarian Court more "democratic."

Besides seeking out unfamiliar perspectives and analogies new to the law, all judges should also consider the human consequences of their decisions in difference cases, rather than insulating themselves in abstractions. Such engagement encourages the judge to fill in textual gaps based on his or her own experiences. It may seem paradoxical to urge those who judge to bring their own experiences to the problems before them, after identifying the dangerous ways in which we all confuse our own perceptions and interests for reality. In the process of personal reflection, however, the judge may stretch faculties for connection while engaging in dialogue with the parties over their legal arguments and analogies. I petition all judges to open up to the chance that someone may move them – the experience will not tell them what to do, but it may give them a way outside routinized categories to forge new approaches to the problem at hand.

This call to be open, to canvas personal experience, applies to all legal controversies, but it is especially important in the context of cases that present the dilemma of difference. Here the judicial mainstays of neutrality and distance prove most risky, for they blind judges to their own involvement in recreating the negative meanings of difference. Yet the dangers of making differences matter also argue against categorical solutions. By struggling to respond humanly to the dilemma in each particular context, the judge can supply the possibility of connection otherwise missing in the categorical treatments of difference.

C Choosing among divergent demands

Urging judges to allow themselves to be moved by the arguments may seem misguided. A judge who identifies with every perspective may simply feel indecisive and overburdened. Would feeling the tugs in all directions render us powerless to choose? It may be just this fear that explains our attachment to simplifying categories, stereotypes, and fixed ways of thought. Some of us may fear being overwhelmed by the world, others fear being too moved by it, others fear being powerless before it. Challenging familiar categories and styles of reasoning may threaten the search for order, decisiveness, and manageability that maintain the predictability in our lives. But there are other ways to hold things together than the methods we have used in the past.

Some may aspire to a jurisprudence of individualism, never treating any individual as a member of a group. Yet, resonant as it is with many American traditions, individualization is a myth: Because our language is shared and our categories communally invented, any word I use to describe your uniqueness draws you into the classes of people sharing your traits. Even if ultimately I produce enough words so that the intersection of all classes you belong in contains only one member – you – we understand this through a language of comparison with others. This language, however, seems to embroil us in the dilemma of difference.

What could we do instead? I believe we should welcome complexity and challenge complacency

– and stop fearing that we will be unable to make judgments. We can and do make judgments all the time, in a way committed to making meaning, rather than recreating or ignoring difference. We make commitments when we make decisions; we reconfirm or remake current understandings by reflecting so deeply and particularly about a new situation that we challenge presumptive solutions. Instead of trying continually to fit people into categories, and to enforce or deny rights on that basis, we can and do make decisions by immersing in particulars to renew commitments to a fair world.

Thus, one reason we can still decide, amid powerfully competing claims, is that immersion in particulars does not require the relinquishment of general commitments. The struggle is not over the validity of principles and generalizations – it is over which ones should prevail in a given context. The choice from among principles, in turn, implicates choices about which differences, and which similarities, should matter. These are moral choices, choices about which voices should persuade those who judge.

Even when we understand them, some voices will lose. The fundamentalist Christians who supported the Balanced Treatment Act in Louisiana deserve respect and understanding: Their view of the world may well be threatened by the curriculum taught to their children in the public schools. However, this is what the fight is about. Whose view of reality should prevail in public institutions? This deep conundrum involves the conflicts between the worldview animating any rule for the entire society, and the worldviews of subgroups who will never share the dominant views. I am tempted to propose a seemingly "neutral" rule, such as a rule that judges interpreting the commitment to respect difference should make the choice that allows difference to flourish without imposing it on others. If exclusion of their worldview from the biology curriculum creates an intolerable choice for the fundamentalists, they do and they must have the choice to establish their own educational institutions, and their own separate community. Yet this seemingly "neutral" position is a comfortable view for a nonfundamentalist like myself, who cannot appreciate the full impact of the evolution science curriculum as experienced by at least some fundamentalists. Rather than pretending to secure a permanent solution through a "neutral" rule, I must acknowledge the tragedy of nonneutrality – and admit that our very commitment to tolerance yields intolerance toward some views. If the fundamentalists lose in this case, they can continue to struggle to challenge the meaning of the commitment to separate church and state, and they may convince the rest of us in the next round. Although it may be little solace for the minority group, its challenge achieves something even when it loses, by reminding the nation of our commitment to diversity, and our inability, thus far, to achieve it fully.

Thus, choices from among competing commitments do not end after the Court announces its judgment. Continuing skepticism about the reality endorsed by the Court – or any source of governmental power – is the only guard against tyranny.

The continuing process of debate over deeply held but conflicting commitments is both the mechanism and the promise of our governmental system. Within that system, the Supreme Court's power depends upon persuasion. As Hannah Arendt wrote: "The thinking process which is active in judging something is not, like the thought process of pure reasoning, a dialogue between me and myself, but finds itself always and primarily, even if I am quite alone in making up my mind, in an anticipated communication with others with whom I know I must finally come to some agreement."[58] The important question is, with whom must you come to agreement? In a society of diversity with legacies of discrimination, within a polity committed to self-governance, the judiciary becomes a critical arena for demands of inclusion. I see the judicial arena as a forum for contests over competing realities. The question remains, however, whose definitions of realities will govern in a given case and over time.

Court judgments endow some perspectives, rather than others, with power. Judicial power is least accountable when judges leave unstated – and treat as a given – the perspective they select. Litigation before the Supreme Court sometimes highlights individuals who otherwise seldom imprint their perspective on the polity. In eliciting these perspectives and accepting their challenge to the version of reality the justices otherwise would take for granted, the Court advances the fundamental constitutional commitment to require reasons before exercises of power, whether public or private. Growing from our history, wrought from many struggles, is the

tradition we have invented, and it is a tradition that declares that the status quo cannot be immune from demands for justification. Litigation over the meanings of difference represents demands for such accountability. By asking how power influences knowledge, the Court can address whether a "difference" has been assigned through past domination or as a remedy for past domination. In this way, the Court can solicit information about contrasting views of reality without casting off the moorings of historical experience, and in this inquiry, the Court can assess the risk of creating new patterns of domination while remedying inequalities of the past. As we compete for power to give reality to our visions, we confront tragic limits in our abilities to make meaning together. Yet we must continue to seek a language to speak across conflicting affiliations.

We need settings in which to engage in the clash of realities that breaks us out of settled and complacent meanings and creates opportunities for insight and growth. This is the special burden and opportunity for the Court: to enact and preside over the dialogue through which we remake the normative endowment that shapes current understandings.

When the Court performs these roles, it engenders justice. Justice is engendered when judges admit the limitations of their own viewpoints, when judges reach beyond those limits by trying to see from contrasting perspectives, and when people seek to exercise power to nurture differences, not to assign and control them. Rather than securing an illusory universality and objectivity, law is a medium through which particular people can engage in the continuous work of making justice. The law "is part of a distinctive manner of imagining the real."[59] Legal decisions engrave upon our culture the stories we tell to and about ourselves, the meanings that constitute the traditions we invent. Searching for words to describe realities too multiple and complex to be contained by their language, litigants and judges struggle over what will be revealed and what will be concealed in the inevitable partiality of human judgment. Through deliberate attention to our own partiality, we can begin to acknowledge the dangers of pretended impartiality. By taking difference into account, we can overcome our pretended indifference to difference, and people our worlds with those who can surprise and enrich one another. As we make audible, in official arenas, the struggles over which version of reality will secure power, we disrupt the silence of one perspective, imposed as if universal. Admitting the partiality of the perspective that temporarily gains official endorsement may embolden resistance to announced rules. But only by admitting that rules are resistible – and by justifying to the governed their calls for adherence – can justice be done in a democracy. "It is only through the variety of relations constructed by the plurality of beings that truth can be known and community constructed."[60] Then we constitute ourselves as members of conflicting communities with enough reciprocal regard to talk across differences. We engender mutual regard for pain we know and pain we do not understand.

Notes

For resolving any doubts about the possibility that people can take the perspective of another, the author thanks Joe Singer, Karol Dean, David Fernandez, Mary Joe Frug, Maura Kelley, Catharine Krupnick, Frank Michelman, Peter Rubin, Elizabeth Schneider, Avi Soifer, Elizabeth Spelman, Kathleen Sullivan, Cass Sunstein, and Stephen Wieder.

1   107 S. Ct. 683 (1987).
2   California Fair Employment and Housing Act, Cal. Gov't Code Ann. § 12945(b)(2) (West 1980).
3   See 107 S. Ct. at 691. In the Pregnancy Discrimination Act of 1978 (PDA), Pub. L. No. 95–555, 92 Stat. 2076 (1978) (codified at 42 U.S.C. § 2000e(k) (1978)), Congress amended Title VII to include discrimination on the basis of pregnancy, rejecting the Supreme Court's contrary ruling in General Electric Co. v. Gilbert, 429 U.S. 125 (1976).
4   107 S. Ct. at 692 (quoting Cal Fed, 758 F.2d 390, 396 (9th Cir. 1985)).
5   Id. at 691, n. 17. In Cal Fed, the Court tried to avoid the problems of stereotyping by characterizing pregnancy solely as a physical disability – ignoring alternative characterizations that analogize women's role in pregnancy to veterans' role in national defense – a role justifying preferential treatment in employment. See Littleton, Reconstructing Sexual Equality, 75 Calif. L. Rev. 201 (forthcoming 1987).
6   See 107 S. Ct. at 694.
7   107 S. Ct. at 698 (White, J., dissenting.) The dissent rejected the claim that employers could comply with both statutes by providing benefits to both women and men in comparable situations, because that approach would extend the scope of the state statute beyond its express language and because the federal statute did not require programs where none currently existed. See id. at 701.
8   Id. at 700. See 107 S. Ct. at 694 (opinion of the Court).
9   107 S. Ct. 2022 (1987).
10 107 S. Ct. 2019 (1987).
11 785 F.2d 523, 527 (4th Cir. 1986).
12 Id. at 529 (Wilkinson, J., concurring in part and dissenting in part). Judge Wilkinson explained: "It is an understatement to note that attempts to place individuals in distinct racial groups frequently serve only to facilitate continued discrimination and postpone the day when all individuals will be addressed as such" (id. at 533).
13 107 S. Ct. 2573 (1987).
14 See 107 S. Ct. at 2576; id. at 2600–5 (Scalia, J., dissenting).
15 Id. at 2582; accord id. at 2587 (Powell, J., concurring).
16 107 S. Ct. 1046 (1987).
17 Id. at 1048 (quoting Fla. Stat. § 443.021 (1985)).
18 See 107 S. Ct at 1051 and n.11.
19 107 S. Ct. 821 (1987).
20 26 U.S.C. § 3304(a)(12)(1982).
21 107 S. Ct. at 825.
22 107 S. Ct. 1756 (1987).
23 107 S. Ct. at 1778, n. 37.
24 Id. at 1791; accord id. at 1806 (Stevens, J., dissenting); id. at 1805 (Blackmun, J., dissenting) ("If a grant of relief to [McCleskey] were to lead to a closer examination of the effects of racial considerations throughout the criminal-justice system, the system, and hence society, might benefit.").
25 Id. at 1806 (Stevens, J., dissenting).
26 107 S. Ct. 2862 (1987).
27 107 S. Ct. at 2874 (O'Connor, J., concurring in the judgment).
28 Christian, The Race for Theory, Cultural Critique, Spring 1987, at 51, 54.
29 G. Gunn, The Interpretation of Otherness: Literature, Religion, and the American Imagination 177 (1979).
30 J. Bruner, Actual Minds, Possible Worlds 110 (1986) (paraphrasing Robert Woodworth). Similarly, Albert Einstein said. "It is the theory which decides what we can observe." D. Bell. The Coming of Post-Industrial Society 9 (1973) (quoting Einstein).
31 Gould, The Woman Question: Philosophy of Liberation and the Liberation of Philosophy, in Women and Philosophy: Toward a Theory of Liberation 21 (C. Gould and M. Wartofsky eds. 1976).
32 E. Keller. A Feeling for the Organism: The Life

and Work of Barbara McClintock 150 (1983).

33 W. James, *What Makes a Life Significant*, in On Some of Life's Ideals, at 49, 81.

34 Soifer, at 409.

35 It is not clear whether Justice Scalia looked at the Balanced Treatment Act in *Edwards* from the vantage point of fundamentalist parents, or instead from the vantage point of state legislators.

36 City of Cleburne v. Cleburne Living Center, 473 U.S. 432, 455 (1985) (Stevens, J., concurring).

37 *See* Lau v. Nichols, 414 U.S. 563, 566 (1974).

38 163 U.S. 537, 552 (1896) (Harlan, J., dissenting).

39 Brief for the Plaintiff, *Plessy v. Ferguson*, reprinted in Civil Rights and the American Negro 298, 303–4 (A. Blaustein and R. Zangrando eds. 1968).

40 *See* R. Wiebe, The Search for Order, 1877–1920, at 111–13 (1967).

41 *See, e.g.*, Castaneda v. Partida, 430 U.S. 482, 503 (1977) (Marshall, J., concurring).

42 M. Douglas, Implicit Meanings: Essays in Anthropology 224 (1975).

43 Burns, *Apologia for the Status Quo* (Book Review), 74 Geo. L.J. 1791, 1819 (1986).

44 *See* Ozawa v. United States, 260 U.S. 178 (1922).

45 *See, e.g.*, C. Gilligan. In a Different Voice (1982), at 151–74 (linking a vision of maturity to a complementary and productive tension between (feminine) ethos of care and a (masculine) ethic of rights).

46 *See* M. Nussbaum, The Fragility of Goodness (1986), at 314. Nussbaum adds that the someone should be committed to "the value of the passions, and the incommensurability of the values that will tend to approve of this particular sort of judge as a guide" (*id* at 311). The point is that a judge must have a plurality of attachments and do justice in the tension among them (*id.* at 314).

47 C.S. Peirce, *Some Consequences of Four Incapacities*, in 5 Collected Papers at 157 (C. Hartshorne and P. Weiss eds. 1931).

48 Lorde, *The Master's Tools Will Never Dismantle the Master's House*, in This Bridge Called My Back: Writings by Radical Women of Color 98 (C. Moraga and G. Anzaldua eds. 1981). This is not sympathy, tolerance, or even compassion, each of which leaves the viewer's understanding fundamentally unchanged.

49 Keyes v. School Dist. No. 1, 576 F. Supp. 1503, 1520 (D. Colo. 1983) (Matsch. J.).

50 Cornell, *The Poststructuralist Challenge to the Ideal of Community*, 8 Cardozo L.R. 989–90 (1987).

51 Michelman, *The Supreme Court, 1985 Term – Forward*, 100 Harv. L.R. 1, at 76 (1986).

52 Johnson v. Transportation Agency 107 S. Ct. 1442 (1987). In Hobble v. Unemployment Appeals Commission, 107 S. Ct. 1046, 1051 (1987), however, the Court's majority was sympathetic about constraints on choice, arguing that it is unlawful coercion to force an employee to choose between fidelity to religious beliefs and continued employment.

53 *See* E. Levi, An Introduction to Legal Reasoning (1972), at 8.

54 F. Capra, The Tao of Physics xii (1984) (quoting Werner Weisenberg); *cf.* S. Harding, at 235: "Analogies are not aids to the establishment of theories; they are an utterly essential part of theories, without which theories would be completely valueless and unworthy of the name" (quoting N. Campbell, Physics, the Elements (1920)).

55 B. Johnson, A World of Difference (1987) at 83 (emphasis in original).

56 *See* Brief Amici Curiae, of National Abortion Rights Action League et al., Thornburgh v. American College of Obstetricians & Gynecologists, 476 U.S. 747 (1986) (no. 84–495 and 84–1379).

57 208 U.S. 412 (1908).

58 H. Arendt, Between Past and Future 220 (1961).

59 C. Geertz, Local Knowledge (1983), at 184.

60 N. Hartsock, at 254 (describing the view of Hannah Arendt), Money, Sex, & Power: Toward a Feminist Historical Materialism (1983).

32

Humanity and Justice in Global Perspective

Brian Barry

This chapter has three sections. The first argues that considerations of humanity require that rich countries give aid to poor ones. The second argues that considerations of justice also require transfers from rich countries to poor ones. The third picks up the distinction between aid and transfer and argues that, when we get into detail, the obligations imposed by humanity and justice are different, although not incompatible.

1 Humanity

Introduction

What is it to act in a way called for by humanity? A humane act is a beneficent act, but not every beneficent act is a humane one. To do something that helps to make someone who is already very happy even happier is certainly beneficent, but it would not naturally be described as an act called for by considerations of humanity.

The *Oxford English Dictionary* defines humanity as "Disposition to treat human beings and animals with consideration and compassion, and to relieve their distresses; kindness, benevolence."[1] In this essay I shall understand by "humanity" the relief of distress. As a matter of usage, it seems to me that the *OED* is right to put this before the more extended sense of kindness or benevolence in general. In any case, it is this notion that I want to

discuss, and the word "humanity" is the closest representation of it in common use.

There are three questions to be dealt with. First, is it morally obligatory to behave humanely, or is it simply laudable but not morally delinquent to fail so to act? Second, if it is morally obligatory, what implications does it have, if any, for the obligations of rich countries to aid poor ones? Third, if (as I shall suggest) rich countries have a humanitarian obligation to aid poor ones, on what criterion can we determine how much sacrifice the rich countries should be prepared to make?

The obligation of humanity

I shall begin my discussion by taking up and considering the argument put forward by Peter Singer in his article "Famine, Affluence and Morality."[2] Singer puts forward a simple, clear, and forceful case for a humanitarian obligation for those in rich countries to give economic aid to those in poor countries. The premises of his argument are as follows. The first is "that suffering and death from lack of food, shelter, and medical care are bad."[3] The second is given in two alternative forms. One is that "if it is in our power to prevent something bad from happening, without thereby sacrificing anything of comparable moral importance, we ought, morally, to do it."[4] The other, and weaker, form is that "if it is in our power to prevent something very bad from happening, without sacrificing anything morally significant, we ought, morally, to do it."[5] He goes on to say that "an application of this principle [i.e., the second version] would be as follows: if I

Originally published in *Nomos XXIV: Ethics, Economics and the Law*, ed. J. R. Pennock and J. W. Chapman (1982), 219–52. Reprinted by permission of New York University Press.

am walking past a shallow pond and see a child drowning in it, I ought to wade in and pull the child out. This will mean getting my clothes muddy, but this is insignificant, while the death of the child would presumably be a very bad thing."[6] All that has to be added is that the application of the second premise is unaffected by proximity or distance and "makes no distinction between cases in which I am the only person who could possibly do anything and cases in which I am just one among millions in the same position."[7] If we accept these premises, we are committed, Singer claims, to the conclusion that people in the rich countries have a moral obligation to help those in the poor countries.

For the purpose of this chapter, I am going to take it as common ground that one would indeed be doing wrong to walk past Peter Singer's drowning child and do nothing to save it. This of course entails that, at least in the most favorable cases, duties of humanity must exist. In the space available, it hardly makes sense to try to argue for a complete theory of morality from which this can be deduced, and in any case I myself am more sure of the conclusion than of any of the alternative premises from which it would follow. Anyone who disagrees with the claim that there is an obligation to rescue the child in the case as stated will not find what follows persuasive, since I certainly do not think that the case for international aid on humanitarian grounds is *stronger* than the case for rescuing the drowning child.

Does the drowning child case extend to international aid?

The extension of the drowning child case may be challenged along several lines. Here I can only state them and say briefly why I do not think they undercut the basic idea that the case for an obligation to save the drowning child applies also to giving international aid. The appearance of dogmatism is purely a result of compression.

The first argument is that the child may be supposed not to be responsible for his plight (or at any rate it may be on that supposition that the example gets to us) but that countries are responsible for their economic problems. My comments here are two. First, even if it were true that the death by disease and or starvation of somebody in a poor country were to some degree the result of past acts or omissions by the entire population, that scarcely makes it morally decent to hold the individual responsible for his plight; nor, similarly, if his predicament could have been avoided had the policies of his government been different.

Let us move on to consider another way in which a challenge may be mounted to Singer's extension of the argument for a duty to aid from the case of the drowning child to that of famine relief. It may be recalled that Singer explicitly made the shift from one case to the other via the statement that neither proximity nor the one-to-one relation between the victim and the potential rescuer makes any moral difference. Clearly, if this claim is denied, we can again agree on the duty to rescue the drowning child but deny that this is an appropriate analogue to the putative duty of people in rich countries to aid those in poor ones. A number of philosophers have tried to drive a wedge between the cases in this way, but I have to say that I am not very impressed by their efforts. The argument for proximity as a relevant factor is that, if we posit a duty to rescue those near at hand, we keep the duty within narrow bounds and thus do not let it interfere with people's life plans; but, if we allow the duty to range over the whole of mankind, it becomes too demanding. Although some people see merit in this, it appears to me that it is invoked simply because it provides a way of arbitrarily truncating the application of the principle so as to arrive at a convenient answer. I shall go on later to agree that there are limits to what people can be required to sacrifice. But I see no ethically defensible reason for saying that, if we can't (or can't be required to) do anything we might, we should simply contract the sphere of operation of the principle that we are obliged to relieve suffering. Perhaps we should channel our limited humanitarian efforts to where they are most needed, which, if we live in a relatively rich country, is likely to be outside its boundaries.

Singer also made it explicit that, if the case of the drowning child were to be extended to international aid, one would have to rule out the one-to-one relation between the rescuer and potential rescuee as a morally relevant factor. Attempts have been made to do so, but they likewise seem to me to lack merit. If there are several people who could save the drowning child, it is sometimes said that none of them is particularly responsible for saving it. But if the child drowns because none of them saves it, they are all, I would suggest, morally responsible for its death. Conversely, suppose that several people are drowning at some distance from one another and there is only one person around to save them. It has been argued that since that person cannot do his duty, if that is defined as saving all those whom he might save (assuming that he could save any one of them but cannot save more than one), no such duty exists. The obvious reply to this is that the duty has been incorrectly defined: the duty in this case is to save one, and his duty is not affected by the fact that there are others who cannot be saved.

Finally, it might be accepted that the case of the drowning child would extend to international aid if the aid would do any good, but then denied that it will. The main lines of this argument are two. The first is the one from waste and inefficiency: aid does not get to the right people; development projects are a disaster; and so on. But I would claim that even if waste is endemic in aid to poor (and probably ill-organized) countries, the difference it makes to health and nutrition is sufficient to make it worth giving if only part of it gets to the people it is supposed to get to. And if, as is all too true, aid in the past has often been inappropriate, the answer is not to withhold aid but to make it more appropriate: no more massive dams, electricity generating stations, or steel mills, but cheaper, less complex, and more decentralized technology.

The second line of argument is the neo-Malthusian: that the only effect of aid in the long run is to lead to population increase and thus to even more suffering. I agree that if this is the only effect of aid, the humanitarian case for it falls to the ground. But it is clear that economic development combined with appropriate social policies and the widespread availability of contraception can actually reduce the rate of population growth. The implication is thus that aid should be given in large amounts where the social and political conditions are right, so as to get countries through the demographic transition from high birthrate and high death rate to low birthrate and low death rate as rapidly as possible.

Where ideological or religious dogmas result in pronatalist government policies or rejection of contraception by the population, one might conclude that aid would be better withheld, since the only foreseeable effect of economic improvement will be to increase numbers. But can we really be so sure that attitudes will not change? The election of a relatively young and doctrinally reactionary pope does not encourage hopes of any early change in official doctrine. But even without any change at that level, it is striking how, in the developed countries, the practices of Roman Catholics have altered dramatically in just a couple of decades. For example, in the Province of Quebec, which had for more than two centuries a birthrate close to the physical maximum, with families of more than 10 children quite common, has now one of the lowest birthrates in North America.

How far does the obligation extend?

If we accept the conclusion that the rich have some obligation on humanitarian grounds to provide economic aid to the poor, the next question is, How much sacrifice is required? In my view, no simple and determinate criterion is available. This is a problem of the obligation of humanity in general, not a peculiarity of the international context. In the standard case of rescuing someone in danger of drowning, the usual guidance one gets from moral philosophers is that the obligation does not extend to risking one's life, though it does require that one suffer a fair amount of inconvenience. However, the decision in such cases, like that of Singer's drowning child, characteristically has clear and finite limits to its implications. But, given the failure of most people or governments in rich countries to give much aid, it would clearly be possible for individuals to give up a high proportion of their incomes without risking their lives and still leave millions of savable lives in poor countries unsaved. Thus, the question of limits is pressing.

There is an answer that is, in principle, straightforward. It is the one embodied in Singer's claim that one is obliged to help up to the point at which one is sacrificing something of "comparable moral importance." This is, of course, a maximizing form of consequentialism. If you say that pains and pleasures are what is of moral importance, you get Benthamite utilitarianism (in the traditional interpretation, anyway); if you say it is the enjoyment of beauty and personal relationships, you get G.E. Moore's ideal consequentialism; and so on. The trouble with this is, needless to say, that most of us do not see any reason for accepting an obligation to maximize the total amount of good in the universe.

Singer's weaker principle that we should give aid up to the point at which we are sacrificing anything of moral importance seems to me useless: for a Benthamite utilitarian, for example, even getting one's trousers muddy would be in itself an evil – not one comparable to the death of a child, but an evil none the less. Even Singer's chosen case would therefore be eliminated on this criterion, let alone any more strenuous sacrifices.

Conclusion

I conclude, provisionally and in the absence of any plausible alternative, that there is no firm criterion for the amount of sacrifice required to relieve distress. This does not mean that nothing can be said. I think it is fairly clear that there is a greater obligation the more severe the distress, the better off the potential helper would still be after helping, and the higher the ratio of benefit to cost. What is indefinite is where the line is to be drawn. In the words of C.D. Broad, in what may be the best single article in philosophical ethics ever written, "it is no objection to say that it is totally impossible to determine exactly where this point comes in any particular case. This is quite true, but it is too common a difficulty in ethics to worry us, and we know that we are lucky in ethical questions if we can state upper and lower limits that are not too ridiculously far apart."[8]

What, in any case, are we talking about here as the range? We could perhaps wonder whether the level of aid from a country like the United States should be 3 percent of GNP (the level of Marshall aid) or 10 or 25 percent. But, unless we reject the idea of an obligation to aid those in distress altogether, we can hardly doubt that one quarter of 1 percent is grotesquely too little.

2 Justice

The concept of justice

"Are we not trying to pack too much into the concept of justice and the correlative concept of rights? The question whether it is *wrong* to act in certain ways is not the same question as whether it is *unjust* so to act."[9] I think the answer to Passmore's rhetorical question is in the affirmative. We should not expect to get out of "justice" a blueprint for the good society – nor should we wish to, since that degree of specificity would inevitably limit potential applicability. Surely it ought to be possible for a just society to be rich or poor, cultivated or philistine, religious or secular

and (within limits that are inherent in justice itself) to have more or less of liberty, equality, and fraternity.

Up to this point, I have studiously avoided any reference to justice. I have been talking about the obligation to relieve suffering as a matter of humanity. The fact that the obligation is not derived from justice does not make it a matter of generosity, nor does it entail that it should be left to voluntary action to adhere to it. It is an obligation that it would be wrong not to carry out and that could quite properly be enforced upon rich countries if the world political system made this feasible. And the core of the discussion has been the claim that the obligation to help (and a fortiori the obligation not to harm) is not limited in its application to those who form a single political community.

It is of course open to anyone who wishes to do so to argue that, if the rich have a properly enforceable obligation to give, this is all we need in order to be able to say that the rich must give to the poor as a matter of justice. I have no way of proving that it is a mistake to use the term "just" to mark out the line between, on the one hand, what is morally required and, on the other, what is praiseworthy to do but not wrong to omit doing. All I can say is that such a way of talking seems to me to result in the blunting of our moral vocabulary and therefore to a loss of precision in our moral thinking. Justice, I wish to maintain, is not merely one end of a monochromatic scale that has at the other end sacrifice of self-interest for the good of others to a heroic or saintly degree. Rather, it points to a particular set of reasons why people (or societies) may have duties to one another and to particular features of institutions that make them morally condemnable.[10]

I shall return to the distinction between humanity and justice in Section 3, where I shall be able to refer to the results of my discussions of each of them. My plan is to analyze justice under two heads. The first is justice as reciprocity; the second, justice as equal rights. These are both familiar ideas though I shall give the second a slightly unfamiliar twist. Justice as reciprocity I will discuss in three aspects: justice as fidelity, justice as requital, and justice as fair play.

Justice as fidelity

The notion of justice as fidelity is that of keeping faith. In addition to covering contract and promises, it extends, in a rather indefinite way, to meeting legitimate expectations not derived from explicit voluntary agreement. Clearly it is an essentially conservative principle and tends if anything to operate contrary to the interests of poor countries, insofar as they often find themselves in the position of seeking to renegotiate disadvantageous deals with transnational corporations within their territories.

Justice as requital

Justice as requital is also a basically conservative principle but can, on occasion, have revisionist implications vis-à-vis justice as fidelity. No simple rule governs what happens when they conflict. Henry Sidgwick, with characteristic caution, said that we have two standards of justice, as the customary distribution and as the ideal distribution, and added that "it is the reconciliation between these two views which is the problem of political justice."[11] I shall not take up that challenge here, but explore the possible implications of justice as requital for international distribution.

The idea of justice as requital is that of a fair return: a fair exchange, a fair share of benefits from some common endeavor, and so on. The most obvious application in the relations between rich and poor countries is whether poor countries are getting fair prices for their exports and paying fair prices for their imports. This, of course, raises the obvious question of what the criterion of a "fair price" is. Suppose, however, that we say, minimally, that it is the prevailing world price. Then it seems clear that, even on this criterion, many poor countries have legitimate complaints about the transfer pricing of transnational corporations. For example, when in the late 1960s the Andean Pact countries (Bolivia, Colombia, Ecuador, and Peru) started taking a serious interest in the pricing policies of transnational corporations operating within their territories, they found overpricing of imports to be the norm, sometimes by factors of hundreds of percent, and, less spectacularly, underpricing of the value of exports.[12] This enabled the companies to attain rates of return on capital of often more than 100 percent while at the same time evading government limits on repatriation of profits. Since the Andean Pact countries have been politically independent for a century and a half and have relatively sophisticated bureaucracies compared with most countries in the Third World, it is inconceivable that similar practices do not obtain in other, more vulnerable countries.

When we turn to the structure of world prices itself, the criterion of justice as requital becomes less helpful. The countries of the Third World, as part of their demands for a "New International Economic Order" have demanded an "Integrated Program" of commodity management that would be designed to push up the prices of raw materials in relation to manufactured products.

The success of the Organization of Petroleum Exporting Countries (OPEC) is, of course, significant here in providing a dazzling example of the effectiveness of a producer cartel. Oil, however, seems to be unique in that it is so cheap to extract and worth so much to consumers. This means that it has always, since the days of the Pennsylvania oilfields, yielded enormous economic rents. The only question has been who captured them. And clearly, until 1973, the Middle Eastern oil producers were getting only a small proportion of the economic rent.

Other commodities are not like oil. It may indeed be possible to push up the prices by restricting supply, but substitution or recycling is likely to set in. From the long-run point of view of the world, this pressure toward conservation would be desirable, no doubt, but the point is that it does not spell a bonanza for the raw material producers.

Clearly, this is only scratching the surface, but I think that it is, at any rate, important to keep in mind that, even if commodity prices could be raised substantially across the board, this would not make most poor countries *appreciably* better off; and it would make some, including the important cases of India and Bangladesh, worse off. Whatever conclusion one wishes to draw, therefore, about the applicability to world prices of justice as requital, the implications are not going to be such as to solve the problem of poor countries that are also resource poor.

Justice as fair play

We still have to see if any redistributive implications flow from the third branch of justice as reciprocity: justice as fair play. The idea here is that if one benefits (or stands to benefit) from some cooperative practice, one should not be a "free rider" by taking the benefits (or being ready to take them if the occasion arises) while failing to do one's part in sustaining the practice when it is one's turn to do so. Thus, if others burn smoke-less fuel in their fireplaces, pack their litter out of the backcountry, or clean up after their dogs, it is unfair for you to refuse to do the same.

The principle of fair play has a potentiality for underwriting a certain amount of redistribution from rich to poor insofar as one practice that might be regarded as prospectively beneficial to all concerned would be the practice of helping those in need. If such a practice existed, it would operate analogously to insurance, which is a con-tractual way of transferring money from those who have not suffered from certain specified calamities to those who have. The principle of fair play would then hold that it would be unfair to be a free rider on a scheme of helping those in need by refusing to do your part when called upon.

The invocation of this notion of what the sociobiologists call "reciprocal altruism" may appear to provide a new way of distinguishing the drowning child case from that of international aid. Perhaps what motivates us in agreeing that there is an obligation to rescue the child is an unarticulated contextual assumption that the child belongs to our community (however widely we may conceive that "community") and that there are norms within that community calling for low-cost rescue from which we stand to gain if ever we find ourselves in need of rescue. Such feelings of obligation as we have in this case can therefore be adequately explained by supposing that they arise from the application of the princi-ple of fair play. It was, thus, an error to have taken it for granted that an acknowledgment of an obligation to help in the drowning child case must show that we accepted a general principle of an obligation to aid those in distress.

I believe that the objection is formally valid. That is to say, it is possible by invoking the prin-ciple of fair play to underwrite the obligation to rescue the drowning child without committing oneself to a universal obligation to rescue. One could respond to this by arguing that the conclu-sions in Section 1 of this essay can be reinstated by deriving universal obligations from the exis-tence of world community. I shall consider this argument below. But before doing so, I should like to follow an alternative and more aggressive line.

The point to observe is that, although we may indeed be motivated to agree that we ought to rescue the drowning child by considerations of justice as reciprocity, it does not follow that we are motivated solely by those considerations. Suppose that you are briefly visiting a foreign country, with an entirely alien culture, and have no idea about the local norms of rescue. Would you, if you came across Singer's drowning child, have an obligation to wade in and rescue it? I think that most people would say yes in answer to that question. And, clearly, those who do are acknowledging obligations of humanity as distinct from obligations of justice.

None of this, of course, is intended to suggest that the difficulties in moving from a general obligation of humanity to an obligation on the part of rich countries to give economic aid to poor ones is any less problematic than it appeared ear-lier. But it does fend off a possible challenge to the move from the drowning child case to the universal obligation to aid. The view I want to maintain is that the answer in the drowning child case is overdetermined where the duty of fair play also underwrites rescue. The strength of the obligation depends upon the circumstances, but it never disappears. Both psychologically and morally, the obligation to aid would be strongest if there were an explicit and generally observed agreement among a group of parents to keep an eye on one another's children: humanity, fidelity, and fair play would then coincide and reinforce each other. The obligation would be perhaps a lit-tle less strong but still very strong in a small, sta-ble, and close-knit community with a well-developed tradition of "neighborliness," since the obligation of fair play would here have maximum force. It would be less strong if the norm of rescue were more widely diffused over a whole society, and would of course vary accord-ing to the society. (New Zealand would rate much higher than the United States on the strength of the norm of helping strangers within the society, for example.) And, finally, in the absence of any established practice of aiding strangers that would give rise to obligations of fair play, there is still, I am suggesting, an obligation of humanity that does not in any way depend upon considerations of reciprocity.[13]

I have been taking for granted that the exis-tence of a practice of rescue does give rise to an obligation to play one's part. This can be ques-tioned. Somebody might say: "Why should I cooperate with the scheme if I'm willing to renounce any benefits that might be due to me under it?"[14] But the cogency of the objection depends upon the existence of stringent conditions of publicity: it must be possible to make this known to all those in the scheme, and it must be remembered perhaps for decades. (This is essential, since many transfers to those in need are going to be predominantly from the young and middle-aged to the old, so it would undermine the integrity of any such cooperative scheme if people could change their minds about its value as they got older.) Neither condition is generally met. Consider a practice of rescuing the victims of accidents – drowning swimmers are the usually cited case. If this practice exists in a whole society, it is not feasible for those who wish to opt out to notify everybody else in advance. And how many could be counted on to be strong-minded enough to wave away a would-be rescuer when they were in need of help themselves? Even if they could, in many cases the rescuer has to incur the trouble and risk in order to get there (as with rescuing a swimmer) or the victim may be unconscious and thus incapable of spurning help.

It is crucially important to notice, however, that the principle of fair play is conditional; that is to say, it stipulates that it is unfair to be a free rider on an actually existing cooperative practice, and that it *would* be unfair to free ride on other mutually beneficial practices if they did exist. But it does not say that it is unfair for a practice that would, if it existed, be mutually beneficial, not to exist.

As anyone familiar with Rawls's theory of justice will have been aware for some time, we are here on the edge of deep waters. For one strand of Rawls's theory is precisely the notion of justice as reciprocity that is embodied in the principle of fair play. According to Rawls, a society is a scheme of social cooperation, and from this fact we can generate, via the notion of fair play, principles of justice. But, clearly, any actual society simply generates whatever is generated by its actual cooperative practice. If it provides retirement pensions out of social security taxes, it is unfair to be a free rider on the scheme by dodging your share of the cost. And so on. But if I am right about the applicability of the principle of fair play, the most Rawls can say about a society that does not have such a scheme is that it suffers from collective irrationality in that it is passing up a chance to do itself some good. He cannot, I suggest, employ the principle as a step in an argument that such a society is unjust.

I make this point because Charles Beitz, in the last part of his admirable book, *Political Philosophy and International Relations*,[15] has argued, within a Rawlsian framework, for a global difference principle. That is to say, income should be redistributed internationally so that the worst-off representative individual in the world is as well off as possible. Beitz acknowledges that he is taking for granted the general validity of Rawls's theory and is simply arguing from within its basic premises for the dropping of Rawls's restriction on the application of the two principles of justice to societies. I have been suggesting that, even within a society, one cannot use the fact that it is a cooperative scheme to argue that it is unfair not to have more extensive cooperation, though not to do so may be collectively irrational. But the international scene presents two further difficulties. First, I think that Rawls is broadly right in (implicitly) denying that the whole world constitutes a single cooperative partnership in the required sense. Second, I do not think that international redistribution can plausibly be said to be advantageous to rich as well as poor countries. Rawls is therefore probably correct in deducing from his system only nonaggression, diplomatic immunity, and the like as mutually advantageous to countries and thus, on his side of the principle of fair play, just. If I am right, however, they are simply collectively rational and give rise to duties of fair play only to the extent that they are instantiated in actual practice.

Beitz's argument for extending the Rawlsian difference principle is in essence that the network of international trade is sufficiently extensive to draw all countries together in a single cooperative scheme. But it seems to be that trade, however multilateral, does not constitute a cooperative scheme of the relevant kind. Trade, if freely undertaken, is (presumably) beneficial to the exchanging parties, but it is not, it seems to me, the kind of relationship that gives rise to duties of fair play. To the extent that justice is involved it is, I would say, justice as requital, that is, giving a fair return. Justice as fair play arises not from simple exchange but from either the provision of public goods that are collectively enjoyed (parks; defense; a litter-free, or unpolluted, environment; and so on) or from quasi-insurance schemes for mutual aid of the kind just discussed. Trade in pottery, ornamentation, and weapons can be traced back to prehistoric times, but we would hardly feel inclined to think of, say, the Beaker Folk as forming a single cooperative enterprise with their trading partners. No more did the spice trade unite East and West.

To the extent that we are inclined to think of the world as more of a cooperative enterprise now, this is, in my judgment, not because trade is more extensive or multilateral, but because there really are rudimentary organs of international cooperation in the form of United Nations agencies and such entities as the International Monetary Fund (IMF) and the World Bank. But the resulting relationships clearly fall short of those of mutual dependence found within societies. And my second point comes in here to draw attention to the fact that the extent of increased cooperation that would really be mutually beneficial is probably quite limited. In particular, redistribution on the insurance principle seems to have little appeal to rich countries. In the foreseeable future, aid to the needy is going to flow from, say, the United States to Bangladesh rather than vice versa. The conditions for reciprocity – that all the parties stand prospectively to benefit from the scheme – simply do not exist. One could, of course, again retreat behind the "veil of ignorance" and argue that, if people did not know to which society they belonged, they would surely choose something like a global difference principle – or at any rate a floor below which nobody should be allowed to fall. And this seems plausible enough. (I have argued it myself in an earlier work.[16]) But this move clearly points up even more sharply than in the case of a single society the degree to which inserting the "veil of ignorance" takes us away from the sphere of the principle of fair play.

Justice as equal rights

In his well-known article, "Are There Any Natural Rights?"[17] H.L.A. Hart argued that special rights must presuppose general rights. Before people can act in ways that modify their, and others', rights (paradigmatically by promising), they must, as a matter of elementary logic, have rights that do not stem from such modifications. Putting this in terms of the present discussion, we can say that justice as reciprocity needs a prior assignment of rights before it can get off the ground.

Now we might try to solve the problem of sanctifying the status quo. We could, in other words, simply declare that we are going to push the principle of justice as the fulfillment of reasonable expectations to the limit and say that what-

ever rights somebody now has are to be taken as the baseline in relation to which all future developments must satisfy the requirements of fidelity, requital, and fair play. If we note that the conservation of value is akin to the Pareto principle, we may observe that this would give us the Virginia school of political economy, especially associated with James Buchanan.

I have criticized his approach elsewhere,[18] and I shall not repeat my criticisms here. But it is surely enough for the present purpose to draw attention to the fact that on the principle of the unquestioned justice of the status quo, the most grotesque features of the existing allocation of rights would be frozen in place forever unless those who suffered from them could find some quid pro quo that would make it worth the while of, say, a shah of Iran or a General Somoza to accept change. But that would be, if it could be found, an improvement in efficiency arising from the reallocation of the existing rights. It would not face the real problem, which was, of course, the injustice of the initial allocation of rights.

Hart's answer to his own question is that the general right that is presupposed by any special rights is an equal right to liberty. He does not give any explicit argument, as far as I can see, for its being equal. But I take it the point is that since a general right is something that is necessarily anterior to any act giving rise to a special right, there is simply no basis for discriminating among people in respect of general rights. In order to discriminate, one would either have to do so on the basis of some quality that is obviously irrelevant to the assignment of rights (e.g., skin color) or on the basis of something the person has done (e.g., made a promise) that provides a reason for attributing different rights to him. But then we get back to the original point, namely that such a differentiation in rights entails that we have an idea of the proper distribution of rights without the special factor adduced. And that must, it seems, be an equal distribution.

In this essay I want to take this idea and apply it to the case of natural resources. I shall suggest that they fit all the requirements for being the subjects of a general right and that therefore everyone has an equal right to enjoy their benefits.

As Hillel Steiner has remarked, "Nozick rightly insists that our commonsense view of what is just – of what is owed to individuals by right – is inextricably bound up with what they *have done* . . . [but] unlike other objects, the objects of appropriative rights . . . are *not* the results of individuals' past actions. . . . Appropriative claims, and the rules governing them, can have nothing to do with desert."[19] Consider, for example, Bruce Ackerman's fable of the spaceship and the manna. One of the claimants, "Rusher," says: "I say that the first person who grabs a piece of manna should be recognized as its true owner" and, when asked for a reason, says, "Because people who grab first are better than people who grab second."[20] That, I think, illustrates my point. What exactly is supposed to be the virtue of getting there first, or even worse, in merely having some ancestor who got there first?

The position with regard to countries is parallel to that of individuals. Today the basis of state sovereignty over natural resources is convention reinforced by international declarations such as votes of the United Nations General Assembly in 1970, 1972, and 1974 to the effect that each country has "permanent sovereignty over natural resources" within its territory.[21] It is easy enough to see the basis of the convention. It has a transcendent simplicity and definiteness that must recommend it in international relations. For, in the absence of a "common power," stability depends heavily on conventions that leave the minimum amount of room for interpretation. Within a municipal legal system, by contrast, it is possible to introduce and enforce complex rules limiting the rights of individual appropriation (e.g., restricting the amount of water that can be drawn off from a river) and transferring a portion of the economic rent from the property owner to the state. Moreover, in the absence of a "common power" it is a convention that is relatively easy to enforce – at any rate easier than any alternative. For a state may be presumed, other things being equal, to be in a better position to control the appropriation of the natural resources of its own territory than to control those of some other country.

In practice, of course, things are not always equal, and many Third World countries have found that controlling foreign companies that own their natural resources is no easy matter: an unholy alliance of multinational corporations and their patron governments (for most, this is the United States) stand ready to organize international boycotts, to manipulate institutions such as the World Bank and the IMF against them; and, if all else fails, go in for "destabilization" on the Chilean model. The problem is exacerbated when a country seeks to gain control of the exploitation of its own natural resources by expropriating the foreign-based companies that have been there, often long before the country became independent. For the issue of compensation then arises, and this is likely to be contentious, not only because of the possibility of dispute about the current value of the investment, but also because the country may claim compensation for inadequate (or no) royalties paid on extraction in the past, a claim that (as we noted above) falls under the head of justice as requital.

However, as far as I am aware, no body of opinion in either the North or the South is averse to the principle that each country is entitled to benefit exclusively from its own natural resources, and to decide whether they should be exploited and, if so, at what rate and in what order. And even the practice has come a long way in the last twenty years. The OPEC is of course the outstanding illustration, but the same pattern of improved royalties and more control over the amount extracted and the way in which it is done obtains also in other countries and other commodities.

It would hardly be surprising if, when the principle of national sovereignty over natural resources has been so recently and precariously established, Third World countries should be highly suspicious of any suggestion that natural resources should in future be treated as collective international property. They may well wonder whether this is anything more than a cover for the reintroduction of colonialism. I do not see how such doubts can be allayed by mere assertion. Clearly, everything would depend on the principle's being applied across the board rather than in a one-sided way that lets the industrialized countries act on the maxim "What's yours is mine and what's mine is my own." So far, that is precisely how it has been used, as in the proposals of American chauvinists such as Robert Tucker that the United States should be prepared to occupy the Saudi Arabian oilfields by military force in order to maintain the flow of oil at a "reasonable" price, so that Americans can continue to use up a grossly disproportionate share of the world's oil. Since the United States, if it used only domestically produced oil, would still have one of the world's highest per capita levels of consumption, the effrontery of this proposal for the international control of other countries' oil would be hard to beat.

If the Third World countries were too weak to do anything more than hang on to the present position of national sovereignty over natural resources, we would, it seems to me, have to regard that as the best outcome that can be obtained. It is clearly preferable to the earlier setup, in which countries with the power to do so controlled the natural resources of others. For, although the distribution of natural resources is entirely arbitrary from a moral point of view, it has at any rate the kind of fairness displayed by a lottery. That is presumably better than a situation in which the weak are despoiled of their prizes by force and fraud.

In spite of these forebodings about the potential misuse of the principle that natural resources are the joint possession of the human race as a whole, I think it is worth pursuing. For it is scarcely possible to be satisfied with the present situation from any angle except that of extreme pessimism about the chances of changing it for the better rather than for the worse. The overwhelming fact about the existing system is, obviously, that it makes the economic prospects of a country depend, to a significant degree, on something for which its inhabitants (present or past) can take absolutely no credit and lay no just claim to its exclusive benefits, namely its natural resources – including in this land, water, minerals, sunlight, and so on. The claims of collectivities to appropriate natural resources rest, as do those of individuals, on convention or on law (in this case, such quasi-law as the United Nations resolutions cited above). No doubt, the point has been impressed on people in the West by examples such as Kuwait, the United Arab Emirates, or Saudi Arabia, and it may be that such small numbers of people have never before become so rich without any effort on their own part, simply as a result of sitting on top of rich deposits. But I see no coherent way of saying why there is anything grotesque about, say, the case of Kuwait, without acknowledging that the fault lies in the whole principle of national sovereignty over natural resources. If it were simply a matter of a few million people hitting the jackpot, things would not be bad, but of course the obverse of that is countries that have poor land, or little land per head, and few mineral resources or other sources of energy such as hydroelectric power.

Obviously, some countries are richer than others for many reasons, and some, like Japan, are among the more affluent in spite of having to import almost all their oil and the greatest part of many other natural resources. What, then, about the other advantages that the people in the rich countries inherit – productive capital, good systems of communications, orderly administration, well-developed systems of education and training, and so on? If the point about special rights is that someone must have done something to acquire a special right, what have the fortunate inheritors of all the advantages done to give them an exclusive claim to the benefits flowing from them?

The answer that the defenders of property rights normally give at this point is that, although the inheritors have done nothing to establish any special rights, those who left it to them did do something (namely, help to create the advantages) and had a right to dispose of it to some rather than to others. The special rights of those in the present generation thus derive from the use made by those in the previous generation of *their* special rights.

I cannot, in this already long chapter, undertake here to ask how far this answer takes us. We would have to get into questions that seem to me very difficult, such as the extent to which the fact that people who are no longer alive wanted something to happen, and perhaps even made sacrifices in order to insure that it could happen, provides any basis in justice for determining what those now alive now should do. I shall simply say here that I regard any claims that those now alive can make to special advantages derived from the efforts of their ancestors as quite limited. First, the inheritance must itself have been justly acquired in the first place, and that cannot be said of any country that violated the equal claims of all on natural resources – which means almost all industrial countries. Second, the claims to inheritance seem to me to attenuate with time, so that, although the present generation might legitimately derive some special advantages from the efforts of the preceding one, and perhaps the one before that, the part of what they passed on that was in turn inherited from their predecessors should, I think, be regarded as by now forming part of the common heritage.

Obviously, making this case out would require elaboration beyond the space available. But I do want to emphasize that what follows constitutes, in my view, a minimalist strategy. That is to say, whatever obligations of justice follow from it represent the absolutely rock-bottom requirements of justice in international affairs. To the extent that other advantages can be brought within the net of the principle of equal rights, the obligations of rich countries go beyond what is argued for here.

International institutions

It would be ridiculous to spend time here on a blueprint for a scheme to put into effect the principle that I have been advancing. Its implementation on a worldwide scale, if it happens at all, is going to occur over a period measured in decades and, indeed, centuries. It will depend on both fundamental changes in outlook and on the development of international organs capable of taking decisions and carrying them out with reasonable efficiency and honesty.

The history of domestic redistribution is, I think, very much to the point here in suggesting that there is a virtuous circle in which the existence of redistributive institutions and beliefs in the legitimacy of redistribution are mutually reinforcing and have a strong tendency to become more extensive together over time. When Hume discussed redistribution in the *Enquiry*, the only form of it that he considered was "perfect equality of possessions."[22] The notion of continuous redistribution of income through a system of progressive taxation does not seem to have occurred to him. The Poor Law did, of course, provide a minimum of relief to the indigent, but it was organized by parishes and it is doubtful that the amateurish and nepotistic central administration of the eighteenth century could have handled a national scheme. The introduction of unemployment and sickness benefits and old age pensions in one Western European country after another in the late nineteenth century and early twentieth century was made possible by the development of competent national administrations.

At the same time, these programs constituted a political response to the extension of the suffrage, or perhaps one might more precisely say a response to conditions that, among other things, made the extension of the suffrage necessary for the continued legitimacy of the state. A certain measure of redistribution was the price the privileged were prepared to pay for mass acceptance of their remaining advantages. Once in place, however, such programs have shown a universal tendency to take on a life of their own and to grow incrementally as gaps in the original coverage are

filled in and the whole level of benefits is gradually raised. Indeed, it has been found in cross-national studies that the best predictor of the relative size of a given program (say, aid to the blind) within the whole welfare system is the amount of time the program has been running compared with others. In the long run, the programs seem to generate supporting sentiments, so that even Margaret Thatcher and Ronald Reagan proposed only reductions of a few percentage points in programs that even thirty years previously would have seemed quite ambitious.

I do not want to drive the comparison with the international arena into the ground, but I think that, if nothing else, reflecting on domestic experience ought to lead us to look at international transfers from an appropriate time perspective. The United Nations Organization obviously has a lot wrong with it, for example, but its administration is probably less corrupt, self-serving, and inefficient than that which served Sir Robert Walpole. If one takes a time span of thirty years, it is, I suggest, more remarkable that the network of international cooperation has developed as far as it has than that it has not gone further. And in the realm of ideas the notion that poor countries have claims of one sort or another to aid from rich ones has moved from being quite exotic to one that is widely accepted in principle. At any rate in public, the representatives of the rich countries on international bodies no longer deny such a responsibility. They merely seek to evade any binding commitment based on it. But in the long run what is professed in public makes a difference to what gets done because it sets the terms of the discussion.

International taxation

It is not at all difficult to come up with proposals for a system by which revenues would be raised on a regular basis from the rich countries and transferred to the poor ones. Accordingly, no elaborate discussion is needed here. If any such scheme ever gained enough momentum to be a serious international issue, economists and accountants would no doubt have a field day arguing about the details. There is no point in anticipating such arguments, even in outline here. However, the relative brevity of treatment here should not lead to any underestimation of its importance. It is in fact the centerpiece of what is being put forward in this essay.

Now, broadly speaking, two alternative approaches are possible. One would be to take up each of the aspects of international justice that have been discussed – and whatever others might be raised – and to base a system of taxes and receipts upon each. This would be messy and endlessly contentious. The alternative, which is, I predict, the only way in which any systematic redistribution will ever take place, if it ever does, is to have one or two comprehensive taxes and distribute the proceeds according to some relatively simple formula among the poor countries.

The most obvious, and in my view the best, would be a tax on the governments of rich countries, assessed as a proportion of gross national product that increases with per capita income, the proceeds to be distributed to poor countries on a parallel basis of negative income tax. Gross national product reflects, roughly, the use of irreplaceable natural resources, the burden on the ecosphere, and advantages derived from the efforts of past generations, and past exploitation of other countries. Ideally, this tax would be supplemented by a severance tax on the extraction of mineral resources and a shadow tax on the value of land and similar resources. (States could be left to collect the money by any means they chose. But their aggregate liability would be assessed by valuing the taxable base and applying the set rate). This would certainly be required to take care of some glaring inequities that would still otherwise remain. But the simple system of transfer based on gross national product would be such an advance over the status quo that it would be a mistake to miss any chance to implement it by pursuing further refinements.

I believe that any other kinds of general tax, that is to say, taxes not related specifically to some aspect of justice, should be rejected. For example, a tax on foreign trade, or on foreign trade in fossil fuels has been proposed.[23] This is so obviously arbitrary that it is hard to see how anyone can have considered it worth mooting. It has the manifest effect of penalizing small countries and countries that export (or import, if one believes that the tax on exports of fossil fuel would be shifted forward) coal and oil. It conversely has an absurdly favorable effect on very large countries that import and export little in relation to the size of the GNPs and are relatively self-sufficient in energy derived from fossil fuels. No doubt the State Department loves it, but why anyone else should be imposed on is a mystery to me.

I have assumed without discussion that resources transferred to satisfy the requirements of justice should go straight to poor countries rather than being channeled through international agencies and dispensed in the form of aid for specific projects. I shall spell out the rationale for this in the next section. But I will simply remark here that nothing I have said about justice rules out additional humanitarian transfers. And these would appropriately be administered by international organizations. The basis for raising such revenues for humanitarian aid would very reasonably be a progressive international shadow income tax, since this would perfectly reflect ability to pay. We might thus envisage a dual system of international taxation – one part, corresponding to the requirements of justice, going directly to poor countries to be spent at their own discretion; the other going to the World Bank or some successor organization less dominated by the donor countries.

3 The Relations Between Humanity and Justice

Introduction

I have been arguing that both humanity and justice require a substantial expansion in the scale of economic transfers from rich countries to poor ones. I should now like to show that, as the two rationales are very different, so are their practical implications. This point is, I think, worth emphasizing because those who pride themselves on the possession of sturdy Anglo-Saxon "common sense" tend to conclude that, if we agree on the humanitarian obligation, we are wasting our breath in arguing about claims of injustice – claims for the rectification of alleged unrequited transfers from poor to rich countries in the past that are hard to assess and impossible to quantify or involving more or less abstruse doctrines about the nature of justice in the contemporary world. If we recognize the case for action on simple and straightforward humanitarian grounds, the idea goes, shouldn't we concentrate on putting into place the appropriate aid policies, rather than allow ourselves to get sidetracked into fruitless wrangles about justice? In this context it is often said that the demands made by the countries of the South are "symbolic" or "ideological" and have the effect only of making more difficult the real, practical task of negotiating actual concessions by the countries of the North. The question that seems to me of more import is the following: If an obligation of humanity is accepted, under whatever name, how much difference does it make whether or not the kinds of claims I have been discussing under the heading of "justice" are also conceded?

Rights and goals

The answer is, I believe, that it makes a great deal of difference. Putting it in the most abstract terms, the obligations of humanity are goal-based, whereas those of justice are rights-based.[24] I would once have expressed the distinction between humanity and justice as one between an aggregative principle and a distributive principle.[25] I now, however, regard that distinction as less fundamental than the one I wish to mark by talking of goal-based and rights-based obligations. The point is that humanity and justice are not simply alternative prescriptions with respect to the same thing. Rather, they have different subject matters.

Humanity, understood as a principle that directs us not to cause suffering and to relieve it where it occurs, is a leading member of a family of principles concerned with what happens to people (and other sentient creatures) – with what I shall call their well-being, intending to include in this such notions as welfare, happiness, self-fulfillment, freedom from malnutrition and disease, and satisfaction of basic needs. Justice, by contrast, is not directly concerned with such matters at all. As well as principles that tell us what are good and bad states of affairs and what responsibilities we have to foster the one and to avert the other, we also have principles that tell us how control over resources should be allocated. If we understand "resources" in a very wide sense, so that it includes all kinds of rights to act without interference from others, to constrain the actions of others, and to bring about changes in the nonhuman environment, then we can say that the subject matter of justice (at any rate, in modern usage) is the distribution of control over material resources. At this high level of generality, it is complemented by the principle of equal liberty, which is concerned with the control over nonmaterial resources. To put it in a slogan, which has the advantages as well as the disadvantages of any slogan, humanity is a question of doing good; justice is a question of power.

When the contrast is stated in those terms, it might seem that bothering about justice is indeed a waste of time and that the bluff Anglo-Saxon advocates of commonsensical utilitarianism have the best of it after all. Why, it may naturally be asked, should we care about the distribution of *stuff* as against the distribution of *welfare*? Isn't this simply commodity fetishism in a new guise?

The easy but inadequate answer is that the concept of justice is, of course, concerned not only with old stuff but the kind of stuff that has the capacity to provide those who use it with the material means of well-being: food, housing, clothing, medical care, and so on. This is correct as far as it goes and shows that being concerned with justice is not irrational. But it is inadequate because it leaves the supporter of justice open to an obvious flanking movement. His opponent may reply: "You say that the only reason for concern about the distribution of the things whose proper allocation constitutes the subject matter of justice is that they are the means to well-being. Very well. But are you not then in effect conceding that your 'deep theory' is goal-based? For what you are saying is that we really are ultimately concerned with the distribution of well-being. We simply take an interest in the distribution of the means of well-being because they are what we can actually allocate. But this means that justice is a derivative principle."

There are two lines of response open at this point. One is to concede that criteria for the distribution of resources are ultimately to be referred to the goal of well-being, but at the same time to deny that it follows from that concession that we can cut out the middleman (or put in the Michelman) and set out our principles for the allocation of resources with an eye directly on the well-being they are likely to produce. Or, more precisely, we may say that among the constituents of well-being is autonomy, and autonomy includes the power to choose frivolously or imprudently. Thus, on one (admittedly controversial) interpretation, Mill's talk of justice in Book V of *Utilitarianism* and his presentation of the "simple principle" of *On Liberty* in terms of rights is all consistent with an underlying utilitarian commitment if we allow for the importance to people of being able to plan their own lives and make their own decisions.

I think that this is by no means an unreasonable view and has more to be said for it than is, perhaps, fashionable to admit. Anyone who wishes at all costs to hold up a monistic ethical position is, I suspect, almost bound to finish up by trying to make some such argument as this. But I think that it is, nevertheless, in the last analysis a heroic attempt to fudge the issue by using the concept of autonomy to smuggle a basically foreign idea into the goal-based notion of advancing well-being.

The alternative is to deny that, in conceding that control over resources is important only because of the connection between resources and well-being, one is thereby committed to the view that principles for the distribution of resources are derivative. According to this view, there simply are two separate kinds of question. One concerns the deployment of resources to promote happiness and reduce misery. The other concerns the ethically defensible basis for allocating control over resources. Neither is reducible, even circuitously, to the other. When they conflict, we get hard questions, such as those involved in the whole issue of paternalism. But there is no overarching criterion within which such conflicts can be solved, as is offered (at least in principle) by the idea that autonomy is an important, but not the only, ingredient in well-being.

As may be gathered, this is the position that I hold. In what follows, I want to show what difference it makes to employ an independent principle of justice in considering issues of international distribution. To make the discussion as clear as possible, I shall draw my contrast with a principle of humanity understood in the kind of pretty straightforward way exemplified in Section 1 of this chapter. The contrast would be softened the more weight we were to give to autonomy as a component in well-being. Note, however, that even those who might wish to emphasize the importance of individual autonomy are likely to doubt the value to individual well-being of autonomy for states; yet it is precisely the question of autonomy for states that is going to turn out to be the main dividing line between humanity and justice at the international level.

International applications

The point is one of control. The rich countries already mostly concede, at least in verbal declarations, that they have a humanitarian obligation to assist the poor countries economically. The importance to the future of the world of their beginning to live up to those declarations can scarcely be overestimated. I trust that nothing in this chapter will be taken as disparaging humanitarian aid. To the extent that it does in fact relieve problems of poverty, disease, malnutrition, and population growth it is, obviously, of enormous value.

But to see its limitations, let us be really utopian about humanitarian aid. Let us imagine that it is collected on a regular and automatic basis from rich countries according to some formula that more or less reflects ability to pay; for example, a shadow tax on GNP graduated by the level of GNP per capita. And suppose that the proceeds were pooled and dispersed through agencies of the United Nations, according to general criteria for entitlement to assistance.

Now, undoubtedly such a world would be an immense improvement over the present one, just as the modern welfare state has transformed, say, Henry Mayhew's London. But it would still have the division between the donor countries, free to spend "their" incomes as they pleased and the recipient countries, which would have to spend their incomes "responsibly." No doubt, this would be less objectionable if the criteria were drawn up in partnership between donor and recipient countries rather than, as now, being laid down by bodies such as the IMF and the World Bank in whose governing councils the rich countries have a preponderant voice. But funds earmarked and conditional upon approved use would still be basically different from income of the usual kind.

In contrast, transfers that were consequential upon considerations of justice would simply reduce the resources of one set of countries and augment those of another set. The distribution of control of resources would actually be shifted. It is therefore easy to see that the question of justice in the relations between rich and poor countries is by no means a purely "symbolic" one. Real issues are at stake, and it is no self-delusion that leads the poor countries to press for a recognition of the claims of justice and the rich countries to resist.

The conclusion we have reached, then, is that the crucial characteristic of justice is that the obligation to make the transfers required by it does not depend upon the use made of them by the recipient. At this point, I find that the following kinds of objection are usually made: What if the recipient country wastes the resources transferred to it? What if it is going to spend the money on armaments? What if it has a very unequal distribution of income and the additional income will be divided in the same unequal way? Such objections illustrate how difficult it is to get across the idea that if some share of resources is justly owed to a country, then it is (even before it has been actually transferred) as much that country's as it is now normally thought that what a country produces belongs to that country.

The answer that I give is that there are extreme circumstances in which the international community or some particular donor country would be justified in withholding resources owed as a matter of justice to some country. But these are exactly the same extreme conditions under which it would also be justifiable to refuse to pay debts to it or to freeze its assets overseas.

One could envisage a world in which there were indeed an international authority that allowed countries to keep only that income that would be justly distributed internally and used in approved, nonwasteful ways. Such a world would not be at all like ours, since it would accept no principle of national autonomy. It would be a world in which a presently nonexisting world society had inscribed on its banner: "From each according to his ability, to each according to his needs."

The alternative is a world in which the general presumption is of national autonomy, with countries being treated as units capable of determining the use of those resources to which they were justly entitled. This is the world that we now have, and the only modification in the status quo I am arguing for is a redefinition of what justly belongs to a country. It inevitably, as the price of autonomy, permits countries to use their resources in wasteful ways ("theirs," on my interpretation, being of course those in their own territories plus or minus transfers required by justice) and does not insist that a country that allows some to live in luxury while others have basic needs unfulfilled should lose income to which it is entitled as a matter of justice.

My point is that both of the models I have sketched are internally consistent. We could have a system in which there are no entitlements based on justice and in which, assuming that states are still the administrative intermediaries, funds are allocated for worthy purposes and cut off if they are misspent, just as in the United States the federal government cuts off funds to state and local governments that do not comply with various guidelines. Or we could have a world in which, once the demands of just distribution between countries are satisfied, we say that we have justice at the world level, and the question of domestic distribution and national priorities then becomes one for each country to decide for itself.

What is not consistent is to have a world in which those countries that are required by international justice to be donors live under the second system while those that are recipients live under the stern dispensation of the first. If the idea is going to be that countries should have their entitlements reduced if they are wasteful and fail in internal equity, then the obvious place to start is not with some poor country in sub-Saharan Africa or South Asia but with, say, a country that burns one ninth of the world's daily oil consumption on its roads alone and that, in spite of having a quarter of the world's GNP, is unable to provide for much of its population decent medical care, while a substantial proportion live in material conditions of abject squalor that (except for being more dirty and dangerous) recall the cities of Germany and Britain in the aftermath of World War II.

None of this, of course, denies the independent significance of humanity as a criterion in international morality. But we cannot sensibly talk about humanity unless we have a baseline set by justice. To talk about what I ought, as a matter of humanity, to do with what is mine makes no sense until we have established what is mine in the first place. If I have stolen what is rightfully somebody else's property, or if I have borrowed from him and refuse to repay the debt when it is due, and as a result he is destitute, it would be unbecoming on my part to dole out some part of the money that should belong to him, with various strings attached as to the way in which he should spend it, and then go around posing as a great humanitarian. That is, in my judgment, an exact description of the position in which the rich countries have currently placed themselves.

The need for humanitarian aid would be reduced in a world that had a basically just international distribution. It would be required still to meet special problems caused by crop failure owing to drought, destruction owing to floods and earthquakes, and similar losses resulting from other natural disasters. It would also, unhappily, continue to be required to cope with the massive refugee problems that periodically arise from political upheavals.

Beyond that, humanitarian aid in the form of food, technical assistance, or plain money is always a good thing, of course. How much the rich countries would be obliged to give depends first on the extent of redistribution we hold to be required by justice and, second, on the stringency that we assign to the obligation of humanity – how much sacrifice can be demanded to deal with what level of need.

As will be clear, this chapter is concerned only with a preliminary investigation of the principles relevant to an ethical appraisal of international distribution and redistribution. I must therefore leave any more precise statement of implications for future discussions – and not necessarily by me. Ultimately, if anything is to be done, it will require a widespread shift in ideas. Greater precision can be expected to develop *pari passu* with such a shift. I very much doubt the value of single-handed attempts to produce a blueprint in advance of that.

Notes

1 *Oxford English Dictionary*, sub. Humanity, 3b. In the light of the central example to be discussed below, it is interesting to note that the title of a society founded in England for the rescuing of drowning persons in 1774 was the Humane Society (*OED*, sub. Humane, 1c).

2 1 *Philosophy & Public Affairs*, 229–43 (1972). See, for a briefer and more recent statement of the same basic case, Peter Singer, *Practical Ethics* (Cambridge: Cambridge University Press, 1979), ch. 8, pp. 158–81.

3 *Ibid.*, p. 231.

4 *Ibid.*

5 *Ibid.*

6 *Ibid.*

7 *Ibid.*

8 C.D. Broad, "On the Function of False Hypotheses in Ethics," 26 *International Journal of Ethics* 377–97, at 389–90 (1916).

9 John Passmore, "Civil Justice and Its Rivals," in Eugene Kamenka and Alice Erh-Soon Tay, *Justice* (London: Edward Arnold, 1979) pp. 25–49, at 47 [italics in original].

10 For a sustained argument along these lines, see T.D. Campbell, "Humanity before Justice," 4 *British Journal of Political Science* 1–16 (1974).

11 Henry Sidgwick, *The Methods of Ethics* (London: Macmillan, 1907), p. 273.

12 Constantine V. Vaitsos, *Intercountry Income Distribution and Transnational Enterprises* (Oxford: Clarendon Press, 1974), esp. ch. 4.

13 See for an elaboration of these remarks "And Who Is My Neighbor?" 88 *Yale L.J.* 629–58 (1979).

14 Adam Smith expressed this view: "As a man doth, so it shall be done to him, and retaliation seems to be the great law which is dictated to us by nature. Beneficence and generosity we think due to the generous and beneficent. Those whose hearts never open to the feelings of humanity should, we think, be shut out in the same manner, from the affections of all their fellow-creatures, and be allowed to live in the midst of society, as in a great desert, where there is nobody to care for them, or to enquire after them." Adam Smith, *The Theory of Moral Sentiments* (Indianapolis: Liberty Classics, n.d.), p. 160.

15 Princeton, N.J.: Princeton University Press, 1979. The part of the book in question was first published in substantially the same form as "Justice and International Relations," 4 *Philosophy & Public Affairs* 360–89 (1975).

16 *The Liberal Theory of Justice* (Oxford: Clarendon Press, 1973), ch. 12.

17 H.L.A. Hart, "Are There Any Natural Rights?" 64 *Philosophical Review* 175–91 (1955).

18 See my extended review in 12 *Theory and Decision*, 95–106 (1980).

19 Hillel Steiner, "The Natural Right to the Means of Production," 27 *The Philosophical Quarterly* 41–49, at 44–45 (1977). The reference to Nozick is to *Anarchy, State, and Utopia* (New York: Basic Books, 1974), p. 154.

20 Bruce A. Ackerman, *Social Justice in the Liberal State* (New Haven: Yale University Press, 1980), p. 38.

21 Oscar Schachter, *Sharing the World's Resources* (New York: Columbia University Press, 1977), p. 124, references n, 52, p. 159.

22 David Hume, *An Enquiry Concerning the Principles of Morals*, 3rd ed. (Oxford: Clarendon Press, 1975), pp. 193–94.

23 Eleanor B. Steinberg and Joseph Y. Yager, eds., *New Means of Financing International Needs* (Washington, D.C.: The Brookings Institution, 1978), ch. 3.

24 For a distinction stated in these terms see Ronald Dworkin, "The Original Position," 4 *Chi. L. Rev.*, 500–33 (1973), reprinted in Norman Daniels, ed., *Reading Rawls* (Oxford: Basil Blackwell, 1975) pp. 16–53. The relevant discussion is on pp. 38–40 of this reprint.

25 *Political Argument* (London: Routledge and Kegan Paul, 1965), pp. 43–44.

PART VII

Oppression

33

Power, Right, Truth

Michel Foucault

The course of study that I have been following until now – roughly since 1970/71 – has been concerned with the *how* of power. I have tried, that is, to relate its mechanisms to two points of reference, two limits: on the one hand, to the rules of right that provide a formal delimitation of power; on the other, to the effects of truth that this power produces and transmits, and which in their turn reproduce this power. Hence we have a triangle: power, right, truth.

Schematically, we can formulate the traditional question of political philosophy in the following terms: how is the discourse of truth, or quite simply, philosophy as that discourse which *par excellence* is concerned with truth, able to fix limits to the rights of power? That is the traditional question. The one I would prefer to pose is rather different. Compared to the traditional, noble and philosophic question it is much more down to earth and concrete. My problem is rather this: what rules of right are implemented by the relations of power in the production of discourses of truth? Or alternatively, what type of power is susceptible of producing discourses of truth that in a society such as ours are endowed with such potent effects? What I mean is this: in a society such as ours, but basically in any society, there are manifold relations of power which permeate, characterise and constitute the social body, and these relations of power cannot themselves be established, consolidated nor implemented without the production, accumulation, circulation and functioning of a discourse. There can be no possible exercise of power without a certain economy of discourses of truth which operates through and on the basis of this association. We are subjected to the production of truth through power and we cannot exercise power except through the production of truth. This is the case for every society, but I believe that in ours the relationship between power, right and truth is organised in a highly specific fashion. If I were to characterise, not its mechanism itself, but its intensity and constancy, I would say that we are forced to produce the truth of power that our society demands, of which it has need, in order to function: we *must* speak the truth; we are constrained or condemned to confess or to discover the truth. Power never ceases its interrogation, its inquisition, its registration of truth: it institutionalises, professionalises and rewards its pursuit. In the last analysis, we must produce truth as we must produce wealth, indeed we must produce truth in order to produce wealth in the first place. In another way, we are also subjected to truth in the sense in which it is truth that makes the laws, that produces the true discourse which, at least partially, decides, transmits and itself extends upon the effects of power. In the end, we are judged, condemned, classified, determined in our undertakings, destined to a certain mode of living or dying, as a function of the true discourses which are the bearers of the specific effects of power.

So, it is the rules of right, the mechanisms of power, the effects of truth or if you like, the rules of power and the powers of true discourses, that can be said more or less to have formed the

Originally published in *Power/Knowledge*, ed. Colin Gordon (Harvester, 1980), 92–108. Copyright © 1972, 1975, 1976, 1977 by Michel Foucault. Reprinted by permission of Prentice Hall.

general terrain of my concern, even if, as I know full well, I have traversed it only partially and in a very zig-zag fashion. I should like to speak briefly about this course of research, about what I have considered as being its guiding principle and about the methodological imperatives and precautions which I have sought to adopt. As regards the general principle involved in a study of the relations between right and power, it seems to me that in Western societies since Medieval times it has been royal power that has provided the essential focus around which legal thought has been elaborated. It is in reponse to the demands of royal power, for its profit and to serve as its instrument or justification, that the juridical edifice of our own society has been developed. Right in the West is the King's right. Naturally everyone is familiar with the famous, celebrated, repeatedly emphasised role of the jurists in the organisation of royal power. We must not forget that the re-vitalisation of Roman Law in the twelfth century was the major event around which, and on whose basis, the juridical edifice which had collapsed after the fall of the Roman Empire was reconstructed. This resurrection of Roman Law had in effect a technical and constitutive role to play in the establishment of the authoritarian, administrative, and, in the final analysis, absolute power of the monarchy. And when this legal edifice escapes in later centuries from the control of the monarch, when, more accurately, it is turned against that control, it is always the limits of this sovereign power that are put in question, its prerogatives that are challenged. In other words, I believe that the King remains the central personage in the whole legal edifice of the West. When it comes to the general organisation of the legal system in the West, it is essentially with the King, his rights, his power and its eventual limitations, that one is dealing. Whether the jurists were the King's henchmen or his adversaries, it is of royal power that we are speaking in every case when we speak of these grandiose edifices of legal thought and knowledge.

There are two ways in which we do so speak. Either we do so in order to show the nature of the juridical armoury that invested royal power, to reveal the monarch as the effective embodiment of sovereignty, to demonstrate that his power, for all that it was absolute, was exactly that which befitted his fundamental right. Or, by contrast, we do so in order to show the necessity of impos-

ing limits upon this sovereign power, of submitting it to certain rules of right, within whose confines it had to be exercised in order for it to remain legitimate. The essential role of the theory of right, from medieval times onwards, was to fix the legitimacy of power; that is the major problem around which the whole theory of right and sovereignty is organised.

When we say that sovereignty is the central problem of right in Western societies, what we mean basically is that the essential function of the discourse and techniques of right has been to efface the domination intrinsic to power in order to present the latter at the level of appearance under two different aspects: on the one hand, as the legitimate rights of sovereignty, and on the other, as the legal obligation to obey it. The system of right is centred entirely upon the King, and it is therefore designed to eliminate the fact of domination and its consequences.

My general project over the past few years has been, in essence, to reverse the mode of analysis followed by the entire discourse of right from the time of the Middle Ages. My aim, therefore, was to invert it, to give due weight, that is, to the fact of domination, to expose both its latent nature and its brutality. I then wanted to show not only how right is, in a general way, the instrument of this domination – which scarcely needs saying – but also to show the extent to which, and the forms in which, right (not simply the laws but the whole complex of apparatuses, institutions and regulations responsible for their application) transmits and puts in motion relations that are not relations of sovereignty, but of domination. Moreover, in speaking of domination I do not have in mind that solid and global kind of domination that one person exercises over others, or one group over another, but the manifold forms of domination that can be exercised within society. Not the domination of the King in his central position, therefore, but that of his subjects in their mutual relations: not the uniform edifice of sovereignty, but the multiple forms of subjugation that have a place and function within the social organism.

The system of right, the domain of the law, are permanent agents of these relations of domination, these polymorphous techniques of subjugation. Right should be viewed, I believe, not in terms of a legitimacy to be established, but in terms of the methods of subjugation that it instigates.

The problem for me is how to avoid this question, central to the theme of right, regarding sovereignty and the obedience of individual subjects in order that I may substitute the problem of domination and subjugation for that of sovereignty and obedience. Given that this was to be the general line of my analysis, there were a certain number of methodological precautions that seemed requisite to its pursuit. In the very first place, it seemed important to accept that the analysis in question should not concern itself with the regulated and legitimate forms of power in their central locations, with the general mechanisms through which they operate, and the continual effects of these. On the contrary, it should be concerned with power at its extremities, in its ultimate destinations, with those points where it becomes capillary, that is, in its more regional and local forms and institutions. Its paramount concern, in fact, should be with the point where power surmounts the rules of right which organise and delimit it and extends itself beyond them, invests itself in institutions, becomes embodied in techniques, and equips itself with instruments and eventually even violent means of material intervention. To give an example: rather than try to discover where and how the right of punishment is founded on sovereignty, how it is presented in the theory of monarchical right or in that of democratic right, I have tried to see in what ways punishment and the power of punishment are effectively embodied in a certain number of local, regional, material institutions, which are concerned with torture or imprisonment, and to place these in the climate – at once institutional and physical, regulated and violent – of the effective apparatuses of punishment. In other words, one should try to locate power at the extreme points of its exercise, where it is always less legal in character.

A second methodological precaution urged that the analysis should not concern itself with power at the level of conscious intention or decision; that it should not attempt to consider power from its internal point of view and that it should refrain from posing the labyrinthine and unanswerable question: 'Who then has power and what has he in mind? What is the aim of someone who possesses power?' Instead, it is a case of studying power at the point where its intention, if it has one, is completely invested in its real and effective practices. What is needed is a study of power in its external visage, at the point where it is in direct and immediate relationship with that which we can provisionally call its object, its target, its field of application, there – that is to say – where it installs itself and produces its real effects.

Let us not, therefore, ask why certain people want to dominate, what they seek, what is their overall strategy. Let us ask, instead, how things work at the level of on-going subjugation, at the level of those continuous and uninterrupted processes which subject our bodies, govern our gestures, dictate our behaviours etc. In other words, rather than ask ourselves how the sovereign appears to us in his lofty isolation, we should try to discover how it is that subjects are gradually, progressively, really and materially constituted through a multiplicity of organisms, forces, energies, materials, desires, thoughts etc. We should try to grasp subjection in its material instance as a constitution of subjects. This would be the exact opposite of Hobbes' project in *Leviathan*, and of that, I believe, of all jurists for whom the problem is the distillation of a single will – or rather, the constitution of a unitary, singular body animated by the spirit of sovereignty – from the particular wills of a multiplicity of individuals. Think of the scheme of Leviathan: insofar as he is a fabricated man, Leviathan is no other than the amalgamation of a certain number of separate individualities, who find themselves reunited by the complex of elements that go to compose the State; but at the heart of the State, or rather, at its head, there exists something which constitutes it as such, and this is sovereignty, which Hobbes says is precisely the spirit of Leviathan. Well, rather than worry about the problem of the central spirit, I believe that we must attempt to study the myriad of bodies which are constituted as peripheral *subjects* as a result of the effects of power.

A third methodological precaution relates to the fact that power is not to be taken to be a phenomenon of one individual's consolidated and homogeneous domination over others, or that of one group or class over others. What, by contrast, should always be kept in mind is that power, if we do not take too distant a view of it, is not that which makes the difference between those who exclusively possess and retain it, and those who do not have it and submit to it. Power must be analysed as something which circulates, or rather as something which only functions in the form of a chain. It is never localised here or there, never in anybody's hands, never appropriated as a commodity or piece of wealth. Power is employed and exercised through a net-like organisation. And not only do individuals circulate between its threads; they are always in the position of simultaneously undergoing and exercising this power. They are not only its inert or consenting target; they are always also the elements of its articulation. In other words, individuals are the vehicles of power, not its points of application.

The individual is not to be conceived as a sort of elementary nucleus, a primitive atom, a multiple and inert material on which power comes to fasten or against which it happens to strike, and in so doing subdues or crushes individuals. In fact, it is already one of the prime effects of power that certain bodies, certain gestures, certain discourses, certain desires, come to be identified and constituted as individuals. The individual, that is, is not the *vis-à-vis* of power; it is, I believe, one of its prime effects. The individual is an effect of power, and at the same time, or precisely to the extent to which it is that effect, it is the element of its articulation. The individual which power has constituted is at the same time its vehicle.

There is a fourth methodological precaution that follows from this: when I say that power establishes a network through which it freely circulates, this is true only up to a certain point. In much the same fashion we could say that therefore we all have a fascism in our heads, or, more profoundly, that we all have a power in our bodies. But I do not believe that one should conclude from that that power is the best distributed thing in the world, although in some sense that is indeed so. We are not dealing with a sort of democratic or anarchic distribution of power through bodies. That is to say, it seems to me – and this then would be the fourth methodological precaution – that the important thing is not to attempt some kind of deduction of power starting from its centre and aimed at the discovery of the extent to which it permeates into the base, of the degree to which it reproduces itself down to and including the most molecular elements of society. One must rather conduct an *ascending* analysis of power, starting, that is, from its infinitesimal mechanisms, which each have their own history, their own trajectory, their own techniques and tactics, and then see how these mechanisms of power have been – and continue to be – invested, colonised, utilised, involuted, transformed, displaced, extended etc., by ever more general

mechanisms and by forms of global domination. It is not that this global domination extends itself right to the base in a plurality of repercussions: I believe that the manner in which the phenomena, the techniques and the procedures of power enter into play at the most basic levels must be analysed, that the way in which these procedures are displaced, extended and altered must certainly be demonstrated; but above all what must be shown is the manner in which they are invested and annexed by more global phenomena and the subtle fashion in which more general powers or economic interests are able to engage with these technologies that are at once both relatively autonomous of power and act as its infinitesimal elements. In order to make this clearer, one might cite the example of madness. The descending type of analysis, the one of which I believe one ought to be wary, will say that the bourgeoisie has, since the sixteenth or seventeenth century, been the dominant class; from this premise, it will then set out to deduce the internment of the insane. One can always make this deduction, it is always easily done and that is precisely what I would hold against it. It is in fact a simple matter to show that since lunatics are precisely those persons who are useless to industrial production, one is obliged to dispense with them. One could argue similarly in regard to infantile sexuality – and several thinkers, including Wilhelm Reich have indeed sought to do so up to a certain point. Given the domination of the bourgeois class, how can one understand the repression of infantile sexuality? Well, very simply – given that the human body had become essentially a force of production from the time of the seventeenth and eighteenth century, all the forms of its expenditure which did not lend themselves to the constitution of the productive forces – and were therefore exposed as redundant – were banned, excluded and repressed. These kinds of deduction are always possible. They are simultaneously correct and false. Above all they are too glib, because one can always do exactly the opposite and show, precisely by appeal to the principle of the dominance of the bourgeois class, that the forms of control of infantile sexuality could in no way have been predicted. On the contrary, it is equally plausible to suggest that what was needed was sexual training, the encouragement of a sexual precociousness, given that what was fundamentally at stake was the constitution of a labour force whose optimal state, as we well know, at least at the beginning of the nineteenth century, was to be infinite: the greater the labour force, the better able would the system of capitalist production have been to fulfil and improve its functions.

I believe that anything can be deduced from the general phenomenon of the domination of the bourgeois class. What needs to be done is something quite different. One needs to investigate historically, and beginning from the lowest level, how mechanisms of power have been able to function. In regard to the confinement of the insane, for example, or the repression and interdiction of sexuality, we need to see the manner in which, at the effective level of the family, of the immediate environment, of the cells and most basic units of society, these phenomena of repression or exclusion possessed their instruments and their logic, in response to a certain number of needs. We need to identify the agents responsible for them, their real agents (those which constituted the immediate social *entourage*, the family, parents, doctors etc.), and not be content to lump them under the formula of a generalised bourgeoisie. We need to see how these mechanisms of power, at a given moment, in a precise conjuncture and by means of a certain number of transformations, have begun to become economically advantageous and politically useful. I think that in this way one could easily manage to demonstrate that what the bourgeoisie needed, or that in which its system discovered its real interests, was not the exclusion of the mad or the surveillance and prohibition of infantile masturbation (for, to repeat, such a system can perfectly well tolerate quite opposite practices), but rather, the techniques and procedures themselves of such an exclusion. It is the mechanisms of that exclusion that are necessary, the apparatuses of surveillance, the medicalisation of sexuality, of madness, of delinquency, all the micro-mechanisms of power, that came, from a certain moment in time, to represent the interests of the bourgeoisie. Or even better, we could say that to the extent to which this view of the bourgeoisie and of its interests appears to lack content, at least in regard to the problems with which we are here concerned, it reflects the fact that it was not the bourgeoisie itself which thought that madness had to be excluded or infantile sexuality repressed. What in fact happened instead was that the mechanisms of the exclusion of madness, and of the surveillance of infantile sexuality,

began from a particular point in time, and for reasons which need to be studied, to reveal their political usefulness and to lend themselves to economic profit, and that as a natural consequence, all of a sudden, they came to be colonised and maintained by global mechanisms and the entire State system. It is only if we grasp these techniques of power and demonstrate the economic advantages or political utility that derives from them in a given context for specific reasons, that we can understand how these mechanisms come to be effectively incorporated into the social whole.

To put this somewhat differently: the bourgeoisie has never had any use for the insane; but the procedures it has employed to exclude them have revealed and realised – from the nineteenth century onwards, and again on the basis of certain transformations – a political advantage, on occasion even a certain economic utility, which have consolidated the system and contributed to its overall functioning. The bourgeoisie is interested in power, not in madness, in the system of control of infantile sexuality, not in that phenomenon itself. The bourgeoisie could not care less about delinquents, about their punishment and rehabilitation, which economically have little importance, but it is concerned about the complex of mechanisms with which delinquency is controlled, pursued, punished and reformed etc.

As for our fifth methodological precaution: it is quite possible that the major mechanisms of power have been accompanied by ideological productions. There has, for example, probably been an ideology of education, an ideology of the monarchy, an ideology of parliamentary democracy etc ; but basically I do not believe that what has taken place can be said to be ideological. It is both much more and much less than ideology. It is the production of effective instruments for the formation and accumulation of knowledge – methods of observation, techniques of registration, procedures for investigation and research, apparatuses of control. All this means that power, when it is exercised through these subtle mechanisms, cannot but evolve, organise and put into circulation a knowledge, or rather apparatuses of knowledge, which are not ideological constructs.

By way of summarising these five methodological precautions, I would say that we should direct our researches on the nature of power not towards the juridical edifice of sovereignty, the State apparatuses and the ideologies which accompany them, but towards domination and the material operators of power, towards forms of subjection and the inflections and utilisations of their localised systems, and towards strategic apparatuses. We must eschew the model of Leviathan in the study of power. We must escape from the limited field of juridical sovereignty and State institutions, and instead base our analysis of power on the study of the techniques and tactics of domination.

This, in its general outline, is the methodological course that I believe must be followed, and which I have tried to pursue in the various researches that we have conducted over recent years on psychiatric power, on infantile sexuality, on political systems, etc. Now as one explores these fields of investigation, observing the methodological precautions I have mentioned, I believe that what then comes into view is a solid body of historical fact, which will ultimately bring us into confrontation with the problems of which I want to speak this year.

This solid, historical body of fact is the juridical-political theory of sovereignty of which I spoke a moment ago, a theory which has had four roles to play. In the first place, it has been used to refer to a mechanism of power that was effective under the feudal monarchy. In the second place, it has served as instrument and even as justification for the construction of the large scale administrative monarchies. Again, from the time of the sixteenth century and more than ever from the seventeenth century onwards, but already at the time of the wars of religion, the theory of sovereignty has been a weapon which has circulated from one camp to another, which has been utilised in one sense or another, either to limit or else to reinforce royal power: we find it among Catholic monarchists and Protestant anti-monarchists, among Protestant and more-or-less liberal monarchists, but also among Catholic partisans of regicide or dynastic transformation. It functions both in the hands of aristocrats and in the hands of parliamentarians. It is found among the representatives of royal power and among the last feudatories. In short, it was the major instrument of political and theoretical struggle around systems of power of the sixteenth and seventeenth centuries. Finally, in the eighteenth century, it is again this same theory of sovereignty, re-activated through the doctrine of Roman Law, that we find in its essentials in Rousseau and his contemporaries, but now with a fourth role to play:

now it is concerned with the construction, in opposition to the administrative, authoritarian and absolutist monarchies, of an alternative model, that of parliamentary democracy. And it is still this role that it plays at the moment of the Revolution.

Well, it seems to me that if we investigate these four roles there is a definite conclusion to be drawn: as long as a feudal type of society survived, the problems to which the theory of sovereignty was addressed were in effect confined to the general mechanisms of power, to the way in which its forms of existence at the higher level of society influenced its exercise at the lowest levels. In other words, the relationship of sovereignty, whether interpreted in a wider or a narrower sense, encompasses the totality of the social body. In effect, the mode in which power was exercised could be defined in its essentials in terms of the relationship sovereign – subject. But in the seventeenth and eighteenth centuries, we have the production of an important phenomenon, the emergence, or rather the invention, of a new mechanism of power possessed of highly specific procedural techniques, completely novel instruments, quite different apparatuses, and which is also, I believe, absolutely incompatible with the relations of sovereignty.

This new mechanism of power is more dependent upon bodies and what they do than upon the Earth and its products. It is a mechanism of power which permits time and labour, rather than wealth and commodities, to be extracted from bodies. It is a type of power which is constantly exercised by means of surveillance rather than in a discontinuous manner by means of a system of levies or obligations distributed over time. It presupposes a tightly knit grid of material coercions rather than the physical existence of a sovereign. It is ultimately dependent upon the principle, which introduces a genuinely new economy of power, that one must be able simultaneously both to increase the subjected forces and to improve the force and efficacy of that which subjects them.

This type of power is in every aspect the antithesis of that mechanism of power which the theory of sovereignty described or sought to transcribe. The latter is linked to a form of power that is exercised over the Earth and its products, much more than over human bodies and their operations. The theory of sovereignty is something which refers to the displacement and appropriation on the part of power, not of time and labour, but of goods and wealth. It allows discontinuous obligations distributed over time to be given legal expression but it does not allow for the codification of a continuous surveillance. It enables power to be founded in the physical existence of the sovereign, but not in continuous and permanent systems of surveillance. The theory of sovereignty permits the foundation of an absolute power in the absolute expenditure of power. It does not allow for a calculation of power in terms of the minimum expenditure for the maximum return.

This new type of power, which can no longer be formulated in terms of sovereignty, is, I believe, one of the great inventions of bourgeois society. It has been a fundamental instrument in the constitution of industrial capitalism and of the type of society that is its accompaniment. This non-sovereign power, which lies outside the form of sovereignty, is disciplinary power. Impossible to describe in the terminology of the theory of sovereignty from which it differs so radically, this disciplinary power ought by rights to have led to the disappearance of the grand juridical edifice created by that theory. But in reality, the theory of sovereignty has continued not only to exist as an ideology of right, but also to provide the organising principle of the legal codes which Europe acquired in the nineteenth century, beginning with the Napoleonic Code.

Why has the theory of sovereignty persisted in this fashion as an ideology and an organising principle of these major legal codes? For two reasons, I believe. On the one hand, it has been, in the eighteenth and again in the nineteenth century, a permanent instrument of criticism of the monarchy and of all the obstacles that can thwart the development of disciplinary society. But at the same time, the theory of sovereignty, and the organisation of a legal code centred upon it, have allowed a system of right to be superimposed upon the mechanisms of discipline in such a way as to conceal its actual procedures, the element of domination inherent in its techniques, and to guarantee to everyone, by virtue of the sovereignty of the State, the exercise of his proper sovereign rights. The juridical systems – and this applies both to their codification and to their theorisation – have enabled sovereignty to be democratised through the constitution of a public right articulated upon collective sovereignty, while at the same time this democratisation of sovereignty was fundamentally determined by and grounded in mechanisms of disciplinary coercion.

To put this in more rigorous terms, one might say that once it became necessary for disciplinary constraints to be exercised through mechanisms of domination and yet at the same time for their effective exercise of power to be disguised, a theory of sovereignty was required to make an appearance at the level of the legal apparatus, and to re-emerge in its codes. Modern society, then, from the nineteenth century up to our own day, has been characterised on the one hand, by a legislation, a discourse, an organisation based on public right, whose principle of articulation is the social body and the delegative status of each citizen; and, on the other hand, by a closely linked grid of disciplinary coercions whose purpose is in fact to assure the cohesion of this same social body. Though a theory of right is a necessary companion to this grid, it cannot in any event provide the terms of its endorsement. Hence these two limits, a right of sovereignty and a mechanism of discipline, which define, I believe, the arena in which power is exercised. But these two limits are so heterogeneous that they cannot possibly be reduced to each other. The powers of modern society are exercised through, on the basis of, and by virtue of, this very heterogeneity between a public right of sovereignty and a polymorphous disciplinary mechanism. This is not to suggest that there is on the one hand an explicit and scholarly system of right which is that of sovereignty, and, on the other hand, obscure and unspoken disciplines which carry out their shadowy operations in the depths, and thus constitute the bedrock of the great mechanism of power. In reality, the disciplines have their own discourse. They engender, for the reasons of which we spoke earlier, apparatuses of knowledge (*savoir*) and a multiplicity of new domains of understanding. They are extraordinarily inventive participants in the order of these knowledge-producing apparatuses. Disciplines are the bearers of a discourse, but this cannot be the discourse of right. The discourse of discipline has nothing in common with that of law, rule, or sovereign will. The disciplines may well be the carriers of a discourse that speaks of a rule, but this is not the juridical rule deriving from sovereignty, but a natural rule, a norm. The code they come to define is not that of law but that of normalisation. Their reference is to a theoretical horizon which of necessity has nothing in common with the edifice of right. It is human science which constitutes their domain, and clinical knowledge their jurisprudence.

In short, what I have wanted to demonstrate in the course of the last few years is not the manner in which at the advance front of the exact sciences the uncertain, recalcitrant, confused dominion of human behaviour has little by little been annexed to science: it is not through some advancement in the rationality of the exact sciences that the human sciences are gradually constituted. I believe that the process which has really rendered the discourse of the human sciences possible is the juxtaposition, the encounter between two lines of approach, two mechanisms, two absolutely heterogeneous types of discourse: on the one hand there is the re-organisation of right that invests sovereignty, and on the other, the mechanics of the coercive forces whose exercise takes a disciplinary form. And I believe that in our own times power is exercised simultaneously through this right and these techniques and that these techniques and these discourses, to which the disciplines give rise invade the area of right so that the procedures of normalisation come to be ever more constantly engaged in the colonisation of those of law. I believe that all this can explain the global functioning of what I would call a *society of normalisation*. I mean, more precisely, that disciplinary normalisations come into ever greater conflict with the juridical systems of sovereignty: their incompatibility with each other is ever more acutely felt and apparent; some kind of arbitrating discourse is made ever more necessary, a type of power and of knowledge that the sanctity of science would render neutral. It is precisely in the extension of medicine that we see, in some sense, not so much the linking as the perpetual exchange or encounter of mechanisms of discipline with the principle of right. The developments of medicine, the general medicalisation of behaviours, conducts, discourses, desires etc., take place at the point of intersection between the two heterogeneous levels of discipline and sovereignty. For this reason, against these usurpations by the disciplinary mechanisms, against this ascent of a

power that is tied to scientific knowledge, we find that there is no solid recourse available to us today, such being our situation, except that which lies precisely in the return to a theory of right organised around sovereignty and articulated upon its ancient principle. When today one wants to object in some way to the disciplines and all the effects of power and knowledge that are linked to them, what is it that one does, concretely, in real life, what do the Magistrates Union[1] or other similar institutions do, if not precisely appeal to this canon of right, this famous, formal right, that is said to be bourgeois, and which in reality is the right of sovereignty? But I believe that we find ourselves here in a kind of blind alley: it is not through recourse to sovereignty against discipline that the effects of disciplinary power can be limited, because sovereignty and disciplinary mechanisms are two absolutely integral constituents of the general mechanism of power in our society.

If one wants to look for a non-disciplinary form of power, or rather, to struggle against disciplines and disciplinary power, it is not towards the ancient right of sovereignty that one should turn, but towards the possibility of a new form of right, one which must indeed be anti-disciplinarian, but at the same time liberated from the principle of sovereignty. It is at this point that we once more come up against the notion of repression, whose use in this context I believe to be doubly unfortunate. On the one hand, it contains an obscure reference to a certain theory of sovereignty, the sovereignty of the sovereign rights of the individual, and on the other hand, its usage introduces a system of psychological reference points borrowed from the human sciences, that is to say, from discourses and practices that belong to the disciplinary realm. I believe that the notion of repression remains a juridical-disciplinary notion whatever the critical use one would make of it. To this extent the critical application of the notion of repression is found to be vitiated and nullified from the outset by the two-fold juridical and disciplinary reference it contains to sovereignty on the one hand and to normalisation on the other.

Notes

1   This Union, established after 1968, has adopted a radical line on civil rights, the law and the prisons.

34

Bearing the Consequences of Belief

Peter Jones

1 The Issue

Should people suffer social disadvantage because of their beliefs? There is a strong element in the liberal tradition which holds that they should not. According to that tradition, people should be free to adopt and to live in accordance with whatever beliefs they find persuasive. People can be considered 'free' to adopt and to live in accordance with a set of beliefs only if they are not subject to persecution and harassment for holding those beliefs. If there are any 'settled convictions' of liberalism, this commitment to freedom of belief is surely one of them. One offshoot of that conviction is an antipathy to discrimination against people on grounds of religious faith in matters such as employment and education. In some societies discrimination against people on grounds of religious faith is legally prohibited along with discrimination on other grounds such as race and sex. In other societies, religious discrimination remains legally unproscribed but is still frowned upon in their official and unofficial cultures and may well become the subject of legislative action in the near future. Yet just what ought to count as 'discrimination' in relation to religious belief and just what 'toleration' requires of us are often far from clear. Consider the following celebrated case.[1]

Mr Ahmad, a devout Muslim, was employed as a full-time school teacher by the Inner London Education Authority (ILEA). His faith required

Originally published in *Journal of Political Philosophy*, 2 (1994), 24–43. Reprinted by permission of Blackwell Publishers.

that, if possible, he should attend a mosque for prayers on Friday afternoons. At first Mr Ahmad taught in a district too far from a mosque to enable him to fulfil this injunction. But when he was transferred by ILEA to a district within reasonable distance of a mosque, he insisted that, thenceforth, he should attend the mosque each Friday afternoon. His doing so meant that he was absent for the first three-quarters of an hour of teaching time on Friday afternoons and his absence had to be covered by other teachers. ILEA advised the head-teachers of the schools at which Mr Ahmad taught that he should not be given permission to absent himself in this way. However, Mr Ahmad continued to attend the mosque.[2] Eventually ILEA informed Mr Ahmad that, if he insisted on absenting himself on Friday afternoons, he would have to relinquish his appointment as a full-time teacher. The Authority offered to re-employ him as a part-time teacher for $4\frac{1}{2}$ days a week though, of course, that would have meant a commensurate reduction in his salary. Mr Ahmad found the offer of part-time employment unacceptable and resigned from his full-time post.

Mr Ahmad contended that his treatment by ILEA amounted to unfair dismissal and appealed to an industrial tribunal. The tribunal dismissed his appeal, a decision that was subsequently upheld by the Employment Appeal Tribunal. Mr Ahmad then took his case to the Court of Appeal where, by a majority decision, his appeal was again rejected, the dissenting judgment in his favour coming from Scarman L.J. Finally Mr Ahmad petitioned the European Court of Human Rights but still without success; his application was found by the European Commission to be manifestly ill-founded and declared inadmissible.[3]

Was Mr Ahmad treated fairly? My concern here is not with the legal niceties of his case which turned, in large part, upon the precise interpretation that should be placed upon section 30 of the British 1944 Education Act and section 9 of ILEA's staff code, both of which made provision for the religious convictions of teachers. Rather I want to focus on the general point of principle underlying the case. In part, this was a question of what constituted equitable treatment of different faiths. This was a worry expressed by Scarman L.J. in the Court of Appeal who pointed out that the established five-day working week created no problem for Jewish teachers in relation to Saturday or for Christian teachers in relation to Sundays. But a rigid adherence to the five-day working week would mean that a devout Muslim, who took seriously his duty to attend Friday prayers, could never become a full-time teacher.[4]

However, beneath this question of equity lay a more fundamental issue. On whom should the 'costs' of belief fall? Who should bear the consequences of belief? Should the inconvenience and the loss of working time involved in a teacher's attending an act of worship during the working day be borne by the education authority? Or should the costs consequent upon belief fall upon the believer himself? In the Court of Appeal, Lord Denning M.R. and Scarman L.J. differed not only in their interpretation of the legal details that bore upon the case but also in their general approach to this question. Lord Denning, while 'upholding religious freedom to the full', clearly regarded the demands of Mr Ahmad's beliefs as a burden that Mr Ahmad should bear and construed his claim that he should be able to attend the mosque, on full pay, as a demand that the Muslim community be given 'preferential treatment over the great majority of the people'.[5] By contrast, Scarman L.J. argued that the educational system should be sufficiently flexible to accommodate the beliefs and observances of all religions and held that, if it did not accommodate a demand like Mr Ahmad's, Muslims could properly complain of 'discrimination'.[6]

In Mr Ahmad's case, then, it is not enough to be told that we should not engage in religious discrimination for it is not clear what should count as 'discrimination' in a case like his. Nor is anything settled by insisting that all religious beliefs

should be 'tolerated', for the issue here is not so much whether or why we should tolerate Mr Ahmad's beliefs, but rather of 'how' his beliefs should be tolerated, of what toleration itself requires. Is it enough that we simply leave Mr Ahmad to pursue his faith and to bear whatever burdens that brings his way? Or should a society arrange things so that believers are spared the incidental but adverse effects that might otherwise be consequent upon their beliefs?

The general issue underlying Mr Ahmad's case arises in many other forms in the contemporary world. For example, is it acceptable that orthodox Jews should find their employment opportunities curtailed because they refuse to work on Saturdays? Should Christian Sabbatarian traders have to suffer commercial disadvantage, relative to their non-Sabbatarian competitors, because they refuse to trade on Sundays or should law prohibit all commercial activity on Sundays so that Sabbatarians and non-Sabbatarians enjoy 'equal terms of trade'?[7] Should churches be taxed like other organisations or should they receive tax concessions so that their members do not incur financial burdens because they possess religious beliefs? Should people be safeguarded from conduct which they find offensive because of their religious beliefs, or should their offended condition be regarded as a consequence of their beliefs which they should therefore have to endure? Should religious groups who want their children to be separately educated be required to meet the additional expense that that involves, or should their separate education be financed entirely from the public purse?

In contemporary western societies these issues are likely to arise most frequently in relation to minorities, several of whom will be ethnic as well as religious minorities. It is worth noting therefore that the question of beliefs and their consequences is not inherently one about the status of minorities. In principle, it could be a majority that is required to suffer disadvantages consequent upon its beliefs. For example, in a society in which the majority were Sabbatarians and in which people were required to bear the consequences of their beliefs, it would be the majority that would find itself commercially disadvantaged relative to the minority.

Nor is this issue limited to religious belief. In this article, I shall confine myself to the case of religious belief since the issue of consequences arises particularly obviously and acutely in relation to that form of belief. But the question of who should bear the consequences can arise in relation to any sort of belief that is treated as a matter of private conviction. 'Private' here obviously does not mean 'behind closed doors'; people can and do make public expressions of the beliefs with which I am concerned. Nor does 'private' necessarily mean 'individual'. We might treat groups rather than individuals as the bearers of beliefs; that would make no material difference to the issue of consequences. Rather, these beliefs are appropriately described as 'private' only because and in so far as a society treats them as outside the proper realm of public decision.

A society cannot remove all matters of belief from the public domain. Some matters have to be the subject of public decision and the outcomes of those decisions must be regarded as matters of public responsibility. Suppose, for example, that the majority of a society believes that, for reasons of social justice, taxation should be increased while the minority strongly opposes any such increase. If taxation is then increased, it will hardly do for the minority to argue that, since the increase in taxation is a consequence of the beliefs of the majority, only the majority should have to pay that increase. That would not do because taxation is properly a matter of public decision and public decisions properly apply to all members of the public. Henceforth, when I use the term 'belief' I shall use it to refer only to those beliefs that a society treats as matters of private conviction. I shall pass over the question of why we should not treat all matters of belief as properly the subjects of public decision.

Generally the liberal tradition has held, or perhaps taken for granted, that people should bear the consequences of their beliefs. John Rawls will serve as an example.[8] Indeed, Rawls is a particularly apt example since he is willing to go a considerable way in requiring the members of a society to take responsibility for one another's well-being. He regards the distribution of natural abilities amongst people as morally arbitrary; no-one has a claim to a better lot in life merely because he or she has been favoured by nature. Thus, a just society would distribute its resources so that those of its members who had been least favoured by nature were not materially disadvantaged because of that fact about themselves. In particular, Rawls's difference principle allows inequality in the distribution of income and wealth only in so far as that inequality works to the advantage of the least well-off group in society. So Rawls does not allow that individuals should have simply to endure whatever consequences happen to follow upon their possessing or not possessing natural abilities.

However, he handles people's beliefs quite differently from their natural abilities. He places individuals' beliefs, including their religious beliefs, within what he calls their 'conceptions of the good'. In Rawls's scheme of things, the basic rules of a society are set without reference to the different content of people's conceptions of the good. Subject to the difference principle, liberties and resources are apportioned to people equally. People are then at liberty, within the structure established by that just distribution, to pursue whatever conception of the good they choose. That may mean, of course, that some conceptions of the good – those demanding more resources or more than one's allotted portion of liberty – are more difficult to fulfil than others. But individuals must take responsibility for their conceptions of the good and there can be no complaint of 'injustice' merely because a more demanding conception is harder to realise than a less demanding conception.[9] Thus, if some beliefs turn out to be more demanding than others, and therefore less easy to fulfil, that is an outcome that the believers have to endure. By the same token, individuals have to look to themselves and to other like-minded individuals to cope with the consequences of their beliefs. They cannot, in fairness, impose those consequences upon others.

Why should that be? Why should people bear the consequences of their beliefs? Why does justice not require us to even out those consequences so that no body of believers is more or less well placed than any other?

2 Foundations

Belief and choice

One consideration which may be invoked to justify our making people bear the consequences of their beliefs is choice. People do not choose their race or their sex and it is unfair that their opportunities in life should be prejudiced by these unchosen features of themselves. Similarly people do not choose their abilities and talents – in so far as those abilities and talents are determined by each individual's genetic endowment rather than by the subsequent development of that endowment. We might argue therefore, like Rawls, that a society should try to arrange things so that those who have not been favoured in the genetic lottery do not suffer economic and social disadvantage as a consequence of their having been disadvantaged by nature. By contrast, people's beliefs are not a given part of themselves like their race or sex or genetic make-up. People choose what they believe and they can therefore be held responsible for what they believe and, by extension, for the consequences of what they believe. The consequences of people's beliefs are the consequences of their choices; they must therefore shoulder the burden of those consequences themselves rather than expect that burden to be shouldered by others.[10]

In some ways the language of choice goes quite naturally with that of belief. For example, we might casually remark to someone, 'if that is what you choose to believe, that is up to you'. But there is also reason to question whether people can really be said to 'choose' what they believe.

Firstly, people are greatly influenced in what they believe by the social context in which they develop. In reality, it might be said, people do not adopt beliefs via a process of autonomous, critical reflection. They simply imbibe beliefs from the social and cultural context in which they find themselves. Thus, although people do not come into the world already possessed of beliefs, the process of socialisation ensures that their beliefs are just as 'unchosen' as their race or their sex.[11]

This is a large and complicated matter. In so far as the link between socialisation and belief is an empirical matter, different things are likely to be true of different circumstances and different individuals and, perhaps also, different beliefs. There is reason to resist the claim that, in Richard Rorty's phrase, socialisation 'goes all the way down' for everyone, everywhere.[12] Clearly many people can and do shed beliefs which were part of their upbringing, and they can and do adopt beliefs that were not a part of their upbringing. This fluidity is more likely to characterise the sort of society with which we are concerned here: a plural society which, just because it is plural, causes its members to be aware of beliefs other than those which form their immediate context. However I can do little to settle this issue here and I do not wish to deny the tremendous importance of socialisation in the formation of beliefs. I suggest only that there is reason to

hesitate before accepting that people are the entirely helpless victims of inherited systems of belief.

How we regard this issue is likely to be biased by how we conceptualise it. I have characterised it in terms of beliefs, but nowadays it is also likely to be characterised by reference to 'cultures'. It is part of the idea of a 'culture' that it is something which envelops those who belong to it. Individuals do not make their own cultures, nor do they choose a culture. Their culture is something that they find themselves within and the culture to which they belong constitutes part of their given identity. The idea of 'choosing' a culture has the same absurdity about it as the idea of deciding to start a tradition. Cultures and traditions do not work like that. Thus, in so far as we treat people's beliefs as ingredients of their culture, we will be predisposed to treat those beliefs as part of their given identity rather than features of their lives over which they have control.

However, we should not allow our thought to be tyrannised by concepts like 'culture'. That term takes in a large array of very different aspects of people's lives – their language, diet, manners, mores, dress, and so on. Some of these, such as language and dress, would not normally be objects of critical reflection. But beliefs have epistemic content. They make claims about the way the world is and about how we should behave in it. They can be assessed as true or false, more or less supported by evidence, more or less plausible, and so on. Beliefs are therefore open to critical appraisal in a way that is quite irrelevant to many of the other ingredients of culture. Anyone who takes his beliefs seriously must be concerned about the truth or merit of their content. He cannot regard his own beliefs as a mere quirk of culture. A person's culture may be invoked in a *causal* explanation of his beliefs, but it cannot be offered by the believer himself as a *reason* for his believing what he does. In addition, the notion, which has been voiced in some quarters recently, that it is somehow disloyal and traitorous to do other than accept the truth or the rightness of the beliefs that form a part of one's inherited culture is both silly and sinister.[13]

Once again, I do not mean to be dismissive of the significance of culture. I mean only to question whether societies and cultures imprison their members in systems of belief from which there is no escape. At the very least, the appeals to socialisation and culture would seem insufficiently conclusive to remove all reason for holding people responsible for their beliefs.

However, there is a second and less contingent way in which the idea of 'choosing beliefs' may be questioned. Do I 'choose' what to believe? Do I not simply believe? I do not choose to believe Pythagoras's theorem; I simply believe it. I do not choose to believe that New York is in the United States; I just believe that that is where it is. The use of 'choice' in conjunction with 'belief' implies an act of choosing which is separate from that of believing: we choose what to believe and then we believe it. But that is not how belief works. I can choose to go to France for a holiday and that act of choosing can be distinguished from my subsequently going to France. I can decide to buy a car and that act of deciding can be distinguished from my actually buying the car. But there is not a similar act of choosing or deciding to believe which is distinguishable from a subsequent and separate act of believing. There is just believing. I may, of course, gradually come to believe something and my beliefs may be the outcome of a long process of deliberation. But 'coming to believe' is not the same as choosing to believe something and then going on to believe it.

In addition, 'choosing to believe' implies an optionality of a sort that is not normally a part of the believing process. I choose to go to France for a holiday when I might have chosen to go to Spain or Italy. Similarly I choose to buy a car when I might have chosen to buy a yacht or to have spent my money on something else. But it is not similarly open to me to choose to believe that the square on the hypotenuse is not equal to the sum of the squares of the two other sides of a right-angled triangle. Nor can I simply opt to believe that New York is in Canada or Mexico rather than in the USA. Thus, when people are told that their beliefs are the offspring of their choices, they may reasonably object that, on the contrary, they have no choice about what they believe. They cannot but believe what seems to them to be the case. Their beliefs are no more at their disposal than their physical make-up.

At this point, it may be that we should begin to distinguish between different sorts of belief. What is morally right or what is religiously true are not, it might be said, matters on which people find themselves confronted with indisputable states of affairs which they cannot but recognise. Thus, in these areas, there remains a significant element of choice. Even if there is no scope for people to choose what to believe about Pythagoras's theorem or about the location of New York, there is scope for them to choose which God or gods to believe in. However, even that is disputable. Some believers would protest that their religious beliefs are so manifestly true to themselves, even if not to others, that they have no choice but to believe. Those who accept that there is scope for different people to arrive intelligibly at different beliefs in religious matters might still object that the language of choice misdescribes the process by which particular individuals come to hold particular beliefs.[14] Since the role of choice, or of processes akin to choice, in believing is likely to remain controversial, let me add one further comment on the alleged centrality of choice to the issue of consequences.

Even if some feature of a person is a product of that person's choice, it does not follow that others are justified in treating that person any old how in respect of that choice. Suppose we accept that I have the right to adopt any religion that I 'choose'; it does not follow that others are free to persecute me for my religious beliefs just because those beliefs are 'chosen'. On the contrary, it is implicit in my having a *right* to adopt the religion I choose that others are duty-bound not to persecute me in that way. If we move from outright persecution to discrimination, we may still say that my having chosen a particular religion does not justify others' discriminating against me in matters such as employment and education. If I have the right to adopt whatever religion I choose, my choice ought to be respected and others ought not to deprive me of opportunities because they dislike the particular choice I have made.

Of course, much depends on how we define the right at issue here. Assuming that the right to adopt and to pursue a religion is, in jurisprudential terminology, a claim as well as a liberty, the scope of that claim can be drawn more or less generously. Libertarians, for example, would normally accept that the right to religious liberty constitutes a claim upon others to refrain from religious persecution, but not a claim which properly limits the freedom of employers to hire and fire whomsoever they choose, for whatever reason they choose. We should note, however, that the libertarian's objection centres on the right of private employers to determine the make-up of their own workforce. It is not therefore special to laws prohibiting religious discrimination and counts equally against the legal prohibition of racial and sexual discrimination.[15] But, if we do not share this general aversion to antidiscrimination measures, it does not seem extravagant to hold that, if the freedom to adopt and to pursue a religion has the status of a fundamental right, people should not have to suffer unfavourable treatment because of the use they make of that fundamental right. But that, in turn, simply takes us back to the question of what is to count as 'suffering unfavourable treatment'. If people have a right to hold the beliefs they do – whether or not those beliefs are 'chosen' – does requiring them to bear the consequences of their beliefs amount to a violation of that right? We may find a clearer answer to that question if we shift our focus from the idea of choice to that of freedom of belief.

Freedom of belief

I shall simply take for granted that people should be accorded freedom of belief and leave unstated the many cogent arguments that may be urged in favour of that freedom. That people should possess freedom of belief is not an extravagant assumption in this context for, in the absence of that freedom, the issue of who should bear the diverse consequences of diverse beliefs could hardly arise. By 'freedom of belief' I understand not only the liberty to believe but also the liberty to act upon one's beliefs. Limits may have to be imposed upon that freedom and, in a plural society, just where those limits should fall, and why, are likely to be controversial matters. Again, I shall not pursue those matters here. Rather, I want to suggest that, if we accord people freedom of belief, it is reasonable to require them to bear the consequences of what they believe.

Freedom of belief, I have said, includes not just the freedom to believe but also the freedom to shape one's life in accordance with one's belief. Indeed, it is the latter freedom that has been the more significant in that it has been the more vulnerable. It is, of course, possible to control what people believe – sadly, more so in this century than in any other. But, for the most part, what goes on in the recesses of people's minds has been of less concern to others and less vulnerable to interference and suppression than the external manifestations of belief. In particular, given that our concern is with the consequences of belief, it is not merely believing but 'practising' one's belief that is more pertinent.

Now as long as my beliefs shape only my life, I can reasonably keep others at bay. My beliefs, I can protest, are properly no-one's concern but my own. In particular, as long as I bear the consequences of my belief, I can maintain that my beliefs remain purely my affair. However, if I expect others to bear those consequences, that ceases to be true. What I believe then affects lives other than my own. The more burdensome the consequences of my beliefs, the more those beliefs will burden the lives of others. That provides reason for others having some control over what I believe. Of course, they may be unable to alter what I believe and it may be highly undesirable that they should if they could. But they are capable of controlling how far I *act* on my beliefs and, if they are going to have to meet the costs of my actions, why should they not spare themselves that expense by preventing my acting in costly ways? In other words, why should they not be entitled to limit my freedom rather than bear its consequences? If my acting on my beliefs significantly affects the lives of others, it becomes implausible for me to claim an inviolable and exclusive right to determine how I should behave in matters of religious faith. The force of this line of argument is all the greater for its arising in a context of conflicting beliefs. It is bad enough that others should have to bear the costs of my freely chosen actions. How much worse that they should have to bear the consequences of my beliefs, which beliefs they may reckon (perhaps with good reason) to be false, wrong or evil. How much stronger the case for protecting people from becoming the unwilling 'victims' of another's freedom.

It will not do to reply that any such pre-emptive strategy should be vetoed in the name of 'freedom', for it is not just my freedom that is at stake. If others have to bear the consequences of my beliefs, my use of my freedom can unilaterally diminish the freedom of others. We should be concerned not only with freedom but also with its equitable distribution and it is difficult to see how an arrangement which places the freedom of some at the mercy of the freedom of others can be consistent with any standard of equitable distribution.

Thus, I suggest, the reason why people should bear the consequences of their beliefs is that that is a natural concomitant of their enjoying freedom of belief. Those who claim that freedom must accept responsibility for the use they make of it. We could, of course, turn this around and argue that people have to bear the consequence of one another's beliefs and that freedom of belief should be curtailed accordingly. But that, I suspect, is an option which will appeal to no-one.[16]

Promoting diversity

The argument I have developed here may be regarded as altogether too negative in spirit. Is not the diversity of a plural society something that we should cherish and celebrate rather than merely tolerate? It is enough merely to refrain from persecuting or impeding ways of life other than our own? Should we not take positive steps to see that all ways of life flourish? This more positive, promotive approach to diversity might be used to argue that the consequences of belief should be treated as a burden to be borne by society as a whole. By taking collective responsibility for those consequences, we will ensure that no system of belief labours under any special disadvantage and that a hundred flowers can bloom.

There are many forms of human diversity and many of those forms are quite intelligibly cherished and fostered. A society may be said to be richer for having a diversity of forms of literature, of music, of food, and so on. It may therefore be in the interests of all of us that we should ensure that that diversity should continue and develop; if that requires a sharing of costs, so be it. But what are we to say to a diversity of beliefs about the true, the right and the good? Can we similarly celebrate the propagation and proliferation of beliefs which we ourselves believe to be erroneous, evil, and wrong? It is one thing to refrain from preventing people holding and acting upon beliefs which we ourselves believe to be false. It is quite another positively to contribute towards the maintenance and promotion of those erroneous beliefs. It borders on absurdity to suppose that a group of people with a system of belief about the true and the right should welcome and feel dutybound to support a rival system of belief which they hold to be false and wrong.

This objection is likely to be felt particularly keenly by those who possess a religious faith. Atheists, of course, can regard religious beliefs as pernicious as well as false. But the non-believer might also take a more relaxed and benign view of religion. He might regard it as a relatively harmless delusion which adds to the range of human experience and which has some fortunate social and cultural side-effects. He might therefore be relatively undisturbed by having to play some small part in its continuance. But it is hard to see how the religious adherent could be similarly relaxed about his having to sustain a rival system of belief – unless he subscribes to the rather odd belief that all religions, without distinction, are equally valid and valuable paths to God (or the gods?). Imagine how Muslims and Hindus in contemporary India would respond to the suggestion that they should help to maintain and promote one another's beliefs. At a minimum they would be likely to react with indignation and incredulity and I, for my part, could not fault those reactions.

However, there is another sort of argument that might be used to justify our adopting a more positive attitude and assisting with the consequences of others' beliefs. Instead of appealing to an alleged collective interest that we all have in the maintenance of a diversity of beliefs, we might focus upon each person's 'good' and how that good is related to that person's beliefs. People, it might be argued, should be able to flourish in whatever lives they lead and a society ought to ensure that all of its members have genuinely equal opportunities to lead equally fulfilled lives. What constitutes 'flourishing' and 'fulfilment' for individuals or groups must be tied to their fundamental beliefs. That is, they can flourish and find fulfilment only in forms of life to which they themselves are committed. We have to accept that people believe what they believe and work from there. Thus a society ought to do its utmost to assist its members to maintain and promote their beliefs, not because that society has a collective interest in the continuance of all of those beliefs, but because its members ought to flourish equally in whatever lives they themselves believe to be right.[17]

This argument raises large and fundamental issues about the character of a just society and here I can do no more than point to various reasons for rejecting it. Notice that it is an argument which demands far more than that we should cancel out whatever material inequalities happen to be consequent upon differences in belief. It shifts the focus of justice from the distribution of resources to the relative levels of individuals' fulfilment. A just society ceases to be one which distributes resources fairly amongst people and then leaves them to use those resources in the pursuit of whatever goals they think good, right or desirable.

Instead it becomes one in which a society is made responsible for ensuring that people attain equal levels of fulfilment in whatever forms of life they commit themselves to.

There would clearly be massive practical problems in implementing this principle of equal fulfilment. Large philosophical doubts must also hang over the intelligibility of 'equal fulfilment' in the context of radically different forms of life. The most obvious candidate for reducing different forms of life to commensurability would be some form of utilitarianism, but a utilitarian measure would be both inappropriate and improper in the context of forms of life which were non-utilitarian in character.[18] Even if equal fulfilment were feasible, we might still question whether it would be just. If people are left free to pursue any form of life, should some have to suffer because of the extravagant, eccentric or ill-judged use that others make of that freedom? As I argued earlier, if some have to pay the price for the use that others make of their freedom, including their freedom of belief, the legitimacy of that freedom is very much in doubt. In addition, the view that people's 'good' consists in fulfilment in *whatever* form of life they pursue is obviously a highly contestable form of perfectionism and is a conception of the good which is most unlikely to be shared by the members of a religiously plural society.[19]

There is much more to be said on the ideal of equal fulfilment, but I hope that these brief remarks are sufficient to intimate why a society should not assume collective responsibility for securing equal levels of 'belief fulfilment' for each of its members.

3 Identifying Consequences

Even if we accept that, in principle, people should bear the consequences of their beliefs, we are not yet out of the woods. We have still to establish what *are*, or what are to *count as*, the consequences of belief. That is far from straightforward.

Consider Mr Ahmad's position. His predicament arose not merely from his duty (as he understood it) to attend a mosque on Friday afternoons. It arose because Friday afternoon forms part of the normal working week in Britain. If the working week had run from Sundays to Thursdays, with Fridays and Saturdays counting as the 'week-end', Mr Ahmad's beliefs would not

have had problematic consequences. It would then have been Christian Sabbatarians who would have been in trouble. So was Mr Ahmad's inability to perform his teaching duties to the full a consequence of his beliefs? Might he not claim that it was rather a consequence of the particular set of days that children were required to attend school in Britain?

In some cases we may be able to say that an outcome is a 'natural' consequence of a belief such that no-one but the believer can be held responsible for that outcome. For example, if a Jehovah's Witness contracts an illness which can be cured only by a blood transfusion and if he refuses to receive a transfusion, his death can be characterised as a natural consequence of his belief.[20] But most controversial cases will not be like that. They will result not from a conjunction of beliefs and 'nature' but from a confluence of beliefs and humanly established circumstances.

Here it may help to distinguish between two different ways in which systems of belief can make demands upon their adherents. Demands which are intrinsic to a system of belief I shall call *burdens* of belief. Those which are extrinsic to the system of belief I shall call *consequences* of belief. The 'burden' of a belief is intrinsic to the belief in that it is imposed by the belief itself. Thus it is part of the burden of Islamic belief that one must pray five times a day. It is part of the burden of Catholic belief that one should attend Mass on Sundays. It is part of the burden of orthodox Judaism that one should not work between nightfall on Friday and nightfall on Saturday. (What I describe as a 'burden' of belief may, of course, be experienced as joyous rather than onerous by the believer.) By contrast what I label the 'consequences' of belief are distinct from the belief itself in that they are not essential requirements of the belief even though that belief is essential to their occurrence. If, for the sake of argument, we accept Mr Ahmad's own interpretation of the demands of his faith, it is part of the 'burden' of his belief that he should attend a mosque on Friday afternoons, but it is not a part of that burden that he should refrain from performing the duties of a full-time teacher. That is simply a 'consequence' of his belief which arises in the context of the British educational system. Similarly, refraining from working on the Lord's Day is part of the 'burden' of Sabbatarian belief, but suffering commercial disadvantage is not; that may be a 'consequence' of Sabbatarian belief but 'suffering commercial disadvantage' is not something enjoined by Sabbatarianism itself.

Given all that I have argued up to now and, in particular, assuming that we reject the equal fulfilment principle, we should require people to bear the 'burdens' of their beliefs for those burdens are imposed only by their beliefs. But assigning responsibility for what I have distinguished as the 'consequences' of belief is altogether more complicated since those consequences are not uniquely determined by belief. Let me identify two fundamentally different approaches to this issue.

The first possibility is that we establish a set of social arrangements independently of people's religious beliefs. Those arrangements would be set according to certain standards of fairness or rightfulness and would constitute a 'fixed background'. People would then be free to live according to their beliefs within the constraints set by that background. Whatever consequences, advantageous or disadvantageous, arose from the conjunction of a particular set of beliefs with those background arrangements would have to be borne by believers themselves. This approach is implicit in the work of liberal theorists such as Rawls and Ackerman.[21]

The second possibility is more even-handed in character. If an outcome is the result of two (or more) factors, it would hold both (or all) factors responsible for the outcome and proceed accordingly. Believers should be held jointly rather than solely responsible for the consequences which emanate from the conjunction of their beliefs and social circumstances. That points to a policy of compromise, mutual accommodation or cost-sharing or, where no such middle way is possible, a decision which is reached only after due weight has been given to all of the interests involved, including those of religious believers.

For the sake of clarity it might help to mention a third approach which would be the obverse of the first: beliefs should be treated as fixed features of the social landscape and believers should bear no responsibility at all for consequences which emanate from the interaction of those beliefs with social circumstances. The purpose of the second part of this article was to rule out this third approach. But how should we decide between the first and second?

That question is not easy to answer within the limits of this article, or indeed outside of them, since it turns not on the status to be given to beliefs and to the demands of belief, but on the status to be given to the circumstances and arrangements which combine with beliefs to yield consequences. Thus where one stands on this issue will depend upon where one stands on some of the most fundamental questions of political philosophy. People of significantly different political persuasions will give significantly different answers not because they give different values to belief and to the demands of belief, but because of their different evaluations of the social and political contexts in which beliefs are held and acted upon. It is not therefore easy to make progress in this area. Here I shall confine myself to pointing out that the two approaches I have described need not be thought of as mutually exclusive and that some mix of the two has considerable appeal.

Suppose a religion requires that a temple be constructed for the glory and worship of God. According to the distinction I made a moment ago, it will be part of the 'burden' of belief of that religion that a temple should be constructed. Constructing the temple will take time, effort and money. But the expenditure of that time, effort and money is not itself part of the 'burden' of belief. It is a 'consequence' of the belief. The belief requires only that there be a temple; it does not prescribe that its adherents, and its adherents alone, must sacrifice specific amounts of time, effort and money to construct the temple. Those costs arise for the believers only because non-believers will not share in financing the temple and/or because, and to the extent that, people charge for the expenditure of labour and for materials in the society concerned. Now we have shown that believers should not be entirely absolved of responsibility for the consequences of their beliefs. The temple should not, therefore, be financed wholly out of general taxation. But might we argue that, since the costs of constructing the temple arise only in part because the faithful believe it ought to be constructed, and since they arise also because people are unwilling to provide labour and materials at less than the going rates, those costs are jointly brought about by believers and non-believers and therefore should be met jointly by the two groups? The temple might then be financed partly from the private funds of believers and partly from general taxation.

That proposal would not, I suspect, win much approval – from either believers or non-believers. The reason is not that current rates for labour and materials (whether fixed by the market or by the state) contribute nothing causally to the costs incurred in building the temple. Clearly they do. Rather it is because material and labour costs set a 'background' against which people are to make decisions about their lives and against which, in the ordinary course of things, they are required to take responsibility for the costs of their own projects. Of course, what that 'background' should be is open to disputes of a familiar sort – a range of possibilities is on offer from the libertarian to the liberal socialist. But, given that those background arrangements are 'just', believers should have to bear the financial consequences of having to construct temples, to go on pilgrimages, to stage festivals, and the like. For moral and political purposes, those consequences are to be deemed exclusively consequences of belief.

I myself would respond to Sabbatarianism in this way. Other things being equal,[22] people should be free to enter into whatever voluntary arrangements they choose, with whom they choose, when they choose. If some people possess beliefs according to which it is wrong to trade or work on Saturdays or Sundays, they should be free to abstain from trading and working on those days. But any commercial disadvantage they suffer as a consequence should be regarded as a consequence of their beliefs and not as a consequence of others not sharing those beliefs. That disadvantage should not therefore rank as a reason for removing or limiting the freedom of non-Sabbatarians to trade and work as they see fit and it would be quite wrong to deal with this issue in a utilitarian, or quasi-utilitarian, fashion by simply weighing up the competing interests involved.

But, however one sets those background constraints, there may also be cases which arise *within* them, cases in which private or public projects are at odds with, or in competition with, the demands of religious belief and which are properly dealt with by weighing and, if possible, accommodating the competing interests involved. Consider the once contentious issue of Sikhs and motor-cycle crash helmets. In 1972 the British Parliament passed a law empowering the Minister of Transport to require all motor-cyclists to wear crash helmets, which he duly did. That caused problems for biking Sikhs who would not remove their turbans. In 1976 the law was amended to exempt Sikhs from this requirement. Should Sikhs have been accommodated in that way?

In a case that went to trial before the law was amended, a Sikh claimed that his religious beliefs provided adequate excuse for his not wearing a crash helmet. In response a judge presiding at the trial commented that no-one was bound to ride a motor-cycle and the law prescribed simply that, if you rode a motor-cycle, you had to wear a crash helmet; members of the Sikh community might find themselves unable to ride motor-cycles but they were prevented 'not because of the English law but by the requirements of their religion'.[23] In other words, a Sikh's inability to ride a motor-cycle was to be deemed a consequence not of the law but of his beliefs. But that construction seems much less plausible in this case. Why? In part, no doubt, the answer is that compelling people to wear crash helmets is a largely paternalistic measure and Sikhs have a reason, special to themselves, for taking a different view of what is for their good. However, that is not the only consideration. Other-regarding interests are also at stake in this issue but those interests do not seem sufficiently special to trump all competing considerations.[24] Consequently, in this sort of case, it seems appropriate that interests should be weighed and the law adjusted accordingly.

One further comment on this alternative. An argument commonly used in relation to religiously plural societies is that their constitutions and policies should not be grounded upon religious principles. The justification usually given is that public rules and public policies should be based upon reasons of a kind that are accessible to, and that can be acknowledged by, all members of the public; in a religiously diverse society, religious doctrine cannot provide that shared form of reason.[25] But that argument does not require that public decisions should ignore the interests that people have as holders of religious beliefs, nor does it require that any non-religious concern should routinely trump any interest that has its foundation in a religious belief. It does not therefore require us to adopt the 'background' approach to the complete exclusion of the approach that I have just described.

However, as I have already indicated, I cannot settle the question of how beliefs should rank alongside other factors which contribute to consequences. All I have sought to establish is that a society does not have a *general* duty to relieve people of the consequences of their beliefs. If, in a particular instance, there is a case for relief, that case must be grounded not in any such general duty but in a claim that, morally as well as empirically, the relevant consequence is not to be considered a consequence of belief alone.

Since I began with the case of Mr Ahmad, perhaps I should conclude with it. Applied to that case, the thrust of my argument is that Mr Ahmad had no general claim, *qua* believer, that others should bear the consequences of his not being available for teaching on Friday afternoons. However, there is obviously more to be said. Mr Ahmad's beliefs caused difficulty only in the context of the working week in Britain. The pattern of that week cannot pretend to be a fact of nature nor can the use of Sunday as a day of rest pretend to be religiously neutral either in effect or, more importantly, in intention. For those who take the view that Britain and other western societies are, or ought to be, 'Christian societies' there is nothing untoward in that; those societies' arrangements are rightly Christian in character and other religions have to take their chances against that background. In so far as Saturdays are also non-working days for many people in Christian soci-

eties, that is simply fortunate for members of the Jewish faith; in so far as Fridays are working days for almost everyone in Christian societies, that is simply unfortunate for members of the Islamic faith. (*Mutatis mutandis*, the same might be said of Islamic or Jewish societies.) But for those who hold that, in its laws and its public policy, a society should aspire to be neutral between religions, the 'inequitable' character of the British week must be a source of concern. It would of course be possible to make the non-working day neutral between religions by shifting it to, say, Tuesday or Wednesday, or by altering its frequency, so that it would be equally inconvenient for all religions. But to invert the Pareto principle in that way ('make some people worse off while making no-one better off') would seem entirely without merit. As long as Sundays retain their traditional status in societies like Britain, Mr Ahmad and Muslims like him have some claim to be accommodated.[26] Whether, all things considered, they should be accommodated must depend upon the feasibility and the costs of that accommodation.

Notes

An earlier version of this article was given to a seminar on 'Political Theory and Toleration' organised by Sally Jenkinson and Preston King for the annual conference of the Political Studies Association of the United Kingdom, 1991. I am grateful to both of them and to the other participants in the seminar, particularly Mark Goldie, John Horton and Deborah Fitzmaurice, for their comments on the paper. I am also grateful for their helpful advice to Kay Black, Robert Goodin, Tim Gray and Albert Weale.

1 *Ahmad v. Inner London Education Authority.* Employment Appeal Tribunal: [1976] I.C.R. 461. Court of Appeal: [1978] 1 Q.B. 36, [1977] 3 W.L.R. 396. The case is described in detail in Sebastian Poulter, *English Law and Ethnic Minority Customs* (London: Butterworths, 1986), pp. 247–52. See also St John A. Robilliard, *Religion and the Law* (Manchester: Manchester University Press, 1984).

2 Whether the demands of employment provide sufficient reason for not attending Friday prayers seems to be disputed within the Muslim community. ILEA pointed out that it employed hundreds of Muslim teachers none of whom had made the same request as Mr Ahmad; [1978] 1 Q.B. 39, 40–1, 43–4.

3 *X v. United Kingdom*, (1981) 22 Decisions and Reports of the European Commission 27.

4 [1978] 1 Q.B. 47, 50.

5 [1978] 1 Q.B. 11.

6 [1978] 1 Q.B. 48, 50. See also Lord Scarman, 'Toleration and the law', *On Toleration*, ed. S. Mendus and D. Edwards (Oxford: Clarendon Press, 1987), pp. 49–62.

Mr Ahmad's case is not unique in English law. For another case arising from a conflict between patterns of work and Muslim religious obligations, see *Hussain v. London Country Bus Services Ltd*, Incomes Data Services (IDS) Brief 263 (Aug 1984) p. 5. For similar cases, concerning other faiths, see *London Borough of Tower Hamlets v. Rabin*, IDS Brief 406 (Oct 1989) p. 12, and *Fluss v. Grant Thornton Chartered Accountants*, IDS Brief 360 (1987) p. 6 (both concerning Jews); *Esson v. London Transport Executive*, [1975] I.R.L.R. 48 (concerning a Seventh Day Adventist); *Post Office v. Mayers*, IDS Brief 397 (May 1989) p. 4 (concerning a member of the World Wide Church of God). There have also been a number of notable cases concerning specific religious festivals; see *Ostreicher v. Secretary of State for the Environment*, [1978] 1 All ER 591, [1978] 3 All ER 82 (C.A.); *Prais v. EC Council*, [1977] ICR 284; *Naiz v. Ryman Ltd*, IDS Brief 376 (July 1988) p. 6.

Currently law in the United Kingdom prohibits direct and indirect discrimination on grounds of race and sex but, with the exception of Northern Ireland, not on grounds of religious faith.

However, in the case of groups such as Jews and Sikhs, a high degree of coincidence between ethnic identity and religious belief means that, under the 1976 Race Relations Act, those groups do receive a measure of legal protection against adverse treatment related to their religious beliefs. The House of Lords ruled that Sikhs were a racial group (by reference to their 'ethnic origins') within the meaning of the Race Relations Act 1976, in *Mandla v. Dowell Lee*; [1983] 2 A.C. 548. Lord Fraser gave 'a common religion' as one of several characteristics that might contribute to the identification of a community as an 'ethnic group' (562). In the same case, the Court of Appeal had previously ruled that Sikhs were a religious rather than a racial group who therefore, *qua* Sikhs, fell outside the protection afforded by the Race Relations Act; [1982] W.L.R. 932. In a recent unreported case, *Dawkins v. The Crown Suppliers (P.S.A.)*, a tribunal decided that Rastafarians were an ethnic group, rather than merely a religious group, and therefore came within the provisions of the Act; see Dave Marrington, 'Legal decisions', *New Community*, 16 (1990) 296–8. However, that decision was subsequently overturned; [1991] I.R.L.R. 327; [1993] I.R.L.R. 284.

If British law had provided against religious discrimination on the model of current British laws prohibiting racial and sexual discrimination, Mr Ahmad could not have complained of direct discrimination since he did not lose his full-time post because he was a Muslim. Rather he lost his post because he failed to comply fully with ILEA's requirement to teach on Friday afternoons. But he might well have complained of indirect discrimination in respect of that requirement since he, and Muslims like him, were prevented by their religious beliefs from complying fully with that requirement and suffered disadvantage as a consequence. It would then have been open to ILEA to have shown that that requirement was 'justifiable' in spite of its disadvantageous effect for devout Muslims.

For two significant American cases, raising issues similar in character to the case of Mr Ahmad, see *T.W.A. v. Hardison*, 432 U.S. 63 (1977), and *Ansonia Board of Education v. Philbrook*, 55 USLW 4019 (1986). For investigations of these issues in the context of American law, see David E. Retter, 'The rise and fall of Title VII's requirement of reasonable accommodation for religious employees', *Columbia Human Rights Law Review* 11 (1979), 63–86; Michael W. McConnell, 'Accommodation of Religion', *The Supreme Court Review*, ed. P. Kurland, G. Casper, D.J. Hutchinson (Chicago: University of Chicago Press, 1986), pp. 1–59; William L. Kandel, 'Current developments in EEO: religious accom-

modation after *Philbrook*', *Employee Relations Law Journal* 12 (1987), 690–7; and Gloria T. Beckley and Paul Burstein, 'Religious pluralism, equal opportunity, and the state', *Western Political Quarterly* 44 (1991), 185–208.

7   cf. Albert Weale, 'Toleration, individual differences and respect for persons', *Aspects of Toleration*, ed. J. Horton and S. Mendus (London: Methuen, 1985), pp. 16–35 at p. 27; and Susan Mendus, *Toleration and the Limits of Liberalism* (Basingstoke: Macmillan, 1989), p. 84. There are, of course, many arguments for and against keeping Sundays 'special' which do not turn on the issue that I am concerned with here.

8   John Rawls, *A Theory of Justice* (Oxford: Oxford University Press, 1972).

9   Rawls has underlined this feature of his theory in articles that he has written since the publication of *A Theory of Justice*. See especially, 'Fairness to goodness', *Philosophical Review* 84 (1975), 536–54; 'Justice as fairness: political not metaphysical', *Philosophy and Public Affairs* 14 (1985), 223–51; 'The priority of right and ideas of the good', *Philosophy and Public Affairs* 17 (1988), 251–76.

10   That religious faith, unlike race, is a 'chosen' rather than an 'unalterable' feature of people was a consideration that weighed with the English Court of Appeal in reaching its decision, in *Mandla v. Dowell Lee*, that Sikhs did not constitute an 'ethnic group'. In particular, Oliver L.J. thought the expression 'ethnic group' was 'entirely inappropriate to describe a group into and out of which anyone may travel as a matter of free choice; and freedom of choice – to join, to remain or to leave – is inherent in the whole philosophy of Sikhism'; [1982] W.L.R. 932 at 941–2; see also the similar views of Kerr L.J. at 945–9. The House of Lords recognised that people may convert into and out of Sikhism but held that that did not preclude Sikhs being an ethnic group; [1983] 2 A.C, 548 at 562–3, 569.

11   cf. Susan Mendus, 'The tigers of wrath and the horses of instruction', *Free Speech*, ed. B. Parekh (London: Commission for Racial Equality, 1990), pp. 3–17.

12   Richard Rorty, *Contingency, Irony and Solidarity* (Cambridge: Cambridge University Press, 1989), p. xiii.

13   cf. Ali A. Mazrui, 'The Satanic Verses or a satanic novel? Moral dilemmas of the Rushdie affair', *Free Speech*, ed. B. Parekh (London: Commission for Racial Equality, 1990), pp. 79–103 at pp. 80–1, 101.

14   cf. Mendus, *Toleration and the Limits of Liberalism*, pp. 32–5.

15   Even the libertarian need not be wholly indifferent to discrimination. Firstly, to say that employers have an unlimited right to decide whom they

employ is not to say that they cannot be criticised for the use they make of that right. Secondly, even in the minimal state there will be a public sector and the libertarian's claim that anti-discrimination measures violate the rights of private employers has no obvious equivalent in that sector.

16 For a British case which comes close to this alternative, see *Singh v. British Rail Engineering Ltd*, [1986] I.C.R. 22. Singh was not allowed to continue with his job because he refused to remove his turban so that he could wear a hard hat. Part of the justification offered by the employer was that, if Singh continued with the job wearing only his turban and then incurred injury, the fact that the injury was a consequence of Singh's beliefs would not absolve the employer of legal liability for that injury. In other words, that the employer would have to bear the financial consequences of Singh's acting on his beliefs – that is, the costs that would be consequent upon Singh's sustaining injury through wearing a turban rather than a hard hat – became a reason for depriving Singh of the freedom to continue with his job while wearing a turban.

17 cf. Charles Taylor, 'Atomism', in his *Philosophy and the Human Sciences*, vol. 2 (Cambridge: Cambridge University Press, 1985), pp. 187–210.

18 For a close examination of the idea of equal fulfilment, see Ronald Dworkin, 'What is equality? Part I: equality of welfare', *Philosophy and Public Affairs*, 10 (1981), 185–246. See also my 'The Ideal of the Neutral State', *Liberal Neutrality*, ed. R.E. Goodin and A. Reeve, pp. 9–38 at pp. 14–17. For a defence of a utilitarian form of 'equal fulfilment', but one cast only in terms of 'preferences', see Richard J. Arneson, 'Liberalism, distributive subjectivism, and equal opportunity for welfare', *Philosophy and Public Affairs*, 19 (1990), 158–94; see also his 'Neutrality and utility', *Canadian Journal of Philosophy* 20 (1990), 215–40.

19 See further my 'Liberalism, belief and doubt', *Liberalism and Recent Social and Political Philosophy*, ed. R. Bellamy, ARSP, Beiheft 36 (Stuttgart: Steiner, 1989), pp. 51–69 at pp. 63–8. I use the term 'perfectionism' in the special sense given to it by Rawls, *Theory of Justice*, pp. 25, 325–32.

20 One could resist that only by claiming that others were duty-bound to override the Jehovah's Witness's freedom of belief and to force a blood transfusion upon him; his death could then be characterised as a consequence of their failure to perform that duty.

21 Bruce A. Ackerman, *Social Justice in the Liberal State* (New Haven: Yale University Press, 1980).

22 I include this phrase only to provide for restrictions upon freedom of contract other than those at issue here.

23 *R v. Aylesbury Crown Court ex parte Chahal*, [1976] R.T.R. 489 at 492.

24 I have in mind here the distress caused to those involved in accidents causing serious injury to others. Hospital treatment and other supportive public expenditure following injury are also at issue, although those are not always straightforwardly unpaternalistic in character; see my 'Toleration, harm, and moral effect', *Aspects of Toleration*, ed. Horton and Mendus, pp. 136–57.

25 The exclusion of religious reasons from public policy is implicit in the approaches of Rawls and Ackerman. See also Jeremy Waldron, 'Theoretical foundations of liberalism', *Philosophical Quarterly* 37 (1987), 127–50, and Thomas Nagel, 'Moral conflict and political legitimacy', *Philosophy and Public Affairs* 16 (1987), 215–40. For critical examinations of this approach, see Kent Greenawalt, *Religious Convictions and Political Choice* (New York: Oxford University Press, 1988), and Joseph Raz, 'Facing diversity: the case of epistemic abstinence', *Philosophy and Public Affairs* 19 (1990), 3–46.

26 The number of those within a religious group making demands like Mr Ahmad's has implications which point in opposite directions. The smaller the number, the more easily they can be accommodated. But, the smaller the number, the greater must also be doubts about whether they *rightly* make that demand. Suppose Mr Ahmad were *mistaken* in believing that, within Islam, the exigencies of employment did not provide adequate reason for not attending a mosque (on which see note 2 above). Should that make a difference? In principle, surely it should, since Mr Ahmad's claims about what his own religion required of him would be false. In practice, public bodies would probably be reluctant to become embroiled in questions of correct doctrine. This is one respect in which a 'group' approach might yield a different answer from an 'individual' approach, i.e. an approach which identifies beliefs and the demands of belief by reference to groups rather than individuals. This issue arose in Britain in *Saggers v. British Railways Board*, a case concerning exemption from a trade union closed shop on grounds of religious belief; [1977] I.R.L.R. 266. Saggers, a Jehovah's Witness, believed that his religion was incompatible with his membership of a trade union even though membership of trade unions was not proscribed by the doctrine of Jehovah's Witnesses. The Employment Appeal Tribunal ruled that (as far as the law relevant to that case was concerned) 'belief' referred to the belief of the relevant individual and not to the established creed or dogma of the religious body of which that individual was a member.

35

Exploitation, Alternatives and Socialism

John E. Roemer

How can one understand the formation of inequality, strata and classes, and perhaps exploitation, in socialist society? Among Marxists there is no widely accepted materialist theory of the development of classes and inequality under socialism. Perhaps more noticeably, there is no widely accepted theory of the political behaviour of socialist states. Indeed, the response of many or most Marxists to wars between socialist states, for example, is that at least one of the countries involved is not socialist. This argument is tautological and not scientific: since two socialist countries could never fight each other, therefore the major premise (that they are both socialist) must be false.

The example of wars between socialist countries is given to point out the nature of a crisis in Marxian theory: that theory, formulated in the late nineteenth century to explain the development of nineteenth century capitalism, does not seem useful when applied to late twentieth century socialism (and capitalism, perhaps). Marxists cannot, for instance, agree on the nature of Soviet society. Is it socialist, capitalist, state capitalist, or transitional? What definitions might one give to decide? Taking a cue from the Marxian approach to capitalism, one might seek to define a notion of exploitation relevant to socialist society. From such a beginning could follow a theory of class, and finally a political theory of socialist society as corollary to the theory of class. This paper is an attempt to approach this set of problems in the

way indicated, by proposing a general theory of exploitation, of which socialist exploitation will be a special case. The task of providing a theory of exploitation relevant to socialist economies has much in common with the problem Marx faced in providing a theory of exploitation for capitalist economies. The economic problem for Marx was to explain how the gross inequities of capitalism could be reproduced in an economy characterised by voluntary exchange. In feudal and slave economies, there was no mystery to the locus of surplus appropriation, since the institution of labour exchange was coercive: one could clearly speak of serf and slave labour as being forcibly expropriated due to those social relations. Under capitalism, where the institution for labour exchange is non-coercive, how could one speak of exploitation, or expropriation of any commodity, including labour power? Marx's effort was to resolve this paradox by providing a theory of value which claimed that *despite* the non-coerciveness of the institution of labour exchange, that exchange was exploitative. Thus, he claimed that exploitation was a phenomenon which was robust when one relaxes the requirement that institutions for labour exchange be coercive. It is at this point that neoclassical and Marxian theory part company, for as will be shown, neoclassical economics claims that competitive allocations are not exploitative precisely because market institutions are competitive and noncoercive.

In facing socialist society, we must relax the institutional dimension labelled 'private ownership of the means of production', just as Marx had to relax the institutional dimension labelled 'coerciveness of labour exchange'. A nineteenth

Originally published in *Economic Journal*, 92 (1982), 87–107. Reprinted by permission of Blackwell Publishers.

century Marxist might have thought that when the means of production are no longer differentially (and privately) owned, then exploitation would be a meaningless concept. I wish to claim such is not the case: that, indeed, a generalisation of the Marxian theory of exploitation exists in which the phenomenon remains viable even when the means of production are socialised.

This paper proposes a general taxonomy of exploitation, which will have as special cases feudal exploitation, capitalist exploitation, and socialist exploitation. This taxonomy constitutes a general definition of exploitation. Although one intention is to apply the taxonomy to understand socialist development, as has been briefly described, there are several other applications. It provides a common language with which social scientists can contrast different conceptions of exploitation. Neoclassical economists often challenge Marxists to defend their notion of exploitation: granted, surplus value (if one wants to call it that) exists, but why should its existence entail exploitation? It is shown below how both the neoclassical conception of exploitation and the Marxian conception are special cases of the general taxonomy. The inherent normative disagreement between neoclassicals and Marxists on this issue can be stated precisely.

A third application of the general theory of exploitation is a characterisation of Marxian exploitation which, I believe, is in many ways superior to the classical approach via the labour theory of value. The key to the present approach is property relations, not labour value, and although the two are related, the property relations approach is more general and resolves many classical problems which have inflicted the labour theory of value approach to exploitation.

The outline of the paper is as follows. In section 1, a game-theoretic formulation of the concept of exploitation is proposed. Sections 2 and 3 define the games which characterise feudal and capitalistic exploitation; it is argued that the form of inequality which neoclassicals consider exploitative is akin to feudal exploitation, while Marxian exploitation is equivalent to capitalist exploitation. Section 4 defines another game which characterises socialist exploitation. Section 5 investigates the issue of socially necessary exploitation, and states some claims of the theory of historical materialism in the language of the theory of exploitation, although it does not argue for those claims. Section 6 indicates briefly the

application of the theory to inequality in existing socialist societies (which is a more subtle project than simply defining socialist exploitation), and section 7 summarises.

1 Exploitation and Alternatives

In virtually every society or economic mechanism, there is inequality. Yet not all inequality is viewed by a society as exploitative; nor will all people agree whether a given form of inequality is exploitative. Certainly, however, the notion of exploitation involves inequality in some way. What forms of inequality does a particular society (or person) view as exploitative? The inequality of master and slave was viewed as just and non-exploitative by many in ancient society, as was the inequality of lord and serf in feudal society, although today most of us consider both of these relationships exploitative. Similarly, Marxists view the inequality in the capitalist-worker relationship as exploitative, although this inequality is conceived of as non-exploitative by many people in capitalist society today. I wish to propose a theoretical device for clarifying the criteria according to which a type of economic inequality is evaluated as exploitative or not so.

What is meant when one says a person or group is exploited in a certain situation? I propose a concept of exploitation which entails these conditions. A coalition S, in a larger society N, is exploited if and only if:

(1)   There is an alternative, which we may conceive of as hypothetically feasible, in which S would be better off than in its present situation;

(2)   Under this alternative, the complement to S, the coalition $N - S = S'$, would be worse off than at present;

The formal analysis in this paper will take exploitation to be characterised by (1) and (2), although a third condition is also necessary to rule out certain bizarre examples, namely:

(3) S' is in a 'relationship of dominance' to S.

Precisely how to specify the alternative is left open for the moment. The general claim is that this device can be applied whenever people use the word 'exploit' referring to the human condition. If two people disagree on whether a group is exploited in some situation, then the device leads us to ask: Are they specifying the alternative for the group differently? Different *specifications of the alternative* will be proposed which will define different concepts of exploitation.

What is accomplished by the conditions (1)–(3) above? Condition (1) has an obvious meaning. Condition (2) is necessary for exploitation since it must be the case that the exploited coalition S is exploited by other people, not by nature or technology, for instance. (Thus, exploitation as here used is to be distinguished from the exploitation of natural resources.) Condition (3) is sociological, and is not formally modelled, nor will dominance be defined. It will be indicated in a footnote below why (3) is not redundant with (1) and (2).

Formally, we can model (1) and (2) by specifying a game played by coalitions of agents in the economy. To define the game, it is specified what any coalition can achieve on its own, if it 'withdraws' from the economy. The alternative to participating in the economy is for a coalition to withdraw, taking its payoff or dowry, under the definition of the game. If a coalition S can do better for its members under the alternative of withdrawing, and if the complementary coalition to it, S', does worse after S's withdrawal, then S is *exploited* under that particular specification of the rules of the game.[1]

To make this more concrete, consider as an example the usual notion of the core of a private ownership exchange economy. The core is the set of allocations which no coalition can improve upon by withdrawing under the following rule: that it can take with it the private endowments of its members. Under these particular withdrawal rules, there is a certain utility frontier available to any coalition, and we could say a coalition is exploited if it is receiving utilities which can be dominated by a vector of utilities achievable by the coalition acting cooperatively on its own, given those withdrawal rules. In addition, for exploitation to occur, it must be the case that the complementary coalition fares worse after the original coalition withdraws with its endowments. More generally, if we adopt a different rule of withdrawal, which is to say a different way of specifying the payoffs achievable by the various coalitions on their own, a different game with a different core will result. Our definition implies this: exploitation occurs, at a given allocation, if that allocation is not in the core of the game defined by the particular withdrawal specification under consideration. That is, a coalition is exploited if and

only if it can 'block' an allocation, under the rules of the game. This will be proved presently.

This device captures the idea that exploitation involves the possibility of a better alternative. My proposal for what constitutes feudal exploitation, capitalist exploitation, and socialist exploitation amounts to naming three different specifications of withdrawal rules, three different games. One can then compare different concepts of exploitation by comparing the different rule specifications which define their respective games. A particular concept of exploitation is exhibited in explicit or canonical form as it were, as the rules of a game.

A formal definition of the concept follows. Let an economy be sustaining an allocation $\{z^1, \ldots, z^N\}$. That is, z^ν is the payoff that the νth agent is receiving. (z^ν can be an amount of money, or a bundle of goods and leisure, or a utility level.) Suppose we specify a game for this economy by stipulating a *characteristic function* v which assigns to every coalition S of agents in the economy a payoff $v(S)$. The value $v(S)$ should, of course, be in the same space as the values z^ν. $v(S)$ is to be thought of as the payoff available to the coalition S should it choose to exercise its right to withdraw from the parent economy; it is the dowry assigned to it by society as a whole. We do not assume that institutional arrangements exist in the parent economy for actually giving S an amount $v(S)$ should it choose to withdraw; for instance, the function v may define what some observer considers the just entitlement to coalitions should be, were they to opt out of society. Given this structure, we say a coalition S is *exploited at an allocation* $\{z^1, \ldots, z^N\}$ *with respect to alternative* v if[2]

$$\sum_{\nu \in S} z^\nu < v(S), \tag{1}$$

$$\sum_{\nu \in S'} z^\nu > v(S'). \tag{2}$$

We assume at this point that the coalition can distribute the dowry to its members so that each member ν receives a share v^ν such that $z^\nu < v^\nu$, which is certainly algebraically possible if (1) holds. (Thus, there are no considerations of incentives and strategy within the coalition, an important complication avoided here. Within the coalition, there is cooperative behaviour.)

Notice exploitation is defined with respect to a *specific conception* of an alternative. The actual allocation is $\{z^1, \ldots, z^N\}$, the alternative is defined by the function $v(S)$. There are, of course both interesting and silly ways of specifying v: the task will be to specify particular functions v which capture intelligible and historically cogent types of exploitation. For instance, one might wish to require of a specification v that it permit the possibility of no exploitation. That is, given v, is there an allocation of the economy at which no agent or coalition is exploited? If not, then v would seem to suggest the impossible, if we take as v's suggested ethical imperative the elimination of its associated form of exploitation. A sufficient condition that v permit a non-exploitative allocation is that the game v have a non-empty core (there should be an allocation $\{z^1, \ldots, z^N\}$ which no coalition S can block, according to (1)). The different games in characteristic function form v which are proposed in this paper all have non-empty cores.

We define the *exploiting* coalitions with respect to an alternative v as the complementary coalitions to the exploited coalitions. S is an exploiting coalition if and only if the inequalities (1) and (2) hold, but with the inequality signs reversed in each.

We now observe, under reasonable assumptions, the non-exploitative allocations are precisely the core of the game v.

THEOREM 1: *Let v be a superadditive game, and let the allocation $\{z^1, \ldots, z^N\}$ be Pareto optimal: $v(N) \leqq \sum_N z^v$. Then a coalition S is exploited if and only if $v(S) > \sum_S z^v$. Likewise a coalition T is exploiting if and only if $v(T) > \sum_T z^v$. Hence the core of v is precisely the set of non-exploitative allocations.*

Proof: The necessity of the condition holds by definition. To prove sufficiency, suppose S is not exploited but:

$$v(S) > \sum_S z^v. \tag{4}$$

Then S's failure to be exploited can only be due to:

$$v(S') \geqq \sum_{S'} z^v. \tag{5}$$

Adding (4) and (5) gives

$$v(S) + v(S') > \sum_N z^v \geqq v(N). \tag{6}$$

But the superadditivity of v implies $v(S) + v(S') \leqq v(N)$, for any coalition S. Hence S must be exploited if (4) holds.

The second statement follows since the complements of exploiting sets are exploited sets.

We remark further on why condition (2) is required for the definition of exploitation. As

mentioned, it is to guarantee that when a coalition is exploited, it is exploited *by someone*. If we required only (1) for S to be exploited, then it would be possible for both S and its complement to be exploited. Symmetrically, if we required only $\sum z^v > v(S)$ for S to be exploiting, then both S and S' could be exploiting. Consider, for instance, an economy with increasing returns to scale, and let $v(S)$ be the income a coalition S would attain by withdrawing with its own assets. Because of the returns to scale, it is possible that both S and S' satisfy $\sum_S z^v > v(S)$: but we would not wish to consider them to be exploiting coalitions at the allocation $\{z^1, \ldots, z^N\}$. Rather, they are each benefitting from (or exploiting) the scale economies present. (Similarly, an economy with decreasing returns would identify many coalitions and their complements as exploited, if only inequality (1) were insisted upon.) Defining exploitation as consisting of (1) and (2) guarantees that every exploited coalition has as its complement an exploiting coalition, and conversely. Thus, exploitation must involve some coalition's benefitting at another coalition's expense – rather than benefits or expenses accruing from a purely natural or technological phenomenon, such as scale economies.[3]

Thus, the device for defining exploitation conceives of agents as exploited at a particular allocation, with respect to a particular alternative. The alternative is specified by a characteristic function which defines the entitlements of agents and coalitions of agents. The formulation ignores, for the time being, these sorts of problems: Is realisation of pay-offs $v(S)$ in some way feasible? What are the costs of coalition formation? How will the coalition S arrange to distribute $v(S)$ among its members?[4]

2 Feudal Exploitation

I will not be historically precise concerning the underlying model of feudal economy. Think of agents with various endowments, who are engaged in production and consumption under feudal relations. A coalition is *feudally exploited* if it can improve its lot by withdrawing under the following rule: the coalition can take with it its own endowments. Thus, feudally non-exploitative allocations are, in fact, precisely the usual core of the exchange game, as conventionally defined, for a private ownership economy.

(See, for one of many references, Varian (1978).) This withdrawal specification, it is claimed, is the correct one for capturing feudal exploitation as it gives the result that serfs are exploited and lords are exploiters, which is the result we wish to capture. Moreover, non-serf proletarians will not be an exploited coalition, under these rules, and so the definition captures *only* feudal exploitation.

To verify this claim, we will make a cavalier assumption, that the serf's family plot was part of his own endowment. Clearly demarcated property rights in these plots did not in general exist under feudalism, but the history will be simplified, for the sake of making a point, to say that the essence of feudalism was bondage which required the serf to perform labour on the lord's demesne and corvée labour, *in spite* of his access to the means of subsistence for his family which included the family plot. Thus, a crucial distinction between proletarians and serfs is that the former must exchange their labour to acquire access to their means of sustenance, while the latter must exchange their labour despite their access to the means of sustenance. This distinction accounts for the coerciveness of labour extraction relations under feudalism, as contrasted with the voluntary labour market under capitalism.[5]

Thus, were a group of serfs to be allowed to withdraw from feudal society with their endowments, in which we include the family plots, they would have been better off, having access to the same means of production, but providing no labour for the demesne and corvée. Withdrawal, under these rules, amounts to withdrawal from feudal bondage, and that only. There is, however, a counterargument, which could have been put forth by a feudal ideologue: serfs would not be better off, he might say, by withdrawing with their own endowments, because they receive various benefits from the lord which they cannot produce on their own, the most obvious being military protection. The argument concerning military protection is an important one, and it introduces the difficulties in analysing exploitation as here defined when non-convexities are present. These are treated at length elsewhere (Roemer, 1982); the essential point is that when non-convexities are present, it is not relevant to ask whether individuals (or small coalitions) are exploited. (Indeed, if one serf withdraws under rules of the feudal game, he may be worse off, and so will the complementary coalition. Thus, he is not feudally exploited.)

If sufficiently large coalitions of serfs had withdrawn with their plots, they could have provided for their own defence, and hence have been better off; clearly the complementary coalition would be worse off, not benefitting from the serfs' surplus labour. The serfs as a class were feudally exploited and the lords were feudal exploiters.[6]

Secondly, the feudal ideologue might assert the lord possessed certain skills or abilities to organise manor life, without which the serfs would have been worse off. This argument is put forth by North and Thomas (1973), who claim that the serf's demesne and corvée labour was the *quid pro quo*, and a fair one (or implicitly agreed upon), for access to the benefits of feudal society. The claim is rebutted by Brenner (1976), and will not be further discussed here. Suffice to say, the disagreement between North and Thomas and Marxists concerns the proper specification of the characteristic function: that is, what income would the serfs have enjoyed had they seceded from feudal society, even supposing the immediate costs of withdrawal need not be counted? This disagreement will be taken up briefly below, when the concept of *socially necessary exploitation* is discussed.

To say serfs would be better off were they to withdraw from bondage and preserve their access to technology and land is to invoke a static notion of welfare comparison, which is purposeful at this point. What should be conveyed is that the ex-serfs could enjoy a bundle of leisure and goods which strictly dominated the bundle they received under feudal bondage. If the problem is treated dynamically, one is forced to ask other questions. Suppose, after withdrawal from serfdom, the peasant eventually becomes a proletarian, after being impoverished by his ineffectiveness in competitive agricultural capitalism which develops after feudalism's demise. As a proletarian, is he now better off than he was on the manor?

The general definition of exploitation purposely ignores these dynamic issues in constructing the counterfactual against which to judge the current allocation. The alternative we pose to the feudal allocation of society's income is an allocation which agents could hypothetically realise for themselves, through cooperative agreement, in an economy where private property is respected, but no ties of bondage or coercive dues arising therefrom exist. Thus the inequality viewed as feudally exploitative is that inequality which is specifically feudal in origin – as opposed, for instance, to inequality which is capitalist in origin, discussed next.

3 Capitalist Exploitation

To test whether a coalition of agents is capitalistically exploited, a different set of withdrawal rules is specified to define the game. When a coalition 'withdraws', it takes with it the coalition's *per capita* share of society's alienable, non-human property, and its *own* inalienable assets. That is, a coalition can block a particular allocation if that allocation can be improved upon by the coalition, when the initial endowment of alienable assets is an equal division, egalitarian endowment of property. While the test for feudal exploitation amounts to equalising every agent's access to personal freedom in constructing the alternative against which a current allocation is judged, the test for capitalist exploitation amounts to equalising every agent's access to society's alienable property (non-human means of production) in constructing the hypothetical alternative. Under feudalism, it is asked how well agents do if relations of feudal bondage are abolished; under capitalism, we ask how they fare if property relations in alienable property are changed so that each agent possesses the same amount. Given this phrasing of the alternative, it is not surprising that capitalist exploitation, as here defined, is equivalent to the usual Marxian definition of exploitation in terms of socially necessary labour time and surplus value.[7]

This is, indeed, a theorem, which space does not permit me to formulate precisely, as such formulation requires that Marxian exploitation be exhibited in explicit economic models. Suffice to say that in a variety of such models, Marxian exploitation is equivalent to capitalist exploitation as here defined. That is: the expropriation or transfer of surplus value from workers to capitalists occurs, in the Marxian framework, precisely because workers do not have access to alienable means of production. In the counterfactual posited by the game posed above, workers are imagined to withdraw with their proportionate share of society's alienable assets, thus eliminating the necessity to trade their 'surplus' labour for access to that capital. The coalitions which are Marxian-exploited are precisely the ones which are capitalistically exploited; i.e., which can block

an allocation under the rules of the game assigning coalitions proportionate shares of society's aggregate alienable assets. Moreover, the game-theoretic definition of capitalist exploitation applies more generally than Marxian exploitation: the test for capitalist exploitation can be applied even if labour is heterogeneous and other non-produced factors exist, a production environment in which the classical definition of Marxian exploitation, depending as it does on the labour theory of value, encounters severe if not intractable problems.[8]

In most summary form, the specification of the games which define feudal and capitalist exploitation capture what is meant when we say feudal exploitation is that inequality which comes about because of specifically feudal relations, and capitalist exploitation is that inequality which is the consequence of relations of private property in the alienable means of production (capitalist relations of property).

Just as the feudal ideologue argued that, in fact, serfs would not have been better off had they withdrawn with their own endowments, so a bourgeois ideologue might argue that those who are Marxian-exploited (that is, whose surplus value is appropriated by others) would not, in fact, be better off were they to withdraw with their per capita share of society's alienable assets. The surplus value which workers contribute to the capitalist is, perhaps, a return to a scarce *skill* possessed by him, necessary for organising production. The bourgeois ideologue's argument is in theory a correct one: if, in fact equalisation of alienable assets would not be sufficient to make Marxian-exploited workers better off on their own, then they are not capitalistically exploited. This non-trivial bone of contention between Marxist and bourgeois thinkers will be called the subtle disagreement on the existence of capitalist exploitation under capitalism.

There is, however, a less subtle disagreement also. A common neoclassical position is that exploitation cannot be said to exist at a competitive equilibrium, because everyone has gained from trade as much as possible. How can one say μ is exploiting v if v has voluntarily entered in to trade with μ? Now the models of Marxian-exploitation which have been referred to, show that *gains from trade and Marxian exploitation are not mutually exclusive.* (The proletarian gains from trading his labour power, since otherwise he cannot reproduce, but his surplus labour time is nevertheless transferred.) What is at issue here is precisely the difference between feudal and capitalist exploitation. The statement that no coalition can gain further from trade amounts to saying the allocation is in the core of the feudal game: no group of agents, withdrawing with *its endowments*, can trade to a superior allocation for its members. Hence, the neoclassical position says 'There is no feudal exploitation under capitalism', a statement which is true by the well-known fact that competitive equilibria lie in the private ownership core of the economy, that is, the core of the game defined by private ownership withdrawal rules.

It is not always obvious whether objections to the Marxian notion of exploitation are of the subtle form (in which case there is a substantial disagreement about the contribution of agents' inalienable assets to production), or of the non-subtle form (in which case there are two different varieties of exploitation under discussion). In the non-subtle case, the antagonists are adopting different specifications of the hypothetical alternative which they respectively view as normatively cogent for testing 'exploitation'. Although, in the case of the non-subtle disagreement, the difference between the two positions may be unambiguous, that does not mean it is simply resolved: there are still substantial disagreements concerning what kind of property entitlements are acceptable or just. I would argue that the non-subtle disagreement is quite prevalent. In particular, if both parties to the discussion agree to model agents as differing only in their ownership rights of produced goods, then the disagreement must be of the non-subtle variety. When the neoclassical party says that the proletarian is not exploited by the capitalist because the latter requires a return to his capital (being, we insist, alienable assets, not skills) for whatever reason, what is in fact being said is that ownership rights of produced means of production must be respected, and therefore the test for capitalist exploitation is not appropriate.

To be more precise in discussions of this nature, it is convenient to differentiate between *entrepreneurs* and *coupon-clippers* among the class of capitalists. Entrepreneurs presumably earn a high return to their inalienable endowments, while coupon-clippers earn a return only to their alienable endowments. If we conceive of the capitalist class as predominantly composed of the former, then the statement 'exploitation does not exist under capitalism' can be consistently interpreted as referring to *capitalist* exploitation; if the latter, then that statement can only refer to feudal exploitation.

There is, however, one most important piece of circumstantial evidence against the hypothesis that the prevailing disagreement about exploitation under capitalism is of the subtle variety. Prevailing norms of neoclassical (liberal, pluralist) social science respect private property in the means of production. (In contrast, they do not respect relations of personal bondage of either the slave or feudal type.) Consequently, prevailing liberal philosophy cannot accept the test for capitalist exploitation which has been proposed, for that test nullifies property relations. Note that a proponent of the existence of capitalist exploitation would not judge *all* inequality under capitalism as being of the capitalistically exploiting type but only that part of it which could be eliminated by an egalitarian distribution of endowments of *alienable* resources.

I therefore conclude that a fair summary of prevailing liberal opinion, which argues against applying the term exploitation to the idealised equilibria of a private ownership market economy, is, in terms of this taxonomy: 'There is no feudal exploitation under capitalism.' This is a true statement, at least of a competitive equilibrium. Marxists would argue, however, that there is capitalist exploitation under capitalism, although – and this is critical – not all inequality would be eliminated by abolishing private ownership of the means of production.

The implicit alternative against which neoclassical economists evaluate an allocation is the 'free trade' alternative, and agents or coalitions are exploited if they could be doing better under that alternative. The culprits in a neoclassically exploitation allocation are barriers to the competitive operation of markets. We can, indeed, link up another traditional neoclassical notion of exploitation with our characterisation of it as feudal exploitation. Joe Ostroy (1980) has shown that in large economies, the allocations in the private ownership core of an exchange economy (i.e. feudally non-exploitative allocations) are precisely those allocations at which every agent is receiving his marginal product, properly defined.

On the other hand, the implicit alternative against which a Marxist evaluates an allocation is not one of free trade, but of 'free' alienable property.

I close this section by noting that the specification of the communal game, which defines capitalist exploitation, has the advantage of capturing the Marxian theory of exploitation without reference to the labour theory of value. It is property relations which occupy centre stage in the definition, not the transfer of labour. This immediately clarifies the different ethical positions which lie behind neoclassical and Marxist conceptions of exploitation, as they are exhibited transparently in the rules of the game which define the two concepts.[9]

4 Socialist Exploitation

I now pose the rules of the game which define *socialist exploitation*. Some endowments were not hypothetically equalised in formulating the rules of the game to test for capitalist exploitation: endowments of inalienable assets, skills. Let us picture an idyllic socialist economy where private property is not held in alienable assets which are accessible to all, but inalienable assets are still held by individuals. Under market arrangements, those with scarce skills will be better off than the unskilled. This inequality is not, however, capitalist exploitation, as all have equal access to alienable property, and so no coalition can improve its position by withdrawing with its per capita share of society's alienable means of production. We may, however, wish to refer to this inequality as socialist exploitation, characterised as follows. Let a coalition withdraw, taking with it its per capita share of *all* endowments, alienable and inalienable. If it can improve the position of its members, and if the complementary coalition is worse off under such an arrangement, then it is socialistically exploited at the allocation in question.

There are, of course, formidable incentive problems with carrying out this procedure, as has been discussed by parties to the Rawlsian debate over talent pooling. (See, for example, Kronman (1980).) How can talents be pooled without destroying them and so on? Although the potential *realisation* of the alternative is problematic, as a hypothetical test it can be specified, and for the sake of concreteness, a model is presented in the appendix.

Thus, if all individual endowments are of either the alienable or inalienable type, then an allocation is free of socialist exploitation precisely

when it is in the equal-division core. One should note how a certain classical conception of socialism and communism is reflected in this definition. The historical task of the socialist revolution is to bring about a regime where each labours according to his ability and is paid according to his work, while the communist revolution (from socialism) transforms the formula so that each is paid according to his need. Thus, socialist exploitation is to be expected under socialism: the elimination of differential rewards to ability is not socialism's historical task, only the elimination of differential reward to property ownership. The communist revolution is the one which eliminates socialist exploitation. This is as it should be, following the historical parallels of the demise of feudal exploitation in the capitalist revolution, and of capitalist exploitation in the socialist revolution.

Hence the rules of the latest game seem to fit classical definitions. The troublesome question is: To what extent can we attribute inequality in real socialist economies to 'socialist exploitation?'

5 Socially Necessary Exploitation and Historical Materialism

From the names given to the various forms of exploitation – feudal, capitalist, socialist – it appears that history, according to the historical materialist conception, necessarily eliminates the various forms of exploitation, in a certain order, until communism is reached, a society whose distribution, according to the *Critique of the Gotha Program*, is characterised by 'from each according to his ability, to each according to his need.' There is a temptation to claim that, in the language of historical materialism, the historical task of a given epoch is to eliminate its concomitant form of exploitation, as here named. Yet a more careful reading of historical materialism shows this is not its claim: rather, the historical task of an epoch is to remove fetters on the development of the productive forces, which is not necessarily the same as producing a situation in which the direct producers are 'better off'.

To approach this question somewhat more carefully, socially necessary exploitation is now defined. It was assumed in the initial definition of exploitation that when a coalition withdraws, the incentive structure which its members face in the alternative economy set up by the coalition does not differ from the incentive structure in the original economy. In general, this is false. Consider proletarians under early capitalism. Had they withdrawn with their per capita share of the produced assets of society, they may very well not have worked long enough to make the income that they had as proletarians; instead they might have chosen to take more leisure and less income. Assuming capitalist property relations were necessary to bring about accumulation and technical innovation in the early period of capitalism, then the coalition which has withdrawn will soon fall behind the capitalist society because of the absence of incentives to innovate. Even the proletarians under capitalism will eventually enjoy an income-leisure bundle superior to the bundle of independent utopian socialists who have retired into the hills with their share of the capital, assuming enough of the benefits of increased productivity pass down to the proletarians, as has historically been the case. Thus, a more precise phrasing of the criterion is: *were* a coalition able to preserve the same incentive structure, and, by withdrawing with its per capita share of produced assets thereby improve the lot of its members, then it is capitalistically exploited in the current allocation. If, however, the incentive structure cannot be maintained, and in addition, as a consequence, the coalition will immediately be worse off, then the capitalist exploitation which it endures is *socially necessary in the static sense*. Suppose, however, the coalition is initially better off after exercising its withdrawal option, even allowing for incentive effects, but then 'soon' it becomes worse off, due for instance to the lack of incentives to develop the forces of production. In this case, I will say the exploitation was *socially necessary in the dynamic sense*.

There are, in the Marxist reading of history, many examples of the implementation of regimes entailing dynamically socially necessary exploitation, which brought about an inferior income-leisure bundle for the direct producers. Two will be mentioned. Marx approved of the British conquest of India, despite the misery it brought to the direct producers, because of its role in developing the productive forces. Thus, the contention is proletarians in India would have been better off, statically, in the alternative without imperialist interference, but dynamically British imperialist exploitation was socially necessary to bring about the development of the productive forces, eventually improving the income-leisure bundles

of the producers (or their children) over what they would have been. (For a discussion of this point, see Brenkert (1979).) A second example is taken from Brenner's (1976) discussion of the development of capitalism in England as contrasted with France. In England, agrarian capitalists succeeded in breaking the power of the yeoman peasantry, and the productive forces in agriculture were developed under the capitalists' aegis. In France, the independent peasantry remained strong, did not develop the productive forces, and chose a bundle of leisure and income which was doubtless superior to that of their English counterparts, in the short run.[10] The development of productive forces in agriculture was not synonymous with the improved welfare of the peasantry. Eventually, the British agricultural proletarians were better off (in our sense) than their French counterparts.

Why does Marxism maintain capitalist exploitation was dynamically socially necessary in early capitalism, otherwise phrased, that capitalism was initially a progressive system, an optimal economic structure for furthering the development of the productive forces at a certain stage in their development?[11] First, it is claimed to be socially necessary only in the dynamic sense: that without capitalist property relations, innovation and the development of labour productivity would have stagnated, and workers would consequently eventually have been worse off. Secondly, and worthy of note, it is relations of private property which were socially necessary not particular individual capitalists as such. It is not the contention that private property was necessary to coax certain specific individuals in possession of scarce skills to employ them (entrepreneurial ability, inventiveness); rather, it was the *system* of private property in the means of production which stimulated innovation. Anyone could have played the role of capitalist, but someone had to. This is not to deny that the skills of capitalists may be somewhat scarce – it is just that they are not *that* scarce. Within the population of proletarians there are plenty of potential capitalists, that is, persons capable of performing that role, but who do not, because of their lack of access to the means of production.

There is a difference between maintaining that capitalist exploitation exists, but is socially necessary, and the argument of the bourgeois ideologue that capitalist exploitation does not exist. For he is maintaining that capitalists' profits are a return to scarce skills they possess, and hence the income losses workers would suffer in the coalition, when they withdraw with their per capita share of alienable assets, are not due to incentive problems, but rather to their lack of accessibility to the skills of capitalists. The bourgeois ideologue claims the workers under capitalism are experiencing *socialist* exploitation, not capitalist exploitation. This is quite different from maintaining that capitalists possess no skills which do not also exist in the large pool of proletarians (even though they may be scarce!), but that the regime of private ownership relations in the means of production produces certain behaviour (of competition leading to innovation) which would be absent without those relations. In the second view, it does not matter who the capitalists are, but the workers will be better off if someone is a capitalist. Capitalism is socially necessary, but particular individual capitalists are dispensable.

The social necessity of socialist exploitation in early socialism may appear to differ from this, in that the skills which are specially remunerated are embodied in particular people. Not only may socialist exploitation be necessary, but particular socialist exploiters may be. Viewed dynamically, however, this may not be (and I believe is not) the case. If skills are a consequence of nurture only, the result of prior status exploitation, perhaps, then anyone can be the vessel for them, although someone must be.[12] It is, again, not the particular person who must be discovered, and will so be with the offer of a special wage, but rather that the special wage creates a system where a certain fraction of people will train themselves. Once trained, the particular skilled person will be of special value to society, but the same may be true of particular capitalists, like Henry Ford II, who acquire their class status by virtue of birth, but eventually do learn to run capitalist empires.

According to historical materialism, feudal, capitalist and socialist exploitation all exist under feudalism. At some point feudal relations become a fetter on the development of the productive forces, and they are eliminated by the bourgeois revolution. Feudal exploitation is outlawed under capitalism. Although the proletarians might not immediately appear to be better off than the serfs, because of the non-comparability of their income-leisure bundles, one can assert that quite rapidly (in a generation, perhaps) they are better off due to the rapid development of the produc-

tive forces and the increase in the real wage.[13] Thus, feudal relations were eliminated when they became *socially unnecessary in the dynamic sense*. Under capitalism, only capitalist and socialist exploitation continue to exist. Capitalist exploitation in the beginning is socially necessary, as discussed; eventually, however, it becomes a fetter on the development of productive forces. Large coalitions of proletarians could be (dynamically) better off by withdrawing with their per capita share of the produced means of production, and organising themselves in a socialist way, because capitalism no longer performs a progressive innovating function, compared to what society is capable of accomplishing under socialist organisation. Capitalist exploitation becomes socially unnecessary, and is eliminated by socialist revolution. Under socialism, capitalist exploitation is outlawed, but socialist exploitation exists and, most would argue, is socially necessary, at least in the early period.

Historical materialism, in summary, claims that *history progresses by the successive elimination of forms of exploitation which are socially unnecessary in the dynamic sense.*[14] It is important to reiterate this does not mean the exploited agents will immediately be better off (in terms of the income-leisure bundle) after the revolution. Nor has the historical mechanism been discussed here which might lead to this pattern. The above is a translation of the technological determinist aspect of historical materialist theory into the language of the theory of exploitation.

In summary, the purpose of this section has been to exhibit how some claims of historical materialism can be stated in the language of the taxonomy of exploitation. I must underscore it has not been the intention to argue for the theory of historical materialism, which would be a much more subtle undertaking.

6 Exploitation in Existing Socialism

I take up, briefly, the question posed at the end of section 4. The first relevant, important phenomenon is the existence of inequality in socialist countries which comes about by virtue of *status* such as Communist Party membership. To the extent that status is itself a 'competitive' remuneration to skill, it can be viewed as the conduit (or signal) which permits differential remuneration to skill. In principle, party members possess some scarce skills (the ability to lead the revolution, and so on), but there will be little debate here if I claim that not all (or even most) of the remuneration to status can be explained by remuneration to skill. How then, should we treat inequalities due to that part of status which is not a signal for skill? Formally, this is most appropriately viewed as feudal exploitation, which is precisely exploitation by virtue of status. If we ask whether a coalition under socialism could improve the position of its members if the rights of status were abolished, the test is the same as for feudal exploitation. (Some of the product of low-status individuals goes to high-status individuals; if the low-status ones could exempt themselves from their dues of status, they would be better off. If in fact the high-status people are not especially skilled, the low-status people will be better off simply by withdrawing with their own endowments.)

Why does status exploitation exist under socialism? A conjecture is because of the absence of markets in current socialist mechanisms. A long literature testifies to the belief that if the market is not used, bureaucratic power must replace it. (A pithy Marx statement, albeit from another context: 'Rob the thing [money] of this social power, and you must give it to persons to exercise over other persons' (Marx (1973); pp. 157–8).) Hence the question whether status exploitation must necessarily be concomitant with socialism is, under this conjecture, equivalent to the more familiar question of whether the practice of socialism conflicts with the use of a market mechanism.

Suppose status exploitation exists in socialist countries; it may nevertheless be socially necessary in the sense of section 5, as follows. To eliminate status exploitation may entail the elimination of the bureaucracy, replacing it by the market. Under the market, capitalist exploitation may regenerate, thus making the coalitions who are status-exploited even worse off. Hence, the social necessity of status exploitation. Those who attack étatisme (such as Branco Horvat) argue against the social necessity of status exploitation. The debate between self-management and central planning can be seen, in part, as concerning whether it is better to take the socially necessary dose of inequality in the form of status exploitation, or as capitalist exploitation which will accompany a system giving sufficient leeway to markets. (The inequalities between rich and poor

firms in Yugoslavia are an example of capitalist exploitation, according to the game-theoretic criterion.)

A second important question, with respect to the applicability of the theoretical characterisation of socialist exploitation to current socialist inequality, is this: has socialism abolished capitalist exploitation? If a coalition of socialist workers were to withdraw, taking with them their *per capita* share of society's *alienable* assets, could they perhaps improve their position? The reason this question emerges forcefully is that alienable assets are not distributed in an egalitarian manner to individuals under socialism – as they would be under a syndicalist or anarchist mechanism – but are centralised in the hands of the state. This, indeed, is precisely the left-anarchist critique of socialism: in our terms, that capitalist exploitation will not be abolished so long as property is not in the hands of individual producers, because there is no guarantee that the state will follow the best interests of the direct producers. Proponents of the thesis that *state capitalism* is the proper way to describe the Soviet state are also saying that the state apparatus is controlled by a stratum which employs the means of production in its own interest. As with the previous question, it is beyond our scope to pursue this further.

The taxonomy of exploitation suggests a sense in which socialism is an inherently unstable arrangement. Under capitalism, agents are allowed to reap the benefits from all their assets. Under communism (hypothetically), agents are not allowed differential remuneration due either to alienable or inalienable assets which they possess. Socialism takes a compromise stance: it allows agents differential remuneration to skill, but it forbids the capitalisation of those rewards into alienable assets, for that would give rise to capitalist exploitation. The difficulty of maintaining this posture may explain, to some extent, the necessity for authority under socialism.

7 Concluding Remarks

Some conclusions with respect to four questions will be indicated.

(1) With respect to the *debate between neoclassicals and Marxists* concerning exploitation, the taxonomy of exploitation proposed allows the antagonists to formulate the disagreements precisely. It is claimed that the neoclassical and

Marxian conceptions of exploitation correspond to two different hypothetical alternatives, two different games. Neoclassicals pose feudal exploitation as the relevant concept, Marxians pose capitalist exploitation. (If, however, the antagonists disagree on the contribution of entrepreneurial skill to production, the disagreement is of another sort.)

(2) Concerning the *Marxian theory of exploitation*, the game-theoretic property relations approach allows a considerably more general definition than the labour-theory-of-value approach. I believe the property relations approach is superior for several reasons. First, it makes explicit the alternative of which Marxists are conceiving when they say surplus value is expropriated, is *unpaid* labour. Secondly, it is applicable with general production sets, while the labour-theory approach is not. Thirdly, it allows one to distinguish between different forms of 'expropriation of unpaid labour' – those resulting from feudalism, capitalism, and socialism, as the labour-theory by itself does not.

(3) With regard to *historical materialism*, the taxonomy of exploitation allows a statement of its major claims in analytical terms. The link between two great Marxian theories is exhibited. An analytic statement of historical materialism should allow critical discussion of its claimed theorems to proceed.

(4) With reference to *inequality in existing socialism*, the theory proposes a decomposition into three types of exploitation. Marxist theory has long recognised the social necessity of socialist exploitation in early socialism; capitalist exploitation in existing socialism can be more carefully discussed if the definitions here are applied; on the social necessity of status exploitation there has been the least theory, although the debate on the plan versus the market touches on that issue.

Perhaps the main influence this theory should have on our evaluation of existing socialist societies is to teach us not to expect too much of them, with respect to the elimination of inequality. In each epoch, revolutionaries have believed that the elimination of the major prevailing form of exploitation would bring about a free society. The French revolutionaries thought the ending of feudal exploitation would entail 'liberté, fraternité, égalité'; they underestimated the effects of capitalist exploitation. Socialist revolutionaries have believed that the elimination of capitalist exploitation would bring about the conditions for the free development of all, underestimating, perhaps, the significance of socialist and status exploitation. That these forms of exploitation exist in socialist countries should not necessarily be cause for condemning them. In particular, both socialist and status exploitation exist in capitalism also. While capitalism's advertisement has been that status exploitation does not exist as the market rewards only real contributions and ruthlessly casts aside all remnants of feudal privilege, this is clearly not the case. It seems quite possible that status exploitation in existing capitalism is more severe than in existing socialism.

Appendix: A Schematic Model of Socialist Exploitation

A model will be presented to illustrate the difference between socialist and capitalist exploitation, and the advantage of using the game-theoretic definition of exploitation over the Marxian definition in terms of surplus value. For simplicity, the model is of an imaginary 'socialist subsistence' economy, which uses markets.

There are N producers, each of whom wishes to minimise labour expended, subject to producing a bundle of goods which he can trade, at going prices, for some required subsistence vector b. Assume there is a single indecomposable, productive Leontief technology (A, L), with $L > 0$, and n sectors, but that each producer has access to only some subset of the n processes. A is the material input matrix, and L the vector of labour inputs. Producer v has knowledge of sectors indexed by integers in the set $\mathcal{J} \subseteq \{1, \ldots, n\}$. This models the idea that producers have different skills. Note, however, that each producer possesses some socially necessary skill, since the economy is indecomposable. A more general model might posit an activity analysis technology with many processes, and some producers would have knowledge of only inferior processes. Such a model would necessitate a more complicated definition of socially necessary labour time.

The socialist nature of the economy is modelled by remarking that there is no capital constraint on a producer's production; in a capitalist economy, the production choices open to a producer are constrained by the availability of capital to him. (For models of a capitalist economy showing this, see Roemer (1982).) Any inputs the producer needs are available from the centre without interest. Thus producers are not constrained by their access to alienable assets in this economy. It is perhaps convenient to think of a producer as a socialist collective, a worker-managed firm, which has access to the produced means of production. Collectives will differ, however, according to their technological know-how, or skill.

Each producer seeks to minimise labour time expended subject to his informational constraint on technological knowledge, or his 'skill'. His program is:

$$\text{choose } \mathbf{x}^v \in R_+^n \quad \text{to} \quad \min \mathbf{Lx}^v$$
$$\text{subject to } \mathbf{px}^v - \mathbf{pAx}^v \geqq \mathbf{pb}$$
$$\mathbf{Lx}^v \leqq \mathbf{I}$$
$$x_j^v = 0 \text{ for } j \notin \mathcal{F}.$$

The purchases of inputs are $\mathbf{pAx}^v$ and $\mathbf{pb}$ is the value of subsistence, so the constraint expresses the fact that the value of gross product is sufficient to pay these two costs. Let $A^v(\mathbf{p})$ be the set of solutions to v's program.

Definition. A price vector $\mathbf{p}$ and activity vectors $\mathbf{x}^1, \ldots \mathbf{x}^N$ constitute a *reproducible solution* for the socialist subsistence economy with N producers if:

$$(1) \ \mathbf{x}^v \in A^v(\mathbf{p}), \text{ for all } v$$
$$(2) \ \mathbf{x} = \Sigma \mathbf{x}^v \text{ and } (\mathbf{I} - \mathbf{A}) \mathbf{x} \geqq N\mathbf{b}.$$

A reproducible solution allows each producer to optimise, and social net output is sufficient to feed everyone. That is, what inputs are used up ($\mathbf{Ax}$) are replaced. It follows that:

THEOREM 2. *At a reproducible solution* (RS) *aggregate work time is*:

$$\mathbf{Lx} = N\mathbf{L}(\mathbf{I} - \mathbf{A})^{-1}\mathbf{b} \equiv N\Lambda\mathbf{b}$$

where $\Lambda = \mathbf{L}(\mathbf{I} - \mathbf{A})^{-1}$.

Proof: At a RS, $(\mathbf{I} - \mathbf{A}) \mathbf{x} \geqq N\mathbf{b}$ and so $\mathbf{x} \geqq N(\mathbf{I} - \mathbf{A})^{-1}\mathbf{b}$, implying $\mathbf{x} > 0$ since $\mathbf{A}$ is indecomposable so $(\mathbf{I} - \mathbf{A})^{-1} > 0$. This implies $\mathbf{p} \geqq \mathbf{pA}$: for a sector j with $p_j - \mathbf{pA}_j < 0$ would never operate (examine the producer's program). But $\mathbf{p} \geqq \mathbf{pA}$ implies $\mathbf{p} > 0$ by indecomposability of $\mathbf{A}$, and the fact that $\mathbf{A}$ is a productive matrix.

At an individual optimum, $\mathbf{x}^v \in A^v(\mathbf{p})$, it is clear from the program each producer sets

$$\mathbf{p}(\mathbf{I} - \mathbf{A}) \mathbf{x}^v = \mathbf{pb};$$

for if $\mathbf{p}(\mathbf{I} - \mathbf{A}) \mathbf{x}^v > \mathbf{pb}$ then v could reduce his labour time further since $\mathbf{L} > 0$. Hence summing

these equality constraints over all v gives:

$$\mathbf{p}(\mathbf{I} - \mathbf{A}) \mathbf{x} = N\mathbf{pb}. \tag{a}$$

However $(\mathbf{I} - \mathbf{A}) \mathbf{x} \geqq N\mathbf{b}$ by reproducibility; it follows from (a), and because $\mathbf{p} > 0$, that $(\mathbf{I} - \mathbf{A}) \mathbf{x} = N\mathbf{b}$. The result follows.

We identify $\Lambda\mathbf{b}$ as socially necessary labour time, for reasons with which the reader is familiar. Theorem 2 thus informs us that at a RS, society as a whole works socially necessary labour time.

However, it is possible that some producers work longer than $\Lambda\mathbf{b}$ and some less than $\Lambda\mathbf{b}$. Such *inegalitarian* reproducible solutions virtually always exist. If

$$\mathbf{Lx}^v > \Lambda\mathbf{b} > \mathbf{Lx}^\mu, \tag{b}$$

a Marxist might be tempted to say v is exploited and μ is an exploiter, as surplus labour is being appropriated by μ from v. Note that such inegalitarianism is an explicitly social phenomenon, in this sense. Suppose μ has knowledge of the whole matrix $(\mathbf{A}, \mathbf{L})$, but v has knowledge only of certain columns, and they are the only two producers in the economy. Then inequality (b) may very well be the case at a reproducible solution. (In particular, μ can never work longer than v at a RS.) Now suppose v leaves the economy. Without v, μ can reproduce himself, but he must work $\Lambda\mathbf{b}$ time to fulfil $(\mathbf{I} - \mathbf{A}) \mathbf{x} \geqq \mathbf{b}$ (note $N = 1$, now). Hence μ becomes worse off with v's departure. Thus μ is better off because of v's presence; one might argue surplus value is being transferred from v to μ through the exchange mechanism, and be tempted to call such expropriation of surplus value, exploitation.

According to our taxonomic device, this inegalitarianism is not *capitalist* exploitation. Indeed, if v withdraws in a coalition of one, no matter what alienable assets he is assigned he cannot improve his position. (This is clear, since alienable assets are available in unlimited amount from the centre in this economy.) In fact, he cannot even reproduce himself on his own, as he does not have knowledge of the whole technology.

However, this inequality is *socialist* exploitation. How do we formulate the withdrawal rule for a coalition to test for socialist exploitation? We allow the coalition to take with it its per capita share of society's inalienable assets. Precisely, each member of a withdrawing coalition is assigned the ability to operate each individual's technology for $1/N$ of the day. Under this average or composite technology, we easily show:

THEOREM 3. *Let* $(\mathbf{p}, \mathbf{x}^1, \ldots, \mathbf{x}^N)$ *be a RS. Then* μ *is socialistically exploited if and only if* $\mathbf{L}\mathbf{x}^\mu > \Lambda\mathbf{b}$.

Proof: Let $\mathbf{L}\mathbf{x}^\mu > \Lambda\mathbf{b}$. At the RS, $(\mathbf{I} - \mathbf{A}) \mathbf{x} = N\mathbf{b}$, so $(1/N) (\mathbf{I} - \mathbf{A}) \mathbf{x} = \mathbf{b}$. But this means that μ can produce for himself the net output vector $\mathbf{b}$ with the composite technology which he has been assigned, as he has precisely the capabilities of $1/N$ of society in the aggregate. Thus he operates activity levels $(1/N)\Sigma\mathbf{x}^v$ and reproduces himself,

working time $\mathbf{L}[(1/N)\mathbf{x}] = \Lambda\mathbf{b}$, thus improving his situation.

The converse is immediate.

In fact, the same proof shows a slightly more general proposition, that a coalition S of producers is socialistically exploited if and only if

$$\sum_{v \in S} \mathbf{L}\mathbf{x}^v > |S| \Lambda\mathbf{b}.$$

Similarly, a coalition S is socialistically exploiting if and only if

$$\sum_{S} \mathbf{L}\mathbf{x}^v < |S| \Lambda\mathbf{b}.$$

Notes

This work has been carried out with support from the John Simon Guggenheim Memorial Foundation. Many people have given me valuable comments on this paper, in particular Zvi Adar, G.A. Cohen, Meghnad Desai, Jon Elster, Victor Goldberg, Serge-Christophe Kolm, Andreu Mas-Colell and Amartya Sen.

1 A formal definition of exploitation is given below.

2 From now on, reference to the dominance requirement is omitted. For the body of the paper, (3) is assumed to hold whenever (1) and (2) do. In a footnote below, a perverse example is given in which this would not be the case. For most practical purposes, however, (1) and (2) together are a satisfactory definition of exploitation. As well, it is assumed that we have transferable utility, so that payoffs can be treated additively within coalitions.

3 My first pass at a definition of exploitation involved requiring only inequality (1). I am indebted to Jon Elster and Serge-Christophe Kolm for criticising the lack of interaction between agents in that formulation. In the current formulation, interaction is necessary for exploitation to the extent that exploiting and exploited coalitions always appear as complements. Interaction is also assured by the dominance requirement (3).

4 I now indicate why the dominance condition (3) is needed to eliminate certain perverse cases. Consider an invalid, supported with costly medical services by the rest of society. Suppose we specify the game as withdrawal with one's own assets. Then the invalid will be worse off and the rest of society better off (if, at least, we do not count the pain society may feel for the death of the invalid after his withdrawal). This might lead one to conclude, according to (1) and (2), that the invalid is exploiting the rest of society according to this specification of the alternative. The dominance condition (3) eliminates this perverse conclusion since the relation of dominance is the other way around. Despite this case, I think conditions (1) and (2) suffice to characterise economic exploitation for most practical purposes.

5 For discussion see Brenner (1977) and Marx, *Capital*, Volume III (1966, pp. 790–1), in the section on labour rent.

6 For the precise resolution of the treatment of exploitation in the presence of increasing returns the reader is referred to Roemer (1982), Chapter 7. In brief, the approach is this. An agent is considered *vulnerable* if he is a member of a minimal exploited coalition, and *culpable* if he is a member of a minimal exploiting coalition. With increasing returns, the minimal exploited coalitions will have many members. Vulnerability and culpability become the relevant characteristics of agents with non-constant returns.

7 In the models for which capitalist exploitation is proved to be equivalent to Marxian exploitation, there are no externalities or public goods. Admitting these features, which complicate property relations, will surely complicate the game-theoretic test for exploitation, and consequently the theorem referred to. Nevertheless, some types of externality (such as increasing returns to scale) can be successfully handled as the previous note indicates.

8 The definitions of Marxian and capitalist exploitation are equivalent in the standard models which have been used to study Marxian exploitation in a formal way. There are, however, situations in which the two definitions render different judgements concerning the exploitation status of some coalitions. In these cases, I think the property relations definition is superior to the surplus labour definition, as its verdict on exploitation conforms more to the intuitive judgements of Marxists.

9 The confrontation between the surplus labour (Marxian) definition of exploitation and the property relations definition of capitalist exploitation can be made sharper, in this sense. There are situations in which the Marxian definition diagnoses certain coalitions as exploited who are not capitalistically exploited according to the property rights

definition. In these cases, it is the property relations definition which renders the intuitively correct judgement. The surplus labour approach fails essentially because it takes too micro an approach, concentrating on what is happening in one market (the labour market) rather than evaluating the macro alternatives under different regimes of property.

10 Perhaps 'doubtless' is not the word, for neoclassical interpreters such as North and Thomas (1973) would say that the English agricultural proletarians voluntarily contracted with their capitalists to enter into relations of wage labour, so that the capitalists would force them to work, prevent them from shirking, thereby improving their welfare. See Brenner (1976) for arguments against the neoclassical implicit contract interpretation.

11 For discussion of what is meant by an economic structure being optimal for the level of development of productive forces, see Cohen (1978), especially chapter 6, and Elster and Hylland (1980).

12 Those with high status have access to educational facilities for their children. (See Section 6.)

13 Lindert and Williamson (1980) claim, on the basis of new statistical evidence, that workers in the cities of mid nineteenth-century England were better off, in terms of real wages, life expectancy and other quality-of-life indicators, than rural unskilled labourers of 1780. Their work challenges the conventional Marxist view that the 'satanic mills' were an unmitigated disaster for the working class over the period of the industrial revolution. It is nevertheless true that at any point in time until the 1880s or so life expectancy was lower for urban workers. They also assert that at any point in time urban workers felt subjectively better off than they had as country dwellers, that is, the higher urban wage compensated for the disamenities of city life.

14 The precise claim is that history progresses by eliminating property relations which fetter the productive forces: but it is further claimed that the fettering of the productive forces makes the direct producers worse off than they would be with the further development of the productive forces, since enough of the benefits of increased productivity will return to them in the form of better living standards. These two claims together imply the statement to which this note is attached.

References

Brenkert, George G. (1979). 'Freedom and private property in Marx.' *Philosophy and Public Affairs*, vol. 8, no. 2.

Brenner, Robert. (1976). 'Agrarian class structure and economic development in pre-industrial Europe,' *Past and Present*, vol. 70.

——(1977). 'The origins of capitalist development: a critique of neo-Smithian Marxism.' *New Left Review*, 104.

Cohen, G.A. (1978). *Karl Marx's Theory of History: A Defence*. Princeton: Princeton University Press.

Elster, Jon and Hylland, Aanund. (1980). 'The contradiction between forces and relations of production.' Oslo: Historisk Institutt, University of Oslo (unpublished paper).

Kronman, Anthony. (1981). 'Talent Pooling.' *Nomos XXIII: Human Rights*, ed. J.R. Pennock and J.W. Chapman. New York: New York University Press, pp. 58–79.

Lindert, Peter and Williamson, Jeffrey. (1980). 'English workers' living standards during the industrial revolution: a new look.' Davis: University of California, Department of Economics Working Paper 144.

Marx. Karl. (1966). *Capital*, Volume III. Moscow: Progress Publishers.

——(1973). *Grundrisse*.

North, Douglass and Thomas, Robert. (1973). *The Rise of the Western World*. Cambridge: Cambridge University Press.

Ostroy, Joseph, (1980). 'The no-surplus condition as a characterization of perfectly competitive equilibrium.' *Journal of Economic Theory*, vol. 22, pp. 183–207.

Roemer, John E. (1982). *A General Theory of Exploitation and Class*. Cambridge, Ma.: Harvard University Press.

Varian, Hal. (1978). *Microeconomic Theory*. New York: Norton.

36

Racism, Sexism, and Preferential Treatment: An Approach to the Topics

Richard A. Wasserstrom

Introduction

Racism and sexism are two central issues that engage the attention of many persons living within the United States today. But while there is relatively little disagreement about their importance as topics, there is substantial, vehement, and apparently intractable disagreement about what individuals, practices, ideas, and institutions are either racist or sexist – and for what reasons. In dispute are a number of related questions concerning how individuals and institutions ought to regard and respond to matters relating to race or sex.

One particularly contemporary example concerns those programs variously called programs of "affirmative action," "preferential treatment," or "reverse discrimination" that are a feature of much of our institutional life. Attitudes and beliefs about these programs are diverse. Some persons are convinced that all such programs in virtually all of their forms are themselves racist and sexist and are for these among other reasons indefensible.[1] The programs are causally explicable, perhaps, but morally reprehensible. Other persons – a majority, I suspect – are sorely troubled by these programs. They are convinced that some features of some programs, *e.g.*, quotas, are indefensible and wrong. Other features and programs are tolerated, but not with fervor or enthusiasm. They are seen as a kind of moral compromise, as, perhaps, a lesser evil among a set

Originally published in *UCLA Law Review*, 24 (1977), 581–622. Copyright © 1977 by The Regents of the University of California. Reprinted by permission of UCLA Law Review.

of unappealing options.[2] They are reluctantly perceived and implemented as a covert, euphemistic way to do what would clearly be wrong – even racist or sexist – to do overtly and with candor. And still a third group has a very different view. They think these programs are important and appropriate. They do not see these programs, quotas included, as racist or sexist, and they see much about the dominant societal institutions that is.[3] They regard the racism and sexism of the society as accounting in substantial measure for the failure or refusal to adopt such programs willingly and to press vigorously for their full implementation.

I think that much of the confusion in thinking and arguing about racism, sexism and affirmative action results from a failure to see that there are three different perspectives within which the topics of racism, sexism and affirmative action can most usefully be examined. The first of these perspectives concentrates on what in fact is true of the culture, on what can be called the social realities. Here the fundamental question concerns the way the culture is: What are its institutions, attitudes and ideologies in respect to matters of race and sex?[4]

The second perspective is concerned with the way things ought to be. From this perspective, analysis focuses very largely on possible, desirable states of affairs. Here the fundamental question concerns ideals: What would the good society – in terms of its institutions, its attitudes, and its values – look like in respect to matters involving race and sex?[5]

The third perspective looks forward to the means by which the ideal may be achieved. Its focus is on the question: What is the best or most appropriate way to move from the existing social realities, whatever they happen to be, to a closer approximation of the ideal society? This perspective is concerned with instrumentalities.[6]

Many of the debates over affirmative action and over what things are racist and sexist are unilluminating because they neglect to take into account these three perspectives, which are important and must be considered separately. While I do not claim that all the significant normative and conceptual questions concerning race, sex, or affirmative action can be made to disappear, I do believe that an awareness and use of these perspectives can produce valuable insights that contribute to their resolution. In particular, it can almost immediately be seen that the question of whether something is racist or sexist is not as straightforward or unambiguous as may appear at first. The question may be about social realities, about how the categories of race or sex in fact function in the culture and to what effect. Or the question may be about ideals, about what the good society would make of race or sex. Or the question may be about instrumentalities, about how, given the social realities as to race and sex, to achieve a closer approximation of the ideal. It can also be seen, therefore, that what might be an impermissible way to take race or sex into account in the ideal society, may also be a desirable and appropriate way to take race or sex into account, given the social realities.

It is these three different perspectives and these underlying issues that I am interested in exploring. This framework is used to clarify a number of the central matters that are involved in thinking clearly about the topics of racism, sexism and affirmative action. Within this framework, some of the analogies and disanalogies between racism and sexism are explored – the ways they are and are not analytically interchangeable phenomena. I also provide an analytic scheme for distinguishing different respects in which a complex institution such as the legal system might plausibly be seen to be racist or sexist. And I examine some of the key arguments that most often arise whenever these topics are considered. In respect to programs of affirmative action, or preferential treatment, I argue specifically that much of the opposition to such programs is not justifiable. It rests upon confusion in thinking about the relevant issues and upon a failure to perceive and appreciate some of the ways in which our society is racist and sexist. I argue that there is much to be said for the view that such programs, even when they include quotas, are defensible and right. My central focus is not, however, on affirmative action per se, but rather on how a consideration of affirmative action is linked to a deepened understanding of these larger, related issues.

1 Social Realities

One way to think and talk about racism and sexism is to concentrate upon the perspective of the social realities. Here one must begin by insisting that to talk about either is to talk about a particular social and cultural context. In this section I concentrate upon two questions that can be asked about the social realities of our culture. First, I consider the position of blacks and females in the culture vis-à-vis the position of those who are white, and those who are male. And second, I provide an analysis of the different ways in which a complex institution, such as our legal system, can be seen to be racist or sexist. The analysis is offered as a schematic account of the possible types of racism or sexism.

A The position of blacks and women

In our own culture the first thing to observe is that race and sex are socially important categories. They are so in virtue of the fact that we live in a culture which has, throughout its existence, made race and sex extremely important characteristics of and for all the people living in the culture.[7]

It is surely possible to imagine a culture in which race would be an unimportant, insignificant characteristic of individuals. In such a culture race would be largely if not exclusively a matter of superficial physiology; a matter, we might say, simply of the way one looked. And if it were, then any analysis of race and racism would necessarily assume very different dimensions from what they do in our society. In such a culture, the meaning of the term "race" would itself have to change substantially. This can be seen by the fact that in such a culture it would literally make no sense to say of a person that he or she was "passing."[8] This is something that can be said and understood in our own culture and it shows at least that to talk of race is to talk of more than the way one looks.[9]

Sometimes when people talk about what is

wrong with affirmative action programs, or programs of preferential hiring, they say that what is wrong with such programs is that they take a thing as superficial as an individual's race and turn it into something important.[10] They say that a person's race doesn't matter; other things do, such as qualifications. Whatever else may be said of statements such as these, as descriptions of the social realities they seem to be simply false. One complex but true empirical fact about our society is that the race of an individual is much more than a fact of superficial physiology. It is, instead, one of the dominant characteristics that affects both the way the individual looks at the world and the way the world looks at the individual. As I have said, that need not be the case. It may in fact be very important that we work toward a society in which that would not be the case, but it is the case now and it must be understood in any adequate and complete discussion of racism. That is why, too, it does not make much sense when people sometimes say, in talking about the fact that they are not racists, that they would not care if an individual were green and came from Mars, they would treat that individual the same way they treat people exactly like themselves. For part of *our* social and cultural history is to treat people of certain races in a certain way, and we do not have a social or cultural history of treating green people from Mars in any particular way. To put it simply, it is to misunderstand the social realities of race and racism to think of them simply as questions of how some people respond to other people whose skins are of different hues, irrespective of the social context.

I can put the point another way: Race does not function in our culture as does eye color. Eye color is an irrelevant category; nobody cares what color people's eyes are; it is not an important cultural fact; nothing turns on what eye color you have. It is important to see that race is not like that at all. And this truth affects what will and will not count as cases of racism. In our culture to be nonwhite – and especially to be black[11] – is to be treated and seen to be a member of a group that is different from and inferior to the group of standard, fully developed persons, the adult white males. To be black is to be a member of what was a despised minority and what is still a disliked and oppressed one.[12] That is simply part of the awful truth of our cultural and social history, and a significant feature of the social reality of our culture today.

We can see fairly easily that the two sexual categories, like the racial ones, are themselves in important respects products of the society. Like one's race, one's sex is not merely or even primarily a matter of physiology. To see this we need only realize that we can understand the idea of a transsexual. A transsexual is someone who would describe himself or herself either as a person who is essentially a female but through some accident of nature is trapped in a male body, or a person who is essentially a male but through some accident of nature is trapped in the body of a female. His (or her) description is some kind of a shorthand way of saying that he (or she) is more comfortable with the role allocated by the culture to people who are physiologically of the opposite sex. The fact that we regard this assertion of the transsexual as intelligible seems to me to show how deep the notion of sexual identity is in our culture and how little it has to do with physiological differences between males and females. Because people do pass in the context of race and because we can understand what passing means; because people are transsexuals and because we can understand what transsexuality means, we can see that the existing social categories of both race and sex are in this sense creations of the culture.

It is even clearer in the case of sex than in the case of race that one's sexual identity is a centrally important, crucially relevant category within our culture. I think, in fact, that it is more important and more fundamental than one's race. It is evident that there are substantially different role expectations and role assignments to persons in accordance with their sexual physiology, and that the positions of the two sexes in the culture are distinct. We do have a patriarchal society in which it matters enormously whether one is a male or a female.[13] By almost all important measures it is more advantageous to be a male rather than a female.

Women and men are socialized differently. We learn very early and forcefully that we are either males or females and that much turns upon which sex we are. The evidence seems to be overwhelming and well-documented that sex roles play a fundamental role in the way persons think of themselves and the world – to say nothing of the way the world thinks of them.[14] Men and women are taught to see men as independent, capable, and powerful; men and women are taught to see women as dependent, limited in abilities, and passive. A woman's success or failure in life is defined largely in terms of her activities within the family. It is important for her that she marry, and when she does she is expected to take responsibility for the wifely tasks: the housework, the child care, and the general emotional welfare of the husband and children.[15] Her status in society is determined in substantial measure by the vocation and success of her husband.[16] Economically, women are substantially worse off than men. They do not receive any pay for the work that is done in the home. As members of the labor force their wages are significantly lower than those paid to men, even when they are engaged in similar work and have similar educational backgrounds.[17] The higher the prestige or the salary of the job, the less present women are in the labor force. And, of course, women are conspicuously absent from most positions of authority and power in the major economic and political institutions of our society.

As is true for race, it is also a significant social fact that to be a female is to be an entity or creature viewed as different from the standard, fully developed person who is male as well as white. But to be female, as opposed to being black, is not to be conceived of as simply a creature of less worth. That is one important thing that differentiates sexism from racism: The ideology of sex, as opposed to the ideology of race, is a good deal more complex and confusing. Women are both put on a pedestal and deemed not fully developed persons. They are idealized; their approval and admiration is sought; and they are at the same time regarded as less competent than men and less able to live fully developed, fully human lives – for that is what men do.[18] At best, they are viewed and treated as having properties and attributes that are valuable and admirable for humans of this type. For example, they may be viewed as especially empathetic, intuitive, loving, and nurturing. At best, these qualities are viewed as good properties for women to have, and, provided they are properly muted, are sometimes valued within the more well-rounded male. Because the sexual ideology is complex, confusing, and variable, it does not unambiguously proclaim the lesser value attached to being female rather than being male, nor does it unambiguously correspond to the existing social realities. For these, among other reasons, sexism could plausibly be regarded as a deeper phenomenon than racism. It is more deeply embedded in the culture, and thus less visible. Being harder to detect, it is harder to eradicate. Moreover, it is less unequivocally regarded as unjust and unjustifiable. That is to say, there is less agreement within the dominant ideology that sexism even implies an unjustifiable practice or attitude. Hence, many persons announce, without regret or embarrassment, that they are sexists or male chauvinists; very few announce openly that they are racists.[19] For all of these reasons sexism may be a more insidious evil than racism, but there is little merit in trying to decide between two seriously objectionable practices which one is worse.

While I do not think that I have made very controversial claims about either our cultural history or our present-day culture, I am aware of the fact that they have been stated very imprecisely and that I have offered little evidence to substantiate them. In a crude way we ought to be able both to understand the claims and to see that they are correct if we reflect seriously and critically upon our own cultural institutions, attitudes, and practices. But in a more refined, theoretical way, I am imagining that a more precise and correct description of the social reality in respect to race and sex would be derivable from a composite, descriptive account of our society which utilized the relevant social sciences to examine such things as the society's institutions, practices, attitudes and ideology[20] – if the social sciences could be value-free and unaffected in outlook or approach by the fact that they, themselves, are largely composed of persons who are white and male.[21]

Viewed from the perspective of social reality it should be clear, too, that racism and sexism should not be thought of as phenomena that consist simply in taking a person's race or sex into account, or even simply in taking a person's race or sex into account in an arbitrary way. Instead, racism and sexism consist in taking race and sex into account in a certain way, in the context of a specific set of institutional arrangements and a specific ideology which together create and maintain a *system* of unjust institutions and unwarranted beliefs and attitudes. That system is and has been one in which political, economic, and social power and advantage are concentrated in the hands of those who are white and male.

One way to bring this out, as well as to show another respect in which racism and sexism are different, concerns segregated bathrooms – a topic that may seem silly and trivial but which is certainly illuminating and probably important. We know, for instance, that it is wrong, clearly racist, to have racially segregated bathrooms. There is, however, no common conception that it is wrong, clearly sexist, to have sexually segregated ones. How is this to be accounted for? The answer to the question of why it was and is racist to have racially segregated bathrooms can be discovered through a consideration of the role that this practice played in that system of racial segregation we had in the United States – from, in other words, an examination of the social realities. For racially segregated bathrooms were an important part of that system. And that system had an ideology; it was complex and perhaps not even wholly internally consistent. A significant feature of the ideology was that blacks were not only less than fully developed humans, but that they were also dirty and impure. They were the sorts of creatures who could and would contaminate white persons if they came into certain kinds of contact with them – in the bathroom, at the dinner table, or in bed, although it was appropriate for blacks to prepare and handle food, and even to nurse white infants. This ideology was intimately related to a set of institutional arrangements and power relationships in which whites were politically, economically, and socially dominant. The ideology supported the institutional arrangements, and the institutional arrangements reinforced the ideology. The net effect was that racially segregated bathrooms were both a part of the institutional mechanism of oppression and an instantiation of this ideology of racial taint. The point of maintaining racially segregated bathrooms was not in any simple or direct sense to keep both whites and blacks from using each other's bathrooms; it was to make sure that blacks would not contaminate bathrooms used by whites. The practice also taught both whites and blacks that certain kinds of contacts were forbidden because whites would be degraded by the contact with the blacks.

The failure to understand the character of these institutions of racial oppression is what makes some of the judicial reasoning about racial discrimination against blacks so confusing and unsatisfactory. At times when the courts have tried to explain what is constitutionally wrong with racial segregation, they have said that the problem is that race is an inherently suspect category. What they have meant by this, or have been thought to mean, is that any differentiation among human beings on the basis of racial identity is inherently unjust, because arbitrary, and therefore any particular case of racial differentiation must be shown to be fully rational and justifiable.[22] But the primary evil of the various schemes of racial segregation against blacks that the courts were being called upon to assess was not that such schemes were a capricious and irrational way of allocating public benefits and burdens. That might well be the primary wrong with racial segregation if we lived in a society very different from the one we have. The primary evil of these schemes was instead that they designedly and effectively marked off all black persons as degraded, dirty, less than fully developed persons who were unfit for full membership in the political, social, and moral community.[23]

It is worth observing that the social reality of sexually segregated bathrooms appears to be different. The idea behind such sexual segregation seems to have more to do with the mutual undesirability of the use by both sexes of the same bathroom at the same time. There is no notion of the possibility of contamination; or even directly of inferiority and superiority. What seems to be involved – at least in part – is the importance of inculcating and preserving a sense of secrecy concerning the genitalia of the opposite sex. What seems to be at stake is the maintenance of that same sense of mystery or forbiddenness about the other sex's sexuality which is fostered by the general prohibition upon public nudity and the unashamed viewing of genitalia.

Sexually segregated bathrooms simply play a different role in our culture than did racially segregated ones. But that is not to say that the role they play is either benign or unobjectionable – only that it is different. Sexually segregated bathrooms may well be objectionable, but here too, the objection is not on the ground that they are prima facie capricious or arbitrary. Rather, the case against them now would rest on the ground that they are, perhaps, one small part of that scheme of sex-role differentiation which uses the mystery of sexual anatomy, among other things, to maintain the primacy of heterosexual sexual attraction central to that version of the patriarchal system of power relationships we have today.[24] Whether sexually segregated bathrooms would be objectionable, because irrational, in the good society depends once again upon what the good society would look like in respect to sexual differentiation.

Richard A. Wasserstrom

B Types of racism or sexism

Another recurring question that can profitably be examined within the perspective of social realities is whether the legal system is racist or sexist. Indeed, it seems to me essential that the social realities of the relationships and ideologies concerning race and sex be kept in mind whenever one is trying to assess claims that are made about the racism or sexism of important institutions such as the legal system. It is also of considerable importance in assessing such claims to understand that even within the perspective of social reality, racism or sexism can manifest itself, or be understood, in different ways. That these are both important points can be seen through a brief examination of the different, distinctive ways in which our own legal system might plausibly be understood to be racist. The mode of analysis I propose serves as well, I believe, for an analogous analysis of the sexism of the legal system, although I do not undertake the latter analysis in this paper.

The first type of racism is the simplest and the least controversial. It is the case of overt racism, in which a law or a legal institution expressly takes into account the race of individuals in order to assign benefits and burdens in such a way as to bestow an unjustified benefit upon a member or members of the racially dominant group or an unjustified burden upon members of the racial groups that are oppressed. We no longer have many, if any, cases of overt racism in our legal system today, although we certainly had a number in the past. Indeed, the historical system of formal, racial segregation was both buttressed by, and constituted of, a number of overtly racist laws and practices. At different times in our history, racism included laws and practices which dealt with such things as the exclusion of non-whites from the franchise, from decent primary and secondary schools and most professional schools, and the prohibition against interracial marriages.

The second type of racism is very similar to overt racism. It is covert, but intentional, racism, in which a law or a legal institution has as its purpose the allocation of benefits and burdens in order to support the power of the dominant race, but does not use race specifically as a basis for allocating these benefits and burdens. One particularly good historical example involves the use of grandfather clauses which were inserted in

statutes governing voter registration in a number of states after passage of the fifteenth amendment.[25]

Covert racism within the law is not entirely a thing of the past. Many instances of de facto school segregation in the North and West are cases of covert racism. At times certain school boards – virtually all of which are overwhelmingly white in composition – quite consciously try to maintain exclusively or predominantly white schools within a school district. The classifications such school boards use are not ostensibly racial, but are based upon the places of residence of the affected students. These categories provide the opportunity for covert racism in engineering the racial composition of individual schools within the board's jurisdiction.[26]

What has been said so far is surely neither novel nor controversial. What is interesting, however, is that a number of persons appear to believe that as long as the legal system is not overtly or covertly racist, there is nothing to the charge that it is racist. So, for example, Mr. Justice Powell said in a speech a few years ago:

It is of course true that we have witnessed racial injustice in the past, as has every other country with significant racial diversity. But no one can fairly question the present national commitment to full equality and justice. Racial discrimination, by state action, is now proscribed by laws and court decisions which protect civil liberties more broadly than in any other country. But laws alone are not enough. Racial prejudice in the hearts of men cannot be legislated out of existence; it will pass only in time, and as human beings of all races learn in humility to respect each other – a process not furthered by recrimination or undue self-accusation.[27]

I believe it is a mistake to think about the problem of racism in terms of overt or covert racial discrimination by state action, which is now banished, and racial prejudice, which still lingers, but only in the hearts of persons. For there is another, more subtle kind of racism – unintentional, perhaps, but effective – which is as much a part of the legal system as are overt and covert racist laws and practices. It is what some critics of the legal system probably mean when they talk about the "institutional racism" of the legal system.[28]

There are at least two kinds of institutional racism. The first is the racism of sub-institutions within the legal system such as the jury, or the racism of practices built upon or countenanced by the law. These institutions and practices very often, if not always, reflect in important and serious ways a variety of dominant values in the operation of what is apparently a neutral legal mechanism. The result is the maintenance and reenforcement of a system in which whites dominate over nonwhites. One relatively uninteresting (because familiar) example is the case of de facto school segregation. As observed above, some cases of de facto segregation are examples of covert racism. But even in school districts where there is no intention to divide pupils on grounds of race so as to maintain existing power relationships along racial lines, school attendance zones are utilized which are based on the geographical location of the pupil. Because it is a fact in our culture that there is racial discrimination against black people in respect to housing, it is also a fact that any geographical allocation of pupils – unless one pays a lot of attention to housing patterns – will have the effect of continuing to segregate minority pupils very largely on grounds of race. It is perfectly appropriate to regard this effect as a case of racism in public education.[29]

A less familiar, and hence perhaps more instructive, example concerns the question of the importance of having blacks on juries, especially in cases in which blacks are criminal defendants. The orthodox view within the law is that it is unfair to try a black defendant before an all-white jury if blacks were overtly or covertly excluded from the jury rolls used to provide the jury panel, but not otherwise.[30] One reason that is often given is that the systematic exclusion of blacks increases too greatly the chance of racial prejudice operating against the black defendant.[31] The problem with this way of thinking about things is that it does not make much sense. If whites are apt to be prejudiced against blacks, then an all-white jury is just as apt to be prejudiced against a black defendant, irrespective of whether blacks were systematically excluded from the jury rolls. I suspect that the rule has developed in the way it has because the courts think that many, if not most, whites are not prejudiced against blacks, unless, perhaps, they happen to live in an area where there is systematic exclusion of blacks from the jury rolls. Hence prejudice is the chief worry, and a sectional, if not historical, one at that.

White prejudice against blacks is, I think, a problem, and not just a sectional one. However, the existence or nonexistence of prejudice against blacks does not go to the heart of the matter. It is a worry, but it is not the chief worry. A black person may not be able to get a fair trial from an all-white jury even though the jurors are disposed to be fair and impartial, because the whites may unknowingly bring into the jury box a view about a variety of matters which affects in very fundamental respects the way they will look at and assess the facts. Thus, for example, it is not, I suspect, part of the experience of most white persons who serve on juries that police often lie in their dealings with people and the courts. Indeed, it is probably not part of their experience that persons lie about serious matters except on rare occasions. And they themselves tend to take truth telling very seriously. As a result, white persons for whom these facts about police and lying are a part of their social reality will have very great difficulty taking seriously the possibility that the inculpatory testimony of a police witness is a deliberate untruth. However, it may also be a part of the social reality that many black persons, just because they are black, have had encounters with the police in which the police were at best indifferent to whether they, the police, were speaking the truth. And even more black persons may have known a friend or a relative who has had such an experience. As a result, a black juror would be more likely than his or her white counterpart to approach skeptically the testimony of ostensibly neutral, reliable witnesses such as police officers. The point is not that all police officers lie; nor is the point that all whites always believe everything police say, and blacks never do. The point is that because the world we live in is the way it is, it is likely that whites and blacks will on the whole be disposed to view the credibility of police officers very differently. If so, the legal system's election to ignore this reality, and to regard as fair and above reproach the common occurrence of all-white juries (and white judges) passing on the guilt or innocence of black defendants is a decision in fact to permit and to perpetuate a kind of institutional racism within the law.[32]

The second type of institutional racism is what I will call "conceptual" institutional racism. We have a variety of ways of thinking about the legal system, and we have a variety of ways of thinking within the legal system about certain problems. We use concepts. Quite often without realizing it, the concepts used take for granted certain objectionable aspects of racist ideology without our being aware of it. The second *Brown* case (*Brown II*) provides an example.[33] There was a second *Brown* case because, having decided that the existing system of racially segregated public education was unconstitutional (*Brown I*),[34] the Supreme Court gave legitimacy to a second issue – the nature of the relief to be granted – by treating it as a distinct question to be considered and decided separately. That in itself was striking because in most cases, once the Supreme Court has found unconstitutionality, there has been no problem about relief (apart from questions of retroactivity): The unconstitutional practices and acts are to cease. As is well known, the Court in *Brown II* concluded that the desegregation of public education had to proceed "with all deliberate speed."[35] The Court said that there were "complexities arising from the transition to a system of public education freed from racial discrimination."[36] More specifically, time might be necessary to carry out the ruling because of

> problems related to administration, arising from the physical condition of the school plant, the school transportation system personnel, revision of school districts and attendance areas into compact units to achieve a system of determining admission to the public school on a non-racial basis, and revision of local laws and regulations which may be necessary in solving the foregoing problems.[37]

Now, I do not know whether the Court believed what it said in this passage, but it is a fantastic bit of nonsense that is, for my purposes, most instructive. Why? Because there was nothing complicated about most of the dual school systems of the southern states. Many counties, especially the rural ones, had one high school, typically called either "Booker T. Washington High School" or "George Washington Carver High School," where all the black children in the county went; another school, often called "Sidney Lanier High School" or "Robert E. Lee High School," was attended by all the white children in the county. There was nothing difficult about deciding that – as of the day after the decision – half of the children in the county, say all those who lived in the southern part of the county, would go to Robert E. Lee High School, and all those who lived in the northern half would go to

Booker T. Washington High School. *Brown I* could have been implemented the day after the Court reached its decision. But it was also true that the black schools throughout the South were utterly wretched when compared to the white schools. There never had been any system of separate but equal education. In almost every measurable respect, the black schools were inferior. One possibility is that, without being explicitly aware of it, the members of the Supreme Court made use of some assumptions that were a significant feature of the dominant racist ideology. If the assumptions had been made explicit, the reasoning would have gone something like this: Those black schools are wretched. We cannot order white children to go to those schools, especially when they have gone to better schools in the past. So while it is unfair to deprive blacks, to make them go to these awful, segregated schools, they will have to wait until the black schools either are eliminated or are sufficiently improved so that there are good schools for everybody to attend.

What seems to me to be most objectionable, and racist, about *Brown II* is the uncritical acceptance of the idea that during this process of change, black schoolchildren would have to suffer by continuing to attend inadequate schools. The Supreme Court's solution assumed that the correct way to deal with this problem was to continue to have the black children go to their schools until the black schools were brought up to par or eliminated. That is a kind of conceptual racism in which the legal system accepts the dominant racist ideology, which holds that the claims of black children are worth less than the claims of white children in those cases in which conflict is inevitable.[38] It seems to me that any minimally fair solution would have required that during the interim process, if anybody had to go to an inadequate school, it would have been the white children, since they were the ones who had previously had the benefit of the good schools. But this is simply not the way racial matters are thought about within the dominant ideology.

A study of *Brown II* is instructive because it is a good illustration of conceptual racism within the legal system. It also reflects another kind of conceptual racism – conceptual racism about the system. *Brown I* and *II* typically are thought of by our culture, and especially by our educational institutions, as representing one of the high points in the legal system's fight against racism.

The dominant way of thinking about the desegregation cases is that the legal system was functioning at its very best. Yet, as I have indicated, there are important respects in which the legal system's response to the then existing system of racially segregated education was defective and hence should hardly be taken as a model of the just, institutional way of dealing with this problem of racial oppression. But the fact that we have, as well as inculcate, these attitudes of effusive praise toward *Brown I* and *II* and its progeny reveals a kind of persistent conceptual racism in talk about the character of the legal system, and what constitutes the right way to have dealt with the social reality of American racial oppression of black people.[39]

In theory, the foregoing analytic scheme can be applied as readily to the social realities of sexual oppression as to racism. Given an understanding of the social realities in respect to sex – the ways in which the system of patriarchy inequitably distributes important benefits and burdens for the benefit of males, and the ideology which is a part of that patriarchal system and supportive of it – one can examine the different types of sexism that exist within the legal system. In practice the task is more difficult because we are inclined to take as appropriate even overt instances of sexist laws, *e.g.*, that it is appropriately a part of the definition of rape that a man cannot rape his wife.[40] The task is also more difficult because sexism is, as I have suggested, a "deeper" phenomenon than racism.[41] As a result, there is less awareness of the significance of much of the social reality, *e.g.*, that the language we use to talk about the world and ourselves has embedded within it ideological assumptions and preferences that support the existing patriarchal system.[42] Cases of institutional sexism will therefore be systematically harder to detect. But these difficulties to one side, the mode of analysis seems to me to be in principle equally applicable to sexism, although, as I indicate in the next section on ideals, a complete account of the sexism of the legal system necessarily awaits a determination of what is the correct picture of the good society in respect to sexual differences.

2 Ideals

A second perspective is also important for an understanding and analysis of racism and sexism. It is the perspective of the ideal. Just as we can and must ask what is involved today in our culture in being of one race or of one sex rather than the other, and how individuals are in fact viewed and treated, we can also ask different questions: What would the good or just society make of race and sex, and to what degree, if at all, would racial and sexual distinctions ever be taken into account? Indeed, it could plausibly be argued that we could not have an adequate idea of whether a society was racist or sexist unless we had some conception of what a thoroughly nonracist or nonsexist society would look like. This perspective is an extremely instructive as well as an often neglected one. Comparatively little theoretical literature dealing with either racism or sexism has concerned itself in a systematic way with this perspective.[43] Moreover, as I shall try to demonstrate, it is on occasion introduced in an inappropriate context, *e.g.*, in discussions of the relevance of the biological differences between males and females.

To understand more precisely what some of the possible ideals are in respect to racial or sexual differentiation, it is necessary to distinguish in a crude way among three levels or areas of social and political arrangements and activities.[44] First, there is the area of basic political rights and obligations, including the right to vote and to travel and the obligation to pay taxes. Second, there is the area of important, nongovernmental institutional benefits and burdens. Examples are access to and employment in the significant economic markets, the opportunity to acquire and enjoy housing in the setting of one's choice, the right of persons who want to marry each other to do so, and the duties (nonlegal as well as legal) that persons acquire in getting married. Third, there is the area of individual, social interaction, including such matters as whom one will have as friends, and what aesthetic preferences one will cultivate and enjoy.

As to each of these three areas we can ask whether in a nonracist society it would be thought appropriate ever to take the race of the individuals into account. Thus, one picture of a nonracist society is that which is captured by what I call the assimilationist ideal: A nonracist society would be one in which the race of an individual would be the functional equivalent of the eye color of individuals in our society today.[45] In our society no basic political rights and obligations are determined on the basis of eye color. No important institutional benefits and burdens are connected with eye color. Indeed, except for the mildest sort of aesthetic preferences, a person would be thought odd who even made private, social decisions by taking eye color into account. And for reasons that we could fairly readily state, we could explain why it would be wrong to permit anything but the mildest, most trivial aesthetic preference to turn on eye color. The reasons would concern the irrelevance of eye color for any political or social institution, practice or arrangement. It would, of course, be equally odd for a person to say that while he or she looked blue-eyed, he or she regarded himself or herself as really a brown-eyed person. That is, because eye color functions differently in our culture than does race or sex, there is no analogue in respect to eye color to passing or transsexuality. According to the assimilationist ideal, a nonracist society would be one in which an individual's race was of no more significance in any of these three areas than is eye color today.

The assimilationist ideal is not, however, the only possible plausible ideal. There are two others that are closely related, but distinguishable. One is the ideal of diversity; the other, the ideal of tolerance. Both can be understood by considering how religion, rather than eye color, tends to be thought about in our culture. According to the ideal of diversity, heterodoxy in respect to religious belief and practice is regarded as a positive good. In this view there would be a loss – it would be a worse society – were everyone to be a member of the same religion. According to the other view, the ideal of tolerance, heterodoxy in respect to religious belief and practice would be seen more as a necessary, lesser evil. In this view there is nothing intrinsically better about diversity in respect to religion, but the evils of achieving anything like homogeneity far outweigh the possible benefits.

Now, whatever differences there might be between the ideals of diversity and tolerance, the similarities are more striking. Under neither ideal would it be thought that the allocation of basic political rights and duties should take an individual's religion into account. We would want equalitarianism or nondiscrimination even in respect to most important institutional benefits and burdens – for example, access to employment in the desirable vocations. Nonetheless, on both views it would be deemed appropriate to have some institutions (typically those which are connected in an intimate way with these religions) which do in a variety of ways take the religion of members of the society into account. For example, it might be thought permissible and appropriate for members of a religious group to join together in collective associations which have religious, educational and social dimensions. And on the individual, interpersonal level, it might be thought unobjectionable, or on the diversity view, even admirable, were persons to select their associates, friends, and mates on the basis of their religious orientation. So there are two possible and plausible ideals of what the good society would look like in respect to religion in which religious differences would be to some degree maintained because the variety of religions was seen either as a valuable feature of the society, or as one to be tolerated. The picture is a more complex, less easily describable one than that of the assimilationist ideal.

The point of all this is its relevance to the case of sexism. One central and difficult question is what the ideal society would look like in respect to sex. The assimilationist ideal does not seem to be as readily plausible and obviously attractive here as it is in the case of race. Many persons invoke the possible realization of the assimilationist ideal as a reason for rejecting the equal rights amendment and indeed the idea of women's liberation itself. My view is that the assimilationist ideal may be just as good and just as important an ideal in respect to sex as it is in respect to race.[46] But many persons think there are good reasons why an assimilationist society in respect to sex would not be desirable. One reason for their view might be that to make the assimilationist ideal a reality in respect to sex would involve more profound and fundamental revisions of our institutions and our attitudes than would be the case in respect to race. It is certainly true that on the institutional level we would have to alter radically our practices concerning the family and marriage. If a nonsexist society is a society in which one's sex is no more significant than eye color in our society today, then laws which require the persons who are being married to be of different sexes would clearly be sexist laws. Insofar as they are based upon the desirability of unifying the distinctive features of one male and one female, laws and institutions which conceive of the nuclear family as ideally composed of two and only two adults should also be thought of as anachronistic as well as sexist laws and institutions.

On the attitudinal and conceptual level, the assimilationist ideal would require the eradication of all sex-role differentiation. It would never teach about the inevitable or essential attributes of masculinity or femininity; it would never encourage or discourage the ideas of sisterhood or brotherhood; and it would be unintelligible to talk about the virtues as well as disabilities of being a woman or a man. Were sex like eye color, these things would make no sense. A nonsexist world might conceivably tolerate both homosexuality and heterosexuality (as peculiar kinds of personal erotic preference), but any kind of sexually *exclusive* preference would be either as anomalous or as statistically fortuitous as is a sexual preference connected with eye color in our society today. Just as the normal, typical adult is virtually oblivious to the eye color of other persons for all major interpersonal relationships, so the normal, typical adult in this kind of nonsexist society would be indifferent to the sexual, physiological differences of other persons for all interpersonal relationships. Bisexuality, not heterosexuality or homosexuality, would be the norm for intimate, sexual relationships in the ideal society that was assimilationist in respect to sex.

All of this seems to me to be worth talking about because unless and until we are clear about issues such as these we cannot be wholly certain about whether, from the perspective of the ideal, some of the institutions in our own culture are or are not sexist. We know that racially segregated bathrooms are racist. We know that laws that prohibit persons of different races from marrying are racist. But throughout our society we have sexually segregated bathrooms, and we have laws which prohibit individuals of the same sex from marrying. As I have argued above,[47] from the perspective of the existing social reality there are important ways to distinguish the racial from the sexual cases and to criticize both practices. But that still leaves open the question of whether in the good society these sexual distinctions, or others, would be thought worth preserving either because they were meritorious, or at least to be tolerated because they were necessary.

As I have indicated, it may be that the problem is with the assimilationist ideal. It may be that in respect to sex (and conceivably, even in respect to race) something more like either of the ideals in respect to religion – pluralistic ideals founded on diversity or tolerance – is the right one. But the problem then – and it is a very substantial one – is to specify with a good deal of precision and care what that ideal really comes to. Which legal, institutional and personal differentiations are permissible and which are not? Which attitudes and beliefs concerning sexual identification and difference are properly introduced and maintained and which are not? Part, but by no means all, of the attractiveness of the assimilationist ideal is its clarity and simplicity. In the good society of the assimilationist sort we would be able to tell easily and unequivocally whether any law, practice or attitude was in any respect either racist or sexist. Part, but by no means all, of the unattractiveness of any pluralistic ideal is that it makes the question of what is racist or sexist a much more difficult and complicated one to answer. But although simplicity and lack of ambiguity may be virtues, they are not the only virtues to be taken into account in deciding among competing ideals. We quite appropriately take other considerations to be relevant to an assessment of the value and worth of alternative nonracist and nonsexist societies.

Nor do I even mean to suggest that all persons who reject the assimilationist ideal in respect to sex would necessarily embrace either something like the ideal of tolerance or the ideal of diversity. Some persons might think the right ideal was one in which substantially greater sexual differentiation and sex-role identification was retained than would be the case under either of these conceptions. Thus, someone might believe that the good society was, perhaps, essentially like the one they think we now have in respect to sex: equality of political rights, such as the right to vote, but all of the sexual differentiation in both legal and nonlegal institutions that is characteristic of the way in which our society has been and still is ordered. And someone might also believe that the usual ideological justifications for these arrangements are the correct and appropriate ones.[48] This could, of course, be regarded as a version of the ideal of diversity, with the emphasis upon the extensive character of the institutional and personal difference connected with sexual identity. Whether it is a kind of ideal of diversity or a different ideal altogether turns, I think, upon two things: first, how pervasive the sexual differentiation is; second, whether the ideal contains a conception of the appropriateness of significant institutional and interpersonal inequality, *e.g.*, that the woman's job is in large measure to serve and be dominated by the male. The more this latter feature is present, the clearer the case for regarding this as a distinctively different ideal.

The question of whether something is a plausible and attractive ideal turns in part on the nature of the empirical world. If it is true, for example, that race is not only a socially significant category in our culture but also largely a socially created one, then many ostensible objections to the assimilationist ideal appear to disappear immediately. What I mean is this: It is obvious that we could formulate and use some sort of a crude, incredibly imprecise physiological concept of race. In this sense we could even say that race is a naturally occurring rather than a socially created feature of the world. There are diverse skin colors and related physiological characteristics distributed among human beings, But the fact is that except for skin hue and the related physiological characteristics, race is a socially created category. And skin hue, as I have shown, is neither a necessary nor a sufficient condition for being classified as black in our culture.[49] Race as a naturally occurring characteristic is also a socially irrelevant category. There do not in fact appear to be any characteristics that are part of this natural concept of race and that are in any plausible way even relevant to the appropriate distribution of any political, institutional, or interpersonal concerns in the good society. Because in this sense race is like eye color, there is no plausible case to be made on this ground against the assimilationist ideal.[50]

There is, of course, the social reality of race. In creating and tolerating a society in which race matters, we must recognize that we have created a vastly more complex concept of race which includes what might be called the idea of ethnicity as well – a set of attitudes, traditions, beliefs, etc., which the society has made part of what it means to be of a race. It may be, therefore, that one could argue that a form of the pluralist ideal ought to be preserved in respect to race, in the socially created sense, for reasons similar to those that might be offered in support of the desirability of some version of the pluralist ideal in respect to religion. As I have indicated, I am skeptical, but for the purposes of this essay it can well be left an open question.

Despite appearances, the case of sex is more like that of race than is often thought. What opponents of assimilationism seize upon is that sexual difference appears to be a naturally occurring category of obvious and inevitable social

relevance in a way, or to a degree, which race is not. The problems with this way of thinking are twofold. To begin with, an analysis of the social realities reveals that it is the socially created sexual differences which tend in fact to matter the most. It is sex-role differentiation, not gender per se,[51] that makes men and women as different as they are from each other, and it is sex-role differences which are invoked to justify most sexual differentiation at any of the levels of society.[52]

More importantly, even if naturally occurring sexual differences were of such a nature that they were of obvious prima facie social relevance, this would by no means settle the question of whether in the good society sex should or should not be as minimally significant as eye color. Even though there are biological differences between men and women in nature, this fact does not determine the question of what the good society can and should make of these differences. I have difficulty understanding why so many persons seem to think that it does settle the question adversely to anything like the assimilationist ideal. They might think it does settle the question for two different reasons. In the first place, they might think the differences are of such a character that they substantially affect what would be possible within a good society of human persons. Just as the fact that humans are mortal necessarily limits the features of any possible good society, so, they might argue, the fact that males and females are physiologically different limits the features of any possible good society.

In the second place, they might think the differences are of such a character that they are relevant to the question of what would be desirable in the good society. That is to say, they might not think that the differences *determine* to a substantial degree what is possible, but that the differences ought to be taken into account in any rational construction of an ideal social existence.

The second reason seems to me to be a good deal more plausible than the first. For there appear to be very few, if any, respects in which the ineradicable, naturally occurring differences between males and females *must* be taken into account. The industrial revolution has certainly made any of the general differences in strength between the sexes capable of being ignored by the good society in virtually all activities.[53] And it is sex-role acculturation, not biology, that mistakenly leads many persons to the view that women are both naturally and necessarily better suited than men to be assigned the primary responsibilities of child rearing. Indeed, the only fact that seems required to be taken into account is the fact that reproduction of the human species requires that the fetus develop *in utero* for a period of months. Sexual intercourse is not necessary, for artificial insemination is available. Neither marriage nor the family is required for conception or child rearing. Given the present state of medical knowledge and the natural realities of female pregnancy, it is difficult to see why any important institutional or interpersonal arrangements *must* take the existing gender difference of *in utero* pregnancy into account.

But, as I have said, this is still to leave it a wholly open question to what degree the good society *ought* to build upon any ineradicable gender differences to construct institutions which would maintain a substantial degree of sexual differentiation. The arguments are typically far less persuasive for doing so than appears upon the initial statement of this possibility. Someone might argue that the fact of menstruation, for instance, could be used as a premise upon which to predicate different social roles for females than for males. But this could only plausibly be proposed if two things were true: first, that menstruation would be debilitating to women and hence relevant to social role even in a culture which did not teach women to view menstruation as a sign of uncleanliness or as a curse,[54] and second, that the way in which menstruation necessarily affected some or all women was in fact related in an important way to the role in question. But even if both of these were true, it would still be an open question whether any sexual differentiation ought to be built upon these facts. The society could still elect to develop institutions that would nullify the effect of the natural differences. And suppose, for example, what seems implausible – that some or all women will not be able to perform a particular task while menstruating, *e.g.*, guard a border. It would be easy enough, if the society wanted to, to arrange for substitute guards for the women who were incapacitated. We know that persons are not good guards when they are sleepy, and we make arrangements so that persons alternate guard duty to avoid fatigue. The same could be done for menstruating women, even given these implausibly strong assumptions about menstruation. At the risk of belaboring the obvious, what I think it important to see is that the case against the assimilationist ideal – if it is

to be a good one – must rest on arguments concerned to show why some other ideal would be preferable; it cannot plausibly rest on the claim that it is either necessary or inevitable.

There is, however, at least one more argument based upon nature, or at least the "natural," that is worth mentioning. Someone might argue that significant sex-role differentiation is natural not in the sense that it is biologically determined but only in the sense that it is a virtually universal phenomenon in human culture. By itself, this claim of virtual universality, even if accurate, does not directly establish anything about the desirability or undesirability of any particular ideal. But it can be made into an argument by the addition of the proposition that where there is a virtually universal social practice, there is probably some good or important purpose served by the practice. Hence, given the fact of sex-role differentiation in all, or almost all, cultures, we have some reason to think that substantial sex role differentiation serves some important purpose for and in human society.

This is an argument, but I see no reason to be impressed by it. The premise which turns the fact of sex-role differentiation into any kind of a strong reason for sex-role differentiation is the premise of conservatism. And it is no more convincing here than elsewhere. There are any number of practices that are typical and yet upon reflection seem without significant social purpose. Slavery was once such a practice; war perhaps still is.

More to the point, perhaps, the concept of "purpose" is ambiguous. It can mean in a descriptive sense "plays some role" or "is causally relevant." Or it can mean in a prescriptive sense "does something desirable" or "has some useful function." If "purpose" is used prescriptively in the conservative premise, then there is no reason to think that premise is true.

To put it another way, the question is whether it is desirable to have a society in which sex-role differences are to be retained at all. The straightforward way to think about that question is to ask what would be good and what would be bad about a society in which sex functioned like eye color does in our society. We can imagine what such a society would look like and how it would work. It is hard to see how our thinking is substantially advanced by reference to what has typically or always been the case. If it is true, as I think it is, that the sex-role differentiated societies we have had so far have tended to concentrate power in the hands of males, have developed institutions and ideologies that have perpetuated that concentration and have restricted and prevented women from living the kinds of lives that persons ought to be able to live for themselves, then this says far more about what may be wrong with any nonassimilationist ideal than does the conservative premise say what may be right about any nonassimilationist ideal.

Nor is this all that can be said in favor of the assimilationist ideal. For it seems to me that the strongest affirmative moral argument on its behalf is that it provides for a kind of individual autonomy that a nonassimilationist society cannot attain. Any nonassimilationist society will have sex roles. Any nonassimilationist society will have some institutions that distinguish between individuals by virtue of their gender, and any such society will necessarily teach the desirability of doing so. Any substantially nonassimilationist society will make one's sexual identity an important characteristic, so that there are substantial psychological, role, and status differences between persons who are males and those who are females. Even if these could be attained without systemic dominance of one sex over the other, they would, I think, be objectionable on the ground that they necessarily impaired an individual's ability to develop his or her own characteristics, talents and capacities to the fullest extent to which he or she might desire. Sex roles, and all that accompany them, necessarily impose limits – restrictions on what one can do, be or become. As such, they are, I think, at least prima facie wrong.

To some degree, all role-differentiated living is restrictive in this sense. Perhaps, therefore, all role-differentiation in society is to some degree troublesome, and perhaps all strongly role-differentiated societies are objectionable. But the case against sexual differentiation need not rest upon this more controversial point. For one thing that distinguishes sex roles from many other roles is that they are wholly involuntarily assumed. One has no choice whatsoever about whether one shall be born a male or female. And if it is a consequence of one's being born a male or a female that one's subsequent emotional, intellectual, and material development will be substantially controlled by this fact, then substantial, permanent, and involuntarily assumed restraints have been imposed on the most central factors concerning the way one will shape and live one's life.[55] The

point to be emphasized is that this would necessarily be the case, even in the unlikely event that substantial sexual differentiation could be maintained without one sex or the other becoming dominant and developing institutions and an ideology to support that dominance.

I do not believe that all I have said in this section shows in any conclusive fashion the desirability of the assimilationist ideal in respect to sex. I have tried to show why some typical arguments against the assimilationist ideal are not persuasive,[56] and why some of the central ones in support of that ideal are persuasive. But I have not provided a complete account, or a complete analysis. At a minimum, what I have shown is how thinking about this topic ought to proceed, and what kinds of arguments need to be marshalled and considered before a serious and informed discussion of alternative conceptions of a nonsexist society can even take place. Once assembled, these arguments need to be individually and carefully assessed before any final, reflective choice among the competing ideals can be made. There does, however, seem to me to be a strong presumptive case for something very close to, if not identical with, the assimilationist ideal.

3 Instrumentalities

The instrumental perspective does not require much theoretical attention beyond what has already been said. It is concerned with the question of what would be the best way to move from the social realities to the ideal. The most salient considerations are, therefore, empirical ones – although of a complex sort.

Affirmative action programs, even those which require explicit racial and sexual minimum quotas, are most plausibly assessed from within this perspective.[57] If the social reality is one of racial and sexual oppression – as I think it is – and if, for example, the most defensible picture of a nonracist, nonsexist society is the one captured by the assimilationist ideal, then the chief and perhaps only question to be asked of such programs is whether they are well suited to bring about movement from the existing state of affairs to a closer approximation of the assimilationist ideal.[58] If it turns out, for example, that explicit racial quotas will in fact exacerbate racial prejudice and hostility,[59] thereby making it harder rather than easier to achieve an assimilationist society, that is a reason which counts against the instrumental desirability of racial quotas. This would not settle the matter, of course, for there might also be respects in which racial quotas would advance the coming of the assimilationist society, *e.g.*, by redistributing wealth and positions of power and authority to blacks, thereby creating previously unavailable role models, and by putting persons with different perspectives and interests in a position more directly to influence the course of social change.

But persons might be unhappy with this way of thinking about affirmative action – and especially about quotas. They might have three different but related objections. The first objection would be that there are more questions to be asked about means or instruments than whether they will work to bring about a certain end. In particular, there is also the question of the *way* they will work as means to bring about the end. Some means may be morally objectionable as means, no matter how noble or desirable the end. That is the good sense in the slogan: The ends do not justify the means.

I certainly agree with this general point. It is the application to particular cases, for example this one, that vitiates the force of the objection. Indeed, given the way I have formulated the instrumental perspective, I have left a good deal of room for the moral assessment of means to be built in. That is to say, I have described the question as one of the instrumental "desirability," not just the "efficaciousness" in any narrow sense, of the means that are selected.

The second objection is rather more sophisticated. Someone might say something like this: it is just wrong in principle ever to take an individual's race or sex into account.[60] Persons just have a right never to have race or sex considered. No reasons need be given; we just know they have that right. This is a common way of talking today in moral philosophy,[61] but I find nothing persuasive or attractive about it. I do not know that persons have such a right. I do not "see" it. Instead, I think I can give and have given reasons in my discussion of the social realities as well as my discussion of ideals for why they might be said to have rights not to be treated in certain ways. That is to say, I have tried to show something of what was wrong about the way blacks and women were and are treated in our culture.[62] I have not simply proclaimed the existence of a right.

Another form of this objection is more convincing. The opponent of quotas and affirmative

action programs might argue that any proponent of them is guilty of intellectual inconsistency, if not racism or sexism. At times past, employers, universities, and many social institutions did have racial or sexual quotas, when they did not practice overt racial or sexual exclusion, and it was clear that these quotas were pernicious. What is more, many of those who were most concerned to bring about the eradication of those racial quotas are now untroubled by the new programs which reinstitute them. And this is just a terrible sort of intellectual inconsistency which at worst panders to the fashion of the present moment and at best replaces intellectual honesty and integrity with understandable but misguided sympathy. The assimilationist ideal requires ignoring race and sex as distinguishing features of people.

Such an argument is a useful means by which to bring out the way in which the analysis I am proposing can respond. The racial quotas and practices of racial exclusion that were an integral part of the fabric of our culture, and which are still to some degree a part of it, were pernicious. They were a grievous wrong and it was and is important that all morally concerned individuals work for their eradication from our social universe. The racial quotas that are a part of contemporary affirmative action programs are, I think, commendable and right. But even if I am mistaken about the latter, the point is that there is no inconsistency involved in holding both views. For even if contemporary schemes of racial quotas are wrong, they are wrong for reasons very different from those that made quotas against blacks wrong.

As I have argued,[63] the fundamental evil of programs that discriminated against blacks or women was that these programs were a part of a larger social universe which systematically maintained an unwarranted and unjust scheme which concentrated power, authority, and goods in the hands of white males. Programs which excluded or limited the access of blacks and women into these institutions were wrong both because of the direct consequences of these programs on the individuals most affected and because the system of racial and sexual superiority of which they were constituents was an immoral one in that it severely and without any adequate justification restricted the capacities, autonomy, and happiness of those who were members of the less favored categories.

Whatever may be wrong with today's affirmative

action programs and quota systems, it should be clear that the evil, if any, is not the same. Racial and sexual minorities do not constitute the dominant social group. Nor is the conception of who is a fully developed member of the moral and social community one of an individual who is either female or black. Quotas which prefer women or blacks do not add to the already relatively overabundant supply of resources and opportunities at the disposal of white males. If racial quotas are to be condemned or if affirmative action programs are to be abandoned, it should be because they will not work well to achieve the desired result. It is not because they seek either to perpetuate an unjust society or to realize a corrupt ideal.

Still a third version of this objection might be that when used in affirmative action programs, race and sex are categories that are too broad in scope. They include some persons who do not have the appropriate characteristics and exclude some persons who do. If affirmative action programs made race and sex the sole criteria of selection, this would certainly be a plausible objection, although even here it is very important to see that the objection is no different in kind from that which applies to all legislation and rules. For example, in restricting the franchise to those who are eighteen and older, we exclude some who have all the relevant qualifications for voting and we include some who lack them. The fit can never be precise. Affirmative action programs almost always make race or sex a *relevant* condition, not a conclusive one. As such, they function the way all other classificatory schemes do. The defect, if there is one, is generic, and not peculiar to programs such as these.

There is finally the third objection: that affirmative action programs are wrong because they take race and sex into account rather than the only thing that matters – an individual's qualifications. Someone might argue that what is wrong with these programs is that they deprive persons who are more qualifed by bestowing benefits on those who are less qualified in virtue of their being either black or female.

There are many things wrong with the objection based on qualifications. Not the least of them is that we do not live in a society in which there is even the serious pretense of a qualification requirement for many jobs of substantial power and authority. Would anyone claim that the persons who comprise the judiciary are there because they are the most qualified lawyers or the most

qualified persons to be judges? Would anyone claim that Henry Ford II was the head of the Ford Motor Company because he was the most qualified person for the job? Or that the one hundred men who are Senators are the most qualified persons to be Senators? Part of what is wrong with even talking about qualifications and merit is that the argument derives some of its force from the erroneous notion that we would have a meritocracy were it not for affirmative action.[64]

But there is a theoretical difficulty as well, which cuts much more deeply into the argument about qualifications. The argument cannot be that the most qualified ought to be selected because the most qualified will perform most efficiently, for this instrumental approach was what the opponent of affirmative action thought was wrong with taking the instrumental perspective in the first place. To be at all persuasive, the argument must be that those who are the most qualified *deserve* to receive the benefits (the job, the place in law school, etc.) because they are the most qualified. And there is just no reason to think that this is a correct premise. There is a logical gap in the inference that the person who is most qualified to perform a task, *e.g.*, be a good student, deserves to be admitted as a student. Of course, those who deserve to be admitted should be admitted. But why do the most qualified deserve anything? There is just no necessary connection between academic merit (in the sense of qualification) and deserving to be a member of a student body. Suppose, for instance, that there is only one tennis court in the community. Is it clear that the two best tennis players ought to be the ones permitted to use it? Why not those who were there first? Or those who will enjoy playing the most? Or those who are the worst and therefore need the greatest opportunity to practice? Or those who have the chance to play least frequently?

We might, of course, have a rule that says that the best tennis players get to use the court before the others. Under such a rule, the best players would deserve the court more than the poorer ones. But that is just to push the inquiry back one stage. Is there any reason to think that good tennis players are entitled to such a rule? Indeed, the arguments that might be given for or against such a rule are many and varied. And few if any of the arguments that might support the rule would depend upon a connection between ability and desert.

Someone might reply that the most able students deserve to be admitted to the university because all of their earlier schooling was a kind of competition, with university admission being the prize awarded to the winners. They deserve to be admitted because that is what the rule of the competition provides. In addition, it would be unfair now to exclude them in favor of others, given the reasonable expectations they developed about the way in which their industry and performance would be rewarded. Minority admission programs, which inevitably prefer some who are less qualified over some who are more qualified, all possess this flaw.

There are several problems with this argument. The most substantial of them is that it is an empirically implausible picture of our social world. Most of what are regarded as the decisive characteristics for higher education have a great deal to do with things over which the individual has neither control nor responsibility: such things as home environment, socioeconomic class of parents, and, of course, the quality of the primary and secondary schools attended. Since individuals do not deserve having had any of these things vis-à-vis other individuals, they do not, for the most part, deserve their qualifications. And since they do not deserve their abilities they do not in any strong sense deserve to be admitted because of their abilities.

To be sure, if there is a rule which connects, say, performance at high school with admission to college, then there is a weak sense in which those who do well at high school deserve, for that reason alone, to be admitted to college. But then, as I have said, the merits of this rule need to be explored and defended. In addition, if persons have built up or relied upon their reasonable expectations concerning performance and admission, they have a claim to be admitted on this ground as well. But it is certainly not obvious that these claims of desert are any stronger or more compelling than competing claims based upon the needs of or advantages to women or blacks.[65]

Qualifications are also potentially relevant in at least three other respects. In the first place, there is some minimal set of qualifications without which the benefits of participation in higher education cannot be obtained by the individuals involved. In the second place, the qualifications of the students within the university will affect to some degree or other the benefits obtainable to anyone within it. And finally, the qualifications of students within the university may also affect the way the university functions vis-à-vis the rest of the world. The university will do some things better and some things worse, depending upon the qualifications of those who make it up. If the students are "less qualified," teachers may have to spend more time with them and less time on research. Some teachers may find teaching now more interesting. Others may find it less so. But all these considerations only establish that qualifications, in this sense, are relevant, not that they are decisive. This is wholly consistent with the claim that minority group membership is also a relevant but not a decisive consideration when it comes to matters of admission.[66] And that is all that virtually any preferential treatment program – even one with quotas – has ever tried to claim.

I do not think I have shown programs of preferential treatment to be right and desirable, because I have not sought to answer all of the empirical questions that may be relevant. But I have, I hope, shown that it is wrong to think that contemporary affirmative action programs are racist or sexist in the centrally important sense in which many past and present features of our society have been and are racist and sexist. The social realities do make a fundamental difference. It is also wrong to think that these programs are in any strong sense either unjust or unprincipled. The case for programs of preferential treatment can plausibly rest on the view that the programs are not unfair (except in the weak sense described above) to white males, and on the view that it is unfair to continue the present set of unjust – often racist and sexist – institutions that comprise the social reality. The case for these programs also rests on the thesis that it is fair, given the distribution of power and influence in the United States, to redistribute in this way, and that such programs may reasonably be viewed as useful means by which to achieve very significant social ideals.

Conclusion

I do not think that the topics of racism, sexism, and preferential treatment are easily penetrable. Indeed, I have tried to show that they contain complicated issues which must be carefully distinguished and discussed. But I also believe, and have tried to show, that the topics are susceptible to rational analysis. There is a difference between problems that are difficult because confusion is present, and problems that are difficult because a number of distinct ideas and arguments must be considered. It is my ambition to have moved

thinking about the topics and issues in question some distance from the first to the second of these categories.

Notes

Richard A. Wasserstrom is Professor of Law and Professor of Philosophy, University of California, Los Angeles. Copyright © 1977 by Richard A. Wasserstrom.

1   Such a view appears to be held in, *e.g.*, Brief for the Anti-Defamation League of the B'nai B'rith as Amicus Curiae on Appeal, DeFunis v. Odegaard, 416 U.S. 312 (1974): "Discrimination on the basis of race is illegal, immoral, unconstitutional, and inherently wrong." *Id.* at 16–17; Mr. Justice Douglas' dissent in *DeFunis* (above): "There is no superior person by constitutional standards. A DeFunis who is white is entitled to no advantage by reason of that fact; nor is he subject to any disability, no matter what his race or color. Whatever his race, he has a constitutional right to have his application considered on its individual merits in a racially neutral manner," *id.* at 337; Anderson v. San Francisco Unified School Dist., 357 F. Supp. 248 (N.D. Cal. 1972): Preferential treatment "under the guise of 'affirmative action' is the imposition of . . . racial discrimination," *id.* at 249; Bakke v. Regents of the Univ. of Cal., 18 Cal. 3d 34, 553 P. 2d 1152, 132 Cal. Rptr. 680 (1976), *cert. granted*, L.A. Daily Jour., Feb. 23, 1977, at 1, col. 2 (No. 76–811): "We cannot agree with the proposition that deprivation based on race is subject to a less demanding standard of review under the Fourteenth Amendment if the race discriminated against is the majority rather than a minority. We have found no case so holding, and we do not hesitate to reject the notion that racial discrimination may be more easily justified against one race rather than another," *id.* at 50, 553 P. 2d at 1163, 132, Cal. Rptr. at 691 (footnotes omitted); Graglia, *Special Admission of the "Culturally Deprived" to Law School*, 119 U. Pa. L. Rev. 351 (1970); Lavinsky, *DeFunis v. Odegaard: The Non-Decision with a Message*, 75 Colum. L. Rev. 520 (1975).

I say such a view "appears to be held" because it is never wholly clear within the context of constitutional adjudication and commentary whether the claim is that it is wrong to take race into account in these ways or that it is forbidden by the Constitution so to take race into account. The two claims are intimately related. What one thinks about the rightness or wrongness of a practice or program will, appropriately, influence the way in

which a constitutional provision – particularly one as general as the equal protection clause of the 14th amendment – is interpreted. And, in fact, it does appear that those who think these programs are unconstitutional also believe that it is good that the Constitution prohibits such programs, because they independently believe that it is wrong to have programs such as these that take race into account. But the two claims are also distinguishable. Legislative history, prior judicial decisions, and various doctrinal considerations, such as standing and state action, are also appropriately taken into account in interpreting and applying the Constitution to particular cases and practices.

The inquiry I conduct in this paper is not directed to the constitutional question, but to broader questions concerning a number of moral, conceptual and methodological issues involving race and sex. Since the two kinds of questions are related, my comments have relevance, I believe, within and for the constitutional context. The focus of my inquiry is not the constitutional question, however. I therefore do not seek to elucidate doctrine or even to discuss cases and commentaries dealing with these matters in the way or to the degree one might otherwise expect.

2   *See, e.g.*, Nagel, *Equal Treatment and Compensatory Discrimination*, 2 Phil. & Pub. Aff. 348, 362 (1973).

3   Among those who have defended such programs, in one form or another, are Askin, *The Case for Compensatory Treatment*, 24 Rut. L. Rev. 65 (1964); Bell, *In Defense of Minority Admissions Programs: A Reply to Professor Graglia*, 119 U. Pa. L. Rev. 364 (1970); Ely, *The Constitutionality of Reverse Discrimination*, 41 U. Chi. L. Rev. 723 (1974); Hughes, *Reparations for Blacks*, 43 N.Y.U. L. Rev. 1063 (1968). The precise programs defended vary greatly, as do the reasons offered to justify them.

4   This perspective is discussed in Part 1.

5   This perspective is discussed in Part 2.

6   This perspective is discussed in Part 3.

7   In asserting the importance of one's race and sex in our culture I do not mean to deny the importance of other characteristics – in particular, socioeconomic class. I do think that in our culture race and sex are two very important facts about a person, and I am skeptical of theories which "reduce" the importance of these features to a single, more basic

one, *e.g.*, class. But apart from this one bit of skepticism I think that all of what I have to say is compatible with several different theories concerning why race and sex are so important – including, for instance, most versions of Marxism. *See, e.g.*, the account provided in J. Mitchell, Woman's Estate (1971). The correct causal explanation for the social realities I describe is certainly an important question, both in its own right and for some of the issues I address. It is particularly significant for the issue of how to alter the social realities to bring them closer to the ideal. *See* Part 3. Nonetheless, I have limited the scope of my inquiry to exclude a consideration of this large, difficult topic.

8   Passing is the phenomenon in which a person who in some sense knows himself or herself to be black "passes" as white because he or she looks white. A version of this is described in Sinclair Lewis' novel Kingsblood Royal (1947), where the protagonist discovers when he is an adult that he, his father, and his father's mother are black (or, in the idiom of the late 1940's, Negro) in virtue of the fact that his great grandfather was black. His grandmother knew this and was consciously passing. When he learns about his ancestry, one decision he has to make is whether to continue to pass, or to acknowledge to the world that he is in fact "Negro."

9   That looking black is not in our culture a necessary condition for being black can be seen from the phenomenon of passing. That it is not a sufficient condition can be seen from the book Black Like Me (1960), by John Howard Griffin, where "looking black" is easily understood by the reader to be different from being black. I suspect that the concept of being black is, in our culture, one which combines both physiological and ancestral criteria in some moderately complex fashion.

10   Mr. Justice Douglas suggests something like this in his dissent in *DeFunis*: "The consideration of race as a measure of an applicant's qualification normally introduces a capricious and irrelevant factor working an invidious discrimination." DeFunis v. Odegaard, 416 U.S. 312, 333 (1974).

11   There are significant respects in which the important racial distinction is between being white and being nonwhite, and there are other significant respects in which the fact of being black has its own special meaning and importance. My analysis is conducted largely in terms of what is involved in being black. To a considerable extent, however, what I say directly applies to the more inclusive category of being nonwhite. To the extent to which what I say does not apply to the other nonwhite racial distinctions, the analysis of those distinctions should, of course, be undertaken separately.

12   *See, e.g.*, J. Baldwin, The Fire Next Time (1963);

W.E.B. DuBois, The Souls of Black Folks (1903); R. Ellison, Invisible Man (1952); J. Franklin, From Slavery to Freedom (3rd ed. 1968); C. Hamilton and S. Carmichael, Black Power (1967); Report of the U.S. Commission on Civil Disorders (1968); Kilson, *Whither Integration?*, 45 Am. Scholar 360 (1976); and hundreds, if not thousands of other books and articles, both literary and empirical. These sources describe a great variety of features of the black experience in America: such things as the historical as well as the present day material realities, and the historical as well as present day ideological realities, the way black people have been and are thought about within the culture. In Kingsblood Royal (above) note 8, Lewis provides a powerful account of what he calls the "American Credo" about the Negro, circa 1946. *Id.* at 194–97.

13   The best general account I have read of the structure of patriarchy and of its major dimensions and attributes is that found in Sexual Politics in the chapter, "Theory of Sexual Politics." K. Millett, Sexual Politics 23–58 (1970). The essay seems to me to be truly a major contribution to an understanding of the subject. Something of the essence of the thesis is contained in the following:

[A] disinterested examination of our system of sexual relationship must point out that the situation between the sexes now, and throughout history, is a case of that phenomenon Max Weber defined as *herrschaft*, a relationship of dominance and subordinance. What goes largely unexamined, often even unacknowledged (yet is institutionalized nonetheless) in our social order, is the birthright priority whereby males rule females. Through this system a most ingenious form of "interior colonization" has been achieved. It is one which tends moreover to be sturdier than any form of segregation and more rigorous than class stratification, more uniform, certainly more enduring. However muted its present appearance may be, sexual dominion obtains nevertheless as perhaps the most pervasive ideology of our culture and provides its most fundamental concept of power.

This is so because our society, like all other historical civilizations, is a patriarchy. The fact is evident at once if one recalls that the military, industry, technology, universities, science, political office, and finance – in short, every avenue of power within the society, including the coercive force of the police, is entirely in male hands . . . .

Sexual politics obtains consent through the "socialization" of both sexes to basic patriarchal politics with regard to temperament, role, and status. As to status, a pervasive assent to the prejudice of male superiority guarantees superior status in the male, inferior in the female. The first item, temperament, involves the formation of human personality along stereotyped lines of sex category ("masculine" and "feminine"), based on the needs and values of the dominant group and dictated by what its members cherish in themselves and find convenient in subordinates: aggression, intelligence, force and efficacy in the male; passivity, ignorance, docility, "virtue," and ineffectuality in the female. This is complemented by a second factor, sex role, which decrees a consonant and highly elaborate code of conduct, gesture and attitude for each sex. In terms of activity, sex role assigns domestic service and attendance upon infants to the female, the rest of human achievement, interest and ambition to the male. . . . Were one to analyze the three categories one might designate status as the political component, role as the sociological, and temperament as the psychological – yet their interdependence is unquestionable and they form a chain.

Id. at 24–26 (footnotes omitted).

14 *See, e.g.,* Hochschild, *A Review of Sex Role Research,* 78 Am. J. Soc. 1011 (1973), which reviews and very usefully categorizes the enormous volume of literature on this topic. *See also* Stewart, *Social Influences on Sex Differences in Behavior,* in Sex Differences 138 (M. Teitelbaum ed. 1976); Weitzman, *Sex-Role Socialization,* in Women: A Feminist Perspective 105 (J. Freeman ed. 1975). A number of the other pieces in Women: A Feminist Perspective also describe and analyze the role of women in the culture, including the way they are thought of by the culture. I return to consider further the question of what accounts for the existing psychological and sociological sex differences in section 2 below.

15 For the married woman, her husband and children must always come first; her own needs and desires, last. When the children reach school age, they no longer require constant attention. The emotional-expressive function assigned to the woman is still required of her. Called the "stroking function" by sociologist Jessie Bernard, it consists of showing solidarity, raising the status of others, giving help, rewarding, agreeing, concurring, complying, understanding, and passively accepting. The woman is expected to give emotional support and comfort to other family members, to make them feel like good and worthwhile human beings.

B. Deckard, The Women's Movement 59 (1975), *citing* J. Bernard, Women and the Public Interest 88 (1971).

Patriarchy's chief institution is the family. It is

both a mirror of and a connection with the larger society; a patriarchal unit within a patriarchal whole. Mediating between the individual and the social structure, the family effects control and conformity where political and other authorities are insufficient.

K. Millett note 13 (above), at 33.

16 Even if the couple consciously try to attain an egalitarian marriage, so long as the traditional division of labor is maintained, the husband will be "more equal." He is the provider not only of money but of status. Especially if he is successful, society values what he does; she is just a housewife. Their friends are likely to be his friends and co-workers; in their company, she is just his wife. Because his provider function is essential for the family's survival, major family decisions are made in terms of how they affect his career. He need not and usually does not act like the authoritarian paterfamilius [*sic*] of the Victorian age. His power and status are derived from his function in the family and are secure so long as the traditional division of labor is maintained.

B. Deckard note 15 (above), at 62.

17 In 1970, women workers were, on the average, paid only 59 percent of men's wages. And when wages of persons with similar educational levels are compared, women still were paid over 40 percent less than men. *Id.* at 79–81.

18 It is generally accepted that Western patriarchy has been much softened by the concepts of courtly and romantic love. While this is certainly true, such influence has also been vastly overestimated. In comparison with the candor of "machismo" or oriental behavior, one realizes how much of a concession traditional chivalrous behavior represents – a sporting kind of reparation to allow the subordinate female certain means of saving face. While a palliative to the injustice of woman's social position, chivalry is also a technique for disguising it. One must acknowledge that the chivalrous stance is a game the master group plays in elevating its subject to pedestal level. Historians of courtly love stress the fact that the raptures of the poets had no effect upon the legal or economic standing of women, and very little upon their social status. As the sociologist Hugo Beigel has observed, both the courtly and the romantic versions of love are "grants" which the male concedes out of his total powers. Both have the effect of obscuring the patriarchal character of Western culture and in their general tendency to attribute impossible virtues to women, have ended by confining them in a narrow and often remarkably conscribing sphere of behavior. It

was a Victorian habit, for example, to insist the female assume the function of serving as the male's conscience and living the life of goodness he found tedious but felt someone ought to do anyway.

K. Millett note 13 (above), at 36–37.

19 Thus, even after his "joke" about black persons became known to the public, the former Secretary of Agriculture, Earl Butz, took great pains to insist that this in no way showed that he was a racist. This is understandable, given the strongly condemnatory feature of being described as a racist.

Equally illuminating was the behavior of Butz's associates and superiors. Then-President Ford, for example, criticized Butz for the joke, but did not demand Butz's removal until there was a strong public outcry. It was as though Butz's problem was that he had been indiscreet; he had done something rude like belching in public. What Ford, Butz, and others apparently failed to grasp is that it is just as wrong to tell these jokes in private because to tell a joke of this sort is to have a view about what black people are like: that they can appropriately be ridiculed as being creatures who care only about intercourse, shoes, and defecation. What these persons also failed to grasp is how implausible it is to believe that one can hold these views about black people and at the same time deal with them in a nonracist fashion.

20 At a minimum, this account would include: (1) a description of the economic, political, and social positions of blacks and whites, males and females in the culture; (2) a description of the sexual and racial roles, i.e., the rules, conventions and expectations concerning how males and females, blacks and whites, should behave, and the attitudes and responses produced by these roles; and (3) a description of the de facto ideology of racial and sexual differences. This would include popular beliefs about how males and females, blacks and whites, differ, as well as the beliefs as to what accounts for these differences, roles, and economic, political and social realities.

21 The problem of empirical objectivity is compounded by the fact that part of the dominant, white male ideology is that white males are the one group in society whose members are able to be genuinely detached and objective when it comes to things like an understanding of the place of race and sex in the culture. Thus, for example, when a sex-discrimination suit was brought against a law firm and the case was assigned to Judge Constance Motley, the defendant filed a motion that she be disqualified partly because, as a woman judge, she would be biased in favor of the plaintiff. Judge Motley denied the motion. Bank v. Sullivan & Cromwell, 418 F. Supp. 1 (S.D.N.Y. 1975), *writ of mandamus denied sub nom.* Sullivan & Cromwell v.

Motley, No. 75–3045 (2d Cir. Aug. 26, 1975). Explaining her decision, Judge Motley stated: "[I]f background or sex or race of each judge were, *by definition*, sufficient grounds for removal, no judge on this court could hear this case, or many others, by virtue of the fact that all of them were attorneys, of a sex, often with distinguished law firm or public service backgrounds." 418 F. Supp. at 4 (emphasis added).

22 Thus, in Bolling v. Sharpe, 347 U.S. 497 (1953), the Supreme Court said that what was wrong with preventing black children from attending the all white schools of the District of Columbia was that

> [s]egregation in public education is not reasonably related to any proper governmental objective, and thus it imposes on Negro children of the District of Columbia a burden that constitutes an arbitrary deprivation of their liberty in violation of the Due Process Clause.

Id. at 500. I ignore those cases in which the courts decline to formulate a view about racial differentiation because the behavior involved is not the sort that the law thinks it appropriate to deal with, e.g., "private" racial discrimination.

23 Others have made this general point about the nature of the evil of racial segregation in the United States. See, e.g., Ely, note 3 (above); Fiss, *Groups and Equal Protection*, 5 Phil. & Pub. Aff. 107 (1976), Thalberg, *Reverse Discrimination and the Future*, 5 Phil. F. 268 (1973).

The failure fully to understand this general point seems to me to be one of the things wrong with Weschler's famous article, *Toward Neutral Principles of Constitutional Interpretation*, 73 Harv. L. Rev. 1 (1959). Near the very end of the piece Weschler reports, "In the days when I joined with Charles H. Houston [a well-known black lawyer] in a litigation in the Supreme Court, before the present building was constructed, he did not suffer more than I in knowing that we had to go to Union Station to lunch together during the recess." *Id.* at 34. If the stress in that sentence is wholly on the fact of *knowing*, no one can say for certain that Weschler is wrong. But what is certain is that Charles H. Houston suffered more than Weschler from *living* in a system in which he could only lunch at Union Station.

24 This conjecture about the role of sexually segregated bathrooms may well be inaccurate or incomplete. The sexual segregation of bathrooms may have more to do with privacy than with patriarchy. However, if so, it is at least odd that what the institution makes relevant is sex rather than merely the ability to perform the eliminatory acts in private.

25 See, e.g., Guinn v. United States, 238 U.S. 347 (1915). Such statutes provided that the grandchild of someone who had been registered to vote in the

state was permitted to vote in that state; but the grandchild of somebody who had never been registered to vote in the state had to take a special test in order to become qualified to vote. It does not take much knowledge of history to know that in most of the southern states few if any black people had grandparents who before the Civil War were registered to vote. And the persons who enacted these laws knew it too. So even though race was not made a category by the described laws, they effectively divided people on grounds of race into those who were qualified to vote without more, and those who had to submit to substantially more rigorous tests before they could exercise the franchise. All of this was done, as is well known, so as to perpetuate the control of the franchise by whites.

26 *See, e.g.*, Crawford v. Board of Educ., 17 Cal. 3d 280 (1976); Jackson v. Pasadena City School Dist., 59 Cal. 2d 876, 382 P.2d 878, 31 Cal. Rptr. 606 (1963).

27 N.Y. Times, Aug. 31, 1972, § 1, at 33, col. 3.

28 All of the laws, institutional arrangements, etc., that I analyze are, I think, cases of racism and not, for example, cases of prejudice. The latter concept I take to refer more specifically to the defective, incomplete or objectionable beliefs and attitudes of individuals. Prejudiced individuals often engage in racist acts, enact racist laws and participate in racist institutions. But they need not. Nor is it true that the only persons connected with racist acts, laws, or institutions need be prejudiced individuals.

A perceptive account of the differences between prejudice and racism, and of the different kinds of racism, including institutional racism of the sorts I discuss below, can be found in M. Jones, Prejudice and Racism (1972). *See especially id.* at 60–115 (ch. 4, "Perspectives on Prejudice"); *id.* at 116–67 (ch. 5, "Realities of Racism"). A somewhat analogous set of distinctions concerning sexism is made in Jaggar, *On Sexual Equality*, 84 Ethics 275, 276–77 (1974).

29 One example of what may have been an instance of genuine de facto racism in a noneducational setting is found in Gregory v. Litton Systems, Inc., 316 F. Supp. 401 (C.D. Cal. 1970), *modified*, 472 F.2d 631 (9th Cir. 1972). Litton Systems had a policy of refusing to employ persons who had been frequently arrested. The court found this to violate Title VII of the Civil Rights Act of 1964, 42 U.S.C. § 2000e (1970):

Negroes are arrested substantially more frequently than whites in proportion to their numbers. The evidence on this question was overwhelming and utterly convincing. For example, negroes nationally comprise some 11% of the population and account for 27% of reported arrests and 45% of arrests reported as

"suspicious arrests". Thus, any policy that disqualifies prospective employees because of having been arrested once, or more than once, discriminates in fact against negro applicants. This discrimination exists even though such a policy is objectively and fairly applied as between applicants of various races. A substantial and disproportionately large number of negroes are excluded from employment opportunities by Defendant's policy.

316 F. Supp. at 403.

30 Whitus v. Georgia, 385 U.S. 545 (1967), Avery v. Georgia, 345 U.S. 559 (1953), and Strauder v. West Virginia, 100 U.S. 303 (1880), are three of the many cases declaring it unconstitutional to exclude blacks systematically from the jury rolls when the defendant is black. Swain v. Alabama, 380 U.S. 202 (1965), is one of the many cases declaring that it is not unconstitutional that no blacks were in fact on the jury that tried the defendant.

31 *See, e.g.*, Peters v. Kiff, 407 U.S. 493, 508–09 (Burger, C.J., dissenting).

32 I discuss this particular situation in somewhat more detail in Wasserstrom, *The University and the Case for Preferential Treatment*, 13 Am. Phil. Q. 165, 169–70 (1976). Mr. Justice Marshall expresses a view that I take to be reasonably close to mine in Peters v. Kiff, 407 U.S. 493 (1972). The case involved the question whether a white defendant could challenge the systematic exclusion of blacks from the jury rolls. Mr. Justice Marshall held that he could:

[W]e are unwilling to make the assumption that the exclusion of Negroes has relevance only for issues involving race. When any large and identifiable segment of the community is excluded from jury service, the effect is to remove from the jury room qualities of human nature and varieties of human experience, the range of which is unknown and perhaps unknowable. It is not necessary to assume that the excluded group will consistently vote as a class in order to conclude, as we do, that its exclusion deprives the jury of a perspective on human events that may have unsuspected importance in any case that may be presented.

Id. at 503–04 (footnote omitted).

Given my analysis, I think any defendant is disadvantaged by the absence of blacks from the jury, where, for instance, the testimony of a police officer is a significant part of the prosecution case. Because police are more apt to lie about black defendants, and because black jurors are more apt to be sensitive to this possibility, black defendants are, I think, especially likely to be tried unfairly by many all-white juries. What matters in terms of fairness is that blacks be represented on particular juries; nonexclusion from the jury rolls is certainly not obviously sufficient.

33 Brown v. Board of Educ., 349 U.S. 294 (1955).

34 Brown v. Board of Educ., 347 U.S. 483 (1954).

35 349 U.S. at 301.

36 *Id.* at 299.

37 *Id.*, at 300–01.

38 The unusual character of *Brown II* was recognized by Mr. Justice Goldberg in Watson v. City of Memphis, 373 U.S. 526 (1963):

> Most importantly, of course, it must be recognized that even the delay countenanced by *Brown* was a necessary, albeit significant, adaptation of the usual principle that any deprivation of constitutional rights calls for prompt rectification. The rights here asserted are, like all such rights, *present* rights; they are not merely hopes to some *future* enjoyment of some formalistic constitutional promise. The basic guarantees of our Constitution are warrants for the here and now and, unless there is an overwhelmingly compelling reason, they are to be promptly fulfilled. The second *Brown* decision is but a narrowly drawn, and carefully limited, qualification upon usual precepts of constitutional adjudication . . . .

Id. at 532–33 (emphasis in original; footnote omitted). As I have indicated, the problem with Brown II is that there was no "overwhelmingly compelling reason" to delay. It might be argued though, that the Court deliberately opted for "all deliberate speed" and all that meant about the dreary pace of desegregation because it believed the country would not accept full, immediate implementation of Brown I. If this was the reasoning, it is equally pernicious. It is sound, only if the country is identified with white people; blacks were surely willing to accept the immediate elimination of the system of racial segregation.

But someone might still say that the Court was just dealing sensibly with the political realities. The white power structure would not have accepted anything more drastic. Arguments such as these are developed at considerable length by A. Bickel, The Least Dangerous Branch 247–54 (1962). The problem with this is twofold. First, what is deemed a drastic solution has a lot to do with whether whites or blacks are being affected, and how. It was and is thought to be drastic for force and the criminal law to be used against whites to secure compliance with laws relating to segregation. It was and is thought to be much less drastic to use force and the criminal law against blacks who object vigorously and sometimes violently to the system of racial oppression. The sim-

ple truth is that when the executive branch, as well as the judiciary, thought about these issues it typically weighed the claims of whites very differently from the claims of blacks. The history of the enforcement of civil rights by the federal government in the 1950's and early 1960's is largely a history of the consistent overvaluation of the claims and concerns of whites vis-à-vis blacks. I have suggested some of the ways this was true of the Civil Rights Division of the Department of Justice. See Wasserstrom, Book Review, 33 U. Chi. L. Rev. 406, 409–13 (1966); Wasserstrom, Postscript: Lawyers and Revolution, 30 U. Pitt. L. Rev. 125, 131 (1968).

Second, whether the decision would have been "accepted" is in large measure a function of what the United States government would have been prepared to do to get the decision implemented. During this same era things that were viewed as absolutely unacceptable or as not feasible suddenly became acceptable and feasible without any substantial change in material circumstances, e.g., the passage of the 1965 Voting Rights Act, 42 U.S.C. §§ 1973 et seq. (1970). It mysteriously became acceptable to the Congress, enforceable by the government and accepted by the South when Reverend Reeb and Mrs. Liuzzo were murdered during the time of the Selma march, and former President Johnson declared his determination to see the law enacted and enforced.

39 A discussion of some of these same kinds of issues concerning ideology can be found in Thalberg, *Justifications for Institutional Racism*, 5 Phil. F. 243 (1973).

40 In California, rape was traditionally defined as "an act of sexual intercourse, accomplished with a female *not the wife of the perpetrator*, under either of the following circumstances. . . ." Cal. Penal Code § 261 (West Supp. 1976) (emphasis added).

41 For an example of a kind of analysis that is beginning to show some of the ways in which the law builds upon and supports the patriarchal system of marriage, see Johnston, *Sex and Property: The Common Law Tradition, The Law School Curriculum, and Developments Toward Equality*, 47 N.Y.U. L. Rev. 1033, 1071–89 (1972). Another very rich source is the recent casebook on sex discrimination by B. Babcock, A. Freedman, E. Norton and S. Ross, Sex Discrimination and the Law – Causes and Remedies (1975).

42 *See, e.g.*, R. Lakoff, Language and Woman's Place (1975); Baker, *"Pricks" and "Chicks": A Plea for "Persons"*, in Philosophy and Sex 45 (R. Baker and F. Elliston eds. 1975); Moulton, *Sex and Reference* in *id.* at 34.

43 One thorough and very valuable exploration of this and a number of the other topics discussed in this section is Alison Jaggar's *On Sexual Equality*, note

28. The article also contains a very useful analysis of the views of a number of other feminists who have dealt with this issue.

44 An analysis of the social realities of an existing society can also divide things up into these three areas.

45 There is a danger in calling this ideal the "assimilationist" ideal. That term suggests the idea of incorporating oneself, one's values, and the like into the dominant group and its practices and values. I want to make it clear that no part of that idea is meant to be captured by my use of this term. Mine is a stipulative definition.

46 Jaggar describes something fairly close to the assimilationist view in this way:

> The traditional feminist answer to this question [of what the features of a nonsexist society would be] has been that a sexually egalitarian society is one in which virtually no public recognition is given to the fact that there is a physiological sex difference between persons. This is not to say that the different reproductive function of each sex should be unacknowledged in such a society nor that there should be no physicians specializing in female and male complaints, etc. But it is to say that, except in this sort of context, the question whether someone is female or male should have no significance.
> . . . .
> . . . In the mainstream tradition, the non-sexist society is one which is totally integrated sexually, one in which sexual differences have ceased to be a matter of public concern.
> Jaggar, note 28 (above), at 276–77.

47 *See* section 1. A above.

48 Thus, for example, a column appeared a few years ago in the *Washington Star* concerning the decision of the Cosmos Club to continue to refuse to permit women to be members. The author of the column (and a member of the club) defended the decision on the ground that women appropriately had a different status in the society. Their true distinction was to be achieved by being faithful spouses and devoted mothers. The column closed with this paragraph:

> In these days of broken homes, derision of marriage, reluctance to bear children, contempt for the institution of the family – a phase in our national life when it seems more honorable to be a policewoman, or a model, or an accountant than to be a wife or mother – there is a need to reassert a traditional scale of values in which the vocation of homemaker is as honorable and distinguished as any in political or professional life. Such women, as wives and widows of members, now enjoy in the club the privileges of their sta-

tus, which includes [*sic*] their own drawing rooms, and it is of interest that they have been among the most outspoken opponents of the proposed changes in club structure.

Groseclose, *Now – Shall We Join the Ladies?*, Washington Star, Mar. 13, 1975.

The same view may be held by Senator Daniel Moynihan. It is his view, apparently, that the United States government ought to work primarily to strengthen the institution of the family. Moynihan is quoted as saying:

> If the family is strong, the economy will be productive. If the family is strong, law will be respected and crime will decrease. If the family is strong, the welfare rolls will shrink. . . . All this is true, and its truth has been confirmed and reconfirmed by the evidence of history, of social science, of direct observation, and of simple common sense.

Buckley, *The Main Event East*, N.Y. Times, Oct. 31, 1976, § 6 (Magazine), at 16, 57.

For the reasons that I give in the remainder of section 2, I think any version of this ideal is seriously flawed. But it is one that is certainly much more widely held in respect to sex than is a comparable one held today in respect to race.

49 *See* note 9 (above).

50 This is not to deny that certain people believe that race is linked with characteristics that prima facie are relevant. Such beliefs persist. They are, however, unjustified by the evidence. *See, e.g.*, Block and Dworkin, *IQ, Heritability and Inequality* (pts. 1–2), 3 Phil. & Pub. Aff. 331, 4 *id.* 40 (1974). More to the point, even if it were true that such a linkage existed, none of the characteristics suggested would require that political or social institutions, or inter-personal relationships, would have to be structured in a certain way.

51 The term "gender" may be used in a number of different senses. I use it to refer to those anatomical, physiological, and other differences (if any) that are naturally occurring in the sense described above. Some persons refer to these differences as "sex differences," but that seems to me confusing. In any event, I am giving a stipulative definition to "gender."

52 *See, e.g.*, authorities cited in note 14 (above); M. Mead, Sex and Temperament in Three Primitive Societies (1935):

> These three situations [the cultures of the Anapesh, the Mundugumor, and the Tchambuli] suggest, then, a very definite conclusion. If those temperamental attitudes which we have traditionally regarded as feminine – such as passivity, responsiveness, and a willing-

ness to cherish children – can so easily be set up as the masculine pattern in one tribe, and in another to be outlawed for the majority of women as well as for the majority of men, we no longer have any basis for regarding such aspects of behaviour as sex-linked . . . .

. . . We are forced to conclude that human nature is almost unbelievably malleable, responding accurately and contrastingly to contrasting cultural conditions. . . . Standardized personality differences between the sexes are of this order, cultural creations to which each generation, male and female is trained to conform. *Id.* at 190–91.

A somewhat different view is expressed in J. Sherman, On the Psychology of Women (1971). There, the author suggests that there are "natural" differences of a psychological sort between men and women, the chief ones being aggressiveness and strength of sex drive. See id. at 238. However, even if she is correct as to these biologically based differences, this does little to establish what the good society should look like, as argued in the remainder of section 2.

Almost certainly the most complete discussion of this topic is E. Macoby and C. Jacklin, The Psychology of Sex Differences (1974). The authors conclude that the sex differences which are, in their words, "fairly well established," are: (1) that girls have greater verbal ability than boys; (2) that boys excel in visual-spatial ability; (3) that boys excel in mathematical ability; and (4) that males are aggressive. Id. at 351–52. They conclude, in respect to the etiology of these psychological sex differences, that there appears to be a biological component to the greater visual-spatial ability of males and to their greater aggressiveness. Id. at 360.

53 As Sherman observes,

Each sex has its own special physical assets and liabilities. The principal female liability of less muscular strength is not ordinarily a handicap in a civilized, mechanized, society. . . . There is nothing in the biological evidence to prevent women from taking a role of equality in a civilized society.

J. Sherman note 52 (above), at 11.

There are, of course, some activities that would be sexually differentiated in the assimilationist society; namely, those that were specifically directed toward, say, measuring unaided physical strength. Thus, I think it likely that even in this ideal society, weight lifting contests and boxing matches would in fact be dominated, perhaps exclusively so, by men. But it is hard to find any significant activities or institutions that are analogous. And it is not clear that such insignificant activities would

be thought worth continuing, especially since sports function in existing patriarchal societies to help maintain the dominance of males. See K. Millett note 13 (above), at 48–49.

It is possible that there are some nontrivial activities or occupations that depend sufficiently directly upon unaided physical strength that most if not all women would be excluded. Perhaps being a lifeguard at the ocean is an example. Even here, though, it would be important to see whether the way lifeguarding had traditionally been done could be changed to render such physical strength unimportant. If it could be changed, then the question would simply be one of whether the increased cost (or loss of efficiency) was worth the gain in terms of equality and the avoidance of sex-role differentiation. In a nonpatriarchal society very different from ours, where sex was not a dominant social category, the argument from efficiency might well prevail. What is important, once again, is to see how infrequent and peripheral such occupational cases are.

54 *See, e.g.,* Paige, *Women Learn to Sing the Menstrual Blues,* in The Female Experience 17 (C. Tavis ed. 1973).

I have come to believe that the "raging hormones" theory of menstrual distress simply isn't adequate. All women have the raging hormones, but not all women have menstrual symptoms, nor do they have the same symptoms for the same reasons. Nor do I agree with the "raging neurosis" theory, which argues that women who have menstrual symptoms are merely whining neurotics, who need only a kind pat on the head to cure their problems.

We must instead consider the problem from the perspective of women's subordinate social position, and of the cultural ideology that so narrowly defines the behaviors and emotions that are appropriately "feminine." Women have perfectly good reasons to react emotionally to reproductive events. Menstruation, pregnancy and childbirth – so sacred, yet so unclean – are the woman's primary avenues of achievement and self-expression. Her reproductive abilities define her femininity; other routes to success are only second-best in this society. . . .

. . . .

. . . My current research on a sample of 114 societies around the world indicates that ritual observances and taboos about menstruation are a method of controlling women and their fertility. Men apparently use such rituals, along with those surrounding pregnancy and childbirth, to assert their claims to women and their children.

. . . The hormone theory isn't giving us much mileage, and it's time to turn it in for a better model, one that looks to our beliefs about menstruation and women. It is no mere coincidence

that women get the blue meanies along with an event they consider embarrassing, unclean – and a curse.
Id. at 21.

55 One article that explores this point in some detail is Hill, *Self-Determination and Autonomy*, in Today's Moral Problems 171 (Wasserstrom ed. 1975). *See also* Jaggar note 28 (above), at 289–91.

56 Still other arguments against something like the assimilationist ideal and in favor of something like the idea of diversity are considered by Jaggar and shown by her to be unpersuasive. *See* Jaggar note 28 (above), at 281–91.

57 Although ostensibly empirical, the question of whether and to what extent affirmative action programs "work" has a substantial nonempirical component. There are many variables that can plausibly be taken into account, and many differing weights to be assigned to these variables. Consequently, how one marshalls and assesses the "evidence" concerning which programs "work" and which do not, has at least as much to do with whether one believes that the programs are or are not justifiable on other grounds as it does with a disinterested marshalling of the "facts." *See, e.g.,* T. Sowell, Affirmative Action Reconsidered 34–40 (1975); N. Glazer, Affirmative Discrimination: Ethnic Inequality and Public Policy (1975). This also is a feature of Mr. Justice Mosk's analysis where he asserts, for example, that "[t]he overemphasis upon race as a criterion will *undoubtedly* be counterproductive." Bakke v. Regents of the Univ. of Cal., 18 Cal. 3d 34, 62, 553 P.2d 1152, 1171, 132 Cal. Rptr. 680, 699 (1976) (emphasis added), *cert. granted*, L.A. Daily Jour., Feb. 23, 1977, at 1, col. 2 (No. 76–811).

The general point is related to my discussion of *Brown II*, note 39 (above) A tremendous amount does turn in this area on who defines the nature of the problem and how the problem gets defined. My own analysis, to the degree to which it has endeavored to be empirical is, of course, subject to this same potential distortion.

58 It is here that an understanding of the *causes* of the position of blacks and women is most important. Such an understanding is crucial to an ability to make the kinds of changes and interventions that will successfully make real and lasting differences in the status quo. *See* note 7 and accompanying text (above).

59 *See* Bakke v. Regents of the Univ. of Cal., 18 Cal. 3d 34, 62, 553 P.2d 1152, 1171, 132 Cal. Rptr. 680, 699 (1976), *cert. granted*, 45 U.S.L.W. 3437 (U.S. Dec. 14, 1976) (No. 76–811).

60 *See, e.g.,* the sources cited in note 1 (above).

61 For example, such an approach seems, at least at times, to underlie the writings of R. Nozick, Anarchy, State and Utopia (1974).

62 I have also tried to discuss some of these matters, although not with anything like complete success, in Wasserstrom, *Rights, Human Rights, and Racial Discrimination*, 61 J. Phil. 628 (1964).

63 *See* Part 1.

64 The point is a more general one than the few random examples suggest. The more prestige, power, wealth or influence is attached to the job, the less likely it is that there are specifiable qualifications that make it easy to determine who in fact is the most qualified. There are, to be sure, minimum qualifications. But these are satisfied by a large number of individuals. Moreover, for most of these positions the notion simply does not exist that the most qualified individuals from among this large class are the ones who deserve to be selected, *e.g.,* the dean of a college or the head of a federal agency.

65 I prefer to focus on these aspects of desert and considerations of fairness rather than principles of compensation and reparation because I can thereby bypass the claim that compensation or reparation is being exacted from the wrong individuals, because they are innocent of any wrongdoing, and causally unconnected with the injuries suffered. I do think the causal link is often present and the claim of innocence often suspect. But my analysis puts these issues to one side. For a discussion of some of the literature that discusses the issues of compensation and reparation, see, *e.g.,* Boxill, *The Morality of Reparation*, 2 Soc. Theory & Prac. 113 (1972).

66 The preceding six paragraphs appear in substantially the same form in Wasserstrom, note 32 (above), at 166–67.

37

Moral Woman and Immoral Man: A Consideration of the Public–Private Split and Its Political Ramifications

Jean Bethke Elshtain

It is a part of the common wisdom of our political and historic past that the fight for female suffrage failed to alter significantly the system of social constraints which intertwined to oppress women in both the economic and political spheres. Admittedly, the majority of Suffragists were engaged in a struggle for formal-legalistic equality only – many in the hope that other changes would quickly follow upon the heels of reform in statutes discriminating against women in the holding of property, in bringing action in civil suits, and in exercising the franchise. It is my contention, however, that the Suffragists failed, even on their own terms, and that this failure can be traced, first, to the manner in which they initially analyzed their dilemma and, second, to the proposed remedies which followed from their original conceptualization. Indeed, I shall argue that, with few exceptions, the Suffragists did not confront the full scope and basis of one of our system's basic incoherencies or "crimes of birth"[1] (that is, flaws of construction) and thus they were incapable of moving beyond the symptomatic surface of sexual inequality.

An appreciation of all that is implied by the inadequacies of Suffragist thought and action necessitates a critical exploration of the theoretical and ideological split between what has come to be the public, political realm of immoral man and the private, apolitical realm of moral woman. To get at these antipodes I will first examine the defining contours of a *public person* and a *private person*; the relationship of these persons to systems of *public* and *private morality*; and the link of both to *politics* and that which is *not-politics*. I begin with the conceptual categories of Aristotle's *Politics*.

For Aristotle, the good life was possible only through participation in the life of the *polis*, the "final and perfect association."[2] Man himself was "by nature an animal intended to live in a *polis*."[3] Although all associations aimed at some good, it was in the *polis* that the highest good was actualized; therefore, only those persons who were its citizens achieved complete good.[4] Women, slaves, and children did not partake in the full realization of goodness and rationality which defined the co-equal participants in the perfect association. There was an "essential" difference between greater (free, male) and lesser (unfree, female) persons, but these two classes of persons were nonetheless linked together in relationships of *necessary* superordination and subordination. A nexus between "the naturally ruling element with the element which is naturally ruled" was essential to "the preservation of both."[5]

Aristotle argued against the notion that power over others was *automatically* tied to goodness. He urged instead that "the superior in goodness ought to rule over inferiors"; that power must be accompanied by goodness before it can become an element in a *legitimate* relationship between

Originally published in *Politics and Society*, 4 (1974), 453–73. Reprinted by permission of Sage Publications Inc.

master and slave, or male and female; nevertheless, because the mere *fact* of such rule implied
the existence of superior goodness in the superor-
dinate party, that is, a man could not be the slave
of another were he not "capable" of becoming
another's property and of "apprehending" the
full reason and goodness in his master which he
himself lacked,[6] power over another was (tauto-
logically) accompanied by goodness in Aristotle's
ideal state.

The household constituted the non-public
sphere within which the female was subsumed
and which therefore defined her. Because the
good at which the household aimed was a lesser
good than that which was the end of the *polis*, the
wife-mother achieved only the limited goodness
of the "naturally ruled," a goodness different in
kind from that of the naturally ruling.[7] (Females
possessed reason in a similarly incomplete,
"inconclusive" form.) Aristotle states:

> The ruler, accordingly, must possess moral
> goodness in its full and perfect form (i.e., the
> form based on rational deliberation), because
> his function, regarded absolutely and in its full
> nature, demands a master-artificer, and reason
> is such a master-artificer; but all other persons
> need only possess moral goodness to the extent
> required of them (by their particular position).[8]

Aristotle's theory of citizenship emerges from
his normative presumption that the life of the
polis is superior to any other. A citizen in the
strict sense (after paring away certain disqualifica-
tions or defects of youth, age, infirmity, and so
on), is "best defined by the one criterion, 'a man
who shares in the administration of justice and in
the holding of office.'"[9] The state "in its simplest
terms" is a "body of such persons adequate . . .
for achieving a selfsufficient existence."[10] A good
citizen isn't necessarily coterminous with a good
man – not because there are divergent notions of
"goodness", but because concepts of citizenship
differ from state-to-state. The two can be linked,
however, in the paradigm case of the good citizen
living under an ideal constitution.

Where do "lesser" persons fit into this scheme
of things? Aristotle makes a distinction between
women, children, slaves, "mechanics and labourers", and citizens. The latter alone comprise the
"integral parts" of the state. The former are its
"necessary conditions" who, although they do not
share in public life *per se*, nevertheless provide the

basis or precondition upon which that public life
rests.[11] Aristotle compares rulers and subjects to
flute-players and flute-makers; one makes use of
what the other makes.[12]

What, to summarize thus far, emerges from
Aristotle's discussion in terms of the questions
posed at the outset concerning public and private
persons, morality, and the connection of both to
politics? Aristotle radically bifurcates public
(political) from private (apolitical) realms. There
are greater (public) associations and lesser (private) associations. Fully realized moral goodness
and reason are attainable only through participation in public life, and this involvement is
reserved to free, adult males. Women *share* in
goodness and rationality in the limited sense
appropriate to their confinement in a lesser association, the household. Their relationship to the
public realm is that of one of its "necessary" conditions rather than its "integral parts." Indeed, it
can be said with no exaggeration that women in
Aristotle's schema are *idiots* in the Greek sense of
the word, that is, persons who do not participate
in the *polis*.[13] Politics, the life of rationality,
responsibility, and the highest system of justice is
that activity which defines the *polis*. Aristotle's
paradigm can be set forth as a series of
dichotomies or "typologies" of persons, moralities, and public and private life.[14]

Public (Political)
Public persons are responsible, rational persons
who share fully in both private life *and* the life
of the *polis* and its *integral* elements (citizens).
As citizens, such persons participate in the
highest moral good and system of justice. In
the ideal state, the good man and the good citizen are coterminous. The life of the whole is
superior in nature, intent, and purpose to that
of all lesser associations.

Private (Not-Political)
Private persons are those who (for whatever
reason) are not fully rational and who can only
share in the limited goodness appropriate to
their spheres. They are confined to these
spheres and as such form a *necessary* condition
for the superior public realm. The life of lesser
associations, including the household, is inferior in nature, intent, and purpose to that of
the more inclusive association.

The above bifurcations are necessary ones given

Aristotle's conceptual system which entails a rigid differentiation between all phenomena – biological and social – according to his principle of entelechy. In Aristotelian philosophy, entelechy means *completed actuality* as opposed to *potentiality*.[15] In simplest terms, what *is* is what *ought to be* because whatever *ought to be* has been actualized, that is, *is*.

The normative import of Aristotle's theories in terms of the actual operation of Greek politics lies in the fact that his concepts could be utilized to justify slavery, to defend the dominance of women by men, and to support as well the subordination of certain "underclasses". His concepts additionally underpinned the notion that Athenians, as superior participants in the ideal state, had a right to extend their sway over certain lesser, barbarous peoples.[16]

It is my contention that Aristotelian typologies still predominate in most discussions of public and private realms and of political personhood. Having put the proposition baldly, I would first like to lodge a partial caveat which should add to the complexity of my analysis. A presumptive shift did occur in the work of post-medieval political theorists from a controlling definition of the political realm as an arena which constituted *per se* a sphere with intrinsic moral purposes, governed at least in part by moral rules and considerations, to one in which force alone constituted the final political appeal. Early modern political theorists, of whom Bodin and Machiavelli were the most important, responding to the growth in power and complexity of states governed by rulers increasingly freed from intervention in affairs of state by the Church, elaborated grandiose conceptions of political sovereignty and *raison d'état*. These theories, in turn, were used to rationalize and justify sovereign power and the use of force and as such they became constitutive elements in its exercise.

The recognition that force is or can be the *ultima ratio* of politics was not, of course, new. St. Augustine observed it and, before him, Thrasymachus.[17] But with Bodin and Machiavelli politics was celebrated as the use of force *par excellence*. The state for Jean Bodin was an entity possessing perpetual, absolute sovereignty (*puissance souveraine*)[18] with unlimited authority to make laws. The perspective which had prevailed in medieval political theory as well as in the thought of Aristotle, Plato, and the Stoic philosophers, did not involve bifurcation of the exercise

of politics from knowledge and pursuit of the good. The new definition of politics as the exercise of force on the highest levels, and of the state as (above all else) an organization of violence, tempered perhaps by law, reinforced Aristotelian distinctions between public and private persons and spheres, but invited an additional bifurcation not present in Aristotelian thought: the divorce of politics from moral considerations.

In order to be politically "good," that is, efficacious in the exercise of force, Machiavelli's prince had to be capable of being "bad" according to the standards of Christian morality which still predominated in the early modern period. Machiavelli adjured that a good prince was one who could "deliver the goods." This meant that a man could be a good ruler and a perfectly horrid person if "private" morality were set up as the criterion by which to judge his "public" actions – something Machiavelli rejected.[19] Rules of conduct appropriate to the one sphere (public) were inappropriate to the other (private), and the obverse also pertained. The (im)morality of the public sphere as a competing system of morality – a "new" morality of politics, of rules appropriate to holding and exercising power on the macro-level, received full elaboration.[20] "Good" and "bad", as these terms related to what was public and private, political and non-political, lost any universalizable meaning.

If the public and private spheres are definitionally bifurcated, two divergent sets of standards by which conduct in either realm is to be judged may be erected. Indeed, the two realms become, in a real sense, incommensurable. But there is a complication in the taxonomy: individuals do not share equally in both spheres. Man, for example, has two statuses: as a public person and as a private person; therefore, men are subject to two disparate judgments in their capacities as public and private persons.

Woman, however, is totally immersed in the private, non-public realm and is judged by the single standard appropriate to that realm alone. She does not share in public life, hence she does not participate in the "good" (the competing standard of morality) of that life. As Hegel put it:

In a household of the ethical kind, a woman's relationships are not based on a reference to this particular husband, this particular child, but to a husband, to children in general – not to feeling, but to the general. The distinction between her ethical life (Sittlichkeit), (while it determines her particular existence and brings her pleasure), and that of her husband consists just in this and is quite alien to the impulsive condition of the mere particular desire. On the other hand, *in the husband these two aspects get separated; and since he possesses, as a citizen, the self-conscious power belonging to the general life of the community, the life of the social whole, he acquires thereby the rights of desire, and keeps himself at the same time in detachment from it.*[21] (emphasis mine)

According to this system, if a woman should "go public" (or attempt to) she is still to be judged as a *private* person. All that women were in private (kind, virtuous, loving, responsible) men could attempt to become with the aid and succor of women; but women could not "become" what men were (responsible public persons) without forsaking their womanhood by definition.[22]

The combined Aristotelian-power politics paradigm, a male dominant system, is a set of partial or whole antinomies, each dependent on the other.

Public (Im)Morality

A "bad" man can be a "good" politician but he can also be a "good" man in private. What is moral in the public realm cannot be judged by the standards of private moral conduct; therefore, public persons are judged one way in their capacity as public persons and another way in their existence as private persons.

Politics

Politics is the realm of public power, the sphere of justice, and systems of law. The state is a body of citizens subject to laws. Political leaders are also subject to laws but not necessarily bound by them in the exercise of power. Women are not part of politics *per se*, but provide, in their capacities in the private sphere, a refuge from public life for men when they share in the private sphere.

Private Morality

A "good" woman makes a "bad" citizen by definition. The woman who is a "good" citizen cannot, in the private sphere, be a "good" woman. She is judged in each instance by standards of so-called private morality. She is not to share in public (im)morality. Women are

morally "superior" because they are publicly inferior.

Non-Politics

Non-politics is a private realm of feeling and sentiment, or moral suasion, not subject to laws and not judged by rational standards. If there is power in this sphere it is power as covert manipulation, deceit, and cunning. This realm is not properly part of the public sphere but provides a base for it. Women are part of non-politics, and so are men in their "private" capacities.

The political effect of the powerful typologies set forth above are incalculable. The bifurcations were seen as necessary in order to maintain politics, law, order, justice, and sovereignty on the one hand, and to protect the innocent and helpless, preserve the home and its private virtues, and provide succor for those (men) seeking respite from the public world on the other. I shall now explore the ramifications of the paradigm in terms of the woman's suffrage movement.

On what terms did the Suffragists lodge their battle for formal-legalistic equality? In what categories did they analyze their dilemma and propose remedies? With few exceptions, the Suffragists accepted (implicitly if not explicitly) the presumptions of the Aristotelian-power politics paradigm – they simply placed a different interpretation on certain of its constituent elements. Their arguments for the franchise involved some shifting and rearranging of terms but did not entail a paradigm shift.[23] By thus proceeding from the assumptions of their opponents, the Suffragists perpetuated the very mystifications and unexamined presumptions which served to rig the system against them.

The following, for example, is a typical anti-Suffragist argument:

Man assumed the direction of government and war, woman of the domestic and family affairs and the care and training of the child. . . . It has been so from the beginning, throughout the whole history of man, and it will continue to be so to the end, because it is in conformity to nature and its laws, and is sustained and confirmed by the experience and reason of six thousand years. . . . The domestic altar is a sacred flame where woman is the high and officiating priestess. . . . To keep her in that condition of purity, it is necessary that she should be separated from the exercise of suffrage and from all those stern and contaminating and demoralizing duties that devolves upon the hardier sex – man.[24]

The statement sets into crystal relief the antipodal notions that man and woman are different in essence and hence must have separate spheres of activity. (Or, man and woman have separate spheres of activity *because* they are different in essence.) Politics is by definition the man's sphere; it follows, *a fortiori*, that woman has nothing to do with politics. To the man alone lies those "stern . . . contaminating . . . demoralizing" duties.

Women had more important duties. Rev. N.J. Danforth, in a treatise called *The Ladies Casket*, proclaimed: "Oh, mother, acquit thyself well in thy humble sphere, for thou mayest affect the world." And one Rev. Harrington felt assured that most women, rejecting the Suffragists, would cry: "Let the men take care of politics, we will take care of the children!"[25] Those women who moved outside the private realm were "semi-women, mental hermaphrodites."

Women were separate but equal.[26] Suffrage opponents elaborated on this theme:

The Creator has assigned to woman very laborious and responsible duties, by no means less important than those imposed upon the male sex, though entirely different in their character. . . . While the man is contending with the sterner duties of life, the whole time of the noble, affectionate and true woman is required in the discharge of her delicate and difficult duties assigned her in the family circle, in her relations and in the society where her lot is cast. . . . I believe that they [women] are better than men, but I do not believe that they are adapted to the political work of this world I would not, and I say it deliberately, degrade woman by giving her the right of suffrage. I mean the word in its full signification, because I believe that woman as she is today, the queen of home and of hearts, is above the political collisions of this world, and should always be kept above them.[27]

What was the response of the Suffragists to arguments that woman was pure, private, and apolitical and man was immoral, public, and political (because his sphere was)? Rather than rejecting the conceptual system from which these dichotomies were a predictable outgrowth, the Suffragists simply turned anti-Suffrage arguments upside down to serve as the basis for a pro-Suffrage plea. Yes, man was evil and bad and he had made something nasty out of politics. True, woman was purer and more virtuous – look at the way she had ennobled the private sphere. What must be done, therefore, is to throw the mantle of private morality *over* the public sphere by drawing women *into* it. Women would be politicized and politics would be transformed in one fell swoop.[28]

Elizabeth Cady Stanton, the most important of the early Suffrage theorists, espoused the female-superiority view with vehemence.

The male element is a destructive force, stern, selfish, aggrandizing, loving war, violence, conquest, acquisition, breeding in the material and moral world alike discord, disorder, disease and death. See what a record of blood and cruelty the pages of history reveal! Through what slavery, and slaughter, and sacrifice, through what inquisitions and imprisonments, pains and persecutions, black codes and gloomy creeds, the soul of humanity has struggled for the centuries, while mercy has veiled her face and all hearts have been dead alike to love and hope! The male element has held high carnival thus far, it has fairly run riot from the beginning, overpowering the feminine element everywhere, crushing out the diviner qualities in human nature until we know but little of true manhood and womanhood, of the latter comparatively nothing, for it has scarce been recognized as a power until within the last century. . . . The need of this hour is not territory, gold mines, railroads, or specie payments, but a new evangel of womanhood, to exalt purity, virtue, morality, true religion, to lift man up into the higher realms of thought and action . . . .[29]

The image enunciated by Stanton holds that the male element – destructive and selfish – is in control. The female element – loving and virtuous – is enslaved and intimidated. If social chaos is to be prevented, the balance must be tipped to the feminine element.

Theodore Parker, a male Suffragist and a member of that group of New England transcendentalists which included Margaret Fuller, cast a backward glance at human history and observed that things would have been much different had women exerted political control.

> If the affairs of the nation had been under woman's joint control. I doubt that we should have butchered the Indians with such exterminating savagery, that, in fifty years, we should have spent seven hundred millions of dollars for war, and now, in time of peace, send twenty annual millions more to the same waste. I doubt that we should have spread slavery into nine new States, and made it national. I think the Fugitive Slave Bill would never have been an act. Woman has some respect for the natural law of God.[30]

The following excerpts, from arguments for suffrage made in 1898 and 1905 respectively, echo one another in their categorization of woman's unique superior nature and sphere and what her entry into politics would mean.

> Wherever the State touches the personal life of the infant, the child, the youth, or the aged, helpless, defective in mind, . . . there the State enters "woman's peculiar sphere", her sphere of motherly succor and training . . . .[31]
>
> Does an intelligent interest in the education of a child render a woman less a mother? Does the housekeeping instinct of woman, manifested in a desire for clean streets, pure water and unadulterated food, destroy her efficiency as a home-maker? Does a desire for an environment of moral and civic purity show neglect for the highest good of the family?[32]

As the Suffrage fight progressed women increasingly proclaimed their purity in religious terms and flatly contended that Christ himself received his "sweet, tender, suffering humanity . . . wholly from woman." Women, consequently, "have a greater share of Him than men have."[33] If elected to public office, women would "far more effectively guard the morals of society, and the sanitary conditions of cities."[34] There were Suffragists who admitted that the vote for women would not cure all society's ills, but they believed it would mean that governments responsible to women would be more likely to conserve life and preserve morals. Even the remedy for the evil of the liquor traffic lay in woman's suffrage. The social triumph of Christ's Golden Rule would be a corollary achievement.[35]

Why did the Suffragists feel constrained to celebrate their nobility and the purity of women? Why did they make such outrageous claims for the power of the ballot and their abilities, armed with the ballot, to transform public life? They readily admitted to being "dreamers" (again the adoption of an epithet turned on its head to create a presumed virtue): "We are told that to assume that women will help purify political life and develop a more ideal government but proves us to be dreamers of dreams. Yes, we are in a goodly company of dreamers, of Confucius, of Buddha, of Jesus, of the English Commons fighting for the Magna Charta . . .", etc.[36] The answer to these troubling questions becomes somewhat clearer if one remembers that the dominant paradigm set forth controlling presumptions for both politics and the private realm. For women to reject its terms would have meant a rejection of the Victorian version of marriage and family life which revolved around the image of a saintly, sexless, Wife-Mother.

The sexual Manicheanism[37] of the nineteenth century, reinforced by the typologies I have explored, was so deeply entrenched that the Suffragists could not and did not consider the manner in which this image served to reinforce male dominance.

Certain scholars see the increased emphasis by the Suffragists on their superior virtue as one indication of a shift in the movement from arguments for the vote based on "justice" to arguments based on "expedience." Aileen Kraditor contends that the early Suffragist arguments demanded political equality "on the same ground as that on which men had based their demand for political equality with their English rulers two generations before."[38] I agree with Kraditor that a shift in emphasis did occur. But I do not see this, as she apparently does, as a major qualitative change; rather, it seems to me at best an altered and quite predictable emphasis within a single tradition.

Kraditor herself points out that most of the Suffragists belonged to the same native-born white, middle to upper-middle class, Anglo-Saxon Protestant group as the male-dominant group of American society. She sees the expedience argument as one put forth to appeal to that group. Because the Suffragists shared the same class status as the dominant males, they also shared identical class prejudices – without, however, sharing in the political power of the males of their class. The following statements are representative of the "expediency" approach to votes for women.

You did not trust the Southern freedman to the arbitrary will of courts and States! Why send your mothers, wives and daughters to the unwashed unlettered, unthinking masses that carry popular elections?[39]

We ask for the ballot for the good of the race. . . . When you debar from your councils and legislative halls the purity, the spirituality and the love of woman, those councils are apt to become coarse and brutal. God gave us to you to help you in this little journey to a better land, and by our love and our intellect to help make our country pure and noble. . . .[40]

Woman's vote is needed for the good of others. Our horizon is misty with apparent dangers. Woman may aid in dispelling them. . . . She desires the homes of the land to be pure and sober; with her help they may become so . . . .[41]

"Real democracy" has not yet existed and "never will" until women receive the ballot. Instead, "the dangerous experiment has been made of enfranchising the vast proportion of crime, intemperance, immorality and dishonesty, and barring absolutely from the suffrage the great proportion of temperance, morality, religion, and conscientiousness; that, in other words, the worst elements have been put into the ballot-boxes and the best elements kept out."[42]

We point to the official statistics for proof that there are more white women in the United States than colored men and women together; that there are more American-born women than foreign-born men and women combined; that women form only one-eleventh of the criminals in the jails and penitentiaries, that they compose more than two-thirds of the church membership, and that the percentage of illiteracy is very much less among women than among men. Therefore we urge that this large proportion of patriotism, temperance, morality, religion and intelligence be allowed to impress itself upon the government through the medium of the ballot-box.[43]

The shift in emphasis to expedience rationales for women's suffrage is further evidence, I believe, of the effects on women of the inequality necessitated by the terms of the Aristotelian-power politics paradigm. The way in which the original justice argument was framed contained

the seeds of the expediency justification because it meant the Suffragists had implicity accepted a set of beliefs about themselves and their society. Their failure lay in an initial conceptualization which was tied to the dominant ideology. With the achievement of suffrage, this ideology remained and served to gloss over the inequalities of the system with the claim that these inequalities emerged "naturally" and therefore lay outside the sphere of politics. The Suffragists accepted their de-materialization, the terms of sexual Manicheanism. They wished to draw "their" men into this rarified realm and to exclude the more "bestial" and animalistic underclasses (whose "overbreeding" constituted a clear and present danger to Anglo-Saxon dominance.) De-materialization was a function of both their sex and their social class.

Political power – associated with war, force, and violence – was anathema to the Suffragists. Such power was an aspect of the public, male sphere they wished to join and by joining, transform. Rosemary Radford Ruether points out that by the mid-nineteenth century and the beginning of Suffragist protest, the splits between public and private spheres and moralities had already had a devastating, impoverishing effect on both realms.[44] Moral virtues had been so "sentimentalized and privatized they ceased to have serious public power."[45] Morality was identified with the feminine sphere. In the rough and tumble world of politics, such morality was deemed "unrealistic."

The political world demanded "hard, practical aggressivity, devoid of sentiment or moralizing." A male participates in this world during the day; in the evening he repairs "to the idealized world of the 'Home' where all moral and spiritual values are confined."[46] What the Suffragists did by accepting a definition of themselves which arose out of their powerlessness (which meant embracing their purity and suffering) was to reinforce a set of presumptions which were strongly arrayed against female political participation and socio-economic equality.[47]

Suffragist insistence on their purity and their dependence upon moral suasion as the means to reform meant they could gloss over a hard look at political power: What was it? How was it gained? To what ends was it (could it be) used? In their scheme of things, if women gained political power, that power would be transformed automatically into a moral force. Women would therefore never have to face issues arising from those ambiguous situations in which political judgments were made with no clear-cut array of the "good" and the "bad" on one side or the other. Women would use the votes to change society, but the vote would not change women.

> That woman will, by voting, lose nothing of man's courteous, chivalric attention and respect is admirably proven by the manner in which both houses of congress, in the midst of the most anxious and perplexing presidential conflict in our history, received their appeals from twenty-three States for a sixteenth amendment protecting the rights of women.[48]
> I will say to woman's credit she has not sought office, she is not a natural office-seeker, but she desires to vote . . . .[49]
> Woman's work during the nation's various wars showed that "women were clearer and more exalted than the men, because their moral feelings and political instincts were not so much affected by selfishness, or business, or party consideration . . . ."[50]

Because the Suffragists assumed that moral high-mindedness was almost exclusively a female trait, they could treat obliquely (or not at all) the argument that moving into public life would force women into a change of habits, attitudes, and standards. Women would remain guileless. Once the private had become public, politics in the traditional sense would come to an end.

Operating within the male-dominant paradigm, the form, language, and mode of Suffragist protest was set not so much by the objective conditions of female oppression as by their response to the idealizations and mystifications and legalities which rationalized continuance of the *status quo*. This led, for example, to the fallacy of attributing the political position of men to their position *under the law*. Political power was seen as something which automatically flowed out of legal "power." Legal change, therefore, was the path to political goals. The Suffragists (with a few notable exceptions) failed to recognize that men could use the law in this way because of a set of economic and social conditions which lay outside the law itself but which provided, as it were, the substructure on which the law was erected.

The power of men to achieve their objectives was power with a legal component (or legal gloss) but the law itself was not the root of that power.

That Suffragists concentrated upon the trappings rather than the substance of male power indicates that the paradigm was functioning successfully. The end result was the failure of the Suffragists to achieve an original political vision. The Suffragists said they wanted equality within the extant structure. But that structure was one of sex dominance by definition. They therefore were proposing change with a presupposition of stasis or stability. They apparently did not see through the fact that the ideal of "woman" which they celebrated included the idea of "man" which they denigrated, that these concepts were necessarily connected. The controlling images of "woman" and "man," in turn, were linked to a larger matrix, a social structure within which these relations made sense. As Winch has pointed out, the idea we form of an object includes the idea of connections between it and other objects.[51]

The Suffragists' ultimate conclusions were that private morality could be reified to the macro-level; that public persons ought to be judged by the rigorous standards of the private sphere; that the public (im)moral qualities men exhibited were probably innate to the male character, but that men, too, could be transformed as could public life by the entry of women into it; that the qualities women exhibited were innate and were not merely an outgrowth of their enforced domesticity; that these same qualities were the qualities which would invest the political sphere with a sanctified aura. In the Suffragist future, if a man wished to be a "good" citizen he would have to take on the cloak of selflessness and private virtue. None of the Suffragist conclusions, taken singly or together, comprised an *important* conceptual shift in the Aristotelian-power politics paradigm. Most Suffragists simply wanted to take the identifying terms of the private sphere in the paradigm and ramify these terms into the public sphere.

A demoralization set in among Suffragists when votes for women did not achieve all the miracles they had claimed it would. Women could vote, but the system was largely unchanged; indeed, both the ideas and the economic and political realities underpinning it retained their viability. Women did not vote as a bloc nor organize into political movements to promote their "interests" by translating certain needs into interests. All of this is unsurprising given the assumption that women were to stay pure and to purify politics at the same time.

When the vote for women did not see the victory of private morality in the public sphere, it led to a reversion to the full defining terms of the paradigm with the single exception that women could vote without completely losing their "femininity" or claims to private virtue. (Participation beyond the level of the vote did present such a danger, however.)

What has the split between public and private, morality and politics, meant for political inquiry? American political scientists work within a polity in which the macro-system has been systematically denuded of a set of public moral values; a polity in which "self-interest" is the penultimate guide to political activity and political behavior; a polity in which vast inequities in the distribution of goods and services is considered normal; a polity in which sex and race inequality are part of the *status quo*; and, finally, a polity in which the private sphere retains its importance both as a haven and solace for (mostly male) adults from the harsh realities of the competitive work-a-day world and as the one arena within which expression of sentiment and moral "values" is acceptable.

Given the interrelated set of presumptions or conditions I have set forth, what outcomes for politics should I expect? Does mainstream political science, for example, consciously or unconsciously, adopt certain norms or desired outcomes on these issues? I see the following as a partial list of the normative conclusions which flow from the typologies of politics and morality I have discussed.

Normative Import of Aristotelian-Power Politics [Paradigm]

P-i. Continued dominance of public-political life by men and categorization of that life as the amoral pursuit and exercise of power. Leads to exertion by the powerful of unintended power in the private realm as well. Women continue as apolitical, private, largely innocent creatures. They are victims of unintended power for whom no one is held responsible.

P-ii. Responsibilities and privileges under the law (participation in the highest system of justice) are available only to those who act responsibly, i.e., publicly. Privatized persons receive revocable privileges but do not have the full rights and responsibilities of public persons.

P-iii. That certain political interests are served is hidden behind a gloss of professed concern for the sanctity of the private realm. The paradigm supports limiting the scope of politics to public consideration of those issues not threatening to dominant groups. Groups not organized into "interests" are presumed to have none. Women become covert participants in this process by their acceptance of the split upon which it is based.

P-iv. Moral values remain trivialized and privatized and are seen as merely emotive desiderata or personal preferences. A movement towards a set of public moral values is considered to be a confusion of the two spheres or an attempt to create a (probably dangerous) ideology.

I would anticipate, minimally, that an analyst who accepts all or a major portion of the dichotomies of the paradigm would urge (a) a definition of politics which either has a clearly defined cut-off point for where politics and the private sphere begin and end, or would, in some other manner, definitionally exclude the familial, "private" sphere within which most women are located from open political consideration, (b) a concept of political participation which involves some standard of an "active" and aware political citizen and goes on to judge individuals against that norm without giving consideration to the factors which mitigate against participation or, having looked at those factors, decides that participation isn't necessarily desirable for all, (c) a focus on political interest groups (given the liberal dogma of politics as the sphere for the achievement of individual self-interest),[52] (d) a trivialization of moral concerns or values as they relate to public, political matters, (e) a justification or rationalization of the various systems of stratification in a society (sex, race, class, age) so long as systems stability is unthreatened.

The conceptual and ideological system which together forms the Aristotelian-power politics paradigm serves to perpetuate an arbitrary bifurcation between that which is politics and that which is not and to promote an ideology which severs politics from coherent moral consideration and moral issues from that which is explicitly political (public). Implicit within the paradigm is a concept of persons which admits into the privileges of full personhood – the notion of an individual who is rational, responsible, makes choices, and is judged according to a known set of rules and standards – only those individuals who hold dual statuses as both public and private persons and denies such personhood to those individuals with a single private status.[53] (The single-status individuals are assessed as if they were fully public persons, however, in order to point out their "inherent" limitations and inadequacies.) Women face a perpetual double-bind. Concerns which arise "naturally" from their position in the private sphere, including the health, education, and welfare of children, are deemed private expressions of personal values, but any "hard-nosed," realistic talk about power from women means they have forfeited the right to represent to the public sphere the private world which they have presumably forsaken.

Notes

1   Abigail L. Rosenthal, "Feminism Without Contradictions." *The Monist* (Vol. 57, No. 1, January, 1973, pp. 28–42), p. 42.
2   Ernest Barker, ed. *The Politics of Aristotle* (New York: Oxford University Press, 1962), p. 4.
3   *Ibid.*, p. 5.
4   Cf. Alasdair MacIntyre, *A Short History of Ethics* (New York: The MacMillan Co., 1971), p. 63. "The good of man is defined as the activity of the soul in accordance with virtue, or if there are a number of human excellences or virtues, in accordance with the best and most perfect of them."
5   *The Politics*, p. 3.
6   *Ibid.*, p. 15, including footnotes #1 and #3.
7   *Ibid.*, p. 34.
8   *Ibid.*, pp. 35–36.
9   *Ibid.*, p. 93.
10 *Ibid.*, p. 95.
11 *Ibid.*, p. 108.
12 *Ibid.*, p. 106.
13 Although the term was intended as an epithet for men who withdrew from the administration of justice and holding of public office, all women within Aristotle's system are appropriately termed idiots because they are exclusively private people.
14 I contrast "typologies" with a divergent mode of structuring reality which I label the "populational" approach. These categories – the typological and populational – go back at least as far as the logic and natural history of Aristotle and Plato's concept of plenitude. A typological thinker sees individuals, first, as members of a category – "women", "Jews" or "blacks". Each ideal type or class possesses its own set of traits. It follows that individuals within each "type" are defined by the characteristics of the collective category. "Woman", for Aristotle, is a typological category isolated from a political context. There is a separate "goodness" for women, slaves, and children; therefore, individuals from these categories or "types" can never possess the full qualities which individuals of another type, e.g., free males, participants in the *polis*, share. Typological thinking is a form of essentialism – the narrow positivist fallacy that one can somehow know an object in itself and that this object can be isolated and defined apart from social context and relationships. Typological concepts about persons are inherent in the belief that individuals are somehow "naturally" predestined for one slot or another in systems of stratification, a conviction linked to conservative political ideology. Populational concepts, including the Kantian precept that every human being is an end in himself, or the socialist conviction that each person, as a human being, is entitled to have certain basic needs met without having to first "prove" merit or desert, are linked to aspects of liberal, reformist, and radical thinking.

   If, as Arthur O. Lovejoy contends in his ground-breaking study in the history of ideas, *The Great Chain of Being*, Romanticism wrought a major change in the prevailing intellectual assumptions of the West, or what Lovejoy calls the substitution of diversitarianism for uniformitarianism in most of the normative provinces of thought, my use of the terms would be weak and perhaps unnecessary. Lovejoy, I believe, overstates the intellectual transformation. Diversitarianism may have been victorious in post-Darwinian and post-Mendelian biology and genetics, but uniformitarianism (or typological thinking) in its various guises, including functionalism, still prevails in much social and political theory.

15 Cf. Thomas S. Kuhn, *The Structure of Scientific Revolutions* (2nd edition) (Chicago: University of Chicago Press, 1973), p. 104. In his discussion of Newton's work, Kuhn points out that its impact on seventeenth century science was abetted by the fact that scientists in the previous century "had at last succeeded in rejecting Aristotelian and scholastic explanations expressed in terms of the essences of material bodies. To say that a stone fell because its 'nature' drove it toward the center of the universe had been made to look a mere tautological word-play. . . . " I contend that Aristotle's concepts of the "natures" of women, men, and politics are similar tautologies.

16 I am indebted to an article by William E. Connolly, "Theoretical Self-Consciousness," *Polity* (Volume VI, Number 1, Fall, 1973, pp. 5–35), for many of the perspectives which underlie this paper. See especially pp. 22–23 of the

paper in which Connolly sets forth the manner in which "presumptions, concepts, theory, test procedures, and normative conclusions" interconnect.

17　Although St. Augustine believed that earthly peace and security, the good at which earthly society aimed, was a real good, he added that true justice and true peace were unobtainable in that society. A "kind of commonwealth" existed even in a robber band. The lust of dominion is omnipresent and political control on all levels is the result of sin. The lofty and ennobling purpose of politics is missing from the pages of Augustine. Later medieval theorists were not unaware of politics as force and violence – they simply rejected this point of view as one degrading to man as a moral being. Medieval theorists did recognize justifications for overriding the higher law on grounds of necessity, but they labelled these emergency measures regrettable and (probably) sinful – never "normal" political behavior. The idea of emancipating politics from theology, or moral from political behavior, was anathema to the medieval world-view.

18　Jean Bodin, *Six Books of the Commonwealth*, trans. by M.A. Tooley (Oxford: Basil Blackwell, 1956), *passim*. Bodin also urges that the power, authority, and command a husband has over his wife is "allowed by both divine and positive law to be honourable and right." The Father, as the image of God on earth, has a "natural right to command." Whatever is contrary to nature, Bodin argues following Aristotle, "cannot endure and since subjection of women has always pertained" it must be according to nature. *Contra* Aristotle, Bodin argues against the "naturalness" of slavery, however. (pp. 10–12). Cf Alexander Passerin d'Entrèves, *The Notion of the State. An Introduction to Political Theory* (Oxford: Clarendon Press, 1967), p. 6. Bodin's definition of the state comprises what d'Entrèves calls the "state of legal theorizing," i.e., the presumption that politics is power as force qualified by law but not necessarily bound by it.

19　Niccolò Machiavelli, *The Prince and the Discourses* (New York: Modern Library Edition, 1950), *passim*. See also an article celebrating Machiavelli's "public morality" by Isaiah Berlin, "The Question of Machiavelli," *New York Review of Books* (Vol. XVII, No. 7, Nov. 4, 1971, pp. 20–32).

20　For Machiavelli and Bodin this meant open justification of amoral politics. For others, including natural law theorists in the Catholic tradition, it involved an unfortunate, occasional need to transgress the higher law for reasons of state. Two modern theorists in the *realpolitiker* tradition, Reinhold Niebuhr and Hans Morgenthau, purport to hold the second point of view. But this view is easily drawn into an unabashed celebration of politics as force, for it is an image redolent with the same presumptions concerning the nature of man and political society which Machiavelli and Bodin espoused. At what point does a series of assertions that only "power can catch power"; that conflict is inevitable; that collective man cannot be moral (Niebuhr speaks of the "brutal character" of all groups and collectivities); that politics is rooted, as Morgenthau would have it, in an *animus dominandi*, a "lust for power"; that one cannot disavow *a priori* a political policy which "can be proved to be an efficacious instrument" for the achievement of certain ends although that policy may, on its own terms, be "evil," percolate so thoroughly in and through a conceptual system that, despite all the disclaimers about "lesser evils," the image has taken on so many of the defining contours of an unadulterated *realpolitik* position that it is analytically indistinguishable from it. Cf. Reinhold Niebuhr, *Moral Man and Immoral Society* (New York: Charles Scribners' Sons, 1932), *passim*, and Hans Morgenthau, *Scientific Man vs. Power Politics* (Chicago: University of Chicago Press, 4th ed., 1962), *passim*.

21　Carl J. Friedrich, ed. *The Philosophy of Hegel* (New York: Modern Library, 1951), p. 425. (From "The Phenomenology of the Spirit.")

22　These concepts are not archaic. In what was touted as a "major" work on women in American history, the historian Page Smith, notes the following:

Women are "private," men are "public". A woman's life turns inward. Her "internality," her privateness, is symbolized if not directly related to the fact that her sex organs and above all, her womb, are interior. Man's external organs symbolize his "externality," his outwardness, his "publicness." He must be authenticated by an audience, listeners, critics, acclaimers, otherwise he has, ultimately no power to sustain his creativity. A woman can go on creating for a lifetime for her own private pleasure. Her acts are thus much "purer," the symbols of her bountifulness. . . . But the point I would come back to is that women (or perhaps I should say uncorrupted women) generally speaking do things for their pleasure and the pleasure of those they love; men seek fame and are thus far more ambitious and competitive. To be public means certainly to be competitive and while this competitiveness undoubtedly very often improves the quality of the work done, it makes men much more susceptible to fads and fashions. . . . A woman "is"; a man is always in the process of becoming, and this latter process as we have suggested elsewhere is a much more precarious one; hence the need for support, admiration, authentication. A man wishes an audience of millions, a woman will create for the one man she loves. (From *Daughters of the Promised Land* (Boston: Little, Brown & Company, 1970), p. 317)

23 As J.G.A. Pocock points out in his essay, "Languages and Their Implications: The Transformation of the Study of Political Thought," which appears on pp. 3–41 of *Politics, Language and Time* (New York: Atheneum, 1973), paradigms must be thought of as existing in many contexts and on many levels simultaneously. (p. 18)

24 Elizabeth Cady Stanton, Susan B. Anthony and Matilda Joslyn Gage, eds. *History of Woman Suffrage*, Vol. 1 (Rochester, New York: Charles Mann, 1881), p. 145.

25 Barbara Welter, "The Cult of True Womanhood, 1820–1860," in Ronald W. Hogeland, ed. *Women and Womanhood in America* (Lexington, Massachusetts: D.C. Heath and Co., 1973, pp. 103–113), p. 111.

26 Alexis de Tocqueville also developed a separate but equal view of the sexes. He was pleased that Americans, unlike his European contemporaries "who would make man and woman into beings not only equal but alike," agreed with him that true sex equality lay in allowing each sex to fulfill its own innate capacities to the highest extent. The separate but equal argument served as a mainstay of anti-Suffragist ideology. That argument, as it relates to women, holds that biological sex differences not only *do* but necessarily *must* lead to social, political, and occupational distinctions between the sexes: the Aristotelian paradigm. In the "separate but equal" formula each sex is regarded as equal in some lofty realm beyond ordinary understanding: meta-equality one might uncharitably call it. American women, within their domestic sphere, were equal to, but never the same as men. It is necessary for those who adhere to the natural difference hypothesis regarding the sexes to contrive an image of the woman as a creature of monovalent capacities and concerns whereas the man is replete with polyvalent qualities. An *imbecillitas sexus* defines woman even as it "ennobles" her. See Alexis de Tocqueville, *Democracy in America II* ed. Phillips Bradley (New York: Vintage Books, 1945), pp. 222–223; 225.

27 Susan B. Anthony and Ida Husted Harper, ed. *History of Woman Suffrage*, Vol. IV (Indianapolis, Indiana: Hollenbeck Press, 1902), pp. 95–96, 106–108. The first two sentences are drawn from an 1887 anti-suffrage speech by Sen. George Vest; the remainder are taken from a similar speech by Sen. Joseph E. Brown.

28 Ann Battle-Sister, "Conjectures on the Female Culture Question," *Journal of Marriage and the Family* (Vol 33, No. 3, August, 1971, pp. 411–420), points to the pitfalls involved in operating from the presumptions of one's opponent. The five standards replies to the argument that women are "different" from men are all potentially harmful. These include: (1) True, but not all of us are like that, (2) We're just like you, (3) True, but so what?, (4) True, but in the past we were dominant, (5) True, but our way is right. The fifth approach leads to the mystification that an oppressed group somehow deserves more power because of its oppression.

29 Elizabeth Cady Stanton, Susan B. Anthony and Matilda Joslyn Gage, eds. *History of Woman Suffrage*, Vol. II (Rochester, New York: Charles Mann, 1891), pp. 351–352.

30 Stanton, *et. al.*, *Woman Suffrage*, I, p. 126.

31 Anthony and Harper, *Woman Suffrage*, IV, pp. 308–309.

32 Ida Husted Harper, ed. *History of Woman Suffrage*, Vol. V (New York: J.J. Little and Ives Co., 1922), p. 125.

33 Stanton, *et. al.*, *Woman Suffrage*, II, p. 785.

34 Stanton, *et. al.*, *Woman Suffrage*, I, pp. 19–20.

35 Emma Goldman, a committed socialist-anarchist, placed middle-class Feminism within its larger social context. She adamantly rejected both universal suffrage as a political panacea and the notion of woman's unique nature. Universal suffrage had become a "modern fetich" [sic]. Women had yet to realize "that suffrage is an evil, that it has only helped to enslave people, that it has closed their eyes that they may not see how craftily they are made to submit. Not only is suffrage a hoax, but American women believe they will "purify politics." To Goldman, this is dangerous nonsense. Politics is not susceptible to purification. The Suffragists, by insisting on woman's purity, served to magnify the mystification surrounding woman, who is always regarded either as an angel or a devil, but never as merely human. Goldman condemns Suffragists for their prudery and hypocrisy and herself falls into the typological mode when she avers that woman is "essentially a purist . . . naturally bigoted and relentless in her effort to make others as good as she thinks they ought to be." (Goldman's ire had been roused by women in Idaho who wanted to disenfranchise women-of-the-streets). Feminist hypocrisy is evident when they demand the same rights as men, on the one hand, but still want him to behave towards them as if they were delicate creatures and ladies. The middle-class American woman "not only considers herself the equal of man, but his superior, especially in her purity, goodness and morality. Small wonder that the American suffragist claims for her vote the most miraculous power. In her exalted conceit she does not see how truly enslaved she is, not so much by man, as by her own silly notions and traditions." See Emma Goldman, *The Traffic in Women and Other Essays in Feminism* (New York: Times Change Press, 1970), *passim*.

36 Harper, ed. *Woman Suffrage*, V, p. 126.

37 Manicheans believed in the ultimate principle of a

dualism between good and evil, God and matter. According to their theory there were two ultimate principles which were both eternal and in mutual conflict. See Frederick Copleston, S.J., *A History of Philosophy*, Vol. II (Garden City, New York: Doubleday and Co., Image Book, 1962), *passim*. Victorian Manicheanism revolved around the sexless immateriality of women and the flesh-bound materiality of men. The lower classes *in toto* (males and females) were also seen as creatures "of the flesh" and, as such, they were invidiously compared with the loftier, less matter-bound Victorian upper-classes.

Men have never known whether to praise women as sexless or damn them as seductive fleshpots. Either approach constitutes an idealization (positive, in the one case, negative in the other) and both serve to reinforce the paradigm. The medievalists both praised and damned women. The cult of the Virgin and the chivalric code existed side-by-side with condemnations of women as "sinful, fleshy," as sources of evil and temptation. Tertullian, a second century churchman, proclaimed: "And do you not know that you are Eve? God's sentence hangs still over all your sex and His punishment weighs down upon you. You are the devil's gateway; you are she who first violated the forbidden tree and broke the law of God." From Julia O'Faolain and Lauro Martines, eds. *Not in God's Image. Women in History from the Greeks to the Victorians* (New York: Harper Torchbooks, 1973), p. 132. See also G. Rattray Taylor, *Sex in History* (New York: Harper Torchbooks, 1973), p. 209. Sexual Manicheanism continues as a theme in contemporary Feminist analysis. Simone de Beauvoir bifurcates the male (Transcendant) from the female (Immanent) realms. She wants women to achieve Transcendance. See her *The Second Sex*, trans by H.M. Parshley (New York: Alfred A. Knopf, 1953), *passim*. Cf. Germaine Greer, *The Female Eunuch* (New York: McGraw Hill, 1970), pp. 168, 315.

38 Aileen S. Kraditor, *The Ideas of the Woman Suffrage Movement 1890–1920* (New York: Doubleday Anchor Book, 1971), pp. 38–39.

39 Elizabeth Cady Stanton, Susan B. Anthony and Matilda Joslyn Gage, eds. *History of Woman Suffrage*, Vol. III (Rochester, New York: Charles Mann Printing Co., 1881), p. 88.

40 Anthony and Harper, *Woman Suffrage*, IV, p. 39.

41 *Ibid.*, p. 84.

42 *Ibid.*, p. XXXVI.

43 Harper, *Woman Suffrage*, V, p. 77.

44 Consider the ostensible silliness and naivete of the following: The mother of a political leader notorious for his villainy and chicanery parries a question concerning her son with the comment: "But he's a *good* boy." The statement makes perfect sense. He may indeed be a "good" boy according to the set of standards used by the privatized mother to judge him.

45 Rosemary Radford Ruether, "The Cult of True Womanhood," *Commonweal* (Vol. XXXXCIX, No. 6, Nov. 9, 1973, pp. 127–132), p. 131.

46 *Ibid.*

47 Rosenthal, "Feminism Without Contradictions," *op. cit.*, p. 29. As Rosenthal points out, a victim is "supposed to have moral authority or purity because the exploitative terms in which her suppression is couched have been imposed on her by others. Her real voice has been silenced . . ." The majority of Suffragists did not "break the silence" by speaking with their real voices. Instead they made, in Hegelian terms, a virtue out of historic necessity by celebrating the qualities which arose from their oppression. That the Suffragists could urge that those same qualities would purify and transform the system which had created them (in their stereotypical form) demonstrates how deeply entrenched were the interrelated elements of the Aristotelian-power politics paradigm.

48 Stanton, *et. al.*, *Woman Suffrage*, III, p. 67.

49 Anthony and Harper, *Woman Suffrage*, IV, pp. 116–117.

50 Stanton, *et. al.*, *Woman Suffrage*, II, p. 17.

51 Peter Winch, *The Idea of a Social Science* (London: Routledge and Kegan Paul, 1958), p. 124.

52 See William E. Connolly, ed., *The Bias of Pluralism* (Chicago/New York: Aldine/Atherton, 1972) for a series of critiques on pluralist theory, especially the article by Peter Bachrach and Morton S. Baratz, "Two Faces of Power," pp. 51–66.

53 Cf. Stuart Hampshire, *Thought and Action* (New York: Viking Press, 1967), pp. 236–237. Hampshire notes: "Two sides in an argument about the goodness or badness of a man cannot differ totally in the facts they take to be relevant. At the very least they are anchored by the concept of a man to the recognition of certain activities and performances as unavoidably to be mentioned. . . . There is no possibility that a man's family relationships, his knowledge and mental skills, the effects of his actions on his society, his loyalties and friendships, his tendency to tell the truth, his sense of justice, his good faith in keeping contracts, should be dismissed as altogether irrelevant to his goodness or badness as a human being. . . . Criticism and comparison of men must at least be a comparison of their activities and performances, in the widest sense of these words, within this constant framework of comparison." It is perhaps unnecessary to observe that the range of comparison (utilizing Hampshire's minimal criteria set forth above) and hence grounds for moral judgment on human goodness or badness, is severely restricted for women who have traditionally been cut off from the "public" activities Hampshire cites as features in the conceptual contours of the "good man."

38

"Dependency" Demystified: Inscriptions of Power in a Keyword of the Welfare State

Nancy Fraser and Linda Gordon

"Dependency" is the single most crucial term in the current U.S. debate about welfare reform. "Welfare dependent" in the United States means someone who relies on one of the stigmatized programs of public assistance, as distinguished from honorable programs such as old age insurance, which are not called "welfare." The paradigmatic "dependent" is the poor solo mother who collects benefits from the stingy and politically unpopular program, Aid to Families with Dependent Children (AFDC). "Welfare reform" today means reducing "dependency" by getting claimants off the rolls.

Few concepts in U.S. social policy discussions do as much ideological work as "dependency." The term leaks a profusion of stigmatizing connotations – racial, sexual, misogynist, and more. It alludes implicitly to a normative state of "independence," which will itself not withstand critical scrutiny. Naming the problems of poor solo mothers and their children "dependency," moreover, tends to make them appear to be individual rather than social problems, as much moral or psychological as economic. The word carries strong emotive and visual associations and a powerful pejorative charge. The most common image is a "welfare mother," typically figured as a young unmarried black woman of uncontrolled sexuality and fertility. This stereotype haunts even the

most neutral-sounding talk about dependency in discussions of welfare reform.

Why does the word "dependency" carry so much ideological weight? Part of the reason, we suggest, is historical. The term carries the debris of several centuries of poor relief policies that relieved hunger while stigmatizing recipients, often actually impeding their escape from the dole into wage labor. Branding welfare recipients as "dependents" continues a long tradition of opposing dependence to independence. Both terms were redefined in the last few centuries in ways that helped adapt old traditions of gender, race, and class domination to new social and economic conditions. But the fundamental opposition remains: "independence" is strong, virtuous, white, and male, while "dependence" is weak, disreputable, colored, and/or female. In the last half-century, as "dependency" became associated particularly with AFDC, it has intensified disrespect for women's unpaid labor.

Tracing the historical career of "dependency," then, can illuminate contemporary social policy debates.[1] In this article we analyze the term as a keyword of the U.S. welfare state and we reconstruct its genealogy.[2] We excavate broad historical shifts in the term's usage, and in the assumptions undergirding its usage, in order to advance a critique of the present. By historicizing "dependency," we aim to defamiliarize it, to render explicit assumptions and connotations that usually go without saying (e.g., assumptions about human nature, gender roles, the causes of

Originally published in *Social Politics*, 1 (1994), 4–31. Copyright © 1994 by Nancy Fraser and Linda Gordon. Reprinted by permission of the authors.

poverty, the sources of entitlement, and what counts as work and as a contribution to society).

This article is a critique of U.S. welfare ideology in the form of a critical political semantics. The project of analyzing "dependency" as a "keyword of the welfare state" owes much to Raymond Williams's *Keywords: A Vocabulary of Culture and Society* (1976), which mapped some major currents of modern English culture by studying shifts in the usage, and in the assumptions and experiences undergirding usage, of some salient cultural terms. We share with Williams the premise that the terms used to describe social life are also active forces shaping it. These terms contain sedimented traces of past usages and function as vehicles through which the past influences the present. Some words become sites at which the meaning of social experience is negotiated and contested. Studies of their shifting usages in the past, then, can illuminate social conflict in the present.

The aim of our genealogy is activist. When ideological assumptions are tacitly inscribed in social policy discourse, they are difficult to challenge. Policy discourse then becomes a medium through which political hegemony is reproduced. To render explicit such assumptions, in contrast, is to render them contestable and to challenge their power. Thus, by constructing a genealogy of "dependency" we provide a challenge to ideology. We show how unreflective mainstream uses of this keyword serve to enshrine certain interpretations of social life as authoritative and to delegitimate or obscure others, usually to the advantage of dominant groups in society and the disadvantage of subordinates.

Such a critique is not merely negative. By questioning the terms in which social problems are named, we expand the collective capacity to imagine solutions. A genealogy of "dependency" should encourage rethinking welfare from a feminist and democratic perspective.

Reviling welfare recipients serves not only to dishonor those individuals, but also to mystify and legitimate inequalities that affect us all. Giving and receiving welfare will remain a necessary aspect of citizenship for a long time. To prevent welfare programs from being used by conservatives to promote hostility to feminism, single mothers, minorities, and poor people, we must imbue our public language with different meanings and associations. We will need to develop alternative meanings for "welfare," "dependence," and "independence." It is in this spirit that we offer a genealogy of "dependency." After charting the term's history and current uses, we sketch the beginnings of an alternative semantics premised on the inescapable fact of human interdependence.

Registers of Meaning

In its root meaning, the verb "to depend" refers to a physical relationship in which one thing hangs from another. The more abstract meanings — social, economic, psychological, and political — were originally metaphorical. In current usage, we find four registers in which the meanings of dependency reverberate. The first is an economic register, in which one depends on some other person(s) or institution for subsistence. In a second register, the term denotes a socio-legal status, the lack of a separate legal or public identity, as in the status of married women created by coverture. The third register is political: dependency means subjection to an external ruling power and may be predicated of a colony or subject caste of noncitizen residents. The fourth register we call the moral/psychological; dependency in this sense is an individual character trait similar to lack of will power or excessive emotional neediness.

To be sure, not every use of "dependency" fits neatly into one and only one of these registers. By distinguishing them analytically, however, we present a matrix on which to plot the historical adventures of the term. In what follows, we shall trace the shift from a patriarchal preindustrial usage in which women, however subordinate, shared a condition of dependency with many men to a modern, industrial, male supremacist usage that constructed a specifically feminine sense of dependency. That usage is now giving way, we contend, to a postindustrial usage in which growing numbers of relatively prosperous women claim the same kind of independence that men do while a more stigmatized but still feminized sense of dependency attaches to groups considered deviant and superfluous. Not just gender but also racializing practices play a major role in these shifts, as do changes in the organization and meaning of labor.

Preindustrial "Dependency"

In preindustrial English usage, the most common meaning of "dependency" was subordination.

The economic, socio-legal, and political registers were relatively undifferentiated, reflecting the fusion of various forms of hierarchy in state and society. Further, the moral/psychological use of the term barely existed. The earliest social definition of the verb "to depend (on)" in the *Oxford English Dictionary* (*OED*) is "to be connected within a relation of subordination." A "dependent," from at least 1588, was one "who depends on another for support, position, etc.; a retainer, attendant, subordinate, servant." A "dependency" was either a retinue or body of servants or a foreign territorial possession or colony. This family of terms applied widely in a hierarchical social context in which nearly everyone was subordinate to someone else but did not incur individual stigma thereby (Gundersen 1987).

We can appreciate just how common dependency was in preindustrial society by examining its opposite. The term "independence" at first applied primarily to aggregate entities, not to individuals; thus in the seventeenth century a nation or a church congregation could be independent. By the eighteenth century, however, an individual could be said to have an "independency," meaning an ownership of property, a fortune that made it possible to live without laboring. (This sense of the term, which we would today call economic, survives in our expressions "to be independently wealthy" and "a person of independent means.") To be independent, in contrast, was to gain one's livelihood by working for someone else. This of course was the condition of most people, of wage laborers as well as serfs and slaves, of most men as well as most women.[3]

Dependency, therefore, was a normal, as opposed to a deviant, condition; a social relation, as opposed to an individual trait. Thus, it did not carry any moral opprobrium.[4] Yet it did mean status inferiority and legal coverture, being a part of a unit headed by someone else who had legal standing. In a world of status hierarchies dominated by great landowners and their retainers, all members of a household other than its "head" were dependents, as were peasants, free or bound. They were, as Peter Laslett wrote, "caught up, so to speak, 'subsumed' . . . into the personalities of their fathers and masters" (1971, 21).

Dependency also had what today we would call political consequences. While the term did not mean precisely "unfree," its context was a social order in which subjection, not citizenship, was the norm. Throughout most of the European development of representative government, independence in the sense of property ownership was a prerequisite for political rights. When dependents began to claim rights and liberty, they perforce became revolutionaries.

"Dependency" was not then applied uniquely to characterize the relation of a wife to her husband. Women's dependency, like children's, meant being on a lower rung in a long social ladder; their husbands and fathers were above them but below others. For the agrarian majority, moreover, there was no implication of unilateral economic dependency, because women's and children's labor was recognized as essential to the family economy. Women's dependency in preindustrial society was similar in kind to that of subordinate men, only multiplied. But so too were the lives of children, servants, and the elderly overlaid with multiple layers of dependency.[5]

Nevertheless, dependency was not universally approved or uncontested. It was subject, rather, to principled challenges since at least the seventeenth century, when liberal-individualist political arguments became common. The terms "dependence" and "independence" often figured centrally in political debates in this period.[6] Sometimes they even became key signifiers of social crisis, as in the seventeenth-century English controversy about "out-of-doors" servants, hired help who did not reside in the homes of their masters and who were not bound by indentures or similar legal understandings. In the discourse of the time, the anomalous "independence" of these men served as a general symbol for social disorder, a lightning rod focusing diffuse cultural anxieties – much as the anomalous "dependence" of "welfare mothers" does today.

Industrial "Dependency": The Worker and his Negatives

With the rise of industrial capitalism, the semantic geography of dependency shifted significantly. What in preindustrial society had been a normal and unstigmatized condition became deviant and stigmatized. More precisely, certain dependencies became shameful while others were deemed natural and proper. In particular, as eighteenth- and nineteenth-century political culture intensified gender difference, new, specifically gendered uses of dependency appeared – considered proper for women, but degrading for men. Likewise, emergent racial constructions made some forms of dependency appropriate for the "dark races," but intolerable for "whites." Such differentiated valuations became possible as the term's preindustrial usage fractured. No longer designating only generalized subordination, "dependency" in the industrial era could be socio-legal, political, or economic. With these distinctions came another major semantic shift: "dependency" need not always refer to a social relation; it could also designate an individual character trait. Thus, the moral/psychological register was born.

These redefinitions were greatly influenced by Radical Protestantism, which elaborated a new positive image of individual independence and a critique of socio-legal and political dependency. From this perspective, status hierarchies no longer appeared natural or just, and subjection and subsumption were increasingly objectionable. These beliefs informed a variety of radical movements throughout the industrial era, including abolition of slavery, feminism, and labor organizing, with substantial successes. In the nineteenth century these movements abolished slavery and some of the legal disabilities of women. More thoroughgoing victories were won in the United States by white male workers who, in the eighteenth and nineteenth centuries, threw off their socio-legal and political dependency and won civil and electoral rights. In the age of democratic revolutions, the newly developing concept of citizenship rested on independence; dependency was deemed antithetical to citizenship.

Changes in the civil and political landscape of dependence and independence were accompanied by even more dramatic changes in the economic register. When white workingmen demanded civil and electoral rights, they claimed to be independent. This entailed reinterpreting the meaning of wage labor so as to divest it of the association with dependency. That in turn required a shift in focus – from the experience or means of labor (e.g., ownership of tools or land, control of skills, and the organization of work) to its remuneration and how that was spent. As a result of the struggles of radical workingmen, economic independence came eventually to encompass the ideal of earning a family wage, a wage sufficient to maintain a household and support a dependent wife and children. Thus, workingmen expanded the meaning of economic

independence to include wage labor in addition to property ownership and self-employment.[7]

This shift in the meaning of independence also transformed the meanings of dependency. As wage labor became increasingly normative – and increasingly associated with independence – it was precisely those excluded from wage labor who appeared to personify dependency. In the new industrial semantics, three principal icons of dependency emerged, all effectively negatives of the dominant image of "the worker," and each embodying a different aspect of non-independence.

The first icon of industrial dependency was "the pauper," who lived not on wages but on poor relief.[8] In the strenuous new culture of emergent capitalism, the figure of the pauper was like a bad double of the upstanding workingman, threatening the worker should he lag. The image of the pauper was elaborated largely in an emerging new register of dependency discourse – the moral/psychological register. Paupers were not simply poor but degraded, their character corrupted and their will sapped through reliance on charity. Toward the end of the nineteenth century, as hereditarian (eugenic) thought caught on, the pauper's character defects were given a basis in biology. The pauper's dependency was figured as unlike the serf's in that it was unilateral, not reciprocal. To be a pauper was not to be subordinate within a system of productive labor; it was to be outside such a system altogether.

A second icon of industrial dependency was embodied alternately in the figures of the "colonial native" and the "slave." They, of course, were very much inside the economic system; their labor was often fundamental to the development of capital and industry. Whereas the pauper personified economic dependency, natives and slaves personified political subjection.[9] Their images as "savage," "childlike," and "submissive" became salient as the old, territorial sense of dependency as a colony was intertwined with a new, racist discourse developed to justify colonialism and slavery.[10] There emerged a drift from an older sense of dependency as a relation of subjection imposed by an imperial power on an indigenous population to a newer sense of dependency as an inherent property or character trait of the people so subjected. In earlier usage, colonials were dependent because they had been conquered; in nineteenth-century imperialist culture, they were conquered because they were dependent. In this new conception, the intrinsic, essential dependency of natives and slaves justified their colonization and enslavement. Racialist thought was the linchpin for this reasoning.

Like paupers, natives and slaves were excluded from wage labor and thus were negatives of the image of the "worker." They shared that characteristic, if little else, with the third major icon of dependency in the industrial era: the newly invented figure of "the housewife." As we saw, the independence of white workingmen presupposed the ideal of the family wage, a wage sufficient to maintain a household and support a (non-employed) wife and children. Thus, for wage labor to create (white male) independence, (white) female economic dependence was required. Women were thus transformed "from partners to parasites" (Land 1980, 57; Boydston, 1991). This transformation was by no means universal; since few husbands actually were able to support a family single-handedly, most families continued to depend on the labor of women and children.[11]

Several different registers of dependency converged in the figure of the housewife. This figure melded woman's traditional socio-legal and political dependency with her more recent economic dependency in the industrial order.[12] In addition, the connotations of female dependency were altered. Although erstwhile dependent white men gained political rights, most white women remained legally and politically dependent. The result was to feminize – and stigmatize – socio-legal and political dependency.

Together, then, a series of new personifications of dependency combined to constitute the underside of the workingman's independence. Henceforth, those who aspired to full membership in society would have to distinguish themselves from the pauper, native, slave, and housewife in order to construct their independence. In a social order in which wage labor was becoming hegemonic, all of these distinctions could be encapsulated simultaneously in the ideal of the family wage. On the one hand, and most overtly, that ideal premised the white workingman's independence on his wife's subordination and economic dependence. On the other hand, it simultaneously contrasted with counterimages of dependent men – first with degraded male paupers on poor relief and later with racist stereotypes of black men unable to dominate black women. The family wage, therefore, was a vehicle

for elaborating meanings of dependence and independence that were deeply inflected by gender, race, and class.

In this new industrial semantics, white workingmen appeared to be economically independent, but their independence was largely illusory and ideological. Since few actually earned enough to single-handedly support a family, most depended in fact – if not in word – on their wives' and children's contributions. Equally important, dominant understandings of wage labor in capitalism denied workers' dependence on their employers, thereby veiling their status as subordinates in a unit headed by someone else. Thus, the hierarchy that had been relatively explicit and visible in the peasant-landlord relation was mystified in the relationship of factory operative to factory owner. There was a sense, then, in which the economic dependency of white workingmen was spirited away through linguistic sleight of hand – somewhat like reducing the number of poor people by lowering the official poverty demarcating line.

By definition, then, economic inequality among white men no longer created dependency. But noneconomic hierarchy among white men was considered unacceptable in the United States. Thus, "dependency" was redefined to refer exclusively to those noneconomic relations of subordination deemed suitable only for people of color and white women. Whereas all relations of subordination had previously counted as dependency relations, now capital–labor relations were exempted. Socio-legal and political hierarchy appeared to diverge from economic hierarchy, and only the first two seemed incompatible with hegemonic views of society. It seemed to follow, moreover, that were socio-legal dependency and political dependency ever to be formally abolished, no social-structural dependency would remain. Any dependency that did persist could only be moral or psychological.

The Rise of American "Welfare Dependency": 1890–1945

Informed by these general features of industrial-era semantics, a distinctive welfare-related use of "dependency" developed in the United States. Originating in the late nineteenth-century discourse of pauperism, modified in the Progressive Era, and stabilized in the period of the New Deal, this use of the term was fundamentally ambiguous, slipping easily and repeatedly from an economic meaning to a moral/psychological meaning.

As we saw, the most general definition of economic dependency in this era was simply non-wage-earning. By the end of the nineteenth century, however, that definition had divided into a "good" household dependency, predicated on children's and wives' relation to the male bread-winner, and an increasingly "bad" (or at least dubious) charity dependency, predicated on recipients of relief. Both definitions used as their reference point the ideal of the family wage, and both were eventually incorporated into the discourse of the national state. The good, household definition was elaborated by the census (Folbre 1991) and Internal Revenue Service, which installed the category of dependent as the norm for wives. Meanwhile, the stigma of dependence on charity or public assistance continued and was often intensified by "scientific charity" late in the nineteenth century.

Ironically, reformers in the 1890s introduced the word "dependent" into relief discourse as a substitute for the older pejorative "pauper" precisely in order to destigmatize the receipt of help. They first applied the new word to children, the paradigmatic "innocent" victims of poverty (Warner 1894–1930; Abbott and Breckinridge 1921, 7; National Conference of Charities and Correction 1890s–1920s). Then, in the early twentieth century, Progressive Era reformers began to apply the term to adults, again to rid them of stigma. Only after World War II did "dependent" become the hegemonic word for a recipient of aid (Brown 1940; Bruno 1948; Howard 1943).

The attempt to get rid of stigma by replacing "pauperism" with "dependency" failed. Discourse about economic dependency repeatedly slid into condemnation of moral/psychological dependency. Even during the depression of the 1930s, experts worried that receipt of relief would create "habits of dependence," or "a belligerent dependency, an attitude of having a right and title to relief" (Brandt 1932, 23–24; Vaile 1934, 26; Gibbons 1933). Many needy people accepted public aid only after much hesitation and with great shame, so strong was the stigma of dependency (Bakke 1940a; Bakke 1940b).

Most important, the New Deal intensified the dishonor of receiving help by consolidating a two-track welfare system. First-track social insur-

ance programs such as unemployment and old age insurance offered aid as an entitlement, without stigma or supervision and hence without dependency. Such programs were deliberately designed to create the appearance that beneficiaries merely got back what they put in. They constructed an honorable status for recipients; today no one calls these programs "welfare." Intended to replace temporarily the family wage, first-track programs excluded most women and minorities. In contrast, second-track public assistance programs (among which Aid to Dependent Children [ADC], later Aid to Families with Dependent Children [AFDC], became the biggest and most well-known) continued the private charity tradition of searching out the deserving among the chiselers. Funded from general tax revenues instead of earmarked wage deductions, these programs created the appearance that claimants were getting something for nothing (Fraser and Gordon 1992). They established entirely different conditions for receiving aid: means-testing, morals-testing, moral and household supervision, home visits, extremely low stipends – in short, they humiliated, infantilized, and thus created the "welfare dependency" they feared (Fraser 1987; Gordon 1990b; Nelson 1990).

The racial and sexual exclusions of the first-track programs were not accidental. They were designed to win the support of southern legislators who wanted to keep blacks dependent in another sense – on low wages or sharecropping (Quadagno 1988). Equally deliberate was the construction of the differential in legitimacy between the two tracks of the welfare system.[13] Most Americans today still distinguish between "welfare" and "non-welfare" forms of public provision and view only the former as creating dependency. The assumptions underlying these distinctions, however, had to be constructed politically. Older people became privileged (non-welfare) recipients only through decades of militant organization and lobbying. All programs of public provision, whether they are called welfare or not, shore up some dependencies and discourage others. Social Security subverted adults' sense of responsibility for their parents, for example. Public assistance programs, by contrast, aimed to buttress the dependence of the poor on low-wage labor, wives on husbands, and children on their parents.

The conditions of second-track assistance made recipients view their dependence on public assistance as inferior to the supposed independence of wage labor (Pope 1989, 73, 144; West 1981; Milwaukee County Welfare Rights Organization 1972). But the designers of ADC did not initially intend to drive white solo mothers into paid employment. Rather, they wanted to protect the norm of the family wage by making dependence on a male breadwinner continue to seem preferable to dependence on the state (Gordon 1992). ADC occupied the strategic semantic space where the good, household sense of dependency and the bad, relief sense of dependency intersected. It enforced at the same time the positive connotations of the first and the negative connotations of the second.

Thus, the poor solo mother was enshrined as the quintessential "welfare dependent."[14] That designation has become significant not only for what it includes, but also for what it excludes and occludes. Although it appears to mean relying on the government for economic support, not all recipients of public funds are equally considered dependent. Hardly anyone today calls recipients of Social Security retirement insurance "dependents." Similarly, persons receiving unemployment insurance, agricultural loans, and home mortgage assistance are excluded from that categorization, as indeed are defense contractors and the beneficiaries of corporate bail-outs and regressive taxation.

Postindustrial Society and the Disappearance of "Good" Dependency

With the transition to a postindustrial phase of capitalism, the semantic map of dependency is being redrawn yet again. Whereas industrial usage had cast some forms of dependency as natural and proper, postindustrial usage casts all forms as avoidable and blameworthy; and it focuses even more intensely on the traits of individuals. One major influence is the formal abolition of much of the gender- and race-based legal and political dependency that was endemic to industrial society. Housewives, paupers, natives, and the descendants of slaves are no longer formally excluded from most civil and political rights; neither their subsumption nor their subjection is viewed as legitimate. Thus, major forms of dependency deemed proper in industrial usage are now considered objectionable, and postindustrial uses of the term carry a stronger negative charge.

A second major shift in the geography of postin-

dustrial dependency is affecting the economic register. This is the decentering of the ideal of the family wage, which had been the gravitational center of industrial usage. The relative deindustrialization of the United States is restructuring the political economy, making the single-earner family even more mythical. The loss of higher paid "male" manufacturing jobs and the massive entry of women into low-wage service work is meanwhile altering the gender composition of employment (Smith 1984). At the same time, divorce is common and, thanks in large part to the feminist and gay and lesbian liberation movements, changing gender norms are helping to proliferate new family forms, making the male breadwinner/female homemaker model less attractive to many (Stacey 1987; Stacey 1990; Weston 1991). It no longer goes without saying that a woman should rely on a man for economic support, nor that mothers should not also be "workers." Thus, another major form of dependency that was positively inflected in industrial semantics has become contested if not simply negative.

The combined result of these developments is to increase the stigma of dependency. With all legal and political dependency now illegitimate, and with wives' economic dependency now contested, there is no longer any self-evidently "good" adult dependency in postindustrial society. Rather, all dependency is suspect, and independence is enjoined upon everyone. Independence, however, remains identified with wage labor. Everyone is expected to "work" and be "self-supporting." Any adult not perceived as a worker shoulders a heavier burden of self-justification.

With the formal dismantling of coverture and Jim Crow, it has become possible to claim that equality of opportunity exists and that individual merit determines outcomes. With capitalist economic dependency already abolished by definition, and with legal and political dependency now abolished by law, postindustrial society appears to some conservatives and liberals to have eliminated every social-structural basis of dependency. Whatever dependency remains, therefore, can be interpreted as the fault of individuals.

Welfare Dependency as Postindustrial Pathology

The worsening connotations of "welfare dependency" have been nourished by several streams from outside the field of welfare. New postindustrial medical and psychological discourses have associated dependency with pathology. Social scientists began in the 1980s to write about "chemical," "alcohol," and "drug dependency," euphemisms for addiction (e.g., Haynes 1988). Because welfare claimants are often – falsely – assumed to be addicts, the pathological connotations of "drug dependency" tend also to infect "welfare dependency," increasing stigmatization.

A second important postindustrial current is the rise of new psychological meanings of dependency, which have very strong feminine associations. In the 1950s, social workers influenced by psychiatry began to diagnose dependence as a form of immaturity common among women, particularly among solo mothers (who were often, of course, welfare claimants). The problem was that women were supposed to be just dependent enough, and it was easy to tip over into excess in either direction.[15]

Psychologized dependency became the target of some of the earliest second-wave feminism. Betty Friedan's 1963 classic, *The Feminine Mystique*, provided a phenomenological account of the housewife's psychological dependency and drew from it a political critique of her social subordination. More recently, however, a burgeoning cultural-feminist, postfeminist, and antifeminist self-help and pop-psychology literature has obfuscated the link between the psychological and the political. In Colette Dowling's 1981 book, *The Cinderella Complex*, women's dependency was hypostatized as a depth-psychological gender structure: "women's hidden fear of independence" or the "wish to be saved." The late 1980s saw a spate of books about "co-dependency," a supposedly prototypically female syndrome of supporting or "enabling" the dependency of someone else. In a metaphor that reflects the drug hysteria of the period, dependency in this case, too, is an addiction. Apparently, even if a woman manages to escape her gender's predilection to dependency, she is still liable to incur the blame for facilitating the dependency of her husband or children. This completes the vicious circle: the increased stigmatizing of dependency in the culture at large has also deepened contempt for those who care for dependents (Sapiro 1990).

The 1980s saw a cultural panic about dependency. In 1980, the American Psychiatric Association codified "Dependent Personality Disorder" (DPD) as an official psychopathology. According to the 1987 edition of the *Diagnostic and Statistical Manual of Mental Disorders (DSM-III-R)*, "the essential feature of this disorder is a pervasive pattern of dependent and submissive behavior beginning by early childhood. . . . People with this disorder are unable to make everyday decisions without an excessive amount of advice and reassurance from others, and will even allow others to make most of their important decisions. . . . The disorder is apparently common and is diagnosed more frequently in females" (American Psychiatric Association 1987, 353–54).

The codification of DPD as an official psychopathology represents a new stage in the history of the moral/psychological register. Here the social relations of dependency disappear entirely into the (individual) personality of the dependent. Overt moralism also disappears in the apparently neutral, scientific, medicalized formulation. Thus, although the defining traits of the dependent personality match point for point the traits traditionally ascribed to housewives, paupers, natives, and slaves, all links to subordination have vanished. The only remaining trace of those themes is the flat, categorical, and uninterpreted observation that DPD is "diagnosed more frequently in females."

If psychological discourse has further feminized and individualized dependency, other postindustrial developments have further racialized it. The increased stigmatization of welfare dependency followed a general increase in public provision in the United States, the removal of some discriminatory practices that had previously excluded minority women from participation in AFDC, especially in the South, and the transfer of many white women to first-track programs as social insurance coverage expanded. By the 1970s the figure of the black solo mother had come to epitomize welfare dependency. As a result, the new discourse about welfare draws on older symbolic currents that linked dependency with racist ideologies.

The ground was laid by a long, somewhat contradictory stream of discourses about "the black family," in which African American gender and kinship relations were measured against white middle-class norms and deemed pathological. One supposedly pathological element was "the excessive independence" of black women, an ideologically distorted allusion to long traditions of wage work, educational achievement, and community activism. The 1960s and 1970s discourse about poverty recapitulated traditions of misogyny toward African American women; in Daniel Moynihan's diagnosis, for example, "matriarchal" families had "emasculated" black men and created a "culture of poverty" based on a "tangle of [family] pathology" (Rainwater and Yancey 1967). This discourse placed black AFDC claimants in a double bind: they were pathologically independent with respect to men and pathologically dependent with respect to government.

By the 1980s, however, the racial imagery of dependency had shifted. The black welfare mother that haunted the white imagination ceased to be the powerful matriarch. Now the preeminent stereotype is the unmarried teenage mother caught in the "welfare trap" and rendered drone-like and passive. This new icon of welfare dependency is younger and weaker than the matriarch. She is often evoked in the phrase "children having children," which can express feminist sympathy or antifeminist contempt, black appeals for parental control or white racist eugenic anxieties.

Many of these postindustrial discourses coalesced in the early 1990s. Then Vice President Dan Quayle brought together the pathologized, feminized, and racialized currents in his comment on the May 1992 Los Angeles riot: "Our inner cities are filled with children having children . . . with people who are dependent on drugs and on the narcotic of welfare" (Quayle 1992).

Thus postindustrial culture has called up a new personification of dependency: the black, unmarried, teenaged, welfare dependent mother. This image has usurped the symbolic space previously occupied by the housewife, pauper, native, and slave, while absorbing and condensing their connotations. Black, female, a pauper, not a worker, a housewife and mother, yet practically a child herself – this new stereotype partakes of virtually every quality that has been coded historically as antithetical to independence. Condensing multiple, often contradictory meanings of dependency, it is a powerful ideological trope that simultaneously organizes diffuse cultural anxieties and dissimulates their social bases.

Postindustrial Policy and the Politics of Dependency

Contemporary policy discourse about welfare dependency is thoroughly inflected by these assumptions. It divides into two major streams. The first continues the rhetoric of pauperism and the culture of poverty. It is used in both conservative and liberal, victim-blaming or non-victim-blaming ways, depending on the causal structure of the argument. The contention is that poor, dependent people have something more than lack of money wrong with them. Conservatives, such as George Gilder (1981) and Lawrence Mead (1986), argue that welfare causes moral/psychological dependency. Some liberals, such as William Julius Wilson (1987) and Christopher Jencks (1992), blame social and economic influences but agree that claimants' culture and behavior are problematic.

A second stream of thought draws on neoclassical economic premises. It assumes a "rational man" facing choices in which welfare and work are both options. For these policy analysts, the moral/psychological meanings of dependency are accepted, not interrogated, assumed to be undesirable. Liberals of this school grant that welfare inevitably has some bad, dependency-creating effects, but claim that these are outweighed by other, good effects such as improved conditions for children, increased societal stability, and relief of suffering (Pearce 1990). Conservatives of this school, such as Charles Murray (1984), believe the negative effects of welfare outweigh the positive. The two camps argue above all about the question of incentives. Do AFDC stipends encourage women to have out-of-wedlock children? Do they discourage them from accepting jobs? Can reducing or withholding stipends serve as a stick to encourage recipients to stay in school, keep their children in school, get married?

Certainly, there are real and significant differences here, but there are also important similarities. Liberals and conservatives of both schools rarely situate the notion of dependency in its historical or economic context; nor do they interrogate its presuppositions. Neither group questions the assumption that independence is an unmitigated good nor its identification with wage labor. Many poverty and welfare analysts equivocate between an official position that "dependency" is a value-neutral term for receipt of (or need for) welfare and a usage that makes it a synonym for "pauperism."

These assumptions permeate the public sphere. In the current discussion of welfare dependency, it is increasingly claimed that "welfare mothers ought to work," a usage that tacitly defines work as wage-earning and child-raising as nonwork. Here we run up against a contradiction in the discourse of dependency: when the subject under consideration is teenage pregnancy, these mothers are cast as children; when the subject is welfare, they become adults who should be self-supporting.

None of the negative imagery about welfare dependency has gone uncontested, of course. Much of it was directly challenged in the mid-1960s by an organization of women welfare claimants, the National Welfare Rights Organization. NWRO women cast their relation with the welfare system as active rather than passive, a matter of claiming rights rather than receiving charity. They also insisted that their domestic labor was socially necessary and praiseworthy. Their perspective helped reconstruct the arguments for welfare, spurring poverty lawyers and radical intellectuals to develop a legal and political-theoretical basis for welfare as an entitlement and right. Edward Sparer, a legal strategist for the welfare rights movement, challenged the dominant understanding of dependency: "The charge of antiwelfare politicians is that welfare makes the recipient 'dependent.' What this means is that the recipient depends on the welfare check for his [sic] material subsistence rather than upon some other source. . . . Whether that is good or bad depends on whether a better source of income is available. . . . The real problem . . . is something entirely different. The recipient and the applicant traditionally have been dependent on the whim of the caseworker" (Sparer 1970–71, 71). The cure for welfare dependency, then, was welfare rights (Goodin 1988). Had the NWRO not been greatly weakened in the late 1970s, the revived discourse of pauperism in the 1980s could not have become hegemonic.

Even in the absence of a powerful National Welfare Rights Organization, many AFDC recipients maintained their own oppositional interpretation of welfare dependency. In their view, it is a social condition, not a psychological state or what a left-wing English dictionary of social welfare calls "enforced dependency," "the creation of a dependent class" as a result of "enforced reliance . . . for necessary psychological or material resources" (Timms and Timms 1982, 55–56).

Meanwhile, during the period in which NWRO activism was at its height, New Left revisionist historians developed an interpretation of the welfare state as an apparatus of social control. They argued that what apologists portrayed as helping practices were actually modes of domination that created enforced dependency.[16] Another challenge to mainstream uses of "dependency" arose from a New Left school of international political economy. The context was the realization, after the first heady days of postwar decolonization, that politically independent former colonies remained economically dependent. In "dependency theory," radical theorists of "underdevelopment" used the concept of dependency to analyze the global neocolonial economic order from an antiracist and anti-imperialist perspective. In so doing, they resurrected the old preindustrial meaning of dependency as a subjected territory, seeking thereby to divest the term of its newer moral/psychological accretions and to retrieve the occluded dimensions of subjection and subordination.

What all these oppositional discourses share is a rejection of the dominant emphasis on dependency as an individual trait: they seek to shift the focus back to the social relations of subordination. But they no longer have much impact on mainstream discussion about welfare in the United States. On the contrary, with economic dependency now a synonym for poverty, and moral/psychological dependency now a personality disorder, talk of dependency as a social relation of subordination has become increasingly rare. Power and domination tend to disappear.[17]

Recapitulation

"Dependency," once a general term for all social relations of subordination, is now differentiated into several analytically distinct registers. In the economic register, its meaning has shifted from gaining one's livelihood by working for someone else to relying on charity or welfare for support; wage labor now confers independence. In the socio-legal register, the meaning of dependency as subsumption is unchanged, but its scope of reference and connotations have altered: once a socially approved majority condition, it became first a group-based status deemed proper for some classes of persons but not others and then shifted to designate (except in the case of children) an anomalous, highly stigmatized status of deviant and incompetent individuals. In the political register, dependency's meaning as subjection to an external governing power has remained relatively constant, but its evaluative connotations worsened as individual political rights and national sovereignty became normative. Meanwhile, with the emergence of a newer moral/psychological register, properties once ascribed to social relations were posited instead as inherent character traits of individuals or groups, and the connotations here, too, have worsened. This last register now claims an increasingly large proportion of the discourse, as if the social relations of dependency were being absorbed into personality. Symptomatically, erstwhile relational understandings have been hypostatized in a veritable portrait gallery of dependent personalities: first, housewives, paupers, natives, and slaves; then poor black teenage solo mothers.

These shifts in the semantics of dependency reflect some major socio-historical developments. One is the progressive differentiation of the official economy – that which is counted in the gross domestic product (GDP) – as a seemingly autonomous system that dominates social life. Before the rise of capitalism, any particular dependency was part of a net of dependencies, a single, continuous fabric of social hierarchies. Although women were subordinated and their labor often controlled by others, their labor was more visible, understood, and formally valued. With the emergence of religious and secular individualism, on the one hand, and industrial capitalism, on the other, a sharp, new dichotomy was constructed in which economic dependency and economic independence were opposed to one another. A crucial corollary of this dichotomy, and of the hegemony of wage labor in general, was the occlusion and devaluation of women's unpaid domestic and parenting labor.

The genealogy of dependency also expresses the modern emphasis on individual personality. Fear of dependency, both explicit and implicit, posits an ideal, independent personality in contrast to which those considered dependent are deviant. This contrast bears traces of a sexual division of labor that assigns men primary responsibility as providers or breadwinners and women primary responsibility as caretakers and nurturers and then treats the derivative personality patterns as fundamental. It is as if male breadwinners absorbed into their personalities the independence associated with their ideologically interpreted economic role, whereas the persons of female nurturers became saturated with the dependency of those for whom they care. The opposition between the independent and dependent personalities maps onto a whole series of hierarchical oppositions and dichotomies that are central in modern culture: masculine/feminine, public/private, work/care-giving, success/love, individual/community, economy/family, and competitive/self-sacrificing.

Toward Interdependence

Often, though not always, the various registers of dependency discourse are associated with political positions. Today the moral/psychological critique is associated with neoconservatism, the focus on the economic with liberalism. The Left is more likely to deny the existence of dependency as a problem and to presume that, given economic justice and freedom from domination, poor women would assume their "independent" potential. Feminists are just beginning to generate what we might call a transvaluative critique, influenced primarily by the welfare rights movement, which questions the opposition between dependence and independence. We conclude with some modest efforts at developing that feminist vision.

A genealogy of dependency, obviously, does not automatically produce a political strategy. But it does suggest the limits of a response that presupposes, rather than challenges, the definition of the problem implicit in the expression "welfare dependency." An adequate response would need to question our received valuations and definitions of "dependency" and "independence" in order to allow new, emancipatory social visions to emerge.

We might start from the insight that all versions of the opposition between dependence and independence are ideological; these versions simultaneously reflect and dissimulate male-supremacist social organization. The feminist activist and scholar Diana Pearce formulates this point:

The campaign against women's poverty should not be premised, implicitly or explicitly, on a false distinction between those who are economically "independent" and those who are "dependent." Frequently this contrast is drawn between women whose work is in the home, either unpaid or poorly paid (such as housekeepers and child-care workers), versus those whose work is in the marketplace, including some women as well as most men. Those in paid employment outside the home environment could not be "independent" without the support system provided by the home or its surrogates, such as "housewives" and day care centers. Such workers' "independence" could not occur without the hidden and unrecognized dependence the workers have on others. At the heart of this false dichotomy, of course, is the devaluation of the work that women perform, as those who take care of "dependents" as well as "independents." (Pearce 1990, 275)

Pearce's formulation suggests that one crucial element of a feminist response is to revalue the devalued side of the dichotomy (i.e., to rehabilitate dependency as a normal, even valuable, human quality). This sort of approach has been articulated relatively widely in the moral/psychological register, in feminist work that reconsiders the moral and social value of personality traits such as interpersonal sensitivity. We have been reminded that every pejoratively coded feminine trait can be positively recoded (e.g., worrying about the opinion of others is also sensitivity; being "other-directed" is also being good at building relationships; gossip is also the nurturing of social networks). Conversely, the canonical masculine-coded characteristics of independence, such as ambition and bravery, can be recoded perjoratively as ruthlessness, insensitivity, and inability to build intimate relationships. Dependency, thus, can be re-described as a virtue.

We must do this re-describing cautiously. We are reminded, often by welfare recipients themselves, that the existing conditions of claiming AFDC are wretched and damaging. "Welfare" in the United States – as opposed to dignified ways of getting help from the state – really does reduce self-esteem and autonomy. Re-describing the program will not change that.

Moreover, the contemporary feminist debate about the work of Carol Gilligan (1982), and particularly her suggestion that women have different moral approaches and ego development, reminds us of how easy it is to romanticize women's adaptations to powerlessness (Kittay and Meyers 1987; Kerber et al. 1986; Flanagan and Jackson 1987). It will not do to argue, as the Sears Corporation did several years ago in a much publicized sex discrimination case, that women were stuck in low-paying jobs because they did not aspire to more competitive, higher-paying jobs. Not only have such gender differences evidently been primarily conditioned by women's subordination, but it is dubious that they have rendered women morally superior, as our Victorian ancestors claimed. In addition, when women have developed their own ambitiousness, that very quality is likely to be perceived more negatively, as abrasiveness, than when it is displayed in men. All of this suggests that a simple revaluative strategy will not suffice.

To avoid these distortions, we might borrow a conceptual strategy from Herbert Marcuse. In *Eros and Civilization* (1955), he distinguished between "socially necessary repression" and "surplus repression". "Necessary repression" was defined as the quantity and quality of repression that any society – however libertarian, egalitarian, and democratic – would have to impose on unsocialized infants in the process of socialization. "Surplus repression," in contrast, was repression in excess – quantitative and qualitative – of the inevitable minimum, hence repression rooted in unjust and potentially remediable social institutions. Likewise, feminists interested in developing a transvaluative critique of dependence might distinguish socially necessary dependence from surplus dependence. Socially necessary dependence would be the sort of dependence, or need for others' care, that is an inescapable feature of the human condition, experienced particularly intensely in the beginning and end of the life cycle, as well as frequently in between. Surplus dependence, in contrast, would be dependence that is rooted in unjust and potentially remediable social institutions.

On the basis of this distinction, feminists could safely argue to revalue socially necessary dependence. This means challenging the hyperbolic masculinist-capitalist view that the normal human condition is independence and that dependence is deviant. It entails building and institutionalizing respect for the activity of caring for those who are necessarily dependent (i.e., children, older persons, the sick, the troubled). Then, what is now the unpaid and unrecognized care-giving work of women would be revealed as crucial to society, and the surplus dependence that currently adheres to those who perform this work would be eliminated. The utopian end would be abolition of the current link between caring for dependents and thereby being rendered dependent oneself (Kittay 1993; Sapiro 1990).

A second, more far-reaching task is overcoming the dependence/independence dichotomy altogether. This dichotomy is negated by the most essential characteristics of the modern world, which create ever higher relations of interdependence, based on an ever increasing division of labor, from the global to the neighborhood level. Yet many existing welfare programs replicate or reinforce the dichotomy even in their administration. For example, AFDC rules prohibit sharing, insisting on dyadic relations between identified recipients and the bureaucracy; and many welfare systems ideologically identify some people as 100 percent dependent and others as 100 percent independent. It is in our broad social interest to do the opposite: to spread responsibility and the freedom to take help from others. We know, for example, that children are less likely to be abused or neglected when more than one adult contributes to their welfare; that women with large circles of friends and acquaintances are much less vulnerable to abuse. Moreover, only by challenging this fundamental dichotomy can we appreciate giving and taking help without losing that which is valuable in the work ethic. "Dependency" cannot be redefined without also redefining "work," for otherwise welfare programs meet strenuous political opposition from those who are aware that they work hard and earn little while others seem to them lazy and irresponsible. We need, in fact, to historicize work and redefine it so that it is understood to include non-wage-earning labor; to elaborate historical change in what has counted as work, reconsidering a variety of labor such as housework and child care, children's activity in attending school, the labor of artists, and the effort that goes into nurturance of friends and maintenance of social networks. This means overcoming not only arbitrary divisions of labor but also arbitrary divisions of labor's meanings.

Some contemporary U.S. welfare rights activists have adopted this strategy, continuing the NWRO tradition. Pat Gowens, for example, expresses such a feminist reinterpretation of "dependency": "The vast majority of mothers of *all classes and all educational levels* 'depends' on another income. It may come from child support . . . or from a husband who earns $20,000 while she averages $7,000. But 'dependence' more accurately defines dads who count on women's unwaged labor to raise children and care for the home. Surely, 'dependence' doesn't define the single mom who does it all: child-rearing, home-making, and bring in the money (one way or another). When caregiving is valued and paid, when dependence is not a dirty word, and interdependence is the norm – only then will we make a dent in poverty" (Gowens 1991, 90–91).

Notes

This is a revised version of "A Genealogy of *Dependency*: Tracing a Keyword of the U.S. Welfare State," an article published in *Signs: Journal of Women in Culture and Society* 19, no. 2 (Winter 1994). Nancy Fraser is grateful for research support from the Center for Urban Affairs and Policy Research, Northwestern University; the Newberry Library/National Endowment for the Humanities; and the American Council of Learned Societies. Linda Gordon thanks the University of Wisconsin Graduate School, Vilas Trust, and the Institute for Research on Poverty. We both thank the Rockefeller Foundation Research and Study Center, Bellagio, Italy. We are also grateful for helpful comments from Lisa Brush, Robert Entman, Joel Handler, Dirk Hartog, Barbara Hobson, Allen Hunter, Eva Kittay, Felicia Kornbluh, Jenny Mansbridge, Linda Nicholson, Erik Wright, and Eli Zaretsky.

1   Another part of the story, of course, concerns the word "welfare." In this article, our focus is U.S. political culture and thus U.S. English usage. Our findings should be of more general interest, however, as some other languages have similar meanings embedded in analogous words. In this article we have of necessity used British sources for the early stages of our genealogy, which spans the sixteenth and seventeenth centuries. We assume that these meanings of "dependency" were brought to the "New World" and were formative for the early stages of U.S. political culture.

2   The term "genealogy" is today associated with Michel Foucault (1984). Our approach differs from Foucault's, however, in two crucial respects: we seek to contextualize discursive shifts in relation to broad institutional and socio-structural shifts, and we welcome normative political reflection (Fraser 1989).

3   In preindustrial society, moreover, the reverse dependence of the master upon his men was widely recognized. The historian Christopher Hill

evoked that understanding when he characterized the "essence" of feudal society as "the bond of loyalty and dependence between lord and man" (1972, 32). Here "dependence" means interdependence.

4   Neither English nor U.S. dictionaries report any pejorative uses of the term before the early twentieth century. In fact, some leading preindustrial definitions were explicitly positive, implying trusting, relying, or counting on another, the predecessors of today's "dependable."

5   In practice, of course, these preindustrial arrangements did not always provide satisfactorily for the poor. In the fourteenth century, new, stronger states began to limit the freedom of movement of the destitute and codify older informal distinctions between those worthy and unworthy of assistance. When the English Poor Law of 1601 confirmed this latter distinction, it was already considered shameful to ask for public help. But the culture neither disapproved of dependency nor valorized individual independence. Rather, the aim of the statutes was to return the mobile, uprooted, and excessively "independent" poor to their local parishes or communities, and hence to enforce their traditional dependencies.

6   For example, they were central to the Putney Debates of the English Civil War.

7   One might say that this redefinition foregrounded wage labor as a new form of property, namely property in one's own labor power. This conception was premised on what C.B. Macpherson called "possessive individualism," the assumption of an individual's property in his [sic] own person (1962). Leading to the construction of wages as an entitlement, this approach was overwhelmingly male. It represented a loss of systemic critique, a sense of independence gained by narrowing the focus to the individual worker and leaving behind aspirations for collective independence from capital.

8   In the sixteenth century the term "pauper" had meant simply a poor person and, in law, one who was allowed to sue or defend in court without paying costs (OED). Two centuries later, it took on a more restricted definition, denoting a new class of persons who subsisted on poor relief instead of wages and who were held to be deviant and blameworthy.

9   Actually, there are many variants within the family of images that personify subjection in the industrial era. Among these are related but not identical stereotypes of the Russian serf, the Caribbean slave, the slave in the United States, and Native Americans. Moreover, there are distinct male and female stereotypes within each of those categories. We simplify here in order to highlight the features that are common to all these images, notably the idea of natural subjection rooted in race. We focus especially on stereotypes that portray African Americans as personifications of dependency because of their historic importance and contemporary resonance in the U.S. language of social welfare.

10   The evolution of the term "native" neatly encapsulates this process. Its original meaning in English, dating from about 1450, was tied to dependency: "one born in bondage; a born thrall," but without racial meaning. Two centuries later it carried the additional meaning of colored or black (OED).

11   In the United States, the family wage ideal held greater sway among whites than among blacks, and was at variance with actual practice for all of the poor and working classes. Moreover, both employed and non-employed wives continued to perform work once considered crucial to a family economy.

12   Continuing from preindustrial usage was the assumption that fathers headed households and that other household members were represented by them, as codified in the legal doctrine of coverture. The socio-legal and political dependency of wives enforced their new economic dependency, since under coverture even married women who were wage workers could not legally control their wages.

13   The Social Security Board propagandized for Social Security Old Age Insurance (the program today called "Social Security") precisely because, at first, it did not seem more earned or dignified than public assistance. To make Social Security more acceptable, the Board worked to stigmatize public assistance, even pressuring states to keep stipends low (Cates 1983).

14   Men on "general relief" are sometimes also included in that designation; their treatment by the welfare system is usually as bad or worse.

15   The norm, moreover, was racially marked, as white women were usually portrayed as erring on the side of excessive dependence, while black women were typically charged with excessive independence.

16   The New Left critique bore some resemblance to the NWRO critique, but the overlap was only partial. The historians of social control told their story mainly from the perspective of the "helpers" and cast recipients as almost entirely passive. They thereby occluded the agency of actual or potential welfare claimants in articulating needs, demanding rights, and making claims. For a fuller discussion of the social control critique, see Gordon (1990b). On needs claims, see Fraser (1990) and Nelson (1990).

17   For an argument that President Clinton's recent neo-liberal discourse continues to individualize dependency, see Fraser (1993).

References

Abbott, Edith, and Sophonisba P. Breckinridge. 1921. *The Administration of the Aid-to-Mothers Law in Illinois*. Publication no. 82. Washington, D.C.: U.S. Children's Bureau.

American Psychiatric Association. 1987. *Diagnostic and Statistical Manual of Mental Disorders*, 3rd ed. Washington, D.C.: American Psychiatric Association.

Bakke, E. Wight. 1940a. *Citizens without Work: A Study of the Effects of Unemployment upon Workers' Social Relations and Practices*. New Haven: Yale University Press.

———. 1940b. *The Unemployed Worker: A Study of the Task of Making a Living without a Job*. New Haven: Yale University Press.

Boydston, Jeanne. 1991. *Home and Work: Housework, Wages, and the Ideology of Labor in the Early Republic*. New York: Oxford.

Brandt, Lilian. 1932. *An Impressionistic View of the Winter of 1930–31 in New York City*. New York: Welfare Council of New York City.

Brown, Josephine Chapin. 1940. *Public Relief, 1929–1939*. New York: Henry Holt.

Bruno, Frank J. 1948. *Trends in Social Work*. New York: Columbia University Press.

Cates, Jerry R. 1983. *Insuring Inequality: Administrative Leadership in Social Security, 1935–54*. Ann Arbor: University of Michigan Press.

Dowling, Colette. 1981. *The Cinderella Complex: Women's Hidden Fear of Independence*. New York: Summit Books.

Flanagan, Owen, and Kathryn Jackson. 1987. "Justice, Care, and Gender: The Kohlberg-Gilligan Debate Revisited." *Ethics* 97: 622–37.

Folbre, Nancy. 1991. "The Unproductive Housewife: Her Evolution in Nineteenth-Century Economic Thought." *Signs: Journal of Women in Culture and Society* 16, no. 3: 463–84.

Foucault, Michel. 1984. "Nietzsche, Genealogy, History." Pp. 76–100 in *The Foucault Reader*, ed. Paul Rabinow. New York: Pantheon.

Fraser, Nancy. 1987. "Women, Welfare, and the Politics of Need Interpretation." *Hypatia: A Journal of Feminist Philosophy* 2, no. 1: 103–21.

———. 1989. *Unruly Practices: Power, Discourse, and Gender in Contemporary Social Theory*. Minneapolis: University of Minnesota Press.

———. 1990. "Struggle over Needs: Outline of a Socialist-Feminist Critical Theory of Late-Capitalist Political Culture." Pp. 199–225 in *Women*, ed. Gordon.

———. 1993. "Clintonism, Welfare, and the Antisocial Wage: The Emergence of a Neoliberal Political Imaginary." *Rethinking Marxism* 6, no. 1: 9–23.

Fraser, Nancy, and Linda Gordon. 1992. "Contract versus Charity: Why Is There No Social Citizenship in the United States?" *Socialist Review* 22, no. 3: 45–68.

Friedan, Betty. 1963. *The Feminine Mystique*. New York: Norton.

Gibbons, Mary L. 1933. "Family Life Today and Tomorrow." *Proceedings* (National Conference of Catholic Charities) 19:133–68.

Gilder, George. 1981. *Wealth and Poverty*. New York: Basic Books.

Gilligan, Carol. 1982. *In a Different Voice: Psychological Theory and Women's Development*. Cambridge, Mass.: Harvard University Press.

Goodin, Robert E. 1988. *Reasons for Welfare: The Political Theory of the Welfare State*. Princeton, N.J.: Princeton University Press.

Gordon, Linda, ed. 1990a. *Women, the State, and Welfare*. Madison: University of Wisconsin Press.

———. 1990b. "The New Feminist Scholarship on the Welfare State." Pp. 9–35 in *Women*, ed. Gordon.

———. 1992. "Social Insurance and Public Assistance: The Influence of Gender in Welfare Thought in the United States, 1890–1935." *American Historical Review* 97, no. 1: 19–54.

Gowens, Pat. 1991. "Welfare, Learnfare – Unfair! A Letter to My Governor." *Ms.* (Sept.–Oct.), 90–91.

Gundersen, Joan R. 1987. "Independence, Citizenship, and the American Revolution." *Signs: Journal of Women in Culture and Society* 13, no. 1: 59–77.

Haynes, M. 1988. "Pharmacist Involvement in a Chemical-Dependency Rehabilitation Program." *American Journal of Hospital Pharmacy* 45, no. 10: 2099–101.

Hill, Christopher. 1972. *The World Turned Upside Down: Radical Ideas during the English Revolution*. New York: Viking.

Howard, Donald S. 1943. *The WPA and Federal Relief Policy*. New York: Russell Sage.

Jencks, Christopher. 1992. *Rethinking Social Policy: Race, Poverty, and the Underclass*. Cambridge, Mass.: Harvard University Press.

Kerber, Linda K., Catherine G. Green, Eleanor E. Maccoby, Zella Luria, Carol B. Stack, and Carol Gilligan. 1986. "On *In a Different Voice*: An Interdisciplinary Forum." *Signs: Journal of Women in Culture and Society* 11, no. 2: 304–33.

Kittay, Eva. 1993. We Are All Some Mother's Child: Vulnerability, Equality, and the Dependency Worker. Unpublished manuscript.

Kittay, Eva, and Diana T. Meyers, eds. 1987. *Women and Moral Theory*. Totowa, N.J.: Rowman and Littlefield.

Land, Hilary. 1980. "The Family Wage." *Feminist Review* 6:55–77.

Laslett, Peter. 1971. *The World We Have Lost: England before the Industrial Age*. New York: Charles Scribner.

Macpherson, C.B. 1962. *The Political Theory of Possessive Individualism: Hobbes to Locke.* Oxford: Oxford University Press.

Marcuse, Herbert. 1955. *Eros and Civilization: A Philosophical Inquiry into Freud.* Boston: Beacon Press.

Mead, Lawrence. 1986. *Beyond Entitlement: The Social Obligations of Citizenship.* New York: Free Press.

Milwaukee County Welfare Rights Organization. 1972. *Welfare Mothers Speak Out.* New York: Norton.

Murray, Charles. 1984. *Losing Ground: American Social Policy, 1950–1980.* New York: Basic Books.

National Conference of Charities and Correction. 1890s–1920s. *Proceedings.*

Nelson, Barbara J. 1990. "The Origins of the Two-Channel Welfare State: Workmen's Compensation and Mothers' Aid." Pp. 123–51 in *Women*, ed. Gordon.

Pearce, Diana. 1990. "Welfare Is Not *for* Women: Why the War on Poverty Cannot Conquer the Feminization of Poverty." Pp. 265–79 in *Women*, ed. Gordon.

Pope, Jacqueline. 1989. *Biting the Hand That Feeds Them: Organizing Women on Welfare at the Grass Roots Level.* New York: Praeger.

Quadagno, Jill. 1988. "From Old-Age Assistance to Supplemental Social Security Income: The Political Economy of Relief in the South, 1935–1972." Pp. 235–63 in *The Politics of Social Policy in the United States*, ed. Margaret Weir, Ann Shola Orloff, and Theda Skocpol. Princeton, N.J.: Princeton University Press.

Quayle, Dan. 1992. "Excerpts from Vice President's Speech on Cities and Poverty." *New York Times*, May 20.

Rainwater, Lee, and William L. Yancey. 1967. *The Moynihan Report and the Politics of Controversy.* Cambridge, Mass.: MIT Press.

Sapiro, Virginia. 1990. "The Gender Basis of American Social Policy." Pp. 36–54 in *Women*, ed. Gordon.

Smith, Joan. 1984. "The Paradox of Women's Poverty: Wage-Earning Women and Economic Transformation." *Signs: Journal of Women in Culture and Society* 10, no. 2: 291–310.

Sparer, Edward V. 1970–71. "The Right to Welfare." Pp. 65–93 in *The Rights of Americans: What They Are – What They Should Be*, ed. Norman Dorsen. New York: Pantheon.

Stacey, Judith. 1987. "Sexism by a Subtler Name? Postindustrial Conditions and Postfeminist Consciousness in the Silicon Valley." *Socialist Review* 96:7–28.

——. 1990. *Brave New Families: Stories of Domestic Upheaval in Late Twentieth Century America.* New York: Basic Books.

Timms, Noel, and Rita Timms. 1982. *Dictionary of Social Welfare.* London: Routledge and Kegan Paul.

Vaile, Gertrude. 1934. "Public Relief." Pp. 19–40 in *College Women and the Social Sciences*, ed. Herbert Elmer Mills. New York: John Day.

Warner, Amos Griswold. 1894–1930 editions. *American Charities and Social Work.* New York: Thomas Y. Crowell.

West, Guida. 1981. *The National Welfare Rights Movement: The Social Protest of Poor Women.* New York: Praeger.

Weston, Kath. 1991. *Families We Choose: Lesbians, Gays, Kinship.* New York: Columbia University Press.

Williams, Raymond. 1976. *Keywords: A Vocabulary of Culture and Society.* Oxford: Oxford University Press.

Wilson, William Julius. 1987. *The Truly Disadvantaged: The Inner City, the Underclass, and Public Policy.* Chicago: University of Chicago Press.

Index

Note: Figures in **bold** refer to chapters written by the named author.

Index